F. B. MEYER
BIBLE COMMENTARY

F. B. MEYER
BIBLE COMMENTARY

TYNDALE HOUSE PUBLISHERS, INC. WHEATON, ILLINOIS

All Scripture quotations
are from the King James Version
unless otherwise indicated.

This material was originally published
in seven volumes by American
Sunday-School Union, Philadelphia,
and was titled
Through the Bible Day by Day.

Library of Congress Catalog Card
Number 78-66196.
ISBN 0-8423-4250-8, cloth.
First Tyndale House printing,
September 1979.
Printed in the United States of
America.

CONTENTS

Introduction 7
Preface 9

THE OLD TESTAMENT

Genesis 13
Exodus 35
Leviticus 53
Numbers 63
Deuteronomy 77
Joshua 89
Judges 99
Ruth 111
1 Samuel 115
2 Samuel 133
1 Kings 149
2 Kings 167
1 & 2 Chronicles 187

Ezra 197
Nehemiah 203
Esther 209
Job 215
Psalms 229
Proverbs 279
Ecclesiastes 289
Isaiah 293
Jeremiah 313
The Lamentations of
 Jeremiah 319
Ezekiel 321
Daniel 327

Hosea 335
Joel 343
Amos 347
Obadiah 353
Jonah 357
Micah 361
Nahum 365
Habakkuk 369
Zephaniah 373
Haggai 377
Zechariah 381
Malachi 387

THE NEW TESTAMENT

The Gospel
 According to
 Matthew 393

The Gospel
 According to Mark
 419

The Gospel
 According to Luke
 431

The Gospel According to John 455	Ephesians 547	Hebrews 597
	Philippians 555	James 607
	Colossians 561	1 Peter 613
The Acts of the Apostles 481	1 Thessalonians 567	2 Peter 619
	2 Thessalonians 573	The Epistles of John 623
Romans 503	1 Timothy 577	
1 Corinthians 517	2 Timothy 583	Jude 629
2 Corinthians 529	Titus 589	The Revelation 633
Galatians 539	Philemon 593	

INTRODUCTION

THERE IS NEED EVERYWHERE FOR THE CULTIVATION OF THE habit of reading some portion of God's Word *each day*. Such reading should be *consecutive*, for only thus can continuous interest be maintained. It may also be greatly helped by an interpreter who could explain what is obscure as well as suggest applications of the message to the daily life.

To meet such a need, this commentary provides an arrangement of the books of the Bible in daily portions, with concise devotional comments. It includes all portions of the Bible most suitable for daily reading, either individually or in family groups. You will notice that not every Bible paragraph is discussed. In fact, one entire book, the Song of Solomon, is not included in this volume. However, those passages covered are representative of the Bible books studied.

As a commentary on the whole Bible, this book will be found valuable because it omits points of merely scholarly interest and fixes attention upon the central message of each passage and its application to daily needs. There are frequent references to other parts of Scripture, especially from Old Testament truths to their New Testament fulfillment and interpretation.

Mr. Meyer's lifelong experience in teaching the Bible to laymen made him preeminently fitted for this book—"a crowning one in his worldwide ministry by voice and pen," said the original publisher.

It is hoped that this work will prove of much value to Sunday school teachers and adult scholars, promote profitable Bible reading in connection with both family and private devotions, and everywhere deepen a love for and an intelligent acquaintance with the one Book which can provide a fresh and helpful message for the needs of each new day.

PREFACE

THE BIBLE IS FULL OF GOD'S WISDOM. IT IS THE WORD OF GOD. We must read it not only with our head, but with our heart. An analysis of its contents is good and desirable; but when all this is done, we need to allow time for the inner wisdom, power, and grace which are stored in the Book to soak into our inner consciousness. Therefore, it is better to have a shorter portion for daily study, to give us time to get all the juice and marrow out of what we read.

This is the method followed in this book. Busy people, students, businessmen, Sunday school workers and older scholars, soldiers and sailors, people on the hills and on the prairies, living on the edge of the great tides of human activity, will find these passages, selected for daily reading, ample to furnish a daily meal of truth, and yet deep and wide enough for profound inquiry and interest.

It has always seemed to me that the true way to know the Bible is to read it through from beginning to end. It is only so that we can follow the unveiling of the divine purpose, from the dawn of Genesis to the perfect day of the divine writings of John. It is only so that we can obtain a connected view of the wide scope of revelation. To read in different, unconnected passages, now of poetry, now of history, now of doctrine, prevents the mind from getting proper focus. We are apt by that method to concentrate on a few familiar passages, instead of listening to *all* that God has spoken to men's hearts. There is probably nothing more vital to an accurate knowledge of the Bible than the good old practice of reading it thoughtfully and steadily through with such brief notes as this volume provides.

But let it always be remembered that the profoundest knowledge of the Word comes from the illuminating grace of the Holy Spirit. Ask him to unlock and unfold its sacred mysteries. Ask him to reveal the glories of our Lord in every chapter. Ask him to enable you to read, mark, learn, and inwardly digest. Ask him, finally, to enable you to become not a forgetful hearer or reader, but a doer of the Word. See to it that your reading is combined with the faith that claims from God the fulfillment, in your own experience, of all he has promised. No prayer, therefore, is more salutary, as you open your Bible morning by morning, than the familiar old words of the psalmist: "Open thou mine eyes, that I may behold wondrous things out of thy law."

F. B. Meyer

THE OLD TESTAMENT

THE BOOK OF
GENESIS

THE BEGINNINGS OF THE RACE AND OF THE CHOSEN FAMILY

I. GOD AND THE RACE *1:1—11:26*
   A. The beginnings of the world and of man *1:1—2:25*
   B. The beginning and spread of evil *3:1—6:7*
   C. The judgment and renewal of the earth *6:8—11:26*

II. GOD AND THE CHOSEN FAMILY *11:27—50:26*
   A. The history of Abraham and his son Isaac *11:27—25:11*
      (The line of Ishmael, Hagar's son) *25:12-18*
   B. The history of Isaac and Jacob *25:19—35:29*
      (The line of Esau, who sold his birthright) *36:1—37:1*
   C. The history of Jacob's sons, Joseph and his brothers *37:2—50:26*
      1. Joseph sold into Egypt *37:1-36*
         (Judah's sin) *38:1-30*
      2. Joseph's servitude in Egypt *39—41*
      3. The journeys of Joseph's brothers to Egypt *42—45*
      4. Jacob goes to Egypt. He and Joseph die there *46—50*

INTRODUCTION

The name "Genesis" is the Greek word for "beginning," and was selected by the translators of the Hebrew Scriptures into Greek. This version was known as the Septuagint (frequently indicated by LXX), because it was said the translators numbered seventy men. It was made for the Jews of "the Dispersion" dwelling in Egypt and elsewhere, who had become unfamiliar with the language of their fathers.

The word "generations" indicates the successive divisions of the book and the gradual concentration of the divine purpose in one special line of ancestry, leading to the development of the knowledge of Jehovah through Israel. Notice this word in 2:4; 5:1; 6:9; 10:1; 11:10; 11:27; 25:12; 25:19; 36:1; 37:2. Each of these verses introduces a new section, in which is traced the "generations" or issue of the person it names. Ishmael and Esau are sidelines from which the history promptly returns to the line of promise through Isaac and Jacob.

Genesis is the first of the five books of Moses, known as the Pentateuch and also called "the Law" (see Luke 24:44). The unanimous testimony of the New Testament is to ascribe the authorship to Moses. See Matt. 19:8; Mark 12:26; Luke 16:31; John 5:46. But he doubtless incorporated sacred traditions handed down from the patriarchs, and there are traces of an editor's hand, probably Ezra's.

COMMENTARY

GENESIS 1:1-5

Beginnings. All beginnings must begin with God. Always put God first. The first stone in every building, our first thought every morning, the first aim and purpose of all activity ought to be for him. Begin the book of the year with God, and you will end it with the glory of the new Jerusalem. At first, as in the physical creation, your heart and life may seem to be "without form and void." Do not be discouraged. The Spirit of God is within you, brooding amid the darkness, and presently his Light will shine through. It is the blessed presence of the Lord Jesus that stirs in your heart and will presently rule your life (John 1:4). His presence divides between good and evil. You must distinguish between Christ and self. Follow the gleam and you shall not walk in darkness, but have the light of life. God's days begin in evenings, and always end in mornings.

GENESIS 1:6-19

Sky, Earth, Seasons. There were successive stages in creation. The days probably represent long periods. It is so with the new creation in our hearts (see 2 Cor. 5:17). In Nature the clouds that float above us are separated from the waters at our feet; so in Christian experience we must seek to quench our thirst not only from below, but from above. See Col. 3:1-4. Our wells must be filled from Heaven. Notice how in creation there are repeated separations, as between day and night, seas and lands; so as we live in the Spirit, we are quicker to distinguish not only between white and black, but the different shades of gray. The test of plant life is the power of reproducing their kind; we are always reproducing ourselves in others, and sowing wheat or poppies. If God maintains suns and planets in bright and ordered beauty, he can keep us (Isa. 40:26, 27).

GENESIS 1:20-31

Man—Creation's Crown. Creation reveals God's nature, as the picture the artist. His eternal power and Godhead are visible in his works. See Rom. 1:20. And all things and beings were made through Jesus Christ (Col. 1:15, 16). The hands of the Son of God wove the blue curtains above us and filled them with luminaries. The seas are his; he made them and filled them with living creatures. The woodlands are the outcome of his mind, and he filled them with flowers and birds. He taught them to live without worry. He filled the tiny heart of the mother bird with love for her young. His are the cattle on a thousand hills. He molded the red earth into his own likeness and made man. We were made to have dominion. See Psalm 8:6-8. Ask God to put all things, especially all the evil things of your heart, under your feet. The world is good, and if you are good you find it so.

GENESIS 2:1-17

Man in Eden. Innocence. The first paragraph belongs to the previous chapter, as is clear from the use of the same term for God—*Elohim.* God's rest was not from weariness or exhaustion, but because his work of creation was finished. He is ever at work; remember John 5:17. We enter into his rest when we cease to worry and rather trust him in all and for all. In the fourth verse, Moses incorporates another of those wonderful God-given narratives which had been handed down from the lips of the patriarchs. It is marked by the use of another term for God—*Jehovah Elohim.* Every man is entrusted with a garden, that he may keep it. God's goodness is no excuse for idleness. Whether your heart and life shall produce weeds or flowers and fruits depends on you. Ponder Prov. 4:23; 24:30, 31.

GENESIS 2:18—3:8

Man and Woman. Temptation. Love is God's best gift to man. Without it, even Eden would not be Paradise. That Adam was able to name the animals, affixing a title suggested by some peculiarity or characteristic, indicated his royal supremacy; and insofar as we live in God, that supremacy is restored. See Dan. 6:22; Mark 1:13. But what is power without love, or a throne without a consort? Eve was, therefore, given to crown Adam's bliss; taken from his side, as afterward the Church from the opened side of Christ. See John 19:34 and Eph. 5:25.

The order of temptation is always the same: the tempter without, and within the strong desire for sensual gratification, with the secret hope that somehow the consequences may be avoided. The eye inflames passion; passion masters the resistance of the will; the body obeys its impulse; the act of gratification is followed immediately by remorse and guilt. Then we need the second Adam!

GENESIS 3:9-21

God's Condemnation of Adam and Eve. God does not wait for Adam to find his own way back, but hastens in search of him. "Where art thou?" is rendered in one version, "Alas for thee."

Jesus met the tempter not in a garden, but in the wilderness. He suffered being tempted, but has become to all who obey him a life-giving spirit and the author of eternal salvation. Read 1 Cor. 15:45 and Heb. 5:9. The penalty is gone, borne by him in his own body on the cross. So Paul affirms in Rom. 5:14ff. Our bias toward evil is counteracted by his indwelling through the Holy Spirit; so we are taught in Rom. 8:1-4. He bruises Satan beneath the feet of those who trust him. Such is his own assurance in Luke 10:19 and Mark 16:17, 18. He transforms the other results of sin. Through pain, the mother's love is drawn out to her child. Hard work is educative and ennobling. Death is the gate of life. Where sin abounded, grace abounds much more.

GENESIS 3:22—4:8

Offerings by Cain and Abel. It was good that man should be driven from Eden. Soft comfort enervates. Man goes forth from the Eden of innocence, of home, of the land of his birth, to create gardens out of deserts and to become a pilgrim to the abiding City of God. Angels of love forbid our return. Heaven lies before us; the City gleams with light on the far horizon. For the tree of life, see Rev. 2:7.

The inner motive of Cain's ruthless deed is supplied in 1 John 3:12. Abel, deeply conscious of sin, felt that a sacrifice was needed; therefore, his faith saved him and links him with all who believe. See Heb. 11:4. Cain had no sense of sin and thought a gift of produce enough. But all the while sin was crouching at the door, like a hungry tiger, waiting for the chance to enter. Watch and pray, lest ye enter into temptation!

GENESIS 4:9-26

Cain's Career. God's first question is, "Adam, where art thou?" The next, "Where is thy brother?" We *are* our brother's keepers. All related to us, within our reach or needing our help, have a claim. We must not take advantage of them. Their well-being and our own are inseparable. God keeps an inventory of his saints and will avenge them. Their blood will cry to God against those who have wronged them. There is only one cry in the world which is stronger—"the blood of Jesus." See Heb. 12:24.

A numerous family sprang from our first parents, and as these intermarried a large population began to people the early seat of human life. Cain founded a city, dedicated to all that ministered to sensuous enjoyment. This was "the way of Cain," brilliant but godless, away from the presence of the Lord.

GENESIS 5:1-24

Posterity of Adam. In contrast to Cain's line in the previous chapter, we have Seth's in this. Note the curious similarity in the names in the two lines, as though the Cainites professed all that the Sethites held, but lacked the reality and power. There have always been these two families in the world—tares and wheat, goats and sheep. This is an old-world cemetery; we walk among old monuments with time-worn inscriptions. Though the Sethites were God-fearers, they were tinged with Adam's sin. He was made in God's image, but they in his as well. "That which is born of the flesh is flesh." We need what is described in Col. 3:10 and Eph. 4:23.

The birth of Methuselah seems to have had a profound influence on his father. *After* that he walked with God. Faith will enable us to do the same, because it makes the unseen visible and God real. Go God's way. Keep God's pace. Talk to him aloud and constantly as the great Companion.

GENESIS 5:25—6:8

The Wickedness of Men. When a son was born to Lamech, he named him Noah, which means "rest." He thought that the boy would grow up to share and alleviate the strain of daily toil. But his hope was premature; rest was not yet. The Deluge would soon sweep over the works of men. The world must await the true Rest-giver who said, "Come unto me."

It was an age of abounding wickedness, but the language describing it is obscure. Some think that "the sons of God" were fallen angels; others that the seed of Seth became joined in marriage with the daughters of Cain. But God's Spirit strove with man and though a limit was put to his pleadings, yet he sought men with yearning remonstrance, until he received the final negative and turned away disappointed and grieved. There was considerable delay. For 120 years the Spirit of God waited. See 1 Pet. 3:20. But he will not wait forever (Luke 13:9).

GENESIS 6:9–22

Noah Builds the Ark. Human sin had reached an awful climax. Sooner or later its results would certainly have swept the human race from the earth, as smallpox will slay every native on some infected island. God only hastened by the Flood the inevitable result of wrongdoing. Amid the universal corruption and violence, one man stood out as precious in the sight of God. His name meant "rest." He was righteous toward man and "perfect" or blameless toward God; he walked in fellowship with God; his ear was quick to detect, and his hand deft to fulfill, the divine will. "By faith Noah . . ." (Heb. 11:7). Such is the character to which God reveals his secrets and with which he enters into covenant. If we live thus, we shall cross the flood of death into the resurrection life (2 Pet. 2:5). Not only shall we be saved, but we shall save others.

GENESIS 7:1–24

The Great Flood. What anguish! They climbed the highest story of their towers, then to the hills, but the greedy waters followed them, until the last crag was covered and all living things except those in the ark had perished. Equally sudden and unexpected shall be the days of the Son of man. See Luke 17:26; 2 Pet. 3:7.

But what drowns other men only lifts the child of God nearer his home. The waters bear up the ark. When the loftiest refuges of lies and pride are submerged, and the whole landscape is covered with a monotonous waste of trouble, God says to the soul, "Come into the ark." It is as though he is inside and wants us to enter into close fellowship with himself. See Psalm 27:5. When God shuts the door behind us, no power can force, no skeleton key can unlock, no wedge can pry the door.

For the extent of the Deluge it is appropriate to consider Luke 2:1–3. In the Genesis, as in the Luke, passage "all" may be used in a general rather than an absolute sense.

GENESIS 8:1–22

Noah Leaves the Ark. Traditions of the Flood are found in every country, from the tablets of Babylon to the rude carvings of the Aztecs, proving man's common origin. "God remembered Noah." He could not forget, because he had entered into covenant with him and his. Though the floods have been abroad on your life for long years, God has not forgotten you. Sooner might a woman forget her babe!

Noah's window only looked upward. It had no outlook on the waters; therefore, he sent forth the birds. Dove and raven issued from the same window, as the child of God and the wayward, willful child may issue from the same family. But the former cannot find satisfaction with what satisfies the other, but wings its flight back to God. See Psalm 116:7. Through God's grace Noah stepped out into the new world—the world of resurrection. His first act was the burnt offering of consecration, which was followed immediately by promise. See Rom. 12:1, 2.

GENESIS 9:1–17

God's Covenant with Noah. As the human race started afresh on its career, God blessed it, as at the first. God always stands with us in a new start. The prohibition against the use of blood in food is often repeated. See Lev. 17:10-12; Acts 15:29. In a very deep sense, the blood is the life. When we speak of being redeemed by the blood of Jesus, we mean that we have been saved by his sacrificed life. The blood makes atonement for the soul. But while animal life might be used for food or sacrifice, human life was surrounded by the most solemn sanctions.

A covenant is a promise or undertaking resting on certain conditions, with a sign or token attached to it. The rainbow in the cloud, the Lord's Supper, the wedding ring are signs and seals of their respective covenants. Never witness a rainbow without remembering that as God has sworn that the waters of Noah shall no more go over the earth, so he will not withdraw his kindness. See Isa. 54:9.

GENESIS 9:18-29

Noah's Three Sons. Noah's sin reminds us how weak are the best of men; liable to fall, even after the most marvelous deliverances. The love of strong drink will drag a preacher of righteousness into the dust. But if our brethren sin, let us not parade or tell their faults, but cover them with the mantle of divine love. We may abhor the sin, but let us restore such an one in the spirit of meekness, remembering that we also may be tempted. See Gal. 6:1-4.

The *Semitic* races have been the source of religious light and teaching to the world. God has been known in their tents. The *Japhetic* races are the great colonizers and populators of the world, overflowing their own boundaries and participating in the religious privileges of the Shemites or Semites. The progressive ideas of the race of Japheth, which of course includes the Indo-European race, have also pervaded the world. The *Hamitic* races, of which Canaan was one, have always gravitated downward.

GENESIS 11:1-9

The Confusion of Tongues. Driven by the fear of another deluge, though God had given distinct assurances to the contrary, and impelled by the desire to perpetuate their name and memory to coming generations, Noah's descendants began to build on the plain of Shinar—a fertile valley watered by the Euphrates and Tigris. Babel, Babylon, and Babylon the Great—such is the lineage of the apostasy which has ever opposed the Church of God, like a shadow, stealing along the wall at our side. To Babel we must oppose Abraham; to Babylon, Jerusalem; to Babylon the Great, the Bride, the Lamb's wife. "Come out of her, my people," is the cry that rings down the ages.

God comes down to see! From him no secrets are hid. All things are naked and open to his eyes. The one *language* or lip refers to the pronunciation; *speech* to the stock of words. God touched the *lips.* When disunion prevails, destruction follows. But Pentecost and Heaven will undo the wreck of Babel. See Rev. 7:9.

GENESIS 11:10-32

The Generations until Abram. The reason for the movement of Terah's clan from Ur is given in Acts 7:3. Apparently his father was unwilling for Abram to go alone on his long pilgrimage, and so the whole family moved along the valley of the Euphrates to the famous ford of Haran. There was no other easy way by which travelers could strike the route for Canaan. But Terah never advanced beyond that point; and it was only when his father was dead that Abram resumed his march (Acts 7:4). Let us beware lest the ties of human affection withhold us from entire obedience to the call of God.

The word *Hebrew* means "one who has crossed over." It was specially applicable to Abraham. See Genesis 14:13. It may be that you are living on the world's side of the cross. Come over, though you should have to break dear associations. Be one who has passed through death to resurrection. See Col. 3:1-4.

GENESIS 12:1-9

God's Call and Promise to Abram. God's commands are always associated with promises. Count the "shalls" and "wills" here. He does not give his reasons, but he is generous with his promises. The keynote of Abram's life was *separation,* step by step, until country, kindred, Lot, worldly alliances, and fleshly expedients were one by one cast aside and he stood alone with God! Though he knew not whither he went, the father of the faithful obeyed and crossed the wide and perilous deserts. It was this absolute and unquestioning obedience that endeared him to God. Let us ever obey and step out, though it seems as though there were naught but seething mist. We shall find it is solid under the tread of faith. Read Rom. 4:16; Heb. 11:8. Notice the combination of the tent and altar. The tent-life is natural to the man whose portion is God; and where he pitches his tent, he will rear his altar.

GENESIS 12:10-20

Abram and Sarai in Egypt. It is a comfort that the Holy Spirit permits us to trace the successive stages through which the father of those who believe made his way to the maturity of faith.

GENESIS

We all stumble as we step out on the difficult path. But God is patient with his dull scholars and protects them. See Psalm 105:15. It was certain that no weapon formed against him could prosper, nor God's promise fail; yet Abram meanly sacrificed Sarai with his pitiful proposition, for his own safety. This doubting outbreak would never have occurred unless the patriarch had gone down to Egypt, which in Scripture stands for creature-confidence. See Isa. 30:1. The God of glory, who had sent him forth, was responsible for his care in Canaan, even though famine prevailed. He ought to have stayed quietly in the position to which God had called him, leaving the Almighty to provide. Live with God in the heights; and do not go *down* into Egypt.

GENESIS 13:1-13

Abram and Lot Part. The patriarch, like a restored backslider, made his way back to the old spot on the highlands of Bethel, where his first tent and altar had stood. Through his wanderings hitherto there had been a depressing element of worldliness in his camp, through the presence of Lot, who, like many more, was swept along by his uncle's religion, but had little of his own. Feeling that separation was inevitable and that God would surely care for him, Abram offered Lot his choice. See Psa. 16:5. The younger man chose according to the sight of his eyes. In his judgment he gained the world—but see 2 Pet. 2:7, 8. The world is full of Lots—shallow, impulsive, doomed to be revealed by their choice and end. "Let there be no strife!" Blessed are the peacemakers! Wherever the interests of peace can be conserved through the sacrifice of your own interests, be prepared to forfeit the advantage; but stand like a rock when God's truth is in balance.

GENESIS 13:14—14:12

Abram at Hebron; Lot Taken Captive. Lot lifted up his eyes for himself. But when the last of Lot's followers had streamed out of the camp, God bade Abram lift up his eyes, not to choose, but to behold what God had chosen for him. He must first estimate his possessions, and then enjoy them. Let us count up our treasures in Christ, and use them. Lot grasped at and lost his all. Abram left and inherited all. Notice how abundant God's provision is. "*All* the land ... *for ever* ... *as* the dust ... the length *and* breadth." It was a far cry from the valley of the Euphrates to Sodom. The little confederate kings dared to rebel against Chedorlaomer, who swept over their lands like a sirocco and marched up the valley of the Jordan, laden with booty and carrying Lot. You cannot have the sweets of the world and miss its bitters. The path of separation is the only way of safety and peace!

GENESIS 14:13-24

Abram and Melchizedek. Recently discovered monuments confirm this narrative of the confederacy of the kings, but do not tell of their overthrow. Abram might fairly have left Lot to reap as he had sown, but his soul yearned over his weak and entrapped relative, and he set himself to deliver him. Men of faith and prayer are still able to rescue those who are taken captive by the devil at his will. Faith subdues kingdoms. The moment of success is always one of danger. The king of Sodom insidiously proposed that they should share the spoils! But how could Abram live as a pensioner on God's care if he feathered his nest with the tainted wealth of Sodom?

A previous interview had taken place which made Abram strong. Melchizedek was king and priest of the tribe which held Jerusalem. Read Heb. 7. He brought bread and wine, and a fresh revelation of the character of God on which Abram rested his soul. What had he to do with Sodom who was the child of such a Father? Christ always anticipates Satan. See Luke 22:31.

GENESIS 15:1-21

Abram's Vision of the Future. Abram had good reason to fear the vengeance of the defeated kings; but the divine Voice reassured him. For all of us there is need of a shield, because the world hates us. God will be our compensation for every sacrifice we have made. Refuse to take even the shoe-latchets of Sodom, and God will be your exceeding great reward. The patriarch addressed God as *Adonai Jehovah*, which occurs only twice more in the Pentateuch. While he was pouring out the bitterness of his soul, the stars came out. "Count these," said his Almighty Friend. "So shall your seed be." And he "believed." For the first time that mighty word occurs in Scripture. The apostle makes much of it. See Rom. 4:9; Gal. 3:6. It was as good as done.

Henceforth the patriarch reckoned on God's faithfulness. In olden times covenants were ratified by the parties passing between the pieces of the sacrifice. To give strong consolation, the Almighty confirmed his word with an oath. See Heb. 6:17. But God must wait until the hour for fulfillment is fully come.

GENESIS 16:1-16

Abram's Son Ishmael. Poor Hagar! What contrasts met in her life! Bought in an Egyptian slave-mart, but destined to be the mother of a great people! She is not the last to suffer from the mistakes and sins of God's children, but she was abundantly recompensed. Abram did her a great wrong. Human policy will often suggest a course which seems right in our own eyes, but the end is death. How remarkable is the advice given to Hagar by the angel: return and submit! Does not the child of God often seek to evade the cross! "Let me but get away from this intolerable trouble," we cry. But God meets us. "No stranger he to all our wanderings wild!" We have to take up the cross and sit down again on the hard stool. Someday we shall be permitted to go out, but not until we have learned our lesson perfectly. In the meanwhile, we are assured that our life shall be prolific in great results. In an outburst of awe and joy, the slave-girl learned that God sees and hears. Note 2 Chron. 16:9; 1 Pet. 3:12.

GENESIS 17:1-14

God's Covenant with Abraham. At least thirteen years had passed since the promise of Isaac was first made, years of sorrow and discipline. But God had not forgotten. Always under such circumstances the eternal Voice bids us to walk before him and be perfect. Our surrender must be complete, our obedience absolute, our faith fixed steadfastly on the Promiser. So only can God fulfill his covenant, which includes fruitfulness, the salvation of our households, the inheritance and abundance of spiritual reproductiveness.

These promises were made to Abram, being yet uncircumcised, when he was yet a Gentile, proving that they were irrespective of any mere Hebrew interpretation. See Rom. 4:11. But the rite was the sign and seal of the national covenant with the Hebrew race. Spiritually it stands for the separation of the believer; and though as a religious rite it has existed only within Judaism, its spiritual significance is permanent. See Col. 2:11.

GENESIS 17:15-27

Isaac Is Promised. There are two allusions to laughter in these chapters. Sarah's was the laugh of incredulity, (Gen. 18:12). But Abraham's was the laugh of happy confidence which reckoned on God. As the R.V. puts it, he looked his difficulties in the face and then turned away to the promise of God and wavered not, but waxed strong, giving glory to God. Ponder Rom. 4:20, 21. Therefore, he obtained promises for his wife, for Ishmael, and for the coming child, which was to bear the name of "laughter," partly because of that hour and also because he would bring sunshine into the old man's life.

His heart had entwined about Ishmael. As he had watched the masterful and clever youth, he had said to himself, "He will hold the camp together when I am gone." But the divine covenant could not be with one that had slave-blood in his veins and was not to abide in the house forever. See John 8:35; Gal. 4:22. The covenant is always with Isaac.

GENESIS 18:1-15

Abraham Entertains Heavenly Visitors. The Son of God is the central figure here. He loves the homes of men. It has ever been his wont to visit the homes and hearts of those who love him. See Prov. 8:31. Abraham knew well that the High and Lofty One, who inhabits eternity, had come to dwell with him. Others might see only three men, but he recognized his divine friend, addressing him as "My Lord." And when the two angels went forward alone to do their awful work in Sodom, he entered into close converse with the wondrous central figure, who remained with him still.

He gave personal service, and so did Sarah. They gave their very best—"fine, tender, good." And in their love the Lord found satisfaction and rest. But remember that he still stands at the door and knocks. Ponder John 14:23; Rev. 3:20. Christ tells his secrets to those he loves. His proposals and promises are so great that we can almost laugh with incredulity, but the question of v. 14 is answered by Jer. 32:17. Reckon on God's faithfulness; he cannot fail those who trust him.

GENESIS 18:16-33

Abraham Pleads for Sodom. Christ had visited Abraham's tent, but he did more. He trusted him with his secrets, and led him almost unconsciously to a degree of faith and prayer that was far beyond what he had hitherto attained. Abraham *seemed* to be driving the Blessed One from point to point, but as a matter of fact he was being drawn forward. God's love and willingness to bless far exceeded Abraham's faith, and when he had gone as far as he dared, the divine love went farther and saved Lot from the overthrow.

We can never go into the realms of love and

compassion without finding the footsteps of the Redeemer. See Heb. 10:22. Amid all the mysteries of God's moral government we must always believe that he is just and righteous. His throne is encircled by the rainbow, but it is founded in unimpeachable integrity. How low Abraham lay in his self-estimate! They who know most of God do not presume on their knowledge, but esteem themselves the least of saints.

GENESIS 19:1–11

Angels with Lot in Sodom. This chapter withdraws the veil from the ministry of angels. The Lord of angels stayed with Abraham on the heights. He also, in future ages, was to descend into human Sodoms to seek and save the lost; but at present he delegated this work to angels until the fullness of the time was come. The visit of the angels was due to Abraham's prayer. How often do angels speed to our dear ones for whom we have prayed! To that ship laboring in the storm, to that deep, dark forest, to that new settlement, into the slums of that wicked city! Two Gospel references to this scene show how carefully it was being watched by the pure and holy eyes of the Son of man. In Matt. 11:23, 24, it seems as though he knew well those streets, and would gladly have passed through them, healing and saving. In Luke 17:28 he adds some further particulars of the careless unconcern of those who would not heed the warnings implied in the story of Genesis 14.

GENESIS 19:12–25

Sodom and Gomorrah Destroyed. It was a very weak nature that Heaven was so eager to rescue. Though described as a "righteous" man, Lot was a very weak one. He had pitched his tent toward Sodom, but apparently had been unable to resist its attractions and had gone to live within its precincts. It would almost appear that he had become one of its leading citizens. Therefore, his testimony for God was invalidated and worthless. He seemed as one that mocked, even to his own family.

How the angels must have loved this work. There were four people to be saved, and between them, in the human forms they had assumed, there were four hands—one for each. Is not this work in which we all should share? Let us hasten the lingerers! It is fatal to look behind. All our past is strewn with the memories of our sins and failures. There is but one hope. Escape to the cross of the Divine Redeemer! Take shelter in the cleft Rock of Ages! Hasten to the open arms of the Father!

GENESIS 19:26–38

Lot and His Daughters Rescued. God had mercy on Lot for Abraham's sake. A missionary told me that when, writing home to his mother, he narrated his miraculous deliverance from an infuriated mob, she replied by quoting a special entry in her diary to the effect that during those exact hours she was detained before God in a perfect agony of intercession for him. Lot was saved from Sodom, but took Sodom with him. He was saved so as by fire, but his lifework was burnt up. See 1 Cor. 3:15. Even his wife might have been saved, but her heart was inveterately wedded to the city.

In modern cities there are traces of the sins that doomed Sodom. Let us bear witness against them, that we may arrest inevitable judgment. Jude tells us that in the fate of these cities we have an example of eternal fire. Have a place where you stand before God. Only from that eminence can you venture to look out on the awful retribution of human rebellion.

GENESIS 20:1–18

Abraham Again Denies His Wife. It is amazing that Abraham should fall like this. He had walked with God for so many years and experienced so many deliverances that we would expect him to have reached an unassailable position. But the best of men are men at best; and God, who knows us better than we know ourselves, remembers that we are dust. He often steps in by his providence to intercept the full consequences of our wrongdoing, provided always that our heart is really true to him.

There is delightful reassurance in the words, "I withheld thee." God may have to chastise his children for their backslidings, but he will not hand them over to the will of their enemies, nor allow his covenant to fail. He rebukes kings for the sake of his people. See Psalm 105:14. There is a high-toned morality in some who are outside our Christian circles, which may put us to shame. It crops up in unexpected places, as here in Abimelech's remonstrance. It was terrible that he was compelled to address Abraham as in v. 9. God has direct dealings with such men, but they need our prayer and help. See vv. 3, 17.

GENESIS 21:1–8

Birth of Isaac. God is faithful. Heaven and earth may pass, but his word cannot fail. We may wait until all human hopes have died and then, at God's "set time," the child is born. Abraham laughed at the first announcement of this event (Gen. 17:17). Later, as Sarah listened to the conversation between her husband and his mysterious guests, she laughed with incredulity (18:12-15). But now, in the joy of long-deferred motherhood, she found that "the Lord had prepared laughter for her," and so named her child Isaac (see R.V. margin).

Be of good cheer. The Lord has prepared laughter for you also, some few miles ahead on life's journey. Light is sown for the righteous, and gladness for the upright. O you afflicted, he shall lay your stones in fair colors! And when your joy comes, rejoice in it. "Thou shalt rejoice in every good thing which the Lord thy God giveth thee." But in those hours think kindly of others, and do not forget that some, like Hagar, may be disappointed by what gives you joy!

GENESIS 21:9-21

Hagar and Ishmael Cast Out. Poor Hagar! She thought that she had given Abraham his heir, but now she found herself and her boy outcasts on the desert waste. The water soon spent, she little dreamed that a fountain was so near. Cry to God; he will open fountains in the midst of your deserts. Beneath their sad lot a divine purpose was running.

This is the teaching of Scripture: our lives are being ordered and our steps prepared. All we need to be anxious about is the finding of the path. Let us ask God to open our eyes to see the fountains beside us and the way before us. And after all, was not the wilderness a better training-ground for the lad than the comparative luxury of Abraham's tent? "He became an archer." Isaac would have been the better after a touch of the desert-life. The Holy Spirit, through Paul, gives the inner significance of this incident in Gal. 5:1. See also John 8:36.

GENESIS 21:22-34

Abraham and Abimelech Make a Covenant. Abimelech was impressed with Abraham's growing prosperity. He felt that it could not be explained on merely natural grounds. "God is with thee in all that thou doest." He sought, therefore, to secure the well-being of himself and his kingdom by forming an amicable treaty. Abraham immediately indicated that while willing to meet him, they must first have a clear understanding about a certain injustice which he had suffered. As our Lord taught afterward, he showed Abimelech his fault as between them alone (Matt. 18:15). The matter was easily adjusted by the king's frank disavowal of his servants' action. In lieu of written documents the seven lambs would be a perpetual sign and token of Abraham's claim to the well, henceforth known as Beersheba, "the well of the oath." The tamarisk was the second of these natural title-deeds. Wherever the religious man dwells he should pray, and leave behind him trees and wells.

GENESIS 22:1-13

Abraham Ready to Offer Isaac. Faith must be proved. Only in trial does she put forth her strength or dare the impossible. Satan tempts to bring forth the bad; God tests to call forth into exercise our highest and best. God went every step of the way with his servant, who was called into closer fellowship with himself than any other of the human race. Moriah was a miniature of Calvary, where God spared not his only Son.

Abraham's obedience was *immediate.* He arose early in the morning. It was *exact.* It was performed in the spirit of *worship.* It was *contagious,* for Isaac used the same expression to his father, as he to God—"Here am I." Apparently he had no need to acquaint Sarah with the object of his journey, he was so sure that the divine promise could not fail. He said to his young men, *"We* will come unto you." If it were necessary, he knew that God would raise him from the dead (Heb. 11:19). Isaac asked, "Where is the lamb?" John the Baptist answered in John 1:29.

GENESIS 22:14-24

The Promise Sealed with an Oath. It was only at the last moment that the ram was shown and substituted. It is when we get to the mount of sacrifice that God's deliverance is seen. It was when Pharaoh had almost overtaken Israel that their way was cleft through the Red Sea. It was in the early dawn that Jesus came walking on the water. The angel delivered Peter just before the time of his execution. God is never a moment too soon, or too late. What an outburst of blessing!

When we have obeyed God to the uttermost and glorified him in the fires, there is no limit to the fruitfulness or increase with which we shall become enriched. God puts his key into the hands of the faith that absolutely trusts him, saying, "Take what you will." Let us not forget that, as the children of Abraham by faith, we are his heirs and may reverently lay claim to a share in these glorious promises. See Gal. 3:9.

GENESIS 23:1-20

Abraham Buys a Burial Place. Death is an ever-constant reminder that this world is not our home. We rise up from before our dead to confess that we are only strangers and sojourners on the earth. Though the whole country, by God's deed and gift, belonged to Abraham, it had not as yet been made over; hence the necessity for this deliberate purchase with all the stately formalities of the leisured East. Abraham's insistence on buying this grave, and the care with which the negotiations were pursued, show that he realized that his descendants would come again into that land and possess it. It was as though he felt that he and Sarah should lie there awaiting the return of their children and their children's children. See also Gen. 49:29, 30. In the same way, the graves of martyrs and of missionaries who have fallen at the post of duty are the silent outposts that hold those lands for Christ, as the graves of the saints await the Second Advent.

GENESIS 24:1-9

A Wife Sought for Isaac. It is all-important that the children of God's people should marry only in the Lord. See 1 Cor. 7:39. Those who live in fellowship with him may confidently count on his help in this. Every marriage should be a matter for profound concern and much prayer, both for the parents of each, as well as for those that are to be wed. What wonder that so many marriages turn out to be a disappointment and a curse when they are entered upon so lightly and thoughtlessly!

In this graphic chapter we may find a close analogy to the work of the Holy Spirit, who has come forth during the present age to seek a bride for the Son of God; namely, the Church that he is gathering out of the world. There is always a "peradventure" that the soul may be unwilling at first, but he confronts it with overwhelming arguments, as we shall see.

GENESIS 24:10-27

Rebekah Meets Abraham's Servant. As we enter upon a new day, or a fresh undertaking, it is always wise and right to ask for good speed. Good speed is Godspeed. Praying times are not lost times. The reaper saves time when he stops to whet his scythe. Eliezer had learned a sincere respect for his master's piety and felt that his name had sure acceptance with God. How much more may we ask in the name of Jesus (John 14:13).

What a concentration of heaven-contrived circumstances gathered around this event! Abraham planning, the servant praying and waiting expectantly, the Angel of God leading, the very camels kneeling patiently beside the well as though they counted on the troughs being filled, the damsel coming at the precise hour! It is thus that all our daily life might be aglow with the presence and help of God. Such things take place, but, alas, our eyes are holden! Compare "prosper" in Gen. 24:21, 40, 42, 56 with Psalm 1:3. See Acts 10:17 also.

GENESIS 24:28-49

Abraham's Servant Fulfills His Mission. This worthy man was almost garrulous about his master. Count the number of times in which he contrives to introduce those two words, "my master." He put the errand on which he had come before his necessary food and poured out his story in a stream of crystal utterance of the highest eloquence. This identification of his thought and speech with his master's interests is full of teaching for us all. He could talk of nothing else, was only anxious not to fail for Abraham's sake, and took the favorable reply as kindness shown to him whom he represented. We, too, are called to be ambassadors, as though God did beseech men by us. If we are in the way of God's will, be sure that the Lord will not only lead, but lead "in the right way," and will create for us a sympathetic reception wherever we go.

GENESIS 24:50-67

Rebekah Marries Isaac. Rebekah's relatives recognized the hand of God in what had taken place and could not demur. The maiden herself was not asked, according to oriental custom, but in her readiness on the following morning to start forthwith, it was clear that her heart had been already won. This favorable reply prostrated Eliezer to the earth with thankfulness. Would that we were always as eager to praise as to pray. The precious gifts with which the whole family were enriched remind us of those gifts and graces with which the Holy Spirit, the Divine Wooer, enriches the soul that accepts his invitation to yield itself to the Divine Master, Christ. When her friends suggested delay, Rebekah would not hear of it. With his jewels on her person, the young girl longed to see the bridegroom himself. Her "I will go" settled the matter. The foretastes of our heavenly inheritance whet our appetite to see and be with him whom, not having seen, we love.

GENESIS 25:1-18

Abraham's Death and Burial. After being for sixteen years contemporary with his grandsons, Esau and Jacob, Abraham died without owning a foot of land except the cave for which he had paid, as a stranger might. But all was his. He was persuaded of God's faithfulness and earnestly reached out his hands toward the City with foundations. See Heb. 11:10. He was *full*. Those who had known him in Ur might have looked on his life as a huge failure and have spoken of him as a fanatic who had sacrificed all for nothing. But he was satisfied.

He was "gathered unto his people," a phrase which does not refer to the body, for his people were far away across the desert, but to the recognition and welcome that awaited him on the other side of death. His sons, Isaac and Ishmael, differed widely. The one dwelt by the well, engaged in pastoral pursuits, while the other lived by his own strong hand in the desert expanse. But they met in their common respect and grief. Births and deaths unite families.

GENESIS 25:19-34

Jacob and Esau, Twin Brothers. In the thought of that age, the birthright carried with it the spiritual leadership of the tribe. To be the priest of the family, to stand between the Most High and the rest of the household, to receive divine communications and execute the divine will, and to be in the direct line of the Messiah —such were some of the privileges that gathered around this position. They were nought in Esau's estimation, and he was quite content to part with all they implied, if only he might have the immediate gratification of appetite. The steaming fragrance of the lentil pottage was sweet in the nostrils of the hungry hunter.

We have all passed through such an experience. On the one hand, our self-respect, our true advantage, our God; on the other, passionate desire crying, "Give, give." In days and hours like that, beware. For you may say a word or do an act that shall determine your future, and like Esau you will find no loophole for altering the cast of the die. See Heb. 12:16, 17.

GENESIS 26:1-17

Isaac Is Blessed and Grows Rich. There was no harm in Isaac's going to Gerar, as he had a distinct command to that effect, vv. 2, 3. But he does not seem to have been strong enough to stand the test of residence there. He might have received into his soul that sufficient grace which is always within the reach of tempted men; but like so many of us, he looked down and not up. What could have been more reassuring than the promises of the divine presence and blessing! But he was guilty of incredible meanness to the woman who had come so far to be his wife, and of deceit to Abimelech.

Notice how the sins of the fathers repeat themselves in the children! It was a disappointing lapse from the glorious height on which he had stood when he yielded himself to God's call on Mount Moriah! But we have experienced the same contrasts within ourselves. Now on the mount of transfiguration, asking to live there, and then in the valley, quarreling for preeminence. But, notwithstanding all, God's lovingkindness does not fail. See v. 12.

GENESIS 26:18-35

Isaac's Wells and Covenant. It is interesting to follow Isaac in his well-digging. Let us also dig wells and set streams flowing which will bless men long after we have gone home to Heaven. The first well was *Esek*—"strife." The second, *Sitnah*—"hatred." The third, *Rehoboth*—"room." Thus is human life, too often, till it ends with *Sheba*—"oath or covenant." But even the outward repose to which life may attain, as the result of the struggles of earlier life, may be interrupted by anxiety and trial caused by children or grandchildren. Esau's marriage brought endless trouble in its train. And grief of mind will sow life with thorns.

Let children take care lest they give needless pain to those who love them. That which hurts tender and true hearts is not likely to carry with it the blessing of God. As soon as a wandering soul gets back to God, even his enemies make peace with him; he is at least secure from their hurt. See Proverbs 16:7.

GENESIS 27:1-17

Rebekah Plans to Cheat Isaac. This chapter narrates a sad story of the chosen family. Esau is the only character which elicits universal sympathy. Isaac appears to have sunk into premature senility. It seems hardly credible that he who had borne the wood for the offering on Mount Moriah, and had yielded himself so absolutely to the divine will, would have become so keen a sensualist. He could only be reached now through the senses. Perhaps this was due to the prosperity and smooth sailing of his life. It is better, after all, to live the strenuous life, with its uphill climb, than to rest in the ease of the valley.

The birthright had been already promised to Jacob, and there was no need for him to win it by fraud. And Rebekah was truly blameworthy in that she deceived her husband, showed partiality toward her children, and acted unworthily. Who would have expected that out of such a family God was about to produce the religious leaders of the world! Pharaoh would one day crave a blessing from those kid-lined hands!

GENESIS 27:18-29

Jacob Gets Esau's Blessing. It is better not to attempt to justify Jacob in this act of treachery. But we may learn the deep and helpful lesson that if God was able to make a saint out of such material as this, he also can take our poor lives with all their sin and failure and make something of them for his glory.

Notice how one lie led to another! Few who enter on a course of deception stop at one falsehood; and how terrible it was to add blasphemy to lying, as when he said that God brought him his quarry in the hunt. Luther wonders how Jacob was able to brazen it out, adding, "I should probably have run away in terror and let the dish fall."

Rebekah kept her son's garments well perfumed with the aromatic plants of Palestine, and their odor awoke the sleeping poetry and fire of the aged father. He compared them to a field of Paradise, filled with the sweet presence of God. Let us see to it that we carry everywhere the fragrance of Christ. See 2 Cor. 2:15.

GENESIS 27:30-45

Esau's Grief and Anger. Esau apparently had awakened to realize the value of the blessing of the birthright which he had treated so lightly. His exceeding great and bitter cry expressed the anguish of one who awakes to discover that he has forfeited the *best* for a trifle. But obviously he was only being held to his own original contract with Jacob.

There are similar events in all our lives when we take some irrevocable step under the sway of evil passion, and it affects the whole future. There is "no place for repentance"—i.e., no opportunity of altering the decisive effect of that act. See Heb. 12:17. We may obtain some lower and inferior blessing, as Esau did, acquiring something of the fatness of the earth and the dew of Heaven, living by our sword, and finally, after long years, shaking the yoke from our neck. But we can never be what we might have been! We can never undo that moment of sowing to the flesh. See Gal. 6:7, 8.

GENESIS 27:46—28:9

Jacob Sent Away from Home. Esau deferred the execution of his murderous purpose because of the near approach, as he supposed, of his father's death. But Isaac lived for forty years after this. Esau's secret purpose, however, became known to Rebekah. See Prov. 29:11.

The ostensible reason for Jacob's expatriation which Rebekah gave her husband was not the real one. He was sent to Haran, not primarily for a wife, but to escape his brother. Does not this constant duplicity explain the reason for Rebekah's heart-weariness? It seems probable that she never saw her favorite son again.

The benediction already pronounced on Jacob was repeated with greater amplitude and tenderness as he left his father's tent. Sad as he was at the inevitable separation, the star of hope shone in the sky, beckoning him onward. It was necessary that he should be taken from under his mother's influence into that greater world where, through pain and disappointment, he should become a prince with God. Often our nest is broken up that we may learn to fly.

GENESIS 28:10-22

Jacob's Vision at Bethel. This is the "ladder chapter," in which a wayward, weak man is seen holding fellowship with the Eternal God who loves us, notwithstanding our unworthiness, and desires to lead us into a life of power and blessedness. It is all wonderful! Notice the four "Beholds" (vv. 12-15).

Sunset. Overtaken on a moor by the swift fall of the oriental night, Jacob had no alternative than to sleep in the open. But he slept to see! *Night.* There is an open way between Heaven and earth for each of us. The movement of the tide and circulation of the blood are not more regular than the intercommunication between Heaven and earth. Jacob may have thought that God was local; now he found him to be omnipresent. Every lonely spot was his house, filled with angels. *Morning.* Worship, consecration, the vows of God. Put down your foot on God's promises. He will do more than he has said. You shall come to your Father's house in peace.

GENESIS 29:1-20

Jacob in Laban's Home. Well might Jacob "lift up his feet" (see margin). When we are sure of God, we receive strength that enables us to "run with patience the race that is set before us." The steps of a good man are ordered by the Lord, and we have a special claim on his guidance in our matrimonial alliances—the most solemn and momentous step of all. There were many good qualities in Rachel, fitting her to be a good wife. Her humility and industry, her patience under the oppression of the unmannerly shepherds, her haste to share her joy with her father—all these elicited Jacob's love.

What a touch of old-world and new-world poetry is in those words of verse 20! Where Love is queen, time is too short, labor never hard, distance never long, sacrifice unheard of! Oh, that we so loved our Lord that for the missionary toiling through long years and the invalid condemned to a life of pain, affliction might appear light and but for a moment.

GENESIS 29:21-35

Jacob Marries Leah and Rachel. The chief lesson of this paragraph is its illustration of the awful nemesis which accompanies wrongdoing. No thoughtful person can watch the events of history or experience without realizing that we are already standing before the judgment-seat of God, and that his sentences are in process of being executed. Jacob deceived his father, and was himself deceived. "With what measure ye mete, it shall be measured to you again."

What disappointments there are in life! We think that we are to be given Rachel, and lo! Leah is substituted. But in later days Jacob spoke of Reuben as his might, the beginning of his dignity and excellency. The names of Leah's sons suggest the blessings that accrue through heartbreak. For the Leahs of the world there are great compensations. God remembers and hears them. Brokenhearted and forsaken, they live again in the lives of those whom they have borne either naturally or spiritually.

GENESIS 30:1-24

Sons Born to Jacob. The details of this paragraph are given with great detail, because they concern the twelve sons of Jacob, the forefathers of Israel. After all, history is made in the nursery, and we are very much what our mothers have made us in the formative years. An old Spanish proverb says, "An ounce of mother is worth a pound of clergy." Leah's influence on her boys, as judged by their subsequent life, was anything but healthy. Yet with Jacob being the man he was, there was poor chance for them to realize the highest ideals.

Rachel's anguish of heart led her to earnest prayer. Compare vv. 1, 22. Wait on God, anguished ones; you shall surely have reason to praise him. Was it not worth waiting for, to bear a Joseph, whose branches were to run over the wall in blessing? There are more compensations in life than we think. If Rachel had her husband's love, Leah had a large family of boys. In the saddest lives there are glints of sunshine.

GENESIS 30:25-43

Jacob's Flocks Increase. There is little in this story to the credit of Jacob, and nothing to choose between him and Laban. They are well matched one against another; and if anything, Jacob excelled in cunning. The heir of the promises (Jacob) deals with the child of this world (Laban) on principles which men of honor refuse to use. We feel inclined to pity Laban, who had never seen the angel-ladder or shared the great promises which had surrounded the path of his relative. He trusted this man of the chosen tribe, but was to be woefully deceived.

But are there not many professing Christians who are playing Jacob's part today? While holding high positions in the religious world, they stoop to practices to which men of the world would be no parties. We hear but little more of Laban, but Jacob is destined to pass through the fire of trouble, by which the dross will be consumed and his soul made white and pure.

GENESIS 31:1-21

Jacob Leaves Laban. Jacob was a remarkable mixture. He had an eminently religious nature and had intimate dealings with God. Note vv. 3, 5, 7. But he grossly misrepresented God's dealings with him when he gave his wives the reasons on which he proposed flight. Note vv. 9-13. So the flesh and spirit struggle for mastery within us all, and only as the grace of God enters our hearts can we come into the absolute supremacy of the spiritual and divine (Gal. 5:17).

The secret departure was very undignified and unworthy of the heir of the promises. The command to return was of God, and what he commands he becomes responsible for. Besides, had not the Almighty promised to keep him in all places? See 28:15. When we are on God's plan, we may reckon on him absolutely.

GENESIS 31:22-42

The Dispute between Laban and Jacob. These chapters afford a remarkable insight into God's forbearance. He knew what was in Jacob's heart, and could see all its weakness and deceit. There was not a thought in his heart or a word on his tongue, but God knew them altogether. Yet God cast the mantle of forgiveness and defense around this most unworthy soul, bidding Laban not to speak to him either good or bad. Indeed, in a later book we are told, "He hath not beheld iniquity in Jacob, neither hath he seen perverseness in Israel." Not that the holy God was unaware of the evil traits in his child, but he refused to dwell on them or to allow himself to be turned away from his purposes of grace. Rachel secretly carried with her the teraphim, which wrought evil throughout the home in later years, as we shall see. The "fear of Isaac" (v. 42) was on Jacob's lips, but too little of it in his character and surroundings!

GENESIS 31:43-55

The Covenant between Jacob and Laban. In our time covenants are engrossed on parchment, so that there may be written documentary evidence accessible to prove that certain transactions have taken place. Then the same object was accomplished (the art of writing confined to the few) by the erection of monuments whose existence was associated with the agreements into which men had entered with one another.

Though these two men were far below the Christian ideal of character, it is evident that they lived in an habitual recognition of God and the eternal sanction of his presence. The Lord was to watch between them. God was to be witness and judge. They looked back on the days of Abraham with reverential awe and loyalty, and commemorated Abraham's God.

GENESIS 32:1-12

Jacob Fears to Meet Esau. Before we encounter our Esaus, we are sure to meet God's angels. If only our eyes are not held shut, we shall perceive them. The world is full of angel help! There are more for us than against us! The Captain of the Lord's hosts is as near us as he was to Joshua, and his squadrons await our cry. "Thinkest thou," said our Lord, "that I cannot beseech my Father, and he shall even now send more than twelve legions of angels!"

In times of trial we run to God and are justified in claiming his protection, so long as we can show that we are on his plan and doing his will. It was the news brought by his messengers of Esau's approach that elicited from Jacob this marvelous prayer; but his prayer did not prevent him making what plans he could for the safety of his dear ones.

GENESIS 32:13-32

Jacob Wrestles and Prevails. There is a flattery in Jacob's address to Esau which sounds inconsistent with the noblest manhood and the firmest faith. Why should he speak of "my lord" Esau and endeavor to appease his wrath with soft speeches and rich gifts? Evidently much had to be effected in Jacob's character before he could become one of the great spiritual forces of the world, and his supreme discipline came in that midnight wrestle.

The Angel who wrestled with him could have been none other than the Son of man, who is also the Angel of the Covenant and Son of God. It was not that Jacob wrestled with the Angel, but that the Angel wrestled with him, as though to discover and reveal his weakness, and to constrain him to quit reliance on his own strength and to learn to cling with the tenacious grip of a lame man who dare not let go, lest he fall to the earth. Ah, it is well to be maimed, if through the withered thigh we may learn to lay hold on the everlasting strength of God and learn his secret Name!

GENESIS 33:1-17

Jacob and Esau Reconciled. Many things, like this meeting with Esau, are worse in anticipation than in actuality. The brothers were on the same old terms as before that filching of Isaac's blessing. The holy transactions of the previous night had induced this change in the atmosphere. If our ways please the Lord, he will make our enemies to be at peace with us. We must win power with God, by yielding to him, before we can have power with our Esaus and prevail.

When you fear man's wrath, do not run hither and thither for defense; be still and fear not. Commit your way to the Lord and read Psalm 37. When the enemy comes in like a flood, the Lord shall lift up a standard against him. Surely Jacob needed not to fear, or make these lame excuses and promises. He never intended to go to Esau, to Seir. As soon as the last ranks of his brother's men were lost in the desert haze, he turned to go in the contrary direction. This duplicity was not worthy of the heir of the promises; but too many of us would have done the same, even on the morrow of the Jabbok-wrestle.

GENESIS 33:18—34:17

Jacob with the Shechemites. Jacob was tempted by the fat pastures of Shechem, without thought or care of the character of its people, and he lived to bitterly rue his choice. How many religious parents have made the same mistake! They first encamp near the world, pitching their tent doors in that direction; then they buy a parcel of land, and finally their children contract alliances that end in shame and disaster. He who came of a pilgrim race, and to whom the whole land had been given by promise, bought real estate right next to Shechem, one of the worst cities in the country.

Like Lot, Jacob bid high for wealth and worldly advancement, risked the highest for the lowest, and was saved as by fire. Poor Dinah! Yet she was more sinned against than sinning. Jacob had put her in jeopardy by his selfish policy; and Leah was not blameless, for she had let her go unwarned and unaccompanied into the midst of that furnace of trial.

GENESIS 34:18–31

Jacob's Sons Spoil the Shechemites. It is not easy to steer our family life amid the rocks and quicksands of present-day worldliness; but we shall not prosper by using the world's weapons of duplicity and craft. The true way is to make our homes so attractive that our children will not be tempted to court the alliances that are offered by those whose only portion is in this life. Our Ruths would not leave our fields if we dropped more handfuls on purpose for them.

The treachery of these two brethren was absolutely inexcusable. On his deathbed Jacob reverted to it, and pronounced their scattering in Israel. Though Levi undid that curse by his obedience and devotion, Simeon seems to have made no effort in that direction and soon became as water absorbed by the desert sands. But see Rev. 7:7. What an awful thing it is when our conduct is such as to make religion offensive to those who observe our behavior (verse 30).

GENESIS 35:1–15

Jacob Blessed at Bethel. Thirty years before, Jacob was at Bethel. Life was young then. He had only his staff. The future was unshaped and unknown. It was on the occasion of his first night from home, and he made many vows. How much had happened since then! Marriage, prosperity, children! But he had drifted down the stream and had traveled into the far country from God. It was well that he should get back to Bethel and consider the whole story of his life, as you may trace a river from source to mouth from an overlooking hill. The divine summons is always bidding us be clean and change our garments, and be rid of idols.

There God gave Jacob the great new name of Israel and took to himself the reassuring name of El-Shaddai. It was as though, as the Almighty, he pledged himself to realize the highest and best. Let us take heart! God will make us fruitful, will give us the land, and will ward off the results of our misdeeds (v. 5).

GENESIS 35:16—36:8

Jacob's Sons; Esau's Sons; Isaac's Death. From Bethel to Bethlehem is not far. The one, the "house of God"; the other, the "house of Bread." We need them both if we are to bear up under the repeated shocks of life, such as the death of the old nurse Deborah, the death of our beloved Rachels, the sins of our children, and the breakup of the old home, as when our father is borne to his grave. Well was it for Jacob that he had got right with God before these repeated waves broke over him.

Isaac had not lived a great life, but his full years gave him a claim on the veneration of his sons, who forgot their jealousies and feuds as they stood together at his bier. But how greatly men misjudge death. It is not the end, but the beginning. We find hereafter Isaac associated with Abraham and Jacob, as welcoming the saints homeward. Death makes good men great.

GENESIS 37:1–11

Joseph Loved and Hated; His Dreams. It is a mistake for parents to show favoritism; but we can hardly wonder at Jacob's partiality for the lad, who reminded him so vividly of the beloved Rachel. Besides, there was a purity and an elevation of spirit in Joseph that stood out in welcome contrast to the coarse brutality and impurity of the others. He was separate from his brethren (49:26). The coat of many colors was, as the RV margin indicates, a long garment of delicate texture with sleeves, fitting for young princes or nobles, who were not called to the menial toil of the field or household.

The dreams of youth are proverbial and prophetic. In this case it would have been wiser for the lad to have kept his secrets locked in his own heart, though it was a tribute to his childlike simplicity and innocence that he disclosed them. The suggestion of coming greatness aroused his brothers' sharpest envy, but the hands of the Mighty One upheld the lad (49:23, 24).

GENESIS 37:12–24

Joseph's Brothers Plot His Death. Throughout, Joseph was a very remarkable type of our Lord. There was, first, this mission of the beloved son to inquire after the well-being of his brethren, which reminds us so vividly of the advent of God's beloved and only begotten Son, who brought us the Father's greeting and came to see and know by personal inquiry how we fared. Dothan was in the northern portion of the land, and the journey must have taken time and strength; but he persisted until he found them and came where they were.

Their plot against their helpless brother was as the plot of Caiaphas and the rest against our Lord. Pilate knew that for envy they had delivered him into his hands. The pit was one of those rock-hewn cisterns that abound in Palestine, and as there was no water in it Joseph's life

GENESIS

was not sacrificed. There he awaited what was a kind of resurrection. The scene at the pit's mouth was never forgotten by the others (42:21, 22).

GENESIS 37:25–36

Joseph Sold into Egypt. It was not chance, but providence that brought these Midianites to the pit at that hour. They had, of course, fixed their time of departure from their native land, the pace at which their camels were to travel, and the amount of time which they would spend at the fairs and markets *en route*, quite irrespectively of all other considerations but their own profit and convenience. Yet quite unconsciously they were moving according to a divine timetable. Everything in life is directed, superintended, and controlled by divine forethought. Let us live in constant recognition of this!

You may be in a pit of dark misery, but God knows that you are there and times the moments. Only continue to trust and do not be afraid! Blessed are they that believe; to them there shall be precise provision. Months ago a caravan started, which will arrive at the precise hour when intervention will best serve you.

GENESIS 39:1–18

Joseph in Potiphar's House. Ungodly families and employers owe more than they realize to the presence in their homes and businesses of those who love God; for God comes with his servants. See vv. 2, 21, 23, and Acts 7:9. But those who would enjoy that accompanying Presence must resist and overcome the appeals of the flesh. Days of outward prosperity are those in which we are most keenly tempted. The most venomous serpents coil in the damp heat of tropical forests. When temptation and opportunity meet, our case is hard indeed. At such times only God's grace can hold us back.

As temptation presents itself again and again, it gives us opportunities of continued growth in strength and grace. Joseph had probably wrought out his noble answer in his own secret heart and had lived by it, weeks before he flashed it forth. In the critical hour the mouth blurts out what the heart has been meditating. They who can rule themselves will be presently trusted to rule others.

GENESIS 39:19—40:8

Joseph Fares Well in Prison. These two men remind us of the two thieves crucified beside our Lord; to the one he was a savor of life, to the other of death. Jeremy Taylor says that he must be in love with peevishness who chooses to sit down on his little handful of thorns when there are so many causes that call for him. Wherever in the world we are, there is a fellowship of sad and lonely hearts for us to cultivate. Like Joseph, let us set about helping others, and so find solace and help for ourselves. We must move in and out among our fellows with "a glorious morning face." Keep your sorrows for your Lord and yourself, but learn from your own experiences how to comfort those who are in any sorrow by the comfort with which you yourself have been comforted of God. How quick Joseph was to detect the added anxiety on the two faces! It was because he had known similar experiences. See 2 Cor. 1:4.

GENESIS 40:9–23

Joseph Interprets Two Dreams. Joseph as an interpreter was one in a thousand. Because his pure heart was open to God, he could unriddle the mysteries of human life. Very often those who walk with God can solve and explain the dark riddles of human life for the less enlightened. Joseph was keenly alive to God's presence. It filled the prison with glory. He knew that thence must come all their hope and expectation; and God was "in the shadow, keeping watch above his own." He was contriving and superintending the chain of events which were to set his young servant on the throne. Man had despised and rejected him, but God had already prepared for him a position of honor and usefulness, to which his ministry to these men was as rungs in the upward ladder.

Do not neglect small acts of ministry. Faithfulness in the very little leads to the throne-life. The butler's forgetfulness reminds us of our shameful forgetfulness of the Redeemer, who has brought us up out of the pit and redeemed us with precious blood. Yet he said: "This do in remembrance of me."

GENESIS 41:1–13

Pharaoh Dreams of Cattle and of Ears of Grain. This chapter tells of ascension and exaltation, and affords an inimitable type of our Lord's humiliation and death. Like Joseph, he went and preached to spirits in prison, and then God highly exalted him and gave him a name above every name. Rejected by his brethren, refused by those to whom he was sent, falsely accused and condemned, classed with the wicked, thrust into prison, rescuing one of his poor associates, called to a throne—it would be possible in almost every particular to substitute the name of Jesus for that of Joseph. What a corroboration of those great words of Asaph, "For promotion cometh neither from the east, nor from the west, nor from the south. But God is the judge" (Psalm 75:6, 7). When sorrow falls, how quickly the world remembers the child of God and turns to him! Those that despise and forget will seek you out some day.

GENESIS 41:14–36

Pharaoh's Dreams Interpreted. Notwithstanding the great urgency of the royal summons, and the speed with which the great events of his life crowded on one another, Joseph was kept in perfect peace. He found time to shave and to change his raiment. Let us be at rest in God. He that believeth does not make needless haste.

One of the loveliest traits in Joseph's character was his humility. He did not take on airs, nor assume superiority, nor pose as a superior and injured person. He said simply, "It is not in me; God will give." These words might have been uttered by our Lord; they are so perfectly in harmony with the tenor of his life. Surely we should appropriate them. At the best we are but God's almsgivers, passing on to others the good things of which he has made us the stewards. Joseph was set on using all he had, not for himself, but for others; therefore he had more and more to give.

GENESIS 41:37–57

Joseph, Exalted, Prepares for Famine. The Spirit of God was evidently in Joseph, but so far from rendering him a mere visionary it made him eminently practical. Have your visions of God, but descend from your housetop to answer the men who knock at your door! See Acts 10. In this story we see reflected the glories of our Lord, who was raised to the throne to become a Prince and a Savior, the Giver of the bread of life to the perishing souls of men. But he distributes without money and without price!

Joseph's marriage to an Egyptian bride reminds us of our Lord's union with the Gentile Church, on the significance of which Paul so strenuously insists. If you live for God, he will see to your interests. Such joy will be yours that you will forget your sorrows (Manasseh) and become fruitful in the land of affliction (Ephraim).

GENESIS 42:1–17

Joseph Sees His Ten Brothers. The true interpretation of Joseph's treatment of his brethren is to be found in the supposition that he repeated toward them, as nearly as possible, the behavior that they had shown to himself at the pit's mouth, and this with no thought of retaliation, but that their consciences might be awakened, and that he might discover if they would deal differently with Benjamin than they had dealt with him. He needed to be sure of their repentance before he could trust himself to them again. His purpose, therefore, was in part secured when he heard them saying to each other in the dear old home-tongue, which they never expected him to understand, "We are verily guilty because of our brother."

So God deals with us. The east wind blows bitterly in our faces, the famine is behind, and the harsh governor before. All these things are hard to bear; but behind them is the tenderest love, which struggles with its tears and is only eager to get us right before entrusting itself to us.

GENESIS 42:18–38

Simeon Held; the Others Sent Home. The behavior of this great Egyptian official—for so the brethren deemed him—must have seemed very hard and tyrannical to the trembling shepherds from the far land of Canaan. They had no idea that he understood what they said, and turned away to weep. But we can read his inner meaning. He must secure their return, so he kept Simeon bound. He wanted to see the beloved Benjamin, and to test their behavior to him, so he threatened that they should not see his face unless their youngest brother accompanied them. He gave to them kindly care in the gift of provisions and the return of their money. It was natural that the old father heard their story with failing heart—"All these things are against me." Nay, in all these things was the life of the Spirit, and in all these things we are more than conquerors. See Rom. 8:37.

> *Judge not the Lord with feeble sense,*
> *But trust him for his grace;*
> *Behind a frowning providence*
> *He hides a smiling face.*

GENESIS 43:1–15

The Brothers Return with Benjamin. Joseph, in giving corn to save his own brethren and the Egyptians from starvation, is a type of our Lord, who gives the bread of life to Jew and Gentile—to all that come to him in their hopeless need. And in this return of the full money in the sacks we are reminded that salvation is without money and without price. Whatever we bring to enrich Christ, he returns to us. His gifts are all of his unmerited grace and favor.

Very often we move forward with dread into the unknown; but that dread is the child of ignorance. If only we realized that love is waiting for us there, which does not ask for balm and honey, for spices and myrrh, but just for ourselves, how much happier life would become! Lift up your hearts; a feast awaits you!

GENESIS 43:16-34

Joseph Feasts His Brothers. Our Savior, of whom Joseph was such a striking emblem, knows all about us. Though we may fear him with a great fear, he is providing for us with a thoughtful tenderness which adapts itself to our every need. There is water for traveled feet; the benediction of peace for troubled hearts; a feast for hungry souls; tears of love for Benjamin; and a consideration of our very sitting at his table, which reveals his perfect knowledge of us. He waits to manifest himself, as he does not to the world. The only thing that can separate is unconfessed sin. But just so soon as this is put away, the floodgates are opened and heart commingles with heart. Do not his mercies lead us to repentance?

GENESIS 44:1-17

Joseph's Cup in Benjamin's Sack. It is a terrible revelation when our Benjamins are found possessed of the cup. They have been so loved, so favored, so screened; they have never been guilty of the excesses of Reuben and Judah; they have given no rise to evil reports, like the sons of Bilhah and Zilpah, 37:2. Now when *they* are convicted of sin, the surprise of their brethren is only equaled by their own remorse. This accounts for the soul agony of men like Cyprian, Augustine, Bunyan, and Spurgeon.

What transitions there are in life! At the close of the previous chapter the brothers were as happy as they could be, and here plunged into the deepest anguish. But the intensity of their pain and sorrow, like fire, melted and cleansed them, and prepared for the great reconciliation.

GENESIS 44:18-34

Judah Pleads for Benjamin. No portion in Genesis would be more suitable for Good Friday. Judah's proposal to give himself instead of Benjamin reminds us of him who freely gave himself up for us all. It was with such love, but of infinite intensity, that Christ loved us. In Judah's words we find the loftiest type of pleading which man has ever put forth for man. It is extraordinary to get this glimpse of the strong and noble emotions that slumber in hearts where we should least expect them! But these words are poor and cold compared with those that Jesus utters on our behalf. It must have required extraordinary self-command on Joseph's part to make his brethren suffer thus. But he dared to enforce it, because he knew the goal they were approaching. Christ often turns aside to hide his sorrow at our griefs, which are the necessary pathway to where all tears are wiped away.

GENESIS 45:1-15

Joseph Makes Himself Known to His Brothers. It may be that we have here an exact representation of a scene which shall be transacted some day, when our Lord makes himself known to his brethren, the Jews. The Apostle Paul tells us that ultimately all Israel shall be saved; and may not this be brought about when Christ says to them, "I am Jesus, your brother, whom you delivered up and denied in the presence of Pilate"? Was not Joseph's wife rejoiced by his joy, and will not the Church of the redeemed be glad when that great reconciliation takes effect?

What a beautiful interpretation Joseph put on their act of treachery—"God did send me before you." Let us always trace God's plan in the malevolence and opposition of men. They could have no power at all unless it were given them from above. Joseph supplied all their needs—wagons to carry, food to nourish, raiment to clothe, and greetings to welcome!

GENESIS 45:16-28

Joseph Sends for His Father. This is an Easter lesson. It must have seemed to Jacob and his children as though Joseph were indeed risen from the dead. Hardly more startling were the appearances of the risen Lord than the news carried back to Jacob that his long-lost and much-mourned son was the prime minister of Egypt. Joseph had not forgotten his father. His one desire was to bring him to share his glory. For this he sent the wagons to transport the whole family to his side. At first Jacob was incredulous. It seemed too good to be true. But when he saw the wagons that Joseph had sent, that touch of delicate thoughtfulness, in such striking contrast to the cheerless isolation and loneliness of the last few years, caused his aged spirit to revive. Let us talk of the glory of our risen and ascended Lord, and specially of his desire that where he is we may be also. Now let us thank him that he is not only willing to receive us, but provides the grace and help of the Spirit to transport us thither.

GENESIS 46:1-27

Jacob and His Family Go to Egypt. Evidently Joseph's invitation to his father to come to him in Egypt aroused very earnest questionings in Jacob's soul. Was it a wise step for him to take? Perhaps he remembered what we read in Genesis 15:13 and dreaded to take the risk. Under these circumstances he went to Beersheba, "the well of the oath," so intimately associated with the lives of Abraham and Isaac, and from which he had gone forth on his life's pilgrimage. There he offered special sacrifices and received special directions and promises. He was not only to go down into Egypt, but to go there under divine guidance and protection.

When we visit Egypt at our own impulse we shall land ourselves, as Abraham and Isaac did, in temptation and failure; but when God bids us go, we may make the journey with absolute impunity. Though we walk through the dark valley, we need not fear, if he be with us.

GENESIS 46:28—47:12

Pharaoh Welcomes Joseph's Relatives. What a meeting between father and son! If the old man were sitting in the corner of the lumbering wagon, weary with the long journey, how he must have started up when they said, "Joseph is coming!" What pathos there is in the expression, "wept a good while," as though the long pent-up streams took a long time to exhaust themselves. Had Joseph been less noble he might have shrunk from introducing his lowly relatives to the mighty Pharaoh! But such thoughts were submerged in the great love which claimed that withered, aged, halting man as his father. Let us never be ashamed of our Savior, who has done more for us than even Jacob for his sons. The confession that the days of his pilgrimage had been few and evil is set to a sad minor chord; and to the superficial gaze Esau had enjoyed a much more prosperous career. But when Jacob stood before Pharaoh, the mighty monarch recognized his moral supremacy and bent beneath his benediction. Surely the lesser is blessed of the greater. Here was the harvest of Jacob's tears!

GENESIS 47:13-26

Egyptians Saved in Famine. The slender stores of the Egyptians were soon exhausted, and had it not been for Joseph the streets would have been filled with the dying and dead. His Egyptian name means "the savior of the world"; and the confession of the Egyptians proved how true it was: "Thou hast saved our lives."

How closely the parallel holds! Joseph rose from the pit and the prison to save his brethren as well as the myriads of his adopted fellow-countrymen. Jesus rose from the grave to be a Prince and a Savior. Joseph's bread cost him nothing, while Jesus gave us that which cost him Calvary. Joseph sold his corn for money; our Lord gave himself without money or price. You may go to him without reluctance, though your sack is empty and you have no money in your hand; but he will give and give again, without stint.

GENESIS 47:27—48:7

Joseph Visits His Dying Father. How inexorable is the *must* of death! For many years Jacob had exceeded the ordinary span of human life, and now, like the last apple on the tree, he must be gathered. For seventeen years he had been familiar with Egypt's splendid temples, obelisks, and pyramids. He had been surrounded with all the comforts that filial love could devise; but nothing could make him forget that distant cave in the land of Canaan. In his judgment Egypt's most splendid pyramid was not to be compared with that humble sepulchre where the mortal remains of Abraham and Sarah, of Isaac and Rebekah, and of the faithful Leah awaited his. On Joseph's second visit he was weaker, and with an effort nerved himself for the interview. The angel-ladder and Rachel's death stood prominently before the dying eyes. When he returned from this pathetic reverie he turned to the two boys who stood awestruck beside him and adopted them, for their beloved father's sake.

GENESIS 48:8-22

Jacob Blesses Joseph's Sons. By his act in blessing them, Jacob reversed the verdict of birth and gave the younger the birthright. Probably there were qualities in Ephraim which naturally put him in the foremost place. The Bible is full of hope for younger sons. He spoke of the Angel, Jehovah, so often referred to in the Old Testament, and who can be no other than the Son of God. He also is *our* Shepherd, Guardian, and Friend. He will feed and tend us all our life long. He will redeem us from all evil and bring us to a blessed end in peace. Be of good cheer! He cared for you in your helpless infancy and will do no less in your helpless old age. If any lads hear this portion read, let them notice that old Jacob prayed God to bless the lads. Evidently then, no little lad is too small for God to notice and bless! Though the fathers die, God lives and will bring us again to "the land of your fathers."

GENESIS 49:1-12

Jacob Foretells the Future of His Sons. Once more Joseph visited his father's deathbed. This was the third time and the last. He stood as one of twelve strong bearded men, gathered around the aged form, whose face was shadowed by death but aglow with the light of prophecy. How intense their silent awe as they heard their names called one by one by the old man's trembling voice, speaking with difficulty! The character of each was delineated with unerring insight, the outstanding incidents of their past history enumerated, and their future forecasted. The scene was an anticipation of the final judgment, where men shall hear their lives reviewed and the sentence passed. "Shiloh" means Peace-giver. What a fragrant name for our Lord! What wonder that he shall gather the nations to his cross and throne!

GENESIS 49:13-27

Joseph Specially Blessed. The position of Zebulun and the following tribes in the land of promise is accurately foretold. Compare the allotments of Joshua 18. Notice the exclamation of the dying man in v. 18. Such a spirit of waiting cannot be disappointed. See Isaiah 26:8, 9. Joseph's blessing is preeminently beautiful: "Fruitful!" This is mentioned twice, reminding us of John 15:8. But fruitfulness is only possible where there is the *wall* for separation, and the *well* for communion. When these are present, the branches droop over the wall with clusters of blessings to a thirsty world. Let us seek divine strength and ask that the mighty hands of the God of Jacob may be placed under our own poor weak hands! See Psalm 144:1. The separated life is the crowned life. To the heart of the dying man came the memory of his native land and its mountains. What mountains are to a country, God is to his people!

GENESIS 49:28—50:3

Jacob's Last Directions and Death. Jacob gave a final charge as to his burial in Machpelah—that his dust at least should be there to welcome his children and his children's children when they came thither in due course, as God had promised. Then the weary pilgrim gathered up those tired feet, which had paced out their last mile, into the bed and gave up his spirit to God. When we are told that he was gathered to his people, it must mean more than that his dust mingled with their dust in the place of burial. There are great gatherings of loving friends awaiting us on the other side. See Heb. 11:40. At the ladder-scene in Bethel, God had told him that he would not leave him till he had done what he promised, and surely not one good thing had failed. Life may be hard and sad, but God will end it rightly. Be of good cheer; trust God.

GENESIS 50:4-14

Jacob Mourned and Buried. The days of mourning for Jacob were only two less in number than for a king. Three hundred miles were traversed by that splendid funeral cavalcade, which included not only the family of Israel, but the magnates of Egypt. The words, "beyond Jordan" (v. 10), indicate that this book was finished on the further side of Jordan, where Moses afterward died.

The evident grief with which the precious remains were laid beside the great dead reminds us that when God wills to do honor to any servant of his, he can secure it in remarkable ways—and ways which are entirely independent of human methods and reasonings. "Precious in the sight of the Lord is the death of his saints." At birth he cared for your helpless body; when you die he will see to its sepulchre. The bones of the saints hold the earth for the ultimate reign of Christ!

GENESIS 50:15-26

Joseph Loves Until His Death. The fear of Joseph's brethren illustrates the insecurity of a position which is conceded only at the bidding of the tender caprice of love, apart from satisfaction based on satisfied justice. As Joseph had pardoned, so he might retract his pardon. No satisfaction, beyond tears, had been rendered for that faraway sin. Might he not even now require it! So fears might legitimately arise in our own hearts, had not divine forgiveness been based on the finished work of the cross!

How significant that sentence: "God meant it unto good!" There are *meanings* in life. Things do not happen by chance, and what happens is meant for good. All things work together for good for them that love God.

Ninety-three years had passed since he was lifted from the pit; sixty since he buried his father. Finally Joseph's end came. His bones were not buried, but awaited the summons for the Exodus. That coffin seemed to be the end of all. Nay! It was the seed of the coming harvest.

THE BOOK OF EXODUS

THE NATION DELIVERED AND ORGANIZED

INTRODUCTION *1:1–7*

I. ISRAEL IN EGYPT *1:8—12:36*
   A. Oppression *1:8–22*
   B. The deliverer raised up and called *2:1—4:31*
   C. The plagues and the Passover *5:1—12:36*

II. FROM EGYPT TO SINAI *12:37—18:27*
   A. The departure *12:37–42*
   B. The laws of the Passover and of the firstborn *12:43—13:22*
   C. The passage of the Red Sea and the song of deliverance *14:1—15:19*
   D. Marah, Elim, and the manna *15:20—16:36*
   E. Murmuring; victory; Jethro's visit *17:1—18:27*

III. ISRAEL AT SINAI *19:1—40:38*
   A. The covenant proposed and the people prepared *19:1–25*
   B. The Ten Commandments and other laws *20:1—23:33*
   C. Ratification of the covenant of the Law *24:1–11*
   D. Moses in the Mount; directions for the Tabernacle *24:12—31:18*
   E. The golden calf; penalty; Moses' intercession *32:1—33:23*
   F. Moses again in the Mount; the covenant renewed *34:1–35*
   G. Construction and erection of the Tabernacle *35:1—40:38*

INTRODUCTION

The word means "going out," and was given by the Greek translators, as in the case of Genesis.

The book embraces 145 years, and may be divided into three principal parts: (1) The deliverance of Israel from Egypt: 1:1—12:36. (2) The journey to Sinai: 12:37—18:27. (3) The manifestation of God's will for his people, especially in the legislation of Sinai: 19:1—40:38.

Its authorship by Moses is distinctly asserted by our Lord. See Mark 12:26; Luke 20:37. The parallel between the pilgrimage of the hosts of Israel and the experiences of the soul is obvious and instructive, and we do well to read it with this parallel in mind; but the book is also of the greatest historical importance, and the increasing knowledge of Egyptian customs and of the conditions of life in the Sinaitic peninsula confirm the exactness and accuracy of the narrative. It could only have been written by one who, like Moses, had an intimate acquaintance with both Egypt and the wilderness.

COMMENTARY

EXODUS 1:1-14

The Children of Israel Afflicted. The buried seed began to bear an abundant harvest, notwithstanding the efforts of Pharaoh and his people. The kings of the earth take counsel together to thwart the divine purpose. They might as well work to arrest the incoming tide. The days of persecution and opposition have always been the growing days of the Church.

The new king probably belonged to a great dynasty, intent on preventing the recurrence of shepherd domination. The first move of the new policy was to embitter Israel's existence by cruel bondage. The pictured walls of the Pyramids bear witness to sufferings inflicted on slaves of a Hebrew cast of face by taskmasters armed with whips. Pharaoh and his counselors had to learn that they were not only dealing with a subject nation, but with the Eternal God.

EXODUS 1:15-22

God Protects Hebrew Babes from Pharaoh's Decree. Egypt's second stroke of policy was to begin with the children. Pharaoh and Herod set us an example in turning their attention to young life. There is nothing which so closely and instantly touches national well-being as the treatment of the children.

It is wonderful to notice what unexpected instruments God uses to defeat the purposes of his enemies. Of all people these two women seemed the unlikeliest. It may be that these two women were Egyptians who had recently learned to fear God; but if so, their conduct was even more remarkable. God, who makes of soft sand a strong barrier against the billows, can restrain man's wrath by the humblest instruments. You may be obscure and weak, but if you fear God he will make use of you, write your name in the book of life, and multiply your spiritual children.

EXODUS 2:1-10

Moses Preserved by Pharaoh's Daughter. When matters had reached their worst in respect to Israel's condition, God was preparing a deliverer. The child was more than ordinarily beautiful, Acts 7:20. His parents hid him by faith, Heb. 11:23. Perhaps they had received a special revelation of his great future, on the strength of which they became strong to resist the royal command. They launched the ark, not on the Nile only, but on God's providence. He would be captain, steersman, and convoy of the tiny bark. Miriam stood to watch. There was no fear of fatal consequences, only the quiet expectancy that God would do something worthy of himself. They reckoned on God's faithfulness, and they were amply rewarded when the daughter of their greatest foe became the babe's patroness. See Psalm 76:10.

EXODUS 2:11-25

Moses Slays an Egyptian and Flees to Midian. Amid all the allurements of Pharaoh's court, the heart of Moses beat true to his own people. Neither the treasures of Egypt, nor the pleasures of sin, the attraction of human love, nor the glamor of the world's smile could turn him aside from his own folk. A light shone for him over the humble huts of Goshen, before which that of Pharaoh's palaces paled. Some glimmering knowledge of the promised Christ appears to have been present to his mind; and he esteemed that hope to be greater riches than the treasures of Egypt, Heb. 11:26.

He had, however, much to learn. By strength no man can prevail. The battle is not to the strong, nor the race to the swift. The salvation of Israel from their untold miseries must be due, from first to last, to the outstretched hand of their Almighty Protector. Hence the failure of Moses' first attempt. Instead of looking "this way and that," he must look *upward*.

EXODUS 3:1-12

God's Message from the Bush. The learning of Egypt was not sufficient to equip Moses for his lifework. He is taken to the solitudes of the wilderness. *That* is God's college. All who have done the greatest work in the world have graduated there—Elijah at Horeb, Ezekiel at Chebar, Paul in Arabia, John in Patmos. God's workers may take their arts course in the universities, but must take their divinity course alone with him. Often in the midst of daily duty we come on the outshining of his Presence. Let us be on the outlook for it, and take off our shoes.

This burning bush has generally been taken as the emblem of the Church amid the fires of tribulation; but there is a deeper meaning. The fire was the token of God's presence. The bush was unconsumed, because God's love is its own fuel. Notice the successive steps: "I have seen"; "heard"; "know"; "am come down"; "will send." The "cry" of the previous chapter is answered by the "coming down" of this. See Luke 18:7.

EXODUS 3:13-22

Moses Sent to Deliver Israel. How unlike this Moses was to the man who, forty years before, had acted with such impulsive haste, Acts 7:23, 24. He had learned much since then, and most about himself. But there should be no shrinking when God says "I am." Fill in this blank check with whatever you need for life or godliness, and God will do that and more also, with exceeding abundance.

Had we been called upon to demonstrate life beyond death from the Old Testament, we should hardly have turned to this chapter. But our Lord read the profound significance of these august words, Matthew 22:31, 32. Evidently the patriarchs must have been all living when God spoke, or he would never have described himself as being still their God. Had they ceased to exist he must have said, not I *am*, but I *was* the God of the fathers.

EXODUS 4:1-9

God's Signs to Confirm Moses' Words. This wonderful chapter tells us how Moses' three misgivings were tenderly and sufficiently dealt with by his heavenly Friend. To his first misgiving God made answer by giving him three signs. Here first we meet with that *rod* which was so often stretched out, over the land of Egypt, over the sea, and during the sojourn in the wilderness. Moses was but a rod, but what cannot a rod do if handled by an Almighty hand!

Leprosy was the type for sin, and the cleansed hand suggests God's marvelous power in cleansing, and so qualifying for service, all who yield themselves to him. The third sign of the *water turned to blood* was not less significant, revealing the divine power operating through this feeble human instrument to produce wonderful effects in the world of Nature. We must not live on signs, but on the Holy Spirit, though the outward sign reassures and strengthens us.

EXODUS 4:10-17

God's Promises Overcome Moses' Reluctance. To Moses' second misgiving God made a promise of exceeding beauty, which all who speak for God should consider. Compare v. 12 with Jer. 1:7-9 and 1 Cor. 2:4. If we looked at our natural powers as Paul used to do, we should glory in our lack of eloquence as affording a better platform on which God might work. See 2 Cor. 12:9, 10.

In answer to the third misgiving, God gave him his brother as assistant. Indeed, he was already on his way; but he was a weak man, and gave to Moses a great amount of anxiety and pain. After all, it is best for a man to lean only on God for counsel and ready help. If we step forth with this supreme alliance, we shall escape the hampering association with Aarons. We may as well get all we need firsthand.

EXODUS 4:18-31

Moses and Aaron Announce God's Purpose to Israel. So often the keenest tests of a man's fitness for his lifework are furnished by his behavior in his home. It may be that Zipporah had resisted the earlier imposition on her son of the initial rite of the Jewish faith and her proud soul had to yield. No man who has put his hand to God's plow can take counsel with flesh and blood, or look back. At whatever cost, we must set our own house in order before we can emancipate a nation.

When God designs it, he will contrive for us to meet the man, or men, who are to help us in our life mission. Our paths meet in the Mount of God. When the Alps were bored for the railway track, the work started on either side and the workers met in the middle. Help is coming to you from unexpected quarters, and will meet you when you need it most.

EXODUS 5:1-14

The Request to Worship Jehovah Answered by Oppression. The bondage of Israel in Egypt is an apt type of our bondage to sin. See John 8:34-36; Rom. 7:23-25. The weary tyranny of our besetting sins; the imperious demands of Satan; the absence of all reward to our hopeless toils—these are striking points of analogy. Though we weep and struggle, there is no help for us but in God.

No straw! No lessening of the tally of bricks! The charge of idleness! Cruel beatings! Deliverance apparently more distant than ever! But the darkest hour precedes dawn.

The hue and cry is always raised when a prisoner is escaping. The tyrant, who has so long held his prey, is not minded to surrender it without a struggle. The devil convulsed the child as he was about to depart. Moreover, Israel must be taught to look beyond Moses or Aaron to the Eternal Jehovah.

EXODUS 5:15—6:1

Moses Appeals from Pharaoh to God. God's way is to bring men to an end of themselves before he arises to their help. Our efforts to deliver ourselves only end in increasing our perplexities. The quota of bricks is doubled; the burdens augment; the strength of our purpose is broken; we are brought to the edge of despair. Probably this was the darkest hour in the life of the great leader. But from all the obloquy that was heaped on him, he took refuge in God. There is no other refuge for a limited man than "to return unto the Lord," v. 22. Return unto the Lord with your story of failure! Return unto him for fresh instructions! Return unto him with your appeal for his interposition! Be perfectly natural with your Heavenly Father! Humble yourself under his mighty hand! Even dare to reason with him, saying: "Why!" Then the Lord will say to you, as to Moses: "Now thou shalt see what I will do."

EXODUS 6:2-9

God's Name Confirms His Promises. The statement of verse 3 is at first sight startling, because we remember several passages in Genesis where that sacred name appears. But this arises from the fact that much of Genesis was composed long after the people had left these sad experiences behind them; and it was natural to apply to God the name which was familiar to them all at the time of writing. To the patriarchs God was *El*, the Strong; to their descendants he was the unchanging *Jehovah*, who fulfilled promises made centuries before. See Mal. 3:6. Notice the seven "I wills," and the three "I Ams." How often with us, as with Israel in v. 9, our faith and hope are hindered by physical or temporal circumstances. But our God knows our frame and is touched with the feeling of our infirmities. Therefore, he can make allowances.

EXODUS 6:10-27

The Line of Descent of God's Spokesmen. Here is an inventory of God's jewels, in the day when he counted them up. We are reminded of Mal. 3:17. Before he led forth the flock, the Good Shepherd counted them, that not one might be missing. There is a peculiar emphasis on the mention of Moses and Aaron in verse 26: "These are *that* Moses and Aaron." It was as though we were led to the hole of the pit whence they were digged, and a very poor hole it was, for their parentage and estate were quite humble and ordinary. But by means of them the Almighty wrought the deliverance of his people. It was through such feeble instruments as these that he spoke to the greatest monarch of the time, the mighty Pharaoh, whose remains are with us to this day. It is his method to choose the weak and foolish things to bring to naught and confound the strong and wise, that no flesh should glory in his presence.

EXODUS 6:28—7:13

Pharaoh Stubborn Against Israel's Release. How often we say in a similar tone, "I am of uncircumcised lips, and how shall Pharaoh hearken unto me?" Forty years in the wilderness, in absolute solitude, had robbed Moses of the eloquence with which Stephen credits him in earlier life. Like Jeremiah, he felt himself a child and unable to speak.

It is an awful moment when the human will sets itself in antagonism to the divine. If it will not bend, it must break. For once the scion of an imperial race had met his superior. It were better for the potsherd to strive with the potsherds of the earth! But God is not unreasonable. At the outset he endeavored to prove to Pharaoh who and what he was. One of the chief reasons for the plagues, as well as of these miracles, was to establish the fact that the Jehovah of the Hebrews was the great Being who lives behind the whole apparatus of nature.

EXODUS 7:14–25

Sign of the Waters Turned to Blood. Satan will mimic God's work up to a point. We are told that Jannes and Jambres withstood Moses; but even then Moses' rod swallowed their rods. They were defeated in their own realm, that Pharaoh's faith in them might be shaken. But it was in their predictions of what was coming that the Hebrew brethren specially attested their superiority. The sky was roseate with the blush of dawn as Pharaoh, accompanied by his court, came to perform his customary ablutions or to worship at the brink of the Nile. Moses met him with the peremptory summons, "Let my people go." In accordance with his prediction the Nile became as blood. But since by their clever legerdemain the magicians appeared able to do as much, Pharaoh's heart was hardened—i.e., "neither did he set his heart to this." In other words, he would not consider the message sent to him by the hand of God's accredited messengers.

EXODUS 8:1–15

The Plague of Frogs and Its Removal. Probably the plagues followed in rapid succession, so that the impression of one had not passed away before another succeeded. The whole conflict was probably completed in nine or ten months. The frog was a goddess; hence the plague was aggravated, as it was unlawful to destroy one. This stroke elicited the first symptom of surrender. Though the magicians counterfeited the coming of the frogs, they failed to remove them, and the king did not hope for such help from them. Pharaoh implored the intercession of the great Hebrew brethren, who, to make the power of God and the efficacy of prayer more manifest, asked the king to fix the time. They who know God and obey him absolutely can reckon on him with perfect certainty and confidence. Our God delights in the faith that dares to pledge his willingness and power, and he will not fail the soul that ventures wholly on his all-sufficiency.

EXODUS 8:16–32

The Plagues of Lice and of Flies. Verse 22 gives us the clue to these successive visitations—"To the end thou mayest know." The Egyptians worshiped the river from which the frogs came, were extremely punctilious in their purity by perpetual bathing, and sacrificed to the deities who presided over the noisome insect tribes. It was necessary to prove, therefore, that these gods were no gods, "but that the Lord made the heavens." The just and righteous Jehovah could not expect Pharaoh to obey his voice until he had shown himself to be God of gods and Lord of lords, and that he was Lord "in the midst of the earth." He is not an absentee, but nearer than breathing.

Notice the severance in verse 22! We do not belong to this world, because we have been crucified to it in Christ, and in him have risen to the heavenly places.

EXODUS 9:1–12

The Plague on Cattle and the Plague of Boils. The curse on the cattle reminds us that the whole creation groans and travails from the effects of human sin. See Romans 8:22. But those groans are the cries of birth, not of death, and herald a happier day when the creation shall be delivered from the bondage of corruption into the glorious liberty of the sons of God. There is a hint of this here, for the children of Israel lost not so much as one of their cattle from this pestilence. The Lord knoweth how to deliver his own, and our religion should make a difference for the living things of our firesides and farms.

How terribly does sin affect our physical health! These boils and blains on man and beast remind us of the inevitable brand with which sin marks its slaves. Let us read again Psalm 91, in the light of this passage. The souls that shelter under God's wing, from the charmed circle of his presence look, unharmed and unfearful, on pestilence and plague.

EXODUS 9:13–35

Mighty Thunderings and Hail. This paragraph recalls Rev. 7:3. The great angel there commanded that no wind should blow on the earth, or on the sea, or upon any tree until the servants of God had been sealed on their foreheads. Only when this had been effected did the

EXODUS

trumpets give signal of the disasters that broke successively on the earth. See Rev. 8:7ff. The only spot in which the soul is safe is within the encircling provisions of the covenant. Israel stood there and was safe, not only from the hail but from the destroying sword. It was as safe a spot as the center of a cyclone is said to be. God had bound himself by the most solemn sanctions to be a God to his people and deliver them. It was in pursuance of this pledge that he was their pavilion and canopy in this awful hour, catching the hailstones on his wings, and securing them from hurt. When we trust in Christ, he becomes our hiding-place from the storms of judgment and condemnation.

EXODUS 10:1-11

Pharaoh Still Refuses to Submit. Pharaoh was capable of being a noble and glorious soul, through which God might have shown forth all his power and glory, 9:16. But he refused, and the profanation of the best made him the worst. There is a crisis in every soul-history up to which God's methods appear likely to turn the proud to himself; but if that is passed, those methods seem only to harden. Just as in winter the thaw of the noon makes harder ice during the night, so if the love of God fails to soften, it hardens. In this sense God seemed to harden Pharaoh's heart. The real conflict lay with Pharaoh's stubborn will, which would not yield, v. 3, although his servants advised him to let the people go, v. 7. The only result was that the king recalled the Hebrew leaders and made another effort at compromise—"Go now ye that are *men.*" The children are always the key to the situation.

EXODUS 10:12-29

The Plagues of Locusts and of Darkness. The locust is the most terrible plague of Eastern lands. The heat is intense, the air languid, the sound as of a strong breeze, the sun darkened by a cloud of living things which cover the earth several inches thick and devour every green thing, v. 15. Notice the extorted confession, at last, of sin, v. 16. Many hearts and lives are devastated by these locusts, which eat up all the blades of promise. At the first trace of genuine repentance, however, they are borne away.

The Hebrew word for "darkness" is the same that is used in Gen. 1:2. The sun was one of the chief deities of Egypt; hence the horror that paralyzed her population, v. 23. But there was light in Goshen. See Psalm 112:4 and John 8:12. Pharaoh proposed one last compromise. See v. 24. Moses made a grand answer. The whole universe shall share in our redemption, Rom. 8:20, 21. Jesus will be content with nothing less than all the purchased possession.

EXODUS 11:1-10

The Death of the Firstborn Threatened. "One plague more." These are ominous words! This final act of judgment would smite the fetters from Israel's neck forever. It is vain for man to enter into conflict with God. God does not crush him at once, because he is long-suffering and forgiving. See 2 Peter 3:9. But if man persists, the inevitable blow falls. See Psalm 7:12. The word "borrow" is better rendered "ask," v. 2. The Hebrew phrase has no suggestion of a return being expected. This was befitting payment for their long and unrewarded labor.

The "great cry," v. 6, recalls the piercing wail that rings through an Eastern home when death takes place. The world shall hear one other such cry, as we learn from Rev. 1:7. There is no difference between God's people and others when sin is concerned. All have come short of God's glory. Nor is there difference in his redeeming grace. But there is *all* the difference between those who shelter under the blood of the Lamb and those who refuse.

EXODUS 12:1-14

The Passover Lamb and Its Sprinkled Blood. Henceforth, for Israel, there was to be a new beginning of the year. We should date our birthdays not from the cradle, but from the cross. The Paschal Lamb was an evident foreshadowing of Christ. See 1 Cor. 5:7. (1) He was without blemish. Searched by friend and foe, no fault was found in him. (2) He was in his prime when he laid down his life. (3) Set apart at the opening of his ministry, it took three years to consummate his purpose. (4) His blood—that phrase being equivalent to his sacrificial death—speaks of the satisfaction of the just claims of inviolable law, where his flesh is "meat indeed." (5) Roasting with fire, unleavened bread and bitter herbs denote the intensity of his sufferings, and the chastened spirit with which we draw nigh. And does not the pilgrim's attitude bespeak the attitude of the Church, which at any moment may be summoned to go forth at the trumpet sounding? See 1 Cor. 15:52.

EXODUS 12:15-28

The Feast of Unleavened Bread. The inmate of the house did not see the sprinkled blood. It was not necessary to be always going forth to look at it. It was clearly not a matter for his emotion or his intelligence. It was an accomplished fact, and it was enough for God to see it: "When *I* see the blood, I will pass over." Abide in Christ. It is not necessary to try to understand or feel; just be quiet and trust the finished work and the sworn promise of God. He has said: "Whosoever believeth shall not perish." The Lamb slain is in the midst of the throne; it is enough.

Let us keep the feast, not with the leavened bread of malice and wickedness, but with the unleavened bread of sincerity and truth. Remember that you must put away all ferment and all that partakes of disease, decay, or death, that God may be able to tarry in the house of your life and be your fellow-pilgrim in the march of life.

EXODUS 12:29–36

The Firstborn of Egypt Slain. It was night, the time for peace, rest, and silence. None anticipated evil, unless some few among the Egyptians had begun to believe in the veracity of Moses, that man of God. Suddenly, without warning, there was death everywhere. Death can enter the palace, elude the sentinels, pass locked doors, and smite the son of Pharaoh. The lowly obscurity of the woman grinding corn and the captive in the dungeon will not save them from his blow. There is no difference between us all in the fact of our sinnership, or the inevitableness of penalty, unless redeemed, as Israel was, by sacrifice.

Pharaoh's surrender was complete. Children? *Yes!* Flocks and herds? *Yes!* There was also a great popular uprising, and the people readily supplied the Israelites with whatever they asked—their wages for long unpaid servitude. They went forth as a triumphant host, "more than conquerors" through him who loved them.

EXODUS 12:37–51

Israel Led Out of Egypt. The 600,000 were males above twenty years of age, Numbers 1:3–46. This would make the entire body not less than 2,000,000 people of all ages. Succoth was the first rallying point on which the various bands converged. It stood in open country, over which their flocks and herds spread themselves. It was, indeed, a night to be observed when the Exodus took place, because, as Bunsen says, it was the beginning of history. And we may almost say further that it was the hour when Israel was born as a nation. God called his son out of Egypt. At that moment also the period of which Abraham had been apprised ran out. See Gen. 15:13; Gal. 3:17; and v. 40 here.

Notice the stress laid on circumcision, which was the type of putting away the sins of the flesh. See Col. 2:11. We must be separated from sin before we can claim our portion in the Paschal Lamb or join the Exodus.

EXODUS 13:1–16

The Firstborn Set Apart unto Jehovah. Two Hebrew customs dated from the Exodus—first, the dedication of the firstborn to God's service; and second, the Feast of Unleavened Bread, when the Passover must be killed. See Luke 22:7. The firstborn had been specially redeemed and so were specially God's. On them all was branded the one brief word *Mine*. What a lesson for us all who have been redeemed by the precious blood of Christ. We are his by right of purchase; we ought to be his by our own choice as well. Whenever we take up this position with regard to God, we may count on his strong hand. In later years the firstborn sons, who performed the priestly rites, were replaced by Levites, Num. 3:11–13; but still they were ransomed by a slain lamb. Every firstborn son lived because a lamb died. In this he stood on the same level as the firstling of an ass. What a parable is here! See Rom. 3:22 and 10:12.

EXODUS 13:17—14:9

The People Are Led Out and Pursued. There were two routes to Canaan, the nearest through the land of the Philistines; but to take that would have exposed the Hebrews to the very sights that so dismayed the twelve spies. See Num. 33. They might have had to fight every mile of advance. This would have been too great an ordeal for their young faith. So God, like the mother eagle, bore them on his wings. The Angel who conducted the march in the cloud chariot "led the people about." Thus God deals with us still, tempering the wind to the shorn lamb. Patience and faith are still severely tested by the circuitous and laborious route, but when in the afterwards we understand God's reasons, we are satisfied. There are many lessons learned on the wilderness route. How often God leads us into what seem to be impossible positions, that in our absolute extremity there may be room for him to work. All is love. See Psalm 136.

EXODUS 14:10–20

The Murmuring People Encouraged. We cannot wonder at their consternation. Before, the surf of the beach; behind, the crowded ranks of Egypt's army; on either side, impassable cliffs. It seemed a veritable death-trap. But Moses reckoned confidently on the salvation of God.

EXODUS

All they had to do, in the first instance, was to stand still and see it. It is hard to stand still when the situation becomes acute. If you don't know what to do, stand still until you do; it is God's business to direct and defend the believing soul. Let God do the fighting, v. 14. This Angel, Stephen tells us, was our Lord, Acts 7:38. He always puts himself between us and our strong enemies. Note v. 19. The ordinary man puts circumstances between himself and God, but the consecrated soul inserts God between himself and circumstances. When God says *Forward!* he will open the path and lead his people, as a shepherd leads his flock, by a way they know not.

EXODUS 14:21-31

The Egyptians Destroyed in the Sea. As the front ranks of Israel approached the surf, the billows parted. The very waves they dreaded became a wall. By faith Israel passed through the Red Sea as on dry land. They went through the flood on foot. So shalt thou, oh frightened child of God! Behind thee, the terror of the foe; before thee, the horror of the unknown. But God is with thee. The sheen of the Presence-Cloud shines upon and before thee. Be of good cheer—though thou passest through the waters, thou shalt not be overwhelmed. See Ps. 66:6; 78:13; Isa. 43:2.

The Egyptians owed their safety at first to the presence of Israel, but it was only for a time. The ungodly owe more to the presence of God's children than they realize. See Gen. 19:22. On which side of God's cloud are you? In Christ we may stand without fear before the searchlight of God! Compare v. 24 with Heb. 4:13 and Rev. 6:16.

EXODUS 15:1-21

Moses' Song of Praise to Jehovah. This sublime ode falls into three divisions. We learn, first, what God is. *Strength* in the day of battle; *song* in victory; *salvation* always. He is the God of our fathers, and our own; the mighty champion of his people. Notice that the Spirit of Inspiration gives but a line or two to Israel's murmurings, but records this happy song with elaborate care. Praise is comely!

We discover, second, what God is to his foes. They are covered by the engulfing waves of destruction. As well might thorns fight fire as a man succeed against God.

We are taught, third, what God does for his friends. He leads forth the people whom he has redeemed. He guides them in his strength to their home. He who brought them out brings them in, and plants them in the place he has prepared. Claim that he should do this for you. He who brought you out from Egypt can bring you into Canaan.

EXODUS 15:22-27

Marah's Waters Sweetened; Elim's Rest. How rapid are the transitions of life! Today the song of victory, tomorrow the bitter wells of Marah, and the next the shadow of Elim's palms! One moment we are singing the joyous song of victory on the shores of the Red Sea, strewn with the bodies of foes, which we believe that we have seen for the last time; and then, by a sudden change, we find ourselves standing beside Marah waters of pain and disappointment. We, however, learn more of God at Marah than at Elim, because he reveals to us the tree of the cross. It was there that our Lord gave up his will absolutely to the Father. See Heb. 10:5-7. "He bare our sins in his own body on the *tree."* Now, for us, there is but one way to bear sorrow and to extract its sweetness. We must yield our will to God; we must accept what he permits; we must do what he bids. So we come to find that *dis*appointments are *his* appointments.

EXODUS 16:1-12

Murmuring for Food Rebuked. Moses made a double promise to the Israelites in God's name. In the evening they were to have flesh to eat, and in the morning bread to the full. But before these gifts could be received, notice must be taken of their conduct toward the two brothers whose authority had been impugned by the events of the morning. Hence the appearance of the divine glory in the cloud, v. 10. After this a vast flight of quails, a migratory bird which often crosses the Red Sea at this very spot, fell to the ground in the near neighborhood of the Hebrew camp and lay there in an exhausted condition, which allowed of their being captured by hand. How striking are those words: "The Lord hath heard your murmurings." We should remember them when next we are tempted to doubt God's love and to complain of his dealings with us. Let God's faithful servants take courage; he will vindicate them.

EXODUS 16:13-26

The Manna in the Wilderness. The manna was typical of Christ. See John 6:31-34. He came down from Heaven to bring God's life within the reach of man. It is not enough that God has made so rich and plentiful a provision for us; we must appropriate it by our daily prayer and faith. Our Lord calls himself "the bread of life," not only to teach us what he is in himself in relation to our soul-need, but to remind us that he must be inwardly appropriated, fed upon, and made part of our very selves. Only so can he impart strength and joy to our hearts. It was not enough that the manna, sparkling like pearls in the morning sunshine, lay within their reach; the Israelites must gather it. The dew speaks not only of the Holy Spirit, but of the dawn. There is no time like the early morning for fellowship with Jesus! You cannot have too much. Gather all you may, you will have none to spare; but if we are pressed with needful duty, a little of Christ will go a long way, you shall have no lack.

EXODUS 16:27-36

Daily Food and Its Memorial. Wherever the cloud broods, the manna falls. If we are true to God's leadings and pitch our tents in obedience to his guiding cloud, we may confidently reckon on him to provide our daily food. It will come "day by day." Each man must gather, not only for himself, but for his own household. We are not to hoard up against tomorrow, because God, who *has* provided, *will* provide. And we are not to break in on the rest-day, or on the rest of our soul, by perpetual fret and care about our physical needs. God who opens his hand to supply the hunger of every living thing will not neglect his children. Give yourself up to holy fellowship; roll your anxieties on him; take what he provides now, and trust him for all coming days. Your bread shall be given you, and more than that. Remember that he gave quails in the desert and fish to the 5,000!

EXODUS 17:1-16

Water from the Rock; Victory over Amalek. From the smitten rock flowed the water for the thirsty hosts. So the Rock of Ages was smitten, and from his riven side has flowed out blood and water for the sin and thirst of the world. He that eateth his flesh and drinketh his blood, spiritually, hath eternal life. Such refreshment is in preparation for warfare. *Then* came Amalek! When our physical needs are satisfied, there is always the fear of Amalek who, in the typology of Scripture, stands for the flesh. Between this wilderness tribe and Israel the conflict was long and bitter. The old Adam, said Luther, is too strong for the young Melanchthon. But let the Lord fight for you! Lift up your hands with opened palms to him; he will not fail. See Matt. 1:21. But guard the rear, and ask that Jesus shall beset you behind as well as before. See Deut. 25:17, 18.

EXODUS 18:1-12

Moses Tells Jethro of God's Goodness. The names that Moses gave his two sons betray the drift of his thoughts during the forty years of his shepherd life. May we ever remember that we are strangers here, and our only help is in God. How humble Moses was in attributing to God all the glory of the Exodus! This is the sure cure of pride; and what are we but the axe that lies at the tree-foot, or the dry jawbone of an ass! Jethro belonged to another type of the religious life. He was not one of the chosen people, nor did he follow the methods of Jewish worship. But holy souls recognize their kinship the world over, and in loving embrace disregard the minor disagreements. "Grace be with *all* those who love the Lord Jesus Christ in sincerity."

EXODUS 18:13-27

Moses Appoints Rulers to Judge Israel. Jethro's frank acknowledgment of God's supremacy and loving-kindness was extremely beautiful. Oh, for more wisdom to discern, and humble reverence to acknowledge the divine goodness wherever we encounter it. His advice also was most sagacious. It is far better to set a thousand people to work than attempt to do the work of a thousand. The greatest and most useful men are those who know how to delegate to others work for which these are quite competent, while they themselves concentrate on matters of the highest moment, which the others cannot undertake. Thus, character is created. It is the highest service of all to bring men's requests and causes to God, and then to show them the way in which they should walk and the work they should do. In the best sense this is what Jesus does for us all.

EXODUS 19:1-15

Moses Receives Jehovah's Words in the Mount. The plain beneath Sinai, where Israel encamped, has been identified, and the reader should study the books of travelers which afford a mental conception of the scene. The brilliant colors, in which red sandstone predominates; the shattered, thunder-stricken peaks; the awful silence; the utter absence of vegetation; the level plain giving abundant opportunity for all to hear and see—all these deserve notice. The tenderness of the divine address is very touching. Nor are *we* excluded from these promises, if we are among Abraham's spiritual children. See Rom. 4:16. If God could carry this multitude of people, he is sufficient for us and our burdens.

EXODUS

We also may be his peculiar treasure and a kingdom of priests.

But Israel's solemn pledge was a profound mistake. Had they known themselves better, they would never have made it, and one design of the Decalogue was to show how absolutely impossible it is for any to be justified by the works of the Law. Pentecost, which Whitsuntide commemorates, took place on the anniversary of this august scene.

EXODUS 19:16-25

The People Warned Not to Approach the Mount. The holiness of God was taught in object lessons. The people must wash their garments, the mount must be fenced in, not a beast might graze upon the slopes, not a hand might touch the holy soil. Moses must twice descend to warn the people, vv. 14, 21, 25. Only he and Aaron might ascend. All was done to convince the people of the vast distance that intervened between themselves and God. It was the awe engendered by such provisions, and which pervaded the ancient dispensation, that led Peter to cry, when the divine glory of Jesus smote upon him, "Depart from me, for I am a sinful man, O Lord."

Dare to believe that beneath every cloud of soul-anguish, bereavement, and trial you will find the burning love of God. Clouds and darkness may be round about him, but faithfulness and truth, judgment and mercy are at the foundation of his throne. Listen to the voice that bids you enter the pavilion, and remember Heb. 12:18ff.

EXODUS 20:1-17

The "Ten Words" Spoken at Sinai. The Law was given by the disposition of angels, through the medium of Moses. See John 1:17; Acts 7:53. It tells us, not what God is, for that is only shown in Jesus Christ, but what man should be. It combines in a concise form that moral code which is part of the nature of things and is written on man's conscience. See Rom. 2:15. Even the Fourth Commandment is deeply graven on our physical nature. These laws are mostly negative, but their positive side is stated in Matt. 5. For practical purposes this divine code consists of two divisions or tables; the first, of our duties toward God; the second, of those to man; but these are summed up in the one great law of love. See Mark 12:29-31; Rom. 13:8-10; Gal. 5:14. Our Lord Jesus stands surety for us at the bar of Sinai. By his righteousness imputed and imparted, by his obedience and death, by the gracious indwelling of his Spirit, he comes "not to destroy, but to fulfill." See Matt. 5:17; Rom. 8:4.

EXODUS 20:18-26

The People Fear; Idols and Altars. When our Lord was on earth, he was so attractive and winsome that the publicans and sinners drew near to hear him, penitents wept at his feet, children loved him. But even then there were some who desired him to depart out of their coasts. So here, while Moses drew near, the people stood afar off. Let us not be among those who avoid the near presence of God, but of those who are made nigh by the blood of Christ. Let us exercise our right to draw near to the throne of grace and stand in the very presence of our Father-God, because we have a great High Priest who is passed through the heavens.

At the 22nd verse we begin the Book of the Covenant, which extends to 23:33, containing a series of wholesome laws. The first enactment deals with the worship of the Most High. Note that in *all* places he will record his Name. Everywhere we may worship him. The altar had to be of earth, teaching us the lessons of humility, simplicity, and self-abasement. See Heb. 13:10. But always the adjustment with God precedes rightness toward man.

EXODUS 23:1-19

Laws of Conduct and Worship. We may apply these various precepts to our own hearts. Many of them breathe the very spirit of Christ. We must watch our speech, so that no man's character may suffer by our gossip or slander. We must dare to stand for the truth, though we stand absolutely alone. With all kindness and goodwill we must save our neighbor from damage, even though he has vented on us his spleen. It is never for us to take advantage of him; God will deal with him on our behalf, and in his own time and way. Let us not fret ourselves to do evil. David's example in refusing to injure Saul when his bitter enemy was within his reach is an inspiring example for us to follow. We must hold an even balance for just and honorable dealing with all men, and cultivate the Sabbath-keeping of the heart. In every life, also, there should be perpetual memory of Calvary, the resurrection, and Pentecost—the three feasts of the soul!

EXODUS 23:20-33

Promise of Entrance into Canaan. This Angel must have been the Lord himself, for Stephen said expressly that the Angel was with Moses at the burning bush, where Jehovah revealed himself and the very ground was holy. Besides, we are told here that God's Name—*i.e.*, his nature—was in him. The Son of God, therefore, must have been the leader of that pilgrim host, preceding the march and preparing for their needs.

Notice that God would also send the hornet before his people, v. 28. The Presence, which is an Angel for God's children, becomes a hornet to the rebellious and ungodly. To one it is a savor of life, and to the other of death. The sun that bleaches linen white tans the hands that expose it; the cloud which is light to Israel is thick darkness to Egypt. Grieve not the Holy One, who will overcome your enemies and satisfy your soul with goodness, if you will obey his voice.

EXODUS 24:1-11

The Covenant Made and Sealed by Blood. Moses remained in communion with God while receiving the laws of the preceding chapters. When they were concluded, he descended to ratify with all solemnity the covenant between Jehovah and Israel. If the altar represented God's side of the transaction, the twelve pillars stood for Israel. The young men filled the priestly office according to 13:2, until the Levites were appointed. It must have been a solemn spectacle as the sprinkled blood sealed the covenant. But let us turn from that first covenant, sealed with the blood of beasts, to the new covenant, by which all the Church of the redeemed are bound to God, and which was sealed by the shedding of the precious blood of Christ. "This is my blood of the covenant," said Jesus, when handing round the wine. See Heb. 9:18-20 and 13:20. The Lord's Supper is a perpetual reminder of our obligations.

EXODUS 24:12—25:9

Moses Shown God's Plan for the Tabernacle. There were four concentric circles, so to speak, represented as gathered around the burning center of the Divine Presence. In the outer circle, the people, 24:2, 17; next, the seventy elders, 24:9, 14; then, Joshua, 24:13; 32:17; and lastly, Moses, 24:18. These represent, respectively, the unenlightened; those whose religious life is hindered by their excessive devotion to the flesh; the few whose fellowship is liable to be interrupted by the war-clarion; and those who have been made nigh unto God in Jesus Christ our Lord, and have been baptized into the Holy Spirit.

To which group have we attained? We are invited to draw nigh; let us act on the invitation. See Heb. 10:19, 20. There is always room at the top, and there we may stand, beholding, as in a glass, the glory of the Lord. Notice that God said, Come up unto *me*. He longs to have our love and faith. His delights are with the sons of men; at great cost he has opened the door of access, Rom. 5:1, 2. We need God, but God wants us; and therefore the construction of the Tabernacle is next arranged, that he may dwell with man upon the earth.

EXODUS 25:10-22

The Ark and the Mercy Seat. The Tabernacle was full of symbolical teaching of which the full meaning is unfolded in the Epistle to the Hebrews, where we are distinctly told that the Holy Spirit inspired the plan of the various parts. See Heb. 9:8. Well would it be for us if we built our lives as Moses the Tabernacle, only on the divine plan. Note 25:9, 40; 26:30; 27:8; Heb. 8:5. The *Ark* was the symbol of the Covenant between Jehovah and his people.

The golden slab, known as the mercy seat, supplied the meeting-place between God and man. It was there that the high priest sprinkled the blood of atonement once a year. It is alluded to by the apostles, Paul and John, as the "propitiation." We might insert *Mercy seat* in each passage. See Rom. 3:25; 1 John 2:2. Angel forms bent on either side, with their faces downward. See 1 Peter 1:12. The tables of the Law lay written beneath, because divine righteousness underlies all God's dealings with men.

EXODUS 25:23-40

The Table of Showbread and the Lampstand. The Table of the Showbread, or Presence-bread, held twelve loaves, which represented the tribes of Israel. It was three feet long, one foot, six inches broad, and two feet, three inches high. The border or edging of gold around the top kept its contents from falling off. The loaves were changed each week, and when removed were eaten only by the priests. See Mark 2:26. Surely the suggestion of this table, standing as it did immediately before the veil on the outer side, was intended to teach that the purity and devotion of Israel were as bread to God. He takes pleasure in them that fear him. We also feed with God on the beauty and glory of our Savior's obedience unto death.

The candlestick, with its seven branches, cost a tremendous fortune and is a type of Christ, the Light of the World, and of the people of God when illuminated by the Divine Fire and shining amid the darkness around. See Zech. 4:2; John 8:12; Rev. 1:13.

EXODUS 26:1-25

The Curtains and Boards of the Tabernacle. The Tabernacle was constructed of upright boards, over which four sets of curtains were thrown. The innermost set, which made the ceiling, was of tapestry, embroidered with cherubim in various colors—blue, scarlet and purple—the cunning work of a damask weaver. Over these was a second set, of goats' hair, longer and broader, so as to protect them, while the third and fourth sets were of rams' and seals' skins respectively to protect the whole from the weather.

In these curtains we may find profound teaching concerning the human nature of our Lord; for we are told that the Word of God became flesh and *tabernacled* among us. That phrase naturally suggests that his human body was the tent or tabernacle in which his spirit dwelt. See John 1:14, margin. In the fine-twined linen his holiness; in the blue his heavenly origin; in the purple his majesty; in the scarlet his sufferings.

EXODUS 26:26-37

The Veil and the Screen. The boards that made the sides and back of the Tabernacle were of wood covered with gold, and set in sockets of silver. They were knit together by the five long bars that passed through the rings, parallel with the ground. The veil typified the separation between man and God, the awful barrier that sin has caused, which shuts out from the enjoyment of God all save those who can enter into the Holiest by the blood of Jesus. Men had impressed on them their unworthiness to approach God. The cherubic forms woven on the veil reminded them of what is recorded in Gen. 3:24. They were led to anticipate the hour when a new and living way would be opened.

The division of the Tabernacle suggests two degrees of nearness to God, or two stages in Christian living. You may know the great brazen altar which is Calvary, and the showbread table and candlestick; but there is something beyond these for those who have learned the meaning of the rent veil and the cross! See Matt. 27:51; Gal. 2:20.

EXODUS 27:1-19

The Altar and the Court. The brazen altar is dealt with long before any particular mention is made of the altar of incense, because the question of our relationship with God, through the death of our Lord on the cross, must precede our fellowship with him and our successful intercession. Each of these altars was made of the same kind of wood, but in the case of the altar we are now considering, and which stood in front of the Tabernacle, the wood was encased in brass, that metal suggesting the severity of the sacrificial flame that burnt at the crucifixion, when Christ our Passover was sacrificed for us. Let us distinguish between these altars. We have passed beyond the one; we are called to minister perpetually at the other. The court was fifty yards long by twenty-five broad, and was formed by curtains of fine-twined yarn. There must be separation between God's priests and the world. See 1 Pet. 2:5.

EXODUS 27:20—28:14

The Beaten Oil; the Ephod. Always in Scripture oil is an emblem of the Holy Spirit. It is his grace communicated to the wick of our character and life, which makes them capable of giving a bright light for God. This oil was *pure,* because none shine brightly for God who are not pure in heart and poor in spirit. It was *beaten,* because our best work is often the result of our sorrows. McCheyne used to say, "Beaten oil for the sanctuary," referring to the care with which ministers and teachers should prepare for their work. Get your oil direct! See Zech. 4:2, 3.

It is befitting that we should consider the priestly garments. We minister within the curtained court, order the lamp of testimony till daybreak, and stand before the altar of incense. It is meet that we should be arrayed in the beauty of holiness. Our Lord bears our names, graven indelibly and eternally, and we are accepted in the Beloved.

EXODUS 28:15-30

The Breastplate and Its Stones. The breastplate bore twelve precious stones, on each of which the name of a tribe was engraved—the smallest as well as the greatest, Benjamin as well as Judah, Simeon which faded in the desert, as well as Ephraim which occupied the center of the Promised Land. Whatever might be their sins and failures, their chastenings and penalties, nothing could remove them from that sacred place. They might even be at enmity among themselves, but still they would abide there in perfect unity.

So it is with ourselves. Our names are engraven on the heart of Jesus, and ever presented before God. Neither life nor death can separate us from his love. Do not look at your shortcomings and failures, but at your standing in Christ Jesus. You cannot be forgotten by God. The dark waters may flow over your soul, the voice of the accuser may be hoarse in your ear, your heart and your flesh may fail, but you are precious in God's sight and sparkle in his light like a jasper or sapphire.

EXODUS 28:31-43

Aaron's Holy Garments. The robe was worn under the ephod. It was of blue, the color of Heaven, of deep lakes, of the gentian and the forget-me-not. It was of one piece. See John 19:23. It ended in a fringe, in which bells and pomegranates alternated. We are as the skirts of his garments, and the holy oil will reach us there, so the psalmist says. See Ps. 133:2. We may receive the unction of the holy Christ. The Spirit so richly given to him may anoint even us, and he will reveal himself in the *fruit* of the pomegranate and the *sweetness* of the golden bell. Aaron's headplate bore an inscription, which the prophet tells us should be written also on our commonest duties and most prosaic service. See Zech.14:20, 21. For ordinary priests the clothing was very simple. Pure white linen! Such is the garb which befits us all! See Rev. 19:8.

EXODUS 29:1-18

The Priests Prepared for Consecration. The consecration of the priests was an elaborate and impressive ceremony. Notice how Aaron and his sons are classed together, as though to remind us that Jesus and we stand together forevermore. He is the faithful High Priest, but we also have been made priests unto God. First came the washing with water, intimating the necessity for personal purity. See Heb. 10:22. Then the donning of official robes; for God's priests must be arrayed in the beauty of holiness. See Ps. 110:3.

The anointing oil is the emblem of the Holy Spirit. See Ps. 132 and 1 John 2:27. It is not enough to have the Holy Spirit in us for character; his anointing must be on us for service. The slain bullock, as sin offering, reminds us of the contrast between our Lord and us. He knew no sin; we require the propitiation for sin. The burnt offering reminds us of Rom. 12:1, 2.

EXODUS 29:19-30

The Consecration Offerings. The second ram of the consecration ceremony yielded its blood to be placed on ear and hand and foot. We are thus taught that our senses, deeds, and goings are to be dedicated to God. Though the garments, which had just been put on, were perfectly new, they were besprinkled with blood and oil from head to foot. To our eyes that is a grievous disfigurement; but the Holy Spirit thus signified that even beauty is subordinate to the necessity for God's forgiveness and anointing. Whenever the priest beheld his dress he was reminded of his unworthiness, and of the abundant grace of God. Of course, the Lord Jesus needed no such preparation. He was holy, harmless, and separate from sinners.

Part of the flesh was waved heavenward and burned, as though God fed on it, while part was eaten by the priests. It was as though God and they feasted together in one holy sacrament, the symbol of their at-one-ment.

EXODUS 29:31-46

The Continual Daily Offerings. The consecration ceremony was repeated on seven succeeding days, and must have produced a profound impression. Thus line was upon line; and we may magnify God's patience, in being willing through these repeated ordinances to educate the Hebrew people to the sublimest spirituality.

Notice the injunctions for daily services! No religious life can thrive without its regular hours and habits of devotion, such as these offerings suggest. Morning and evening prayers have been the custom in all ages. With the one we go forth to our labor till the evening, asking our Father to give guidance and protection. With the other we entreat forgiveness and mercy. See Psalm 55:17; Daniel 6:10. The chapter ends with many great and precious promises, which we who believe in Jesus may claim and enjoy.

EXODUS 30:1-10

The Altar of Incense. The incense-altar's being mentioned now seems late in the story of the Tabernacle. But it is not unsuitable, because intercessory prayer, which it represents, is the crown and climax of the religious life. When our Lord had finished his sacrificial death, he passed into the heavens to make intercession for us. In Rev. 8:3, 4, the veil is lifted and we are allowed to behold him, standing by the golden altar in heaven and adding much incense to the prayers of *all* saints. What a wealth of prayer is ever passing through those gracious hands and that loving heart! John 17 is the golden altar of Scripture; let us often worship there. But, alas, these earthly altars soon get defiled, even by our prayers, and need the blood that speaketh peace. All our prayer requires the blood of at-one-ment.

EXODUS 30:11-21

The Atonement Money and the Laver. The atonement money was paid by all alike, to remind them that they were a redeemed race and that so far as their value was concerned, neither rank, nor age, nor money made any difference. See Rom. 3:22-24; 10:12, 13. The rich might not give more, lest he be made proud; the poor must not give less, so that he might be leveled up by the common mercy of God.

The laver reminds us of our need of daily washing. See John 13. It is very necessary to our peace and strength to retreat constantly to Christ with confession and prayer. See 1 John 1:6, 7. The laver was made out of the looking-glasses of the women. See Ex. 38:8. It was a good use for them and was altogether appropriate, for the Word of God is compared to a mirror for its revealing qualities, and to water for cleansing. See Jas. 1:23; Eph. 5:26.

EXODUS 30:22-38

The Anointing Oil and the Incense. The anointing oil was extremely rich and costly. Pure myrrh, sweet cinnamon (imported probably from Sumatra or China), sweet calamus (the product of India or Mesopotamia), cassia (from Java) were the principal ingredients. Such a combination must have produced a delightful fragrance! The use of this oil was restricted to the holy service of the Tabernacle and reminds us of "the unction of the Holy One"—*i.e.*, the anointing by the Holy Spirit. See Lev. 8:10-12 and 1 John 2:20.

Christ is the Anointed, and he sheds the oil of joy on our heads as one by one we yield ourselves to his service. See Acts 2:33. The oil was not to be poured "upon man's flesh." We must deny the flesh with its affections and lusts, that we may be filled with the Spirit. Calvary before Pentecost!

The incense also was carefully prepared, and thus we are taught that prayers should not be uttered rashly or lightly, but with reverence, deliberation, and forethought.

EXODUS 31:1-18

Wise Workmen for the Tabernacle. Whenever there is special work to be done, God will find and endow the men who are to do it. "I have called, . . . I have filled, . . . I have appointed," etc. There is a niche for each of us in God's service, to each a special work is given; and for each those talents are imparted which are requisite and adequate. "Created unto good works," says the apostle, "which God hath before ordained that we should walk in them," Eph. 2:10. The talent for the sphere and the sphere for the talent—God's call binds the two with golden clasps.

But amid all our work for God there should be Sabbath-keeping—*i.e.*, the inner rest of the soul. We are by nature full of our own works and schemes and plans; but when the spirit of rest enters us, all this is altered. Then we are not agents, but instruments; we do not work for God, but God works through us; we enter into his rest, and cease from ourselves. See Heb. 4:10.

EXODUS 32:1-14

Aaron's Golden Calf Offends the Lord. The people never thought of taking Aaron as a substitute for Moses, because they instinctively recognized his moral weakness. Though he was dressed in the garments of the high priest, he was essentially a weak man. This came into evidence:

(1) *By his reply to the people.* When they demanded the calf, he ought to have met them with an indignant negative. But instead, to prevent the unpopularity which such an attitude might have evoked, he contented himself with putting difficulties in the way of their project. "Surely," he thought, "they will never go on with their mad scheme if they have to pay for it with their jewels." But the event did not justify his expectations.

(2) *By his reply to Moses.* "There came out this calf." "It was the furnace, not I, that did it." *Blame my heredity, environment, companions,* says the wrongdoer. The weak becomes the sinful one. Strong Son of God, help us! Make us strong! See Jer. 15:20.

EXODUS 32:15-24

Moses Breaks the Tables and Burns the Calf. There was no weak compromise on the part of Moses. He cast the tables from his hands as though he felt that the covenant between God and the Hebrew race was hopelessly broken. He remonstrated with Aaron, destroyed the calf, and appointed the tribe of Levi as the executors of divine justice. How striking the act that forced the people to drink the dust of the golden calf! Men *always* have to drink the dust of their idolatries. You cannot make an idol without growing into the likeness of your idol and becoming, someday, nauseated with it.

As Israel turned from the splendors that shone on the summit of Sinai to fashion the calf, and found that the end of those things was misery, so those who turn from the Savior, who is the brightness of the Father's glory and the express image of his Person, pierce themselves through with many sorrows and perish. See Heb. 12:25.

EXODUS 32:25–35

Moses Punishes Idolaters and Prays for the People. The heart of Moses was full of that wonderful new word, *atonement.* For many days Jehovah had been speaking to him about it. But he seemed to feel that on this occasion, the blood of goats and bulls could not avail to put away the transgression of his people. Then there arose within him the noble resolve to which he gave expression when he returned by the well-worn path to the summit of Sinai.

His voice was very broken as he commenced to plead. Mark that unfinished sentence, "If thou wilt forgive their sin—!" It was arrested by a burst of uncontrollable emotion. Can we finish it? "If thou wilt forgive, thou wilt act worthily of thyself and bind us to thee forever; but if not, and if the blood of beasts does not avail, let me be their atoning sacrifice, and blot me from thy book!" See Rom. 9:1–3.

EXODUS 33:1–11

The Angel Leader and the Human Intercessor. Moses knew that his people were forgiven, but it hurt him to hear that an angel was henceforth to lead them. See 32:34. The burden of two and a half million people was too heavy for him to carry, even with angel help. He must somehow secure the withdrawal of that sentence, "I will not go up in the midst of thee." He spoke of it to the people, who awoke to realize what their sin had forfeited, and put off their jewels. But their leader gave himself to prayer. Since Sinai was too far to climb, he seems to have pitched his own tent outside the camp as a temporary meeting-place with God; and when he entered it the people said, "Look! he is going to pray for us"; and he spake with God face to face, as we may, of what was in his heart. See John 16:26, 27.

EXODUS 33:12–23

God's Presence Promised and His Glory Shown. When Moses found himself alone with God, he made two outstanding requests:

(1) *For God's presence.* "If thou dost not go with me, I cannot go; angels are not enough. They are fair, and sweet, and strong, but I want thee. Wilt thou leave me—a lonely man—to thread these desert wastes with this people? Thou hast put the burden on me, and thou canst not leave me to carry it alone!" It is good when a man gets to close grips with God, and Moses was answered according to his faith. See v. 14.

(2) *For a vision of God's glory.* Again the answer came as he asked—"I will put thee in a cleft of the rock." The sides of the mountains are rent and scarred; but who can tell the anguish of him who was "marred" for us? Yet, in the cleft wound of his side there is room for us to hide. "Rock of Ages, cleft for me!" On Calvary, a niche was hollowed out in which a world of sinners may find shelter.

EXODUS 34:1–17

The Covenant of the Law Renewed. Before we can behold the vision of Eternal Love, we must be willing to fulfill three conditions: (1) *Earliness:* "Be ready in the morning." (2) *Solitude:* "No man shall come up with thee." (3) *The open heart:* "And I will write . . ." God is always passing by and covering us with the shadow of his hand, and proclaiming his loving-kindness and tender mercy. He keeps mercy for thousands, and limits the consequence of sin to the third and fourth generation.

Whenever we get near to God, we should begin to think of and pray for others. As the last notes of the divine procession were dying away, Moses bowed his head and worshiped, saying, "Let the Lord go in the midst of us and forgive." It was as though he said, "If thou art a God like that, thou art the God that stiff-necked people need. Go with us, therefore, for thou canst bear with us." He went on to ask that they might be pardoned, and that God would account them his heritage. His request was more than granted! God entered into covenant with them and promised to drive out their enemies on conditions which he proceeded to enumerate.

EXODUS 34:18–35

Moses Brings the Renewed Tables of the Law. For forty days, with no sustenance from bread or water, Moses abode on the Mount—absorbed with a passion of love and awe—not counting the hours, which passed like a dream. He talked with God as a man face to face with his friend; but he was completely unaware of the marvelous transformation which this holy intercourse was effecting. At God's dictation he wrote out the covenant, as we have it in this Book, and finally God gave him the two tables of stone, on which he had imprinted his autograph.

With these in his hand Moses descended to the plain, unaware that his face shone. See 2 Cor. 3:18. The apostle urges that we, as Christians, should first behold, and then reflect the glory of Jesus. We must be mirrors, for the purpose of shedding his light among our fellowmen; and in the effort to do this, we shall become transfigured into his glorious beauty from one degree to another. The crowning glory of that transfiguration will be our unawareness: "Moses wist not."

EXODUS 35:1-19

The Sabbath and Offerings to God. Very significantly this chapter commences with the reiteration of the Rest-day. Perhaps the people needed to be reminded that amid all the din of preparation for the new Tabernacle, they were not to allow their work, however noble the object, to break in on the Sabbath-keeping of the camp. Moses then proceeded to enumerate the character of the gifts that were required. Those who had costly heirlooms had nothing too good; and they who could only bring the acacia wood of the desert were welcome to bring that. Women who were clever with their hands might spin the flax or weave the soft white wool of the Angora goat. A wide variety of work was offered, which reminds us of 1 Cor. 12:4 and following. Repeatedly he urged the word "willing-hearted," and the Hebrew phrase signifies a heart driven by a holy purpose. Tennyson uses the phrase, "Whose heart drove him on like a goad." There was no crack of the taskmaster's whip. "The love of God constrained." "O love that will not let me go!"

EXODUS 35:20-29

Free Gifts for the Tabernacle. The people departed to think over their response to Moses' appeal, and then returned. How long had elapsed? Did Moses speak in the morning, and did they return in the cool of the evening? And what a rich profusion of gifts did they contribute! Here one of the princes brought a priceless jewel; here again were crowds of ordinary people bringing precious amulets, earrings, nose-rings, and other jewelry in which Orientals take great delight. Large numbers of women brought their metal mirrors, and out of them the laver was afterward constructed. These things were piled in heaps, and we are told that the Spirit drove the people to give till the artificers exclaimed that they had more than enough.

But what would the gifts have availed apart from the divinely designated artists! We, too, are called to build the temple of God. Ask the Spirit of God to show you your place and equip you for it. Some sphere will be probably indicated by your natural aptitude; but be sure that you are filled with the Spirit of God.

EXODUS 35:30—36:8

Wise-hearted Workers for the Tabernacle. What were the driving motives of this marvelous outburst of generosity? They remembered that Jehovah had brought them forth from Egypt, destroying their foes and liberating them from slavery. Again they heard the rattle of the pursuing chariots and the clash of arms! Again they thought of the march through the oozy bottom of the sea, while the walls of water stood on either side, irradiated with the glow of the cloud of fire!

With full hearts they turned to God, saying, "The best we have is thine. Thou art worthy to receive glory and honor and riches and power and blessing, for thou hast redeemed us." Upon the heels of that thought came the remembrance of the constant provision for their daily needs. The manna had fallen; the water had gushed from the flinty rock; Amalek had fled! These were the fountains that fed the springs of generosity. But have we not similar reason? "I beseech you, therefore, brethren, *by the mercies of God,* yield yourselves." See Rom. 12:1, 2.

EXODUS 39:32-43

The Tabernacle and Its Furniture. Ten times over we are told that all the work was done, "as the Lord commanded Moses." See v. 43. Their obedience had been minute and exact; and the blessing of the Lawgiver was the outward and audible assurance of the divine "Well done." We are carried forward in thought to anticipate the verdict which will be passed upon our own lifework. Will our Lord, when he beholds it, be able to say that it has all been wrought according to his pattern and in obedience to his command? Alas, that is too much to expect! We have been, too often, disobedient and unprofitable. We would love to hear the Master say, "Well done! I know thy works, and charity, and service, and faith, and thy patience, and thy works; and the last to be more than the first." But is there not reason to fear that he may say: "I have not found thy works perfect before God"? See Rev. 2:19; 3:2. Let us repent, seek forgiveness, and start again!

EXODUS 40:1-16

Directions for Erecting the Tabernacle. On the new year's day of the second year of the exodus, Moses was bidden to rear up the Tabernacle and with his own hand to place each article in its specified position. With what joy must those commands have fallen on his ears! We are reminded of the words of Robert Moffat, when he was completing the translation of the entire

Bible into the language of the Bechuanas: "When I had finished the last verse, I could hardly believe that I was in the world. My emotions found vent by my falling on my knees and thanking God for his grace and goodness in giving me strength to accomplish my task." Under similar circumstances Dr. Paton says that he pitched his hat into the air and danced round and round his printing press. Let us build our life, piece by piece, in the same spirit —not with wood, hay and stubble, but with gold, silver, and precious stones—so that at the close we may be able to say, "I have glorified thee on the earth: I have finished the work which thou gavest me to do."

EXODUS 40:17-38

The Tabernacle Set Up and Dedicated. At the time of the offering of the evening sacrifice all was finished. Moses had placed the table on the right and the candlestick on the left of the holy place; had set the incense-altar near the veil; had washed in the laver, and had anointed it and all its vessels. The Ark had been hidden behind the veil, and Aaron invested in his robes. Then the congregation, deeply moved, retired to their tents and night settled on the mountains. Moses also retired from the scene, full of thankfulness. See Ps. 90:16, 17.

They had hardly left the structure when the cloud that had guided their march settled down upon it, and the glory of the Lord— "the Shekinah"—shone within the Tabernacle itself. Moses immediately hastened back, and found the Presence of God so manifestly in possession that he dared not enter. Behold! the tabernacle of God was with men. So in after years the Divine Word dwelt in the mortal body of Jesus. See John 1:14; 2 Cor. 5:1; Rev. 21:3. This is the worthy close of this great book of the Exodus.

THE BOOK OF
LEVITICUS
A MANUAL OF WORSHIP AT THE TABERNACLE

I. DIRECTIONS REGARDING THE OFFERING OF SACRIFICES *1—7*
   A. The five offerings   *1:1—6:7*
      Burnt: 1; meal: 2; peace: 3; sin: 4; trespass: 5:1—6:7
   B. The laws regarding the disposal of each of these offerings *6:8—7:38*

II. THE CONSECRATION OF AARON AND HIS SONS TO THE PRIESTHOOD   *8—10*
   A. Their consecration by Moses   *8*
   B. Aaron's offerings for himself and the people   *9*
   C. Sin of Nadab and Abihu and the Law as to eating holy things   *10*

III. LAWS REGARDING CEREMONIAL PURITY   *11—16*
   A. Clean and unclean beasts, fishes, and fowls   *11*
   B. The purification of women and their offerings   *12*
   C. Leprosy—laws, signs, sacrifices   *13, 14*
   D. Cleansing from bodily uncleanness   *15*
   E. The great annual atonement for sin   *16*

IV. THE LAWS OF HOLINESS AND SACRED FESTIVALS   *17—26*
   A. Various laws regarding holiness of life   *17—22, 24*
   B. The yearly religious festivals   *23*
      (1) Passover, (2) firstfruits, (3) trumpets, (4) tabernacles
   C. Sabbatical year and year of jubilee   *25*
   D. Blessings for obedience; chastisement for disobedience   *26*

V. APPENDIX ON VOWS, TITHES, AND THINGS DEVOTED   *27*

INTRODUCTION

This name was also given by the Greek translators, and is the equivalent of the opening Hebrew word. The book treats the laws relating to the ritual, services, and sacrifices of the Hebrew religion, the superintendence of which was in the hands of the Levitical priesthood. It is principally concerned with the duties of the priests.

Several passages plainly indicate the wilderness as the place of writing, as 19:23; others that the settlement in Canaan had taken place, as 18:27. The former were probably in the first draft by Moses, while Samuel and others were doubtless responsible for recording further enactments.

COMMENTARY

LEVITICUS 1:1–17

Burnt Offerings of the Herd, Flocks, and Fowls. Jehovah speaks with Moses, not from Sinai's summit, but from the Tabernacle, because he has come to dwell with men on the earth. Compare Exodus 20:22 and 25:8. The early chapters of this book contain the Law of the offerings. He who was to be worshiped prescribed the manner in which he was to be approached. These sacrifices also were intended to typify the great offering which our Lord would one day, in the fullness of time, consummate on Calvary.

Here we have the burnt offering, presenting the more general aspect of our Lord's self-giving. It represents his entire surrender to the Father's will. See Heb. 10:8, 9. The principal feature of this offering was that the whole body of the victim was consumed and ascended in fire and smoke. The Hebrew word comes from a root which means "to ascend." Three grades of this offering were permitted—herd, flock, fowl—to bring it within the means of all, and to typify the varying degrees in which men apprehend and value Christ.

LEVITICUS 2:1–16

Meal Offerings with Oil and Incense. The meal offering, which is described in this chapter, portrayed in emblem the perfect character of our Lord. He was as fine flour, of the best quality, without grit or coarseness. There was nothing uneven, nothing rough and harsh, nothing unseemly or forbidding in him. He was anointed with the oil of the Holy Spirit; his perfect obedience was fragrant to the Father, and should be so to us; there was no leaven of guile or hypocrisy in his constitution. See Eph. 5:2. We should feed on his holy character by meditation and resemble it in daily living. The interposition of the priest was an essential feature of the ancient ritual, informing us that our prayer and self-surrender are acceptable to God through our Savior. We are also reminded by verse 14 that we are called to be a kind of firstfruits of his creatures to the Creator. See Jas. 1:18.

LEVITICUS 3:1–17

Peace Offerings from the Herd and the Flocks. The Lord Jesus has been set forth in Chapter 1 as the burnt offering in relation to God, and in Chapter 2 as the meal offering in relation to man. We are now to regard him as the peace offering, to rectify the disturbed relations between God and man. It supplied food for God in the fat devoured by the sacred fire upon the altar. It fed the priests in those parts specially reserved for them, Lev. 7:33, 34. But the worshiper also might participate, 7:15. Thus, it was a feast that brought into close relations God, priest, and people, and it furnished a beautiful typical picture of the truth taught in 1 John 1:3: "Our fellowship is with the Father, and with his Son Jesus Christ."

Before sitting at the sacrificial feast the offerer laid his hand on the victim's head, as though to transfer his sins; and we are reminded that we cannot feast on Christ as our Passover unless we have been first pardoned and justified through his death.

LEVITICUS 4:1-21

Sin Offerings for Priests and Congregation. The sweet savor offerings have now been considered. They are all concerned with consecration and communion. We now approach the sacrifices for sin, and first, for sins of ignorance. Here provision is made for the anointed priest, for the whole assembly, for the ruler, and for one of the common people. Do we realize sufficiently the sinfulness of our sins of omission—*i. e.,* of coming short of God's glory? See how much they cost! The innocent victim had to suffer; as afterward our Lord suffered without the gate, that he might make an atonement and sanctify his people with his own blood. We learn what the apostle meant when he described our Lord as being "made sin for us."

After certain portions had been placed upon the altar of burnt offering, the remainder of the carcass was burned without the camp, as though it were an altogether polluted thing. Note that the sin of the priest was deemed to require a more costly offering than that of the ordinary man, because he had sinned against fuller light.

LEVITICUS 4:22-35

Sin Offerings for Rulers and People. The character of the sin for which the sin offering was presented is expressed by the words, repeated again and again, "through ignorance," or "unwittingly," or "through error." It is the word used of the unintentional manslayer who without premeditation might kill another. See Num. 35. God's Word distinguishes deliberate, willful sin from that of which it may be said, "they know not what they do"; or, "I wot that through ignorance ye did it." See Luke 23:34; Acts 3:17. While the blood of the offering for the priest and the congregation was brought into the holy place and sprinkled seven times before the Lord, the blood of the offerings for the ruler or the individual was sprinkled only on the horns of the altar. The hue of the sin was not so dark in the latter case as where there was greater knowledge of God's will. In Luke 12:47, 48, our Lord makes a similar distinction.

LEVITICUS 5:1-13

Trespass Offerings for Various Sins. The sin offering was closely resembled by the trespass offering; but they differed in this: that the former was meant to fix the thought of the sinner rather on the evil of his *character,* and that there was within him a root of bitterness and a poisonous fountain. But the latter deals with the *acts* of transgression to which this evil character gives rise, and more specially with the harm which it inflicts on others. We need to confess our trespasses as often as we eat our daily bread; and it is very reassuring that, through the blood of Jesus, God forgives all our trespasses. See Col. 2:13.

It is very touching to notice the provision made for the very poor. Mary, the mother of our Lord, had to content herself with the two pigeons or turtledoves of verse 11. But none of us are exempted. We cannot come to the close of any day without kneeling to confess our sins and asking that we may be sprinkled from an evil conscience.

LEVITICUS 5:14—6:7

Trespass Offerings and Restitution. The root idea of the Hebrew word for *trespass* is "failure of duty through negligence." In addition to the sin itself, which is against God as the august Custodian of the law and order of the universe, the injury which such negligence inflicts upon one's neighbor must be met by a compensation and fine. Any sum which another has lost through us should, of course, be repaid, and a fifth part added, if required. But probably the main lesson of the trespass offering is that we cannot injure any fellow-creature without offending God. Our offense penetrates beyond the thin veil of humanity and the visible universe into the unseen Holy.

In dealing with all failures in regard to our fellows, there are three points, therefore, always to bear in mind: First, we must confess the sin to God. Second, we must seek out our brother and confess to him and ask his forgiveness, that we may win him as our Lord said, Matt. 18:15. And third, we must make restitution, with an addition. This was the teaching under the Law. Should it be less under the gospel of love?

LEVITICUS 6:8-23

Law of the Burnt Offering. Notice well the teaching of this paragraph, which has special reference to the fire which was to be kept always burning upon the altar. Thrice is the injunction repeated, vv. 9, 12, 13. As it originally descended from God, 9:24, so it was to be ever maintained by the watchful care of the priests.

It is interesting to notice that a different Hebrew word is used for the fire that burnt on the great brazen altar within the sacred enclosure from that which consumed the sin offering without the camp, 4:12. That symbolized the wrath of God against sin, while this symbolizes his love and grace, which descend to burn in human hearts. The apostle was very conscious of the latter when he said, "The love of Christ constraineth us." Whenever you feel the glow of that fire in your heart, be sure to nurse it. Ask that it may burn hotly. See Song of Sol. 8:6. It must be fed by the continual fuel of God's Word, consumed and absorbed in meditation. But remember the teaching of the latter part of this paragraph: Only holy souls may partake of the Heavenly Bread. "Let a man examine himself!"

LEVITICUS 6:24—7:10

Laws of the Sin and Trespass Offerings. The peculiar sanctity of the flesh of the sin and trespass offerings is clearly emphasized throughout this paragraph. Notice the repeated phrase, "it is most holy." This seems intended to emphasize the holiness of our Lord, who though he became a sin offering for us all knew no sin, neither was guile found in his mouth. He was searched with the minutest scrutiny, but Pilate, Herod, and Judas agreed in asserting that in him there was no fault. He was holy, harmless, and separate from sin.

Never was our Lord more absolutely "the Holy One of God" than when he was numbered with the transgressors and bare the sin of many. The cross was the climax of his obedience. How watchful we should be against anything that might soil us in our handling of sin in its infinite ramifications. As the priests who dealt with these offerings were permitted to eat of the flesh, are we not reminded that we derive the richest sustenance of our spiritual life by humble, penitent, and thankful meditation on the finished work of the cross?

LEVITICUS 7:11-21

Law of the Peace Offering. Here begins the law of the peace offerings, containing additional directions to those given in Chapter 3. They are classified as (1) thank offerings, (2) vow offerings, and (3) voluntary offerings. When the soul is full of gratitude, as was Hannah when Samuel was granted her in answer to prayer, what is more natural than that it should render some tangible recognition to him from whom cometh every good and perfect gift!

We are ready enough to cry to God in times of great sorrow, but are too forgetful of his benefits when the cloud passes and the sun shines again. In Israel the recognition took the form of a feast, in which the divine fire and the suppliant seem to feed together. The careful prohibition of the flesh remaining over was probably to teach that fresh mercies call for new songs. It had the further result of enforcing a liberal distribution of food among the poor. See also the connection of this thought with Ps. 16:10.

LEVITICUS 7:22-38

Things Forbidden; the Portion of the Priests. The eating of the fat and the blood was prohibited; the first probably during the pilgrimage, the latter in perpetuity. See Lev. 3:17. When we are told that the disobedient soul must be cut off, it refers probably to the excommunication which the priest pronounced until the offender had repented and was reinstated in the privileges of God's house. The *waving* of parts of the victim consisted in the priest placing his hands beneath those of the offerer, who held the piece to be waved, and moving them slowly backward and forward before the Lord, to and from the altar. The *heaving* was performed by slowly lifting the pieces upward and downward. These movements signified that the pieces, though not burnt at the altar, were specially consecrated to God's service.

The shoulder is the emblem of government and strength, the breast of the affections. We specially need to meditate on these aspects of our Lord's character. It may be that the action referred to in Acts 13:3 meant that the Church waved the two first missionaries as a votive offering to God.

LEVITICUS 8:1-17

Aaron and His Sons Consecrated. Here we have our Lord's eternal priesthood presented in miniature. The whole congregation had to be present, because each had a claim on Aaron's services, as each believer has a claim on Christ's. Each portion of Aaron's dress told of some trait or feature in Jesus' fitness to stand for us—the girdle, of his zeal; the robe and ephod, of his beauty and glory; the breastplate, that our names are written on his heart; the Urim and Thummim, of his wisdom to direct; the mitre, of his holiness.

The garments of the priests, the sons of Aaron, remind us of the spotless dress in which we should live, ever remembering that in the lowliest act we may minister to God. We, too, must be anointed, as Jesus was, with the fresh oil of Pentecost. The identification of our Lord with his people is typically set forth in the joint laying of hands on the victims. Jesus had no sins of his own, but he bore our sins and stood with us in the sinner's place, that he might raise us to his throne.

LEVITICUS 8:18–36

Offerings at Their Consecration. The blood of the ram of consecration was used in a remarkable way to symbolize deep truths. On Aaron's ear to express Christ's obedience unto death. On the right thumb to express Christ's willingness to do all that the Father required of him. On the right toe to express that all his ways pleased God. Our Lord was washed in his baptism, anointed with oil on the Mount of Transfiguration, and received the final baptism of consecration in blood on the cross. The sons of Aaron were treated in like manner, to show that in all these things Christians are called to be like Christ. See Matt. 20:22, 23. This remark specially applies to those who have been called to lead the flock.

Consecration, according to the Hebrew word, means "filling the hand." Too many of us suppose that the consecrated soul renounces all—nay, it *receives* all. The nets are full of fish; the baskets are full of the broken pieces; the soul is full of grace and glory. Let us keep the charge of the Lord till the daybreak, and we enter the Most Holy Place beyond the veil!

LEVITICUS 9:1–21

Aaron's Offerings for Himself and the People. In the concluding verses of Chapter 8, we read of Aaron and his sons feeding together on the flesh of the consecration offering for seven days, during which time they were not permitted to leave the Tabernacle—a striking figure of the present position of our Lord and his own during this dispensation, shut in with God, awaiting the manifestation of his glory.

May not this eighth day, on which the glory of the Lord appeared, be an emblem of that bright millennial morning when the congregation of Israel shall behold the true Priest issuing from the sanctuary, where he is now hidden from the eyes of men? And with him, when he is manifested, we shall be manifested also, "the companions of his retirement, and the happy participators of his glory." Oh, that none of us may miss that share in his epiphany, and that now our life may be hidden with Christ in glory! See Col. 3:1–4.

LEVITICUS 9:22—10:20

A Deed That Turned Joy into Grief. There was a double blessing. Aaron blessed the people when he stood against the altar, v. 22, and afterward when he came out of the Tabernacle, v. 23. We find here an illustration of the double blessing which our Lord gives his own. When he came from offering his supreme sacrifice on Calvary, which was burnt offering, peace offering, sin and trespass offerings combined, he blessed his own. We are told that as he blessed them he was borne upward to Heaven, Luke 24:51. But we expect another blessing from him, when he shall come forth out of the heavenly temple and extend his hands in benediction, using perhaps the very words of the ancient benediction.

But take care lest you ever introduce strange fire into your worship—*i.e.,* the fire of your own emotions, enthusiasm, and excitement. Ponder those mighty words in Lev. 10:1–3. We must not rush carelessly into the divine presence, though by the blood of Jesus we have been made nigh, Eph. 2:13.

LEVITICUS 11:1–23, 41–47

The Distinction Between Clean and Unclean. There were good and sufficient reasons for excluding certain animals from Israel's diet. Devout medical men insist that this is the finest sanitary code in existence, and that many of the diseases of modern life would disappear if it were universally adopted. God made these distinctions matters of religion, that the well-being of his people might be doubly assured. These restrictions were also imposed to erect strong barriers between the Chosen People and the heathen. So long as they obeyed, it was clearly impossible to participate in the heathen festivals, where many of these animals were partaken of.

We are not now bound by these enactments. Our Lord made all meats clean, Mark 7:19. Peter was bidden to kill and eat all manner of creeping things, and his protest was overborne by the assurance that God had cleansed all. See Acts 10:11–16. Religion consists not in outward rites, but in the inward temper. See Heb. 9:9, 10. Note that touching was forbidden, because the least contact with evil hurts the soul.

LEVITICUS 12:1–8

Purification after Childbearing. The birth of a boy involved seven days' ceremonial defilement; of a girl, fourteen. Not the child, but the mother was adjudged to be unclean, securing her a period of retirement and rest.

The gracious gradation in the sacrifices made

it possible for the poorest to obey, and it is a memorable fact that the mother of our Lord brought two pigeons or doves—fit emblems of her gentle nature—when she presented her babe in the Temple. See Luke 2:24. Our Lord became poor, that through his poverty we might be eternally enriched. In the light of this ceremonial, we are led back to Ps. 51:5, which we must personally and sadly ponder.

The initial rite of the Hebrew religion stood for separation. The parent taught the child to remember that he belonged to a separated race. It was impossible for him to consort with those who were aliens from the commonwealth of Israel. We all need to undergo the circumcision of Christ, which consists in putting away the sins of the flesh and ceasing to trust in our own energy. See Col. 2:11, 12.

LEVITICUS 13:1-59

The Test of Leprosy. Leprosy was a sort of living death, involving exclusion from the fellowship of the living and from the sanctuary. Consequently the process of restoration consisted of two stages: readmission, through the cure of disease, into the fellowship of the living, 13:1-59, and then to the camp and sanctuary through the due performance of prescribed rites, 14:1-32. The enumeration of the symptoms is very deliberate. The priest was required to conduct his examination with the greatest care, lest he should pronounce that to be leprosy which was not really so.

How different this to the sweeping and hasty judgments that we pass on each other! We judge by appearances only, and are not specially concerned to judge righteously. Sin, of which leprosy is the type, is not a superficial disease; it is "deeper than the skin." See vv. 3, 4, 25, 30, 31, 32, 34. They who know us best are not aware of the secret springs of impure motive, and the polluted things that hold empire within the soul. But the body of sin must be brought to an end at the cross. See Rom. 6:6.

LEVITICUS 14:1-20

The Law of the Cleansed Leper. The penalty, when leprosy had unmistakably declared itself, included compulsory severance from the camp, the rent garments, the bare head, the covered lip, the cry "unclean," 13:45. Sin severs us from fellowship with God and his saints, and makes us a source of contamination to all in contact with us, though they may not realize that we are defiling them.

Being cured, the leper was first *restored to the camp,* vv. 1-9. The birds are striking types of death and resurrection. Notice that the blood of one was mingled with fresh, *i.e.,* running, water, because of the perennial freshness of the blood of Christ; and that the ascension of the other, when liberated, is significant of the freedom from the law of sin and death which the soul of the believer experiences through the power of the Holy Spirit. See Rom. 8:1-4.

Secondly, the leper was *restored to the sanctuary,* vv. 1-20. On the eighth day of resurrection, the blood and oil were placed on thumb and toe and ear, because all our senses have been purchased and consecrated to the service of God. Let us, in gratitude for our own cleansing from sin, consecrate ourselves anew to God!

LEVITICUS 16:1-14

The Offerings for Atonement Day. This chapter contains the ritual of the great Day of Atonement, when the high priest entered within the veil. In virtue of the blood sprinkled upon the mercy seat, and still more of the faith exercised therein, Israel was cleansed from every sin before the Lord, 16:30. The death of his two sons acted as a solemn warning that Aaron should not deviate from the prescribed ceremonial in the smallest particular.

Every step is worthy of notice, each illustrates some feature in the sacrifice of Calvary, each is meant by the Holy Spirit of God to signify something. See Heb. 9:8, 9. The first goat was "for the Lord," representing the work of Christ in its Godward aspect. The second, like the second bird in Lev. 14:6, signified its manward aspect. It is necessary that we should personally avail ourselves of its efficacy. Our faith must "lay its hand on that dear head of thine." It was necessary that Aaron, as himself a sinner, must first offer for his own sins; and his offerings had to be repeated every year. See the triumphant contrast of Heb. 9:24.

LEVITICUS 16:15-34

The Scapegoat. The loneliness of the high priest, v. 17; the sprinkling of blood within the veil upon the mercy seat, v. 15; the fragrant incense, emblematic of a well-pleasing offering, v. 13; the confession of sin and its bearing away into a solitary land, v. 22; the linen garments of simplicity and humility, v. 23; the destruction of the carcasses of the beasts "without the camp," v. 27; the ultimate coming forth of the high priest to bless the people, bringing them the assurance of a finished and accepted work, v. 24 (compare Heb. 9:28)—all these points are carefully elaborated in the Epistle to the Hebrews.

The fate of the scapegoat was very moving! Laden with the sins of the people, it is led forth through the crowd of penitents, innocent yet execrated under the doom of the sinbearer, escaping death by the knife, to be forsaken even unto death! So Jesus died, with the cry of "Forsaken" on his lips.

LEVITICUS 17:1-16

"The Life of the Flesh Is in the Blood." Every animal that was slain for food was regarded as a kind of peace offering, and was therefore slain at the door of the Tabernacle. This Law, though it expressed a great principle, was only provisional. It was kept as long as Israel dwelt in the wilderness, but repealed when they entered the Land of Promise, where their numbers and diffusion would have rendered its strict observance impossible. See Deut. 12:15-24.

Very earnest insistence is laid on the prohibition of blood as an article of diet. See v. 10ff. The reason of this is in the repeated announcement that the life (or soul) is in the blood, vv. 11 and 14. When we are told that the blood maketh atonement, we learn that it does so because it represents the soul of the victim. Life is given for life, soul for soul.

Thus our Lord gave his blood, *i.e.,* his life or soul, a ransom for many. "He hath poured out his soul unto death" (Isa. 53:12). It was his blood, not as it was in his veins, but as poured out, that effected the reconciliation. See Eph. 1:7. It is the death of Christ in which the sinner finds peace. Compare Lev. 16:30 and 1 John 1:7.

LEVITICUS 23:1-14

Sabbath, Passover, and Firstfruits. The year of Israel's national life was marked out by high and blessed convocations, which preserved its unity, kept the people in mind of the great past, and kindled high ideals and enthusiasm. There is a divine precedent, therefore, in the observance of the Christian Year, with its holy services and commemorations. In its earlier stages the religious life requires the help of special times and seasons, when it may realize itself and catch sight of the Golden City.

A pause must be called in life's busy haste, and families should have an opportunity of gathering at solemn ceremonials, participation in which will leave lasting memories with the coming generation. Probably the mature soul outgrows these and ceases to observe days. See Col. 2:16. Remember that the absence of the temple in the new Jerusalem did not imply that there was no worship, but that every moment was worship.

LEVITICUS 23:15-32

Wave Loaves, Trumpets, and Atonement. The Hebrew feasts divide themselves into two groups, connected with the Passover and the Day of Atonement respectively, and occurring in the first and seventh months of the year. First came the Passover, on the fourteenth day of the first month, followed closely by the Week of Unleavened Bread, and at a distance of seven weeks further on by the Feast of Pentecost. (Pentecost is the Greek word for "fifty"; see v. 16.)

These three form the first group. Six months afterward, on the tenth day of the seventh month, came the most solemn day in the whole year—the Day of Atonement. It was preceded by the Feast of Trumpets, and followed closely by the Feast of Tabernacles. This was the second group. But each group set forth a distinct aspect of redemption. In the Passover, we are reminded that we were redeemed *from sin.* In the Atonement, we are redeemed *to God.* Do not forget to find Christ's resurrection in v. 11, and the firstfruits of the Spirit in v. 17.

LEVITICUS 23:33-44

The Feast of Tabernacles. The annual Feast of Tabernacles was a beautiful custom, when the whole people removed from their dwellings to spend the days and nights in booths constructed out of the verdant boughs gathered from woodland and forest. How the children must have reveled in the experience, and what a healthy change it made for them all! The great lesson, of course, was to recall the wilderness experience of their fathers, during which the Almighty was their fellow-pilgrim.

In figure they confessed that they were still pilgrims and strangers on the earth and had no abiding city, but sought one to come. It was the custom of the feast in later years to pour water, drawn from Siloam, on the Temple pavement, in memory of the water supplies of the wilderness—the rock that followed them. And it was on that occasion that Jesus uttered his memorable appeal. See John 7:37.

LEVITICUS 24:1-23

Light and Bread and the Holy Name. The words "Before the Lord" are twice repeated in the opening paragraph. The pure lamplight, emblematic of the influence of a religious life, and the showbread, set on the golden table, emblematic of lives of obedience and devotion, which are well-pleasing to God, are both said to be "before the Lord." We are reminded of the command to Abram, "Walk *before me* and be thou perfect"; and of the words of the dying Jacob, "The God *before whom* my fathers, Abraham and Isaac, did walk." This implies the continual consciousness of the presence of God. We all possess what may be termed a subconsciousness, which lies beneath our ordinary sense. Let that be God-filled!

What a pitiable condition that half-breed (v. 10) was in! May we be Israelites indeed, in whom is no guile! How they reverenced the very name of God. See 3 John 7.

LEVITICUS 25:1–17

The Sabbatic Year and the Jubilee. As the weekly Sabbath was to give rest for man and beast, so the sabbatical year, returning after six years of unbroken harvest, was to be a rest for the land "unto the Lord." The year of jubilee, at the end of seven weeks of years, gave an opportunity of restoration for the poor and those who had been compelled to alienate their lands. The year of jubilee points onward to the "redemption of the purchased possession," Eph. 1:14, when all the disabilities which have befallen us shall be made good, and we shall regain all that glorious inheritance which was ours in the divine purpose, but which we have alienated by our sin.

With what joy must thousands have heard the notes of that trumpet sounding out over the land! Yes, and the trumpet shall sound, and the dead shall be raised incorruptible, and we shall be changed. Then incorruption shall inherit the kingdom of God! See 1 Cor. 15:52.

LEVITICUS 25:18–34

Consideration for the Poor. It was good for the land to lie fallow for one year in seven; and it was a wise provision that it should not be sold in perpetuity. This enactment prevented the stamping out of the small landowners and the accumulation of the land in the hands of a few wealthy families. Though a man might be compelled by stress of circumstances to sell his little farm to a wealthy creditor, when the fiftieth year came around it returned to his possession and there was no further claim on the part of the creditor against him and his estate.

With what joy must debtors and bond servants have heard the notes of the trumpet ring out. For us, the lesson is that our Lord has proclaimed "the acceptable year of the Lord." All that we lost in Adam is restored to us in the redemption; that is, in Christ Jesus. Nay, we have greatly gained! Where sin abounded, grace has superabounded. For innocence, we have purity; for a garden, a city; for the evening fellowship with God, the knowledge that we are sons and heirs.

LEVITICUS 25:35–55

Freedom in the Year of Jubilee. If a man, through misfortune, were forced to sell himself into serfdom to meet his debts, he could not be legally retained after the trumpet had sounded, but was free to return to his home and family. His rich neighbor, during the time of his distress, was not to exact usury on any loan that he might make, but must give him food, lodging, and help without charge. The poor man was to be treated not as a slave, but as a hired servant and fellow-citizen whose engagement was of a temporary character, and who might be redeemed at any time before the jubilee through friendly interposition of a relative.

Nothing in modern legislation equals the jubilee in the interests of religion, social order, and liberty. Is it to be believed that when we, in our various distresses, go to our Heavenly Father, we shall fare any worse than the poor peasant did at the hands of his rich neighbor? And in Jesus have we not one nigh of kin who will redeem us at all costs?

LEVITICUS 26:1–20

Results of Obedience and Disobedience. There is a vast contrast between the ideal life of the first thirteen verses of this chapter and the remainder, just the distinction which God ever makes between a life of obedience and faith and one of disobedience and disbelief. In our inner life we also may have that blessed rain of spiritual grace, the fruitfulness and the peace, the safety and the victory, the old store reaching to the new, the breaking of our bars, and the snapping of our yoke.

If these privileges are not yours, think back on your past to ascertain whether you are walking in all God's commandments, or are in anything walking contrary to them. Confess your sins and return, and dare to believe that he will bring you again, if penitent and believing, into the old glad position. But if "ye will not," vv. 14, 18, 21, 23, 27, heavy penalties must befall. God loves us too well to allow us to drift, unwarned and unrestrained, to perdition.

LEVITICUS 26:21–46

Desolation and Captivity for the Stubborn. Notwithstanding the solemn and appalling pictures placed before Israel in Chapter 26, they forsook the Lord and served other gods. Thus, they brought upon themselves the sore judgments threatened against them, consisting of defeat, scarcity, wild beasts, pestilence and famine, the horrors of siege, and desolation, followed by dispersion to the four winds of Heaven. The book of Judges illustrates the first and the destruction of Jerusalem, as told by Josephus, the last of these plagues.

Under the curse of this chapter, the Chosen People are suffering to this very hour. Scattered, wasted, and outcast, they are monuments of God's truthfulness to his word. They teach an impressive lesson which the nations of the world would do well to lay to heart. Note that remarkable expression about accepting their punishment as the necessary condition of forgiveness and restoration. The same condition always holds.

THE BOOK OF NUMBERS

THE EXPERIENCES IN THE WILDERNESS

I. THE CAMP AT SINAI   *1:1—10:10*
   A. The first numbering and location of the tribes   *1, 2*
   B. Location and duties of the Levites   *3, 4*
   C. Laws regarding lepers, marital jealousy, and the Nazirites   *5, 6*
   D. Offerings of the princes   *7*
   E. The golden lamps and the consecration of the Levites   *8*
   F. The Passover and the cloudy pillar   *9:1—10:10*

II. FROM SINAI TO THE JORDAN   *10:11—22:1*
   A. The departure, the seventy elders, and "the graves of lust"   *10:11—11:35*
   B. The jealousy of Miriam and Aaron   *12*
   C. The spies sent from Kadesh; their reports and God's sentence   *13—15*
   D. Korah's rebellion; Aaron's rod   *16, 17*
   E. Duties of priests and Levites; the water of purification   *18, 19*
   F. Again at Kadesh; Moses' sin; Edom's opposition; Aaron's death   *20*
   G. The Canaanites; the fiery serpent; the Amorities conquered   *21—22:1*

III. IN THE PLAINS OF MOAB   *22:2—36*
   A. Balak and Balaam   *22—24*
   B. Baal-peor and the zeal of Phinehas   *25*
   C. The second numbering; Joshua chosen   *26, 27*
   D. The offerings for the different holy days and the laws of vows   *28—30*
   E. The conquest of Midian   *31*
   F. Division of the land; Aaron's death; Levitical cities; cities of refuge   *32—35*
   G. Additional laws of inheritance   *36*

INTRODUCTION

In the Hebrew this book is called "In the desert." The ordinary name by which we know it is derived from the two "numberings" of Israel, the former (Chapters 1 to 4) in the second year of their journey, the latter (Chapter 26) on the borders of Canaan, thirty-eight years afterward.

The early part (Chapters 1 to 10) appears as a supplement to Leviticus, being occupied with the appointment of the three great families of Levites to their respective departments in the sacred offices. The narrative of the march through the wilderness is then given as far as 21:20, after which the story of the conquest of the country east of the Jordan is narrated. The long years during which the generation that refused to respond to the faith of Joshua and Caleb were dying off in the wilderness lie between Chapters 19 and 20, ending with the reassembling of the congregation at Kadesh for another forward movement. The form of the book is that of a journal in which all the passing occurrences of interest and importance were recorded.

COMMENTARY

NUMBERS 1:1-4, 16-19, 44-54

Numbered for War; Set Apart for Worship. This book records two numberings of the host; the first at Sinai, and the second, thirty-eight years after, on the threshold of Canaan. It is also the book of the wilderness wanderings and contains the story of journeys, service, and vicissitude. It is therefore a valuable guidebook to the Church in her present stage.

For us, too, there is a census. God numbers his jewels. He keeps an inventory of his people. Not one of them is omitted, however weak or unworthy. "In thy book *all* my members are written." We must be able to tell our pedigree; *i. e.*, we must be assured of our regeneration into God's family. If we are doubtful about our being children of God, we shall be fit for neither campaigning nor fighting. The secret of failure always lies here. The Levites were not included because, in a very special sense, they belonged to God. He therefore was responsible for their well-being as he is for all of us who are united by faith with Christ—the true Aaron.

NUMBERS 3:1-13, 44-51

The Substitute for the Firstborn. The Levites were taken, instead of the firstborn sons of Israel, to perform the service of the Tabernacle. There were nearly as many Levites as firstborn, and the difference was made good by the payment of redemption money on the part of the surplus, vv. 45-48. So each of us has been redeemed by the blood of the Lamb to belong to God and to minister to him! Aaron's family provided the priesthood, vv. 9, 10. The rest of the tribe performed the more irksome duties of ministry and transport.

The Gershonites, as eldest, pitched westward of the Tabernacle and cared for the hangings and curtains. The Kohathites, because related to Aaron, pitched southward and had charge of the sacred vessels. The Merarites pitched northward and had charge of the boards and sockets. It was enough for each to know that his place and charge were God-appointed. Even to carry a pin became honorable when God had allotted that to a man as his share.

NUMBERS 6:1-12

The Vow of Separation. The law of the Nazirite is full of instruction, because he is a type of the child of God who is separated from evil, that he may be wholly surrendered and given over to the divine service. Three rules were enjoined. *Not to touch any product of the vine.* If we must have exhilaration and stimulus, let us seek it in the Holy Spirit, not in worldly excitement, Eph. 5:18, 19. *Not to cut the hair.* The unshorn locks signified the dedication of the natural powers to God's service. Let us beware of Delilah. Many are the razors waiting to deprive us of our crown, Judges 16:19. *Not to touch the dead, however dear.* The kingdom of God must supersede all earthly ties.

If our separation breaks down, vv. 9–12, we must seek forgiveness and restoration; but the former days will not count. One sin may mar the power of a whole life of saintly testimony.

NUMBERS 6:13–27

The Nazirite Offering; the Priestly Blessing. Take heed, O Christian soul who hast dedicated thyself to some lofty purpose; be warned by the law of the Nazirite! Thy God expects of thee a more careful walk than is required of others. The cups of gaiety of which they drink are not for thee. Shame and rebuke may fall to thy lot, from which they escape. Thou art specially to beware against defiling contact with aught that savors of death—those who are dead in trespasses and sins. Go with them only to save them, but never to participate in their ways.

If the Nazirite vows were violated, even by accident, the time that had elapsed was canceled. Ah, how many of our days we have rendered void! The beautiful benediction with which the chapter closes has its counterpart in 2 Cor. 13:14. What the human lips spoke on earth, God authenticated from Heaven, v. 27. Be very careful for the honor of the Name! See 3 John 7.

NUMBERS 7:1–11, 89

Princely Generosity; the Voice of God. This and the two following chapters conclude the account of the stay at Sinai. The transport of the furniture of the Tabernacle was committed to the Levites, and the wagons, enumerated here, made their work much simpler. Two were assigned for hangings and drapery, and four for the more solid and cumbersome portions. The sacred vessels were borne on the shoulders of living men—the Kohathites.

Instead of bulking together these twelve gifts, the divine Spirit lingers lovingly over each. In God's book of remembrance each alabaster box is noted by itself. Note that the vessels were not only costly, but filled! "Both of them were full," v. 13ff.

Ponder v. 89. Would that our ears were opened that we might ever hear that voice speaking from between the cherubim, directing in perplexity and revealing the deep things of God!

NUMBERS 8:1–13

Lights in God's House; Clean Workmen. It is strange to come on this paragraph about the candlestick amid the preparations for leaving Sinai. But typically it is appropriate, because the people of God are called, in their earthly pilgrimage, to shine as lights in the world.

The beaten work of gold is significant of persecution, and the one lump of gold indicates the essential unity of the Church. The Levites were symbolically cleansed by the water and the razor. This was required for those who were sprung from a stock so cruel, Gen. 49:7.

Next they were offered to God; *i.e.,* Israel transferred to them the obligations of ministry, which up to this time had been performed by the firstborn. As the priest was wont to wave a portion of the sacrifice before God, so Aaron, v. 11. The counterpart of this is Acts 13:3. Missionaries, teachers, and others who perform certain functions for us all may be regarded as wave offerings.

NUMBERS 8:14–26

Consecrated to God's Service. The Levites may be taken to represent the Church as distinguished from the rest of mankind, or the little band of pastors, teachers, and missionaries set apart for the service of the Church. In any case, they needed to be perpetually reminded that sin mingled with the holiest ceremonial, and required the perpetual cleansing of sacrifice. After our holiest services we need to remember that we are unprofitable servants.

From thirty to fifty is the prime of human life. There is no inconsistency between Num. 4:3 and v. 24 here, because a five years' novitiate was required. When we can no longer bear the strain of mind and body, we may still keep the holy charge and minister before the altar of incense, vv. 25, 26. So it was with Zacharias in Luke 1:7, 9. We can intercede as long as we live, and our maintenance will only cease with our lifework.

NUMBERS 9:1–14

Keeping the Passover. The Passover was celebrated in Egypt, Exod. 12; in the wilderness; and in the land of Canaan, Joshua 5. The thought of our redemption must underpin *all* the great movements of individuals and the Church. This one was specially memorable, because it led to the institution of "the little Passover," vv. 6, 7. Moses did not hasten to give an answer of his own, but waited upon God. The divine nature makes allowance for disabilities over which we have no control. See 2 Chron. 30:13–20.

In the welcome given to strangers, we discover the wideness of God's mercy. We, too, were strangers and foreigners, Eph. 2:19-21. My soul, never forget how thou wast once a stranger to the covenant of promise! Thine were the crumbs of the feast! But God has made thee sit with the children and included thee in the gracious provisions of his covenant!

NUMBERS 9:15-23

The Cloud Upon the Tabernacle. We do not know the shape of this cloud, whether it was a great cumulus, or spread out over the camp like an umbrella so as to shelter the people from the sun's glare. As night fell, the shekinah-fire that burnt at its heart became apparent. But whether it sheltered by day or illumined by night, it was always the symbol of the divine Presence. All this prefigured the guidance and shelter that are afforded to his people by our Lord. Compare John 8:12.

Friends may urge you to make a change. The scarcity of your resources and the pressure of your foes may appear to force a move. A nameless fear may suggest that you will never hold your ground. But so long as the cloud doesn't move, you must tarry where you are. Where the cloud broods, the manna falls. "My soul, wait thou only upon God!" Never go in front of God, nor lag behind, nor hesitate to strike your tent if he leads on.

NUMBERS 10:1-16

The Trumpets Sound the March. Each trumpet was made of a solid piece of silver. They fulfilled several purposes: summoning an assembly, sounding the march, gathering for battle. They are referred to symbolically in Matthew 24:31 and 1 Cor. 15:52. We are constantly being called to arise and depart! Is not the trumpet calling today to a slumbering Church to move out to the evangelization of the world? For a whole year Israel had sojourned under Sinai. They left Egypt an undisciplined crowd; they had become a nation and a marshaled host. Each knew his credentials and standard; every tribe had its appointed place. The soul must visit Sinai, but not live there. It must journey forth to Hermon, Olivet, Calvary. The Church is moving on! Find thy place in the great procession and keep it. You are remembered by God and saved from your enemies! Compare v. 9 and Isaiah 52:12.

NUMBERS 10:17-36

"Come Thou With Us." The invitation of Moses to Hobab is one that we may all give to our friends: "We are journeying to the place of which the Lord hath spoken." We should always be on the alert for those who are not formally united to the Church, and we can always promise that we can do them good. Only good awaits those who travel with their backs to Egypt and their faces toward the Heavenly City. God has prepared for those who love him such good things as it is beyond words to declare. See 1 Cor. 2:9.

And how much we may benefit by such companionships! Hobab was probably Moses' brother-in-law, and Jethro having returned to Midian he was all the more needed to lead Israel to the best routes and the most suitable halting-places, where shade and water could be found. Such a guide would be invaluable. Ministers are such! For Hobab's reward see Judges 1:16 and 4:11. Who would not follow where the Ark of the Covenant leads, and rest where the cloud broods? See John 10:4.

NUMBERS 11:1-15

The Murmuring Flesh-lovers. We cannot wonder at the people's murmuring. They were unaccustomed to the fatigues of the desert, and had not realized the length of the journey. Let us beware of querulous complaints. See 1 Cor. 10:10. Let us also guard against familiarity with those who have never known God's regenerating grace. "The mixed multitude" was largely composed of Egyptians whose evil example spread to the chosen people, Ex. 12:38. When our religious life is low, we tire of angels' food and our hearts turn back to the world we have left.

Moses' outcry is hardly to be wondered at. He was thoroughly overstrained by the immense demands of his life. But he ought not to have spoken as though the entire weight of the pilgrimage rested on him. His Almighty Friend was bearing and carrying them during "all the days of old." See Isa. 63:9. We must never look at our responsibilities apart from him who makes all grace abound, 2 Cor. 9:8.

NUMBERS 11:16-25

God's Spirit Upon the Seventy. God's considerateness for his overwrought servant was very tender. He knows our frame and remembers that we are dust. He does not chide, nor keep his anger forever. The remedy for the situation was provided in the appointment and enduement of the seventy elders, who became the germ of the Sanhedrin.

Moses' depression led to unbelief. It seemed

impossible to suppose that God could provide a table in the wilderness, of such magnitude that in it the whole host could participate. Unbelief says, Can God? Faith answers, God can! See Ps. 78:19. Child of God, God's hand is not short, that it cannot reach to you. Even if we believe not, he remains faithful, 2 Tim. 2:13. This equipping of the elders, v. 25, reminds us that we, too, need to receive the Holy Spirit, first for our sanctification in character, and then for our service and office. This is the special characteristic of Pentecost, Acts 2:1-4.

NUMBERS 11:26-35

"The Graves of Lust." It is delightful to note the proof of the nobility of Moses' nature in the answer he gave to the tidings concerning Eldad and Medad. They might not be of the designated group of elders, and might not have gone out to the Tabernacle, as in v. 16. They remind us of the unordained and simple disciples of Acts 11:19ff. But there was no envy in Moses' nature. He would have been only thankful if all had reached a degree of grace even beyond his own attainment.

The quails came. They flew in prodigious flocks which darkened the air. Exhausted by their long flight, they hovered within three feet of the ground, and so were easily captured. But the passionate haste in eating brought its own terrible nemesis to the Israelites. The story became engraved in the very name given to their halting-place, Ps. 106:15. My soul, beware lest thou also be precipitated by thy passionate desires into that grave! See Gal. 5:17.

NUMBERS 12:1-15

God Protects Moses Against Criticism. This Ethiopian wife may have been Zipporah, or some other woman whom Moses married after his first wife's death. That Moses, the great lawgiver and leader who could rule a turbulent multitude and face the great king of Egypt, should take the taunts of his brother and sister so quietly, indicates how deep and far-reaching had been the transformation of his character. Compare Exodus 2:12ff. "Fret not thyself because of evildoers... Rest in the Lord, and wait patiently for him," Ps. 37:1, 7.

When we hand our cause over to God he comes down, v. 5. He rebukes the enemy and avenger. Be faithful to him and you may reckon on his faithfulness to you! That commendation of faithfulness which Moses received may be won by all! See Matthew 25:21.

Our intercession may bring pardon and healing; but sin leaves its mark, v. 15. You are shut out of the enjoyment of the camp, and the march is delayed. Ponder James 3:5, 6.

NUMBERS 12:16—13:20

The Spies Sent to Canaan. By comparing the opening verses with Deut. 1:19-22, it appears that the suggestion about the spies emanated from the people, and that their proposal was graciously accepted by God. But let us remember that it is a profound mistake to spy out or criticize the land or lot into which we are being led. We are almost certain to see the difficulties apart from the grace, and they sometimes appear to be insurmountable.

It is better to await with calm trust the unfoldings of divine providence. The book of the future is in the hands of the Lamb that was slain, Rev. 5:7, 8. Take no thought for tomorrow! Go steadily on! God will go before you, and cleave your way! Unbelief sees giants and spells them with "G"; faith sees God, and spells giants with "g." Abraham "staggered not at the promise of God," Rom. 4:20.

NUMBERS 13:21-33

The Majority and Minority Reports. It was August. Eshcol lay southeast of Hebron. Its sloping hills were covered with choice grapevines, the clusters of which weighed ten to twelve pounds. The tall, muscular Canaanites presented a strong contrast to the more diminutive Egyptians the Israelites had left behind. The spies compared the Canaanites with themselves, instead of with Almighty God. Do not look at God through circumstances, but at circumstances through God. There is no land worth possessing which has not its giants; but, like Caleb, faith looks not at giants, but to the living God. See 14:8. The doubters said, Can God? Caleb affirmed, God can! Only follow God fully! Be utterly yielded to him. Present yourself to God as alive from the dead, and eternally united to the living Christ; then he will bruise Satan under your feet and make you tread upon the lion and adder. See Ps. 91:13; Rom. 16:20.

NUMBERS 14:1-12

An Unbelieving and Rebellious People. What in any other nation would have been described as a panic of fear was, in the case of Israel, a panic of unbelief, which deserved the reproachful expostulation of Jehovah in v. 11. The transition is easy from unbelief to open rebellion against God, as expressed in the words, "Let us make a captain, and let us return into Egypt." The connection between the fearful and unbelieving is very close, Rev. 21:8. On the other hand, we have the exhortation of 2 Pet. 1:5, "Add to your faith virtue [or courage]," as exemplified in the language of Joshua and Caleb. But their words of faith and encouragement only elicited hatred and murder.

Compare v. 10 with Gen. 4:4 and Heb. 11:4. God's two stalwart witnesses did not minimize the strength or the numbers of the foe, but magnified the mighty power pledged to fulfill the ancient covenant with Abraham: "The Lord is with us: fear them not." He cannot fail the trustful soul!

NUMBERS 14:13-25

Pardon by Moses' Intercession. Moses was free from selfish ambition. His one thought was for the glory of God. When for a moment the suggestion presented itself to his mind that his own seed should take the place of this rebellious race, he instantly dismissed it. It was not to be entertained for a moment, lest the Egyptians make capital of it. He had no desire to be the ancestor of a great nation, if it would tarnish the divine honor. He would rather be consigned to oblivion himself than that one jewel in the glorious galaxy of God's glory should be bedimmed.

There were three arguments in his intercession: God's reputation, God's consistency with himself, and God's mercy. Methinks I hear the voice of the Supreme Mediator behind these pleadings! His prayer was heard, but the generation that believed not could not enter the land. You may escape Egypt and yet miss Canaan. See Heb. 3:12-19.

NUMBERS 14:26-45

The Penalty of Unbelief and Rashness. The old translation in verse 34 was unfortunate. "Breach of promise" is better rendered "my alienation." It is still better to notice the marginal reading, "the revoking of my promise." But even this hardly gives us the true meaning of the words, which teach us that God's promises are conditional on our faith. He cannot do what we fail to trust him to do.

The key of faith will unlock every drawer and cupboard in the divine treasury, but we must use it. If we will not trust God with our life, we shall be left to perish in the wilderness of drought, of restlessness, and of peril. Unbelief paralyzes God's arm. See Matt. 13:58. And let us learn from the closing paragraph that the might of our own right hand will never avail to accomplish what is forfeited by unbelief. "It shall not prosper."

NUMBERS 15:27-41

Exemplary Punishment for Sabbath-breaking. This chapter resembles a sweet flute-like melody inserted between two fierce strains. It reminds us that in the midst of wrath, God remembers mercy. The stranger—whether pilgrim, emigrant, or slave—was to be included in burnt offerings and sacrifices, a preview of the time when all holy souls shall be reckoned in the household of God, Eph. 2:19.

Sins of ignorance may be forgiven, vv. 22-29. They are sins. *Debts* of shortcoming need pardon equally as do trespasses. But, as Paul teaches us, we may confidently count on forgiveness for evil things done unwittingly. See 1 Tim. 1:12-14; Heb. 5:2. It is quite otherwise with *sins of presumption*, vv. 30-36. If persisted in, these induce death. See 1 John 5:16.

We have something better than the memorial fringe, the ministry of the Holy Spirit, John 14:26.

NUMBERS 16:1-19

The Rebellion of Korah. This was a very serious revolt, because so many princes associated themselves with the Levites. Jealousy was at the root of the entire movement. "All the congregation are holy," they said. "Wherefore lift ye up yourselves?" There is no root of bitterness that needs such careful watching as jealousy! If it is in your heart you must, like Samuel of old and General Gordon in our own times, "hew Agag in pieces before the Lord."

The record of Moses' meekness precedes this story of his testing. Whatever is strongest and best in us will be searched as by fire. Even Moses was ruffled by these gross charges. See v. 15. The best of men are but men at best. Only Jesus was without a flaw.

What a beautiful thought is expressed in vv. 5, 7, 9. There are holy and blessed souls who have special right of access into God's presence-chamber. See Zech. 3:7.

NUMBERS 16:20-35

Divine Judgment upon the Rebels. It was wise of Moses not to attempt to vindicate himself, but to let God maintain his cause. He is not slow to undertake the vindication of those who entrust their reputation with him. To take the sword is to perish by the sword. "Wait on the Lord and keep his way, and he will exalt thee to inherit the land."

The doom of Korah and his fellow-conspirators was very terrible; but if they had been spared, the whole camp would have been infected, and God's purposes frustrated. Those who suffer from the bubonic plague must be instantly separated from their fellows, for the sake of society! Remember, as Jude says, that the pit still devours, v. 11. In these last days of the present age, and in view of the terrible records of this chapter, we may well ponder the summons of Rev. 18:4. The congregation was spared because of the divine compassion of which Moses had a true conception. Their prayer only reflected the divine thought, v. 22.

NUMBERS 16:36-50

"Between the Dead and the Living." The censers served as plates for the altar. Even evil men and evil things will be made to subserve the divine purposes. See Acts 2:23. What a wonderful anticipation of our Lord's eternal priesthood and intercession is furnished by this picture of Aaron waving his censer between the living and the dead, and arresting the plague! On which side do you stand? Are you among the living, or among the dead? Is Christ to you a savor of life unto life or of death unto death? Awake thou that sleepest and arise from the dead, and Christ shall enlighten thee.

The priesthood and the incense offering had been usurped by Korah to his destruction; but as exercised by God's appointed priest, they brought life. It is an awful thing for mortal man to intrude into the sacred prerogatives of Christ. See 1 Tim. 2:5.

NUMBERS 17:1-13

The Budding of Aaron's Rod. The controversy about the priesthood needed authoritative settlement, and to remove all grounds of dissension a notable sign was wrought on Aaron's rod. "The man's rod, whom I shall choose, shall blossom." This is an eternal principle. There is an indissoluble connection between God's choice and our fruitfulness. "I have chosen you, and ordained you," said our Lord, "that ye should go and bring forth fruit."

In the Epistle to the Hebrews we learn that Aaron's budding rod symbolized our Lord's unwithering priesthood. See Heb. 7:24. He seemed as a root out of the dry ground; but in the grave the rod of Jesse began to bud and blossom and bear fruit. We may seem to be mere bare rods, but if we become united to Christ by a living faith we shall partake of his strength and beauty. "A man can receive nothing, except it be given him from heaven." "From me is thy fruit found," Hos. 14:8.

NUMBERS 18:21-32

Give God the Best. The inner service of the Tabernacle was assigned to the priests, who must be of the house of Aaron. The Levites were joined to the house of Aaron for the more menial service. In vv. 5-20, the maintenance of the priests is provided for; and in vv. 21-32, the maintenance of the Levites. A tithe of the heave offerings of Israel was assigned to them. It had been Levi's doom to be scattered in Israel, Gen. 49:7. But the curse was transmuted to blessing. They were summoned to perform the priestly office of the firstborn, and God was not unmindful to reward them for their arduous labors. He himself became their inheritance.

But though the Levite's sustenance was assured from the gifts of Israel, he was not absolved from the privilege and duty of contributing to the service of God. He, too, must offer a tithe for the support of the priests. "We are members one of another."

NUMBERS 19:1-22

Purification for Uncleanness. We might have expected this chapter to occur in Leviticus. Is it not incongruous in this narrative of the pilgrimage? Nay; this is the most appropriate place, since in the desert march we are more exposed to the touch of defilement, such as needs daily cleansing lest we be shut out from fellowship with God.

The ashes of an heifer are emblematic of the work of our Lord. See Heb. 9:13, 14. No blemish; never a yoke; slain without the camp; counted an unclean thing! It was easy for the Jew to contract ceremonial defilement. To walk over a grave was enough. But the ashes of the heifer mingled with spring—or running—water restored the polluted soul to the family and the Tabernacle. So as we confess our sins, we are sprinkled from an evil conscience, we are restored to unity with God and his people, and we walk in newness of life.

NUMBERS 20:1-13

The Sin of Moses and Aaron. Again the people, as the long years of their wilderness life drew to an end, gathered around the Tabernacle at Kadesh. Again the murmuring spirit broke out, as it had done forty years before. To the end we shall be liable to the outbreak of the old sins, and can never relax our vigilance or sheathe the sword.

Moses was to *speak* to the rock, not smite it. See Exod. 17:6. The Rock of Ages was smitten only once. "It is appointed unto men *once* to die," and "Christ was *once* offered to bear the sins of many." It is now only needful for the soul to speak to him, though in the lowest and most faltering accents, to elicit streams of help and salvation.

It was lack of faith that led Moses to smite the rock twice. Speaking seemed too slight an effort for the production of such a marvel! He forgot that neither rod nor speech effected the result, but the power of God that wrought through and with him. See 1 Cor. 3:4. The woman only "touched the hem of his garment" (Matt. 9:20).

NUMBERS 20:14-29

Edom Refuses Passage; Aaron Dies. It was an ungracious act on the part of the Edomites—descendants of Esau, Jacob's brother—to forbid the passage of the Chosen People through their territory; and it was never forgotten. It is referred to again and again in the strongest terms by prophet and psalmist. See Deut. 2:4, 8; 23:7; Amos 1:11; Obad. 10, 12; Ps. 137:7.

Aaron's death was arranged so as to give him a distant glimpse of the Land which had so long beckoned him onward. But he was not suffered to continue. His death is quoted in evidence of the imperfection of the Aaronic priesthood, in contrast to the indissoluble priesthood of our Lord, Heb. 7:16.

This is a sad chapter! Moses' failure, Aaron's and Miriam's death, Edom's refusal! But God's purpose moved steadily on. He wrought for his own sake, because of the covenant.

NUMBERS 21:1-20

The Brazen Serpent; Journeying to Pisgah. It often falls to our lot to circle the land of Edom! It is bad enough to have to fight the desert tribes, but it is harder to traverse the long circuitous route, which a little kindness on our brother's part might have rendered needless. What discouragement, heartbreak, and fainting we cause one another!

The story of the brazen serpent was quoted by our Lord to Nicodemus, John 3:14. It exemplifies the law that like cures like. Our Lord came in the likeness of sinful flesh and for sin, and as such was nailed to the tree, that the progress of sin and death might be arrested. Whosoever directs to him the look of faith shall have everlasting life.

Near the pole-foot sprang up the brook, vv. 17, 18. We are reminded of the connection between the cross and Pentecost. Spring up, O well of the Holy Spirit, in our hearts and churches and schools! The living water is within; summon it!

NUMBERS 21:21-35

Victory Over the Amorites. Two great victories opened the eastern lands to the possession and settlement of two tribes and a half. It is not enough to know our heritage in Christ; we must possess our possessions.

Sihon, the king of the Amorites, made an unprovoked attack on Israel; and his action was the less excusable, because he had himself been an invader. As a proof of this, a passage is quoted from one of their national songs, in which the poet describes his invasion of the land, the burning of Heshbon and Ar, and the erection of new cities in their stead, vv. 27-30. See also Judges 11:13-27. Sihon and Og suffered the same fate at the hands of Israel. General Gordon, when crossing the Sudan to attack the slave trader, often heard these words in his heart: "Fear him not: for I have delivered him into thy hand." See Ps. 135:11; 136:19, 20. Behind all history is divine and everlasting love!

NUMBERS 22:1-20

Balaam Sent for, to Curse Israel. These chapters present a surprising contrast between the covetous prophet and his sublime prophecies. It is clearly possible to be the mouthpiece of truth, and yet have neither part nor lot in it.

Balak, as had been predicted, was sore afraid. Compare v. 3 with Exod. 15:15. The elders of Midian were his friends and allies. It was very important for them to stand together. The journey across the desert to Mesopotamia, where Balaam lived, was long and tedious, but he was a famous magician who could marshall unseen forces into the battle by his incantations. He knew the only true God, but loved the wages of unrighteousness and erred for reward. See 2 Pet. 2:14-16; Jude 11.

He made up his mind to win Balak's promised gifts, and sought to persuade God to become his accomplice, first, by letting him go and, secondly, by letting him say what Balak wished said. But God demands our loyalty and unison with him, and will not swerve from the path of truth and righteousness by a hair's-breadth to help our desires and ambitions.

NUMBERS 22:21-40

Balaam Warned What to Speak. If only Balaam had abided by his first answer to Balak's request, he would have been saved from the disgrace and suffering which ensued. But he seemed to think that it was possible to alter God's mind; hence his request to the second company of messengers that they give him time to ascertain God's will. Already that will had been clearly made known to him; what object had he in pressing for a further response?

When finally he was told that he might go, he rose up in the morning, saddled his ass, and started posthaste. He was trying to serve two masters—to speak as God bade him, but to please Balak and pocket his gold.

How many agencies God uses to arrest our evil courses! Peter specially refers to this incident, 2 Peter 2:16. Many futile cries are raised to stop the boat that is caught in the rapids above Niagara! Thus the way of transgressors is stopped by the love of God!

NUMBERS 22:41—23:12

A Blessing Instead of a Curse. Notice the position of these chapters, preceding the awful story of Baal-peor. Presently the Israelites will be perpetrating such terrible sins that it might seem impossible for God to continue to acknowledge them; yet here God stands for them and restrains the spirit of evil. He will take their chastisement, when needed, into his own hands.

With all his might Balaam strove to earn the royal gifts. Ah, thought he, that I could really feel that I was the organ of the divine malediction! But he could not feel in his heart that God's Spirit was urging him in the direction that Balak wished. The stream of destiny was not running that way. On the contrary, he could forge no weapon against Israel that could prosper, and when he tried to raise his tongue in judgment against the people of God he was condemned. It was as if God said, "Touch not mine anointed," Ps. 105:15. See Isa. 54:17; Rom. 8:31.

NUMBERS 23:13-30

No Enchantment Against Israel. Balak was surprised and disappointed. He therefore bethought himself of limiting the seer's vision, so that he might see an attenuated Israel from a height that commanded only a partial view of the camp. How often we try to see only what we want to see! How often we shut our eyes to a rival's real merits! Instead of entering into God's great thoughts, we shut ourselves up in a tiny limited world. We will not acknowledge what our pride does not want to acknowledge. We are like children building sandcastles against the tide. You had better bring your mind to harmonize with God's facts than minimize or evade their truth. You are hurting yourself and can never alter them. Take God's way and be at peace!

Let us ponder verse 21—it is as we are in God's purpose; and verse 23—when faced by our enemies; and verse 24—when most convinced of our helplessness.

NUMBERS 24:1-14

Balaam's Vision of Israel's Prosperity. In these remarkable words, Balaam describes the condition and prospects of God's people. They reveal the innermost thought which even a bad, double-dealing man has of the saint. Balaam had his times of illumination, when he touched the very truth of things. A man may know and speak truth which he does not himself obey. Would that we all realized the high ideals which sinful men have of religion!

We are intended to be as gardens by the river, aloe trees planted by the Lord, cedars fed by perennial streams. Oh, for more of exalted royalty of soul, the invincible strength, the victory that eats up the adversary, and actually feeds on what threatens to destroy! We can only attain to such an ideal by a close union with the risen Savior. Let us live on the plane which is ours in him and for which he imparts the Holy Spirit!

NUMBERS 24:15-25

The "Star out of Jacob." When your heart is dismayed because of the hatred and opposition of Satan, the great accuser, turn to this chapter. If he stands up to resist, the Son of God stands in your defense. The eternal God is on your side, not because you are perfect, but because you have linked your little life with Jesus Christ in his glory and beauty. In Deut. 23:5 we learn the blessed secret that explained Balaam's failure.

Balaam describes in glowing anticipation Israel's future, and his forecast is marvelously accurate. It is clear that a man may speak the truth of which his soul is destitute, as a marble fountain may dispense water which it does not taste.

Balaam started for his home, but never reached it. You may long to die the death of the righteous, but it is a vain dream unless you live their life. Compare Num. 23:10 with 31:8.

NUMBERS 25:1-18

The Zeal of Phinehas Against Impurity. Unable to curse Israel directly, Balaam suggested to Balak the device of destroying the union between Israel and their divine Protector by enticing them into sin. Once bring license and passion into play and let the seductions of evil prevail, and surely the holiness of God would compel him to withdraw his protection! This was a diabolical suggestion to gain his wage. See Rev. 2:14.

The women of the land, notorious for their wantonness, seduced the men of Israel to join in the sensual rites of their worship. All did not fall into this sin. See Deut. 4:3, 4. But it brought terrible chastisement on the offenders, 1 Cor. 10:8. You must amputate a gangrened limb.

Let us come out of the world, cleansing ourselves from its filthiness, 2 Cor. 6:14. There are crises when love for God's honor demands strenuous action, which never fails, as in the case of Phinehas, to bring abounding recognition, v. 12.

NUMBERS 26:1-4, 51-65

The Census of the Nation. The terrible visitation of the preceding chapter swept away the survivors of the old generation. See Ps. 95:11. This new census was very important, partly as showing the numbers to which Israel had grown, and partly as fixing families and clans preparatory to their entrance into Canaan.

The census of the Levites was taken separately, and conducted on different principles. It showed an increase of 1,000 since the numbering forty years before, 3:39. That this was no greater was probably due to Korah's rebellion.

God is ever writing up his people. Can we claim to be included in the divine enumeration and enrolled in the Lamb's book of life? Compare Ps. 87:5, 6; Rev. 3:5. We are born to a great inheritance, but must claim it by faith.

NUMBERS 27:1-23

Joshua Appointed Moses' Successor. Up to the last Moses was faithful as a servant to him that had appointed him in all his house, Heb. 3:2. Notice that he did not attempt to legislate for these young girls, who pleaded for a possession in their father's right; but he brought their case before God. It was ever "as the Lord commanded Moses," vv. 11 and 22. And when he was bidden to ascend the mountain and die, his main anxiety was to secure a successor to shepherd the people. Notice that expressive phrase, "the God of the spirits of all flesh." See Heb. 12:9.

The great lawgiver may bring the people to the borders of the land of rest, but there he must resign his charge. The Law, with its demands for an obedience which we cannot give, cannot bring the soul to rest. That is the prerogative of Joshua—or in Greek, Jesus, Heb. 4:8.

NUMBERS 31:1-20

The Destruction of the Midianites. In reading such a chapter as this, we must remember that the Bible is the history of the slow advance of a nation toward the knowledge of God, and its preparation to become one of the greatest of spiritual forces. That process could only be a prolonged one. Only by slow degrees could the grossness of the period be eliminated. Our Lord distinctly said that certain things were allowed for a time because of the hardness of their hearts. See Matt. 19:8. Many times he made the clear distinction between what "they of old" had said and what he said. See Matt. 5:21, 27, 33, 38, 43. The *highest* law for dealing with our enemies is found in his teachings.

The first steps of purification had to do with the women who might introduce heathen vices into Israelite homes, and the leisurely dealing with spoils and captives, so that passion might have time to cool.

NUMBERS 31:21-54

The Disposition of the Spoils of War. This law, which subjected the victors to a whole week of separation and to special purification, instead of an immediate welcome into the camp, was intended to wean the Hebrews from the practice of war, giving them a higher standard than that of surrounding nations. Thus God educates us, by placing before us an ever higher standard, as we are able to obey it. It is easy to say hard things against this treatment of Midian, but extermination is sometimes the only way to safety.

For us the lesson is one of rigid separation. Some may be able to stand God's searching fire; but others cannot bear that flame. Yet these may not go altogether free. See v. 23. As strangers and pilgrims, we must abstain from fleshly lusts. God demands our holiness, but discriminates in the method of producing it.

NUMBERS 32:1-19

Seeking Inheritance Beyond Jordan. Reuben and Gad were contiguous to each other when the host encamped. They had, therefore, many opportunities for conference, and finally united in asking permission to settle on the east of Jordan, where vast tracks of pasturage were eminently suited to their flocks. They have been held up as types of those whose "multitude of cattle" hinder the realization to the full of the heavenly inheritance. Certainly many professing Christians live on the world's side of the cross. They have no desire to share in the crucifixion of the self-life, if only they may build sheepcotes and cities and provide for their little ones. "It is easier for a camel to go through the eye of a needle than . . ."

At first Moses was indignant at the request, thinking that they desired to evade the hardships, but their explanation modified his wrath. Be swift to hear, slow to speak!

NUMBERS 32:20-42

Warning Against Forsaking Their Brethren. These two and a half tribes never entered the national life as did those on the other side of Jordan. They were far from the center of religious life, first at Shiloh and then at Jerusalem. On them first the tide of invasion broke, sweeping them and their cattle into captivity.

In Deborah's great song Reuben is rebuked for sitting "among the sheepfolds to hear the pipings for the flocks," instead of coming to the help of the Lord against the mighty. The Brahmins say that the holy man dies to every other sin earlier and easier than to the love of money. Their cattle kept these tribes on the wrong side of the river of separation! Let us beware of the cares of this world if we are poor, and of the deceitfulness of riches if we are rich. Better lose all than the soul. See Matt. 16:26.

NUMBERS 33:1-37

The Itinerary of the Wanderings. This record of ineffectual marches is full of pathetic interest and warning. If these halting-places had been in the straight line of march for the Land of Promise, there would be little room for regret. But they were not. They recall journeys that need never to have been taken. The tribes crossed and recrossed the desert, marking time while the bodies of the murmurers fell in the wilderness and were wrapped about with the desert sands.

Such is the doom of unbelief. To effect nothing, to miss the rest of God, and to perish on the threshold of achievement—such is the experience of the soul described in James 1:6. God has given us in Christ the promise of rest, victory, and satisfaction; let us enter upon our inheritance!

NUMBERS 33:38-56

No Compromise with Idolatry. Aaron's death must have been deeply felt by his brother Moses. During the great crisis of Hebrew history they had been so closely associated that the wrench must have been very considerable. In addition, there was the recollection of the sin which had excluded the two brothers from Canaan. In the Epistle to the Hebrews the death of Aaron is recorded to set forth the eternal priesthood of Christ, 7:17. Our High Priest has no successor; his office cannot be passed to another. It is not after Aaron, but Melchizedek.

The last paragraph, vv. 50–56, is especially impressive. There must be no complicity with evil; for if there be, it will eat out the very heart of our character and happiness. It is much better to root out evil with a strong hand than to suffer it in any form, for like the boomerang of the savage, our sinful permissions will come back on ourselves.

NUMBERS 34:1-18

The Borders of the Promised Land. Here are set out the borders of the Promised Land, which were never fully reached in the days of Israel's occupation, except perhaps for one brief period in Solomon's glorious reign. God's ideal for his people far exceeded their realization of it. But is it not always so! Does not his peace pass understanding? Is not his joy unspeakable and full of glory? Does not the love of Christ pass knowledge? Jesus Christ is our inheritance; let us possess our possessions. Let us follow on to know the Lord; and remember that there is an allotted space for each of us in Christ, to which no other soul has a right.

It is a great honor to be chosen to divide the lots. Year by year we ought to set forth the believer's rights in Christ, that a divine discontent may urge to higher heights and deeper experiences.

NUMBERS 35:1-15

The Cities of Refuge for the Manslayer. This chapter is full of provision for the Levites, the chosen ministers of God's house. They who serve there may be at rest about their needs. He is not unrighteous to forget their labor of love.

These forty-eight cities must have been centers of religious influence throughout the land. As cities set on a hill that could not be hid, as salt staying corruption, as lights along a rockbound coast—so must they have stood in the Holy Land. So should our homes be in our land.

Six of the Levite cities were set apart for those who were guilty of manslaughter—*i.e.,* those who had killed some one unwittingly.

They were within easy access from all parts of the land and offered sanctuary until a judicial inquiry could be held. In Jesus we find refuge, Heb. 6:18. No avenger following the track of past sin can hurt the soul that shelters in him. Only we must never venture beyond the precincts of his salvation.

NUMBERS 35:16-34

The Penalty for the Murderer. For murder the penalty was death, vv. 30, 31; but for accidental homicide there was freedom within the city limits until the death of the high priest, when all these refugees might return to their homes with impunity. The institution of the blood-avenger was almost a necessity in those lands of scattered population and without communal organization. Here, without destroying the practice, it has been placed under careful limitations. We are our brethren's keepers, and instead of passing on a slander we should stand for them against those who have wrongfully maligned them.

What an exquisite promise is contained in verse 34! To think that Jehovah actually dwelt in the Holy Land! He dwells also in each assembly of his saints and in our hearts. See Ezekiel 48:35; Matt. 18:20; 2 Cor. 6:16; Rev. 21:3.

THE BOOK OF DEUTERONOMY

THE LAW REPEATED FOR THE NEW GENERATION

I. FIRST DISCOURSE OF MOSES   *1—4*
  A. Review of Israel's history from Sinai to the Jordan   *1—3*
  B. Appeal to the people to faithfully observe God's commands   *4:1-40*
  C. Supplementary historical statement   *4:41-49*

II. MOSES' SECOND DISCOURSE   *5—28*
  A. Repetition of the Decalogue and exhortation to cleave unto God   *5—11*
  B. Laws regulating the religious and social life of the people   *12—26*
  C. The Law to be written on plastered stones; the cursings and the blessings   *27:1—28:6*
  D. Consequences that will follow obedience and disobedience   *28:7-68*

III. THE THIRD DISCOURSE   *29, 30*
  The covenant renewed and enforced with promises and threatenings

IV. THE FINAL SCENES IN MOSES' CAREER   *31—34*
  A. Joshua charged and commissioned   *31:1-23*
  B. The Book of the Law delivered to the priests   *31:24-29*
  C. The song of Moses and directions to ascend Nebo   *31:30—32:52*
  D. Moses' final blessing   *33*
  E. The death of Moses   *34*

INTRODUCTION

This is again the Greek name for this book, and signifies the "second giving of the Law." It contains the records of public addresses to Israel, delivered in the eleventh month of the fortieth year of their wanderings through the wilderness. As Moses uttered them on the eve of his own speedy removal, he was able to speak with unusual emphasis and urgency. The allusions to the natural features amidst which these addresses were given are consistent with the place and speaker. It has been shown also by competent scholarship that Deuteronomy has all the peculiarities of Moses' style; and any differences of hortatory entreaty and appeal may be accounted for by the mellowing effect of age.

The special references to this book in the New Testament are very significant. Our Lord quoted from it thrice in his temptation, Matt. 4:4, 7, 10. See also Rom. 10:19; Acts 3:22; 7:37. There are touches by a later writer, and an appendix, Chapter 34; but the origin of the treatise as a whole must be ascribed to the great lawgiver.

COMMENTARY

DEUTERONOMY 1:1-18

Moses Recalls the Start from Horeb. To this new generation Moses spake the holy law of God, since they had not heard it at Sinai. In view of the great lawgiver's approaching decease, it was necessary to re-edit it. The name of this book means "the second giving of the Law."

"The Red Sea" in v. 1 must be replaced by "Suph." Evidently it was somewhere in the neighborhood of Pisgah. It is meet for us on a birthday, or some such anniversary, to review the way that the Lord our God has conducted us. He is the God of our fathers and of the covenant. Before us is set the land of our inheritance. God calls us to go in and possess it. He hath "blessed us with all spiritual blessings . . . in Christ," but we must appropriate and possess by faith. And the faith that claims depends on the obedience that conforms to the divine Law. See Eph. 1:3; 2 Peter 1:3.

DEUTERONOMY 1:19-40

The Penalty of Unbelief. There is little to distinguish Kadesh-barnea among the sand dunes of the desert. It was situated on the frontier where Canaan fades into the southern desert. But it is a notable place in the spiritual chart, and few are they that have not passed through some notable experience there. It was there that Israel thought more of their enemies and difficulties than of the right hand of the Most High. When we look at circumstances apart from God; when we account our temptations and inbred corruptions too masterful to be subdued; when giants bulk bigger than the ascended Christ, we also turn back from the rest of God to the barren wanderings of the waste. God allows these difficulties as a threat to his power and grace, and to train us to high attainments.

DEUTERONOMY 1:41—2:15

Journeying and Dying in the Wilderness. We cannot obtain by our impetuosity and insistence what God offers only as a free gift to our faith. The Land of Promise is not to be obtained by strength of hand, but by the soul that lives in the will of God. Even when we are rebellious and unbelieving, God does not forget nor forsake us, 2:7. He knows our walking through the great wilderness which we have chosen. Through all the forty years he goes with his people as their fellow-pilgrim. Even under such circumstances they lack nothing that is necessary to a complete and blessed life.

Edom was not to be injured, because of the ancient grant, Gen. 32:3. So with Moab. The gifts and calling of God are without repentance by him. He will remember his Abrahams and his Lots long after they have passed from this mortal sphere, and will care for their children and children's children. See Isa. 59:21.

DEUTERONOMY 2:16-37

Conquering Beyond Jordan. In the earlier verses of this portion we catch a glimpse of the former history of Palestine, with the wars of conquest and changes of tenure that swept over it. The Almighty Governor of the world was, as the Apostle Paul said afterward, determining seasons and frontiers. Nations enervated by their sins are continually being judged by the Prince of the kings of the earth. See Lev. 18:28; Acts 17:26, 27; Rev. 1:5; Matt. 25:32.

A pacific and fair offer, in all good faith, was made to Sihon, which he refused to accept. The heart which is already hardened by sin becomes harder with every fresh rejection of God's love. In that sense we understand how the Lord hardened his heart. No ice is so hard as that which freezes at night after a day of thaw. The sun that melts wax, hardens clay; but the fault is not with the sun, but with the clay.

DEUTERONOMY 3:1-22

The Inheritance of Reuben, Gad, and Manasseh. Sihon's defeat, described in the previous chapter, compelled his ally Og to take the field and oppose the further advance of Israel. "He came out" against them. Perhaps also Josh. 24:12 affords a clue. Swarms of hornets harassed him and his people, and drove them out of their stone houses and fortifications; they preferred meeting the chosen race in the open to the scourge of these formidable creatures. When God says, "Fear not," he fights on our side.

Recent discoveries confirm these references to the many stone cities of Bashan, mentioned in v. 4. The country is covered with ruins. Porter says that 500 ruined places attest the might of the Amorites. The royal bedstead is thought to mean coffin or bier. Its length of 13½ feet would infer a stature of 11 or 12 feet.

These victories opened fertile and beautiful pasturelands, including Hermon and Gilead. "The Lord delivered," "and we took."

DEUTERONOMY 3:23—4:14

"Take Heed to Thyself." Strong faith was required by the two and a half tribes to leave their wives and children while they went to succor their brethren. But God's commands and assurances foreclosed all arguments. Whenever we are summoned to special service, we may consign the care of our personal interests to God. Seek first the kingdom, and all other things will be added.

Notice that Moses referred to the wondrous acts of the Exodus as only the *beginning* of God's wondrous works, 3:24. Probably in the countless ages of eternity we shall always feel that we are witnessing only the beginning of God's self-revelation.

Moses, like Paul afterward, tried to reverse the divine decision. Compare 3:23-25 and 2 Cor. 12:8, 9. Do not pray against God's will, but with it, 1 John 5:14. When God says No, there are always tender compensations, such as the view from Pisgah.

Israel's tenure of Canaan depended on obedience to God's will in *statutes*, including the ordinances of religion, and in *judgments* relating to civil matters.

DEUTERONOMY 4:15-31

Jehovah "a Jealous God." How often Moses repeats, "take heed." We must watch as well as pray and keep our souls diligently. We must specially beware of idols—that is, any visible thing which takes the place of the unseen and eternal, veiling it from our view. The soul must learn to lean on the everlasting arm.

How true that description of the iron furnace! The metaphor is derived from the process of smelting metal. We have had our Egypts, where by trials the real ore of character was disintegrated from its rocky matrix. But though God may remove us from outward affliction, he is himself the furnace of purification, by his Spirit and Word, and in the secrets of our hearts, v. 24. But his fire burns our bonds, while our heads are unsinged, Daniel 3:25.

If these words meet the eyes of any who are among the scattered and vanished ones, let them seek God again and they shall certainly find him. He is merciful, he will not fail or destroy, nor forget the covenant, vv. 30, 31.

DEUTERONOMY 4:32-49

Israel's Peculiar Privileges. Every argument that love and wisdom, the great past and the miracles of the Exodus could suggest was brought to bear on the hearts of the Chosen People, fortifying them against the temptations to backslide. They were bidden to ask from ancient history and from one end of Heaven to another if any such wonders had ever been known in the history of the nations. But it must be sorrowfully confessed that memory and wonder are not enough to permanently fortify the heart against the insidious entrance of evil. Only the Holy Spirit can do that. See Rom. 8:1-4; Gal. 5:16.

So eager is the divine heart that none should perish but that all should come to repentance, that guideposts to refuge are carefully multiplied. Here again their names and locations are specified, lest any should not have met with former notifications. See Num. 35:6, 14; 2 Peter 3:9.

DEUTERONOMY 5:1-21

The Decalogue Repeated. The Law of God is for "*all* Israel." None are exempt. "Not with our fathers" means not with them *only;* Moses also uses the expression because many of the references of the Decalogue were to the settled life of Canaan. "Face to face" means not in dark visions, but clearly and lucidly, Job 4:12, 13. Our "face-to-face" vision is yet to come. See 1 Cor. 13:12; Rev. 22:4. Notice in Deut. 5:5 the ideal mediator. See Gal. 3:19; 1 Tim. 2:5.

Every soul has two givings of the Law. First, we stand under Sinai to be judged, condemned, and shut up to Christ as our only hope; then we come to it a second time, asking that the Holy Spirit should write it in our hearts, and make us to walk in obedience to its precepts. See Gal. 3:23; Rom. 8:4.

Adolphe Monod, on his deathbed, said: "Sin has two divisions; the evil that we have done and the good that we have left undone. As to the first, there is not a single command that I have not transgressed in letter or spirit; as to the second, it weighs on me even more than the first."

DEUTERONOMY 5:22-33

Moses Between God and the People. "He added no more"—*i. e.,* the Law is perfect. It is written in stone, and therefore is permanent. When the conscience has not learned the efficacy of the blood of Jesus, it shrinks from contact with God's holiness, vv. 24-26. But such fear does not save us from going back to our calf-making and license.

Turn from Moses to our blessed Lord, who went into the midst of the thunder and lightning which our sin had incurred. On him the full force of the storm broke, and we were delivered. Adolphe Monod said: "I have a firm and peaceful confidence in the redemption of Jesus Christ, in his blood and sacrifice, accepted before God, taking the place of the good which I have not done and repairing the evil that I have done."

Note the yearning of verse 29. It repeats itself elsewhere: Isa. 48:18; Matt. 23:37. See also Ezekiel 36:26.

DEUTERONOMY 6:1-19

How to Treat God's Words. Obedience is still the one condition of true prosperity and success. Lands still flow with milk and honey; and they live long who live well. Lives are measured by heart-throbs, and not by figures on the dial.

The fourth verse is reckoned by pious Jews as one of the choicest portions of Scripture. They write it on their phylacteries and repeat it, with other verses, at least twice a day. Note the various methods for maintaining the religious atmosphere: (1) by meditation; (2) by the religious training of children; (3) by pious discourse and conversation; (4) by the persistent study of Scripture. When books are scarce, use wall-texts; but never substitute stray snippets, however sweet, for the whole meal of Scripture.

Let us not forget how many of our present privileges and spiritual advantages must be credited to the prayers and the tears, the labors and the sufferings of those who have left these precious inheritances to us, their children and heirs! We drink of cisterns we never hewed!

DEUTERONOMY 6:20—7:11

No Compromise with Idolatry. The great lawgiver had his eye constantly on the coming generation. It is good when the children are so arrested by our religious life that they come to ask us to tell them the reasons that account for it. Seek to live so purely and devoutly, and yet so attractively, that the young people around will be compelled to inquire after your secret, Luke 11:1.

We are not only to teach the children, but to guard them against forming friendships and making marriage alliances with those who might divert them from God. In the New Testament, Christians are forbidden to marry except "in the Lord," and equally stringent are prohibitions against worldly intercourse, 1 Cor. 7:39; 2 Cor. 6:14.

God can break the seven-fold power of sin in the heart of those who are absolutely given over to him and are willing to surrender their evil ways. This is pledged to us by his fidelity and love, 7:8, 9.

DEUTERONOMY 7:12-26

What the Lord Does for His People. The promises to obedience are enlarged upon with touching copiousness. Love, blessing, keeping, peace, multiplication, fruit, and health lie along the narrow pathway entered by the strait gate of the cross. However forbidding its entrance, it "leadeth unto life." May Christ secure in us this obedience which he, too, demands and achieves by his Spirit! See John 14:15.

Whatever be the strength of the Amalekites and Hittites of the heart, let us not fear. We have been "reconciled by his death" and shall be "saved by his life," Rom. 5:10. "Little by little" is the law of progressive sanctification. The Holy Spirit shows us the next portion to be taken and the enemies that resist our prayers. But as we advance, they are driven out, Isa. 54:17.

We resemble what we admire. Let us set our affections above. To abhor the evil and pursue the good casts a glory on our face. Compare verse 26; Psa. 115:8; 2 Cor. 3:18.

DEUTERONOMY 8:1-20

Beware of Forgetting God. "Thou shalt remember," v. 2; "thou shalt consider," v. 5; "thou shalt bless," v. 10.

The lessons of hunger, vv. 1-9: "Suffered to hunger." "Blessed are they that hunger." "Man doth not live by bread only"; he hungers for knowledge, opportunity, society, love. How many wan faces around us bear witness to the gnawing within. But the Father suffered his Son to fast; and so he deals with us, to prove us. It is only through the discipline of the soul, in learning to go without, that it can be trusted with spiritual opulence and power. See vv. 7-9.

The perils of prosperity, vv. 10-20: It is harder to walk with God in the sunshine of success than in the nipping frosts of failure. When Paul said, "I know both how to be abased, and I know how to abound," he put the hardest last. The one secret is to give all the glory to God, and to look always to the cross where we were crucified to the pride of the flesh, Phil. 2:5-11; 4:12.

DEUTERONOMY 9:1-14

Offending the Righteous God. Who can read this chapter without emotion and admiration for its sublime eloquence! It is one of the most striking and moving chapters in this book!

Moses sets himself to convince the people that they must not suppose that their easy entrance to Canaan was due to conspicuous virtue, but rather to God's covenant with their fathers, and also to the sinful practices of the Canaanites. Compare verse 5 with Gen. 15:16. The contagion of these sins might have infected and poisoned humanity; therefore, they had to be extirpated. Whatever we enjoy is due, not to our merit, but to the infinite grace of God in Jesus Christ, 1 Cor. 15:10.

Ah, my soul, ponder this, for this is true of thee also! All thy past has been filled with failure and rebellion. If thou art still used for God's service, and art credited with a good name among his people, remember the reason is in the sovereign grace of Jehovah!

A debtor to mercy alone,
Of covenant mercy I sing.

DEUTERONOMY 9:15-29

Moses' Intercession for a Rebellious People. During the remainder of this chapter, Moses continues to remind the people of their rebellions. It is well, when we are tempted to self-adulation, to listen to that faithful monitor, conscience, recording our evil past. We are apt to forget our many provocations of God, especially when the smart of the rod is over. But we have all had our Horebs, Taberahs, Marahs, Kibroth-hataavahs, and Kadesh-barneas, 1 Cor. 10:11.

Again and again would the people have been destroyed, if human justice had decided their case. But Moses, the mediator, knew the holy love of God's heart, and expressed it in his prayers on their behalf. See vv. 18, 20, 25-29. We are reminded of him who ever liveth to make intercession for us within the veil, Heb. 6:19, 20; 7:26, 27; 9:24. Let us imitate Moses in his life of intercessions, and mark well his arguments that we may use them for ourselves and others.

DEUTERONOMY 10:1-22

What the Lord Requires of Us. The second writing of the Law reminds us of the work wrought in us by the Holy Spirit. When first we hear the Law, we are condemned; but when we have repented and believed, God writes it on the fleshly tablets of our hearts, Heb. 8:10. Together with this deepening love and delight in God's Law, we enter into the spiritual equivalent of Levi's calling, standing to minister and blessing in God's name.

Every word of the magnificent instruction from verse 12 deserves careful pondering. Let us learn what God requires and then ask him to create such things in us. As Augustine puts it: "Give what thou commandest, and then command what thou wilt." But we must be willing to enter into the inner significance of the initial Jewish rite, which is also taught in baptism, Rom. 2:26-29; Col. 2:11, 12. The separation of Calvary's cross leads to the filling of Pentecost!

DEUTERONOMY 11:1-17

The Rewards of Obedience. In this chapter the introductory portion of this book closes, and two final arguments are brought to bear on the Chosen People, to induce them to love God and keep his charge. The one has already been referred to, consisting of those awful judgments with which God had punished the stiff-neckedness of Pharaoh and the rebellions of the wilderness. We may as well learn sooner than later that God will have us holy, and if we will not yield to his loving solicitations we must suffer his stern chastisements.

The other argument is derived from the blessings which they would inherit by obedience. In Egypt the irrigation of the land was laboriously effected by the tread-wheels that raised the water from the Nile level, but in Canaan there were two annual rainy seasons—the former, September-October; the latter, March-April. The regularity of these seasons depended on Israel's loyal obedience. We are reminded of John 4:14. May we not ask ourselves which of these typifies our religious life? See Heb. 4:1.

DEUTERONOMY 11:18-32

The Blessing and the Curse. Never in this world do we reach a position from which it is impossible to fall away. The dew and the rain of God's blessing are contingent on obedience; and one of the strongest incentives to obedience is devout meditation on the Word of God. It is through the letter that we arrive at the spirit, and through the written words at the Eternal Word. We must store up the sacred words of God as a farmer stores up his grain, keeping them before us, making them the familiar topics of home-talk, and exercising ourselves in them. Let us specially ponder verses 22, 23, 24, 25, appropriating them in a spiritual sense and claiming their equivalents in the inner life.

All along our lives are Ebals and Gerizims, with their "Come, ye blessed" and "Depart, ye cursed." Always we are arriving at the crossways, on the one of which lies the smile and on the other the frown of God. Let us be attracted by the one and dissuaded from the other, till we climb the spiral staircase into the land where there is no cooling love or faltering faith.

DEUTERONOMY 13:1-18

Cut Out the Plague Spot. How to exterminate sources of disease is a main question with the modern world; but the stamping out of possible sources of temptation must not less energetically be pursued by each religious soul. The prophet, the beloved associate, the community that endeavored to turn Israel aside from God might have no mercy shown. There was no room for those liberal views, in vogue today, that smile on the greatest divergencies of belief if only their advocates are sincere.

For ourselves the lesson is clear enough. We must dissociate ourselves from companionships, however affectionate, which exert a deleterious effect on our characters and draw us away from God. There is only one alternative—that we should overcome evil with good and lift our friends to our own ideals. If that be impossible, our course is clear. Our eye must not pity, nor our hand spare. Jesus left no other alternative. See Mark 9:42, 43.

DEUTERONOMY 18:1-22

The Prophet Who Was to Come. Those that serve the altar may live by the altar. Let us not forget the needs of those who serve us in holy things. It is a blessed thing when an individual desires "the place which the Lord shall choose" (v. 6). Let us be true to the inner prompting, at whatever cost. We shall be fully repaid. When Peter loaned his boat Jesus returned it, filled with fish!

We are to be "perfect with the Lord" (v. 13) —*i.e.*, we are not knowingly to permit things that hurt or grieve his Holy Spirit. If the question should arise how we are to know God's way, we must take our question to the true Prophet. See Acts 3:22; 7:37. He can answer our hard question; but we are strictly forbidden to go to crystal-gazers, palmists, fortune-tellers, and those who profess to read the future. How serious is their fault who refuse him! Compare verse 19 with Heb. 10:28, 29. Let thy Urim and Thummim be with the Holy One! See 1 Sam. 23:11, 12; 30:7, 8.

DEUTERONOMY 26:1-19

Firstfruits and Tithes. The Israelites were God's tenants-at-will. The entire land and its produce were his; and they were required to acknowledge his ownership by the payment of firstfruits—both at Passover and at Pentecost, Lev. 2:14; Num. 28:26—and of tithes.

All we possess and all we earn are equally the gift of God. Let us acknowledge this by setting apart a fixed proportion of the results of our daily work, whether wages, or crops, or brood, or herd. The words of this ancient collect, with very slight modifications, will suit us well, vv. 5-10. Note the injunction of verse 11. There is not enough joy in our lives or faces. Nothing so quickly commends our religion as the gladness which the world can neither give nor take. To joy let us add intercession, v. 15; and let us never forget to renew our vows of consecration when we bring our gifts, v. 16.

DEUTERONOMY 27:1-26

Curses Upon Evildoers. Mount Gerizim and Mount Ebal were two masses of limestone rock, reaching 2,700 and 2,000 feet above sea level. Between them lay a beautiful valley, about 300 yards wide. At the foot and on the lower slopes of Gerizim stood the descendants of Rachel and Leah; on those of Ebal, the descendants of Zilpah and Bilhah, together with Zebulun and Reuben, who had forfeited the rights of the firstborn. The priests and the Levites, grouped beside the Ark in the valley, uttered both the benedictions and the solemn denunciations of the Law, each item eliciting the responsive "Amens."

Notice the sensitiveness of the divine Spirit! To make a blind man wander out of his way and to wrest justice from the fatherless was held to be as reprehensible as to commit those terrible breaches of the Law of purity. Nothing in life is insignificant or trivial when weighed in the balance of eternal justice. We can only rejoice when we realize that we are accepted in the Beloved, and that he has stood for us, Rom. 3:20; 5:1-3, 9.

DEUTERONOMY 28:1-19

Blessings Upon the Obedient. This remarkable chapter gives the summary of what Israel might have been, contrasted with what she became! It is on account of the transgressions that the centuries have augmented her sum of misery. Oh, that we may never have to lament what we might have been!

These opening verses contain the Beatitudes of the Old Testament. They have their counterparts in the New. Remember that God bends over your life, rejoicing to do you good, and finding pleasure in whatever may enrich your life or flow through it to enrich others. Ask especially that in his great power and grace he shall smite your enemies before you, and establish you unto himself, and open to you his good treasure. If you are in Christ, all things are yours. Possess your possessions, 1 Cor. 3:21, 22; Obadiah 17-20.

DEUTERONOMY 28:20-46

The Fearful Results of Disobedience. If we compare this chapter with Exodus 23:20-23 and Leviticus 26, we shall see how Moses resumes and amplifies the promises and threatenings already set forth in the earlier editions of the Law. The blessings are declared in fourteen verses, while the curses require four times as much space. This is due to God's eagerness that men should be warned from courses that injure, and shut up to those that lead to blessedness. Note the language, which rises to the sublimest level, especially in the latter part. The forecasts of the dispersion and the degradation of the Hebrew people are specially remarkable.

It is not only that God goes out of his way to reward the obedient and to punish the ungodly, but these rewards and punishments are part of the nature of things, just as fire stings and burns when we transgress its laws, but blesses when we obey. If we are at one with God, through Jesus Christ, we are at one with the universe. But if not, "the stars in their courses" fight against us, Judg. 5:20.

DEUTERONOMY 28:47-68

The Bitter Fruits of Disobeying God. These predictions against the Hebrew people were partially fulfilled in such invasions as those of Nebuchadnezzar and his generals; but it is to the Roman conquest of Judea that we must look for complete fulfillment. One only needs to compare these words with the narrative of Josephus to see the exact accomplishment which took place during the wars of Vespasian and Titus. The Jews themselves admit this. Verse 68 was literally fulfilled when Titus transported myriads of Jews to Egypt to be employed in the public works or to fight in the amphitheater.

But if the punishments have been so heavily suffered during these weary centuries, what shall not be the joy when the Lord shall bring back his people to their own land, and all Israel shall be saved! What is this new Euphrates Valley railway but the preparing of the road for their return from the Eastern portions of the world! In the near future, our children, if not we, shall see a fulfillment of Isaiah 60 and 61. See Acts 3:19, 20.

DEUTERONOMY 29:1-13

The Covenant That Brings Prosperity. In one great final convocation, Moses rehearsed the covenant and endeavored to bind the people to its provisions. It becomes us all from time to time to look into the vows that we have made, reviewing them to see if we have carefully observed and kept our pledges. We need also to enlarge their scope as one new department after another is added to the experience of our souls. A review also of God's great love and care through past years should constrain us, as by the mercies of God, to present ourselves anew to him as a "living sacrifice," Rom. 12:1, 2.

Notice the double aspect of verses 12 and 13. It is not enough for us to be willing to enter into a covenant with God and to take his oath; we need that God should "establish" us unto himself that we may become his peculiar people. The established heart and character are the very special gifts of the Holy Spirit, 1 Thess. 3:13; 1 Peter 5:10.

DEUTERONOMY 29:14-29

The Penalty of Serving False Gods. Verse 15 clearly refers to the future generations, who were included in this solemn act. The word "gall," verse 18, indicates the poisonous character of idolatry. The application of this passage to any man who falls short of the grace of God shows that the tendency to idolatry has its root in the apostasy of the heart, Heb. 12:15.

We cannot say that religion is a matter of indifference; or if we say it, we are destined to a terrible awakening. A man may say, "I shall have peace," etc., verse 19, but there is no peace short of the peace of God, Isa. 48:22; Rom. 5:1, 2.

With respect to verse 24, the infidel Volney wrote of the present condition of Palestine: "Why is not the ancient population reproduced and perpetuated? God has doubtless pronounced a secret malediction against this land." This is one of his "secret things"! Compare verse 29 with Romans 11:33.

DEUTERONOMY 30:1-10

Promises to Returning Wanderers. The Hebrew people have often turned to this chapter in the belief that the day must come when God will pity their forlorn condition and restore them from "the outmost parts of heaven." They do not consider that the promise was fulfilled in the return of a handful of their race under Nehemiah and Ezra.

The precious promise of verse 6, where the initial rite of Judaism is to have its spiritual fulfillment, should be compared with Isaiah 52:1. The time is coming when all Israel shall be saved from the mere external badge of their national prerogative, and shall be converted to true faith in Christ as their Messiah and Savior. See Rom. 2:28, 29; Col. 2:11. Then will God rejoice over them for good. Even now, as the true Israel of God, we may claim this rejoicing for ourselves!

DEUTERONOMY 30:11-20

The Supreme Choice. The immediate purpose of this passage is to encourage the people by reminding them that all things needful for a holy life are within their reach. Paul refers to it for the same purpose, Rom. 10:6.

The love and grace of God are not concealed as hidden mysteries might be. There is no need to undertake a long and dangerous journey like that which brought the eastern Magi to the manger-bed of Bethlehem. The Word of God, which is another name for our Lord, is very nigh to us all. We have only to lift the heart to him in simple faith and confess him as our Savior and Lord, and we are assured of salvation from the penalty and power of sin.

Love to God and compliance with his will is the only way of life and peace. Let us choose this narrow path. The gate is strait, but the way becomes always easier. It is narrow, but pleasant.

DEUTERONOMY 31:1-13

The Great Lawgiver's Parting Instructions. This chapter is a link between sunset and sunrise. God buries his workers, but carries on his work. None are indispensable. Moses is succeeded by Joshua, Stephen by Paul. "The grass withereth, . . . but the word of the Lord endureth for ever."

The old lawgiver passes on the assurances on which he had rested. After all, men are but the figureheads of movements which are greater than themselves. God goes before; God destroys; God accompanies and delivers. Let timid souls take courage. When the Good Shepherd puts them forth he precedes them, John 10:4. The iron gates stand open at his summons, and the big stones are rolled from the door of the sepulchres, Acts 12:10; Mark 16:3, 4. "He will not fail thee," etc., reappears in Hebrews 13:5 as the right of all believers. It is for me and thee!

DEUTERONOMY 31:14-29

The Charge to His Successor. Moses had already announced that Joshua would succeed him; but in view of the great difficulties which confronted the new leader, it was expedient that the guiding pillar should give him the symbol and pledge of God's endorsement.

Two other sources of the people's allegiance were proposed. First, *a song*. National songs lay hold on memory and have a powerful effect in stirring the deepest emotions. This song, composed under the divine impulse, embodied the substance of the preceding pleadings and exhortations, and was suitable to be taught to the generations that followed. Be sure that nothing more efficiently preserves religion than noble hymns! Learn and teach them! Secondly, *the book.* See verse 24ff. We have already heard of this. See Exod. 17:14; 24:4-7. No doubt it was to this necessity of recording the Law and chronicling the story of the Exodus that we owe the origin of the sacred books which bear the name of Moses. See John 5:46.

DEUTERONOMY 31:30—32:14

Moses' Song: The Lord's Favor Upon Israel. The song of Moses, like the fabled song of the swan, was his last and sweetest. It is probably the noblest ode in the whole Bible, and is the source from which subsequent singers derived suggestions for their noblest outbursts. The marginal references prove how deeply it dyed the national sentiment.

It excels in the names and designations of the Almighty. He is the Rock: verses 4, 15, 18, 30, 31; Jehovah: verse 6; Father: verse 6; the Most High: verse 8; God (El, the strong): verse 15, etc. What a study are the names of God, scattered through the Bible! Each was coined to meet some need of the human soul. What the rocks of the desert are to its shifting sands, God is amid the changes of this mortal existence.

This earlier part of the song is very tender. We are God's portion; the apple of his eye; as young eaglets, whom the mother bird is carefully teaching to fly; the favored recipients of God's richest gifts.

DEUTERONOMY 32:15-35

Moses' Song: Israel's Response. "Jeshurun" is a pet name for Israel, implying affection and endearment. The metaphor employed is derived from a pampered animal which in consequence of rich and plentiful feeding becomes mischievous and vicious.

Let us be warned by these denunciations against backsliding and willful sin. The greatness of our privileges will be the measure of the anguish of our doom. They who can arrive at Heaven will be cast down to Hades if they refuse and reject. The most fervent love becomes the hottest fire when it turns to jealousy. O my soul, it becomes thee to fear God as well as love him. Remember Heb. 10:26.

But what privileges await those who obey! When we abide in God, no enemy can stand against us. Five, strong in his miraculous fellowship, can chase a hundred, and a hundred ten thousand. See Lev. 26:8; also 1 Sam. 14. God shows "himself strong in the behalf of them whose heart is perfect toward him," 2 Chron. 16:9.

DEUTERONOMY 32:36-52

Moses Views What Others Shall Possess. Sometimes God leaves us to ourselves that we may learn our weakness and sinfulness. Then, when our power is gone and we seem destined to be destroyed, we begin to repent of our idolatry and apostasy and to long after our former blessed experiences. At such times he draws graciously near to us again, to heal, to quicken, and to deliver. He renders swift vengeance to the evils that have desolated us, and is merciful with a great compassion. See verse 43. In that remarkable verse, quoted in Rom. 15:10, the appeal goes forth to all the world to join with God's people in glad acknowledgment of his saving mercy.

This noble song declares for all ages the way of life and peace as contrasted with soul-death and misery. Every line of it has been fulfilled in the history of the Jews. May we not hope, also, that the time is not far distant when Jew and Gentile shall rejoice together in the bonds of common Christian fellowship? Note verses 46, 47. The love and service of God are life.

DEUTERONOMY 33:1-17

The Blessing of the Chosen People. The glorious nature of God is the opening theme here. The reference is to the giving of the Law when, amid fire and the mediation of angels, God descended on Sinai, Psa. 18:7-9; Hab. 3:3, 4. Oh, that we, too, may sit as pupils in God's school and receive his words, verse 3.

Though Reuben could not excel, he was not forgotten. Simeon is omitted because of Numbers 25:14. Judah was to receive prosperity in prayer, in work, and in war. Some render the benediction thus: "Bring him in safety from his wars!" But our warfare is different, Eph. 6:12.

Levi receives special blessing. Note the alternate translation: "Thy Thummim and thy Urim are with him whom thou lovest." This is the white diamond-stone flashing with God's "Yes" or dimming with his "No," Rev. 2:17. Exod. 32:26 was never forgotten. But God forgets our sins, Heb. 8:12. Benjamin's portion may be yours. The precious things of Joseph's heritage pale to insignificance when contrasted with the riches of God's grace, Eph. 1:18.

DEUTERONOMY 33:18-29

Israel's Happy Future Promised. Zebulun and Issachar, sons of Leah, were neighbors in Canaan and, being on the seaboard, became wealthy by commerce. The calling of the peoples may refer to the Gentile proselytes who were influenced by these tribes, 1 Kings 5:1-6; Mark 7:26.

The blessing of the other tribes is suggested by their position in Canaan: Gad, the leader of the west; Dan, standing on the southern fron-

DEUTERONOMY

tier, like a lion at bay; Naphtali, possessing the sea of Galilee, see margin; Asher on the northwest, with mountain barriers against invasion. "Iron and brass!"

Let your soul dwell in the timeless, changeless, tireless God. There is none like him. He will ride through Heaven to help you, will thrust out the enemies that resist your progress, will be your fountain and dew, your corn and wine, and will place beneath you arms as tender as they are loving. However low you fall, they will always be underneath. As your day, so your strength!

DEUTERONOMY 34:1–12

The Great Leader's Exodus. What inimitable beauty in this closing scene! The majestic withdrawal of the illustrious lawgiver in view of the assembled nation! The panorama that greeted his undimmed gaze! The Lord's showing of it to him! The kiss, according to the ancient tradition, in which his spirit passed rapturously to its reward! The burial of his body with proper honor, Jude 9! Well might the people weep!

There is dispensational truth here also. Moses represented God's Law, which never shows signs of age; but it cannot lead the soul into the rest of God, nor give victory over our spiritual foes. For the world and each soul Moses must give place to Joshua,—that is, Jesus.

Be ours that face-to-face fellowship, that doing of his will, those divine credentials of the mighty hand, of deeds wrought in God! See Psa. 90:16, 17.

THE BOOK OF JOSHUA

POSSESSING THE PROMISED LAND

I. ENTRANCE TO CANAAN   *1—5*
   A. God's charge to Joshua; spies sent to Jericho   *1, 2*
   B. The Jordan crossed; memorial stones; circumcision and the Passover   *3—5*

II. THE CONQUEST OF CANAAN   *6—12*
   A. The fall of Jericho   *6*
   B. Achan and Ai   *7—8:29*
   C. Confirmation of the covenant at Ebal and Gerizim   *8:30—9:27*
   D. The southern and northern campaigns   *10, 11*
   E. Summary of the conquest   *12*

III. THE DISTRIBUTION AND PARTITION OF CANAAN   *13—21*
   A. The borders of the tribes beyond the Jordan   *13*
   B. The land allotted to the other tribes   *14—19*
   C. The cities of refuge   *20*
   D. Cities for the Levites   *21*

IV. SETTLEMENT AND ESTABLISHMENT   *22—24*
   A. The two and a half tribes' return beyond Jordan; the altar of witness   *22*
   B. Joshua's farewell address   *23—24:15*
   C. The covenant renewed at Shechem; Joshua's death   *24:16—33*

INTRODUCTION

Though there are evident traces of the hand of an editing scribe, probably Ezra, there are many indications that the substance of this book was written while the events were still recent. There is therefore no good reason for doubting that the book in its original form was written by Joshua, as Jewish tradition alleges.

This book is to the Old Testament what the Acts of the Apostles is to the New. The name "Joshua" is equivalent to Jesus, and means "he shall save," Heb. 4:8. The Jericho of the early Church was Jerusalem, which they compassed through ten days of prayer as Israel compassed Jericho in seven days of marching. At Pentecost the walls of prejudice fell flat. Ananias and Sapphira were the Achan of the first days. The victories of the Church at Samaria, Antioch, and elsewhere recall the conquests of Joshua. And the failure of the Church to go forward to the conquest of the nations finds a bitter parallel in the story of Israel's apathy toward driving out the Canaanites.

COMMENTARY

JOSHUA 1:1-9

The New Leader's Commission. Joshua was a prince of the tribe of Ephraim, and was born in Egypt. After the Exodus he became captain of the host, Exod. 17:9. With Caleb he brought back a good report of the land of Canaan, Num. 14:7. Having been found faithful in the smaller sphere, he was promoted to the wider one. As we have seen, one of Moses' closing acts was to give him a charge. He represents the Lord Jesus in his risen glory, as the Captain and Leader of the Church.

The land of Canaan was Israel's by deed of gift; but Israel had to go up to possess it. Similarly, God's grace is ours, but we must claim it by putting the foot of our faith on God's promises. Though Hittites—our old evil habits—revolt, if we meet them in the power of the Holy Spirit they must yield. God is with us. Verse 5 is the claim of all believers. See Heb. 13:5, 6. But note that the weapon of successful conflict is God's Word. It is our sword, Eph. 6:17. See also Jer. 15:16.

JOSHUA 1:10-18

Provisioned and United for Conquest. It was enough that God had spoken and promised. Nothing more was necessary. Joshua took immediate steps, dictated by sanctified common sense, to prepare the people for the great step in advance to which God was calling them. We are not to throw away prudent foresight when we go forth on God's errands. Faith does not supersede precaution and preparation, where these are possible, although it does not rely on them, but on the living God.

When Joshua addressed the two tribes and a half, there was no faltering in his tone. He was absolutely certain that God would fulfill his promise, verse 15. This inspired the people with similar courage. It was very helpful to have the reassurance of those who were least likely to be enthusiastic, since the campaign must sever them from their families. God often speaks to us through the lips of others. Can we utter verse 16 to our Lord?

JOSHUA 2:1-14

A Heathen Woman's Act of Faith. To "view the land" was a hazardous undertaking. The physiognomy of the Hebrews would certainly betray them, and it did. The sacred writer does not commend Rahab's mode of life, nor her lies. Her morality was faulty enough, but beneath it, slowly smoldering, was a spark of pure love and faith, and this would consume the rubbish and burn clear, Heb. 11:31.

The stalks of flax were probably laid out on the roof to dry. She believed, on the ground of the wonders wrought in Egypt, that Jehovah was the true God, and that his word was sure. Her faith proved itself in her works—in her efforts to save others, and in the confidence with which she rested behind her scarlet cord. That she was sneered at and persecuted is quite likely, but she persisted and became an ancestress of Christ, Matt. 1:5. How faith greatens the soul! See James 2:25.

JOSHUA 2:15-24

The Escape and Report of the Spies. Rahab's trust in the promise of the spies, and in the efficacy of the scarlet line around her window is a striking type of the faith that relies on the promise of God that those who are united with Christ shall be saved in this world and the next. Her faith was not the result of impulse, but of a considerate review of the story of the Exodus. If you would have faith, soak your soul in the fact and teachings of Christ.

Note the strict conditions exacted by the spies as to the extent of their responsibility. Amid the general destruction, only those sheltered in the precincts of Rahab's house would escape. To be outside, though related to her, would not avail. So the great salvation of Jesus is available only to those who are found "in him," having upon them the divine righteousness, Phil. 3:9.

JOSHUA 3:1-17

The Jordan Safely Crossed. For three days the host faced that swollen river. It was enough to appall them, except that, like Abraham, they dared to behold it in the light of the divine promise. Every method was adopted to impress on them that the river was cleft by and for the Ark. The distance between the people and the advancing priests was purposely widened that there might be no doubt about the miracle. Whenever we step out on the unknown path, the Ark of the Covenant, which symbolizes Christ, precedes, Isa. 52:12.

The waters far up the stream were arrested and formed themselves into a vast lake. The bed of the river became dry for miles. The priests stood still till all Israel was safely over—not only the leaders and priests, but the rank and file. Each of the blood-bought is dear to God. They shall not come into judgment, John 5:24.

JOSHUA 4:1-24

The Memorial Stones. Twelve stones were brought up from the Jordan and erected in Gilgal. They gave fathers the opportunity of telling their children of the miraculous passage of the river. We, too, through our Lord, have passed through the waters of death on to resurrection-ground. Let the great deliverances of God wrought for our fatherland, as well as those wrought for us personally in Christ, be frequent subjects of family talk.

Twelve other stones were placed in the river-bed and would be visible when the waters were low. There was a visible demonstration, therefore, that Israel was really once in these depths. We must not forget the Rock out of which we were hewn, Isa. 51:1; 1 Cor. 6:11. Let us never cease to magnify God's grace, Psa. 40:2.

The presence of the Ark alone restrained the piled-up waters. Thus Jesus stands between us and whatever would overwhelm us, especially sin and death, Heb. 2:14. Do not, in rejecting him, reject your only screen.

JOSHUA 5:1-12

Renewing the Covenant with God. Evidently the people of Canaan realized that they were entering into conflict with God Almighty. This made their bitter resistance less excusable. But before Israel could go forward into the campaign, they must undergo that initial rite which from the days of Abraham had separated them unto God, Gen. 17. The outbreak at Kadesh had practically annulled that relationship, which now must be renewed, Num. 14.

Before we can serve God's high purposes in the world, we must be separated from sin. The old nature must be denied and put away, and the new nature, which is holy, harmless, and separate from sin, must become ours. Nothing but death can meet the case, Col. 2:11-15; 2 Cor. 7:1.

The circumcised soul alone may eat of the Passover, which is Christ. We need to feed on him, keeping the daily feast with joy, 1 Cor. 5:7, 8; John 6:51, 54.

JOSHUA 5:13—6:11

The Commander and His Plan of Campaign. When the heart is perfect with God, we may count on his presence and help. It is to the separated and obedient servant that the vision of Christ, as Ally and Captain, is given. Here were three hosts marshaled at Jericho—of the Canaanites, of Israel, and of the heavenly armies, waiting to war against the evil spirits which ruled the darkness of the land, Eph. 6:12.

The answer to Joshua's question depended on whether Israel was prepared to accept God's plan of campaign, which was very humbling to the flesh. The Lord is with us, if we are with him, 7:11, 12; 2 Chron. 15:2. As Jericho was the key to Canaan, and its fall was to be the earnest of complete victory, the program was carefully planned to give God his rightful position. From first to last, its capture was the result of the

JOSHUA

interposition of him who dwelt in the bush. Therefore, the Ark was borne around the city as the symbol of his presence, Num. 10:35.

JOSHUA 6:12-21

Jericho Taken and "Consecrated." "By faith the walls of Jericho fell down," Heb. 11:30. Whose faith? To some extent it was the faith of the people who marched around them day by day in full assurance that God would not fail. But Joshua and Caleb preeminently were deeply concerned in the wonderful result. See Mark 11:23, 24.

To the citizens, the action of the Israelite invaders must have appeared incomprehensible and even ludicrous. What do these feeble folk? But God's people were being daily trained in patience, obedience, and humility. Let God perform all things for you! Many strongholds of the enemy which now remain obstinate would fall if only all the Church would encompass them in faith, 2 Cor. 10:4.

The utter destruction of the city and its people was in keeping with the usage of that age. Without doubt the city might have been a prolific source of infection. Still, its fate was terrible. We learn that God can lift human ideals by very slow, protracted processes.

JOSHUA 6:22-27

Spared When Others Perished. It is not the amount of truth that we know which saves us, but the grasp with which we hold it. All that Rahab knew was very slight and partial, but she held to it with all the tenacity of her soul, and it was accounted to her for righteousness, Rom. 4:5. Also, her works proved her faith. She identified herself with Israel by the scarlet thread, gathered her kinsfolk under her roof, and waited in anticipation of deliverance, Jas. 2:25.

She had yet to be delivered from falsehood and lying, but that God-consciousness which is the first ray of dawn had broken upon her, and would necessarily result in perfect day. Poor outcast though she was, she became incorporated with Israel and the type of Gentile sinners who are permitted to sit with Christ in heavenly places. See Eph. 2:17, 18.

The city was given over to destruction, lest the microbe of corruption should, through Israel, infect the world. See 1 Kings 16:34. But remember Luke 19:1-10.

JOSHUA 7:1-15

The First Defeat and Its Cause. Israel was taught that victory is possible only where there are exact obedience and sincere consecration. We cannot cope with our foes unless we live in unclouded fellowship with God. See 2 Chron. 15:2. Our spiritual allies in the heavenly places cannot cooperate while evil is harbored. Canaan was a gift to faith, and a strong spiritual life was necessary. The gold and silver of Jericho were consecrated to God, so that Achan committed sacrilege as well as theft.

Ai (see Gen. 12:8; 13:3) lay two miles north of Jericho and was a comparatively small place; but without God the smallest opposition is too great for us. Joshua seemed more concerned for the disgrace brought on the divine Name than for the disaster to his men. Let us always look at our failures from God's side! We must not lie too long in the dust of despair, but arise to detect and put away the hidden cause of our defeat, Hosea 5:15; 6:1, 2.

JOSHUA 7:16-26

The Troubler Found and Removed. When God deals with sin, he traces its genealogy. Twice over we have the list of Achan's ancestors, vv. 1, 18. To deal with sin thoroughly we need to go back to its sources. See James 1:14, 15.

How Achan's heart must have stood still as he beheld the closer approach of detection, like the contracting walls of a chamber of horrors. One by one we pass before the eye of Omniscience, as a ship's company before the quarantine officer. We cannot hide ourselves behind parents, lineage, or religious ancestors. Each must give an account of himself, 2 Cor. 5:10.

Achan's family had been privy to his crime. It could hardly have been otherwise, since the goods were buried in the common tent. They were probably grown men and women. The notions of justice were stronger and harsher in that day than with us who have been taught by Christ. When the evil is put away, the door of hope stands wide, Hosea 2:15.

JOSHUA 8:1-17

Ai Again Attacked. Now that the evil was put away, the people were assured of victory: "I have given," etc. But the assurance of faith is not inconsistent with the call for action: "Arise, go up." Though he was thus secure of victory, Joshua adopted such measures as his soldier training suggested. Notice the place which our preparations should occupy. Not to shut God out, but to make the pathway along which his help may travel.

The restrictions as to the spoil which had been in force and which had led to Achan's undoing were now removed. God often tests us before allowing us to enjoy. Certain injunctions or prohibitions may be given to prove us, but are removed when our lesson is learned, Deut. 8:2.

Up the long, desolate pass Israel marched. There they could see Achan's tent, and there the scenes of their recent defeat. Their hearts were chastened. In all humility and faith they marched forward, and they were not ashamed, Joel 2:26.

JOSHUA 8:18–29

The Enemy Completely Destroyed. Joshua's preparations were skillfully made, and in that very place where Israel had been so disastrously defeated they scored a great victory and took large spoil, especially cattle, which they drove in triumph to the camp at Gilgal.

Be of good cheer, you that have been repeatedly overwhelmed by your strong enemies! Your failure arises from some hidden evil lurking in your soul! Put that away! Cast it out as a cancer! Where you were defeated, you shall be more than conqueror through the grace of Christ.

JOSHUA 8:30–35

Recording and Reading the Law. After the fall of Ai, the war was suspended for a time. The divine hand restrained the Canaanites from interfering with Israel's obedience to the Mosaic code. The whole nation was marshaled in the valley between Ebal and Gerizim, to hear the Law recited and to respond with the thunder of their "Amen," Deut. 27:15. Ebal carried a curse. It was appropriate that the altar should be there, Gal. 3:13.

Remember that even when we enter the land of rest, through faith in Jesus, we cannot get away from God's holy Law; nay, it is even more perfectly fulfilled as we walk after the Spirit, Rom. 8:1–4. Let us go further and ask that as the Law was written on those mighty stones, so it may be engraven on the tablets of our hearts, Heb. 8:10.

In the hour of complete triumph we need to stand before the Lord! It was in this spot that the incident of John 4 took place. Jesus transformed it into a valley of blesssing!

JOSHUA 9:1–15

Deceived by the Gibeonites. The presence of common peril forced the nations of Canaan to combine for self-preservation. Would that the various sections of the visible Church might see their way to a similar policy in view of the evil in the world!

Gibeon lay five miles north of Jerusalem. The name means "built on a hill." The Church has suffered more from the *wiles* of the devil than from his attacks. The deceitfulness of sin is most to be dreaded. Better to meet Caiaphas than Judas.

How often we act without asking the counsel of God! Yet when once an oath is taken which does not absolutely conflict with morality, God holds us to it, 2 Sam. 21:1. By this impressive instance we are taught to wait on God before making our decisions, which are apt to become irrevocable.

JOSHUA 9:16–27

"Hewers of Wood and Drawers of Water." The faith of these people was so far rewarded that while their deception was punished by their relegation to the most menial tasks, yet their lives were spared; and to a certain degree they were incorporated with Israel and associated with the service of God's house. This position made them as unlikely as possible to seduce Israel from loyalty to Jehovah.

The Gibeonites were afterward known as Nethinim—that is, "given". See 1 Chron. 9:2; Ezra 2:43; 8:20. If in the earlier part of your life you have made some great mistake which threatens to limit your influence for good, do not sit down in despair, but get service out of it. Let it hew your wood and draw your water!

JOSHUA 10:1–14

"The Lord Fought for Israel." The honor of Israel was implicated in this attack on their confederates, and Joshua went to their assistance. The deception which had been practiced on him did not alienate his help. Before he started he was assured of victory, but this did not make him slothful. See verse 7. But it was by *his* faith, courage, and obedience that this and other victories were won. What may not one man do when God is with him! Paganini once broke all his strings but one; then, holding up his violin, he said, "One string and Paganini."

A terrific storm burst on the fugitives as they crossed the high ridge of Beth-horon and descended in full flight to the plain. We are not called upon to explain the miracle of the sun and moon. The prolongation of daylight was probably due to some cause like that which yields the afterglow of sunset and the optical refractions seen in high latitudes.

JOSHUA 10:15–27, 40–43

Joshua's Victories Over Israel's Foes. The cave of Makkedah was a perpetual reminder of this wonderful victory which God gave his people.

The details as to the placing of the princes' feet on the necks of their foes are related with this precision to indicate the completeness of the conquest. So at the end of this age; see 1 Cor. 15:25. We may therefore appropriate Joshua's words about the enemies of the Church and ourselves. See verse 25.

Joshua's career was one of unbroken success, because the Lord went before him, delivering kings and armies, cities and peoples into his hands. It was a war of utter extermination; but God's justice had waited long, Gen. 15:16, and this was the only way of stamping out the infection. The lesson for us is that no quarter can be given in the inner war. *All* our thoughts must be brought into captivity, 2 Cor. 10:5.

JOSHUA 11:1-15

Joshua's Obedience to the Lord's Commands. The scene is removed to the waters of Merom, near the sources of the Jordan. Hazor was the capital of the region; Jabin, like Pharaoh, was an hereditary title, Judges 4:2. All the northern nations combined. Joshua's heart might well have failed, had it not been for the divine promise on the night before the battle, verse 6.

His attack under cover of night was like the falling of a thunderbolt. The effect was immediate. The huge host dissolved. The hamstringing of the horses disabled them, so that Israel was not tempted to trust in chariots and horses, Deut. 17:16; Isa. 31:1. God's will was literally carried out. But what a noble record is given of this simple-minded soldier! "He left nothing undone," v. 15. It is only as we literally obey that we can count on such success as his. See 2 Tim. 4:7.

JOSHUA 11:16-23; 13:1-7

Much Land Yet to Be Possessed. We do not know how long the war lasted. Probably about seven years, 14:10 (forty-five less thirty-eight). It was only in David's reign that the Canaanites were finally subdued. Note that Joshua took the land and then gave it to Israel. So Christ received the fullness of the Spirit and all spiritual blessings as the Trustee of those who believe; but we must claim and appropriate our heritage. So at last there will be rest, v. 23.

With 13:1 begins the second division of this book, a Domesday Book! How significant is the sentence, "Much land to be possessed." This is true of sections of the Bible, seldom read by the average Christian; of regions of experience, such as those alluded to in Col. 3:1-4; and of countries in the world which have never been trodden by the feet of the missionary! Read also 13:13. What pathos it contains! Either they did not believe in God's assurances, or were too indolent to claim them!

JOSHUA 14:1-15

The Man Who Wholly Followed His God. The lot was doubtless adopted to obviate cause for jealousy or charges of favoritism. It denoted God's choice, Prov. 16:33; 18:18. It could be used only with very evident reliance on him, and in our day has been superseded by the sending of the Comforter to teach us all things, John 16:13.

It was long since Caleb had cut down the bunch of grapes near the spot of his choice, but he had never forgotten it; and now God, who had read his purpose, arranged that what his heart loved best his hand should hold and keep: "Him will I bring into the land whereinto he went," Num. 14:24.

Out of entire surrender to God springs a faith that dares to claim the realization of an olden promise, v. 12. The fact that the Anakim held Hebron did not stagger the old veteran. It was enough that God had promised! How strong and vigorous are those who walk with God, Isa. 40:31!

JOSHUA 15:13-19, 63

Rewards of Courage. Arba was the greatest among the Anakim or giants, 14:15. His three grandsons were equally formidable, 15:14. But Caleb subdued them through an omnipotent faith, 1 John 5:4, 5. Jesus can give us victory over the Anakim of our hearts; the only condition is faith.

Twice in Scripture we are told this story of Achsah. See Judges 1:13. With fatherly generosity Caleb gave her the upper and the nether springs. When men are right with God, they can distribute living water to others. Let us never rest content with the lower, but aspire to the highest, John 3:12, remembering that it is our Father's good pleasure to give.

Alas for the record of verse 63! Centuries passed till David came and subdued the city, 2 Sam. 5:6. But there would have been no waiting had Judah gone up in the power of God. See Psa. 60:5*ff.*

JOSHUA 17:14-18

An Enlarged Inheritance. The greatness of the children of Joseph did not arise from their numbers; for according to Numbers 26, the two tribes, united, did not much exceed the tribe of Judah. Also, one-half of Manasseh was already settled on the other side of Jordan. But they based their claims on the special promises made decades before to Joseph, Deut. 33:13.

Very rightly Joshua bade them prove their greatness by their deeds. It is a vast misfortune when children live in the achievements of their parents instead of standing on their own feet. Besides, they had land enough, if only they would drive out the Canaanites and cut down the shaggy forests that encumbered the soil. All around us are uncleared forests! What a precious promise for us all in v. 18. Let us cut down the wood!

JOSHUA 18:1-10; 19:49-51

Dividing the Remaining Territory. The Tabernacle had remained in Gilgal. It must now be removed to Shiloh, a site selected by God himself, Deut. 12:11; Psa. 78:60. Shiloh means "rest," and it commemorated the ending of the war. The honor of having God's dwelling-place within its border was probably given to Ephraim as the tribe to which Joshua belonged.

As an inducement to occupy the land, this further commission was sent forth. How many of us are equally slack to appropriate the blessings stored up in the Savior! Well is it that God, through the ages, has sent pioneers to tell us what we are missing and to stimulate our zeal.

The veteran leader had earned a good reward. His portion was called "the portion of the sun," probably because of its aspect. Let us live and walk in the light.

JOSHUA 20:1-9

Cities of Refuge. These arrangements carried out Numbers 35:9-34. Remember the distinction between deliberate murder and unintentional homicide. Only those who had committed the latter were eligible for refuge.

The fugitive told his story at the gate and was admitted provisionally, v. 4. His case was afterward investigated by the citizens or their delegates; and if his story were found correct, he might stay till the death of the high priest. This functionary was a type of our Lord; and thus the death of each high priest pre-signified that death by which captive souls are freed and the remembrance of sin made to cease.

The cities were placed so as to be within easy access from all parts of the country. See Prov. 18:10; Heb. 6:18. It is an urgent question for us all: Are we within the city, the walls and bulwarks of which are salvation?

JOSHUA 21:1-3, 40-45

The Lord's Promises Fulfilled. After the cities of refuge had been provided, those to be set apart for priests and Levites were next allotted, Num. 35:1-8. Forty-two cities were set apart in addition to the six cities of refuge. The priests and the Levites were not the sole possessors of those towns, but dwelt in them, receiving freely their dwellings and pasturelands. The closing verses represent the position of affairs at Joshua's death. So far as God's promises went, there had been no failure. The chronicler repeatedly affirms that. It is right to distinguish, says Calvin, between the clear, certain, and unwavering fidelity of God and the weakness and the indolence of his people, which cause God's gifts to slip from their hands.

At the end of life, when we review it from our last halting-place, we shall accept as absolutely true the conclusion of v. 45, and much more but alas for our failures to use his gifts to the full!

JOSHUA 22:1-20

Averting War between Brethren. There was generous appreciation of services rendered as Joshua dismissed the warriors. Something like "Well-done, good and faithful servant" rings through his words. But he takes care to remind them that the tenure of their lands depends wholly on their obedience. This will explain the brief and transient existence of the trans-Jordanic tribes.

The altar was probably erected on the east of the Jordan. It was "over against" the land of Canaan, and was perhaps a facsimile of that at Shiloh. The prompting motive was to cement the union between themselves and the other tribes. But that end would have been better served had they obeyed the divine command in assembling annually with them. You can secure unity, not by external symbols, but by spiritual affinity and fellowship.

JOSHUA 22:21-34

The Altar of Witness. Phinehas and the ten princes did their work well. It was politic as well as true to remind the departing warriors that they could not rebel against God without involving the whole nation. So deeply did the spirit of love work in their hearts that Phinehas and his men even proposed to share the land of western Canaan with them, rather than that they should drift away from the Law of God. There was a gentleness, a desire to conciliate, a yearning over their brethren which were quite after the mind of Christ, and which had the desired effect in a frank disavowal of any of those unworthy motives that their brethren had imputed.

So is it always. Let us lay aside the sword for the olive branch. Before proceeding to severer measures, whether as individuals or as nations, let us ever try to restore our brethren "in the spirit of meekness." Let us count it a greater gain to *win* a brother than to conquer him. As we grow older, may we become more mellow! See Matt. 18:15; Gal. 6:1-5.

JOSHUA 23:1-16

Joshua's Farewell Address. Joshua's anxiety for the welfare of his people after his death has New Testament parallels. See Acts 20:29; 2 Peter 1:13-15; and especially John 13—15. As always, he lays stress on what the Lord had done, vv. 3, 5, 9. Not one ray of glory is stolen for himself.

He argues for their steadfastness on three grounds: There are the promises of v. 5; the threatenings of vv. 11-13; the exhortations of vv. 14-16. Our failure to drive out the foes of our heart is due to our failure to follow the Lord. A lack of wholehearted surrender lies at the root of all failure. Cleaving to the Lord is the Old Testament way of saying "abide in Christ," John 15.

In contrast to man's inconstancy and infidelity, notice the sublime testimony to God's faithfulness. "Not one thing hath failed," v. 14. When at last we review our life, we too shall be able to say as much, if only by his grace we are kept faithful and obedient. We cannot keep the old covenant, but the new stands forever, Jer. 31:31-34.

JOSHUA 24:1-15

The Lesson of Israel's History. The previous chapter contains Joshua's own last words of warning to Israel; here he is God's mouthpiece: "Thus saith the Lord God of Israel." There is, first, the recapitulation of past mercy. From time to time we should definitely recall, for our children's sake, the divine interpositions in our national and domestic life.

It is interesting in the opening words to learn that Abraham was called out of an idolatrous family. This was the pit whence he had been digged, Isa. 51:1. He was a Gentile before he became a Jew, and was familiar with all the seductions of a lower religious type before he definitely stood for the only true God. It took long to eradicate this evil strain from Israel. During their sojourn in Egypt they had yielded to the fascinations of idolatry, v. 14. Joshua at least had made his choice! What a blessed thing for a family when the parents make the avowal of v. 15. Why not from henceforth?

JOSHUA 24:16-33

Joshua's Last Service to His People. Joshua did well to discourage their proud vauntings, and to show that the people could not in their own might realize God's ideal, Psa. 105:4. The book of Judges is a bitter commentary on these lofty words.

What the stone of witness was to Israel, the ordinances of the Lord's Supper and baptism are to the Church and to the world. The walls of our private chambers have listened to our prayers and tears. God help us to be true to them!

Joshua and the elders, while they lived, were a steadying influence to Israel. Such was the influence of the apostles on the early Church. Let us learn the value of character. Compare v. 32 with Gen. 50:25 and Exod. 13:19. Take heart! The fulfillment of God's promise may tarry, but his word is sure as the morning light, Hosea 6:1-3.

THE BOOK OF JUDGES

ISRAEL'S APOSTASIES AND DELIVERANCES

I. INTRODUCTION *1:1—3:4*
    A. The movements of the tribes *1:1–36*
    B. The angel of the covenant *2:1–5*
    C. The passing of Joshua and his generation *2:6–10*
    D. The history in outline *2:11—3:4*

II. RULE OF THE JUDGES *3:5—16:31*
    A. From the king of Mesopotamia by Othniel *3:5–11*
    B. From the king of Moab by Ehud *3:12–30*
        (Shamgar) *3:31*
    C. From the king of Canaan by Deborah and Barak *4—5*
    D. From the kings of Midian by Gideon *6—8*
        (Story of Gideon's sons *9:1–57*
        Rule of Tola and Jair) *10:1–5*
    E. From the king of Ammon by Jephthah *10:6—12:7*
        (Rule of Ibzan, Elon, and Abdon) *12:8–15*
    F. From the Philistines by Samson *13—16*

APPENDICES *17—21*
    The migration of the Danites and the story of Micah *17—18*
    The outrage at Gibeah and the war between Israel and Benjamin *19—21*

INTRODUCTION

This is a history of the Chosen People during the 400 or 450 years which intervened between the death of Joshua and the time of Eli, Acts 13:20. It is not a connected history, but a collection of outstanding incidents which determined the fortunes of the chosen people, and gave special illustrations of the power of faith in God. The chief lesson of the book is the intimate connection between loyalty or disloyalty to God and the corresponding results in well-being or misery. This is distinctly stated in 2:11–23.

The judges were extraordinary agents of the divine pity and helpfulness, raised up as the urgency of the people's need demanded, to deliver Israel from their oppressors, to reform religion, and to administer justice. Their administration was generally local, as Barak among the northern tribes, Samson in the extreme south, and Jephthah across the Jordan in Gilead.

It must not be supposed that Israel perpetrated an unbroken series of apostasies. Though these and their special deliverances occupy the major part of the book, there were evidently long interspaces of fidelity and prosperity. And in the darkest hours, there were probably large numbers who amid the abominations sighed and cried for a better day.

There are two appendices, relating events which took place not long after Joshua's death, and therefore preceding the greater part of the history. We may almost consider the book of Ruth as the third. The touches of human characteristics are very vivid and instinctive, and the book deserves much more attention than it receives from the average reader.

COMMENTARY

JUDGES 1:1—15

Renewing the Conquest. The land had been given. There could be no doubt about that. In the ancient covenant which Jehovah had made with Abram, he said: "Unto thy seed have I given this land," Gen. 15:18. It had also been conquered and divided by lot, as we learn in Joshua 14:1–5. The portion of Judah is specified in Joshua 15. But notwithstanding all, each tribe had to possess its own, first by the sword, and ultimately by the plow and the spade.

It is not enough to be assured that "we are blessed with all spiritual blessings in Christ." We must possess our possessions. By faith, and patience, and daily use, we must appropriate the resources which are stored up in Christ Jesus. See Obadiah 17; Eph. 1:3. Let us not be content with the nether springs of ordinary experience, but let us seek the upper springs that arise hard by the throne of God!

Build thee more stately mansions, O my soul,
As the swift seasons roll!
Till thou at length art free,
Leaving thine outgrown shell by life's unresting
    sea!

JUDGES 1:16—2:5

Flagging in Their Great Task. The conquest of Canaan was very partial. Israel dwelt among the ancient inhabitants of the land, much as the Normans did among the Anglo-Saxons whom they found in England; and the mixture of the two peoples was the beginning of moral degeneracy and decline in the chosen race. Wherever there was the old-time faith in God, as in the case of Caleb, the land was cleared of the Canaanite; but where God was *out,* the Canaanite was *in.*

So it is in the life of the soul. It is intended that the whole should be yielded to Christ, that no evil passion should reign, that no besetting sin should enthrall. But how often Christian people give up the fight! They say that the old Adam is too strong for them, and settle down to a joint-occupation. Let us not yield to reasoning like this! The Lion of Judah can break every chain. By faith in him we can be more than conquerors! The Holy Spirit strives with the flesh, so that we may not do as otherwise we would. Only give him the right of way! Sin shall not reign in your mortal body!

JUDGES 2:6—15

A Generation That Knew Not Jehovah. What a thrilling experience it must have been to hear Joshua and Caleb talk of Egypt, the Red Sea, and Sinai! The younger men would stand awe-struck as the veterans narrated their experiences of God. Open your diaries of the past, ye older saints, and tell what the Lord hath done for you. It will hearten us for the fight, Mal. 3:16.

Joshua was carried to his last resting-place in his inheritance—"the portion of the sun"—amid the respect and affection of the entire people. Like Moses, he had deserved to be known as "the servant of the Lord." The elders, who had witnessed the conquest of Canaan, took up his testimony and told of Jericho and the valley of Ajalon. But these also were "gathered unto their fathers," which implies more than burial. They joined the great throng of holy ones who are gathering around our Lord, awaiting the hour when as a radiant throng they shall issue forth with him to take up the kingdom of the world. What a gathering that will be! Whatever else we miss, let us see to it that we stand in our lot, "at the end of the days," Dan. 12:13. See Gen. 49:33.

JUDGES 2:16-23

Ineffectual Penitence. This paragraph is a summary of this book, which covers some 450 years, Acts 13:20. Israel lacks unity and kingship, and in that reminds us of the heart which has not become united under the reign of Jesus. See 17:6; 18:1. Such rites as were associated with Baal and Ashtaroth were both cruel and demoralizing. A distressing picture is given in Psalm 106:34-45 of the condition of Israel at this period. What wonder that such practices ate out the heart of the people, and left them exposed to the surrounding nations! When the blood becomes thin and impoverished, we can no longer repel the pestilence that walketh in darkness, nor the temptations that assail us at noonday!

Notice God's great patience and pity. He was against the people when they sinned, but as soon as the groans of their misery arose, they touched him to the quick and he raised up a deliverer. Note Psa. 18:26, 27. "Many times did he deliver them; but they provoked him with their counsel ... nevertheless he regarded their affliction ... and remembered them for his covenant" (Psa. 106:43-45). Herein we may take heart of hope for ourselves!

JUDGES 3:1-14

Delivered from Mesopotamian Oppression. Our sins and failures will sometimes be so overruled as to promote the growth of our souls in the true knowledge of ourselves and of God. It would be better to acquire these great lessons and virtues by the regular advance of an obedient and believing life. But where this method fails, God will teach us through our faults. The presence of the Canaanite taught Israel war and self-knowledge. See vv. 2 and 4.

Othniel had a noble estate of his own, which might have made him indifferent to the national crisis. But he and Achsah were animated by the high courage of Caleb, the lion cub. See Judges 1:12, 13. Let us be quick to feel the impulse of the Spirit of the Lord, and yield to it when it prompts us to go forth to war in some sacred cause. No thought of our own comfort or ease must hold us when there is a wrong to right or an oppressor to beat to the ground! Dare to trust the unseen Christ who summons you, and as you step out the air will be rock beneath your feet.

JUDGES 3:15-31

The "Message from God." The sword is usually worn at the left hand, and Ehud escaped suspicion because his was girded under his raiment on his right thigh. Eglon was also the more ready to listen to him and give a secret audience because he had just received a tribute from Ehud's hand. It was a terrible deed of vengeance, which must not be judged by our ethical standards. But can we not understand how the hatred of a downtrodden and high-spirited race would express itself in just this manner?

That dagger, thrust in up to the hilt, was indeed a message from God, for it ended Eglon's life and summoned his soul to stand at the bar of divine judgment. A supreme tragedy cannot befall except by the divine permission. Though God's silent permission of evil cannot be construed as acquiescence, yet the results of an evil deed may be wrought into the scheme of his providence, as in the case of Genesis 50:20, 21 and Acts 2:23. It is our frequent experience to have thrusts made at us; let us ask if they may not be messages from God! There is no chance in life.

JUDGES 4:1-13

A Woman's Deliverance. The scene changes to the northern part of Canaan. Deborah probably belonged to Issachar, 5:15; but her seat of government was removed to the hill country of Ephraim, probably for greater security. Her spirit was susceptible to God, and she recognized that the hour for the emancipation of her suffering country was at hand. Indeed, the command had gone forth, v. 6. But the divine method is ever to link command and promise, as we discover in v. 7. Barak had true faith, Heb. 11:32; but it needed inspiration and stimulus, as a dying fire calls for the bellows.

Kedesh, the gathering-place, was not far from the shores of the Lake of Galilee. From the tableland on the top of Tabor, these two

JUDGES

heroic souls watched the gathering of Sisera's vast host, far away to the slopes of Carmel and the banks of Kishon, soon to be encrimsoned with blood. What a moment that was when Deborah summoned Barak to arise, because the Lord had already gone forth! Who of us need fear and who need hesitate in the face of difficulty, if we are simply called upon to go in the wake of our Lord?

JUDGES 4:14-24

A Woman Executioner. "The Lord discomfited Sisera and all his host." When General Gordon rode off alone on his camel to break up the camps of the Arab slave-drivers, he realized, as he went over the desert with Thomas à Kempis' immortal book in his hand, that God was already discomfiting them; and as he rode into their midst, he discovered that God had made the way perfectly clear. Yes, it is as Deborah sang, in words afterward quoted by our Lord, "Let them that love him be as the sun when he goeth forth in his might," 5:31; Matt. 13:43. The soul that is united to Christ is irresistible.

Jael's deed is narrated at length again in 5:24. It was a most unusual breach of Arab hospitality. Was it that she was aggrieved by Sisera's treatment of her sex, 5:30? Or was it the expression of her faith in Jehovah and of her identification with his people? If the latter, may we not believe that then, as always, the Almighty understood the impulse that lay beneath the crude expression? How often we give blundering expression to noble impulses, which Jesus interprets truly! Ah, how blessed it is to have a Savior who understands the motives of our hearts!

JUDGES 5:1-11

The Song of a "Mother in Israel." Here is one of the noblest odes in literature! It celebrates a mighty victory, through the enthusiastic consecration of the people who laid themselves as freewill offerings on the altar of their country's deliverance, vv. 2 and 9. There is a greater cause that summons us today, for we fight "not against flesh and blood, but . . . against the rulers of the darkness of this world," Eph. 6:12.

The singer recites the mighty deeds of the Exodus, vv. 4 and 5. She feels that the present hour is not less full of God. Let us dare to believe that today is as sublime as any day of the past, and live as though it were. She describes the desolations caused by the foe: the divested caravans, the deserted roads, the defenseless, weaponless people, vv. 6-8. She tells how men mustered in the city gates to take their part in the great effort to which she called them, vv.

9-11. Ye daughters of Deborah, who know God, wake again and sing till your hearts grow hot again; and ye brethren of Barak, arm yourselves for battle against the lies, fashions, and sins that curse both the Church and the world!

JUDGES 5:12-23

"The Stars in Their Courses." This noble psalm contains memorable sentences. The "captivity" phrase in v. 12 is quoted in Psalm 68:18 and Ephesians 4:8, and in the latter is applied to the ascension of our Lord. He led in captivity those evil powers which had for so long held mankind in captivity. Let us not fear death, or the grave, or Hades. They have been bound to the chariot wheels of our Lord, and their keys hang at his girdle, Rev. 1:18.

Levies and reinforcements poured in from the hill-country of Ephraim, once owned by Amalek, 12:15; from little Benjamin; from the northern tribes. But the main brunt of the war of liberation fell on Zebulun and others adjacent to the plain of Esdraelon, one of the great battlefields of history. Megiddo stands to the south of this famous site and has given its name to the last momentous struggle of Armageddon. Clearly Deborah refers to a terrific storm that broke, perhaps at night, upon the plain, flooding the river Kishon and the adjacent lands, so that Sisera's chariots were rendered useless. O my soul, thou too mayest tread under foot thy foes, v. 21. But be sure never to refuse, as Meroz did, to respond when God needs thy help, v. 23.

JUDGES 5:24—6:6

At the Mercy of Midian. What a contrast our reading suggests between those that love the Lord and go from strength to strength in the undimming lustre and influence of their life, and the evil that once more brought the tyrant's yoke upon the neck of Israel! Yet these alternations have too often befallen *us*. At one moment Sisera and his hosts are chased before us as sheep before the dog; then a reaction sets in and the hand of Midian prevails against us. Why are we not always glad, strong, victorious? Is it not because we look to our moods, we relax our close walk with God, we set up the images of Baal in our hearts? We are then reduced to the plight described here and in Haggai 1:6. Why are there not more conversions in the Church? Why is there so little difference between the Church and the world? Why is so much of our Sunday school teaching ineffective? Ah, the Midianite is in our midst and we acquiesce! The urgent, primal need of the present day is for the Church to realize her true condition and cry mightily unto God for help. Note v. 6 and Joel 1:14.

JUDGES 6:7-18

A Farmer Called to Be Deliverer. God is not content with sending a prophet to condemn our sins; he commissions an angel to bring help. Surely there is truth in the old belief that the Angel-Jehovah, designated here, was our Lord, whose delights were ever with the sons of men. Compare Isa. 63:9 and Acts 7:30 with Exod. 3:2, 6. He still comes to us, not visibly to the eye, but sensibly to the heart. There is a peculiar burning at the heart, which those who love him understand, when he manifests himself to them as not to the world. See Luke 24:32 and John 14:21.

Gideon was the youngest son of a poor family, which had suffered greatly at the hands of Midian. Contrast this with 8:18. He was compelled to thresh his wheat in the winepress, below the surface of the ground, lest the Midianites should descend on it and carry it off. He seemed the least likely to be the chosen deliverer. But remember the apostle's words, 1 Cor. 1:26. There is a might that no human valor can impart; it is that which is communicated directly from Christ, as in v. 14. And when Jesus looks and speaks, the young soul that stands in all humility before him knows that it can do all things through him who strengthens, Phil. 4:13.

JUDGES 6:19-27

Face to Face with the "Angel of Jehovah." Gideon realized the momentous character of that interview. He only wanted to be sure that it was no dream or fancy. Hence the proposal of the flesh and broth. As the fire started forth at the Angel's touch, he knew that the veil of the unseen world had been rent to send him direction and help. At first he was startled, and then the peace of God fell upon his soul. He heard the Voice that uttered a similar benediction in Dan. 10:19 and John 20:26. The peace of God henceforth kept his heart and mind.

On Gideon's side, God required an act of immediate obedience: the destruction—though they stood on his father's property—of the hideous emblems of cruel and unclean rites and the substitution of an altar to the Lord. Ten of his household servants, beneath the spell of his personality, aided him in this heroic deed, which exposed him to disownment by his family and the forfeiture of his life by the townsfolk. God demands that we should love him best, Luke 14:26, 27, 33. But when our heart is perfect toward him, he shows himself strong in our behalf, 2 Chron. 16:9.

JUDGES 6:28-40

Beginning Reform at Home. The good sense of Joash saved his son. "Of what use is Baal to us," said he, "if he cannot take care of himself?" Gideon had stood the divine test; can you wonder that the Spirit of Jehovah, whom we know as the Holy Spirit, came upon Gideon and wrought mightily through his submitted life? Oh, to be pliant to the Spirit of Christ, as clothes to the body! With heroic courage he blew the trumpet of revolt, regardless of Midian, and at its notes the whole country aroused as from the spell of a bad enchantment.

But amid the excitement of the hour, the young leader craved one more assurance. He asked two questions. Was it possible that the Spirit had come on him in a special manner? The answer was in the affirmative, for the fleece —which represented himself—contained a bowlful of water, while the floor was dry. Was it possible, also, that the same Spirit that had come on himself would descend on the people who should gather to his summons? Again the answer was in the affirmative, for the floor was wet. God's promises are always "Yea" and "Amen." He cannot fail you. See 2 Cor. 1:18-22.

JUDGES 7:1-8

Quantity versus Quality. "There is no king saved by the multitude of a host," Psa. 33:16. God does not need multitudes. It is false to say that he is "on the side of the heaviest battalions." Read 2 Chron. 14 and 23. Those that are fearful and trembling, because they look at the might of their enemies rather than to the eternal God, had better depart to their *homes;* they are an impediment and hindrance, and may, by an evil telepathy, slacken the faith of others. Those also who forget that they are soldiers, who put the ease of the body before the strenuous attitude of the soul, who think most and first of their physical indulgence, are of no use to God for great exploits. Send them to their *tents;* they can assist in the secondary work of pursuit.

It was a very little act—the attitude in drinking—but how much it meant! The 300 who caught up the water in the hollow of their hands showed that they could not forget the foe; that they were resolved to subordinate bodily appetite to the spirit and dared not relax their girded loins. These are the men that God can use! But 300 of these are enough to rout 135,000, vv. 8, 9. Live in the Spirit; walk in the Spirit; be always in touch with the Spirit, and make no provision for the flesh, Rom. 13:14; Gal. 5:16. And be faithful, also, in very little actions.

JUDGES 7:9-23

"The Sword of Jehovah and of Gideon." Gideon asked for the sign of the fleece, but God, without his asking, gave him that of the barley cake. It was only barley bread, the cheapest and commonest kind of food, but it overthrew a tent. Gideon was quick to recognize the symbol of his weakness and helplessness, but he recognized also the presage of victory. Lying there in the moonless night, with his head toward that tent, he worshiped and hastened back to his camp. We remember what Jesus made of barley loaves. See John 6:9, 13.

The blare of the trumpets, the breaking of the pitchers, the flashing of the lights, and the shouting from three sides of the camp startled the sleeping host into panic. Surely this scene was in Paul's thought when he said that God's light had shone forth on the midnight darkness of that age, and then confessed that the light was contained in the earthen vessel of mortality, "that the excellency of the power may be of God." Let us not be too greatly disturbed when the sorrows and persecutions of earth break up our peace and strength; this is the breaking of the earthen vessel. Our business must be to see that the torch burns within, 2 Cor. 4:6*ff.*

JUDGES 7:24—8:12

"A Soft Answer Turneth Away Wrath." The fleeing host made for the three fords of the Jordan, and with all haste Gideon summoned the tribes to anticipate them. The way of the victor was not without its drawbacks and discouragements. Ephraim was wroth; Succoth and Penuel were contemptuous; his own men were faint, though pursuing. But the faith that had won the great victory never wavered. Gideon "endured as seeing him who is invisible." From the eternal source of patience and hope he derived the grace of continuance. This is what Paul also learned and taught in after-years, 2 Cor. 6:4*ff.*

When the soul is leaning on God, drawing on his resources, and affirming his sufficient grace, it can afford to answer Ephraim pleasantly; it will not shrink from rebuking cowardice in Penuel and Succoth; and it will hold on its victorious way, until the last enemy is destroyed and it enters the presence of God to receive the "Well done!" Discouraged soul, get alone, shut your door on all other thoughts, and say over and over to God the words with which the good Asaph ends Psalm 73, vv. 23-28. Let these fill your heart with music till you are strong again.

JUDGES 8:13-28

The Snare of Success. Clearly Gideon's family had passed through some terrible tragedy previous to this war of emancipation. He had not learned our Lord's teaching of forgiveness and rather acted on the usual maxims of his age. Possibly, also, he felt that he was the executioner of God's vengeance upon these chiefs, whose names, "Immolation" and "Trouble," were derived from their desperate deeds. As they stood anticipating death, they uttered a memorable sentence: "As the man is, so is his strength." The usefulness of our lives is not to be gauged by what we say or have or think, but by what we *are*. It is not gift, but grace that leaves the deepest dint upon other lives. If you want to be strong in the arm, you must be pure and true at heart.

The gold and purple of the spoil enabled Gideon to make an ephod, presumably on the pattern of that described in Exodus 28. It was not exactly an idol but a kind of fetish, and it diverted the thoughts of the people from Shiloh and the spiritual worship of the unseen and eternal God. So apt is the human heart to cling to some outward emblem—it may be a crucifix, a wafer, or a church—and miss that worship in spirit and in truth for which the Father seeks.

JUDGES 8:29—9:6

Through Slaughter to a Throne. The children of Israel were guilty of great fickleness and instability. They soon relapsed into Baal worship and forgot to show kindness to the family of their great leader. But such is the frailty of the human heart. However hot we may be for Christ today, we may be cold and distant tomorrow. It seems as if the great adversary taunts us with this, as he did John Bunyan to whom he kept whispering, "I'll cool you, I'll cool you." We must take our fickle hearts to our Lord, asking him to keep us true and hot in our love. There are times when his friendship is the most real thing in life, but then the rainbow-glory fades in the sky. Let it not be so any more, O Lord, we beseech thee!

The terrible crime of Abimelech was extenuated by the people of Shechem, because his mother was one of themselves. Compare 8:31 with 9:1, 18. But the mills of God were grinding out awful trouble for them all, vv. 56, 57.

Surely, in his lack of self-control, Gideon had much to answer for, 8:30! The evil that men do lives after them.

JUDGES 9:7-21

The Bramble King. Men must have leadership. The reason lies deep in human nature. The French revolutionaries destroyed the royal family, but Robespierre, Danton, and Marat were practically enthroned in the position from which Louis was hurled. In Oliver Cromwell's commonwealth, he exercised the royal prerogative. Some of us enthrone the fatness of the *olive,* some the sweetness of the *fig,* and some the good cheer of the *vine.* In other words, the guiding ideal of some souls is prosperity, of others love, of others pleasure. And yet others choose the *bramble*—with its prickly thorns—which, when scorched by the summer heat, is near unto burning, Heb. 6:8. It stands, therefore, for the useless and perilous life, which is doomed to the scrap heap. See 1 Cor. 9:27.

In the meanwhile, Jesus waits to become the crowned King of each soul. He "adventured" his life and delivered us from the hand of the enemy, to whom we had sold ourselves. Do we deal truly and uprightly with him in allowing other lords to rule over us while we crown *him* with thorns? See vv. 17 and 19.

JUDGES 9:22-40

The Kindling Fire. Although this is a sordid story, it is set out at length to teach us that God's judgments upon sin are not reserved for some future date, but are continually being administered. The Father hath committed all judgment to the Son, and throughout the ages of human history he has been dividing men and nations, as the shepherd divides the sheep from the goats. Peter tells us, for instance, that the cities of Sodom and Gomorrah were condemned to destruction as an example to those who live "ungodly," 2 Pet. 2:6. Adonibezek bore witness to the same great law, Judges 1:7. The Psalms are full of it—see Psalm 7:15-17. Here it is also. Shechem rued the evil agreement with Abimelech, and the fratricide. Contention and bloodshed were their plentiful reward.

Let us keep calm and quiet, when wicked men attain to great power and spread themselves as "a green tree in its native soil." We need not fret ourselves to do evil. Rest in the Lord and wait patiently for him, for the Lord loveth judgment and forsaketh not his saints. They are preserved forever, but the seed of the wicked shall be cut off. See Psalm 37.

JUDGES 9:41-57

The Burning of the Bramble. Terrible deeds like these give tokens of the power of the god of this world, the spirit that now worketh in the children of disobedience. Alas, similar atrocities are being perpetrated still, after all these centuries of what is called Christian civilization. But this Christianity is only a very shallow veneer, and when national passions break loose there is little difference between war today and in pre-Christian ages.

Men have no right to attribute the sins, cruelties, barbarities, and enormities of the present day to Christianity. They are due to its absence. The whole gospel of the Son of man protests against them. We must sadly admit that his enemy hath done this. And there will be no real cessation of the evils beneath which the world groans until the King comes to his own and sets up his everlasting Kingdom. What has happened of late in Europe (editor's note: World War I), notwithstanding all the efforts toward arbitration and peace, proves that something new must be brought to pass before the Father's kingdom can come and his will be done on earth.

JUDGES 10:1-16

Inveterate Idolatry. The scene is now removed to the tribes across the Jordan, especially those settled in Gilead and its vicinity. The children of Ammon were the aggressors, and acquired such boldness as even to cross the Jordan and fight against Judah and Ephraim. "Israel was sore distressed." Almost spontaneously we say, "Surely it served them right." It seems incredible that after all they had suffered on account of their idolatry, they should again relapse to Baal and add further the gods of Zidon, of Moab, of Ammon, and of Philistia. If Jehovah had finally cast them off, could they have complained? But as the psalmist puts it in his touching words, "God regarded their affliction, when he heard their cry," Psalm 106:44.

All these things were written for our example and instruction. Israel did not forsake God more often than we have done. Life has been full of fits and starts, of backsliding and recommencement, of sin and repentance. We have nothing to say against Israel; let us look at home, and search our hearts, and thank the Lord that his mercy endureth forever, Psalm 136.

JUDGES 10:17—11:11

Turning to a Rejected Leader. The life of Jephthah is a great consolation to those whose birth has been irregular. The sin of his parents was not allowed permanently to injure his career. He is also distinctly mentioned in Hebrews 11 as one of the heroes of faith. See Ezekiel 18:14-17.

Driven from his home, Jephthah took to the life of a bandit-chieftain, probably in much the same fashion as David in after-years when he protected, for payment, the cattle of the Hebrews from Ammonite forays. Jephthah's wife apparently had died; but his sweet and noble daughter grew up amid that wild horde, and they were all in all to each other. As David influenced a similar band, so did this father and child lift the tone and morale of their followers until the story of it filled the land and brought the elders, who years before had sided with Jephthah's brethren, to entreat him to lead the fight for freedom. What a beautiful suggestion of our Lord! He came to his own and they crucified him. He comes to us and we at first refuse him. But his love never faileth. Being reviled, he blesses; being persecuted, he endures; being defamed, he entreats, 1 Cor. 4:12.

JUDGES 11:12-28

A Warning from History. Jephthah acted with great prudence. Before rushing into war, he endeavored to argue the matter at issue in peaceful and courteous terms. In answer to the contention that Ammon was only trying to regain its own territories, he insisted that when Israel came on the scene they wrested the land, not from Ammon, but from the Amorites. Besides, the occupation of 300 years, which had never before been challenged, surely disproved the claim of the Ammonite king.

When a nation has right and justice on its side and is fighting against aggression, especially when the choice between two ideals is in the scale, there is every reason why it should appeal to the Lord, the Judge, to vindicate its cause. It was a question whether the worship of Jehovah or of Chemosh should dominate the country; on that issue there could be no vacillation nor hesitancy. It is interesting to notice how accurately Jephthah had studied the sacred annals of his people and how reverently he alludes to God. There is more religion in the hearts of men like Jephthah than certain Pharisees and priests give them credit for!

JUDGES 11:29-40

A Shadowed Victory. All the nations around were accustomed to offer those dearest to them in sacrifice to their cruel national deities. This was preeminently the case with the neighboring country of Moab, which the prophet Micah rebuked, 6:6-8. But in all that wild border country, there was then no prophetic voice to arrest Jephthah, who probably felt that Chemosh should not claim from the king of Ammon more than *he* would surrender to Jehovah. Out of this arose, not the rash but the deliberate though mistaken vow of v. 31. Before you judge him, ask whether you would be willing for your dearest to become a missionary in a heathen land. Have you ever yielded your all to the Man of Calvary? Do you love him better than the best? You would not carry out your vow as probably Jephthah did, but are you as absolute in your dedication?

The reply of Jephthah's daughter is one of the noblest on record. Compare it with Luke 1:38. Her heart was full of filial love and patriotic passion as she stood there, timbrel in hand; but the love of God overmastered all else and made her willing to yield all. See 2 Cor. 5:14.

JUDGES 12:1-15

At the Fords of Ephraim. In this second war, Jephthah showed the same conciliatory spirit as he had showed to Ammon. He parleyed sensibly and courteously before he went into the conflict. A great many Christians are less Christian than this. They ignore Christ's strict injunction, Matt. 18:15. Ephraim had acted in the same manner to Gideon, 8:1. In each case, that tribe wanted to retain its primacy without the sacrifice which leadership involves; and it was angry when deliverance had arisen from another source. Leadership must be won, not inherited. Ephraim, therefore, was clearly in the wrong; and when her troops, which had crossed the Jordan into Gilead, were hurled back, the slaughter at the ford fell as a national judgment. The omission of a letter in their speech betrayed them. Alas, Christians have martyred their fellows for even less!

Jephthah died soon after. Probably he died, not of age nor the brunt of war, but of a broken heart. The sweet voice of his child was always calling him. But the Spirit of God wrote on his memorial tablet, "By faith Jephthah."

JUDGES 13:1-14

The Promise of a Nazarite Champion. The secret of Samson's strength was a puzzle to his contemporaries. Even Delilah could not account for it, 16:5, 6. Clearly, then, it did not depend on his great height, nor his brawny chest and arms, nor his muscular development. It was due, as Hebrews 11:32 explains, to his faith, which opened his nature to the Spirit of God. See Judges 14:6, 19; 15:14. But faith is always in direct proportion to consecration. The soul cannot give itself in two directions, nor serve two masters; and if it draws its energy from the eternal God, there must be strict discipline exercised on the gateways of sense.

This was the intention of the Nazarite vow, which was generally taken for a limited period, but in this case for life. Its three particulars are enumerated in Numbers 6:4-9. Modern physiology has laid heavy emphasis on the necessity for a mother's careful regimen. How blessed it would be if not mothers only, but fathers and indeed all who influence young life would, for the sake of Christ and the children, abstain from alcohol! Is this price too much for love to give? See Mark 9:42.

JUDGES 13:15-25

The Promise Fulfilled. Manoah's wife comforted her husband with admirable tact. How often her words come back to us, at the different stages of life! The fact that God continues to bless and use, to answer prayer and give revelations of himself, may be quoted as a reason for believing that he has not cast us off. Would he have showed us such things as these and then kill us? His love in time past forbids us to think so.

Samson means "sunny." A happy, laughing lad, with his profuse crown of unshorn hair—is it any wonder that the soldiers of the garrison, situated on the Dan frontier, welcomed him? And the Spirit of God began to play on his young soul, as a minstrel plays on his harp. Such is the literal rendering of "began to move." Oh, happy are they whose natures lie open to God's touch, so that the least movement produces a quick and glad answer! As the aeolian harp will respond to the kiss of a light breeze or the moan of the rising storm, so be it with our hearts and lives. Thus our unconscious influence may become as songs without words.

JUDGES 14:1-14

A Self-willed Youth. Timnath lay just across the frontier, in the Philistine country. It was a bad match and the beginning of trouble. Young people cannot be too careful as to their first love match. Pray over it before you let your heart go. Take the advice of parents and friends. Whatever you do, marry only "in the Lord." For a Christian to marry one who is destitute of the divine life is not only to set Christ's Law at defiance, but to incur the misery of perpetual discord. It is impossible to have perfect fellowship with one who is not agreed with you in your deepest nature, 1 Cor. 7:39.

This young lion, on the path between the vineyards, seems to have been the means of awakening Samson to claim that divine strength which had awaited his appeal, but until that moment had been undiscovered. May it not be that lions have been allowed to roar at you that you might be driven back upon God, and compelled to avail yourself of those infinite resources which reside in the ever-living Savior?

JUDGES 14:15—15:8

In Bad Company. What strong confirmation is afforded, by Samson's experience, of the misery of a mixed marriage! This Philistine wife had no real love for him, and was more readily influenced by her own people than by her husband. How could she enter into his desire to emancipate Israel? To carry out his life-purpose of freeing Israel, he must break with her. Notice how this poor wife was visited with the very chastisement from which she hoped, by treachery, to save herself. Compare 14:15 and 15:6.

Samson's riddle is constantly being verified. We all have to encounter lions. Happy are we if we rend them in the power of the Holy Spirit! And have we not often discovered that the very sorrow, trial, or temptation which we dreaded most and which threatened to destroy us has yielded the strength and sweetness, the meat and honey which have enriched us for later times? Samson shared these with his mother and father. Let us never keep to ourselves those glorious lessons and results which we may have won in conflicts and sorrows that only the eye of God has witnessed. Let others share their benefit.

JUDGES 15:9-20

Mighty against the Foe. To how low a depth had the men of Judah descended, that they should hand over their champion to their hereditary foes. The northern tribes that arose at the call of Gideon rebuked such cowardly treachery. There are things worse than defeat or death. To forfeit honor, to shirk duty, to fail in the supreme call of friendship and loyalty—these are the crimes that belittle the soul and court disgrace. What shall it profit, though we gain the whole world, if we lose our souls?

How inspiring is the thought that on us also the Spirit of the Lord may come "mightily"! There is no limit to his gracious and irresistible operations, save that imposed by the narrowness of our faith. Notice how the apostle piles up his words in Ephesians 1:19. Whatever be the cords of evil habits, woven through long years, and however entangling your circumstances, God's indwelling power can set you free. Yes, and that is not all. At the place where you have won your victories, there shall arise that fountain of water which is fed from the throne of God; and the soul, exhausted by its effort, shall drink and be revived. Lord, cause us so to drink!

JUDGES 16:1–14

Playing with the Enemy. Three women, one after another, brought Samson down. If only a noble woman could have influenced him, as Deborah did Barak, how different his record would have been. Let those who are eminent in spiritual capacity guard against the swing of their nature to the opposite, sensual side.

It is clear that Samson's strength was not wholly accounted for by huge stature nor massive muscles, else Delilah would not have needed to ask his secret. He lost his strength, not merely because the razor deprived him of his hitherto unshorn locks, which lay in glossy ringlets at the feet of his temptress, but because he had yielded to her seductive wiles. We should have supposed that one or two experiences of her shameful treachery would have sufficed to put him on his guard and lead him to flee from the spot, as did Joseph, Gen. 39:12. But Samson lingered, as the moth which seems unable to resist the fascination of the flame, although already it has singed its wings, Prov. 1:10–19. There is always a way of escape, but we must take it with instant eagerness, Gen. 19:17–22.

JUDGES 16:15–31

Dying with the Philistines. It may be that the razor has already severed your union with Christ. If we abide not in living union with him, we are cast out as branches from the vine, and wither. This is bad enough, but it is still worse when we are not aware of it. See Hosea 7:9.

We may be blind and captive, yet for us also the hair that was cut may begin to grow again. The old faith and love, the old consecration and surrender, the old power with God and man may come again. Do not turn away from him, penitent soul, for God is willing to take you back again into the secret of his power. "He hateth putting away," Mal. 2:16. See Isa. 50:1. Out of your sorrowful heart, send up Samson's prayer! But do not ask to be strengthened only this once. God will do it not for once, but for many times, if only you will trust him absolutely, 2 Kings 13:19. And do not ask to die; believe that life shall again become bright, strong, and victorious.

THE BOOK OF
RUTH

THE ORIGIN OF THE HOUSE OF DAVID

I. The sojourn of Elimelech and his family in Moab   *1:1–5*
II. The return of Naomi, accompanied by Ruth   *1:6–22*
III. Ruth gleans in the field of Boaz   *2*
IV. Ruth makes herself known to her kinsman   *3*
V. The marriage of Ruth and Boaz   *4:1–12*
VI. The ancestry of David   *4:13–22*

INTRODUCTION

This exquisite idyll is united as a supplement to the book of Judges by the word translated "now," with which it opens. It was evidently written after the monarchy was established. It has been ascribed to the prophet Samuel, and it is easy to understand the special interest with which he would narrate the origin of the family of the youth whom he had anointed as future king.

It is clear, however, from the need of explaining a custom which had become obsolete, that the events narrated took place in the early settlement of Israel in the Land of Promise, and probably before the judgeship of Gideon. The story gives a graphic and admirable picture of the simplicity and beauty of the home life of those early years; and it teaches us that we need never despair of our life, for in ways we know not of, God is bringing good out of evil, and sunshine from the dark and cloudy sky.

COMMENTARY

RUTH 1:1-14

Back to Bethlehem. It was a mistake for Elimelech and his family to have left Bethlehem; God would have sent them bread. The path became darker and darker. Mahlon means "pining" and Chilion "consumption." Three graves in a strange land! All the laughter and hope that had given Naomi her name of "pleasant" had turned to sadness; she longed to see the dear village of her childhood and early married life, and to drink the water of the well, 2 Sam. 23:15. It is thus that the banished soul comes back to God. Moab's fascination palls on the taste, its cisterns are broken and will hold no water. See Psalm 63.

The two younger women climbed the road with Naomi, till they reached the point where the last glimpse could be taken of Moab. There Naomi uttered this remarkable address, urging her daughters to return. It was very thoughtful and tender, and touched chords of bitter memory and deep pathos. But the saddest undertone was not regret for the dead past; it was the feeling that the hand of the Lord had been against her. Nay, dear soul, that hand is already engaged in making all things work together for good. A few more months and your sorrow will be turned into joy, 4:16.

RUTH 1:15-22

Love's Steadfast Choice. This young woman was to be an ancestor of David and in the line of our Lord's descent. Moabite though she was by birth, Ruth was designated for the high honor of introducing a new strain into the Hebrew race that was to enrich it, and through it the world. Indeed, we may almost detect in her noble and beautiful words some anticipation of the Psalms, which have gone singing down the ages. But how stern is the discipline through which those must pass who are called to the highest tasks! The death of her husband in their early married life, the anguish of Naomi, the separation from her own people, the loneliness of a foreign land—these were part of the great price that Ruth paid.

May not something also be said for the mother? It was because of her that Ruth was led to her supreme self-giving. She had never seen a suffering soul bear itself so heroically. She felt that in the Hebrew faith there was something which Chemosh had never imparted to *her* people; she craved for herself some of the holy radiance that lingered on the worn face of Naomi. More people watch our bearing than we think. Let us attract them to Jesus!

RUTH 2:1-13

Gleaning after the Reapers. In great desolation of soul, Naomi had returned. She was no longer the happy woman of earlier days. Ruth also must sometimes have experienced the depression of homesickness, which often steals over the heart of the stranger. But the two women found solace where sad hearts will always find it, first in God and then in ministry to each other, 2 Cor. 1:4; 7:6. In fact, Ruth's devotion to her mother became the common talk of the village, v. 11.

Notice the beautiful old-time salutations between the employer and his employees. The omission of these courteous greetings is one of the mistakes of our modern civilization. We live in a time when the relations between master and servant, between mistress and maid, are strangely altered, being largely financial and selfish. Each tries to get as much as possible out of the other, and thus the personal touch is absent. Is it to be wondered at that the human machine runs hard and sometimes breaks down? But Boaz was clearly a good man. He had won the respect of the whole neighborhood, and his tender words to the young stranger, saluting her as a nestling under the wings of Jehovah, indicated that he dwelt "in the secret place of the Most High."

RUTH 2:14-23

Kindness to the Stranger. From the time of the Exodus, kind and thoughtful references are made to the strangers within the gates, Deut. 5:14; 10:19. These injunctions found beautiful exemplification in Boaz. How careful should be we who live on a higher level, so far as the knowledge of God is concerned, that we exceed the ancient Hebrews in tender regard for the lonely and bereaved! A desolate woman whose husband had met with an accident said the other day to a visitor whom God had sent on an errand of mercy, "I thought nobody cared." Like Boaz, it is our business to speak kindly to such, though not of our kith and kin, and who can know how far our words may travel!

We have a glimpse into Naomi's soul in v. 20. It would seem as if she had come to the conclusion that God had forgotten and forsaken her. But when Ruth repeated the words of Boaz, the human love rekindled her faith in God's love. She began to see God's purpose shaping itself. The rainbow shone on the retreating cloud of her tears. What an opportunity is presented, each day we live, of bringing the consciousness of God to weary and heavy-laden lives!

RUTH 3:1-18

"The Part of a Kinsman." According to the old Hebrew law, Ruth was already married to Boaz, on the supposition that he was next of kin. Naomi apparently had no knowledge of a nearer kinsman than he. Compare 2:20; 3:12; Deut. 25:5-10. There was therefore no immodesty in Naomi's proposals, though they are foreign to our modern practice. But clearly Boaz acted with admirable self-restraint. His earnest concern was for the good name of the young girl who had thrown herself on his protection, vv. 11, 14. Next to God's grace, the one thought which helps us in the hour of testing is to put the interests of another before our own. Love to our neighbor is ultimately love to ourselves.

What confidence these two helpless women reposed in Boaz! The words with which Naomi closed their conversation suggest a character of absolute reliableness. His word was his bond. He was prompt, decisive, and instant in carrying out any measure to which he felt himself pledged. Procrastination will wear out the heart of those who trust us. Let us finish promptly what we undertake! "Diligent in business, fervent in spirit!" Remember that when you trust Christ with anything, he also will not rest till he has finished it.

RUTH 4:1-22

In the Line of David's Ancestry. We are admitted here to a graphic picture of the old world. Men's memories were longer and stronger than ours; and what was done publicly in the Gate, the place of public concourse, had the seal of permanence irrevocably attached to it. The transference of the shoe indicated the inferior position of woman, though she was honored in Israel more than in the neighboring nations.

What a happy ending! The gleaner need never again tread the fields, following the reaper's footsteps. All the broad acres were now hers, since she had become one with the owner. When we are one with Christ, we no longer work for redemption; but being redeemed, we bring forth fruit unto God, Rom. 7:4. The curtain falls on a blessed group. The tiny babe lies on Naomi's bosom. The women who had gone together into the valley of the shadow of death stand together in the light of the mountaintop. God turns mourning into gladness, Psa. 30:11. And let us Gentiles learn that we too have a part in Christ. In him is neither Jew nor Greek, Col. 3:11.

THE FIRST BOOK OF SAMUEL

THE ESTABLISHMENT OF THE MONARCHY

1. FROM THE BIRTH OF SAMUEL TO THE ANOINTING OF SAUL   *1—8*
   - A. Hannah's prayer and its answer   *1*
   - B. Samuel's consecration to Jehovah   *2:1-21*
   - C. The evil conduct of Eli's sons   *2:22-36*
   - D. Their punishment revealed to Samuel   *3*
   - E. The death of Eli and his sons; the capture of the Ark   *4*
   - F. The sojourn of the Ark in Philistia   *5*
   - G. The return of the Ark to Israel   *6—7*
   - H. The demand for a king   *8*

II. FROM THE ANOINTING OF SAUL TO THE ANOINTING OF DAVID   *9—15*
   - A. The meeting of Saul and Samuel   *9*
   - B. Samuel anoints Saul king of Israel   *10:1-16*
   - C. Saul proclaimed king by the people   *10:17-27*
   - D. Saul rescues Jabesh-gilead from the Ammonites   *11*
   - E. Samuel's farewell address   *12*
   - F. Saul's wars with the Philistines   *13—14*
   - G. Saul's failure to destroy the Amalekites; his rejection   *15*

III. FROM THE ANOINTING OF DAVID TO THE DEATH OF SAUL   *16—31*
   - A. Samuel anoints David to succeed Saul   *16*
   - B. David's victory over Goliath   *17*
   - C. The friendship of David and Jonathan   *18—20*
   - D. Saul pursues David to slay him   *21—26*
   - E. David goes over to the Philistines   *27*
   - F. Saul consults the witch of Endor   *28*
   - G. David withdraws from Philistia and conquers the Amalekites   *29—30*
   - H. Saul's last stand against the Philistines   *31*

INTRODUCTION

The two books of Samuel were originally one in Hebrew. The division was first made when the Old Testament was translated into Greek, the amount of space required by that language making it impracticable to write the entire book upon a single roll.

The authorship of these books cannot be determined, but there is abundant evidence that they embody the report of eyewitnesses. Some of the more prominent characters in the scenes described are named as writers in 1 Chronicles 29:29.

The First Book of Samuel records the rise of a new political and spiritual order represented by the kings and the prophets. The establishment of the monarchy, with Saul as the first king, is an epochal event in the development of Israel's national life.

Of no less importance is the appearance of the "schools of the prophets" under the leadership of Samuel. In these institutions we see the beginning of the movement which made Israel spiritually supreme among the nations.

COMMENTARY

1 SAMUEL 1:1-11

Hannah's Prayer and Vow. Elkanah was evidently a kind husband to Hannah, but marriage had suffered from the general relaxation of morals, and the bitter effects of polygamy are illustrated here. Because Hannah was specially loved, Peninnah hated her.

The grief of the childless wife drove Hannah to God. There she found her only resource. When the heart is nigh to breaking, what else can we do than pour out our complaint before the One who is ever ready to hear our cry? We may trust God with our secrets; he will keep sacred our confidence. Elkanah's love may go a long way, but we have for the most part to tread the winepress alone. After we have eaten and drunk before our friends in such a way that they cannot guess what is happening within, we must have a spot where we can unbend and open the sluice-gates of grief. And what place is so good as the mercy seat? We need not vow our vows to bribe God to help us. The gifts of his love are more blessed for him to give than for us to receive. But out of love we can vow what we will.

1 SAMUEL 1:12-28

The Child Dedicated to God. Here is a delightful specimen of secret fellowship with God, and its results. Many were coming and going in the Tabernacle court. It was no place for private prayer; and this sad woman had no opportunity for audible petition, so she spoke in her heart. We may all do that amid the crowds that sweep gaily past us in their lighthearted way. Let us not grow weary. "She continued praying before the Lord." People may misunderstand and reproach you. The Elis that judge superficially may leap to hasty conclusions, but pray on! Pray on, though the prayer seem impossible of answer! Pray on, though heart and flesh fail! Pray on, for God will yet raise the poor from the dust and the beggar from the dunghill! When you have committed your cause to God, go in peace and be no more sad.

"The Lord remembered her." Of course he did. He has graven us on the palms of his hands, and the ruined walls of our peace are ever before him. The hour will come when, like Hannah, you will stand on the very spot where the prayer was offered, to confess that God has given you the petition that you asked of him. God cannot fail, and his gifts are sweetest and safest when they are returned to him by his children.

1 SAMUEL 2:1-11

The God of the Lowly. Hannah's song was to inspire David, the Virgin Mother, and countless others to sing hymns of praise. So the song of a bird will set the whole woodland ringing with the music of a feathered chorus. We, too, shall sing someday! God will turn the waters of our tears, which fill the jars to their brim, into the wine of joy. You also, my friend, shall someday take your harp from the willows and get from it music which will go through the world to stir men's sad hearts.

How full of the Lord the song is! The overflowing heart ascribes its rapture to the Rock of Ages. He saves; he is holy; he knows; he weighs; he kills and makes alive; he brings down to the grave and up; he will vindicate our trust. We do not prevail by strength, but by yielding ourselves into his hands. God answers our prayers thoroughly. The gifts that come from above are good and perfect. Bereaved mother, your little child is yours still, though hidden from your eyes! Try to think of your beloved one as ministering to the Lord in the eternal temple!

1 SAMUEL 2:12-21

Growing before the Lord. Not only were Eli's sons strangers to the power of religion in the heart, but they had gone to great lengths of profligacy. They had seized on a larger share of the offering than was prescribed, and their rapacity had made men abhor the sacred rites. It is an awful thing when the inconsistencies of professing Christians cause men to abhor the service of Christ. It will go very hard with them at the last. The Master says that it would have been better for a millstone to be hanged about their neck; and one cannot but think that great allowance will be made at the last for those who have fallen over these stumbling-blocks.

What love and prayer Hannah must have wrought into that little coat! Every stitch was put in with such motherly pride. It was hard to give the boy up, but at least she could do something for him. How nice he would look in it! How proud she was that every year's new one had to be larger! Thus parents still make the clothes that their children wear. The little ones almost unconsciously become arrayed in the character that is constantly being shown before their quick and inquisitive eyes.

1 SAMUEL 2:22-36

The Penalty of Dishonoring God. Eli was held responsible for the excesses of his sons. He was a mild and gentle old man, but there are times when mildness and gentleness are out of place. We must be stern and strong when the occasion demands. It is always necessary to be on the alert, lest flabbiness and weakness should pass under the designation of Christian graces. Moreover, severer measures might have restrained his sons, 3:13. Therefore, in the message of judgment Eli was included, vv. 27-36. He is classed with his sons and reckoned as an accomplice with them in their sin against God, vv. 29, 30.

Notice that prediction of the "faithful priest," vv. 35, 36. In its first reference Samuel may be seen, but beyond him rises the figure of Another who ever lives to intercede, and is expressly designated as "faithful." Eli and his sons lived in the Temple, where the burning holiness of God was reflected in every service; but they seem never to have heard the chant of the seraphim, nor to have cried, "Woe is me, for I am undone," nor to have felt the burning coal on their lips. Do not trifle with the sacred privileges of God's house! They will condemn where they do not uplift.

1 SAMUEL 3:1-9

"Speak, Lord; for Thy Servant Heareth." As we read again these familiar verses, we are taken back in thought to the dear scenes of childhood, to the home we remember so well and to the mother's voice, perhaps now silent. This story, which was our favorite then, is hardly less dear to us now that we are well advanced on the pathway toward the home beyond.

The dying lamp of the Tabernacle, the glimmering dawn, the silence and awe of the Holy Place were in strict accord with the boy's attentive ear and opened heart. The rug or couch on which he lay was not too lowly for the eternal God to visit. Stooping from his high Heaven, he came, and stood, and called. He was not angry because the child did not understand; nor did he, impatient of the delay, close the interview because he was not recognized. He knew that once Samuel understood, his heart would be eager to obey the call. With all of us there is ignorance as well as mistake. In our confusion we run hither and thither. It is best to lie still, even though the heart throbs and the attention is alert, until the knock is again heard on the door.

1 SAMUEL 3:10-21

A Message through a Child. It was a heavy burden that the young boy had to carry. To remind Eli of his sons' shameful sin; to reprove him for his neglect; to utter a judgment which no sacrifice could avert—all this was so painful that Samuel seems to have lain with wide-open eyes till daybreak. Then he appears to have gone quietly about his usual duties, as if still unwilling to disturb the quiet serenity of old age. It almost seems that Samuel realized the implicit rejection of Eli and his family, since he, and not Eli, had received the divine message.

Samuel's delicacy in trying to save Eli's feelings is as beautiful as the old man's resignation in hearing the awful disclosure of judgment; and in many a trying hour in after-life, he must have remembered Eli's reverent expression of submission: "It is the Lord: let him do what seemeth him good." The secret of a blessed life is to say Yes to God, and as sons to receive the discipline of his chastening and refining providence, Heb. 12:7.

1 SAMUEL 4:1–11

Trusting in the Ark, Not in God. The predictions against Eli's house now began to be fulfilled. It was fitting for Israel to institute an inquiry into the causes of defeat. This is always the first step toward victory. There was no doubt as to the ancient covenant with Israel; the one question was to ascertain what had suddenly neutralized that divine assistance which in former days had always been forthcoming. Failure often indicates that something has happened to cut off the supply of God's saving help.

In this instance, however, Israel did not carry the inquiry into God's presence, but endeavored to supply the lapse of divine help by introducing the symbol of the covenant. "Fetch the Ark!" they cried. They supposed that in some mysterious way it would bring God into their camp and ally him with their arms. In the same manner a brigand might expect an amulet or charm to preserve his life, while violating the laws of God and man. These views of the Israelites' relations with God had to be corrected; and hence defeat ensued. Our only safety lies, not in an outward act or token, but in simple, pure-hearted, and unbroken fellowship with God. Then we become invincible.

1 SAMUEL 4:12–22

The Glory Departed from Israel. Notwithstanding their high hopes, disaster again overtook the hosts of Israel. No symbols of God will help us until we have put away our idols and laid our hearts bare before him.

The bad news traveled quickly over the land and everywhere brought dismay. The death of Eli and that of his daughter-in-law were tragedies, but in each case there was a beautiful touch of true devotion to God's holy cause. The old man succumbed only when the messenger told of the capture of the Ark; while the mother could not be rallied from her death-swoon, even by the cry of her child, because, with the Ark, the glory of her people had passed away. May we not all pray to be equally devoted to the cause of Jesus Christ, so that its victories or its delays may touch us to the quick? The glory of our lives, as of the Church, should ever consist in the possession, not of the symbol, but of the real presence of our Lord, recognized, revered, loved, and enshrined in our tenderest emotions.

1 SAMUEL 5:1–12

The Captured Ark Brings Trouble. Dagon's fall before the Ark of God has a sublime significance. In the evening, as the priests left the temple, the hideous image stood erect on its pedestal; in the morning it was found prostrate before the sacred symbol. A repetition of the incident proved that it was no coincidence. So shall it be with all the idols of the heathen. They shall be utterly abolished, and the demons of whom they are the grotesque representations, together with the devil whom they obey, shall be cast into the "bottomless pit," Rev. 20:3. Thus has it been in many countries already. They have "cast their idols . . . to the moles and bats," Isa. 2:20.

Let this scene be reproduced in your heart! Let Jesus enter, and the dearest idols you have known will yield before him. The presence of Christ, which brings terror to his foes, will bring blessing and deliverance to those that love him. The dying thief passes from his cross to Paradise, while Judas goes to his own place. Dare to admit the Savior into the secret place of your heart. He will utterly destroy the works of Satan, and will drive out the evil things that have too long infested it.

1 SAMUEL 6:1–12

Returned with a Trespass Offering. There is reason to suppose that when the Philistines got possession of the Ark, they destroyed Shiloh. See Psa. 78:60, 64; Jer. 26:9. They could not imagine how to rid themselves of the sacred emblem, which brought only destruction in its train, until they had consulted the priests. These priests appear to have been well acquainted with the previous history of the Israelites, though centuries had passed since the passage of the Red Sea. How ignorantly men think of God! He is not their enemy, but the enemy of their sin.

What a striking illustration is afforded by these lowing kine! Their maternal instincts yearned for their young, detained behind; but they were urged forward by a supernatural impulse. So the missionary may leave wife and child, that he may carry the gospel to the heathen; so the slum-worker may abandon all that others hold dear, in order to change some wretched district into a city of God. Our weak heart clings, but the love of Christ constrains us, and we go forward, urged by a divine and overmastering motive.

1 SAMUEL 6:13-21; 7:1-4

Rashness Punished; Reverence Blessed. The new cart, with its precious burden, must have come upon the men of Beth-shemesh like an apparition. The Ark was welcomed by them, after its seven months' of absence, with great joy. But privilege entails responsibility; and their wanton curiosity and irreverence could not be permitted. Reverence for God himself demanded the most careful behavior toward the Ark of his Presence and when this was lacking, swift judgment ensued. See Num. 1:50, 51; 4:5, 16-30.

It is interesting to notice that when the Israelites were weaned from the Ark, their hearts lamented "after the Lord," 7:2. We cannot be permanently happy without God. Seasons of apathy and irreligion will sooner or later be succeeded by faith and love, as the frost of winter yields to the touch of spring. In this case, the revival was due to the patient labor of Samuel, and he did splendid service in urging the people to deal drastically with the idols of Canaan which had cut them off from God as clouds hide the sun.

1 SAMUEL 7:5-17

Leading the Nation in God's Ways. We are here taught the successive steps that must be taken if revival is to be granted to either Church or individual. (1) *Unity.* All Israel was gathered. The divisions and jealousies of preceding years were renounced. (2) *Confession.* The people poured out their hearts before the Lord. (3) *The abandonment of false gods.* They "put away Baalim and Ashtaroth, and served the Lord only" (7:4). (4) *Intercessory prayer.* The one condition of revival is to get back to prayer. "Cease not to cry unto the Lord our God for us." (5) *Full surrender,* as set forth in Samuel's burnt offering. Yield thyself to God, and the Philistines will fall back discomfited, and thou shalt raise thine Eben-ezer.

So Israel proved. There was immediate evidence that God had accepted them. Natural phenomena fought on their side. The very spot which had been the scene of defeat became the scene of glorious victory. Compare 4:1; 7:12. Here is great encouragement for us, for at certain spots in our life-experience we have been defeated; but just in these same spots, when the barriers which have intercepted God's help are leveled, we shall become more than conquerors.

1 SAMUEL 8:1-9

Seeking a King Like Other Nations. The sin that Samuel, as a lad, rebuked in Eli reappeared in his own family and undermined his influence. The names of Samuel's sons are suggestive of his own piety—"Jehovah is God" and "Jehovah is my Father." But, alas, they failed to walk in his steps! It was a mistake to delegate authority to men whose character was corrupt, and this precipitated the desire of Israel for a king. They failed to value the glory and strength of their position as a theocracy, a nation *directly* ruled by God, and craved to be as other nations. This finally led to their undoing. Be not conformed to the world, or you will share in its condemnation as well as in its penalty, Hos. 13:9-11.

Samuel felt the rebuff keenly, but ultimately he took the one wise step of laying the whole matter before the Lord. It is a good example! When the heart is overwhelmed; when we are hemmed in by difficulty; when men rise up and breathe out cruelty against us, let us roll back our trouble on our Lord and Savior who has identified himself with our life. Tell him all, though your heart is almost too broken for utterance. "He will be very gracious unto thee at the voice of thy cry," Isa. 30:19.

1 SAMUEL 8:10-22

Rejecting the Prophet's Warning. The people had entreated Samuel to cry unto God in their behalf; and now we see him going to and fro between the people and God, as a true mediator and intercessor. He "told all the words of the Lord unto the people," v. 10; and, "he rehearsed [all the words of the people] in the ears of the Lord," v. 21. See also v. 22. Samuel is fitly described in the Psalter as one who called upon God's name, Psa. 99:6. How much we may influence the life of a nation or of an individual if we will only pray with persistent and believing earnestness! We cannot dispense with our statesmen, but our prophets—the Samuels and the Elijahs—are the most efficient chariots and horsemen of protection, 2 Kings 2:12.

The people could not answer Samuel's grave and graphic words. They contented themselves with repeating their request, and soon they learned the bitterness of imposing their own will upon God. They *would* have a king, and God gave them their hearts' desire, but see Psalm 106:15. When Samuel had received God's reply, he set himself, with all his power, to further the matter, at all cost to himself. We are reminded of that noble reply of the Baptist in

1 SAMUEL

John 3:30, 31. God's will must be ever first and supreme!

1 SAMUEL 9:1-14

Saul Is Led to Find Samuel. As a king was demanded by the people, one was selected to suit their taste, "a choice young man, and a goodly." But the king after God's own heart was selected for other qualities, 16:7. Saul's character lacked important elements. His ignorance about Samuel was surprising; even his servant knew better. This did not promise well for a successful reign, Dan. 11:32b.

But how should Saul and Samuel be brought together? A succession of trifling and ordinary events proved to be the links in the divinely constructed chain. The lost asses, the prolonged search, the fear of the effect of anxiety upon Kish, the timely suggestion of the servant and his possession of a few coins which would serve as an introduction, the greeting of the young girls on their way to the well—what accidents they seem! Nay, but they are providences! All things work together to execute God's purpose. Nothing is too trivial to be part of the divine plan. Let us follow the indications of God's will; they lead to the waiting seat, the reserved portion, and the ultimate throne.

1 SAMUEL 9:15-27

The Prophet Meets the Coming King. There are some favored souls to whom God reveals his secrets, Psa. 25:14; John 15:15. Covet, above all things, that habitual nearness to God in which God may speak as a man to his friend. Eye hath not seen, nor ear heard, nor the heart of man conceived what God has prepared for those who love him; but he reveals them by his Spirit. Even when Samuel encountered Saul in the street, Samuel's guidance by God continued, v. 17. His fellowship with the Eternal was like a deep-flowing current; his meeting with Saul was a leaf dropped on its surface.

The prophet did not meet the young man as a rival. The life which is lived in God's presence is so filled with his light and his love that it is not disturbed by the fickle fancies of the crowd. Samuel was quite ready to be abased and to see another exalted, if God willed it, Phil. 4:12. It is good, when we are in partnership with God, to allow him, at the critical moment, to send the man or woman whom he has selected. "To-morrow . . . I will send thee a man." Such may come on quite another errand, but God will give us divine guidance and discernment, so that we may be ready to receive and welcome him.

1 SAMUEL 10:1-13

Anointed with Oil and the Spirit. In the gray dawn the prophet sketched to Saul the events which were to happen on that day and succeeding days. All were made known to the designated king ere they arrived, and in each case he was to act as the occasion demanded. Thus our life-course, day by day, lies open before God. He has planned or permitted the incidents, but leaves us to will and enact the appropriate response. If we turn to him to ask how we should act, he will guide us with his eye; but alas, all too seldom do we turn to him. We lean too much to our own understanding and follow "the devices and desires of our own hearts." We have been "created unto good works, which he has before ordained that we should walk in them." Instead of prying into the future, let us wait for him to unveil it as we advance. Let us most eagerly seek the sacred anointing of the Holy Spirit at the spring of the day. His sacred unction will teach us all things that we need to know. We must have the clean, new heart created, and the right spirit renewed, v. 9.

1 SAMUEL 10:14-27

The People Have Their Desire. Samuel dealt faithfully with the people, reminding them once more of their guilty mistake in demanding a king; and indeed they came to rue their choice. But as they would have it, so it was ordered. We may well ask God not to give us what we desire so earnestly, except as it accords with his purposes of love and wisdom. We have known and believed the love that God hath to us. Sometimes we *know* his will; at other times we have to trust in it blindly.

Saul's modesty was very commendable. There were many beautiful traits in his character in those early days, but as we shall see, all the music was finally silenced when that terrible monster, jealousy, stole into his heart. Among other evidences of a naturally noble disposition was his determination not to heed the detracting voices which challenged his elevation to the throne. Note the alternate translation of v. 27—"he was as though he were deaf." It was both wise and magnanimous. So for us all. When we are sure that we are in the line of God's purpose, and sincerely desire to do his will, we may be deaf to all other voices. "Fret not thyself because of evil-doers," Psalm 37:1.

1 SAMUEL 11:1-15

The New King's Good Beginning. A hundred years before, the Ammonites had been defeated by Jephthah; now they were beleaguering Jabesh-gilead. Help seemed impossible. But when the Spirit of God comes upon a man, what cannot that man do! That was Saul's blessed experience. He aroused the country, after the manner of the Scottish chieftains with their fiery cross. Then he sent a message of hope to the agonized city; and, finally, as morning broke over the quiet pasturelands, with his army of deliverance he burst upon the Ammonite camp.

Was there not a connection between Saul's previous self-control and his present victory? And must not that connection always be realized? Each of us must fight against heredity, environment, and habit; against self within and Satan without. The measure of our success will be the measure of our ability to help others. The mountain of temptation in the life of our Lord was followed in due course by his freeing the bodies and souls of men. In the hour of victory, Saul was borne to the throne. His success was the stairway to his coronation. We remember that when our Lord had destroyed and broken our foes, he took his seat, amid the acclaim of Heaven, at the right hand of power.

1 SAMUEL 12:1-13

Samuel's Last Message to Israel. An end must come to the longest and most useful service. Before his long sleep Samuel made protestation of his innocence before God and the people. The long sleep will come to us all, and happy are they who before they lay down their heads upon the pillow of death are able to extend their hands and to bare their hearts before those who have known them best and say, "These are clean." The people bore double witness to the truth of Samuel's challenge, and the old man was comforted. Yes, God was witness, as well as the people, to his absolute integrity. See Acts 24:16.

Then Samuel pressed home, upon that dense mass of people, the sin of which they had been guilty in demanding a king instead of waiting for a heaven-sent deliverer. But we are liable to the same mistake. We look to the visible and forget the invisible. We forget that the invisible Christ stands waiting to succor, prepared to save unto the uttermost. In this faith the apostle found his abiding peace and steadfastness. See 2 Cor. 1:10. Let us set our hope on him who has delivered, and will deliver.

1 SAMUEL 12:14-25

His Warning Confirmed from Heaven. Having handed his office over to Saul, who henceforth was to shepherd and lead the Chosen People, Samuel assured them that the Lord would not forsake them, "for his great name's sake," v. 22. Oh, take these words to heart, and let them linger like a strain of sweet music in your memory! You may have missed the mark, lost your way, and drifted from the ancient moorings, but the love of God has not forsaken you. Being disappointed, it lingers; being repelled, it returns; being buffeted, it entreats. God's name—that is, his honor—is at stake. See Josh. 7:9; Isa. 48:9, 11.

Terrified by the thunderstorm, which was God's endorsement of his servant's faith, the people entreated for Samuel's continued prayers; and the aged seer assured them that he would count it a great sin if he ceased to pray for them. Prayerlessness is not only an evidence of a besotted and demoralized nature, but is in itself a sin which requires confession and cleansing. When the heart is right with God, prayer arises like a fountain, from unseen depths.

1 SAMUEL 13:1-12

Saul's First Act of Folly. This is the story of a great tragedy! Here was the overcasting of a bright sunrise. The king was certainly subjected to a tremendous test. He had been bidden to wait until Samuel came before offering the sacrifice, because from the first it was understood that Saul was on the throne only as the nominee and vice-regent of Jehovah. And Saul did wait, with growing impatience, for seven weary days. Then, when the allotted period had nearly expired, he "forced" himself and offered the sacrifice. Apparently he had done this within half an hour of Samuel's arrival, because the offering would hardly have taken longer.

The one lesson for us is that the man after God's own heart will obey God to the uttermost, will wait till the last moment with assured faith, will dare to stand amid a dwindling army and with disaster imminent for the lack of marching orders. Man thinks God slow, behind the appointed time, and forgetful. Nay, but God is waiting to be gracious—waiting for the precise moment when he can intervene with most effect, Isa. 30:15, 18.

1 SAMUEL 13:13-23

Left in the Spoilers' Hands. Sternly and sorrowfully the old prophet pronounced the sentence of Saul's deposition, and suggested that already God had sought and found another prince for his people. In Jesse's home was found the stripling who in after-years would say, "Wait on the Lord: be of good courage, and he shall strengthen thine heart: wait, I say, on the Lord," Psa. 27:14.

Wait thou thy Lord's leisure! Bid thy heart stay its feverish beating, and thy pulse subside! To act prematurely and in self-will would mar the divine purpose, and set in motion stones that could not be stopped. "Let your moderation be known unto all men; the Lord is at hand." Never say, "Circumstances compelled me; I had to do it; my hand was forced." No, child of God, thou art greater than circumstances and superior to the crowd of base spirits around thee. Wait thou on God, for he shall yet interpose in thy behalf. Allow no circumstances to provoke or excuse the doing of evil. In quietness and confidence shall be thy strength; in returning and rest shalt thou be saved.

1 SAMUEL 14:1-15

Jonathan's Exploit for the Lord. Jonathan was a true knight of God. He was the Hebrew Galahad, a soldier without fear and without reproach. His life was pure, his word was true, he was faithful to the high claims of human love, and he followed the Christ, though as yet he knew him not.

He had entered into the spirit of the divine covenant, and could not believe that God had forgotten and forsaken. Was not the old promise true that "one [should] chase a thousand, and two put ten thousand to flight" (Deut. 32:30)? Happy are they who can rise above depression and misfortune into the clear heaven of fellowship with God, allying their weakness with his might, their ignorance with his wisdom! "It may be that the Lord will work for us," said Jonathan, "for there is no restraint to the Lord to save by many or by few." Then he offered himself as the humble instrument of God's will. The people recognized this. They said: "He hath wrought with God this day" (14:45). And the soul that reckons on God cannot be ashamed. "The Lord saved Israel that day," 14:23. In such works God and man cooperate. See John 3:21.

1 SAMUEL 14:16-35

Victory Shadowed by Saul's Errors. Saul's unwise prohibition had a terrible sequel: first, in the pursuit of his troops; and, second, in the rushing of the hungry upon the spoil without the proper separation of blood. Then, as the day closed in, the divine oracle was dumb. Evidently some sin had interposed its dark shadow between the king and the Eternal Light. See v. 37. Saul knew this, but he refused to look for the sin in his own heart, even when he and Jonathan stood alone. See v. 42.

The cause of the discomfiture and silence was not in Jonathan. Saul was alone to blame. In that, the good sense of the people decided rightly. Not only had the king marred and missed the greatest opportunity of his life, but he was already enwrapping his soul in that jealousy, moroseness of temper, and impetuosity of judgment which ruined his later career. In Paul's expressive phrase, he became a castaway, and was flung from the mighty hand which longed to make him a vessel unto honor, meet for every noble work. See 1 Cor. 9:27; 2 Tim. 2:21.

1 SAMUEL 14:36-52

The Man Who Wrought with God Rescued. In this case the voice of the people was the voice of God. If a man dares to stand alone with God, he cannot be put to shame. If he says of the Lord, "He is my refuge and my fortress; my God, in whom I trust," ten thousand voices answer: "He shall cover thee with his feathers, and under his wings shalt thou trust . . . Thou shalt not be afraid." "No weapon that is formed against thee shall prosper; and every tongue that shall rise against thee in judgment thou shalt condemn." One with God is always on the stronger side.

How safe are they who do God's commandments, hearkening to the voice of his word! When our Lord was arrested, he stood boldly before his captors and, interposing between them and his timid disciples, said, "If ye seek me, let these go their way." This is his invariable method. As the mother bird interposes for her helpless young; as the ring of fire intercepts the night attack of the wild beast; as the broad river and its streams bar the progress of the foe, so the Lord is round about his people forever!

1 SAMUEL 15:1-16

Leading the People in Disobedience. Several years intervened between the preceding chapter and this. The kingdom had become strong and prosperous. It seemed as though Samuel's sentence of deposition had been forgotten. But even in hot summer weather, the taint of autumn decay may be in the air. The speck of corruption was slowly eating into Saul's heart and at last, when this charge came concerning Amalek, the evil was revealed to all. Amalek was under a curse, and the existence of the tribe was a standing menace to the peace and prosperity of the surrounding nations; hence the edict for its destruction, Exod. 17:16.

Even in this world God judges the nations and condemns such as have ceased to fulfil his purpose. In spite of God's distinct command, Saul connived for the reservation of the choicest and best of the spoils, and this brought about his rejection. It is noticeable, also, that an Amalekite claimed to have dispatched him on the field of Gilboa, 2 Sam. 1:1–10. If we spare what God has commanded us to destroy, it may later destroy us. Take care in your obedience; you serve an exacting though loving God!

1 SAMUEL 15:17–35

Shallow Repentance Unavailing. Samuel was deeply moved when he heard of Saul's failure, "and he cried unto the Lord all night," 15:11. Thus he was prepared to accost the sinful king. Finney tells of a minister who was so burdened with the souls of men that he could do but little preaching, his whole time and strength being given to prayer. It is only in that spirit that men like Samuel can undertake their solemn duty.

Saul's response was very unsatisfactory. He began by laying the blame on the people, v. 21. He pretended that the object of sparing the cattle, etc., was to sacrifice them to God—a very hypocritical excuse. Without any deep consciousness of sin, he lightly professed sorrow and hoped to pacify Samuel by asking that they might kneel together in worship, v. 25. When the old prophet refused to let him off so easily, the only thing that Saul cared for was that the elders should still honor him, v. 30. How hardened Saul had become! This was the beginning of the sin unto death.

1 SAMUEL 16:1–13

God's Choice of His Anointed. The anointing of the young shepherd, with his ruddy cheeks and deep, poetic eyes, is a beautiful episode, in very marked contrast to the events preceding. He had already given proof of his indomitable courage, 17:34–36. They had to fetch him from his sheep, which he was pasturing beside the still waters and on the hillside. God had found him beforehand, Psa. 89:20. "He chose David also his servant, and took him from the sheepfolds . . . to feed Jacob his people, and Israel his inheritance," Psa. 78:70, 71.

The procession of David's brethren before Samuel was very impressive. They probably remembered that Saul had been chosen for his splendid physique, and each held himself high and proud. "Surely," said Jesse to himself, "one of them will captivate the prophet's eye." But no! God chooses by the inward temper and disposition. He knew that David was a man after his own heart. The lad had been faithful in a few things and was now to be made ruler over many. The anointing oil reminds us of the anointing for service which was given to our Lord at his baptism. In David's case it was accompanied by a glorious Pentecost, v. 13.

1 SAMUEL 16:14–23

The Young Harpist before the Dejected King. In one sentence we are told of the Spirit of the Lord coming upon David, v. 13, and in the next of the departure of the Spirit from Saul. This does not necessarily imply that all religious sensibility had become extinct, but that the special enduement which had fitted him for his kingly office had been withdrawn. An evil spirit "from the Lord" troubled him; that is, God permitted this spirit to enter. The garrison of peace and love had been willfully dismissed by Saul, and by the inevitable operation of the divine law. As he had banished the light, he was necessarily left in darkness. God gave him up to a reprobate mind, Rom. 1:24, 26, 28.

The king's depression demanded an antidote, which was provided by music. Philip V of Spain was helped in the same fashion. The minstrel here was none other than the young shepherd so recently anointed. A directing Providence superintends every incident in life. That a servant of Saul's had seen David in some country contest was only a link in the chain, v. 18. God has a plan for each life. "All things work together for good to them that love God," Rom. 8:28.

1 SAMUEL 17:1–16

Israel Defied by the Philistine Champion. When their king lost the special consciousness of God's presence and power, the whole kingdom became demoralized, and the Hebrews had the humiliation of hearing in silence a defiant challenge to "the armies of the living God," 17:26. It looked as if the answer would have to go by default, that Jehovah was a God who could not save. The impotence of the Israelites made Goliath still more defiant. At first he came down from the ranks of his own camp on the southern side of the valley and walked vaingloriously through the level plain between the two hosts; but after forty days had passed, he became bolder and came up the slopes where Israel stood. At his approach they fled in terror. Measuring nine feet, nine inches, covered with mail and carrying a spear, the head of which

1 SAMUEL

weighed eighteen pounds, the giant must have seemed very formidable to the men of Israel. And are there not giants equally determined and terrible that threaten us, in national and individual experience, and find us unable to cope with them? We need David's God and David's faith!

1 SAMUEL 17:17–30

David Unawed by the Giant. At this juncture David arrived in the camp, sent by Jesse to inquire after the welfare of his three elder sons, who had followed Saul to the war. He also brought them provisions, and a present for the captain of their troop. On arriving at the trenches, he found the army in battle array, but not daring to advance. When the whole story was detailed to the young shepherd, he looked at the incident and challenge from the spiritual side. This event, therefore, marked a turning point not only in his own history, but in that of his people. One, at least, was found in their ranks who looked at things from God's standpoint, counted on the God of the ancient covenant, and was prepared to venture all on faith, vv. 26, 36, 37.

His brother imputed to him a restless ambition, an unworthy curiosity. Much in the same way the kinsfolk of our Savior misunderstood his motives and sought to interrupt his work. But David was undaunted and answering his brother kindly and gently, he pressed on with his inquiries and protests until the tidings of the young champion reached the king. The victory over himself when Eliab reproached him was part of his preparation for the coming conflict.

1 SAMUEL 17:31–40

David Trusts His Former Deliverer. David was conducted into Saul's presence—his soul aglow with heroic faith—avowing that he was willing to go alone to fight the Philistine. Saul, however, had no thought of power save that which comes from long practice, 17:33, or from helmets and coats of mail, 17:38, 39; so he endeavored to dissuade the stripling. It was no small temptation to David to take a lower ground and retreat from his offer. Let us never listen to flesh and blood! They always say to us, after the manner of Peter at Caesarea Philippi, when our Lord spoke of his crucifixion and death, "This shall not be unto thee," Matt. 16:22.

The point of David's narrative of his encounter with the lion and the bear was entirely lost on Saul. The king regarded these exploits as solely the result of superior agility and sinewy strength. He did not fathom David's meaning when the lad ascribed his success to the direct interposition of Jehovah, v. 37. Already the underlying note of Psalm 27 may have been haunting the young psalmist's soul. Saul had no idea that faith opens new sources of power, touches new stops in the great organ, and accomplishes alliance with the Almighty. See Psa. 20:7, 8.

1 SAMUEL 17:41–54

He Wins the Lord's Battle. David did not wait until his enemy had crossed the valley, but hastened to the stream to select the pebbles needed for his sling. Goliath scouted such a champion and cursed him. To this boasting and blaspheming, David opposed the name of Jehovah of Hosts—the unseen hosts of Heaven, the twelve legions of angels of which our Lord spoke. That God—the God of Israel—would assuredly take up the challenge, and vindicate his servant's faith. Thus all Gentile nations would see that the God of Israel was a living reality, while Israel also would learn the too long forgotten lesson that Jehovah saveth not by sword or spear.

So confident was the Philistine that he did not trouble to draw his sword nor let down the visor of his helmet. One thrust of his heavy spear, he reckoned, was all that would be required. But in a moment more Goliath was lying helpless on the ground. It is thus that God's champions, in every age, have gone out against giant wrongs, as Luther against Tetzel, or Garrison against slavery; and it is thus that we may confidently overthrow the inbred sins that claim supremacy over our lives.

1 SAMUEL 17:55–58; 18:1–9

A Loyal Friend and a Jealous Enemy. These verses make very good reading. They present the one ray of light in a story which, from this point on, becomes more and more somber. David's bearing in the hour of victory was so modest and unaffected that Jonathan's heart leaped out to greet him as a kindred soul, while his advances awoke in David a love almost womanly in its tenderness. When we see Jonathan arraying his newfound friend in his own raiment, we are reminded of our Lord's great exchange with us. He was made sin, that we might become the righteousness of God in him, 2 Cor. 5:21.

David's harp was now, for the most part, exchanged for the sword, and he became a popular hero. It was the refrain of the women's ode of victory that opened Saul's soul to the poisonous dart of jealousy. The milk of human kindness suddenly turned sour. "Saul eyed David from that day," not with affectionate admiration, but always with desire to place a malicious construction on every act and word and look. With terrible accuracy James shows the certain progress and development of such an attitude, 1:14, 15.

1 SAMUEL 18:10-21

Protected from Dastardly Assaults. The Lord was evidently with David. Mark how the sacred chronicle keeps this fact in view, vv. 12, 14, 28. And David behaved himself "wisely," vv. 5, 14, 15, 30. How judicious it would have been for Saul to bind David to himself! Instead of this, he cherished his mad passion until it broke out in irresistible fury. Oh, beware of jealousy! It opens the soul's door to the devil. The best way of meeting it, apart from prayer, is to compel yourself to take an interest in your rival, and to put yourself loyally in his place. Overcome your mean and wicked soul, in the power of the Lord Jesus. "Put ye on the Lord Jesus Christ, and make not provision for the flesh," Rom. 13:14.

The evil spirit that possessed Saul is said to have come from God; that is, God permitted it to come. It came according to the ordered rule of the universe. "God," it has been said, "must be *something* to us; *what* he shall be depends on ourselves and on what we are to him." See Psa. 18:25, 26. The king, having failed to murder David, encouraged him in dangerous undertakings. But if David had fallen in battle, his death would still have been justly laid at Saul's door.

1 SAMUEL 18:22-30

Prospered in Spite of Plots. The affection of Michal for the young warrior suggested a way of luring David into personal conflict with the Philistines. Saul's secret hope was that he might fall a victim to their prowess. David at first took no notice of the royal proposals, because the king had already failed to keep his word; but when the courtiers explained the terms, David accepted the challenge. Saul was playing his game with great adroitness. His attendants genuinely believed that he delighted in David and desired the alliance. See his true motive in v. 25.

Once more Saul was foiled, for within the appointed time David secured double the king's requirement, and Michal became his wife. If jealous people would only ponder this story, they would discover the uselessness of setting themselves athwart God's manifest purpose in another's life. See Psa. 7:11-13, 16. Don't sulk, don't detract, don't sow suspicions. Take your father's side, you elder brother! Go into the banqueting-hall, salute your younger brother, and enter into the general joy. If you choose the generous course and affirm it, you will find the joy welling in your heart. Stand your ground in Christ against your unworthy, selfish, lower self!

1 SAMUEL 19:1-12

Noble Intercession; Implacable Hate. Not content with exchanging his dress and weapons with his friend, Jonathan pleaded David's cause at court. He had the royal ear and spoke as David's defender. As he touched upon his brother-in-law's devotion, modesty, and courage, his father's heart relented. We must not, however, take Jonathan's interposition as illustrating our Lord's, because Jesus stands for us in the presence of One whose love requires no argument. But learn to abide in "the secret place of the Most High," and hide thyself until thou hast learned what thou shouldst do, v. 2.

While Saul's troops were watching the house on the outside, the psalmist was appealing to God as his strength, and hiding in him as his strong tower. See Psa. 59:9, 17. Wait on God during the hours when your enemy is waiting for you. We must not only pray for God's help, but expect and look out for it. All true waiting must be combined with singing. Sing, persecuted soul, in sure confidence that the glorious deliverance awaiting you is near at hand! Notice that Holy Scripture never conceals and never palliates wrongdoing. It does not excuse "lies of necessity." See Lev. 19:11; Col. 3:9.

1 SAMUEL 19:13-24

Saul Checked by the Spirit of God. David hastened to apprise Samuel of the turn that events were taking, and of his suspicions that Saul was endangering his life. For greater security the prophet led him to a cluster of booths, woven probably of osiers or willows (hence the name Naioth), where a number of young men were being trained for the prophetic office. This gives us an insight into the constructive work in which Samuel was engaged during the later years of his life. They were living in an atmosphere which seemed charged with spiritual electricity. Into this sacred assembly Saul forced three successive bands of messengers to arrest David—and finally went himself.

Before he reached the place he also was overcome, and lay on the ground in a trance which lasted all that day and night. Such scenes were not uncommon in the days of the Wesleys and Jonathan Edwards. But there was a vast gulf separating Saul from David in this matter. Between David and the prophetic Spirit there was

1 SAMUEL

a real affinity. In purity and simplicity he had yielded himself to God. Saul was another man for the time, but not a new man. The Spirit was *on,* but not *in* him. He had gifts, but not grace. There was no root, and the plant withered away.

1 SAMUEL 20:1–16

Friendship's Covenant. Life becomes intolerable when suspense is long drawn out; hence David's appeal to his friend. Besides, he yearned for one more glimpse of the dear home at Bethlehem, and to drink of "the well which was by the gate." The talk between the friends was heartbreaking to both. Only those who have experienced the severance of loving communion and intercourse can fathom the depth and bitterness of the waters that began to roll between the two friends.

Jonathan is one of the noblest types of manhood presented in Scripture biography. Whether in private or public life, he shone with peerless beauty, as a star in a dark sky. David said of him that he was "lovely and pleasant." Jonathan had a clear prevision of David's coming greatness, but it gave him no pang of jealousy. He loved his friend better than himself, so much, indeed, that it was a richer ecstasy for Jonathan to see David crowned and exalted than to ascend the throne himself. Love casts out jealousy. This friendship was ideal; and we can only ask that we may realize something of its sweetness, and know the love of Christ after the same fashion.

1 SAMUEL 20:17–34

A Friend at Court. Jonathan must have been strongly tempted to ally himself with his friend, that they might face the world together; but he clung loyally to his father's fortunes, though he knew that he was courting failure and overthrow. At the same time he stood nobly forth at the banquet in defense of his friend. What a rebuke for some of us! The Prince of the kings of the earth is not ashamed to call us brethren, but alas, how often we shrink from acknowledging and confessing him when in company which refuses to own his supremacy. We are silent when his honor is flouted; we flinch before the rising storm. If we do not take sides against him, we at least do not speak up on his behalf. Such cowards are we in spite of our covenants!

Saul's jealousy broke out with volcanic vehemence. The king and father abused his son with vile epithets. He demanded David's instant execution, and ended by seeking to take Jonathan's life. Truly it may be said of him, as was afterward said of Judas, Satan had entered into him. Be watchful not to give the smallest foothold to the devil.

1 SAMUEL 20:35–42

The Sign of the Arrow. It had become clear that the arrows were against David. It was useless to endeavor to fight against the force of irresistible circumstances. We are to hold our ground till the Captain, by an indubitable sign, tells us that we may retire. But when the hour of parting came, the two fond hearts were well-nigh broken. How little the lad realized the tragedy which was taking place beneath the calm beauty of that morning dawn! The birds were singing and the flowers unfolding to the sun as usual; but to the two friends the sun was darkened and a pall lay over Nature. Yet God was leading David forth to lay the foundations of the kingdom of the Messiah, and the two were still joined in God. The Lord was between them, as the ocean is between the United States and Great Britain, not as a divider, but as a medium of communication.

Are the arrows beyond thee? Be of good cheer; there is something beyond their farthest reach. God is beyond, a kingdom is beyond, songs of overflowing ecstasy are beyond! Arise and go forth into the unknown. If thou shalt take the wings of the morning, thou canst not outstrip the love of God.

1 SAMUEL 21:1–15

Food and Weapon: a Side Step. David fled to Nob, at the north of the Mount of Olives, where Ahimelech presided over the relics of the ancient sanctuary. His suspicions were removed by an evasion on David's part, which he must have regretted to the end of his life. If we are right with God and know ourselves to be on the predestined path, we need not resort to deceit nor subterfuge; if we adopt such means, the results are likely to be disastrous to ourselves and others, our innocent fellow-sufferers.

It was the Sabbath day, for the showbread had just been removed from the table, Lev. 24:5–8. This was the perquisite of the priest, but in subordinating the ceremonial to the urgency of human need, Ahimelech acted in strict harmony with the spirit of the Mosaic legislation. This is the distinct teaching of Mark 2:25–27, and of our Lord's insistence on his right to heal on the Sabbath day. Read Psalms 34 and 56 with the closing paragraph of the chapter. David's behavior was unworthy, yet in his heart he was hiding in God. We must not judge by appearances, but with discerning judgment. There is a large measure of humanity in all God's saints.

1 SAMUEL 22:1-10

Captain of an Outlawed Band. What a striking analogy there is between the gathering of these outlawed men to David, and the attraction of publicans and sinners, in all ages, to Christ! He also is outlawed by "the prince of this world." To find Christ, we must go outside the camp, where he has set up the standard of his cross. How many of those who were in distress or in debt, or who were "bitter of soul," v. 2, alternate translation, have gathered to him and have been received! Rejected by all others, they have found an asylum in his heart of love, and out of such refugees he is founding a kingdom that can never be moved, and forming an army that will break forever the power of evil.

Notice David's care for his parents. Our love to God should make us not less but more attentive to those to whom we are bound by Nature's ties. It is probable that David's descent from Ruth, the Moabitess, may have suggested Moab as a suitable asylum; but in any case it was a wise precaution to shield the aged pair in the land of a neutral nation. In our experience, the warning of the prophet Gad has its counterpart in the gracious impressions of the Holy Spirit.

1 SAMUEL 22:11-23

The Slaughter of David's Friends. The Apostle James says that "the tongue is set on fire of hell." Surely this was the case when Saul, encamped on the height above Gibeah, scattered his biting words like firebrands. They met with a ready response in Doeg's evil heart, and the two perpetrated one of the most atrocious tragedies of history.

This black act—the blackest of Saul's life—was not to be extenuated, although it executed the malediction, uttered long before in the days of Eli, against the latter's evil house. That Saul's footmen refused to execute the king's sentence should have made him hesitate. Doeg's tale was true in its statement, but false in its implications.

There is nothing to alleviate the lurid horror of this incident, except David's welcome to Abiathar. Are not such words addressed by our Lord to all who escape to him? "Abide with me" may be understood in the light of John 15. With Christ there is safeguard. "Your life is hid with Christ in God." Fear not, trembling soul; Christ stands surety for thee! See Psalm 52, where David predicts Doeg's fate and contrasts it with his own happy lot.

1 SAMUEL 23:1-14

Success and Safety under God's Guidance. We learn here that those who are called to walk in the maze of human life need to look constantly upward for direction. "It is not in man that walketh to direct his steps." Our eyes need to be fixed constantly on the Lord. "Lean not unto thine own understanding. In all thy ways acknowledge him, and he shall direct thy paths." We have no priestly ephod to direct us. But if we roll the responsibility of our way on God and wait for him, the conviction of his plan will steal into our hearts, and this will be corroborated by the advice of experienced friends and the trend of circumstances.

The recompense of the people of Keilah for David's noble interposition on their behalf was very base, and warns us not to trust in human safeguards, which are so liable to be broken down. The only place of absolute security is in God. Blessed are they whose life is "hid with Christ in God." David knew that, and in these sad and difficult days, when he was hunted as a partridge on the mountains, he was composing some of his most helpful psalms. See the 11th, the 54th, and the 57th. In our own troubled times, how good it is that we should listen to the sweet music of the eternal world which surrounds this one and in which the harried soul may have its abiding-place.

1 SAMUEL 23:15-29

A Relentless Pursuit Foiled. Amid outward strife, God is sure to provide some stream of human love—a tender friendship, a Jonathan. This is the mission of a friend—to strengthen our hands in God, whisper words of hope, and enter into renewed covenants with us. Is not this what our best Friend does? He finds us out in the deepest woods and whispers his "Fear not." There is no hunted soul to whom Jesus will not come to pour in the oil and wine of his presence.

Let us always strengthen our friends' hands in God. We sometimes weaken their good resolutions by our timid entreaties, as Peter did when he urged the Lord to spare himself, Matt. 16:22. No, you must always help your friend to be his noblest and strongest. The angel strengthened the Redeemer in the garden. The one word for us to pass on is, "O man, greatly beloved, fear not; peace be unto thee; be strong, yea, be strong," Dan. 10:19.

The Ziphites made a direct bid for Saul's

favor, but their plot miscarried. When a man puts his life into God's hands, he has no need to fear "the arrow by day nor the terror by night." Whatever difficulties threaten him, there is ever a way of escape.

1 SAMUEL 24:1-15

Returning Good for Evil. Engedi is situated on the western shore of the Dead Sea. As Saul entered the cave, a very insidious temptation presented itself to David. Why not rid the kingdom of this cruel and oppressive monarch? Would it not confer a public benefit? Had not Samuel promised David the kingdom? Even if he himself did not strike the blow, why not let his men, who were not so squeamish, do so? But the man of God must not yield to such suggestions. He insisted on waiting the Lord's own time. He would not anticipate, by a single hour, the fulfillment of the great word on which he had been taught to rest through these weary years. The sensitiveness of his conscience was indicated in his compunction at having cut off a piece of the royal robe.

Never forget that opportunity does not make a wrong thing right. That the ship was waiting to sail to Tarshish did not make it right for Jonah to take passage. Our actions must not be determined by the opening of the door of circumstance, but by conscience, faith, obedience, and the high sense of Christian honor.

1 SAMUEL 24:16—25:1

Kindness Wakens a Better Spirit. David's noble self-restraint, followed as it was by no less noble words, awoke the best side of Saul's nature. Chords began to vibrate that had long been silent. The memory of happier days, before their communion had become clouded by jealousy and hatred, came trooping back, and Saul was himself again. Indeed, David's appeal called forth from Saul a confession of his sin; and he went so far as to ask David to spare his house in the coming days when David would assuredly be king. But as the sequel proved, this better spirit was but temporary. It was a change of mood, not of will. Let us not form the habit of trusting in our emotional life. Nothing is permanent save the will that is energized by the will of God. Psalm 142 throws a light on David's state of heart at this period.

The death of a good man is a serious loss at any time, but to Israel, governed by a cruel, wayward king, Samuel's death was cause for special lamentation. His holy life, his fearless denunciation of wrong, his self-sacrifice for the people's welfare, and especially his power in intercessory prayer made him one of the most important national assets. Let us so live that we may be missed when we go home!

1 SAMUEL 25:2-17

A Rich Man's Churlishness. This Carmel was a city in the mountains of Judah, ten miles south of Hebron. See Josh. 15:55. Though a descendant of Caleb, Nabal had none of that hero's spirit. He had great wealth, but little wit. Today the Arab tribe which guards the shepherd or caravan, or restrains itself from plundering, expects some acknowledgment. It was unfair that the rich sheep-master should take all the advantage and make no return and worse, cap injustice with a coarse jest. Nabal's shepherds were quite explicit in their testimony to the benefits they had received, vv. 7, 15, 16. His jibes and churlishness justified the general estimate entertained by those who knew him best.

For David to take the sword to avenge the insult stands out in striking contrast to him who "when he was reviled, reviled not again." Revenge for an insult where one has personally suffered has no place in Christ's teaching, and is separated by a whole heaven from the magisterial use of the sword referred to in Rom. 13:4. In later years David must have been very thankful for the interposition, through Abigail, of God's grace that arrested his hand. See Rom. 12:17.

1 SAMUEL 25:18-31

A Wise Woman's Plea. What a contrast between the sordid Nabal and his beautiful wife, as lovely in disposition as in face! What a terrible trial for such a woman to be united with a man of whom his servant did not hesitate to speak to his wife in the words of v. 17! With what admirable tact did Abigail treat the whole situation! She did not talk to her husband while he was drunk; she took the matter in hand without a moment's delay and marshaled her arguments with commendable sagacity.

It is a blessed partnership when husband and wife are so united that they are animated by a common purpose; but where this is not the case, let not the evil disposition of the one hinder the devotion and grace of the other. In the home life, as in redemption, where sin abounds grace should much more abound, that where the former reigns unto death, the latter may reign in life, Rom. 5:21. Never let the difficulties of your home lead you to abdicate your throne. Do not step down to the level of your circumstances, but life these to your own high calling in Jesus Christ. "Be not conformed . . . be transformed," Rom. 12:1, 2.

1 SAMUEL 25:32–44

The End of Selfish Indulgence. The lowly obeisance of this beautiful woman at the young soldier's feet, her frank confession of the injustice done him, her thankfulness that he had been withheld from hasty vengeance, her appreciation of his desire to fight only as a soldier of the Lord brought David back to his best self.

What a revelation is here given of the agencies by which God seeks to turn us from our evil ways! Those that enter our lives as sweet human ministries are arresting influences of the Holy Spirit, pleading with us, striving against our passion and selfishness, and calling us to a nobler, better life. Blessed Spirit, come down more often by the covert of the hill, and stay us in our mad career. Let us not press past thee to take our own wild way, and we shall review thy gracious arrest with ceaseless gratitude.

The idyll ended happily. Nabal died in an apoplectic fit, caused by his debauch and anger. Then David made proposals of marriage to the woman to whom he owed so much, and she gracefully but humbly accepted, declaring herself unworthy. Verse 35 is our Lord's answer to every soul that casts itself upon him, and every such soul becomes married to him, when the former husband is dead. See Rom. 7:4.

1 SAMUEL 26:1–12

Sparing His Enemy's Life. The Ziphites' treachery served as a foil to the intrinsic nobility of David's character. God made the wrath of man to praise him and restrained the remainder, Psa. 76:10, so that his servant escaped as a bird out of the fowler's snare. Read Psalm 54.

It was a bold act for David and Abishai to thread their way between watch-fires and sentries, and talk in whispers over the prostrate body of the sleeping monarch. As David says in one of the Psalms, "By thee I have run through a troop; and by my God have I leaped over a wall." The special share attributed here to God is the deep sleep which had fallen on the camp, v. 12. The Lord who put the resolve into David's mind cooperated in its execution. We are sometimes led by a divine impulse, and God will set his seal on our act; but we should not throw ourselves into peril unless the occasion plainly requires it. We are not at liberty to cast ourselves down from the mountain, unless it is clearly God's will. In David's case, there was sufficient reason for this adventure; first, that Saul might be warned once more and second, that the integrity of the young outlaw might be established.

1 SAMUEL 26:13–25

Facing the Truth at Last. It is good to notice David's frequent references to the living Lord. See vv. 10, 16, 23. The fact is, he was always waiting on God. See Psalm 40, which may have emanated from this period in his life. David would take no mean advantage of his adversary. He would not retaliate, nor avenge his wrongs. He refused to admit the specious argument that opportunity means permission, and license liberty. He quieted the fever of his soul, resisted the subtle temptation of the adversary, and elected to wait for the slow unfolding of the divine purpose. Calm thyself; God is working out the plan of thy life! In his own time—the best time—he will give thee thy heart's desire!

When David gave such unmistakable evidences of his loyalty, innocence, and affection, Saul was overcome with emotion and confessed that he had played the fool. It is thus that we may win men still. The man who can watch with God shows that he is possessed of spiritual strength which others must acknowledge. Fret not thyself because of evildoers; trust in the Lord; delight in the Lord; roll the way of thy life on the Lord, and wait patiently for him.

1 SAMUEL 27:1–12

Substituting Policy for Trust. David had every assurance that he would be king. From Samuel, Jonathan, and Saul he had heard predictions of his coming exaltation; yet suddenly he seems to have had a fainting spell and to have concluded that he would after all perish by the hand of Saul. It was thus with Elijah under the juniper bush, when he asked God to take away his life; and thus with the Baptist, when from prison he sent to ask whether Jesus was the Christ. Let us not sink into despair when the shadow of discouragement falls across our path. Let us believe that God's word shall stand though the heavens fall. Let us especially beware of taking our own measures of self-defense. The caves of Adullam are safer for the child of God than the land of the Philistines. David was driven to ruthless cruelty; he went about under the constant fear of discovery and lived a perpetual lie. It was a life of deceit that was wholly unworthy of a servant of the Most High, and must have had a fatal effect on David's followers. And in the end Ziklag was destroyed, and the exile's heart was well-nigh broken. See 30:1–4. "The way of the transgressor is hard!" No psalms can be traced to this period.

1 SAMUEL

1 SAMUEL 28:1-14

Resorting to a Familiar Spirit. This chapter records the climax to which Saul's sins led, and which sealed his fate. See 1 Chron. 10:13, 14. He went back to that which he had put away and sought counsel of a familiar spirit, 2 Peter 2:20-22.

The soul cannot live apart from the unseen world. It is its native element. Divorce it from God, and it will fill the empty space with demons. When the king could get no answer to his questions by the usual means, he sent his servants, in desperation, to seek for a medium. Had he been right with God, there would have been no need for this. It is the decay of the old religious spirit that nowadays gives occasion for the rise of crystal-gazing, palmistry, and seances. What a tragedy was presented that night in the witch's hut, and how terrible must have been Saul's long tramp to and fro, between his own encampment and Endor, which lay in the rear of the Philistine host! It is an evil thing and a bitter to forsake the fountain of living waters and hew out "broken cisterns, that can hold no water," Jer. 2:13, 19.

1 SAMUEL 28:15-25

Listening to His Own Doom. That there should be an apparition of Samuel occasions no difficulty, for as Moses and Elijah were permitted to speak with our Lord of the "decease" to be accomplished at Jerusalem, so God may have specially permitted the prophet to speak with Saul. We may believe that these sentences passed between them without any aid on the part of the medium. From the lips of the prophet came no words of comfort or hope. Nothing could avert the descending avalanche of destruction. As Saul had sown, so must he reap; as he had fallen, so must he lie.

While the king sat on that divan, what memories must have passed through his mind: The first happy days of his reign, Jabesh-gilead, the loyalty of his people. Then he saw how, step by step, that cursed jealousy of David had dragged him down into the turbid current that was now bearing him to a suicide's end. It is one of the most pitiful spectacles in history. But let *us* be warned; let us watch and pray; let us guard against the first tiny rift within the mortar of life!

1 SAMUEL 29:1-11

Under Just Suspicion. David was in a strait! To what a plight had eighteen months of deceit brought him! He had no alternative other than to follow King Achish to battle, but it must have been with a sinking heart. It looked as if he would be forced to fight Saul, the Lord's anointed, and Jonathan, his friend, and the people whom he was one day to rule. Probably he turned in an agony of prayer to God, that he might be extricated from the net which his sins had woven. Read Deut. 30:4.

An unexpected door opened in the valley of Achor. The Philistine lords took offense at David's position in the rear with the king, and insisted on his returning with his men to Ziklag. In the end Achish had to yield, though with great reluctance. He little realized the profound sense of relief with which David heard the royal order. As David stole off in the gray dawn with his men on the homeward journey, he must have broken into the words of Psalm 124:7.

1 SAMUEL 30:1-15

A Blow That Led Back to God. As David was leaving the battlefield, a number of men of Manasseh joined with him, 1 Chron. 12:20, so his following was greatly increased. It was as if God had anticipated his coming trial and prepared him to encounter it. But what a mercy it was that he had been sent back, that no garrison had been left to guard the women, which might have irritated the invaders, and that nobody had been killed, v. 2!

In the first outburst of grief and horror, only divine and gracious interposition could have saved David's life. But this was the hour of his return to God. With the charred embers at his feet and anxiety gnawing at his heart, with the threat of violence in his ears and bitter compunction of conscience, "he encouraged himself in the Lord his God." From that hour he was his old, strong, glad, noble self. After months of neglect, he bade Abiathar bring him the ephod, and he inquired the will of God. Then with marvelous vigor he went in pursuit and recovered all. He had been brought out of a horrible pit, and again his feet were on the rock, Psa. 40:2. His "goings" could now be established.

1 SAMUEL 30:16-31

Sharing the Spoil. He that lays hold on God's strength will be courteous in his behavior to the weak and weary, and will not quail before the clamor of men of Belial. Thus we are not surprised to learn that David kindly inquired of the 200 as to their welfare, v. 21, and insisted that they should share equally with those who went to battle. This was a beautiful instance of sanctified common sense, and the reasonableness of the decision appealed to his followers. The gains and losses of the whole band must be shared equally by those at the front and in the rear. This is God's rule! He that receives the prophet shall have the prophet's reward. Girls who stay at home to care for aged mothers, instead of becoming missionaries; young men who maintain orphaned brothers and sisters; invalids confined to their rooms—let such take heart. They shall share in the victory of their Lord. David's thankful joy yielded practical fruit in his generous gifts to those who had showed him kindness in his adversity. Gratitude is the trait of a noble nature. Let us share our possessions with others less favored and increase our own enjoyment, 2 Cor. 8:14, 15.

1 SAMUEL 31:1–13

One Brave Deed on a Dark Day. This defeat meant something more than a temporary reverse. It was symptomatic of national decay. Saul's reign had brought moral degeneracy to his people. Their moral fibre was impaired, their life-blood impoverished. As king and people were weighed in the divine balances (which are ever testing us), they were found wanting. Men seldom sin alone! Sin becomes an epidemic!

Much had happened since Saul's designation as king. Alas, that so bright a dawn should have clouded in such a sunset! Like a noble tree, Saul fell before the storm. He fell because he had never prayed, as David did, to be cleansed from secret faults and to be held back from presumptuous sins. The only gleam of light on that terrible day was the chivalrous deed of Jabesh-gilead. Her sons could never forget Saul's valorous exploit on their behalf. After the manner of Joseph and Nicodemus at the death of our Lord, they identified themselves with what seemed a lost cause. Would that every reader of these lines was equally grateful and generous in confessing him who delivered us from a yet greater death!

THE SECOND BOOK OF SAMUEL

THE REIGN OF DAVID

I. DAVID'S EARLY REIGN OVER JUDAH   *1—4*
  A. David's lament over the death of Saul and Jonathan   *1*
  B. The contest between David and Ish-bosheth   *2:1—3:5*
  C. Abner, estranged from Ish-bosheth, joins David   *3:6–21*
  D. The murder of Abner by Joab   *3:22–39*
  E. The overthrow of the house of Saul   *4*

II. DAVID'S LATER REIGN OVER ALL ISRAEL   *5—20*
  A. David proclaimed king by all the tribes   *5*
  B. David's care for the Ark   *6, 7*
  C. David's conquests   *8*
  D. David's kindness to the remnant of the house of Saul   *9*
  E. The war with Ammon and the siege of Rabbah   *10—12*
  F. Absalom's crime, banishment, and return   *13, 14*
  G. Absalom's rebellion and death   *15—18*
  H. David's return and the revolt of Sheba   *19, 20*

III. APPENDIX: UNDATED INCIDENTS, REGISTERS, AND PSALMS   *21—24*
  A. The story of Rizpah; deeds of the Philistine wars   *21*
  B. The words of David   *22:1—23:7*
  C. Register of the mighty men   *23:8–39*
  D. The numbering of the people; the pestilence   *24*

INTRODUCTION

The Second Book of Samuel is devoted entirely to the reign of David. His coronation, first by Judah and then by all of the tribes, his wars and conquests, his care for the religious life of the people, his sins, and the calamities he suffered are impartially set forth in vivid and convincing narrative.

"A very notable thing in the books of Samuel," says James Robertson, "is the prominence given to music and song. There is in these books an unusual number of poetical pieces ascribed to this period, and all the indications put together give ample justification for the fame of David as the sweet singer of Israel, and for the ascription to him of the origin of that volume of sacred song which never ceased in Israel, and has become embodied in the Psalms."

COMMENTARY

2 SAMUEL 1:1-16

"The Lord's Anointed." The scene changes from Gilboa to Ziklag, whither the tidings were carried by an Amalekite. It is remarkable to notice how David received them. Though he had spent years in the rough life of a plunderer, surrounded by coarse and hardened men, he had not lost the delicacy and refinement of his earlier days. To men like Nabal, he seemed an outlaw; but those who were admitted to the inner circle of David's friendship knew that there was a whole heaven of difference between him and the men who followed him. Let us see to it that by fellowship with God, we keep our nature uncontaminated by the world, its fine edge not blunted, its bloom not brushed off.

It was genuine grief that made David rend his clothes, and a genuine emotion of horror that led to the execution of this self-confessed regicide. Then from the depths of a guileless heart there poured forth the "Song of the Bow," one of the noblest elegies in any tongue. Let us speak tenderly of the dead. Let God in his infinite pity judge them, while we scatter rose leaves on their graves.

2 SAMUEL 1:17-27

"The Song of the Bow." This noble poem is unrivaled. It is a perfect model of a funeral dirge. It is in poetry what Handel's *Dead March in Saul* is in music. The psalmist is borne along both by art and affection. He could not have composed this song unless he had been a consummate artist, and unless he had drunk deep of that divine love which believes, bears, hopes, and endures all things and never fails.

He forgets all that he has suffered. His love refuses to consider anything but what has been pleasant and lovely in his liege lord. And for Jonathan there is a special stanza. The Philistines had felt David's might, but his friend had tasted his sweetness, terrible as a whirlwind in flight, yet winsome as a woman! But if human love can impute only good to those who are the objects of its affection, what will not God's love say of us, feel toward us, and impute to us! Here is a clue to the exceeding riches of the love with which he loved us, even when we were dead in sins!

2 SAMUEL 2:1-11

A Divided People. David's habit of inquiring of the Lord was not discontinued when he ascended the throne. He allowed his steps still to be ordered by the Lord, who delighted in his servant's way. From how many blunders might we be saved if we leaned less on our own understanding and trusted him with all our hearts! Those who believe like this need not make haste.

This anointing in Hebron—the second in David's life—is parallel with the unction of the

Holy One received by our Lord on his ascension. "Having received of the Father the promise of the Holy Spirit," said Peter on the day of Pentecost, "he hath shed forth this." The house of Saul was still determined to rule. Its seat was across the Jordan. Is it not a type of the fashion of this world, which is destined to pass away? Between those who refuse and those who accept the cross, with its separating death, there can be no peace. The war will be long and painful, but the result must end in the victory of the house of David, of which our Lord is both root and offspring, Rev. 22:16.

2 SAMUEL 2:12-23

Swordplay to the Death. For seven and a half years David reigned over the house of Judah. He was in the prime of life, thirty years of age, and seems to have given himself to the consolidation of his kingdom and the quiet sanctities of the home. He maintained throughout those years that spirit of quiet expectancy of which his psalms so often speak. In this, he reminds us of our Lord, who is depicted as sitting at his Father's side till his foes become his footstool.

From Hebron, the city of fellowship, bands of mighty men went forth to fight with Ish-bosheth, just as the warriors of the cross have, in every age, gone forth to engage in deadly conflict with unbelief and sin. Asahel's death reminds us of Stephen's martyrdom. But the end is not yet! The Church's warfare is not against flesh and blood, but against the wicked spirits that rule the darkness of the world. Her weapons, therefore, are not carnal but spiritual, and particularly that of "all prayer," Eph. 6:10-20.

2 SAMUEL 2:24-32

"Shall the Sword Devour for Ever?" The longer the sword devours, the more bitter the hatred engendered. Early that morning, each of twenty-four young men had buried his sword in his antagonist's heart; and as the hours passed, the flame of mutual hate had become hotter. There was no telling to what it might lead. Hatred is like a prairie fire in its rapid spread and remorseless destruction.

When night fell Abner, alarmed by the prospects of slaughter, asked Joab to stay the pursuit. Otherwise, Joab would have fought through the night. However, he drew off his men, and Abner, still dreading his wrath, by a forced march crossed the Jordan that night.

Abner's reference to the insatiate lust of the sword for human life reminds us, by force of contrast, of the hunger of Christ to seek and to save that which is lost. His appetite to save is a consuming passion. It is his meat and drink to win souls to the eternal life that he is commissioned to impart.

2 SAMUEL 3:1-11

A Split in the Enemy's Ranks. Abner's career reveals the principles on which ambitious men build their lives. He was, according to David's estimate, a great man and a prince, but his soul was eager for his own advancement. "He made himself strong for the house of Saul," v. 6. He knew that David was God's appointed king and that through him the divine purpose would move, vv. 10, 18; but yet, because it seemed likely to insure his own advancement, he set Ish-bosheth on the throne. It was a deliberate attempt to thwart God's will, and it failed miserably. "Woe to him that striveth with his Maker!"

Ish-bosheth was a poor weak soul, a mere puppet king who was set on the throne because he was likely to be pliant in the hands of his great general. Yet even he was aroused to protest when Abner threatened to desert him. And so the alliance between ambition and weakness was broken, and the way was made for David to come to the throne of all Israel. In the meantime he ruled at Hebron, waiting, as our Lord waits at the Father's right hand till his enemies should be made his footstool, Acts 2:34, 35.

2 SAMUEL 3:12-21

Abner Wins David's Favor. We cannot defend David's request for Michal to be restored to him. It inflicted bitter pain on an apparently happy pair, and Michal's revenge stung him to the quick, 2 Sam. 6:20. But he may have felt it right to insist on his legal status as son-in-law to the late king. It was, however, a needless precaution, as they who wait on God can dispense with expedients which are esteemed by worldly prudence.

With this exception David maintained a passive policy. The overtures for the transference of the kingdom were made by Abner. It was he who communicated with Israel and Benjamin, and then with David. Thus great events may move around us while we live in the center of God's will in perfect peace. We must be willing to respond to the stirring bugle call to action, but we must also have our waiting-times, when the soul is learning to possess itself in patience. The long summer days are needed to prepare for the autumn ingatherings; and the hours

2 SAMUEL

spent in Horeb and Carmel prepare for the stirring part that God's servants must play in the history of their time.

2 SAMUEL 3:22-30

A Treacherous Revenge. There is no doubt that Abner was guilty of disloyalty and treachery, but this did not excuse Joab's dastardly act. He could not claim the right to act as *goel*—blood avenger—for his dead brother, because Asahel had died a soldier's death in open war. Joab was probably actuated by jealousy of the military talents, the vast influence, and the widespread popularity of the rival general whom he murdered in cold blood, just outside the city of refuge. Evidently he was a fierce, cruel, unscrupulous man, who hurt David more than he helped him, v. 39. But Joab also was destined to suffer similar punishment in later years, 1 Kings 2:28-34.

This world is governed according to a plan. We need not try to climb into the judgment-seat. God is there already. His rewards and punishments befall with greater certainty than we always believe. Whether their schemes are hidden amid the intricacies of state, or open to all eyes, let us be sure that evil men reap as they have sown, and suffer evils similar to those which they endeavor to inflict upon others. We all get our deserts.

2 SAMUEL 3:31-39

David's Lament over Abner. It was a noble spectacle when David followed the bier of Abner and wept at his grave. He forgot that this man had been his persistent foe, and remembered only his great personal qualities. The chaplet of elegiacs that he wove for Abner's grave was only second to that which he prepared for Saul's. It is not strange that all the people took notice of it and that it pleased them. We should be particularly careful to disavow all complicity in the evil doings of those with whom we happen to be associated, and to stand clear of the wreckage that floats around us. The honor of God's cause must be dearer to us than life.

The cultivation of a noble and generous spirit, like that which David manifested toward Saul and Abner, is an aim to which we should set ourselves with patient care. It is the outgrowth of years of self-discipline, of prayer, of fellowship with God. Life is too short to allow it to be consumed by evil and vindictive thoughts. Hand over to God all thoughts of retaliation! Certainly you must withstand the wrongdoer when the weak and defenseless are in jeopardy; but for yourself, love and conquer!

2 SAMUEL 4:1-12

Another Treacherous Deed and Its Penalty. Abner's death rendered hopeless the cause of Ish-bosheth. Two captains incurred lasting shame and deserved punishment by their dastardly act of murder. Their act was the more despicable because of their prince's trust.

How little do coarse natures understand the workings of a really religious nature! These men knew that if they were in David's place, nothing would please them better than the removal of the last obstacle to the throne. They reasoned that David would feel thus and reward them munificently. But to their astonishment, he turned on them with honest indignation. We must dare to act apart from self-interest, as in the light and fire of the Eternal Throne.

Notice David's devout spirit. He ascribed his redemption to God's tender mercy, v. 9. His first thought was always of God's love and grace and help. Ah, Christian soul, you too will one day attain the sunny heights, standing on which you also will be able to say, "He hath redeemed my soul from all adversity." The night may be long, but the day-spring is at hand.

2 SAMUEL 5:1-12

David King in Jerusalem. David was anointed thrice: by Samuel in his home, by the men of Judah, and here. So our Lord has been crowned in the Father's purpose and by his Church. There awaits another day, when he will be recognized as King by the entire universe, Rev. 11:15. The reasons for David's coronation apply equally to our Lord: (1) kinship; (2) power to lead; (3) God's eternal purpose.

Because of its impregnable position, it was wise policy to secure Jerusalem as the site of the capital. Here was the beginning of new prosperity for Israel, and for Jerusalem as well, which was now to become "the joy of the whole earth." See 1 Chron. 12:23. David's influence increased by leaps and bounds, v. 10. There broke on his mind a perception of the divine purpose, v. 12. Often we are unable to see this in the earlier stages of our life. We see no meaning, no purpose. But as year is added to year, God's great scheme begins to unfold. Only be sure that any position or opportunity is intended, not for us alone, but for his people's sake.

2 SAMUEL 5:13-25

Jehovah's Victories over the Philistines. David's prosperity led to luxurious living and sensual indulgence, out of which sprang the troubles of his later life, v. 13.

The Philistines watched the acquisition of Jerusalem with profound anxiety. It was against their policy for David to be the head of a united nation. It would seem that their first onset drove him back to the cave of Adullam, v. 17. This was a startling reversal of fortune, but it was salutary that, now as ever, David should learn how dependent he was on God, and that God, who had given him so much, might at any time withdraw his gifts. Loneliness, failure, solitude are necessary for us all! Twice David sought direction as to the ordering of the fight. On the first occasion, the command was, "Go up." On the second, it was, "Thou shalt not go up." In the first battle the Philistine position was carried by assault; in the second it was turned by ambush. The movement in the trees suggests the footfalls of angel squadrons. Oh, for the quick ear to detect the goings-forth of God's help, and grace to bestir ourselves to follow!

2 SAMUEL 6:1-11

The Return of the Ark Interrupted. We have heard nothing of the Ark since it left the land of the Philistines, 1 Sam. 7:1, 2. The spiritual life of the nation was low, else this holy symbol of God's presence would not have been thus neglected. David wished to make the new capital the religious as well as the political center of his kingdom. It was necessary, therefore, that the Ark be removed thither.

The sacredness of the Ark lay in its association with Jehovah Sabaoth, "the Lord of Hosts." It was his seat or throne. "He dwelt between the cherubim." The clear order was that it should be borne on the shoulders of the Levites, and David had no right to substitute a new cart, after the manner of the Philistines, Num. 7:9; 1 Chron. 15:12-15. The death of Uzzah and the blessing on the house of Obed-edom illustrate the severity and the goodness of God. Not one jot or tittle of the Law can fail; therefore the least violation must bring suffering on the part of those who offend, while reverence, obedience, and faith secure an immediate response of the divine favor and love. God can and will take care of his own. We need not fear for the safety of his Church.

2 SAMUEL 6:12-23

The Ark Tabernacled in the City of David. Josephus tells us that from the moment the Ark rested beneath Obed-edom's roof, a tide of golden prosperity set in, and he passed from poverty to wealth. But 1 Chronicles 26:4, 5 sheds a new light on the subject, for there we learn that the whole family became attached to the service of the Lord's house, and even the grandchildren became mighty. If only we would open our homes to God's Ark—that is, if we maintained the observances of religion for our children and dependents—for us also there would be similar blessing. One likes to imagine the reverence and joy with which those boys and girls lay down to sleep at night, feeling that the symbol of God's presence was in the house.

This time the prescribed ritual was minutely observed. The warning given by Uzzah's death had aroused the entire nation to a realization of their indifference and neglect. The stroke had been terrible, but the effect was eminently salutary. It seemed as if the floodgates of David's joy had been thrown wide open, and he could not contain his ecstasy. Then from an overflowing heart, he turned to bless his people. The one event that marred the day was poor Michal's bitter speech. There is no perfect joy in this world; every rose has its thorn.

2 SAMUEL 7:1-17

The Glorious Future of David's House. Always do better for the cause of God than for yourself. You have no right to dwell in cedar, while God's Ark is under curtains. Also, beware of giving directions or advice, unless you have first consulted God. You may be as good as Nathan, but if you speak apart from the divine Spirit, you will probably be compelled, on the following morning, to eat your words.

David's intention was good, but neither was he the man nor was that the time for temple-building. See 1 Chron. 22:8. The sword could not yet be exchanged for the trowel, but in the meantime the will was accepted in lieu of the act. It was then God's turn to pour out a perfect avalanche of blessing, which must have made David forget those weary years of waiting and wandering. Do not be anxious about the future. Use your life and all its resources for God, and he will care for you. No tongue can exaggerate the goodness and mercy which God lays up for them that trust in him before the sons of men. And it is because he loves that he does not hesitate to chasten.

2 SAMUEL 7:18-29

David's Humble and Grateful Prayer. The promise made through Nathan was threefold: (1) that David's house should reign forever; (2) that his seed should build the Temple; (3) that the kingdom of Israel should be made sure. These glowing words were fulfilled in shadow in the literal story of Judah, but in substance in him whom David foresaw, Acts 2:30. There is only One whose reign is permanent, whose kingdom is without end, and who can bring rest to the hearts of men. See Zech. 6:12.

Take time to *sit* before God. It is good to kneel or stand; but have moments of reverie, when you shall expose the sensitive plate of your soul to receive his imprint. It is good for us all to take up God's holy words of promise and turn them back on himself, saying, "Do as thou hast said." Learn to put your finger on this or the other promise, turning each check into the cash of its daily use for daily thanksgiving. There is no exercise in which mortal man can engage more strengthening, more prolific of good, more glorifying to God.

2 SAMUEL 8:1-18

Victorious on Every Side. Twice in this chapter we are told that the Lord gave victory to David "whithersoever he went," vv. 6, 14. Indeed, he was more than a conqueror, for he obtained not only victory but the spoils of his foes, of which he afterward made large donations to the house of God. We are reminded of those great words: "Now thanks be unto God, which always leadeth us to triumph in Christ"; and, "They also shall overcome that are with him [the Lamb], called and chosen and faithful," 2 Cor. 2:14; Rev. 17:14, alternate translation.

Never in this world shall we be able to lay down our weapons. Often temptations that we thought had passed out of our lives will revive in their old vigor and present themselves with even greater subtlety and force. Resolutions and vows will fail us. We shall be constantly kept in mind of our weakness and dependence. The only victory which is permanent is our faith, which receives from him what we cannot achieve for ourselves. It is a very humbling experience, but it is our safeguard against presumptuous pride.

2 SAMUEL 9:1-13

"Kindness for Jonathan's Sake." This poor cripple at Lodebar never supposed that David would show him favor. Did he not belong to the rejected house of Saul? What could he expect from one whom his grandfather had hunted like a partridge on the mountains? Besides, his lameness made him unfit for court life. We, like him, are the children of an apostate race; we have neither beauty nor worth to commend us. We may class together those two sentences: "What is thy servant, that thou shouldest look upon such a dead dog as I am?" and, "Depart from me, for I am a sinful man, O Lord," v. 8 and Luke 5:8.

But Mephibosheth had been included in a covenant. He might be unaware of it, but David could not forget, 1 Sam. 20:14-16. For the sake of the beloved Jonathan, David treated his son as a blood relation. Nothing in the course of events could alter the sacred word that David had sworn to his departed friend. Our own case is similar. We were chosen in Christ before the world began, predestined to be sons, included in the covenant between the Father and our Surety. Let us join with Paul in Ephesians 1:3.

2 SAMUEL 10:1-19

The Penalty of Rejecting Kindness. A Jewish tradition tells us that Nahash, Hanun's father, had shown kindness to David by sheltering one of his brothers when the king of Moab treacherously massacred the rest of the family. Civility is the daughter of piety. The son had inherited his father's throne, but not his spirit. He was misled by foolish advisers to offer a gross insult, not only to the ambassadors, but to the king and nation whom they represented.

Let us, however, contrast our Lord's dealings with those who ill-treated him in the person of his disciples. When they had been refused by a certain village of the Samaritans, they appealed for fire from Heaven; but Jesus reminded them that the dispensation in which Elijah had lived was past. The disciples were the children of a new age, and the only fire with which they could deal was that of love, Luke 9:51-56. Yes, and afterward the baptism of the Holy Spirit was given to Samaria, perhaps to those very villages, Acts 8. It used to be said that the best way to secure the tenderest kindness of the great and saintly Archbishop Leighton was to show him a discourtesy. He had not followed his great Master in vain.

2 SAMUEL 11:1-13

Giving Rein to Self-indulgence. This was not an isolated sin. For some time, backsliding had been eating out David's heart. The cankerworm takes its toll before the noble tree crashes to the ground. Joab and his brave soldiers were in the thick of a great conflict. Rabbah was being besieged and had not fallen. It was a time when kings went out to battle, but David tarried at home. It was a fatal lethargy. If the king had been in his place, this sin would never have besmirched his character.

A look, as in Eve's case, opened the door to the devil. "Turn away mine eyes from beholding vanity." However great our attainments and however high our standing, we are all liable to attack and failure; but when we abide in Christ, no weapon that hell can forge can hurt us. When we have sinned, our only safety is in instant confession. This David delayed for a year and till forced to it. He was more eager to evade the consequences than to deal with his transgression. Sober David was far worse, here, than drunken Uriah. The singular self-restraint of the soldier threw the sin of the king into terrible and disgraceful prominence.

2 SAMUEL 11:14-27

Adding Bloodguiltiness to Adultery. Joab must have smiled grimly to himself when he received his master's letter. "This king of ours can sing psalms with the best, but I have to do his dirty work. He wants to rid himself of Uriah—I wonder why? Well, I'll help him to it. At any rate, he will not be able to talk to me about Abner!" See 3:27. It is an awful thing when the servants of God give the enemy such occasion to blaspheme.

Uriah was set in the battleline and left to die. The king was duly notified and, on hearing the news, must have given a sigh of relief. The child could be born under cover of lawful wedlock. There was, however, a fatal flaw in the whole arrangement: "The thing that David had done displeased the Lord." David and the world would hear of it again. But, oh, the bitter sorrow, that he who had spoken of walking in his house with a perfect heart, who had so great a faculty for divine fellowship should have fallen into this double sin! Psalmist, king, lover of God—all trampled in the mud by one passionate act of self-indulgence!

2 SAMUEL 12:1-14

"Thou Art the Man." A year followed on his sin, but David gave no sign. He describes his condition during that awful time in Psalm 32:3, 4. Conscience scourged him incessantly, but he did not return to God until Nathan had been sent to fetch him. The Good Shepherd went after that which was lost until he found it. "He restoreth my soul!" But soul-agony is not enough, keen though it be; there must be confession.

Nathan's parable was the mirror in which the true enormity of the king's sin was held up to his face. He was judged, and he judged himself. By the manifestation of the truth, Nathan commended himself to the king's conscience, as in the sight of God. And finally came the final thrust—"Thou art the man." Words of confession were immediate and deeply sincere. There was no thought of the human wrongs he had done. All were included in the great sin against God. "Against thee, thee only, have I sinned." And the confession was met, as it always is, by an instant assurance of pardon—"The Lord also hath put away thy sin."

2 SAMUEL 12:15-31

Accepting the Lord's Judgment. When Nathan had gone, David beat out his brief confession into Psalm 51. He knew that he was clean, because purged with hyssop, Exod. 12:22; that he was whiter than snow, because the hand of the Redeemer had touched him, and the joy of God's salvation had been restored. And now he bowed himself before the train of evil consequences that must ensue. Sin may be forgiven, but the Father must needs chasten his child.

The little babe died. It cuts us to the quick when innocent children suffer for our wrongdoing. Two years after, David's sin was repeated by one of his sons, while another sought to dispossess his father of the throne. In Amnon's offense David beheld the features of his own passion, and in Absalom's revenge his own bloodguiltiness. Psalms 41 and 55 are supposed to record his sufferings during those dreary years, when it seemed as if the sunshine had passed forever from his life. The wonder is that he treated Rabbah so harshly; but it may be, as some think, that its fate was decided during the months which preceded his confession, when the misery of his soul made him petulant and exacting.

2 SAMUEL 13:1-14

Sin in David's Household. The law of Moses clearly forbade the union which Amnon sought, Lev. 18:11. It was an infamous passion, and the suggestion of Jonadab, if it was any reflection of his father's character, would show why the Lord had said of Shammah, "Neither hath the Lord chosen this," 1 Sam. 16:9. Passion is deaf to the remonstrances and pleadings of its victim, and strangles pity and honor. Let us walk in the Spirit, that he may save us from ourselves; for there is no knowing to what lengths we may go if not kept by the grace of God.

It seems difficult to believe that this was the home life of the man that wrote the Psalms. It had been better to remain in the valley of the wild goat than amid the luxury of Jerusalem, which made so great an inroad upon the peace and purity of his home. We prosper better amid the bleak climate of the mountains than in the enervating atmosphere of the plains.

Thus David's sin began to bear the entail of misery to his own household. None of us can limit the far-reaching harvests of the seeds that we drop upon the flowing stream.

2 SAMUEL 13:15-27

Absalom Executes Judgment. When men yield to irregular passion, they go from one extreme to the other—from wicked love to wicked hate. If women would but realize this, how often it would save them from lives of misery. To yield to a man's impulse is not to secure his loyalty, but to alienate and perhaps destroy it.

Absalom was Tamar's own brother and since her father had failed her, was therefore her natural protector. Recommending her to hold her peace, Absalom quietly awaited a suitable opportunity for wreaking vengeance; but she, poor girl, had to face a blighted life. The crime of her betrayal would hang over it as a dark cloud which even the vengeance that Absalom was about to take could never remove. How many myriads of girls have had to face the same sad lot!

It was David's duty, as her father, to punish the evildoer. The Law enjoined the penalty of death for such an offense, Lev. 18:9, 29. But David's hands were not clean. He had himself incurred the same penalty, and could not condemn in another what he had condoned in himself. Besides this, the Septuagint adds, "he loved Amnon, because he was his firstborn." How tortuous are the ways of sin!

2 SAMUEL 13:28-39

Absalom Flees While David Mourns. For two years Absalom nursed his anger. Time did not alter his resolve, though it lulled to sleep any suspicion that might have been excited if he had taken immediate steps to get Amnon into his power. Then came the festival of a sheep-shearing, the enticement of Amnon from the shelter of the palace and his murder, the rumor that reached David, and the flight of the murderer to his mother's father, Talmai, the king of Geshur. Of course, if David had insisted upon his surrender, Absalom would have had to be handed over for punishment; but again, the memory of his own sin withheld David's hand. Had he not treacherously plotted Uriah's death? How could he punish the avenger of a sister's wrong? His own sin had come home to roost.

The punishment of sin is much more swift and certain than many seem to suppose, not only in the next life, but also in this. We need not climb the throne to exercise vengeance. That is God's part, and it is carried out by the inevitable working of law. What a man sows, he is invariably called to reap.

2 SAMUEL 14:1-17

Joab's Plea for the Fugitive. Joab had ends of his own to serve in securing the return of Absalom. Were the two sworn together to hatch a great plot? Or was Absalom shrewdly using Joab to advance his own selfish interests? David hesitated. If he recalled Absalom without punishment, the foundations of law and order would be shaken throughout the kingdom. Joab saw that in some way he must satisfy this natural conflict in the royal mind; and it was for this purpose that he summoned from Tekoa, a village twelve miles south of Jerusalem, this woman of unusual intelligence. By an apt parable she showed that on occasions even murder might be condoned.

In her discourse she dropped the golden sentence that even God devises means that his banished be not expelled. Yes, God has devised means, but how much they cost! In David's case there was no attempt to meet the demands of a broken Law, but God's means include this. In the person of the Son of his love, he has satisfied the demands of law and honored them by Jesus' obedience unto the death of the cross! He is just and the Justifier! Righteousness and peace kissed each other at the cross of Jesus. See Psa. 85:10.

2 SAMUEL 14:18-33

Restored Though Unrepentant. Joab knew perfectly that David was well-pleased to recall Absalom in response, as it appeared, to the request of the most powerful of his subjects. But Joab was equally satisfied that Absalom was now in a position to execute plans for personal advancement. His refusal to meet Absalom was perhaps only a blind. David, at least, was bitterly to rue his weakness in restoring his wayward son without the latter's penitence.

Absalom's behavior was base in the extreme. Beauty of body and deformity of soul often coexist in the same individual. A flower-covered grave may hide gross corruption. See in his case an illustration of what would happen if sin could be forgiven apart from repentance and regeneration. Justification without sanctification would turn Heaven into hell. There must be deep soul-work if we are to come forth into the light of the love of God. The barley field, set on fire to bring about this meeting between Absalom and Joab, suggests how often God has to fire our choice possessions, that as the flame flares up to Heaven we may be induced to seek the presence of him whom we have deeply wronged.

2 SAMUEL 15:1-12

The Plot of the Ambitious Son. David's government had become lax. Many causes were awaiting trial. Cases demanding his royal decision had accumulated. Suitors could get nothing done. Discontent was rife. The king had forfeited the former love and respect of his people. Perhaps the story of his sin had leaked out. It is thought, also, that at this time he was smitten by disease and that Psalms 41 and 55 record the sufferings of those withered years. Meanwhile, Absalom was undermining the throne and dividing the heart of the people.

How soon the heart may become alienated from its rightful king! The Absaloms ingratiate themselves, and wean away our loyalty and love from Jesus. Is there a favorite that fawns on you and entices you to a lower level than you occupied in earlier, happier days? If so, your King may be driven from the citadel of your soul, and you may be left to mourn over the tragedy caused by the transference of your heart's affections. Be warned ere it be too late. Deal sternly with Absalom!

2 SAMUEL 15:13-23

The Loyal Stranger. David was conscious of ill desert; hence his resolve to flee. How different his bearing now from that great hour when Goliath fell before him! Ah, conscience doth make cowards of us all! And yet there was a beautiful spirit of resignation welling up amid the salt waves of his bitter sorrow. When we are called to pass through dark hours, we cannot do better than repeat the words of this royal penitent: "Behold, here am I; let him [God] do to me as seemeth good to him," v. 26. What thoughtfulness of Ittai! What pathos in the king's words to Zadok! What humility as he climbed Olivet! What trust still in God to turn the counsel of Ahithophel into foolishness! It is an impressive picture of the resignation of a broken and a contrite heart.

They were noble words that Ittai uttered! His name associates him with David's residence in Gath, among the Philistines. He was a stranger and an exile in Israel, but the king's friendship had made a home for him. In these days of our Lord's humiliation, let us address him in the chivalrous and noble words of v. 21. See John 12:26; 1 Thess. 5:10.

2 SAMUEL 15:24-37

The Friends of the Fleeing King. Outside the story of our Lord, the Bible records nothing more admirable than David's behavior as he passed through this thicket of thorns. He never appeared to better advantage than during those awful days. Tribulation had wrought patience, and patience experience, and experience hope, and his hope was destined not to be ashamed. The psalms in which he embalms these experiences are the heritage of the saints. Among them are 3, 4, 26, 27, 28, and probably 62. The procession reminds us of another—only that was still more sorrowful—led by his Son and Lord, Matt. 26.

Adversity sifts out the false from the true, the spurious from the genuine. The trusted counselor turns traitor, v. 31; but against this must be set the loyalty of Zadok and Abiathar, and the devotion of Hushai. There are indications that Bathsheba was Ahithophel's granddaughter. This would explain why Absalom sent for him, why he was so bitter, and why he committed suicide. The cross has been the touchstone of trial to myriads! Have you been true to your exiled King? Let us go forth to him without the camp, bearing his reproach, Heb. 13:13.

2 SAMUEL 16:1-12

A Day That Revealed Character. There may have been some truth in Ziba's statement, but we should balance it with 2 Sam. 19:24. Shimei vented the spleen of the house of Saul. He probably referred to the recent execution of the sons of Rizpah, and perhaps suggested that David had been guilty of all the disaster that had befallen Saul's house from the day of Gilboa. When men curse us, whether we deserve it or not, let us look past them to the permissive will of God. "Let him curse; for the Lord hath bidden him!"

When, through the treachery of Judas, the bitter cup came to the lips of our Lord, he said, "It is the cup that my Father hath given me to drink." Pain and sorrow, treachery and hard speeches may be devised against us by the malignity of an Ahithophel, a Shimei, or a Judas; but by the time these have passed, through the permissive will of God, we may receive them as the strokes of his chastening rod, that we may partake of his holiness. We are not the sport of chance or human caprice. God deals with us as with sons.

2 SAMUEL 16:13-23

The True King's Loyal Friend. There are always some alleviations in our trials. Every cloud is edged with a silver or golden fringe. Shimei may curse, but Ittai swears allegiance; Zadok and Abiathar forget their ancient rivalry in a common sorrow; Ahithophel's defection may cut us to the quick, but Hushai is willing to plead our cause.

Beware of any advice which complies with and gratifies the impulses of your own lower nature. He who begins by counseling you to do what is morally wrong can never be trusted as an adviser in matters that require consummate prudence. He is no oracle of God who does not take his stand on righteousness and purity. "The wisdom which is from above is first *pure,* then peaceable, ... and without hypocrisy," Jas. 3:17. Let us not run hither and thither to seek counsel of man. If any lack wisdom, let him ask of God, who giveth to all liberally, and upbraideth not. The one characteristic of a heaven-guided man is his calm decision and deliberateness. They that believe do not make haste!

2 SAMUEL 17:1-14

Tripped by Hushai's Counsel. What a contrast to the plottings of David's foes was his own state of mind, as disclosed in Psalms 3 and 4, written at this time! At Jerusalem they were taking counsel against him. Ahithophel describes the deposed king as weary and weak-handed, and shows how easily he may be smitten, while Hushai pictures him as chafed and savage. Choosing to believe Hushai, Absalom sends messengers on their way, lest he should be swallowed up. But David betakes himself to God.

He knows that God is a shield unto him, so that there is no need to be afraid of ten thousands of people. He lies down in peace and sleeps, because God makes him to dwell in safety. He knows that God hath set him apart for himself, and will answer to his call. He said all this, though he knew that these disasters were the result of his sin. But this is the prerogative of all whose iniquity is forgiven and whose sin is covered. Though we continue to blame ourselves as we remember the past, yet we absolutely accept our Lord's assurances that he will deliver us from the complications caused by our sins, and act as our rear guard against the consequences.

2 SAMUEL 17:15-29

The Helpers of the King. The two young men were narrowly watched, and had it not been for the deception practiced on Absalom's servants by the mistress of the house at Bahurim, they would probably not have reached David in time to put him on his guard. That her device secured his safety does not extenuate nor justify her falsehood. God could have found some other method of delivering his servant. Let us remember the warning voices that speak to us, bidding us beware of temptation. There is a river that we also may put between us and our pursuers. It is the Jordan of Calvary—the cross of our Savior. Reckon yourselves dead unto sin!

As Ahithophel foreshadowed Judas in his treachery, so did he in his end. See Psa. 41:9; Matt. 27:5. He was not only mortified by the refusal of his advice, but clearly saw therein the inevitable triumph of David's cause and the punishment that would follow. On the farther bank, friends awaited the fugitives. For Shobi, see 10:1, 2; Machir, 9:4. But Psalms 42 and 43 reflect David's feelings at this sad hour. Even in the night God's song was with him.

2 SAMUEL 18:1-15

The End of a Rebellious Son. Absalom's army was soon across the river under Amasa, David's nephew, 17:25, 26. Though political reasons constrained David to flight, his heart bled for his wrong-headed and evil-hearted son, and he gave urgent directions for his safety. Let us here learn something of God's own heart of love. We may have been heartless and thoughtless, have defied his authority and refused to give him his rightful place; but he gives charge concerning us, desires that we may be spared the full results of our actions, and yearns for our return.

The eastern tribes had rallied so enthusiastically around David's standard that he soon found himself at the head of a great army which, to judge from v. 12, was absolutely loyal to him. But Joab saw farther than the ordinary soldiers and knew that there could be no peace while Absalom lived. He had forfeited his life, according to Deut. 21:18, 21, 23. See also 2 Sam. 17:2, 4. His head being caught in the fork of a tree, it seemed, indeed, as if he were cursed according to the law, Gal. 3:13; Deut. 21:23.

2 SAMUEL 18:16-30

Tidings That Failed to Bring Joy. Ahimaaz was far-famed for his swift running. He had already served the royal cause, and his family was intimate with the king, 15:36; 17:17. Joab was therefore unwilling to entrust the youth with tidings which must give the king bitter sorrow, and perhaps cause him to associate them ever after with the bearer. Perhaps Joab also feared that the part which he himself had taken in Absalom's death would be exposed by Ahimaaz. The tidings were therefore entrusted to an Ethiopian slave. He ran along the straight road to Mahanaim, but the young priest took the way of the plain and outran him.

Tidings are constantly pouring in upon us, some by the stranger, some by the friend. But if we trust in the Lord we shall not be afraid of them, Psa. 112:7. Only let our heart be "fixed." For us also there shall arise light in the darkness, our heart shall be established, and we shall not be moved. When next you break the seal of the dreaded letter, lift your heart to God. He will bring good out of evil.

2 SAMUEL 18:31-33

Mourning Too Late. What an awful day that was for David, seated between the inner and outer gates, scanning the landscape, and speaking now and again to the sentry posted above him. Did not the Spirit work an even deeper repentance than ever before, recalling the self-indulgence, the failure to watch, the lapse of fellowship? But was it not also an hour when David put his finger on the covenant and asked God, notwithstanding all, to do as he had said, 7:15?

As David waited, his heart interceded for Absalom. How exactly his attitude is that of many who read these words, who are unable to join in the activities of life, and who spend days and nights in uttering one dear name before God! But he loves our Absaloms more than we do! David wished that he might have died for his son, and you have felt the same. But did not Jesus die for the ungodly? We must leave all with him, the Judge of all the earth, but also its Redeemer and Savior.

2 SAMUEL 19:1-20

Bringing the King Back. Joab's remonstrance, though expressed in rough and uncourteous phrase, was perfectly just. The royal troops, instead of being welcomed with acclamation, had slunk into the city as if defeated. Immediate steps must be taken to counteract their depression. Private grief must yield to public interests.

The restoration of loyalty to David began with the ten tribes; but the concurrence of Judah was essential, and it was secured by the mission of the two priests and by the overtures of Amasa. These turned the scale, and Judah welcomed the king with joy, v. 14. What a glimpse all this gives of the change that will be wrought when our Lord comes again—and apparently his advent is very nigh! Previous verdicts will be reversed. Shimeis will sue for mercy. Mephibosheths will be justified and Barzillais rewarded. What are we doing as individuals to secure the return of the King? Compare v. 10 with 2 Peter 3:12. Have we brought the King back to his throne in our own hearts?

2 SAMUEL 19:21-30

A Day to Forget Injuries. Abishai's reprobation of Shimei's disloyalty was very natural; but at that supreme moment of triumph, David could afford to be magnanimous, and so he accepted Shimei's abject apology and pleading. Evidently there was a growing alienation between the king and the sons of Zeruiah.

Mephibosheth urged that Ziba had shamefully wronged and misrepresented him, taking away the ass on which he had intended to accompany the king into exile, and imputing his laxity to the hope that he might be restored to his grandfather's throne. He pointed to his disordered appearance as evidence of his intense grief. Clearly, however, David was not altogether satisfied and, desiring not to make Ziba his enemy, ruled that the estate should be divided between them. But Mephibosheth professed his willingness for his late servant to own it all. He might well feel repaid and satisfied, now that he had seen David's face once again in peace, Phil. 3:8.

2 SAMUEL 19:31-43

Returning over Jordan. David would willingly have taken Barzillai to his palace, but the famous Gileadite respectfully declined the invitation, alleging the infirmities of old age. However, the overtures which he refused for himself he gladly accepted for his son Chimham, who accompanied the king to the city and was treated with every consideration. In himself, the youth had no claims upon David, but he stood in the merits of another—his father. His title to the king's favor consisted entirely in his being the son of Barzillai. Similarly, the believer in Jesus, who is united to him by a living faith, is "accepted in the beloved." We are as near and as dear to God as Jesus is, and for his sake may stand in the palace.

The invitation for David's return had originated in the ten tribes, but through some mismanagement the actual welcome was given by Judah. This led to a renewed manifestation of the rivalry that at length brought about the division of the kingdom.

2 SAMUEL 20:1-13

Pursuing Another Rebel. Like Shimei, Sheba belonged to the tribe of Benjamin. The old "Saul faction" was always breaking out in rebellion, and Nathan's prediction that the sword would never cease from David's house was literally fulfilled. We must always watch against the return of our old sins.

Amasa's appointment was a mistake. He had already proved his incompetence under Absalom, and now his delay threatened disaster. David had chosen him only because he wished, at any cost, to rid himself of Joab. He could not forgive that general for slaying Absalom. The proud spirit of the old leader, however, would not brook the division of the military command, and Joab treated Amasa as he had treated Abner. An attempt was afterward made to justify the deed by casting suspicion on Amasa's loyalty. See v. 11. But jealousy will catch at a straw to justify its crimes.

We turn from these deeds of blood, mindful that the heart of man is still capable of them. We are daily taught in the present European crisis (Note: World War I), to what lengths men will go. The heart is deceitful above all things and desperately wicked. Only God knows it, only God can cleanse it, and only God can create a clean heart and renew a right spirit.

2 SAMUEL 20:14-26

One Head Saves Many. This wise woman, by her intervention, saved many lives, and reminds us of the value of presence of mind in a great crisis. She gave Joab to understand, first, that he ought to have given the inhabitants of Abel the opportunity of saying whether or not they intended to fight for Sheba, Deut. 20:10; and, secondly, that he ought to have taken into account the peaceableness and fidelity of the citizens of that city. A great deal of misunderstanding and bloodshed would be prevented if contending parties would only confer with each other. There is crying and universal need for boards of compulsory arbitration.

Sheba's head saved the city. Bishop Hall says: "Spiritually the case is ours; every man's breast is a city enclosed; every sin is a traitor that lurks within the walls. If we love the head of one traitor above the life of our soul, we shall justly perish. We cannot be more willing to part with our sin than our merciful God is to withdraw his judgments." Oh, that every reader of these lines would heed the command of the Savior, Matt. 5:29, 30, so as to enter into everlasting life!

2 SAMUEL 21:1-9

A Devoted Mother. The time of this famine cannot be fixed with certainty. Probably it took place before Absalom's rebellion. The reason for it was found in Saul's slaughter of the Gibeonites. See v. 1; 1 Sam. 22:19. Though their fathers had obtained the promise of immunity from Joshua and the princes by fraud, yet it was regarded as binding, and its violation was looked upon as a grave offense, involving the whole nation in the charge of perjury. The remnant of the Gibeonites were therefore allowed to fix their own terms. This tendency to connect a national calamity with a national crime has always obtained. There seems to be a universal consciousness that uncaused judgments do not befall.

Note that Merab should be substituted for Michal, v. 8; 1 Sam. 18:19. Out of all the scenes of cruelty and blood with which this age was characterized, the love of motherhood shines forth undimmed. It is one of the most precious of God's gifts to man. But what shall we not say of that divine love which clings to us in our most hopeless condition?

2 SAMUEL 21:10-22

More Giants Slain. It was in unsettled weather that Rizpah began her watch; but no hardship daunted her, no cost was too great. She shielded the dear remains from bird and beast till the falling rain gave assurance that the long famine was ended, v. 10. Her devotion seems to have aroused David to treat with similar honor the remains of Saul and Jonathan, and all were buried together in the sepulchre of Kish.

Love ignites love, as fire kindles fire, without impoverishment. How often a voice raised in prayerful and passionate affection to Jesus has made volcanic fires leap out where all had seemed extinct! Do not stint your alabasterboxes, for though they drive a Judas to desperation, they will stimulate a David or a Peter to a forgotten duty.

Monstrous sin stalked the world in the person of these giants, vv. 16-22. They beset the old age of David, as they did his youth. Though we may not be assailed by the identical temptations as at first, there never will be a time when the progeny of sin will not molest us; if not passion, then jealousy, or avarice, or pride.

2 SAMUEL 23:1-7

David's Last Song. Let us place our lips at God's disposal, that he may speak by them, and let his words be on our tongues. God's love is to our souls like morning light. It stole over our hearts in childhood so gently that we did not know when first it came. The happy experiences of those pure and holy years were like the grass-blades that glisten across the lawns soaked in dew. "Thou hast the dew of thy youth."

When our heart is breaking with domestic or public anxiety, what a comfort it is to look away to the covenant, ordered in all things and sure. Sometimes, indeed, God's purpose in our lives seems to come to a standstill. "... he make it not to grow," 23:5. But beneath the scaffolding the building is rising, and under the ground the harvest seeds are swelling.

These verses indicate David's ideal for himself which he had not fully attained. The harp became jangled, and the strain lost its music. There is only one King who can realize all that we ask or think, our fair dream. That King is our Lord Jesus.

2 SAMUEL 23:8-17

David's Mighty Men. David's yearning for the water of the well of Bethlehem was very natural. He could almost see the ancient wellhead where as a lad he had gone with his mother to draw water. In the scorching heat that beat down on the hillside that sultry afternoon, nothing seemed so desirable as a draught from those cool depths. So does the exile yearn for home, and the backslider for his early blessedness. But, thank God, we cannot wish for the Water of Life—if we wish with all our heart—without having it. To wish is to enjoy. Our Mighty Savior has broken through the Philistines, and has won for us access to the springs of eternal blessedness.

It was very noble of David to refuse to drink that which had been obtained at such cost. Self-control and thoughtfulness for others are graces that bind men's hearts to their leaders. Moreover, David's example suggests a quite different call which modern conditions make upon us for the exercise of similar self-control. Should we not refuse to make any use of wine and strong drink which have cost, and are costing, the lives of myriads? God forbid that any of us should enjoy, for our selfish pleasures, a foe of human happiness, purity, and hope.

2 SAMUEL 23:18-39

Men with a Record. What marvels may be wrought by the inspiration of a single life! We remember the hour when an unknown youth stepped out of the affrighted hosts of Israel to face Goliath. Alone, so far as human help went, David encountered and defeated that terrible antagonist. But after some fourteen or fifteen years had run their course, he no longer stood alone. Scores of heroes, animated by his spirit and exercising his faith, stepped forth on the new path which he had opened.

Thus the lives of great men light up and inspire the lives of others. They mold their contemporaries. Wesley's career has raised a great army of preachers and evangelists. The enthusiasm of a Brainerd, a Finney, a Moody has stirred tens of thousands with kindred passion for the souls of men. The companions of our Lord became his Apostles (his missionaries). His own life of sacrifice for men has become the beacon-fire which has summoned myriads from the sloth and indulgence of the valleys to the surrender, the self-denial, the anguish of his cross, if only they might be permitted to follow in his steps. Is there anything in *our* lives that is inspiring others?

2 SAMUEL 24:1-14

A Proud Heart Humbled. The sin of numbering the people lay in its *motive.* David was animated by a spirit of pride and vainglory. He was eager to make a fine showing among the surrounding nations, and to impress them with such a conception of Israel's greatness that they would not dare to attack any point of the long frontier line. He yielded to the temptation of trusting in chariots and horses, instead of in the victories of faith.

When the enumeration was nearly complete, David's heart smote him. He saw how far he had swerved from the idea of the theocracy, in which God's will was the sole guide of national policy. He had substituted his own wisdom for the divine edict. A night of anguish followed on this self-discovery, but David submitted himself to God's dealings.

It was wise to choose to fall into the hands of God. They are very loving and tender hands, but David viewed them as punitive and not redemptive; and the plague, which devastated the people, cut him to the quick.

2 SAMUEL 24:15-25

Judgment Stayed by Sacrifice. The pestilence swept through the land like cholera or the black death in modern times. At last it approached the Holy City. It seemed as if the angel of the Lord were hovering over it, sword in hand, awaiting the final order. All this is spoken after the manner of men. It is clear, however, that in answer to David's penitent faith, a great change came over the scene. If the same faith had been exercised before the plague reached Jerusalem, may we not believe that an arrest would have come previously? As soon as David was prepared, as in v. 17, to suffer instead of his people, his love and contrition and faith were accepted on their behalf.

Then, on Mount Moriah, where centuries before Abraham's uplifted knife was stayed, the angel now stayed his act of judgment. The threshing-floor of Araunah became the site of an altar, while afterward on that spot stood the Temple, the center of national worship and the scene of the manifestation of the Son of man. The lesson for us is that when we take the true attitude toward God, we can exercise, by our faith, prayer, and self-sacrifice, a wonderful influence in behalf of cities and nations.

THE FIRST BOOK OF
KINGS

NATIONAL DEVELOPMENT UNDER THE MONARCHY

I. THE UNITED KINGDOM   *1—11*
- A. The rebellion of Adonijah and the coronation of Solomon   *1*
- B. Solomon's establishment in power, wealth, and wisdom   *2—4*
- C. The building and dedication of the Temple   *5:1—9:25*
- D. Solomon's commerce; visit of the Queen of Sheba   *9:26—10:29*
- E. Solomon's polygamy, apostasy, and death   *11:1-43*

II. THE DIVIDED KINGDOM   *12—22*
- A. Rehoboam alienates the ten tribes, who choose Jeroboam   *12:1-24*
- B. The reign of Jeroboam   *12:25—14:20*
- C. The reign of Rehoboam   *14:21-31*
- D. The reigns of Nadab, Baasha, Elah, Zimri, and Omri in Israel; and the reigns of Abijam and Asa in Judah   *15:1—16:28*
- E. The reigns of Ahab and Jehoshaphat and the work of Elijah   *16:29—22:53*
  1. The season of drought   *17:1—18:16*
  2. The contest on Mount Carmel   *18:17-46*
  3. The revelation at Mount Sinai   *19:1-18*
  4. The call of Elisha   *19:19-21*
  5. The doom of Ahab   *20:1—22:40*
  6. Summary of Jehoshaphat's reign   *22:41-53*

INTRODUCTION

Originally Samuel, Kings, and Chronicles were regarded as one series and called the Books of Kings. In the Septuagint (the Greek version of the Old Testament, made during the period between the Testaments), each of these books was divided into two parts, and what we term First Kings was called the Third Book of Kings.

It is impossible to fix accurately either the date when this book was compiled, or the name of the writer. From the fact that the last chapter of 2 Kings records the release of Jehoiachin from captivity, which took place 562, B.C., but makes no mention of the decree of Cyrus, 538, B.C., with which the return of the Jews from captivity began, it is concluded that the book was compiled some time between these dates.

The sources from which the compiler drew were three: the Book of the Acts of Solomon, 1 Kings 11:41; the Book of the Chronicles of the Kings of Judah, 14:29; and the Book of the Chronicles of the Kings of Israel, 14:19. The Chronicles here referred to are not the books called Chronicles in the Bible, but separate works which are now lost.

The history of the nation is recorded from the close of the reign of David to the middle of the reign of Ahaziah. In its highest glory under Solomon, the kingdom foreshadows the millennial kingdom of our Lord. The prosperity of the nation rises or falls according to the character of the ruler and his people, illustrating for us the important truth that obedience is the condition of blessing.

COMMENTARY

1 KINGS 1:1–14

A Self-seeker's Scheme. Adonijah was the fourth son of David, but probably the oldest of those who survived. He was born after Absalom, and like him was goodly in appearance, ambitious in spirit, and equally spoiled by his father's indulgence, v. 6. His attempt to usurp the kingdom reminds us of another great usurper. Satan, we know, in one last desperate effort will try to secure the empire of the world. But when the people rage and the rulers devise, Psa. 2:1, 2, 4, Heaven will laugh at them. The Lamb that was slain is the destined King of men, Rev. 11:15. The book of destiny is in the pierced hand. The government is upon Christ's shoulders. He declares the decree, "The Lord said unto my Lord, Sit thou at my right hand, until I make thine enemies thy footstool," Psa. 110:1.

We look out on the world which is rent by revolt. The prince of this world is attracting to himself the Joabs and Abiathars. They make merry, but do not realize that the hour is at hand when they shall cry to the rocks and the hills to fall on them and hide them from the wrath of the Lamb, Rev. 6:16. Remember the counsel of Augustine, "If you would flee from God, flee to him!"

1 KINGS 1:15–27

Learning the King's Will. The attempt of the usurper was met and defeated through Nathan's prompt action, and by the concerted appeal that he and Bath-sheba made to the king, who seems to have sunk into premature old age. Bath-sheba and David probably met for the last time on this dark day, and each of them must have remembered the solemn promise given them years before, through Nathan, who was still with them as friend and counselor. Much had happened since, but amid all the changes in human affairs the Word of God is immutable and the promise of 1 Chronicles 22:9 must stand.

Probably only Bath-sheba and Nathan knew of that solemn compact; and, knowing it, they at once took action. It is not enough that God should make a promise to his people; they must claim its fulfilment and put themselves at his disposal, that it may be fulfilled through them. The ancient prediction that the kingdoms of this world shall become the kingdom of our Lord is true, but we must pray for and hasten its advent.

1 KINGS 1:28–40

Anointing the Chosen One. David aroused himself and acted with commendable prudence and swiftness. The crisis required promptness of decision and energy in execution. The whole nation was waiting to know the king's will regarding the succession to the throne, and David left no doubt as to his choice. His orders were quickly carried out by Nathan, Zadok, and Benaiah, and the royal action was also endorsed by popular acclaim.

What tumultuous joy burst over Jerusalem when Solomon was enthroned! The earth rang again with jubilant shouts which struck terror among the guests at Adonijah's feast. But all such opposition shall be forgotten in that day for which the whole creation—groaning in travail, Rom. 8:22—waits, when Jesus shall be manifested and those who love him shall be manifested with him in glory, Col. 3:4. Then we shall hear that new song, in which ten thousand times ten thousand voices shall acknowledge that Jesus is worthy to receive power and riches and wisdom and strength and honor and glory and blessing. *He must reign!* See Rev. 5:12.

1 KINGS 1:41-53

Justice and Brotherhood the Foundations of the State. According to popular usage, Adonijah was the rightful heir to the throne. He was handsome and kingly in appearance and behavior. He was also in his prime, while Solomon was just out of his teens. So plausible was his address that the nation was bewildered, and old retainers of David's throne were seduced. We are reminded in all this of the god of this world, 2 Cor. 4:4, who blinds the eyes of those who believe not, lest the light of the glorious knowledge of God should shine in upon them.

Solomon displayed remarkable clemency in dealing with Adonijah. He was willing to let bygones be bygones. He promised that if Adonijah proved himself a worthy man, no harm should befall him. But as the following chapter records, the evil that wrought in Adonijah came out in a further plot to secure the throne, and he paid the death penalty. Let us see to it that we walk, not according to the course of this world or the spirit that works in the children of disobedience, but remembering that we have been quickened together with Christ and made to sit with him in heavenly places, let us walk worthy of our high calling.

1 KINGS 2:1-9

New Responsibilities for the New King. 1 Chronicles 28 and 29 should be read as coming between this and the preceding chapter. It was with a ripe knowledge of life that David urged Solomon to keep God's charge, to walk in his ways and do his commandments as the sure road to prosperity. The guiding star of David's life—2 Sam. 7:25—shone over him in death. God never goes back on a word that he has once spoken. He continues his word; only we must walk before him in obedience and faith that it may have free course.

At first sight, we might suppose that the old king cherished bitter feelings against those named in this parting charge; but it should be remembered that he speaks here from a public, rather than a private, standpoint. He knew that these men constituted a grave peril to the peace and stability of the state; and indeed his fears were abundantly justified, for each of them was discovered in acts of treachery, on account of which, and not because of David's words, he suffered death. David held that the claims of gratitude were not less binding than those of justice; hence his warm recommendation of Barzillai. "Show thyself a man" was good advice to a youth called to rule in turbulent times.

1 KINGS 2:10-25

A Foolish and Fatal Petition. So David's troubled life came to a close, but he has never ceased to lead the praises of the saints.

At the very beginning of his reign, Solomon was confronted by a difficult problem. There was so close a connection in public opinion between the title to the crown and the possession of a deceased monarch's harem that it would have been impossible to grant Adonijah's request without giving strong encouragement to his pretensions. Solomon treated Bathsheba with profound respect, but his love for her did not blind him to his duty to his realm, Prov. 20:26.

Notice that solemn declaration, "As Jehovah liveth," v. 24. It was common to the godly of those days. See 1 Kings 17:1. They would not use the phrase lightly nor flippantly, but with a profound realization of standing in the presence of God. Let us recall those words of our Lord, "As the living Father sent me, and I live by the Father," John 6:57, and let us draw daily on his life, so that we may live, yet not we, but he in us and we in him, Gal. 2:20.

1 KINGS 2:26-35

Paying Penalty for Bloody Deeds. The removal of Abiathar from the office of high priest and the execution of Joab quenched the last faint hopes of the house of Saul. In the case of Abiathar, note the remarkable fulfilment of the divine prediction, 1 Sam. 2:31-35. God does not fail to keep his word, whether of threatening or of promise.

Joab fled to the altar. Men who throughout their life have disregarded or despised religion will often turn to it in their extremity. Those who blaspheme when the seas are smooth will

1 KINGS

be the first to cry for mercy when the storm winds lash the waters into foam.

Joab's attempt to find mercy through the altar was futile; but no sinner ever flees to the cross in vain. If he fulfills the conditions of repentance and faith, the sword of the avenger cannot touch him there. If we confess and forsake our sins, and humbly trust in the mercy of the Redeemer, no weapon that is formed against us can prosper, and every tongue that rises in judgment is condemned. "This is the heritage of the servants of the Lord," Isa. 54:17.

1 KINGS 2:36-46

Presuming and Perishing. Shimei broke the one condition on which his life had been given back to him, and could have no just cause of complaint against the king. It may be argued that his offense was a trifling and excusable one, but we must remember that it was committed not only against the royal commandment, but against the oath of God, v. 43. By this one act he forfeited all claim upon Solomon's clemency.

We are here reminded of the parable of the two debtors in Matt. 18:28*ff.* The debtor who owed the most had been released, and we naturally look to see the forgiven man's glad forgiveness of his brother, who was in turn indebted to him. But, so far from forgiveness, there was rough retaliation. This canceled the first offer of pardon and it was withdrawn. So this act on the part of Shimei was fatal in its effect. The Jews were doubtful as to the forgivableness of presumptuous sins, and our Lord also taught that there is a sin against the Holy Spirit which cannot be forgiven.

1 KINGS 3:1-15

The Young King's Wise Choice. The chapter opens doubtfully. The affinity with Pharaoh, and the two "onlys" of vv. 2 and 3 are not promising. See Deut. 12:13, 14. Yet there were hopeful features in Solomon's love for God, and the devotion and obedience by which it was proved. It remained, however, to be seen which of these influences was to triumph in the outworking of his character. That is always the most urgent question in life. With too many the early dew and morning cloud pass away, leaving no trace, Hosea 6:4.

There is an inner wisdom which is of the heart rather than of the head, and which God's Spirit bestows on those who love him. Having this, we possess the key to all things in Heaven and on earth. See 1 Cor. 2:5*ff.* When a man seeks first the kingdom, all else is added, Matt. 6:33. Only the man who delights in God can be trusted with the gratification of his heart's desires, Psa. 37:4.

Live deep in God. Do not be dazzled or fascinated by outward things. Be concerned to know God's will and become the organ of his purpose. He will add to you all else that is needful for the fulfillment of your life-course.

1 KINGS 3:16-28

A Discerning Judgment. The incident gave convincing proof of the gift of wisdom. This is the most esteemed endowment of an Eastern potentate, who is called upon to arbitrate in cases that defy the labored processes of law and precedent. How could so difficult a case be decided? There were no witnesses on either side. But Solomon appealed to the instincts of a mother's love. The proposal to divide the child at once revealed the mother, who would rather expose herself to a life of anguish than see her child suffer or its life extinguished.

Bishop Hall, commenting on this incident, says, "Truth demands entireness; falsehood is satisfied with less. Satan, who has no right to the heart, is content with a piece of it; God, who made the heart, will have either all or none."

But surely there is a still deeper lesson. When we truly belong to Christ, sharing his nature and having fellowship in his kingdom, we shall live in quick sympathy with everything that touches his honor. The child of God instinctively winces whenever his Father's character is challenged, or a foul suggestion is made to his own soul. This is evidence of sonship.

1 KINGS 4:1-7, 20-28

A Prosperous Nation. What a picture is here given of national contentment and prosperity! We can almost hear the gladsome voice of the myriad-peopled land, teeming with young life and laden with golden harvests. It was the summer of their national existence. The sacred scribe enumerates first the high officials of the court, then the daily provision of the king, his studies, and his fame. Abundant proof was yielded by all these circumstances to the manner in which God kept the pledges which had been made to David, his father.

Here is Solomon "in all his glory," but as we turn from him to the lowly carpenter of Nazareth, who had nowhere to lay his head, who found his friends among the poor, and who ultimately laid down his life a ransom for many, we realize that even apart from his divine nature, his was the nobler ideal and the richer existence. "A greater than Solomon is here." Who can measure his empire or resources? What tongue can recount his wisdom? Happy and safe are they that sit at his table, hear his words, and are joint-heirs with him in his kingdom! See Rom. 8:17.

1 KINGS 4:29—5:6

The Wise King's Great Purpose. David, before his death, had made great preparations for building the Temple, but had not been permitted to proceed with its construction. "Thou didst well in that it was in thine heart," 2 Chron. 6:8. God credits us with what we would have done, had it been in our power. But now war on every side had been exchanged for peace, and the time for temple-building had come. A great principle is here involved which has many applications.

It is true of the *Church at large.* When the Church throughout all Judea and Galilee had peace, it was edified; and as it walked in the fear of the Lord and in the comfort of the Holy Spirit, it was multiplied, Acts 9:31. When the love of God reigns amid professing Christians, and they neither war against nor vex each other, then the world believes, and the very Hirams help to build.

It is also true of the *inner life.* The days of peace are those in which the heart thrives. See 1 Thess. 5:23 and Heb. 13:20, 21. God is not in the earthquake nor in the fire, but in the "still small voice." Cultivate a quiet heart, as did Mary, at the feet of Christ. It will result in deeds to be spoken of throughout the whole world, Luke 10:39 and Matt. 26:13.

1 KINGS 5:7-18

Preparations for the Great Task. It was good for Hiram and his Tyrians to be associated with the servants of Solomon. Together they hewed immense blocks of stone, some of which were thirty feet in length and six feet in breadth, and which still form foundations on the ancient Temple site. Together they hewed down and fashioned the cedar and fir trees on the slopes of Lebanon. May we not learn from this partnership that Gentiles are to be associated with Jews in that one holy Temple, which through the ages is growing into a habitation of God by his Spirit? Read Eph. 2:21, 22. In Christ there is neither Jew nor Greek, circumcision nor uncircumcision.

The treaty between the two kingdoms was eminently wise, because they differed so widely —the one being pastoral, the other commercial. It was wise for Peter and John to enter into close friendship and together ascend the steps to the Beautiful Gate of the Temple, Acts 3:1-3. Be content to be a hewer on the mountains, shaping rough blocks of granite, but do something toward building the Temple of God, which arises slowly amid the wreck of all human structures.

1 KINGS 6:1-13

The Plan of the Lord's House. The Temple was twice the size of the Tabernacle, ninety feet long by thirty feet broad, and forty-five feet high. The plan had been given to David by revelation, 1 Chron. 28:11, 12. Seven years and a half were consumed in its erection. It was completed in sacred silence, v. 7. The awful sanctity of the shrine would have been violated if its construction had been marred by the harsh and violent sounds that generally accompany the mason's toil. "Like some tall palm the noiseless fabric sprang." In Nature, God works so silently that we do not realize his activities.

The central motive was to provide a place worthy to be called the house of God. Israel was now ruled by a king, but he was viewed as the organ and instrument of Jehovah. It was fitting, therefore, that the King of kings should have a dwelling-place among the people of Israel. The tabernacle of God was with men. He dwelt with them on the earth. The Temple was, moreover, the type, first of the body of Jesus, John 2:21, then of each believer, 1 Cor. 3:16, and lastly of the whole Church, Eph. 2:21, 22. Each of these is the dwelling-place of God, and the innermost chamber—the Holy of Holies—is meant to be the throne-room of the Shekinah of his presence, Lev. 16:2.

1 KINGS 6:14-28

The Oracle in the Midst. In the Temple the general design of the Tabernacle was perpetuated by the division between the Holy Place and the Most Holy Place, but there were several additions. For instance, there was a lofty porch in front of the Temple, beneath which the priests passed to the entrance. Also, on the other three sides were rooms, built one above the other in three stories. They were needed for storage purposes.

Inside no stones were visible. All was of gilded cedar, olive, and cypress wood, variously carved and tapestried by embroidered hangings. It was "exceeding magnificent." The Holy of Holies was plunged in darkness, save as the Shekinah shone from the mercy seat over the Ark and between the cherubim. Over this venerable relic of the wilderness pilgrimage, Solomon set up two cherubim. Each was ten cubits high and their outstretched wings, which touched each other above the Ark, also touched the walls on either side. These symbolized the highest forms of creature-life, reverently attendant upon their Creator.

1 KINGS 6:29-38

Carved; Overlaid; Finished. The meaning of v. 31 is uncertain. We gather that the door of the inner shrine was made of wild-olive wood and in two parts, and that it occupied a fifth of the cedar partition which separated the two chambers. This wooden door was carved with cherubim, palm trees, and open flowers and was overlaid with gold. One part was always open, but the interior was concealed from view by a veil of blue, purple, and crimson, 2 Chron. 3:14. In front of this were hung festoons of golden chains. Thus it was signified that the way into the Holiest was not then open. But *we* have boldness to enter, through the new and living way which Jesus consecrated for us. The surrendered will, the cleansed life, the meek and humble faith—these are the path, Heb. 10:19, 20.

The erection occupied seven and a half years, and the completed Temple stood for upward of four centuries, until destroyed by Nebuchadnezzar. The construction of character, after God's ideal, may take long, but it advances to completion. First the stone, hewn with difficulty; then cedar and olive; lastly gold.

1 KINGS 7:1-12

Other Splendid Structures. Solomon's house took nearly twice as long to build as did the Temple, because there was not the same urgency for it. His house and that for the queen were probably built around large open courts and stood, after the manner of the East, on either side of the central hall where public business was transacted.

The royal hall in Jerusalem was called the "House of the Forest of Lebanon," because its many pillars resembled a forest of cedar wood. In front of this building was a colonnade, and in front of this again, the King's Gate.

It is more than likely that the area of Mount Zion was greatly enlarged by walls built up from the valley and filled in with earth. This furnished room for the many splendid buildings named in this paragraph. Traces of these cyclopean walls can still be seen. In order to estimate the real value of all this splendor, we have only to turn to the earliest chapters of Ecclesiastes, where we read how little it satisfied the hunger of Solomon's soul. He turned away from it all, as unsatisfied as the prodigal from the husks of the swine. We were made for God and only God can suffice.

1 KINGS 7:13-26

Pillars of Security and Strength. Hiram, the artificer, was remarkably gifted. From his father he had inherited all the genius of Tyre, while on his mother's side he was of the tribe of Naphtali and thus inherited the religious genius of the Hebrew people. The twin pillars were made of the brass taken from the king of Zobah, 1 Chron. 18:8, 9. Each would stand to a height of forty feet. Their names were symbolical, and indicated their strength and durability. Wreaths of golden chainwork hung from them, while beautiful ornaments adorned the heads of these noble columns. *Jachin*—"he shall establish"—and *Boaz*—"in him is strength"—combined with the beauty of the "lily work" to remind us that strength and beauty are in God's sanctuary and blend in the character of his people.

The molten sea was substituted for the ancient laver, that soul, mind, and strength may be full of love and light.

1 KINGS 8:1-21

The Builder's Dedication Address. Solomon, standing on the great platform within view of the vast, thronging multitudes, recited the steps that had led them to that illustrious hour. His whole speech was of God's dealings. Why do we not speak of God more often, as the most important factor in life! It is a blessed thing to trace the connection between what God has promised and what he has fulfilled, v. 15. "The Lord hath performed his word that he spake," v. 20. Many of us could say that, and we ought to say it.

Solomon brought out clearly in this address that God took account of David's good intentions. "Thou didst well that it was in thine heart," v. 18. Circumstances may prevent the execution of a desire and a purpose with which, years ago, our hearts were filled. God, however, will never forget it, and will see that the project is carried out in some other way, perhaps by another instrument. It was well that it was in thine heart to become a foreign missionary, though the need of widowed mother, or the claims of home rendered literal obedience impossible. Thou shalt have the missionary's place and crown hereafter, for it was in thine heart.

1 KINGS 8:22-32

God Greater Than Any Temple. Solomon's different attitudes are specially mentioned. First he stood with hands outspread, v. 22; then, as indicated by v. 54, he came to his knees. These attitudes show expectant faith, as well as profound humility and reverence. The more we know of God and experience the blessing of fellowship with him, the lower becomes our self-estimate. Confidence in God always enhances reverence, Heb. 12:28. The man who is lowest on his knees before God stands most erect to bless others, v. 55.

The prayer began with *an ascription of glory to God.* In this it resembles the Lord's Prayer, which begins with "Hallowed be thy Name." Compare Psa. 115:1. Let us form our own prayers on this model. Then it acknowledges *God's fidelity to his promises.* As he speaks, so he fulfils. But it is our part always to say with Solomon, "Keep that thou promisedst," v. 25, and "Let thy word be verified," v. 26. When we stand on this sure footing with God, we can look out on all possible ills that may confront us—whether drought, famine, pestilence, defeat, or captivity—and be absolutely sure that he will hear, answer, and forgive. Heaven cannot contain him, but he dwells in the contrite heart, Isa. 57:15.

1 KINGS 8:33-43

Appeals to the God of Mercy. Solomon's prayer is evidently based on the book of Deuteronomy and tends to confirm the old belief that, with the rest of the Pentateuch, this book came from the hand of Moses. In 2 Chron. 20:7-9, Jehoshaphat pleaded this prayer as though it were substantially a promise, and therefore all needy souls who find their case described here may plead it on their own behalf.

Notice how frequently Solomon speaks of prayer, even in the land of captivity and exile, as being directed toward the Temple, v. 38, etc. It reminds us of the grave need of maintaining unimpaired our spiritual frontage. It has been truly said that the direction of the soul's outlook is the preliminary question in religion. Whether our home looks south or north, whether it faces sunless alleys or sunny fields is an important physical consideration with us. It is likewise of great importance that the mind or soul should face the right way. The difference between spiritual health and disease is very largely one of the way in which we face. For us, Temple, altar, and mercy seat are all summed up in Jesus Christ. Our life must be spent looking unto him, Heb. 12:2.

1 KINGS 8:44-53

A Plea for National Righteousness. How true it is that there is no man that sinneth not, v. 46! Only one who ever walked this earth was holy, guileless, and undefiled, Heb. 7:26. When we fail to watch and abide in Christ, we are easily carried into captivity. How many of God's children are thus taken captive! They are in bondage to some besetting sin, to some evil habit, to some degrading business, or to some unseemly alliance. Like blind Samson, they grind in the prison house.

Let any such, who long for freedom, take home to their souls the infinite comfort which God's Word affords. Let them bethink themselves of the holy and blessed days of the past. Let them repent—that is, in their heart and in practice put away the evil thing which is the outward badge of their sad condition. Let them turn again to the Savior, who has passed into the Holiest that he may intercede in the presence of God for us all. There will be an immediate response. God will hearken in all that they call unto him for, will forgive transgression and sin, and will restore his people to become again his own inheritance for his glory and praise.

1 KINGS 8:54-66

Petition and Sacrifice. The man, as we have seen, who kneels most humbly before God is empowered to bless the people in God's name. What an august and noble testimony the king bore: "There hath not failed one word of all his good promise," v. 56. Joshua had said that before Solomon, Josh. 23:14. Myriads have borne similar witness, and as we are passing hence we shall say the same. We have failed, but not God; we have left him, but he has never cast us away. The mountains may depart and the hills remove, but he will not alter nor falter in his everlasting kindness. Let us ask him to incline our hearts unto him, v. 58.

Notice the marginal reading in verse 59 of the phrase, "as the matter shall require"—"the thing of a day in its day." Whatever may be the requirement for any day, the abundance of grace needed is provided, but you must look up for it and use it. It is they who receive the abundance of grace that reign in life. But you cannot receive unless your heart is perfect with God and you walk in his statutes and keep his commandments.

1 KINGS 9:1-14

A Searching Word to the Wise. God's second revelation of himself to Solomon had a double ob-

1 KINGS

ject. In the first place, it assured the king that his prayer was heard and that the new building was accepted. It is always thus. When we yield ourselves to God, desiring to be his alone, he makes us his possession, hallowing, infilling, and guaranteeing our security. In the second place, God laid down the conditions on which both king and people might be assured of permanent prosperity. We must be wholehearted, not in the *miles* but in the *steps* of our daily walk. Obedience to the inner voice is essential. The child of God distinguishes his Father's voice from every other sound and call, because it is definite and unvarying.

It was a pity that after such loyal cooperation, Hiram was disappointed with his recompense. Happy are they who as they work for God look for no reward from their fellows, because they are the servants of a Master whose generous gifts do not need to be eked out by additions from any other quarter. Do right because it *is* right, and not because you are looking for any gift or reward from human hands.

1 KINGS 9:15–28

Prosperity and Wealth. Solomon was a great builder and employed vast numbers of Canaanites, the old inhabitants of the land, as forced laborers. They performed the drudgery, while the Israelites filled the more honorable and lucrative posts. See Isa. 60:10. There are Amorites and Perizzites in our lives. Let us not be mastered by them, but compel them to subserve our own growth in grace.

Millo was the key to the fortifications of Jerusalem; Hazor and Megiddo, Baalath and Tadmor guarded the northern frontier. On the extreme south, the navies visited distant realms and returned laden with gold. Such were Israel's midsummer days. But as in the latter days of summer there is the faint odor of decay in the air, and we know that autumn comes apace, so beneath all this splendor and imperial glory, as we turn to the earlier chapters of Ecclesiastes we learn that decadence was at its heart.

1 KINGS 10:1–13

"The Half Was Not Told Me." Sheba, to the Jewish mind, was at the ends of the earth, Matt. 12:42. It probably lay in southern Arabia, 1,500 miles from Jerusalem. The queen brought munificent presents of spices, gold, precious stones, and sweet-scented wood. The last-named Solomon used for musical instruments and for stairs in his Temple and palace, 2 Chron. 9:11. But the queen's heart was set on plying him with hard questions, for which she had sought in vain a satisfactory solution.

We may come to "a greater than Solomon," Matt. 12:42. Our native country may lie far away, but he will receive us and give us the right to live forever in his palace, listening to his words and beholding his face. Let us bring him, as our gifts, the faith, love, and loyalty of our hearts. Above all, let us lay before him our perplexities and questions. He may not immediately reveal an answer, as Solomon did, but will put his Spirit into our hearts. And having the anointing of the Spirit, we shall know all things, 1 John 2:27. Though the mind cannot grasp, the heart will be at rest. The Bible, as someone says, does not teach us philosophy, but makes us philosophers. Be sure to obtain and use *your* share of his royal bounty.

1 KINGS 10:14–29

"Solomon in All His Glory." How dazzling is this description of Solomon's glory! And yet our Lord said that it was excelled by a single lily of the field, Matt. 6:28, 29. Solomon's glory was put on from without; the real beauty is that which unfolds from within. If only your soul is planted in the soil of God's grace, it will array itself in the beauties of a holy life. The stainless robes are those which are washed in the blood of the Lamb.

Observe again—this was not the glory of June, but of October. Already the germs of disease were in Solomon's heart; already the autumn decay was in the air. The secret is told in the significant words of Neh. 13:26. Among many nations there was none like him and he was beloved of his God, but strange women were turning away his heart. It was a true statement that our Lord made concerning the rich, that with difficulty they enter the kingdom. A holy man had good reason to pray earnestly for a young believer who had suddenly come into a large estate.

1 KINGS 11:1–13

A Heart Turned Away from God. The practice of mixed marriages was in direct violation of the divine Law, Deut. 7:3, 4, and it led to idolatry. All around the Holy City arose heathen temples. It seems almost incredible that Solomon should have lent himself to such unblushing patronage of idolatry. His sin was aggravated by the great privileges he had enjoyed, v. 9, and there was no escape from chastisement, 2 Sam. 7:14. The more privileged we are, the more disastrous our fall and the more inevitable the penalty. If God loved us less, he might be more sparing of the rod. We are often punished with the rod of men—that is, we suffer at their hands; but God does not cease to love us. The father will listen at the door of the room of the child whom he has been compelled to chastise to detect the first sign of brokenhearted grief.

It is sad to witness the breakup of a noble ship. Listen to the boom of the successive waves: "His heart was not perfect" . . . "Did that which was evil" . . . "The Lord was angry" . . . "Behold, I will rend the kingdom." But out of loving regard to David's memory, one tribe was left. See vv. 12, 32, 34, 38, 39. Your children's children will benefit as the result of your consecrated life. God will not forget.

1 KINGS 11:14–25

Adversaries of the Recreant King. Two of the instruments of Solomon's chastisement are enumerated in this paragraph.

First, Hadad the Edomite, vv. 14–22. Notice the importance of a little child. All the male representatives of the royal family of Edom had perished; but in this child, the line was preserved and perpetuated, to be through long years a formidable menace to Israel. Never neglect a little child. You never know what good or ill may be hidden in a tiny bud. Mark in this man Hadad the trace of those strange impulses which determine destiny. He could not assign the reason that led him to leave Egypt, but he knew he must go, v. 22. Thus migratory birds feel the call of southern lands.

Second, Rezon, who "abhorred Israel," vv. 23–25. It is an awful thing when such hatred arises between two peoples. We as Christians must use all our power to arrest and allay it. Only love and goodwill can guarantee a lasting peace. It was by these two human "rods" that God chastened Solomon. Let us live in such conformity to his will that he may not need to chasten us as individuals or as a nation. "Our God is a consuming fire!"

1 KINGS 11:26–40

The Kingdom Promised to His Servant. The opening chapters of Jeroboam's life were very promising. He sprang from the ranks of the toilers, but his business talent attracted the notice of Solomon, who set him over the forced labor which was levied from the great tribes of Manasseh and Ephraim. Whether Jeroboam had entertained the prospect of rulership before the prophet met him, we cannot tell, but after that interview his whole life was altered. And if only he had observed the injunction of v. 38, he might have lifted Israel to a level of prosperity and glory that would have blessed the world. But, alas, he sinned and made Israel to sin, 12:30; 13:34; 14:16; 16:2, 26.

When God has given you your place, do not devise things out of your own heart in order to retain it, 12:33. The plans that Jeroboam laid to secure the stability of his throne led to its undoing, and covered his name with undying infamy. "Trust in the Lord and do good; so shalt thou dwell in the land." "Fret not thyself in any wise to do evil." "*Thou* maintainest my lot." Let those who feel compelled to do wrong in order to keep their business or position dare to stand with God against the temptation. He will honor those who honor him, 1 Sam. 2:30.

1 KINGS 11:41—12:11

The Wise King's Foolish Son. Solomon's reign had been splendid but very oppressive, and it was reasonable to ask for some relief. The people felt that the accession of the new king gave them their opportunity, and apparently they took the first step in this momentous crisis. We are expressly told that Rehoboam came to Shechem. If this mighty gathering had been called by himself or his court, the people would have had to come to him at Jerusalem. Here was the muttering of the rising storm.

There was much wisdom in the counsel of the older men: "Serve them . . . then they will be thy servants for ever." This principle underlay the sacrifice of Calvary. "Thou art worthy to take the book, for thou wast slain," Rev. 5:9. It is because Jesus girded himself with humility and washed our sins in his own precious blood that he has ascended to the throne, not only of God, but of our hearts and lives. And he has taught us that whosoever would become great must begin by being the servant of all. The proud and lofty in this world are served often enough with the eye-service that gives superficial obedience for wages and rewards, Eph. 6:6, but what is this compared with that which is yielded by gratitude and love!

1 KINGS 12:12–24

The Kingdom Rent in Twain. Rehoboam richly deserved his fate. He was forty-one years old, 2 Chron. 12:13, and ought to have known better. His speech betrayed the despot. He had no right to speak with such arrogant insolence to a great and liberty-loving people. It is only a weak man who boasts of deeds he cannot perform, and there was a rasping flavor in his comparison which indicated the malice of an unregenerate heart. We have heard people speak like this to those whom they counted their inferiors, but all such words are the scattering of thistledown, which will spoil the harvests of their own fields. Learn to speak civilly or not at all. Insist that young lads and girls keep a civil tongue in their heads. Curses are like boomerangs; they come back on the man that utters them.

Twice over we are told that it was a thing brought about by God, vv. 15, 24. Beneath all political changes and revolutions you will find the slow evolving of a divine purpose. God does not instigate sin. This arises from man's abuse of his own free will. But God will so control the warring wills of men that the plan of his eternal counsel and foreknowledge shall not be interfered with, but furthered.

1 KINGS 12:25-33

Manmade Religion. Jeroboam knew better than to make these two calves. The prophet had clearly told him that the stability of his throne was contingent upon his obedience, 11:38. It was definitely promised that if he would hearken to do all that was commanded him, God would be with him and build him a sure house. But he was not content with this.

Fearing that if his people went up to the annual feasts at Jerusalem they would return to their ancient loyalty to David's throne and kill him, Jeroboam set up the worship of Jehovah under the semblance of these two calves. He thus broke not the First but the Second Commandment, and sowed seeds from which his descendants were destined to reap a succession of bitter harvests. He was like the foolish man of our Lord's parable who heard and did not, and whose house, however carefully it might have been constructed, was destroyed by the rising waters. Expediency always deceives those who turn from God and rely on the devices of their own hearts. It seems that Jeroboam constituted himself priest as well as king. There is no knowing to what lengths men may drift when they lose their moorings in God.

1 KINGS 13:1-10

Judgment upon Worthless Worship. What a noble title for any one to bear—"a man of God!" Yet we all might so bear the impress of God in our character, that those who come in contact with us might feel that ineffable something which you cannot define, which does not need advertising, but which tells that the person who bears it is truly a child of God.

The altar by which Jeroboam expected to consolidate his kingdom was the cause of its overthrow and disaster, until at last Israel was carried into captivity. When we turn from the fountain of living waters and hew out for ourselves broken cisterns that can hold no water, we start on a course of unfailing disaster and loss.

Literal obedience to God is indispensable to those who would carry his messages. It was a fit and proper answer that the prophet, in the first instance, gave the king. He rightly told Jeroboam that he must abide by the exact terms of his commission, and that the bribe of half of Jeroboam's house would not induce him to tarry even so long as to take a meal at the royal table. This minute and rigorous obedience stood out in striking contrast to the conduct of Jeroboam. God is exact and requires exact obedience.

1 KINGS 13:11-19

Led Astray by a False Messenger. The unnamed prophet from Judah had received distinct instructions not to eat bread nor drink water while on his divinely-commissioned errand. He was therefore justified in refusing the royal invitation; and it would have been well with him had he also refused the invitation of the old prophet, who followed him with the persistent invitation to return with him to his house. But the younger prophet failed, because the older man professed to speak by divine warrant and because the invitation chimed in with his own inclinations. As he sat there under the oak, tired and hungry, he was only too willing to believe that the prophet's message was true, although it was altogether contrary to his own impression.

When God has spoken to us, let us not dare to turn aside on the advice of others, however good they seem, even though their proposals may be draped with a show of religious phraseology. God does not say Yea or Nay; but all his commands, like all his promises, are Yea and Amen in Christ. In him is no variableness, nor shadow cast by turning.

1 KINGS 13:20-34

Sign upon Sign Unheeded. There is a tragic note in this paragraph. The man of God had performed God's errand bravely and well, and his words were verified by the result; but he perished as a castaway. See 1 Cor. 9:27. If only he had obeyed God's word, as it came directly to himself, he might have been entrusted with many similar errands; but "Alas, my brother!" was a true elegy on the part of the man who had led to his downfall. How careful we should be never to dissuade a young soul from some heroic purpose which has formed itself in his imagination! Too many young men have perished on the threshold of their lifework because older prophets have cried, "Spare thyself; have mercy on thy flesh."

God never goes back on his first instructions. If he has clearly spoken to your soul, refuse to take your marching orders from others. No man, however aged or holy, has any right to intrude into the sacred dealings of God and the individual disciple. We may always detect the false voice, because its suggestions so exactly chime in with the weakness of our nature, in its desire to eat bread, drink water, and enjoy the society of our fellows.

1 KINGS 14:1-16

The Blind Prophet Sees Jeroboam's Doom. How blind we become when we sin against our conscience! Each act of willful sin puts another shade on the window of the soul. "Their foolish heart was darkened," Rom. 1:21. Surely if the prophet were able to predict the issue of this sickness, he would be able to penetrate the mother's disguise, although she brought only the gifts of a poor peasant woman. Jeroboam had devised this ruse, partly because he did not wish the nation to know that he was consulting a prophet of Jehovah—an act which might invalidate his new temple and the calves, and also because he wanted to get a more favorable answer than that which he anticipated in case the prophet recognized the inquirer. We may disguise ourselves as we will, but we cannot cheat God, and no dissembling can ever turn away the arrow that speeds straight to the guilty heart.

Jewish historians say that the exception was made in Abijah's case, v. 13, because he interceded with his father that all Israelites who wished might be allowed to go to the feasts at Jerusalem without being penalized. There is always discrimination in the divine judgments. How often God has brought beautiful lives out of foul surroundings, as the pure lily cup out of a muddy pond!

1 KINGS 14:17-31

South Rivals North in Sinning. Rehoboam's mother's name signifies *beauty*, and she may have been attractive in her person; but we are twice told that she was an Ammonitess, as if to emphasize the disastrous influence which she exercised over her son, vv. 21, 31. In the earlier part of the chapter, there are tender reminiscences of David—that he kept God's commandments, followed him with all his heart, did what was right in his eyes. How dear is such a life to God! How he keeps it in remembrance! How he holds it up to veneration, notwithstanding a serious lapse! But this only serves by contrast to make the corruption of later times the more terrible.

The national sins compelled God to withdraw his environing protection. He no longer went out with their armies. The deterioration in the metal from gold to brass is an apt illustration of how the fine gold of character had become dimmed, Lam. 4:1. To what may we not come if the grace of God is withdrawn! Well may the apostle beseech us not to receive it in vain! When corruption sets in, the best and ripest becomes the worst. Traditional goodness —that of our parents—cannot save the soul from the inevitable drift. We must have our personal anchorage in God!

1 KINGS 15:1-15

A Better Day Dawns. Again we meet with those references to David that we found in the previous chapter. See vv. 3, 4, 5, 11. His name lingers as sweet fragrance in the air, or as the afterglow of sundown. But Abijam's mother was descended from Absalom, and it is hardly surprising that the unhappy ancestry conflicted with the other holier influence. Though the lamp burned low, however, it was not entirely extinguished. What a pathetic touch that is in v. 5! One moment of passion may be a long regret to God and to the soul! Yet there is forgiveness with God, that he may be feared, Psa. 130:4.

For Asa's reign, we must turn to the book of Chronicles, where further evidence is given of his truly religious character—at least during the earlier portion of his rule. Even his grandmother was removed from her position. Compare vv. 2 and 10; the words "father" and "mother" are used loosely, as may be seen in v. 3. On the whole, Asa's policy was directed to the overthrow of the heathen worship, but he seems to have shrunk from a root-and-branch extermination of the evil, v. 14. The result was personal deterioration and the springing up again of idolatry. Our Lord asks us never to compromise. The right hand that offends must be cut off. The brood of the viper must be stamped out to the last egg.

1 KINGS 15:16-34

Warring Brethren. We obtain a fuller view of the events described in the earlier part of this passage by reference to 2 Chron. 16:1-6. Asa's early piety, which shone out in his drastic purging of idolatry and of the corruptions which sprang up like fungi on a damp soil, cannot be questioned. Strange that such a man who by faith in God had driven back Zerah's formidable invasion should in later years succumb to the craven methods of mere expediency in his conflict with Baasha.

This league with Ben-hadad arose from unbelief. Even true believers are sometimes hard pressed to maintain their integrity, because the trials of faith tend to increase. When Peter looked at the rising billows, his heart became troubled and he began to sink. To Asa's alliance with this heathen king may be traced the beginning of the downfall of both kingdoms—of the ten tribes and of Judah. Palestine was no longer a neutral state, but became involved in the political combinations of the time. Those that honor God are honored, 1 Sam. 2:30; those that put their trust elsewhere rue it all their days.

1 KINGS 16:1-14

Executioners of Evildoers. A noble figure crosses the canvas for a moment. It is Jehu, the son of Hanani, shining like a star in the night. No age has been without its prophets; no life, however abandoned, has been without some remonstrating voice; no soul goes over the falls without a warning cry. And these messages, answering to the voice of conscience within, reveal the pitying love of the Father, not willing that any should perish, Ezek. 18:23. Hanani, Jehu's father, had been a prophet, 2 Chron. 16:7, and Jehu held the same office for a long period, 2 Chron. 19:2; 20:34.

Baasha died in peace and was buried in state. But such an end is not the end and points forward to another life, since God is God, Psa. 17:14, 15. Elah and the remainder of the royal house were cut off by Zimri, and the extermination was so complete that none of his avengers were left. But Zimri, after a reign of seven days, was similarly treated, 2 Kings 9:31. Seven days are long enough to test a man, and in that brief space Zimri found time to walk in the way of Jeroboam and his sin, vv. 15, 19. Such is the course of this world. Happy are they who, amid political convulsion, live the life of the quiet in the land, 1 Thess. 4:11, and receive the kingdom that cannot be moved, Heb. 12:27.

1 KINGS 16:15-28

Persistence in Sinful Ways. These chapters afford a dreary record of apostasy and revolution, of idolatry and national disaster. Perhaps the great mass of the people—the peasantry—were not greatly affected by these dynastic changes, though severe judgments of famine and drought were soon to make the nation realize what an evil and bitter thing it is to desert the Fountain of living waters for broken cisterns that can hold no water, Jer. 2:13. Four times in this chapter we meet the phrase, "provoke to anger," vv. 7, 13, 26, 33. To idolatry was added intemperance, v. 9, and the fruit was suicide, anarchy, and civil war, vv. 18, 21, 22. But great as these evils were, they were to be surpassed, v. 30.

The one sufficient bulwark against universal anarchy is the maintenance of true religion. People talk with glib tongues against the Puritan conscience and demand the secularization of the Lord's day, but they are surely imperiling the stability and order of the commonwealth. More than is ordinarily realized are the relations between man and man affected by the relation between the nation and God. The writings of Voltaire helped to bring on the French Revolution, while the religious revivals of the eighteenth century, both in England and in America, contributed greatly to solid national progress.

1 KINGS 16:29—17:7

Sin's Climax Summons Jehovah's Prophet. From the beginning of his reign, Ahab set aside both the First and the Second Commandment. His marriage with Jezebel, the young and beautiful Sidonian princess, plunged him and his kingdom into yet deeper darkness. In addition to Jeroboam's calves the worship of Baal, the sun-god, was shamelessly introduced, and his temple was served by hundreds of priests. The inspired artist does not hesitate to paint with Rembrandt colors, and the illustrious glory of Elijah shows clearly against the dark background. The darkest hour precedes the dawn; the keenest pain ushers in birth. First Ahab and Jezebel, then Elijah.

Gilead was far from court or temple—God trains his workers in his own school. The prophet's name—"Jehovah is my strength"—suggests where he abode and whence he derived his power. He stood before God for the uniting and the uplifting of a divided people. The drought was the result of prayer. Elijah felt that nothing less could arrest king and people, Jas. 5:17. The man who stands before God is not afraid to stand before Ahab. Now and again God bids his servants hide themselves toward the sunrise, but in these periods of enforced seclusion he makes himself responsible for their supplies.

1 KINGS 17:8-16

The Jar of Meal That Wasted Not. Even at Cherith we cannot be exempt from trial, and it is hard to sit beside a gradually dwindling brook. But God always provides. None of them that trust in him shall be desolate. Whether the visible agents be ravens, or a poor heathen widow ready to perish, it matters little. God's majestic "I have commanded" is enough. Whether it be ordinary or extraordinary, natural or supernatural, through Jew or Gentile, God's purpose does not tarry.

Gentile help supplied what Israel might not give, Luke 4:25, 26. God uses the weak and foolish things as well as those which are not, 1 Cor. 1:28. Yet there were noble qualities in this woman. She did not complain, but went at once for the water; she was generous and hospitable, and believed that God would supply their need. How little did she realize the greatness of her reward, Matt. 10:41, 42! But her faith was great. She stood the test of making Elijah's cake first, believing that afterward there would be enough for herself and her son. Though she little understood it, she had within her a spark of the same fire that burned in the soul of the great prophet; and therefore, when we all stand in our lot at the end of the days, Dan. 12:13, her portion will be with the great prophets and heroes of faith.

1 KINGS 17:17-24

New Life for the Dead. It must have been a severe trial to Elijah's faith, first to note the gradual diminishing of the brook, then the abject poverty of the woman to whom he was directed, and finally the illness and death of her child. But through it all, he held fast to the living God. It was still, "O Lord *my* God," v. 20. Affliction is no proof that we are off the path of duty. The way of obedience is sometimes paved with thorns, as every servant of God has discovered. But the difficulties only give room for the exercise of greater faith, and reveal more of the delivering power of the Almighty Friend.

The true physician bends over the little child of the poor, eager to save a human life; but his power is limited. To faith and prayer, however, other forces are available which accomplish what no skill or medicine can. When we have confessed and put away sin which the hour of anguish has brought to light, room is made for the exercise of that divine power which is always within the reach of hands that are lifted without fear or doubting.

1 KINGS 18:1-15

"Behold, Elijah!" "The word of the Lord came" to Elijah on four successive occasions—17:2, 8; 18:1; 19:9. God has many things to say to us, if we will only listen. His word may find us in very different places and direct us to varied duties; but to live by it is to execute the perfect plan of life.

Obadiah was a good man, but weak. He did his best to shield the prophets and to keep the true light from becoming extinguished, v. 13. But court favor had corrupted him. He stood before Ahab, while Elijah stood before God. Our Lord said that "soft raiment" and the king's court go together, Luke 7:25; and in the enervating atmosphere of a palace, it is granted to very few to retain the spirit and power of Elijah or of the Baptist. Who would not rather be Elijah than Obadiah! Elijah dared confront Ahab as the troubler of Israel, while Obadiah daily feared for his own life. Elijah rooted up idolatry, while Obadiah endeavored only to check its excesses. Obadiah sought grass for the royal steeds, but Elijah's prayer brought the rain. Let us dare to stand for God, though we stand alone!

1 KINGS 18:16-29

The God That Answereth Not. "The God that answereth by fire, let him be God." We are thrilled as we read these words. Our altars stand unkindled, our sacrifices are unconsumed, our churches do not witness the descending of the holy flame, our sermons are damp tinder. It ought not so to be. The Baptist said that our Lord would baptize with the Holy Spirit as by fire, Matt. 3:11, and Jesus himself taught that he came to kindle fire on the earth, Luke 12:49. The seven lamps burn evermore before the throne, Rev. 4:5. It was as fire that the Holy Spirit fell on the sitting group in the upper room—*sitting* because they had reached an end of praying, and were now only waiting for the fulfillment of the promise, Acts 2:2, 3.

Nothing is needed more absolutely than the answer by fire. There are many who, like the prophets of Baal, endeavor to kindle it. But when prevented from putting their own false fire into the stack of wood, they are paralyzed. The frantic entreaties, the self-inflicted wounds, the monotonous chant are insufficient. They are carnal and arouse only the worst emotions. Spiritual conditions have to be fulfilled, as Elijah showed; then God bears witness "by signs and wonders" and by gifts of the Holy Spirit, according to his own will.

1 KINGS 18:30-40

"The God That Answereth by Fire." Too many "halt," or limp, between two opinions. The altar of consecration to Christ has been thrown down, v. 30. The worship of Baal, which stands for creature-energy, has secretly stolen away our allegiance from him who is very jealous of any strange affinities; and as the necessary result, our heart is drought-smitten and our sphere of service is like a parched land. The idolatrous priests had everything in their favor, for at noon the sun-god was on his throne; but there was no voice. It is an awful thing when a man listens for his god to speak and there is no reply!

Elijah built again the ruined altar which for long years had stood on Carmel's height, 19:10. Let us build again the altars of personal consecration, of family piety, and of national religion. Elijah prayed; as the apostle expressed it, Jas. 5:17, he put all the passion of his mighty nature into prayer. As a result, because they had been shown to be deceivers, he destroyed the prophets of Baal with a ruthless hand. These are the conditions of revival and refreshing. Let any church give itself to consecration, fervent prayer, and the expulsion of wrong, and there need be no anxiety as to the result; there will be an abundance of rain.

1 KINGS 18:41—19:8

Exaltation and Depression. When the priests had been executed, the quick ear of the prophet detected the hurrying rain clouds. Note the contrast between Ahab and the prophet. The one ascended from the Kishon gorge to eat and drink in his pavilion until the darkened heavens made him drive post-haste to Jezreel; the other went up to pray! Which do we care for most—to eat and drink or to pray? God help us! The answer that our hearts utter is far from satisfactory. But what praying was this! So humble, so intense, so expectant. Six times the servant came down from the spur, saying, "There is nothing," and a seventh time he was sent back to watch the Mediterranean skyline,—this time, not in vain!

But why that sudden change to despair? Was it the overstrain of that day on Carmel, which induced a terrible reaction? Was it that swift run from Carmel to Jezreel, in front of Ahab's fiery steeds? Was it that threat of Jezebel? She, at least, was neither awed nor checkmated by the massacre of her favorite priests. Did he lose sight of God in that dark hour? Elijah was but mortal! His feet had almost gone; his steps had well-nigh slipped, Psa. 73:2.

1 KINGS 19:9-14

Learning How God Works. God knew how to treat his servant, resting beneath the juniper tree. He steeped his nature in refreshing sleep, fed his exhausted energies, caused angel hands to minister to him, and finally conducted him across the desert to that sacred mountain where Moses in the old time had stood in the divine audience-chamber. There the forces of Nature spoke to Elijah's varying moods. In the fire, the earthquake, and the tempest, he heard the voices of his own soul. They expressed what he would say, and relieved him in the expression. Then the accents of the "still small voice" fell upon his ear, calming, quieting, soothing. Best of all, the voice of God commissioned him once more with the words, "Go, return." The vacated post was open still; the crown of the lifework could be worthily placed; the gate was open through which he might serve the land he loved.

Often we lie down on the desert sands and think that death is near. But it is not so. God does not judge us by our moods. He knows the faithful heart that is true to him, and he wants to bestow the crown of life. Not the winding-sheet of the desert sands, but the chariot of fire to the Homeland was to be the portion of God's faithful prophet.

1 KINGS 19:15-21

Appointing Jehovah's Instruments. Elijah was never reinstated in quite the position that he had occupied before his fatal flight. True, he was bidden to return, and work was given him to do. But that work consisted in anointing three men who were to share the ministry which he might have fulfilled if only he had been true to his opportunities and faithful to his God. God's work must go forward, if not by us, then by others brought in to fill our place.

Hazael, king of Syria; Jehu, the rude captain; and Elisha, the young farmer. Each was as different as possible from the others; yet each had his special sphere in dealing with the idolatries and impurities that were destroying the chosen race. God's nets are not all constructed with the same size of meshes. Men may escape some of the bigger ones, but be caught by the smaller ones. But God so orders the lives of men that once at least each encounters a mesh that cannot be evaded. What a comfort it is to think that God is at work in the world, and that while statistics tell a sad tale, there may still be 7,000 secret disciples for every Elijah!

1 KINGS 20:1-15

Boasting Before the Battle. Ben-hadad's insolent demand indicated how low Israel had sunk. The worship of Jezebel's gods had wrought moral degeneracy. Let us never forget this lesson. When national religion fades and our churches are deserted; when the Bible loses place in education, and family prayer fades out of the home, dry rot and decay eat away the strength of the national heart.

Ahab's answer was better than might have been expected from such a man, but it would have amounted to little beyond a stalwart boast if there had not been other influences at work on the behalf of the chosen race. It may be that at this crisis, ceaseless prayer was being offered in the schools of the prophets. Elijah, certainly, was not silent, but on mountain heights or by the Cherith brook was no doubt pouring out his mighty soul. The advent of a prophet, v. 13, unasked, was a harbinger of good. Notice how God's loving-kindness follows us into a far country. He does not forget, but woos us back. His tools of help, however, are not what we should expect, but ever the weakest and least likely, that no flesh should glory, 1 Cor. 1:27.

1 KINGS 20:16-30

The God Both of Hills and Valleys. What is God to us? Is he only the God of the hills? We expect religion to serve us when we come to the great summits of experience. There are times of rapture and of vision when we seem naturally to stand with God on the holy mountains. We have our Moriah, our Pisgah, our Tabor, our Hermon. But is that all?

No! God is with us in the valleys. When we descend into the valley of weeping, Psa. 84:6, the valley of the shadow of death, the valley of obscurity and loneliness, the valley of conflict, we can say with the psalmist, "Thou art with me," Psa. 23:4. Most of us, perhaps, spend the larger part of life in the valleys, walking among commonplace duties. Let us see to it that in these shadowed days we walk in close companionship with the Divine Friend; that when the path ascends and the mountain breeze is on our faces and the view widens, we may stand with God on our high places as with hinds' feet. See Hab. 3:19.

1 KINGS 20:31-43

Losing the Man God Put into His Hand. Ahab's easygoing good nature was criminal, and indicated the evil that was enervating and cankering his heart. Whatever may have been his private feelings and sympathy, it is plain that these had no right to control his action as king when national interests were at stake. The judge may be subject to tender compassion toward those on whom his office requires him to pass sentence, but he should be governed by consideration of the good of all. This unwise clemency on the part of Ahab resulted, in later days, in Israel's suffering at the hand of Syria.

"Busy here and there!" It is true of us all. We are so occupied that we have hardly time to think. We do not realize the opportunities which are placed in our hands and which, if not made immediate use of, depart never to return. The bald head of departing opportunity, said the Greeks, has not even one lock of hair by which we can catch it and drag it back. Let us be diligent in the King's business, remembering that to him we must render an account.

1 KINGS 21:1-16

Breaking Three Commandments. From a worldly point of view Naboth might have done a good stroke of business by selling his estate to Ahab. A royal price and assured favor might have been his, but he had a conscience! Above the persuasive tones of the monarch's offer sounded the voice of God: "The land shall not be sold for ever: for the land is mine," Lev. 25:23. See Num. 36:7; Ezek. 46:18.

Ahab knew perfectly well that Jezebel could not give him the property of another except by foul means, but he took pains not to inquire. Though the direct orders for Naboth's death did not come from him, yet by his silence he was an accomplice and an accessory; and divine justice penetrates all such specious excuses. God holds us responsible for wrongs which we do not arrest, though we have the power. The crime was blacker because of the pretext of religion, as suggested by a fast. See also 2 Kings 9:26. The blood of murdered innocence cries to God and his requital, though delayed, is inevitable. See Rev. 6:9, 10.

1 KINGS 21:17-29

Humbled by the Prophet's Rebuke. Once before, when his presence had been urgently needed, Elijah had fled for his life. But there was no vacillation now. He dared face not only Ahab, but his two ruthless captains. He acted as an incarnate conscience. Ahab had perhaps solaced himself with the idea that he was not a murderer. How should *he* know what Jezebel had done with his seal! But the crime was not

1 KINGS

Jezebel's alone; it was his also. "Thus saith the Lord, Hast *thou* killed?"

Though the king knew it not, Elijah was his best friend, while Jezebel was his direst foe. Sin distorts everything. Let us not be surprised if men hate us and count us their enemies when we charge them with their sins! "Blessed are ye, when men shall revile you, . . . and shall say all manner of evil against you falsely." Each of the woes which the prophet foretold came true. Ahab postponed their fulfillment for some three years by a partial repentance; but at the end of that time he went back to his evil ways, and every item was fulfilled. God is faithful. He bears witness to his witnesses. His mills grind slowly, but they grind to powder!

1 KINGS 22:1-12

Entering into a New Partnership. It seems strange that so good a man as the king of Judah should have entered into such an alliance. It began with the marriage of Jehoram, son of Jehoshaphat, and Athaliah, Ahab's daughter; but it was a terrible descent from the high standing of a servant of Jehovah for Jehoshaphat to say to a practically heathen king: "I am as thou art, my people as thy people, my horses as thy horses." Partnerships like this, either in marriage or in business, are not only absolutely forbidden, but are disastrous in their ultimate outworking. "Be ye not unequally yoked together with unbelievers," 2 Cor. 6:14.

Micaiah stands out in splendid contrast. His was the proud honor of being hated by Ahab, as was John the Baptist by Herod. But the prophet in his dungeon, with the bread and water of affliction, was a happier man by far than the king, though clad in royal robes and held in high respect. Is it not clear that Ahab, in his heart of hearts, feared this man of God? We shall see that he put off his royal robes and dressed in a common uniform, that he might evade the death that Micaiah predicted as his fate. Of course it did not avail. God cannot be evaded in that way. His purpose is irresistible.

1 KINGS 22:13-28

"What Jehovah Saith . . . That Will I Speak." Ramoth was one of the cities of refuge, situated across the Jordan. The false prophets spake as they knew would please the king and gain the popular ear. But Micaiah did not hesitate to say that the spirit of a demon was making use of their lips for the utterance of beguiling falsehood. He was evidently speaking metaphorically. By an ironical method of speech he suggested that the voices of such prophets were not to be accepted as truth. He knew well enough God's living voice. In the silence and solitude of his prison, shut away from all the world besides, he had learned to detect the accent of truth, and could easily discriminate between it and the lying boasts of the false prophets. We must try the spirits, whether they be of God, 1 John 4:1. Beware of being beguiled by every voice that speaks in your heart. God's voice almost always calls you to take up the cross and stand alone against the crowd. It summons to the straight gate and the narrow way.

"Carry him back!" cried the king. He hated the man of God, as the thief dreads a watchdog. But better a thousand times be in that dungeon with Micaiah than faring sumptuously at Ahab's table. Do not hide yourself from the truth. Let it search, though it hurt you. It will save you from the unerring arrow.

1 KINGS 22:29-40

The Bow Executes God's Sentence. The cup of Ahab's sins was full, and the arrow executed divine retribution. Had Micaiah not spoken, men would have attributed this apparently chance arrow to misfortune; now, however, it became invested with quite another significance. There is no such thing as chance in this world. The bird does not fall to the ground, the arrow does not find its way to the heart, without a superintending Providence. Whether you live or die, your life is under the immediate supervision of the Almighty. In the battlefield, not a single bullet can hit your beloved, apart from the permitting providence of God. All is under law.

Put on the whole armor of God, that you may be able to stand in the evil day. Take the shield of faith, as covering your whole being, lest the joints of the armor open to the fiery darts of your foe. Watch and pray that you enter not into temptation. Note the contrast in the end of these men. The one went to his own place; no disguise could avert his doom. The other seems to have returned to God, v. 32 and 2 Chron. 18:31, and God gave him years of rest, victory, and prosperity, of which further details are given in 2 Chron. 19 and 20.

1 KINGS 22:41-53

"Broken Ships." Further details of Jehoshaphat's good reign are given in 2 Chron. 17—20. He made strenuous efforts to rid the land of the more obvious evils that disgraced it, though some of the abuses seemed too deeply rooted even for his strong hand, v. 43. The great defect

of Jehoshaphat's character was the ease with which he associated himself with Ahab and his family; for this, subsequent generations paid a heavy penalty, 2 Kings 11.

Jehoshaphat attempted to reopen sea commerce with Ophir, and entered into partnership with Ahaziah to build ships in Solomon's old port of Ezion-geber, to make the circuit of Africa *en route* for Spain. But as we learn from 2 Chron. 20:37, a prophet of Jehovah remonstrated with him for renewing the alliance with the king of Israel. The storm that shattered the ships on the rocks before they set sail gave evidence of the displeasure of the Almighty. Let us beware of these alliances and partnerships with the ungodly. Sooner or later they meet with disaster. God blocks our path and defeats our plans; and if only we are led to repentance, our broken ships may give us cause for thanksgiving in eternity.

THE SECOND BOOK OF
KINGS
THE DECLINE & FALL OF ISRAEL AND JUDAH

I. FROM THE REIGN OF AHAZIAH TO THE FALL OF SAMARIA
  2 Kings 1–17; 18:9–12
  A. The reign of Ahaziah. *1:1–18*
  B. The translation of Elijah *2*
  C. The work of Elisha *3:1—9:10*
   1. Victory of Israel and Judah over Moab *3*
   2. The widow's oil multiplied *4:1–7*
   3. The son of the Shunammite restored to life *4:8–44*
   4. The healing of Naaman *5*
   5. The discomfiture of the Syrians *6:1–23*
   6. The siege of Samaria *6:24—7:20*
   7. The property of the Shunammite restored *8:1–6*
   8. Elisha and Hazael *8:7–15*
      (Reigns of Jehoram and Ahaziah in Judah, and Jehoram in Israel) *8:16–29*
   9. Elisha and the anointing of Jehu *9:1–10*
  D. The reign of Jehu *9:11—10:36*
  E. The reign of Joash in Judah *11, 12*
  F. The reigns of Jehoahaz and Jehoash in Israel and Amaziah in Judah *13:1—14:20*
  G. The reign of Jeroboam II *14:23–29*
  H. The reign of Azariah in Judah, and the reigns of Zachariah, Shallum, Menahem, Pekahiah, and Pekah in Israel *14:21, 22; , 15:1–29*
  I. The reign of Hoshea in Israel, and the reigns of Jotham and Ahaz in Judah *15:30—16:20*
  J. The fall of Samaria *17; 18:9–12*

II. FROM THE FALL OF SAMARIA TO THE FALL OF JERUSALEM   *18—25*
   A. The reign of Hezekiah   *18:1-8, 13-37; 19; 20*
   B. The reign of Manasseh   *21*
   C. The reign of Josiah   *22:1—23:30*
   D. Egypt surrenders Judah to Babylon   *23:31—24:9*
   E. The fall of Jerusalem   *24:10—25:30*

INTRODUCTION

The Second Book of Kings is a continuation of the First. It records the reigns of fifteen kings in Judah and of eleven kings in Israel. In Judah the dynasty of David continued to the end, while in Israel there were nine changes of dynasty.

The northern kingdom maintained an unbroken course of idolatry, until the nation was ripe for destruction. The end came in 722 B.C., when Samaria was taken by the Assyrians. Judah continued her course for nearly 150 years longer. But in spite of the efforts of prophets and good kings, the tide of idolatry could not be stayed, and Jerusalem fell before the Babylonians, 586 B.C. Nothing but the Exile could avail to purify the nation and restore the spirit of true worship.

COMMENTARY

2 KINGS 1:1–8

A Message from the True God. The king's accident was probably due to the giving way of the balustrade that surrounded the roof of his palace. The Law expressly provided that this latticework should be made very strong to obviate just such an occurrence, Deut. 22:8. Let us be careful to maintain the barriers of good custom, whether of purity, or total abstinence, or the observance of the Lord's day. In this manner we shall preserve our children and ourselves from peril. All good habits are strong battlements.

To reach Ekron the messengers must pass Jerusalem. What a direct insult to Jehovah! Even Ahab had some regard for Micaiah, but Ahaziah went beyond his father in openly flouting the religion of David and Moses. In the interests of the whole nation, this insult could not be passed over in silence, and at God's bidding Elijah appeared upon the scene. He rebuked the messengers for their idolatrous quest and told them that the king would surely die. They returned with the report that a man clad in a hairy garment had met them, and had said that the king would not recover. It was enough. The apprehensions of Ahaziah's guilty conscience were confirmed, and he said, "It is Elijah the Tishbite!"

2 KINGS 1:9–18

Consuming Fire. An awful fate overtook the first two captains; but it must be noted that they were extremely violent and arrogant in their behavior and speech. The altered tone of the last captain wrought an instant alteration in the prophet's attitude and response. That there was no personal malice in Elijah is clear from his willingness to accompany the third captain into the royal presence. Our Lord expressly cautioned his followers from attempting to imitate this episode. We belong to another dispensation, which savors of forbearance and meekness. See Luke 9:54–56.

On a former day Jezebel's message made the prophet flee; but now he does not hesitate to pass through the crowded streets of the capital and to enter the palace of the king. Elijah was dwelling in the secret place of the Most High and standing before Jehovah, as aforetime. His faith was able to avail itself of the panoply of God. He quenched the violence of fire, escaped the edge of the sword, and out of weakness was made strong. Let us admire the loving forbearance of God who restores the wavering ones, brings them up from the grave, holds them as stars in his right hand, Rev. 1:16, and uses them once more in his glorious service.

2 KINGS 2:1-12

Fitted to Succeed His Master. We are at a loss whether to admire most the humility of Elijah or the pertinacity of Elisha. The humility of the former is very beautiful. An ordinary man would have blazoned abroad the honor to be conferred upon him. He would have taken care to secure witnesses, that it might not be unrecognized and unknown. Instead of this, Elijah sought to be alone, that no eye might see the chariot sent specially from Heaven for his conveyance.

But the determination of Elisha is equally beautiful, and only they who stand such tests can behold and inherit the things which God hath prepared for them that love him. At Gilgal, Beth-el, and Jericho, Elisha might have stayed his steps at the call of indolence or love of ease; but the divine promptings would not allow him to remain. Do not allow yourself to be put back by apparent rebuffs. The Divine Spirit is only testing your mettle. Be ready with your request when he says: "Ask what I shall do for thee." But you must have communion with the Spirit if you would have the double portion of the eldest son. They two went on; they two stood by Jordan; they two went over on dry ground; they two still went on and talked. Apply that to your intercourse with your Savior!

2 KINGS 2:13-25

Elijah's Spirit on Elisha. We, too, may have a double portion of Elijah's spirit, but everything depends on the purity of our hearts. Only the pure in heart can see, and if we can see into the spiritual it is proof that our hearts are pure enough to be used by the Holy Spirit. Had Elisha been unable to see the translation of his friend, his nature would have been shown to be gross and sensual, and how should such a one have God's supreme gift?

When we receive this power, we must begin to use it at once. Whether we feel possessed of a fresh accession of spiritual dynamic or not is immaterial. We must reckon that we have received, and must proceed to use; and as we make the attempt, the parting water will prove not only to ourselves, but to others, the reality of our experience. The reception of spiritual power is a quiet, secret act, known only to God and the soul; but the results are manifest to all. Hear these young men talk! Has God ever been known to take up a man and then cast him away on valley or mountain? That is not his way of dealing with those whom he loves and would honor.

2 KINGS 3:1-12

An Unwise Alliance. Jehoram's reign over the ten tribes was marked by some measures of reform. He discountenanced Baal worship, though, in defiance of the Second Commandment, he clave to Jeroboam's calves. Therefore, Jehoshaphat was ill-advised to enter into alliance with him. The servant of Jehovah had no right to say to such a man, "I am as thou art," etc. He had said this before, and narrowly escaped with his life. It was very bad, therefore, to repeat a policy which was already discredited. See 1 Kings 22:4.

How often we rush into alliances and undertake engagements without prayer for guidance, and begin to seek God only when faced with disappointment! In the day of sore trouble, when it seemed likely that kings and troops would perish in the waterless desert, Judah sought divine help. But it was foolish and wrong to charge the Lord with their disasters, as in v. 10. When the curtains of night are drawn, sailors steer by the stars; and often it is the pressure of dark trials that drives men to seek the advice and help of the servants of God. They know where to find such helpers when they want them, though in their prosperity they ignore and deride. He who is willing to pour water, as a servant, will not be inflated with pride when three kings visit him.

2 KINGS 3:13-27

Defeat and a Desperate Sacrifice. Jehoshaphat, though erring, was still God's child, and deliverance came to him. The heights of our senseless folly and the depths of our waywardness will not succeed in severing us from God's love. Elisha used the very words of Elijah, v. 14 and 1 Kings 17:1. Notice how men of different mold and mission, the Elijahs and the Elishas, derive their inspiration and strength in the same way. As a great Christian general put it, "Every morning I stand at attention before my Maker." Note the effect of music in soothing the soul, v. 15.

In all God's gifts there is need for our cooperation. He alone can send the water, but we must trench the ground. Our expectant faith creates the capacity to receive God's gifts; but when we have gone to our limit and the valley is filled with ditches, he is able to do exceeding abundantly beyond. The answer came at the hour of morning prayer, and probably at the prophet's intercession, 1 Kings 8:44. God's answers are often too deep and inward to give outward sign. There is sound of neither wind nor rain; but our prayers are answered to the

2 KINGS 4:1-7

full. Many of the points in this narrative—notably v. 27—have been corroborated by recent explorations in Moab.

2 KINGS 4:1-7

Every Vessel Filled. Elisha's ministry was not startling. It was redemptive and constructive. Widows came to him for help against their creditors; mothers appealed on behalf of their children; poison was rendered powerless; and loaves were multiplied. Do not judge power by the noise it makes. The dew excites less notice than a thunderstorm, but it may be more refreshing. A life filled with quiet ministry will bear comparison with one whose outbursts of passion are followed by reaction and depression. Twelve hours of daily sunshine, year in and year out, are preferable to the summer of daylight in the Arctic Circle, followed by months of midnight.

When our need is urgent and we spread it before God, the question is never about the amount of oil, but of the empty vessels. We fear that there will not be enough oil; God is concerned lest we fail to bring sufficient vessels to hold all he wants to give. The oil was multiplied in the pouring, as the meal of the other widow was increased in the spending. God's oil will never be exhausted so long as we can receive and impart. According to our faith will it be done. It is not a question of how much God can give, but how much we can use.

2 KINGS 4:8-24

Entertaining a Prophet. The real man needs a very small supply of outward comfort, because his life is hid in God. It does not consist in the abundance of things that he possesses, but in faith, love, and hope. What a noble testimony it would be to our character if people who saw us going to and fro became convinced that "this is a holy man of God," v. 9!

Sunstroke in the tropics is a frequent cause of death, Psa. 121:6. When a child is taken sick, it is the mother who is the best comforter; but there are limits to a mother's power to help. This woman of Shunem must be referred to in Hebrews 11:35. She was so sure of the life-restoring prayers of the great prophet that she did not feel it necessary to tell her husband what had befallen. Why should she grieve him, when the child would soon be given back to them! In noble confidence she dared to say that all would be well, and God did not disappoint nor fail. Shunem was fifteen miles from Carmel, and there was not an inch of the road which was not covered by the mother's splendid faith that God would make all grace abound toward her.

2 KINGS 4:25-37

The Dead Boy Restored to Life. There is fine illustration in this chapter of a noble reverence for goodness, of a good man's gratitude, and of the large reward that never fails those who deal kindly with God's children.

It is not enough to put the staff, even though it be the prophet's, on the cold, sweet face of a child. Our doctrine and precept may be quite good and straight, but something more is needed. There must be not a staff, not a servant, not an intermediary, but ourselves, our heart against the heart that is still, our lips against the dear, cold lips. It is as we give ourselves to the children, imparting our tenderest, strongest sympathy, that new life will come to them.

Walk to and fro in your house! Shut the door on yourself and the child! Pray to the Lord! Give yourself to the great work of saving the soul from death! Let the mother be praying in the room downstairs! Call to the little soul to awake and live! Your faith and prayer cannot fail of an answer.

2 KINGS 4:38-44

"They Shall Eat." This miracle, it has been justly remarked, is a faint foreshadowing of our Lord's marvelous feeding of thousands with even scantier materials. As Elijah was a type of John the Baptist, so Elisha was, in many respects, a type of our Lord. In his peaceful, human life, his mild and gentle character, his constant travels, his many miracles of mercy, he resembles, more than any other prophet, the Messiah.

We have also, in this miracle, the great province of the gospel to counteract the ancient curse of a forfeited Paradise and meet the hunger of the soul. The grace of God will turn an evil into a blessing and multiply a little to feed a multitude. See Mark 16:18; Psa. 132:15. Can there be any doubt that to faith and prayer resources are open which are closed to all else? If Nature contained all we need, ready to our hand, of what use would prayer be? The very injunctions to prayer and the success of those who have prayed prove that God has forces available which can operate in behalf of those who love him and are the called according to his purpose.

2 KINGS 5:1-14

The Cure for Leprosy. From Assyrian monuments we learn that at this period Syria regained her independence from under the yoke of Assyria, and probably it was during this struggle that Naaman gained his great victories. Note the suggestiveness of the phrase, "The Lord had given," which teaches that the hand of God was guiding heathen as well as Hebrew history. The realm of God's providence is as long as time, and as broad as the earth.

The destruction of this poor child's home and her captivity must, at the time, have seemed to be an unexplainable disaster from which there could be no relief; and yet it enabled her to bring about a great deliverance, which has shone on the page of Scripture, giving inspiration to tens of thousands. She rose above her sorrows, and by faith wrought victory out of defeat. By preferring his own way to God's, Naaman came dangerously near returning home unhealed. We must adopt God's method of salvation, however humbling to our pride. "I thought," will wreck us; "To thee, O Lamb of God, I come," will save us. Note the combination of a warrior's strength with the flesh of a little child, strength married to purity and simplicity.

2 KINGS 5:15-27

The Penalty of Greed. Naaman was so grateful that he came twenty miles out of his way to render thanks to the man of God, bringing a great sum as a gift. Notice his whole-souled desire to worship Jehovah, as shown in his fear lest his official connection with idolatry might be held to compromise him; and in his ready beneficence toward Gehazi, who, he supposed, had come in Elisha's name. All these are symptoms of a noble soul on whom the Holy Spirit had been at work. We are here reminded of Cornelius, Naaman's counterpart in the New Testament, Acts 10:1. What a comfort it is to believe that God has been influencing men like this in all the centuries, fashioning them, though they knew him not, till the hour arrived when he spoke to them through prophet or apostle.

Gehazi is the sad counterpart of Judas. Like the traitor, he revealed the hardening effect that association with pure goodness may have on the human conscience. If it does not produce life unto life, it issues in death unto death. The same sun that bleaches linen tans the hand that exposes it to the sunlight.

2 KINGS 6:1-13

The Servant of the Lord of Battles. To us, the first of these miracles may appear somewhat trivial, but we must remember the value of an iron axe-head at that time, the inconvenience and delay caused to the builders, and the slur accruing to religion if it were irreparably lost. The story shows how keen was the sympathy of the great prophet for a poor man overtaken by an ordinary trouble, and how ready Elisha was to seek the help of God to redress the mischief. See John 2:1-11. It is right to go to God about matters of this kind, as well as greater issues. What wonders faith can do! Hearts may be as heavy as lead at the bottom of the stream, but when a splinter of the cross of Calvary is inserted, they rise to the surface and swim.

The king believed that Elisha could wield superhuman power and knowledge, yet he thought to secure him with chariots and horses. He acknowledged that Elisha was a servant of the Most High God, yet he expected to take him captive by sending a mighty host! To such folly men descend when they begin to fight against the Most High!

2 KINGS 6:14-23

Opened Eyes. This is an acted parable of extreme beauty and suggestiveness. First, the stroke of trouble—swift, unlooked for, and apparently insurmountable; then the vivid contrast between the despair of the man of this world and the undaunted faith of him to whom the unseen is as real as the visible, because he possesses the second-sight of faith. Faith visualizes the unseen and eternal. A good man's intercession will still obtain spiritual vision for those who are spiritually blind. For many whom we love we may breathe Elisha's prayer, v. 17. Notice that the last sentence of v. 19 should begin with "and." The objective of the Syrian army was the king of Israel, and Elisha led them to him.

The lesson of this narrative is the proximity of God's guardian hosts. They are a cordon of protection to his children. The mountain is full of them. Elisha had seen them convoy his master home; he never expected that *he* would have the honor of their care. We do not need more help than is already within reach, but we do need grace to see the things that are freely given to us of God, John 4:10.

2 KINGS 6:24-33

The Dire Straits of Those Who Forsake God. This siege was the result of Ahab's foolish and misplaced leniency. See 1 Kings 20:42. The children are often called to suffer for the misdeeds and follies of their parents. Let us bear this in mind. "No man liveth to himself." Conduct yourself so that none may be offended through long years after you have passed from earth.

Apparently Elisha had counseled the king not to surrender, with the further assurance of deliverance on condition of his repentance. Jehoram therefore assumed the signs of penitence and contrition without the reality; and when the promised deliverance was not forthcoming, he put the blame of Israel's calamities on the prophet and vowed vengeance against his life. The elders were gathered with Elisha, perhaps for prayer, when Elisha apprised them of the advent of the king's messenger, with his announcement of the royal determination not to wait for God any longer. The trial of our patience is more precious than of gold, but how few of us can endure it!

2 KINGS 7:1-11

"Windows in Heaven." There is a sore famine just now over the whole world, a famine of God's Word. For some years the Church has felt its growing severity, but there are two classes within her borders: they who believe that God can open the windows of Heaven and pour down such a blessing that there will not be room to receive it, Mal. 3:10; and those who, like the unbelieving courtier, jeer at the hope of the saints. Let us answer the skeptic's "Can God?" by the positive achievements of faith.

When God sends blessings to his people, he rarely takes methods that we might expect. Rather, he chooses the weak and foolish things, yea, those that are not, to confound those that are, so as to prevent flesh from glorying in his presence. Whenever, in the first glint of the morning light, you discover the divine answer to your prayers, in all its plenteous abundance, do not keep the good news to yourself lest punishment overtake you, but be sure to bear the glad tidings to others. When it is a day of good tidings, be sure to act upon them in faith and patience, counting it a sin to hold your peace.

2 KINGS 7:12-20

The Prophet's Word Fulfilled. The lepers were first in the deserted camp. The abundance was awaiting the starving populace, but only a few outcasts tasted it. So Christ's wealth and unsearchable riches are for all, but often the outcasts gathered by the Salvation Army know more about them than the children of the Church. The cottager who early opens his window for his sick child knows more of the summer morning than does the millionaire who sleeps within curtained windows. But be sure you tell out what you know, else you sin against God and man. There is enough for all. To scatter is to increase.

Though this plenty had been predicted, it seemed too good to be believed. Send out your scouts, O Church of God! As the result of our Lord's victory at Calvary, the roads—north, south, east, and west—have been trodden by your fleeing foes and are strewn with spoil. But beware lest in the day of the Lord's deliverance you see with your eyes but are unable, through unbelief, to partake, Luke 13:28. Man's unbelief cannot hinder God's purpose, but it excludes the unbeliever, who perishes amid abundance.

2 KINGS 8:1-15

The Power behind the Throne. Nothing happens in our life or in the world apart from the divine appointment or permission. Behind every event and incident there is divine providence. The Shunammite who had done so much for Elisha was remembered and cared for years afterward. The King has a wonderful memory for those who fed him when he was hungry, and ministered to him when he was in need. "When saw we thee . . . ? Inasmuch as . . .," Matt. 25:37. This conversation between the king and Gehazi might have seemed an accident, but it was a providence. If we abide in the will of God, life will be sown with divine coincidences.

Here is another instance: Elisha comes to Damascus, evidently at God's bidding, just when Ben-hadad is sick. That sickness would not be mortal, but he would die prematurely from another cause. Would that men of God today had more of this gift of weeping over sinners and their destiny! No one resented hearing D. L. Moody talk of hell, because his voice always faltered. The prophet read Hazael's destiny from the Book of God, not from his set face, and how astounding it was! Ah, what depths of wickedness there are of which we are capable! "Keep back thy servant from presumptuous sins."

2 KINGS 8:16-29

Athaliah's Wicked Husband and Son. Jehoram's history furnishes an example of how an ill marriage may mar a man's life. He had a good father, but a bad wife, and the latter more strongly influenced him than the former, 2 Chron. 21:6. The fuller story of Jehoram's reign, and the apparent extinction of the royal family, is told in 2 Chronicles 22. But notice especially v. 19. The lamp was kept burning for David's sake, Psa. 132:17. Surely the grace of

God can keep that same lamp burning in the hearts of our children. A lamp, as we learned from the Chicago fire, may make a very great conflagration.

Ahaziah followed in the steps of his parents. What could be expected from the training of such a mother! Misled by her, he followed the dreary steps of Ahab. The close intimacy between the two houses led to alliance in war and a common fate. Little did Jehoshaphat realize all the evil that would result from his dealings with Ahab, 1 Kings 22:4. The story told in these pages is sad reading, but through it all God's purpose moves on. See Matt. 1:8. As a water lily grows from a muddy bottom, so the pure life of Christ came, on the human side, out of this family. God's purpose shall finally emerge from this present strife in a further revelation of the Son of man.

2 KINGS 9:1–13

The Avenger of Blood Anointed. Youth is always being called upon to gird up its loins and dare to fulfil its commissions without fear of man. We are not to tarry to hear what men say of us. The King's business requires haste. Do your work and flee, before the world can scare you by its threats or cajole you by its blandishments. You have one Master, one errand: do it, and get back into his presence!

God has his appointed instruments to carry out his plans, 1 Kings 19:17. The King will avenge his own elect, though he bear long with their oppressors. Sooner or later his sentence will be executed. His servants are often accounted mad, but whether we be beside ourselves, it is to God, 2 Cor. 5:13. Naturally his fellow-officers were astonished that Jehu should have dealings with one whose garb and bearing indicated his religious character. It is not usual for God's servants to penetrate a camp with such a message; and yet how striking would be the effect if only we could announce to the strong, swift-acting, vehement-hearted leaders of the age that a higher vocation awaited them than they had ever conceived, and that God's anointing was within their reach. "I have anointed thee king."

2 KINGS 9:14–26

"The Driving of Jehu." Many times in this chapter the question is asked, though in varying tones, "Is it peace?" The horsemen ask it of the furious driver; the king asks it of his captain; Jezebel asks it of the executioners of her son. Is not the human heart always asking the same question? If there is the slightest tremor in the air, the inquiry is at once started, "Will this make or mar our peace?" The heart of man is ill at ease. Deeply conscious that all is not right between itself and God, anxious that its efforts to reassure itself should not be disturbed, dreading lest an earthquake or a flood may detect the foundation on sand, the soul asks eagerly, "Is it peace?"

There can be no peace for man till he has put away the evil things associated with the name of Jezebel. Let us not forget those solemn words of the Holy Spirit, "I have against thee that thou sufferest that woman Jezebel." We have to do with One who searches the reins and hearts of professing Christians. See Rev. 2:18–29. We are all in danger of being seduced by the soft caresses of the world and the honeyed flattery of false professors. There is no peace apart from true repentance and faith in the Lord Jesus, Rom. 5:1.

2 KINGS 9:27–37

"The Word of the Lord by Elijah." Let us read again 1 Kings 21:23. How those words came back to the two men who had heard them from the lips of God's servant years before! God's mills grind slowly, but to powder. In a deep sense Ahab's blood was licked by dogs, as it flowed from the gaping wounds of his son. As a man sows he reaps, and when his children follow his steps, they too reap. But Ezekiel makes it perfectly clear that a godly son may break the entail of his father's iniquities. See Ezekiel 18, which has a most important bearing on the modern doctrine of heredity.

Jezebel's heart was proud and unbroken. She thought to make the conqueror the slave of her charms. When these failed, she taunted him with the fate of Zimri, so closely associated with the rise of Ahab's family to the throne. His reign of seven days was thrown in Jehu's teeth, 1 Kings 16:15. But Jezebel could not avert her fate. Her very chamberlains turned against her. How often does God's representative ask the same question, "Who is on my side?" Let us heed the challenge and dare to "look out" in answer! There is service appointed for us all, and we must not fail to render it.

2 KINGS 10:1–11

The Doom of the House of Ahab. What an iconoclast was this Jehu! Before his strong hand the whole structure of Baal-worship received its deathblow. And as we meet Elijah's name in this chapter, connecting him with these events, we turn back to the story of Horeb, with its solemn words: "And it shall come to pass that

2 KINGS

him that escapeth from the sword of Hazael shall Jehu slay: and him that escapeth from the sword of Jehu shall Elisha slay." God has many nets, and if the fish escape one set of meshes, they will be caught by another; none shall finally escape. "Every one shall give an account of himself to God." See v. 10.

It is a searching thought! Because men escape one judgment, they count themselves immune; but it is not so. He that escapes Hazael shall meet Jehu. "As if a man did flee from a lion, and a bear met him; or went into the house, and leaned his hand on the wall, and a serpent bit him," Amos 5:19. "There shall fall unto the earth nothing . . . which the Lord spake," v. 10. "How shall we escape if we neglect so great salvation," and trifle with such a God, whose love is as searching as his chastening wrath? See Jer. 16:16, 17.

2 KINGS 10:12-24

Wiping Out Baal Worship. For the well-being of the race it is sometimes necessary to cut off evildoers, lest they spread such a contagion of evil as to involve the whole body politic. The actual brethren of Ahaziah were slain by the Arabians, 2 Chron. 22:1. Jehu's work seems to have been complemented by an invasion of the Bedouins. The men mentioned here were probably, as the margin suggests, cousins or acquaintances. "Brethren" is a wide word, covering many degrees of blood-relationship.

Jehonadab was head of a remarkable tribe, and himself a man of unusual strength of character. The influence of his example and precepts left its mark on following generations, 1 Chron. 2:55; Jer. 35. Jehu evidently respected Jehonadab's good opinion, and was careful to advertise his own zeal for Jehovah. But the really good man has no need to parade his excellencies; and certainly Jehu could not count that his manner of going to work would be acceptable to the Most High. He might have achieved the same results by less objectionable methods. We must, of course, remember that this Baal worship was very licentious, and that every Israelite who entered that temple did so in direct defiance of repeated warnings from Elijah and others.

2 KINGS 10:25-36

Jehu's Own Failure. Jehu was earnest enough in uprooting all traces of Baal worship, but he permitted the worship of the calves and was careless in the matter of personal religion, v. 31. How much easier it is to see and rebuke the sins of others than to take heed to our own ways! It is comparatively easy to detect and destroy the sinner, without personally yielding to the claims of God ourselves. The judge who administers the law may be a transgressor of it, and all the more keen in inflicting penalty as if to satisfy his own uneasy conscience. We who utter God's solemn warnings against sin must not yield in thought to the sins that we denounce in act.

The Israelites were short in their duty to God, and God cut them short in territory, in wealth, and in power. Hazael thus fulfilled Elisha's anticipations, 2 Kings 8:12. Those eastern tribes that were attracted by the fatness of the land and settled there first were the first to suffer. Those who choose for this life only are the first to deteriorate and perish. It was so with Lot!

2 KINGS 11:1-12

Crowning the Boy-king. Athaliah well deserves the title given her in 2 Chron. 24:7. She usurped the throne, and played in Judah the part of her mother Jezebel. Joram was a wicked man and a bad king, but he recognized the value of piety and chose the good priest Jehoiada as the husband of his daughter. The husband neutralized the evil influences of his wife's upbringing and led her into a noble and useful career, the chief episode of which was the rescue of the youngest son of Ahaziah. His nurse and he were hidden in a room where the mattresses were kept in case of a sudden influx of priests at festal times. Is not this hidden king a type of the hiding of the true Prince in the recesses of our hearts, while some Athaliah occupies too large a share of government? There is no alternative but that the evil self-life, our Athaliah, should be stoned.

It was a glad moment when the hidden prince was produced. Many loyal hearts had renounced all hope of again seeing a scion of David's line. But God kept his promise. The Word of God was a befitting gift to place in the hands of the young prince, v. 12. Compare Deut. 17:18, 19. But what a revelation will it be when Jesus assumes the government of the earth, and its kingdoms become the kingdom of God and his Christ! He is now hidden, but he shall be manifested, Col. 3:4.

2 KINGS 11:13-20

Covenanting to Be the Lord's People. The death of Athaliah led the way to a thorough change throughout the kingdom. There was a double covenant, first, between the Lord on the one hand and the king and the people on the other, and second, between the king and the people; then the demolition of the Baal-house, which had sadly profaned the Holy City; and finally regulations for the proper performance of divine worship. These led the way to the public enthronement of the boy-king. The joy and quiet which ensued always follow the casting out of evil. Adjust a nation or an individual to the claims of God, and at once peace and joy succeed. The Lord Jesus, who is now hidden, shall one day be manifested, as we have seen. Those that hate him shall be put to shame. Then shall come salvation and the kingdom of God. Every evil that exalts itself against him shall be cast out, and the nations shall rejoice and be quiet because they have discovered their rightful ruler. Notice the alliance between the young king and the aged priest. It was necessary, under the old covenant, that the functions of king and priest should be fulfilled by different individuals. The civil and religious elements demanded separate expression, but in Jesus they perfectly blend. He is "a priest upon his throne," Zech. 6:13.

2 KINGS 11:21—12:16

Money for the Lord's House. So long as the good priest lived, the young king did well. How much we owe to the presence of wise, strong men to advise and assist us! But neither king nor priest dared to go to the furthest limit of reform, 12:3. This failure bore disastrous fruit in later years. It is a mistake to cut off weeds on the surface; they will sprout again and give trouble. If thy right hand cause thee to offend, cut it off.

The Temple had suffered terribly under Athaliah, 2 Chron. 24:7. The king might well take an interest in its reconstruction, because of the shelter it had afforded him from his enemies. The first attempt to raise a renovation fund was a failure. It was in the wrong hands. The priests appear to have appropriated for their own use offerings intended for Temple repair. A change was therefore required, and their receipts were limited to the sin offerings. As soon as a clear chance was given to the people, their free-will gifts totaled a large amount, which justified the resumption of the work. Certainly the promptness and integrity of the men who did the work put to shame the lethargy and peculation of the priests. Trust the people! This is not the last time that the heart of the masses was more to be trusted than the priestly caste.

2 KINGS 12:17—13:9

Inglorious Ends. As long as we are with the Lord, he is with us. Then our enemies are his enemies, and he shows himself strong on the behalf of those whose heart is perfect toward him. See 2 Chron. 15:2. So Joash found it in the earlier part of his reign. We need to ponder the blessings set out in Psalm 81:14-16, as guaranteed to the life which is at one with God. But when directly Joash listened to the princes and forsook the house of God and gave license to the Asherim and idols, God was turned against the people and became their enemy. See 2 Chron. 24:23-25. The reign that commenced in sunshine was sadly overcast, and the king perished by the hands of conspirators and never came to the sepulcher of the kings.

Then disaster after disaster befell the nation. They had to learn that they had been chosen for a special service in the world and could not be as others. Yet amid these dark days, what gleams of light there were! The Lord hearkened, 13:4; he gave Israel a savior, v. 5; he was gracious and had compassion and would not cast them from his presence, 13:23. Even when the Lord chastens us sore, he does not give us over unto death, Psa. 118:18. There is a "needs be," but there is also a "thus far and no farther."

2 KINGS 13:10-25

"The Arrow of the Lord's Deliverance." A good man is a great defense to his country. Mary, Queen of Scots, dreaded the prayers of Knox more than the armies of the king of France. Perhaps the king expected that Elisha also might pass home to God in a chariot of fire, as Elijah had done.

Notice how much Israel missed through the unbelief of her king. If only he had smitten five or six times, Syria would have been consumed; but he was content with striking only three times. Let us not ask small things of God, or be content with a partial deliverance. Nothing pleases him more than to be greatly trusted. For those who ask and expect the most, he will always go beyond all that they ask or think. Strike on the ground, child of God, nor stay thy striking. Claim the absolute overthrow of the power of Satan, which antagonizes and resists the coming of the kingdom. Claim the salvation of your fatherland from the tyranny of drink, gambling, and impurity! Open the windows heavenward and Godward; strike within and shoot without. It is not enough to do either without the other. And remember that unseen

2 KINGS 14:1-14

The Penalty of Pride. There were good traits in Amaziah's character, such as humanity to the children of his father's murderers, and his willingness to forfeit the aid of the army of Israel because of the prophet's remonstrance. See 2 Chron. 25. But he fell a victim to Edom's idols, though he conquered Edom that worshiped them; and from that moment God's Spirit and guidance seemed to desert him. He was puffed up with pride and vainglory, challenged the king of Israel to battle, and brought disaster on his people and himself.

But what a profound lesson is presented by his life! Do we never become elated with success, so that our heart is lifted up? Do we not fling ourselves in an hour of self-confidence from the Temple terrace, and find that no hand of might and love is stretched out to intercept our fall and make us alight uninjured on the ground? Let those who are successful and prosperous remember the Giver of every good and perfect gift and walk humbly with God. When we are evidently summoned to a supreme conflict with our foes, no weapon formed against us prospers. But if we are foolhardy, we are left to the results of our folly.

2 KINGS 14:15-29

Outward Prosperity without Inward Renewal. Azariah is elsewhere called Uzziah. See 2 Chron. 26:1-23; Isa. 6:1. The two names mean respectively, "whom Jehovah assists" and "the strength of Jehovah." After the death of his father, he finished the conquest of Edom by conquering Elath and restoring it to Judah. This was the beginning of a long and in some respects remarkable reign, though with a sad ending, as we shall see.

The reign of Jeroboam II was the longest and outwardly the most prosperous of any of the kings of Israel; for he regained possession of the land in the north and east which had been lost, v. 25, and made the Syrians tributary, v. 28. During his long reign, Hosea and Amos were sent to Israel, reproving their idolatry, warning them of the folly of relying on foreign help, and foretelling their overthrow by Assyria if they persisted in their sins. At the same time they did not cease to open the doors of God's forgiveness and mercy, if Israel would repent. God could not forget the time when Israel was a child, and he loved him and brought him out of Egypt, Hosea 11:1. The memory of our early years, with their holy promise, is lovingly cherished by our Father.

2 KINGS 15:1-12

"A Leper unto the Day of His Death." The reign of Azariah, or Uzziah, in Judah was very splendid. Fifty-two years of almost unbroken prosperity! The story is told in the glowing periods of 2 Chron. 26. Here, too, we learn that his sun suffered an eclipse because he persisted in the sacrilegious endeavor to combine the office of king and priest—the exclusive prerogative of Messiah. See Zech. 6:13. As a leper he was excluded from all contact with his fellows and dwelt in a separate house, while his son Jotham acted as his viceroy.

For more than thirty years preceding its dissolution, the Northern Kingdom was terribly distracted. Anarchy, idolatry, high-handed crime, and immorality of a flagrant description swept like a hurricane over all classes. Rent by these evils and with no strong men like Hezekiah and Isaiah, then in Judah, to place their hands on the helm, the kingdom drifted to destruction. The sacred books give but brief and disjointed accounts of the last times of the kingdom of Israel, because God has no pleasure in the process of decay. He has no pleasure in the death of individuals or in the nation that dieth, but rather that "they should turn unto him and live."

2 KINGS 15:13-22

Buying Temporary Relief. The usurping murderer Shallum enjoyed but a very brief reign, occupying the throne for one month only and then being slain by Menahem, who according to Josephus was commander of his forces. Menahem carried his arms as far as Tiphsah, which apparently resisted this red-handed assassin. The ruthless cruelty which he showed toward the hapless citizens attracted the notice of the Assyrian monarch, and led ultimately to that invasion of Israel which terminated in its destruction. God has ever sat as Judge over the nations. His judgments and sentences are exact. With what measure we mete, it shall be measured to us again.

Menahem obtained a temporary respite by the gift of 1,000 talents, which secured the alliance of the king of Assyria, turning him from an avenger into a patron. See Hos. 5:13. This was the confederacy to which Isaiah probably refers in his 8th chapter, when he alludes to a confederacy that seemed to bode no good. But on the bosom of this cloud of menace shone, as always, the rainbow of promise which is implied in the name "Immanuel."

2 KINGS 15:23-38

Usurpers and Invaders. The dissolution of Israel proceeded rapidly, for nothing could avert the steady advance of the Assyrian. According to the usual policy of Eastern conquerors, the flower of the nation was sent beyond the Euphrates to people the thinly inhabited portions of the Assyrian empire; and when this process was completed, new settlers were brought from Assyria to occupy the depopulated land, 17:24. The cuneiform inscriptions discovered at Nineveh contain remarkable corroborations of the Bible records. This was the *first* captivity, or exile, of Israel.

The ten tribes never returned to Palestine to any appreciable degree; but their terrible discipline became the enriching of the world. They planted synagogues on foreign soil, and disseminated in many lands the knowledge of Jehovah and their Scriptures. They were represented at Jerusalem by their descendants on the day of Pentecost; and the Apostle John counted their myriads among the redeemed, Rev. 7.

2 KINGS 16:1-9

Seeking Help from Wrong Sources. Ahaz was one of the most wicked kings of Judah. He not only passed his children through the lines of fire, but seems to have burnt some of them, 2 Chron. 28:3. He filled Judah with the abominations of the heathen. The hills and woodlands of the Holy Land were contaminated by all the excesses of Nature worship. When therefore Syria and Israel confederated against him, Ahaz naturally turned to creature aid. In spite of the remonstrances of Isaiah, he offered a bribe to the king of Assyria to do what God Almighty would have done, under happier conditions. This was the first step toward the utter undoing of Judah.

The first ten or twelve chapters of Isaiah cast a flood of light on the inner politics of this dark epoch. They give a glimpse also of Isaiah's profound emotions at the evils that threatened his fatherland. No servant of God can view the present state of civilization without grave concern, and we are bound to resist, so far as we can, the influences which are engaged in the work of moral disintegration. We are citizens of Heaven, but also of earth, and must render to Caesar such things as naturally belong to him.

2 KINGS 16:10-20

High-handed Idolatry. The calling in of the king of Assyria was fraught with disastrous consequences. "He distressed him, but strengthened him not," 2 Chron. 28:20. Well may the apostle warn us not to be yoked with unbelievers. Such alliances always result in the undoing of God's children. We cannot serve two masters. Thus in the hour of distress, notwithstanding the increasing and noble remonstrances of Isaiah, this same king Ahaz trespassed yet more against Jehovah.

It is remarkable, as showing the folly of the human heart, that in the lowest hour of his degradation before his conqueror Ahaz imitated the altar which he saw at Damascus. For this, the ancient brazen altar in Jehovah's Temple was displaced; and upon it in the sacred Temple sacrifices were offered to the gods of the heathen. Alas, there is too much of this in the present day! Men are going back from the simplicity and spirituality of Christ to exploded philosophies and systems which have failed in the past to satisfy soul-hunger. Let us beware of the vacuum of the soul into which such evil things intrude. It is only as we are filled by the indwelling Spirit that we are immune against these temptations.

2 KINGS 17:1-12

The Cause of Israel's Weakness. This chapter reads like a page from the books of the great white throne. Hoshea, the last king of Israel, did not follow in all the evil deeds of his eighteen predecessors, but the degeneracy of the nation was too far advanced for anything to arrest its collapse. The dry rot had eaten its way through the specious covering. Worldly policy was the immediate cause of the nation's downfall. Had they obeyed God simply and absolutely, they could have trusted him to maintain their independence. But they chose to enter into alliances, now with Syria and then with Egypt, and so became entangled in the wars of their allies. See Hos. 7:11; 9:3, 6; 12:1.

Let us read carefully the bill of divorce which the Heavenly Husband gave to the recreant people whom he put away. It is a pathetic document from v. 7 onward; but none can say that Jehovah had not good and sufficient cause for acting as he did. The wonder is that he bore so long with the apostate race. Read the first three chapters of Hosea to learn how the divine heart was rent when the hour of separation came. But let us not forget the assurances of Romans 11, that the true Israel shall ultimately be saved.

2 KINGS 17:13-26

The End of Stiff-necked Disobedience. There are three leading counts in this terrible indictment against Judah and Israel: (1) idolatry; (2) the ignoring of the Law; and (3) disregard of the many warnings brought them by prophets and seers. And all were aggravated by the fact that they sinned against the Lord their God, who had brought them up out of the land of Egypt. How greatly the complexion of our sins is deepened when we remember the anguish by which we have been redeemed!

Interwoven with the black catalogue of sin are golden threads of tender love, v. 13. But note the remarkable expression of v. 15, that we resemble the objects we adore, Psa. 115:8. Israel, as we have seen, was never restored. Those that returned to Judah with Ezra were for the most part Jews. Yet many Hebrews became believers in Christ, and were added to the Church at Pentecost and afterward, 1 Peter 1:1, 2. Paul gives us a far horizon in Romans 11:25-27. Who can tell whether we are not very near that hour of the restoration of Israel and the restitution of all things!

2 KINGS 17:27-41

"They Feared the Lord, and Served Their Own Gods." The policy of peopling Israel with other races was intended to keep the land under cultivation and to break the ties of fatherland, which are the spring of patriotism. Men will not fight for a land which does not pull at their heartstrings. These newly-imported peoples believed that each country was under the care of its own local deity. They therefore deemed it advisable that without renouncing their own gods, they should give the God of Israel some sort of recognition. Samaritan religion of this kind is still very popular. Too many people feel that they ought to do something to show their respect for God. They attend to the outward forms of worship, lest they should lose status; but in their hearts they enthrone worldly and worthless ideals.

The Jews, as we learn from John 4:9, hated the Samaritans, as a kind of mongrel race. But how generous was the Savior, ministering to the woman of Sychar, healing the Samaritan leper, and making one of this despised people the central figure in his parable of mercy, thus compelling the world to speak of the *good* Samaritan!

2 KINGS 18:1-12

A Resolute Religious Reformer. It is wonderful that such a man as Ahaz should have had so good a son, but it is likely that Hezekiah had a good mother. See 2 Chron. 29:1; 26:5. No doubt the fall of Samaria was a great incentive with the king and his advisers to root out idolatry. There is no better way of neutralizing evil than by accentuating good, and Hezekiah was wise to reopen and purify the Temple at the very beginning of his reign. See 2 Chron. 29:3, 19, 21-35. It has been supposed that the prophecy of Micah 3:12 and Jeremiah 26:18 was made effective by the power of the Holy Spirit.

When a soul is all for God, God is all to it. "The eyes of the Lord run to and fro throughout the whole earth, to show himself strong in the behalf of them whose heart is perfect toward him." See v. 7. Let us see to it that we follow the suggestion of Psalm 1 and strike our roots deep into the Word of God, pondering it carefully and obeying it reverently; then our leaf shall not fade, and whatsoever we do shall prosper. It is a good thing to cleave to God and keep his commandments. Compare v. 6 with Deut. 10:20.

2 KINGS 18:13-25

Threatened by Worldly Might. It is an interesting fact that this siege of Lachish is mentioned on the Assyrian monuments, and Sennacherib is depicted as giving orders for its destruction. Also the names and Jewish physiognomy of these ambassadors are clearly recognizable. It was a mistake to bribe the foe; the bribes only excited his cupidity. You may as well come to blows with Apollyon as soon as he straddles across your path; sooner or later the conflict will have to come to a head. Three years afterward, Rabshakeh appeared before the gates of Jerusalem.

It has been suggested that this bold blasphemer was an apostate Jew. He drew a false inference from the recent destructions of altars, etc., which had been reported to him. His taunts were barbed with biting satire. He spoke contemptuously of the little army that was absolutely unable to cope with the disciplined troops of Assyria. It seemed a most unequal conflict which could end only in one way. But he failed to take into account the covenant mercy of God and the heavenly forces which were allied with Hezekiah.

2 KINGS 18:26-37

Silent before the Boaster. The Jews met the taunts of Rabshakeh with silence. It was wise policy. It is infinitely better to hand over our cause to God, and leave him to answer for us and avenge our wrongs. He will undertake our case, if we will but leave it unreservedly in his hands. The only exception is when some simple explanation will relieve the cause we love from any evil imputation. Rabshakeh could not have been made to understand the attitude of king and people. See Isa. 37:22. Men of the world cannot read the secrets of the heart that is stayed upon Jehovah. God's hidden ones are as great a mystery as was our Lord. Their life is hid with Christ in God, but some day he will be manifested, and they shall be manifested with him in glory.

When our Lord was threatened, he remained calm and quiet. "As a sheep before her shearers is dumb, so he openeth not his mouth," Isa. 53:7. We are bidden to follow his steps and to do as he did, silently committing our cause to him who never fails to vindicate those who put their trust in him.

2 KINGS 19:1-13

Facing the Enemy's Threatenings. That bowed form of Hezekiah before the altar of God, while his servants and elders were conferring with Isaiah, is a beautiful emblem of the true way of meeting trouble. And it is very blessed when our cause is so closely identified with God's that we can appeal to him to intervene for his own sake, v. 4.

All through this crisis, Isaiah acted the part of a patriot and a saint. His intrepid figure stands out in bold relief amid the storm. He even dared to compose a funeral ode for the burial of this imperious tyrant. In all literature there is nothing more sublime than Isaiah 10:11-14. When bitter and threatening words are flung at us, let us go up to the house of God. See Psa. 73:17. Let us get in touch with some holy soul, of the type of Isaiah, and ask for his prayers on our behalf. The prayer of a righteous man is very effectual. To stand in God's secret place is to be in the calm center of the cyclone. Around us the elements may rage and the people imagine a vain thing; but they shall pass away as the chaff of the threshing-floor, while not a hair of our head shall perish.

2 KINGS 19:14-24

Spreading the Case before the Lord. That bowed form of King Hezekiah, kneeling before God with this insolent and blasphemous overflow spread out before him, is a beautiful suggestion of our duty under similar circumstances. When we receive letters of rebuke and unkindness, whether they are signed or anonymous, let us treat them as Hezekiah treated this one. Let us spread them before God, and plead with him to interpose for his holy Name's sake. How blessed it is when our lot is so identified with God's that we can forget ourselves in the one sincere desire that his character shall be vindicated and his Name honored! The selfish element has been so strong in our praying and doing!

In all Scripture there is nothing finer than the magnificent answer to Sennacherib's challenge which God gave through Isaiah. The phrase, "virgin daughter," fittingly indicates that the foreign invader was not to set his foot in the Holy City. Listen to her gleeful laughter as, strong in the Lord of hosts, she derides her foes, v. 21*ff.* But that faith may be ours. Others who have not made God their trust are like the green herb that withers in the drought. But they who are planted in God send their roots deep down to the moist earth and draw perennial freshness and strength.

2 KINGS 19:25-37

The Answer of the King of Kings. These verses, taken with Isaiah 10:5-15, form a most suggestive and sublime comment on the words, "the Lord reigneth." They show us God using the Assyrian as "the rod of his anger," and working personally and mightily through the politics of the world. Isaiah's faith, through all this terrible crisis, was the one bulwark behind which king and people lay entrenched. What a gift one such man is to an entire people! His heart is fixed, trusting in the Lord, and he cannot be made afraid by evil tidings.

It has been suggested that this was a Sabbatic year, the produce of which sufficed for two years, v. 29. In any case, the Sabbatic peace and calm had entered Isaiah's soul. They who have learned to stay themselves on God may sing triumphal odes, in sure conviction of coming victory. Thus, also, it befell. The angel of God's deliverance wrought triumph through some terrible outbreak of plague, and thus the tents were strewn with the silent corpses of men who had yesterday been full of manly vigor. The Lord was Judge, Lawgiver, and King. He saved his people, as the mother bird with outspread wing protects her brood against the hawk. God's presence, like an invisible river, surrounded and saved his people. "The Lord of hosts is with us; the God of Jacob is our refuge," Ps. 46:11.

2 KINGS 20:1-11

The Shadow Turned Back on Life's Dial. What a contrast between Hezekiah and the Apostle Paul! To the great Christian hero, death seemed infinitely desirable. He was ready to be offered; it would be gain to depart and be with Christ. But Hezekiah, who had walked before God in truth and with a perfect heart, turned his face to the wall and wept as the shadow of death fell upon him. Could anything prove more conclusively how much we owe to the Lord Jesus, who abolished death for those who trust him?

Who does not know what it is to turn the face to the wall in unutterable anguish? There are moments when we are face to face with a blank wall, and only God can open a door in it. But he did for Hezekiah and he will for you. Only have faith and reckon on God's faithfulness. Has the shadow gone down on your dial? Has the day of your earnest zeal for God begun to wane? Have the bright promises of the morning become overcast? Then turn to God with true repentance! Let him see thy tears of heart-sorrow, and he will restore the years that the cankerworm has eaten. It shall be with thee as in the past. The shadow shall return on the dial and the days of thy youth shall be renewed. There is a sense in which our sun never goes down, but leads our days forward, when the Lord becomes our Everlasting Light.

2 KINGS 20:12-21

A Mistake and Its Penalty. God does not always prolong life in answer to prayer, and we should always leave such things submissively to him, because he may see reasons why it would be far better for us to be removed from this world of temptation and sorrow. If Hezekiah had been taken away by early death, he would never have incurred the terrible sentence of v.16*ff.*

Let us watch against the sin of ostentation. It was a foolish act on the part of the king, because he aroused in these ambassadors desire and greed, which they communicated to their sovereign. There is too much of this spirit in us all. What a solemn inquiry that is, "What have they seen in thine house?" If that inquiry were put to us, we should too often have to confess that our visitors have not seen our piety, our family worship, the decorous behavior of our children, our love and devotion; but that they have seen our dresses and our ornaments, our best linen and our china. Alas for us if these are our treasures, and we have nothing behind them of the priceless jewels and wealth of Christian character! At the best we are only caretakers and stewards; we have nothing that we have not received! See 1 Cor. 4:7. Let us remember that at any time the Master of the House may arrive! See Matt. 24:44.

2 KINGS 21:1-15

An Evil Leader's Terrible Influence. It seems incredible that the good Hezekiah should have had such a son; but the young prince was evidently under the power of that reactionary party which, during Hezekiah's reign, had been kept in check only by the strong influence of Isaiah. Hence, on becoming king, Manasseh reintroduced the worst forms of idolatry which had disgraced the nations of Canaan and were rife in neighboring countries. It was the height of presumptuous impiety to place an Asherah, such as Ahab made, 1 Kings 16:32, in the very precincts of the Temple, and to patronize the Chaldean astrologers who poured into the country from Babylon. See Ezekiel 8.

Vigorous protests were raised against these shameful abominations by Hosea, Joel, Nahum, Habakkuk, and Isaiah; but in vain. Nothing could stay the mad fanaticism of the people for licentious rites, and their doom became inevitable. The gentle voice of love was of none avail, and the brazen clangor of Babylonian captivity must speak in tones that could not be silenced. For Manasseh's end, consult 2 Chron. 33. Surely none need despair, since he found mercy. But alas, nothing can restore the years that the locust hath eaten.

2 KINGS 21:16-26

Like Father, Like Son. Manasseh shed much innocent blood, and among others, tradition has it that Isaiah was sawn asunder at his command, Heb. 11:37. Amon followed in his father's steps. Here is the horror of sin! A man may repent and turn to God, but he cannot undo the effect of his evil course on those whom he has seduced. Probably, on his conversion to God, Manasseh used all the power at his command to induce Amon to avoid the sins of his own early life and to follow the example of his later years. But Amon would not listen. "He walked in all the way that his father walked in!"

No man sins by himself. The evil of his deeds is far-reaching. When once you have scattered thistledown, as you have sown, so will you reap. Christ's heaviest denunciations were launched against those who put an occasion to fall in the way of one of his little ones. God forgive us if we are making life's battle harder for any soul, especially for our own child. "Take the safe path, father!" said a little boy as they were climbing a steep place. "Remember that I am coming behind you."

2 KINGS 22:1-13

Finding the Lost Law. In the midst of a dissolute court, Josiah's young life grew as a palm on the desert waste. At the age of sixteen he sought the Lord, and at eighteen he became even more earnest and devoted, as though some special quickening had passed over his soul and led him to set about the repair of the Temple. In this he was greatly aided by Hilkiah. It was a fair sunrise, though the day was prematurely overcast.

During the process of renovation a copy of the Book of the Law was discovered, and Shaphan read it before the king. It is supposed that the passage which he recited and which so greatly moved his soul was Deuteronomy 28 to 30, where are enumerated the awful consequences that would follow the failure to observe God's Law. What ruthless havoc had Manasseh wrought, that all the copies of the Law had become destroyed! It reminds us of the wholesale burning of the Bible in Tyndale's day! The burglar is always careful to extinguish the light that might reveal his presence and lead to his identification. Let us not hesitate to preach the whole counsel of God, and not hide the inevitable doom of the ungodly. It is by the Word that the Holy Spirit convicts of sin.

2 KINGS 22:14—23:4

Hearkening to the Message. Josiah's fears were deeply stirred by the evils which the Law of the Lord clearly indicated as imminent, and he immediately sent for advice to the prophetess Huldah, who was held in great veneration. Her answer was full of gentle kindness. Though the king's punishment could not be averted, it could nevertheless be postponed. How quick is God to notice the tears of genuine contrition and to meet the soul that seeks to do his will! If only the whole nation had been equally repentant, its fate would have doubtless been altered.

It is remarkable, however, that even in Josiah's case the prediction of the prophetess was not realized. He died in battle, and his dead body was brought to Jerusalem amid mourning, 23:30. Why this apparent breach of promise? The answer is suggested by our Lord's temptation. He refused to make bread of stones because of his absolute faith in God, and when Satan tempted him still further to manifest that faith by casting himself from the Temple crag, he again refused because such an act was not in the scope of the Father's plan. On the other hand, Josiah, disregarding all counsels to the contrary, needlessly flung himself into the fray between Egypt and Babylon and there lost his life. "Thou shalt not tempt the Lord thy God!"

2 KINGS 23:5-14

Destroying Inducements to Evil. Encouraged by the prophets Zephaniah, Urijah, and perhaps Jeremiah, Josiah set himself to the work of thorough reform, in which he endeavored to carry his people. The various items mentioned here prove how deeply the heart of the nation had become corrupted. In the very Temple itself were altars and vessels for the unholy rites of Baal and Ashtaroth. Multitudes of black-hooded priests filled the streets. At the Temple gates were the horses and chariots of sun worship. Around the hills glittered idol shrines. These were all swept away.

In all our lives there are times when we should carefully examine ourselves, not by our own conceptions of what may be right or wrong, nor by the conventional standards which are accepted by our neighbors, but by the high and holy standards of the New Testament, the example and precepts of our Lord. We are too prone to suit our conceptions of what he requires to the fancies or choices of our own desires, instead of testing ourselves by "the pattern given in the Mount." If hand or foot or eye cause us to offend, we must show ourselves no mercy.

2 KINGS 23:15-25

Proving His Wholeheartedness. Josiah carried his drastic reforms even to Samaria, thus fulfilling a prophecy uttered 350 years before. See 1 Kings 13:2, 3. The old leaven having now been cleared out, the Passover could be celebrated. We cannot keep the feast of joy and worship till the work of self-purification has been undertaken. See 1 Cor. 5:7. In that great feast some of the ten tribes also joined. There was therefore an affirmation of the spiritual unity of the entire nation, though, like the professing Church of today, it was outwardly in fragments. We must never let go of our belief in the Holy Universal Church, however distracted and divided to outward appearance it may be.

Though these reforms were carried through by the king's strong hand, the generality of the nation remained idolatrous and corrupt and yielded a feigned rather than a felt repentance. See Jer. 3:10; 4:3, 4, 14; 5:1-3. Therefore, judgment could not be averted. External reformation is not enough to secure the permanence of national life. We must rend our hearts rather than our garments, Joel 2:13. There is a sorrow that needs not to be repented of, and a sorrow which "worketh death," 2 Cor. 7:10.

2 KINGS 23:26-37

In the Hands of Heathen Foes. Josiah's life ended in terrible disaster. He persisted in measuring himself in battle against the king of Egypt in a quarrel which was none of his, and thus met his death. The events of this paragraph are fully narrated in 2 Chron. 35, and are corroborated by the Greek historian Herodotus and by the sculptures on this Pharaoh's tomb. The story of Jehoiakim should also be studied in the pages of Jeremiah 22, 26, 36, which cast a flood of light on these last days, when the sands in the hourglass of repentance were running out.

It is extraordinary that notwithstanding the earnest expostulations of Jeremiah and others, and the awful example furnished by the fate of the ten tribes, the kings of Judah and their people should be so persistent in wrongdoing. But their hearts were fully set upon evil. In our own time the history of alcoholic abuse furnishes a parallel. Its evils stand confessed, as they touch individuals and nations, and yet neither individuals nor nations seem able to cast off the coils of this serpent. The Hebrew race had to pass through terrible fires to become fitted for their mission to the world, and surely the present anguish of conflict is our parallel!

2 KINGS 24:1-9

The Price of Innocent Blood. Note the entail of Manasseh's sin. He had lived, had been forgiven, and had died years before, but Judah was irretrievably implicated in his sins. The poison had eaten into the national heart, and for the innocent blood which had been shed like water there had been no amends. Notice the emphatic statement that Nebuchadnezzar and the other enemies who came against the land were deliberately carrying out the divine chastenings. They were, as Isaiah puts it, the rod of God's anger and the staff of his indignation, 10:5. How often does God still use evil men as his instruments to chasten us! The best way of escaping them is to commit ourselves to God.

Jehoiakim was blatant in his blasphemy, Jer. 36:23. He was a very contemptible prince, and was carried in chains to Babylon, Dan. 1:1, 2. Apparently he was temporarily restored to his throne, but in the end he perished ignominiously, Jer. 36:30.

What sorrows befell the Holy City! Though God would have gathered her under the wings of his protecting care, she would not, and therefore the times of the Gentiles began, which would now seem to be hastening to their end, Luke 21:24.

2 KINGS 24:10-20

The Captivity Begins. Jehoiachin followed the evil path of his predecessors. Again Jerusalem was besieged and Deuteronomy 28:48 began to be fulfilled. The ill-advised revolt of the young king ended in bitter disappointment, as Jeremiah had foretold, 22:24, 25. The final tragedy came on apace, in spite of the insistence of the false prophets that the sacred vessels of the Temple should be returned from Babylon, Jer. 27:16. Finally, a sad procession issued from the gate of the doomed city, and the king and his nobles and officials presented themselves before the enemy, sitting on the ground, clothed in black, their faces covered in their mantles, Jer. 13:18. They were at once deported to Babylon, with thousands more. The treasures in the Temple and the palace were plundered, and a cry of agony and astonishment arose from Jeremiah and the whole land. See Jer. 22:24, 28; some add Psalms 42 and 43.

Zedekiah, Josiah's youngest son, enticed into a league with neighboring nations against the conqueror, brought upon himself and his people a yet more disastrous overthrow. How foolish man's wisdom becomes when he departs from the living God! "A wave of the sea driven with the wind and tossed," Jas. 1:6.

2 KINGS 25:1-12

The Captivity Made Complete. As the final catastrophe approaches, the historian becomes more minute in his dates, marking the month and the day. From Ezekiel 24:1 we gather that on the very day when the foe made his appearance before Jerusalem, the fact was revealed to Ezekiel in Babylon and the fate of the city made clear. Jeremiah besought Zedekiah to submit, but to no purpose, Jer. 38:17-19. The siege lasted eighteen months, and its calamities may be gathered from Lamentations 2:20, 21; 4:3-20. Finally famine triumphed, Lam. 4:8, 10; Ezek. 5:10. A third of the population perished of hunger and plague, Ezek. 5:12.

Such is the divine judgment upon sin. God pleads long with man, but if man will not turn, then God whets his sword and becomes terrible in his retribution. Amid all this catastrophe, however, we recall the tears of the book of Lamentations, like those of Jesus afterward. There is that in God which sorrows as he chastises and causes him to say, "How shall I make thee as Admah, and set thee as Zeboim?" (Deut. 29:23; Hos. 11:8). Notice how, in putting out the eyes of Zedekiah, two prophecies which appeared to be contradictory were reconciled and fulfilled, Jer. 32:5; 34:3 and Ezek. 12:13.

2 KINGS 25:13-21

The Temple Despoiled. The Temple, after 420 years of varying fortune, was burned to the ground, and the remainder of its treasures carried off. A few years after, Nebuchadnezzar set up an image of gold on the plains of Dura, Dan. 3:1. It has been suggested that this image was probably made from the metal removed from the Holy City; and this may have been an additional reason for the refusal of the Jews to worship as the king demanded.

We have no information respecting the disposition of the Ark. It may have been hidden by Jeremiah or by some other pious priest who took the precaution of conveying it and the sacred documents it contained to a place of safety. How wonderful it would be if remains of the Ark of the Covenant should yet be discovered in connection with the vast subterranean vaults beneath the Temple site!

These tragic events are a powerful commentary upon the ancient text that sin is a reproach to any people, Prov. 14:34. Let modern cities and civilizations beware; for if God spared not the natural branches, neither will he spare those which have been grafted in among them. See Rom. 11:18-25.

2 KINGS 25:22-30

The Remnant Flee to Egypt. Thus at last the city which had been full of people sat solitary, bewailed by Jeremiah in exquisite elegies. The poorest only were left, under Gedaliah, the constant friend of Jeremiah. See Jer. 40:6. His brief rule brought a gleam of light, a transient relief from the long monotony of disaster and despair. But the dastardly murder of this noble man by Ishmael, who was jealous of him, added the last bitter ingredient to the already bitter cup of the harried remnant, Jer. 40 and 41. Notwithstanding Jeremiah's earnest protestations, they finally deserted their own land, and settled in Egypt, Jer. 44:1.

Thus ended the kingdom of Judah, and thereafter the Jews became a scattered people. Though the return under Ezra seemed likely to renew their kingdom, this also was a transient dream which ended in their final overthrow in A.D. 70. Note how pathetically, in his last paragraph, the chronicler snatches at the one small crumb of comfort left, in the pity providentially shown to Jehoiachin by the Babylonian king. God had not forgotten the sure mercies of David!

THE FIRST & SECOND BOOK OF CHRONICLES

THE HISTORY OF THE COVENANT

I. THE GENEALOGIES OF THE TRIBES OF ISRAEL   *1 Chron. 1—9*
II. THE KINGS OF THE UNITED KINGDOM
   1 Chron. 10—2 Chron. 9
   - A. Saul   *1 Chron. 10*
   - B. David   *1 Chron. 11—29*
   - C. Solomon   *2 Chron. 1—9*
III. THE KINGS OF JUDAH   *2 Chron. 10—36*
   - A. Rehoboam   *10—12*
   - B. Abijah   *13*
   - C. Asa   *14—16*
   - D. Jehoshaphat   *17—20*
   - E. Jehoram   *21*
   - F. Ahaziah   *22*
   - G. Joash   *23, 24*
   - H. Amaziah   *25*
   - I. Uzziah   *26*
   - J. Jotham   *27*
   - K. Ahaz   *28*
   - L. Hezekiah   *29—32*
   - M. Manasseh   *33*
   - N. Josiah   *34, 35*
   - O. Jehoahaz   *36:1-3*
   - P. Jehoiakim   *36:4-8*
   - Q. Jehoiachin   *36:9, 10*
   - R. Zedekiah   *36:11-13*
   - S. The captivity   *36:14-21*
   - T. The decree of Cyrus   *36:22, 23*

INTRODUCTION

The books of Kings and Chronicles are often regarded as much alike, but there are marked differences between them. The books of Kings present mainly political annals from the time of Solomon to the fall of Jerusalem. The northern and southern kingdoms receive equal attention. The books of Chronicles cover a much longer period, longer indeed than that surveyed by any other portion of Scripture. They are a summary of religious history from the creation of the world down to the time when they were written, subsequent to the Captivity. From the time of the division of the kingdom, the history of Judah only is recorded, the writer's purpose excluding any account of apostate Israel.

The books are drawn from a great variety of sources, many of which are named in the text. Though it is impossible to determine the author with certainty, probability strongly favors Ezra.

Because most of 1 and 2 Chronicles consists of genealogical information, etc. which is of great historical value, it does not lend itself to the devotional format of this book. Thus, only 2 Chronicles 26—36 is discussed.

COMMENTARY

2 CHRON. 26:1-15

"God Made Him to Prosper." The reign of Uzziah was, to all appearance, extremely prosperous; but his personal character deteriorated, as though it could not bear an unbroken succession of prosperity. Proofs of his genius for empire are furnished by his successful wars, vv. 6, 7; his widespread fame, v. 8; his buildings and husbandry, vv. 9, 10; and his armies and engines of war, vv. 11, 15. In all these "he was marvelously helped." How many can bear the same glad witness concerning God's dealings with them! The best preventive of pride is to recognize all blessing as coming from the marvelous help of God.

When we review our earlier life and think of the position to which God has raised us, can we do other than cry, "Marvelous! Marvelous!" We cannot understand why God has so signally favored us, but we are persuaded that only by his grace we are as we are. Let us not forget that we are made strong in order to help the weak. Whatever we have must be viewed as a precious talent for helping advance the everlasting kingdom of the Lord Jesus. The secret of prosperity is given in Psalm 1:3.

2 CHRON. 26:16-23

The Penalty of Pride. The offices of priest and king were rigorously kept apart throughout the history of Israel. Melchizedek's dual office is typical of the priestly reign of Christ, and had no counterpart in the Mosaic and Levitical ritual. Zechariah's prediction indicated an absolutely new era, Zech. 6:12, 13. The rash act of Uzziah was resisted by the priests, and the issue was decided by the terrible brand of leprosy which appeared suddenly upon his forehead. As the result of his attempt to flout the solemn sanctions of divine origin and authority, he lost even the religious privileges which he had enjoyed before.

However great God's goodness, and whatever be the position of usefulness to which we may attain, there are prescribed limits beyond which we may not go. We must not cast ourselves in willful abandonment from the pinnacle of the Temple. God's dearest children must not presume on their familiarity and take liberties with his rules and ways.

2 CHRON. 27:1-9

Ordering His Way before God. This story of Jotham is memorable if only for one sentence: that he "became mighty because he prepared his ways before the Lord his God." We should order our lives as we order our prayers. First things must come first. We should always consider, in anticipating any course of action, how best to promote God's glory and the interests of his kingdom. As far as lies in our power, we should adopt and follow some plan or program, such as he will reveal to us. *An ordered life is a mighty life.* The people that make themselves felt in the world are those who can say with Paul, "This one thing I do." They are invulnerable and invincible. Repressed in one place, they break out in another; cast down, they are not destroyed; perplexed, they are not in despair. *An ordered and mighty life draws its supplies from God.* However well-laid our plans or single our purpose, nothing avails apart from God. It is by him that we become strong; and his power, allied with us and working through us, makes us more than conquerors.

2 CHRON. 28:1-11

Smitten for Forsaking the Lord. The reign of Ahaz was marked by terrible and rapid degeneration. He not only restored idolatry and offered his children to Moloch, but as the difficulties of his reign increased he made an alliance with the king of Assyria, notwithstanding the vehement protests of Isaiah. His extreme wickedness made him notorious. "This is that king Ahaz," v. 22. The instruments used for his punishment were the kings of Syria and Israel, vv. 5, 6; and his sin led to the suffering of his people, carried from their homes to Samaria. When a nation or an individual life turns from the love and life of God, it becomes at once a prey to enemies that are lurking near, as an anemic constitution is liable to the microbes of disease.

It was a noble act on the part of the prophet Oded to denounce the captivity of so many brethren and sisters; and his splendid protest touched the finest chords in the conquerors' hearts. We must never flinch from holding up God's standard before the minds of our contemporaries. It will often arrest evil and incite nobleness of action.

2 CHRON. 28:12-27

A Wicked King's Blind Folly. This sending of the captives home, clothed, shod, and anointed, was a beautiful act and anticipates the spirit of Christianity. This is the true way of making and maintaining peace. Magnanimity is, after all, the best solvent of national hatred, and lays the foundations of enduring brotherhood. The Edomites and Philistines smote Judah and weakened it, but they were only the instruments. We are distinctly told that the Lord brought Judah low, v. 19. The relief bought from the king of Assyria at so great a sacrifice secured a temporary respite. See 2 Kings 16:7-9. In the end, however, it only added to his distress, v. 20. None can help the man who has forfeited the help of God. If he is against us, who can be for us!

The more distressed Ahaz was, the more he trespassed. See Isa. 1:5, 6. With blind infatuation he went step by step farther from God, sacrificed to the gods of Damascus, and offered wanton insult to God's house. The detestation of the people was evidenced in their treatment of his remains. See Proverbs 10:7.

2 CHRON. 29:1-11

A Revival of Righteousness. It was a blessing for Judah that Ahaz left as successor a son who inherited none of his father's traits. Hezekiah ranks as one of the best kings that occupied the throne of David. This chapter is full of illustrative and interesting description. In the first month of his reign, the young king began his work of reform by assembling to his help the priests and Levites, and bidding them make all possible speed to cleanse the Temple.

The clarion call of this exhortation rings yet and bids us cleanse the inner shrine of our heart from all filthiness of the flesh and spirit. Let us hasten to open the doors, kindle the lamps, and burn incense in the inner prayer chamber of the heart. And what is true for the individual applies equally to the national conscience. Religion is the safeguard of our prosperity; and they who secure a healthy religious sentiment contribute as much to the well-being of their fatherland as the statesmen and politicians of worldwide fame.

2 CHRON. 29:12-24

Removing Uncleanness. The names of the assisting Levites are specially mentioned, because their obedient cooperation counted for so much in the national reconstruction. For eight days the priests and they wrought in the great work of cleansing the Temple of the filthiness which had accumulated through neglect. The drift of the sandstorm, the havoc of weeds, the multitudes of living things that come from the air and the earth to brood and breed in neglected buildings had wrought sad disfigurement and dilapidation in the holy and beautiful house which David and Solomon had built for God. Deterioration of heart and life, of church and state is the sure result of neglect. The garden of the sluggard could hardly be more useless or perilous to the ordered cultivation around than is the heart of man when it neglects the cultivation of its spiritual affinities. We were made for God and cannot be perfectly healthy or happy apart from him. These sins must be expiated by blood. A deep lesson is contained in vv. 20-24. See Heb. 9:22.

2 CHRON. 29:25-36

Sacrifice and Song. Among the usual sacrifices following the cleansing, the burnt offering occupied a conspicuous place, as expressive of sincere and entire devotion to God. Notice that as the burnt offering began, the song began also. Self-sacrifice and the surrender of heart and life to God always lead to joy. First cleansing, then forgiveness and the blotting out of sin, and finally reconsecration to God—such are the inevitable steps that conduct the soul from the depths of depression into the joy of God's salvation. It is the self-absorbed and self-contained life which is miserable. Notice how contagious the joy of God is. From Hezekiah it spread to his people and led to the uplift of the entire nation. It is interesting to learn that this happy outbreak of religious fervor sprang from a divine preparation which had long been working below the surface of the national life.

2 CHRON. 30:1-12

A Summons to the Nation. Though it was one of the most important feasts, the Passover had long been neglected. When a spiritual revival takes place, men naturally begin to observe the old sacred institutions through which religious feeling can express itself. As the proper month for observing it had gone, rather than miss the whole year, the king and his people resolved to observe their annual festival in the second month, as provided in Numbers 9:10, 11. The quickened life of Judah revealed itself in a fervent yearning for national unity, and the invitation to share in celebrating the Passover was distributed from Dan to Beersheba. Many mocked, imputing Hezekiah's appeal to low motives of ambition and self-aggrandizement. We cannot doubt that Isaiah prompted the king to suggest that if Israel would accept the invitation and join in a common act of penitence and faith, it would probably lead to the rehabilitation of their national life. In putting aside this suggestion, Israel not only flouted the royal proposal, but destroyed one of the last methods of undoing the ruin which had already commenced in the Northern Kingdom.

2 CHRON. 30:13-27

Wholehearted Seeking of God. As a necessary preliminary to the right observance of the approaching feast, the removal of the altars erected by Ahaz was resolved upon. The feast and its antitype can be observed only as the leaven of evil is put away, 1 Cor. 5:7. So great was the zeal of the people that it shamed the priests and Levites into a new earnestness. There were irregularities in the celebration; for instance, the Levites slaughtered the paschal victims for every one that had not passed through the usual process of ceremonial cleansing. But the intention of the crowds was right, and in answer to Hezekiah's prayer no penalty was inflicted for these violations of the prescribed ritual. Another proof is thus afforded that the main thing with God is the attitude of the heart, Psa. 69:31.

When spiritual captivities are turned, there is an outburst of singing. Each great revival has had its Gregorian chants, its Luther's hymns, its Charles Wesley, its Havergal, its Sankey.

The immense numbers of slaughtered beasts were necessitated by the presence of vast multitudes of people, who needed to be supported while at Jerusalem. Only a small portion of the animal was presented on the altar, the remainder being eaten by the offerers.

2 CHRON. 31:1-10

Abundant Giving to God. This Passover left a permanent impression on the nation, and led to the complete overthrow of idolatry. The pure worship of God was now established throughout the land, and the people returned to their homes in confident expectation that a long period of national prosperity was now in store. Hezekiah therefore turned his attention to provide for the maintenance of the Temple worship and the proper provision of revenues for the priests and Levites. As an example to his people, the king followed in the steps of David and Solomon, providing out of his own purse for the expenses of the altar.

Following on this good example, a proclamation was made to the nation, with the result that contributions of firstfruits and tithes poured in with great liberality from the children of Israel, as well as Judah. There had been an abundant harvest, as the great heaps testified. It is not often that ministers of religion are in the same happy condition as Azariah was, but they are partly to blame for not instructing their people to give systematically. Everyone should set apart a stated portion of his income for God.

2 CHRON. 31:11-21

Order and Prosperity. There are several noticeable expressions in this paragraph. We are told that they brought in the dedicated things "faithfully," v. 12; and that the small as well as the great received their share, even as the daily portion of each required, v. 16, margin; also that the priests sanctified themselves in holiness, v. 18, as though touched and quickened by the generous gifts of the people. And in consequence of their entire devotion to the service of the sanctuary, adequate provision was made for their wives and children, while officers were appointed to distribute equal rations to all in the cities of the priests who, from age or other reasons, were not able to serve in the Temple.

The closing expression about Hezekiah, that he began nothing into which he did not put his heart and that God placed the crown of prosperity on him and his work, presents a striking contrast to the tale of disaster in the reign of Ahaz, and is an incentive to all of us to go and do likewise. See Rom. 12:11.

2 CHRON. 32:1-15

Prepared to Meet the Foe. We might have supposed that Hezekiah's faithfulness in cleansing the Temple and restoring the worship of Jehovah would have secured for him and his people complete immunity from invasion. Surely for such a loyal servant, God would graciously interpose and defend from Sennacherib's encampment on the sacred soil of the south country. We are taught the lesson that faith is not rewarded by the unbroken summer of prosperity, but tried, tested, and matured by the stormy blasts of attack and peril. The great Husbandman pruned Hezekiah that he might bring forth more fruit.

These careful preparations made by the king and his people for cutting off the water supply and equipping the soldiers and fortifications against attack were perfectly consistent with a true faith. Hezekiah's ultimate confidence was not in these things, but in that Greater One who was undoubtedly with them, vv. 7, 8. There was considerable subtlety in Sennacherib's messages, but he did not understand how much that "one altar" meant, and how different Jehovah was from the idols of the nations, vv. 12 and 15.

2 CHRON. 32:16-23

The Cry to Heaven Answered. Sennacherib's generals were even more insolent than himself. Their aim was to discourage the people and undermine their faith. To destroy confidence in God is the surest method of attack and victory. A significant description of their braggart boastfulness is given in v. 19. The only effect, however, was to drive the king and the prophet to prayer, v. 20. This is the talisman of victory. Isaiah tells how Hezekiah spread out the blasphemous letter of the invader before God and asked his help, that the kingdoms of the earth might know his power, inasmuch as his character was at stake before the heathen.

One angel sufficed for the work of deliverance and Sennacherib returned home a discredited man, to be murdered by his own children. The Lord not only saved Israel, but "guided them on every side." Shall we not claim similar treatment? And when we are true to God, we may rely on him to give us favor with men and enrich our lives with his hid treasures. "Them that honor me, I will honor."

2 CHRON. 32:24-33

One Flaw in a Good Life. What this sign was is more clearly told in Isaiah 38:1-8. Great interpositions on the part of God impose corresponding responsibilities. If you have received special benefits, be sure to render again according to the benefit done. When visited by the Babylonian ambassadors, as in 2 Kings 20:13, Hezekiah received them in a spirit of vanity—all too natural to most of us—and displayed a conceit in his acquisitions which shut out such acknowledgment of the divine love and care as was due. In man's view, that was merely a little weakness, something to be smiled at and excused, but it was inconsistent with the intimacy into which Hezekiah had been introduced by his heavenly Friend.

However pious and devoted a man may be, if he does not walk carefully he will break down in some crucial test. It is easier to withstand the invasion of Sennacherib than the flattery of Babylon. We need to guard against pride of heart. Compare vv. 25 and 31. Hezekiah's ostentatious display of his wealth and treasure excited the cupidity of the Babylonian envoys and sowed the seed of Nebuchadnezzar's invasion, though the blow was temporarily averted by the repentance of the king and nation, v. 26.

2 CHRON. 33:1-13

Affliction Teaches Humility. Because of his youth Manasseh was probably the more easily influenced by the reactionary party, who came back to power on Hezekiah's death; but afterward, in his early manhood, he pursued still further these evil courses and made Judah and Jerusalem to err. Warning voices protested in vain, until there was no alternative save the hooks and fetters of the king of Assyria. But in his dungeon in the far country he came to himself and God.

The words describing his penitence are very

strong, suggesting long-continued tortures of conscience and much agony of remorse. How quickly God heard him, and how incredible was his restoration! Here was a captive for life, as it seemed; yet he is not only set free, but actually restored to his kingdom and established on his throne. There is much hope for us all in this. If we truly repent of our sins, we shall be forgiven, and not only forgiven but restored again to our kingdom. Let us believe that God not only casts away our sins, but restores our soul.

2 CHRON. 33:14-25

Humbled Father, but Self-willed Son. Manasseh apparently did his best to undo the evil he had wrought in Jerusalem. So far as the idols and other symbols of idolatry were concerned, it was comparatively easy to take them away. But notwithstanding all his endeavors, the people still sacrificed in high places; and his son Amon perpetuated the memory of his father's sins, making no effort to repeat his repentance and tears. Though Manasseh "commanded" Judah to serve the Lord, the people continued to worship amid the impure and degrading associations to which he had accustomed them.

It is easier to scatter thistledown than gather it up. There are great thistle tracts in Australia which would never have arisen but for the careless act of a Scotch settler, who imported from his native land one specimen of the national emblem. Take care of your influence. It is easier to set stones rolling than to stop them. It is recorded of a dean of St. Paul's in London that he was never seen to smile, because in his early life he had written verses of a sensual character, the circulation of which he was unable to arrest.

2 CHRON. 34:1-11

A Young King's Noble Leadership. Josiah was as much better than his father Amon, as Manasseh had been worse than Hezekiah. How strange to find such a pure young soul in the heart of Amon's court! What led the boy to such moral and religious attainments? Perhaps his grandfather, Manasseh, unable to change his son, focused his prayers and influence on his grandson. It is probable, also, that considerable influence for good resulted from the discovery that he had been the subject of prophecy. See 1 Kings 13:2. He felt encouraged to apprehend that for which he had been apprehended years before. Though no prophet's voice has predicted the program and attainments of our lives, they are well known in Heaven, and we are summoned to realize God's great ideals for us.

The call of Jeremiah, also, so nearly coincides with the commencement of Josiah's reforms that we can scarcely regard the two facts as unconnected. At any rate, the king's earlier efforts seem to have been coincident with the first appearance of the prophet-statesman in the king's court at Jerusalem.

2 CHRON. 34:12-21

A Disturbing Discovery. The finding of the roll of the Law was a very significant incident. That it should have become so rare—apparently this was the only copy extant—was doubtless due to the destructive and desecrating efforts of Manasseh and other kings. Some pious hand had concealed it from the search of the inquisitors, and the secret had never been divulged. It is small wonder that the king's heart misgave him when he compared the divine ideal with the actual condition of things in Judah and Jerusalem. Here is an illustration of the way in which conscience may awake to the demands of God, which have long been buried amid the drift and rubbish of our lives, ignored and disobeyed. One day this neglect is brought suddenly and sadly home to us, and we cry out in an agony of conviction.

Let us read God's Word carefully and reverently until we come on something which accuses us, and then stop to listen. We must submit ourselves to its scrutiny. We must allow it to divide between soul and spirit. We must enthrone it, at whatever cost, as the critic of our lives. We must follow its leadings wherever it points the way.

2 CHRON. 34:22-33

Renewing the Covenant. The tender heart is a humble one, v. 27. To admit that God is right and we are wrong, and to take home his rebuke, is an admirable position. The penitential tear is like the baptism of dew on foliage parched by the scorching heat. But the tender heart does not confine itself to emotion; it acts. The king gathered all the elders of Judah and Jerusalem, went up to the house of the Lord, and caused all the people to stand to the covenant he proposed. He "made all that were present in Israel," though they were outside his jurisdiction, "to serve the Lord their God." Evidently Josiah was one of those men who have a compelling force because they appeal to the conscience in the heart of all men, and are themselves in close touch with God. Why not surrender yourself wholly to God! There are temples which need repairing, priests and people who require direction and leadership, nations which must be brought back to the God of their fathers. Only be tender, humble, and trustful. The world has yet to learn what God can do by those wholly devoted to him.

2 CHRON. 35:1–15

A Memorable Passover. This Passover was memorable, not only for the imposing grandeur of the ceremonial and the concourse of worshipers, but because of the strict adherence, even in minute particulars, to the prescriptions of the Law. Josiah was the soul and life of the movement. First the Levites were addressed and reminded that as they were not required to carry the Ark from place to place, as in the days of the Exodus, they might fitly undertake other work and assist the priests, who were likely to be overwhelmed by the demands of the approaching celebration. Let us not cling to stereotyped conditions, but adapt ourselves cheerfully to new demands. One of their first duties was to bring the Ark out of the side chamber to which neglect had relegated it, and reestablish it in the Most Holy Place.

Vast preparations were made for the poor and those unable to provide for themselves. Munificent offerings were made by the king and the princes. True love to God is always accompanied by unselfish care for others. If you really love God, you will desire to promote the knowledge of, and participation in, his love. Never forget to leave a place for worship and praise!

2 CHRON. 35:16–27

A Fatal Conflict. The huge masses of people were admitted according to their families into the sacred courts, and the gates were closed as soon as these were filled. Thus all the fathers' houses came, one after another, in solemn procession to the altar, offering such part of the sacred victims as was required and receiving part for their own use. While this was in progress the Levite choir chanted Psalms 113—118.

What a misfortune that so auspicious a reign should end so disastrously! Josiah opposed Pharoah because Palestine was under the tutelage of Babylon and had become the cockpit of the two warring nations, which were then contending for the mastery of the world. It would seem from v. 21 as if the Egyptian kings acknowledged the supremacy of one overruling Deity and considered that they were inspired by him. Blame appears to be attached to Josiah for not recognizing the voice of God. The lamentation over his death became proverbial for its excessive grief, Zech. 12:11. Josiah's reign was the last gleam of light in his doomed country, but it was good for him to be removed before the storm burst.

2 CHRON. 36:1–10

At the Mercy of the Foe. The narrative here runs parallel with 2 Kings, but the events are described with a certain gravity of warning which enforces the lesson of history. Here was the final catastrophe. Long predicted, at last it fell. The Jewish kings named here were mere puppets, and instead of turning to Jehovah, followed each other in persistent idolatry. Jehoahaz was deposed by Necho, who hoped for a more obsequious tool in his brother Jehoiakim; and the latter in his turn was deposed by Nebuchadnezzar, because he was Necho's nominee. Jehoiachin was carried into captivity because he was the choice of the people, and Zedekiah because he rebelled. These are the superficial reasons for the changes that followed each other with such terrible rapidity. But the pages of Jeremiah and Ezekiel reveal other and deeper reasons, alluded to subsequently in this chapter.

It was a long process of pruning through which Israel had to pass before this stock could bear that one pure flower, the mother of our Lord, who was to give the human side of his holy nature to the world.

2 CHRON. 36:11–23

Defeat and Exile. It is expressly stated in Ezekiel 17:13 that Nebuchadnezzar administered to Zedekiah an oath of fealty in the presence of Jehovah. Hence by his rebellion, he not only broke his promise to the king of Babylon, but profaned the name of God. It is in reference to this profanation of his oath that Zedekiah is addressed in Ezekiel 21:25 as "thou, profane wicked prince . . . whose day is come."

It also appears that toward the close of this reign idolatrous rites of various kinds intruded upon the sacred precincts of the Temple. Hebrew women bewailed Tammuz; elders burned incense to the forms of beasts portrayed on the walls; and men, turning their backs on the sanctuary, worshiped the sun. There was no remedy but exile.

It had been distinctly predicted that if the

Hebrew people disobeyed, their land should become a desolation and their cities a waste, until the soil had enjoyed the rest which they had failed to give it. Compare Lev. 25:4 with 26:34, 35. There was a point beyond which the divine judgment would not go. God loved the people whom he chastened; the recreant nation, at the instigation of Cyrus, had one further opportunity of fulfilling their great mission to mankind.

THE BOOK OF
EZRA

RETURN AND RECONSTRUCTION

I. THE RETURN UNDER ZERUBBABEL *1—6*
   - A. The proclamation and provision of Cyrus *1*
   - B. The census of the return *2:1-67*
   - C. The offerings of the people *2:68—3:7*
   - D. The building of the Temple *3:8—6:22*

II. THE RETURN UNDER EZRA *7—10*
   - A. The commission and gifts of Artaxerxes *7*
   - B. The census of the return *8:1-20*
   - C. The journey, and the delivery of the treasure *8:21-36*
   - D. Ezra annuls strange marriages *9, 10*

INTRODUCTION

Ezra was a Jew, sprung from the race of Aaron and descended from the high priest who was slain at the capture of Jerusalem, 2 Kings 25:18–21. This book is not a continuous narrative, but consists of two parts separated by several years. The first part, chapters 1—6, contains a narrative of the return of the first caravan of Jews from Babylon, under the leadership of Zerubbabel and Jeshua. The second part, chapters 7—10, is an account of an expedition, sixty years after the first, conducted by Ezra himself, accompanied by large numbers of his fellow-countrymen and empowered to reestablish order and religion.

This book is supposed to have been written by Ezra, who was a great student of the holy writings, and a ready scribe in the Law of Moses. He must have been a man of note among the Jewish captives to have won the favor and trust of the king of Persia. There is an absence of the miraculous, and a great similarity to the books of Chronicles. It shows enthusiasm characterizing the beginnings of work for God; then coldness and apathy follow in face of opposition. But when men get back to foundation principles, the work is carried forward to completion.

COMMENTARY

EZRA 1

God's Promises Fulfilled. God will ever be mindful of his covenant. There were also many remembrancers such as Daniel and other likeminded exiles who gave him no rest and were ever asking him for David's sake to bring his people from captivity. See Isa. 62:6, 7. The Lord stirred up the spirit of Cyrus, v. 1, and the spirits of the people, v. 5. How clearly the minds of men are subject to his promptings! May we never be disobedient to the heavenly visions that visit us, but always on the alert to work out with fear and trembling whatsoever he may work in.

Whenever we yield to the divine promptings, it is remarkable how everything seems to cooperate with us. The stars in their courses fight for us. All things serve the man who serves Christ. In the present instance, all that were round about strengthened their hands. Cyrus brought forth the vessels of the house of the Lord, which had been in safekeeping during those years of anarchy and confusion, like the precious manuscripts of Scripture during the Middle Ages. But when they were needed, God brought them out of their hiding place. Trust in him; he makes no mistakes.

EZRA 2:61—3:7

The Building of the Altar. Throughout their history the true Israelites were eager to maintain their genealogy; wherever they were scattered, they carefully guarded their national registers. Each of us should be able to establish his descent and to vindicate his claim to be considered a child of God, a joint-heir with Christ, a partaker in the inheritance which God has promised to them that love him. If you cannot establish your sonship, you may doubt your right to the spiritual blessings which are a part of the family estates. This is clearly illustrated by the prohibition issued against the eating of the most holy things by the priests whose names were not found in the register. They must wait till the Urim and Thummin attested that they were Israelites indeed. What that witness was in olden days, the testimony of the Holy Spirit is within us. He witnesses with our spirit that we are born of God.

The first act of the restored Jews was to set up the House of God. For this they gave willingly and after their ability. The altar was the center of their religion. So the cross of Jesus is the center of our life and worship, reminding us of his work for us in justification, or his claims in sanctification.

EZRA 3:8–13

The Foundation of the Temple Laid. Foundation laying is not always pleasant work. It means toil under ground, down in the trenches, unnoticed and unknown, and those who begin are often not permitted to finish. But amid all, the minstrel Hope brought her harp and sang her sweet strains of encouragement. In spite of the fewness and poverty of the builders, the voice of Inspiration had assured them that the glory of the latter house should surpass that of the former. So by the reckoning of faith, in sure anticipation that God would keep his word, the builders encircled their foundations with their songs. But the same event excited tears and shoutings. The old men looked back, and as they contrasted the impoverished and diminished condition of their people with the opulent crowds that had thronged the courts of Solomon's Temple, they could not restrain their tears. The young, new generation had not the same retrospect or ideals, and filled with hope of that which was to be, they could not restrain their shouts, which were heard afar off. "We have been," said the graybeards, "and the good old times were better than these." "We shall be," said the young, "and we will make the coming days better than any that have been since the beginning of the world!"

EZRA 4:1-10

The Building of the Temple Opposed. So long as you lead a languid and unaggressive life, the enemy will leave you alone, but directly you begin to build God's Temple, you may count on his strenuous opposition. When we are permitted to go on from day to day without much temptation, we may fear that we are doing little to destroy evil and construct good. But the virulent hate of the wicked one is a comfortable sign that his kingdom is suffering serious damage. Let us so live that we may give the devil good reason to fear and hate us. There is a stronger than he.

We must beware of the proposal to join in with the ungodly. Their arguments may sound very fair and appeal to a false liberality of sentiment, but the golden cup contains poison, and beneath the kiss is the traitor's hand. This is why so many fair enterprises have miscarried. They have seemed to afford common ground for cooperation with the false and counterfeit Israel, but they have ended in disillusionment and disappointment. Though the Jews excited the intense hatred and opposition of their would-be helpers, their policy of exclusiveness was amply justified by the result. The old proverb reminds us that we must never trust our enemies when they offer blandishments and gifts.

EZRA 4:11-24

The Enemy's Short-lived Triumph. The promoters of this letter were descendants of the heathen colonists who had been sent into the land by the Assyrians, 2 Kings 17:24. It was written to the then reigning monarch, Artaxerxes, which Ezra seems to have copied from the records of Persia, because it stands in the original in the Chaldee language. Notice that now the Israelites are first called Jews, i.e., Judahites, v. 12. The enemies urge that the Temple-building should be stayed for the king's own sake. Secret enmity to God's kingdom is often hidden under pretended devotion to Caesar, John 19:12. We, too, have our maintenance from the God of Heaven, we have eaten the salt of the palace, v. 14; and we should never allow his name to be dishonored without doing our best to prevent it. The king was imposed upon by their representations, and ordered the work to cease. But it is probable that something was due to the supineness of the Jews, who were already half-hearted in their endeavors, Hag. 1:2-9. The rebuilding of the Temple stopped during the reigns of Cambyses and the Magia Smerdis; but in the second year of Darius Hystaspes it was recommenced, and was then finished in four years, or nineteen years after its commencement, Zech. 8:9; Hag. 2:18.

EZRA 5

The Mission of Haggai and Zechariah. It is necessary to read the books of Haggai and Zechariah to see what difficulties the leaders of the people had to meet, and how much they needed the help of the prophets. At last matters were brought to an issue by the failure of the crops, which gave the prophets additional arguments. When God's judgments are abroad in the earth, men learn righteousness. As soon as the rebuilding began after a lapse of fifteen years, another letter was sent to the metropolis for advice. Tatnai appears to have been incited by the Samaritans, and he made a visit for personal inspection. His account of the proceedings is very graphic. The eye of God is on those whose hearts are perfect toward him, v. 5; 2 Chron. 16:9; Ps. 33:18. It is very well to imitate these elders in giving an answer in meekness and fear, but not terrified by our adversaries, 1 Pet. 3:12, 15. If God has clearly set us to do work for him, let us go through with it in spite of all human opposition. Storms are the methods by which he reveals our weakness and his all-sufficiency. The walls of the spiritual temple are built in troublous times, but the work goeth fast on. The rulers of this world cannot understand and gnash impotently with their teeth. God's plan shall stand, though earth be in arms to resist it.

EZRA 6

Prospered in a Difficult Work. How much depended on the finding of that roll! But God knew where it was, and led them to discover it, and inclined Darius to ratify it. When we are anxious and troubled about our relations to our fellowmen, we do little by worrying, we do much by trusting. Missing documents, alien hearts, tangled skeins, all yield before the hand of our Father working for us. The difficulty raised by their foes really reacted for the benefit of the Jews, for the king decreed that their expenses should be met and their needs supplied. When we are living upon God's plan and need material resources for his work, he will see that they are forthcoming from the most unlikely sources, and the revenues of heathen monarchs shall be laid under contribution.

When the house was finished it was dedicated, v. 16. What joy was there, but amid all, a solemn memory of the sin of the whole people of Israel. Though scattered to the four winds, they could not forget that in God's sight they were one still. It is highly probable that Psalms 146-150 were composed at this time. In the Septuagint they are called "the Psalms of Haggai." Burnt offering and song go together, 2 Chron. 29:27. After the dedication, the Passover. Separation must ever precede our feasting on God's Paschal Lamb, and out of this state of heart influences proceed which produce the true unity and drawing together of the children of God.

EZRA 7:1-18

A Missionary Journey. An interval of sixty years intervened between the events of chapters 6 and 7, and in that time the history recorded in the book of Esther took place. This chapter is full of helpful thoughts. Note the description of Ezra's character—"a ready scribe," v. 6. He not only knew the Law, but he set his heart to "seek ... and do," v. 10. The only way to understand Scripture is to be prepared to do it. What a contrast to Matthew 23:3! Let us not resemble the signpost, which directs the traveler but stirs not a step along the road it points. Note the secret of Ezra's success, "the good hand of his God." This is a characteristic phrase of Ezra and Nehemiah. That hand answers prayer, v. 6; speeds our way, as much in railway trains as in caravans, v. 9; and strengthens us for service, v. 28. The strong, tender hand of God is laid on our hands, as a father's on those of the son learning to draw a bow, Gen. 49:24. And when God's hand is on us, it is also on others, preparing them to cooperate. When God needs an instrument, he will come to men of Ezra's spirit.

EZRA 7:19-28

A King's Bounty. Ezra's commission was very ample. Those who officiated or assisted in Temple service were exonerated from taxation. Full permission was given to take all voluntary gifts of money. Orders were issued for the supply of food and other necessities. He was also appointed governor of all Jews west of the Euphrates. The royal bounty was very generous. Here was the harvest of Daniel's prayers and tears. God did exceeding abundantly unto his people beyond all that they had asked or thought. Notice how Ezra's love for God's Law impressed Artaxerxes with the conviction that it was perfect. He commanded that the will of God should be the supreme court of reference to Ezra and his brethren in the disposal of the free-will offerings. He further enjoined that they should do exactly the commands of the God of Heaven, and ordained that all who refused should be punished. So great was his respect for the Law that he left Ezra to do very much as he thought best. This reverence on the part of a heathen monarch for God's Law shames us. Let us make more of it ourselves! Let us be people of the Book and exalt it as we are exalted by it, in the judgment even of those who do not revere it!

EZRA 8:1-23

United Prayer for Guidance. The number of men who accompanied Ezra amounted to 1,754, but the women and children would bring up the gross total to about 7,000. The lack of Levites was very serious. These should have been among the very first. A deputation was therefore sent to the place where they were being trained, and here again is the mention of "the good hand of God." Sometimes hearts are ready and waiting for service, needing just a word or appeal to complete their plans. There is always special interest in this paragraph for those who are venturing forth on the untried and unknown. We see the camp at Ahava; the sending for the priests; the waiting for their coming; the recognition of God's good hand in sending a man of discretion; and then the fast and prayer for protection. We can almost see the little band on the point of plunging into the inhospitable and dangerous desert, spending hours in prayer, and restrained from requesting an escort, lest they might invalidate their leader's trustful boast. How careful we should be to do nothing inconsistent with the proud position that faith gives us in the keeping power of God! Seek him, O soul of mine, and he will be found, and his hand shall be upon thee for good.

EZRA 8:24-36

Thanksgiving for Safety and Success. Into our hands also is committed first the rich treasure and solemn trust of our own souls, and next the great deposit of the gospel, 1 Tim. 1:11; 6:20. In order to fulfill this sacred charge there must be purity, "Ye are holy"; and sleepless vigilance, "Watch ye." There were ambushes and designs on their safety, but the foe was unable to break through the divine environment, v. 31. How safe are we who live in God! What joy as the little band weighed the vessels and rendered up their charge, Luke 19:16. Is not this a picture of our entrance into Heaven, when we also shall acknowledge the good hand of the Lord and sacrifice our burnt offerings of thanksgiving? This incident is no exception. Similar care will be surely and blessedly experienced by all those who trust under the shadow of God's wing. It is credibly affirmed that in the American Civil War none of the Quakers, who of course were pacifists, suffered any damage from the troops of either side. "The angel of the Lord encampeth round about them that fear him, and delivereth them." Let those who fast and pray for God's help be sure to return him thanks when it has been given.

EZRA 9

A Leader's Sorrows for His People's Sins. The mingling of the holy seed with heathen peoples was always the curse of Israel, and it has been the temptation of God's children in every age. Do we sufficiently tremble at the words of the God of Israel because of our sins or those of others? The humiliation and anguish of soul experienced by Ezra and his associates are a great rebuke to us. We are indignant, but we do not view sin from God's standpoint. Notice the humility of his prayer, "I blush to lift up my face"; its vicarious confession of sin; its acknowledgment of God's grace in giving a little reviving; its recital of the aggravation which had dyed their sin of a deeper hue. Israel was intended to live in Canaan as a separated people. The land itself could not yield its good, or remain their permanent inheritance on condition of their fidelity to God. When confession of sin has been made, let us stand before God claiming forgiveness, acceptance, and cleansing through the precious blood of Christ, 1 John 1:7.

EZRA 10

Putting Away Strange Marriages. The people seem to have been more impressed by Ezra's intense grief of soul than they could have been by his severest condemnation. Is not this the secret of winning men from their evil ways? But we must not expend all our force in tears; we must act when we have opportunity. Shechaniah was not implicated, but his father and other near relatives were, v. 26. His words may be appropriated by us all, v. 2. There is always hope for the man who repents and puts away evil. It is a great encouragement when brave men will stand by the reformer, but whether they do or not, there is One who neither leaves nor forsakes, Heb. 13:5, 6. A drastic remedy was required; it seemed very hard and must have occasioned many heartbreaks. Probably if a wife had truly turned to the God of Israel, she would have been retained. God demands the sacrifice of anything which comes between us and him, however dear, Mark 9:43; Matt. 10:37. There is no warrant for such action in our days. The process of the gospel is given in 1 Cor. 7:12, 13. A solemn assembly was convened in the month of December, the coldest and rainiest time of the year. A court of inquiry was finally appointed, who continued their labors for about a quarter of a year. The offense seems to have been temporarily eradicated, though we meet with it again, Neh. 13:23; Mal. 2:11. Each generation repeats the sins of its predecessors, unwarned by their bitter experiences. Not the study of history, but the Spirit of God is needed to deal with and subdue individual and national sins.

THE BOOK OF NEHEMIAH

RECONSTRUCTION AND REFORM

I. THE BUILDING OF THE WALL   *1—7*
    A. The expedition of Nehemiah to Jerusalem   *1, 2*
    B. The assigning of the workers and their tasks   *3*
    C. The opposition of Tobiah, Sanballat, and Geshem   *4, 6*
    D. Nehemiah's reform of unjust usury among the Jews   *5*
    E. The completion of the wall and census of the city   *7*

II. RENEWING THE RELIGIOUS LIFE; REFORM   *8—13*
    A. The public reading of the Law; Feast of Tabernacles   *8*
    B. The renewing of the covenant   *9—10*
        1. The national fast   *9:1-3*
        2. The prayer of the Levites   *9:4-37*
        3. The sealing of the covenant   *9:38—10:39*
    C. Distribution of population; census of the priests   *11:1—12:26*
    D. The dedication of the wall   *12:27-47*
    E. The cleansing of the Temple; Sabbath and marriage reforms   *13*

INTRODUCTION

Ezra continued his labors in Jerusalem for some twelve years after the events recorded in his narrative, and actively cooperated with Nehemiah, to whose history we now turn. Indeed, though this book was largely written by him whose name it bears, certain portions of it were probably written by the ready scribe, Ezra, who spent the closing years of his life in collecting the sacred books into one volume, and completing the canon of Scripture. Nehemiah was born in exile. In early life he was exposed to great temptation, although the appointment which he held in the Persian court was an honorable one. But he remained faithful, devout, simple-hearted, patriotic, and godly; he was evidently valued by the heathen monarch as a good and faithful servant—"an Israelite indeed, in whom was no guile."

He arrived at Jerusalem thirteen years after Ezra, with the rank of governor of the province, and with full authority to rebuild the walls, which, notwithstanding the erection of the Temple, still lay waste. His administration lasted some thirty-six years. The secret of his efficiency lay in his constant bringing of all the problems before God, and of this habit we shall have abundant evidence as we proceed. The book abounds in expressions of his sincerity. Nehemiah was a simple-hearted man, characterized chiefly by humility and purity of motive, and revealing the mighty power that can be exerted by one who has no purpose in life and no power that is not centered in God.

COMMENTARY

NEHEMIAH 1

A Patriot's Prayer. Though living in luxury, in the winter palace of the Persian kings, Nehemiah's heart was keenly sensitive to all that affected his people. But he turned from tears to prayer, from man to God. Oh, that we could cry and sigh for the rents and breaches in the Church of God. We should deal much more successfully with men if, like Nehemiah, we dealt more largely with God. Gordon used to say that he had met and conquered his enemies before he saw them. This prayer of Nehemiah's is very beautiful, saturated as it is with quotations from Scripture, and so effective with God because based on his own Word. It was steeped in tears of contrition for sin, and offered without ceasing "day and night." Nor was it solitary, for there seems to have been a little band of others united with him, v. 11. Lord, teach us to pray thus, till others are found kneeling with us. Here is a good petition for us as we go forth to our daily calling, in which so much depends on the attitude of our fellowmen. "Prosper thy servant this day and grant him mercy in the sight of this man."

NEHEMIAH 2:1-11

A Patriot's Self-sacrifice. The seventh month answers to our March or April, so that four months had passed since Nehemiah had set himself to special prayer. Between the king's second question and Nehemiah's answer, the simple-hearted cupbearer found time to pray to the God of Heaven. Then, with the assurance that God was with him, he did not hesitate to ask great things: that he might be sent to the city of his fathers to build it, and that he might receive all the materials necessary for its construction. But he is careful to record that his requests were granted, not by the clemency of the king, but according to the good hand of God. Do we recognize that good hand enough? We get glimpses here into the inner workings of this man's heart. He felt that God had put his holy purpose there. He did not hesitate to confess this to the Jews and amid the opposition and scorn of their foes, he strengthened himself in his God, sure that he would not have brought him so far to put him to shame. Be sure you are on God's side, and nothing will be impossible to you.

NEHEMIAH 2:12-20; 4:1-12

Braving Ridicule and Treachery. Suspicion, 2:12-20. Sanballat was probably a Moabite, a native of Horonaim; Tobiah had been a slave. There are many descendants of these two men in all our Christian communities today, hindering God's work. This heroic soul met their scorn and the depression of the people by unwavering faith and calm confidence in the good hand of God, v. 18. How small do our difficulties seem when brought into the sight of the God of

Heaven! *Reproach,* 4:1-6. Whenever God's work revives, there is sure to be evil-speaking and reproach. It is a mistake to reply. Let us hand over our cause to God, and go on with his work. It matters very little what men say, as long as *he* is pleased. Had Nehemiah had the message of Christ, he would not have prayed as in v. 5. Our Lord taught us to intercede for our enemies, Matt. 5:44. But let us emulate Nehemiah's zeal for the name of God, and let us remember that increased light means increased responsibility, Matt. 11:11. *Active opposition,* vv. 7-12. In time of hostility, our friends and allies are apt to grow discouraged and to advise the suspension of our work. "We are not able"; but faith looks to God alone and triumphantly holds on its way.

NEHEMIAH 4:13-23

The Triumph of Courage and Devotion. The work of rebuilding the ruins of Zion is typical of our efforts as Christians to counteract the deterioration which is ever at work in our own hearts, in the professing Church, and in society. No one who attempts this work will escape hostility, covert or manifested. That is a suggestive attitude pictured here; the girded sword, the spear in one hand, and the trowel in the other. So they wrought, with ear intent for the trumpet sound, ready for any emergency, and yet sure that God would fight for them. All the people of God should make common cause against a common foe. We stand or fall together, v. 20. Our hands must be familiar with the sword against the attack of our spiritual enemies, and with the trowel to contribute our bit of work toward God's building.

NEHEMIAH 5

Securing Justice for the Poor. The prospects of the poor people among the returned exiles were deplorable. There had been deficient rains and poor harvests, Hag. 1:6-11. They had mortgaged their lands to their richer brethren, and had even sold their children to pay the royal taxes and procure means of subsistence. The rich had taken advantage of their necessities, oppressing them with grievous exactions and heavy usury. When Nehemiah heard of it, he seems to have withstood the wrong with strenuous protest, depending on his God for support. And in a great assembly he carried the day against selfishness and greed. There is nothing here to condemn mortgages or interest in themselves. Each is a legitimate method of trade, except when undue advantage is taken of a brother's necessities. Verses 14-19 were evidently added at a subsequent period to the rest of the chapter, and relate the habits of Nehemiah's administration. How full is this book of ejaculatory prayer! Even from his writing table, this true-hearted man would lift up his eyes to God.

NEHEMIAH 6

A Great Task—A Safeguard from Danger. How often Satan tries to call us off from our work for God! He cannot endure to see us engaged so eagerly on our Master's business and therefore raises up all sorts of hindrances and hostilities. Amid all these we have but one duty to perform. We must lose ourselves in our work. Ours is but to reply, "I am doing a great work, I cannot come down; why should the work cease?" If we will see to God's business, he will see to our safety. False friends, who prophesy in God's name, are more to be dreaded than open foes. We must learn to discern the spirits. The counsel which savors of self is always to be suspected. Note that Nehemiah considered that to have fear would have been to sin. But God was with the little band through dangers, and the wall was finished in spite of all opposition, 1 Cor. 15:58.

NEHEMIAH 7:1-8, 36-73

Public-spirited Citizens. It is probable that Nehemiah returned to the Persian court on the completion of the first part of his enterprise, the building of the walls, and that he left Hananiah and his brother in charge until he had been able to obtain a prolongation of his mission. Hananiah's character is very aptly described in v. 2. These are splendid characteristics—the fear of God and faithfulness, 1 Cor. 4:2. Sound common sense, through which God wrought, dictated the policy of appointing each man to guard his own property, v. 3. The extent of the city walls had evidently been marked out in faith, as directed in Zechariah 8. Registration seems to have engrossed much of the care of these returned exiles, and it was necessary, not only that each might inherit his ancestral property, but that the descent of our Lord might be easily traced to David. We ought to be very sure that we and our dear ones are included in God's register. We cannot lay claim to our inheritance unless we are heirs through the new birth, Rom. 8:16, 17.

NEHEMIAH 8

New Light from God's Law. Surely this was the first public Bible-reading! When will the people be again as hungry for the Word of God as these

Jews who stood in the open space from early dawn till the scorching noon? What reverence for the Word! "When Ezra opened the book, all the people stood up." What holy worship! "Ezra blessed the Lord, the great God. And all the people answered, Amen, amen!" What a model to us all! "They gave the sense, and caused them to understand." What searching of heart! "The people wept, when they heard the words of the law."

There is nothing which weakens us so much as does unrestrained remorse. Contriteness of heart is wholesome and helpful, but excessive grief incapacitates us for our duties. It is well therefore to cultivate holy joy; the joy of sin forgiven, of acceptance with God, of hope that anchors us to the unseen and cannot be ashamed. You may not be able to joy in yourself or your surroundings, but you may always rejoice in the Lord.

NEHEMIAH 9:1-21

God's Hand in History. What a blessed result of the Bible study of the previous chapter. It led to confession, separation from evil association, and worship. It is good to review the dealings of God with us and with our people in bygone days. There are hilltops in our experience where the air is clear, and we can see the way by which we have been led. At such times we look beyond second causes to the great Orderer of our lives, and our history is one perpetual assertion of "Thou." The history of God's dealings with Israel is a summary of his dealings with ourselves. The choice in Ur, the redemption from Egypt, the wilderness wanderings, the land of rest—all these have their counterparts in our life-story. Side by side with the story of God's care runs the story of transgression, vv. 16-18. The gold and black strands are closely interwoven. In the midst of God's best gifts, we break out into sin; yet he still gives us his good spirit, and withholds not the manna which he promised, v. 20.

NEHEMIAH 9:22-38

The Penalty of Ingratitude and Disobedience. The theme of this prayer is the covenant mercy of God. However great the provocation of the Chosen People, he never swerved from his ancient promise to their fathers. He testified against them by his Spirit and chastened them for their sins. He allowed them to be oppressed by their enemies and carried into captivity. But when they returned and cried for his help, they found his manifold mercies waiting to welcome, forgive, and restore them. They were conscious that there was nothing in themselves or even in their fathers to explain these wonderful dealings, and the secret had ever to be found in "thy mercies." In this hour of distress, they turned back to him and bound themselves by a faithful covenant. But, alas, even written promises will not hold the wayward heart of man. What a picture this is of our own lives, and how often have all these experiences been repeated in us! Fortunately for us we are represented now, not by our promises and prayers, but by Jesus Christ, in whom we stand and are accepted and kept.

NEHEMIAH 10:28-39

A Pledge of Better Service. Chapter 10 opens with a list of the signers of the covenant, which was signed on behalf of the people. The consecration covenant involved: first, obedience; then, the purity of the holy seed from intermarriage with heathen peoples; next, the observance of the Sabbath, and of the Sabbatic year. In addition there was the yearly charge for the maintenance of divine worship.

The great lack among Christian people is system in the apportioning of their incomes. They leave their giving to impulse, and thus often give the merest fraction of their possessions to the cause of God. We should at least give a tenth, and as much more as we can afford. If only all who read these words would resolve to imitate these impoverished exiles, and to set aside the tithe of all they earn or receive, they would discover the luxury of giving, and a new zest in receiving. The firstfruits of increased wages and revenue should also be given to God, as a tribute of thanksgiving. Let the first produce of henroost, orchard, and field be his. Do not neglect or forsake God's house, v. 39.

NEHEMIAH 12:44—13:14

Neglect of Religious Duties. In v. 44-47 we have recorded the care that was manifested for the worthy maintenance of those who ministered in sacred things. As a result there were glad outbursts of minstrelsy and holy joy. Make room in your life for songs and praises, Ps. 33:1. In the opening of Chapter 13 we see how the Word of God cuts like a two-edged sword against evil. Happy are they who attend to its solemn warnings. The law referred to here was Deuteronomy 23:3-5. Tobiah was an Ammonite, and it was a scandalous thing that the high priest was not only allied to him by marriage, but had cast out the stores of the Temple in order to make room for him in the sacred edifice. Tobiah's influence was so great that the rest shrank from putting the law of separation into operation against him. When Nehemiah returned from a long sojourn in Persia, he cast out all of Tobiah's goods and restored the chamber to its proper use. If we have given up a chamber in our heart to any Tobiah, we must be prepared to do likewise.

NEHEMIAH 13:15–31

A Disobedient and Gainsaying People. Let us remember to keep perpetual Sabbath in the heart, whatever be our outward life. In this life there is a Sabbath rest for the people of God, Heb. 4:9, but we must labor to enter into it and must set God's angel of peace to keep the door against all intruders, Phil. 4:7. Twenty years before, Ezra had dismissed the strange wives, but the evil had risen again. Alas, how sadly do children expose the inconsistencies of their parents and betray the evil of unequal marriages! We see plenty of this around us; and where there is such a union, the balance is almost certain to turn in favor of the world and against vital godliness, Deut. 7:4; 2 Cor. 6:14. Nehemiah did not hesitate to add strong acts to strong words. Josephus says that this expelled priest was Manasseh, and that he went to his father-in-law, Sanballat, who built for him a temple on Mount Gerizim like that at Jerusalem, and that this was the origin of the religious rivalry and hatred between Samaritans and Jews, John 4:20. The faithful servant and the dying thief join in the same petition, v. 31. To be remembered by Jesus Christ is enough reward for any of us!

THE BOOK OF ESTHER

DELIVERANCE FROM NATIONAL DISASTER

I. THE PLOT TO DESTROY THE JEWISH NATION   *1—3*
    A. The deposition of Vashti   *1*
    B. The advancement of Esther   *2:1–18*
    C. Mordecai's service to the king   *2:19–23*
    D. The promotion of Haman   *3:1–6*
    E. Haman's plot against the Jews   *3:7–15*

II. THE PLOT EXPOSED   *4—7*
    A. Mordecai's appeal to Esther   *4*
    B. Esther's appearance before the king   *5:1–8*
    C. Haman anticipates Mordecai's death   *5:9–14*
    D. Haman obliged to honor Mordecai   *6*
    E. Haman's fall and execution   *7*

III. THE PLOT FRUSTRATED   *8—10*
    A. Esther's plea for her people   *8:1–9*
    B. The king's decree for their self-defense   *8:9–17*
    C. The Jews slay their enemies   *9:1–16*
    D. Feast of Purim established   *9:17–32*
    E. The advancement of Mordecai   *10*

INTRODUCTION

This book is a striking record of the divine providence. In the foregoing books we learn how God watched over the Jews who returned from captivity. This tells us how those who remained still in exile, scattered through the great heathen world, were marvelously preserved. Though the name of God does not occur in this book, yet his hand is everywhere manifest. His name does not often occur in the daily press, which records the history of our times; yet we may ask whether the workings of God are not also clearly recorded there. Verily our God sometimes hides himself.

The time occupied by this story falls between the going up of Zerubbabel from Babylon to Jerusalem, and that of Ezra. The Persian empire was at the height of its glory, extending from the Indus to the Mediterranean. It is supposed that the Ahasuerus here mentioned was Xerxes, the invader of Greece. The feast in Chapter 1 corresponds in point of time to the great council he summoned to decide on that invasion. His winter palace was at Shushan, and his court given up to revelry and excess. It is held by some that the book is an extract from the imperial records of the time, and was perhaps drawn up by some pious Jew, Mordecai or another, who was annalist at that time. If this were the case, it would account for many parentheses and explanations which are inserted, which would not have been required by ordinary Jewish readers.

COMMENTARY

ESTHER 1

Vashti's Noble Refusal. The book opens with a royal festival, which lasted for six months, vv. 1–9. Perhaps the princes came up from their governments to partake of it in rotation. It finished with a banquet, open to all the people who dwelt in Shushan, great and small. Whenever men are overcome with wine, there is grave peril for women. Coarseness, indelicacy, impurity troop in at the door which has been unlocked by the excess of wine. Who can tell the anguish which has been caused to women, children, and the dumb creation through the intemperance of man! Here is given a glimpse of a noble woman who respected herself too highly to yield to a demand, wholly foreign to the customs of the time which forbade women to appear in public. Of course the king was incensed, all the more so because he knew that he was in the wrong. He had command over 127 provinces, but he could not rule his own spirit, and the sense of moral weakness is always irritating. He consulted his counselors, who were only too glad to fall in with and humor the royal whims. They counseled that the divorce of Vashti was a public duty, for the repression of wife insubordination throughout the empire. Men are not always to be trusted when they legislate about women, or in respect to their own dignity. When wine is in them, they may be expected to say and do very stupid things. It has been truly said that every Ahasuerus has his Memucan, a man who was sycophant and parasite, who held his influence by humoring caprice and lust.

ESTHER 2

The Service of a Foreigner. Esther's Hebrew name meant "myrtle." It could not have been easy for her to retain her sweet simplicity amid the corruptions of her time, but her Persian name means "a star," as though she were a garden enclosed, encircled by the atmosphere of the divine purity and protection. We must not judge Esther by our own standards, but by the custom of her time. Each of these young girls was considered to be married to the king, was kept under his roof, and was his wife of a lower rank. How great is the influence of Christianity in raising our standards and pervading the world with a loftier morality! She was not bidden to deny her parentage, but only advised not to proclaim it, v. 10. When afterwards she was raised to power, she showed no flinching from identification with her race. So she attained the highest position in the world to which a woman could aspire. God lifted her there to serve a high and noble purpose. Her relative, Mordecai, discovered a plot against the king and told it to his ward, the queen, and she to her royal spouse. The deed was unrewarded; in this, however, the faithful doorkeeper felt no disappointment. He acted not for reward, but from a sense of duty. But the act was registered both in Heaven and on earth, and it bore fruit. It is enough for us to do our duty, and please God.

ESTHER 3

Race Prejudice Breeds Hatred. Josephus says that "Agagite" means a descendant of Agag, the common name for the kings of the Amalekites, Num. 24:7. It is probable that something of the nature of religious homage to Haman was demanded, and this Mordecai could not tolerate for a moment. It would have been as bad as the falling down to worship the golden image of Dura. He, therefore, sturdily refused. What diabolical cruelty was here, to determine to destroy a nation to satisfy a personal grudge! The resolve was taken in the first month, when Esther had been queen for five years; but the lot indicated the twelfth month for its execution, so that Esther had twelve months in which to oppose the plan. The disposing of the lot was evidently God's, Prov. 16:33. The bribe, which Haman hoped to get from the spoils of the slaughtered Jews, without doubt helped to pave his way and make the king favorable to his request. The matter was soon settled, and the messengers were carrying the edict of slaughter to the furthest limits of the realm. It reminds us of the decree for the massacre of the Huguenots. But God was over all. The strongest assaults are vain against him, Ps. 2:4. He will not let high-handed wrong proceed beyond a certain point, 2 Kings 19:28. Let us shelter behind him and be at peace, Isa. 54:14.

ESTHER 4

Opportunity for Patriotic Devotion. It seemed as if the whole nation would suddenly be cut off to satisfy the hatred of Haman, and Mordecai knew that he had been the cause of the plot. Esther was evidently living in close sympathy with her uncle, though now separated from him. In reply to the demand that she should hazard her life for the people, there was at first a natural reluctance. Was her love for her people greater than her love for herself? In her resolve there was surely something of the great love of Christ. We may be quite sure that God will carry out his plans—*with* us, if possible; if not, in spite of us, to our utter loss. We should look upon our position as a sacred trust to be used for others. We are created for good works, which God hath prepared for us to walk in. There can be no presumption in action which is preceded by prayer and heart-searching.

ESTHER 5

Hatred Breeds Crime. Thus the soul clad in the royal garments of Christ's righteousness stands in the throne-room with its request. It has already obtained favor, for has it not been accepted in the beloved? The Lord waits that he may be gracious. Delay is not denial, and in the meanwhile there are things to be seen and heard which fill the soul with rapture. Have you touched the top of the sceptre? Have you claimed unto the half of the kingdom? Have you invited the King himself to your banqueting table? For the King himself is willing to be your guest. We feast at his table, but he also comes and sups with us at ours. In all earthly joy there is alloy, something which detracts from full gratification; a Mordecai for Haman, because of whom all else availed nothing. The joy that this world gives is at the mercy of unfavorable circumstances, but "he that drinketh of the water that I shall give him shall never thirst."

ESTHER 6

Gratitude for a Forgotten Service. There was a divine providence in this royal sleeplessness. On the very next night Haman would be hanging on the gallows, and it would be too late for him to render this honor to the hated Jew. Therefore, on this night the king must be reminded of a forgotten incident, must ask if the chivalrous informant had been rewarded, and must, through Haman, decree his splendid reward. When we are suffering indignity at the hand of enemies who seem to pass out of our lives without making reparation, let us turn to this story and remember that as honor came to Mordecai through Haman, so honor and reparation shall accrue through the very circumstances and people that seem most threatening. The wrath of man is made to praise God.

ESTHER 7

Craft Overreaches Itself. Esther had prayed, as we have seen, 4:16, but she acted also. She took such measures as were possible to gain the king's favor, to awaken his curiosity, and to appeal for his help. All the money that Haman could pour into the royal treasury could not compensate for the loss of an entire people. In his anguish of soul, Haman adopted an attitude of entreaty which seemed to the king a gross impertinence, and this sealed his fate. His face was covered as though he were no longer worthy to behold the king. The chamberlain sent to summon Haman had probably seen the gallows on that errand; and thus it befell that the wicked was taken in his own trap, Ps. 9:15. It may be that we are to see in our modern world, on a national scale, the counterpart of this extraordinary reversal. Watch events transpiring in Palestine!

ESTHER 8

Courage Rewarded. The ring symbolized royal power and authority; by this sign Mordecai was suddenly raised to the position formerly held by Haman. He also managed for Esther the large estate which had come into her possession. Because of the permanence of the customs and laws of the Medes, it was impossible to reverse the royal proclamation, which had decreed that the Hebrew people should be exterminated. So the king granted Mordecai permission to send letters to his people, allowing them to arm and defend themselves. The speed with which the circulation of the royal decree was carried out is a rebuke to the Church of God which has been entrusted with the gospel of salvation. More than 1,900 years have passed, and still immense multitudes have never heard the name of Christ or the love of God. Let us at least strain every nerve to pass on the joyful news, overtaking the tidings of death.

ESTHER 9:1–19

Deliverance by the Sword. When the fateful day arrived, the Jews throughout the empire stood on the defense. As it appears from v. 16, 75,000 of their assailants fell in the provinces and 500 in Shushan alone. Among these were the ten sons of Haman. No attempt at plunder was made by the victors. The second day was asked for probably to confirm the settled policy of Ahasuerus, and the exposure of the bodies of Haman's sons was rendered necessary by the virulent hatred entertained toward the Jews. Decisive measures were demanded to show their enemies the risk they would incur by pursuing Haman's policy. Haman was an Amalekite, and in this light we may recall Exodus 17:14, 16; Deuteronomy 25:19. In all this, especially in this terrible act of vengeance, we are reminded repeatedly of the change that Christ's coming made in the world, even among religious people. Contrast Esther and Mary of Bethany!

ESTHER 9:20—10:3

The Feast of Purim. The Feast of Purim—so called from 3:7—was held on the 14th and 15th of Adar, our February. The whole of this book was read on the previous evening in the synagogue. Whenever Haman's name was pronounced, the whole congregation made a terrible noise, and every voice shouted imprecations such as, "Let his name rot!" The reference to tribute in 10:1 shows that this book is a historical document, preserved in the state archives and probably written by a Jewish chronicler, who may have owed his position to Mordecai himself. The providence of God is clearly discernible in all the incidents recorded here. Through all human governments and events a divine purpose runs; and as God exalted Mordecai to honor and glory, so will he work for those who love him, and so ultimately will he put all enemies under his feet.

THE BOOK OF JOB

THE MYSTERY OF SUFFERING

I. THE PROLOGUE   *1:1—2:13*
  A. Job's prosperity   *1:1–5*
  B. The first council in Heaven   *1:6–12*
  C. Job's adversity   *1:13–22*
  D. The second council in Heaven   *2:1–6*
  E. Job's affliction   *2:7–13*

II. THE POEM   *3:1—42:6*
  A. Job's lament   *3:1–26*
  B. The first colloquy   *4:1—14:22*
  C. The second colloquy   *15:1—21:34*
  D. The third colloquy   *22:1—31:40*
  E. The address of Elihu   *32:1—37:24*
  F. The address of Jehovah   *38:1—41:34*
  G. The submission of Job   *42:1–6*

III. THE EPILOGUE   *42:7–17*
  A. Job and his friends reconciled   *42:7–9*
  B. Job restored to prosperity   *42:10–17*

INTRODUCTION

This is one of the great poems or dramas of the world, founded on historical fact. That Job was a real person may be inferred from Ezekiel 14:14; James 5:11.

Neither the age in which Job lived nor the date of the book itself has ever been definitely determined. The author is unknown. The book is unique in the canon in that it has no immediate connection with the people of Israel or their institutions. The most natural explanation of this fact is that its events antedate the history of Israel.

The problem of the book is as old as the world—how to reconcile the goodness and justice of God with the apparently arbitrary and unequal distribution of affliction and prosperity that we see about us. It shows us how, in the fierce light of reality, men who have prided themselves on their uprightness suddenly become convinced of sin and resigned to God's dealings.

Of its literary character perhaps no one has written better than Carlyle: "I call this book . . . one of the grandest things ever written with pen. One feels indeed as if it were not Hebrew—such a noble universality, different from ignoble patriotism or sectarianism, reigns in it. A noble book, all men's book! It is our first, oldest statement of the never-ending problem—man's destiny and God's ways with him here in this earth. And all in such free, flowing outlines; grand in its sincerity, in its simplicity. . . . Sublime sorrow, sublime reconciliation; oldest choral melody, as of the heart of mankind; so soft and great; as the summer midnight, as the world with its seas and stars! There is nothing written, I think, in the Bible or out of it, of equal literary merit."

COMMENTARY

JOB 1:1–12

Satan Aims at a High Mark. Job is introduced as a man of large possessions, highly honored by all who knew him and of unimpeachable integrity toward God. His piety was specially evinced in the anxiety he experienced for his children, lest any of them should renounce or say farewell to God. What an example this is for parents! We should pray for each child by name and, like Job, we should do so continually.

Satan is well called the "Adversary," margin, because he opposes God and goodness. Compare Zech. 3:1; Rev. 12:10. He admits Job's goodness, but challenges its motive. He suggests that it is by no means disinterested. Satan still considers the saints, and finds out their weak places and secret sins. But he has no power over us save by the divine permission, and if we are tempted, there is always available the needed supply of grace, 2 Cor. 12:9.

JOB 1:13–22

Stripped of Every Possession. There are dark days in our lives when messenger follows on the heel of messenger, and we sit down amid the ruins of our happiness. All that made life gay and beautiful has withered, and we are treading a dreary waste; our soul is almost dead within us and our feet are blistered. Then our friends come and lay the blame on the Chaldeans and lightning, the Sabeans and the hurricane. They pity us as unfortunate and miserable. But we say to ourselves, looking beyond the secondary causes to the Cause beyond them all, "The Lord gave, and the Lord hath taken away." Sometimes we can get no farther than this, but how happy we are when we can go on to say, "Blessed be the name of the Lord." The true soul is reckless of what happens to himself, so long as the glory of the Lord's name remains unsullied and enhanced. Let us, above all, never charge God with foolishness by impeaching his love or the rectitude of his decisions.

JOB 2

"Among the Ashes." It gives God deep pleasure when he can point to one of his servants who has borne fiery trial with unwavering patience and faith. The adversary comes back from his restless, ceaseless rounds, 1 Pet. 5:8; but there is one soul at least which has resisted his worst attacks. Observing Job, the principalities and powers in the heavenly places have learned that God can make a man love him, not for his gifts, but for himself, Eph. 3:10.

The adversary suggests a severe test, and God permits it because he knows his child. A limit, however, is put upon the ordeal, 1 Cor. 10:13. The story is very comforting, because we see that we are not the sport of chance, but in every detail our education is being carried out by our Father's hand. Our dearest friends may advise us to renounce God and die, but in Gethsemane our Lord taught us to take the Father's will at all costs—though it seem to spell death—sure that he will not leave us in the grave, Ps. 16:10.

JOB 3

Is Life Worth Living? In the closing paragraphs of the previous chapter, three friends arrive. Teman is Edom; for Shuah see Genesis 25:2; Naamah is Arabia. The group of spectators, gathered round Job's mound, reverently make way for them.

Job opens his mouth in a curse. But it was not, as Satan had expected, against God. The Hebrew word is different from that used in Job 2:9. He does not curse God, but the day of his birth, and asks that his stripped and suffering existence may be brought to as speedy an end as possible. Job's words are very profitable for all whose way is hid. Is the joy of life fled? Yet its duties remain. Continue in these and the path will lead back to light.

This opening elegy consists of two parts: the first, vv. 1–10, calls on darkness to blot out the day which witnessed the beginning of so sad a life; the second, vv. 11–26, inquires why, if he were doomed to be born, the luxury of instant death had not been also granted. Oh, human heart, of what sore anguish art thou not capable!

JOB 4

"Shall Mortal Man Be More Just Than God?" The first cycle of speeches is opened by Eliphaz. It must be remembered that he and the two others believed that special suffering resulted from and was the sign of special sin. Job's calamities, in the light of that thought, seemed to prove that he who had been considered a paragon of perfection was not what they had supposed. According to their philosophy, if only he would confess his sin, all would be well and the sun would shine again upon his path.

Eliphaz recounts a visitation, in a night vision, from the unseen world, which is described with marvelous power. Emphasis is laid on the infinite distance between God and man, and on the impossibility of a mortal being accounted just in the presence of divine purity. Of course the suggestion is that Job was suffering the penalty of sin which, though it had eluded human eyes, was naked and open before God. An angel seems dark against God's pure light, and if an angel is deficient how much more man!

JOB 5

The Benefits of Chastisement. In this chapter Eliphaz closes his first speech. He had already suggested that Job's sufferings were the result of some secret sin. It could not be otherwise, according to his philosophy. Affliction and trouble did not come by chance. It was as much a law of Nature, so Eliphaz thought, for calamity to follow sin as for sparks to fly upward. However deeply evil men had rooted themselves, they were doomed to be destroyed. Was it not obvious that Job had in some way offended? Let him confess and be restored!

The ideal life which will ensue on a genuine repentance is described in the most thrilling and glowing terms, vv. 8–17. Each sentence is a priceless jewel, and each has been tested by generations of returning prodigals, for whom each promise has been countersigned by the "Yea" of Christ, 2 Cor. 1:20. Paul quotes v. 13 in 1 Corinthians 3:19.

JOB 6

"A Deceitful Brook." The burden of Job's complaint is the ill-treatment meted out by his friends. They had accused him of speaking rashly, but they had not measured the greatness of his pain, v. 4, or they would have seen it to be as natural as the braying and lowing of hungry and suffering beasts, v. 5. A man would not take insipid food without complaint; how much more reason had he to complain whose tears were his meat day and night, vv. 6, 7! So bitter were his pains that he would welcome death and exult in the throes of dissolution, vv. 8–10. It could hardly be otherwise than that he should succumb, since he had only the ordinary strength of mortals, and both strength and wisdom were exhausted, vv. 11–13.

Job next characterizes the assistance of his friends as winter brooks, turbid with melted ice and snow, which bitterly disappoint the travelers who had hoped to find water and perish beside the dry heaps of stones, v. 17. They had found fault with his words which, in the circumstances, were not a true index to his heart, v. 26; but a look into his face would have sufficed to attest his innocence of the sin of which they accused him, vv. 28–30.

From these complaints of faithlessness and disappointment we turn to him who, having been made perfect through suffering, has become "the author of eternal salvation unto all them that obey him," Heb. 5:9.

JOB 7

Longing for the Evening. The servant eagerly longs for the lengthening shadow which tells him that his day of labor is at an end, and we may allow ourselves to anticipate the hour of our reward and deliverance.

In plaintive words, which have so often been on the lips of heavy sufferers, Job tells the story of his sorrow and bitterness. The sufferer addresses God directly—almost suggesting at first that God was persecuting him without cause. Let those who have been disposed to think God unmindful and hard in his dealings, ponder these words. Even this saint of patience has trodden that path before them, and he came out right at last. But a softer tone follows; Job realizes that he has sinned, pleads to be forgiven, and asks that the word of forgiving love may not tarry, lest it be too late. The psalmist uses expressions similar to vv. 17, 18, but with a more wholesome application, Ps. 8:4; 144:3.

Notice that wonderful name for God—"the watcher of men," v. 20, margin. Not to discover their sins, but to learn their sorrows and needs with the intent of helping them with his saving strength.

JOB 8

God Will Not Cast Away. Bildad now takes up the argument, appealing to the experience of former generations to show that special suffering, like Job's, indicated special sin, however deeply concealed. He feels that God could not pervert judgment, and that the sudden destruction of Job's children proved that they had transgressed.

Verses 11-13 are probably quoted from an old poem, embodying the sententious observation of some older generation, which compared the ungodly to the rapid growth and more rapid destruction of the papyrus plant. Verses 14, 15 compare the state of the ungodly to the slight fabric of the spider's web, finespun, flimsy, and insecure. Verses 16-19 employ yet another comparison—that of the weeds, which grow to rank luxuriance, spreading over heaps of stones and even walls, which they are figuratively said to "see" in the distance and creep toward; the very earth is ashamed of them, as presently they lie withered on the path. But notice the assurances that God will uphold all those who return to him. Be of good cheer; thou shalt yet praise him!

JOB 9

"The Daysman." Ponder the sublimity of the conceptions of God given in this magnificent passage. To God are attributed the earthquake that rocks the pillars on which the world rests, v. 6; the eclipse which hides the heavenly bodies, v. 7; the storm in which he moves the heavens and treads majestically on the waves, v. 8; and the creation of the constellations, v. 9. Who can dare to argue with or call to account so great a God as this? See vv. 10-19. Even if a man be outwardly and inwardly righteous (that is, so far as the measure of his light), yet in such a Presence the heart of the most perfect must condemn him. "If we say that we have no sin, we deceive ourselves. . . . God is light, and in him is no darkness at all." We cannot but feel that this old-world thinker had a truer view of that conscious imperfection and sin which must be experienced by every mortal who has a right appreciation of the holiness of God than have those who refuse to say the Lord's Prayer because it contains a petition for forgiveness!

Truly we need that Daysman! But we have him in Jesus our Mediator, who can lay his hand on God and us, v. 33; 1 Tim. 2:5.

JOB 10

Soul Bitterness. In this chapter Job accuses God of persecuting his own workmanship, v. 3; of pursuing him with repeated strokes, as if he had not time enough to wait between them, but must hurry on to achieve his design, v. 5; of reversing the careful providence which had watched over his earlier years, v. 12; of hunting and playing with him as a wild beast with his prey, vv. 16, 17; and asks that he may be allowed speedily to enter the land of Sheol, vv. 18-22.

As we read these complaints, we may remember days in our lives when we uttered similar ones, but we are without excuse. And when we are tempted in this direction, it is for us to remember that probably we are being tried to teach us the manifold wisdom of God, so that the works of God should be made manifest in us, Eph. 3:10; John 9:3. It will enable us to endure if we remember that God has conferred on us high honor by choosing us to show that we can stand the fire, like those iron safes, blackened by smoke, which the makers place in the shop windows to prove the stability of their workmanship.

JOB 11

"Canst Thou by Searching Find Out God?" Zophar waxes vehement as he censures Job's self-justification and his refusal to acknowledge the guilt which his friends attribute to him. There is some truth in his allegations, though it was cruel to goad Job with them, notwithstanding his repeated protestations.

It is quite true that many of us are filled with self-complacency, because we judge our best by others' worst. It may be also that we have a very poor conception of what God is and asks. It is best for us to strike our breasts with the publican and to confess ourselves the chief of sinners.

What a magnificent challenge is that of vv. 7–12! Canst thou reach God's depths, or his perfections, or his heights? But, oh my soul, remember that through all his unsearchable depths God is love. Job had said he could not lift up his face, 10:15, but when sin is put away, we may exchange glances with our Father (compare v. 15).

JOB 12

"Deep Things out of Darkness." Job sets himself to disprove Zophar's contention that wickedness invariably causes insecurity in men's dwellings; and in doing so he bitterly complains that his friends mocked at him so contemptuously. He says that they remind him of those who are glad enough of a torch when their foot is slipping in the dark, but cast it aside when they reach their quarters, v. 5.

Those who rob are often the most prosperous, v. 6, and Nature teaches that the animals and plants which are most sturdy in their self-assertion are most secure. Is not the vulture more secure than the dove, the lion than the ox, the shark than the dolphin, the rose than the thorn which tears it? In all such cases you cannot explain the mystery except by referring it to the will of God, whose reasons are past finding out. Similar mysteries beset human life.

Job still further illustrates his point from human life, showing that the lives of counselors, judges, kings, priests, princes, and elders are exposed to the same apparent anomalies and inequalities of treatment. We know, however, that suffering is purifying to the soul and often redemptive, as Christ's was, for others.

JOB 13

"Though He Slay Me." The sufferer first rebukes his friends, vv. 4–12. Then he makes an appeal to God, affirming that he was no hypocrite and asking that his sins, for which he was suffering, might be identified, v. 23.

When Job said that he knew himself to be righteous, he was clearly speaking of known sin; he knew, so far as a man may know himself, that he had not committed the sins of which his friends charged him. He could bare his life to the inspection of men and angels, being sure that no accusation of which human law courts would take cognizance could be established against him. But this is a very different matter with the divine tribunal. When a fuller light had shone upon him from the face of God, when the patriarch had seen him instead of merely hearing of him by the ear, then he would "abhor himself, and repent in dust and ashes," 42:5, 6.

Verse 15 is almost the greatest sentence ever uttered by mortal lips! Let us ask for grace to affirm it.

JOB 14

Shall Man Live Again? Continuing his appeal, Job looks from his own case to the condition of mankind generally, vv. 1–6. All men are frail and full of trouble, v. 12; why should God bring a creature so weak into judgment with him, v. 3? The sinfulness of man is universal—not one can be proved clean before God, v. 4. Since man is so frail, Job pleads that he may not have such overwhelming affliction, but may get some pleasure, v. 6, margin, out of his brief day.

The anticipation of death as total extinction strengthens Job's appeal, vv. 7–12. Of a tree there is hope that, if cut down, it will sprout again, vv. 7–9. But at present Job sees no such hope for man. He dies and is done with, as waters "fail from the sea," vv. 10–12. This is a gloomy, despairing thought, and one against which the mind rebels as soon as uttered. Against the belief that death is the end of all things every man's better nature revolts. Hence the picture of another life beyond the present immediately rises to Job, vv. 13–15. It may be only a yearning desire, for Job still asks the question, v. 14. Yet this desire, as that for a Daysman, 9:32–34, both suggested by the heart's despair, is equally answered by the gospel.

The hope for a future life is made stronger by the apparent injustices that exist now, vv. 16–22. God's treatment of Job appears to be so severe that Job must perish under his hand, vv. 18-22. A future life is surely necessary to remedy the inequalities of the present. Evidently this is not the place and time of judgment.

JOB 15

"The Heavens Are Not Clean." The second colloquy, like the first, is commenced by Eliphaz. He begins by *rebuking* Job, vv. 1-16. He complains that the words of Job proved him to be unwise, vv. 2, 3, and even irreverent, v. 4. His very speech testified to his iniquity, vv. 5, 6. With something of irony Eliphaz asks upon what Job's claim to superior wisdom rests. Was he the first man, v. 7? Or had he access to the secret counsel of God, v. 8? In refusing the counsel of his friends, vv. 9, 10, and the consolations of God they had offered, v. 11, had he not proved his want of wisdom? He had even proved his folly and his impiety by attempting to assert his innocence before God, vv. 12-14, in whose presence even the heavens were unclean, vv. 15, 16. It is clear that Eliphaz and his friends did not believe the sincerity of Job's protestations of innocence.

Eliphaz then attempts to *instruct* Job, vv. 17-35. His theme is almost the same as that of his former speech. It is the righteousness of God as specially manifested in the punishment of the wicked. He claims that his doctrine is that of the wise men, vv. 17-19; then proceeds to describe the wicked man as troubled in conscience and full of fear, vv. 20-24; attributes this to his bold impiety, vv. 25-28; and predicts his fearful doom, vv. 29-35. The application of such teaching to Job must have been very painful. He insinuated that Job's terrible afflictions were God's testimony against his sin. We know better from John 11:4, 5.

JOB 16

Turning from "Miserable Comforters" unto God. With bitterness the sufferer turns from his comforters to God. He says that if he were in their place and they in his, instead of joining words together and evincing the pride of the immaculate, he would set himself to speak strengthening words and to assuage their grief by tender sympathy.

He compares his pains to the attack of a wild beast, vv. 7-14; and from this he proceeds to describe the anguish of his grief, vv. 15-20. But toward the end of the chapter a new thought begins to shape itself; and from his lowest despair he catches sight of a Vindicator and a vindication that must someday be his. Job wanted a son of man to plead for him; and his prayer has been more than answered in *the* Son of man, who pleads for us "not after the law of a carnal commandment, but after the power of an endless life," Heb. 7:16. "O Lord, thou hast pleaded the causes of my soul," Lam. 3:58.

JOB 17

"The Bars of Sheol." Job's *continued complaint of his friends,* vv. 1-9: He avows that he could bear his awful calamities if only he were delivered from their mockery, and asks that God would arbitrate between him and them. God is the supreme Judge, and Job asks him to become his surety against the recriminations of those who so shamefully misjudged him. There is no other course for hunted souls than appeal from man to God in the person of Jesus. At the close of this paragraph, he insists that amid a whirlwind of trouble the righteous must hold on his way and keep his hands clean. If any should read these words whose path has dipped down into the valley of the shadow, let them hold on their way. Go on doing the will of God, so far as you know it, and it will bring you out under his Heaven of love.

Job's gloomy anticipations of the future, vv. 10-16: For him there was a grave of darkness and gloom. Men had not as yet been begotten again unto a living hope by the resurrection of our Lord Jesus Christ. The soul must descend to "the bars of Sheol," v. 16. What a contrast to our Christian hope! There is no need for us to claim the pit for father and the worm for sister! In the Father's house are many mansions. The sufferings of the present are not worthy to be compared with the glory to be revealed! Our kin are not in the dust. We are surrounded by a great cloud of witnesses.

JOB 18

"Cast into a Net." Bildad's second speech reveals how utterly he failed to understand Job's appeal for a divine witness and surety. The deep things that pass in a heart which is enduring sorrow are incomprehensible to shallow and narrow souls.

His description of the calamities which befall the wicked is terrible: their extinguished light, vv. 5, 6; their awful distress, vv. 7-11; their destruction, vv. 12-17; the horror with which men shall regard their fate, vv. 18-21. All this was, of course, intended for Job. It was very severe. Even if the worst had been true, his extreme sufferings should have elicited more tenderness from his friends. Only the strong, wise hand of love can assuage the wounds that sin has made. We are indebted to Bildad for the phrase, "king of terrors," as applied to death, v. 14. Apart from Christ, it is a significant and appropriate term. Sin has made his monarchy terrible. Yet even he has met his conqueror, John 11:25, 26; Heb. 2:14; 1 Cor. 15:26.

The ancients had a deep presentiment of the punishments which must overtake sin. Probably we make too little of them. The note of fear has almost died out of modern preaching. In this there is a marked divergence from Baxter's "Call to the Unconverted" and from Jonathan Edwards' "Sinners in the Hands of an Angry God." But the doom of sin is terrible for those to whom Calvary has pleaded in vain. A great atonement implies great sin, and a great penalty.

JOB 19

"I Know That My Redeemer Liveth." In Job's melancholy condition his friends seemed only to add vexation and trial. The hirelings who sojourned in his household looked on him with disdain; his kith and kin were alienated; it seemed as if the Almighty had an antipathy against him. So great was his physical suffering that the only sound part of his body seemed to be the skin of his gums and his teeth, v. 20 (that is, all he could do was to speak). Then he suddenly breaks into the majestic utterance of vv. 25 and 26.

Among the Bedouins the institution of the *goel*—or kinsman representative—still exists for the avenging of wrong done to a kinsman. Job believed that his divine *Goel* would one day stand on the earth for his vindication. Yes, and more, he felt that somehow he, too, would arise from the very grave to hear that vindication spoken by those just and true lips. Above all, he would see God himself standing with him—"whom I . . . shall see, on my side," v. 27, margin.

JOB 20

"The Triumphing of the Wicked." Zophar is the man who least of all understood Job. The rebuke which Job had just administered, 19:28, 29, has vexed him, so that he speaks with impatience.

The theme of Zophar's speech is the brevity of the prosperity of the wicked. He claims that this is an acknowledged principle, v. 4, then proceeds to show it by many striking metaphors.

"Hypocrite," v. 5, is literally "godless." In describing the prosperity and speedy destruction of such, vv. 5–11, he manifestly applies his words to Job. He refuses to pay any heed to Job's protestations of innocence. His theology was: God is righteous; he blesses and prospers the good, and destroys the wicked. Job was being destroyed; therefore, Job was wicked. Thus often do we in our ignorance misunderstand God and cruelly misjudge man.

Zophar descends to more particulars. He describes the pleasure which the ungodly has in sin, vv. 12, 13; how his sin becomes his punishment, vv. 14–22; and how terrible destruction at last visits him, vv. 23–28, as his "portion from God," v. 29. Though in all this Zophar was wrong in applying it to Job's case, and equally wrong in supposing that this life is the place of judgment for the wicked, yet it is important to remember that he was right in seeing a very real connection between sin and punishment. However sweet sin may be to the taste, it is sure to become bitter as the gall of asps ere long. The "pleasures of sin" are but "for a season."

JOB 21

"Shall Any Teach God?" After a brief introduction, in which he claims the right to reply, vv. 1–6, Job brings forward a new argument. He affirms that his friends are wrong in assuming that the connection between sin and suffering is invariable. On the contrary, he urges that wicked men often spend their lives in prosperity, on the farm, in the fold, and in the home, vv. 10, 11. Sounds of joy issue from their dwellings, v. 12. They die without prolonged torture, v. 13. From the contention of his friends, Job turns to the passerby for confirmation of his words. Surely, he says, it is a matter of common observation that some wicked men do prosper and die in peace, v. 29.

With Job's answer the second colloquy ends. His friends have gained nothing by their arguments, but Job has learned much by his afflictions. On the dark background of his night the Morning Star has actually begun to shine. He appeals to God with greater confidence and even finds refuge in him; but so far, though arguing his case, he has preserved a humble and reverent attitude.

JOB 22

"Acquaint Thyself with God." Eliphaz opens the third cycle of the discussion with a speech altogether too hard and cruel. He begins with an enumeration of Job's fancied misdeeds, vv. 1–11. The fundamental position with Eliphaz was the absolute, evenhanded justice of God. In contrast with the magnate who is influenced by

gifts, God at least was unimpeachable; and therefore, however Job might affirm the contrary, he must have deserved the chastisement which had befallen him.

Then follows his argument from the Deluge, vv. 12–20. Evil men are always anxious to think that God does not notice them. This was, says Eliphaz, the policy of those who were destroyed by the Flood. They attempted to build society on atheistic lines, though he filled their houses with good things. The inference, of course, was that Job had been guilty of the same offense.

Eliphaz concludes with a tender delineation of a holy life, vv. 21–30. To be reconciled to God, to obey his Word, to put away iniquity and trust in earthly riches are the conditions of blessedness. We shall gain more than we lose, v. 25. We shall inherit the confidence and joy of his presence, v. 26. Our prayers will be answered, we shall walk "in the light," and our ministry to others will be full of helpfulness. Let us, then, acquaint ourselves with God and be at peace!

JOB 23

"He Knoweth the Way That I Take." This chapter is threaded by a sublime faith. Job admitted that his complaint seemed rebellious, but God's hand had been heavy on him. From the misunderstandings of his friends, he longs for the calm, holy presence of God himself.

It seemed as if nothing would content the sufferer but a personal audience with the Almighty. He felt that he could plead his cause there without fear. He was sure that his Almighty Judge would not contend against him with his great power, but would listen to him. Yet it seemed impossible to find him. Job did not realize that he was already in God's audience-room. We are made nigh through Jesus Christ. God hides himself because mortal eyes could not bear the burning glory of his presence. But though we fail to see him, we are never for a moment out of his view. He knows the way that we take. Speak to him, weary, suffering soul; the Lord is at hand!

It was not a mere self-righteous boast that the sufferer made in vv. 7, 11, 12. David also used similar words of himself, Ps. 18:20–23. We are always sinners, needing the precious blood; but we may be very thankful if we have been kept from "the great transgression." Yet the perfect man is still troubled in the divine presence and his heart becomes faint, vv. 15, 16, unless he can claim something more than natural goodness. "On Christ, the solid rock, I stand; all other ground is sinking sand."

JOB 24

Not Here, but Hereafter. Job laments that the times of punishment are not so explained by God, that those who know him may see and understand his reasons. He then turns to describe the life of the ungodly, who do dark deeds with apparent impunity. A very sad catalogue of crimes follows. The oppression of the needy, the driving away of the ass of the fatherless, the taking of the widow's ox for a pledge, the plunder of caravans regardless of the claims of pity, the stealing of oil and wine from those who had labored to produce them, the murdering of the poor laboring man at the dawn, the commission of crimes at night—such are the iniquities which are described. And these crimes are still committed in so-called Christian lands. It is wonderful that God should bear with us, but his long-suffering should lead men to repent. It is only after long forbearing and trial that he cuts down.

In his closing words, vv. 18–21, Job quotes the opinion of his friends as to the condition of the ungodly, that they pass away swiftly as the waters and are snapped as a branch of a tree. And, in opposition, he states his own view, vv. 23–25, that they die in exalted positions—not by a painful and lingering death, but as corn in the maturity of the ear. This also is true. Wicked men do not always meet their deserts in this world. In the next world penalty is inevitable.

JOB 25

How Can Man Be Just before God? Bildad's closing speech adds little to the controversy. He suggests simply that Job's vindications of himself do not imply that he is righteous before God and, acting upon the philosophy of the time, Bildad prefers to consider that Job is guilty of unrealized sins rather than believe that God has permitted suffering to come to him unmerited.

There are some unanswerable questions in this paragraph—suggestions full of helpfulness. God's armies are numberless—ten thousand times ten thousand, and every angel is pledged to our help. His light shines everywhere, even on the saddest hearts. Not one of us can be just before him, but we may avail ourselves of the justifying righteousness of Christ which, as Bunyan says, is always the same, not increased by our good frames of mind or lessened by our bad ones. None born of woman are clean, but the blood of Jesus Christ cleanses from all sin. Moon and stars pale and pass away, but God hath set his heart upon his saints, and hath adopted them into his family.

And when the fabric of Nature shall have decayed, they shall shine as the sun in the kingdom of their Father.

JOB 26

"Parts of His Ways." Job taunts Bildad as having imparted no help or thought. He then proceeds, vv. 5–14, to give a description of God's power as manifested in Hades, in space, in the clouds, in the ocean, and throughout the universe. The spirits of the dead tremble before him; the grave and destruction that veil themselves in night are stripped before his gaze; the world itself is suspended in space by invisible threads (a wonderful foreshadowing of the true theory of the earth); the waters are held in the clouds, which do not burst under their weight but act as the veil of God's throne; the sea owns his authority, hushing under his word or rising in its might; his breath brings the dawn; his hand strangles the dragon, as representing a well-known constellation, Draco. But these are only "parts [lit. outskirts] of his ways." Great as is their acclaim as they circle his throne in thunder and splendor, they are but as a whisper compared with his divine power and Godhead. All that the scientist has known of God is, when compared with his essential nature, what the quiver of a leaf in the breeze is to the crash of the thunderpeal. This, O child of God, is thy Father, and his power is for thy defense.

JOB 27

The Justice of God. Zophar ought now to have taken up the discourse, but as he is silent, Job proceeds. First he renews his protestations of integrity, vv. 1–10. He denies the charge of being ungodly, and says that till he dies he will not put away his integrity. He refuses to justify the accusations of his friends, and demands that they who had spoken against him should suffer the punishments which they had suggested as his due, v. 7. The falsity of their charges was surely evidenced by the fact that he could still delight in the Almighty and call upon his name, v. 10.

Then he speaks of the portion of the wicked, vv. 11–23. Zophar and the rest could hardly have spoken more strongly. Though Job denied the application to himself, he was willing to admit the general truth of these propositions. Through what marvelous alternations the mind of man passes—now on the crest of the wave and again in the trough; arguing, debating, questioning; now antagonizing a position, and then almost accepting it! But be of good cheer! "At eventide it shall be light!" "I have been within the gates," said one brave explorer, "and there is no dark valley."

JOB 28

The Pearl of Great Price. A search for this pearl of great price has occupied men in every age. Job compares it with the search of the miner for the hidden treasures of the earth, vv. 1–12. The shaft into the earth, the miner's exile from the cheerful haunts of human life, his exposure to dangers from foul air, water, and the falling in of the mine, the binding up of the streams are vividly portrayed. But the miner perseveres through all till he obtains his golden spoil. Would that we were as persistent in our quest for the knowledge of God! Paul was a great miner; he went down into caverns of pain and sorrow, that he might bring to light the treasures of God's wisdom and love.

Only God knows God, v. 23. In the depths of his nature, dark with excess of light but hidden from the falcon's eye of human genius, are both knowledge and understanding. He waits to reveal these things to babes, saying, "Fear God, and you will be wise. Depart from evil, and you will understand," v. 28. Christ is the Word and the Wisdom of God, 1 Cor. 1:24.

JOB 29

The Bitter Memory of the Happy Past. How many thousands, looking back on the beautiful dawn of a life which has become overcast, have uttered the thought of the opening words of this chapter. The worldling has no hope of the renewal of that blessed past; but the believer knows that in Christ he belongs to the eternal order, which enters into the devastation wrought by sin, arresting, canceling, and converting evil into good.

If we believe in Jesus Christ, submit to his will, and unite ourselves to his heart, "a statelier Eden" comes back to us. God watches over us for good; his lamp shines on our way; his friendship is in our tent; his love transfigures all things. The graphic description which follows of the life of a godly man is still true when a man's ways please the Lord.

JOB 31

The Clean Life. Job had specially guarded against impurity, for its heritage is one of calamity and disaster. He is sure that even if he were weighed by God himself there would be no iniquity discovered in him. He even goes so far as to invoke the most awful results if he has sinned against the seventh commandment. It is well for us if we are able with similar sincerity to appeal to the verdict of God and of our own heart. Let us ask the Holy Spirit to beget in us purity and separateness from sin, that we may walk with unsullied garments.

Job also protests the evenhandedness of his dealings with his servants, alleging the principle which underlies the whole Christian teaching on the point, that we all have been made by the same Creator. He insists on his benevolence to the widow and the fatherless. He is careful to show that he had not failed in doing all the good that was within his reach. Alas, how few of us can say as much! How many such occasions cross our path every day, which we heedlessly let pass!

With this appeal Job goes into the presence of God, and asks for a reply. In the strong gospel light we are too deeply convicted of sin to dare to do this, and must rely upon the merits of Christ. In these alone can we approach the uncreated light.

JOB 32

Elihu Enters. The controversy between Job and his counselors is now at an end. They have failed in making out their case; but before God himself takes up the argument, there is another side of the case to be presented by the fervid life of a younger generation. The name Elihu means, "My God is he." He had preserved a respectful silence while his elders were speaking; but he was so conscious of the uprising of the divine that he could refrain no longer.

Elihu was greatly indignant, first with Job for not justifying God, v. 2; and then with his friends for their inability to cope with him, v. 5. But in addition to these criticisms, he has some positive contribution to make to the debate, and must needs make it. Silence is golden, but there is a time to speak. Be sure to inbreathe the Spirit of God. Do not speak, as John Woolman says, beyond the divine openings.

JOB 33

The Interpreter. It is not surprising that Elihu has been mistaken for the Mediator himself, so helpfully does he interpose between Job and his Maker. He dwells especially on his own likeness to Job in his manhood, and quotes this as the reason why he could specially help him: "I also am formed out of the clay." So also our High Priest is man. Elihu takes up Job's words protesting his innocence, and he insists that Job was not right in those protestations, or in the conclusions that he drew from them.

Then follows one of the grandest passages in the book. Elihu tells how God speaks in Nature and through conscience, and is often disregarded; and how then he speaks by revelation, opening the ears of men to withdraw them from their purpose. He shows that God often lays a man upon a bed of pain, that he may speak to his heart. Happy is the afflicted if an interpreter stands beside him to point the path to repentance. Finally, broken and penitent, he turns back to God and sees his face with joy, and sings before men the story of his restoration. Thus Elihu argues that affliction is often sent as discipline to read to man God's deepest truth.

JOB 34

The Almighty Must Be Just. Elihu stands in v. 10 as God's apologist. God's absolute and impartial justice is at all times a matter of untold comfort. There will be no cause of ultimate complaint, but from the lips of the holiest beings in the universe, most able to pass an opinion, the cry will ascend, "Great and marvelous are thy works, Lord God Almighty; just and true are thy ways, thou King of saints. . . . Thy judgments are made manifest," Rev. 15:3, 4.

Ponder those last words. God's judgments have not yet been made manifest; it is therefore foolish and wrong to pass judgment upon an unfinished program. Wait, mortal man, until at the great white throne God shall unfold his inner reasons. If it is not fit to say to a king, "Thou art vile," how much less to him who lives through the ages, while the people are shaken and pass away and the mighty are taken away without hand!

JOB 35

Songs in the Night. God is so exalted above man in his nature that he is altogether independent of him. When men sin against him, they hurt not him, but themselves. There is no motive, therefore, of retaliation or revenge in his chastisements. Not for his pleasure, the Holy Ghost says in another place, "but for our profit," Heb. 12:10.

Instead of seeking after God our Maker, who can give songs in the darkest night that ever befell a human spirit, we are too apt to despair. Instead of crying *to* God, we cry *against* him. We murmur and complain. We arraign God. There is our pride, v. 12. We regard iniquity in our heart, and God cannot answer us until we change our note for one of loving, trustful submission. God will not hear vanity, neither will the Almighty regard it.

Let us change our temper and our note. Have done with the proud self-will that chafes and argues and complains. This will not speed thy cause at God's bar. Humble thyself under his

JOB 36

He Despiseth Not Any. God is mighty, but he does not despise thee, though thou be the least of saints. His eyes are upon thee for good, and he will set thee before his throne forever. He will stoop to thy low dungeon, whispering instruction to thine ear and commanding thee to return. There are broad places before thee in which there shall be no straitness; tables await thee full of fatness. They path leads from thy present prison-house into liberty and light.

Remember the unsearchable numbers of his years. Behold the wonderful machinery by which he collects from ocean, lake, and stream the clouds which, like floating cisterns, carry the waters to be bleached in the snow of the hills, and oxidized in the torrent beds! There is more love than terror in creation. Nature's myriad voices proclaim with Scripture, "God is love." He cannot, therefore, be indifferent to the righteous man or neglect him. He may discipline him to make him hate sin; but when this end is attained, he will assuredly withdraw his rod, vv. 10, 11.

JOB 37

The Light in the Clouds. As Elihu spoke, a thunderstorm was gathering, and much of the imagery of this chapter is suggested by that fact. The little group listened to the sound of God's voice in the thunder. Peal followed peal without cessation, v. 4. The lightly falling snow and the drenching showers are alike his work, whether they restrain men from their labor in the fields or drive the beasts to their dens, v. 8. From the storm Elihu turns naturally to the winter, with its ice and snow, and the frost that binds up the flow of the streams, v. 10. All these perform God's bidding in the earth.

How little we know of atmospheric phenomena! Why the north and south winds blow, what is the real nature of the azure, and what the red and gold of the northern lights! We cannot find out the Almighty. He is great and glorious, and cannot be unjust. But let us be more eager to look for the bright light in the clouds. It is always there. A rainbow for every storm; an arbor for every difficult hill; a sure hiding place in every tempest. Such is Jesus to all who love and trust him.

JOB 38:1–18

Divine Power and Human Ignorance. When the storm had ceased and the thunder was hushed, a voice spoke out of the golden splendor of the sky. See Job 37:21, 22. Job had challenged God to answer him and now he is taken at his word. We recall Horeb's ancient cave, where, after wind and earthquake, there came a sound of gentle stillness. "Gird up now thy loins," said the Eternal to Job. In later years, under similar circumstances, the Spirit entered Ezekiel to strengthen him. Surely some such strengthening was forthwith given the patriarch!

A sublime series of questions is now addressed to him, not by a God of judgment and wrath, but by a Father arguing and pleading with his child and pointing out two things: first, the inability of mortal man to understand the ways of God; and second, the minuteness and tenderness of God's providence. Job had thought of him as remote, but he is near and is ordering all things wisely and lovingly. Can he forget his child?

JOB 38:19–41

What Man Cannot Do. In this chapter a number of Nature pictures pass before us. These include the creation of the earth, vv. 4–7; the sea, vv. 8–11; light, vv. 12–15; the mysteries of the unseen, vv. 16–18; snow and rain, vv. 22–30; the constellations of the heavens, vv. 31–38; and the recesses of the forest glades, vv. 39–41.

What does it all mean? Ah! there are times when the voice of God through Nature falls on our hearts like sweet music, and we hardly know whence or how, but we are comforted and strengthened. The peace passes understanding. Besides, the frequent question, "Hast thou?" was intended to turn Job's attention to the great mysteries contained in common and ordinary things. If he could not unravel these, how could he hope to fathom all the wonderful dealings of God with the human soul? His ways are above ours and his thoughts higher than ours; but we are sure from Calvary that he is love. Let us quiet ourselves, therefore, and trust.

JOB 39

"Knowest Thou?" "Canst Thou?" The series of questions is continued, and God asks more especially with respect to animated and organic nature: the wild goats, vv. 1–4; the wild ass, vv. 5–8; the wild ox, vv. 9–12; the peacocks and ostriches, vv. 13–18; the war horse, vv. 19–25; the hawk, vv. 26–30. In each case some special point is asked, hidden from the observation of ordinary men. If Job were unable to know more than they on such matters as these, how could

he expect to know more than they of the reasons that dictate God's dealings with his people?

There is mystery in every part of the universe of God. He hides himself, so that we cannot discover him. His thoughts are deeper, his ways profounder than our mind can fathom. There is not a single pathway leading out of the garden of life along which a man, traversing it, will not come to a point when the track dies away in the grass and there is no further progress. In Nature and in Scripture alike we have to deal with the inscrutability of God's ways. Nor can we wonder, if the God of the Bible and of Nature be the God of providence, that we find mystery also there.

JOB 40

"Hast Thou an Arm Like God?" God seemed to await Job's reply to his questions. Job had protested that he would fill his mouth with arguments, but none was forthcoming. That vision of God had robbed him of self-reliance. He could only humbly acknowledge that he had uttered words enough. He must be led to the further confession, which will come presently, that he had sinned. Compare Job 42:6.

It was as though the Omniscient Eye still saw in Job some trust in himself; God therefore summoned him to array himself in his utmost glory and majesty and to argue his case further. But how impotent man is at best!

The truth is driven home by a magnificent description of the hippopotamus, to whom the strongest and biggest of man's creations are child's play. If you cannot prevail against his creatures, how can you stand against the Creator? But if that Creator is your Father, how safe you are!

JOB 41

The Parable of the Crocodile. The last paragraph described the hippopotamus; the whole of this chapter is devoted to the crocodile. In a series of striking questions the voice of the Almighty suggests his greatness. He is not an animal with whom you can play, or to whom you can speak soft words, or whose skin can be pierced with sharpened weapons. His scales, vv. 12-17; his eyes, mouth, and nostrils, vv. 18-24; his fearlessness of human attack, vv. 25-29; his power to lash the sea into a fury, making it to boil, vv. 30-34—each of these features is described in graphic terms.

As before, it is clear that the object is to throw into strong contrast the puniness and littleness of man. We may not be so much given to speculations about the organic world in which we live. But we are able to appreciate the argument. Surely he who tells the number of the stars and weighs the mountains in scales will have his pathway through the deep and his footsteps in mighty waters. Being all that he is, he cannot but baffle the eye of man, but the heart can fully trust him. We know that he does all things well.

JOB 42

Restored to Right Relations with God. In complete surrender Job bowed before God, confessing his ignorance and owning that he had spoken glibly of things which he understood not. He had retorted to his friends that he was as good as they, but now he confessed, as did the apostle after him, that he was of sinners the chief. It is one thing to hear of God, another to see and know him close at hand. Well may we loathe our proud words and repent in dust and ashes, v. 6.

When Job was right with God, the Almighty took his side against his accusers and silenced them. It was through Job's intercessions that they were forgiven. He himself was not fully forgiven till he could pray for them with loving forgiveness. But immediately he had done so, God turned "the shadow of death into the morning" and gave him the double portion of the firstborn. Thus men, when forgiven and restored, are heirs of riches greater than they had forfeited.

THE BOOK OF
PSALMS
THE TRIUMPH OF FAITH

I. SONGS OF DELIVERANCE *1—41*
II. THE DIVINE JUDGMENTS *42—72*
III. NATIONAL HYMNS OF JUDAH *73—89*
IV. THE OVERRULING KINGDOM *90—106*
V. ANTHEMS OF PRAISE AND THANKSGIVING *107—150*

INTRODUCTION

"The Hebrew Psalms have furnished the bridal hymns, the battle songs, the pilgrim marches, the penitential prayers, and the public praises of every nation of Christendom since Christendom was born" (source unknown).

"At the time of the Reformation," says the great expositor Delitzsch, "the Psalter began to diffuse its odors as in the renewed freshness of a May morning." Von Mueller says that the Psalms can make a life of trial to be a life of joy, while LeFèvre calls them "the marrow of lions."

The Psalter is found in the center of the Bible and contains the heart of revelation. It is sometimes called "the Bible within the Bible," because it summarizes what precedes and anticipates what follows. It is the one book of Scripture for which every other book has a marked affinity.

Most of the Psalms are prayers—not merely forms of devotion, but the heart utterances of men who could not live without God. All of their experiences—whether unheard-of sufferings or unutterable joy—are viewed in relation to the divine will.

A number of the Psalms are songs which celebrate the history of the Hebrew people. While the leading events are depicted in broad outline, there is also a wealth of detail. About one-third are anonymous; seventy-three bear the name of David; twenty-four are attributed to the minstrels of his reign and subsequent singers, some of whom lived in the glorious period of Ezra's restoration.

COMMENTARY

PSALM 1

The Two Ways and the Two Ends. Like a signpost, this psalm points the road to blessedness. The opening word may be read, "Oh, the blessedness!" The psalm begins with the same message as the Sermon on the Mount, Matt. 5. Beneath the lintel of benediction we pass into the temple of praise.

Blessedness is obtainable in two ways: negatively, we may avoid the society of the irreligious; positively, we must enter the company of prophets and kings, of psalmists and historians, and especially of God himself, speaking in Scripture. Do not simply read the Bible; "meditate" upon it. Better one verse really masticated than a whole chapter bolted.

The rewards are: to be planted by rivers, to bear fruit, and to prosper. See Gen. 39:3, 4; 49:22. How blessed it is, also, to realize that God knows and loves! See Ps. 56:8. The sinner begins with ungodliness, goes on to scorning, and ends as chaff, Matt. 13:30.

PSALM 2

God's Son upon His Throne. This is one of the sublimest of the Psalms, and can find its fulfillment only in our Lord. See Acts 4:25; 13:33; Heb. 1:5; 5:5; Rev. 2:27. The mold in which the psalm is cast is highly dramatic.

The determined hate of the peoples, vv. 1–3: "Rage" conveys the idea of gesticulations and cries of frenzy. For v. 2, see Luke 23:12, 13; Acts 4:25, 26.

The divine tranquility, vv. 4–6: The scene shifts to Heaven. In spite of all, the eternal purpose moves on. "Have I set" means "anointed." "Messiah" and "Christ" alike mean "anointed," Acts 10:38.

The manifesto of Messiah, vv. 7–9: Before time began he was the only begotten Son of God, John 17:5. But his Sonship was declared at his resurrection, Acts 13:30–37. The world is his, to be won by the cross and intercession.

Overtures of peace, v. 12: "Kiss the Son." See 1 Sam. 10:1. This psalm closes as the first began, "Oh, the blessedness!"

PSALMS 3 & 4

Morning and Evening Prayers. These psalms probably date from David's flight before Absalom, 2 Sam. 15. It is the perfection of trust to be able to sleep when our foes are many and set upon our destruction. So Jesus slept, Mark 4:38; and Peter, Acts 12:6. Be sure that you are where God would have you to be, and then resign yourself to his loving care. Even though pursued by the results of your sins, you will find that God will save you, on condition of your being contrite.

Let us begin the day and close it with thanksgivings and prayers. "Godly" means having the power to love. Dost thou love God and his saints? Then know that he has set thee apart—

that is, separated thee—for himself. Seek his will alone. Be content to let the world go by. Thou hast no need to envy the prosperous worldling. God suffices for Heaven; why not for earth?

PSALM 5

Protection from the Wicked. The ordering of prayer is very necessary, Gen. 22:9. Our Lord's prayer should be our model. Often our "words" need to be supplemented by our "meditations"; that is, we must make room for the "groanings which cannot be uttered," but which the Spirit understands, Rom. 8:26, 27. Distinct from either of these is the urgent ejaculation for aid which is here described as "the voice of my cry," v. 2. As soon as we awake, let us speak to God. We must keep watch for the answer, v. 3. How many answers we miss, because we get tired of waiting for the return of our ships!

Note the seven expressions for the ungodly, vv. 4–7. "As for me"—the chief of sinners; but see 1 Corinthians 15:10. The Jew in prayer turned toward the Temple, v. 7; Dan. 6:10. Here the Tabernacle, which preceeded it, stood for the same, 1 Sam. 1:9. We look to the Most Holy Place, whither Jesus has entered, Heb. 10:19.

The ungodly are specially characterized by sins of speech, v. 9. Wicked men are like sepulchers which exhale pestilential odors. Their doom is inevitable. Notice the combination of trust, love, and joy, v. 11.

PSALM 6

Deliverance in Trouble. This is the first of the Penitential Psalms, the other six being 32, 38, 51, 102, 130, 143. The earliest verses are a wail, but the psalm ends in a song. It is like a day of rain which clears at evening. "Sheminith" is a musical term signifying "octave."

The elements of the psalmist's sorrow are given in vv. 1–7. The pressure of God's displeasure, soul-anguish, sickness, soul-depression, an enemy's opposition—all these were ingredients in his cup of bitterness. How touching the plea, "I am weak!" How expressive the broken sentence, so often on Calvin's lips, "How long?" That prayer, "O Lord, heal me," includes the mental as well as the physical.

The certainty of deliverance looms in sight in vv. 8–10. The consciousness of having been heard steals over the soul as a glint of light in the hospital ward. The answer may not be at hand, but it is sure, 1 John 5:15. Weeping has a voice: God interprets sighs. The imprecation of v. 10 is really a prediction. When God returns to us, because we return to him, our enemies turn back.

PSALM 7

Refuge in God from Evil Men. This psalm should be compared with 1 Samuel 24. "Cush," or "dark-complexioned," may refer to a Benjamite who made malicious false statements. If David needed deliverance from his foes, how much more do we from Satan, 1 Pet. 5:8, 9.

So far from being guilty of the offense charged against him, David on two occasions had spared Saul's life, 1 Sam. 24 and 26. "Mine honor," v. 5, is probably another word for "soul," Gen. 49:6. It seems as if, vv. 6–9, God has abdicated his throne, and the suppliant is pleading with him to resume it, with no fear as to the verdict.

Evil recoils, like the boomerang, on those who set it in motion. Ralph the Rover perished on the Inchcape Rock, whose warning bell he had destroyed. The hunter falls into the pit prepared in the forest track for his prey, Judg. 1:7. What a noble prayer in v. 9!

PSALM 8

God's Glory in Man's Headship. This exquisite ode can reach perfect fulfillment only in our Lord, Heb. 2:6–9. It was evidently composed at night and probably dates from the early shepherd days, when wild creatures crept around the fold and night birds screamed above, reminding the singer of the animal world over which man was meant to reign.

The *ascription* of vv. 1 and 2 is very fine. Christ is so mighty that when his strength is given to babes, they vanquish and silence his foes, Matt. 21:16; 1 Cor. 1:25. Do not regret your helplessness, 2 Cor. 12:9, 10. The *comparison* of vv. 3 and 4 is striking. It is a great descent from Adonai above the heavens to the son of Adam ("dust"). But the king loves his child more than his palace. What must not be the worth of man, of whom God makes so much! The crown of creation was placed on man's brow. Sin wrecked it, but the Son of man regained it, Matt. 28:18; Isa. 11:6–9; Rom. 8:19–22. The holy soul has the talisman of rule, 1 Cor. 3:22.

PSALM 9

Confidence in the Righteous Judge. The Chaldee version adds to the inscription, "concerning the death of the champion who went out between the camps," referring to the death of Goliath. This is the first of the Acrostic or Alphabetical Psalms, of which there are nine: 9, 10, 25, 34, 37, 111, 112, 119, 145.

There is a predominant note of praise, vv. 1–5, 11, 12, 14. Let memory heap fuel on the altar of praise. In the resurrection of our Lord, God indeed rebuked our archenemy and his strongholds are now wastes, Zech. 3:1, 2; 2 Cor. 10:4; Col. 2:15. *There is a corresponding note of trust,* vv. 7–12. Calamity drives us to God. The more we know, the more we trust him. Doubt is born of ignorance. Leave God to vindicate; he will not forget, v. 12. *There is a petition for further help,* vv. 13, 19, 20. We have been at the gates of death, v. 13; here are the gates of the Holy City, v. 14. Compare v. 15 and Esth. 7:10. God does not forget; forget him not, vv. 12 and 17.

PSALM 10

God Will Not Forget the Lowly. The malice of our foes, and especially of Satan, is powerfully described, vv. 1–11. Now it is the venom beneath the serpent's tongue, v. 7; now the bandit in ambush, v. 8; now the lion in his den, and again the hunter snaring his unsuspecting prey, v. 9. And all the while God is so quiet that it seems as if he has abdicated his throne.

Then the oppressed begin to pray, committing themselves to him, vv. 12–15. May we not rise above the spirit of the old covenant and ask that the venomous evil which is in the heart of our foes may be exterminated, so that it leave no vestiges? And such prayer must be answered. Compare 9:19 with 10:16, 17. True prayer begins with God and returns to him. When he prepares the heart, v. 17, he prepares the answer, which exceeds all, 1 Cor. 2:9.

PSALMS 11 & 12

God Our Refuge and Defense. The first of these is a debate between fear and faith, and dates from Saul's persecutions. Timid friends, anxious for David's safety, urged him to flee to the mountains. Such counsels of expediency are frequently given to the servants of God, Neh. 6. Luther's diaries are full of such references. But unless our duty is finished, we must stand our ground; we "can do no other." We must remember that God's love is with us, and that he always exchanges glances of love with his suffering ones. Compare 11:7 with Exod. 3:7.

The opening words of the next psalm appeal for help in bad and evil days. See Mic. 7:2. "A double heart" is literally "a heart and a heart," v. 2. Let us be true in act and speech, else we forfeit the Spirit of truth, Eph. 4:25; Col. 3:9. Our sighing will make God arise, Acts 7:56. We shall be helped and kept, v. 7 and Isa. 54:17.

PSALMS 13 & 14

The Bounty of God and the Folly of Men. The first of these psalms evidently dates from the Sauline persecutions, 1 Sam. 19:1. Four times the persecuted soul cries, "How long?" The psalm begins in deepest dejection, but clears as it proceeds. Prayer often proves to be the ladder from the deepest dungeon to the more radiant day. We find here depression, vv. 1, 2; supplication, vv. 3, 4; assurance, vv. 5, 6. Do not carry your anxieties in your heart. Remember that Christ is by your side, and leading you through all to the kingdom. Faith begins praise for victory before the fight has reached its worst.

The creed, character, and doom of the atheist are set forth in the next psalm, and the psalm is so important as to demand repetition. See Ps. 53. The root of atheism is in the heart, Rom. 1:21. Its effect on character, speech, and action is disastrous, and it ends in great fear, v. 5. The best answer to atheism is the light and liberty of the children of God, v. 7; Heb. 9:28; 2 Thess. 1:6–10.

PSALMS 15 & 16

The Citizen of Zion and His Inheritance. The first of these psalms was probably composed to celebrate the bringing of the Ark to Mount Zion, 1 Sam. 6:20. It describes the character of those who have fellowship with God and dwell in his house all the days of their earthly lot. To the challenge of the soloist, v. 1, the choir makes response, vv. 2–5, first positively, then negatively. We must act as nonconductors to evil; must mind what company we keep; and must cultivate a spirit of love and self-sacrifice which will never take advantage of others, v. 5. Here is the secret of permanence and peace.

"Michtam" means "golden," and may be truly applied to the next psalm, as also to Psalms 56, 57, 58, 59, and 60. Others explain the word as a "secret." It is the song of the golden secret. The key is furnished in Acts 2:25. The Apostle Paul expressly emphasizes the divine authorship in Acts 13:35–38. Our Lord may have repeated vv. 8–11 when he was descending the dark valley, and so may we.

PSALM 17

God's True Servants Safely Kept. This also dates from the Sauline persecutions. In the earlier verses David protests his innocence, pleads for deliverance from his foes, and ends with glad anticipation of the vision of God. The psalm may have been composed for use at eventide; at least two of its verses point in that direction, 3 and 15.

What a comfort it is to appeal from the accusations of men to the judgment-bar of God! Yet our sufferings at their hands are God's smelting-furnace. The Hebrew word translated "tried" is "melted," v. 3. But we cannot be kept without constant use of God's Word, v. 4. And then how safe we are! "The apple of the eye"—that is, the pupil—is defended by eyelash, lid, brow, bony socket, and uplifted arm. "Thy wings," see Deut. 32:11.

Note the contrast between v. 14 and Psalm 16:5, 11. The worldy are filled with this world—I with thee. They look for the things of this life—I for the unseen and eternal. They are satisfied with "children"—I with "thy likeness."

PSALM 18:1-26

A Wonderful Deliverance. There is another edition of this psalm in 2 Samuel 22. Verse 49 is applied in the New Testament to the Lord Jesus, Rom. 15:9. We begin with *the psalmist's good resolve,* vv. 1-3. No single metaphor can comprehend the whole of God's helpfulness to men; but can we say, "I love thee"? See John 21:17. "Thou knowest!"

The story of the past, vv. 4-19. We also have our Red Seas. In our distress let us also cry. The voice of the sufferer may be weak and solitary, but it reaches through the gates of pearl and moves creation, Luke 8:46.

The confident claim of the righteous, vv. 20-26. We cannot boast a righteousness of our own, but we stand in Christ. We are full of impurity and evil, but we may claim at least integrity of motive. Compare v. 26 with Lev. 26:21-24. The wind blows in one direction; you can walk against it or with it—take your choice.

PSALM 18:27-50

Girded with Strength for Service. God's way is perfect, and if only we will walk with him he will make ours perfect also. Walls and troops cannot stop a man when God leads him through them. We must follow on the line of his purpose, and then the very mountains are a way and our enemies subserve the program, Acts 2:23.

Swift and surefooted when the path is slippery, v. 33; strong in battle, v. 34; great through God's gentle kindness, or as the English Book of Common Prayer renders it, "thy loving correction," v. 35. Severity would never have done for the apostles what Jesus did by his patience and long-suffering.

The closing hallelujah of vv. 46-50 is very fine. It is the *living* Savior that we need. We must restrict our words when we speak of men; but mortal lips, however eloquent, have never exhausted the worth of our King.

PSALM 19

The Works and the Word of God. This is the "Psalm of the Two Books"—Nature and Scripture. If Psalm 8 were written at night, Psalm 19 was surely written by day. In v. 1, God is called *El,* "strong"; in vv. 7, 8, 9, 14, the Hebrew *Jehovah* is translated "Lord," as if his glory as Creator is the stepping-stone to loftier conceptions of the Redeemer.

Nature's silence: "No speech nor language," v. 3. What a picture of the sacred stillness of dawn! Yet the witness-bearing is universal. "Line," v. 4, is "compass" or "territory," but some translate it "chord." Nature's harp is strung to the glory of God. Jesus is our Sun, Mal. 4:2.

Six synonyms are given for Scripture, and twelve qualities ascribed to it, vv. 7-9. How truly does our Lord fit this, v. 10! Let us end with confession and prayer. "Errors," v. 12, see Lev. 4:2, 13. "Dominion," v. 13, see Rom. 6:14. For the seventh time Jehovah is mentioned, v. 14, with two loving epithets! Can we all say "my," claiming all of God?

PSALM 20

The Saving Strength of God's Right Hand. This may have been written on such an occasion as 2 Samuel 10.

The prayer of the soldiers, vv. 1-4. Ready, drawn up for the battle, they salute their king. God's name is his character. The God of Jacob cannot forsake us, though we be unworthy as the patriarch. "Thou worm Jacob," Isa. 41:14.

The resolve, v. 5. Our banners may wave proudly in the breeze, but all is vain if God be not our trust. The Lord is our "banner," Exod. 17:15. We succeed only as we set out in his name and for his glory.

The king's voice, v. 6. "Strength" is plural, signifying the variety and infinity of God's resources, on which we may count.

The final chorus of the host, vv. 7-9. As they look across the field, they contrast the might of their foes with their puny equipment. But as they gaze, those embattled hosts are dispersed, as clouds before a gale. "Save!" is the battle cry.

PSALM 21

Rejoicing in the Strength of Jehovah. This is a companion to the psalm preceding. The blessings there asked for are here gladly acknowledged to have been granted; and bright anticipations are entertained for the future. How much of this psalm is true only of the ideal King—our Lord! Let us read it with special reference to him as he rides forth on his white horse, Rev. 19:11-16.

That which the heart desires, the lips at times find difficulty in expressing. God's help always "prevents" us, that is, "goes before" us, anticipates our needs. The only life that can satisfy is the eternal, but that is ours already if we only knew it. Our beloved dead are more blessed "for ever," because they see him "face to face"; but we also may share their joy. Trust in Christ is the secret of immovability. God has exalted Christ to be a Prince and a Savior, and we shall never be at peace until we have done the same, Acts 5:31.

PSALM 22:1-15

The Cry of the Forsaken. The Hebrew inscription of this exquisite ode is, "The hind of the morning." The hind is the emblem of loveliness; see Song of Songs 2:7, 9. The cruel persecutors are designated as bulls, lions, and dogs. Perhaps the allusion to the morning refers to the daybreak of resurrection-hope.

Of course our blessed Lord is in every syllable. Indeed, the psalm reads more as history than as prophecy. The divine Sufferer seems to have recited it to himself when on the cross; for it begins with "My God, my God, why hast thou forsaken me?" and ends, according to some, with a word in the Hebrew meaning, "It is finished." The psalm is indeed a photograph of Calvary, a memorial of the heartbreak of Jesus.

Sometimes to the soul in agony God seems not to hear; but through those hours of darkness the Easter day is hastening to break in resplendent glory. He will not suffer his holy one to see corruption, Ps. 16:10.

PSALM 22:16-31

The Testimony of the Delivered. In the middle of v. 21 there is a remarkable change from the plaintive to the triumphant: supplication and entreaty break out into exultation; hope saves the broken harp from the hands of despair, restrings it, and extracts from it strains to which angels, on their way home to God, are constrained to listen.

He who had said, "Thou hearest not," v. 2, confesses that all the while God has been hearing and helping. Now Jesus will join the saints in psalms of praise. See John 17:26 (*"will* declare it") and Heb. 2:12. Man may abhor a worm, but God uses worms to thresh mountains, Isa. 41:14, 15.

In the closing verses, there is a sure forecast of the effects of the death on the cross not only upon the Jews, but also upon "the ends of the world"; that is, the Gentiles. The usurper shall be dethroned, v. 28; resurrection shall be accomplished, v. 29; and a spiritual seed shall satisfy the Redeemer's travail, v. 30.

PSALM 23

The Song of the Good Shepherd. A sabbatic rest breathes through this psalm, the children's favorite, while the oldest and holiest confess that it touches an experience which still lies *before* them. Here is no strife, no fear, no denunciation, no self-vindication.

Jehovah is represented as the Shepherd, the Guide, and the Host of his people. We are taught to think less of our attitude toward him and more of his responsibility for us. The flock does not keep the shepherd, but the shepherd keeps the flock. Look away from yourself and trust him with all, in all, and for all.

Let God see to your wants. You need nothing outside of him. His "pastures" are "tender grass"; his "waters," "waters of rest." He refreshes us when exhausted; heals when diseased; restores from wandering; leads in right paths, though steep; accompanies us into the valley with club for our foes and crook for the pits; spreads our table amid hatred; and protects us with the twin angels, goodness and mercy!

PSALM 24

Entering Jehovah's Holy Place. Psalm 22 tells of the cross, Psalm 23 of the crook, Psalm 24 of the crown. This great choral hymn was evidently composed to celebrate the removal of the Ark from the house of Obed-edom to Mount Zion, 2 Sam. 6. It was conducted with music and song to its resting-place, and this psalm was the marching song of the priests, 1 Chron. 15:2-27.

The first two verses were sung by the whole festal crowd, the third by a soloist, the fourth and fifth by the choir, and the sixth by the entire congregation. What a sublime challenge on the part of the approaching host is contained in v. 7, to be answered by a company from within the gates in v. 8! To this again the vast shout of the multitude gives reply in v. 9.

This magnificent ode reached its perfect accomplishment when the mighty Victor over hell and the grave arose on high and sat down at the Father's right hand. Oh, let the gates of your heart open wide to admit him!

PSALM 25

A Prayer for Pardon and Protection. This is an acrostic or alphabetical psalm. The verses begin with the successive letters of the Hebrew alphabet, to aid the memory. So also in Psalms 9, 10, 34, 37, 111, 112, 119, and 145. It repeats the same expressions several or more times, such as "wait," vv. 3, 5, 21; "ashamed," vv. 2, 3, 20; and "teach," vv. 4, 5, 8, 9, 12.

Lift up your soul to God, that its darkness may flee before his light and your maladies be healed by his saving health. If you pray to be led and taught, be quiet and wait "all the day," v. 5. The anointing that you have received is all that you require, 1 John 2:27. God's holiness is no barrier, but an encouragement to repentant sinners. Notice "therefore," v. 8, and compare with Matthew 9:13 and Luke 15:1. What will not God do for the Name! See Isa. 63:14, 16; Ezek. 36:22, 23. For God's "secrets," see Gen. 18:17; 1 Cor. 2:9, 10. Entrust God with the keeping of your soul and you will never be ashamed, Isa. 49:23.

PSALM 26

A Declaration of Loyalty to God. In some respects this psalm resembles the previous one, only instead of entreaties for forgiveness, there are protestations of innocence. It may have been composed during Absalom's rebellion, and contains a strenuous protest against the dissembling and hypocrisy upon which that revolt was based. In these avowals of conscious rectitude, it should be borne in mind that David did not mean to claim absolute sinlessness, but rather to declare his innocence of the specific charges with which he had been assailed.

We all need the laver of purification mentioned in vv. 6, 7. Or better, let us repair to our Lord, who still washes the feet of his disciples, as in John 13. Hatred to evil men is one side of the coin; love to God's house, the reverse. Either implies the other. However firm our foot seems to stand, we all need the redeeming mercy and grace of God. Ah, the riches of his gentle goodness, Eph. 2:7.

PSALM 27

The Song of Fearless Trust in God. This psalm probably dates from the time when the exiled king, surrounded by unscrupulous foes, looked from his hiding place beyond the Jordan to the Holy City, where the Ark abode. "One thing" he desired above all else. "One thing" people are irresistible, Phil. 3:13, 14.

Here we have *assurance,* vv. 1–6. God's house for us is his presence. We may live day by day in the new Jerusalem, which needs no light of sun or candle. We are in it, though we know it not. Oh, that our eyes might be opened to see where we are, 2 Kings 6:20. How beautiful must God be, who has made the world so fair!

Next we have *supplication,* vv. 7–14. The triumphant note changes to sadness. Did the writer look from his Redeemer to the winds and waves? But sometimes God seems to hide his face only to draw us to a point of trust and abandonment which otherwise the soul had never dared to adopt, Mark 7:28. The dearest may forsake, but the Lord gathers, Isa. 40:11.

PSALM 28

A Prayer and Its Answer. This psalm also probably belongs to the time of Absalom's rebellion. Verses 2 and 3 resemble Psalm 26:8, 9.

God is silent sometimes because he loves us unspeakably, Zeph. 3:17, margin; sometimes to test our faith, Matt. 15:23; sometimes because he has already spoken and we have not listened, Matt. 26:62, 63. But let us never go elsewhere for help, 1 Sam. 28:6, 7. Let us wait and pray, lifting up our hands in the dark to touch his hands.

These prayers for the punishment of the wicked should be read as predictions. Do not be afraid of evil or of evildoers. God is "a consuming fire" and destroys all evil. He causes the enemy to be still as a stone until his redeemed have passed over. Therefore, there breaks in on the psalmist the ray of hope which finds expression in vv. 6, 7. Faith cries, "I am helped!" Let us rejoice even before the jailer comes to tell us that we are free, Acts 16:25; and let us send out our prayers for all the Church, v. 9.

PSALM 29

Peace after Storm. This is a perfect specimen of Hebrew poetry, describing the march of a thunderstorm over Palestine from north to south.

The prelude, vv. 1 and 2, is addressed to the angelic hosts, who stand above the tumult of earth and sky. Heaven is viewed as a temple in which the angels are the priests.

The storm, vv. 3–9. The "many waters" are the Mediterranean. The tempest breaks first on Lebanon, the cedars of which sway to and fro before its fury. Each thunderclap is accompanied by forked lightning. The storm passes to Kadesh and the rock-hewn cities of Petra. The beasts are terror-stricken; the trees are stripped of their leafy dress. In the Temple the worshipers respond to the challenge of Nature! Glory to the King! "The voice of the Lord" is mentioned seven times. Compare Rev. 10:3.

The conclusion, vv. 10, 11. This God is our God, and will give us strength and peace. The psalm begins with "glory in the highest" and ends with "peace on earth."

PSALM 30

"Joy Cometh in the Morning." This psalm dates from 2 Samuel 5:11. What a contrast between Adullam's cave and the house of cedar! When God has lifted us up in mercy, we should lift him up in song.

Apparently David had been passing through a time of sickness or intense sorrow, and now he could not be thankful enough for God's redeeming mercy. When shall we realize that God both forgives sin and redeems us from its eternal consequences! "Weeping" is here personified; she is only a lodger who tarries for the brief Eastern night and then, veiled, glides out of the house at daybreak. With the first ray of light Joy comes to abide, and we hear his hearty salutation in the vestibule.

We need more of the joy of the Lord. The first touch of pain makes us "cry," v. 8; but we are slow to put on and wear the girdle and the garments of gladness. Be of good cheer, sad friend; God will yet turn the shadow of death into the morning.

PSALM 31:1-13

A Cry out of Deep Trouble. Some have supposed that this psalm was written during the Sauline persecutions; but it is more likely that it dates from Absalom's rebellion. It alternates between the depths of despondency and the heights of sublime faith, and well befits those who walk in darkness and have no light, Isa. 50:10.

It sounds as if the soul were on a windswept moor, with no shelter from the storm. All is dark and wild, and it dreads to be caught in the entangling net, v. 4. What a magnificent prayer is that of v. 5! It supplied their last words to Stephen, Polycarp, Bernard, Huss, Luther, Melanchton —above all, to our Lord, Luke 23:46; Acts 7:59. The Psalter was our Lord's prayer book. This verse is a suitable petition also as we go forth into the unknown day, 2 Tim. 1:12.

Sin, slander, neglect make the heart break; but God is all-sufficient. Hide in him; that life is safe which is God-encompassed. "Hid with Christ in God," Col. 3:1-4.

PSALM 31:14-24

"Jehovah Preserveth the Faithful." What a change ensues in the spirit of our life when we look from men and things to God! Do not look at God through circumstances, but at circumstances through God's environing presence, as through a golden haze. Our Lord's times were in the hands of the Father, and he would not move an inch until the clock had struck in Heaven, John 2:4, 7:6, 8, 30; 8:20.

As God has laid up coal and ore in the earth, and as explorers in Arctic regions deposit provisions in cairns that those who follow in their steps, or they themselves returning, may be supplied on their march, so unsearchable riches are stored in Christ awaiting our appropriation, 2 Pet. 1:3.

What a hiding place is the secret of his presence! Have you ever been inside that royal withdrawing room? God's pavilion is soundproof; the strife of tongues cannot penetrate.

PSALM 32

The Song of the Forgiven. David wrote this psalm, Rom. 4:6-8. "Maschil" means "to give instruction." We are deeply instructed as to the working of conscience. Compare with Psalm 51. This was one of Luther's favorites.

For some time after his sin, David withheld confession and suffered terribly. But when the wound was opened and the poison pressed from it, he burst out in the words with which the psalm opens: "Oh, the blessedness!" "Sin" means "missing the mark"; "iniquity" is that which is turned aside from its course. "Forgiven, covered, not imputed"—each of these is true in Jesus.

The presence of God is always appreciably nearer when floods are running high. Note those three precious promises of instruction, teaching, and guidance, v. 8. Throw on God the responsibility of indicating your path. Don't wait for the sharp jerk of bit or bridle; let love prompt and inspire your every movement. Haydn said, "When I think on God, the notes dance from my pen." Remember the music and dancing that welcomed the prodigal!

PSALM 33:1-12

"The Word of Jehovah." This psalm is eminently calculated to incite praise. Let us note the subjects which are touched upon, in the hope that presently one may strike a spark at which our cold hearts shall flame up.

The words and works of Jehovah are the first to

pass in review, v. 4. Let us never forget that nothing was made apart from our Lord Jesus. He is emphatically the Word through whom the creative fiat went forth, John 1:3; Col. 1:16; Heb. 1:2. It is good, as we contemplate the beauties and wonders of creation, to turn in praise to him whose parables disclose the secrets which he hid in the works of his hands.

Note the vivid touches with which the work of creation is described in vv. 6–9. Then turn to the description of *God's providential government*, vv. 10–12. We are said to be God's inheritance. See v. 12. Ephesians 1:11 tells us that we inherit him, and v. 18 that he inherits us. Bring every inch of us under thy tillage, Great Occupier.

PSALM 33:13–22

"The Eye of Jehovah." The comprehensiveness of God's providence, vv. 13–15. No one, however lowly or abject, is beneath his notice. It is not that all hearts are alike in their aptitudes or intensity, but that there is not one that does not bear some trace, however defaced, of his image and superscription.

God's watchfulness, vv. 16–19. The preparations that men make against peril and poverty often fail them. "A horse is a vain thing for safety." If God is not with you, his fleet foot will not deliver you in the day of battle, when the enemy bears down on you in force. But God's unslumbering eye watches over them that fear him; and at the moment when he can help them best, he will intervene to deliver. Remember Ps. 20:7.

The certainty of God's help, vv. 20–22. Let us await his time to act. Trust is certain to bear fruit in joy. They that hope in God shall have abundant cause to praise him. Be of good cheer! Even now you can hear the footfall of the advancing angel hosts! Get ready to praise him!

PSALM 34:1–10

"Magnify the Lord with Me." The event associated with this psalm is recorded in 1 Samuel 21. It was not a very creditable incident. David, however, realized the goodness of God, notwithstanding his own failures and mistakes.

In the original the verses begin with the letters of the Hebrew alphabet. Verse 1: "At all times . . . continually." It is a sign of great grace to bless always, in dark as well as bright days. Verse 3: "Birds," says Trapp, "when they come to a full heap of corn, will chirp to call their fellows." Verses 4–6: All the time David was feigning madness, his soul was going out to God in prayer. Verse 7: Compare Acts 12:6–10. Verse 8: Some experiences must be enjoyed to be understood. There are not words adequate to tell of them. Verse 10: "We will leave thee nothing!" said plundering soldiers to a widow. "I care not," returned she. "I shall not want so long as God is in the heavens." Columba, an early Celtic missionary, spent his last afternoon transcribing this psalm, saying when he reached the tenth verse: "I will stop here. The following verse will better suit my successor."

PSALM 34:11–22

The Salvation of the Contrite. Verses 11–14: The gist of this exhortation is quoted by Peter in his first epistle. See 1 Pet. 3:10. We need not fret to defend ourselves or to answer false accusations. Let us refrain our lips, hold our peace, as Jesus did, and go on doing what is right and good. God will see to it that our needs are supplied, that our enemies are silenced, and that our soul is redeemed. Verse 15: Do you feel unable to claim the designation of "righteous"? Remember that Paul was glad to reject his own, that he might be clad in Another's righteousness. That still avails for us. See Phil. 3:9.

Verse 17: We are not kept *from* trouble, but delivered "out of" it. Verse 20: You do not recognize him, but the Great Gardener passes by the plants that have braved the wind and storm, to bend over you who are beaten to the earth. See the literal fulfillment of this in John 19:36. How much we owe to God's continuous care! Verse 22: Observe the present tenses in which the psalmist records God's redeeming love. It never grows old.

PSALM 35:1–17

Rescuing the Poor and Needy. This psalm dates from the Sauline persecution, or else from the disturbed condition of the kingdom in David's later years. Each of the three divisions into which the psalm naturally falls ends with praise, vv. 9, 18, 28.

Throughout the psalm we meet with strong imprecations on the wicked. The spirit of the New Testament inculcates a higher law of love and forgiveness, Luke 9:55, 56. Therefore our Lord rebuked his apostles when they called for fire from heaven. He said, "You do not understand that you have passed out of the old covenant into the new." It has been suggested that the maledictions of these verses should be read as predictions. Thus, "Let them be confounded" would read, "They *will* be confounded," "Their way *will* be dark and slippery," "The angel of the Lord *will* oppose them," etc.

What a thrill passes through the soul when

PSALMS

God whispers the assurance, "I am thy salvation!" "Who is like unto thee?" Exod. 15:11.

PSALM 35:18-28

An Appeal to the Righteous Judge. Verse 20: "The Quiet in the Land" was the title adopted by holy men and women in Germany, during long dark days when religion was under an eclipse. It is beautifully appropriate to those whose life is "hid with Christ in God." "We are in him that is true," Col. 3:1-4; 1 John 5:20.

Verse 24: "Judge me, O Lord!" What a comfort it is to appeal from the judgments of men to the bar of God! We know that the soul's Advocate there will plead its cause with the eloquence of love. His interposition and vindication will clear us. God has seen! God will not keep silence! He is not far away!

Verses 27, 28: We desire that others should join us in praise. One seraph cried to another in Isaiah's vision. There should be a holy emulation in thanksgiving. Oh, that the resolution of the psalmist might characterize us all; and that all our days might be full of praise, instead of the constant murmuring and complaining which are so rife even among God's children!

PSALM 36

God the Fountain of Life. The servant of the Lord, as the superscription tells us, is speaking here. He is horror-stricken at the ways and thoughts of the ungodly. By a bold image, v. 1, transgression is personified as speaking in the heart of the ungodly, as the Delphic oracle in her dark cave; and the answer from that secret oracle is full of smooth but beguiling words. So our first parents found it.

What a blessed thing it is to turn from man to God! Notice God's attributes as here enumerated: "thy mercy," "thy faithfulness," "thy righteousness," "thy judgments." The golden bracelet begins and ends with love. All Nature speaks, to the heart that loves, of the love of God. But they who fly to God find him even better than Nature can proclaim. He is better than banquets for hungry men. Let his life arise in thee as a fountain, and ask for the illumination of his light. Serenely sheltered under the wing, or in the house, of God, the soul may look out, unmoved, on "the wrecks of matter, and the crush of worlds."

PSALM 37:1-17

A Sure Cure for Fretting. This is an acrostic psalm, grappling with the problem of the inequality of human life and the apparent failure of God to reward his servants and punish his enemies as they deserve. Life and immortality, where we know that the balance will be readjusted, had not then been brought to light, and therefore the solution was far harder before the advent of our Lord than for us.

But though the psalmist's solution is therefore not complete, his teaching of the blessedness of absolute trust in God's providence is very delightful. "Fret not thyself"; that is, do not give way to passionate resentment or bitter disappointment. Live in God; find your delight in contemplating his nature and his works; roll on him the decision of your life choices; trust in him to supply all your need and work in your behalf. Be silent and rest!

How dramatically this picture of the happy, restful child of God is contrasted with the wicked and his certain doom—like barren pastures scorched by heat, or thin smoke columns vanishing in the air! Wait and trust!

PSALM 37:18-29

Ways That God Establishes. God takes pleasure in our lives. In each he is working out a plan. Even our failures do not turn him away from us, for he keeps fast hold of our hands, v. 24. Long after his people have passed home, God sees to their children. If they follow in their parents' ways, they are borne along in the stream of providential care; but obviously they may depart from it. What precious promises in vv. 28, 31, 33, 37, 39, and 40! Never forsaken! Always sure of an Advocate in the Divine Presence! Not left to the mercy of our foes! Safely housed in the time of need! Dying in peace! Such are the blessings which accrue to the servant of God. Such has been the observation of one no longer young, v. 25.

When taunted, persecuted, maligned, desperate, go into a silent place and lift your tear-stained face to him. He understands the unspoken language of sighs and tears. Do not hurry him; he has ages to work in. Wait patiently and rest.

PSALM 37:30-40

Steps That Shall Not Slide. How dear this psalm has been to God's saints! It has been peculiarly prized by them in all ages. Gerhardt has paraphrased it in his noble hymn:

> *Give to the winds thy fears,*
> *Hope, and be undismayed.*

When banished from Berlin by the Elector, he turned into a small wayside hostelry, not knowing where to go. Seeing his wife greatly depressed, he turned to find comfort for them both in these verses, and the conception of his hymn broke upon him. That evening messengers arrived from the Duke of Mecklenburg, offering Gerhardt an honorable position in his kingdom.

Among many others, the fifth verse was frequently quoted by David Livingstone. Bishop Coverdale's translation of v. 37 is noteworthy: "Keep innocency and take heed unto the thing that is right, for that shall bring a man peace at the last." But the psalmist repeatedly insists that the fulfillment of God's promises is conditioned by our faith, v. 40. The day may break stormily, but the storms expend themselves before nightfall and the sunset is golden.

PSALM 38

The Cry of the Needy Penitent. Here is a long drawn-out sigh of pain. Some think it should be classed with Psalms 32 and 51, as belonging to the time of David's fall and repentance. It is filled with a sense of God's judgments and the profound consciousness of sin. Perhaps David was suffering physically, or he may be describing his spiritual maladies in terms borrowed from that source. His friends stood apart and his enemies were near. But it was wise to refrain from man and to wait only on God. When we are buffeted and derided, the true attitude is our Lord's. As the dumb sheep before her shearers, he opened not his mouth!

In v. 15 the tone becomes calmer. The soul begins to recover its center of gravity in God. Notice the four-fold repetition of "For," vv. 15-18. Faith marshals her arguments. Out of "stony griefs" she builds "Bethels." Like Samson, she finds honey in the lion's carcass. But God will not forsake. He never for a moment withdraws his close attention. The Refiner sits by the crucible, and will cool down the heat the moment it has done its work.

PSALM 39

The Fleeting Measure of Our Days. In the opening verses David describes the circumstances out of which this psalm arose. The presence and prosperity of the wicked stirred him to the depths, but he carefully refrained from speech. There are hot moments in our lives when we do well not to say what is in our hearts. But if our feelings demand a vent, let us get alone and speak out our hearts to God. A softer tone settles on heart and tongue when we reach his holy presence.

How frail we are, not only in our life, but in our moods! We need not fear men; they are but for a moment, as a breath that curls up in the frosty air, or as a shadow sweeping across the mountainside. Only God abides. Man is vanity; his pride and beauty are like a bursting soap bubble; he is a stranger and pilgrim along this bank and shoal of time. But the child of the Eternal God is a guest with him, v. 12. He travels in our company. He makes himself responsible for our well-being. He will bring us safely home as he did all our "fathers."

PSALM 40:1-10

A Joyous Testimony. This psalm follows appropriately on the two former, in which the psalmist had been detailing his sufferings. Here he celebrates deliverance. But a greater than David is here. Hebrews 10:5-7 puts vv. 6-8 upon the lips of Christ, and we hear his voice speaking through these olden words.

In deep distress, vv. 1-3, what can the soul do but wait patiently until the Lord inclines and hears? The "horrible" pit is a "pit of roaring"; that is, a ravine where the deep waters rush and roar. What Jeremiah experienced literally, 38:6, we pass through spiritually. But God will leave no child of his there; he will lift him to stand on the rock, his mouth filled with songs.

When we are delivered, let us set our gladness to music and embody it in renewed consecration, vv. 4-10. Let us not hide God's love in our hearts, but tell it out. The bored ear, v. 6, in reference to Exodus 21:6, means obedience forever, absolute consecration, the glad submission of the will. This is dearer to God than the most elaborate ceremonial or ritual.

PSALM 40:11-17

A Cry for Deliverance. To the end of life we shall continually need God's "lovingkindness," to deal mercifully with our failures and sins, and his "truth," that is, his faithfulness. The covenant, ordered in all things and sure and that which binds him irrevocably, is the rock of our comfort, whether we are compassed by innumerable evils or overtaken by iniquities, v. 12.

Our sense of sin grows with our increasing knowledge of the holiness and love of God. They who are nearest to the heart of God are least able to forgive themselves, though they know that they are forgiven. But while we think hard thoughts against ourselves, and confess ourselves to be "poor and needy," we may take great comfort in God's thoughts for us, v. 17. They are tender and loving, Jer. 29:11. Poverty and need are never reasons for despair. These things do not alienate God's interest.

They rather attract him, just as a sick child will get more of the mother's care than the healthy members of the home circle.

PSALM 41

"Lord, Heal My Soul." This psalm was probably composed, with the adjacent ones, during the four years in which Absalom's conspiracy was being hatched. Perhaps the anxiety thus caused induced some serious illness, over which David's enemies exulted with unseemly glee. His sensitive nature was evidently greatly pained. But who does not realize the applicability of the psalm to the betrayal of our Lord? Verse 9 is quoted in John 13:18.

In the day of trouble, when enemies oppose, vv. 5-8, and friends prove false, v. 9, God draws near. Look after God's poor and he will care for you in the evil day. The blessings that you have endeavored to communicate will return to your own comfort in the hour of tribulation. God will make (or change) your bed in sickness, v. 3; will heal your soul, v. 4; and will set you before his face forever, v. 12. What a sweet conception of God as nurse in the room where feet must be shod with velvet and voices speak in gentlest tones!

PSALM 42

Thirsting after God. This psalm clearly embalms the holy musings and yearnings of the exiled king during Absalom's rebellion. Their setting to music was left to the sons of Korah, 2 Chron. 20:19. It was a great favorite with the early Church, driven to the Catacombs, on the walls of which are many designs of hunted deer.

"The water brooks," vv. 1-3. The hind suffers much from the sultry heat, but it dare not linger too long at the waterhole, because the wild beasts gather there. We never realize the value of God's house till we are compulsorily separated from its sacred rites. How blessed it is to return to the sanctuary after such separation! "I will come into thy house in the multitude of thy mercy," 5:7.

The blessed past, vv. 4-6. Exiled to the Hermons, beyond the Jordan, the fugitive recalls the festal crowds, wont to gather at the holy feasts. But when such thoughts oppress us, we should turn our hearts to God and in touching him, we cease to be lonely. See Heb. 12:22ff.

The bitter present, vv. 7-11. The day of pain and rebuke, when the heart is pierced, is the day of God! "His lovingkindness"; "his song"; "the God of my life"; "God of my rock"; "the health of my countenance"; "my God"—what a heritage is this!

PSALM 43

"The Health of My Countenance." The exiled king still pours out his soul to God. Already David has addressed him as "God of my life"; here God seems to David the "God of my strength," v. 2, and "God, my exceeding joy," v. 4. Speak well of thy God, even though his back seems turned on thee!

"Thy light and thy truth," v. 3, may refer to the Urim and Thummim. Or we may think of them as two white-vestured angels sent from God's presence-chamber to guide the exile's steps back to his home. "Send them forth, commissioned to find me in this lone land and bring me to thine altar." There seem to be four steps in the approach. "Unto thy holy hill"—this was Mount Zion. "To thy tabernacles," the earthly presence-chamber. "Unto the altar of God." Here is a step in advance. Our altar is the cross where Jesus died, Heb. 13:10. But God's altar is not enough; we need *him.* So we still press on "unto God my exceeding joy." Then the hue of health appears on our faces! See v. 5.

PSALM 44:1-8

Courage from Former Deliverances. This psalm, like Psalm 60, came out of one of the early wars in David's reign, as described in 2 Samuel 8:13, 14. Some refer it to 2 Chronicles 20. It befits the Church when her former prosperous state contrasts sadly with her depressed and suffering condition.

It is a great argument in prayer when we can quote to God the mighty things of the past, and ask that he should do the same again. The great revivals and advances of the past were not achieved by human wisdom or might, but by faith. It is always *God's* right hand and the light of *his* countenance that win the land in possession; but why should he not command similar deliverances again! And what is true of the Church is equally true of the individual. Why not lift thy heart to God, O defeated soul, and claim that he should command "victories for thee," v. 2, margin. Make thy boast in God and thou wilt have reason to give thanks unto him forever! But before we can claim God's deliverances, we must be able to say, "Thou art my King," v. 4.

PSALM 44:9-26

A Plea for Present Help. In vv. 11, 12 God's people are compared to sheep appointed for meat, which are sold by the shepherd for nought, so worthless are they. Before their savage foes, sheep are defenseless and unresisting. Their bitter lot is aggravated by their fear lest the shepherd has forgotten them. The reference in the 19th verse suggests the further picture of a harried and panting flock. It is hardly to be wondered at that God's tender mercies seemed withdrawn from his people!

But notice how the Apostle Paul uses these words in Romans 8:36. He does not complain of forsakenness, nor appeal for help. On the contrary, he declares that in all these things we are more than conquerors, and that nothing can separate us from the love of Christ. This is the lesson of the New Testament—that we conquer when we are defeated; overcome when we are slain; are strongest when we are beaten to the dust; and ascend to the throne only when we lie in the grave where Jesus, our Master, lay! See John 12:24; 2 Cor. 13:3, 4.

PSALM 45

The King's Wedding Song. Though this psalm was probably composed to celebrate Solomon's marriage with Pharaoh's daughter, we must remember that it is distinctly applied to our Lord in Hebrews 1:8. See also Eph. 5:23; Rev. 19:7. What wonder that the psalmist's heart overflowed! It was bubbling up with good matter! His work was for a King! See v. 1.

The Warrior, vv. 2–5. The Word of God rides forth to war, followed by the armies of Heaven. See Rev. 19:13. His glory is the cross; his majesty is in his meekness, his prosperity in his loyalty to truth. His arrows are tipped with love, and those who fall beneath them die that they may live. *The King,* vv. 6–8. The oil of gladness is the anointing of the Holy Spirit, which we also may share. See 1 John 2:20, 27. *The Bridegroom,* vv. 9–17. Clad in glistening raiment, the Church stands by her Lord, who claims her love and loyalty. But these are not inconsistent claims! By nature she was without beauty or dower; but she has won both in him. See to it that you are not missing at that wedding feast (Matt. 7:22, 23).

PSALM 46

"Our Refuge and Strength." The historical origin of this psalm cannot be certainly determined. Probably it was composed when Jerusalem was beleaguered by Sennacherib's hosts, 2 Kings 18. It befits every era in which the Church is in danger from her foes, and foretells the final destruction of Antichrist. It was Luther's favorite psalm, and is rendered into verse in his memorable hymn, *Ein' Feste Burg.* During the sitting of the Diet of Augsburg he sang it every day, playing his lute and standing at the window and looking up to Heaven. The theme of the psalm is the security of God's people, and this is elaborated in three stanzas, each of which ends with "Selah."

Alone among great cities, Jerusalem lacked a river; but God was willing to become all that a river could be and more. Your deficiencies give more room for God's all-sufficiency. Mark the beautiful alternative translation of v. 5, "at the dawn of morning." Your sorrow is limited to a single night. See also Isa. 37:36; Matt. 14:25. Be still, O troubled heart! The God of the nations is your Father! Desolations are the snapping off of the dead branches to prepare for the spring.

PSALM 47

"King over All the Earth." This psalm may have been sung in the valley of Berachah, where Jehoshaphat celebrated his victory over the Moabites. See 2 Chron. 20. When some great deliverance has been granted, we should break out in blessing and praise. Notice vv. 3, 4. They are rightly placed side by side, because God will not subdue our enemies under us unless we have allowed him to choose our life-plan. Live on that plan and you are unconquerable.

In the second division, vv. 5–9, Jehovah is depicted as returning from the war to his dwelling-place in the height of Zion. This seems to anticipate the ascension, when Jesus became the enthroned King of men. They fail to recognize him now, but some day the princes of the people shall be gathered together, and the kingdoms of the world shall have become the one kingdom of the Christ, Rev. 15:4. "The shields of the earth," v. 9, are its princes and leaders. See Hos. 4:18, margin. The kings of wealth, science, art, literature, and power will one day bring their glory and honor into the gates of the new Jerusalem, Rev. 1:5; 21:24.

PSALM 48

"The City of Our God." This psalm also probably dates from 2 Chronicles 20:20. Tekoa was only three hours' march from Jerusalem and commanded an extensive view, so that vv. 4, 5 were literally true.

The psalmist celebrates the beauty and glory of Zion, vv. 1–3. The Church today is the City of the great King. Apart from God, the fairest palace is no refuge; but a cottage becomes a palace if God is known and loved there. Judah's recent deliverance is gratefully commemorated, vv. 4–8. It is a sublime picture: the gathered array; the dismay, flight, and destruction of the foe. Then comes the call to loving thought on God's care and goodness, vv. 9-14. Notice those two sentences—"As we have heard, so we have seen," v. 8; and, "According to thy name, so is thy praise," v. 10. Whatever we have been told by our fathers about God, God is prepared to be and do for us; and our aim should be to praise him worthily. Think of his love till your heart kindles to praise; and remember that this God is yours forever and ever. Let us surrender to him the guidance of every step, until we pass through death into his immediate presence.

PSALM 49

The Folly of Trusting in Riches. Here is a proclamation worthy of the hearing of all the world. The psalmist is listening to voices unheard by ordinary ears. Be sure to listen to God's voice, and then unfold his dark sayings in music. However dark they may seem in their mystery and awe, they may be uttered in song. See Rev. 15:3, 4.

The burden of the psalm is the impotence of wealth. The millionaire cannot prolong the life of his sick child. And even if, like Queen Elizabeth, he cries on his dying bed, "A million of money for a moment of time!" the sand passes unheeding through the hourglass. He must leave stocks and shares, jewels and gold at the summons of Death, described in v. 14 as the shepherd who calls his flock to Sheol. How different the lot of the righteous! As eternity dawns, they are redeemed from the power of the grave and pass to the bosom of God. What are the riches and glory of this world compared with the sense of God's presence in the humble and contrite heart! To have that is to have the essence of all! "Whom have I in heaven but thee? and there is none upon earth that I desire beside thee," Ps. 73:25.

PSALM 50:1-15

Sacrifices Which God Desires. This is one of the most majestic compositions of this book. For literary power it cannot be excelled. The psalmist hears God calling the whole world from east to west. His presence is compared to the dawn and to a tropical storm. When he is seated on his throne, the heavens and the earth bear witness while he judges his people. Then up the crowded aisles his saints advance and stand before him.

There is no need to enlarge upon the spiritual insight of the psalmist, who realizes that God cannot be enriched by anything that we can bring, but insists on the sacrifice of thanksgiving, vows of consecration, and the loud call for help in the day of trouble. These are characteristic of those whose God is the Lord, and of the people whom he has taken for his own inheritance. Let us specially ponder these three conditions of the happy life, vv. 14, 15. What comfort is contained in the blessed promise of v. 15! It is so absolute in its certainty and assurance. God has here bound himself to deliver the soul that calls on him in its trouble and to give it reason to glorify him.

PSALM 50:16-23

God's Warning to the Wicked. These searching words are for us all. We have no right to declare God's statutes if our hearts hide wickedness in their secret chambers. We must not share ill-gotten money. Impurity, deceit, slander must be far from us if we would have fellowship with God in prayer or service. God's silence must not be taken as indifference, for he is carefully watching each word and act; and if we persist, he will arise and set out all these unforgiven sins in order before the quickened vision of the soul.

Notice the two final conditions of a blessed life, v. 23. First, we must offer the sacrifice of praise, for we are priests and must not be slack in presenting the fruit of our lips. See Heb. 13:15. But in addition we must order our behavior, or way, aright. It is a solemn thing to be entrusted with the great opportunity of living. Every passing moment should have something committed to it to keep in store. We dare not live by haphazard or chance. We must order our ways with prayerful deliberation.

PSALM 51:1-10

The Prayer of the Contrite Heart. This psalm is a ladder which climbs from the horrible pit, with its miry clay, into the heights of sunny joy, where the song breaks from the forgiven penitent. Here is the cry of the lost sheep which has been torn by briers, harried by wild dogs, drenched in the morass, but which the shepherd has found and brought home rejoicing. This path has been walked by myriads of penitents. Verse 17 was written on the wall of St. Augustine's cell.

There is no doubt as to the occasion or the authorship of this psalm. It abounds in references to 2 Samuel 11 and 12. It is remarkable that such a confession should have been handed to the chief musician; but the publicity thus given has made it a means of grace to myriads.

Note the epithets for sin: "transgression," "the violation of law"; "iniquity," "crookedness from the straight line of rectitude"; "sin," "missing the mark." However much God longs to forgive, he cannot until confession is made. We must acknowledge our lapse from virtue! "Blot out," as from a record; "wash," as foul stains from linen; "cleanse," as a leper by the touch of Christ. Our only plea is the multitude of God's tender mercies.

PSALM 51:11-19

The Sacrifices God Accepts. It is not enough to be forgiven; the true penitent longs to be kept from breaking out into the old sins. He desires a "clean" heart that abhors the least taint of sin; a "right" or steadfast (margin) spirit, influenced by God's "holy" Spirit, and therefore a "willing" spirit as well. Then shall follow the joy of salvation, success in soul-winning, humility of soul, the blessing of Zion, and the upbuilding of the Church. What glorious results are these —like the fair colors extracted from coal-tar!

There are no sacrifices so dear to God as broken hearts, no offerings so precious as contrite spirits. It would be impossible to compute all the walls that have been built, all the Jerusalems that have been blessed, all the congregations that have been moved, all the revivals that have resulted because sinful men and women have been loved back from the pit of corruption and reinstated into the clear shining of God's forgiveness and favor. Do not be content with forgiveness; seek restoration to the old place and then strive for a better.

PSALM 52

The Boaster and the Truster. The inscription of this psalm describes its origin. The contrast which it presents is full of instruction. The ungodly is often a mighty man in the estimation of the world. He boasts mischief; his tongue resembles the razor, which inflicts sharp and deep wounds; his words devour reputations, family peace, and souls.

What a contrast is presented by the humble believer who trusts, not in wealth which vanishes, but in God's mercy which abides forever, vv. 1 and 8. As the olives grew around the humble forest sanctuary at Nob, where the tragedy which called forth this psalm took place, and were hallowed by the shrine they encompassed, so the believer grows and is safe in loving fellowship with his Almighty Friend. Let us be among God's evergreens, drawing our nutriment from him, as the roots reach into the rich mold. The psalmist is so certain of vindication and so assured of the overthrow of wickedness that he celebrates God's interposition before it takes place, and accounts it as being already accomplished.

PSALMS 53, 54

Sinners All—God Alone Can Help. That Psalm 53 should be a repetition of the 14th, with very few variations, suggests, as does the "verily, verily" of Christ, that the truths contained in these words are worthy of special attention. They supply the apostle, in Romans 3, with his phraseology for describing the state of the ungodly before the searching eye of Omniscience.

We have here a photograph of the human heart. Jew and Gentile are alike in their innermost texture. There is nothing to choose between the Pharisee and the publican, except when either turns the balance by humble confession, as in Luke 18:9ff.

Psalm 54 is probably founded on 1 Samuel 23:19. It is short, as if compressed by the urgency of David's need. Evidently he was in sore straits, though conscious of the rectitude of his cause. Notice how he makes his transition from prayer to praise, v. 4. He affirms, in spite of everything, that God is still his helper. He hears the approaching footsteps of those who are pledged to uphold him, and God is with them. As he speaks thus in the confidence of faith, the storm clears away. He *is* delivered; his eye *has* seen the defeat of his foes.

PSALM 55:1-11

Fleeing the City's Ills. This psalm was suggested by Absalom's rebellion and Ahithophel's treachery. But it contains references which, in their full extent, are chiefly applicable to Judas' treatment of our Lord. The terrors of the unseen, the stealthy tread of the assassin, the treachery of a friend, the drawn sword under unctuous speech—such were the bitter ingredients mingled for this deeply-tried soul. But we have all known something of his disappointment and anguish, and have longed for the swift wings of a dove to escape to the bosom of God.

One of the Puritans says: "My Spouse is ascended higher than the highest heavens, and I, poor soul, am left desolate and disconsolate in this valley of tears. The weight of my weakness and my sins doth so clog and shackle me, so glue and nail me to the earth, that I cannot rise. Let him descend and give me wings whereby I may ascend." "... and *give*"—humility. "... give me *wings*"—celerity. "Like a *dove*"—innocence. "*Fly away*"—aspirations to the Lord, "whom having not seen, we love." "*Rest*"—permanent security.

PSALM 55:12-23

Friends May Forsake, but God Abideth. The streets and open spaces of the city were filled with conspirators. Violence, strife, deceit, and oppression trampled the virtuous and helpless under foot. The treachery of Ahithophel was worse than all. How different the hot anger of David from our Lord's treatment of Judas, when he washed Judas' feet, expostulated with him in the garden, and bade him pause to think to what he had come! Blessed is the soul that retires from the hubbub of the street—as David, Daniel, and all devout Israelites were wont to do—three times a day. Compare v. 17 with Dan. 6:10 and Acts 10:9. He will cover our heads in the day of battle and redeem our souls in peace, if only we will trust him.

As the marginal rendering of v. 22 suggests, "thy burden" is that which God has given thee to carry. It did not come by chance, nor from the evil intent of men. He cast it on thee; cast it back on him. We cannot do our work so long as we stoop beneath the exhausting waste of anxiety and care. Hand all over to thy Father's care. Let no burdens break the Sabbath-keeping of thy heart, Neh. 13:19.

PSALM 56

"What Can Man Do unto Me?" This psalm was composed under the same circumstances as Psalm 34. See 1 Sam. 21. What a strange medley is here shown—David feigning madness and composing psalms! Commenting on v. 3, one commentator says that Isaiah's resolve is still better: "I will trust, and not be afraid," 12:2. Note the magnificent refrain at the close of each of the first two strophes, vv. 4 and 10. The psalmist asks: "What can flesh do?" "Nothing," is the Apostle Paul's emphatic answer. Neither death, nor life, nor angels, nor principalities, nor powers can hurt a man who makes God his stronghold, Rom. 8:31.

Let us use the last verse for our life-prayer. Live as one on whom God's vows rest. Thank him that by his cross and passion he has delivered thy soul from death. Could he have done so much at such cost, and then fail? Surely he must deliver our feet from falling, 116:8, or all the past will have been in vain. Whenever the shadows gather and past sins threaten and the enemies of your soul seek to overthrow, plead this prayer: "Thou hast . . . wilt not thou?"

PSALM 57

"In the Shadow of Thy Wings." This is one of the choicest psalms. It dates from Adullam or Engedi. It consists of two sections, each of which ends with the same refrain, vv. 5, 11.

First strophe, vv. 1-5: The fugitive in a rocky wilderness hears the roar of the wild beast, but lies quietly in his hiding place. God's angels will shut lions' mouths. As the wings of a mother bird intercept the danger that menaces her nestlings, so the loving care of God protects his people. Is there not here a trace of words uttered earlier by David's ancestors? See Ruth 2:12; Deut. 32:11.

Second strophe, vv. 6-11: Before we can awake and sing, we must be conscious that we are touching bedrock. If we are without assurance of salvation, we shall be songless and joyless. In this short psalm the singer has sung himself clear into the blue heaven. He awakes the dawn with his notes. God's mercy and truth —or faithfulness—like guardian angels in the meanwhile keep watch.

PSALM 58

"He Is a God That Judgeth." This psalm is launched against wicked rulers. It may have been occasioned by the attitude of Abner and others of Saul's party, who accounted David as a rebel and outlaw and urged vindictive measures against him.

Their sin, vv. 1-5: "Poison" is literally "burning heat." Such is the effect of venomous words, into which the malice of the great serpent is infused. Evil men, capable of such speech, resemble the snake which will respond only to the shrillest notes. Hot speech to man and deaf ears to God go together.

Their doom, vv. 6-9: For "let them" read "they shall," v. 7. The imperative and predictive future are in Hebrew expressed by similar words. Note the remarkable comparisons—the lion's broken jaw-tooth, the ebbing tide, the snail scorched by intense heat, the untimely birth, the quickly expiring fire, the cyclone! Sin inevitably brings penalty, and herein is God's moral government vindicated.

The contrast, vv. 10, 11: As the weary traveler is refreshed when his feet are washed, so the saints are glad to see God's vindication of the righteous. There is a wide difference between the gratification of personal vengeance, and a consuming zeal to uphold God's character.

PSALM 59

"God Is My Defence." This is the fifth of the *Michtams*, or "Golden Psalms." Compare Psalms 16, 56, 57, 58. The contents correspond to the title and to 1 Samuel 19:11.

The most noticeable feature is the twice-repeated refrain of vv. 9 and 17. In each case

David appeals to God as "my strength," and describes him as "my defence" and "the God of my mercy." The possessive pronoun *my* is very remarkable. Each of us needs mercy of a very special sort. *My* mercy would not help you, nor would *yours* help me. Note also that God's mercy "prevents," that is, "goes in front," v. 10. As the mother's thought prepares beforehand for the child, so God thinks ahead for us, and leads us into the good things which he has prepared for them that love him, 1 Cor. 2:9; Ps. 31:19.

In the first refrain David says, "I will wait upon thee"; in the second, "I will sing of thy power and mercy." Waiting on God leads to singing. All night Saul's emissaries might prowl around David's home, like the wild dogs of an Eastern city. But within he was singing aloud of God's mercy, and when the morning broke he was in safety.

PSALM 60

Prayer for Help against Foes. This was a national psalm to be taught to the people. See title; also Deut. 31:19. A strong coalition had been formed against David at that time. See 2 Sam. 10:6, 8, 17, 19; 1 Chron. 18:12-25. Israel was threatened with disaster. It was as if an earthquake had rent the soil. But the king-psalmist argued that God had given his people a mission in the world, which could not be forfeited. First, Israel carried a banner for the truth, v. 4. In addition, God had "spoken in his holiness" and had promised that the seed of Abraham should possess Canaan. Standing on a hill-summit, the psalmist sees the Land of Promise outspread before him. Shechem and Succoth, v. 6, one west, the other east of the Jordan, indicate the breadth of the land. All had been made over to Israel by covenant, and therefore the surrounding peoples must become subject.

As yet the strong city of Petra, rock-girded, v. 9, had laughed David to scorn; but he had confidence that God would lead him within its mighty walls, to tread down his adversaries, Num. 24:18. Man could not, but God could. The question is never, Can God? but always, Can we trust and follow him?

PSALM 61

Safe under God's Protection. This psalm was probably composed at the time of Absalom's rebellion, when David was a fugitive from the Tabernacle that he loved. There are two stanzas.

Prayer, vv. 1-4: The king was only across the Jordan, yet it seemed the end of the earth. He was at the end of human help. In overwhelming floods trouble poured all around, but in the distance he perceived the rock that towered above the waters. If he could but reach it, he would be safe. What rock is this save the Rock of Ages that was cleft for us! We cannot reach or climb it by ourselves, but need to be led and lifted thither. And God answers, "I will put thee," Exod. 33:22.

Confidence, vv. 5-8: The psalmist quotes the great assurance of 2 Samuel 7:12-16, and turns it into prayer. Faith presents God's pledges to himself, and affirms her confidence in their fulfillment. Thus we advance from step to step on the predestined road, knowing that lovingkindness and truth have gone before us to prepare the way of our steps and to discover themes for endless praise.

PSALM 62

Our Only Rock and Refuge. This is the "Only" Psalm. It consists of three stanzas, each of which includes that word and ends with "Selah." It was probably composed during Absalom's rebellion.

Waiting, vv. 1-4: They who wait for God, and God alone, cannot wait in vain. Though ringed around by men who hide their malice under specious words, the soul is not greatly moved. Their fence of hate totters to its fall, but the inner wall of God's care is steadfast.

Silence, vv. 5-8: "Wait" here, and in v. 1, may be rendered "is silent," "be silent." There are times when God seems so near that we cannot speak aloud, but are just silent before him and breathe out our thoughts and desires.

Not disappointed, vv. 9-12: Men and money are less than vanity, but God endures. His performances, unlike man's, weigh heavier than his promises. They who trust him will be satisfied with an abundance of power and mercy, which are open to the poorest, but which gold can never buy.

PSALM 63

The Longing Soul Abundantly Satisfied. Ever since the third century this has been the morning song of the Church. The superscription tells us that it was written in the wilderness of Judah, probably during the events recorded in 2 Samuel 15:23-28; 16:2; 17:16. Notice the many references to the life of the soul. These are the many considerations of our mortal pilgrimage! "My soul thirsteth; my soul longeth; my soul shall be satisfied; my soul followeth hard after thee."

The soul thirsting, vv. 1-4: Let us be on the alert to see God's power and glory, not only in the sanctuary, but in dry and thirsty lands. How sad and weary is life without God!

The soul satisfied, vv. 5-7: To desire God is to have him. To long for him is to be at the wellhead. To remember him on the bed rests us. To meditate on him in the night is to have the dawn. The shadow of his wings is absolute safety.

The soul in hot pursuit, vv. 8-11: God is always in front of us. The Savior went before; we must follow in his steps, but there ought to be as little space as possible between us. Another turn of the road, and you will see him!

PSALM 64

Deliverance from Powerful Foes. This is another of the psalms dating from Saul's persecution. There are two stanzas.

Prayer for preservation, vv. 1-6: Insult, sarcasm, and slander still fall to the lot of those who will live godly in this world. Very few of us are safe from poisoned arrows. Because the world is so full of evil men, who are disposed to put the worst construction on every act, we should be constantly on our guard to give no needless cause to the enemy to blaspheme, 2 Sam. 12:14. Daniel gives us an admirable illustration of this, since his enemies had no cause against him, save as it concerned the law of his God, 6:5.

Assurance of divine vindication, vv. 7-10: David felt that God had undertaken to be his champion. His arrows were flying through the air thick and fast. Curses came home to roost, and the overthrow of wickedness by the floating mines set to wreck the righteous is evidence of God's government of the world. Let the righteous look forward with quiet confidence to the time when the world shall be righted, and when the waterpots that are now filled to the brim with tears shall yield the wine of the wedding feast.

PSALM 65

Abundant Favor from Our Gracious God. This joyous hymn was probably composed for use in the sanctuary at one of the great annual festivals. It deals expressly with God's bounty in the fertility of the earth.

The Temple courts, vv. 1-4: God hears our prayer, purges away our transgressions, chooses us, causes us to approach. Let us ask him to "cause" us to approach and to make us dwell in the consciousness of his presence. If iniquities prevail and transgressions shame us, there is provision for these also. God shall purge them away. For such condescending love all flesh shall ultimately come to his footstool.

Terrible things, vv. 5-7: Thunder tones and lightning flashes, inaccessible mountains and roaring seas—such are the darker aspects of Nature. But beneath all, like a sweet refrain, we hear God praised as the God of salvation. Make him your confidence, by land and sea.

The beauty and order of the world, vv. 8-13: Brimming rivers, soft spring showers, golden harvests, the hum of the bees in mountain pastures, the call of the ewes to their lambs—all bespeak God's goodness. Let us ask him to visit our hearts with the throb of springtime.

PSALM 66:1-15

"Come and See the Works of God." Some of the old expositors speak of this psalm as "the Lord's prayer in the Old Testament."

A summons to praise, vv. 1-4: The devout soul cannot be glad alone. It demands sympathy in its raptures. All the earth is not too great for an orchestra, nor all mankind for a choir. God's power may compel a feigned obedience, v. 3, but the divine Spirit changes the heart.

Divine deliverance, vv. 5-12: "Come and see." Compare John 1:39, 40. Let us never forget the great past. The Red Sea and the Jordan have their counterparts in all lives. How often God has turned our seas into dry land, and cleaved paths through our rivers! "Through the flood on foot" is a miracle of daily experience. The rebels exalt themselves, but we are unmoved. We are tried in the fire, but no atom perishes. We go through persecution and oppression, but we come forth into abundance.

The payment of vows, vv. 13-15: Let us pay under bright skies what we vowed under dark ones. Pay your vows; declare what God has done for you. Offer not beasts, but offer yourself as a living sacrifice unto God! See Rom. 12:1.

PSALM 66:16—67:7

"Let All the People Praise Thee." "Come and hear," vv. 16-20: The psalm began with "Come and see," v. 5. Compare Mark 5:19, 20; John 4:29. It will be one of the employments of Heaven to go from group to group to tell what God has done for us. But each hearer will have a tale as wonderful as ours. We must praise without stint, and pray with pure and unselfish motives. From such prayers God will not turn away.

Psalm 67, like Psalm 65, was composed for use at an annual festival. "Bless us," say the saints in yearning prayer. "God shall bless us," is the certain answer of faith, vv. 1, 7. We desire blessing, not to hoard for ourselves, but that all mankind may share with us. Ask for God's smile on yourself alone and you will miss it; ask for it that you may reflect and pass it on, and the Lord will become your everlasting light, and the days of your mourning will be ended.

Four times the psalmist cries, "Let the people [or peoples] praise thee." In answer to his appeal, it seemed as if the whole world had broken out into fresh fertility. "Our own God," v. 6, has given himself to us, and each may have the whole of the fullness as an estate of boundless extent and wealth, Num. 18:20; Ps. 16:5.

PSALM 68:1-11

The Leader of His People. This is one of the grandest odes in literature. It was probably composed when the Ark was brought in triumph from the house of Obed-edom to the newly acquired hill of the Lord, 2 Sam. 6. It is evidently a processional hymn, intended to be sung by bands of white-robed priests and Levites. In this paragraph the Ark was lifted to the shoulders of its bearers, while a measured strain was chanted, vv. 1-6. Then, as the procession moved forward, the march through the wilderness was recited, vv. 7-11.

"Let God arise!" These opening words are borrowed from the formula used by Moses, Num. 10:35. Through the smoke of many a battlefield have they rung out! Cromwell's "Ironsides" charged to their music. In vv. 5, 6 we learn that God has a special care for lonely people and prisoners. The former he introduces to families, John 19:26, 27. The latter are brought out into prosperity. Verse 11 (alternate translation) seems to have a modern fulfillment in the exodus of noble women from happy homes in Christian lands to publish the gospel of Christ to the heathen.

PSALM 68:12-25

Their Mighty Deliverer. The processional march still continues. Presently Mount Zion comes in sight, and the neighboring hills are depicted as eyeing it enviously for its selection in preference to themselves. In vv. 17, 18 the glad throng begins to climb the sacred slopes of Zion, amid still more triumphant strains; and in v. 19ff. the gates of the sanctuary stand wide open to welcome the festal crowds.

How great the contrast between the blackened appearance of a smoky caldron, and the lustrous sheen of a bird's wings as they flash in the sunlight, v. 13. Yet that is the contrast between what we were, and what we now are. "Salmon," v. 14, is perhaps a reference to the wooded hill near Shechem, mentioned in Judges 9:48. The hostile kings were scattered as snowflakes are driven before the wind and melt in the sun. The hill "Bashan," v. 15, is a snow-clad summit, but Zion is greater, since God is there. In the triumphant words of v. 18, the singer quotes Judges 5:12, and they are applied in Ephesians 4:8 to our Lord's ascension. Note the alternate rendering of v. 19—that the Lord "daily beareth our burdens." Singers, minstrels, and girls with timbrels, v. 25—all have a share in the Church's joy.

PSALM 68:26-35

The God of the Whole Earth. The constituent parts of the procession are now described, and in these closing verses the triumphal note rings out. It tells of the confidence of Israel in her ultimate dominance of the world, which was to be not physical, but moral and spiritual.

The psalmist sees tribe after tribe passing into the sanctuary, and indicates each as it goes by. Zebulun and Naphtali were mentioned in Deborah's song, already quoted. They are specially noticed here, because they who have done well in the wars of the Lord will ever be rewarded. Among the results of God's enthronement among his people is the submission of the kings of unnamed lands. In v. 30, "the beast of the reeds" (alternate translation) is probably the crocodile, and refers to Egypt. "Bulls" and "calves" refer to the princes of surrounding nations and their subjects. Ethiopia reaches out her hands, offering tribute. The whole world is subdued to worship before the great God of Israel. "He giveth strength and power unto his people." Let us avail ourselves of his gracious provisions. Let us ask him to command our strength, vv. 28, 35.

PSALM 69:1-17

A Cry out of Deep Waters. This psalm and the 22nd are quoted most often in the New Testament as referring to our Lord. Psalm 69 is very sad. Throughout we detect a heartbreak. There are many grounds on which the sufferer bases his plea for salvation. First, his imminent danger from inrushing waters and the deep mire like that in which Jeremiah sank. There are also failing strength, the dried throat, and the drooping eyes. Mighty foes, too, who hate wrongfully, are plotting his ruin. The consciousness of sin and the dread that others may be made ashamed through his failure are also bitter ingredients in his cup. And in addition he bore the reproach of those who hated God. What a combination of misery! In some, though not in all, of these sources of grief, our Savior had a share, and therefore he can be a sympathizing High Priest.

But out of his misery the psalmist builds his altar of prayer. His plea is in God's lovingkindness and tender mercies. Here is the master-argument with God. He can do no other than redeem the soul that clings to him with such unfaltering faith. It reminds us of the olden resolve, "Though he slay me, yet will I trust in him," Job 13:15, and also recalls the persistence of the Syrophoenician woman, Mark 7:26. Such souls need not fear that they can be cast away.

PSALM 69:18-36

"Jehovah Heareth the Poor." In vv. 19-21 the psalmist again spreads out his griefs before God. He had looked for pity, but his foes only aggravated his sufferings. Both Matthew and John had these verses in mind in describing our Lord's sufferings on the cross, Matt. 27:48; John 19:29. The next section, vv. 22-28, is full of imprecations. We cannot bring these terrible words within the scope of our Lord's teachings. They show, like a pillar which marks the farthest recession of the tide, how great a difference there is between the standard of the Old Testament ethics and that by which we shall be judged.

Verses 29-36 are full of anticipation of deliverance and vows of thanksgiving. The psalmist is sure that God's salvation will lift him above his enemies, and that his thanks will be sweeter to God than any sacrifice. Notice that sudden address to seekers after God, v. 32. Let us draw lessons from our own experiences of God that will hearten others. Seekers will certainly be finders where God is concerned! See Matt. 7:7. The news of God's restoring power will circle out in ever-widening waves of glory, till heaven and earth and sea catch up the story and respond.

PSALM 70

"My Help and My Deliverer." This psalm repeats the closing verses of Psalm 40. It is a song of remembrance to remind Jehovah of his suffering ones. See Isa. 43:26; 62:6, 7.

Verse 1: God's help is often delayed till the morning watch, but it is never too late. He is hastening on the wings of the wind and walking across the waves to the tossing boat. Verses 2, 3: Wicked spirits, as well as evil men, seek after our soul to destroy it. But *our* shame would be *God's* dishonor. We may therefore plead for his name's sake.

Verse 4: Before we actually find God, we are blessed in the act of seeking him. If you are only a seeker, you may rejoice. If only we had Mary's heart of love, we could join in her "Magnificat," Luke 1:46-55, and add similar songs of our own. Verse 5: Happy are they who have learned to glory in their infirmities and to use them as arguments with God. Are you poor and needy? Turn to Psalm 72:4, and learn that a Helper and Deliverer is provided. The more helpless you are, the better your recourse with God in prayer.

PSALM 71:1-12

"My Trust from My Youth." Some commentators ascribe this psalm to Jeremiah. His pensive, plaintive tone is certainly present in it. But whoever the author, he must have written in his old age, vv. 9, 17, 18. One keynote is "great" and "greatly," vv. 19-21, 23; another is "all the day," vv. 8, 15, 24.

Old men need have no failure in their buoyancy and gladness, if they will fix their thoughts where the psalmist fixed his. Other subjects will soon wear out, but they who make God's righteousness and salvation their theme will ever have material for meditation and praise. We have here an inexhaustible subject, and one which will keep us young. Let us ask for help, that we may disappoint the calculations of those who hate us, whether men or demons. It is a piteous spectacle when apparently prosperous careers are overclouded and age is overwhelmed in catastrophes which there is no time to surmount. But such is not God's way with his loyal servants. His rivers do not end in swamps and marshes, but broaden and deepen till they kiss the mighty ocean.

PSALM 71:13-24

The Greatest of All Workers. The singer glances both backward and forward. He goes back in thought to the time when he was cast on God at birth, and acknowledges that God has taught him from his youth and has enabled him to declare God's wondrous works. We may make the same retrospect, and as we muse on all that God has been to us, we may be assured that he will not forsake the work of his own hands, 138:8. His deliverances will give cause for endless praise, even when our eyes are closing and the heart waxes feeble in death.

But let us also think of those who are following us, and see to it that we leave behind some record of God's righteousness and salvation. Let us place a flaming torch in the hands of our children for them in turn to pass on. Let us show God's strength and power to those who are to come.

The best occupation for the aged is praise, vv. 8, 14, 22, 23. Thy mouth shall be filled . . . shall tell . . . shall talk. When our hearts are bubbling over with good matter, 45:1, we can leave our speech to take care of itself. Love will not lack for means of expression.

PSALM 72:1-11

"King of Kings." Solomon's reign opened as a morning without clouds. Much of the imagery of this royal ode is derived from the circumstances of his life. Compare vv. 1-4 with his prayer for the listening heart, 1 Kings 3:9; the anticipations of peace, vv. 3, 7, with his name, "the peaceful one"; the rule from sea to sea, v. 8, with 1 Kings 4:24; the presents from Sheba, v. 10, with 1 Kings 10. But Solomon's failure to realize his ideals compelled men to anticipate with great desire the advent of a greater Prince of Peace. Of Jesus alone is this psalm true in its details.

Notice the *foundations* of Jesus' reign, vv. 1-4; the *perpetuity* of his kingdom, vv. 5-7, and its *universality,* vv. 8-11. The poor are his care. The peace he gives is in abundance and it passes understanding. Sun and moon may fail, but his love is unaffected by the flight of ages. The rain on mown grass and the distilling of the dew are not more gentle than his work in human souls that lie open to his approach. Take this glorious psalm and claim it, verse by verse, as true for you.

PSALM 72:12-20

"His Name Shall Endure for Ever." How is it that lands so distant as Tarshish, by the Strait of Gibraltar; so rich as Sheba and Seba in south Arabia; tribes so wild as the Bedouin of the desert; and nations so imperial as those beyond the River, shall own the sway of Christ? The answer is given in v. 12. The world is full of sorrow and injustice, and he who can stanch flowing wounds and mete out justice to the oppressed will win all hearts and become the acknowledged Leader of mankind.

"He shall live!" We cannot forget our Lord's own words: "I am he that liveth, and was dead; and behold, I am alive for evermore," Rev. 1:18. Jesus is possessed of the ageless life of the eternal Word, of the human life which he bore through his sojourn on earth, and of that indissoluble life in virtue of which he exercises his priesthood, Heb. 7:17.

"We pray for Christ," says Augustine, "when we pray for his Church, because it is his body; and when we say, 'Thy kingdom come.'" "His name shall have issue," v. 17, margin. It will reproduce itself. The children of "the Name" are found in every land, and will ultimately people the world.

PSALM 73:1-15

Deceptive Prosperity. The opening psalms of this third Book of Psalms are by Asaph; see 2 Chron. 29:30. "Truly" can be translated "only" in v. 1. There is none good but God and God is only good. "His every act pure goodness is; his path unsullied light." "Israel," as here intended, is not after the flesh, but after the Spirit. See John 1:47 and Rom. 2:28, 29.

We have in these verses a good man's temptation. In every age God's people have asked whether God can possibly know all that is taking place on the earth, and if he does know, why he allows evil to prosper. The dark spirit who is ever at our elbow whispers that we should have done as well, and better, if we had not been quite so scrupulous in our business dealings; and we are held back from giving expression to our thoughts only by the fear that we might cause God's weaker children to stumble. This reticence is, of course, wholly commendable.

PSALM 73:16-28

"Their End—Destruction." The true place in which to form a right estimate of life is where Asaph found it—in the sanctuary of God. From its elevation and the purity of its atmosphere, one can take into view the unseen as well as the seen, the eternal as well as the transient. If in this life only we have hope in Christ, we may dwell upon our losses with disappointment and regret, 1 Cor. 15:19. But if the future is taken into consideration, what Lazarus would exchange his lot with Dives (Luke 16:19-31)? When once the soul crosses the frontier between this life and the next, it finds that the coin on this side is valueless on that.

One day as Asaph, more bowed down than usual, entered the sanctuary, deliverance came. Whether it was when the sacrifice was being offered, or when the holy psalm was being sung, the clouds suddenly broke and the burden rolled away. He saw that God did not reward goodness with *things,* but with *himself,* and he turned to him with adoring love. Even in the present life the righteous may count on the constant presence of God. His hand holds them; his counsel guides. He is our strength and our portion; and when we change worlds,

PSALMS

we shall only enter more fully and absolutely into our inheritance.

> *Why should the soul a drop bemoan,*
> *That has an ocean near?*

PSALM 74:1-11

The Sanctuary of God Profaned. This psalm probably dates from the time when the Chaldeans destroyed the Temple and the city of Jerusalem. Compare v. 8 with Jer. 3:13-17. The main emphasis of the opening verse lies in the argument which arose from Israel's close relationship with God. Were they not *his* congregation? Was not the Temple *his* own chosen sanctuary? Did not these facts constitute the reason why he should come with swift footsteps to undo the evils that their foes were inflicting? The invaders were his ("thine") adversaries. The Temple was the dwelling-place of his ("thy") name. The whole psalm is dominated by this note. It says very little of the sufferings which the enemy has inflicted, but constantly recurs to the insult and reproach done to God.

When we live only for Jesus Christ, so that our case and his have become one, we can use language like this. But this position is not acquired lightly, nor without much watchfulness and prayer. We by nature watch out for our own dignity and welfare much more quickly than for the interests of God's kingdom and glory. When, however, we are absolutely identified with the kingdom and glory of Jesus, our argument for deliverance is omnipotent.

PSALM 74:12-23

"Plead Thine Own Cause, O God." "Yet," v. 12, margin. There is always some compensating and consolatory thought. God is in the background of our thought. Not only *the* King, but "my King," ever working salvation in the midst of the earth. Faith is quickened as she reviews the marvels of the past, or considers the constant putting forth of God's power in Nature. See vv. 12-15.

The dove is a tender emblem of the Church in her simplicity, weakness, and defenselessness; and there is no plea so potent as to remind God of his covenant, which has been sealed with the blood of the cross. Though we are utterly unworthy, he cannot deny himself. Every time we put the cup to our lips in the Holy Supper, we say in effect, "Have respect unto the covenant," v. 20. This is an invincible argument with God. Go over the different items of that covenant enumerated in Hebrews 8. Place your finger on the one that fits your case and present that at the bank of Heaven, endorsed by the countersign of our Lord. See to it that your cause is so identified with God's that in soliciting his help, you may be able to add: "Arise, O God; plead thine own cause," v. 22. God is faithful to those whom he has called into the fellowship of his Son.

PSALM 75

God Putteth Down and Lifteth Up. This psalm dates probably from Sennacherib's invasion, and therefore the north is omitted in v. 6, that being the quarter from which the enemy came.

God is near, vv. 1-3. There are high moments in life when we realize how real and near God is. The ground on which we stand is holy. We know that we are safe in the pavilion of our Father's care. Then we give repeated thanks, v. 1. Presently God speaks and assures us that when the earth and its inhabitants dissolve, he will sustain its pillars. What an encouragement is this when the whole world seems about to be dissolved!

Turning from God to man, the psalmist rebukes his enemies and bids them cease their arrogant talk and behavior, v. 4. The horn is the strength of certain beasts and is a symbol of power, Deut. 33:17; Dan. 7:7. But God is the supreme Ruler of men. Our position or promotion in life is his arrangement, to be held as a sacred trust for him. Let us, amid a world in arms, be lighthearted and sing. God will take care of those who trust him.

PSALM 76

"The Wrath of Man Shall Praise Thee." In the 2nd verse "tabernacle" may be rendered "covert," and "dwelling place" "lair." God is compared to the lion, that dreaded monarch of beasts who finds his home in a den into which no inferior animal may intrude. Even the hunter's bows and arrows are broken in pursuit of him. As the mountains yielded prey to the young lion, so the hills around Jerusalem, where Sennacherib had pitched his camp, would be full of Assyrian spoil for the armies of the Lion of Judah. The stouthearted captains of Assyria would there sleep their last sleep, v. 5.

Some of the meek of the earth may read these lines, v. 9. They do not avenge themselves. Weak and helpless, they turn their eyes to God, who cannot fail them. When he speaks his sentence of acquittal, no voice will be raised to dispute it. For when he arises in judgment he will save all the meek of the earth. There is a "thus far and no farther" to the wrath of man. God will not allow it to go beyond certain limits, and it is remarkable how he is able to make man's wrath to subserve his purposes. Bring God the gift of your love. Fear not, ye humble souls, but let your enemies be in fear!

PSALM 77:1-10

"Doth His Promise Fail?" There is a strong resemblance between this psalm and Habbakuk 3. It may be divided at the Selahs.

The psalmist's anguish, vv. 1-3. It is well to give expression to grief. Do not lock it in your breast. Even in the thick darkness reach out your hands toward God. Your fingertips will find themselves touched by the divine response. Refuse to be comforted by Christian work, or by the diversions of society and business, or by the exercise of a strong will. Open the wound to God; he will heal it and wipe away your tears.

The contrast between past and present, vv. 4-9. In the scarcity of his comfort, David was glad to live on his old stores, as are bees in winter. He specially recalled his "song in the night," which is probably the equivalent of that glorying in tribulation of which the New Testament is full. Let us answer those questions of the psalmist: "Will the Lord cast off?" No; Rom. 11:1. "Will he be favourable?" Yes; Lam. 3:32. "Is his mercy clean gone?" No; 103:17. "Doth his promise fail?" No; Heb. 6:18. "Hath God forgotten to be gracious?" No; Exod. 34:6. "Hath he shut up his mercies?" No; Lam. 3:22, 23. He is Jehovah, and changes not.

PSALM 77:11-20

"The God That Doest Wonders." Go back to the past. Consider the manner in which God has stood by his saints in the days of old, in the years of ancient time. What he did for them he is prepared to do again. He cannot cast us off. When once he begins, he will continue. The train may be lost in a dark tunnel, but it will shoot out again into the radiant daylight. Through the hard wilderness God led his people into the land of milk and honey. It is thy infirmity that leads thee to doubt him. Like John the Baptist, thou mayst be enclosed in a dungeon-cell of adverse circumstances, but remember the long years in which the right hand of the Most High has wrought for his people.

Compare vv. 13 and 19. God's way is in the sea—it is impossible to track his footsteps—but it is also in the sanctuary! In other words, however perplexing his providences may appear, they are governed by his redeeming love for his own, and are consistent with his perfect holiness. His ways may be veiled in mystery, but he leads his people as the shepherd his flock. Do not look down at your path, but up into his face.

PSALM 78:1-12

Learning from the Fathers. This psalm is said to have arisen from a strong controversy between Judah and Ephraim as to the location of God's sanctuary, and its final transfer within the limits of the tribe of Judah. The psalmist enumerates the moral and spiritual considerations that led to the choice. See vv. 67, 68. The great message of the psalm is the inconstancy of the people, which so often manifested itself. "Whose spirit was not stedfast with God," v. 8. "They turned back in the day of battle," v. 9. See also vv. 17, 37, 41, 57. It may be that the psalmist implies that these failures were for the most part Ephraim's, and that therefore Judah was chosen. Surely, however, there was not much to choose between them, and whatever favor was shown to either of them was wholly attributable to God's unchanging mercy.

This hymn was probably intended to be learned by the children in the Hebrew home, that they might set their hearts on God and not forget his works. It is a good practice to store the fresh memories of the young with the words of Scripture, which will often return later in hours of temptation and distress. The memorizing of the Word of God is a most valuable habit. The wheels of the mind and heart must grind; let them grind wheat!

PSALM 78:13-24

"A Table in the Wilderness." Throughout this wonderful recital there is a perpetual contrast between God's unswerving goodness and the incessant backsliding of his people; and as we read it, we learn that sin is not simply the violation of the divine Law, but a source of pain and trouble to our Heavenly Father's heart. For us he cleaves the seas, leads us in the daytime, builds his watch fires around us at night, and brings streams of blessing from the rocks. But we tempt him by our incessant unbelief. We say, "He certainly *did* thus and thus, but can he, will he, *do* this or that?" "Can God furnish?" "Can God give bread?"

When shall we dare to believe in our Lord's assurances, first, that "with God all things are possible"; and second, that "all things are possible to him that believeth"? But we must live habitually in fellowship with God before we are able to exercise this faith. As we nourish our souls by feeding on the promises and studying what he has done in the lives of others, our faith removes all the boundaries with which it had limited the Holy One and cries, "Thou canst and thou wilt!"

PSALM 78:25-37

Blessed Yet Ungrateful. God our Father is prepared to do "exceeding abundantly" for his children; but too often we become so engrossed with his gifts as to forget and neglect the Giver. We allow ourselves enjoyment to the point of satiety; and then, by an inevitable revulsion, we begin to suffer. Always acknowledge God while enjoying his gifts. Do not separate the gifts of his grace and those of his providence. *All* good and perfect gifts are from him, and are to be received with equal thanksgiving. Do not use them in excess, but in moderation; and let not the enjoyment of their sweetness be your main object, but that you may be fitted to play your part and do your work in the world.

It must greatly wound the love of God that we need to be placed on short rations in order to bring us back to himself. But how true is v. 34 of us all! We sadly require to have the steadfast heart, and to be faithful to our side of the covenant, for we must all confess to the sin of fickleness and changeableness in our religious life. Our constant prayer should be that of Psalm 51:10, "Renew a right spirit within me." But how can this be ours, except by the dwelling and uprising within us of the life of God?

PSALM 78:38-48

"Signs in Egypt." God takes into account the frailty and infirmity of our natures. "The Spirit ... helpeth our infirmities," Rom. 8:26. In the words of Hosea, God teaches us "to go"; that is, he puts his hands under our armpits, that we may learn how to walk. In the process there are many failures, but he distinguishes between the willful breach of his commands and the blunders that are due to the frailty of our natures. Being full of compassion, he forgives; he remembers that we are but flesh.

Let us not limit the Holy One, v. 41. He waits to do marvelous things for us and by us. But how often we confine his power within the narrow channel of our own little faith. We do not like to trouble him too often. We say in effect that as he has done this, we can hardly expect him to do the other. We bring a limited number of vessels to be filled with the sacred oil. We strike but three times on the ground, and not until the seventh time of perfection. He cannot do many mighty things for us because of our unbelief. Let us quicken our souls to larger thoughts of God by recounting, as in this paragraph, his wonders of old.

PSALM 78:49-58

Safely Led, Yet Bent on Wandering. This section of the psalm deals largely with the books of Joshua and Judges. The failures that had characterized the wilderness crossed the Jordan with the Chosen People, and were the reason of their sufferings and captivities in what might otherwise have been a period of uninterrupted blessedness. In fact, the sins of the Land of Promise were even more disastrous. The Israelites were intended to be to Jehovah what the bow is to the huntsman or warrior; but they absolutely failed him. "They were turned aside like a deceitful bow," v. 57.

The lesson for older believers is very searching. Some readers of these words may recall that at a notable period in the past, they crossed the river of death to sin and life unto God. Jordan stands for consecration. It should be remembered, however, that no matter how rich and lofty have been the experiences of past blessing, we cannot be immune from failures, unless we watch and pray and live in abiding fellowship with Jesus Christ. The soul which has passed the Jordan is attacked by the principalities and powers in the heavenlies, Eph. 6:12, and has an even harder time of it. The nearer the Captain, the more perilous the position.

PSALM 78:59-72

God Raises Up His Shepherd David. This paragraph continues the history of the judges, and tells the story of what befell after the battle in which Eli's sons were slain. See 1 Sam. 4. It is difficult to estimate the despair which that disaster caused, because Israel seemed the lightbearer of the world. What hope was there for mankind, if its lamp of testimony was extinguished!

It inspires great confidence, however, to read in v. 65 of God's awakening. The language, of course, is highly metaphorical, because he neither slumbers nor sleeps. But there have been many times in the history of the Church when he has seemed to be indifferent. Sin and evil have held undisputed sway. Then a time of revival has suddenly set in. Some David or Daniel, some Athanasius or Augustine, some Wycliffe or Luther, some Spurgeon or Moody has been brought from an obscure family—"one of the least of the thousands of Judah"—and has led the host of God with unerring accuracy and success. Even at this hour, amid the sheepfolds or the far-spreading acres of the Western world, God is probably training the ardently looked-for leaders of his Church.

PSALM 79

"Help Us, O God of Our Salvation." It was the period of the Chaldean invasion. This cry of horror went forth from the heart of the Chosen People, who had looked upon the sacred shrine as inviolable. They could not believe that the tide of invasion could break in upon Jerusalem, or that the Holy City should be defiled by the profane feet of the heathen. This psalm should be compared with the book of Lamentations. We there find the same horror, the same anguish, the same sense of surprise, the same hatred of the foe, the same cry to God.

Does it seem as if God were angry with you? Have the heathen forced their way into the inner shrine and city of your heart? Are you "brought very low" and near unto death? Then begin to inquire whether some sin may not have alienated God from you. Confess it and put it away. Turn to God with a free and glad faith. Ask that his mercies may "prevent" (literally, "go before") and his help succor you, for his name's sake. The sighing of the captive and the greatness of God's power, v. 11, are in close affinity; and when you are delivered, remember your vows and show forth his praise to all within your reach.

PSALM 80:1–7

"Turn Us Again, O God." The ten tribes were in captivity and the hearts of their brethren, still living at Jerusalem under the reign of David's line, seem to have turned with great longing toward them. This psalm is full of intercession on their behalf. Three times, at the turning points of the psalm, the refrain is repeated that God would turn them again and cause them to be saved, vv. 3, 7, 19. Note the ascending climax: "God; God of Hosts; Jehovah, God of Hosts."

In Jacob's blessing of Joseph, God is appealed to as Shepherd, Gen. 49:24. To sit enthroned above the cherubim is an emblem of omnipotence. Notice how the gentleness of the Shepherd blends with his almightiness. In the wilderness march the three great tribes of Ephraim, Benjamin, and Manasseh immediately followed the Ark, which was borne by the priests. This ancient litany surely befits the present condition of the Church when she is rent by internal divisions or infected with a spirit of skepticism and unable to exorcise the demons that possess society. Let us plead with God to enlighten us by his face and quicken us by his Spirit. God must defend his cause, else there is no help for it.

PSALM 80:8–19

"Cause Thy Face to Shine." The imagery of the vine is taken from Jacob's dying words, in which he compared Joseph to a fruitful bough which had grown over the wall, Gen. 49:22. It is therefore a very apt and appropriate figure in this psalm, of which the northern tribes are the special subject. The figure of the vine is wrought out with extreme beauty. The book of Exodus tells of the transplanting, and those of Joshua and Judges of the ground that was cleared to receive it. In the days of Solomon, the boughs of the kingdom reached to the Euphrates on the east, and the Great Sea (the Mediterranean) on the west. But the walls were broken down by invasion, and the vine lay at the mercy of every passerby or the wild creatures of the forest.

We, too, know the havoc which ensues when the Church no longer lives within the fence of God's care. Revive us! Restore us! "Cause thy face to shine!" "The man of thy right hand," v. 17, may be another term for Israel. But our Lord alone can fulfill this description; and God's power is pledged to arrest the advance of the enemy, and to cause the true Vine and its branches to cover the earth. We must turn to John 15 to find the antitype of Israel, in the relation between Christ and his Church.

PSALM 81:1–7

Sing unto God, the Deliverer. It is supposed that this psalm was composed for use at the great Hebrew festivals and especially at the Passover, which is referred to in vv. 5–7, 10. See also 2 Chron. 30:21. Let us remember to celebrate the redemption of the cross, where our Paschal Lamb was sacrificed. We must celebrate, here and hereafter, the love that rescued us from the burden and the basket, at Sinai and Meribah. Baskets have been found in the sepulchral vaults at Thebes, and were doubtless used for carrying the clay or the manufactured bricks. They are symbols of the drudgery and slavery of sin, when we served a hard taskmaster whose wages is death.

If we are in trouble, let us quote v. 7, call on God, and reckon on his delivering helpfulness. He will answer from "his thunder-covert." He comes out of his secret place. Especially when the thunder of a broken law is in our ears, let

PSALMS

us hasten to the Redeemer, who has fulfilled the law in our stead. Let us maintain by faith our standing in him; then we shall be as they who look down from the high mountains on the thunderstorm at our feet.

PSALM 81:8-16

"If Thou Wilt Hearken unto Me." God wants our emptiness, which seems to him like the gaping beak of the young fledgling, v. 10. "Give me room!" seems to be his incessant appeal. It must be the wonder of eternity, and it will certainly be our regret when we come to review our life, that we have asked so little. "Give me room!" cries the river as it comes with a rush to the plains. "Give me room!" cries the wind as it searches the narrow courts and alleys of the slums. "Give me room!" says the Spirit of God as he breathes around the house of our heart, seeking by any tiny crack to enter.

In the closing verses, 13-16, we have an enumeration of all the blessings which would be ours if only we would open our mouths wide. God would constitute himself as our champion in subduing our enemies—the temptations from without and the inward warrings of selfishness and passion. He would give us unbroken and enduring blessedness. He would allow us to eat of his flesh and drink of his blood, which are meat and drink indeed. He would surely satisfy us with the sweet honey of his love. Let us begin to claim these benefits!

PSALM 82

The Just Judge of All. Those described here as "gods" are evidently the judges and magistrates of Israel. See John 10:34. They were intended to be the mouthpiece and representatives of God; but instead they thought only of their own interests and sought personal aggrandizement. But the psalmist beheld what was veiled from ordinary view—God standing in the midst of his people, judging them himself and judging their judges.

We may have done wrongs of which no judge has convicted us. But God has seen and unless there is confession, leading to forgiveness, he will certainly punish. Or we may have been grossly misjudged, and in that case he will vindicate us. Go to Jesus, to whom the Father has committed all judgment, and remember that while all things are naked and open to his eyes, he also is the High Priest who is touched with the feeling of our infirmities, and the Lamb that takes away sin. When the foundations of the earth are out of course, let us remember that we belong to a kingdom that cannot be moved, Heb. 12:28.

PSALM 83

"The Most High over All the Earth." This psalm was composed on the occasion described in 2 Chronicles 20, where we learn that at a great crisis the Spirit of God came on Jahaziel, one of the sons of Asaph, v. 14. It was written to be sung before the battle, in anticipation of certain victory. The Levites chanted it with a loud voice on high as Jehoshaphat's army marched out against the great confederacy of nations which threatened the very existence of Israel. There were strong reasons for God's interposition, for Israel's foes were God's foes also. It was *his* people that were the target of this crafty conspiracy. Were they not his "hidden ones," v. 3? Could a hostile world pluck them from the hollow of his hand? When our life is "hid with Christ in God," we may confidently appeal for his safekeeping.

The fate here imprecated savors of Moses rather than of Jesus Christ, vv. 9-18. Our Lord's way is to seek the conversion of the heathen. At the same time it may at least be urged that Israel did not pray thus to gratify a personal vindictiveness, but that the great world of men might know God to be Jehovah. Out of the mighty convulsions that sweep across society, we know that the coming of the divine kingdom is somehow being prepared. God can make even the wrath of man to praise him, 76:10.

PSALM 84

Longing for the House of God. One of the sweetest of the Psalms, David probably composed it during his absence from Jerusalem at the time of Absalom's rebellion, though its final form may have been due to the sons of Korah. It is divided into three parts by the Selahs.

"They that dwell in thy house," vv. 1-4. The psalmist envies the wingèd things that rest in those hallowed precincts, and how much more the priests and Levites who serve there! Foxes have holes and birds have nests, but man can rest only in God. *Those in whose hearts are the ways of Zion,* vv. 5-8. We may not be able actually to walk along those ways, but it is good to tread them in living sympathy with the saints, and to unite ourselves to the pilgrim hosts. Those absent from God's house may in their heart join the great congregation. Thus, dry and desolate valleys may become filled with water springs, making them green and beautiful. When the heart is right with God, the desert becomes a

temple, and tears are exchanged for smiles. *"The man that trusteth in thee,"* vv. 9–12. God is better than his sanctuary. He is a Sun in dark hours and a Shadow in scorching ones. "Grace" is his unmerited pardon and blessing to sinners, "glory" the irradiation of his character, into the likeness of which we shall be changed.

PSALM 85

A Prayer for the Nation. This psalm is the counterpart of the 80th. There we see petitions ascending; here thanksgivings are returned. Evidently there had been granted some great national deliverance, which filled the land with thanksgiving. The restoration of the captives from Babylon was such an event; but the words well befit glad days of revival. They might have been sung on the first Easter day, when mercy and truth met at the cross, and there was a wedding of earth and sky. Reversed captivity, forgiven and buried sin, the dark clouds of estrangement dispelled, the speaking of peace—these are great themes and all have their counterparts in Christian experience.

There is exquisite beauty in vv. 10 and 11. What a meeting of the divine attributes! The cross is their trysting-place. It resembles the family gathering of brothers and sisters in the old homestead. Notice that Heaven must combine with earth in the production of Christian grace. Truth can spring up in the soil of our heart only when righteousness looks down with benignant love from heaven. But she does even more; she shows us how to walk in the way of God's steps.

PSALM 86

A Prayer to the God of Mercy. This psalm is largely composed of quotations. When the soul is in great need, it is not concerned with inventing new forms of address to God, but avails itself of well-known and well-worn phrases. Our Lord in Gethsemane "prayed the same words." The background of the psalm is faith which reckons on God's goodness. "Thou art good," v. 5; "thou art great," v. 10; "thou art full of compassion, and gracious," v. 15. Be sure to build prayer upon the revelation of God's nature as given by Christ.

Verses 1–5: That we are indeed poor and needy is our strongest plea with God. That we are holy is true only so far as we present Christ as our righteousness. That we cry all the day is a plea which God honors. But the best of all is the plenteousness of his loving-kindness.

Verses 6–13: Again, in this strophe, there is the cry of need; and faith is helped by remembering that God's power is sufficient. God is so great that he can include our little life in his microscopic care. Verses 14–17: We can readily imagine the rabble that beset the psalmist, for we are similarly beset; but nearer than they can come is the calm and holy inner presence of God.

PSALM 87

Citizens of Zion. This psalm blends in one great congregation the ancient foes of Israel and the Chosen People. It is a vision of the Holy Universal Church. The Selahs divide it into three parts:

Verses 1–3: An outburst of rapturous praise. Zion's foundations are in the mountains, and her gates are dear to God. Far and wide men recount her glories and triumphs. But how much greater is the glory of the Church, which is founded on Christ's finished work and ruled by him from Heaven. The Church is indwelt by the Holy Spirit, and a light shines from her into all the world.

Verses 4–6: The ancient enemies of Zion contribute their children to the Church. Egypt or Rahab are no longer dreaded and despised; Babylon no longer detested for its tyranny; Philistia and Ethiopia, once far off, now made nigh. They come from the east and west, and sit down at the feast of fat things of which Isaiah sang, Isa. 25:6.

Verse 7: A triumphal procession passes before us, confessing that the springs of the true life are to be found in the Church, because they are fed from the great depths of eternal love and life.

PSALM 88

A Cry from the Waves. Most of the psalms which begin in sorrow end in exuberant joy and praise. This is an exception. There seems to be no break in the monotony of grief and despair. In vv. 1–8 it would appear that the psalmist was oppressed by some loathsome disorder which made even his friends shrink from companionship. But it is a hopeful sign when, even in such circumstances, a man can still speak of God as "the God of *my* salvation."

In vv. 9–18 the psalmist combats his despair by reminding God and himself that his has been a praying soul. Surely the Almighty will not forget his outstretched hands, nor the prayers that have anticipated the morning! It is a true argument. That you can pray at all is a sure sign that the divine Spirit is within your heart. From unknown depths he is helping your infirmity, and this proves that God has not forgotten or forsaken you. If just now life's ship is overwhelmed with difficulty, God rules the waves. The storm wind will presently subside at his rebuke. Lover and friend will again stand round about you, and your soul will come back into light. God's days are not like man's—from morning to evening—but from dark to dawn.

PSALM 89:1-18

No God Like Our God. To understand this psalm we must turn to 2 Samuel 7, where God guaranteed that David's kingdom should be continued to his descendants. Nathan's words are quoted in vv. 3 and 4. But in contrast with these promises, which were conditional upon the faithful obedience of David's descendants, the psalmist sorrowfully recites the disobedience of the Chosen People. There could be no doubt as to the divine faithfulness to covenant engagements. See vv. 1, 2, 5, 8, and 14. The object of this psalm is to inquire whether that faithfulness does not include the recall and restoration of a sinful nation, as it most certainly does include the continued blessing of an obedient one.

In the first division, vv. 1-18, the singer enumerates the divine attributes. God's mercy is conceived as a stately mansion which is being reared, story by story, throughout the centuries. The enduring heavens, the mightiest natural forces, such as the tides, the glorious mountains, are emblems of qualities in God's nature. He is described as going forth in a triumphal procession, preceded by mercy and truth; and we are invited to accompany him, and to walk in the light of his countenance.

PSALM 89:19-37

The Covenant with David. In this section the psalmist draws out, in detail, the fundamental prophecy by Nathan already mentioned; first, in the promises given to David, vv. 19-27; and second, in those relating to his descendants, vv. 28-37.

David's origin was very humble. His dignity and power were all of God. But our Father never sets a man in any position and fails to supply the gifts needed for it. When he chooses, he anoints, strengthens, and protects. Victory also is granted over the man's enemies, because God's faithfulness and mercy are beside him, v. 24. The relationship between the soul and God is very intimate; on the one hand you have v. 26, and on the other v. 27.

What a precious promise is v. 28! From this point the psalmist turns to expand the promises to David's line. They may be chastened, but not permanently rejected. In v. 33 the twin attributes of mercy and faithfulness are again blended as the ground of hope of sinful and unworthy men. God's word, once spoken, is inviolable. He is bound by his oath. Sin cannot alter his promise or the obligations under which he has laid himself. His unchangeableness is a bedrock upon which we may build with certitude.

PSALM 89:38-52

A Consuming Fire. Here the psalmist falls into expostulation and lament. Whether he alludes to the time when Jerusalem was taken by Shishak in the days of Rehoboam, 1 Kings 14:25, 26, or when the youthful prince Jehoiachin was deposed by Nebuchadnezzar, 2 Kings 24:10-16, it is impossible to say; but it seemed as if God's faithfulness had failed. The psalmist dwells sorrowfully upon the contrast between God's ancient covenant and the sad reality. The family that had been promised perpetual duration and dominion had lost its luster and had become like a dying lamp.

Then the psalmist betakes himself to prayer, and bases his argument upon the brevity of the age. There is but a little while during which God has the opportunity of manifesting his love and truth. Literally the words are, "Remember—what a transitoriness!" (v. 47). In the last three verses another plea is presented—that dishonor will accrue to God if he does not arrest the continuance of disaster. The insults and reproaches that are hurled against the servants are really directed against their God; therefore he is entreated, in vindicating them, to vindicate himself.

PSALM 90

The Message of the Passing Years. The majestic music of this great psalm separates it from all the rest. It is like the deep bass stop of a mighty organ. Moses' authorship is stamped upon it. It is worthy of the man who had seen God.

Verses 1-6: The transitoriness of human life is contrasted with the stability of God. He is the asylum and home of all the generations of mankind, Deut. 33:27. The earth and its mountains, the universe and its worlds were born of him; but he himself had no origin, no beginning. Time is but a sigh, a breath, the swift rush of the mountain torrent, a tale told by the campfire at night, the grass of a morning's growth.

Verses 7-12: A wail is borne in these verses from the forty years of wanderings. The ceaseless succession of graves was the bitter harvest of Israel's rebellions. Oh, that we might apply our hearts to wisdom, that we may not fail of God's rest!

Verses 13–17: In the closing words Moses utters a sublime prayer which includes us all. Let us seek to do some good work before we go, and may our children be a nobler generation than ourselves! But all beauty of character and permanence of work must emanate from God.

PSALM 91

Security in Trusting the Lord. In harmony with the new light cast upon it by recent translations, this psalm has been divided as follows: vv. 1, 2, a soliloquy in which the believer states the blessedness of dwelling under God's sheltering care, and encourages his heart to exercise personal faith; vv. 3–8, the assurance of a chorus of voices, which emphasize the safety of those who believe; v. 9a, an exclamation in which the believer again expresses his resolve to exercise this personal faith; vv. 9b–13, the second assurance of a chorus of reassuring voices; vv. 14–16, God's ratification of the whole attitude and expressions of the psalmist and his friends.

The psalm abounds in metaphors familiar to the East: the lion with its roar and leap in the open; the adder with its stealthy glide through the grass; the nocturnal assault; the devastating plague; the fowler's snare; the eagle's wing; the transitory tent. This is the traveler's psalm and may well be read in private or with the family, whenever we are starting on a journey.

But notice those closing verses, 14–16. Our conceptions of God's care are too narrow. We fail to make enough use of the power, love, and presence of his fatherhood, which is waiting and longing to be called upon. Only we must exercise an appropriating faith.

PSALM 92

Gladness and Growth. The inscription alludes to the suitability of this psalm for the Sabbath day. Verses 1–3 contain the general statement of the desirability of praise and thanksgiving. Verses 4, 5 suggest that God's work in creation, providence, and grace should elicit perpetual thanksgiving, but that the thoughts and purposes which underlie them are too deep for our fathoming.

Two classes of men are here mentioned: the brutish and wicked, vv. 6–9; the servants of God, vv. 10–15. The former are like grass, which soon grows to maturity and is then cut down; the latter are as the palm and cedar. There is no part of the palm which is not utilized in some way. The cedar is one of the largest of living trees. A thousand years is no uncommon duration, and its fiber is practically incorruptible.

The witness of an aged saint to the faithfulness of God is very delightful. When Charles H. Spurgeon was a young man, he was preaching upon this subject in his grandfather's pulpit. Halfway through the sermon, the veteran man of God advanced to the front and said, "My grandson is preaching what he has read and heard about; but I have proved for eighty-four years that God is faithful to his servants and true to his Word."

PSALM 93:1—94:5

The Lord Who Ruleth over All. It is thought that these two psalms date from the Assyrian invasion in Hezekiah's time, and that the psalmist compares the strength of Sennacherib and his hosts to the mighty breakers of the sea. But they well befit all times of anxiety and opposition. It is interesting to remember, also, that these and the six psalms which follow have always been applied by the Jews to the days of the Messiah. Surely, then, we may apply them to our own time.

It is an infinite comfort to know that above and beyond all that distresses and hinders the Church or our individual lives, there exists the great fact of our Lord's sovereignty. This encourages us in conflict and makes us steadfast and unmovable. We can almost hear the dash of successive breakers with foam and fury around the throne of God, which, however, stands without a tremor. The miracle of Jesus in quieting the storm has a symbolic and far-reaching meaning. He is in our hearts, in the world, and in his Church, as it is tossed on the surface of the storm-swept water—and Jesus rules the waves. He must vindicate the law of righteousness and save his people.

PSALM 94:6-23

The Lord Our Defense against Evildoers. Let us ponder all the great things that God will do for them that trust him. He planted the ear, and will detect the sigh, sob, or broken utterance of his child, v. 9. He formed the eye, and he knows our sorrows. He watches the sparrow's fall, and his child is of more value than many sparrows. He corrects us; shall we not be in subjection to the Father of spirits and live, v. 10? He knows our thoughts; let us ask him to purify and restrain them, v. 11. He teaches out of his Law; let us be diligent students of the Scriptures, v. 12. He will neither cast us off nor forsake us, v. 14.

The Lord is our help, and the soul that trusts him shall not be silenced, v. 17. He holds us up when our foot slips, v. 18. Whatever thoughts may startle or affright us, God has a comfort suited to counteract each of them. His comforts delight the soul. They bring joy and hope with them, v. 19. He defends us against the charges laid at our door, and is a rock on which we may stand steadily, amid the seething waters, v. 22. If God be for us, who can be against us, or who can separate us from his love? See Rom. 8:31.

PSALM 95

Praise the Lord and Tempt Him Not. This psalm is deeply inwoven into the life of the Church, because of the worshipful strain which pervades it, and also because of the illuminating manner in which it is introduced into the argument of Hebrews 3 and 4. The works of God in creation are specially enumerated as incentives to praise. The sea, the hills, the deep places of the earth have often inspired the minstrel, but how much more the devout soul!

Let us remember, also, when we are tossed on the seas of life, or are called to descend into valleys of shadow, that faith will still dare to sing. But in the second stanza of the psalm, from v. 6 onward, we are confronted with the sad story of Exodus 17. There are Meribahs and Massahs in all lives, where we murmur against God's dealings and lose our inward rest. There is a sabbath of the heart when the will is yielded to God's will and the heart is cleansed from its wayward whims, when the very peace that fills the divine nature settles down on the heart. That experience is an entrance into God's rest. It remains unexhausted for all the people of God. Let us not miss it through default of faith!

PSALM 96

"The Lord Reigneth." This psalm is found also in 1 Chronicles 16. Note the thrice-repeated command, "Sing, sing, sing," vv. 1 and 2; the corresponding, thrice-repeated, "Give, give, give," vv. 7 and 8; the triple call for joy from Heaven, sea, and land, vv. 11 and 12. It is good to read these psalms; they impart the burning devotion of these olden saints. They break on our lethargy as the bugle call on the sleeping soldier. Notice that we call men to a *Jubilate*, not a *Miserere*, when we invite them to come home to God.

What a stately procession escorts the King to the throne of the world! He comes to reign in equity. Righteousness and truth which had fled the world return with him. Honor and majesty are his couriers. Strength and beauty stand in his court circle. When we are brought into the divine kingdom, and are at one with God, we detect the unison of Nature in her song of praise. The seas provide the bass; the quivering leaves, the song of buds, the hum of insect life provide the tenors and altos; while the stars in their courses sing the treble. To the anointed ear, the new song has already begun.

PSALM 97

"Rejoice in the Lord." The keynote here is the reign of God. To the wicked, it spells misery; to the believer, it is the inauguration of harmony and joy. It is as though herald-angels step from isle to isle, from mountain peak to mountain peak with glad tidings of great joy. It is not always easy to trace its advent. Clouds and darkness are around God. The eye of sense cannot penetrate the black enclosing pall, but faith is ever certain that righteousness and judgment are the foundation of his throne.

Sometimes God comes in fire, v. 3, as at Sinai, or on the day of Pentecost, which took place on the anniversary of the giving of the Law. Days come like that on which Jerusalem fell, or when the Turks took Constantinople, or when Napoleon was shattered at Waterloo. Then hills melt like wax. But through all dark and terrible dispensations the kingdom is secretly growing, the Lord is being exalted, light is being sown for his people, v. 11. So, believer, your tears and fightings, as they pass, are absorbing Heaven's love and power, which they will hold in reserve through long buried in the dark. Days of unspeakable gladness are at hand. Be of good cheer.

PSALM 98

Worthy of Praise from All the Earth. This psalm is parallel to the 96th. That dealt with the reign of God; this deals with the victory on which that reign is based, v. 1. God could create without restraint, but before he could redeem he had to quell the resistance of evil and to overcome the prince of this world. Hence the long conflict; but salvation was wrought by that holy arm which was outstretched on the cross, and by the right hand which gave itself to the nails. In the resurrection and ascension our Lord's righteousness and salvation were openly manifested. See Col. 2:15.

The "Hallelujah Chorus" of vv. 4–9 well befits the triumph of Christ. Earth that shared in the fall of man shall participate in his redemption. See Isa. 32. Too long has Nature groaned and travailed, like an imprisoned captive; but she shall have her rebirth. When Jesus is King, seas and floods, mountains and hills are filled with music. Nature is like a stringed instrument that awaits tuning and the touch of a master-hand. Revelation 5 gives the counterpart of the psalmist's summons; there the apostle tells us that the song which started from the elders was echoed back from all things in Heaven, on earth, and in the sea, and all that is in them. Be optimistic. Eat your meat with gladness and singleness of heart. You are on the winning and singing side.

PSALM 99

Worship the Great and Holy One. This psalm has its counterpart in Psalm 97. There Jehovah's reign is associated with the gladness of faith, here with the trembling of mortal and sinful hearts. Thrice we are reminded that he is holy, vv. 3, 5, 9. This threefold ascription of earth concerning the holiness of God answers the threefold ascription of Heaven, where one seraph cries to the rest, saying, "Holy, holy, holy, is the Lord of hosts: the whole earth is full of his glory," Isa. 6:3.

God's holiness is terrible to sinners. It inspires even his own people with awe. However near we come to him in Christ, we always must remember that we are sinful men who have no right to stand before him, save through the mediation and in the righteousness of his Son.

How great God must be, who can reckon Moses, Aaron, and Samuel as his servants! And we, too, though beneath them in personal character and gift, are permitted to be among his priests, to call upon his name, to hear him speaking from the pillar of cloud. Let us all walk worthy of our high calling! Let us fear this great and holy God, who cannot tolerate sin in his children and will not hesitate to inflict pain if sin is persisted in. He does forgive—glory to his name!—but he will not hesitate to chasten us for sins which we presumptuously and knowingly permit.

PSALM 100

Universal Praise. If we could enter into the spirit of this psalm, every day would be a Thanksgiving Day. The psalmist invites all the earth to enter into the courts of God's house with joyful songs. In many of the Psalms the minor chords overpower the major ones, and weeping prevails over rejoicing. But this psalm is full of unclouded sunlight. The reason for this gladness is suggested in the words, "We are his." His by creation, by providence, and by grace; and his also by the glad consecration of our hearts to his service. We belong to him by right; it is for us to see to it that we are also his by choice. And his ownership involves his shepherd-care. We are his flock; it is for him to lead us into green pastures and beside still waters.

To the psalmist's eye the nations of the world pour into the Temple through the wide-open portals. "Hark!" he cries. "Listen to the burst of thanksgivings which roll forth from the mighty throng!" The great attraction is the goodness of Jehovah, and the everlastingness of his love and troth. This psalm reveals the true genius of religion. We cannot be satisfied till all men share our knowledge of the love of God. There is nothing which will better promote the true happiness and gladness of mankind.

PSALM 101

My Righteous Purpose. This psalm, as the title indicates, was composed by David, probably at the commencement of his reign. It contains a number of resolutions upon which he was prepared to act. First, he made up his mind that he would give heed to "a perfect way," and would walk in his house in the integrity of his heart, v. 2. Next, he made up his mind to choose his friends with rigorous care, that froward hearts and evil persons should depart from him; that he would not enter into close relations with those that slandered their neighbors, or that gave evidence by their high looks of proud hearts. Deceit and falsehood were alike to be banished from his palace, while faithful souls, who also walked in "a perfect way," should minister to him. Finally, he made up his mind to carry out his rule in the public state that the wicked might be put out of the way and the righteous exalted.

It was an excellent program, and happy would he have been if throughout his life he had rigorously adhered to it. It is not possible for us to exercise David's absolute power in the selection of our environment. It is often necessary for us to work in places of business among those whom we would not choose as associates. But we can, at least, forbear making any of these our intimates, or the friends with whom we spend our leisure and recreative hours, 1 Cor. 5:9-11.

PSALM 102:1-11

The Cry of the Afflicted. This is the fifth of the Penitential Psalms. Some hold that it is one of the later psalms, asking for deliverance from captivity; others, emphasizing certain Davidic characteristics, ascribe it to the hand of the royal psalmist. Its actual authorship, however, is of comparatively small consequence; the main thing is to notice what adequate expression it gives to the sorrow of an almost broken heart.

The psalmist bases his cry for a speedy answer on the swiftness with which his days are passing away, like smoke escaping from a chimney. His bones are calcined; his heart withers like Jonah's gourd; he is worn to a skeleton by his long and passionate lamentations. He finds his likeness in solitude-loving creatures, such as the pelican and the owl. Still another element in his suffering is the mockery of his foes. He cannot get away from it; it haunts him. Ashes, the token of his mourning, are his food, and tears fill his cup. But the bitterest element of all is the consciousness of God's displeasure. It seems as if God's hand is against him, and in the accumulated weight of grief he deems that the day of his life must expire. However, in the concluding portion of the psalm his hope is renewed.

PSALM 102:12–28

The Time to Have Mercy upon Zion. We must remember that the Holy Spirit appropriates the closing words of this psalm as addressed to our Lord. See Heb. 1:10–12. This gives new point to these petitions. The psalmist's sorrows, described in the previous paragraph, had their source in the desolations of Zion rather than in personal afflictions; and when the soul feels such oppression, it is a sign that deliverance is near. Finney, the great evangelist, tells of a woman who came to her pastor under such concern for the perishing that she could neither eat nor sleep. She entreated him to appoint an inquirers' meeting, and though there had been no signs of a revival it suddenly broke out. When Christians take pity on the stones and dust of the Church, the time has come for God to arise to her help.

Behold the unchanging Christ! Creation may wax old, the heavens and earth may be laid aside as an outworn garment, the old order may give place to new; but beneath all the changes Jesus Christ remains the same yesterday, today, and forever. How delightful are those immortal words, "But thou, O Lord, shalt endure." And if he endures, his servants shall continue also, and their children after them.

PSALM 103:1–12

The Lord's Abundant Mercies. David's name heads this peerless psalm, which expresses, as none other, the soul of the universal Church and of the individual Christian. Notice the present tenses throughout these verses. God's tender dealings run parallel with our lives. He is never weary nor exhausted. When once he begins, he keeps on. Let us enumerate the blessings that he gives in such unbroken abundance, and as the fingers tell the successive beads, praise him: forgiveness; healing, Exod. 15:26; redemption from perils and accidents, seen and unseen; the crowns that he places on our unworthy heads; entire satisfaction, Ps. 36:8 and Isa. 58:11; perennial youth.

It was a proverb among Orientals that the eagle literally grows younger. This is the psalmist's reference in v. 5. For us it means that the life which is fed from the eternal springs is eagle-like in royal strength and sunward flight. "Ways" or plans are revealed to the inner circle; the ordinary congregation knows only "acts." The Father does chide, but only till we put sin away. Conceive the infinite spaces of east and west; such is the distance of forgiven sin from us. It is impossible that the blame or curse of it should ever return upon the redeemed soul.

PSALM 103:13–22

Everlasting Lovingkindness. The psalmist comes from the far-reaching sky to the down-to-earth image of a father's pity. God is a great King, the mighty Creator, but the Spirit witnesses that we are his "children" and teaches us to say, "Abba, Father." The idea of "dust" is that of frailty. Made of dust and fragile as an earthen vessel, man by his weakness appeals to Jehovah's compassion. The thought of frailty and helplessness is still further impressed by the figure of the fading flower, scorched by the hot desert wind. By force of contrast, the psalmist passes from man's brief span of life to God's eternal years. And God's love is as his life. Because God is eternal, his love is eternal. When once he loves, he loves always; he never wearies, never cools, never lets go. A parent who fears God may leave a legacy of priceless worth to his children's children. See v. 17.

From v. 19 to the end, the psalmist pulls out all the stops in the great organ of existence. Angels and hosts of other intelligent beings who perform the Lord's will, all his works animate and inanimate, all saints, all souls, stars and suns, oceans, and mountains—*all* must join the "Hallelujah Chorus."

PSALM 104:1–12

The Lord's Wondrous Handiwork. The opening verses of this psalm appear to describe in sublime poetry the creation of the world. God is very great, because he created the heavens and the earth. He is clothed with honor and majesty, and yet he stooped to brood over the chaos and darkness which preceded the order and beauty of our earth. When he said, "Let there be light," he robed himself in its texture. The firmament of Genesis 1:8 was the curtain of his tent. The clouds above and the seas beneath yielded his chariot and hid for him the joists of his palace. See Gen. 1:9, 10. Compare v. 4 and Heb. 1:7.

The psalmist in v. 6 seems to see the process which is described briefly and graphically in Genesis 1:10. The waters had covered the world with their storm and turmoil; but at God's command they poured down the mountain slopes to the ocean bed, there to be retained by banks of sand. What exquisite thoughtfulness is disclosed in God's provision of the springs! He thinks for the wild asses and the fowls, and how much more will he care for you, O ye of little faith!

PSALM 104:13-23

A Habitation for Beast and Man. Where there is true love for God, there will be a glad and rejoicing heart that takes pleasure in the study of his works. The loving child of a great artist lingers about his studio, watches with eager interest the development of picture or statute, and speaks with delight to others of her father's work. It is in such a spirit that those who know God in daily fellowship and communion follow the psalmist to mountain streams, to the pastures and the meadows, the grainfields and the orchards, the high mountains with their dark pines and firs.

There is no pen that has more eloquently portrayed these scenes than Ruskin's. He had a natural love for beauty, and an unrivaled genius for vivid description; but it was as a boy at his mother's knee that he learned from these Scriptures to connect the glories of the natural world with the devout adoration of the Creator. His books reflect this early training.

This psalm may be called a divine commentary on God's earliest book—the world which lies around us.

PSALM 104:24-35

The Almighty's Open Hand. The psalmist says nothing of the operation of the great laws of Nature, but passes behind and beyond to the Great Hand which opens to fill and satisfy all living things with good. The personality of God is the moving force behind the thin veil of outward appearance. This is in striking contrast with much of the thinking and speaking of the present day, which practically exclude the Creator from his own creation. But there is no real opposition between the two conceptions. Natural law is only another way of stating the usual method of God's working. There is no variableness in him, nor shadow cast by turning; and it is because we can count on his unaltering methods that human life can develop regularly and successfully.

While all creation waits on the opening of God's hand, man alone can adore him. We stand in the midst of creation as its high priest and interpreter. We can say to God what Nature longs to express but cannot. Amid the beauty and magnificence of natural scenery, let us sing the "Te Deum"; and let us believe that he who rejoices in his works comes very near us in our joy, which proves that our nature and his are closely akin.

PSALM 105:1-15

The Lord's Covenant with Israel. This psalm and the next are a pair, probably composed during the Exile in Babylon. They are evidently derived in part from the old Tabernacle service, in which is found the beginning of this psalm and the end of the next, 1 Chron. 16. Here we have the story of Jehovah's faithfulness to his covenant and of Israel's ingratitude.

It is right to make known God's doings. Nothing touches men more quickly, or excites faith and hope more certainly, than to hear what others have experienced of God's saving health. Let us talk more often of his marvelous works. If God has forgiven you, even to 10,000 talents, confess it. If you have learned more of Christ's patience in his bearing with your sins and failures, tell it out. The salient points which stand out in our record of the past may be summarized under the same general headings as those of the psalmist. God has been mindful of his covenant, ratified by the blood of his Son. He has shown his independence of human standards in choosing us, though we are absolutely unworthy to inherit his kingdom. How often he has interposed in our behalf, even when we have deserved the worst, saying, "Touch not mine anointed!"

PSALM 105:16-30

Wonders in Egypt. The psalmist retells the story of Joseph, as a link in the chain of providences which secured the fulfillment of the covenant. It may be that it was also introduced to comfort Israel amid the afflictions of the Captivity. Another reading of the second clause of v. 18 is, "The iron entered his soul." This is what pain does for us all; it puts iron into our blood. In v. 19 we learn that God's promise, while unfulfilled and apparently contradicted by present facts, serves as a test of a man's reliance upon God. It brings into clear relief his unwavering faith. Joseph was tested and not found wanting.

Verses 23-27 carry us a step farther in the unfolding of God's purpose. The sojourn in Egypt, with its terrible hardships and the trouble that befell the tyrant, is quoted with direct reference to the action and interposition of the Almighty. The psalmist sees only one hand at work. He does not hesitate to ascribe to God even the hatred which the Egyptians entertained toward Israel and which, in Pharaoh's case, meant the hardening of his heart. Such is the inevitable effect when man's pride conflicts with divine tenderness and love. Let us believe that God is in all the incidents of our daily life and of human history.

PSALM 105:31-45

Led by a Mighty Hand. Notice in this enumeration of the plagues that the emphasis in each is laid on God's direct act. *He* is the great agent of his own purposes. The tenth plague, v. 36, is followed by the triumphant exodus, when Israel went forth, enriched with treasure and strong for the march. However sad and weary our life may be, it will one day be rich and strong as it goes forth to serve under new and loftier conditions. How good it is to realize that God hath prepared for us things that surpass human thought, and which are proportioned not according to intellect but according to heart; not according to deeds, but according to character!

God is all-sufficient for us. He was everything that Israel needed. Can he not suffice for us? We have good hope, not because of our merit, but because of the covenant into which he has entered with our Savior, who is our representative and federal head. Not for *our* sakes, but for his holy name's sake, God has pledged himself to make us his heirs, joint-heirs with his Son, and sharers in all that joy and bliss which await us on the other side. Ought we not, then, to love him and to keep his statutes and laws? Hallelujah!

PSALM 106:1-15

Unfailing Loving-kindness. "Who can utter?" That is an unanswered question. Not even the leader of the heavenly choir can answer it. But what blessedness it brings to the heart of one who begins to recite the goodness and lovingkindness of God! When prayer goes heavily, begin to praise.

The theme of this psalm is God's redeeming grace. It contains a gruesome catalog of sin. "We have sinned . . . we have committed iniquity . . . our fathers understood not . . . they remembered not . . . but provoked . . . they soon forgat . . . they waited not . . . but lusted exceedingly . . . and tempted God." But side by side were divine love and mercy: *"Nevertheless* he saved them for his name's sake," v. 8. God is bound to keep his covenant, even to the children's children. He must act worthily of himself. "Truth" is another spelling of "troth." When God has pledged his troth, as he did to Abraham and has also to us, he cannot fail.

Notice the pathetic prayer of v. 4. Though we are more or less implicated in the sins of those around us, we, as Christians, may claim special favor and help, in order to be placed in a stronger position when we come to intercede for others.

PSALM 106:16-33

Judgment Restrained by Intercession. The strife between the ungodly and the servants of God has characterized all the centuries. These verses record some of its phases. Moses is called God's chosen, Aaron his saint, while Phinehas is held in honor as one to whom his noble deed was counted for righteousness. But such men are always envied, refused, resisted. Men hate them, but God loves and vindicates them for their loyalty and uncompromising righteousness.

It is beautiful to notice how, so far from human hatred inducing such leaders to turn from their persecutors, it seems to drive them to more intense and ceaseless intercession for them. They stand in the breach, to turn away deserved wrath. From the days of Abraham, who prayed for Sodom, right down the stream of time, the people of God have been his remembrancers, giving him no rest. Let us cultivate the great art of intercession; and if there is need, let us, like Phinehas, not hesitate to strike strongly in the interests of purity. But while thus standing before men, we must cultivate the grace of humility. We are only servants at the most and must not assume more for ourselves. Our authority is only delegated. This is where Moses failed, Num. 20:2-13.

PSALM 106:34-48

Regarded When They Cried. Israel's conquest of Canaan did not fulfill the divine mandate. The inhabitants, whose sins had become a menace to mankind, were allowed to exist side by side with the Hebrew immigrants; and, as is often the case, the conquerors were conquered, and the invaders were contaminated by the morals of the invaded. Intermarriage poured a large admixture of alien blood into Israel, and the excesses of idolatry, even to the hideous practice of human sacrifices, became intensified by the ties of kinship and neighborhood.

The whole history of Israel is summed up as alternating cycles of sin and punishment, repentance and deliverance; and we are left wondering, first at the inveterate evil of the human heart, which learns nothing from experience, and next at the inexhaustible long-suffering of God, which, while justice strikes, yet finds some way of alleviating the smart of the stroke, v. 46. The love of God persists all through human sin and outreaches it.

The prayer of v. 47 shows that this psalm was written in exile. The psalmist hopes and believes that one result of his people's restoration will be thankfulness and the expression upon grateful lips of never-ending praise. So ends the fourth book of the Psalter.

PSALM 107:1-16

"Wonderful Works to the Children of Men." In this psalm those who have been redeemed by the gracious interpositions of God are summoned to praise him for a love which endures through all our rebuffs and backslidings. Note how this refrain breaks out in vv. 8, 15, 21, and 31. The psalmist passes before us a series of pictures, selected from the stories of human suffering which have been repeated in all ages of human history. Travelers who have lost their way, captives, sick men, storm-tossed sailors are presented in as many panels or pictures. The psalmist says that whatever our trouble, there is only one way out of it—to cry to God. This is never in vain. There is always the saving help of his right hand; and there is always, therefore, the obligation of praise.

The first scene is of a caravan in the desert, with depleted water-skins, emptied supplies, exhausted strength. How many have lost their way in life and are in this plight! These details are true not only physically, but spiritually. The second scene is of a prison-house, and the suggestion is that in all our lives there are imprisoning circumstances and limitations which compel us to call for help from him who said, "He hath sent me to proclaim liberty to the captives."

PSALM 107:17-32

"His Wonders in the Deep." Sickness yields the third type of suffering. Emphasis is laid on the cause of the suffering, which in the view of the writer is transgression and sin. We shall be justified, therefore, in confining our view of this section to the pain which is directly traceable to wrongdoing. Men ruin their health by evil courses, and the sinner drags down his punishment with his own hands. The portals of death had already opened to receive the sick men, but before they passed through they cried to Jehovah, and though their voice was feeble, they were heard. May we not make our own application of v. 20, by referring it to that Word of God through whom God's love and healing came to sinners in the days of his flesh?

The storm at sea is the next tableau. We have the sudden gale, the high waves, the ship now on the crest and then in the trough; the terror of the crew; the failure of the helm; the desperation of the sailors; and finally the voice of God above and through the storm. The sudden subsidence of the tempest is a grateful change to the sailors and the crew; and what gladness is theirs when they reach the harbor which they had longed for, but had never thought to see again! Such is life, and such will be, by God's mercy, our coming into harbor. "Safe into the haven guide."

PSALM 107:33-43

"The Lovingkindness of the Lord." The measure changes here. From v. 33 the psalmist drops the refrain and describes, not deliverance from peril or pain, but the sudden alternations wrought by God's providence. Lands pass from fertility to barrenness, and human lives from prosperity to trouble, and back again. But through all these vicissitudes runs the same lovingkindness, as is clearly discerned by those who have eyes to see and hearts to take heed. How little did Joseph's brethren realize that behind all the strange experiences they had with his steward, in his house and in the matter of the cup, a brother's heart was yearning to reach a moment when all disguise might be laid aside! Similarly we fail to believe that love is above and through and in all things.

Life resembles this psalm, so full is it of change and trying experiences. Few enjoy unbroken years of prosperity. We are poured from vessel to vessel, and are forbidden to settle on our lees. Our nests are stirred up to teach us how to fly. For most there is the wilderness, the cell, sickness, and the tossing of the ocean waves. But always believe in the love of God. Do not forget to cry; and when your cry has brought an answer of peace, do not forget to praise.

PSALM 108

Victorious through God. Two fragments of Davidic psalms are here joined together with very slight alterations. Verses 1-5 are from Psalm

57:7-11, and vv. 6-18 from Psalm 60:5-12. We need the fixed heart, ever constant to God, as is the needle to the pole. When we are right with God, we go through the world awakening song and hope in forlorn hearts. Note the themes for constant adoration, vv. 3-5.

Apparently David stood in imagination at the beginning of those conquests which made Israel great and extended her frontiers to the great river Euphrates. He felt that God had spoken in his holiness, and had already given him the territories here enumerated. All that remained for him to do was to occupy and possess what the Almighty had allotted. There is a close analogy here to our appropriation of those heavenly blessings which are ours in the risen Lord. It is not we who can tread down our adversaries. They are too strong and insidious. But when our heart is fixed, God goes before us, vanquishing our foes, and we have but to follow after, gathering in the spoils. In our inner conflicts, vain is human help, even the best. Go before us, Great Shepherd, with thy rod and staff!

PSALM 109:1-16

The Persecutor of the Needy. This psalm is like a patch of the Sahara amid a smiling Eden. But terrible as the words are, remember that they were written by the man who on two occasions spared the life of his persecutor and who, when the field of Gilboa was wet with Saul's lifeblood, sang the loveliest of elegies to his memory. These maledictions do not express personal vindictiveness. Probably they should be read as depicting the doom of the wrongdoer. The Apostle Peter, quoting this psalm, expressly says that the Spirit of Inspiration spoke before by the mouth of David, Acts 1:16. The imperative "let" might better be translated by the future "shall." This would be in perfect conformity with Hebrew usage.

Notice in v. 4 that by omitting the three words in italics, a beautiful suggestion is made of the life of prayer: "But I—prayer." The only response of the psalmist to the hatred of his enemies was to give himself more absolutely to prayer. His whole being was consumed in the one intense appeal to God. Such times come to us all. Such prayers always end in praise and thanksgiving, v. 30. Happy are we who also can count on the Advocate with the Father, v. 31. Jesus prays our prayers with us.

PSALM 109:17-31

The Deliverer of the Needy. This psalm emphasizes the difference, indicated by our Lord, between his teaching and that addressed to "them of old time," especially on the point of forgiveness. It is in such teaching as this that the psalmist's mood is distinctly inferior to that which has now become the law for devout men. This at least may be said, that these ancient saints did not desire vengeance for private injuries, but that God's name and character might be vindicated. Devout men could not but long for the triumph of good and the defeat and destruction of its opposite.

The closing paragraph voices some of those lowly, sad petitions for help which occur in so many of the Psalms. This combination of devout meekness and trust with the fiery imprecations or predictions at the core of this psalm substantiates what has been said above as to the spirit in which the psalm was conceived. It is not personal, but the voice of the Church asking God to make known the righteousness of his government. The psalm begins and ends with praise. It starts by picturing an adversary at the right hand of the wicked, v. 6, and closes with assurance that Jehovah stands at the right hand of his afflicted servant to deliver him. "I have set the Lord always before me: because he is at my right hand, I shall not be moved," Ps. 16:8.

PSALM 110

Our Priest-King at God's Right Hand. Luther describes this psalm as "the true, high, main psalm of our beloved Lord Jesus Christ." Our Lord attributed it to David, in the power of the Holy Spirit; and there is no portion of the Old Testament more frequently quoted in the New. See Matt. 22:44; 1 Cor. 15:25; Heb. 1:3, 13; 5:6, 10; 7:17, 21. David speaks of the Messiah as "my Lord." The inference as to the deity of our Lord is incontestable. His mighty scepter, the symbol of his rule, reaches from Zion to the utmost limits of space and time. He waits till all his enemies are his footstool. Their character is evident in their attire—"the beauties of holiness." They are as numerous and refreshing as dewdrops on parched meadows. There is an infinite attractiveness between our Savior and young life—"thy youth."

The offices of priest and king were jealously kept apart in the old Hebrew monarchy; so the psalmist has to travel into the childhood of the world to find the type of a priest-king. Jesus is King and Priest after a more ancient and abiding order, which, it is testified, is based on a timeless life. Our Lord shall come to the throne from the battlefield. He shall bruise the serpent's head, but he needs the refreshment of our love and faith. That is the wayside brook.

PSALM 111

The Works of the Lord. A fresh series of psalms begins here, of which the dominant note is "Hallelujah" ("Praise the Lord"). This and the next are similar in construction, each being alphabetical; that is, the verses begin with the letters of the Hebrew alphabet. The first is a hymn of praise and thanksgiving at the contemplation of Jehovah's works; and the second describes the righteousness which his chosen derive from him. They are the work of an unknown minstrel, but anonymity is characteristic of the highest work. When a man has achieved a really noble and beautiful work, he is indifferent to the judgment and praise of his fellows.

Let us, as the 2nd verse suggests, take pleasure in God's works and seek them out. It is well to acquaint ourselves with some branch of natural study for this purpose. But the wealth of truth hidden in the precepts of the Word of God, v. 7, will still better repay us. God's works in Nature, providence, and grace will be our theme and joy for eternal ages. A veil, however, is now on our eyes and a lethargy on our tongues. What precious phrases are scattered through this psalm! "Full of compassion; meat unto them that fear him; ever mindful of his covenant; sent redemption to his people; commanded his covenant for ever." What strong consolation for those who have fled for refuge! In the closing verses wisdom is used, as in Solomon's time, of the intuitions of the pure heart.

PSALM 112

Prosperity in Serving the Lord. Here are the two conditions of the blessed life: first, to fear the Lord; second, to delight greatly in his commandments. And then the blessed results: a mighty seed; a blessed generation; wealth and riches; enduring influence; light amid darkness; and many suchlike things. The psalm is replete with the beatitudes that alight on the heart of the man who lives for God alone.

Around us may be the encircling gloom, in which evil men and tidings lurk as savages in the shadow of the forest, but within there is the blessed sense of the presence of God, like the circle of fire within which the traveler is secure. The voice of God assures him that he shall never be moved, and the heart is so established that it cannot yield to fear. It is good to have that quiet, unperturbed confidence in God. Moses had it at the Red Sea, Exod. 14:13; Asa, before the overwhelming hosts that threatened to submerge his little army, 2 Chron. 14:9–12; Jehoshaphat, when confronted by the hordes of Ammon, 2 Chron. 20:12; and Hezekiah, when the Assyrian threatened to invade Judah, 2 Chron. 32:6–8. Such a life is full of the "Hallelujah Chorus," in accord with the opening note of the psalm.

PSALMS 113 & 114

The Mighty God Uplifteth the Lowly. We detect the song of Samuel's mother in the first of these psalms. She sang the Old Testament "Magnificat" and it was passed on to us by the psalmist here. Thus it passed into the psalter of the Church. Note the universality of this ascription of praise: for all time, v. 2; through all the earth, v. 3; and above all heavens, v. 4. What a wonderful God is ours! Heaven cannot contain him, but he lifts the poor and needy out of the dust. Largeness is not greatness, and the babe in the cot is more important than the palace.

In Psalm 114 Egypt represents the tyranny of sin; but we have been redeemed. Like Israel we have gone forth. We belong no more to the present world with its strange tongue. Ours is the language of Canaan, our home. This exodus of ours has made us the temple and sanctuary of God. If once the Church realized that she is God-possessed, she would become irresistible. Seas would divide, rivers would move back, mountains would cleave, and the hills would remove. "Impossible" would be blotted from our vocabulary. The power that made Sinai tremble gave earth water springs. When the soul finds its all in God, the world ceases to affright or attract it, and the rocks yield refreshing streams.

PSALM 115

Powerless Idols; Our Powerful God. Evidently this psalm was intended to be sung by various voices: vv. 1–8 by the whole congregation in unison, while the sacrifice was being offered; vv. 9–11, by a solo voice giving the first line of each couplet, the whole audience chanting the refrain; vv. 12–15, by the priest as a benediction; vv. 16–18, by the whole congregation, which now breaks into glad hallelujahs.

It was composed during the early days of the return from Babylon, when the small groups of settlers were surrounded by the jeers and scoffs of their enemies. This was their reply, as they brought out the scathing contrast between the idols of their neighbors and the majesty of Jehovah. We are reminded of Isaiah's description of an idol factory. The idols had outward semblance and *no* power. Jehovah had no outward semblance, but *all* power. Let us take to heart the threefold invitation to faith in vv. 9–11, and reckon on God as our help in the battle and our shield against our foes. The smallest may get his blessing as well as the greatest, v. 13. We can never impose a strain on the resources of God, however great our demands.

PSALM 116:1-11

He Delivered My Soul. Throughout this psalm we meet the pronoun in the first person. Only in two verses, 15 and 19, does it not so occur. There is no fear of egotism, however, when the heart of the singer overflows with divine love.

Verses 1-4: The psalmist here compares himself to some wild animal ensnared by the hunter and bound by the sharp cords which make free movement impossible. How many of God's saints have felt the deep incision of these cords! It has been with them as with Joseph when let down into the pit. But there is no pit so deep that a cry from it may not reach the heart of God.

Verses 5-11: When the quiet faith of answered prayer is ours, the fluttering soul seems to settle down to its nest in peace. The feet which were slipping now walk in the paths of life. Notice the prayer of v. 4 and the reply of v. 8. God does more than deliver; he wipes the tears from our faces and holds us as does a mother who places her hands under the armpits of her child, teaching it to walk. Paul quotes v. 10 in 2 Corinthians 4:13. How often must this psalm have been in his thought and on his lips! Do not speak hastily. An eminent religious leader said once, "I shall have good hopes of you when you can speak and move slowly."

PSALM 116:12—117

Praise Him for All His Benefits. The psalmist dwells joyfully on his enslavement to God, because in and through it he had found perfect liberty. "Thou hast loosed my bonds." They who become enslaved to Christ are set free from all other restraints. See John 8:31-36. Do not forget to "pay" your vows! In trouble we make promises, which when the trouble has passed we find convenient to forget. See Gen. 40:23.

Psalm 117 is the shortest chapter in the Bible and its center; but small as it is, it breathes a worldwide spirit and reaches out to all nations. "It is a dewdrop reflecting the universe." The apostle quotes it in Romans 15:11 as foretelling the call of the Gentiles. Here, as in Isaiah 11:10 and elsewhere, the spirit of the singer overleaps all national exclusiveness and comprehends *all* people and *all* time.

Let us learn to exercise the spirit of praise in our daily sphere. Surely we also can say that God's loving-kindness has been, and is, "great toward us." "Where sin abounded, grace did much more abound." The permanence of this love is guaranteed by God's faithfulness; for his truth is his troth. The shortest prayer of praise should find room for Hallelujah! See Rev. 19:4.

PSALM 118:1-14

Trust in God Brings Strength. It is generally agreed that this psalm dates back to the restoration from Babylon. It was probably used as a processional hymn for the first time at the great Feast of Tabernacles mentioned in Nehemiah 8:13-18. The structure of the psalm is as follows: vv. 1-4, the summons of the full choir to the constituent parts of the procession; vv. 5-14, the song of the soloist; vv. 15, 16, the answer of the choir; vv. 17-19, the soloist. At this point the procession reaches the Temple gates. Verse 20 is the response of priests and Levites, the custodians of the sacred edifice, who lay stress on the character of those who tread its courts. Verse 21, the soloist; vv. 22-27, the full chorus; v. 28, the soloist; v. 29, the concluding doxology.

Luther says of this psalm, "This is mine, the one which I love." As it was included in the great Hallel we infer that our Lord sang it before he went forth to die, Matt. 26:30. It will be sung once more on that coming day for which we wait. See Isa. 25:9; Matt. 23:39. When we identify ourselves with God's great cause, we may absolutely count on God as our strength in the conflict, and our song in assured victory.

PSALM 118:15-29

A New Way in a New Day. As we draw near the mellowing light of the sanctuary, we see more deeply into the divine meaning of our experiences. In v. 13, "Thou [the enemy] hast thrust sore at me," but in v. 18, "The Lord hath chastened me sore." Our Lord and his apostles made much use of v. 22. See Matt. 21:42; Acts 4:11; Eph. 2:20; 1 Pet. 2:4-7. It probably refers to an incident in the building of the Temple, when a rejected stone was sought to complete the structure. Its rejection and recovery were "the Lord's doing," as a parable of other and more momentous events.

Verse 27 is peculiarly beautiful. As soon as God gives you light, make use of it for a fuller consecration and the renewal of sacrifice. New light means the discovery of fresh opportunities for divine service. Let light and life keep step! Pass from the altar to the cross, at which Jesus stands to welcome and endorse your new act of surrender. Behold there the golden cord of love, the silver cord of hope, and the crimson cord of his redeeming sacrifice for you. The confession of such a life will be that God is good, that his service is bliss, and that his mercy never fails.

PSALM 119:1–16

God's Word an Inner Power. This long and noble psalm is devoted to the praise of God's Word, which is mentioned in every verse but vv. 121, 122. Probably if we were to substitute "will" for "Word" (or its equivalent), we should not be far wrong. The earnest desire of the writer was that his will should be brought into blessed and unbroken union with the divine purpose in his life.

In its structure the psalm is an elaborate acrostic. In the original, each verse in a given section begins with the same letter, so that the twenty-two sections present the complete Hebrew alphabet.

It needs to be often used to be understood and valued. Chrysostom, Ambrose, Augustine, and Luther have left on record high tributes to its worth. There are several key expressions, which recur again and again, such as "quicken" and "teach me thy statutes." It is interesting, also, to construct the psalmist's biography from his confessions. He had gone astray like a lost sheep, was small and despised, had many adversaries, was like a bottle in the smoke; but he accounted God's will and service more than food or gold, and his one desire was to be taught to do that will.

PSALM 119:17–32

A Prayer for Understanding. These verses are full of yearning and unsatisfied desire. The soul "breaks for longing," "cleaves to the dust," "melts for heaviness." We are reminded of the complaint of a godly man, uttered two centuries and a half ago: "If God had not said, 'Blessed are those that hunger,' I know not what could keep weak Christians from sinking into despair. Many times all I can do is to complain that I want him and wish to recover him."

We learn from this psalm to pour out before God such desires. If we can do nothing else, we can complain that we are lacking in delight, in the sense of his nearness, and in the comfort of holy prayer. The expression of desire for God is prayer, which he accepts and will answer. "He will fulfil the desire of them that fear him; he also will hear their cry, and will save them," 145:19. When the father of the prodigal first saw him, he was a long way off, but love could not wait till the son had traversed that intervening distance. He ran to meet him, and kissed him while the words of confession were trembling on his lips. So God will draw near to quicken, strengthen, teach, and cause us to understand. Then we shall run where now we limp.

PSALM 119:33–48

Love for God's Commands. Twice over the psalmist says, "thy commandments, which I have loved," and then proceeds to give the key to perfect love of them in the words, "I will meditate in thy statutes." Fugitive moments spent over God's Word will never lead to a deep and fervent affection for it. If you look cursorily at a great painting, you will fail to become enthralled with it. In the Dresden gallery connoisseurs will spend hours before a single painting by Raphael. They go away and return the next day. They make the painting their own by prolonged communion with its matchless forms. One of them said: "I could spend an hour every day, for years, upon that assemblage of human, angelic, and divine ideals, and on the last day of the last year discover some new beauty and a new joy." But what thoughts, what ideals can genius express in a painting which can be compared with those great thoughts of God, of Heaven, and of eternity which are given on the page of Scripture! Surely we cannot hope to spring into possession of such thoughts in less time than lovers of art spend on a masterpiece! We must meditate!

PSALM 119:49–64

Comforted by God's Judgments. Rays of comfort begin to steal into the psalmist's heart. "Thou hast caused me to hope; this is my comfort in my affliction; thy statutes have been my songs; at midnight I will rise to give thanks." Often prayer clears itself as it proceeds. It is the repeated testimony of all who have become proficient in the art of prayer that the seasons which begin with a struggle against depression, gloom, and the sense of absence end in triumphant joy. Jeremy Taylor puts it thus: "So have I seen a lark rising from his bed of grass and soaring upward, singing as he rises, and hoping to get to Heaven and climb above the clouds; but the poor bird was beaten back by the loud sighings of an eastern wind. His motion became inconstant and irregular, till the little creature was forced to sit down and pant, and stay till the storm was over; and then it made a prosperous flight, and did rise and sing, as if it had learned music and motion from an angel, as he was passing through the air about his ministries of mercy."

PSALM 119:65-80

Profiting from Affliction. "Before I was afflicted I went astray; it is good for me that I have been afflicted; thou in faithfulness hast afflicted me." Here is the far-off interest of our tears. God measures out our sorrows and the trials which cause them. But our condition requires a stern and bitter regimen. The stone must be cut by the lapidary. The heavy clouds, with their drenching showers, must hang over the landscape. The fire must cleanse the metal. If need be, ye suffer heaviness through many temptations. Yes, there is a need-be, and only if need be, for he doth not afflict willingly nor grieve the children of men. It is "his strange work," Isa. 28:21. The very least and the very greatest sorrows that befall us are provided, or permitted, by his unspeakable love. If we be without chastisement, whereof all children are partakers, then are we bastards and not sons, Heb. 12:8. But amid the affliction, his loving-kindness always waits upon our comfort, v. 76. "God, that comforteth those that are cast down," says the apostle, "comforted us by the coming of Titus," 2 Cor. 7:6.

PSALM 119:81-96

The Word That Stands Fast. They persecute wrongfully; they dig pits; they have almost consumed; they have waited to destroy; but thy Word abides steadfast. The driven soul flees to the cleft of the Rock and hides there.

At the beginning of our religious life, we rest on the assurances of others. Our parents, teachers, ministers—all insist on the truth of Scripture and the certainty of the facts which it reveals; but as life goes on we change our foundations and advance to the personal and experimental conviction which has been wrought in us by years of testing the Word of God for ourselves.

The famous Scotch clergyman, Thomas Erskine, said that no demolition of outward authority, even if such demolition were possible, could deprive him of the conviction of the divine origin and authority of the Bible, because it so exactly coincided with the experiences of his life and had been verified in so many remarkable instances. We have experienced God's faithfulness to his promises too often to be afraid of any attack upon the truth of Scripture. It is settled in Heaven, v. 89.

PSALM 119:97-112

"Thy Word Is a Lamp unto My Feet." The psalmist cries, "O how love I thy law!" He then proceeds to say that he has become wiser than his enemies and has more understanding than all his teachers. But this is not to be wondered at, because love is so quick and unerring in its intuitions. They who love, know. We have two organs of knowledge, the head and the heart. The latter is the swifter and truer of the two; and it lies open to love, human and divine, as the lyre to the musician's hand. The study of God's Word by a loving heart gives, to simple and unlearned people, an understanding which no college learning can impart. They have a lamp that lights them unerringly on the devious tracks of this mortal life.

There is also this advantage: the soul which is deeply instructed in God's Word hates every false way. It is not simply warned against taking it; it does not want to take it. A distaste for sin is the result of Bible love and Bible study. We may not retain all that we read, but the water that percolates through a sieve cleanses it.

PSALM 119:113-128

"Time for the Lord to Work." There is an unmistakable difference between the child of God and evildoers, and the believer does not want to be involved in their fate. Therefore he bids them depart from him. But though we know that in the end the wicked shall be put away as the dross, there seem to be long periods of divine inaction. Sin grows and flourishes like the green bay tree, 37:35. Wicked men are prosperous and at ease. The divine procedure of judgment seems to be arrested; and we set ourselves to awaken it with the reminding suggestion that it is time for God to work, because men are making void his law, v. 126. Our eyes fail with long watching for his salvation and the award of righteousness, v. 123.

In the meantime let us not lose heart. Let us continue to keep the commandments of God. Let us prize the precepts and promises of God above fine gold; and let us dare to regard all his precepts as right. Thus shall we nurse our souls in patience and faith, Luke 21:19, conscious that though we cannot be God's timekeepers, yet the Judge will come and will not tarry, Heb. 10:37.

PSALM 119:129-144

Why Love God's Word? What a beautiful soul this is that utters itself in these stanzas! The psalmist acknowledges his simplicity; is quite content to be among the unknown and despised of men. He is very anxious to be free from iniquity and transgression. He sheds bitter tears as he beholds the sin around him. He humbly asks only to be remembered, taught, and cared for. Nothing is left to him but what is God's or of God. God is his own desire, God's Word his stay and comfort, God's love his solace. God is the one goal and purpose of his search.

And his whole nature glows with love. He opens his mouth and pants with pure desire for God. He wants only that face to shine which fills Heaven with brightness. The very purity of the Word only stirs again the embers of his true affection. He is one, therefore, with all the saints of every age, for humble, meek, merciful, and loving souls are everywhere of one religion; and when death has taken off the mask, as William Penn put it, they will know one another, though the various garb they wear here make them strangers.

PSALM 119:145-160

The Joy of Communion with God. There is great eagerness in the psalmist's prayerfulness. He calls with his whole heart; he awakes before the dawn and continues long after the fall of night; he asks that his case may be considered, his cause pleaded, and his soul quickened. When we draw near to God in prayer, our prayers must not be vague or languid. Jeremy Taylor says: "Easiness of desire is a great enemy to the success of a good man's prayer. It must be an intent, zealous, busy, operative prayer. For consider what a huge indecency it is that a man should speak to God for a thing that he values not. Our prayers upbraid our spirits when we beg tamely for those things for which we ought to die." But when we pray after the manner of the psalmist, we become aware that God is near. "Thou art near, O Jehovah," v. 151. This is the crowning moment in prayer, when we cease speaking and almost hold our breath because we are suddenly aware of a presence, the dear and awful presence of our Lord.

PSALM 119:161-176

Jehovah Inspires Continual Praise. What a noble conclusion we reach in these closing stanzas! "I rejoice at thy word; thy law do I love; seven times a day do I praise thee; my lips shall utter praise; my tongue shall speak; let my soul live, and it shall praise thee." There are many beautiful things in the world around us. We eat and drink and sleep; we read and meditate; we walk in the pleasant fields of Nature. We have our homes, our loved ones, the respect and goodwill of many. But, above all, we have God and his Word, our eternal hope, and blessed foretastes of the Heaven that is to be. Surely we should be less peevish and morose! We should rejoice in every good thing that the Lord our God gives us. We should take the cup brimming with salvation and praise his holy name. "He that hath so many causes of joy must be very much in love with sorrow who chooses to turn aside and sit upon his little handful of thorns." And is not this the most wonderful of all, that though we were going astray like lost sheep, the Great Shepherd himself came to seek and to save? *Te Deum laudamus!*

PSALM 120

Where to Find Help. This is the first of the "Songs of Degrees." It has been suggested that they were pilgrim songs for the journeys from all parts of the country to the great annual feasts. They have been associated with the reign of the good Hezekiah. "Mesech" and "Kedar" are typical enemies, who forced their way into the kingdom of Judah and vexed the people of God. They are compared to sharp swords and arrows in Psalm 57:4 and 64:3, but now in turn they shall be pierced and scorched. How many who start on a pilgrimage to the Celestial City must run a similar gauntlet! Their enemies arise from their own household. In such distress of soul, prayer is our only hope, v. 1.

PSALM 121

The keynote of this psalm is the word "keep," which occurs in one form or another six times. In vv. 1 and 2 the soloist suggests that in hours of trial we should look beyond mountains and hills to the Lord who made them all. In vv. 3-8 the chorus endorses and commends the choice. All the saints of every dispensation add their cumulative testimony to the wisdom of entrusting the keeping of soul and body to our faithful Creator. Notice the exquisite sequence of phrases: "neither slumber nor sleep; by day, by night; thee . . . thy soul; thy going out and thy coming in; this time forth and for evermore." The meshes are woven very closely.

PSALM 122

Joy in God's House. As in the other psalms of the series, there is here alternation between soloist and choir. In v. 1 the soloist rejoices in the proposal made to go on a pilgrimage. The chorus announces that the journey is already accomplished, vv. 2-5. The Church of Christ is compacted, built together, by his tears and blood and risen power. In v. 6, margin, the soloist bids the company salute Jerusalem, and the chorus replies. In vv. 7-9 the soloist announces three reasons why they should pray for Jerusalem's peace: They who love her prosper; those who reside within her precincts are our brethren and companions; hers is the house of God built for his habitation.

PSALM 123

The life of the pilgrim is full of sharp contrasts. Yesterday he was rejoicing in Jerusalem and sharing her peace. Today he is grieved with the contempt of her foes. Hence this tiny psalm, which has been compared to "a sigh, an upward look, a sigh." The oriental servant is adept at reading the meaning of his master's slightest gesture, v. 2. Let us live, as our Savior did, with our eye fixed on the least indication of God's will. See Acts 16:1-10.

PSALM 124

The Christian's Fortress. Here are three instances of escaped peril. In v. 3 is an allusion to Korah and his company; see Num. 16:32, 33. Why are *we* spared when others have been overwhelmed by swift disasters? In vv. 4 and 5, as the morning breaks we see the proud waters that have burst their banks and are inundating the low-lying lands. Why did *our* house escape? In vv. 6 and 7 we have the metaphor of the ensnared bird; and as the fluttering fledgling, when freed, leaps into the sunny air, so do we rejoice when God frees us. But why should *we* escape when so many never break loose?

PSALM 125

Jerusalem lies on a broad and high mountain range, shut in by two deep valleys. But the surrounding hills are higher, and made her almost impregnable to the methods of ancient warfare. They who trust in God live within ramparts of his loving care forevermore. The scepter of evil may sometimes cast its gaunt shadow over their lives, but it is always arrested in time. "Crooked ways" are bypaths. The commandments of God are a public thoroughfare. Keep on the highway and no hurt shall assail you.

PSALM 126

"The Lord Hath Done Great Things for Us." The circumstances under which this psalm was written are evident upon its face. The exiles, lately back from Babylon, are rejoicing in the gladness of their return. But their joy was not complete so long as the larger portion of their nation was still in bondage. The metaphor of "streams in the south" is derived from the rapidity with which dry water-courses become flushed with torrent streams. The returned exiles longed to see the vacant solitudes of their land suddenly filled with returning crowds. They asked that their tears might be the seeds of mighty harvests. Let not the Christian worker count as lost the seeds he sows or the tears in which he steeps them. That "doubtless" is God's guarantee.

PSALM 127

This psalm was probably suggested by Ezra's efforts to rebuild the Temple. We cannot succeed apart from God, but must be his fellow-workers. See Prov. 10:22. The "bread of sorrows" is that which is obtained with great difficulty, when labor is severe and the results slow. Beware of needless anxiety. As builders, v. 1, look to God for plan, materials, and cooperation. As watchers, v. 1, commit all keeping to God's watch and ward. As toilers, v. 2, have a little more quiet rest and ease of mind. As parents, vv. 3-5, do not shrink from parental responsibilities; when you are old, your children will answer for you.

PSALM 128

"It Shall Be Well with Thee." This psalm is the portrait of a godly man and his home in the best days of the Hebrew commonwealth. *The husband and father,* vv. 1, 2. He is reverent and devout. Peace is on his face; he is happy in himself and in his home, respected among his fellows, and collects at the end the results of his work. *The wife and mother,* v. 3. She is like the vine surrounding the inner court of an oriental house, yielding shade and refreshment. *The children,* v. 3. The olive is the symbol of enduring prosperity and joy. The young plants will presently be bedded out to become trees of mature growth.

PSALM 129

Past deliverances, vv. 1-4. Israel's youth was spent in Egypt. See Hos. 2:15; 11:1; Jer. 2:6. As the plow tears up the soil, so the lash cuts their quivering flesh. But in such furrows God sows the seed of later blessing. When our case is desperate, God cuts the oxen's binding cords, the plow stands still, and the bitter pain ceases. *Forebodings and predictions,* vv. 5-8. Withered grass, unmourned, fit only for fuel. Such is the fate of those who oppress God's people. The reference is to the scant blades which grow on the flat roof of an Eastern house. The usual benediction on the reaper's toil will never extend to those withered blades.

PSALM 130

"Out of the Depths." The cry, vv. 1, 2. The word "Lord" occurs as often as there are verses. The soul in trouble repeats again and again that precious Name, in which comfort and help are summed up. *The chief cause of anguish,* vv. 3, 4, is the memory of our sins. But our iniquities are not "marked" save by the jewels of forgiveness, like the pearls of an oyster that are set in the place where it was wounded. *The soul's attitude,* vv. 5, 6. It waits! He will surely come, though he seems to tarry. *"Plenteous redemption,"* v. 7, 8. It is not enough for God to forgive. He will abundantly pardon.

PSALM 131

This is the cry of the child-heart. The psalmist said this in all simplicity. He did not "exercise" himself (literally "walk to and fro") in things beyond his powers, but left God to reveal them to him, as he was able to receive them. We are reminded of Matthew 11:25. Clearly he had not reached this position without effort. He had found it necessary to still and quiet himself, as a nurse quiets a fretful babe. There had been a time when he was fed at the breast of the world's consolations. The weaning had been hard, but he had learned to get all from God and to draw on his sustaining grace.

PSALM 132

The Lord's Blessing upon Zion. This psalm evidently dates from the dedication of Solomon's Temple. In the glory of completion God never forgets the toils and anxieties of the builders. When the top stone flashes in the sunlight, the trench-diggers and foundation-makers come in for their deserved praise. The singer recapitulates two memorable scenes in the history of the Ark. "Ephratah" is probably Shiloh, in the tribe of Ephraim, where the Tabernacle was situated in Eli's time. "The fields of the wood" is Kirjath-jearim, whence David brought the sacred emblem to Jerusalem, 1 Chron. 13:5.

The prayer of vv. 8–10 is similar to that of Solomon, 2 Chron. 6:41. For us the ark of God's strength is our Lord's nature, in which God and man meet. We are called to be priests, to lift our hands in intercession, and to fill the earth with praise. Then in vv. 11–18 God seems to take the clauses of that prayer, one by one, and to answer them. His resting-place is in his people. The staves were drawn out from the Ark when it was deposited in the Temple. In Christ there is finality; he is Omega, "the Last."

PSALM 133

Unity Is of God. The word "Behold" suggests that some special manifestation of unity was taking place under the psalmist's eyes, perhaps in connection with some great religious festival; or David may have composed it to celebrate the healing of the breach after the death of Ish-bosheth. We must not only be one in God's purpose, but must be willing to "dwell together," that is, to manifest our unity in outward action. For the "precious ointment," see Exodus 30:20–38 and 1 John 2:27. Our Lord was anointed with the Holy Spirit, and we may share in his Pentecost, Luke 3:21, 22; Acts 2:33.

PSALM 134

This is the last of the "Songs of Degrees." It may have been addressed to the priests who came on duty after the offering of the evening sacrifice. There was evidently a band of choristers and others who were on duty while Jerusalem slept. The psalm ends with the reciprocal blessing of the watchers on the retreating crowds, commending them, during the hours of darkness, to the care of the Lord of Heaven and earth.

PSALM 135:1–12

God's Wonderful Power. This psalm begins and ends with "Hallelujah." It contains choice extracts from various psalms, which have been culled as the flowers of a garden are gathered for one bouquet. The arguments for praise are threefold: God's glory in nature, vv. 5–7; his dealings with Israel, vv. 8–14; the contrast of his glorious nature with idols, vv. 15–21.

Notice the arguments adduced to stimulate our praise: that God is good; that praise-giving is pleasant; that he has chosen his people to be his peculiar treasure; that he is as great as he is good; that he will take our part against our foes, etc. The moral of it all is that if we would praise God aright and with zest, we must carefully gather our materials and meditate on all his dealings with us. These are fuel for the flame. But how many more reasons than the psalmist had are there for us to praise him who have been adopted into his family and made joint-heirs with Christ!

PSALM 135:13-21

Men Become Like the Gods They Serve. What a contrast between our God and idols! His mouth speaks words of grace; his eyes follow our every movement and watch our sleep; his ears are open to the faintest call. Let us who love and adore him resemble him, as the idolater resembles his stony idol.

The fourfold division of the chosen race deserves our thought, vv. 19-21. Some belonged to the great commonwealth of Israel, some to the priestly family of Aaron, some to the humbler ranks of Levi, and some were proselytes who just feared the Lord; but none could be excused from the offering of praise. Whoever and whatever we may be, let us never fail to add our quota of adoration to that song which John tells us he heard arising from all in Heaven, and on earth, and under the earth, and on the sea, Rev. 5:13.

PSALM 136:1-12

A Review of God's Mercies. This is an antiphonal psalm, intended to be sung by two choirs, or by a soloist and the Temple choir. This avowal of the eternity of God's mercy, amid all the fluctuation and change of human affairs, is very striking. When we can look out on the history of our world from God's standpoint, we discover that the black-edged pages have been interleaved with golden pages of mercy. When we review our own lives from the vantage ground of Heaven, we shall see that the mercy of God was the blue sky of background across which the dark clouds floated for but a limited space.

The divisions are as follows: *Creation,* vv. 1-9; *Redemption,* vv. 10-22; *Providence,* vv. 23-26. In the first division the psalmist views the framework of the world and the redemption of Israel from Egypt as equal monuments of divine loving-kindness. It was love that made the theater on which the great revelation of redemption was manifested. The crimson lips of a tulip's petals are his work as well as the crimson blood that flowed at Calvary.

PSALM 136:13-26

Deliverance from Enemies. This psalm is no mere running commentary on the ways of God. It is a song of redemption. Pharaoh, Sihon, Og opposed God's redeeming purpose, though there were abundant evidences throughout the Exodus that it was of supernatural origin, and they came under the divine judgment. It was a mercy for all later ages that their ideals did not prevail. Was there not ineffable wisdom and benevolence in the substitution of monotheism and the honor of womanhood and the assertion of individual rights for the degradation of their type of civilization? We must take large views of God's dealings in Providence and history.

Men are apt to forget us when we are in low estate, but that is the time when God seems more thoughtful, v. 23. He has delivered, does deliver, and will deliver, v. 24. Will God make provision for all living creatures and neglect his children, v. 25? Let us trust in the love of God, which remains constant amid our fluctuations and unaffected by our failures and sins, so long as we return from our backslidings with repentance on our lips. It is very comforting to realize that the essence of this psalm will be sung on the other side. See Rev. 15:3.

PSALM 137

Loyalty in Adversity. It seems as if the exiles had withdrawn from the city, with its distractions, to some natural retreat beside the Euphrates. They had brought their harps with them, but had not the heart to touch their chords. Songs were choked by sobs. Suddenly a band of insolent revelers broke in on the scene, demanding one of those Temple songs for which Hebrew minstrelsy was famed.

But the Lord's song was possible only in the Lord's house. To be separated from the Temple seemed to the Jews like separation from God. When we have been led captive by our sins and have lost the sense of God's presence, we, too, lose the spring of holy joy. Let us make not Jerusalem, but the glory and interests of Christ's kingdom our chief joy. The closing imprecation on Edom reminds one of Jer. 49:7-22; Lam. 4:22; Ezek. 25:12-14. We can understand it, but we must remember that we belong to another covenant. See Luke 9:54-56; Rom. 12:20.

PSALM 138

The Most High Regards the Lowly. This is the first of a cycle of Davidic psalms, based on 2 Samuel 7. God's promised favors are the theme of devout thanksgiving. No idols could have achieved such generous and great results. Even God had outdone himself by magnifying his word above his name. Prayer had played its part, for in the day that it was offered it had been answered. Even kings in their various spheres would add their praises, v. 4. Yet this would be only the beginning of wonders. God can never rest with an incomplete or an unfinished work. When he puts his hand to the salvation of a soul, he pledges himself to perfect the good work until the day of Jesus Christ, Phil. 1:6. Trust God, amid all disappointment and heartache. He will wipe away all tears, explain all mysteries, and place a pinnacle of glory on the structure of your life.

PSALM 139:1-13

The All-seeing God. The psalmist speaks as if there were only two beings in the universe—God and himself. In all literature there is no nobler conception of the divine attributes.

God's omniscience, vv. 1-6. The "downsittings" of life are times of weariness, depression, failure, shortcoming, and inconsistency, when we are far short of our best. Our "uprisings" are our strongest, happiest, holiest moments, when we are at our best. God knows all. He cannot be surprised. He besets us "before"—the future is full of him—and "behind," as the wave follows closely in the wake of the swimmer or the rearguard the march. His hand is laid upon us, shielding and protecting. His winnowing-fan is ever detecting every grain of wheat and extracting it from the chaff.

God's omnipresence, vv. 7-12. It is impossible to flee from God. However thick the foliage, it cannot separate the sinner from those eyes of love and fire. This thought is terrible to those who are not at peace with him, but delightful to those who love. Be of good cheer, lonely one; thy night of sorrow is as the day—full of him.

PSALM 139:14-24

God's Thoughts and Ours. God's creative power, vv. 14-18. The psalmist goes back to the beginning of life and describes the weaving of our physical nature. Here we may discover a suggestive analogy; for the Church, which is the Body of Christ, has been wrought in secret from its earliest beginnings, and its development continues preparatory to the manifestation in complete beauty and glory at the Lord's coming. "When Christ ... shall appear, then shall ye also appear with him in glory" Col. 3:4. Remember, also, that the Christ-life in our hearts is subject to the same secret processes.

The psalm closes with *the saints' antagonism to evil,* vv. 19-24. The more they meditate on the precious thoughts of God, the more they desire to be freed from the tyranny of evil, whether it shows itself in the ways of evil men or in the inward evil of the heart. Our one cry should be that God would lead us in "the way," which is based on eternal principles and which winds ever upward from the lowland valleys, where we have dwelt too long, to those glorious uplands where God himself is Sun.

PSALM 140

Confidence in God's Protection. Here is a picture of a man who is beset by foes. Around are slander and hatred, at his feet stratagems and snares. There is no help save in him who alone can cover the head in the day of battle. Similar experiences befall God's people still. Some are hunted by earthly enemies; others are stung by the fiery darts of the wicked. In vv. 1-5 life is like a path through a forest, where adders hide and where traps are laid. At any moment the foe may break from his ambush. In vv. 6 and 7 faith discovers God, at such a time, as strength, salvation, and protection.

There follows, in vv. 8-12, a terrible outburst. Instead of the "let" of the imperative, many read the "shall" of prediction. We belong to the kingdom of Christ, the teachings of which are given in Matthew 5. The only coals of fire that we can deal with are those of love and mercy, which we heap on the heads of our enemies. The least in the kingdom of love stands on a higher plane than the greatest in the kingdom of law. But let the wicked remember Romans 2:5. The psalm ends in a gladder strain, v. 13. There is an inner sanctuary where we shall be safe!

PSALM 141

Humility. This is an evening psalm. Acceptable prayer is as the smoke of incense rising in the still air, Rev. 5:8; 8:3, 4. Each day we should ask to be delivered from lip sins, life sins, and like sins—especially the last, the dainties of appetite and desire, v. 4.

We owe a great deal to the care of fellow-believers. It may take more love to smite than to soothe. The breaking of the box of precious ointment over our heads may cause a momentary shock; but we must not refuse it, since the contents are so salutary. We can return their well-meant kindness by praying for the righteous when their calamities are multiplied, v. 5. It was a rough time for David, but he kept looking up and committing his soul to God's faithful care. Under similar circumstances Paul struck an even higher note, Rom. 8:36, 37. Go on patiently living up to your ideal. God will surely vindicate you!

PSALM 142

"No Man Cared for My Soul." The cave was dark and shared by rough and lawless men with whom David had little sympathy. His gentle and devout spirit must often have craved for more congenial society. But he never ceased to

cry and make supplication whenever his spirit was overwhelmed. Are you in that plight? Be comforted by the reflection that God knows your path. It is the predestined way, Eph. 2:10. Before the heavens or earth were made, it was prepared. God foreknew all its perplexities and difficulties—how dark the shadows, how fearsome the black current—but he chose it as your best way home. Are all faces averted? Does no one seem to care? Is your soul in prison, and are your persecutors strong? Be of good cheer! Reinforcements of divine grace are on their way; the righteous shall crown themselves because of you; and you will say with your dying breath, "He has dealt bountifully with me."

PSALM 143

The Cry of the Thirsty Soul. This psalm falls into four stanzas of three verses each. *Complaint,* vv. 1-3. Though the enemy has resorted to unwarrantable violence, David realized that his past had been by no means immaculate. The holiest have least confidence in themselves, Job 9:3; Phil. 3:7. Bernard of Clairvaux said: "So far from being able to answer for my sins, I cannot answer even for my righteousness." There is no judgment or condemnation for those who are in Christ, because they were judged in him. Now God's justice is on our side, 1 John 1:9.

Depression, vv. 4-6. Those capable of the sunny heights are capable of the lowest depths. Memory, meditation, musing often lead to melancholy. But reach out after God. To thirst for him is to have him. To desire is to possess. *Entreaty,* vv. 7-9. "Hear me; cause me to hear; cause me to know; deliver me." *Docility,* vv. 10-12: We can trust ourselves absolutely to be led by God's Spirit, because he is good and he brings the soul out of trouble into the land of uprightness, Rom. 8:14.

PSALM 144

God's People Are Happy. This psalm savors of the rocky caverns from which David and his men emerged to fight. Each day the chieftain asked God to teach him to fight, and realized that all his need would be met. The names he gives to God indicate that "all-sided-ness" which becomes the complement of every conceivable necessity on our part.

What a striking conception is found in v. 4! Saul was but a "breath," margin. The persecuting bands were as the shadows that pass across the hills! From them all he appealed to God to bow the heavens and come, to touch the mountains, and to rescue him from the rising waters. And when the storm has passed he sings his new glad song, v. 9. Verses 12-15 were probably added at a later time, when David was established in his kingdom. They describe a summer afternoon of prosperity, when sons have grown from plants to trees, and daughters resemble the carved figures which support the beams of a palace. Now there is no breaking in of the foe, no need to go forth to fight, no outcry of oppression or want, but the peaceful sunset of a well-spent life.

PSALM 145:1-9

God's Unsearchable Greatness. This psalm is an acrostic, the verses beginning with the successive letters of the Hebrew alphabet. The couplet for the fourteenth letter, *Nun,* between vv. 13 and 14, has no place in the text. Some versions have supplied the omission as follows: "The Lord is faithful in all his words and holy in all his works." This is virtually a repetition of v. 17.

The word "all" is characteristic of this psalm, the *Te Deum* of the Hebrew Church. The Jews said that its threefold repetition was the best preparation for the praises of the world to come. Speaking of this psalm and those following, Dr. Gilfillan says: "They are the Beulah of the Book; the sun shineth night and day. Coming at the close of all the prayerful, penitential, and mournful psalms, they unconsciously typify the joy and rest of glory." The theme of the psalm is God. He is "great," v. 3; "gracious," v. 8; "good," v. 9; "upholdeth," v. 14; "is righteous," v. 17; "is nigh," v. 18; "preserveth," v. 20. And the main aspect of his handiwork is the creation and maintenance of a universe of happy beings who subsist on his bountiful care. "His tender mercies are over all his works."

PSALM 145:10-21

God's Bountiful Provision. There is more happiness in the world than we are disposed to think. God's works give praise to him. Take, for instance, the gladness of one summer day, when from the little green lizards upward there is a perfect murmur of enjoyment in the still heat. Shall we not trust God, to whom the care of all things is as easy as the opening of the hand is to us? See 104:28.

Verse 13 is graven in the keystone of a very old building in Damascus, once a Christian church but for many centuries a mosque. The words are still true and are nearer historical fulfillment today than ever. Verse 18, the Lord is always nigh, though we do not perceive or realize his presence, and it is good to affirm it as we pray. To utter these words often during one's daily life is to practice the presence of God, after the manner of the Christian mystics. But some cannot do as much; they can only "desire," v. 19. But he whose love notices the faintest yearning after himself will fulfill it. We shall praise God worthily when we see him as he is!

PSALM 146

"The Lord Loveth the Righteous." This and the four following psalms are the "Hallelujah Psalms." Each begins with that word. They were probably composed for use in the second Temple. In the Septuagint this psalm is ascribed to Zechariah and Haggai. The key to it is v. 5, which is the last of the twenty-six "Blesseds" in the Psalter. What can bring more blessedness into life than the recognition of Jehovah as "help" and "hope"?

Verses 6-10 emphasize the present tense in a way which reminds us of the words of our Lord: "My Father worketh hitherto." It is true that with the oppressed and the prisoners in iron circumstance, the blind and the boweddown, the stranger, the fatherless, and the widowed, the promises appear unfulfilled. This, however, is probably due not only to the failure of God's Church and of themselves to realize that the kingdom has been set up in the unseen sphere, but because we need to appropriate its deliverances by faith. They who receive abundance of grace and righteousness shall reign. But all God's promises, like the great promise of salvation, are contingent on the exercise of faith.

PSALM 147:1-11

Why We Praise the Lord. It has been supposed that this psalm was prepared for use when the new walls of the city were completed in the days of Nehemiah. It contains a further enumeration of God's present tenses. The psalmist never tires of celebrating the immediateness of God. He will not tolerate the intervention of second causes, which are the artifice of scientific explanation. Laws are, after all, only the convenient statement of the regularity of God's methods. The couplets of this psalm are amazingly suggestive. By contrast they complete each other. God builds up the great city of Jerusalem, but his heart goes out to the individual prodigal. He is equally at home in the hospital where broken hearts congregate and among the stars, which he names and counts as a shepherd his flock. He upholds the meek and overthrows the proud. Spring, with its clouds and rain and sprouting grass, is his work; but so also the wild life of the forest, with its beasts and birds. He has no such delight in athletic strength or speed as he has in the reverent worship of his people. There is a perfect balance and rhythm in God's nature.

PSALM 147:12-20

Peace and Prosperity. From v. 12 on there is a more personal address to Jerusalem and Zion. The "thee" and "thou" justify the application of the psalm to the spiritual condition of the Church and the individual. God's work in Nature illustrates his dealings with his children. Are we strengthened against temptation, as a city with bars and bolts, blessed with peace, and filled with the fine flour of gospel truth? It is because he hath so appointed it by his commandment and swiftly-running word. Is it winter, the air full of blinding snowflakes, frost everywhere, as if the frost-king had powdered the earth and bound the waters with his chain? Be of good cheer; God is in it all. Winter is needed to pulverize the soil; but as soon as it has done its necessary work, the warm breath of his manifested love will breathe over desolations, and all the frost and snow will hasten to be gone. Will God give so much thought to garnishing the home in which his children live and neglect *them?* Besides, he has shown us so many wonderful judgments and such discoveries of his character, that he is pledged to us. Hallelujah!

PSALM 148

Creation's Song of Praise. The *"Benedicite"* in the Book of Common Prayer is based on this psalm. The sacred minstrel is not content that he or his people should have a monopoly of praise. He calls to Nature, with her myriad voices, to take up the strain. It is interesting to turn these words from the imperative to the indicative mood, for already the heights and depths around us are vocal. The sun leads the chorus, and the moon plays upon her silver harp. The stars "quire to the young-eyed cherubim." The deeps praise for depths of love, the mountains for its height, the fruit trees for its sweetness, while the great forest monarchs, their branches swaying in the wind, clap their hands. Surely the children of God should awake from their lethargy! Can we be redeemed and dumb, saved and silent, delivered and made near, and no word of gratitude? Let us, as we read this psalm, remember also that there is a praise note for the fire of tribulation and the hail of abusive scorn. The saints have long ago praised God in the fires. The stormy wind of adversity, no less than the zephyrs of prosperity, fulfills his purpose and deserves our trust.

PSALM 149

The Praise Songs of God's People. Israel was formed into a nation and delivered from Babylon, that her singers should lead the praises of mankind and her teachers provide the metaphors and phrases for the world's religious nurture. "This people have I made for myself," said the Most High, "that they might show forth my praise." Is it not also our Christian duty to be joyful in our King? Our religious life has not enough ecstasy and gladness in it to attract the world, which is sad enough beneath its outward gaiety.

PSALM 150

Here is a worthy close to the Psalter. Ten times the summons to praise rings out, and ten is the number of perfection. Think of the tears and groans, the questionings and perplexities, the feeble faith and disappointed aspiration that have preceded! Now it all finishes thus! So life will finish! Our *Misereres* will be forgotten in the outbursting *Jubilates*. The first three books of the Psalter end with "Amen and Amen," the firm expression of faith, the fourth book with "Amen, Hallelujah," as though faith were beginning to be lost in glad realization. But here, at the end of all, there is one abounding and unhesitating Hallelujah!

THE BOOK OF PROVERBS

"THE WORDS OF THE WISE"

I. THE VOICE OF WISDOM *1:1—9:18.*
II. WISDOM AND FOLLY CONTRASTED *10:1—22:16.*
III. THE COUNSEL OF THE WISE *22:17—24:34.*
IV. SIMILES OF LIFE'S VARIED EXPERIENCES *25:1—29:27.*
V. SHORTER COLLECTIONS *30:1—31:31.*
    A. The words of Agur *30:1–33.*
    B. The words of King Lemuel *31:1–9.*
    C. The virtuous woman (acrostic poem) *31:10–31.*

INTRODUCTION

This book occupies an important place in what is called "Hebrew wisdom literature." Other examples are Job, Ecclesiastes, some of the Psalms, and such apocryphal books as the Wisdom of Solomon and Ecclesiasticus.

Certain sections are expressly attributed to Solomon, but elsewhere other sources are referred to. The title of the fourth section, "These also are proverbs of Solomon which the men of Hezekiah, king of Judah, copied out," is proof that the book did not receive its present form till the time of Hezekiah.

The book was written as a guide for the young. The experience of many generations is here presented to the youth who is approaching independence. The form of address throughout is that of a father speaking to his son.

The foundation principle is that the right life is not merely a moral life, but the life that is lived toward God. The supreme folly in life is to leave God out. Hence the book is not simply a collection of homey maxims, but a source of spiritual insight.

The virtues taught are those which make for individual and national strength—honesty, industry, purity, sobriety, moderation, faithfulness, diligence, prudence, impartiality, humility, contentment—and all are based upon the fear of the Lord.

The literary structure is comparatively loose. "We are not," says Bishop Hopkins, "generally to expect any connection of sentences in this book of Proverbs. Other parts of Scripture are like a rich mine, where the precious ore runs along in one continued vein; but this is like a heap of pearls, which, though they are unstrung, are not therefore the less excellent and valuable."

COMMENTARY

PROVERBS 1:1-19

"The Beginning of Knowledge." Notice the perfect balance of each clause, and the duplication of the one thought in the two clauses of each verse.

"Wisdom" as used in this book is more than intellectual learning or cleverness. It represents a moral quality, the result of a pure and a true life. We are conscious that many simpleminded people, who have little enough book-learning, are remarkable for sagacious advice, insight into character, the wise reading of events, an intuitive knowledge—all based on the fear of God. Certain it is that the young who ponder and practice these maxims can hardly fail to have a successful career.

PROVERBS 1:20-33

The Call of Wisdom. The word "Wisdom" and the description of her standing "at the head of the noisy streets"—see v. 21, margin—remind us of our Lord, who as the Word of God stood and cried, John 7:37. It is a remarkable picture of the world as it is today. The streets filled with traffickers, with the bawling of wares, with the crowds of idle sightseers, and amid it all the ringing appeal of Christ to the heart of man! But the scorners deride and mock, while fools hate the speaker and threaten his life. Yet there is no crowded thoroughfare in the world from which the Spirit of God is absent. See Matt. 22:1-10.

The two results that divide the hearers are set forth in words that are always receiving verification. The day of "calamity," when banks suspend payment and the boldest speculators lose heart, breaks suddenly on the worldling. He has no hiding place, no second line of defense, no spiritual treasure, and is like a drowning sailor in a tempestuous sea. But "Wisdom is justified of all her children," for they "dwell safely." See v. 33 and Luke 7:35.

PROVERBS 2

Wisdom Guards from Evil. Several words are reiterated in this chapter, which will unlock its treasures. "Understanding" is seen in vv. 2, 3, 9, 11. If wisdom is a moral quality, leading to intuitive knowledge, understanding may be taken to include something of a prophetic strain. Understanding gathers up and makes use of the results of observation and experience, whether of oneself or of others.

Notice also the word "walk," vv. 7, 13; "way," vv. 8, 12, 13, 15, 20; "paths," vv. 8, 13, 15, 18, 19, 20. See how eager the Divine Teacher is (1) to deliver the unwary from the way of the evil man, v. 12, and from the way of the evil woman, v. 16; and (2) to direct the feet of the young into the ways of the good and into the paths of the righteous, v. 20. The path of safety and permanence is that in which we are perpetually conscious of the presence of the Master, Christ. He is the unseen companion of the soul in its difficult and perilous pilgrimage; and we may, in that companionship, appropriate the "buckler" of v. 7, the preservation of v. 8, and the stability of v. 21.

PROVERBS 3:1-12

The Results of Trusting Jehovah. How replete with helpful instruction on the policy of life is this paragraph! The young of both sexes are invited to be merciful in their judgments or dealings, and faithful in the discharge of their responsibilities or duties. These are two prime qualifications for a right attitude toward God and man.

The *perplexed* are bidden to distrust their own understanding and to trust in God for guidance. If you do not see your way, wait till God reveals it. Notice the repeated word "all"—"all thine heart", "all thy ways." The businessman is urged to honor God, as Abraham did when returning laden with booty from his conflict with the freebooting kings, Gen. 14:23. The *suffering* are urged to look beyond their pain and sorrow to the hand that chastens, vv. 11 and 12. These precious words are endorsed by later Scriptures. See Heb. 12:5, 6 and Rev. 3:19. We can never forget the tender assurance of Job 5:18, 19. There is no chance in life; accept all as by God's appointment or permission.

PROVERBS 3:13-26

Wisdom's Ways of Pleasantness. Wisdom is susceptible of cultivation. It is a *mine* that needs to be worked with patient toil. Compare vv. 13 15 with Job 28:18. It is comparable to a *noble woman* who approaches us with full-handed beneficence, vv. 16, 17. It may be described as a *tree,* requiring tender care and bearing fruit for the patient cultivator, v. 18. And we may turn from our own little lives to see the mighty results of divine wisdom in Creation and Providence. We are made in the image of God, our minds are able to appreciate *his* mind, and we think over again, as Kepler said, the thoughts of God, vv. 19, 20.

Learn the security of the life which is built on the eternal principles of this book. It has no fear. Its repose is unbroken by alarm. It is at peace with itself, with man, and with God. This is not the result of our calculating prudence, but because we exercise ourselves to have consciences void of offense toward God and man, and because the God of patience, of hope, and of peace is with us. See Rom. 15:5, 13, 33.

PROVERBS 3:27—4:9

The Counsels of Experience. Here are many duties! *Be generous!* Of course we must discriminate— "to whom it is due"—and we must be prudent —"when it is in the power of thine hand," v. 27. Moreover, *be prompt,* v. 28. *Don't stir up strife or take a mean advantage,* vv. 29, 30. In the presence of the prosperity of the violent and evil man, *repress envy* and recall Ps. 37.

The word translated "secret" in v. 32 should be rendered "friendship." See Ps. 25:14. Remember that Jesus calls us into this sacred inner circle, John 15:15. *Count on God blessing your home life,* v. 33. *Be lowly and claim your great inheritance,* vv. 34, 35. See Matt. 5:3.

We are next admitted into an ancient Hebrew home, 4:1-9. We can hear the old patriarch advising his son, with deep and fond anxiety, that he should make the best of his life. What a difference would come over the land if fathers spoke more often like this! But to speak thus needs a background of noble living.

PROVERBS 4:10-27

Guideposts on the Way of Life. One or two sentences stand out in this section, demanding special attention. *"The path of the just is as the shining light,"* v. 18. We may compare this beautiful similitude with 2 Samuel 23:4. In the East, where the heavens are for the most part free of cloud, the steadily increasing light of any day to perfect noontide glory is the ordinary experience. Let us so live that the path of our life may become ever more radiant and beneficent in its heat and light.

"Keep thy heart with all diligence," v. 23 ("above all keeping," margin). The gates of the heart need careful scrutiny. When we are careless, thoughts creep in with malign intent. We should imitate the good Nehemiah, Neh. 13:19. Ask that pure and holy angels may stand sentry as at the gates of pearl, Rev. 21:12. If you *think* right, you will *live* right.

"Ponder the path of thy feet," v. 26. "Weigh carefully." Act in haste and repent at leisure! Ask God to keep you back from presumptuous sins; and bear in mind the wise exhortation of Ecclesiastes 5:2.

PROVERBS 5:1-14

Quicksands! Keep Off! It is a matter for great thankfulness that the Bible, which is God's Book rather than man's, deals so strongly and wisely with one great evil which has manifested itself in every age and in every state of society. It speaks boldly and plainly, and all who

PROVERBS

will meditate on its teaching with a prayerful heart will be saved from many a painful snare. If we fall, it will only be due to our having refused to heed the voice that speaks to us from paragraphs like these.

The one great caution that we must all observe is in the control of our thoughts. The soul must never lie open to the tide of suggestive thoughts that break along its beach. As of old the watchman kept the gate of the medieval city so soon as darkness fell, so must the purity of God keep watch and ward at eye-gate, ear-gate, and touch-gate, lest some emissary of evil gain entrance and betray the citadel. Let Christ be the custodian of thy soul, whether thou be man or woman, old or young, and let him impart to thee his own divine and human purity.

PROVERBS 6:1-19

Avoid Suretyship and Sloth. A young man, being entreated by his friend to go bond for him, consents in an easygoing way to become his surety. He promises to be responsible for the other's debt. From that moment he resembles a roe caught by a hunter or a bird snared by a fowler. If any shall have enmeshed himself in an obligation of this kind he is exhorted to spare no pains, to stand on no false pride, but to go with all urgency to the man for whom he has pledged his credit, and get released at all cost. If we can afford to be surety, we can afford to lend the money ourselves. If we cannot do the former, it is weak and foolish to do the latter.

The ants swarm in the woods and fields, and rebuke our laziness and thriftlessness. They work day and night, storing their galleries with food, building mounds which relative to the size of the builders are three or four times larger than the Pyramids. In sickness they nurse one another; in the winter they feed on their supplies. Learn from the ceaseless industry of Nature, and do something worthy before sundown!

PROVERBS 8:1-21

"Better Than Gold." This chapter contains a bewitching picture of Wisdom as a noble matron. Were it not for this feminine touch, we might suppose that the Preacher had become a Prophet and was discerning the qualities of Christ, who in his human life embodied the Divine Wisdom, as indeed he was the Eternal Word.

She stands in the open places; her ringing voice is heard down the streets, appealing to those who are entering the city gates or doors of the houses. There is no muttering or whispering; but the beauty of goodness illuminates all she says. She insists on her own value, as compared with the valuables that men prize. The central point in her promises is that she imparts those great moral qualities which imply the true leadership and right estimate of others. What a precious word is v. 17; but we can never forget that we love "because he first loved us." Oh, the mystery and wonder of it! And can that love ever fail us?

PROVERBS 8:22-36

Finding Wisdom, Finding Life. The world did not come into being by chance. It was created by an intelligent Creator. Nothing is arbitrary or by accident. Law is the expression of the perfect will of God. It is founded on the inherent necessity which is at the heart of all things; and it is according to unchanging law that all things subsist. Yet never forget that God is Redeemer as well as Creator, and reserves to himself the right of suffering because we break his laws, that he may step in to redeem those who are penitent and believing.

It would seem as if in Luke 7:35 our Lord appropriated these sublime words as applicable to himself. How glorious it is that he appropriates v. 31! He does not delight in us only after we are redeemed, but before; and it is on this that he bases his appeal: "Blessed are they that keep my ways," v. 32. Let us watch daily at his gates, and wait at the posts of his doors. To find him is to find eternal life, 1 John 4:9.

PROVERBS 9

Two Contrasted Invitations. There is an age-long competition between Wisdom and Folly, Virtue and Vice. The palace of Wisdom is very attractive—well-built and well-furnished. It is reared upon seven well-hewn marble pillars, in a quadrangular form, the entrance being left wide open. An eternal mansion, it is stable and beautiful. Great preparations are made for the feast, which is open to all—in striking contrast to the private supper to which Vice allures the unwary youth. The beautiful owner also sends forth her maidens into the public thoroughfares to give free invitations to all who will accept them. See Matt. 22:1ff.

Only to the simple or child-hearted, and not to the scorner, is the invitation addressed. Wisdom lets the scorner pass, because a word to him would only recoil on herself, and would add to his wickedness. To scoff at things which are holy and scorn the divine power is to risk the sin that is never forgiven. Such is the man who enters the feast without the wedding garment.

PROVERBS 10:1-16

The Righteous and the Wicked. Wealth has its advantages, which are more than apparent. "The rich man's wealth is his strong city," v. 15; but the treasures which have been obtained by wickedness are soon dissipated. They "profit nothing," v. 2. This book contains the striking thought that ill-earned wealth is never gathered for the benefit of the possessor, but rather for the benefit of the righteous, and must be useless until it gets into hands which will use it benevolently and rightly.

But there is another kind of wealth, which will never take wings to fly away, which no moth can corrupt nor thief steal, and which will avail not only here but hereafter. Note the antithesis of v. 2. If you would increase your wealth, give it away. See v. 4.

The covering work of love, referred to in v. 12, is emphasized in 1 Cor. 13:7; 1 Pet. 4:8; and Jas. 5:20. God covers sin, so that the memory of it is obliterated, Ezek. 33:16.

PROVERBS 10:17-32

"The Blessing of the Lord Maketh Rich." Let us specially avoid talking too much. Silence is golden. See v. 19. Yet "the tongue of the just is as choice silver" and "the lips of the righteous feed many," vv. 20, 21. When we speak, let us say something and let the people to whom we speak feel that their heart is lighter and that the heavenly horizons are nearer and clearer. Whatever you do, beware of uttering slander, v. 18. You know, by your own experience, what is acceptable; see to it that your mouth brings forth wisdom and grace, vv. 31, 32.

But this portion of Scripture deals not only with the speech of the good man, but with his stability. The blessing of God is upon him, enriching him in all manner of ways; and there is no alloy in this gold, no bitterness in God's love, v. 22. The desire of the righteous is granted because it is begotten of the divine Spirit. He is built on the Everlasting Rock, vv. 25, 30. His hope is gladness, v. 28. As he walks in God's way, he gathers strength, v. 29. Though he fall, he is not utterly cast down, for God succors him with his saving strength, Ps. 37:24.

PROVERBS 15:1-17

Kind Words and Glad Hearts. "A soft answer; the tongue of the wise; a wholesome tongue; the lips of the wise; the prayer of the upright"— these key words touch one of the greatest departments of human influence. If we can rule our speech, or at least hand over our tongue and lips to the keeping of God's Spirit, what a world of trouble we should save ourselves and others! And God would keep watch over us and for us. See v. 3.

Notice, also, the inducements to a right and holy life! Treasure in the house; answered prayer; the love of God; a cheerful heart; a contented mind—such are some of the byproducts and experiences of those whose life is "hid with Christ in God." When we put first things in the first place, all else is added.

What a comfort it is that God searcheth our hearts and knoweth them altogether! Yes, and even when he chastens and corrects us, it is well. There is no bliss comparable to that of the forgiven sinner, who is called into "the secret place of the Most High."

PROVERBS 15:18-33

Words in Season. Learn to be slow to anger. This paragraph describes the even temper which is blessed to live with and blessed to die with. Temper is said to be nine-tenths of Christianity. What best proves a Christian is an even temper. It is told of a Japanese gentleman, who was led by a tract to renounce the use of intoxicants and to accept Jesus Christ, that the immediate effect on his temper was so great that his wife, who had often suffered from his uncontrollable fits of anger, said, "If this is the result of Christianity, I want to become a Christian." When the missionaries afterward visited the place, they found her and ten other persons awaiting baptism.

As these proverbs suggest, the quickest method of overcoming and eradicating the wrong is, in the power of God, to cultivate the right. By this we shall tread the way of the wise that goeth upward toward the heavenly life of the angels, and we shall be saved from a hell of misery. See v. 24; Phil. 3:20; Col. 3:1.

PROVERBS 20:1-15

Sobriety; Industry; Honesty. Strong drink is the greatest of all foes to human happiness. It gains an influence over men by fair promises, but when once it is entrenched, it mocks at the misery of its abject slave. It promises strength for the arm, joy for the heart, brilliance for the mind; but those fair promises are not kept, and the end is impotence, misery, and imbecility. Let each reader of these words henceforth utterly abjure it!

The sluggard is depicted throughout this

PROVERBS

book to stir us to diligent industry. After all, it is not by great gifts but by patient persistence that men succeed. Indeed, the highest genius is left behind by the careful plodder, if the one lacks and the other possesses this invaluable quality. "Not slothful in business . . . serving the Lord" (Rom. 12:11).

All our life lies open to the eye of God. He is closely acquainted with the transactions of the bank, the office, the ledger, and the weights in the store. No lapse from perfect honesty escapes his notice; and for every act of deception there is an inevitable nemesis.

PROVERBS 20:16–30

"The Glory of Young Men." What a wonderful thought is given in v. 27! We stand like a row of unlighted candles until God's Spirit kindles us. Has the Divine Nature ever bent over your nature, communicating to it its glow and fire? If so, be very careful that no puff of wind shall extinguish that sacred spark; and see that it is supplied with the daily nutriment it requires. The whole paragraph seems to indicate the clear shining of this light, which must not be hidden under a bushel, but placed on the stand, that it may give light to all who come in. So let your light shine that men may admire neither the lampstand nor the wick, but the glory of the light of God radiating from you.

Such a soul will be true, v. 17; will be wise, v. 18; will eschew talebearing and flattery, v. 19; will honor the parents that gave it birth, v. 20; will win a good inheritance by patient industry, v. 21; will wait on the salvation of God, v. 22; will accept God's guidance, v. 24; will follow mercy and truth, v. 28; will be strong, and pure, and faithful. Such should be the glory of all young men and maidens if their old age shall be beautiful, v. 29.

PROVERBS 22:1–16

"He That Loveth Pureness of Heart." Great riches are not always a great blessing. When they are held in trust for God, they afford the opportunity of giving a vast amount of happiness to the benefactor as well as to those benefited. But we recall other riches, which do not consist in what a man *has,* but in what he *is.* There are four levels of human experience—to have, to do, to know, and to be—and these in their order are like iron, silver, gold, precious stones.

Some of these riches are enumerated here: a good name and loving favor, v. 1; the faith that hides in God, v. 3; true humility and godly fear, v. 4; the child-heart, v. 6; the beautiful eye and open hand, v. 9; purity of heart and thought, v. 11; alacrity and diligence, v. 13. If only we would cultivate the inward graces and gifts of our soul-life, all who feel our influence would be proportionately enriched.

PROVERBS 25:1–14

Words Fitly Spoken. This collection of proverbs was made 250 years after the time of Solomon by the scribes of King Hezekiah. The glory of God is too great to be disclosed to the vulgar eye of mere curiosity, but it will be unfolded to royal souls that seek for it as for hid treasure. The great rulers of the world must have their secret counsels, but they should be freed from evil counselors, as gold from dross. Compare vv. 6 and 7 with Luke 14:8–10. Second thoughts are best; sleep over your plan or letter; be deliberate in planning and prompt in acting on the plan when formed. Don't reveal to another a cause of offense that should be adjusted between yourself and your neighbor, Matt. 18:15. A word happily adapted to a circumstance is like an apple of gold (that is, an orange) in a basket of silver filigree. As drink cooled with snow refreshes the thirsty reaper, so is a messenger who faithfully executes his errand to the master who sent him.

PROVERBS 25:15–28

Self-control and Kindliness. In this paragraph we have good advice as to our dealings with the varied characters with whom we are forced into daily contact. Here is a man hard as a bone; try gentleness, for a soft tongue will win his heart, just because it finds a new and unexpected way of approach which no one else has tried for long years. Beware of honeyed words; you may get stung. Do not make yourself too common, or pry into your neighbor's affairs, or ask his help too often. Keep clear of the talebearer. Be very careful to whom you confide your troubles. Vinegar poured on potash makes it effervesce; so joyous mirth is incongruous to a heavy heart. Even if your love fails to meet your enemy, the Lord will reward you by revealing and communicating his own perfection, Matt. 5:43–48. If you frown on a backbiter, you will silence him. Do not give way to the wicked, lest you become a corrupted spring. Rule over your spirit; nay, better, hand over its keys to Emmanuel, and let him be crowned in Mansoul.

PROVERBS 27:1–22

"Hearty Counsel." The key word in this paragraph is "friends," vv. 6, 9, 10, 14, 17. Friends, according to the original sense of the Hebrew

word, are those who delight in each other's companionship. Either they are useful to each other because the one possesses gifts that the other lacks, or they have certain tastes in common.

It is in friendship that we get to know ourselves, as a man sees his face in the mirror of calm water, v. 19. We unfold to each other; our friend elicits traits of which we were hardly aware. Our sympathy and tenderness are drawn forth by our friend's troubles, as our laughter flashes out to awaken or to answer his high spirits. We shudder to think what cold and undeveloped beings we would be without the sharpening of friendship, v. 17. How sweet human friendships are, v. 9. Why not find equal confidence and sweetness in the greatest Friend of all? Of course, there is a friendship which is wholly hypocritical and worthless. Such a friendship is marked by loud and ostentatious demonstration. See v. 14. Ponder Christ's offer, John 15:14, 15.

PROVERBS 30:1-17

The Advice of a Shrewd Observer. This chapter contains a collection of sayings of one person, Agur, of whom we know nothing further. It is supposed that he lived after the return from the Exile. The opening verses of the chapter may be thus rendered: "The utterance of the man who has questioned and thought, I have wearied after God, I have wearied after God, and am faint; for I am too stupid for a man, and am without reason, and I have not learned wisdom, nor have I knowledge of the All-Holy."

Agur answers his complaint in vv. 5-9. You cannot know God by your own discovery, but he will make himself known to you through the written Word, to which no addition may be made, v. 6. See also John 1:18, which shows our clearest revelation of him. But there are two conditions: We must put away vanity and lies; and we must be satisfied with God's arrangement of our daily food. Notice the following quatrain, vv. 11-14, which is descriptive of four kinds of evil men: the unfilial, the self-righteous, the haughty, and the rapacious. The next quatrain, vv. 15, 16, treats of the insatiable; and this is followed by a further description of the doom of the disobedient. This is strong, wise, shrewd, sanctified sense.

PROVERBS 30:18-33

Lessons from Common Things. We have four more quatrains. 1) There are the four wonders that baffle Agur's understanding. How superficial is our knowledge! How does the eagle mount the air, or the serpent find a hold on the slippery rock, or a ship plow her way across the deep, or a man and woman fall in love by a secret interchange of heart which no one else perceives? And further, how can a sinner continue to sin without experiencing remorse?

2) There are four intolerable conditions: a slave in authority, a pampered fool, a difficult marriage, and a slave-girl, like Hagar, preferred to her mistress.

3) There are four kinds of animals which prove that it is possible to be insignificant and yet be wise: the ant, the cony, the locust, and the spider (lit. lizard).

4) There are four things which give the idea of stateliness in motion: a lion, a greyhound, a he-goat, and a king "against whom there is no rising up."

This remarkable collection ends with an exhortation to the repression of anger. Sometimes to refuse to express one's passion is the surest way of killing it. Treat it like a room on fire. Shut door and window, that it may die for want of air. Ask God's holy sunlight to replace the unholy heat of your soul.

PROVERBS 31:1-9

The Worthy Woman. In these words of King Lemuel, we notice a mother's influence in the education of her son. A woman is never more nobly occupied than in warning her son against the seductions of pleasure and in giving him a high sense of that which is right.

The sins of the flesh have been the peculiar snare of royal personages, preventing them from pleading the cause of the desolate and ministering judgment to the poor and needy. What a contrast to the glory of the sovereignty of Jesus! When Savonarola preached with his burning eloquence in Florence, the people cried, "Jesus is our King, only Jesus!" That is what we all need. He is the King of whom his subjects need never be ashamed.

We cannot interpret vv. 6 and 7 as a divine injunction, but rather as an admission that alcohol imparts a temporary stimulus to the despairing and the dying. We must remember Proverbs 20:1. Still speaking of the king, Lemuel shows how best his influence can be employed, vv. 8 and 9. But the same obligation and privilege rests on us all.

PROVERBS 31:10-31

"Her Works Praise Her." The ideal woman, as portrayed here, is a wife. She is the stay and

confidence of her husband. Not only when she comes as a young bride into his home, in the glory and beauty of her youth, nor only when her womanly beauty holds his admiration, but long after and to the end of life she does him good. She is always busy. She is thrifty in administering his earnings. If he brings the money to her, she expends it economically for their common well-being. When a friend of mine was sixty, his wife came to him with an annuity which she had purchased for them both, by her wise administration of the money entrusted to her through forty years of married life.

It is in the home that the man's strength is gathered for public life. The woman in the home communicates the inspiration and strength which make him "known in the gates." Her secret, unobtrusive loyalty, counsel, and thrift inspire a growing depth of appreciation, so that the man who chose her in the spring will say of her amid the snows of age, "Other women may be good and true, but *thou excellest them all.*"

THE BOOK OF
ECCLESIASTES
THE VANITY AND VALUE OF LIFE

I. THE PROLOGUE *1:1–11.*

II. THE TESTING OF LIFE'S EXPERIENCES *1:12—12:7.*
    A. The preacher's experience *1:12—2:26.*
    B. The preacher's observation *3:1—4:8.*
    C. The preacher's counsel *4:9—7:10.*
    D. The preacher's commendation of wisdom *7:11—9:18.*
    E. Proverbs—life's closing scenes *10:1—12:7.*

III. THE EPILOGUE *12:8–14.*

INTRODUCTION

The word "Ecclesiastes" is from the Greek, and means "Preacher." The book is really a sermon, designed to teach the unsatisfying nature of worldly pleasures and attainments unless God rules the heart and life. The great lesson is that man's true wisdom lies in fearing God and looking forward to the judgment.

The word "vanity," which occurs thirty-eight times, is the keynote of the book. How true happiness may be attained is the problem the author endeavors to solve.

COMMENTARY

ECCLESIASTES 1

The Testimony of an Unsatisfied Soul. "All is vanity!" This cry finds an echo in human hearts of every age and clime. God meant man to be happy. "These things," said our Lord, "I have spoken to you, that your joy may be full." "The fruit of the Spirit is joy." Yet the air is laden with complaint and bitterness. Men are asking constantly, "Is life worth living?" The present age is full of unrest and weariness, of war and strife, of unsatisfied yearnings and desires. The mistake is that men seek to solve the mystery of life and to find their happiness apart from God, who has made us for himself.

This book was written and incorporated in the Bible to show that man's quest for happiness is vain, so long as it is apart from God. Solomon had unbounded opportunities for pursuing his quest. Youth, wealth, wisdom, royalty, human love were his, but when all were mixed in the golden cup of his life, he turned from the draught unsatisfied and sad. Listen to the sigh of the sated voluptuary: "Vanity of vanities!" Let us turn from these bitter experiences to 1 John 2:15-17.

ECCLESIASTES 2:1-17, 24-26

Vain Undertakings. At the beginning of his search for happiness Solomon erected a splendid home and planned all kinds of delights of an artistic and sensuous nature. There were gardens, pools of crystal water, fruit trees, meadows filled with cattle, regal splendor, musicians who poured their sweet melodies into the palace. He went further, adding to architecture and art his intellectual pursuits. But when he had gone to the furthest limit, he turned from it all, with the old gnawing at his heart—"Vanity of vanities!"

A few days before the death of the great Cardinal Mazarin, he was heard by a friend to utter something of the same sad refrain. "I was walking," says this friend, "in one of the apartments of the palace when I recognized the approach of the Cardinal by the sound of his slippered feet, which he dragged one after the other as a man suffering from a mortal malady. I concealed myself behind the tapestry and heard him say, as he looked at one picture and rare treasure after another, 'I must leave all these.' " Let us, in the light of these things, ponder again those words of Christ in Luke 12:33.

ECCLESIASTES 11

Live Not for Today Alone. The casting of bread upon the waters is an allusion to the oriental custom of casting rice grains on the fields, when they lie submerged beneath the annual inundation of such a river as the Nile. To the inexperienced eye, this would seem the prodigality of waste, but the husbandman knows full well that he will meet his seed again with abundant returns. So it is in life, whether we befriend young boys and girls, or distribute tracts, or speak kind and loving words, or invest our money in philanthropic enterprise, we are casting our bread upon the waters to find it after many days in this world or the next.

But how wise the advice not to be always considering the winds and clouds, vv. 3, 4. There is considerable hazard in the life of the farmer. If he waits until all the conditions are favorable, he will never begin. So with our work for God. We must risk something. Often the word spoken at an apparently untoward moment will prove to be the word in season, while that spoken under the most favorable conditions will yield no return at all. God gives it a body as and when and how it pleaseth him.

ECCLESIASTES 12

"The Conclusion of the Matter." This comparison of the human body to a house is extremely beautiful. The inference is obvious that our bodies are not ourselves, but only our tenement. Our sojourn in this world is on a lodger's tenure. "The keepers of the house" are, of course, the arms and hands. "The grinding is low" as in advancing life we lose our teeth. The "door" is the mouth, for in age we talk and laugh less, and our lips become compressed. The voice falters and mutters. The "almond tree," with its white blossoms, is, of course, an appropriate symbol of old age. The lamp of life finally falls with a crash on the floor, and the "wheel" is broken.

What, then, is the conclusion of the whole matter? This: that earthly delights are transient; that all this world can offer is an inn for a lodging—it is not our home; that the soul must go forth on its great quest at the hour of death; and that then the one all-important consideration will be, What has been its attitude toward God? Let us love God with the loving fear of grieving him that casts out the fear which has torment. This is the "whole" matter; that is, the one matter of overshadowing importance.

THE BOOK OF ISAIAH

"THE EVANGELICAL PROPHET"

I. JUDGMENT, RESTORATION, THANKSGIVING   *1—12.*
   A. Introduction   *1.*
   B. Judah and Jerusalem   *2—6.*
   C. The book of Immanuel   *7—12.*

II. THE BURDENS OF THE NATIONS   *13—27.*
   A. Babylon, Assyria, Philistia, Syria, Israel, Egypt, Edom, Tyre   *13—23.*
   B. World judgment and the redemption of Judah   *24—27.*

III. THE SIX WOES   *28—35.*
   (To the drunken; to formalists; to those who hide their plans from God; to those who trust in Egypt; to those who rely on horses and chariots; to the Assyrian destroyer.)

IV. HISTORICAL SECTION   *36—39.*
   A. The deliverance of Jerusalem from Sennacherib   *36, 37.*
   B. Hezekiah's sickness and recovery   *38.*
   C. Embassy of Merodach-baladan   *39.*

V. DIVINE DELIVERANCE FROM SIN AND CAPTIVITY   *40—48.*
   A. Assurance of salvation   *40, 41.*
   B. The riches of grace   *42:1—44:23.*
   C. The mission of Cyrus   *44:24—47:15.*
   D. God's chastisement disciplinary   *48.*

VI. THE SERVANT OF JEHOVAH   *49—57.*
   A. The Servant's mission   *49:1—52:12.*
   B. The Servant's sacrifice and exaltation   *52:13—53:12.*
   C. The fullness and freeness of salvation   *54—57.*

VII. NEW HEAVENS AND A NEW EARTH   *58—66.*
   A. The dawning light   *58—62.*
   B. The redeeming God   *63—66.*

INTRODUCTION

Both as a prophet and as a statesman, Isaiah took an active part in the affairs of Judah during the reigns of Uzziah, Jotham, Ahaz, and Hezekiah. He was contemporary also with the prophets Hosea and Micah. At the lowest estimate his public career extended over a period of forty years. According to tradition he was executed by being sawn asunder during the reign of Manasseh, to which there may be reference in Heb. 11:37.

Much controversy has gathered around the authorship of the book which bears his name. While there are difficulties in the way of attributing the entire book to a single writer, much more serious problems have been created by every attempt to divide the authorship among different writers.

Isaiah is called the "Evangelical Prophet," as a large part of his book is indissolubly bound with the life and work of the Messiah. Philip, finding the Ethiopian eunuch reading from this prophecy, "began at the same scripture, and preached unto him Jesus." The book contains also a wide variety of materials: prophetic oracles concerning the nations, sermons, hymns, apocalypses, narratives, and autobiography. It is commonly regarded as the greatest of the prophecies, and its influence upon the development of Christian thought can hardly be overestimated.

The second section of the book, Chapters 40–66, is "one of the finest poems existing in any language." The author's aim in this part is to encourage the Israelites in their exile by showing that Jehovah is supreme and that, therefore, no obstacle will be able to prevent the restoration of Israel and the overthrow of their enemies. In accomplishing his purpose, God uses the following agents:

1. Cyrus, one "from the east," 41:2, who is also called "my shepherd," 44:28, and Jehovah's "anointed," 45:1, and who is to be God's instrument in overthrowing Babylon and delivering Israel from exile.

2. The "Servant of Jehovah." In several passages, 41:8; 44:1, 2, 21, the nation of Israel is the "Servant of Jehovah," to accomplish his purposes with reference to all peoples. But in many others, the personal, suffering "Servant of Jehovah" is beautifully pictured as God's instrument in the redemption of Israel and in the ingathering of the Gentiles. Through Christ, the Messiah, is to be fulfilled God's promise to Abraham, culminating in an endless kingdom of peace and righteousness.

COMMENTARY

ISAIAH 1:1-9

The Ingratitude of a Favored Nation. This chapter forms the preface to the prophecies of Isaiah. It is a clear and concise statement of the points at issue between Jehovah and his people. Special urgency was given to these appeals, when first uttered, by the fact which was well-known to the Hebrew politicians and people, that Assyria was preparing for a great war of conquest, which would be directed specially against Jerusalem and her allies. This chapter is cast in the form of a trial, a case in which God is both complainant and judge. The conviction of sinfulness which the prophet desired to secure was sought, not by appealing to a code of laws which had been transgressed, but by showing the ingratitude with which Israel had repaid the fatherly love of God. It is the personal element in sin that most quickly convicts men. "Saul, Saul, why persecutest thou me?" "Thou art the man!" "He hath done despite unto the Spirit of grace!"

ISAIAH 1:10-20

Religion without Righteousness Vain. The prophet points out, first the misery that had overtaken the country, vv. 4-9; and then the sins of the ruling classes, vv. 10, 17, 21-23. What may be called personal and private sins, such as drunkenness, vanity, bribery, and the oppression of the poor, are viewed in their public hearing as bringing wrath and disaster on the whole nation. No man can sin by himself. His most private sins react on the whole community. Thistledown floats far and wide. In reply, the nation pointed to the splendid ritual and innumerable sacrifices of the Temple service. But these observances only added to the tale of their sins, because they were formal and perfunctory.

The sacrifice of God is a broken and contrite heart. The outward is absolutely worthless unless it is the expression of the inward and the spiritual. But where a pure and holy spirit is present, the simplest forms are magnificent in their significance and value. To atone becomes the base of a ladder to Heaven, and the thornbush flames with Deity. But forgiveness is freely offered to the guilty. Crimson and scarlet are the most lasting of all colors, and their removal shows the completeness of God's pardoning love.

ISAIAH 1:21-31

A Nation Purged of Dross by Disaster. The great lover of our souls does not abandon his people even when they spurn the first overtures of his appealing pity. Though they refuse to yield to them, he refuses to cast them off, and sets himself by the cleansing judgments of his providence to wean them from the evil ways they have chosen and to win them back to himself. If only Jerusalem had now listened to Isaiah's earnest pleadings, she would never have been carried away into the seventy years' captivity in a land of strangers. This is the cleansing fire referred to in v. 25. Their ground of confidence, whether in themselves or their allies, would be destroyed, vv. 29, 30; the ringleaders of the evil which had brought them to desolation would be exterminated; and there would emerge a new and purified people as in the days of Ezra and Nehemiah. Let us thank God for the cleansing fires in national and personal experience. Let us not fear them when plied by the hand of love. See Mal. 3:3 and John 15:2, 3.

ISAIAH 2:1-11

A Vision of World Peace. This and the four following chapters must be classed together as a distinct portion of this book, belonging to the earliest years of Isaiah's ministry. Their date is 735 B. C., about the time of the accession of Ahaz to the throne. Verses 2-4 are evidently an ancient prophecy by some unknown seer, for Micah also quotes it. This section presents a fair vision of the future, when the beloved city must become the center of the religious life of the world, the seat of the theocracy, the burning nucleus of a reign of love and peace. We cherish this ancient prophecy as our guiding star in the present storm. But it can be realized only when the Son of God, riding forth on his white horse, has subdued his enemies. Then Revelation 21 and 22 will fulfill this ancient dream. The contrast between the ideal city and the actual is terrible, vv. 6–9. But let us not despair. The exalted Lord, from the right hand of power, is hastening the coming of the day of God.

ISAIAH 2:12—3:12

An Exhortation to Humility and Reverence. If men will not repent, they must suffer. If they will not voluntarily put away their idols and sorceries, they will be compelled to do so in the anguish of their disappointment with their helpless deities, v. 20. Nothing in that great civilization would be spared. High towers, fenced walls, ships, treasures, armor—all would perish. Their vaunted faith in man would cease. Life would become elemental in its simplicity amid the shelter of the ragged rocks. In sarcastic phrase the prophet depicts a despairing nation choosing for ruler the first man that came along with a decent coat on his back, v. 6; but in vain. We can almost hear the sob of the prophet's soul in vv. 8 and 9, and recall the tears of a greater than Isaiah who wept over this same Jerusalem 800 years afterward. Patriotism is one of the purest passions that can burn in the heart of man! "Lives there a man, with soul so dead, that never to himself has said, This is my own, my native land?"

ISAIAH 3:13—4:6

Vanity and Selfish Luxury Condemned. This paragraph opens with the majestic figure of Jehovah himself, who arises to judge the misrulers and plead the cause of the poor. The prophet enumerates the trinkets of the women of Israel, who had given themselves up to luxury and corruption. Woman is the priestess and prophetess of the home and religion, and when she forsakes the level of spiritual influence for that of physical adornment, the salt has lost its savor and the whole commonwealth suffers. The manhood of a land is lost, morally and spiritually, when woman falls from her high estate. There could be no hope for Jerusalem until the divine fire had consumed the filth of her daughters and the oppressive selfishness of her sons. Then once more each home in Jerusalem would have the same blessed signs of the Divine Presence as had once been granted to the Tabernacle—the shadowing cloud by day and the gleam of the shekinah-fire by night. Let us claim these for our homes also!

ISAIAH 5:1–17

A Disappointing Harvest. In a picture of great beauty, Isaiah describes a vineyard situated on one of the sunny heights visible from Jerusalem. Every care which an experienced vinedresser could devise had been expended on it, but in vain. The vinedresser himself is introduced, demanding if more could have been done. When God selects a nation, a church, or an individual for high and holy work in the world and expends care and pains on the preparation of the instrument, and his plans miscarry through no failure on his part but through the obstinacy or obtuseness of the human soul, the measure of what might have been is the gauge of its doom. The worst weeds grow on the richest soil. This picture is the counterpart of Paul's dread of being a castaway, 1 Cor. 9:27.

The six woes which follow, arising from drunkenness and avarice, remind us of sorrows that menace the selfish heart. How different such a lot to the blessedness of the humblest soul that possesses God and is possessed by him! "Evil shall slay the wicked: and they that hate the righteous shall be desolate. Jehovah redeemeth the soul of his servants: and none of them that take refuge in him shall be desolate," Ps. 34:21, 22.

ISAIAH 5:18–30

Warning against Pride, Intemperance, and Corruption. The wild grapes of Judah are here continued: blind atheism, vv. 18–20; proud self-conceit, v. 21; drunkenness, v. 22; injustice in the courts, vv. 23, 24. What a terrible description is that given in v. 18 of the inevitable progress of sin! The bacchanalian procession which is seen in v. 14, descending with music and flowers into the open gates of Hades, is described in v. 18 as being drawn down by a cable. Men begin with a thread, but the thread of habit becomes a rope, and the rope grows to a cable which ultimately lands a man in the pit.

From v. 25 onward we have the description of impending judgment. Earthquakes, armed raids, civil strife, famine, the devastating inroads of hostile invasion, a desolate land, and a hungry sea would be the forces of destruction

ISAIAH

which Judah's sin would unloose. Recent events have revealed the terror of such a visitation. Remember that the wrath of love is as severe as a consuming fire.

ISAIAH 6

A Call to Heroic Service. Kings die; Jesus lives. See John 12:41. We are here reminded of Acts 22:17, 18. How great the contrast between the worship of these seraphim and man's perfunctory rites! "Six wings"—two for meditation, two for humility, and two for service. Service should take only a third of our energy. "One cried unto another"—one inspired spirit will awaken others. The threefold repetition of the word "holy" implies the Trinity. If doorposts tremble, much more should the hearts of sinful men! Isaiah, in the previous chapter, had uttered six woes against others, but his seventh and sorest woe is against himself. The sinner, like the leper, cries, "Unclean" (Lev. 13:45). There is only one cure for such need as the prophet's, vv. 9–13. When men refuse God's offered grace, every refusal hardens. It is either "the savour of death unto death" or of "life unto life," 2 Cor. 2:16. The life of the oak and the terebinth only seems to become extinct in winter; there is revival in the spring. Is it winter with you? Pray for the springtime!

ISAIAH 7:1–17

The Sign of Immanuel. A new cycle of prophecy begins here, covering the reign of Ahaz. The complete history which illustrates these chapters is given in 2 Chronicles 28:5. The invasion of Judah by Syria and Samaria was permitted because a severe warning was needed to enforce Isaiah's remonstrances and appeals. See 2 Kings 15:37. The Holy City, as Isaiah predicted, was not to be trodden by the invader, though it would pass through severe suffering and anxiety. This immunity, which neither Ahaz nor his people deserved, was secured by Isaiah's faith and prayer, pleading as he did for God's ancient covenant.

This great prophecy of the coming Immanuel must have greatly encouraged that generation, as it has all succeeding ones. It reminds us of Psalm 46. What greater comfort have we than that Jesus is the companion of our pilgrimage? See Matt. 1:21–23. Though the cornlands were desolate, the cattle on the mountain pastures would yield butter and the wild bees honey; and this would supply the nation's needs till the invader had withdrawn. Though God chastens us, he will not forget our daily bread.

ISAIAH 7:18—8:4

A Foreign Foe—God's Instrument. Ahaz, as we have seen, summoned the king of Assyria to his aid. This policy, dictated by human prudence, was fraught with vast peril. He and his advisers would rue their choice, and would have to pay dearly for introducing Assyria into the complicated politics of these minor states. Though this policy might effect a temporary success, like that which Isaiah indicated in the naming of his newborn child, yet ultimately it would work out disastrously, in the depopulation and desolation of the country. The impoverished peasants would have one cow instead of a herd, and two sheep instead of a flock. Is not this true of all the expedients which we substitute for faith in God? At first they promise well, but they disappoint and fail. It is the old lesson: "Lean not unto thine own understanding," Prov. 3:5.

ISAIAH 8:5–18

Fear God's Power, Not Man's. It seems likely that Syria and Samaria attacked Ahaz because he would not join in a federation against the growing power of Assyria. A strong party seems to have pressed this policy on him, but in all such schemes they repudiated the divine protection, v. 6. Compare Ps. 46:4. Ahaz and the court party on the other hand sought to federate with Assyria. But Isaiah never ceased to urge that the true line of defense was to put away whatever was inconsistent with the fear of God. He would be the sanctuary of defense and hiding in the day of trouble, vv. 13, 14. We learn from Hebrews 2:13 how absolutely, when speaking thus, the prophet was being prompted by the Holy Spirit. If men will not build on God's foundation-stone, they fall over it to their hurt. Compare v. 15 and Matt. 21:44. Are we not all in danger of substituting human alliances for federation and union with the eternal God? Let our fellowship be with the Father and the Son; and let us wait for him till the day dawn and the daystar shines, 2 Pet. 1:19.

ISAIAH 8:19—9:7

The Prince of Peace. When men cease to trust in God and rely on the help of man, they often turn to necromancy and spiritism. The medium takes the place of the Mediator. The seance is sought after instead of the Law and the Testimony. What have God's children to do with back-stair gossip, when their Father's presence-chamber is open to them? What he does not tell us is not worth our knowing.

The land of Galilee was destined to suffer

sorely, but better days would dawn on its mountains and lakes. The joy that was in store is compared to the daybreak, v. 2; to the joy of harvest, v. 3; and to the gladness of the harried tribes when Gideon broke the power of Midian, v. 4. The implements of battle would become fuel for the peasants' cottage-fires.

What titles are these for our Lord! They befit no human babe! Let us place the government of our lives on his shoulders; and as it extends, so shall our peace. Ask God's zeal to do this for thee! In the power of his grace, put the government of all on the wonderful Son of God.

ISAIAH 9:8–17

False Leadership Brings Ruin. The grievous sins of the Chosen People are again enumerated. They defied God, vv. 9, 10. They refused to repent; they were blind and deaf and profane, v. 13. Their religious and political leaders led them astray, v. 16. What could they expect but the letting loose of the judgments of the Almighty!

Isaiah's protests were disregarded, and 2 Kings 15 tells the sequel. It seems very terrible. But what would the forest glades become if there were not the removal of all traces of disease, decay, and death! What is true in the physical is true also in the moral sphere. When a nation has ceased to help, and has commenced to impede the progress of humanity, it must be put out of the way.

ISAIAH 9:18—10:4

Social Injustice Condemned. The terrible indictment of the preceding paragraphs is continued here. Notice the awful monotony of the refrain, 9:12, 17, 21; 10:4. Internal anarchy spread with the rapidity of a prairie fire. Jealousy and distrust awoke murderous hatred. Even the ties of brotherhood would not avail to arrest the knife of the assassin. In the horrors of starvation men would consume their own flesh, v. 20. Civil strife would exhaust the forces which, combined with God's blessing, might have arrested the invader. The weak would become the spoil of the strong, and there would be no appeal. What pathetic questions are suggested in 10:3! "What will ye do?" "To whom will ye flee?" See Heb. 9:26–28. What hope is there for the soul that has known and refused the offer of forgiveness in Jesus? Dear soul, make haste to the cleft of the Rock!

ISAIAH 10:5–19

The Mighty Laid Low. These questions (v. 3) were addressed to the Assyrian invader, described as God's staff and rod. He was the means of inflicting deserved penalty on the world of that age, and especially on the Chosen People. He had no thought of this, but considered himself free to wreak his will without reference to that Higher Power whose agent he was. But the ruthless manner in which he carried out his work was destined to come under the divine judgment, vv. 12–15.

The capture of Jerusalem seemed as sure as the taking of a nest of eggs. The strongest barriers that the nations could oppose to his arms had fallen before the Assyrian king; surely the Hebrew city should not escape. But God had yet to be reckoned with, vv. 16–19. The conception here is borrowed from a forest fire, which begins among the brushwood and presently consumes the loftiest and stoutest trees; so would the fire of destruction be kindled during the attack on the Holy City, which finally would involve the whole Assyrian empire. Let us not fear the wrath of man. God makes some portion of it to praise him, and he restrains the remainder.

ISAIAH 10:20–32

A Remnant Shall Return. Notice the effect of the Assyrian invasion. The survivors would once again learn to "stay" themselves on God, v. 20. It is a remarkable expression! Let us ponder carefully vv. 20 and 21. We are reminded of Cardinal Mercier's famous pastoral letter, written after the desolation of Belgium: "Men long unaccustomed to prayer are turning again to God. Nor is that prayer a word learned by rote; it surges up from the troubled heart, and takes its form at the feet of God by the very sacrifice of life." It is evidently necessary that God, from time to time, should break up the foundations of human society in order that men may be awakened to consider the elemental realities of God and the soul, vv. 24–27. The destruction of Sennacherib is anticipated as resembling the overthrow of Midian by Gideon, and of Egypt in the Red Sea. Then the burden and yoke would be destroyed, so far as Jerusalem was concerned, in answer to the anointed priests who had pleaded for her deliverance. But how much more will the prayer of our anointed Savior bring help to us!

ISAIAH 10:33—11:9

The Kingdom of the Messiah. The advance of the Assyrian along the great north road is graphically described. It was marked by raided villages and towns. The night sky was lurid with flames. But his collapse would be as sudden and irretrievable as the felling of forest timber. As

ISAIAH

the one chapter closes, we can almost hear the crash of the Assyrian tree to the ground, and there is no sprout from his roots. But in the next the prophet descries a fair and healthy branch rising from the trunk of Jesse's line. The vision of the King is then presented, who can be none other than the divine Redeemer on whom rests the sevenfold Spirit of God. The second verse defines the work of the Comforter, and is evidently the model of that royal hymn, *"Veni Creator Spiritus."* But remember that he on whom this divine unction rested longs to share the Pentecostal gift with the least of his disciples, 1 John 2:27. Note that as man's sin brought travail and groaning on all creation, so will his redemption deliver it, Rom. 8:19-25.

ISAIAH 11:10—12:6

A Song of Thanksgiving. The prophet's vision extends. He has seen the effect of redemption, as it emanates from Jesus Christ, upon the whole physical creation; now he beholds also the ingathering of all Israel. The ancient enmity between Ephraim and Judah would pass away. As Paul puts it afterward, "All Israel shall be saved," Rom. 11:26. As they were brought out of Egypt, so shall they be brought from all the countries of the world where they have dwelt during these Christian centuries. The return of the Jews under Ezra included those of one tribe only, and cannot fulfill the great dreams of all the prophets as here of Isaiah.

The following chapter is the counterpart of Exodus 15. When their enemies are overwhelmed in the great battle of Armageddon, the ransomed hosts of Israel shall break forth in this anthem.

The 3rd verse was chanted by the priests on the last day of the Feast of Tabernacles, John 7:37, 38. The little possessive pronoun "my" is the bucket with which we draw water from the depths of God. Our pilgrimage way is lined by these wells of saving help.

ISAIAH 24:1-13

The Desolation of a Guilty World. This and the three following chapters form a single prophecy, describing the calamities about to desolate the land because the inhabitants had "transgressed the laws, changed the ordinance, broken the everlasting covenant." Primarily it describes the experiences of Palestine under the successive invasions from the Euphrates valley, first of Nineveh and then of Babylon. There is a mysterious connection between the condition of a man's soul and the response of surrounding Nature. The very vineyards would sigh in sad accord with the prevailing misery and sin, vv. 7-9; and in the great city silence would reign in streets decimated by plague and war, vv. 10-12. Both in the Old and the New Testament the blessings of sufficiency and comfort are the fruits of holy living; whereas sooner or later evil overtakes wrongdoing. "Trust in the Lord and do good, so shalt thou dwell in the land, and verily thou shalt be fed" is always true.

ISAIAH 24:14-23

The Inescapable Penalty of Sin. There is always a godly remnant, as we are told in vv. 13, 14, remaining in times of shaking, on the topmost boughs. The survivors who had fled across the seas from the judgments would adore Jehovah for his goodness and mercy.

The fires of the East are in contrast to the isles of the West, v. 15. Perhaps they stand for the fires of tribulation, in which we must glorify God. To whatever part of the earth the fugitives fled, they would be compelled to acknowledge the glory of righteousness, or perhaps of the Righteous One. The dispersion of the Church in the early days carried the message and music of the gospel everywhere. Though we may travel to the limits of sorrow, let us glorify our God.

Note the instability of all earthly things, v. 18ff. Woe to those who trust in them! Remember to build within the borders of the everlasting kingdom of Hebrews 12:23-28. When all the world kingdoms are destroyed, that of Israel, God's ancient choice, shall stand, v. 23. May we as the brethren of the King share his glory and reign with him in those great coming days! In the meanwhile, glorify him in the skies.

ISAIAH 25

Sorrow Turned to Gladness. Here is a song of thanksgiving at the fall of Babylon. When she fell, a sigh of relief passed over the whole world, and strong, terrible nations over which she had exerted her tyranny gratefully recognized the goodness and righteousness of Jehovah. We may anticipate, as we read these glowing words, what that song will be when the spiritual Babylon is overthrown, Rev. 19:1-7.

Notice how God suits himself to our need, whether for strength or refuge or shadow. Take from him what you are needing most. As the cloud draws its veil over the burning sunshine to mitigate its heat, so does God interpose to reduce the sufferings of his own. The branch—that is, the exulting song of the terrible ones, their song of triumph—shall be hushed. From

v. 6 we learn that the hunger of man for God can only be satisfied in Jesus; and from v. 7, that the dread of death and the hereafter, which has lain heavily on humanity as a pall, shall be forever ended when Jesus comes the second time unto salvation. Compare 1 Cor. 15:54. God will not only wipe tears from our eyes, but the fountains of tears shall be dried up, Rev. 21:4.

ISAIAH 26:1–10

Peace through Steadfast Trust. No doubt when Babylon fell before Cyrus, the Jewish remnant under Ezra and Nehemiah sang this triumphal ode, which contrasts the respective lots of Babylon and Jerusalem. The one is the city of this world and its children; the other the city and home of the saints. The fate of Babylon is delineated in vv. 5 and 6; but with what glowing words does the prophet dwell on the blessedness of those who are fellow-citizens with the saints and of the household of God, Eph. 2:19. Note in v. 3 one of God's double doors against the intrusion on the soul of a single note of alarm or fear. God is the Rock of Ages, v. 4, margin. Our trust should be as permanent as his love—forever. The weakest foot may trample on the proudest foe when God has laid him in the dust. God levels the path of the just. However difficult your path, dare to believe that you are being directed in righteousness. God cannot make mistakes. Any other path would be impracticable. Only nurse the desires of your soul for God; they are the result of the promptings and drawings of his Spirit.

ISAIAH 26:11–21

Chastened by Suffering. When God ordains our peace, a world in arms cannot disturb us. Our peace results from the conviction that God is going before us and preparing our works. But be careful to make mention of his name; that is, to give him the glory.

Do not be afraid of your enemies. When God brings you back from the ends of the earth, he will free you from their toils and snares. Let us, as v. 16 suggests, pour out our prayers as a vessel its contents, though, as the Hebrew signifies, those prayers are but whispers. It is true that apart from God we work no "deliverance in the earth," v. 18; but when he speaks, even the dead live. Jesus, the resurrection and the life, speaks in v. 19. What comfort results to those who dwell in the dust of self-abasement and despair but look up to the ever-living Christ, from whom streams of life-giving energy come to believing hearts! Arise and sing, thou broken heart. Even now the stone is being rolled from the door of thy sepulcher; the morning dew is distilling upon thee. Cast out by earth, thou shalt be welcomed by Heaven and sheltered in God's secret place till the storm-burst has spent itself.

ISAIAH 27

God's Care for His Vineyard. Throughout these chapters we must remember that the doom of Babylon and the restoration of God's people are symbolical of other events, for which the world is preparing. Then Babylon the Great shall give place to the Holy City, which comes down out of Heaven from God. Egypt and Babylon are represented by the leviathan, a general term applicable to any great water animal. The one had its Nile, the other its Euphrates. Parallel with the destruction of our foes is God's care of his own people. The Church is his vineyard. We do not keep him, but he us. Not for a moment does he relax his care. Those who oppose his purposes are trampled down as briars beneath the booted foot. In v. 6 we have a glimpse of the ultimate mission of the Hebrew race.

Note the difference in vv. 7–11 between punishment and chastisement. The former is irremediable and destructive; the latter is always in measure. The rough wind is stayed in the day of the east wind. Its object is to purge away our sins. After the Captivity, idolatry ceased in Israel. How tenderly God gathers his wanderers—one by one as hand-picked fruit; even those who had wandered farthest and were ready to perish!

ISAIAH 28:1–13

The Decay of an Intemperate People. A new series of prophecies begins here and extends to Isaiah 32:20. Samaria is described as a faded crown or garland on the nation's head because it was disgraced by national drunkenness. See Amos 4:1. So corrupted was she by strong drink and its attendant evils that the Assyrian invader would plunder her as a man gathers ripe figs. But to Judah, that is, the remnant, the Lord would be a crown or garland, not of pride but of glory. His beauty would not be as a fading flower, but a lasting diadem. What wine is to the sensuous man, that God is to the spiritual. See Eph. 5:18. You that have to form right judgments, and you that have to turn the battle from the gate will find all your need in him. In vv. 7 and 8 we have a terrible picture of widespread effects of strong drink; and in v. 9 the prophet recites the ribald remarks addressed to himself by the roisterers of those evil days. He replies that God would himself answer them by the stern accents of the Assyrian tongue, which would sound like stammering, v. 11; and this would befall them because they would not heed the wooing accents of his love, v. 12.

ISAIAH 28:14–29

Truth the Only Refuge. In the beginning of Hezekiah's reign the Jewish leaders had made an alliance with Assyria, on whom they relied to protect them against any and all foes. But the prophet told them plainly that they would be disappointed, and that when the Assyrian scourge passed through the land toward Egypt, it would involve them also in disaster, v. 18. Then he broke out with this sublime description of the only foundation of security that could never fail. The deep meaning of this prediction of the precious cornerstone is unfolded in later Scriptures, Matt. 21:42; Eph. 2:20; 1 Pet. 2:7. Christ was tried by Satan and by man. He is precious; he unites the walls of Jew and Gentile that were at right angles to each other. All our excuses and professions are too short and too narrow when God enters into judgment. Outside of Christ there is neither peace nor safety. See that thou buildest on him a holy character of gold, silver, and precious stones, 1 Cor. 3:10ff.

ISAIAH 30:1–17

Fatal Reliance on Human Aid. Toward the close of the eighth century B. C., Jerusalem sent ambassadors to seek help from Egypt against Assyria, in distinct defiance of God's repeated warnings. Isaiah denounced this as adding sin to sin. Even though their princes reached Zoan and Hanes, capital cities, and succeeded in their object, it would not help them. The beasts of burden might traverse the deserts with presents and bribes, but all would be in vain. These truths, however, were unpalatable, and the politicians endeavored to silence the prophet, vv. 9–11. All sin recoils on the sinner. At first his efforts seem to protect him; but soon the wall begins to bulge, then it totters, finally it falls. The true policy, urged by Isaiah in v. 15, would be to renounce these efforts for Egyptian help and return to rest in the loving care of God. In returning and rest they would be saved! Oh, that we were more quiet and calm in the face of danger, hushing our fears, stilling our throbbing hearts, and leaning back on the everlasting arms! God cannot fail you, ye fearful saints.

ISAIAH 30:18–33

The Goodness of God's Severity. Jerusalem refused God's invitation to return to him and rest; they preferred to trust in Egyptian cavalry. Their almighty Friend knew that this would end in disappointment, but he said that he would wait till they had exhausted every expedient and returned to him. Then would he be gracious and have mercy. The results of repentance and forgiveness are set forth with singular beauty: no more tears; great grace; answered prayer; divine teaching; guidance in the right way; no more idols; good harvests and rich pasturelands; the dumb creation benefiting by man's repentance. Thus in v. 26 we come to the light of the millennial dawn.

In vv. 27–33 Jehovah is represented as coming to avenge his people and to judge their enemies. Their welcoming gladness is compared in v. 29 to the songs of the Hebrew festivals. What a magnificent description in vv. 30 and 31 of Jehovah as a man of war! Every stroke he inflicted on the foe would awaken the music of tabrets and harps in the Temple at Zion. Tophet, near Jerusalem, was the place where refuse was burnt. The spiritual counterpart of its fire is ever burning up the waste products of men and nations.

ISAIAH 31:1—32:8

A Nobler Future for the Nation. Isaiah continues to denounce the contemplated alliance with Egypt. His compatriots put their trust in horses and chariots, and refused the help of their fathers' God. Yet was he not so wise as the Egyptians, and equally as strong! And were they not running a fearful risk in rejecting One who would not recall his words of threatened punishment to those who refused his help? At best, the Egyptians were men and not God, and their cavalry flesh. If only the people would trust him, God would defy their foes, as a lion defies a company of unarmed shepherds, 31:4. The mother bird hovers over her brood to protect it; so would he spread his covering wing over Jerusalem, v. 5. We may have deeply revolted; yet we may turn back to God with the certainty that he will receive and rescue us, v. 6.

Sennacherib fell by the sword of his sons. Compare v. 8 with 2 Kings 19:36, 37. How different is our glorious King, whose many-sided nature meets all our needs, 32:2. Before him all men are unveiled in their true characters. Only those who are royal in heart shall stand before him.

ISAIAH 32:9-20

The Fruits of Righteousness. When Christ's kingdom is set up, it will bring dismay to the poor children of fashion. For more days than there are in the year will they be troubled, v. 10, and will smite on their breasts in lamentation, v. 12. The prediction of vv. 15-20 includes Pentecost and looks forward to the era which lies immediately beyond this travail of the world. What is now reckoned as a fruitful field will be regarded as a barren forest in comparison with what shall then exist. Let us remember that righteousness must precede peace. See Matt. 5:24 and Heb. 7:2. When God's judgments are hurtling through the air, and proud cities are being leveled to the earth, let us take refuge in his loving care. In him are our safe dwellings and our quiet resting-places. But when the world is most unquiet, let us pursue our work of salvation; for when waters overflow the banks of the river, oxen and asses may still be sent forth to make furrows for the harvest seed.

ISAIAH 33:1-12

God Exalted in Judgment. Here we have the final prediction against Sennacherib. He had dealt very treacherously by returning against Jerusalem, though he had taken a heavy ransom to leave it unmolested, 2 Kings 18:16. In v. 2 Isaiah recalls the daily prayer offered by the priests in the Temple, when they heard of the steady advance of the foe. It was quite true that nations had fled before the dreaded Assyrian, v. 3; but in this case those precedents would be reversed, v. 4, because the Lord would appear for his people, v. 5. That was a sweet assurance that the prophet gave to Hezekiah in v. 6—to sustain his spirit through the strain of the invasion described in vv. 7 and 8. God always gives us a promise on the eve of trial. He victuals his ships ere he exposes them to the storm. Though God sometimes seems to sleep, yet when the hour strikes for the deliverance of his people, he will not tarry for a single moment. Be of good cheer; he will ride upon the wings of the wind to succor you!

ISAIAH 33:13-24

The Reward of the Righteous. The devouring fire and everlasting burnings of v. 14 are clearly the emblems of the Divine Presence. The righteous dwell in God as the bush which was baptized in the shekinah-glory and was not consumed. The fire of his holy presence makes them holy at the same time that it protects them from their enemies. Compare with Psalm 15. They are characterized by their walk, speech, the closed fist, the stopped ears, and the shut eyes. They dwell in heights which are inaccessible to the foe, and no oppressor can cut off their supplies of hidden manna or water of life. Hezekiah, Isaiah predicts in v. 17, would soon put off his sackcloth, and the citizens would cease to be penned up in a beleaguered city. They should recall the terror of that hour as a bad dream, recalled to be dismissed and forgotten. Zion had no river, but God would be all that a river was to other cities, without the disadvantages of navigable water which might serve for the passage of a hostile fleet. Be sure to make God your Judge, Lawgiver, and King. Then, notwithstanding that you limp in weakness, you shall gather your share in the great spoils of victory.

ISAIAH 34

Reaping the Whirlwind. This chapter is one prolonged description of the judgments which were to befall the nations at the hand of Assyria and Babylon. The imagery employed is borrowed from the destruction of the cities of the plain. Streams of pitch; dust of brimstone; the ever-ascending smoke of a furnace; the scream of the eagle, hawk, and owl; the invasion of palaces by the thistle; the howl of the wolf; the call of the jackal; the vulture with its mate—such are the illustrations employed to depict the scorching desolations which were impending. Edom or Idumea is especially mentioned as suffering these awful desolations because of her long-standing hatred of Israel. See Ps. 137:7; Ezek. 36:5; Lam. 4:21, 22. These terrible and graphic predictions have been literally fulfilled, but they foreshadow those further and eternal disasters which must overtake willful and designed rejection of the divine purposes and laws. Are not all nations at this hour standing before the Son of man and being judged? See Matt. 25:31ff.

ISAIAH 35

The Rejoicing of the Redeemed. God's judgments change Carmel and Sharon into a waste; but his blessing makes the wilderness and parched land as Carmel and Sharon. Where the smile of God rests, deserts sing and become carpeted with flowers. Your hands may be weak and your knees feeble, but when your helplessness invokes the help of God, he will begin to perform wonderful things that pass expectation. Say over and over to yourself: "My God will come: be strong, my heart, and fear not. He will come and save." Oh, for the quickened sense; the bounding leap of our nature lamed by the fall; the songs from lips that God will touch! Your dreariest desert shall become water springs; the mirage shall no longer disappoint; thirst shall be satisfied, and the dragons of the heart extirpated. Nothing can hurt us while we walk with God in holiness. Dreaded evils may threaten to cast their shadows on our path, but they shall not stay our songs as we come with singing unto the everlasting joy.

ISAIAH 40:1-8

The Cry of Jehovah's Herald. Voices are ever speaking to us from the infinite; let us heed them. (1) There is the voice of forgiveness, v. 2. Are you truly penitent? Have you put away your sin? Have you meekly accepted the chastening rod? Then be of good cheer; this promise is for you. The time of hard service as a conscript (the literal rendering) is accomplished, your iniquity is pardoned, you have received double for all your sins. God speaks comfortably to your heart, that you may be able to comfort others as he does you, 2 Cor. 1:4.

(2) The voice of deliverance, vv. 3, 4. Between Babylon and Canaan lay a great desert of thirty days' journey with mountain ranges, yawning gulfs. But when God arises to deliver his children who cry day and night unto him, crooked places straighten out, rough ones become smooth, and mountains disappear.

(3) The voices of decay, vv. 6-8. The one herald, speaking from his observation of human mortality, describes man and his glory as the "flower of the field." But in contrast to this, another voice seems to break in with the eternal Word of God, which stands forever. The precepts, promises, and invitations of the gospel are as sure as God's throne, 1 Pet. 1:25.

ISAIAH 40:9-17

Creator and Ruler of All the Earth. Zion is bidden to climb the highest mountain within reach, and announce the advent of the Savior-God. When all eyes are turned to behold him, expecting a mighty hero, lo, a shepherd conducts his flock across the wastelands, gathering the weakly lambs to his bosom and gently leading the ewes with their young. Do not be afraid of God; he has a shepherd's heart. Words can never tell out all his tenderness, his pitying, understanding love.

We are next conducted to the Great Sea, v. 12. Remember, says the prophet, that God's hands are so strong that the ocean lies in them as a drop of water in man's. He can place mountains in the scales he holds. So great is he that if all Lebanon's forests were laid as wood on his altar, and all its beasts were consumed as burnt sacrifices, it would not be sufficient to set forth his praise. And this God is our God forever and ever. The Creator of the ends of the earth is our Father.

ISAIAH 40:18-31

The Everlasting God the Giver of Strength. Day changes to night, and as the twilight deepens the stars come out in their myriads, v. 26. To the poetic eye of the watcher, they appear as a vast flock following the shepherd, who calls each by its name. Not one falls out of its place or is lacking. Will Jehovah do so much for stars and nought for men? Will he not have a name for each? Will he not guard and guide each? If he has sustained the orbs of light in their mighty rounds, will he fail the poor soul that clings to his feet?

They that wait on God change their strength. In their earliest days they rely on the energy and vigor of youth, on their blameless, unstained character, in the consciousness of their glorious manhood; but as years pass, they come to count all these as refuse in comparison with Jesus Christ the Lord, Phil. 3:8. Notice the order in v. 31! At first sight we should have expected that it would advance from walking to running, and so to flying. But that order is reversed. It is more difficult to walk than to mount! Every cyclist will tell you that the hardest task is to keep your cycle at walking pace.

ISAIAH 41:1-16

The Lord Upholdeth His Servant. The conception of this passage is superb. Jehovah is represented as summoning the earth to determine whether he or some idol of the heathen is the true God, vv. 4, 22, 23. The test proposed is a simple one! Which can most precisely predict the future? Not, as in Elijah's case, is the appeal made to fire, but to the fitting of prophecy with historical fulfillment.

While this great arbitration is in process, God turns with tender assurances to his own people. They were at this time captives in Babylon. They were poor and needy. They were surrounded by strong and crafty foes, against whom they were as powerless as a worm. But no height, however precipitous, or depth, however profound, could separate them from his love. Heart and flesh might fail, but he would strengthen; difficulties might appear insurmountable, but he would help. He does more. He takes his people, weak as worms, and makes them, if they but yield to him, sharp threshing instruments having teeth before which the powers of evil become as chaff. O man, listen to God saying, "I will make."

ISAIAH 41:17-29

What the Lord's Hand Does for the Needy. Life is not easy for any of us, if we regard external conditions only; but directly we learn the divine secret, rivers flow from bare heights, fountains arise in sterile valleys, and the desert blooms like the forest glade. To the ordinary eye there might appear no outward change in the forbidding circumstance; but faith's eye always beholds a paradise of beauty where other eyes see only straitened circumstances and a trying lot.

Once again our minds are brought back to the great convocation announced in the opening verses of the chapter. The idols are asked to say or do something to prove that they are divine. See vv. 21-23. But there is no response, with the result that a crushing verdict is passed on them as recorded in v. 24. On the other hand, the prophet of the Lord is prepared with his predictions of Cyrus, "the one from the east," (see v. 2 and 44:28), which would be fulfilled before that generation had passed away. Let us give heed to the sure word of prophecy, "as unto a light that shineth in a dark place," 2 Pet. 1:19.

ISAIAH 42:1-13

The Work of the Lord's Servant. We cannot doubt the application of this passage to our Lord, Matt. 12:18-20. The unobtrusiveness of his life and work was clearly demonstrated in every hour of his sojourn among men. He silenced those whom he healed. He stole away from the multitudes for prayer. He stayed in Galilee till his brethren were angry at his reluctance to show himself to the people. He did "not strive, nor cry."

How meek and lowly was our Lord! A "reed" is typical of a heart broken by unkindness or a sense of sin. The "smoking flax" cannot ignite, because it is hardly able to remain aglow. This is the symbol of one whose love is tardy and cold. But such our Lord does not ignore. He can use the commonest and most unlikely materials.

He is never discouraged and cannot fail; and since *he* cannot, neither shall the Church, nor shall we. His love and power are pledged to us. Let us sing to him and of him.

ISAIAH 42:14-25

A Deaf and Blind Messenger. There are times in our lives when God seems to hold his peace. Evil is rife, bad men prosper, society lies under the spell of vice. It is only temporary, however. Then God comes forth out of the silence and shows himself strong on the behalf of them whose heart is perfect toward him. He brings the blind "by a way that they knew not," and makes "crooked things straight."

These wonderful things are wrought not for the wise and holy alone, but for the blind and the deaf, who nevertheless desire to serve him. See v. 19. God's help is not conditioned by our merit, but by our faith. In the eyes of men we may be the least fit to claim divine succor. But our deficiencies and failures constitute our most eloquent claim; God knew what we were before he ever stooped to identify himself with us. He is pleased to help us "for his righteousness' sake." His name and character must be maintained. Therefore, he has magnified the Law and made it honorable by the matchless obedience and death of his only begotten Son. See Gal. 4:4, 5.

ISAIAH 43:1-13

Jehovah's Witnesses. We have still the convocation of mankind summoned to decide whether Jehovah or some idol god shall be recognized as the supreme deity. In the arena are rows of helpless images rich in paint and tinsel, but mute and helpless, vv. 8, 9. Jehovah, to vindicate his claims, calls into the witness box his Chosen People, that they may tell what they have known, tasted, and handled of the Word of life, v. 10.

This special function is not confined to the Hebrew race. By the express words of our Lord it is shared by the Church. See Acts 1:8. As our Lord bore witness to truth, his subjects are summoned to do the same. See 1 Tim. 6:13, 14; Rev. 1:5.

Let us witness to the love that never tires. "Fear not, thou art mine." Let us witness to a purpose that never falters, vv. 1 and 7. Let us witness to a deliverance that never disappoints. We are not saved from fire and water, but are delivered in the midst of them by the never-failing presence of our King. Let us ask for the Spirit of Truth to witness with us, Acts 5:31, 32.

ISAIAH 43:14-28

A Way in the Wilderness. Let us take care lest we thwart God's purpose in our lives. We were made to show forth his praise, v. 21; but we must beware of causing a revoking of his gracious purpose. See Num. 14:34. By prayerlessness, v. 22; by the neglect of little things, v. 23; by the lack of sweetness and tenderness in our

ISAIAH

disposition, v. 24. "Be not high-minded, but fear; for if God spared not the natural branches, take heed lest he also spare not thee," Rom. 11:20, 21.

On the other hand, directly sin is repented of and put away, it is blotted out, v. 25. It is persistence in sin that causes God to turn from us. If we forsake what is evil as soon as we are conscious of it, "the blood of Jesus Christ his son cleanseth us from all sin." It is blotted out as a cloud from the sky and no more remembered against us forever. This is done for God's own sake. The reason for our salvation and deliverance is not in us, but in him. The cross of shame and sorrow was his own expedient, and the Lamb in the midst of the throne is the emblem of the divine Atonement, which was commenced and finished by the inexplicable grace of God.

ISAIAH 44:1-11

"Beside Me There Is No God." What gracious promises are given throughout Scripture, not only to God's children, but to their seed! Here the thirsty soul, longing for love, sympathy, God, is promised an abundant supply. See John 4:13, 14; Rev. 22:17. But notice the extreme beauty of the further response which shall be made by the young followers of our Lord.

One shall say, "I am the Lord's," v. 5. What ecstasy such a declaration causes to a parent's heart! Young friends, do not be satisfied till you have confessed Christ. Say, "I am the Lord's." Another shall write on his hand, "unto the Lord"; that is, he shall dedicate his hand to do God's work in the world. Oh, to write a similar declaration on every member of our body!

Again we have the conflict with the idols of the heathen, vv. 6-11. But what chance have their followers when confronted by the glad and assured testimony of those who have seen the King in his beauty!

ISAIAH 44:12-20

The Folly of Idolatry. We are here conducted to a metal idol factory, v. 12. As we enter, we are forewarned that we shall find the workmen vain and their delectable things unprofitable. With this caution, we watch the image being made beneath the heavy blows of the hammer, wielded by the swarthy smith. After a few hours of work, he becomes tired and thirsty. Surely an idol can never impart perennial energy and help if its manufacturer is so easily exhausted.

Next, we are led into a factory of wooden idols, v. 13, where a carpenter is at work drawing a pattern on a block of timber. The floor is littered with shavings, and the idol that is to receive worship and exercise authority is handled very unceremoniously. Lastly we follow an individual into the forest where he saws part of a tree for firewood and the rest for his household deity. What folly! These men are hungry for some object of worship, but they feed their hunger on ashes; they cannot be made to realize that they are deceiving themselves. The true bread is Christ.

ISAIAH 44:21-28

The Promise of Redemption. What divine comfort there is in these gracious words! Notwithstanding all their wanderings and sins, the Chosen People were Jehovah's elect race. Nothing could make him forget them; he had redeemed them with the saving strength of his right hand. He could never forget *them,* but he would forget their sins. Their transgressions had melted into the blue azure of his love. If sought for, they could not be found. Nature was asked to be one great orchestra of praise. Notice that our redemption brings more glory to Jehovah than our undoing would.

In the following chapter, the people are assured that they would return from captivity to rebuild Jerusalem and reinhabit the cities of Judah. They probably expected that their return would be marked by miracles as marvelous as those through which their fathers emerged from Egyptian bondage. But God never repeats himself; his purposes would work out through a heathen monarch, Cyrus, whom God was preparing as the executor of his purpose, v. 28. "Deep in unfathomable mines of never-failing skill, he treasures up his bright designs, and works his sovereign will."

ISAIAH 45:1-13

Jehovah's Chosen Instrument. Cyrus is one of the noblest figures in ancient history. His character became a model for Greek youth in strength, simplicity, humanity, purity, and self-restraint. We have seen that Jehovah had assured his people that Jerusalem would be restored, 44:26. They probably expected a repetition of the Red Sea and the Exodus. But God does not repeat himself; and their deliverance from captivity was to be achieved through the victories that made Cyrus master of Babylon. See Ezra 1:1-4.

God's plans are achieved through individuals, whom he equips and raises up for their specific work. There is much in all our lives that we cannot account for, and which is due to the girding of the Almighty. We do not always recognize the real sources of our lives. They are hidden in God. He girds us though we do not know him. Let us not gird ourselves in our own strength, but stretch forth our hands unto him, sure that he will neither fail nor forsake. See John 21:18. They who thus utterly yield to God are bidden in the exercise of a daring faith to command, that is, to claim, his saving power.

ISAIAH 45:14-25

A Call to the Ends of the Earth. As the prophet reviews God's method of delivering his people —so unexpected and so wonderful—he cannot restrain the ejaculation, "Thou art a God that hidest thyself!" "Deep in unfathomable mines of never-failing skill, he treasures up his bright designs, and works his sovereign will." You do not see how God is going to save you; but most certainly his Angel will redeem you from all evil.

God contrasts himself with idols, v. 20. We can never seek his face in vain. They that trust in man or their own devices are doomed to disappointment; but faith and prayer make all the difference. He is "a just God and a Savior." This is the wonderful combination that the cross reveals. See Rom. 3:26; 1 John 1:9. Look to him and be saved. Even if you dwell in a far land or at the ends of the earth, and even if you can only look toward him with failing sight, remember that "there is life in a look." Dare to say, "In the Lord have I righteousness and strength." You have none of your own! Your strength is weakness! Your righteousness is full of flaws! Look to him, boast in him, and men shall come to you for your secret.

ISAIAH 46

God's Salvation Shall Not Tarry. Here is a startling contrast! Babylon is broken up. An invading army of stern monotheists have slain the idolatrous priests at their altars and are engaged in carrying out the idols for the bonfire. And as the Jewish remnant is witnessing the extraordinary spectacle, they are reminded that *their* God does not require to be borne. Nay, on the contrary *he* has borne his people from the earliest days and will continue to bear them till the heavens have passed away.

The contrast is a perpetual one. Some people carry their religion; others are carried by it. Some are burdened by minute prescriptions and an external ritual; others yield themselves to God, to be borne by him in old age as they were in the helplessness of childhood. They are persuaded that he will bear them as a man bears his son, in all the way that they go until they come to the prepared place. See Deut. 1:31; Isa. 63:9. God immediately responds to a trust like that, and his salvation does not tarry.

ISAIAH 47

The Penalty of Trusting in Wickedness. Babylon dwelt in careless security. She was given to pleasures, v. 8, and said in her heart that her vast crowd of astrologers, magicians, and priests would certainly warn her of impending evil and deliver her. But nothing could be more absolute than her fall. For centuries she has been buried under mounds of desolation, while the Hebrew people, whom she so cruelly oppressed, are the monument of God's preserving mercy. The fact is that Babylon exceeded her duty. She was used as Jehovah's chastising rod upon the Hebrews, but she was merciless in the extreme in her behavior and for this excess she suffered. Compare v. 6 with Zech. 1:15.

Notice the 4th verse. The prophet turns from the overthrow of the proud city to remind his people that Babylon's tribulation is due to the redeeming arm of God; and we must never forget that in the midst of her overthrow there was a thread of golden mercy. The love that brooded over Nineveh must have been there. See Jonah 4:10, 11.

ISAIAH 48:1-16

The Obstinate and Insincere Rebuked. We are meant to be for God's praise and glory; but we may delay the realization of his high purpose. Our neck iron, our brow brass, we trust in idols and refuse to open our ear. It is necessary, therefore, to send us to Babylon where, as in a furnace for silver, the dross and alloy are purged away. Many of us are in furnaces which have been rendered needful through our evil ways.

Nothwithstanding our sins, God comes to the furnace mouth and chooses us there. For his own sake, he does it that his name may not be polluted. He cannot give his glory to another. You cannot account for God's grace to you personally. He must have known all, from the first. Then dare to believe that the reason that prompted him at the first will suffice to the end. He is not "the son of man that he should repent." He who was the first will be the last. Jesus is Omega as well as Alpha, the end as well as the beginning! Fear not! See Rev. 1:17.

ISAIAH 48:17—49:13

"A Light to the Gentiles." The first division of this second part of Isaiah closes at 48:22, with the phrase "there is no peace unto the wicked."

The second division of Part 2 closes with a similar phrase, 57:21. The first division here ends with the proclamation for Israel to leave Babylon. They need never have gone there. If only they have been obedient in every particular, theirs would have been the happy lot of v. 18, as contrasted with v. 22. But even under such circumstances, in captivity and as slaves of the Chaldeans, the redeeming grace of God would triumph, 48:20; 49:5.

The second great division of Part 2 opens with 49:1. In their first and immediate reference, these verses evidently apply to our Lord. See Acts 13:47ff. In the mission of Jesus, the ideal of the Hebrew race was realized. As the white flower on the stalk he revealed the essential beauty and glory of the root, 49:6. See Hos. 11:1; Matt. 2:1, 2, 14, 15.

There is a secondary sense, also, in which the Christian worker may appropriate many things in this glowing paragraph. Our mouth must be surrendered to God, that he may use it for his own high purposes. But do not dread the shadow of his hand. It is the quiver case in which he keeps his chosen arrows against the battle!

ISAIAH 49:14-26

The Lord Cannot Forget His Own. These assurances were given to the chosen race on the eve of their return from Babylon. They were timid and reluctant to quit the familiar scenes of their captivity; they dreaded the dangers and privations of their way home, and questioned whether the great empire of their captors would ever let them go or allow their city to rise from its ruins. Therefore, the Lord's voice takes on a tone of unusual persuasiveness. Let us ponder his assurances of compassion and comfort, vv. 13, 15, 16.

He will lead us with a shepherd's care, v. 10. He will make obstacles subserve his purpose, v. 11. His love is more than motherhood, v. 15. He treasures the remembrance of his own, v. 16. Zion thinks herself cast away as a derelict, v. 14, but such is not the case. Even her broken walls are ever before God, with a view to their rebuilding, v. 19. God's love is stronger than our strongest enemies, vv. 25, 26. Let us hide in it, standing above the fears that compose the clouds of our soul, in the upper peaks of a strong faith.

ISAIAH 50

Help for Those Who Trust in Him. It is impossible for God to put away the soul that clings to him in penitence and faith. Heaven and earth may be searched, but no bill of divorce can be found. See Deut. 24:1. And he sends his great servant, our Lord, of whom this chapter is full, to deliver and assure our trembling faith.

Verse 4 can be translated, "Jehovah hath given me the tongue of them that are taught, that I may know how to sustain with words him that is weary.... He wakeneth mine ear to hear as they that are taught." This quality of teachableness was primarily true of Jesus. It was the habit of his human life to listen to the secret teaching of the Father, breathed into his heart. See John 8:28, 40. So also must we allow ourselves to be wakened by him, each morning, that we also may know how to help men more efficiently and tenderly.

From the first, Jesus knew that he must die. See Mark 10:34. But he did not turn back. See Heb. 10:5ff. Was not his choice abundantly vindicated? The Father who justified him was always near, John 8:29; 16:22. Let us who may be walking in darkness learn from our King to stay ourselves on God.

ISAIAH 51:1-11

"Awake, O Arm of Jehovah!" This chapter is extremely dramatic. We are conscious that we are nearing a revelation of unparalleled sublimity. As we hear the thrice "Hearken" in vv. 1-8, and the thrice "Awake," v. 9, which follows, we realize that we are traversing the entrance portico of a noble temple. When God says, "Hearken," it is for us to ask him to fulfill—"Awake!"

Recall the loneliness of Abraham. He was alone. Terah died, Lot dropped away, Hagar was thrust out, Isaac was laid on the altar, but the fire that burned in Abraham's heart only grew brighter. Do not despair if you are alone in your stand for God. One acorn, when the life of Nature touches it, may become parent to a forest. These exiled Jews hardly dared to hope that they could escape from their foes. The air was heavy with their revilings, but compare v. 8 with 50:9. With such assurances we may face a world in arms. The forces of evil are strong, but God is stronger. The clouds threaten, but the sun is shining. Don't forget the Lord thy Maker, thy Redeemer, thy Father! He cannot fail or forsake!

ISAIAH 51:12-23

"The Captive Exile Shall Be Loosed." During the Sepoy mutiny in India, when a number of English men and women were shut up in a quarter of Cawnpore, expecting a terrible death by assault or slow starvation, a torn page of the Bible

containing this passage was found on the street pavement and was of unspeakable comfort. Oh, the blessedness of appropriating the 16th verse! See 49:7.

We are too apt to forget that God pleads the cause of his people, even when they have sinned and have reduced themselves to sore straits, vv. 17 and 22. We think more of the earth than of the overarching skies; of the fading grass than of the tree of life; of man than of God. The near obscures the distant, and flaring earth lights obscure the shine of the stars! Root yourself in God! Think of him who sits at the right hand of the throne, the seat of resistless, ceaseless energy! Believe that God has placed himself between you and all enemies and circumstances which threaten. To fear all day is impossible in face of these paragraphs.

ISAIAH 52

"Thy God Reigneth!" It is not God that has become lethargic, but *we* that have slept and need to awake. Being awakened, we discover that two sets of attire are waiting for us. First, his strength, so that we may not be afraid of tens of thousands of people who set themselves round about; and secondly, the beautiful garments of our Lord's character. See Col. 3:9–17.

At last the climax of the long prophetic stairway is reached and the summons for the exodus from Babylon rings out, v. 11. It was God's return to the desolate city, vv. 2 and 8. The stately procession moves slowly and fearlessly. It is not the escape of a band of fugitive slaves, dreading pursuit and recapture, v. 12. Before it speed the heralds, appearing on the sky line as they ascend the mountains which surround the Holy City, publishing peace and salvation, v. 7. The central body is composed of white-robed priests, bearing with reverent care the holy vessels, v. 11, of which Nebuchadnezzar despoiled the Temple, but which Cyrus restored. See Ezra 1:7–11. Thus, also, the Church marches through the world.

ISAIAH 53

The Rejected and Suffering Redeemer. The common lot of man may be summed up in three words: suffering, sin, and death. Our Lord, the Divine Servant, presents a notable exception to the rest of the race; not in his sufferings, v. 3; not in his death, v. 9; but in his perfect innocence and goodness. His sufferings were due to sins not his own, Rom. 5:8. We must make his soul our guilt offering, v. 10. It is the same word as is used in Lev. 5:1–16.

Jesus shall one day be satisfied. In the glory that shall accrue to the Father; in the redemption of untold myriads; in the character of the redeemed; in the destruction of the results of the Fall, we shall hear his sigh of content and see the triumph on his face. We shall witness his transference of the kingdom to the Father, 1 Cor. 15:24. We shall behold the satisfactory termination of the mystery of evil. If he is satisfied, we shall be!

ISAIAH 54

The Wondrous Love of God. We have heard the exiles summoned to leave Babylon, and have beheld the Savior becoming the sin-bearer. Here our attention is recalled to the still desolate condition of Jerusalem. See Neh. 1:3; 2:3, 13–17. Jehovah says, "Sing," but Israel replies that she cannot sing so long as she lies desolate. In reply, God declares his inalienable love: he is their husband still and has sworn that the waters of death and destruction shall never be able to separate them from himself. The kindness of his mercy is everlasting, and his covenant of peace shall outlast the mountains and hills.

In the closing paragraph, vv. 11–17, we behold the chosen city emerging from her heap of ruins. Watched by the eye of the great Architect, wrought by unseen hands, tested by the line and plummet of righteousness, she arises to fulfill her mission to the world. To inspired hearts it seems as though her common stones are jewels. Her children are taught of the Lord. Every accusing voice is hushed. All weapons of destruction are impotent. The new Jerusalem seems to have come down from Heaven.

ISAIAH 55

The Free Offer of Pardoning Grace. "*The Prince of Life,*" v. 4, margin. Four times in the New Testament this title or its equivalent is applied to our Lord, and always in connection with his resurrection. See Acts 3:14, 15; 5:31; Heb. 2:9, 10; 12:2, where the words prince, author, and captain are various translations of the same Greek word. The meaning of the original word is "file leader." He leads out of death into life; out of defeat into victory; out of suffering into perfection; out of the sorrow and pain of discipline into the triumph of the sons of light.

The "everlasting covenant," v. 3. David's sin could not cancel the sure mercies of God. See 2 Sam. 7:14–16 and 23:5. God will never go back on that covenant which includes us! See Heb. 8. God's mercies in Christ are "sure." Listen! Come! Hear! We are not only forever safe, but we are provided against all want.

God's abundant provision is described under several terms: waters, wine, milk, wholesome and satisfying bread, the good, fatness, vv. 1, 2. We are blessed with all spiritual blessings in Christ, Eph. 1:3. And because God's thoughts and ways are not as ours, the result is the transformation of thorns into firs, and briars into myrtles.

ISAIAH 56

The Blessedness of Sabbath-keeping. The bright array of Messianic promises which occupied the preceding chapters is now followed by a portion of lesser interest, seeing that our attention is not now fastened on Christ, but on Israel. Birk calls this sermon "The Middle Ages of Delay," and says: "This new section of advice and warning belongs to the whole period from Isaiah to Christ. The like message applies now to the Church of Christ and its prospect of the Second Advent."

Special emphasis is laid on Sabbath-keeping because it was the special sign of God's connection with Israel. See Exod. 31:13-17; Ezek. 20:12. It was also a type and pledge of the redemption rest, soon to be brought in and perfected by Christ's finished work, Heb. 4:9, 10.

What an ideal is presented here for character and conduct! To keep God's rest in our heart—the rest of faith; to cease from ourselves; to be joined to the Lord by one Spirit; to minister to him; to love his name; to be his servants! What more could we imagine as characteristic of the Christian soul! Let us ask God to bring *us* to his "holy mountain" and to make *us* "joyful" in his "house of prayer."

ISAIAH 57

No Peace to the Wicked. A terrible portrayal is given here of the idolatries and impurities into which the Chosen People had fallen. These scenes under the oaks and in the valleys remind us of the invariable evils associated with idolatry which the great apostle has recorded in Rom. 1:23-28. They refused to retain God in their knowledge, and he gave them over to a reprobate mind; that is, he ceased to restrain them.

But amid the degenerate nation, there was a handful of elect souls; God is always careful against rooting up the tares, lest one stalk of wheat perish. Amid the destruction that must overtake the guilty land, they that trusted in him would not be overlooked. See vv. 13, 14.

With what comfort the chapter closes, v. 15ff. We may have been covetous and froward, and have deserved wrath and chastisement, but God will not always chide. Only return to him! He will revive your heart and "restore comforts" to you. He will heal where he has wounded and will bring you near, through the blood of the cross. See Eph. 2:16, 17.

ISAIAH 58

The Fast That God Has Chosen. The divorce between outward rites and inward piety has been the curse of every age. When the Pharisees were plotting our Lord's death, they refused to enter Pilate's hall. Not the bowed head, but the broken heart; not the sackcloth and ashes of the flesh, but the contrition of the soul is needed.

Notice the three paragraphs descriptive of the experiences of the devout and consecrated soul: (1) The conditions of blessedness, vv. 6, 7; (2) The successive items which go to make a blessed life, vv. 8-12; (3) The true Sabbath-keeping, vv. 13, 14. Primarily it is inward, not outward. Let us be on our watch against the entrance into our hearts of all thoughts that would break the holy inward calm. Remember to imitate Nehemiah's instructions, Neh. 13:16-22. Let the divine peace rule within and be as a sentinel keeping the outward gate, Col. 3:15; Phil. 4:7. Cease to follow your own ways, or find your own pleasures, or speak your own words. Delight yourself in God; so shall you sit with Christ in heavenly places and feed at the heavenly table.

ISAIAH 59:1-15

Iniquities Separate from God. Israel's sins, vv. 1-8. Much of our suffering in life results from our sins, which cut off God's health and help. Let us not blame Providence, but set ourselves to discover the cause of controversy. When the law courts—the fountains of justice—are demoralized, the community is in a hopeless condition, vv. 3, 4. Instead of stamping out evil in the egg, the sinful heart hatches it out, and it yields the poison of vipers, v. 5. Ah, the hapless state of the ungodly! Their feet, and their thoughts, and their paths are fatal to the peace of others and to their own. The way of peace can be entered only at the cross, and maintained only by constant watchfulness. See Luke 1:79.

Israel's confession, vv. 9-15. Here the stricken people pour out their complaint before God, confessing first the bitterness of their sufferings and then the blackness of their sins. The roar of the hungry bear for food and the dove's mourning for her mate, v. 11, are apt descriptions of the complaint of the penitent soul. It is a good

ISAIAH 59:16-21

The Divine Arm Brings Redemption. Israel's Savior. The almighty lover of souls is described as looking round to see if help were forthcoming from any other quarter; there being none, he girds himself for the conflict with the enemies of his people. He dons breastplate and helmet, clothing and cloak, and hastens to deliver, v. 17. This is surely a portrait of our Lord Jesus, who stands up to plead the cause and to achieve the redemption of the penitent and believing soul. When the enemy threatens to pour in like a pent-up stream, look to Jesus to raise the standard against him. Let him fight your battles! Let the blows that are meant for you be caught on his shield!

All parents and grandparents should ponder the precious promises of vv. 20, 21. As God gives us children, let us place our fingers on this sure word of promise and claim that it shall be literally fulfilled in children and children's children. In thousands of godly families there has been an unbroken succession of piety.

ISAIAH 60:1-14

The Lord Glorifies His People. From this chapter and onward, the prophet predicts the glories of the restored Hebrew people. In a secondary sense, they are also true of the Church, for we are "blessed with faithful Abraham." See Gal. 3:8, 9.

The summons to "arise" is addressed to Jerusalem. The seer beholds the flush of dawn on the eastern sky and bids the Holy City catch the earliest beams, vv. 1, 2. While darkness veils the lowlands, the dweller on the plains looks up to the heights of Zion, vv. 3, 4, and finds them bathed in the splendor of dawn. See 2 Cor. 3:18.

There is a marvelous attractiveness in real religion. Where that is present, men need no driving. From the Far East come the camels, laden with priceless treasures, and from the distant west the ships laden with costly merchandise. The wastes of many years are rebuilt by the labor of strangers, while kings vie with each other in ministering to the beauty of the chosen city. When you are right with God, he will raise up help from unexpected quarters and even from former foes, v. 14.

ISAIAH 60:15-22

"The Lord Shall Be Your Everlasting Light." What a graphic delineation is presented in these words of the privileges of the consecrated life! The Mighty One of Israel becomes its Savior. Thenceforth it is ever ascending in the scale of experience, exchanging the period of stone for that of iron, of iron for silver, and of brass for gold. Anxiety and depression are followed by long and happy years of fullness and joy. Violence and destruction, which, like vandals, hewed and burned, are replaced by salvation and praise. The Lord becomes the everlasting light, and the days of mourning are ended.

Do not think that such an experience is too good to last, and so beautiful that it must be evanescent. When once the dawn of perfect surrender and acceptance breaks, there is no sundown, no shadowed sky, no more sorrow or crying, no more heartbreak or hopelessness. The inheritance is forever! The branch is ever green! The strong nation is destined never again to become small!

ISAIAH 61

"The Acceptable Year of the Lord." Messiah's mission, vv. 1-3. At Nazareth our Lord applied these words to himself. Let us care for the outcasts as he did; but to do so, we need to be anointed with the Holy Spirit, who rested so mightily on him. The acceptable year is clearly that of Lev. 25:8-13. Our Lord, when quoting this, stopped at the comma, v. 2, because the day of vengeance is not yet. See Luke 4:19. Mark that it is only for a day! God not only delivers, but anoints and crowns.

Messiah's kingdom, vv. 4-9. In days yet future, the ruined cities of Palestine shall be restored. In a spiritual sense, we also may appropriate this promise. When we receive the Pentecostal gift, we also witness the restoration of the wastes which our sins have caused in our own lives and in the lives of others. Let us clasp to our hearts vv. 7-9.

Messiah's joy, vv. 10-11. Jesus is the true bridegroom of the soul; and we may appropriate our side of these happy words. Note this combination of imputed and imparted righteousness. The one is put on as a garment, v. 10; the other blossoms out from within, v. 11. Oh, that from our lives God would cause righteousness and praise to spring forth!

ISAIAH 62

The Land of Beulah. The Intercessor, vv. 1-4. Messiah is speaking here. Throughout the ages, he ever lives to make intercession. He asks that his Church may be one, that the heathen may be given him for his inheritance, and that Israel may be restored. It is the cry of the unresting Savior. When Jesus pleads for thee, poor soul, thou canst not be desolate and forsaken. God loves, though all hate; God delights, though all abhor; God remains, though all forsake.

Intercessors, vv. 5-7. The Great High Priest calls us to be priests. The unresting Lord calls on us not to rest. He says, "Watch with me." He gives us rest from sin and sorrow, that we may not rest from prayer. We must take no rest and give God no rest. We are to become God's "remembrancers," v. 6, margin.

The divine answer, vv. 8-12. To the prophet's mind the prayer is already answered as soon as spoken. Already the highway must be prepared for the return of the exiles. So to us, who have lain among the ashes, salvation comes apace. Make ready to trail thy Deliverer! Then learn to become the salt and benediction of others!

ISAIAH 63:1-9

The Mighty Savior. For long years there had been virulent hostility between Israel and Edom. It began when Esau and Jacob were lads. It broke out in bitterness when Edom denied Israel the right of passage, Num. 20:20, 21. When Babylon had triumphed over Jerusalem, Edom urged that her walls should be leveled to the ground, Ps. 137:7.

How great the change pictured here! The prophet stands at the division of the two countries, looking south, from the foothills of Judah across the sandy waste. In the distance he beholds the mighty Warrior coming up from Edom, his garments wet, not with his own blood, but with Edom's, henceforth to stand as sentinel between Edom and Israel, so that nevermore need Israel fear invasion.

If Edom stands for sins of passion or for the hatred of unscrupulous foes, see how safe and blessed you are. Jesus, mighty to save, stands between you and your besetting sins, between you and your fears, between you and the power of the adversary, v. 9. "Mention the lovingkindnesses of the Lord!"

ISAIAH 63:10-19

Salvation Obstructed by Rebellion. The exhortation of the apostle against grieving the Holy Spirit is based on v. 10. See Eph. 4:30. There is no limit to the gracious work which the Holy Spirit will do in and for us, if only we will take jealous care of our behavior toward him. Be specially heedful about thy speech! The least uncharitableness hurts him, as frost the spring blossoms.

But God never forgets the blessed past and labors to restore it. See what he will do! His power shall work through a human wrist, v. 12. Before him the waters part and leave a path for his chosen. All that would cause us to stumble is taken out of the way and we are led as on a level plain. As cattle descend into the hollows of the hills at noon, to escape the sultry heat, so will God's Spirit cause us to rest. Oh, claim that these promises be realized! He is Father, Redeemer, the Eternal, the Lover of souls! Even when we believe not and have forfeited all claim on him, he remaineth faithful and cannot deny himself!

ISAIAH 64

A Cry for Pardon. The great past, vv. 1-5. We are introduced to the prophet's oratory and hear the outpourings of his heart. As he recalls the story of bygone days, he asks that God would do as he had done. It is as easy for God to rend the heavens as for us to tear a piece of cloth. Great mountains of difficulty dissolve before him, as a pyramid of snow in a thaw. God works while we wait. When there is no sign of his help, he is hastening toward us. If you go out to meet him, he will quicken his pace and run to embrace you. These are God's ways and in them there is everlasting continuance. See Mal. 3:6.

Confession and prayer, vv. 6-12. The leper, the foul garment, the fading leaf fleeing before the autumn gusts—such emblems become us. If our righteousnesses are black, what must not our sins be! We need him who comes not with water only, but with water and with blood. See 1 John 5:6. Perhaps our greatest sin is our prayerlessness. We do not stir ourselves up to it. God cannot "refrain" his mercy if we cannot refrain our tears!

ISAIAH 65:1-12

A Seed Rescued from Destruction. The prophet now enumerates the reasons that forced the Lord to turn aside from the Chosen People and call in the Gentiles to occupy the place and perform the mission which they had despised and forfeited. Paul makes memorable reference to this passage. See Rom. 10:20, 21. Their gardens were scenes of debauchery; their altars were covered by polluting engravings; they practiced necromancy in the graveyards, and ate swine's flesh, vv. 3, 4. Fortune and destiny were their chosen deities, v. 11, margin. While professing greater holiness than others, the land was filled with abominations.

But the Lord ever discriminates between the righteous and the wicked. Did he not spare Noah and Lot and Caleb? There has always been a faithful remnant, and these become the seed germs of a new nation. Ponder vv. 8–10. Then ask that your life may be like the new young grapes of the vineyard, on which the blessing of God rests!

ISAIAH 65:13–25

A New Earth for God's Servants. Notice the wide difference that religion makes to the soul. The children of God are secured against the evils which visit all others. *They* eat; *they* drink; *they* rejoice; *they* sing; *they* are called by another name, vv. 13–15.

Behold a new creation, vv. 17–25! The present dispensation is ended. Jerusalem, restored to her former glory, sings for joy; and her rejoicing sends a thrill of joy through the nature of God. Long years of life and security of tenure are granted again to man. The red rapine of the forest is ended, for creation is emancipated from its bondage and participates in the glorious liberty of the sons of God. Peace shall reign in the forest glades, never again to abdicate her throne, v. 25. But, best of all, there shall be such unity between man and God that prayer will be anticipated, and the pleading soul shall be conscious of the listening ear of God. Hasten, O day of days, for which creation and the saints groan with inexpressible desire!

ISAIAH 66:1–14

God's People Made a Blessing. The prophet forecasts the advent of a new day, when places and rites would be comparatively unimportant compared with the condition of the heart, vv. 1–4. The opening words were quoted by Stephen when announcing the substitution of spiritual worship for the system which it superseded. See Acts 7:48, 49. What is the outward rite to God when the spirit has fled? It was all one to him whether a man killed a lamb in the Temple, or broke a dog's neck on his farm. His chosen home is not in ornate temples, but in contrite hearts!

The blessedness of God's people is depicted in glowing words, vv. 5–14. God will appear, to the joy of his people and the recompense of their foes. Those times will be characterized by great revivals, and souls will be easily born into the heavenly kingdom. The Jew and Gentile will meet like confluent streams in one blessed channel. But, above all, we shall become aware of the motherhood in God's nature: "as one whom his mother comforteth," v. 13.

ISAIAH 66:15–24

All Flesh Shall Worship the Lord. The prophet makes it clear that whatever blessings accrue in the golden future, they will be apportioned to those alone who are the Israel of God, not merely by descent but in heart and life. They must be what the apostle describes in Phil. 3:3. Those who were bent on practicing idolatrous rites, such as passing in procession, with priests as teachers, through gardens and groves devoted to impurity, or who by partaking of the flesh of animals forbidden in the Levitical law had become as Gentiles, must suffer with the heathen.

Verse 19 suggests that the restored Jewish remnant are to become the future missionaries of the world. The book closes with a vision of the Holy City as the focus and center of the religious life of mankind. It is as though, like John, Isaiah beheld her descending from God out of Heaven, with wide-open gates, through which the kings of the earth bring their glory and honor, v. 20. The lot of all enemies of goodness is depicted in the ever-burning fires of Tophet—the rubbish heaps of which are significant of uselessness, v. 24.

THE BOOK OF
JEREMIAH

THE PROPHET OF JUDAH'S DOWNFALL AND RESTORATION

I. DENUNCIATION OF JUDAH *1—33.*
- A. The prophet's call and commission *1.*
- B. The nation's apostasy *2—20.*
- C. The sins of her leaders *21—23.*
- D. The impending judgment *24—29.*
- E. The promise of restoration *30—33.*

II. THE INFLICTION OF JUDGMENT *34—45.*
- A. The immediate occasion of judgment *34—38.*
- B. The destruction of Jerusalem *39.*
- C. The wretched condition of the remnant *40—45.*

III. PROPHECIES AGAINST THE NATIONS *46—51.*
- A. Egypt *46.*
- B. Philistia *47.*
- C. Moab, Ammon, and Edom *48:1—49:22.*
- D. Syria and Elam *49:23-39.*
- E. Babylon *50, 51.*

APPENDIX (from 2 Kings 24:18—25:30). *52.*

INTRODUCTION

Jeremiah was of priestly descent and was born at Anathoth, a Levitical city a few miles northeast of Jerusalem. His commission was given him in very early life, and continued through the reigns of five kings for forty troubled years. He had neither wife nor child. His love was concentrated on his people, who ill requited it. The men of Anathoth sought his life. He was assailed with misrepresentation, bitter persecution, and murderous hate. He nearly lost his life under the displeasure of the king and princes, at whose command he was cast into a miry dungeon. He lived to see a faint gleam of returning prosperity, overcast by the crimes of Ishmael and his fellow-conspirators.

He was a sensitive, delicately organized man, to whom it must have been a matter of peculiar trial to be called upon to play so prominent a part in those dark and stormy times, and to be "as an iron and brazen wall against the whole land." But he is an evidence of what may be done by a man in whom the Spirit of God resides in mighty, living force. Tradition states that he died in Egypt, stoned by his fellow-countrymen. It has been often said that there are few Old Testament saints who afford more points of likeness to our Lord than does Jeremiah.

COMMENTARY

JEREMIAH 1

Courage Promised to a Fearful Messenger. God has a distinct purpose for each life, and our one aim should be to discover and work out his plan. See Ps. 139:16; Gal. 1:15, 16. The sanctification here referred to applies to office rather than to character, and means "set apart." See John 17:19. Jeremiah was very young and shrank from the responsibility of the great mission entrusted to him. Thus it has been with the noblest, Exod. 4:10. But that is godly fear indeed which casts us back on God. He never gives a commission without assuming the responsibility of its execution in, with, or through, us. Powers of utterance are specially his gift, Isa. 6:7; Acts 6:10; 1 Cor. 1:5. The almond tree in Hebrew is the wakeful tree. It awakes from the winter sleep earlier than others, flowering in January and fruiting in March. It indicated the swiftness of God's movement. The boiling pot is the symbol of war. The promises of vv. 18, 19 are very precious to all who are called to stand in the breach and charge men with their sins.

JEREMIAH 2:1-8, 26-32

Ungrateful Forgetfulness. God regarded Israel as his bride who had responded to his love, or as a vineyard and cornfield which were expected to yield their firstfruits in response to the careful cultivation of the owner. Why had they failed to respond? For the answer, let us question our own hearts. What marvels of perversity and disappointment we are! Who can understand or fathom the reason of our poor response to the yearning love of Christ! The heathen, in their punctilious devotion and lavish sacrifices at their idol shrines, may well shame us. The root of the evil is disclosed in v. 31. We like to be lords, to assume and hold the mastery of our lives. But God has been anything but a wilderness to us. He has given us ornaments, and we owe to his grace the garments of righteousness which he has put on us. In return we have forgotten him days without number, v. 32. Let us ask him to call us back—nay more, to draw us by the chains of love.

JEREMIAH 3:11—4:2

Pleading with Faithless Children. The people of the northern kingdom, to whom this appeal is especially addressed, were more excusable than Judah, because their privileges had been less. God judges us according to our opportunities. How precious the invitation and promise of v. 12! Confession is an essential condition that must be fulfilled by us. See 1 John 1:9. Zion shall yet be the center of a restored Israel, vv. 14 and 18. In vv. 21-25 the voices of the people in confession and prayer mingle with Jehovah's encouraging their return. When we lie down in brokenhearted shame and penitence, we are very near to being lifted to the bosom of God. Compare Jer. 3:25 with 4:1. The return of the

Chosen People to the God of their fathers will be the cause of revival and quickening throughout the earth. Compare Jer. 4:2 with Rom. 11:12.

JEREMIAH 5:1-6, 19-31

Widespread Corruption. Diogenes, the cynic, was discovered one day in Athens in broad daylight, lantern in hand, looking for something. When someone remonstrated with him, he said that he needed all the light possible to enable him to find an honest man. Something like that is in the prophet's thought. God was prepared to spare Jerusalem on lower terms than even Sodom, and yet he was driven to destroy her. Both poor and rich had alike "broken the yoke, and burst the bonds." The description of the onset of the Chaldeans is very graphic. They settle down upon the land as a flock of locusts, but still the Chosen People refuse to connect their punishment with their sin. It never occurred to the Chosen People that the failure of the rain, the withering of their crops, and the assault of their foes were all connected with their sin. There is nothing unusual in this obtuseness, for as we read the history of our own times, men are equally inapt at connecting national disaster with national sin.

How good it would be if the national cry of today were that of v. 24: "Let us now fear the Lord our God." Notice the delightful metaphor of v. 22. When God would stay the wild ocean wave, a barrier of sand will suffice. The martyrs were as sand grains, but wild persecutions were quenched by their heroic patience.

JEREMIAH 8:4-22

False Promises of Peace. This chapter is filled with denunciation of the unreasonable and infatuated obstinacy of Israel. As the horse rushes madly to the fight, so were the people set on evil. The very birds that were sensitive to the laws of migration and obeyed the call of the sunnier clime were more responsive than the Chosen People. God often calls us out of the stormy winter blasts to lands of sunny fellowship, but we will not heed. From v. 10 onward we have a description of the desolation about to visit the land. Notwithstanding the promises of false prophets, the invader overran the country and the exiled people might readily begin to question why such a fate had befallen them. To this there was but one answer. Their sin had cut them off from God's protecting care. Is not this the reason why harvests pass and summers end, and the years roll on, and still you are not saved? There is balm for your wounds and a physician for your healing, but you do not avail yourselves of them. God's love is powerless, however greatly he desires to help you, until you return. The father would do anything for the prodigal, but he has no chance so long as the prodigal remains in a distant land.

JEREMIAH 9:1-16

National Perversity. Verses 1-6: Once the voice of joy and thanksgiving had been heard in Jerusalem, but now on every side there was bloodshed, and the patriot-prophet could only weep incessantly over the slain. A lodge in the wilderness seemed preferable to the most luxurious mansion in the city. Solitude would be better than association with the ungodly perpetrators of such crimes. Yet we must not go out of the fray so long as our Captain wants us to remain in it, in dependence upon him.

Verses 7-16: What a magnificent description of the effect of God's judgments on the land! No bird, no beast, no lowing of cattle, but jackals playing over the ruins of Jerusalem! However fast we shut our doors and windows, death enters our homes. Neither palace nor cottage is exempted. There is no escape for young or old from the judgments of God, except in penitence and faith. The secret of national decay and overthrow is the same in all ages. The tree is rotten at the core before it falls beneath the hurricane. Let us turn to 1 Corinthians 1:18, which belongs to this chapter, and learn how little the wisdom and might of the world can avail us in the dread hour of universal desolation. Stand with the Crucified and glory in his cross; be content to bear his reproach and shame, that you may become a son of the resurrection, and be accounted worthy to escape those things that must come to pass, and at last stand before him.

JEREMIAH 10:1-10, 19-25

The Folly of Idolatry. Verses 1-10: We are here introduced into an idol factory. Contrasted with the manufactured idols is the majesty of our God. There is none like him. His name is great in might, he is the King of the nations, the true and living God, and the everlasting King! Christian, fear not or be dismayed when enemies plot against you. It is a vain device that they frame. To hide in God is a sure defense from all that man can do for our hurt. O thou true and living Savior, in thy wounds harried and faithful souls become strong and brave again.

Verses 19-25: The prophet now bids the people prepare for their captivity. Their city would be as when a shepherd removed his slight and insubstantial tent, leaving no trace.

JEREMIAH

But Jeremiah's soul is lacerated and torn with the message he must needs announce. Are we called to be shepherds? Let us see to it that we seek the Lord; so only shall our flocks not be scattered, v. 21. Are we in perplexity as to our path in life? It is not for us to direct ourselves, but to look up for God's sure guidance, which will be given to the soul that waits for it, v. 23. Are we being corrected? Let us be patient; it is only when we endure without complaining that our trial works out the highest good, and God will not give us more than we can bear, v. 24.

JEREMIAH 11:1–20

The Penalty of a Broken Covenant. This and the following two chapters belong to the earlier ministry of Jeremiah, when he still dwelt in his native home of Anathoth. The prophet refers to the covenant which had been lately renewed by Josiah, 2 Kings 22 and 23, and quotes largely from the book of Deuteronomy, which had been recently read in the hearing of the people. To that covenant the prophet reverently gives his endorsement, v. 5. His amen reminds us of him who is God's Amen, and in whom all the promises of God are ratified forever, 2 Cor. 1:20. Shall we not learn, like our Lord in Matthew 11:26, to look into the Father's face and say, "Even so"? We must do so, that one day we may join with the redeemed in crying, "Amen, Alleluia," Rev. 19:4.

The repeated relapses of Israel into idolatry were in part due to the licentious rites associated with such worship. The people were seduced from their allegiance to Jehovah by the fascination of passion; and herein we are reminded of the many times that we have been beguiled into sinful thoughts and imaginings in spite of God's earnest solicitations and protestation, "rising early and protesting." As long as the soul is wedded to its evil ways, it is impervious to the entrance of God's light and love. "There is a sin unto death," says the apostle, "I do not say that he shall pray for it," a saying which is closely akin to the solemn prohibition of v. 14, "Therefore pray not thou for this people, neither lift up a cry or prayer for them."

JEREMIAH 13:1–11, 20–25

The Parable of the Girdle. This parable of the girdle may really have been transacted. By some such striking symbol before them, the attention of the people must have been powerfully arrested. Or it may be that this is only a vivid style of presentation. Whichever it is, the chief idea is the intimacy of relationship between the Chosen People and their God, v. 11. Oh, that he would cause us to cleave to him! The degradation of the best produces the worst, and nothing more strikingly sets forth the condition to which those may sink who have abused the highest possibilities than the condition of this marred and profitless girdle. Let us beware! Since capable of God's best and highest, we are also liable to the weeping and wailing and gnashing of teeth.

Jerusalem is personified and asked where was the beautiful flock of sister and daughter towns which had gathered under her lead. They had been destroyed, and their people were in captivity. Their destruction had come from those who had been allies and friends, v. 21; but their sin was so deeply seated and inveterate that such a fate was inevitable. There was no hope of reformation, v. 23. It was easier to expect a Negro to become white or for a leopard to change his spots than that Israel should do good. Only Christ can do this for us. He can with a word arrest a Niagara in its fall and bid it leap back. His grace can cause the leprosy of inbred sin to cease its hold, never again to pollute the soul.

JEREMIAH 17:1–14

Human and Divine Help Contrasted. The Jews were always seeking alliance either with Egypt or Babylon. What was true of them applies to us all; but we cannot depend upon human aid without departing from the Lord. The "heath" is probably the juniper, a lonely tree, dwelling in arid wastes, unvisited by dew. The soul that rests on God is watered from his throne. The roots of such are fed from the hidden springs of eternity. The heart is "deceitful"; it tends constantly to substitute the arm of flesh for the living God. "Desperately wicked" means "incurably sick." It was the ancient notion that the partridge stole the eggs of other birds and hatched them as her own. The covetous man is sure to reap disappointment. He steals other people's goods, but is driven off the nest before they hatch out for the benefit of himself. God's glorious throne is a defense to all who trust him, while those who depart from him shall be forgotten, as a sentence written in the sand is obliterated by the next puff of wind. Contrast Job 19:23, 24.

JEREMIAH 23:1–12, 23–32

Shepherds That Mislead God's Flock. It is God's purpose to care for his people through shepherds (pastors) who are responsible to him. Jesus our Lord is the Branch into which we may be grafted. He is our King who saves us and clothes us with his own spotless righteousness. God finds us in him, Phil. 3:9. Because he reigns, we are saved and dwell in safety. When we are brought into contact with false shepherds, whether the failure be in doctrine or example, let us ask for the broken heart of v. 9.

God is everywhere present; as the latter paragraph indicates, he is near at hand to overhear the blasphemy of those who deride religion, and to be a very present help in time of trouble. If he fills Heaven and earth, can he not fill thy heart? If his Word is like fire, let it cleanse thee! If it as a hammer, let it pulverize thy pride! Let those of us who assay to teach and preach not steal our words from our neighbors, or utter our own, but receive them from the source of all truth.

JEREMIAH 24

Two Baskets of Figs. These two baskets represent the different fates that overtook the people at the fall of Jerusalem. The good figs in the first were those who were taken to Babylon with Jeremiah. It was "for their good" that they were transplanted, v. 5. How often we are led into captivity for the same reason. With bitter regrets we turn our backs on our early home, the scenes of our youth, and the faces we have loved. Sometimes we are carried into a strange land, where we find it impossible to sing the Lord's song. But in the absence of all creature aid we find God drawing near to substitute restoration for destruction, building up for pulling down, and planting for uprooting.

Have we profited by our discipline? If so, we are as the ripe figs of June, sweet to the taste of the owner who searches beneath the leaves of profession. Let those who congratulate themselves on their immunity from the troubles that have overtaken others ponder vv. 8-10. In the light of Hebrews 12:9, immunity from chastisement is not to be sought after. The residue of the Jews drifted to their hurt. See Jer. 41 and 42.

JEREMIAH 31:1-9, 15-34

An Everlasting Love. It is all-inclusive: "all the families of Israel." It is patient under provocation. During forty years it bore with Israel. It has a drawing-power which overcomes our obduracy. It longs to restore the old joyous confidence and freedom: "thou shalt go forth in the dances of them that make merry." It will never rest till it has broken down misunderstandings and alienation, so that even Ephraim shall propose to worship at Mount Zion. It meets the heart: "they shall come with weeping." It sets the blind by rivers of waters, and the blind and the lame in a straight way. The effect of such love is still further described in vv. 18, 19—we bemoan our sins with profound remorse. These words, which were so sweet to the prophet, v. 26, are yet to be fulfilled; but in the meantime the covenant is for us all, and each one may claim the fulfillment of the "I wills" of vv. 33, 34. See Matt. 26:28; Heb. 8:8.

JEREMIAH 35

A Lesson from the Rechabites. Among the refugees from the neighboring country who sought asylum within the walls of Jerusalem was a group of Arabs, known as Rechabites. Probably they encamped in one of the open spaces. They clung tenaciously to the regulations promulgated by Jonadab some 300 years before. See Judges 1:16; 2 Kings 10:15; 1 Chron. 2:55. They drank no wine, did not cultivate the ground, and lived in tents. We do well not to touch alcohol; not to strike our roots too deeply into this world, where we are pilgrims and strangers; and to cultivate the pilgrim spirit, which looks for and travels toward the city that hath foundations. Israel had not been as true to the divine precepts as the Rechabites to those of their founder. Therefore, the Chosen People would be dispossessed and scattered, while the Rechabites have preserved their independence to the present day. Obedience is the only source of permanence. "He that doeth the will of God abideth for ever."

JEREMIAH 36

A Vain Attempt To Destroy God's Word. These written words had been directly given from God. The fast was instituted to seek divine help in the approaching conflict with Nebuchadnezzar. But of what good is a fast while the evils of apostasy and disobedience are unredressed? It was against these that Jeremiah protested; and his words were read to a vast concourse of people by Baruch his faithful friend. It was the month of December, and the royal chamber was warmed by a brazier of burning charcoal. As Jehudi read, the godless king cut the roll with a penknife and consigned it to the fire. All down the ages false priests have dealt thus with the Word that condemned them. But a sailor does not escape shipwreck by destroying the chart which indicates the rocks on which he is drifting. God's words are eternal, though the material on which they are written may perish. He who rejects God's truth does so at his peril, while God hides his faithful servants in the secret of his presence, secure from the attacks of enemies.

THE LAMENTATIONS
OF JEREMIAH

COMMENTARY

LAMENTATIONS 3:22–36

The Meaning of Affliction. This book is remarkable for its variety of touching images. The prophet seems to stand amid the ruins of city and Temple, burned with fire, strewn with the ashes of his people. This paragraph, however, is in marked contrast to the rest of the book, containing, as it does, a gleam of hope. If only we would turn from our griefs to the mercies, compassions, and goodness of the Lord, there would be light in our darkest dungeons. It is good to hope and quietly wait; to take Christ's yoke and learn of him; to keep silent in submission and faith. God cannot cast off. He does not willingly afflict; he has no sympathy or pleasure in turning a man aside or subverting his cause. Let us be at least sure of this, that the Lord will neither cast out nor cast off. He may hide his face for a moment, but with everlasting kindness he will have mercy, according to the multitude of his compassions.

THE BOOK OF
EZEKIEL
THE PROPHET OF ISRAEL IN EXILE

I. PROPHECIES REGARDING ISRAEL   *1—24.*
- A. The prophet's call and commission   *1—3.*
- B. The siege of Jerusalem   *4, 5.*
- C. Israel past and present   *6—24.*

II. PROPHECIES REGARDING THE NATIONS   *25—32.*
- A. Ammon, Moab, and Philistia   *25.*
- B. Tyre and Sidon   *26—28.*
- C. Egypt   *29—32.*

III. PROPHECIES REGARDING ISRAEL'S FUTURE   *33—48.*
- A. The fall of Jerusalem   *33:1—34:10.*
- B. The restoration of Israel   *34:11—39:29.*
- C. The new Temple   *40—48.*

INTRODUCTION

Ezekiel's name means, "God will strengthen." Like Jeremiah, he was a priest as well as a prophet. He lived among the Jews who were carried away captive by Nebuchadnezzar and settled on the river Chebar, in the north of Mesopotamia. He began to prophesy about six years before Jerusalem was destroyed, and was therefore contemporary with Jeremiah, prophesying partly before and partly after the destruction of Jerusalem.

COMMENTARY

EZEKIEL 1:1–21

A Vision of God's Majesty. A dark storm cloud approached the prophet, from which an incessant blaze of lightning scintillated. As it drew near, the forms of four living creatures became visible, combining, under various figures, intelligence, strength, patience, and soaring aspiration. The wheels were evidently symbolical of the cycles of divine providence, which cooperate with the ministers of the divine will. The slab of blue expanse supported a human semblance, suggestive of that great later event— God manifest in the flesh. The whole conception impresses us with the reality, order and majesty of the Eternal God. Those holy beings surely represent the intelligent company of innumerable angels and servants, while the wheels represent the material creation. All these are sent forth to minister to the heirs of salvation. Angels and Nature minister to us if we are in union with God. All things serve the servants of the Most High.

EZEKIEL 2:1—3:11

A Hard Commission. The people were impudent and stiff-hearted; their words as briars and thorns; their speech like the poison of scorpions. But the prophet was commissioned to go on with his divine mission, undeterred by their opposition. Under such circumstances we must be sure of a "Thus saith the Lord." But no man can stand against the continual opposition of his fellows unless his strength is renewed, as Ezekiel's was, by eating that which God gives. "Open thy mouth, and eat that I give thee," 2:8. Let us specially consider the divine denunciations of sin, that our words may be sharper than any two-edged sword. Nothing makes us so strong as feeding perpetually upon the roll of the Book, and especially on the Word (Christ) within the words. We must eat the flesh and drink the life of the Son of man if we are to deal aright with the needs of the sons of men.

EZEKIEL 3:12–27

The Watchman's Responsibility. He was bitter because of his message, but hot because God's fire was burning within him. It is a blessed thing for preacher, leader, or Christian worker when the hand of God is strong upon the soul. But whatever your inward condition, you will never be able to do your best work unless you can sit where the people sit. In other words, you must take their attitude, know by experience their circumstances, and share their lot. We must live very near to God, or we shall never hear the word of his mouth. There is no other way of obtaining messages that will effect his purpose. Ponder again v. 17. In v. 20 God is said to lay a stumblingblock only in the sense that he has constituted the world in that way. When the prophet went forth into the plain, God revealed himself. Whether he bids us go to the plain or shut ourselves in the house, the place of obedience and duty will ever be the right one for the manifestation of his glory and the communication of his message. The secret of a successful ministry is to be absolutely yielded in thought and in speech to God.

EZEKIEL 11:5-25

A New Heart Promised. The Spirit of God led the prophet to the east gate of the Temple, where the shekinah had settled, Ezek. 10:19. There he uttered the divine verdict on the priesthood. They had ridiculed Jeremiah's letter to the captives, among whom Ezekiel lived, Jer. 29:1, and had made merry at his comparison between the city and a caldron, Jer. 1:13. It was to these scornful men that Ezekiel uttered the scathing denunciations of vv. 7-18. The sudden death of Pelatiah, the ringleader of the scorners, gave terrible emphasis to the prophet's words. Ezekiel was told to look for his true kinsmen not among the doomed priesthood, but among his fellow-exiles whom they of Jerusalem despised. Spiritual ties must supersede natural ones when the two clash. They might be far removed from the outer Temple, but God would be their asylum and sanctuary. What a sweet promise v. 16 provides for those who are compelled to go far from home! They may always meet their dear ones in God. Note the inclusive promise of v. 19—unity, newness, and sensitiveness to the least touch of the divine nature.

EZEKIEL 14:1-6, 12-23

Reaping as We Sow. It is useless to approach God with prayers and inquiries for guidance as long as our hearts are filled with secret sins and cherished idols. If we regard iniquity in our hearts, God cannot hear us. It often happens when men purpose a certain evil course that everything seems to favor them. For a striking example of this, see 1 Kings 22:6, 15. The second paragraph describes the inveteracy of their sin. Jeremiah had affirmed that Judah's guilt was too great to be pardoned upon the intercession of Moses or of Samuel, Jer. 14:2; 15:1. Ezekiel adds three other revered names. In the four hypothetical cases of famine, noisome beasts, the sword, and pestilence, such men would succeed only in saving their own lives; but even in such cases there would be an elect remnant who would be comforted as they recognized the evidences of the divine rectitude. Yes, as we look back on the history of our race we shall be comforted; we shall feel that God could have done no other; we shall reap the blessing which has been evolved out of events and movements that we had misunderstood or feared.

EZEKIEL 18:14-32

The Reversal of the Divine Judgment. The Jews of Ezekiel's day asserted that God's dealings with their nation were not just because they were suffering, not for their own sins, but for their fathers'. God here makes it clear that he deals with individuals according to their deserts. The guilty son of a good father does not escape punishment because of his father's virtues; and the good son of evil parents reaps the reward of his own goodness. What a well of comfort is supplied by vv. 21 and 22! God pledges himself that forgiven sin shall not even be mentioned. This solemn covenant should be appropriated and its fulfillment claimed by those who through all their lifetime have been subject to bondage because of their past. We must not be content with an outward amendment; there must be, and there can be, through the grace of the Holy Spirit, an inward and radical change. This impossible command drives us to the Holy Spirit, Ps. 51:10, 12. As Augustine puts it: "Give what thou requirest, and require what thou wilt."

EZEKIEL 33:1-16

"Why Will Ye Die?" The prophet depicts the peasantry of a fertile valley as engaged in pastoral pursuits. It is a peaceful, happy scene; but creeping through the mountain passes are their deadliest foes. How necessary that there should be a watchman, trumpet in hand, to give notice; and how unspeakable his guilt if he forbear to sound a warning! We are not responsible for those who refuse to take warning from our announcements, faithfully given; but if we perceive a soul in mortal danger and forbear to warn it, we are not only responsible for its ruin, but we bring awful retribution upon ourselves. Well might Richard Baxter lie awake at night beneath his awful sense of responsibility for the souls of men. God desires our salvation. If only the sinner will confess his sins to the faithful and merciful High Priest, not one of his sins shall be remembered against him.

EZEKIEL 34:1-16

Selfish Shepherds. The shepherds of this chapter were not the religious leaders of the people, but rulers who sought in their government not the good of the people, but their own selfish ends. But the statements made by the prophet may be rightly applied to rapacious priests who care more for the fleece than for the flock. Pastors are required to lead the flock of God, not for filthy lucre, but as examples for the sheep, 1 Pet. 5:2, 3. It is their duty, also, to strengthen the spiritually diseased, heal the sick, bind up the broken in heart, and seek the lost.

Notice the tender manner in which the Lord Jesus himself supplies the deficiencies of his unfaithful servants. In beautiful contrast to their selfish cruelty and rapacity, he sets himself in cloudy and dark days to gather and tend his people, though they had been as scattered sheep, each taking his own way. When the ministers of his Church fail in their duty, the Lord hastens to supply their lack. Without doubt these gracious promises refer primarily to the Lord's Second Advent, when he will seek out and deliver his Chosen People and bring them to their own land. But surely we must not limit the reference thus. We are his sheep, by purchase and by choice. He knows us, as we know him. He has sought and saved us. He feeds us and causes us to lie down beside the waters of rest.

EZEKIEL 34:17-31

"Showers of Blessing." Though God now often seems to make no difference between the oppressors and the oppressed, the time is fast coming when he will make momentous and lasting distinctions, Matt. 25:32, 33. No wrong shall then be unredressed. Note the designation of our Lord as "one Shepherd over them," peerless and matchless in dignity and authority. Once he died to save his flock from the wolf, but he is destined to reign forever as their Great Shepherd in the midst of them, v. 24. They shall be everlastingly exempted from hunger, harm, and reproach. Jesus has been raised up from the dead to be our plant of renown. Planted in the grave of death, he has become with his faithful people a Vine whose shadow covers the hills and enriches the hearts and lives of men with luscious fruit. And because he lives, we shall live also. His resurrection implies and guarantees our own.

EZEKIEL 37:1-14

The Resurrection of a Dead Nation. In this marvelous chapter, the vision is amazingly graphic. Time does not rob it of its significance. Indeed every sign points to speedy fulfillment.* The Jewish nation has long resembled those dry and bleaching bones; and the state of sinners generally may truly be described in the same terms. The condition of many souls and neighborhoods is comparable to the harrowing scenes of a recent battlefield. We may preach so as to effect an outward revolution, but there can be no life until the divine breath passes over them. We must preach the Word, instant in season and out; but we must also call on the Spirit of Life. Those that are in their graves must hear the voice of the Son of God. The promises of vv. 13 and 14 await literal fulfillment in the case of the Jews, but let us plead that they may be also realized in our own congregations and neighborhoods. Revival will assuredly end in unity.

---

*Editor's note: These words were written more than thirty years before the dry bones of Israel again became a nation. Fulfillment of Ezekiel's prophecy has come!

THE BOOK OF DANIEL

THE PROPHET OF WORLD EMPIRES

I. HISTORICAL SECTION   *1—6.*
- A. Daniel and his friends tested   *1.*
- B. Nebuchadnezzar's forgotten dream   *2.*
- C. The golden image and the fiery furnace   *3.*
- D. Nebuchadnezzar's second dream   *4.*
- E. Belshazzar's feast and downfall   *5.*
- F. Daniel delivered from the den of lions   *6.*

II. PROPHETICAL SECTION   *7—12*
- A. The vision of the four beasts   *7.*
- B. The vision of the ram and the he goat   *8.*
- C. Daniel's prayer for Jerusalem and the answer   *9.*
- D. Daniel's vision by the river Hiddekel   *10.*
- E. The conflict of nations   *11.*
- F. The last judgment   *12.*

INTRODUCTION

Daniel and Jonah differ from the other prophets in that their work was among foreign peoples. Their books are also unlike the other books of prophecy, in that they are largely historical. In both books, also, the supernatural element is unusually prominent.

Daniel was a prophet-statesman, and his book deals with Babylon and the empires which should follow it until the coming of the divine kingdom. Of its twelve chapters the first six are narrative; the remainder are devoted to visions. From 2:4—7:28 the Aramaic language is employed; the opening and concluding sections are written in Hebrew. The latter part of the book is written in the first person, and as its unity is not disputed, the whole is to be ascribed to Daniel himself.

It opens with an account of the captivity of Daniel and his three friends, their fearless loyalty to the faith of their fathers, and their advancement in royal favor. While the heroic faith of his friends is manifested in their deliverance from the fiery furnace, Daniel himself is the prominent character in the history. He is distinguished for his ability not only to interpret dreams and visions, but to reproduce such as had been forgotten. In his later life, after Babylon had passed into the hands of Persia, Daniel's courage and faith received striking witness in his deliverance from the den of lions. This is the last recorded event in his life.

The symbolical visions which form the latter half of the book, with the dream of Nebuchadnezzar (Chapter 2), set forth the successive establishment of four empires: Babylon, Persia, Greece, and Rome. The last empire then gives way to smaller kingdoms until the setting up of the kingdom of God, which is to include all the dominions of the earth.

In the vision of a future kingdom of righteousness, the book is at one with all prophecy. In this kingdom even the dead shall share, being raised from the dust of the earth to everlasting life. Much as there is in the book that is hard to understand, the prophecy of Daniel has always ministered to Christian faith, and the climax of its visions is still the hope of the Church.

COMMENTARY

DANIEL 1

Moral Courage Rewarded. These young men of noble Jewish families were brought to Babylon to receive education for civil service. Their names were altered to break, so far as possible, their connection with the past. The food provided probably contravened Lev. 3:17. According to the usual custom it had been presented before an idol, 1 Cor. 8:10. Note those words: "Daniel purposed in his heart." It is all-important to resolve in one's heart that certain things are not possible for us. We ought to realize the extent to which Paul referred when he said, "dead to sin." God always cooperates with his servants when they are true to him. *He* brought Daniel into favor; *he* gave him skill; *he* caused his face and that of his three friends to bear the hue of health. Let us trust him to do his part! This is the secret of continuance, v. 21.

DANIEL 2:1-13

The Forgotten Dream. This was the second year of Nebuchadnezzar's sole reign. At first he was joint-governor with his father. From v. 4b to 7:28 the Syriac or Aramaic language is employed, and as this was the vernacular tongue of the king and his court, it is possible that this part of Daniel's record is based upon documents of state. The king's argument throughout his discussion with the magicians and astrologers was that if they could not recall the past, they certainly could not be trusted to foretell the future; the failure of the wise men provided the opportunity for the greater triumph of the servant of God. The wise men of Babylon said truly that only the gods, whose dwelling is not with flesh, could recover lost dreams. Daniel thought so, too, only he looked to the Lord God of his fathers. Irresponsible power is a temptation to the ruler and perilous to the ruled. No mortal should have despotic power over life and death.

DANIEL 2:14-35

Wisdom Granted in the Hour of Need. The action of Daniel in this supreme crisis is very instructive. He reckoned absolutely on God, and in his chivalrous endeavor to save the lives of the aged men, the heads of the college in which he had been trained, he never doubted that God would be his stay. A prayer meeting was convened to ask for the merciful interposition of the God of Heaven, and at its close Daniel seems to have lain down to sleep in unwavering faith. In this act we are reminded of Jesus sleeping amid the storm. Only a heart so pure and true, so trustful and godly could have slept within the shadow of so terrible a menace. It was "in a night vision" that he beheld the majestic procession of empire, from the gold of absolute monarchy to the clay and metal of constitutional government. Note his care to give all the glory to God and to take the humble position of the mere channel through which the divine message was transmitted to the king.

DANIEL 2:36-49

God's Kingdom Triumphant. Our Lord probably refers to these five empires when he speaks of "the times of the Gentiles." The empire of Babylon was followed by that of Medo-Persia under Cyrus; that by Greece under Alexander the Great; and that in turn by Rome led by the Caesars. Since the dissolution of the Roman Empire, the vast dominions of the east and the west have fallen, generally speaking, into some ten main divisions. There is, therefore, now nothing between us and the final setting up of the kingdom that is not made by human hands and shall never be destroyed. Note the striking anticipation of the outcome of Gentile dominion, in the prostration of supreme human power at the feet of a Jew. Evidently Daniel refused the king's homage, because we are told that Nebuchadnezzar "answered" him. Those who have shared our anxieties and prayers must not be forgotten in our hour of triumph, v. 49. The heart of man may not be able to recall its forgotten dreams, but it will recognize them when presented by the servant of God.

DANIEL 3:1-18

Loyalty Severely Tested. The king, at the close of the foregoing chapter, acknowledged the supremacy of Daniel's God; yet here he erects an image to Bel and to himself, demanding divine honor. Probably there was state policy in this. In so heterogeneous an empire of peoples, nations, and languages, there could be no unity but in universal prostration before one and the same object. Nineteen years had elapsed since the recovery of the lost dream. In that period successful wars had been waged and vast treasures accumulated which made this vast expenditure possible. Imagine the assembled myriads, the glittering array of princes, satraps, viceroys, statesmen, and priests, the grouped bands, and in the background the furnace. The three youths could not have stood alone amid the prostrate throng, had they not been supported by a living faith in the God of their fathers, Heb. 11:33, 34. They would not argue, but they would die if God willed. Their attitude was taken and maintained altogether apart from any expectation of deliverance. Our God whom we serve is able.

DANIEL 3:19-30

Loyalty Rewarded. It is only when we reach the fire that we become aware of the presence of the divine Companion, walking beside us as if treading the dew-besprinkled glades of Paradise. The Good Shepherd was there with his rod and staff. They were "loose," v. 25; that is, the fire had consumed their bonds and nothing else. Hair would soonest catch the flame, but not a hair perished, Luke 12:7; 21:18. The yielded body of v. 28 reminds us of Romans 6:13; 12:1, 2. Let us yield our bodies and souls to our faithful Creator for him to use as he will. He made and redeemed, let him have; and when we are possessed by his Spirit all other fires, whether physical or temperamental, fail to hurt. Of the martyrs, it may be said that upon them also the fire had no power, Isa. 43:2!

DANIEL 4:1-18

"The Decree of the Watchers." Nebuchadnezzar was in the zenith of his fame and power. His wars were over; his prosperity was assured. But he attributed all to his own wisdom and prowess. There was no thought of God, who had raised him up and given him everything. He must be humbled if his soul was to be saved; the whole living world must know that the Most High rules in the kingdom of men and gives it to whomsoever he pleases, v. 17. How gladly worldly men turn in hours of crisis to religious men, who draw upon unseen resources and bear themselves with calm and unruffled peace, v. 9. The greatness of the King is set forth under the figure of a mighty tree, filling the earth and sheltering the nations. There was only one Being who came down, combining in himself watchfulness and holiness. In v. 17 we learn that no destiny is decided apart from the careful sifting of the celestial council chamber. How august is this conception of the matured judgment of Heaven. Where should we stand apart from the pleading of the great High Priest?

DANIEL 4:19-37

Nebuchadnezzar's Humiliation. Beyond doubt Nebuchadnezzar was one of the most illustrious princes the world has ever seen. The discoveries which Layard commenced among the mounds of the Euphrates Valley have afforded striking evidences of his magnificence. Nebuchadnezzar was very conscious of his greatness, and as he looked from the eminence of his throne upon the world at his feet, his heart was lifted up with pride. It would be easy to cite proofs from the stones and bricks of Babylon to corroborate the general tenor of this story; for all the bricks of the ruins in that great province, so far as they have been examined, bear the name of Nebuchadnezzar. Several inscriptions have been found which, in their boastfulness, tally exactly with v. 30. But how marvelous the contrast between those proud and vaunting words and the ascriptions of humble homage and praise in vv. 34–37! If God could produce such a result on the haughty king of Babylon, is there any sinner he cannot subdue? May not the stern discipline to which some lives are subjected be intended to subdue their proud wills and bring them to similar confessions?

DANIEL 5:1–16

The Handwriting on the Wall. The name of Belshazzar has been deciphered in inscriptions found at Babylon, from which it is inferred that he was associated with his father in the kingdom and was left to defend Babylon. He was therefore a grandson of Nebuchadnezzar, the word "father," v. 11, being used in the sense of "ancestor." The great walls of the banqueting hall covered with sculptures and sumptuous decorations, the tablets covered by cuneiform descriptions of the triumphs of former kings—what a feast this was! The thousand lords; the most beautiful women of the land; the concourse of magnates of religion and the state. The wine flowed in rivers, and laughter rang through the vaulted hall. Upon the table stood the vessels of the Temple, and notably the seven-branched candlestick, which cast its radiance on the wall, clearly illumining the fingers of the hand that wrote. The words, though Chaldee, may have been written in Hebrew characters. Conscience filled the king's heart with foreboding. The queen may have been the great Nitocris, wife of Nebuchadnezzar, the ancestor of the present king. God has his own way of bringing his people to the front when he needs them.

DANIEL 5:17–31

Weighed and Found Wanting. Daniel was unperturbed and undismayed. Calm and collected, he recognized his Father's handwriting and read it, as the instructed may decipher a scroll which is illegible to the ordinary gaze. What to him were the baubles of the palace? With the wings of the angel of death overshadowing that awestruck throng, it was of small importance that Belshazzar promised him the purple robe and chain of gold. It seems sometimes as though those fingers were busy still writing their awful sentence on the walls of national revelry. While a nation is drinking deep at its cups and countenancing uncleanness, the divine assay may be in progress and the verdict going forth: "weighed and found wanting." There may be gold and glitter, revelry and mirth, the splendor of state and the profusion of tasty delicacies; but what of these if the people are ignorant, irreligious, and impure? Then, indeed, dry rot has set in! The root sin of all is pride. May the Spirit of God, who ever brings with him light and understanding and excellent wisdom, be found in us as in Daniel.

DANIEL 6:1–15

Fidelity in Worship. Though he was the most distinguished man of his day and full of public business, Daniel managed to find time for prayer in the evening, morning, and at noon, according to the Hebrew custom, Ps. 55:17. He was outwardly a great magnate of the Persian court, but inwardly he was as true as ever to the city of his fathers and to the Temple now in ruins, v. 10. What a marvelous tribute was afforded to his saintly character by his foes, when they could find no fault in him except as concerned his religious life! Time spent in prayer is not lost time to the suppliant. Luther used to say: "I have so much to do today that I cannot get through with less than three hours of prayer." It was customary for the Jews to turn the face toward the Holy City, which for so long had been the center of their great religious system, 1 Kings 8:44; Jonah 2:4. With us, the upturned face and the references we make to the great High Priest are significant of a posture of soul analagous and yet superior to the open window. See to it that your windows are always open toward the new Jerusalem, of which you are a citizen, but from which for a little while you are exiled.

DANIEL 6:16–28

"Persecuted for Righteousness' Sake." The plot was an atrocious one, but it hurt its perpetrators more than the victim of their vindictive hatred, v. 24. They dug a pit into which they fell themselves. They thought to flatter the king and secure Daniel's fall; but their stratagems were like the mines laid at the mouth of a harbor, which are more perilous to those who set them than to others. God still sends his angels to shut the lions' mouths, that they may not hurt his people, strongly conscious of uprightness before God and man. It is not necessary to suppose that Daniel saw the angel, any more than we behold the horses and chariots in the mountains around us. Dare to believe that the ministering angels, though unseen, surround you and intercept the blows and plots of your adversaries. Walk before God in righteousness

and peace, and be sure that you are immortal till your work is done. That a heathen king should publish such a proclamation is a glimpse into the divine wisdom that can make his mighty power known by the strangest circumstances.

DANIEL 7:1-14

God's Everlasting Dominion. This chapter enumerates the succession of world empires and rulers which bridge the gulf of centuries from the Captivity to the Second Advent. The lion represents Babylon, whose cruel and mighty kingdom was animated by marvelous intelligence; the bear, Persia; the leopard, Greece under Alexander the Great; and the fourth beast, with great iron teeth, Rome. The ten horns are ten kings, and these probably represent great European kingdoms which have succeeded, or may yet succeed, to the heritage of the Roman Empire. The Ancient of Days is sitting today upon his throne, his snow-white raiment betokening his purity, the fire of his throne bespeaking his antagonism to all things that offend and work iniquity. The government of the world is on shoulders which are well able to carry it, and he will cause all things to work out his purpose, which is to promote and assure the glory of Christ.

DANIEL 7:15-28

The Destruction of All Rival Powers. The judgment described here is not the last judgment, but that of the nations, which is always in process and in virtue of which one great empire after another is set aside. This constant change must continue until the kingdom of Jesus Christ, which is now a spiritual and hidden one, shall be set up before the eyes of men. This dread persecuting power has been identified with Antiochus and others. But it is better to think of it as that spirit of evil which is always at war with the people of God, assuming different phases in its manifestation. As God's people have suffered from Antichrist in the past, so they may expect some last manifestation of such hatred. But they shall overcome by the blood of Jesus and the word of their testimony, and the kingdom of Christ shall survive the wreck of all others. What a glimpse is afforded of the awful conflict which must go on between the saints of the Most High and the great world powers which desire to wear them out! Are we not now witnessing the judgment of God which is being executed on the nations of the earth?

DANIEL 8:1-14

God's Sanctuary Dishonored. At Shushan, in the palace, by the river Ulai, the prophet beheld in vision the attack which would subsequently be made on the Medo-Persian kingdom by Alexander. The great horn which was broken is, of course, Alexander, and the four notable ones are his four generals who after his death divided up his conquests. The little horn is referred by many to Antiochus, whose conflict with the Maccabees was one of the most significant in later Jewish history. Others refer it to Mohammed and his followers, who have reigned over the same regions. In this case the little horn would stand for the eastern apostasy as distinguished from the western, which is said to be represented by the little horn of the fourth beast, 7:8. The Books of the Maccabees, included in the Apocrypha, should be studied to understand more clearly the history behind vv. 11, 12. The explanation of these obscure verses is also given in vv. 24, 25. Antiochus was obsessed with hatred against the spiritual worship of the Jews and their refusal to admit his image into the Temple. He stopped their sacrifices, though they were restored for a season, to be finally suspended during the present age. The day for a year system, v. 14, may refer to the desolations of the Turkish or Ottoman Empire, of which Antiochus was the representative.

DANIEL 8:15-27

God's Deliverance Is Sure. It does not fall within our study to go into the various fulfillments which have been assigned to the predictions of this chapter—one to the time of the Maccabees, one to our own days, and one to that malign Satanic power which stands up perpetually against the Prince of princes. Let us dwell, rather, on the assertion that whatever sets itself against the kingship of Jesus Christ shall inevitably be broken. The Church of God is menaced today as never before by a vast multiplication of malign influences; but the Master's promise holds good that the gates of Hades shall not prevail against her. They shall be broken without hand. This is our strong confidence with respect to all our foes, and therefore we may possess our souls in patience. It is interesting that Daniel continued to do the king's business, notwithstanding the abundance of the revelations given unto him. However much we may be caught up into the heaven of religious meditation and ecstasy, we must never forget or neglect the interests which are committed to our hands, whether of the home, the business, or the state.

DANIEL 9:1-15

Intercession for a Beloved People. What a prayer is this! In many respects it is a model for us all. *It was based on the divine Word.* The fact that God had promised to restore the desolations of Jerusalem after seventy years did not restrain, but prompted and inspired Daniel's prayers. God's promises are not independent of our faith, but await our appropriation. The blank checks are drawn and signed in our favor, but they must be presented at the bank for payment. *It was very humble.* Fasting, sackcloth, and ashes were the outward works, but notice the tone. "We have sinned . . . and have rebelled. . . . unto us [belongeth] confusion of faces." He confessed his sin and the sin of his people. There is such a thing as vicarious confession, in which some holy soul takes to himself the task of bearing the sins of his people and pouring out the story before God as though the sins were his own. But we hardly need go to our country or people for sins to confess, for we have plenty of our own; and the nearer we come to God's infinite light and holiness, the more we abhor ourselves and repent in dust and ashes.

DANIEL 9:16-27

Renewed Favor in God's Own Time. Verses 17-19 have in them a tone of anguish which reminds us of our Lord's words as to the violence which takes the kingdom of Heaven by force. God loves to see us in dead earnest. It is not long, but strong prayers that prevail with him. He sometimes seems to deny us, that he may draw us out in supplication. Notice the response to such prayer. Before it was spoken, it was granted, v. 23. Before Daniel called, he was answered; and while he was yet speaking, he was heard. Pray on! God is more eager to hear and to bless us than we are to pray. Even now the divine answer is hastening toward thee, swifter than the speed of the morning beams across the vault of space. While we are speaking in prayer, nay, before the beginning of our supplication, the angel is sent out, and he is made to fly very swiftly.

Six purposes were to be effected within 490 years from a specified date. Some refer these to final Jewish restoration, but for this the last week of the seventy has to be separated from the rest and postponed till "the end of the age." It is more natural to understand the passage as describing here Christ's finished work, and thus we avoid impairing the definiteness of the prophecy by indefinitely prolonging it. "The prince that shall come" seems to refer to the Roman emperor Vespasian, whose people destroyed Jerusalem. But many think that v. 27 refers to a future compact between Antichrist and the Jews, previous to their conversion.

DANIEL 10

The Vision by the River. This chapter gives a glimpse into the great conflict which is always in progress between Heaven and hell. For three weeks the radiant being who came to Daniel as he prayed and fasted by the great river was withstood by the mighty fallen spirit who was concerned with the destinies of the kingdom of Persia; and it was only when he was succored and reinforced that he was able to accomplish the divine errand, v. 13. What a revelation is here—that probably each heathen country is ruled by some wicked spirit in the high places; that the fight is at times almost overpowering, even for bright unfallen angels; and that the blessings which are ours are sometimes delayed because of the storms that sweep the ocean through which they come. Perhaps by our prayer we are able to throw an ounce weight into the scale and turn the battle. How reassuring the touch of that hand and tender the address of that voice. Who cannot be strong when strengthened by the right hand of God? Go forth into the fight of another day! God holds thy right hand. Be true and strong; thou canst not fail!

DANIEL 11:1-14

The Rise and Fall of Empires. This chapter foretells the histories of Xerxes, of Alexander the Great, the division of his kingdom on his death, and the long conflicts between the kings of Syria and Egypt. During those years of turmoil and war the eyes of God's faithful servants must often have turned to this page for guidance and comfort. The voice of the prophets was hushed between Malachi 4 and Matthew 1, and therefore the written Word would be more than ordinarily precious. It must have comforted them to be assured that God knew the way they had to travel and would supply all needed help. What a weary monotony of strife, war, and misery is the history of world kingdoms! The heathen rage; the peoples are moved. Earth and sky are wrapped in clouds and darkness. We are reminded of the chaos of the primal condition of our earth, when it was without form and void and darkness was on the face of the deep. But as in creation, so in history: in the darkest hours the divine Spirit is brooding in the heart of the night, and will presently reestablish order and beauty.

DANIEL 11:15-29

The Despoiler Triumphs for a Time. What a picture is presented in this paragraph of the tangled web of earthly politics. They have been too much, and for too long, in the hands of those who sought only their own aggrandizement, to attain which they have been willing to sacrifice their honor, their families, their daughters, their people. The time has arrived when the people themselves, at firsthand, must determine their destinies. These intrigues between the kings of Syria on the north and the kings of Egypt on the south are recorded here as affecting the history of the Chosen People. This enables us to realize that the events of the present hour are being overruled by divine Providence in the interests of the Church of Christ. This alone abides; all else is of secondary importance and is rapidly passing away. The eternal purpose stands forever sure—that the Father has committed the empire of the world to our Lord, and is about to sum all things up in him who is the Head.

DANIEL 11:30-45

Arrogance Overthrown. The career of Antiochus Epiphanes, in persecuting the people of God and plotting against Jehovah and his sanctuary, is so described as to suggest that it also includes further fulfillments, and especially that last Antichrist, of whom Antiochus was the prefigurement. So accurate is the correspondence between this prophecy and its historical fulfillment that Porphyry, the opponent of Christianity, maintained that this description was written after the event. The abomination of v. 31 refers to the idolatrous image or emblem which in succession has been erected on Mount Zion under the auspices of Antiochus, of the Romans, of the Moslems, and shall be set up yet once more by Antichrist. The last clause of v. 32 was marvelously realized in Judas Maccabaeus and his brethren; but it represents the perennial source of strength for all who suffer or serve. The anguish of those who fail under trial has often tended to their greater purification, v. 35, and the white robe is the mark of final victory, Rev. 7:9. God will not allow his people to suffer beyond the determined time, v. 36; Matt. 24:22.

DANIEL 12

Resurrection and Judgment. Michael was the guardian spirit of the Jewish people. When the time of trouble has reached its climax, whether in national or individual life, help is near.

The hope of resurrection, of the life beyond the darkness of their times, animated the hearts of the Chosen People. In the same way the Apostle Paul refers to it, 1 Cor. 15:58. The national resurrection of Israel is without doubt included but the resurrection at the last, when that of the just shall precede that of the unjust by the Millennium, is clearly the topic of these wonderful words. Daniel's prophecies were to be sealed, because their entire fulfillment was not to take place for many days. Three and a half probably stands for three and a half prophetic years, which on the year-day system gives 1,260 days or years, and is therefore equivalent to the forty-two months of Rev. 11:2; 13:5. This is the time of the world power, half the perfect number seven. The supremacy of the Gentile kingdoms is for 2,500 years, of which the latter half has nearly expired. Let us go our way, watch and pray, and at last stand in our lot.

THE BOOK OF
HOSEA

GOD'S LOVE FOR HIS APOSTATE PEOPLE
"How shall I give thee up, Ephraim?" Hos. 11:8.

I. GOMER, UNFAITHFUL BUT BELOVED, A SYMBOL OF ISRAEL *1—3.*
   A. The prophet's wife and family   *1.*
   B. Israel to be judged and restored   *2.*
   C. The return of the prophet's wife   *3:1-3.*
   D. The return of Israel   *3:4, 5.*

II. DIVINE JUDGMENT AND MERCY   *4—14.*
   A. Israel ripe for punishment   *4.*
   B. The guilt of king and priests   *5:1—6:3.*
   C. Israel's depravity and stubbornness   *6:4—7:16.*
   D. Reaping the whirlwind   *8:1—9:9.*
   E. The history of Israel's apostasies   *9:10—11:12.*
   F. The triumph of mercy   *12—14.*

INTRODUCTION

Hosea was probably a native and a subject of the northern kingdom, and exercised his ministry during the turbulent reigns of the last six or seven of its kings—a period of about sixty years. The moral and religious condition of Israel was very corrupt. God and his Word were ignored; the kings and princes were murderers and profligates; idolatrous priests maintained their shameful rites in all parts of the country; the great political parties applied for help now from Assyria and then from Egypt.

It has been supposed that the domestic incidents referred to in the first three chapters are parabolic; but to hold this view is to miss the moving lesson of the suffering which love, whether human or divine, is prepared to undergo, if only the lost can be found and the erring brought back to life and home.

COMMENTARY

HOSEA 1

God Gathers the Outcast. The story of Hosea is a pathetic one. He felt impressed that it was his duty to take as wife one whose earlier life had been unchaste. From this marriage resulted three children, the names of whom are terribly significant. They are as follows:—"God will scatter"; "Not an object of favor"; and "Once my people, but not so now." Here is the history of many a soul. In spite of all God's tender love, we may wander from him into the path of sin.

The chapter closes with brighter prognostications. In part, these latter verses were fulfilled by the return from Babylon, and they will be fulfilled in literal fullness some day—probably sooner than we have been wont to suppose. It is good to lay the emphasis on "in the place ... there." How often we are taken back to the very circumstances in which we appear to have failed most conspicuously, in order that *there* we may receive the crowning blessing of our life, v. 10. Leave God to vindicate you. He will bring you from the land of the enemy and extort this confession from the mouth of your critics and foes, v. 10.

HOSEA 2:1-13

The Bitter Sin of Wandering from God. Hosea is represented as having exhausted his expostulations upon his faithless wife. He has tried every arrow in love's quiver, but in vain; so now he sends his children, worse than motherless, to plead with their mother, before she brings upon them all irretrievable retribution.

Almost insensibly our mind passes from the pleadings of human love to the divine Bridegroom. Often he has to erect thorn hedges about *us*—not that he takes pleasure in thwarting us, but that we may be diverted from ruin. There was no better method of turning Israel from her idols than by withholding that material prosperity which she thought they gave. Has not this been our experience also? Our mirth has ceased and our prosperity has vanished. We have sat amid the wrecks of a happy past. It is not that God has ceased to care for us, but that he longs to wean us back to himself. Have we reached the point of saying, "It was better with me then than now"? Then let us be of good cheer! The dawn is already on the hills, and God's coming to us, in restoring grace, is like the breaking glory of the morning!

HOSEA 2:14—3:5

"A Door of Hope." The valley of Achor was a long wild pass up through the hills. The prophet says that a door of hope would open there, like the Mont Cenis tunnel which leads from the precipices and torrents on the northern slopes of the Alps to the sunny plains of Italy. That door opens hard by the heap of stones beneath which that troubler of Israel, Achan, was laid. We must put away our Achans

before we can see doors of hope swing wide before us.

The prophet was bidden to make one further overture to his truant wife. She had been faithless, but the old love burnt in her husband's soul, and he was prepared to buy her back to himself at half the price of a female slave, Exod. 21:32. His only stipulation was that she should abide with him for many days. This was to be a time of testing, with the assurance that if she were penitent and faithful, she would be perfectly restored.

What a wonderful verse is 3! We are purchased to God by the death of his Son. He only asks us to be for himself and he promises to be for us. "The best of all," cried the dying Wesley, "is that God is for us!" Shall we not close the offer and give ourselves to him?

HOSEA 4:1-10

"Like People, Like Priest." This chapter contains a terrible indictment against the whole kingdom. There was neither truth nor mercy in the land, but swearing, lying, and adultery. Apart from the restraints of religion, such would be the condition of human society today. Even atheists have been known to remove from mining camps where there was no semblance of religion, to places within the sound of the church bell. Notice in v. 3 how man's sin seems to affect even the animals. "The whole creation groaneth and travaileth . . . waiting for the [or our] adoption" as the recognized sons of God, Rom. 8:22, 23.

Rightly enough, the prophet remonstrates with the priests. They were drunken and sensual; they rejected the knowledge and rule of God; they promoted outward ritual in order to fatten on the offerings of the people; and as it was with them, so it became with the deluded worshipers. What a solemn lesson is contained in the proverb which originated in this passage, "Like people, like priest!" It is not what we teach, but what we are that really affects men.

HOSEA 4:11-19

"Joined to Idols." The prophet does not mince his words in describing the morals of his time. We are reminded of Bunyan's words: "My original and inward pollution was my plague. It was always putting itself forth in me, and I was more loathsome in my own eyes than a toad, and I thought I was in God's eyes also. Corruption bubbled up in my heart as naturally as water in a fountain, and I thought that every one had a better heart than I." Of course in Christ "we have redemption through his blood," and that means more than forgiveness; it implies the deliverance of the soul from the love and power of evil. But if the soul of man refuses this obstinately and persistently, a time arrives when God gives him up to reap as he has sown.

The greatest gift we can make to our generation is that of unblemished character. The aged Sir Leslie Stephen, the brilliant agnostic, went back to the grave of an undergraduate who had been his pupil and had died in early life without having distinguished himself in his studies or athletics, but had lived the Christian life with transparent simplicity and lovableness.

HOSEA 5

God's Rebuke of Apostasy. The prophet continues his grave indictment of his people. The court and the priesthood were chiefly responsible for the awful degeneracy that was eating out the national heart. The seductions to idolatry that abounded everywhere resembled the snares and nets set by hunters on the wooded heights of Gilead and Tabor.

Suddenly, within a month, v. 7, an alarm sounds from hill to hill. The foreign invader has entered the country and is slowly marching southward. Even Benjamin is threatened. Ephraim must suffer because of the institutions of Omri and Ahab, v. 11, and Judah, because her princes were grasping and fraudulent. Though message after message was sent to procure the help of Jareb—a symbolical name for Assyria, "the warlike"—he would not be able to avert the approaching dissolution of the Jewish state. You cannot stop the dry rot by grand alliances. Nothing can save a nation in whose heart the worst forms of corruption are being nourished, except a wholesale return to God and a seeking of his face. It is certain that if this lesson were profoundly learned and then practiced, the horrors of a world in arms would come to a speedy and a blessed end.

HOSEA 6

"Let Us Return unto the Lord." How full Scripture is of tender invitations: "Come, and let us return!" This opening verse is closely connected with 5:15. The hand that smote was the Father's who waited to welcome the prodigal nation with healing. When the sun seems to dip below the horizon, we begin to travel toward its rising again. Then we follow on, to behold the glorious dawn of the next day, which is prepared for us. Presently we catch the first glimpse, and soon come into its full splendor. The sun does not move toward us, but we to-

ward it. So when the soul turns toward God, if only it is willing to do his will, it has begun to follow on toward the light of his countenance, which presently will be revealed in its full radiance. God's favor is also compared to the fertilizing rain, for its certainty and refreshment.

While God's love is constant, our religious life is fickle. Emotion is evanescent as the morning clouds, which in Palestine vanish by nine or ten o'clock. Our Lord quoted v. 6 in Matthew 9:13; 12:7. The pomp of outward ritual, however ornate, counts less with God than one contrite sigh or tear.

HOSEA 7

Iniquity Uncovered. The last clause of the previous chapter belongs to this. God desired to turn aside the captivity of his people and to heal Israel, but his pleading was unavailing because of their inveterate sin. This evildoing witnessed against them, v. 2. Their passions did not need incitement, just as an oven retains its heat without the baker's continued attention. The royal birthday was celebrated with drunken orgies, and the national religion had become a confused mixture of Gentile superstition and the old Hebrew faith. In this Israel resembled a cake not turned—crisp on one side, sour and uneatable on the other, v. 8.

What a searching suggestion comes in v. 9! Can it be that strangers have been stealing away our strength, without our realizing that deterioration is creeping steadily through our religious life? Silently the frosty air steals the warmth from boiling water; silently the fungus pitches its tent in the autumn woods; silently old age fastens on the stalwart frame. Thus also our spiritual strength declines, unless we watch and pray; and when it ebbs away, we become foolish as the dove which flies straight into the snare, and useless as the deceitful bow which turns aside in the archer's hand, vv. 11 and 16.

HOSEA 8

Reaping the Whirlwind. A conqueror was at hand who would subdue and punish the whole nation for taking its own course, irrespective of God, vv. 4–8; for seeking foreign alliances which could bring only oppression with them, vv. 9, 10; and for multiplying altars and fortresses which were destined to be destroyed, vv. 11, 14. The circumstances referred to in this chapter seem to point to the reigns of Menahem and Uzziah, 2 Kings 15:19; 2 Chron. 26:6–15.

The 5th verse is very striking. Israel had renounced Jehovah for the likeness of a calf, and now in the misfortunes which had overtaken them their calf had cast them off. What is it that you are putting in the place of God? Power, wealth, the help of influential friends? Sooner or later it will fail you. How different is the One who perpetually encourages us, saying, "I will not fail nor forsake thee." The persistence with which Israel turned to other lovers left God no option but to put them back into a furnace such as Egypt had been, which would finally burn out their apostasy. Only when we walk before God with a perfect heart are we strong and happy. Once entangle yourself with expedients and alliances, and you lay yourself open to many sorrows.

HOSEA 9:1–9

"The Days of Recompence Are Come." The subject of this chapter is the bitterness of the captivity which was awaiting Israel as the result of their unfaithfulness. Their exile would put an effectual end to their idolatrous and sensual feasts. Every pleasure would be removed and every taste would be offended. The contrasts here are very significant. If men choose unclean things when they might have clean, a situation will be created in which only unclean things shall be attainable, v. 3. If they withhold God's offerings when they have plenty, they will presently be reduced to such straits as not to have wherewith to sacrifice or even to sustain life, vv. 4, 5. If we go down to Egypt for help, in Egypt we shall die, vv. 6, 7. In other words, every sin carries within itself the seed of its own avenging. If allowed to work itself out, its harvest is unutterable and irretrievable.

What a privilege Ephraim had within his grasp, as a watchman with God, v. 8! It is to this privilege, also, that our Savior calls all of us. He says to us, as he said to his disciples, "Tarry ye here and watch with me." But too often we refuse to heed the gracious challenge, and allow ourselves to be seduced by the tempter or by the sloth and corruption of our own hearts, vv. 8, 9.

HOSEA 9:10–17

"Wanderers among the Nations." At the Exodus the love and thanks of Israel were as delightful to God as grapes in the desert or as the first ripe figs. But they gave themselves up to the idols of the heathen, and soon became as abominable as the impure gods which they chose.

The prophet does not hesitate to speak plainly of the effects of the awful license of that age. He says that a nation which sins as Israel had sinned must, in the very nature of things, cease to exist. The birthrate declines and family life is stricken at its roots. So long as the home is reverenced and there is a pure and holy love between man and woman, so long and only so long is the nation safe. Sin is like dry rot which eats out the vitality and virility of a people. It is an awful verdict when God says, "They shall bear no fruit," v. 16. We all know the fate of the unfruitful bough. It is only as we yield fruit that we are worth sparing. Will the nations of today learn this lesson? And may we not all question whether the lack of spiritual children does not betoken some degeneracy of our secret life?

HOSEA 10

"Break Up Your Fallow Ground." Israel brought forth fruit, but not such as God could delight in. It was corrupt and evil. How great a disappointment to the Great Cultivator! The land was covered with obelisks and altars, the symbols of idolatry, and the Canaanites themselves had not been more shameless in sin. But notice the terrible judgments that must befall. There would be revolution, for when men say, "We fear not the Lord," they will go on to say, "We fear not the king." Beth-aven, the "house of vanity," would replace Beth-el, the "house of God." The golden calves would be carried off by the conqueror. The king would perish as foam upon the water. The yoke of conquest would be placed on Ephraim's fair neck. The fortresses of Israel would be carried by assault, with all the accompaniments of savage warfare. Is it not "an evil thing and bitter" to forsake the Lord?

Is it not time that we should look into *our* hearts and lives, break up the fallow ground, now covered with thorns and thistles, and begin to sow in righteousness? Let us ask God to drive the plowshares of deep soul-searching and conviction across the hard and sterile acres of our hearts, and cultivate them with his good seed.

HOSEA 11:1–11

"Bands of Love." This is a very tender chapter, full of moving appeals. God looks back on the happy, blessed past as a fond parent on the innocent childhood of a son who is now causing endless pain and grief. He recapitulates the call from Egypt and relates how, in obedience to his appeal, Israel came out of the idolatries of that country. He describes Israel as a tiny child beginning to walk, and says, "I taught him to go." He compares the Israel of those days to horses or oxen, relieved of the yoke, before whom food is set. Let us remember that God is also willing to teach us to go, and to carry us when we are weary.

The blessed childhood of Israel had become like an overcast morning. They were bent on backsliding. But God's love is not easily repelled. What more pathetic words were ever uttered by brokenhearted parents than vv. 8 and 9! That is the motive of our plea still. If we were dealing with a man, we might despair. But we are dealing with One who forgives us according to the riches of his grace. If a backslider should read these touching appeals, let him be encouraged to retrace his steps one by one, sure that the Father waits to welcome him where the path has broken off from the main road.

HOSEA 11:12—12:14

Turn to God, Not to Selfish Gain. Though Judah still ruled with God, 11:12, yet there was grave fault in him and like Ephraim, which had been engaging the prophet's thought, he also must come under the rod. But throughout this paragraph there lingers the sweet music of the previous chapter, and especially the reminiscence of Israel's early days when he had power with the Angel and prevailed. The angel-haunted ideals and resolves of Beth-el could not be forgotten. Tears and weakness are the best arguments with God. He yields to us when we are weak; he yields to our despair. The soul that has been shut up to God and then casts itself at his feet can have what it will. Only beware lest after such an interview with the Angel you deteriorate into a deceitful trader and allow your God-given power to be reduced to making gain.

Notwithstanding all, God was still willing to call his people to the Feast of Tabernacles, the gladdest of all the feasts in the Hebrew year. But even divine love was thwarted by their inveterate sinning. How wonderfully these ancient prophets conceived of the love of God! The Spirit of revelation led them to make declarations that the cross has more than realized!

HOSEA 13:1–14

To Oppose God Is Destruction. Again, here is a very tender chapter. The lips that speak with trembling betray the heart that God can exalt. But when we turn to Baal, the emblem of self-confidence, we pass as the morning cloud, the dew, the chaff, and the smoke.

In v. 4 we again get the sweet strain of early memory. God had not changed and was waiting to save. They had refused his help and had destroyed themselves, and he who would have done his best for them had been constrained to act as though he were a lion, a leopard, or a bear. In the wilderness we are thankful enough for his help, but when we reach the land of the vine and olive, we follow the devices and desires of our own hearts.

What a magnificent outburst is that which declares the divine intention to ransom even from death and the grave! Our Savior by his death destroyed him that had the power of death. He is death's plague and the grave's destruction. The sting of death is sin, but Jesus has borne sin away. The strength of sin is a violated law, but he has fulfilled the law. He is more than conqueror, and the soul that is one with him shall share his triumph.

HOSEA 13:15—14:9

"I Will Heal Their Backsliding." The prophet here ransacks the world of Nature for phrases sufficiently expressive of his transports of joy. The whole world seems to set forth the love of God. The gentle dew, the rich raiment of the lily, the far-reaching spurs and roots of the Lebanon range, the spreading branches of the olive, the fragrant breath of the wind which is laden with the perfume of the land, the golden corn ripe for the sickle, the scent of the vines—these are the images with which the inspired imagination of the prophet teems.

But how deeply the chapter appeals to us! The very words that returning prodigals should adopt are set down. And as we return, we hear the divine voice assuring us that our backslidings shall be healed, that there is no anger and only love, and that God himself shall be the sap of our fruit-bearing life. Our Father wants it to be clearly understood that these promises do not belong to Israel only, but to all who will accept them.

THE BOOK OF JOEL

JUDAH'S JUDGMENT AND EXALTATION

I. THE INFLICTION OF JUDGMENT *1:1—2:17.*
   A. An unparalleled drought and locust plague *1:1–7.*
   B. A call to lamentation *1:8–13.*
   C. A call to repentance *1:14–20.*
   D. The sound of alarm *2:1–11.*
   E. The hope of forgiveness *2:12–17.*

II. THE MANIFESTATION OF MERCY *2:18–32.*
   A. The destruction of the destroyer *2:18–20.*
   B. The restoration of the wasted years *2:21–27.*
   C. The outpouring of the divine Spirit *2:28–32.*

III. JUDAH AND THE NATIONS *3.*
   A. The nations summoned to judgment *3:1–15.*
   B. The exaltation of Judah *3:16–21.*

INTRODUCTION

Of the prophet Joel almost nothing is known. No details of his personal life have come down to us. Even the time when he lived is not known with certainty, though it seems probable that he was one of the first of the prophets. From the frequent references to Judah and Jerusalem it would appear that he was a prophet of the southern kingdom.

The general subject of his prophecy is divine judgment, or the Day of Jehovah. There is first a judgment upon the Chosen People, inflicted through locusts. This is removed through fasting and intercession. A terrible day of final judgment embracing all nations is then described. The faithful will be rewarded while evildoers will be punished. The fulfillment of one of Joel's predictions by the scenes of the day of Pentecost, Acts 2:17–21, has given his book a prominent place in Christian thought.

COMMENTARY

JOEL 1—2:11

A Summons to Penitence. We know nothing of Joel beyond this book. He was content to be God's mouthpiece and remain unknown. His message was one of unparalleled woe. The memory of God's loving-kindness ought to have kept his people faithful and loyal, but since grace and love had failed to affect them, awful judgments were announced. A small insect, the locust, was to prostrate man's boasted power. The four kinds of locusts here described, and which doubtless devastated the country, were also symbols of the four world empires, Assyria, Babylon, Greece, and Rome, which were to lay waste the Holy Land. Such judgments call for acts of repentance, such as fasting, humiliation, and intercession. There are days in national experience when it becomes us to gird ourselves and lament. The ministers and elders of the Church should lead the way. Where there has been infidelity to the great Lover of souls, when the visible Church or the individual member has turned from Christ to the wanton world, then joy withers away, v. 12, spiritual worship ceases, v. 9, and there can be neither peace nor safety until there has been repentance and return.

JOEL 2:12—27

The Averting of Judgment. To rend the *garment* is easy, but a broken and contrite *heart* can be imparted only by the grace of the Holy Spirit. The love of God should bring us to repentance. He takes no pleasure in our miseries, and if men repent and turn from their sin they find an immediate and loving welcome to the Father's heart and home. Joel had called for the trumpet to announce war; he now directs the trumpet blast to summon the people, from the highest to the lowest, to plead for help. Prayer and true repentance and faith bring an immediate answer. As the husband yearns over his erring but repentant wife, and is indignant with those who have maltreated her, so will Jehovah remove from us, when we turn to him, those who have cruelly oppressed us.

The great things Jehovah did against Egypt and Babylon are an earnest of what he will do again. The earth, v. 21, the lower animals, v. 22, and, above all, the children of Zion, literal and spiritual, v. 23, have good reason to rejoice in what awaits them. God promises not only to forgive sin, but to make us happy and well provided as if the locust and cankerworm had never settled upon our lives.

JOEL 2:28—3:21

"The Valley of Decision." Having stated the outward blessings that would follow repentance, Joel unveils the extraordinary spiritual blessings that were in store. The outpouring of the Spirit, described in Acts 2:16, 17, does not exhaust these glorious words. This blessing is for

all whom the Lord our God shall call to himself, and as one to whom his call has come, you have a perfect right to claim your share in Pentecost. The very slaves, the most degraded and despised of men become free when they yield themselves to Jesus, and have an equal right to the same Spirit.

The third chapter refers to the last desperate effort made by the powers of the world against Christ and his people. This will be the closing scene of man's apostasy. But the Lord will vindicate and deliver his oppressed from the hand of their oppressors; and the same judgment will bring them blessing. Having cleansed his people from their stains, Messiah will tabernacle among them, Rev. 21:3.

THE BOOK OF AMOS

"PREPARE TO MEET THY GOD, O ISRAEL," 4:12

I. GOD'S IMPENDING JUDGMENTS   *1, 2.*
   A. Upon the surrounding nations   *1:1—2:5.*
   B. Upon Israel   *2:6–16.*

II. THE STATEMENT OF ISRAEL'S ACCUSATION   *3—6.*
   A. Sins that demand rebuke   *3.*
   B. Defiance of God's judgments   *4.*
   C. Substitution of religious forms for righteousness   *5.*
   D. Luxurious self-indulgence   *6.*

III. SYMBOLIC VISIONS OF ISRAEL'S FUTURE   *7—9.*
   A. Locusts, fire, the plumbline   *7:1–9.*
      (Amos' prophesying provokes resistance)   *7:10–17.*
   B. The basket of summer fruit   *8:1–3.*
      (The accusation renewed)   *8:4–10.*
   C. The famine of the Word of God   *8:11–14.*
   D. The smiting of the Temple pillars   *9:1–10.*
   E. Israel's final restoration   *9:11–15.*

INTRODUCTION

Amos was not a prophet or a prophet's son, but a shepherd and husbandman, 7:14. He was conscious of an irresistible commission, 3:8; 7:15. To this he bore witness when Amaziah, the high priest of idolatry, charged him with conspiracy. God is sovereign and selects as his messengers whom he will. Tekoa, still known by that name, was situated on a noble elevation, six miles south of Bethlehem. From this Judean village Amos was sent on a prophetic mission into the land of Israel. Under the rule of Jeroboam II the nation had reached the high tide of power and prosperity, but corruption and oppression prevailed.

The style of this book is simple, picturesque, and striking. Its illustrations are borrowed from rural scenes and breathe the fresh atmosphere of the country. The allusions to history, such as found in 9:7, as well as the power of consecutive thought here shown, prove that despite the responsible duties of shepherd Amos found time for mental as well as spiritual effort.

COMMENTARY

AMOS 1:1-10

Outside Nations Shall Suffer Judgment. Amos opens his prophecies with predictions against neighboring peoples, that Israel may be led to appreciate her guilt and to bear the approach of God's righteous judgment, Luke 12:47. The formula of "three transgressions... and for four," v. 3, means several or many. Compare Job 5:19.

The order followed is Syria, v. 3; Philistia, v. 6; Tyre, v. 9; Edom, v. 11; Ammon, v. 13; Moab, 2:1. Each of these neighboring kingdoms was successively overwhelmed by the invasion of the great countries that lay in the valley of the Euphrates. Tiglath-pileser began and ultimately Nebuchadnezzar finished the work of desolation. But in turn the conquerors, becoming enervated by uninterrupted success and prosperity, were also swept away. We may be sure that there is One who judges in the earth and that although might may assert its claims to be right, it is but for a moment. The constitution of the universe is in harmony with Bethlehem, Nazareth, Calvary, and only a Christian civilization can be permanent.

AMOS 1:11—2:5

Judah Shall Be Judged Also. "Edom" was Esau; that is, the people were closely akin to Israel. Perhaps for that very reason the hatred on either side became more and more inveterate from the days of the Exodus to the siege and fall of Jerusalem, Ps. 137:7, 8. "Teman" and "Bozrah" were principal cities, the first being named after Esau's grandson, Gen. 36:11. Isaiah, in later years, saw the warrior Angel of Jehovah coming up from Edom to the foothills of Palestine, his garments stained with the blood of the foe whom he had overthrown, 63:1. Thus Jesus Christ has overcome our foes, and now stands sentry between us and them.

"Rabbah" was the capital city of Ammon. The strife between the citizens and the Chosen People smoldered from the days of Saul, flaming out from time to time in terrible intensity. "Moab"—the terrible act referred to here was probably associated with 2 Kings 3:27. Alas that in the divine vengeance Judah should be associated with these heathen peoples! The indictment is not for sins against man, but for those committed against God. We are judged by the greater light and the higher standards that we possess. The fire here threatened was the invasion of Nebuchadnezzar and his Chaldeans, who have their modern counterparts. Man is often used by the Almighty for the chastening and purifying of his fellows.

AMOS 2:6-16

Neither Shall Israel Escape. First, the prophet enumerates Israel's sins. They were unjust to the poor, carrying their extortions to such lengths as to goad the poor to desperation. They were unchaste. They held their idolatrous festivities in idol shrines while they unjustly detained and confiscated the pledges of the poor. They perpetrated shamelessly the enormous crimes for which the Amorites were dispossessed by Joshua and their fathers. But notice nothing is said of that great general and his valiant soldiers; our mind is carried beyond all human agency to the Eternal. "I destroyed," v. 9.

The ripple of the ocean on the beach which you hear and see is due to the action of the sun or moon; so, the changes that men attribute to political combinations must ultimately be traced back to the divine will in its permissive or directive energy. One of the most graphic pictures is in v. 13. We can almost see the heavily laden wagon dragged from the harvest field. The wheels creak and groan; the oxen advance with difficulty; the timbers threaten to succumb. So God bears up the world; and thus did Jesus stoop and sweat great drops of blood under the weight of the sins of the whole world.

AMOS 3

The Lord's Word Must Come True. The closer our relationship with God, the more searching his scrutiny and chastening. The sins of God's children which may seem of slight consequence are rigorously dealt with by their Heavenly Father, who loves them too well to allow their life to be permanently injured. It is because God loves us that he is so quick in detecting the least symptoms of disease. But we must agree (v. 3) with him as to the sinfulness of sin, the need of cleansing, the hopelessness of our old nature, and the world's urgent need both of our sympathy and sacrifice. So only shall we walk with God as Enoch did. The soul that is one with him is on the alert, as is the traveler who hears the lion's roar in the forest. Watch; ye know not the hour!

The nobles of Egypt and Philistia are summoned to view the sins of Samaria and to confirm the justice of her penalty. From all sides the invader would descend on the apostate land. Only a fragment should escape, like the small piece of a lamb rescued from the jaws of the savage beast of prey. The couch of luxury, the bed of sloth, the golden calf of Beth-el—all marked the degeneracy of the Chosen People. May the sorrows through which the world is passing at this hour be the means of cleansing human society from these same evils, that our Christian civilization may escape the penalties that overtook Israel!

AMOS 4:1-11

Calamities Are God's Warnings. Speaking after the imagery of his vocation, Amos the herdsman compares the rich and powerful of Samaria, who were living in luxury and wantonness, to the kine of Bashan, a breed of cattle notorious for strength and stubbornness. They broke through hedges, threw down fences, trespassed on neighboring pastures, and gored lesser cattle. The judges and magistrates were in cruel collusion with the masters who oppressed the serfs; they were willing to condone breaches of the Law for drink. Sacrifices and tithes were rigorously maintained, but the entire religious system was rotten.

Already heavy judgment had fallen upon the degenerate people. There had been famine, occasional rainy seasons, mildew, pestilence, and plague—but all in vain. That God was behind these phenomena was obvious from the fact that rain showers had fallen in one place and not in another. There had been a method in God's dealings that indicated a personal agency. The worst cities had suffered the most. But the people had refused to lay it to heart. Note the sorrowful refrain—"yet have ye not returned unto me, saith the Lord." It may be that some reader of these lines may find herein a clue to the mysterious succession of strokes that have befallen himself and his household.

AMOS 4:12—5:15

"Prepare To Meet Thy God." Worse judgments than those mentioned in the previous verses were in store, but before they are inflicted the entire nation is summoned to the divine bar. Whether we choose or not, "we must all appear before the judgment seat of Christ." Prepare, my soul, to meet him! Note the sublimity of that last verse in Chapter 4. How great is God, who made the mountains; how mysterious, who made the wind; how sublime, who calls to the dawn; how mighty, to whom mountains and peaks are stepping-stones!

But great and holy though God is, we are invited to seek him. He desires to bless, but he must be sought. Were we more diligent in seeking, as the miner for gold or the scientific man for Nature's secrets, we should be marvelously repaid. "Eye hath not seen . . ." Amos speaks as Nature's child. Often as he had tended his flocks, he had watched the Pleiades with their gentle radiance, and Orion, the herald of storm. He had listened to God calling across the waters and had drawn life from him. "Seek and live!" O soul, what a God is thine! Thy springs

AMOS 5:16-27

A Dark Day for Hypocrites. Mighty sins had been committed, and mighty judgments were at hand. The oppression of the poor, v. 11; the erection of elegant dwellings from unrighteous exactions, v. 11; the acceptance of bribes to betray the needy, v. 12—all these must be reckoned with. But if the guilty nation would not seek God and establish judgment in the gate where magistrates sat to dispense justice, the streets would be filled with wailing, and the husbandmen and vine-dressers would be equally affected by the widespread desolation as the dwellers in the cities.

Moreover, bad as Israel's present condition was, it would become infinitely worse, as though a man fleeing from a lion rushed into the arms of a bear, or taking refuge in a house was stung by a serpent that lay hid in a cranny of the wall. Of what avail are religious rites when the heart is alienated from God, v. 21ff? Let us heed well the exhortation of vv. 23 and 24. The martyr Stephen quoted vv. 25-27, which accuse the people of carrying about little shrines and pocket-idols, to serve as amulets averting disaster, Acts 7:43. But they might as well have built a bank of sand to arrest an overflowing flood! The one thing which is going to help us is repentance toward God and faith in our Savior, Jesus Christ.

AMOS 6

"Woe to Them That Are at Ease in Zion!" Zion is included with Samaria in this prophecy, and the nobles are specially condemned for their drunkenness, gluttony, and insolence. The prophet quotes the example of great neighboring peoples as a warning that the abuse of God's good gifts leads to their withdrawal. Calneh, on the Tigris, and Hamath had fallen to Assyria; Gath, also, had been recently overwhelmed. How unlikely, therefore, that Israel, eaten through by extravagance and luxury, could endure. National dissolution is not far away when palaces are filled with riot while the poor rot in neglect. It was thus that Joseph's brethren ate their food at the pit's mouth while Joseph lay beneath. Many professing Christians are similarly "at ease," indifferent to their brother's woe.

The greatness of approaching judgment is illustrated by a simple incident. A household of eleven is smitten by plague; ten die, one only survives. So great has been the mortality that no nearer relative than an uncle is left to carry out the dead for cremation; and when the matter of a funeral service is broached, the suggestion is instantly met by the remark, "Those old customs cannot be observed amid the stress of such a time; we do not now mention God's name." Funeral rites would pass out of use. God's dealings with his people had been as useless as plowing rocks would be.

AMOS 7

The Herdsman's Message. "The king's mowings" were the earliest yield of the grasslands which were exacted by him. Our King also has his mowings, when he takes to himself our dearest and best while the dew of youth is still upon them—but he is only claiming his own.

Three disasters threatened the guilty land—locusts, fire, and plague; but the prophet's intercessions warded off the blow. The Bible often tells a similar story of the power of intercession. If only the Church were united and prayed with one voice, she would be able to secure deliverance for the smitten earth. When God is said to repent, we must not attribute to him changeableness of purpose, but he seems to repent because man has changed his attitude. If you walk against the wind, it resists you; but if you turn and walk in the opposite direction, it helps you. The plumbline, v. 7, is used to discover the extent of the mischief, before the order for destruction is issued.

Amaziah, the chief priest of the national idolatry, found the stalwart witness of the herdsman-prophet extremely inconvenient and wanted to get rid of him. There was great simplicity and dignity in the reply. Like Luther in after years, Amos could "do no other."

AMOS 8

The Worst Famine of All. What is more fragile than summer fruit! It is so beautiful, so refreshing, yet so readily corrupted and diseased. To Amos it was an emblem of the rapidity with which dissolution would overtake his rebellious nation. The end had arrived. The Great Husbandman could do no more. When the harvest has come, separation between good and bad is inevitable. See Isa. 5:4; Matt. 13:30.

The crimes of the ruling class were enormous. Eager to increase their stores, they wearied of time given to religion. They grudged passing a day without opening their salesrooms. They did not hesitate to make their measures ("ephah") small, and to demand a greater weight of money ("shekel") from their clients. These were crimes that could not be passed over. It is an awful sentence when God says, "I will never forget," v. 7. Invasion would sweep the land like an inundation. Since the people would not heed the God-sent messengers, they would be withdrawn. There would be a famine of the Word of God, and those who had most despised it, because enamored with the fascinations of youth, would be smitten with an insatiable appetite for it.

AMOS 9

The Day of Restoration. The guilty will certainly be punished. If they enter the sacred place of worship, even that will not shelter them, v. 1. Flight and concealment will be in vain. Let them climb ever so high or burrow ever so deep, let them scale the loftiest hills or dive into the deepest seas—the consequences of their sins will overtake them, vv. 2, 3. How can sinners hope to escape from him whose chambers are built in the heavens and whose voice governs the tides, v. 6? The great desolations of the past prove the exactness and severity of his judgments, vv. 7, 8. How remarkably v. 9 has been fulfilled! Notwithstanding their scatterings, the Hebrew people have been preserved as a race.

The final paragraph, vv. 11-15, is very reassuring. It is a burst of noble anticipation, quoted by the Apostle James, Acts 15:14-17. The promises made to Abraham and David are yet to be fulfilled. The derision of their foes, of whom Edom was the ringleader, will be silenced. Through the parted curtain, we glimpse the golden age of the future. There is a divine plan working to its conclusion, and Israel shall yet come again to the land given to their fathers.

THE BOOK OF
OBADIAH
THE DOOM OF EDOM

I. THE DESTRUCTION OF THE NATION *1–9.*
II. EDOM'S HEARTLESSNESS TOWARD ISRAEL *10–16.*
II. ISRAEL'S EXALTATION *17–21.*

INTRODUCTION

With regard to the personal life of Obadiah, information is lacking. His prophecy was probably delivered about the time of the fall of Jerusalem, 586 B.C. It is the shortest of the prophetical writings, containing but twenty-one verses. Its theme is the doom of Edom, because that nation mocked Jerusalem when the latter was destroyed. Its predictions have been completely fulfilled.

COMMENTARY

OBADIAH 1-21

The Coming Doom of Edom. A vision was granted to Obadiah of the penalty to be meted out to Edom for his cruelty to his brother Israel. Instead of showing sympathy, the Edomites had feasted their eyes on the misery of their kinsfolk, eagerly watching for their destruction. See Num. 20:14-21 and Ps. 137:7. But the very calamities which had befallen Jacob would visit them.

Since we know not how soon we may be called upon to suffer, we should feel compassion for rather than exultation in the sufferings of others. Malice harbored in any form contains the seed of future suffering. The great day of God is at hand, v. 15, which shall bring retribution to all who have set themselves against the kingdom of God. When our Lord returns he will bring redemption to his saints, and his people shall possess their possessions. This suggests the solemn inquiry whether as the heirs of God we have yet entered upon our inheritance. O happy day when the kingdom shall be the Lord's and we shall reign with him!

THE BOOK OF
JONAH
AN UNWILLING PROPHET OF THE MERCIFUL GOD

I. JONAH'S DISOBEDIENCE *1:1–14.*
II. HIS PUNISHMENT *1:15–17.*
III. HIS PRAYER AND RESCUE *2.*
IV. HIS PREACHING IN NINEVEH *3:1–4.*
V. THE CITY'S REPENTANCE *3:5–10.*
VI. JONAH'S DISPLEASURE; GOD'S MERCY *4.*

INTRODUCTION

Jonah was a native of Gath-hepher in Zebulun. Some think that he was a contemporary and disciple of Elijah, and that he therefore lived about 850 B.C. He is the oldest of the prophets whose writings have come down to us. That the book is historical may be gathered from the references of our Lord in Matthew 12:39–41 and 16:4.

The narrative presents a most striking contrast between the long-suffering mercy of God and the hard indifference of a good man to the fate of a great Gentile city. Probably it indicates the dawn of a better era when the Chosen People shall enter upon that long education, the results of which Paul tells us in Ephesians 2:19–22; 3:1–8.

COMMENTARY

JONAH 1:1-16

Fleeing from God and Duty. Jonah is mentioned in 2 Kings 14:25. He was clearly very patriotic and did not despair of his country in its darkest days. This commission to Nineveh was therefore not to his taste, because he had no desire to see the great heathen city brought to her knees. Another century would have to pass before Isaiah and Micah would proclaim that the heathen world would turn to God, Mic. 4:1, 2; Isa. 2:2.

Rather than go upon this errand of mercy, Jonah hurried down to the one seaport, that he might escape his duty. Sin is always a descent; we always have to pay heavily in tolls and fares when we take our own way instead of God's, and we must never reckon that opportunity implies permission.

Weary with excitement and travel, the prophet is oblivious to the weighing of the anchor. The disasters that block the way of disobedience are harder than our difficulties in performing God's bidding. Note the divine agency in our lives: "the word of the Lord came; the Lord sent out a great wind; the Lord had prepared a great fish." There were, in these heathen sailors, beautiful traits which ought to have abashed the prophet. Their prayer to their idols and their endeavor to save this stranger Jew are as instructive as remarkable.

JONAH 1:17—2:10

A Prayer from the Depths. The great fish was probably a shark. He who sent the storm prepared the fish. Life is full of contrivances on the part of the great Lover of men. To plunge beneath the wave is to fall into his arms. More than once the body of a man has been found in the belly of a shark in the Mediterranean. Even those who hold that this story is an elaborate parable must admit that it is probably founded on such a fact. Our Lord's endorsement of this book and incident is very emphatic, Matt. 12:39-41.

The psalm which follows is very helpful to those who have brought themselves into the depths by their wrongdoing. God will hear such out of the depths of Sheol. When you think you are cast out of his sight forever, if you will look toward his holy temple, you will find that his love is gradually extricating you from the pit. To trust in your own efforts and expedients is to regard lying vanities and to forsake your own mercy. "Salvation is of the Lord." All Nature waits upon his word. The big sharks and the tiny minnows are alike at the behest of God for the help of man. Only "look again" to God, and then be sure to pay your vows when delivered!

JONAH 3

A Repentant City. Peter was not only forgiven, but restored to his office; so also was

Jonah again sent to Nineveh. Thank God for our second chances! There was no hesitancy this time. The prophet arose and went. The story of his deliverance seems to have reached Nineveh and to have prepared its people to receive his word, Luke 11:30. We must deliver God's messages and preach only as he bids us. He will tell us what to say.

Nineveh is said to have been sixty miles in circuit, the distance of a three days' journey. It was full of violence and cruelty. But the sight of that strange figure, clad in a rude sheepskin mantle, smote its conscience. The alarm spread from the streets to the palace. Even the great king felt it within his sculptured chambers. It stirred him to action, so that king and court, peers and people, and even the brute creation became united in one act of common humiliation. The repentance was city-wide in its scope, v. 5; was practical, v. 8; and directed toward God, v. 9. What a contrast to Israel! There, prophet after prophet was exposed to refusal and even to cruel usage. Whatever fear there may have been upon man's side, there was no hesitation upon God's. He abundantly pardoned! See Isa. 55:7.

JONAH 4

The Prophet's Narrowness Rebuked. This chapter marks an era in the development of the outlook of the Hebrew people. Here, upon its repentance, a heathen city was pardoned. Clearly Jehovah was the God, not of Jews only but of Gentiles also. Jonah, however, had no pleasure in the revelation. He clung to the bitter narrowness of national prejudice, fearing that when his own people received tidings of Nineveh's repentance and deliverance, they would be encouraged in their obstinate refusal of God's Law.

How often God puts gourds into our lives to refresh us with their exquisite greenery and to remind us of his thoughtful love! Our fretfulness and petulance are no barriers to his tender mercy. The withering of the gourd brought bitter reproaches from the prophet who would have beheld the destruction of Nineveh without a tear. He did not realize that to God, Nineveh was all and much more than the gourd was to him. Notice the extreme beauty of the concluding verse: the permanence of the city contrasted with the frailty of the gourd; the responsibility of God for Nineveh, which he had made to grow; the preciousness to him, not only of the mature, but of babes and cattle!

THE BOOK OF
MICAH
JUDGMENT SENT FORTH UNTO VICTORY

I. JUDGMENT   *1—3.*
   A. For idolatry   *1.*
   B. For oppression   *2.*
   C. False kings, prophets, and priests   *3.*

II. SALVATION   *4, 5.*
   A. God's reign in Zion   *4.*
   B. The Ruler from Bethlehem   *5.*

III. GOD'S CONTROVERSY WITH HIS PEOPLE   *6.*
   A. A summons to contend before the mountains   *6:1–8.*
   B. Condemnation and judgment   *6:9–16.*

IV. JUDGMENT UNTO VICTORY   *7.*
   A. The appalling national depravity   *7:1–13.*
   B. The triumph of mercy   *7:14–20.*

INTRODUCTION

Micah was a contemporary of Isaiah, but their activities lay far apart. Micah lived in the country and was concerned with both Israel and Judah, while Isaiah's career is closely associated with the fortunes of Jerusalem.

The book of Micah shows a clear understanding of the events of the time. He foresaw the invasions of Shalmaneser and Sennacherib, the dispersion of Israel, and the destruction of Jerusalem. Alone among the prophets he foretells the birth of Christ in Bethlehem, 5:2. "His special office, as a herald of coming judgment, causes a predominant severity of tone; but all harshness is softened into exquisite beauty at the close," says one commentator.

COMMENTARY

MICAH 1

God's Witness against His Chosen. Micah was contemporary with Isaiah and Hosea. Jeremiah quotes from him. Compare 3:12 and Jer. 26:18.

In vv. 1-4 the prophet summons the nations to behold the just punishment which Jehovah would mete out to his faithless people. Verses 5, 6 portray the desolation of Samaria. Destruction would settle on the homes and fields of men, and the prospect of this so affected the prophet that he divested himself of outer garment and sandals, that his disheveled condition might depict the calamities that he announced. Verses 10-16 make clear that Judah also would suffer similar chastisements. Aphrah and Saphir would be hurried into captivity. So universal would be the calamity that Zaanan would not come to bewail with the neighboring city of Beth-ezel.

The prophets were true patriots, and they felt that all good citizens should lament with them, in the hope of averting impending judgments. Are we feeling the sins and sorrows of our time, as Jesus felt those of Jerusalem, when he wept over the city?

MICAH 2

The Harvest of Greed and Injustice. The former chapter dealt with sins against the first table of the law; this deals with those against the second. Evil must sooner or later befall those who devise evil against their neighbors, covet their goods, and oppress their persons. So absolute would be the destruction that estates would no longer descend from father to son or be measured by lot, v. 5; and the people would become hard and callous to the prophet's voice, v. 6. Yet through it all God's Spirit would yearn over his people, vv. 7-13; his words would still comfort humble souls. But the cruelty of men who despoiled their poor neighbors, not only of their ornaments but of the tunic next their skin, would bring disaster upon the entire nation. The guilty people must prepare to arise and depart, for Canaan could no longer be their home.

But even from captivity God would restore his people, breaking the way through walls of difficulty. Our Breaker is the Lord Jesus who broke the way for us from the prison-house of death. Let us follow him as he passes on his way to victory.

MICAH 3

The Punishment of Avarice. The princes who as magistrates should have administered justice to others sat around the caldron, casting in the very flesh and skin of the people whom they were set to rule. Their perversion of justice would lead to their inability to distinguish between evil and good. Sin not only sears the conscience but darkens the understanding, Eph. 4:18. Their punishment would be like their guilt. As they had refused the cry of the oppressed, so would God refuse theirs. The false prophets had willfully misled the people. Their one desire was to get food. For those who provided it, they uttered peace; for those who opposed them, war. Therefore they would be left without a vision; God's Spirit would cease to strive. How great the contrast between them and Micah, who spoke with the consciousness of spiritual power! Oh, that every minister and teacher of God's holy gospel were able to utter v. 8! It may be ours through the Holy Spirit.

MICAH 4

The Promise of Peace. It is not improbable that Isaiah, 2:1-4, and Micah quoted an older prophecy, which in its fullness is yet to be fulfilled. In the millennial age Israel, in her restored beauty, will be the center of a renovated world. That restoration will bring great glory to God and blessing to mankind, Rom. 11:15. The time center of unity is not to be found in creeds or systems, but in the impulse of a common desire after God and common worship. When men have found their unity in God, they will renounce war, and home life will become the preservative of society, v. 4. Verses 6 and 7 foretell the gathering of Israel to their own land. Babylon probably stands not only for the literal nation by which the Jews were carried into captivity, but for all of the Gentile nations that have afflicted the Chosen People. Notice that God's deliverances discover and help us in the midst of our direct affliction.

MICAH 5

The Deliverer from Bethlehem. This name for Bethlehem recalls Genesis 48:7. Though insignificant in size, she would outshine other cities because of Messiah's birth, Matt. 2:6. As man, our Lord comes from David's city; but as Son of God, his goings forth are from eternity. Though the Jewish flock rejected him, he is the Shepherd of men. He is great to the ends of the earth and has made peace by the blood of his cross. What though the Assyrian, whether ancient or modern, threaten us, shepherds and princes shall be raised up as deliverers, v. 5. God's people refresh the world like dew, and are lionlike in strength and courage, v. 8. Horses, chariots, and walled cities are classed with witchcraft, etc., because they weaned away the trust of God's people. "Thou shalt no more worship the work of thine hands."

MICAH 6

"What Doth the Lord Require of Thee?" In vv. 1-4 the prophet returns from his vision of the future to the actual condition of his people, which was utterly desperate. The mountains, as the most enduring monuments of Nature, are summoned as witnesses in the great trial between Jehovah and his people. Like Israel, we have been delivered from the house of bondage with infinite love, but how wayward and willful we have been! Verses 5-8 prove the impotence of a religion which is only external.

Few have known more sublime truth than Baalam, v. 5, but he loved the wages of unrighteousness, and this eclipsed the divine radiance that became overcast and finally overwhelmed. Verses 9-11 reveal the fruitlessness of a life of sin. Sooner or later Nature herself becomes unresponsive—sowing, but no harvest; the treading of the press, but no juice. The only path to real satisfaction and peace is in the love and faithful service of God. Why are we so slow to tread it?

MICAH 7

God's Compassion for an Erring People. Things had come to an awful state in the favored city. Oppression, bribery, and bloodshed were everywhere increasing. Men wrought evil with both hands. Husbands could not trust their wives. At such a time there is no refuge for God's children save in God, vv. 7-13.

When we have learned our lesson, we find God appearing for our help. He brings forth the light and vindicates us. Then those that hated us and suggested that he had forsaken will be compelled to admit that he has completely vindicated us from their reproach. Be of good cheer, believer; wait for God. He will bring out thy righteousness as the light and thy judgment as the noonday, vv. 10-12.

Next the prophet pleads with Israel's Shepherd to repeat the marvels of the Exodus. He knows that God will not only pardon iniquities but "subdue" them, trampling them beneath his feet. This anticipates the ascension, Eph. 1:20-23. When a stone sinks into ocean depths, it cannot be recovered; and when sin is forgiven, God never recalls it either here or hereafter.

THE BOOK OF
NAHUM
THE DOOM OF NINEVEH

I. GOD RESERVES WRATH FOR HIS ADVERSARIES   *1:1—2:2.*
   A. The resistless power of God's judgments   *1:1–8.*
   B. Warning to Assyria; comfort for Judah   *1:9—2:2.*

II. THE CAPITAL OF ASSYRIA SHALL PERISH   *2:3—3:19.*
   A. The siege, capture, and sack of the city   *2:3–12.*
   B. "Behold, I am against thee"   *2:13—3:19.*

INTRODUCTION

The theme of the prophecy of Nahum is the complete and final destruction of Nineveh. Jonah had already warned the city of its danger, and a temporary respite had been gained by repentance. But the people soon returned to their evil ways, and Nahum was sent to declare the doom of the city without promise of relief.

Nineveh was one of the greatest cities of ancient times, the capital of the flourishing Assyrian empire. At the time when Nahum delivered his prophecy, Assurbanipal was at the height of his power. His capital was the center of the trade and commerce of the world. Yet it was a "bloody city, all full of lies and robbery," having plundered the neighboring nations, and was ripe for destruction. Within a short time the prophet's words came true; the great city was laid low, scattered ruins still marking the place where it stood.

COMMENTARY

NAHUM 1

God's Goodness and Righteous Anger. The native city of Nahum was Elkosh, near the Lake of Galilee. The name Capernaum means literally "the village of Nahum." He lived about 150 years after Jonah, who also had been especially concerned with the sins and doom of Nineveh. Though as a Jew he must have dreaded Nineveh, which had already carried Samaria into captivity and was now menacing Jerusalem, he accounted its fate a grievous burden—"the burden of Nineveh." We must never speak of the doom of the ungodly, save from a broken heart.

Verses 1-8 form a magnificent preamble combining the goodness and severity of God. His dealings with mankind are wrapped in mystery, but he is good and the stronghold of his saints. In vv. 9-15 we see how mad Assyria was to enter into conflict with Jehovah. The fate of thorns in fiercely burning flame is the emblem of their doom. Compare v. 14 with Isa. 37:38. When the hour of anguish is past, let us not forget to pay our vows.

NAHUM 2

A Cruel City To Be Overthrown. This is a prophetic foreview of the overthrow of Nineveh by the Medo-Babylonians. God had used her for the chastisement of his people; now, in turn, she must be cast away for her sins. The attacking soldiers wore crimson tunics, and the chariot wheels were armed with scythes that flashed as they revolved. The streets might be filled with chariots mustering for defense, but all must be in vain since the scaling-ladders were already against the walls and the gates of the rivers would soon be opened. Huzzab was Nineveh's queen and represents the condition of the city, going into captivity as a slave, with bare face and legs. Note the comparison of Nineveh to a den of lions filled with bones. Fire and sword completed her ruin. This is the lot of the enemies of God's people. See Isa. 54:16, 17. But if God is true to his threatenings, how much more is he true to his promises!

NAHUM 3

Deserved Doom. This terrible chapter pictures the doom of Nineveh. She had used infamous methods in bringing surrounding nations under her power, and now her shame was to be discovered and exposed. It seemed incredible that so great a city should become desolate, but she is reminded of the populous Thebes especially dedicated to Ammon, the Egyptian Jupiter. As this great city had been overwhelmed by Assyria, so would Nineveh be by the Chaldeans. In spite of her Nile and her tributary nations, Thebes fell, and Nineveh would drink of the same cup. Her fall would be as easy as the plucking of ripe figs. The centuries that have passed since the prophet spoke only lend emphasis to his words. The silence of death still reigns over the desolate mounds that mark the site of the cherished capital. Let us see to it that we are heirs of that kingdom which cannot be shaken, Heb. 12:28.

THE BOOK OF HABAKKUK

"THE JUST SHALL LIVE BY HIS FAITH," 2:4

I. THE PROPHET'S EXPOSTULATION   *1, 2.*
   A. Why are iniquity and injustice permitted to prevail?   *1:1–4.*
      Reply: The Chaldeans will execute judgment   *1:5–11.*
   B. How can power be given to so wicked a people?   *1:12–17.*
      Reply: Their exaltation is but temporary   *2:1–4.*
   C. Five woes against the Chaldeans   *2:5–20.*

II. THE PROPHET'S PRAYER   *3.*
   A. God's mighty works a ground of hope   *3:1–15.*
   B. A declaration of unwavering faith   *3:16–19.*

INTRODUCTION

The prophecy of Habakkuk is concerned with the rise of the Chaldeans to power. Habakkuk had seen this mighty people used in inflicting judgment upon Nineveh, and they appeared to be the very instrument of God. But a problem arose when they were seen to be as wicked as the Assyrians whom they had destroyed. How could God use for any purpose a heartless, cruel nation, bent wholly upon evil? The prophet's answer is that God will make all his dealings clear if we but wait for him. "The just shall live by his faith." When the issues appear confused, the righteous can still remain steadfast and loyal to God—that is their life. "Be true; light will dawn."

The last chapter is a poem of great beauty, remarkable for its expression of unwavering faith. Though all gifts fail, the Giver himself abides, and in him the prophet will rejoice.

COMMENTARY

HABAKKUK 1

The Apparent Prosperity of the Wicked. Habakkuk probably lived toward the beginning of the reign of Jehoiakim, when the Chaldeans were preparing to invade the land. Jerusalem was filled with wickedness. Crimes of violence and lawlessness had become so numerous that the prophet was appalled at the sight. He could only point to the fate of other nations, which must also befall Judah unless the people repented. Paul quotes v. 5 in Acts 13:41. The Chaldeans are compared to the leopard, the evening wolf, and the east wind. The prophet turns to Jehovah in an agony of expostulation and entreaty. Was he not from everlasting? Was he not Israel's Rock? The prophet's solace is the reflection, "We shall not die." An ancient reading is, "Thou canst not die." We are reminded of Revelation 1:18. O thou undying, unchanging, life-giving Savior, we cling to thee amid the storms that sweep the world, as limpets to the rock.

HABAKKUK 2

"The Just Shall Live by His Faith." Having prayed, the prophet expected an answer and looked for it. When it came, there would be no mistaking it. But until we see eye to eye, we must live by simple faith in God. Note that wonderful clause in v. 4, which is referred to so often afterward. See Rom. 1:17; Gal. 2:16; 3:11. Life in this age, as in that, may be obtained and maintained by faith in the ever-living God. Through long waiting-times the only source of continued life is the faith which draws all from God. From v. 5 onwards, the prophet enumerates Babylon's sins: her pride, love of strong drink, rapacity, and violence. It could not be God's will that the mighty city should flourish on the anguish of the world.

From scenes of anarchy and riot which foretell Chaldea's doom, we pass into Jehovah's Temple, where peaceful silence reigns! Let us live in that secret place! "The secret of the Lord is with them that fear him!"

HABAKKUK 3

The Faith That Is Invincible. This psalm was intended to be sung by the captives during the Exile, which was near. In vv. 3–15 there is a recital of the great events in the past. First Sinai, then the victories and deliverances of the Book of Judges, the passage of the Red Sea and Jordan, the divine vengeance on the oppressors. But the prophet could not contemplate the future of the Chosen People without dismay. He longed to be at rest before those terrible Chaldean hosts burst upon the land. At the close he breaks into a sublime refrain which has been the solace and song of myriads of believers. If all God's gifts failed, he would still possess the Giver. He could still triumph in God. Indeed, the divine Savior and Friend is often more apparent when the fields and the farmsteads are bare.

THE BOOK OF ZEPHANIAH

"THE DAY OF THE LORD"

I. A DAY OF JUDGMENT   *1:1—3:8.*
   A. Upon the whole earth   *1:1–3.*
   B. Upon particular nations   *1:4—3:8.*
      1. Judah and Jerusalem   *1:4–18.*
         (Call to repentance)   *2:1–3.*
      2. Philistia, Moab, Ammon, Ethiopia, and Assyria   *2:4–15.*
      3. Princes, prophets, and priests of Jerusalem   *3:1–7.*
         (Call to repentance)   *3:8.*

II. A DAY OF HOPE   *3:9–20.*
   A. All nations to be taught the worship of God   *3:9, 10.*
   B. The cleansing of Israel   *3:11–13.*
   C. God's gracious reign   *3:14–20.*

INTRODUCTION

Zephaniah may have been a great-great-grandson of Hezekiah, 1:1, margin. He prophesied during the reign of Josiah, probably before the discovery of the Book of the Law; the evils which he denounced were removed by the king.

Zephaniah is the prophet of the Day of the Lord. He does not, like Obadiah, Nahum, or Habakkuk, deal with the downfall of any one nation; he is instead a prophet of universal judgment. His message to the nations is parallel to the words of Jesus: "Or those eighteen, upon whom the tower in Siloam fell, and slew them, think ye that they were sinners above all men that dwelt in Jerusalem? I tell you, Nay: but, except ye repent, ye shall all likewise perish," Luke 13:4, 5.

Zephaniah declares that all nations, even Judah itself, will fall under the divine wrath if they continue to defy the divine Law. But his message is more than one of judgment. He shows that God is working for the salvation of mankind, and that following judgment there will be revealed new heavens and a new earth wherein dwells righteousness.

COMMENTARY

ZEPHANIAH 1

"The Great Day of the Lord." Zephaniah means "hidden of the Lord." He lived in Josiah's reign and cooperated with that king in his efforts to put down idolatry. His prophecy deals with the sins that were rife in Judah and the fearful retribution that would be inflicted through the Chaldeans. *Approaching destruction*, vv. 2–6. The "Chemarims" were idolatrous priests dressed in black garments. "Malcham" is Milcom or Moloch. Notice the successive classes of those who were to suffer in the overthrow. They constitute a series of concentric circles, narrowing down at last to those who had turned back, and to those who had never sought the Lord. *The invaders*, vv. 7–18. The guests whom God invited to the banquet were Nebuchadnezzar and his soldiers! They marched in through the Fish Gate; and as they advanced, cry after cry arose from the affrighted populace, driven from quarter to quarter. "Maktesh," v. 11, was probably the Vale of Siloam, where the merchant princes dwelt or pursued their business. None would be able to elude the coming vengeance. Those that affected foreign attire or leaped across the threshold in superstition or practiced deceit would have to pay dearly for their sins. Fulfilled in the overthrow of Jerusalem by Nebuchadnezzar, and afterward by Titus, these words will always stand for the inevitable national sufferings which follow national crimes.

ZEPHANIAH 2

Meekness Saves, Pride Destroys. The nation, on the whole, had no remorse, no desire for God; but there were a few meek and lowly souls, and the hope was held out to them that they would be hidden from the coming overthrow. God discriminates in his judgments, and sends his angels to conduct Lot out of Sodom. The judgment of the surrounding nations occupies vv. 4–18. Philistia, Moab, Ammon, Ethiopia and Assyria are mentioned. God never forgets the treatment meted out to his people by their foes, vv. 8–10. The captivity of Israel would be turned again, but there was no hope of recovery for the peoples that had rejoiced in their overthrow. What a picture is given in v. 11 of famished gods! It seemed incredible that great Nineveh should become a wilderness; yet so it has been for centuries. Whenever an individual or nation dwells carelessly, destruction is not far away.

ZEPHANIAH 3

Fullness of Salvation. The sins of Jerusalem, vv. 1–7. Uninfluenced by judgments upon other nations, Jerusalem pursued her course, morally impure, oppressive, refusing instruction, estranged from God. Yet God still dwelt in the city which he had chosen. Morning by morning his Spirit was appealing for repentance and righteousness. Through his faithful ones he was still shedding the light and glory of a holier civilization throughout the community, but the population at large refused to heed.

The effects of cleansing judgment, vv. 8–20. These closing verses are marked by great tenderness, showing as they do the results that God's dealings are designed to effect: a pure life; wholehearted service; the trust of the afflicted soul in the love of God; the weaning of the heart from all iniquity. What great and lovely results of that long captivity! Let God have his way with you! He will change your sorrow into songs; will cast out your enemies and turn again your captivity; will manifest his infinite love, now in brooding tenderness and then in outbursting songs. Those who have been filled with sorrow and have borne the burden of reproach for God shall be comforted. Even the lame and exiled shall participate and become "a name and a praise." The captives would be liberated and the dispersed would be gathered home.

THE BOOK OF
HAGGAI
THE REBUILDING OF THE TEMPLE

I. APPEAL AND RESPONSE   *1.*
  A. The people admonished for their neglect   *1:1–11.*
  B. Their purpose to make amends   *1:12–15.*

II. CONTRAST BETWEEN THE TWO TEMPLES   *2:1–9.*
  A. As seen by the people   *2:1–3.*
  B. As promised by God   *2:4–9.*

III. REBUKE AND ENCOURAGEMENT   *2:10–19.*
  A. Why God's favor has been denied   *2:10–17.*
  B. How it may be restored   *2:18, 19.*

IV. THE TIMES OF THE END   *2:20–23.*
  A. The overthrow of the nations   *2:20–22.*
  B. The establishment of the house of David   *2:23.*

INTRODUCTION

Haggai returned from exile in Babylon under the leadership of Zerubbabel and Joshua in the year 536 B.C. when Cyrus, moved by the striking prophecies about himself, which had probably been brought under his notice by Daniel, granted the Jews their liberty and provided them with materials for restoring their Temple. This work of rebuilding went on under Cyrus and his successor in spite of the opposition of the Samaritans; but finally these inveterate foes of the returned exiles obtained an edict from Artaxerxes to stay the progress of the rebuilding of the Temple, Ezra 4:7–23. The Jews gave up the work and began to build splendid mansions for themselves, so that the operations on the Temple site were not recommenced, even when there was opportunity for them. For fourteen years the work was discontinued, until Haggai uttered his burning message. He seems to have been an old man when summoned to the prophet's office, and his term of service lasted for only four months. But when a man speaks in the power of God, you cannot measure the effect by chronology. His brief ministry had immediate effect, for within three weeks the people were once more at work.

COMMENTARY

HAGGAI 1:1-11

Selfish and Shortsighted Thrift. Zerubbabel is the Sheshbazzar of Ezra 1:8. He was of the royal line and was appointed governor by Cyrus. Josedech was son of Seraiah, high priest when Jerusalem was taken, 2 Kings 25:18-21. The returned exiles had been experiencing a succession of bad seasons. They had sown much and reaped little; their money ran out of the bag as quickly as they put it in; a drought lay on all the land, and the reason for it was to be found in the neglected Temple. How frequently our disasters and losses in business arise from our failure to remember God's cause. We say that we have not the time, cannot afford the money, and see no necessity for setting apart the Lord's day or the daily period for meditation and prayer. Did we see things as they really are, we should find that this is false economy and wastes more than we save. "There is that which withholdeth more than is meet, but it tendeth to poverty." The mower does not waste time when he stops to whet his scythe.

HAGGAI 1:12—2:9

The True Glory of God's House. One earnest man can arouse an entire community. Let a fire glow in our hearts, and it will spread. Assured of God's presence and favor, Haggai spoke, and within three weeks the whole land was awake. Note the cooperation of God's Spirit with the message of his servant: "the Lord stirred up." Let us ever seek and rely on his cooperation! We are witnesses; so also is the Holy Spirit! Three prophecies occupy the following chapter. In the first, vv. 1-9, the Jews are encouraged to persevere. Although there was no comparison between the glory of Solomon's Temple and the splendor of this, they must not be discouraged. Though they might deplore the absence of the sacred fire of the shekinah, of the Ark with its cherubim, and of the Urim and Thummim, yet the Messiah's presence, which would be associated with the second Temple, would more than compensate for their deficiency, since he was the antitype of them all. If we lack many of the advantages and attractions in which others excel, let us be more than satisfied to possess Christ. And be it always remembered that Christian worship seeks to realize the presence of him who said, "I am in the midst." Without that a cathedral is an empty void; with that, a barn will be Heaven. For vv. 6 and 7, see Heb. 12:26-28. This "little while" in God's arithmetic lasted for 517 years.

HAGGAI 2:10-23

God's Judgment upon the Nations. Two months after the foregoing prophecy, the prophet again remonstrated with the people for still neglecting the Temple, though they appear to have maintained religious rites. As the holy flesh did not sanctify what it touched, so religious observance did not compensate for neglecting the Temple; such neglect would make their service unclean, v. 14. The earnest toils of the people had met with persistent failure because God was against them, but from the moment of their repentance he would bless them, vv. 18, 19. Amid all the upheavals described in 2:7, the Jews would be preserved and their safety guaranteed. Disturbances preceded the Savior's first advent, as they will the second; but amid the shaking and overthrowing that are ushering in the new era, let us not fear. All that cannot be shaken will remain; and as God remembered Noah amid the tossings of the Deluge, he will care for us, not because of our deserts, but because of his grace. We did not choose him, but he us.

THE BOOK OF ZECHARIAH

THE ORACLE OF THE LORD OF HOSTS

INTRODUCTION *1:1–6.*

I. EIGHT VISIONS CONCERNING ISRAEL, JUDAH, AND JERUSALEM *1:7—6:15.*
   A. The horses among the myrtles *1:7–17.*
   B. The four horns and four smiths *1:18–21.*
   C. The man with a measuring line *2.*
   D. The High Priest and the adversary *3.*
   E. The candlestick and two olive trees *4.*
   F. The flying roll *5:1–4.*
   G. The ephah *5:5–11.*
   H. The four chariots *6:1–8.*
      (The coronation of Joshua) *6:9–15*

II. REPLY TO DEPUTATION FROM BETH-EL *7, 8.*
   A. God demands obedience, not fasting *7:1–7.*
   B. Warnings from the past *7:8–14.*
   C. God waiting to show mercy *8:1–17.*
   D. The nations to worship in Jerusalem *8:18–23.*

III. JUDGMENT AND REDEMPTION *9—14.*
   A. Judgments on the nations; the King of peace *9.*
   B. Israel to be saved and strengthened *10.*
   C. The parable of the shepherds *11.*
   D. The siege and deliverance of Jerusalem *12.*
   E. The remnant purified by chastisement *13.*
   F. The exaltation of Jerusalem *14.*

INTRODUCTION

The prophet Zechariah lived at the same time as Haggai and was interested in the same effort: to induce the Jews to carry on the rebuilding of their neglected Temple. The prophecies are dated a few years later than those of Haggai. In contrast to the direct and simple language of Haggai, Zechariah employs many figures and symbols to enforce his message. He especially wished to give encouragement and help to the leader and governor of the people, Zerubbabel, and the priest, Joshua.

In the latter part of the book there are many pictures of the glorious and happy future which God had in store for his people, and of the Deliverer who was to come to rule over them. There will come a great day when "the Lord shall be king over all the earth."

COMMENTARY

ZECHARIAH 1:1-17

A Vision of Pardon and Restoration. Zechariah does not slur over the sins of the past, but lays stress on divine forgiveness. His only fear is lest God should call in vain and the people refuse as their fathers did. Notice the repetition of God's title, "Lord of hosts," five times in the first six verses. The enemy's armies were vast, but the protecting hosts vaster. A glimpse of these hosts is given in the following vision. A green valley filled with myrtles, the emblem of humility, where the prophet may have been wont to meditate, seemed alive with mysterious figures who had been patrolling the earth and announced that it was peace, for these were the days of Cyrus' illustrious reign. Notice the frequent reference to the prophet's celestial friend, 1:9, 14, 19; 4:1, 4, 5; 5:5, 10; 6:4. The future was bright with promise, vv. 16, 17.

ZECHARIAH 1:18—2:13

The Redemption of Jerusalem. The work of Temple-building had ceased for fifteen years, and the new resolve to arise and build might meet with a similar fate. But the four horns met with four carpenters. For Babylon, the carpenter was Cyrus; for Persia, Alexander the Great; for Greece, the Roman; for Rome, the Gaul. No weapon that is formed to thwart God's purposes can prosper. The young man with the measuring line embodied the new spirit animating the returned exiles. But God was intending to give more prosperity and increase than could be contained in walls.

ZECHARIAH 3

Purified for God's Service. The regulation for the maintenance of the priesthood had fallen into disuse, and they had neither robes, vessels, nor proper provision of offerings. Probably also the spiritual life of the priests was at a very low ebb, Mal. 1, 2. Satan is always discovering the weak spots in character and thrusting at them. He is keen as steel and cruel. But we have One who pleads. As the priest Melchizedek, he ever lives to make intercession for us. "The Lord rebuke thee, O Satan."

We are as brands scorched and charred with the burning. But we have been plucked out of the consuming flame. Surely then we are being kept for some high and useful purpose. All the past is an argument for faith. That God has done so much is a pledge that he will perfect that which concerneth us, because his mercy endureth forever. It is not enough to be cleansed from sin; we need the miter of the divine anointing that we may have a place of access among the saints. Whom he justifies, he also glorifies. Let us be content with nothing short of God's best.

ZECHARIAH 4

"Not by Might, Nor by Power." Zerubbabel had faltered in the great work of reconstruction and had practically lost heart. Here he is encouraged to renew his efforts and persevere until the task is finished. He might be weak and flexible as a wick, but none of his deficiencies could hinder him from finishing his lifework, if only his spirit was kindled with divine fire and fed by the grace of the Holy Spirit.

ZECHARIAH 5

The Vision of the Flying Roll. This huge sheet of parchment, thirty by fifteen feet, was covered with the solemn curses of the Law, on one side against the thief and on the other against false swearing. The young community was notorious for these two sins. They brought dry rot with them, v. 4. Their commercial life also, represented by the ephah, was full of wickedness. But it was to be eliminated. The swift stork wings would bear it away.

ZECHARIAH 6

The Vision of the Chariots. This is a vision of protection and deliverance. Four chariots issue from the mountains around Jerusalem. The colors of the horses represent the commission that the drivers were to execute against the nations. Black denoted defeat and despair; the bay acted as a patrol of defense. Note the closing incident, which foreshadowed the union of the offices of priesthood and kingship in the person of our Lord.

ZECHARIAH 7

The Penalty of Injustice and Cruelty. During their captivity the Jews observed four feasts. That of the tenth month recalled the first enclosure of Jerusalem by the enemies' lines; of the fourth the capture of the city; of the fifth the destruction by fire of the Temple; of the seventh the murder of Gedaliah. The national life was depressed by this constant memory of disaster. It seemed incongruous to act thus, when the Holy City was rising from the dust. Surely the lamentations which were befitting in Babylon were out of place now. A deputation was therefore sent to inquire the views of the leaders. Zechariah gave four separate answers to the request. In vv. 4-7 he suggests that as these fasts had been set up by themselves, they were at liberty to discontinue them, and the main question was whether they were pondering the teachings and warnings of the older prophets. In vv. 8-14 he implored them not to yield to the obtuseness and disobedience of their fathers, in order that no second catastrophe should cast them back to the disasters they had suffered.

ZECHARIAH 8:1-17

Truth and Love Must Prevail. In his third answer Zechariah describes at length the prosperity awaiting the chosen city. The Lord had returned to dwell there, and the old men and women who were at the end of life should join with the happy boys and girls who were at the beginning in the enjoyment of the blessings of peace. But with these delightful forecasts ensue reiterated appeals.

ZECHARIAH 8:18-23; 9:1-8

The Nations Will Seek the God of Israel. In his final answer the prophet gives a delightful picture of the future, which was on the eve of complete realization. So entirely would the memory of the past be obliterated that fateful anniversaries would soon fade from their minds. Indeed they would discover that their dark days had been the source and origin of their glad ones. In all subsequent ages, even when persecuting the Jews, the foremost nations have received from their hands, appropriating their sacred writings, venerating their lawgivers, prophets, and saints, and believing in the noblest representative of their race.

The prophet passes his eye over the surrounding nations, showing that his people need fear no more, because their oppressors had been effectually silenced.

ZECHARIAH 9:9-17; 10:1-12

A Lowly Deliverer Brings Peace. Jesus must be King first, then Savior. He is lowly; his steed is not the richly arrayed warhorse, but the humble ass; he needs no weapon to overthrow his foes, because as Priest he speaks peace. The peasantry had taken shelter in the rockhewn mountain cisterns; but they might cherish hope, because they had been redeemed by the blood of the covenant, and God would see to it that that redemption was made effective. Before the advent of the King, the prison doors would open, and at his word the imprisoned should go forth. How great are his goodness and beauty!

In 10:1-12 we have a reference to the successful stand made by Judas Maccabaeus and his brethren against Antiochus. They were to tread them down as the mire of the streets; Joseph and Judah would be reunited and after their far-spread sowing over the world, the scattered tribes would ultimately return as bees to the call of the bee-farmer.

ZECHARIAH 11

"Beauty" and "Bands." The times were very dark when Zechariah felt called upon to act as shepherd to Jehovah's harried flock. Rulers and priests were actuated by selfish greed and mutual antagonism. Three shepherds had already failed. After a brief effort Zechariah renounced the attempt. He broke his staff of Beauty, or Grace, v. 10, margin, as if God's tender love had withdrawn from its struggle with evil; and when he challenged the people to set a value on his services, they weighed him out thirty pieces of silver, the price of a slave. Thereupon he broke the other staff, disrupting the brotherhood between Judah and Israel. In the following paragraph, vv. 15-17, there is an evident reference to the terrible reign of Antiochus whose cruelties led to the heroic uprising of the Maccabees. Five centuries afterwards Jesus was sent to gather the flock with the same result, Matt. 27:9, 10.

ZECHARIAH 12

Jerusalem's Day of Mourning. This vision refers to a time yet future, when the Jews shall have returned to their own land, but still in unbelief, and will be assailed by their foes, though in vain, vv. 2, 3, 6. The Lord will defend them, vv. 7, 8. Then the nation will mourn. Their repentance will be universal, from the highest to the lowest, lonely, and on account of the sufferings they inflicted on Jesus. The Agent of this mourning will be the Holy Spirit, and it will eventuate in the full forgiveness of sin through the blood of atonement and an entire cleansing from idols.

ZECHARIAH 13:1-9; 14:1, 6-9

A Day of Testing. This fountain was opened when the soldier pierced the Savior's side. But it is not enough for God to forgive; he must deal drastically with the waywardness of his people. And so thorough would be the work that parents would rather their son should die than assume for filthy lucre and without the divine call the lucrative profession of a prophet. A town would arise against a man suspected of being a prophet, who in his terror would pretend that he was a tiller of the ground. And if they discovered marks in his body which indicated that he had been previously branded as a false prophet, he would rather assert that his friends had been the cause of his affliction than that he had any sympathy with the prophetic office.

Note that remarkable anticipation, vv. 7-9. See Matt. 26:31. Jesus knew that he was the Father's "fellow." He thought it not robbery to be equal with God. *"We* will come unto him, and make our abode with him." But he is also "the man." By the grace of the one Man, we may reign in life, Rom. 5:17.

ZECHARIAH 14:1-21

"At Evening Time It Shall Be Light." We can hardly doubt that in Chapter 14 Zechariah is anticipating the same events as Ezekiel describes in Chapters 38 and 39 of his remarkable book. At first the attack of the enemies of God's people will be entirely successful; then Jesus will appear to his people and for them. There will be a literal fulfillment of Acts 1:11 and Isa. 25:9, 10. It was when his brethren were in their greatest straits that Joseph made himself known to them, and when the Jews are in dire extremity they will hear the Messiah say, "I am Jesus your Brother." See Gen. 45:1-15. Finally the long stormy days of Israel's history will be over forever, and "at evening time it shall be light." It is clear that Paul's vision in Romans 11 is to be gloriously realized.

THE BOOK OF
MALACHI
THE LORD'S MESSENGER

I. GOD'S UNWEARIED LOVE FOR HIS PEOPLE *1:1–5.*
II. THE SINS OF THE PRIESTS *1:6—2:9.*
III. THE EVILS OF IDOLATRY AND DIVORCE *2:10–16.*
IV. THE COMING JUDGMENT *2:17—3:6.*
V. ROBBING GOD *3:7–12.*
VI. THE BOOK OF REMEMBRANCE *3:13–18.*
VII. THE DAY OF THE LORD *4.*

INTRODUCTION

The name Malachi means "my messenger," so that perhaps we do not know the name of the real author of this book, who hides himself behind his office and his message. Sixty years had passed since the first return of Israel from the land of captivity under Joshua and Zerubbabel, and during this time the holy seed had become mingled with the people of the land. It was necessary, therefore, for a compelling voice to demand the purging and cleansing of the priesthood and the people.

The moral and religious condition of Israel was at a low ebb. They were the slaves of formalism and self-righteousness, satisfied with themselves and not hesitating to blaspheme God's name. Therefore, instead of the language of promise and encouragement used by Haggai and Zechariah, there was need to substitute the reproofs and warnings of this last of the prophets, between whom and the New Testament 400 years were destined to intervene.

COMMENTARY

MALACHI 1

Sincerity of Worship Sought. The love referred to in these opening verses, 1-5, was exemplified in the divine choice, that through Israel the whole world might be blessed. Hate does not mean positive dislike, but a forfeiture of the supreme place of privilege and ministry. Esau's sensuous nature preferred the mess of pottage to the birthright, and this was characteristic of his people. In vv. 6-14 the prophet turns to the priests. They despised God's name and without scruple offered on his altar the lame, the blind, and the sick. They did not hesitate to speak of the routine of Levitical service as a weariness. Notice the pathetic appeal of v. 10, alternate translation: "Oh, that there were one to shut the doors of my house, that ye might not offer vain sacrifices!" In contrast to this indifference, the truly marvelous outlook in v. 11 is very significant. Far away from Jewish altars, God's name was revered in Gentile lands, and sacrifices were offered which he accepted. The words remind us of Acts 10:34, 35.

MALACHI 2

The Transgression of the Covenant. As a contrast to the disgraceful attitude which the prophet had described as characteristic of the priesthood, he paints the picture of the noble priest, whose burning zeal for God's honor averted evil and punishment from the people. It is desirable that each servant of God should seek to exemplify these traits of character, for only they who walk with God in peace and equity can "turn many away from iniquity." The prophet reproves those who had put away their Jewish wives and had contracted marriage with foreigners. In doing this they had ignored the fact that God was the Father of the Hebrew race, of the women as well as the men, in a special sense and he was not the Father of the heathen. In answer to the argument of the Jews who demanded a plurality of wives, Malachi says that God originally made only one woman for one man, though he could have made many. It was a sin, therefore, against the original constitution of the race for a man to have more than one wife, and this is the argument that our Lord employed in Matthew 19:4-8. One man for one woman is the secret of a happy home life and of a godly seed.

MALACHI 3:1-12

A Purging from Evil. The opening verses of this chapter stir the heart like the call of a trumpet. We remember how literally they were fulfilled in the presentation of our Lord in the Temple by his parents. Unnoticed by the crowds, jostled amid the press, borne in the arms of poverty, the King suddenly came to his Temple, even the Messenger of the Covenant. Only two faithful believers, Simeon and Anna, were there to welcome him. But there is another and more personal reference. Let us keep the doors of our hearts wide open to the coming of the King. There may be no blare of trumpet, no flash of jewel, no cry of herald, but into your heart's secret shrine he will come. Is not this just what we need? Make haste, great Lord of all, and in our poor hearts do thy blessed work, that we may be refined as gold and silver, and offer to thee an offering in righteousness. Then will it be a delight to bring all the tithes into the storehouse.

MALACHI 3:13—4:6

Wickedness and Pride Shall Find Judgment. "The day cometh!"—either in the fall of Jerusalem or in some terrible catastrophe yet future. Whenever it comes, may we be reckoned as God's peculiar treasure, preserved as a woman preserves her jewels in the day of calamity, v. 17. Sorrow and disaster are perpetually befalling the proud or those that do wickedly; while on those who fear God's name the dawn of the Sun of righteousness is forever breaking and growing to the perfect day. In the beams of the sun there are not only light and color, but rays which bear health and vitality to the world and to men; so in Jesus there is power to salvation. Notice how the Old Testament ends with the word "curse," while Christ's proclamation opens with "Blessed."

THE NEW TESTAMENT

THE GOSPEL ACCORDING TO
MATTHEW

THE KING OF THE HOUSE OF DAVID

I. THE COMING OF THE KING *1:1—4:11.*
   - A. His genealogy *1:1-17.*
   - B. His birth and early life *1:18—2:23.*
   - C. His baptism *3.*
   - D. His temptation *4:1-11.*

II. PROCLAIMING THE KINGDOM *4:12—16:12.*
   - A. The beginning of the Galilean ministry *4:12-25.*
   - B. The Sermon on the Mount *5:1—7:29.*
   - C. Miracles of healing *8:1—9:35.*
   - D. Sending forth of the Twelve *9:36—10:42.*
   - E. Discourses and kingdom parables *11:1—16:12.*

III. FACING REJECTION *16:13—25:46.*
   - A. Peter's confession—rejection announced *16:13-28.*
   - B. The Transfiguration *17:1-9.*
   - C. Questions, discourses, and parables of judgment *17:10—25:46.*

IV. ENDURING THE CROSS *26:1—27:66.*
   - A. Plots of foes and devotion of friends *26:1-16.*
   - B. The Last Supper and the agony in the Garden *26:17-46.*
   - C. The betrayal *26:47-56.*
   - D. The Jewish and Roman trials *26:57—27:25.*
   - E. The crucifixion and burial *27:26-66.*

V. CONQUERING DEATH *28:1-20.*
   - A. The visit of the women to the empty tomb *28:1-8.*
   - B. The risen Christ *28:9, 10.*
   - C. The testimony of the soldiers *28:11-15.*
   - D. The Great Commission *28:16-20.*

INTRODUCTION

There is no reason to doubt that this Gospel was written by Matthew. It presents the narrative of our Lord's life from the standpoint of the pious Jew; the evident design of the writer is to show how completely and continually our Lord fulfilled the Old Testament Scriptures. No other Gospel contains so many quotations from the Law, the prophets, and the Psalms. In it, the predominant aspect of our Lord's character and work is the Messianic. He was great David's Greater Son. The key phrase of the book is "Behold your King." As King, his line is traced through the kingly race. As King, he proclaims the kingdom of Heaven. As King, he promulgates the laws, describes the subjects, and announces the rewards of the kingdom. When describing his own action at the last, when he sits on his throne and all nations are gathered before him, he speaks of himself as King, Matt. 25:40. It was on his avowal of kingship that he was condemned to die. From every viewpoint this Gospel is one of the most precious documents in the world.

COMMENTARY

MATTHEW 1:1-17

The Line by Which Messiah Came. The enumeration of our Lord's ancestors, with its threefold division into fourteen generations and evident gaps, was probably so arranged to aid the memory. Notice that in unison with the general purpose of the writer, the line is traced to Abraham through David the king. Of course we know that Joseph was only the reputed father of Jesus, v. 18; but in any case this genealogy conformed to Hebrew usage and explained how the birth took place in David's city.

In this list of names the patriarchs, Gentiles, women of doubtful character, good men and bad men, the wise, the illustrious, the unknown —all supply important links. It is as though to teach us that in the Son of man there is a blending of all classes, that he might be the representative and helper of all. Each of us may find some point of contact in this genealogy. Jesus Christ belongs to our race. He knew what was in man by that subtle and intimate knowledge which comes of kinship. In him, therefore, is neither Jew nor Greek exclusively, but all are one in him.

MATTHEW 1:18-25

The Birth of Jesus Christ. The fear that Joseph, being a just man, might withdraw from their contemplated wedlock would have filled Mary's heart with untold anguish had she not been upheld by her faith in God. She felt that God was pledged to vindicate her character. Yield yourself to him for his purposes and leave him to deal with any contingent results! He becomes responsible!

That which happened historically must take place experientially. In each of us Jesus Christ must be born through the direct action of the Holy Spirit. See Gal. 4:1-5. This is what we mean by the new birth; and when he has so entered our hearts, our Lord will become our Savior, not merely from the penalty but from the love and the power of our sins. Claim that this shall be your experience!

Let us seek after that union with God which is the height of blessedness, both in this life and the next, and in virtue of which God becomes the companion of the soul in its earthly pilgrimage. This is the name of names—Emmanuel. See Isa. 7:14; 9:1-7.

MATTHEW 2:1-8

The Wise Men Follow the Star. The expectation of the advent of a great king was far-spread at the time of the Nativity. It was probably founded, so far as the East was concerned, on the prophecies of Balaam and Daniel. See Num. 24:17; Dan. 7:13, 14. There are evidences of the same expectation in the classic literature of the West. Our Lord was the desire of all nations, and the corruption and anarchy of the Roman Empire made the longing still more intense.

God comes to men in the spheres with which they are most familiar; to Zacharias in the Temple, to the shepherds in the fields, to the wise men by a portent in the heavens. He knows just where to find us. Be sure to follow your star, whatever it be; only remember that it must ultimately receive the corroboration of Scripture, as in the present case, v. 5. A miracle may be wrought to awaken and start us on our great quest, but the miraculous is withdrawn where the ordinary methods of inquiry will serve. The news of Jesus always disquiets the children of the world; they know that it means division.

MATTHEW 2:9-15

God Rules and Overrules. The suggestion has been hazarded that "the star" was an unusual combination of three planets; but this would conflict with the disappearance and reappearance of the guiding light. Some experiences during the Welsh Revival seem to point to a connection between high spiritual experiences and a burning glory. Probably only the eyes of the Magi beheld this great light. See Acts 9:3; 26:12-14.

When we follow God's guidance, we may be sure that he will not fail to bring us to our goal. He who brings us out will also bring us in. He will perfect that which concerneth us. These wise men prostrating themselves before the newborn babe were the first of a great procession of the kings of intellect who have followed them to the same spot. After all, does not all true science bend before the mystery of life? We cannot fathom the mystery, but we can adore. We can also present our gifts. Jesus is "worthy to receive riches." It was thus that the Father provided beforehand for the expenses attendant on the approaching visit to Egypt. The Herods of this world are always plotting against the Lord's Christ, but it is in vain. See Psalm 2; Acts 4:25.

MATTHEW 2:16-23

"Out of Egypt Have I Called My Son." The death of those little children was very pathetic. From the first it seemed as though our Lord's advent would bring not peace, but the sword. Their mothers have long since been comforted, but it was a bitter experience. The little ones were the nucleus of the great attendant crowd "which follow the Lamb whithersoever he goeth," Rev. 14:4.

"They are dead which sought the young child's life." Such is the epitaph that may be written for those who have set themselves to oppose the cause of Christ. Voltaire's house in Geneva is now used as a Bible society depot. There is no permanence in destructive criticism. The young child comes up out of Egypt. There is a sense in which the life of Jesus is the epitome of the story of Israel and the experience of each Christian. See that you do not linger in Egypt, but come up in the pathway of separation and consecration to his high purposes.

MATTHEW 3:1-12

The Herald Prepares the Way. Matthew's Gospel heralds the kingdom. We are allowed to see and listen to the forerunner, whose voice again awoke the hearts of men with prophetic utterance after a silence of 400 years. He leaps into the arena with the suddenness of Elijah.

His message was twofold—the need for repentance and the announcement of the nearness of the kingdom. It thrilled his generation with a strange wonder and interest. All of the southern part of the country seemed to empty itself into the Jordan valley. Yes, if a man is not a reed shaken by the wind, not a copy but an original, who speaks what he sees and knows of God, men will come to him in every age.

To us also John the Baptist must come if we shall properly appreciate the Redeemer. We must expose ourselves to the fire, the ax, the winnowing-fan, that we may learn what we really are, and come, like Paul, to reckon our own righteousness as loss if only we may win Christ and be found in him.

MATTHEW 3:13-17

Baptized with the Spirit. While John was denouncing the sins of others, he was very conscious of his own. He melted in holy humility before the one nature in which his keen eye detected no trace of impurity, and he strenuously strove to forbid the incongruity of his polluted hands baptizing so pure a being as he felt Christ to be.

Our Lord accepted the disclaimer, but overruled it. He alone of all holy men had no consciousness of sin. He "did no sin, neither was guile found in his mouth," 1 Pet. 2:22. As God's designated Lamb he was carefully scrutinized, but those who knew the most about him were compelled to attest his innocence and purity. Yet he was baptized, that he might assume the sinner's guilt, standing with him and for him and identifying himself with his lot. Then he was anointed by the Spirit and attested by the Father's voice. Probably only John and he were aware of these celestial tokens. See John 1:32. But let us stand beneath the same chrism as did Christ. See 1 John 2:20, 27.

MATTHEW 4:1-11

Tempted by the Devil. "Then" marks the close connection between the heavenly voice of the baptism and the fiery ordeal of the forty days. Notice that temptation is not in itself sin; only when the evil suggestions of the tempter are harbored do they become sin. Notice also that all around us is a dark region of evil, out of which temptations arise. Whenever you have received a conspicuous revelation, you may expect a time of testing. This is God's way of rooting the trees in the soil, and burning in the fair colors which he paints on the vessels that are being made meet for his use.

The first temptation was that our Lord should use for his physical needs the power which had been entrusted to him, as Son of man, for the service of men. The second was an effort to incite him to act presumptuously, at the dictate of self-will and apart from the clear guidance of God's Spirit. The third was to attain the throne by a wrong method. It was only by the cross that he could win power to rule and save. See Heb. 4:15, 16; 5:8, 9.

MATTHEW 4:12-17

The Light Begins to Shine. Our Lord's earliest ministry seems to have been centered in Jerusalem and its contiguous villages. See John 2 and 3. But on the news of the Baptist's imprisonment, he took up his testimony to the hearers of the heavenly kingdom, which is the reign of God over the hearts and lives of men. Someone has said that it is "the universal awareness of God." Yet there was a difference! At the commencement of his work, the Savior showed a tenderness and a winsomeness which were very inviting to the crowds of harried sheep. See Matt. 9:36. His ministry resembled the gentle, holy dawn that breaks over the mountains and dispels the black shadows of the night. The evangelist quotes the prophet's anticipation of the coming of him who is called "Wonderful, Counsellor, the Mighty God." Oh, do not be afraid when Jesus comes to your heart! You may be as far away from goodness and purity as Naphtali and Zebulun from Jerusalem, but Galilee of the Gentiles is included in John 3:16.

MATTHEW 4:18-25

Opening Works of Mercy and Power. We must read the first chapter of John into the opening paragraph. Already the Lord had met with these first disciples in the Jordan valley, but they had returned to their homes and nets. Their prompt surrender was the result of the power over their hearts which the Master had already won. Their old craft was to be theirs still—only in a nobler form. The patience, courage, tact which had been elicited by their calling were now to be enlisted in the service of souls.

The evangelist then groups together the broad features of the early Galilean ministry. It was a triumphal progress. Notice the reiteration of "all," v. 23. The words struggle to convey the wide comprehensiveness of Christ's influence, even across the border. When the love of God came to our world in the person of Jesus, it immediately began to repair the havoc and damage which sin had caused. There was no hesitation or questioning where it was God's will to heal. Let us always take that for granted for ourselves and others.

MATTHEW 5:1-9

Opening Words of Grace and Truth. There are many doors into the life of blessedness. It does not depend on outward possessions, such as worldly goods or high birth. There is no soul of man, however illiterate, lonely, or poor, that may not step suddenly into this life of beatitude and begin to drink of the river that makes glad the city of God. Our Lord lived this life before he described it. He has opened the doors for us. If you cannot enter by the gate of purity, can you not come in by that which is reserved for those who hunger and thirst?

Note the *passive* side of the blessed life: to be "poor in spirit," that is, to be lowly in one's self-estimate; to be "meek," not always interested in one's rights; to "mourn" for the evils of one's own heart and for the sin and sorrow around; to "hunger and thirst" after Jesus Christ, the Righteous One. These dispositions do not purchase blessedness, but to cultivate them is to be blessed. On the *positive* side are mercy, purity, peace, and willingness to suffer all things for Christ. Here is 1 Cor. 13 anticipated!

MATTHEW 5:10-16

The New Salt and Light of Human Society. We must expect to be persecuted if we hold up the pure light of a consistent life amid the evils of the world. Men hate the light which exposes their misdeeds. They will tolerate you only so long as you leave them alone. But the universal testimony of those who have suffered thus is that the Son of man walks through the furnace beside his faithful martyrs.

Our holy lives ought to act as "salt" to arrest the corruption around us. It is said that the presence of a child has prevented many a crime. A sudden silence should fall on certain kinds of conversation when we enter the room. But it is very easy to lose our saltiness, as did Lot in Sodom and the seven churches of Asia. See also Ezek. 15:2–5. Our lives ought to serve also as "light." The spirit of man is a candle. See Prov. 20:27. We need to be kindled by the nature of God. Men light candles and God will light you. Let us burn and shine as John did, John 5:35. Beware of the "bushel," and ask God to choose your stand.

MATTHEW 5:17–26

New Heart Righteousness. Our Lord's mission was not to destroy, but to construct. As noon fulfills dawn and summer spring, as manhood fulfills childhood and the perfect picture the rude sketch, so does Jesus gather up, realize, and make possible the highest ideals ever inspired in human hearts or written by God's Spirit on the page of inspiration.

Under the terms "the law and the prophets," our Lord includes the entire range of the Old Testament. See Luke 24:44; Acts 13:15. Nothing could exceed our Lord's reverence for the oracles of God. He repeatedly refers to them as of divine authority. His words and teachings are the endorsement of the venerable Scriptures which had nourished his people, preparing them for his further instruction. See Rom. 3:31; 8:4.

The local magistrates' court had the power of life and death, which was inflicted by beheading; the Sanhedrin executed by stoning; the outrageous criminal was cast out to Gehenna, v. 22. In Christ's kingdom unwarranted anger is equivalent to the first, contempt to the second, and vehement passion to the third. To allow hate to smolder is a capital offense.

MATTHEW 5:27–37

Pure Eyes and Clean Speech. The legislation of the old time insisted that no member of the commonwealth should commit adultery and enforced terrible penalties. See Deut. 22:22–24. But the Divine Man, who reads the human heart with perfect accuracy, goes behind the deed to its premonitory stages, legislates about the look that may inflame passion, and condemns the soul that does not instantly turn the eye from that which allures it and to the All-Holy, asking to be cleansed not with tears only but with blood. The first act in the religious life is to detect right and wrong in the thought or intention. If the tempter is arrested there, he is powerless to hurt. Kill the snake in the egg!

The prohibition against swearing does not deal with taking an oath in the law court. During his trial by the high priest, our Lord did not resent being put on his oath. On rare and solemn occasions we may have to bare our heads before God and ask him to corroborate our word. But how different is this from the frequent and flippant use of expletives and extravagances of speech.

MATTHEW 5:38–48

Brotherly Relationship. In mentioning the second mile, our Lord refers to a well-known Eastern custom of forwarding messages by relays of forced labor. We leave our homes on a given morning, anticipating no evil. Suddenly and unexpectedly there are sounds of horses' hoofs and a great demand is thrust upon us. We are sent off in a direction we never contemplated and are "compelled" to go one mile. It is the second that tests character; and your actions with respect to it will determine whether you have entered into the spirit of Christ and are willing to serve others for love's sake and at cost of peril and inconvenience to yourself.

Love to one's neighbor appears in many passages in the Old Testament. See Exod. 23:4, 5. But we have to love "enemies" and resemble God's sun and rain, Matt. 5:45. You say that it is impossible! Remember those sweet old words, "I taught Ephraim to go," Hos. 11:3. Ask your Heavenly Father to teach you to love. Remember Gal. 5:22. Dare to believe that he will perfect what concerneth you.

MATTHEW 6:1–8

Secret Giving and Secret Praying. First we have the general proposition that righteousness, that is, one's religious duties, should not be done for the sake of display. That principle is then applied to alms, prayer, and fasting—the three departments into which the Jews divided personal religion.

The words "take heed" in v. 1 are very searching! We are all likely to put better goods in the window than we have anywhere on our shelves, and to show fairer samples than we can supply in bulk. The Greek word for "hypocrite" means "stage actor." We are tempted to assume on Sunday a religious attire which we certainly do not wear in the home or in business.

In her account of the first Burmese convert, Mrs. Adoniram Judson says: "A few days ago, I was reading with him Matthew 6. He was deeply impressed and solemn. 'These words,' said he, 'take hold of my very heart. They make me tremble. When our people visit the pagodas, they make a great noise with trumpets. But this religion makes the mind fear God.'"

MATTHEW 6:9-18

How to Pray and How to Fast. This might more fitly be termed the "disciples' prayer." As we tread its stately aisles, we cannot but think of the myriads who have stood on the same pavement and have found in every age that these seven brief petitions express sufficiently their deepest and holiest longings. Old men and little children, Roman Catholics and Protestants, the servant and his master, East and West stand together in this noble temple not made with hands.

Prayer should be direct, simple, and earnest. It must be reverent, hallowing God's name, and unselfish, employing, "we," "us," and "our," not "I," "me," "mine." It must breathe the filial spirit which cries, "Abba, Father." It must be conceived in love, breathe forgiveness, and trust for the supply of all the hunger of our nature. When God forgives, he forth-gives; that is, he casts out of his hand and mind and memory every trace of our sin. We may claim that God should repair as well as forgive; but we must be willing to deal with all others as God has dealt with us.

MATTHEW 6:19-26

What to Seek and Whom to Serve. What is in our inner life which answers to the eye of the body? Some have said that it is the intellect; others the heart. But it is truer to say that it is the inner purpose and intention of the soul.

When our physical eye is in an unhealthy condition, the image is doubled and blurred. To use a common expression, it has a squint, such as affected the noble face of Edward Irving, the noted English clergyman. We are told that as a babe he was laid in a wooden cradle, in the side of which was a small hole through which he watched what was going on. This distorted his vision through life. We also may look two ways at once.

The endeavor to serve God and mammon, to stand well with both worlds, to lay up treasures on earth and at the same time be rich toward God is a spiritual squint. John Bunyan tells of Mr. Facing-Both-Ways, who kept one eye on Heaven and the other on earth, who sincerely professed one thing and sincerely did another. He tried to cheat God and devil, but in the end cheated only himself and his neighbors.

MATTHEW 6:27-34

The Cure for Anxious Care. The Lord's tone is gentle and tender when he turns to address the poor. He says three times over, "Don't be anxious." He never forgot that he sprang, according to his human nature, from the ranks of poverty. His references to patching garments, using old bottle-skins, the price of sparrows, and the scanty pittance of a laborer's hire indicate that he was used to the trials of the poor.

There is all the difference between foresight and foreboding. It is the latter that Jesus chides. The farmer must sow in the autumn that he may reap in the summer, but there is no need for him to lie sleepless through the nights of winter, worrying about the yet distant harvest. Do not be anxious about the supply of your needs, whether of body, mind, or heart. God knows what you need. If he has given life, will he not maintain it? Does he not care for the birds and flowers? Did he not give his Son, and will he withhold any good? Trust him and be at peace.

MATTHEW 7:1-12

Judging Self; Asking God; Serving Others. There is abundant need for a right and sound judgment, illumined by the Spirit of truth; but there is a world of difference between it and the censorious and critical opinions which we are apt to form and utter about others. Human nature is fond of climbing up into the judgment-seat and proclaiming its decisions without hearing both sides or calling witnesses. Beware of basing your judgment on idle stories and gossip. In any case, do not utter it if it be adverse unless you have first prayed about it and sought to turn the sinner from the error of his ways. Let God search you before you search another. See Ps. 139:23, 24; 1 Cor. 4:1-5; Heb. 4:12.

We "ask" for a gift; we "seek" for what we have lost; we "knock" for entrance. Only a door stands between us and Christ! He will not give us stones or serpents, even if we clamor for them; but he will never fail to give good things —and above all his Holy Spirit. Only we must ask for them.

The Roman Emperor Severus was so charmed with the Golden Rule that he had it inscribed on the walls of his palace. Let us inscribe it on our hearts and act on it in the power of the Holy Spirit, who sheds God's love abroad in the hearts of those who believe.

MATTHEW 7:13-23

Seeking Life; Testing Leaders. The world is full of shams. Counterfeit coins circulate; paste jewels are worn. Let us take heed against a counterfeit religion. It betrays itself thus:

It does not involve the denial of self. Our Lord compares his way to entrance by a strait gate and walking on a narrow path. It is the way of the cross. We must say "No" to the "I" life which is seated in our soul and which must be ruthlessly denied. We must say of it as Peter did of Jesus, "I do not know the man." The way of self-indulgence begins on a primrose path and ends in a wilderness. The path of self-denial is steep and difficult at the start, but leads to a paradise of joy.

It does not produce good fruit. The worth of the gospel has been attested all down the ages by the characters which it has produced, which have been the world's salt and light. No other teaching has produced such results. Here is the supreme test. There are many new systems of theology, many panaceas are being loudly advertised, but the one test of them all is in the fruit they bear.

MATTHEW 7:24-29

Building on Secure Foundations. In Palestinian summer, when the soil is baked hard by the intense heat, any spot will serve equally well as the site of a house. No one can say whether his neighbor has built well or ill; only the builder knows. But in the winter the rain falls in torrents and the valleys are filled with foaming floods which sap all foundations that have not gripped the living rock.

To believe *about* Christ is not enough; we must believe *in* him. We must come to him as a Living Stone and become living stones, 1 Pet. 2:4-8. We must not only listen to him; we must obey him. There must be living, unbroken unity and fellowship between him and us. Then we may proceed to erect the structure of godly and holy living which shall grow into a holy temple in the Lord, 1 Cor. 3:10-15. May we receive with meekness the engrafting of the Word, which is able to save the soul!

MATTHEW 8:1-10

Rewards of Faith. The Lord can touch thy heart, leprous with impurity, and make its stain depart, so that, as in the case of Naaman, its foulness shall become "like unto the flesh of a little child." See 2 Kings 5:14. The psalmist cried, "Purge me with hyssop, and I shall be clean," alluding to the rite for the cleansing of the leper. Compare Ps. 51:7; Lev. 14:4. But one touch of Christ's hand is enough, for he is the Great High Priest.

He also can heal the paralysis which has limited thy service and pinned thee down in helplessness. As the centurion recognized, because Christ was obedient to the Father's Law he was able to wield the Father's power. He humbled himself and became obedient to the death of the cross; therefore God hath highly exalted him, that he might send tides of living energy into the paralyzed will. The Apostle Paul testified, "I can do all things through Christ which strengtheneth me."

MATTHEW 8:11-17

The Great Physician. A feast was the Hebrew conception of Heaven. The Jews thought they were secure of it because of their descent from Abraham. Grace is not hereditary; to receive it, every man has to exercise a personal faith in Christ. Let us see to it that our religion is absolutely true, lest it land us in hopeless disappointment.

Notice that faith is the measure of divine performance—"as . . . so . . ." Our Lord can deliver from the fever of passion and make the soul calm, quiet, and pure. It was a wonderful thing that the patient could at once arise and minister in Peter's humble home to their great Guest, but it is even more wonderful when a helpless spirit suddenly emerges from the dominion of passion into strength and beauty.

The key to all true service is furnished in v. 17. We must take to ourselves the infirmities, sorrows, and sins of those whom we would really help. This is the law of Christ, Gal. 6:1-4.

MATTHEW 8:18-27

Leader of Men and Ruler of Nature. Christ winnows men. Before any enter upon his service, he places before them the inevitable trials which they must meet, among which loneliness and homelessness bulk large. See that in your heart Christ has a home. Where, however, there is lethargy, the Savior stirs the soul to follow him. Do not mourn about the grave of the past; leave it and enter the life of resurrection and ascension.

Storms must sweep over all our lives. The Master's sleep indicates the peace and security of his nature. What a contrast between our impatience and his infinite serenity! Our Lord was sure that the Father was with him, John 8:29. Near though the enemy may be, the Father is nearer. The everlasting arms are beneath you. You are beset behind and before, but no boat can sink when Christ is on board.

MATTHEW 8:28-34

An Unwelcome Visitor. The demon spirit seems still to tenant the lives of human beings. To what else can we attribute the paroxysms of passion, the awful cruelties and inhumanities of men? There is only one devil, but many demons; only one prince of the power of darkness, but many emissaries. Take heed, lest you open the door of your nature to the spirit of evil and he possess you. Watch and pray, and trust the keeping of your soul to the hands of Christ. He is stronger than the strong man.

Notice that the demon is set upon destruction. If he may not destroy the souls of men, he will destroy swine. This is the mark of evil. It is always destructive; whereas the Spirit of God is constructive and builds up from the ruins of Satan's work a new Heaven and a new earth, both in the soul and in the universe.

All the city besought Jesus to depart, because men count their gains more valuable than his presence. The same spirit rules in the commercial world of today. Let us beware. What shall it profit to gain the world if we lose our souls?

MATTHEW 9:1-8

The Forgiver of Sins. How inventive and ingenious is human love! Not improbably, this was a young man and the others had been his schoolmates and friends for years. They had come to a steadfast faith in Jesus, and it was in response to *their* faith that the miracle was wrought. If only four earnest Christians would take one unbeliever or sinner in hand, we should see new miracles of grace.

Sin lies at the root of all suffering and disease. God's ideal is a fair and healthy body adapted to all the demands we make on it. In this case there was evidently a close connection between the man's paralysis and some former act or acts of sin that lay heavily on conscience and heart. It was as easy for our Lord to utter one sentence as another, and the power which accompanied his utterance in the physical sphere proved that he had equal power in the spirit world.

His critics were perfectly right. Either he blasphemed or he was the Son of God. Note that title, "Son of man." Jesus was the last Adam, the second man. See 1 Cor. 15:45.

MATTHEW 9:9-17

The Friend of Sinners. The name Levi indicates that Matthew sprang from a priestly line. He had lost all self-respect to become the abhorred instrument of the Roman government, collecting dues on the merchandise that crossed the lake. But our Lord sees veins of gold and precious gems in most unlikely places, and he detected the apostle and evangelist in this despised publican.

Wherever a man is found by Christ, he sets himself to find others, and the Lord is willing to cooperate in any effort to bring others to know him. He will sit with perfect grace among publicans and sinners, lifting them to his own pure and holy level. He is always to be found where there are sin-sick souls; and where hearts are famished for love and joy, he is with them as their bridegroom.

But the joy of Christ will make for itself its own impression. The ancient forms will not suffice. The old skin-bottle will not contain the ferment of the new wine. How wonderfully Christ could extract lessons from familiar objects!

MATTHEW 9:18-26

Lord of Life and Death. No grief appeals to Christ in vain. He always arises to follow. Let us as his disciples ever follow where he leads. We are permitted to be his fellow-workers and to help by our sympathy, prayers, and faith.

This poor woman's faith was very imperfect. She believed that there was virtue in his garments, as the ritualist in the emblems of his death. She cared more for her healing than for the Healer. She was full of fear and trembling. But her touch was a magnificent evidence of her faith. It might be as slight as a feather, but it was enough. Not grasping, but lightly touching!

The incident at first fretted Jairus by its delay; but afterward it helped him. Perhaps it was permitted in order to strengthen his faith and thus prepare him to meet the tidings then upon the way to him. Jesus can awake a girl from death as easily as her mother from sleep at morning prime. Let him take the tiny hands of your children in his. Summon them to life and love!

MATTHEW 9:27-34

The Merciful Deliverer. It is thus that the Master speaks to us: "Believe ye" that I am able to make you happy, though you are cut off from the light and gladness of the world? "Believe ye" that I am able to enrich you in poverty, strengthen you in weakness, and raise you even out of death itself, so that the barren rod may bear blossom and fruit? "Believe ye" that I am able to give a knowledge of God which eye hath not seen nor the heart of man conceived?

It may be with a trembling faith that we answer, "Yea, Lord." But how blessed is the soul that dares to say "Yea" to the Master's challenge. Understand that there is no limit to what he will do for you, if only you will trust him. The measure of his giving is according to the measure of your faith, and the measure of your faith will be according to the measure of your abandonment to him. Spread abroad his fame. Pharisees hate him, but demons flee.

MATTHEW 9:35—10:4

Planning the Harvest. A new chapter in our Lord's ministry opens at this point. As he walked amid the crowded towns and villages of Galilee, his heart was deeply moved. His was the shepherd's nature which, ever forgetful of self, expends its all for the flock. Jesus loved the poor people tenderly; those vast multitudes were a scattered, harassed flock. "Fainted" has the meaning of being cast panting on the ground. It was as though they could not move another step. Let us—like our Master—behold, pity, intercede, do our best to send out laborers, and go ourselves, even to a cross, if only we may save.

Pray for laborers, and you will become a laborer. Begin as a disciple, and you will become an apostle. Our Lord is King and if he sends, he gives his signet ring of authority. See Matt. 28:18. How little did these men dream that their names would be engraved on the foundations of the new Jerusalem, Rev. 21:14.

MATTHEW 10:5-15

Missionaries Sent Out. For the present, the Twelve were to confine themselves to Jews, because the Lord's ministry was the climax of the Jewish probation and it was desirable that every opportunity should be given to the lost sheep of the house of Israel to repent. God can never be unmindful of any covenant into which he has entered with the soul. If we believe not, he remaineth faithful.

May we not say that our Lord was the first medical missionary? He has taught us that the healing of disease is often the best way of approaching the soul. The kingdom of God deals not only with our eternal welfare, but with the conditions of human life. On Christ's head are many crowns; social, family, and civic life are departments of his beneficent reign. His servants must be without worldly entanglements and live in absolute dependence upon God to whom they have consecrated their lives. The peace of God goes forth and returns.

MATTHEW 10:16-23

Steadfast under Persecution. The way of the servants and heralds of Christ will never be easy. On the one hand, they are assailed by the rulers and potentates of this world, and on the other by the members of their own homes. See Acts 4:26. But all these experiences are permitted in order to secure an entrance for their message into the most unlikely places, 2 Tim. 4:17. The fact of the disciples being driven from city to city brought the gospel within the reach of a much wider audience than if they had remained in peace in one center. See Acts 11:19.

But when we are persecuted for the Lord's sake, the Father bends over us with tender pity and helpfulness, John 12:26. We are supplied, from the Eternal Light and Love, with a wisdom of speech and an unfailing patience of love that cannot be gainsaid.

MATTHEW 10:24-33

Fearless Confessors of Christ. The more Christlike we are, the more certainly shall we incur the dislike and hatred of men. Only let us take care that they hate us, not on account of our personal peculiarities and pretensions, but solely for the truth's sake. See 1 Kings 22:8; Dan. 6:5.

Christ is often speaking. In the secret chamber of the heart, in the darkness of the night, in the shadowed room of pain and sorrow, in the room which holds all that is mortal of our beloved, hear his voice. It may be in dark sayings, but they are "the dark sayings on a harp," of which the psalmist sings. There are music, tenderness, love notes in these dark sayings. And our hearts can receive lasting impressions in the dark.

Remember that in all your anxiety and pain, the Father is near. His presence encloses you in its gentle, holy embrace. You are of value to him, of more value than you can count, because you were purchased with the precious blood of Christ.

MATTHEW 10:34-42

Receiving Christ's Representatives. In Jesus Christ we acquire a new affinity, stronger than that of family ties. When we enter the family of God, we belong to all his children. They are our brethren and sisters in the most intimate sense. See Matt. 12:48-50. The new love that floods our nature does not make us less but more tender and sympathetic toward our own kith and kin; but if we are compelled to choose, then we must stand with the children of God, though it should rend us from the old happy family life in which we were nurtured.

As to the closing paragraph, may we not illustrate it thus? When the window who sustained Elijah at Zarephath entered Paradise, she found herself standing amid the great prophets of Israel. When she asked the attendant angel whether there was not some mistake, he replied, "Certainly not. In treating the prophet as you did, you proved yourself to be of the same spirit and temper as he; and it is but right that you should share in the prophet's reward."

MATTHEW 11:1-10

How Doubts May Be Solved. The Baptist was languishing in a gloomy dungeon in the castle of Machaerus, on the farther shores of the Dead Sea—like a wild creature of the desert, suddenly entrapped. The darkness of his cell depressed his spirit; it seemed strange, too, if Jesus were the Messiah, that he did not overthrow the tyrant rule of Herod and release his captive friend.

When you are in doubt, go straight to Jesus and ask him to deal with it! Our Lord did not argue with the messengers sent by John, but pointed to the beneficent works that the Father had given him to do. See John 5:36; also Isa. 29:18; 35:5, 6. The influence of Christ on individuals and the world is the best testimony to the validity of his claims. The demonstration of Christianity is to be found in its acceptance and practice.

John's disciples had gone before our Lord uttered this great eulogy on his faithful friend, lest he should be exalted beyond measure and lest his faith should not have room to grow. Ah, downcast soul, who art writing hard things of thyself, it may be that thy merciful Lord is viewing thy life more accurately and estimating it more lovingly than thou knowest!

MATTHEW 11:11-19

The Last of the Prophets. The least in a higher dispensation has great advantages over the greatest in a lower one. A child on a hill can see farther than a giant in the valley. Many have tried to right the world by violence, by the vehemence of their speech and acts. But it is not so that the kingdom comes. Its weapon is not the sword, but the cross. Its advent is not as the thunder shower, but as the summer dew or the opening of the dawn.

Our Lord truly estimated the temper of his age. It was fickle, changeable, hard to please; but beneath its evident superficiality, there was a substratum of rock. They refused John because of his austerity, and they refused Jesus because of his human kindness and gentleness. Never trim your sails for the world's breath. The breeze springs up and soon dies away. Do God's will!

O sinful brother and sister, can we ever estimate enough the assurance that Jesus is the friend of our souls? He does not disown, withdraw, or reproach. He knows what our temptations are, and makes allowances, and loves us steadfastly forever.

MATTHEW 11:20-30

Woe or Welcome. The voice of upbraiding, vv. 20-24. The Judge weeps as he pronounces the doom of those who reject him. They would have crowned him king, but refused to repent. See John 6:15. These cities did not crucify him, but they had been deaf to his warnings and indifferent to his mighty works. Even where there is no direct opposition, indifference will be sufficient to seal our doom.

The voice of thanksgiving, vv. 25-27. He "answered" the voice of God within his breast. Babes are those who mistrust the reasonings of their intellect, but trust the instincts and intuitions of their hearts. The child-heart looks open-eyed into all the mysteries of God. Learn to say "Yea" to all God's dealings. The Spirit reveals the Son, and the Son the Father. Our Lord must be divine, if only God can know him.

The voice of pleading mercy, vv. 28-30. "Labor" is for active manhood; "heavy laden" for suffering, patient womanhood. The invitation is to commit and submit; to come and to bow under the yoke of the Father's will. Submission and obedience are the secrets of the blessed life.

MATTHEW 12:1-14

The Right Use of the Sabbath. The Pharisees had introduced a large number of minute and absurd restrictions on Sabbath observance; so our Lord set himself to recover the day of rest for the use of the people. He never hesitated, therefore, to work miracles of healing on that day, and so set at defiance the Pharisees and their evil amendments. He contended also that all ritual observance must take the secondary place, and that the primary concern must always be the deep and pressing claims of humanity. Thus, it was perfectly legitimate for David to eat the shewbread.

Even if a sheep should fall into a pit on the Sabbath, it would be lifted out by the most punctilious of ritualists. How absurd and illogical it was to prohibit deliverance to this man with his withered hand! Notice that this man's condition is symbolic of many who pose as good Christians, but do nothing. They have the power, but do not use it and it becomes atrophied. That power can be given back by Jesus. Dare to act and you will find yourself able to act.

MATTHEW 12:15-23

The Testimony of Deeds of Mercy. A "reed" is not of much account. You may see hundreds of them encircling a stagnant pond and bending before the breeze. A "bruised reed" is still more worthless to the eye of the world. Yet the Master does not despise a bruised or broken reed. No, he bends over it and tries to restore its shape. He makes out of it a reed-organ for music, or the paper manufacturers weave it into paper on which are printed his messages.

"Flax" does not burn readily. It only smolders. The spark runs feebly up the fibers, and anything like a flame is impossible. Such is our poor love. It sometimes seems but a spark. Yet Jesus does not despise it. So far from quenching it, he breathes on it, places it in the oxygen of his love, and screens it from the wind that would extinguish it.

How gentle, quiet, and unobtrusive is our Master's behavior! He is so frugal of his resources, so careful that nothing be wasted, so eager to make the most of us. And it is out of such materials that he makes his ever-victorious army.

MATTHEW 12:24-37

Slander from Evil Hearts. Spite and hatred absolutely blind the eyes and distort the judgment. They reached their climax in this effort of the Pharisees to discredit Christ. They could not deny his miracles, so they imputed them to a collusion between him and Satan. On the face of it, this charge was absurd. But our Lord showed clearly that in making the allegation, his enemies were violating their spiritual sense and deliberately blinding their eyes and dulling their ears to God's Spirit. This is the sin that hath never forgiveness, because the soul that acts thus ceases to wish for or seek it.

What a glimpse is given of our Savior's sore temptations and glorious victory in v. 29! He had already bound the strong man, and for this reason was able to spoil his house and deliver his captives. Let Jesus into your heart and no foe, though he may batter the door, shall break in to destroy!

The one test that Jesus proposes is "fruit." The nature of a man or doctrine or movement can be rightly estimated only when the results have had time to develop. How splendidly Christianity has stood this test!

MATTHEW 12:38-50

Opposing or Doing God's Will. It was an evil and adulterous age. It had no spiritual appreciation, and was intent on getting an outward and sensible sign. Nineveh itself would have condemned it. The queen of Sheba, without the advantage attaching to the Hebrew race, appreciated Solomon; but the people of this generation had no appreciation of the Christ. They were nearing the last days of corruption and reprobation. They were a deserted palace given over to demons. Seven demons possessed them and urged them, as they did the swine in 8:31, to destruction.

But amid the general apostasy, there were faithful souls who recognized Jesus as the Son of God and drew near to hear his words. They recognized his kinship to the Father and revealed their kinship to him. Let us not look back to Nazareth and Bethany with longing eyes. See Solomon's Song 8:1, 2. We are privileged to occupy a closer relationship than that of natural birth. See John 1:12, 13; Gal. 4:1-6; Rom. 8:16. O Brother Christ, make us more like thee!

MATTHEW 13:1-9

Sowing in Different Soils. The varying results of gospel preaching are due, not primarily to the sower or to the seed, but to the ground. Four classes of hearers are described in this parable: (1) There is the wayside or path, trampled hard as the sower goes to and fro. It was once soft, rich loam like the rest of the field, but in the course of years it has been trodden down by passengers and traffic. The seed falls on the surface, but cannot penetrate. When our heart reaches that condition, we need to ask God to drive through us the plowshare of conviction or sorrow. (2) There is the superficial soil, very light and thin, beneath which lies the rock. How many are easily moved and touched, but refuse to allow God's truth time to root itself and are as quickly moved by some other appeal. (3) There are the rich with their luxuries, and the poor with their cares, in the thorny ground of whose divided hearts there is no chance for the struggling ears of grace. (4) A fourth part of our hearers will receive the implanted Word into true hearts, and their hundredfold will amply repay our toils and tears.

MATTHEW 13:10-23

Teaching for the Teachable. Jesus defended his use of parables. He said that he carefully avoided stating the truths of the kingdom too plainly, so as not to increase the condemnation of those who could not or would not accept them. But where the disciples cared to penetrate below the husk of the story or parable, they would reach the kernel of heavenly significance. It is given to meek and teachable hearts to know the secrets of God. Let us draw near to the great Teacher, the Holy Spirit, asking him to make us know the kernel and heart of the Word of God. See 1 Cor. 2:6ff.

Note these points in our Lord's explanation of his parable: (1) Beware of the evil one, who comes surreptitiously as soon as the sermon is over. (2) The joy of the young convert must be distinguished from that of the superficial hearer. It is joy in Christ, rather than in the novelty and beauty of the words about Christ. (3) Expect tribulation where the gospel is faithfully proclaimed. (4) The cares of poverty hinder as much as the riches of wealth.

MATTHEW 13:24-33

Other Parables of the Kingdom. The tare was a species of rye grass which in its earlier stages closely resembled wheat. In this world, and in the Church, professors are closely mingled with possessors. But there come great times of revealing in the trials and difficulties of life, and in fact Satan and his angels never sleep. Let us beware of them, but be not afraid: Christ is stronger.

The mustard seed and the leaven represent the extensive and intensive, the outward and inward, the objective and subjective aspects of Christianity. Sometimes when the Church is reaching its branches to the farthest, its heart is being corrupted by the slow spread of evil. See 1 Cor. 5:7, 8. See what stress our Lord lays on unnoticed beginnings! What seed is smaller than the mustard! Yet it may be the gateway through which Nature may pour her inner energies, forcing the rootlet down and the green shoot up. And it requires but a very small amount of leaven to permeate a large quantity of meal. Bigness is not greatness. Watch the first speck of sin; cherish each grain of holy impulse.

MATTHEW 13:34-43

Genuine and Counterfeit. Throughout the Synoptic Gospels—Matthew, Mark, and Luke—a consistent distinction is made between the outer ranks of the people, or disciples, and the inner circle of apostles. May we not emphasize the same distinction still? We have among us many who are clearly disciples. They cannot as yet formulate or endorse the full creed of the Church, but if they are true to their convictions and follow the gleam, the Master will bring them to the decision of Peter, Matt. 16:16.

This world is God's field. All the good in it has reached it through Jesus Christ. Fundamentally there are but two classes, for the disciple belongs to Christ, though he has not yet come into the perfect light. Notice that the people who cause stumbling are placed with those who do iniquity, and each class is thrown on the rubbish heap. Ponder the despair with which we shall view wasted opportunities as we look back on them from eternity—weeping for softer natures, and "wailing" for weaker ones. Let us not trifle away the golden chances of life!

MATTHEW 13:44-50

Securing Treasure; Rejecting the Bad. The parables of treasure and pearl are a pair. They describe the various ways we come to know God's truth. Some happen on it suddenly. They are pursuing the ordinary vocations of life when suddenly the plowshare rings against a box of buried treasure. The husbandman is suddenly rich beyond his dreams.

But in other cases religion is the result of diligent search. Man cannot be happy without God. He goes from philosophy to philosophy, from system to system, turning over the pearls on the dealer's trays; but suddenly his listlessness is transformed to eagerness as he discovers the Christ. Here is the pearl of great price. He has sought and found, and is prepared to renounce all. See Phil. 3:7. Is there not, too, a deep sense in which Jesus has renounced all, that he might purchase for himself the Church, his bride? He is the merchant and we the pearl, though only in his eyes—the eyes of love—could we be held worthy of all that he surrendered to win us!

MATTHEW 13:51-58

How Unbelief Hinders. God's truth is always new and always old. It is as fresh as the morning breeze for each coming generation. But however stated, the fundamental facts are invariable. Let us store our minds and hearts with holy and helpful thoughts, so as to deal them out as the occasions serve.

Compare v. 53 with Luke 4:16-30. The question his townspeople put is stated a little differently in Mark 6:3. Till he left home at the age of thirty for his baptism, our Lord evidently worked with his hands. Surely none can despise manual toil when the Son of man wrought at the bench, making, according to the old tradition, implements of husbandry.

Sons and daughters were born to Joseph and Mary, whose names are here given. Alas, that we do not see the glory in common, familiar people and circumstances! Never forget that the absence of expectant faith does more to limit the progress of the gospel than the lack of funds!

MATTHEW 14:1-12

For Righteousness' Sake. In the terror arising from his stricken conscience, Herod made confidants of his slaves, overleaping the barriers of position in his need of some ears into which to pour his fears. He had not finished with John. There is a resurrection of deeds as well as of bodies. The only way to have done with a sinful deed is to confess it and make reparation.

What true nobility John displayed in summoning the king to the bar of eternal justice! He might have said, "It isn't seemly" or "It isn't fair"; but he puts it on more unassailable ground, which Herod's conscience endorsed: "It is not lawful." Herod was luxurious, sensual, superstitious, and weak. He was easily entrapped by the beautiful fiend. To tamper with conscience is like killing the watchdog while the burglar is breaking in.

How splendid the action of John's disciples! Reverent love and grief made them brave the king's hatred. In hours of lonely bereavement, the best policy is to go and tell Jesus.

MATTHEW 14:13-21

Abundance for the Hungry. Jesus sighed for a little quiet and sought it amid the lonely hills across the lake. The crowds saw where his boat was making for and hurried around by shore to greet him. Without a sigh he put away the hope of rest and stillness and set to work to heal and teach the unshepherded sheep.

This is not only a miracle, but a parable. It is thus that the Creator is ever multiplying the slender stores left over from one harvest to produce another. It is thus that he will feed you and yours, if only you will trust him and not run hither and thither in panic. You need not depart from Christ in search of any good thing. All is in him. When he bids us feed the crowds, he makes himself ultimately responsible, but paves the way by forcing home the inadequacy of our resources apart from him. It is as we break and distribute that the living bread multiplies in our hands. The Church is the intermediary between the living Savior and the desperate hunger of the world. You may sit at the world's table and remain hungry. But at Christ's table you are filled. There is always more than enough left for the distributor.

MATTHEW 14:22-36

Help in the Hour of Need. Jesus always comes in the storm. It had been a great relief to escape from the pressure of the crowd to his place of prayer, on heights swept by the evening breeze and lighted by the holy stars. But he tore himself away because his friends needed him. He is watching you also in the storm and will certainly come to your help.

He uses the element we dread as the path for his approach. The waves were endangering the boat, but Jesus walked on them. In our lives are people and circumstances we dread, but it is through these that the greatest blessing of our lives will come, if we look through them to Christ.

His coming is sometimes delayed. The gray dawn was already beginning to spread over the scene. The disciples' strength was spent. He was not too late to be of service, but just in time to save them from despair. Be of good cheer, and if Jesus bids you come to him on the water, always believe that his commands are enabling. Keep looking to him, not at the storm.

MATTHEW 15:1-9

God's Truth above Men's Teaching. The legal washing of hands before eating was specially sacred in the eyes of the Pharisees. "He who does not wash his hands before eating," says the Talmud, "is as bad as a murderer." Jesus had no sympathy with a system that reduced religion to a slavery to outward forms. His new kingdom was in the heart, in loving sonship to God, and in faith. All outward observances had value only as expressions of the inner spirit. He waived aside their deadly pedantry and told his hearers to care above everything for the cleanliness of the heart.

He did more; he accused the Pharisees of putting their commandments on a level with the divine requirements, and so rendering the whole of Israel's worship vain. The divine authority for what *is* commanded is greatly weakened when it is mixed up with the purely human. A multitude of saints' days weakens the claims of the Lord's day. Remember that no gift to God's service is acceptable if you neglect the claims of those who are related to you by natural ties. Morality in God's eyes stands far above ritual.

MATTHEW 15:10-20

What Really Defiles. It is good to study our Lord's list of the sources of soul pollution. "Evil thoughts" come first. We cannot prevent an evil suggestion being presented to our minds, but we can refuse to dwell on it. To resist the inclination to dwell on it strengthens us in the opposite direction; to yield to it is to commit the sin in our heart, which in God's sight is equivalent to the outward act. Notice that unkind and uncharitable speech is on this blacklist.

The "heart," rather than the body, is the source of sin. "Out of the heart!" The body is the gauge on which the soul registers its improvement or deterioration. Do not find fault with your members; look to your heart and keep it beyond keeping, for out of *it* are the issues of life. Ask God to create in you a clean heart. See that you distinguish between the first Adam and the second. Deny what you inherit of human weakness and sin, and affirm all that is of Christ's imparting. The cross of Calvary and the uprising of the living Christ are facts of perpetual experience.

MATTHEW 15:21-28

The Reward of an Outsider's Faith. A crumb from the table of our Lord can make the heart satisfied and glad. But the suppliant must take the right place and give him his right place. This poor Gentile mother had no claim on Jesus as the son of David; he was therefore silent. It was impossible for her to come in by the door of the covenant, but his silence led her to knock at another door and taught her to cry, "Lord, help me."

There was yet another lesson for her to learn, and the Lord knew that she was capable of learning it. She must realize that for the time his ministry was confined to the Chosen People, so that the Gentile claim could be recognized only incidentally. But when she was willing to take the low place under the table and ask for the children's crumbs, he put the key of his unsearchable riches into her hand, saying, "O woman, great is thy faith: be it unto thee even as thou wilt." Those who yield to God most absolutely are able to decree things! See Job 22:28; John 15:7.

MATTHEW 15:29-39

Ministering to the Multitudes. Our Lord's mission of grace and truth was at its height. His help was sought with the utmost eagerness. Large numbers of sick were cast at his feet in hot haste. The crumb was given to the woman of Canaan, but whole loaves were distributed to the crowds of Jews, because it was befitting that they should have a full chance to appreciate and accept Christ. For a brief moment they glorified the God of Israel, but the spasm of gratitude was transient. "His own" rejected Jesus. They would have his miracles, but would not own his claims. Take care that you do not become content with getting his help; love him for himself.

Do not suppose that these miracles were confined to his earthly life. He is still the great storehouse of divine and healing energy. He is still moved with compassion, and longs to help each weary and sin-sick soul. His thought still is "lest they faint in the way." The wilderness can place no bar on "the saving strength of his right hand." Disciples especially are meant to be intermediaries and mediators. They take and give.

MATTHEW 16:1-12

Beware of Evil Influences. The signs of the times in our own day are much as they were in that. Still, men are lovers of pleasure rather than of God. Still, they who will live a godly life must be prepared to suffer persecution. The forms of hatred and dislike of the gospel change, but the hatred of the cross is as inveterate as ever. The sign of Jonah was his resurrection to take up his cry against Nineveh; the resurrection of Jesus is the Father's seal of endorsement. See to it that he shall rise, not only in Joseph's garden, but in thy heart! That is the best evidence of the truth of our holy faith.

There is abroad today much teaching which may be compared to leaven. The germs of hurtful and false doctrine are as thick as microbes. Propagated by the agencies of the spoken address and the written page, they produce fermentation and unrest in the young and unstable. We must judge these pernicious teachings, not by their pleasant and innocent appearance, but by their effect on heart and character.

MATTHEW 16:13-20

"The Son of the Living God." The shadows of Calvary were beginning to gather, and the Lord desired to prepare his friends for all that it stood for. His questions elicited Peter's magnificent confession.

Notice the date of the Church. It was still future when he spoke. "I will build." The materials may have been prepared beforehand, but the actual building began at our Lord's resurrection. He is the Architect. Through the centuries he has been building, and if we are in his Church today we are there because he excavated us out of the first Adam and placed us in the very position we now occupy. The foundations of that Church were not in the apostle *("Petros"),* but in his confession *("petra")* of the divine Sonship of Jesus. See John 5:18. The church's impregnability is attested, for the Lord himself defends it. See Rev. 2:1. The gates of Hades—that is, the unseen world—include all the principalities and powers that are allied against God's people, Eph. 6:12. They cannot prevail.

MATTHEW 16:21-28

Bear the Cross for Jesus. The gospel has two parts: Jesus is the Christ; the Christ must suffer if he shall enter his glory. There had been veiled hints of his death before, as in John 2:19; Matt. 9:15; 12:40; but henceforth it was taught without a veil. The cross had always cast its shadow over our Lord's path. He did not die as the martyr on whom death comes unexpectedly, but he stepped from the throne and became incarnate that he might die. Notice that solemn "must," v. 21.

How soon Peter fell from his high estate! Beware! The voice that bids us spare ourselves is Satan's. Self-pleasing ends in destruction. Self-denial and self-sacrifice are the divine path to life. Let us be more eager to lose ourselves than to find ourselves; more set on the cross than on the glory; more eager to promote the well-being of others than our own. We do not choose or make our cross; Christ gives each a little bit of his true cross to bear as *he* pleases.

MATTHEW 17:1-8

Jesus Shows Divine Glory. Moses' face shone after having absorbed the divine glory, as some diamonds burn with sunlight after being carried into a dark room. Stephen's face shone because for a moment he had seen the Son of man. But the face of our Lord shone, not from without but from within. The shekinah of his heart was for the most part hidden, but here it burst through the frail veil of flesh, John 1:14.

The apostle uses the same word when he says, "Be ye transformed," Rom. 12:2. He does not mean that for a brief moment we should see and reflect our Lord's face. He wants us to enshrine him in our hearts, and then to rid ourselves of all hindering veils, so that the light of the knowledge of the glory of God may make even the common garb of daily drudgery beautiful.

This was the great climax of our Lord's earthly life, when he definitely turned away from the glory that was set before him to endure the cross for our redemption.

MATTHEW 17:9-21

Lack of Faith Rebuked. As Raphael suggests in his great painting, there is a close connection between the mountain and the valley. The glory of the one did not make our Lord indifferent to the bitter need of the other. It seems as though he desired to impress on us the great truth that we must have the seclusion and exaltation of communion with God before we can successfully deal with the anguish and terror that devastate human lives. See v. 21.

In v. 17 our Lord grieves over the unbelief of his disciples. Though they had enjoyed his careful teaching, they had failed to grasp his secret, which he here again elaborates. Faith is openness to God. It is the lifting of the curtain, that the healing light may enter. The tiny seed unlocks its little doorway to welcome the entering life of Nature; and as this continues to enter, it forces the rootlet downward and the green shoot upward. It is thus also with the life of God in the soul. Let this life of God in and there is no limit to what it will effect.

MATTHEW 17:22-27

Pay Tribute Where It Is Due. All Jews were required to pay the half-shekel for the maintenance of the Temple services. See Exod. 30:13. As God's own Son, our Lord might surely have claimed exemption from taxation for his Father's house. But he waived his claims, that he might not put a stumbling block in the way of others. We must often conform to requirements that seem needless, because of the effect of our example on others who have not had the advantages of our illumination.

In the miracle that followed, our Lord sweetly teaches that he is responsible for the expenses of those who have given up other means of livelihood in order to devote themselves to his service. It is as though we are encouraged to go to him to meet the demands made on us for taxes of one kind and another. He will give us what we need, kindly classing himself with us, not in two coins, but in one. Make Christ's interest your aim; he will make your taxes his care. See 1 John 1:3.

MATTHEW 18:1-9

Removing Stumbling Blocks. Our Lord's transfiguration suggested that the time to take up his kingdom was near, and the apostles began to arrange their plans. The Master therefore used a child for his text and preached a sermon on humility. We must not be childish, but childlike. See 1 Cor. 13:11. The beauty of a little child is its humility, simplicity, and faith. Christ's kingdom abounds with the rare blending of the warrior and the child. See 2 Kings 5:14. God's best gifts are placed, not on a high shelf for us to reach up to, but on a low one to which we must stoop.

An offense is anything that makes the path of a holy and useful life more difficult for others. Be sure, in all your actions, to consider the weaker ones who are watching and following you. "Father," said a boy, "take the safe path; I am coming." A man whose arm was caught in a machine saved his boy from being drawn in by severing the arm with a hatchet. All that hurts us or others, however precious, must be severed.

MATTHEW 18:10-20

Saving the Straying. How tenderly the Master speaks of the children! We must turn back to become like them, v. 3. To cause them to stumble is to incur terrible penalties, v. 6. Not one of them is to be despised, v. 10. Each has an angel from the Father's presence-chamber—one of the most exalted—to take charge of him, v. 10. To seek and to save one of these, the Good Shepherd is prepared to traverse the mountain paths, v. 12. It is not the Father's will that one should perish.

When we have sinned against our brother, we must seek him out and be reconciled. See Matt. 5:23, 24. But when our brother has sinned against us, we are to make three efforts before we give him up as hopeless. It is the presence of Jesus with his people that brings them into unison with the unseen world, so that their decisions and prayers are simultaneous with the divine mind. The Advocate-Paraclete in our hearts is at one with the Advocate-Paraclete on the throne, John 14:16.

MATTHEW 18:21-35

Forgiven yet Unforgiving. "Seventy times seven" is illimitable forgiveness. These numbers denote the perfection of perfection; and if God asks so much of us, what is he not prepared to do! Despair of yourself, but never despair of God's forgiving mercy! The cause of soul-ruin is not sin, but the unbelief that thinks sin too great to be forgiven.

The difference between the two amounts of debt named in the parable sets forth the vast difference between our indebtedness to man and to God; and the free pardon of the king teaches us that God desires not only to forgive us, but to wipe out all memory of our sins. We could never pay all, but God will forgive all. Yet notice that this servant forfeited the king's pardon, so that it ceased to operate. Similarly we may shut ourselves out of the benefits of Christ's death—though it has reconciled the world unto God—by an unforgiving and merciless spirit.

MATTHEW 19:1-12

Jesus' View of Marriage. Divorce was common among the Jews of that decadent age, being justified by Deut. 24:1. Concerning this, it should be remembered that this legislation, though in advance of the standards of its age, was a distinct concession to the state of morality which had then been reached. You can legislate only slightly ahead of the general maxims and practices of the people; else you discourage them and bring your laws into disuse.

The Lord takes us back to the original constitution of the family, where the one man was for the one woman. The only act that justifies divorce is the act which violates the marriage vow. Some are debarred from marriage by circumstances, but for such there is provided special grace, if they will seek it. Some refuse marriage in order to be more free for their lifework. Christ does not set these above others. He does not put special honor on celibacy, but in vv. 13, 14 places special emphasis on the beauty of family life.

MATTHEW 19:13-22

How to Enter the Kingdom. Youth, with all its fervor and impetuosity, is very beautiful in itself and very dear to Christ. Here youth was combined with station, wealth, and noble character. It is not necessary that *all* should sell their goods and distribute the proceeds. It is a harder task to retain wealth and administer it for God. But it was necessary that the Master should prove to this young man that he was not fulfilling the Commandments quite so perfectly as he had supposed.

How few would wed poverty today if they had to choose! Yet great riches must lie hidden beneath her rustic dress. Christ chose her as his companion during his human life, and St. Francis of Assisi said that he took her for his bride. In Matthew the beatitude is phrased, "Blessed are the poor in spirit," but in Luke it stands, "Blessed be ye poor." See Jas. 2:5.

MATTHEW 19:23-30

Riches in the Kingdom. Money is not an unmixed good. It brings in its train many temptations. It is easier to bear poverty than wealth—easier to be a saint when life is hard than when prosperity lavishes her gifts.

When the Pope was showing St. Francis of Assisi the treasures of the Vatican, he remarked, "We can hardly say with the apostle, 'Silver and gold have we none.'" Francis replied aptly and incisively, "Yes, holy father, and I suppose we can hardly say either, 'Rise up and walk.' " Often it is in the poverty of earthly circumstances that the soul becomes possessed of an authority which wealth cannot buy.

What compensations there will be hereafter in the times of the restitution of all things! See Acts 3:21. Then the unsatisfied yearnings for husband, wife, or child; the love which craved for love, the lonely, the homeless, the pilgrim will neither hunger nor thirst, because the Lamb will lead him to the fountains of waters of life.

MATTHEW 20:1–16

The Bargaining Spirit Rebuked. This parable originated in Peter's question. He had seen the rich young man go away sorrowful because he could not meet the test which had been put to him, and he contrasted with that great refusal the swift willingness with which he and his fellow apostles had left all to follow the Lord Jesus.

"Take care," said Jesus, "or your bargaining for the rewards of the kingdom will put you down among the lowest, while they who don't bargain will come out at the top." The last made no agreement; they came in at the eleventh hour and were only too glad to take the vineyard path, leaving the vine owner to give what he thought right. The first "agreed," taking care to strike a bargain of so much money for so much work. But they would have done better if they had left the payment to the grace of their employer. "It is of faith, that it may be by grace, to the end the promise might be sure to all the seed," Rom. 4:16.

MATTHEW 20:17–28

Serving Nobler Than Self-seeking. For the third time our Lord foretells his death. In Matt. 16:21, he dwelt especially on the shame of his rejection; in 17:23, he told how the gates of death would open on Easter joy. Now he declares the method of his death and tells how Gentiles would join with his own people in the tragedy of the cross. He was no martyr who went unknowing to his doom. He set his face to go to the cross. Others die because they were born; he was born that he might die.

Many desire the power of the throne without being prepared to pay the price of suffering. Others say glibly and easily, "We can," little realizing what their choice involves, and that nothing but the grace of God can make their vow possible of fulfillment. But it is sufficient! Only claim it. God will not fail you! Notice v. 28. The Lord ministers to us all, daily, patiently, lovingly. He took on him the form of a servant and became obedient. Serve all men for his sake! We have to go down to reach his side.

MATTHEW 20:29—21:7

The Great Healer and the Lowly King. The Lord is always saying: "What will ye that I shall do?" Let us not ask small things. We honor him by making great demands. Our greatest requests come far short of his generosity and resources. It seems as though we are always giving him pain by the meagerness of our expectation. Whatever people say, cry out so much the more! But remember it is not the outcry, but your need and your faith which will arrest his steps.

Our Lord entered the city in fulfillment of prophetic vision, but in great lowliness, along a road carpeted by the loving enthusiasm of the crowds. It was largely a Galilean and popular outburst. The upper classes kept aloof. Remember that ancient prediction quoted here, Isa. 62:11 and especially Zech. 9:9. The King comes, having salvation. That is the divine order! We shall never know the full power of Christ's salvation until we have welcomed him to our hearts as King.

MATTHEW 21:8–17

The Lord of the Temple. It was only a crowd of poor people who escorted Jesus on Palm Sunday to the Holy City; but they sent their hosannas upward to the highest, and their shouts of acclamation and praise are ever ringing down the ages. Let us take them up and pass them on. Hosanna means "Save now." See Psalm 118:25, which formed part of the Great *Hallel*, or Passover Psalms. Thus, one day his Church, and probably the literal Israel of the future, will hail him with transports of joy. See Zech. 2:10. Where Jesus comes, he cleanses. At his word the heart that was filled with the din of worldly care becomes the home of prayer, and children —the emblems of humility, simplicity, and faith—gather. While the needy and the childlike are attracted by our Lord's gentleness, wrongdoers are driven out before the terror of the Lord.

MATTHEW 21:18–22

Fruitlessness Judged and Faith Rewarded. Men have found fault with our Lord for smiting this tree with barrenness. Yet what teacher would not root up a plant, if he desired to teach his pupils some lesson which could be taught only in that manner! Surely Jesus was perfectly justified in making that fig tree the symbol of the judgment that must overtake all who profess but do not possess. Beware lest he seek fruit of thee in vain!

But how wonderful those words on faith! He could speak thus, because he was the "author and perfecter" of faith. Paul lived by "the faith of the Son of God," Gal. 2:20. All things are possible to him that believeth. Faith annihilates time and distance. To her, the unseen is more real than the seen and the distant as near as the things which the hand can touch. She is the open hand of the soul which appropriates and takes from the hand of God. But faith is impossible apart from prayer.

MATTHEW 21:23-32

Authority Which Silenced and Condemned. Our Lord always refused to gratify idle curiosity. When an earnest seeker for truth, like Nicodemus, approached him to know the way of life, he was willing to give time and thought without stint. But of what use was it to endeavor to satisfy these men who had refused to acknowledge the divine mission of the forerunner! They would not speak out their inner convictions, because of the effect it would have on their worldly prospects. For such as these Christ has nothing. At all costs, we must be true to the inner light—that is, to God's Spirit within us.

The parable of the two sons teaches that hard hearts may lie under fair words, while those of whom we expect least and whose first greeting is abrupt and disappointing may later prove to be the most devoted and hopeful disciples. If a man repels the gospel with violence, he is more likely ultimately to be won than he who gives a polite and facile assent.

MATTHEW 21:33-46

Rejecters Themselves Rejected. This parable is based on Isaiah 5:1-7. The husbandmen are the religious leaders of the people. The vineyard is, of course, the Hebrew nation. The servants sent for the produce refer to the prophets and others raised up from time to time to speak for God and to demand "fruits meet for repentance." Notice that when he speaks of the mission of the Son, our Lord severs himself, by the sharpest possible line, from all merely human messengers and claims sonship in the most intimate and lofty sense of the word.

It is said that in the building of Solomon's Temple, a curiously shaped stone, sent from the quarry, was left to lie for many months in the entangled undergrowth, till suddenly its fitness was discovered for a place in the Temple walls. Then it was put into its right position, which it occupied thenceforward. This incident may be referred to in Ps. 118:22. How truly it portrays men's treatment of our Lord! Is he your cornerstone?

MATTHEW 22:1-14

The Penalty of Slighting the Invitation. We have here a continuation of our Lord's teaching on that last great day in the Temple. This day seems to have begun with 21:23, and it continued to 25:46. What wonder that his strength was prematurely exhausted, and that he succumbed so soon under the anguish of his cross!

In this parable he describes his union with his people under the symbolism of marriage. This must have suggested the allusions of Eph. 5:23-32, where the apostle tells us that Christ loved the Church as his bride; and of Rom. 7:1-4, where he encourages us to believe that we may be married to him who was raised from the dead. We can never forget Rev. 21:2, 9. Messenger after messenger was sent to the Hebrew people, but as they would not come the Church was called from the highways and byways of the world to occupy the vacant space. But let us see to it that we are clothed in the spotless robe of his righteousness, in which alone we can stand in the searching light of eternity.

MATTHEW 22:15-22

Duties to God and Society. This reading begins a marvelous cycle of interviews between our Lord and his questioners. First the Herodians, then the Sadducees, and finally the Pharisees were answered and silenced. What inimitable wisdom there was in his replies! How masterfully he turned the battle from the gate and slew them with their own swords!

Theoretically God was King in Israel. Were, then, the Jews justified in paying tribute to Caesar? If our Lord had said so, his enemies would have accused him of treachery to the theocracy. If he had forbidden it, they would have accused him of treachery to their Roman conquerors. Our Lord answered with marvelous wisdom. He tore aside the veil and revealed their hypocrisy. That coin indicated that the Romans were responsible for maintaining law and order. It was surely right that Caesar's dues should be paid. But it was equally right to give to God the souls that he had redeemed. Are we as careful in rendering to God our hearts and lives as we are in paying our taxes and serving the state?

MATTHEW 22:23-33

The Scriptures Teach the Resurrection. The Sadducees professed themselves to be bound by the Pentateuch, and to have searched in vain for evidences of a life beyond. They were greatly startled, therefore, when our Lord proved human immortality from the book of Exodus. He had never passed through their schools and sat at the feet of their great teachers, but he showed them that at the bush the voice of God attested eternal life.

The great I AM would never have spoken of himself as the God of the patriarchs, centuries after their earthly career had closed, unless they had been living somewhere still. It was certain that they were all alive; otherwise God would have said, "I *was* their God." Death is not a chamber, but a passage; not an abiding-place, but a crossing over; not a state, but an act, an experience, a crossing of the bar, a going within the veil. Abraham, Isaac, Jacob, and all the myriads of God's people who have warred and stormed over the earth are living as intensely as ever.

MATTHEW 22:34-46

The Summary of the Law. Our Lord seemed to say: "Here is all Scripture in a nutshell, the whole range of human duty in portable pocket form." We are reminded of Eccles. 12:13. But what a magnificent definition is here given of pure and undefiled religion! The whole Law is gathered up in that one word "love!" See Rom. 13:8-10.

In Mark 12:33 the word "strength" is added. There are four channels of love. The "heart" stands for our emotions, the "soul" for our will and general individuality, the "mind" for our intellect, and "strength" for the activities and energies of our service. Often we cannot feel love, but we can always use our strength for God and show our love by doing things which we would never do except for his sake.

The question which the Master propounded to the scribes can be solved only by the admission of his two natures—divine and human—as existing in his one Person. As David's Lord he is divine; as his son, he was born of the Virgin. See Matt. 1:1.

MATTHEW 23:1-12

Humbling the Self-exalted. These words were addressed to the disciples and the crowds that had gathered around. The Jewish religious leaders divorced morality and religion and insisted that men should respect their office, whatever might be their personal character. The craving for this has been the temptation and bane of Christ's ministers in every age.

But how evidently our Lord condemns clerical and priestly assumption! With the two-edged sword, which pierces to the dividing asunder of soul and spirit, he cuts between the professions and performances of these men. No more awful words were ever spoken! How true is v. 4! The hypocrite always spares himself, but is merciless in his demands on others. The true servant of God never exacts these titles as a rightful homage, or as indicating either superiority or special sanctity. We all have one Master and one Father; and though our talents greatly differ, we stand on an absolute equality so far as saving grace is concerned.

MATTHEW 23:13-26

Woes for the False-hearted. These repeated woes may be translated, "Alas for you!" Our Lord with unfailing accuracy indicates the inevitable doom which such conduct as that of the Pharisees and scribes must incur. He forewarned them that they could expect nothing in the dread future but the judgment of Gehenna—the metaphor being taken from the valley of Hinnom, south of Jerusalem, where fires were kept burning to consume rubbish and refuse.

Hypocrisy hides under a cloak of religion the sins which the ordinary moralist and worldling would condemn. It is very injurious, because it hinders men from entering the kingdom, v. 13. It is punctilious in its exactions, because while it strains out gnats, it swallows camels, vv. 23, 24. It expends itself on outward ritual. The Pharisees would not enter Pilate's hall on the day before the Passover, but they murdered the holy Savior. Above all things, let us be true, professing to be no more than we are!

MATTHEW 23:27-39

Judgment and Lament. True goodness recognizes and rewards good in the living; while the evil-minded cannot, or will not, believe that the people whom they meet daily are purely and sincerely good. They pride themselves on what they would have done if they had lived in the great days of the past, but they miss the opportunities which are always ready at hand. In this they judge and condemn themselves.

How sad is this lament over Jerusalem! The yearning love which longed to intercept descending judgment, as the hen the stroke of danger which menaces her brood, was about to be withdrawn. After striving his best to save them, the world's Redeemer was

MATTHEW 24:1-14

Be Ready to Endure. Successive generations have pored over these words of our Lord with great eagerness, endeavoring to extract from them a clear forecast of the future. In the case of the early Christians, they warned them to flee to Pella and in doing so, to escape the destruction of Jerusalem by Titus. But to all of us they are full of instruction.

It is best to consider these paragraphs as containing a double reference. In the first place, up to v. 28, they evidently deal with the approaching fall of Jerusalem. Our Lord describes the events which were to mark the consummation of the age, v. 3, margin. Antichrists, disturbances of physical and national conditions, the persecutions which the infant Church must encounter, the progress of the gospel, and finally the swoop of the Roman eagles on their prey—all these were to mark the close of the Hebrew dispensation and the birth of the Christian Church.

MATTHEW 24:15-28

Beware of False Christs. The abomination of desolation is explained in Luke 21:20, and probably refers to the Roman ensigns as the symbols of pagan and therefore unclean power. So urgent would be their need of flight that the outside steps of the houses must be used. None might try to save his property. Even the winter's cold must be faced if life is to be saved; and the flight must be farther than could be covered on a Sabbath day—that is, according to Jewish law, less than a mile.

It is a matter of literal fact that there was compressed into the period of the Jewish War an amount of suffering perhaps unparalleled. Josephus' history of the period abounds in references to these false Christs who professed themselves to be the Messiah.

Notice that though the elect may be powerfully tempted, they will repudiate and resist the attack and still remain loyal to their Lord. What a searching word is this! ". . . whom he did predestinate . . . them he also glorified," Rom. 8:30. They may be tempted, tried, almost deceived, but angels will bear them up in their hands and God will keep their feet. See Ps. 91:12; 1 Sam. 2:9.

MATTHEW 24:29-39

Words That Must Be Fulfilled. The preceding portion of this prophecy is by all interpreters applied to the destruction of Jerusalem. But on the portion that follows there is a considerable division of opinion.

Perhaps it is wisest, between vv. 28 and 29, to interpolate the Christian centuries during which the gospel is being preached to the Gentiles, according to Rom. 11:25 (but that whole chapter should be considered). Just as one who looks across a mountainous country may count the successive ranks of sierras or ranges, but does not record the valleys that lie between, so our Lord, who speaks as the last of the Hebrew prophets, does not stop to notice the story of the Church, but confines himself to the events which are specially Hebrew.

Probably the present age will be ushered out by scenes not unlike those of the preceding one; immediately afterward the Lord will set up his reign, and there shall be a new Heaven and a new earth. The Advent will be sudden, v. 36, and will find men unprepared, v. 38. The Jewish people will exist as a people till then, v. 34.

MATTHEW 24:40-51

Watch and Work. There are many comings of the Son of man before the final one to judgment. We may derive the full benefit of our Lord's words, even though we have arrived at no settled opinion as to the precise order of future events. The hour of our death is as uncertain as that of his coming in the clouds. For each, we should be ready!

Watchfulness is keeping awake! We are beset by temptations to sleep. Bunyan said that we are traveling over the Enchanted Ground, the air of which is very heavy and sleep-producing. How dull we are to perceive the unseen, or to meet the great opportunities of life! "Broken up" alludes to the mud or clay house which could not keep out the thief. Death breaks in and carries us away from all of our treasures. See 1 Thess. 5:2, 4.

We had best wait for our Lord while engaged in carefully discharging our appointed tasks. The Church is a big household in which each has his niche. To labor is to pray; to serve is to be ready.

MATTHEW 25:1-13

Be Ready for the Bridegroom. Three remarkable parables occupy this chapter and follow a marked sequence of thought. First, we are called upon to look to ourselves and be sure that we are prepared to enter the wedding feast; that is, to enter into the holiest and closest union with our Lord. Many are called into that union of thought and prayer and service, but, alas, how few there are who approve themselves as chosen for that inner intimacy! We must see to it that our hearts are pure with virginal purity, and that the light is ever burning in our hearts through the continual inpouring of the oil of the Holy Spirit.

How marvelous the power which, from the noisy night procession of an oriental wedding, could bring this exquisite parable of the short, warm Eastern night, the ten girls, the cry, the peace of the prepared, the anguish of the unready, the inside and outside of the door! O blessed Comforter, may we not fail thee, as thou wilt not fail those who in their weakness seek thy help!

MATTHEW 25:14-30

By Faithfulness Win Reward. We are not only guests, but servants who must give an account of their stewardship. Each bondslave has been entrusted with at least one talent. The number of talents varies with our ability to manage them. The Master is not unreasonable, and never overtasks. It is by use that the power to use grows. By carefully employing our opportunities, our sphere of service may be greatly widened, so that at the end of life we shall be able to do twice as much as at the outset.

Christ is always coming to reckon. Every Communion, every birthday is a standing at the judgment-seat of Christ, preliminary to the great white throne, 2 Cor. 5:10. Let those who are entrusted with one talent only be specially on the watch, for they are most exposed to the temptation of saying, "We can do so little, we will do nothing." What you can do best, and which most accords with your circumstances, is probably your talent. If you cannot do much yourself, work with your church and under the direction of your pastor, v. 27.

MATTHEW 25:31-46

Serve Christ by Serving Others. We are called to watch the procedure of God's moral government. This is primarily a forecast of the judgment of *the nations,* v. 32. It would seem as though, in the first instance, their doom will be largely affected by their treatment of the Hebrew people, the brethren of Jesus after the flesh, v. 40.

But the parable has a wider range. Our Lord evidently identifies himself, not so much with great causes as with all who are weary and heavy laden, who are sorrowful or sinful, who have drifted into the hospitals and prisons of the world. None are too desolate and sorrowful to attract his loving notice, and he hails as "blessed" all who sympathize with and help them. In the closing verse, it should be noticed that the word "everlasting" or "eternal" stands in each clause; and it should be remembered that it stands for a quality of existence which is altogether independent of time.

MATTHEW 26:1-13

Love's Fragrant Ministry. How great the contrast between the plotting in the court of Caiaphas and the love-ministry of Bethany! Yet even there, a strain of needless sorrow was added to the cup of our Lord. While his foes were plotting his destruction, it became necessary for him to speak on behalf of the devoted woman who was suffering criticism for his name. It is probable that of all people then living, Mary was the only one who had really entered into the meaning of the Lord's words and had realized the scenes of suffering that lay before him. Through the succeeding hours the aroma of that ointment, lingering still on his person, must have sweetly reminded Jesus how dearly he was loved.

Mary is not named in this Gospel, perhaps because it was written during her lifetime and such a reference might have exposed her to suffering. But in the fourth Gospel she is named, because by that time the whole family had gone into the presence of him whom they so devotedly loved. Do not be deterred by utilitarian calculations from the spontaneous expression of love to Jesus.

MATTHEW 26:14-25

A False Friend Exposed. While Mary sacrificed a large sum of money to show her love to Jesus, Judas sold him for the price of a slave. See Zech. 11:12.

The Lord had a great desire to eat this last meal with his own. It was a proof of his loving anticipation of the strain to which they were to be exposed in soul and body, that he had made arrangements for it with some secret disciple. How glad this loving soul must have been to make the loan of that guest chamber! But have you placed your heart at his disposal? See 1 Cor. 5:7.

It was a time of testing as well as of fellowship. None of us should sit at the Table of the Lord without careful self-examination and confession. We all need to say, "Lord, is it I?" and to ask that we may be clad in the white robes through his precious blood. Remember, also, that they who in all humility and self-distrust fear lest they should commit the deed of treachery are always the ones to whom it will be impossible.

MATTHEW 26:26-35

A Self-confident Disciple Warned. The Passover looked back to the dread hour of the Exodus; the Supper links Calvary with the Second Advent. In partaking of it we should not confine ourselves to either retrospect or anticipation, but should endeavor to feed our souls with the very spirit and heart of our dear Lord, so as to absorb his divine strength, sweetness, and love. We need to feed on his flesh and drink of his blood after a mystical fashion, so that he may become the life of our life. The word "new" is not the same as in Matt. 9:17, but contrasts with the present order of things, being something entirely different. The former things will have passed away—such was our Lord's anticipation!

The new covenant is further explained in Heb. 8. It is good to recite its provisions when we sit at the Table. It is as though God and the believer drink of the cup in pledge of that blessed understanding between them. See how our Shepherd eagerly warns one of the sheep that was dear to him and for which he had pleaded often, Luke 22:31.

MATTHEW 26:36-46

The Hour When the Flesh Was Weak. In human life there is a close connection between our hymns and our olive-presses. We pass from the supper to the garden, from the emblems to the reality. But not all can enter into the fellowship of our Lord's unknown sufferings. Paul longed to do this, that he might realize also the power of his resurrection, Phil. 3:10. Our Lord longs for the sympathy which will keep awake out of love for him, though it may not understand all that is in his heart!

Notice that though the cup seemed to be mixed and presented by human hands, our Lord refused to see in it these alone, but went behind them to the permissive will of God the Father. It is this thought that removes bitterness from the bitterest cup. In the same sentence Jesus bade the disciples sleep on and arise. It was as though he knew and felt that though the past had gone beyond recall, yet further opportunities and testings were awaiting them and him. These they would encounter and share in company. He is always saying to us, however unworthy, "Let us be going."

MATTHEW 26:47-56

Betrayed and Forsaken. We cannot fathom the secret thoughts of the traitor. Did he hope that his act would compel Christ to take the course of self-vindication, which his mighty acts appeared to make possible? It seems unthinkable that there was not some explanation other than mere greed! Yet when we look into our own hearts, can we be altogether surprised? How often have we betrayed the Lord by our reticence, when we should have spoken; by the kiss of the lip, when we were selfishly exploiting our association with him to our own advantage!

Our Lord did not die a martyr's death. The martyr is led to the scaffold or stake because he is overpowered by superior force. But our Lord knew that the invisible world was full of help if only he had expressed the slightest wish. Others die because they are born; he was born that he might die. "He laid down his life, that he might take it again." He would not receive help from the Father, or the angels, or Peter's sword, but poured out his soul unto death because of a love that was stronger than death. See 1 Pet. 2:21ff.

MATTHEW 26:57-66

The True Answer to False Witness. This meeting of the Jewish leaders had been hastily summoned; but their difficulty was to substantiate a charge that would warrant the death sentence. They had to go back to the beginning of Christ's ministry for the one charge that seemed sufficient for their purpose. But see John 2:19; Mark 14:58. In the meanwhile our Lord opened not his mouth. He left his reputation in the care of the Father, to whom he also committed his soul. It is a good example to follow. Do what is right and let God vindicate you!

It was only when Jesus was directly challenged as to his unique relationship to God that he opened his lips. There is an evident reference in his words to Dan. 7:13, 14. The court instantly recognized that in his reply he claimed to be equal with God. To be the Son of God was to be God. See also John 5:18. Note that word "hereafter," which suggests that though it is hidden from us the kingdom is already set up, as was David's even when Saul was still on the throne.

MATTHEW 26:67-75

Ashamed of Jesus! What a shameful travesty of justice! When men yield themselves to violence like this, their passion condemns them as perpetrating the devil's work. But in the whirlwind of abuse and horror, the one thing that hurt our Lord was the defection of Peter, Luke 22:61.

It was love that led Peter to dare to follow to the court. John contrived to get him in, John 18:16. But he stood too near the fire amid that motley group, who were discussing their night adventure. He had been too self-confident, John 13:37; he had not watched unto prayer, Matt. 26:40. The more he cursed and swore, the more he betrayed his Galilean brogue. Ah, the agony that ensued! Did he rush off to Gethsemane and throw himself on the bent grass where the form of the Master had so recently lain prostrate? Did his tears mingle with the sweat of blood? But Jesus loved him still and was preparing a propitiation that would cleanse his sin, as he had already secured that his faith should not fail, Luke 22:32.

MATTHEW 27:1-10

The Betrayer's Remorse and Suicide. It was very early morning when Jesus was led off to Pilate, for he was on the cross by nine. Judas apparently watched the scene from afar. It may be that he was stricken with horror when our Lord did not exert his mighty power in self-deliverance. The only expedient that occurred to the traitor as practicable was to attest the Lord's innocence. What a tribute that was to the absolute purity and beauty of the life which he had known for so long in the closest intimacy! If there had been a flaw, he would have caught at it as justifying his deed; but there was none. See Heb. 7:26, 27.

The money burnt his hands and rang on the marble floor. Who can estimate the despair, the horror, the blackness of darkness that drove him to a suicide's fate? See Acts 1:15ff. Note how punctilious these false priests were, v. 6. It is certain that even after this, if he had repented he would have been forgiven. But despair had seized him. He went to his own place! Each of us is making a place for himself and is going to it.

MATTHEW 27:11-21

Barabbas or Christ? The vacillation of Pilate made him a criminal. Weakness becomes sin. At first he evidently meant to release Jesus, but instead of saying so outright, he strove to bring about his release by indirect means and without committing himself.

First, he sent him to Herod, Luke 23:7, thinking that a Jew would view favorably the position of a fellow-Jew. Then he sought to touch the springs of pity by the anguish of scourging. Finally, he gave the people the choice between Barabbas and Christ, feeling sure that they must choose the liberation of a lover of men rather than that of an outlaw.

None of these expedients succeeded, and he drifted into the very act which his conscience had condemned from the first. He is a specimen of those weak men who want the right thing to be done, but will not adventure their own interests to get it done. There is no chance of such men coming out right. The one hope for us all is to declare ourselves for the right and true, at once and from the start.

MATTHEW 27:22-31

The Stain Water Could Not Wash Away. No judge ought to have asked the crowd what he should do. But every man has to do with Christ. He is ever standing before the bar of conscience, and each of us must accept or condemn, do homage or crucify. If we do not pronounce for him, we pronounce against him; and there is a moment when our verdict becomes irrevocable. "What I have written, I have written." We are all writing our legend and affixing it to the cross for the universe to read, and a day comes when it is irreversible.

We may wash our hands after the deed of treachery is done, but water will not avail for Pilate, for Lady Macbeth, or for us. We need the blood of Christ ere we can be cleansed from all sin, 1 John 5:6.

The King of men must wear a crown of the thorns with which sin is so closely identified. See Gen. 3:18. Only thus can the crown of universal empire be won! The robe of mockery must precede his ascension vesture. The reed is appropriate, for it is through such that he wins and rules. See Isa. 42:3 and 57:15.

MATTHEW 27:32-44

"They Crucified Him." He would not drink what would dull his keen sense of the momentous issues of the cross. Those taunts were true. None who save themselves can save others. The cry of forsakenness, the midday midnight, the yielded spirit, the rent veil, the opened tombs, the sympathy of Nature—all these proved that this was no common death, and were in keeping with everything that Scripture had foretold, 1 Pet. 1:11.

Our Lord was wrapped in midnight, that he might be our "bright and morning star." He became obedient to death, that he might give eternal life. His heel was sorely wounded, that he might break the head of him that had the power of death and might wear forever at his girdle the keys of death and Hades. Make his

MATTHEW

soul an offering for thy sin. Hide in the cleft which the soldier's spear opened in his side. He has made peace by the blood of his cross; we have but to accept and be at rest.

MATTHEW 27:45-56

The Broken Heart and the Rent Veil. With hushed hearts we stand in the presence of that sight. It is the tragedy of time, the one supreme act of self-surrender, the unique unapproachable sacrifice and satisfaction for the sins of the whole world. It is here that myriads of sin-sick, terror-stricken souls in every century have found refuge. It is here that martyrs have been made strong to endure. It is here that Jacob's ladder rested, in the lower places of the earth, for he that ascended is the same also that first "descended into the lower parts of the earth." He became "obedient unto death, even the death of the cross. Wherefore. . . ." See Phil. 2:8.

The centurion had seen other crucified ones die, but never one like this. He recognized the superhuman elements of the scene. But for us, the emotions of this hour are not those of wonder, but of loving gratitude and faith. He "loved me," he "gave himself for me," Gal. 2:20.

MATTHEW 27:57-66

The Closed and Guarded Tomb. Fear not to entrust yourself to God in death. If you yield up your spirit and commend it to the Father's hands, he will provide for it and for your body also. He has his Josephs everywhere. He will provide loving hands for your body, which was the shrine and casket of the precious jewel that he bought at so great a cost. Precious in his sight is the death of his saints, Ps. 116:15.

The kings and princes of this world set themselves to guard the sepulcher of the Son of God by sealing-wax and sentries. They might as well have endeavored to restrain the bursting life of spring. Said the King of Terrors to Captain Corruption, "Take care to keep this Man's body fast." But what did this avail, when it had been ordained that he should not stay in Hades, nor even see corruption? Whatever your foes may do against you will not avail, if only you wait patiently for God. See Ps. 40.

MATTHEW 28:1-10

The Open and Empty Tomb. Ere the sun had risen and while the glory of the dawn was faint in the Eastern sky, the women were well on their way. But he whom they sought had gone. How often we look down into the grave of the dead past, or we peer for help into the diaries, prayers, and rites of departed saints or a moribund church—but we do not find the Lord. The divine Leader of souls is not behind us, but before; not in the grave of the dead past, but in the vanguard of the world's march. Lo, he beckons us on to follow the ascension mountain and the opened Heaven!

The Lord engaged women as messengers of his resurrection. See Ps. 68:11. How eagerly they caught his idea, and with what alacrity they endeavored to fulfill it. And as they went, he for whom they went met them! It is ever thus. We go on his errands, but we do not leave him as we go. On the contrary, he meets us. See Isa. 64:5.

MATTHEW 28:11-20

The Great Commission of the Risen Lord. What absurdity in this fabricated explanation! How could the soldiers know who stole the body if they were asleep? Skeptics have to believe greater marvels than believers. Was it likely that Christ's friends would have wished to unwind the clothes that covered that sacred body? Would his enemies have taken the time, or forfeited the rich shroud that Joseph's love provided? Men will believe any lie rather than God's truth, because their hearts are evil.

This mountain at the conclusion of our Lord's life corresponds to the mountain of temptation at the beginning. There he was offered the empire of the world, if only he would take the easy lower path; here he is acknowledged King of the world because he took the harder one of obedience unto death. This glorious charge to his Church has the ring of universality. It combines the herald and the shepherd, and assures each humble disciple that the day will never dawn, however stormy, on which his Lord will not be near.

THE GOSPEL ACCORDING TO
MARK

"DECLARED TO BE THE SON OF GOD WITH POWER," Rom. 1:4

I. THE BEGINNING OF THE GOSPEL *1:1–13.*
   A. John the Baptist proclaims the coming of One mightier than himself *1:1–8.*
   B. The Voice from Heaven bears witness to Jesus *1:9–11.*
   C. Jesus vanquishes the tempter *1:12, 13.*

II. GROWING AUTHORITY AND GROWING OPPOSITION *1:14—3:6.*
   A. The calling of the first disciples *1:14–20.*
   B. Miracles of healing, and the forgiveness of sins *1:21—2:12*
   C. Opposition of the scribes and Pharisees *2:13—3:6.*

III. THE ABOUNDING MINISTRY *3:7—8:26.*
   ("I must work the work of him that sent me, while it is day.") Teaching, healing, calling of the twelve, parables, preaching, stilling the storm, raising the dead, feeding the multitudes, silencing the scribes and Pharisees.

IV. THE LAST JOURNEY TO JERUSALEM *8:27—10:52.*
   A. The preparation of the disciples *8:27—9:50.*
   Peter's confession, the Transfiguration, healing of demoniac boy, who should be greatest?
   B. Incidents by the way *10:1–52.*
   Questions of Pharisees about divorce, blessing the children, rich young ruler, ambition of James and John.

V. IN THE CITY OF THE GREAT KING *11:1—13:37.*
   Triumphal entry, cleansing of the Temple, questions, parables, warnings, prophecies.

VI. THE TRIUMPH OF SUBMISSION *14:1—15:47.*
   A. The culmination of enmity and of friendship *14:1–11.*
   B. The Last Supper and the agony in the garden *14:12–42.*
   C. The betrayal *14:43–52.*
   D. The Jewish and Roman trials *14:53—15:15.*
   E. The crucifixion and burial *15:16–47.*

VII. CAPTIVITY LED CAPTIVE *16:1–20.*
   A. The visit of the women to the empty tomb *16:1–11.*
   B. The walk to Emmaus *16:12, 13.*
   C. The Great Commission *16:14–20.*

INTRODUCTION

That this Gospel is the briefest and earliest of the four needs no proof. It was written between A.D. 63 and 70, and was primarily intended for the Romans. It has always been believed that Mark was greatly influenced by Peter. This accounts for the many touches which are especially characteristic of Peter. It is usually believed that this Gospel was written in Rome, and we know that Mark is frequently referred to in the epistles as associated with Christian ministry there, 2 Tim. 4:11; Philemon 24; 1 Pet. 5:13.

COMMENTARY

MARK 1:1-20

The Beginning of Jesus' Ministry. The ministry of John the Baptist, vv. 1-8. Always the message of John precedes that of Jesus Christ; first the changed attitude of the will, then faith. The greatness of the Baptist revealed itself in his humility. He saw what we must see, that a negative religion, symbolized by water, is not enough; we need to be set on fire.

The opening pages of Christ's public life, vv. 9-20. Jesus was recognized by the Baptist, who beheld the opened heavens and the descending Spirit. If the Lord was thus anointed ere he commenced his lifework, how much more must we be! Hast thou become united with him in his death, made one with him in his resurrection, and anointed by that same Spirit? Then be sure that thou, too, must be tempted. Sons of men must go the way of the Son of man—now under the opened heavens, then tempted of the devil; on one side the wild beasts, on the other the angels; now driven to loneliness, and then to the crowded street of the cities, there to gather disciples by the energy and beauty of a victorious life.

MARK 1:21-39

The Helper of the Needy. The word "straightway" is typical of our Lord's life. It and such equivalents as "immediately," etc. are the keynote of Mark's Gospel, which is preeminently the Gospel of service. The ancient symbol for this Gospel was the ox. There is comparatively little said in it, as in Matthew, about the King; or, as in Luke, about the details of Jesus' humanity; or, as in John, about his divine Sonship. There are suggestions of all these, but emphasis is laid on the unresting labors of Jesus, who went about doing good. In illustration of this trait in the Master's life, the evangelist narrates the proceedings of two typical days, the one at the beginning, the other at the close of his ministry. The first typical day is recorded in this chapter, vv. 21-38. The morning was spent in the synagogue, where at the close of the service the demon was cast out; the afternoon witnessed the healing of Peter's wife's mother; the evening beheld the throng at the door, whom he healed. Early next day he had gone forth for prayer, and forthwith started on a mission throughout all Galilee. The second typical day is recorded in 11:20 to 13:37.

MARK 1:40—2:22

The Friend of Sinners. The leper, 1:40-45. The news of Christ spread fast and far until it reached the outcasts from Jewish society, the very dregs of humanity. As the story of the wonderful miracles wrought by our Lord was pondered deeply by this man, he concluded that the only question which remained was that of Christ's willingness to hear. As to his power there could be no doubt. But no one of all the religious world of that time had ever thought of extending a helping hand to such as he. Note the instantaneousness of our Lord's response to this appeal. His love and power are commensurate; when you gauge the one, you have measured the other.

The paralytic, 2:1–12. The disease had resulted from sin. It was necessary to deal with the soul before the body could be emancipated. As soon as we sin, God's pardon awaits our asking for it, and of this fact our Lord gave the paralytic man definite assurance. Jesus' right to speak was evidenced by his power to heal. If the latter was effectual, so was the former. *The sinner's friend,* vv. 13–22. They thought to coin a term of reproach, but they added a crown of glory. In eternity the Friend of sinners will surround *his* table with saved sinners who have become his guests.

MARK 2:23—3:19

The Lord of the Sabbath. The ritualist demands the outward, the conventional, the ancient usage of the past. Christ says the needs of man, whether of body or of soul, are greater than ceremonial restriction. Ceremonies are only expressions of life, and where life is wanting they are meaningless and void. *The withered hand,* 3:1–6. Through long disuse of powers which God has given, but which we have refrained from exercising, degeneration may have set in; Christ, however, bids us exert them again. Insofar as we dare to obey, we shall find ourselves able. Dare to speak, or pray, or work, not at the impulse of your nature, but at *his* bidding, and you will suddenly find yourself given power. *The apostolate,* vv. 7–19. On three occasions Christ used the boat as his pulpit. See also Mark 4:1; Luke 5:3. We must be disciples (learners) before we can be apostles (those sent). As the Father sent the Master, so the Master sends us. Our mission is threefold—to bear him company, to perform his errands, and to cast out devils. What infinite variety in the apostolic band: the Boanergic group of four; the group of questioners who were sometimes doubters; and the group of practical men, whose business capacity was a snare at least to one. If there was a traitor even amid the twelve, who can expect to find his fields free from tares?

MARK 3:20—4:9

Brother to All Who Will. The Pharisees circulated this infamous charge, not because they believed it, but to satisfy the questions that were being asked on all sides. What they affirmed, they knew to be untrue; but for selfish reasons they would not confess what they really thought. Such denial of truth is a deadly and unpardonable sin, because it injures the sensitiveness of conscience and produces moral death. *Family ties,* 3:31–35. The family of Jesus needed to be taught, though with the utmost delicacy, that they must not attempt to control his public ministry. All who love God and do his will are welcomed into the divine family circle and become blood relations of the Son of God. *The sower,* 4:1–9. Note the perils of the hearer, that you may guard against the waste of precious seed. There is a grave peril in light, fanciful, wandering thoughts. There is great peril also in a mere emotional response—that which "immediately . . . sprang up," which has no root because the heart is hard. There is danger lest the cares of the poor, the riches of the wealthy, and the too eager pursuit of things by other classes may drain away the strength of the soul, so that the Word of God shall be a slender stalk without ear or fruit. It is not enough to hear the Word; we must accept it and bear fruit. Otherwise the plowing, sowing, and all the operations of Nature are in vain. Live up to what you know. Obedience is the key to understanding.

MARK 4:10-41

Growth in God's Kingdom. How quick the Master was to observe the meaning of natural symbols! To him all things were unfoldings of eternal mystery, and the ways of men unconsciously mirrored the unseen. Are there "bushels" in your life? Use them as lamp stands, not as coverings. All secrets come out; beware of what you say. All measures come back to us; take care how you mete. The mysterious cooperation of God in Nature, and the gradual process of growth, are analogous to the co-working of the Holy Spirit with all faithful sowers of the Word, and the imperceptible stages through which the soul reaches maturity. *The stilling of the storm,* vv. 35–41. They that bear Christ's company must prepare for squalls. Yet, why should we fear when the Master is on board, who can impress his commands on wind and sea—to the wind, "Peace"; to the sea, "Be still!" "The Lord on high is mightier than the waves of the sea." A moment ago he was so weary as to sleep amid the storm, but at a word of appeal from those he loves, he shows himself able to save to the uttermost.

MARK 5:1-20

Power over Unclean Spirits. This poor victim of a dark tyrant was endowed with superhuman strength and scorned restraint. Terrible to others, he endured untold misery himself and sought relief in tears and self-inflicted torture. The evil spirit who inflicted torment was also in dread of torment from the gentle Savior, as one whose eyes are inflamed dreads the light. What an admixture of man and demons—"he answered, We are many!" And how malignant! The demons dread disembodiment and prefer a swine's body to none. Many in our midst are held by a similar diabolic power, against which, because they yielded at first by imperceptible degrees, they now struggle in vain. Yet for such there is absolute deliverance in Christ. The emblem of a sinner, a very Samson in evildoing, this man gives encouragement to all those who are driven to evil by demon power.

Distinguish between the sinner and the evil spirits that have control of him. The demon that torments a man loves mischief and would rather destroy swine than be idle. It was not Christ who destroyed these animals, but the spirit of evil. Hast thou been redeemed? Go forth and win others for thy Lord. Tell them what he has done for thee!

MARK 5:21-43

Hope for the Hopeless We turn from the demon-driven man to this woman, weakened by long disease. For the one there was the outward manifestation of evil, but for the other inward wasting and decay. Let those who are conscious of the ravages of evil in their hearts, destroying their strength, establish connection with Christ as slight as the finger's touch of the garment hem, and forthwith his virtue will enter and stay their inward malady. His power is ever going forth, and faith receives as much as it desires. The reservoir of power is always full, but how few, how very few have learned the secret of tapping it!

Crowds throng him, but only one touches. Proximity to Christ does not necessarily imply the appropriation of Christ. But where there is the faintest touch of faith, there is an instantaneous, may we not say, automatic, response. There may be great weakness, the fingers may be too nerveless to grasp, they can only touch; but the slightest degree of faith saves, because it is the channel by which Christ enters, v. 34. Even children are liable to the havoc caused by sin, vv. 35-43. Death has passed on all, and from the universal blight even the little ones cannot find immunity. But again we turn to the Master of life, whose touch is as gentle as a woman's and whose voice can penetrate the recesses of the unseen.

MARK 6:1-20

The Widening Fields. In the opening paragraph of this chapter, we learn of hatred and rejection of those who had enjoyed the rich privileges of being the neighbors and associates of our Lord from his earliest days. They could not discern the divine in the human, the heavenly under the earthly veil. The Savior, therefore, driven from their towns, goes about the villages, depriving himself of the companionship of his disciples in order to spread the Good News as far as possible. The Lord is still in his Church through the Holy Spirit, but his power is limited and neutralized by our unbelief. It is useless to ask him to put forth his great power and save us, so long as we have made it practically impossible for him to do as we ask. The old-time cry was: "Why shouldst thou be as a mighty man that cannot save?" The answer is supplied here: "He could do no mighty work . . . and he marvelled because of their unbelief." Faith is our capacity for God, and there are several conditions for its nurture and growth.

With what simplicity the twelve were started on their mission, v. 7. But with what authority they spoke! Simplicity and power are closely allied. The truly strong soul is not in need of the external surroundings and circumstances on which others lean. In proportion to our willingness to deprive ourselves of the sources of human confidence, may we lay hold on and possess divine power.

MARK 6:21-29

Martyrdom of a Witness-bearer. Better the dungeon with John than the palace with Herod, for conscience filled the palace with the ghost of the murdered Baptist! A woman brought Herod to that. How careful women should be of the influence they exert over men; how careful men should be of yielding to any but the noblest influence! This family was eaten with lust, usually coupled with cruelty. No vice ever dwells alone. John the Baptist had a brief and tortuous career, for a few months the central figure of the nation and then hurled down into the darkness of the dungeon, like some extinguished torch. No wonder that his specter haunted the heart of Herod, who thought that in Jesus he had become reincarnate. The messenger may fall, but the message is taken up and passed on by a thousand lips. Notice the contrast between John's end and that of our Lord. In John's case the disciples who had hearkened to his every word dispersed. The head had fallen, and the members were scattered. None thought of proclaiming their departed leader as still the living head and center of the movement he had set on foot. But when our Lord died, his true influence over men began. Up to that time he had been the Jewish rabbi; thenceforward he became the Redeemer of the world.

MARK 6:30-56

The Sympathy and Compassion of Jesus. When the apostles returned, they had much to tell. Some were flushed with success, others radiant with victory over demons, others perhaps overstrained and weary, and all needing the quiet, holy influence of repose and silence in the Lord's company. In those quiet hours or days, as the fever passed out of them, he taught them memorable lessons of how he would feed the world by his Church, and how his people would be safe amid the storms that swept the sea, for always he would watch them from the height and come to them at the moment when his help was most needed. Christ sits as host at the great table of the Church, and the meager resources of his servants yield the starting point for his multiplication of bread. He bids us go and consider how little we have, that we may properly estimate the greatness of his help. Notice how the upward look precedes the breaking and giving. There is enough for each, not of bread alone, but of fish; and the disciples are refreshed by another kind of ministry. So the Lord recreates us by turning exhausted energies into new channels. What threatens to overpower us brings Christ to our side. But his footsteps must be arrested if we would have his company. Where Jesus is, storms cease and the sick are made whole.

MARK 7:1-23

Breaking the Bonds of Tradition. The Pharisees laid great stress on ritual. They followed endless rules, both intricate and troublesome, as to ablutions and outward ceremonials. So long as their devotees were careful in the minor observances, they were permitted a wide license so far as the weightier matters of the Law were concerned. This is a natural tendency of the human heart. It is glad to be able to reduce its religious life to an outward and literal obedience, if only its thoughts may be unhampered. In the life of true holiness, everything depends on the control of the thoughts. "As a man thinketh in his heart, so is he." With infinite wisdom the wise man said, "Keep thy heart with all diligence, for out of it are the issues of life," and Jesus put "evil thoughts" first in the black category of the contents of the evil heart. A gang of thieves sometimes put a very small boy through a tiny window that he may unlock the front door. So, one evil thought will often admit an entire crew of evil. Heart of mine, hast thou learned this lesson? Art thou careful enough of thy cleanliness? That the hands should be often washed, that vessels of household use should be kept cleansed, that there should be decorum and neatness in the outward life, all these customs are good. But it becomes thee to inquire whether thou art not more eager for the outward than the inward cleanliness. "Create in me a clean heart," should be thy constant prayer.

MARK 7:24-37

A Mother's Faith Rewarded. Before faith can be fully exercised, we must take the right attitude toward Christ. His mission at that time was to the Jewish people; they were the "children." This woman had no claim as a child, and the question was whether she was prepared to take the lower place. It is the humble soul that has power with God, and when she showed herself prepared to put Jesus in his place as Lord, and to take her own place as willing to accept the children's crumbs, the Lord was able to put the key of his treasure house into her hand and bid her have her desire. Faith can wring blessing from an apparent negative, and use what might seem to be a rebuff to open God's treasuries.

In the following miracle, notice that upward look, that sigh, and that touch. These are the conditions of all successful religious work, and it is a great encouragement to faith that our Lord himself knew what it was by a look to draw down the mighty power of God. That upward look may be ours when it is impossible to kneel for prolonged prayer. When we stand in the light of eternity, we also shall say, as our Lord's contemporaries did, "He hath done all things well."

MARK 8:1-21

The Demand for Signs Rebuked. Notice the Master's tender considerateness, vv. 1-9. He would not have the people faint on their way home. There are distinct differences between this miracle and the feeding of the 5,000. Most of these are evident to the English reader, but that between the baskets used for the fragments is clear only from the original—those used in the case of the 5,000 being quite different from the large ones used here, v. 20; Matt. 15:37. Our Lord never repeats his work.

The Savior sighed in the previous chapter over physical need; here he sighs over moral obtuseness, vv. 10–21. The language is very strong, and gives a glimpse into the Redeemer's heart. Had the Pharisees been as willing to discern the signs of the age as to read the weather, they would have been able to recognize him and his claims; but their foolish heart was darkened. Having sighed over the hard-heartedness of the Pharisees, might he not equally have done so over the obtuseness of the twelve? They thought that he was referring to their carelessness in omitting to take bread. How little they realized that the cause lay far deeper! Let us be quick to read the divine intention in very simple incidents, and to learn that all God's past dealings contain lessons for the present!

MARK 8:22—9:1

The Cost of Following Jesus. Our attention has been drawn to the Master's sighs; here, however, was another characteristic act. He spat on the eyes of the blind man, perhaps to excite his expectation and faith. Repulsive as opthalmia is in the East, it did not repel him nor block the flow of his pity.

We do not at once see everything clearly, but step by step we come unto perfect vision. Here we see through a glass darkly, there face to face. There was a great price to be paid; it was only through suffering and death that Jesus could do his greatest work, in redeeming and cleansing the children of men. He might have been the miracle-worker apart from Calvary; but to be the Savior he must not spare himself, but be willing to pour out his soul even unto death. It was hard for the apostles to learn this lesson; they wanted the Master to spare himself. Peter, especially, sought to dissuade him; but the Lord knew better the desperate need of men and how it must be met. There are three conditions to be fulfilled by those who have resolved to follow the Lamb whithersoever he goeth. (1) We must deny self. (2) Each must take up his cross. (3) We must think more of others than of ourselves. If these are realized, the soul is following Christ and making progress, even though it deems itself stagnant or drifting back.

MARK 9:2–29

Rapture and Service. The apostles had been gladdened by the promise of the coming kingdom. The transfiguring light that shone from our Lord's face differed from the shining of Moses' face. With Moses the light was from without and faded; but with Christ the light shone from within. Surely at that moment he might have stepped back into Heaven by the open door through which the representatives of the Law and the prophets had come; but he turned his back on the joy of the Father's home and set his face to endure the cross, that he might become, not the example only, but the Redeemer of men. What a contrast between that scene on Hermon's slopes, where the glory of Jesus was brighter than the glistening snows about him, and that below where the demoniac child writhed in pain! Raphael does well to group these two incidents in one picture, for we are shown here that the duty of the Church is not to build tabernacles on the mount of vision, but to take her way into the haunts of crime and misery and cope with the power of Satan. Faith is the channel through which the divine power passes. Its quantity is of less importance than its quality. It may be minute as a mustard seed but, like it, must contain the principle of life.

MARK 9:30–50

The Path to Greatness. Such were the hopes awakened by the Transfiguration and the following miracles that the disciples were led to speculate upon their relative position in the kingdom. Jesus therefore took a little child for his text, and preached to them a sermon on humility. How constantly the Master speaks of the little ones! He says that we must be converted to become like them; that to cause them to stumble will involve terrible penalties; that they are not to be despised; that each has an angel of the Father's presence-chamber appointed to his charge; that to seek and to save one, he is prepared as the shepherd to traverse the mountains; that it is not the Father's will that one of them should perish. How infinitely tender and humble was his love for them!

Let us strive to cut off whatever causes us to stumble. It may be a friendship, a pastime, a pursuit, a course of reading; but there must be no quarter given, no excuse accepted. As soon as the soul dares to make this supreme renunciation, there is an accession of life. Whenever the body loses the use of one member, such as the eye, there is an accession of vigor in others; so, to deny the lower is to open the door to the higher and, though maimed, to enter into life. Verses 44–48 evidently refer to the valley of Hinnom, where fires were kept burning to consume waste.

MARK 10:1–22

The Divine Law of Marriage. God made one man for one woman; therefore, divorce is not permissible unless the one act be committed which severs the nuptial tie. Then only is the bond broken by which husband and wife are one.

There should be no compulsory celibacy. Some can live the single life; others cannot. Each must work out his own possibilities, and none may judge another.

It would appear that the fathers brought the little ones. They had a truer perception of the heart of Jesus than the disciples. All through the ages men have supposed that strength, wisdom, and wealth have the greatest attractions for our Lord, whereas it is precisely the reverse. Of "such" is his kingdom.

Youth, with all its fervor and impetuosity, is very beautiful to the Lord Jesus. In this case it was combined with station, high standing, and wealth. It is not necessary that all should sell their goods and give away the proceeds; indeed, it is often harder to retain and administer them rightly for God. But it was necessary for Christ to prove to this young man that he was not living the life of love, as he seemed to suppose. That alone can fulfill the law and secure the highest and most perfect blessedness of which we are capable. It was a severe but necessary test for this young man.

MARK 10:23–52

True Riches and Real Greatness. Wealth brings many temptations. It is not said that rich men cannot get through the gate, but they will have to stoop very low and be stripped of the love of wealth, though not necessarily of wealth itself. In Christ's kingdom, to give all is to get all. The surrendered life needs no pity, for what it loses on the material side is more than compensated by its enormous spiritual gains, vv. 30, 31. Perhaps the request of the two brethren was dictated rather by the desire to be near the Master than by ambition; but in any case there is only one price to be paid. We must know the fellowship of his sufferings if we are to share his glory, 2 Tim. 2:11ff. It is easy to say, "We are able"; but had they not experienced the day of Pentecost, these two aspirants would have certainly failed, Phil. 4:13. If you are not called to suffer with him, then serve. Service like Christ's will bring you near his throne, as will also a share in his suffering. With us as with Bartimaeus, obstacles and difficulties should not daunt, but rather incite to more eager prayers. Only faith could make a blind man cast away his garment, but he knew that he would be able to find it again with the sight that Jesus would certainly bestow.

MARK 11:1–19

Praise and Fear Greet Jesus' Approach. On the first day of Passion Week, a gleam of light fell athwart the Master's path as he rode into Jerusalem. It was a lowly triumph. The humble ass was escorted by poor men, Galilean pilgrims, and children, who excited the haughty criticism of the metropolis. May a similar procession enter your heart and mine! "Lift up your heads, O ye gates; and be ye lift up, ye everlasting doors; and the King of glory shall come in."

With irresistible might the Lord drove forth the buyers and sellers from the Temple. According to the ancient prediction, he sat as a refiner and purifier of silver, to purify the sons of Levi. Whenever he enters the heart, he performs a similar work. He drives out bestial forms of sin, so that the whole nature—spirit, soul, and body—may be surrendered to God. What our Lord said of the Temple should be true of each church of the living God. It should be his residence, where men of all nationalities should come to a unity as they worship, confess sin, and intercede. Certainly God's house must not be a place of merchandise.

MARK 11:20–33

The Conditions of Prayer. The great lesson taught by this stricken tree justified its doom. It was not yet the time of the fig harvest, but some of last year's fruit might still be found; the hope of this was still further aroused by the abundance of young leaves. It was a type of profession without performance. In addition to proclaiming the doom of promise which is not followed by performance, our Lord drew from the miracle the great lesson that faith can absolutely reckon on God's faith, that is, his faithfulness. Throughout his life, as we look into the heart of Jesus we find only forgiving love, humility, faith. Forgiveness and love are the conditions of all successful prayers, vv. 24–26. We do not show sufficient appreciation for our Lord's marvelous intellectual power. He was more than equal to these clever intellects trained for argument. They were beaten at their own game.

MARK 12:1–27

Jesus Silences His Enemies. Our Lord reviews the history of the theocracy. He recounts the long roll of God's servants who had been persecuted and misused from the first to the last, including himself. In doing so, he openly implied that he was the Son of God and made the Pharisees realize how clearly he foresaw the fate which they were preparing for him. They were accustomed to apply Ps. 118:22 to the Messiah, and recognized at once what Jesus meant when he claimed it as an emblem of his own rejection.

How admirably our Lord defined the relations of his kingdom to the civil power! If we accept Caesar's protection and ordered government, we are bound to maintain it by money payment and such other service as conscience permits. This indeed is part of our duty to God; and with equal care we must give him the dues of the spiritual world.

Jesus silenced the Sadducees by a quotation from the Pentateuch, whose authority they admitted. God could not be the God of persons not in existence. Therefore, since he used the present tense for his relationship with the patriarchs when speaking to Moses 300 years after their death, they must have been still in existence.

MARK 12:28-44

The First Commandment. To the young ruler our Lord named one command as great—the love of one's neighbor. Now, in answer to this scribe, he turned with unerring choice, first to Deuteronomy 6:4, 5, and then to Leviticus 19:18, for the two pillars on which the collective and individual life of man must rest. The reverent answer of the scribe proves that he was no ordinary questioner. Our Lord acknowledged this when he told him that a few steps more would bring him into the kingdom of God. Our Lord was David's son by human descent, but as Son of God, proceeding from the Father, he is exalted far above David and all mankind.

In terrible words, vv. 38-40, Christ denounced the moral and religious leaders of the time. They made a pretense and a gain of their religion. How great the contrast between them and this poor widow, who cast into God's treasury all that she had to provide for her day's living! Our Lord is quick to notice acts like these, which give evidence of the true heart.

MARK 13:1-13

Coming Tribulations. Our Lord departed from the Temple, never again to enter its sacred precincts or to open his mouth in public teaching. When he withdrew, the whole system of Judaism was given over to desolation, and the predictions spoken at this time were minutely fulfilled in the fall of Jerusalem under Titus. The Temple was blotted out. Indeed, a plowshare passed over its site; the people were sold into slavery or butchered in the gladiatorial shows; their nationality was obliterated, and their land given to strangers.

Christ's words contain a further reference to his second advent. The signs here mentioned were carefully scanned by the early Christians, as one after another they were fulfilled. They saw the Roman world convulsed by rival claimants for the imperial purple; they knew by bitter experience the brunt of the world's hatred; they realized that by the labors of the great apostle of the Gentiles, and others, the gospel had been preached throughout the known world—and when these signs were being fulfilled, and the Roman eagles gathered to prey on the carcass of Judaism, from which the life had passed, they hastened to flee to Pella, from whence they beheld the collapse of the Jewish state.

MARK 13:14-37

"Watch!" The fall of Jerusalem, vv. 14-23. This abomination had been predicted by Daniel, 9:27. Josephus says that the Romans brought their standards into the Temple, and offered sacrifices to them, and proclaimed Titus emperor. Probably there is to be a yet further fulfillment of these significant words. Houses in the East are, for the most part, provided with staircases outside the wall, so that the occupants, seeing the approach of danger, could flee without going through their homes, v. 15. The ungodly owe more than they realize to the elect who dwell among them, v. 20. Let us not be deceived by the appearance of false doctrines or teachers; there are also false Christs, v. 22. *The Second Advent,* vv. 24-27. These signs may refer to the disorganization of political rule, or to literal convulsions of the elements. The ministry of angels was very real to Jesus, and their function in the future ages is clearly defined. As Enoch was translated before the Deluge, so will the saints be gathered before the final sorrows, 1 Thess. 4:14-17. It would seem as if Christ's coming is to bring "summer" to our world. "This generation" may refer to the fact that the Jewish people would remain as a distinct people. Our Lord had so emptied himself that in his human nature he knew not the hour, and was content to know only as the Father told him. He has now resumed the glory of the knowledge which he had before all worlds. Have we each one found our work? Let us watch!

MARK 14:1-16

An Offering of Love. This beautiful incident took place on the Tuesday evening of Passion Week, while the chief priests were gathered in the house of Caiaphas to plot the Lord's death, Matt. 26:3-5. Simon had probably been healed by Jesus, and the feast was held in his house, as being larger than Martha's. Jesus was intimate with Lazarus and his sisters, and this unnamed woman was Mary, John 12:2, 3. Alabaster resembled white marble, and the perfume was carefully sealed to preserve it. Its cost would amount to about fifty dollars, and would represent the work of three hundred days, Matt. 20:2. Loveless hearts cannot understand the expenditure of love—they count it waste; but how quickly Jesus steps in to vindicate his own! Probably, of all his followers, Mary alone had understood his references to his death, and as she could not be present to perform the last offices of love, she rendered them in advance. Judas, who led the murmuring, seems to have been goaded to this act by the contrast of Mary's spirit with his own, and by Christ's gentle rebuke.

The two sent to prepare the Passover were Peter and John, Luke 22:8. We may often be guided by very trivial incidents—let us look out for them. A straw may indicate the direction of the current. The owner of the room was probably a secret disciple of Jesus, like him who lent the ass. The Revised Version says, "*my* guest chamber." It is very beautiful when the Master feels free to put his hand on our possessions and claim their use. Does he not ask for the guest chamber of our inner life? Is it at his disposal?

MARK 14:17-31

The Last Supper. The two disciples made their preparations, returned to Bethany, and later the whole company came in together. The simple meal, consisting of the Passover lamb, unleavened cakes, bitter herbs, and wine, proceeded in the usual way, interspersed with the singing of the Hallel, Pss. 113—118. How well it is when we do not need the accusation, "Thou art the man," because we utter the inquiry, "Is it I?" Those whose hearts misgive them are not likely to commit the deed of treachery. At the institution of the Lord's Supper, vv. 22-25, Jesus gave thanks for the bread and the wine, Luke 22:19, 20; 1 Cor. 11:24, 25. We must understand his words in v. 22 in the same sense as when he says, "I am the door of the sheep." Those who receive the outward elements worthily partake at the same time spiritually of the things which they signify. Let us never fail to remember at the Lord's Supper that it is the sign and seal of the new covenant into which God has entered with Christ on our behalf. See Heb. 8. For v. 27 compare Zech. 13:7. The energy of our own resolution is not enough to carry us through the supreme ordeals of trial. We need the Holy Spirit for that. Mark alone mentions the warning of the double cock-crow.

MARK 14:32-52

Alone in the Hour of Trial. When the soul is overwhelmed, it seeks to be alone, and yet not too far from human sympathy and help. The three most trusted might enter the enclosure, but even they could not share the depth of the Master's anguish, which was so great as to threaten his very life. He cried to him who could save him from dying before his trial and sentence, and was saved from what he feared. Our Lord did not shrink from physical suffering, but from the horror of becoming sin-bearer for the race and putting away sin by the sacrifice of himself. His disciples failed him, but as he submitted to the Father's will his spirit rose triumphant. "Sleep on now"—the past is irrevocable. The disciples fled as fast as their feet would carry them. If only they had prayed, they would have been steadfast and unmovable. There are good reasons for supposing that the young man mentioned here was Mark himself.

MARK 14:53-72

A Mockery of Justice. A commission of the chief priests awaited the result of the treachery of Judas at the house of Caiaphas. They had made up their minds what to do, but the form of a trial was necessary. The false witnesses were obviously unable to establish a sufficient case, and our Lord maintained a dignified silence. It was too much for Caiaphas, and he put his prisoner on his oath. Our Lord made no attempt to parry the issue or turn aside from the challenge, but replied: "I am: and ye shall see the Son of man sitting on the right hand of power, and coming in the clouds of heaven." See Ps. 110:1; Dan. 7:13. Then followed a shameful scene, v. 65. But our Lord was as self-restrained in the use of his mighty powers as if he had been one of the most helpless of men. The graphic story of the denial, which took place in the servants' hall at the time of the trial, was probably given to the evangelist by Peter himself. What a contrast between the strength of the Master and the weakness of the disciple! Yet Peter was forgiven and made the apostle of Pentecost! We may have hope!

MARK 15:1-21

The Choice of the Multitude. The hurried consultation of the evening was followed by the more formal meeting of the early morning; and even the decision made then had no binding force till ratified by Pilate, the Roman governor, who happened at that time to be in Jerusalem. John gives a more detailed account of this memorable interview, 18:33-38. Our Lord did not plead his own cause, but committed himself to the One who judges righteously, 1 Pet. 2:23. It was only when Pilate asked questions for his own guidance that Jesus sought to help him, and then he relapsed into silence. "As a sheep before her shearers is dumb, so he openeth not his mouth." Men like Barabbas, embodiments of brute force, are ever the darlings of the crowd. By narrowing the people's choice to the murderer and Jesus, Pilate expected to bring them to demand the release of the lover and helper of men. But he failed to gauge the malice of which men are capable. Perhaps he hoped that the marks of extreme suffering would soften their hatred. He might as well have appealed to a pack of hungry wolves! Jesus' "purple" stood for royalty won by blood; "thorns," because his diadem was won by suffering; the "reed," because he can wield the frailest life against momentous issues. Happy is the man who shares Christ's cross! Simon was an African, probably a black man, and this incident changed his life, Rom. 16:13.

MARK 15:22-47

A King upon His Cross. Our Lord refused to drink the potion prepared by the women of Jerusalem, in order to stupefy those who were crucified and so deaden the sense of pain, because he would drain the cup to its dregs. It was nine o'clock in the morning when he was nailed to the cross. His persecutors were, as they thought, destroying the Temple of which he had spoken in John 2:19 and making its restoration impossible. In fact, however, they were giving him the opportunity of fulfilling his great prediction. "He saved others; himself he cannot save." Nature veiled her face from that awful spectacle. Our Redeemer passed under the dark shadow of human sin. The access to the Holy of Holies is now forever free through the entry of our great High Priest. See Heb. 9:7, 8. What love inspired the women, v. 40, to brave the horrors of the scene! And how good it is to see that God cares for the body as well as for the spirit of his beloved! For more on Joseph, see Matt. 27:57 and Luke 23:50, 51. Born of the virgin's womb, our Lord was buried in a virgin tomb.

MARK 16

The Power of His Resurrection. In the dim light the women brave the dangers of an Eastern city and hasten to the grave. How often we seek Christ in the grave of old experiences or of dead and empty rites; and how often we cherish fears for which there are no occasion! In the grave where Christ had lain, a young man was sitting, arrayed in a glistening robe; so out of death comes life. One result of the Savior's resurrection has been that myriads of noble youths, clothed in garments of purity, have gone forth to shine like the dewdrops of the morning sparkling on the bosom of the earth. God's angels are always young. We who are the children of the resurrection in the life of eternity will grow always younger, as here our bodies are ever growing older. The ministry of Galilee and Jerusalem is at an end, but the Master goes forth to new victories in the Acts of the Apostles. Note the mighty power of faith, the signs that follow its manifestation in simplicity and purity; demons cannot resist it, serpents are rendered harmless, and healing streams flow from contact with it. Let us keep our eyes fixed on the risen Christ sitting at the right hand of God, and believe that he is ever working by our side and confirming our words, Heb. 2:4.

THE GOSPEL ACCORDING TO
LUKE

THE HUMAN LIFE OF THE SON OF GOD

PREFACE *1:1-4.*

I. BIRTH AND BEGINNINGS *1:5—2:52.*
   A. Birth of the forerunner *1:5-25, 57-80.*
   B. Birth of Jesus *1:26-56; 2:1-20.*
   C. Infancy and development *2:21-52.*

II. THE LIFE DEVOTED TO HUMAN NEED *3:1—18:30.*
   A. Ministry of the forerunner *3:1-20.*
   B. Baptism and temptation of Jesus *3:21, 22; 4:1-13.*
      (Genealogy, 3:23-38.)
   C. The Galilean ministry *4:14—9:50.*
      Choice of the twelve apostles, sermon on the plain, miracles of many kinds.
   D. Journey toward Jerusalem *9:51—18:30.*
      Sending out of the seventy, parables teaching prayer, mercy, and judgment.

III. THE LIFE REJECTED BY HUMAN HATRED *18:31—22:7.*
   A. Last journey to Jerusalem *18:31—19:27.*
   B. Triumphal entry—cleansing of the Temple *19:28-48.*
   C. Parables of judgment, questions, teaching about last things *20:1—21:38.*
   D. The bargain of Judas *22:1-6.*

IV. THE LIFE SACRIFICED FOR HUMAN SIN *22:7—23:56.*
   A. The Last Supper and the agony in the garden *22:7-46.*
   B. The betrayal *22:47-53.*
   C. The Jewish and Roman trials *22:54—23:25.*
   D. The crucifixion and burial *23:26-56.*

V. THE LIFE REMANIFESTED AND GLORIFIED *24:1-53.*
   A. Visit of women to tomb *24:1-12.*
   B. Walk to Emmaus *24:13-35.*
   C. Appearance to the eleven *24:36-49.*
   D. The ascension *24:50-53.*

INTRODUCTION

The third Gospel is the longest. It was probably written in Greece, for Greek-speaking people, by Luke, a Gentile physician who had not been an eyewitness of the facts he describes, but had taken great pains to acquaint himself with the facts as related to him by eyewitnesses. See 1:1–4. The old tradition is that Luke wrote under the direction of Paul, whose companion he was after the events narrated in Acts 16.

It has been described as the most carefully composed of the three narrative Gospels, and is the reply to questionings that would naturally present themselves to cultured men who had been impressed with the strange beauty of the cross. No one could understand better than the great Apostle Paul the need of an exhaustive reply to such questionings, and of an authoritative history of the rise and progress of the gospel of Christ. Luke dwells specially on the early incidents of our Lord's life, and some have detected in the Greek forms of the sentences the direct recital of Mary as she recounted to Luke those sacred recollections which she pondered in her heart. There are many places where Luke uses medical terms, etc., which the other Gospels do not mention, and which show his training as a physician.

Luke addresses himself to the universality of Christ's gospel. He ignores all privilege of race or caste or training, and traces back our Lord's genealogy to Adam. It is thus that he, of all the evangelists, dwells on the message of the Baptist: "All flesh shall see the salvation of God." In the same spirit he tells the parables of Chapter 15, as well as that of the marriage supper, and contrasts the ingratitude of the nine Jewish lepers with the gratitude of the Samaritan. It is especially the Gospel of hope and love, of pity and faith.

COMMENTARY

LUKE 1:1-12

The Beginning of the Good News. The opening verses are very explicit. They are answer enough to those who question the story of our Lord's supernatural birth and early years. Luke did not grab on to the first legend that floated past him. He made searching inquiry. Weymouth renders the words in v. 3, "having had perfect understanding of all things from the very first" as, "after careful examination of the facts from the commencement."

That our Lord should come into our race under special and supernatural conditions was as it should have been; but the historicity of this story largely rests on the careful investigations of "the beloved physician," who was authenticated by Paul.

The priests were divided into twenty-four groups and shared the Temple services for a week each, the work of each priest being decided by lot, 1 Chron. 24. Sweeter than the incense which he sprinkled on the coals was Zacharias' own prayer, commemorated in the name given to his son, "God's gracious gift," Exod. 30:7, 8; Rev. 8:3, 4.

LUKE 1:13-25

The Forerunner. As we open this Gospel we feel the wealth of a new age. The country was full of anarchy, misrule, and wild passion, but there were many who "spake often one to another," Mal. 3:16. They were the quiet in the land, who looked for redemption of Israel, Luke 2:38.

The separation of the Nazarite was in ordinary cases temporary and voluntary; but Samson, Samuel, and John the Baptist were Nazarites from their birth. As the leper was the living symbol of sin, so was the Nazarite of holiness. No alcohol, no razor, no ceremonial defilement, Num. 6. The mission of the Baptist was to bring back the ancient spirit of religion and prepare Messiah's way.

Notice Gabriel's great and noble position of standing before God, and compare 1 Kings 10:8; 17:1; Luke 21:36. Unbelief robs us of the power of testimony for Jesus. But when faith is in full exercise, the tongue of the dumb sings.

LUKE 1:26-38

The Promised Messiah. The narrative is artlessly simple and natural and is its own complete vindication. No human genius could have invented it. Compare it, for instance, with all the ornate and fantastic pictures of the Annunciation by the great masters! That little children and wise men alike appreciate this story bespeaks its humanness and its divineness.

It is to the humble and childlike maiden that the supreme honor of womanhood is given. The choice was one of pure grace. The Creator-Spirit himself wrought this divine miracle. The appearance of our Savior among mankind was the direct and immediate act of Deity, so far as his body was concerned; but as to his spirit, it was the voluntary emptying on his own part, of which Paul speaks, Phil. 2:7. "The Word was made flesh." It was not a transient assumption of the appearance of humanity, but a real fusion of the divine and the human in that holy thing which was to be born. Here was the beginning of a new humanity, to be reproduced in all that believe, till the earth is filled with "the sons of God," Rom. 8:14.

LUKE 1:39-56

The Song of the Virgin Mother. Zacharias lived in a Levitical city in the hill country of Judah. The narrative evidently implies that there had been no previous communication between the two women of what had happened. In their greeting both were led and taught of the Spirit.

Evidently Mary was living in close familiarity with the Scriptures. Often she had been deeply moved by their radiant promises, and had pleaded that God would at last help his people and send the Savior. Now that this blessing had come to her, she voiced her thanks, not only under the express inspiration of the Holy Spirit, but in the familiar expressions of Scripture. No others would have sufficed. Compare Hannah's song of praise, given under similar circumstances, 1 Sam. 2:1-10. This song is called the *Magnificat,* that being the first word in the Latin version. Wonder and praise, humility and exultation, adoration and congratulation—these colors chase one another in the heart of this jewel.

LUKE 1:57-80

The Song at the Herald's Birth. This song is second only to that of Mary. It is a noble ode, tracing our Lord's advent back to the early covenant of God with the fathers and anticipating its effects to the end of time.

It is wholesome to apply the song to ourselves and ask how far we have participated in these great blessings. Are we experiencing this daily salvation from our spiritual enemies who hate us? Do we serve God without the slavish fear of the serf, and with the loyal allegiance of the child? Are all our days characterized by holiness toward God and righteousness toward man? Has the "dayspring from on high" visited our hearts, and are our feet walking in the way of peace? Solemn questions these, but they must be faced.

LUKE 2:1-14

The Savior of Mankind Is Born. The manger bed and its precious occupant are among the most cherished memories of our childhood; but as we come there in later life, the wonder ever grows. "Great is the mystery of godliness; God was manifest in the flesh," 1 Tim. 3:16.

What company we meet there! Shepherds with their naive wonder; angels from the realms of glory; wise men with their gifts; aged saints like Simeon and Anna. Surely the desire of all nations is here! Let us ask that the Lord of glory will condescend to be born in the mean stable of our heart, transforming it into a palace!

Notice how, to bring Mary to Bethlehem, the Master of all emperors sets on foot the machinery of Providence and history. What can he not do for us and his Church!

LUKE 2:15-24

Welcomed; Named; Presented. From April till the autumn, the flocks pastured at night in the open fields, from which it seems probable that our Lord must have been born much earlier or later than December. No doubt these shepherds were, like Simeon, "waiting for the consolation of Israel," and their purity of life and simplicity of soul well qualified them to receive the blessed tidings of the angels. First simplicity and afterward science, Matt. 2, found their way into the presence of Jesus.

In the act of circumcision, our Lord admitted his obligation to fulfill the whole Law, Gal. 5:3. He was "made under the law, to redeem them that were under the law," Gal. 4:4, 5. Mary could afford only the gift of the poor, Lev. 12:6-8; 5:7-11; 2 Cor. 8:9. The precious name of Jesus—"Savior"—is the name above every name, Acts 4:10-12.

LUKE 2:25-39

The Aged Simeon's Prophetic Blessing. Two aged watchers welcomed the King; but no one else, of all the crowds who went and came, guessed that the Messenger of the Covenant had suddenly come to his Temple, Mal. 3:1-3.

In the Arctic Circle in summer the visitor will behold the magnificent spectacle, on the same sky, of the hues of sunset and of dawn. Dipping only for a brief period beneath the horizon, the setting sun leaves the glorious trail of sunset, and rising bathes the eastern clouds with the radiance of dawn. So, when Simeon embraced Christ, sunset and sunrise met. There was the glory of the age that was passing, and the glory of the new Christian age that shall ever stand at perfect noon.

Note the concentric circles of Simeon's character: "a man"; "a man in Jerusalem"—i.e., a

LUKE 2:40-52

The Boy Jesus in the Temple. "Solitary floweret," says Stier, referring to this incident, "gathered from the wonderful enclosed garden of the thirty years and plucked precisely when the swollen bud, at the age of twelve years, was about to burst into flower."

The incident is specially valuable as indicating so perfect an understanding between our Lord and his mother. He wondered that knowing him as she did, she could have lost him or should have failed to seek him in his Father's house. The stress is on "Wist ye not?" Here, however, he seemed to pass into a new attitude toward his lifework. May we not say that he caught sight of its absorbing character, to which all else must be subordinated?

Let us never "suppose" that we are in the company of Jesus when in fact we may have lost him. Never rest till you and he have found each other!

LUKE 3:1-14

A Preacher of Righteousness. The evangelist sets an emperor, a governor, two high priests, and three tetrarchs in a few lines, as of very subordinate interest compared with the one man, the child of the desert, whose coming dated a new era and to whom he devotes the remainder of the chapter. After all, it is religious men who really make the history of mankind.

"The word of God *came* unto John the Baptist... and he *came.*" That is the true order. Get your message and then come. It is often in the wilderness of life that God's words find us. The man who is going to master men must first master the appetites of his own body. If you seek popularity, you will lose it; if you seek to do God's will, men will almost certainly come to find you. Souls require a clear pane of glass when they look out on the infinite expanse of the sky! Be real! Touch eternal truth for yourself. Fear not the face of man!

LUKE 3:15-23

The Herald Silenced; the Messiah Appears. We are told that the time of John's appearance was the Sabbatic year, when field work was suspended and the people had comparative leisure. In his passion for God, reality, and truth, John asked nothing of men; but men were willing to give him anything. The impression he made on his age was due to his selfless devotion to the coming kingdom and its King. The great cities emptied themselves into the Jordan valley. The youth of Gennesaret left their fishing boats to sit at his feet. The "spirit and power of Elijah" rested on him. All classes felt that he could speak to their needs, and submitted to his direction.

But how abashed his bearing before Jesus! The voice that had swept the crowds like a whirlwind sank to whispers. Our Lord took him into fellowship—"it becometh us," Matt. 3:15. The porter opened the door and recognized that it was the true Shepherd who passed in, John 1:32-34.

LUKE 4:1-13

The Threefold Temptation. As the waters of Jordan bisect the Holy Land, so does our Lord's baptism bisect his holy life. In that act he had identified himself with the world's sin; and now, as the High Priest who was to deal with sin and sinners, he must be "in all points" tempted and tested "like as we are."

He took into the wilderness a perfect humanity of flesh and blood, made in all points like his brethren, though without sin. He elected to fight his great fight, not by the use of the divine attributes, but as Son of man. Where the first Adam fell, the second must stand.

First, he could not use his native power for his own gratification. Second, he would abide strictly within the limitations of the world he had entered, Heb. 2:16, 17. Third, he would win his kingdom by the cross.

LUKE 4:14-30

"His Own Received Him Not." A wide gap occurs here, embracing the important transactions of John 1:29—4:54.

What a flutter in Mary's heart when she saw her son sitting in the teacher's place of his native synagogue; how gratified she was at the reception given to the opening sentences! What a sword pierced her heart at the sudden revulsion of feeling! They were jealous that he performed only a few private miracles; but he could not do more because of their unbelief. See Mark 6:5.

Note that our Lord here sounded forth the silver trumpet of jubilee. Seizing on the imagery of the gladdest festival of Hebrew life, he likened himself to a priest proclaiming "the acceptable year of the Lord." It was not yet the day of vengeance! Compare v. 19 with Isa. 61:1, 2. This is Christ's program for the present age.

LUKE 4:31-44

Healer and Preacher. In later years the evil spirit cried out, "Jesus I know," Acts 19:15. Evidently our Lord was not only "seen of angels," but closely watched by the fallen spirits, who beheld his every act and listened to every word. What a remarkable verdict was that given in v. 34! Those who know most of evil are most certain of the ultimate woe which awaits its doers; and they know genuine goodness when they meet it. Our Lord had overcome the prince of demons, and could therefore command his household.

We need to be delivered from the fever of passion, caught in the low-lying marshes of our lives; to have Christ's hands laid upon our sicknesses and wounds; to be delivered from evil things that haunt our hearts. Then we must help him in similar services to others. But if he must have his quiet prayer times, so must we, v. 42.

LUKE 5:1-11

New Catchers of Men. This was not their first call, recorded in John 1:35-42, but another which preceded their appointment to the apostolate.

The Lord always supersedes us. He superseded Peter in his command of the boat, which he had navigated since he was a lad. There is always a testing-point for the soul. Will you surrender the command and let Christ be captain? If so, in the teeth of great difficulties—for fish are not caught generally in the glare of day—he will fill your boat to the water's edge. He does beyond all we asked or thought.

Christ will be in no man's debt. If you lend him your boat, he will return it filled with silver fish. The boats were filled; the upper room was filled with the Holy Spirit; and all Martha's hospitality was well repaid when Lazarus was raised.

At the day of Pentecost, when Peter's net landed 3,000 souls, was not our Lord's promise fulfilled? "Thrust out a little," is the beginning of long voyages and fishing expeditions with Christ!

LUKE 5:12-26

Cleansing, Power, and Pardon. Jesus did not hesitate to touch the leper, because he could no more be polluted by uncleanness than could a ray of light by passing through a fetid atmosphere. The question is never in can or will as applied to Christ, but whether we will trust him and can believe.

The Mosaic offering was a pair of birds, one of which was killed over running water, while the other, having been dipped into this mingled blood and water, was freed to fly away in its native air. Is not this the meet emblem of the forgiven and cleansed soul? See Lev. 14:2-32.

At first the bed bore the paralytic, but after the power of Jesus had entered into him, he bore the bed. So Jesus pours his energy into our anemic natures, and we master what had mastered us. The miracle in the physical sphere, which men could test, approved his power in the realm of the spiritual, where only the forgiven one could actually "know."

Do not forget to withdraw from the crowd, however eager it is, that you may pray, v. 16.

LUKE 5:27-39

Feasting and Fasting. Matthew in his Gospel says nothing of this great feast; the Spirit of God saw that it should not be forgotten. "When saw we thee an hungered, and fed thee?" Matt. 25:37. Advertise yourself and God will leave you unnoticed. You will have had your reward. Be content to do things as Jesus appointed, and Matthew 6:4 will follow.

Let us not cling to the broken bottle-skins of the past, whether they be outworn ceremonies, creeds, or formulations of truth. Let the ferment of each great religious movement and new era express itself in its own way. We must not encourage the ill-judged speed of those who want to force the pace and fling away the bottle-skins before they are done with. But if the bottle-skins have evidently served their purpose and lie discarded on the ground, that will not affect the vintage, which is reddening on the hills. Go and pick the fruit God is giving you, place it carefully in baskets, and let it have new skins.

LUKE 6:1-11

The Right Use of the Sabbath. It was a brave and bold step for Jesus to set himself against the ritualistic proscriptions of the ruling religious party of his age. How many who had hoped that he would redeem Israel, must have been hurt by what seemed to be ruthless iconoclasm. But there was no hope of the holy thoughts of God ever emerging from the mass of hidebound rules and regulations with which the Pharisees had covered them, unless the frost of literalism was broken up with a strong hand. Christ was not destroying religion, but freeing it from the formalist. Be true and real!

The grave question today is whether, in our revolt from Puritan strictness in observing Sunday, we have not gone to the other extreme.

The Church of God will have to stand for God's day, not only for God's sake, but for the sake of the masses, who are menaced by a seven-day working week. The Sabbath was made for man; he needs it. If God made it for him, let God's children preserve it.

LUKE 6:12-26

New Leaders and New Principles. There are three circles here: First, Christ and his apostles—the men who were to be sent into all the world to preach the gospel and to lay the foundations of the Church. How little did these single men imagine that one day their names would become inscribed on the foundation stones of the new Jerusalem!

The next circle is that of the disciples, v. 17. You must be a disciple before you can be an apostle. You must learn if you are to teach. You must sit at the feet of Jesus, till some day he calls you out from the class and commissions you to the world. The sheep becomes a shepherd.

The third great outer rim is the poor, needy world. What a gathering of sick folk! But if only people knew the distempers of their soul-life, they would gather with equal eagerness to Jesus. How wonderful that secret touch, v. 19. But many still touch him in the crowd.

LUKE 6:27-38

How to Treat Our Fellowmen. Luke's version of the Sermon on the Mount differs from that of Matthew only as each views the great discourse from his own standpoint. By one it is viewed as the manifesto of the King; by the other, as the proclamation of "the Man Christ Jesus" to man.

Notice the secret of blessedness! Here is the portrait of a life of abounding blessing, overflowing with mercy and loving-kindness. With what measure we mete out our love to men, they will measure back their love to us, using our own measures for the purpose.

Each of these Beatitudes is a gateway into blessedness. It is not that blessedness is the reward of virtue, but it is the necessary and invariable result. We must only be good, because it is right and God-pleasing to be so, and the blessedness will be as natural as the bloom on the peach.

LUKE 6:39-49

The Test That Reveals Character. Yes, it is true! Someday we shall be perfected. The long discipline will be over, and we shall be able to close our lesson books and go home. We shall then be found to be like Christ, our Lord. The promise of v. 40 is very beautiful, though it sometimes seems far away.

We need to look at home first before we attempt to judge or condemn others. It is blundering waste to deal with other people's eyes if you have a defect in yours. Color-blind men ought not to run trains. Speech betrayeth men; what they say, that they are. The man who is quickest to judge and discuss the faults of another does so because of his own experience of the same sin. How else could he know so much about it?

The rock is not the Church, nor doctrine, nor even the Bible, but Christ, Isa. 28:16.

LUKE 7:1-10

An Alien's Surprising Faith. It is interesting to find these wild flowers of natural faith, humility, and love growing outside the carefully cultivated garden of the Hebrew religion. God has never been without witnesses among the nations. We recall Cyrus in the Old Testament, Isa. 45:1-7, and Cornelius in the New, Acts 10:1-8. "In every nation," Acts 10:35. But of course the propitiation of Christ underpins the salvation of all men, Rom. 3:25.

Because the centurion was under the authority of Rome and was loyally obedient to it, he was able to exercise authority; and since he was so sure that Christ was obedient and loyal to God, he felt that he, too, was able to exert authority over all other forces, especially those which were injuring and torturing human lives. Let us seek to be such obedient servants that Christ may be able to say to us also, with the absolute certainty that we shall obey, "Go" and "Come" and especially "Do this."

LUKE 7:11-23

"God Hath Visited His People." Nain lay near the plain of Esdraelon, on the slopes of Little Hermon. Two confluent streams met there—those with Christ and those with death, vv. 11 and 12. He wipes away tears by removing the cause. When the young are being borne by their young companions to graves of sin, it is thus that the Master arrests them. See Eph. 5:14. There was a threefold gradation in the power he put forth—to Jairus' daughter, just dead; to this young man, on the way to burial; and to Lazarus, who was three days dead. The depression from John's long confinement in the gloomy fortress of Machaerus, east of the Dead Sea, and the fact that Jesus had not sent to deliver him, were the double root of this sad lapse from the position taken up on the Jordan bank when he recognized and indicated the Lamb of

God. But our Lord did not chide; he understood, Ps. 103:9. His miracles of mercy and power are his best evidences, and he left John to draw his own conclusions, Isa. 35:5, 6. May ours be the blessedness of the unoffended, who will trust Christ even though he does not hasten to deliver them just as they had hoped!

LUKE 7:24–35

A Great Man and a Still Greater. The Master chose the moment of John's fainting fit to give this high eulogy on the Baptist's stalwart character, his indifference to worldly bribes, and his divine commission. When we write hard things against ourselves, he may be judging us with infinite tenderness and wisdom. Heaven does not estimate us by our passing moods. But the least believer in this Christian age has a clearer knowledge of Christ and a closer relationship to him than had the Baptist. He was a servant; we are brothers, sons, heirs, Rom. 8:16, 17.

If we will not accept the lower call of duty, as was manifested in the appeal of the Baptist, we shall never profit by Christ. Accept the dim light of the morning star and it will lead to the dawn.

It ill becomes us to observe the winds of human caprice. If we please one party, we shall displease the other. There is but one path through life, and that is to do the will of God, in which, as Dante puts it, is our peace. But the children of wisdom recognize her alike in the anxiety of the Baptist and in the graces of the Son of man.

LUKE 7:36–50

The Forgiven Sinner's Grateful Love. What a trio! *Christ* stands here as a manifestation of the divine love as it comes among sinners. The love of God is not dependent on our merits; "frankly," v. 42, is "freely." It is not turned away by our sins: "she is a sinner." It ever manifests itself as the clearing of debts. But it demands recognition and service: "thou gavest me no kiss."

The woman represents those who penitently and lovingly recognize the divine love. She was not forgiven because of her love; but her love was the sign that she had been forgiven and recognized it. What will not God's love do! The tropical sun produces rare fruit. What Jesus did for her he can do for your many sins. Pardon will lead to much love, and love becomes the gate of knowledge and the source of obedience.

Simon, the Pharisee, stands for the unloving and self-righteous, who are ignorant of the love of God. They may be respectable in life, rigid in morality, unquestioned in orthodoxy, but what are these without love? See 1 Cor. 13. Note the contrasts between "thou" and "she," "thy" and "her."

LUKE 8:1–15

Various Hearers of the Word of God. Hitherto our Lord had made Capernaum his center; now he started on a circuit through the province of Galilee, going through its cities and villages in a systematic and leisurely manner. It must have been a great opportunity for the instruction of the twelve in his doctrine and methods.

The parable of the sower was suggested by the scenery before the speaker. There is an advance in the stages of reception and growth, indicating the several phases of experience. The success or failure of gospel preaching is determined by the character of the soil. In every crowd there are the hardened, like the trodden path; the impulsive, like the thin layer of earth upon the rock; those with a heart divided by riches or cares, like the thorn-encumbered soil; and those who receive with joy and bear fruit with patience. The Lord veiled his meaning in parables. Increased light would only add to the condemnation of disobedient hearers.

LUKE 8:16–25

Hearing; Doing; Believing. Inconsistency, unkindly words and acts, disobedience to our known duty will prevent our light from shining. If Christ has illumined your wick, see that you trust him to find for you your stand, from which you may emit the clearest rays. You are lighted to shine!

The closest relationship to Jesus is not that of nature, but of grace. To listen in your heart to God's voice, to hear it in his Word and in Providence, and then to do as it decrees will bring you into the closest relationship with your Lord.

Be prepared for storms if you link your lives with Christ. But they cannot hurt you. Men and demons will rage against you; but there is a limit to their power. Jesus rules the waves. "The sea is his and he made it." If only you can include yourself and Christ in that pronoun "we" of v. 24, you can never perish although there be as many demons against you as tiles on the house roofs. So Luther found it. See Isa. 54:17.

LUKE 8:26–39

"Great Things" for One in Great Need. The victim. In referring to but one demoniac the evangelist

LUKE

would probably concentrate attention on the more prominent of the two mentioned by Matthew. There must have been some collusion between the elements of the storm and the demons in this man. Everything seemed to oppose the Lord's assertion of his right to be obeyed. If demons could possess a man with such power, what might not Christ do if we yielded ourselves absolutely to him! There must have been some secret yielding on this man's part, or his heart would never have become a garrison of demons. He mistook Christ's identity, confusing it with that of the demons. Naked; vile; mighty to destroy! What a terrible combination!

His masters. The evil one dreads to be unclothed and would prefer to be in a pig than in the abyss—that word means "without bottom." Once begin to fall, where will it end? The Jews had no right to keep swine, whatever price the Romans were prepared to pay, Lev. 11:7. Christ left Gadara, but left a preacher there. We are not taken out of the world, but sent to witness to it and against it.

LUKE 8:40-56

Tender Ministry to Maid and Woman. The story of the poor woman has been characterized as that of "Nobody, Somebody, and Everybody." *Nobody,* for she was sick and poor and fearful. *Somebody,* for she was worthy of Christ's notice. He healed her and even stayed his progress to the house of Jairus to elicit her frank confession and pronounce a further word of peace. *Everybody,* for her story not only helped Jairus, but has been a blessing to mankind. We also have made the rounds of physicians, but Jesus only has sufficed for our need.

It is a distressing thing to see a child die! Small wonder that Jairus was impatient for Christ's help. The incident of the woman was permitted for his teaching and encouragement. We lose nothing when we await the Lord's leisure. On the contrary, we profit.

Christ needed the companionship of the apostles because their faith counted. Do not mind small numbers; they are often the condition of Christ's mightiest achievements. He will do what man cannot do, and leave man to do his little part. "Give her to eat."

LUKE 9:1-10

Working through His Followers. The Galilean ministry was coming to a close. The light that had shone there was to move southward and set behind the cross. Before finally leaving the district, our Lord made one last effort on its behalf. Calling together the apostles he laid his plans before them, divided the district into sections, and sent them out in pairs. He gave them no outward investiture, but the inward power of casting out evil spirits. Nothing was to distract them from the great object of heralding the kingdom of God.

Here we seem to encounter the origin of medical missions: their object—healing body and mind; their authority—the command of our Savior. George Eliot once said wisely, "The tale of divine pity was never yet believed from lips that had not first been moved by human pity."

Notice how Herod's conscience tormented him! He had begun to feel that scourge which has never failed to find and follow out the murderer, from Cain onward.

LUKE 9:11-17

"Give Ye Them to Eat." Christ feeds the world by his Church. The disciples passed the bread from his hands to those of the hungry crowds. What an honor that though we are least of saints we should have this opportunity of cooperation! But how often are we prepared for our work by being compelled to study the inadequacy of our resources. The only thing for us to do is to place them at his disposal.

But the bread of life is sufficient for all mankind. "They . . . were all filled." There is a universal connection between hunger and bread. Other foods are confined to special countries and districts, but bread is for the educated and ignorant, the rich and poor, the old and young. So with Jesus Christ. To every soul on earth his living, dying love makes its appeal and is enough to satisfy.

The fragments feed the distributors. More was left over than had been possessed at first. To impart to others is to gain for oneself. Fling the seed generously. With what measure ye mete, it shall be measured to you!

LUKE 9:18-27

The True Use of Life. Here and also in v. 28 reference is made to the Master's prayers. He was praying alone, before he broke to his friends the death which awaited him and in which we may have some share. He was praying, too, when the cloud of glory overshadowed him. Would it not be well to begin each new day with the resolve to pray more! If the Lord needed it, surely we do, whether for the cross or the Transfiguration mount.

Into such prayer, petition and intercession must needs enter. But, ah, what prayer that is which is neither of these, but the opening of our nature to the inflowing of the divine nature, which is Love, when the soul recognizes its oneness with God and the whole universe!

Our Lord asked these questions that he might lead the apostles to crystallize their own conceptions in Peter's magnificent affirmation. But they who will follow his footsteps must expect his lot! First, the cross is set up in our heart, and day by day our old self-nature is crucified there; then we have to endure for others the cross of rejection, shame, and death. But it is thus that we gain ourselves and come into possession of our own souls. If we dare take this path, neither here nor hereafter will Christ be ashamed of us.

LUKE 9:28-36

A Glimpse of Glory. From some aspects this was the highest point in our Savior's earthly career. He was the second Adam and had not sinned. There was no reason, therefore, that he should die. He might in a moment have been changed; that which was mortal might have been swallowed up of life. The door through which Moses and Elijah had come stood open, and by it our Lord might have returned. But he could never, under those circumstances, have been the Savior of mankind. He knew this; so he turned his back on the joy set before him and set his face toward Calvary.

Moses came as representing the Law, and Elijah, the prophets. Each of these great departments of divine revelation had anticipated his coming, 24:27, 44. As stars fade in the sunrise, so their mission was now merged in him. They spoke of his "decease" (literally, his "exodus"), and it was from this that Peter caught the term which he applied to his own death, 2 Pet. 1:15. The apostles never forgot this manifestation of the glory of the Lord, 1 John 1:1-4; 2 Pet. 1:17. When you hear that Christ is the Beloved of God, remember Eph. 1:6.

LUKE 9:37-50

The Greatest Serve the Neediest. When the mountain is bathed in the glory of God, we are loath to leave it. But we must not tarry in the enjoyment of its raptures when the plain contains so much misery. Saints and angels on the one hand, demons on the other! The disciples that have not enjoyed the mountain fellowship have no power over the unclean spirits that haunt men. It is easy to denounce demons; we must do more—we must exorcise them.

But let it never be forgotten that if you are able to cope with the devil, in the power of God, you must be prepared for the cross, vv. 44, 45. We cannot die for men, as Jesus did; but we can suffer rebuke and shame with him, and thus "fill up that which is behind" of his afflictions, Col. 1:24.

Let us seek the child-heart! We must distinguish between childishness and childlikeness. One of the loveliest pictures of the coming time is Isa. 11:6. Only childlike souls can tame and conquer the beasts. Let us welcome simple holy souls, and be ourselves of that class; and let us cultivate large-hearted charity toward those who cast out demons, though they be not of our school.

LUKE 9:51-62

The Steadfast Face. The Master's steadfast face rebukes us! Alas, we so often flinch and cannot appropriate Isa. 50:7. But whether we follow afar off or closely, that lithe, alert, eager figure is always in front and taking the upward path.

We need to remember which kingdom we belong to. We have passed out of the sphere of force and war, into the kingdom of the Son of God's love. It is a reversal of the divine plan to go back to the fire of vengeance. The only fire that we can invoke is that of the Holy Spirit; and it is remarkable that one of these two brothers lived to call down that very fire on those same villages. See Acts 8:14-25.

The Lord was ever acting as a winnowing-fan, detecting the wheat and the chaff in human motive. Be prepared to follow your Lord through loneliness, homelessness, the rupture of tender ties, and the plowing of a solitary furrow. But keep your eye fixed on the eternal side of your life!

LUKE 10:1-16

The Forerunners of the Lord. In the appointment of the seventy there was perhaps an allusion to Num. 11:24, 25. In this case, as in that, there was the endowment of conspicuous spiritual power. We can only "prepare" the way for our Lord. No one of us can suffice for the soul of man. We must always say with the Baptist, "There cometh one mightier than I." Would that Christ always came where we had been! See v. 1.

Let us not forget to pray for laborers; but if we pray truly, we shall endeavor to answer our own prayers by going and by inciting others to go. How often a child's life becomes dedicated through hands being laid on the young head by some servant of God who says, "When you grow up, you must work for the Lord Jesus!"

The Lord asks for simplicity. We may not in our particular climate be able to carry out these

LUKE 10:17-24

The Sources of Deepest Joy. How triumphant the return of the evangelist! With faces flushed with pride and hearts high with elation, they returned to the Master with their reports. What wisdom it is to talk our work over with Jesus! Even the demons were subject to his name. The Savior was not surprised. While he had been watching, bearing them up by his intercessions, he had seen an alteration take place in the unseen world. Satan had fallen, as though the work done by these humble men had turned the scale against him. Is it not so still? What we do is of eternal importance.

Then, "in that hour," it seemed as though the floodgates of the Savior's soul were flung open for joy. He rejoiced that babe-like hearts might know the deep things of God; that all things were opened to him in his humanity as in the ages before he became man; and that he was permitted to reveal the Father to those who loved and obeyed him. It was for these, and for us, to know things hidden from prophets and kings.

LUKE 10:25-37

The Man Who Loved His Neighbor. This parable was probably suggested by the journey up to Jerusalem. It may be founded on an actual occurrence. Notice how the Master answered the inquiry, "Who is my neighbour?" He said in effect: The question is not, Who will "neighbor" you? but, Whom will you "neighbor?" You ought to ask, Who wants my help? Neighborhood consists, not in what you receive, but in what you give. It is independent of race, creed, and the ordinary sentiment of pity. Love overleaps all these distinctions and risks its very life in order to render help. In fact, this parable is a very poem of love. It is to be compared with 1 Cor. 13.

Notice those two clauses, "He took care of him" and "Take care of him," vv. 34, 35. It is thus that our Lord deals with us. When we are too far gone to ask for his help, he comes to our side and restores our ebbing life; and he raises up others to do the same. At best, we are pilgrims and refresh ourselves in inns, but the home awaits us yonder! Begin by loving with your "strength" and you will end with the "heart."

precepts precisely and literally. But the inner thought of his words is that we are to be absorbed in giving the message, leaving all things else as a very secondary question and allowing God to care for us and ours.

LUKE 10:38—11:4

Learning the Lord's Secrets. This Bethany idyll follows the story of the Good Samaritan naturally. The village lay at the end of the long pass from Jericho. Love must have its nest and the special objects of its tender care. We cannot live in the inn always; we must come at last to our home, either in this world or the next. He who had welcomed the crowds was now welcomed for his own dear sake. Martha and Mary each gave of her best. Each had her own sphere; one ministered to his physical need, the other to his heart. The mystical and practical are both required in Christ's service, and blend at his feet. Don't live for many things, but for him.

The way to teach people to pray is to pray yourself. It was the habitual prayerfulness of Jesus that made the apostles long to be taught to pray. What an example is here of the power of unconscious influence! If you desire that your children or scholars should pray, pray yourself. The model prayer is full of suggestion as to the order and topics of prayer. Fill in these outlines!

LUKE 11:5-13

Encouragement to Persevering Prayer. The parable of the three friends is very encouraging. We, so to speak, are to act as mediators or intercessors between those who are in sore need and our great Heavenly Friend. They are always coming to us on their journey, and we feel that we have nothing to set before them. Whether their need is for body, mind, or spirit, they find us poor and bankrupt. But at such times let us turn to God with earnest prayer. If persistence in prayer prevails over the churlish and self-indulgent, what will it not achieve with the One who is "rich unto all that call upon him." He will give us just as much as we need.

Notice that "how much more"! Count the stars scattered on the vault of night, or the daisies in the fields, or the myraids of living creatures, sustained as the pensioners of his bounty, and ask yourself if he cannot give enough good gifts, and his Spirit withal, to supply all your need. What would you not do for your helpless little child? "How much more . . ." See Phil. 4:19.

LUKE 11:14-26

For or Against? The strong man of this parable is evidently Satan, who guards the palace of man's nature, to which he has no right. It is the palace of the King, which has been captured by his direst foe. The demon possession of the body is a parable and illustration of the terrible results of the possession of the soul by the demons of jealousy, passion, etc. Satan is strong—stronger than Adam in his innocence or David in his palace. He is armed with the lie, is always on the watch to lull us into false security; but the peace which he promises actually leads to death.

Thank God, Christ is stronger! In the wilderness and on the cross he proved himself so. He took away his foe's armor and bruised his head. When Christ takes up his residence in the heart, Satan may rage outside and fling in horrid suggestions, but the door is kept closed against his return. They are to be pitied who make a reform in their own strength—Satan will return. Only Christ can work permanent deliverance.

LUKE 11:27-32

"The Sign of Jonah." What a tribute this woman paid our Lord! He was full of grace as well as truth; and those who with unbiased and unprejudiced minds saw him moving among men were constrained to confess his inimitable beauty. Notice that the simplest soul that hears and obeys God's Word is equally blessed with his mother, v. 28.

Men will be judged by the opportunities they have had. Every age and every race and every individual on which the sun has ever shone has had a chance. Not our chance, but a chance suited to the spiritual vision of each, John 1:9; Rom. 1:20; 2:5ff. So God will be able to judge all men. But in how many cases will they who have not had our advantages be found in a higher class in the great University of Heaven than some of us who have lived amid the light of Christ!

LUKE 11:33-44

Dark and Foul Within. "The spirit of man is the candle of the Lord," Prov. 20:27. How many unlit candles there are! Will you not ask whether Christ has ever kindled you with his divine light and life? You have the capacity for God, but this is not enough. Christ must give you light, Eph. 5:14. Seek the clear shining of the inner light, and remember that it will grow clearer and brighter just in proportion as it is obeyed and followed. What a glorious conception this is, that the Lord Jesus shall so fill us with the radiance and warmth of his love that there shall be no part dark!

Our Lord's denunciations of the religious leaders of his time reveal the wrath of infinite truth and purity against all that is inconsistent with either. Because he loved his sheep, the Good Shepherd must warn them against wolves. Notice v. 41, which means that our faith, love, and joy are to be shared with others. Let us be generous in self-giving. There is no law of the tithe here! Give all!

LUKE 11:45-54

Searching Words for Hypocrites. The minute oral and written rules promulgated by the Hebrew religious leaders overlaid and almost buried under their weight the simple Mosaic code. They were the subject of incessant disputing and discussion. A vast crowd of copyists, lecturers, teachers, and casuists were always debating them. The lawyer who here addressed Christ was one of this class. He could hardly believe that this revered rabbi could include him and his fellows in these terrible "woes."

Our Lord speaks of himself as "the wisdom of God." Compare v. 49 with Matt. 23:34. For a moment he rises above the low levels of his Incarnation and identifies himself with the Eternal God. But what profound sorrow filled his heart as these stern words were wrung from his lips by the stubborn obduracy of his people! In the Hebrew Scriptures, where the order of the books differs from that of our Old Testament, the death of Abel is related in the first book and that of Zacharias in the last, 2 Chron. 24:20-22. The legend said that the blood of the latter was bubbling up when Nebuchadnezzar took Jerusalem. No sacrifices availed to stop it.

LUKE 12:1-12

The Secret of Fearlessness. The program of this paragraph seems dark. The leaven of evil always at work; the body tortured and killed; confession difficult, denial easy; the trials before synagogues and rulers; the anxiety of witnessing a good confession. The Lord never hesitated in stating the heavy tribulation through which his disciples must come to the kingdom.

But what infinite compensations! Not forgotten by God; our hairs numbered; confessed before the angels; taught how to speak; all sin forgiven! With such comforts, who of us need fear, except only the power of Satan! What infinite sympathy and care our Father has for us! He knows our sorrows, marks every lurch of the boat, and will supply his gracious comfort and help. Why should we flinch before a world in arms so long as the Son of man stands for us, as he did for Stephen, at "the right hand of God"? The outward man may decay, but the inward man is renewed day by day.

LUKE 12:13-21

The Doom of the Money Lover. Our Lord did not come into our world as an earthly judge, adjusting differences between man and man. He lays down great principles, obedience to which will bring Heaven into human lives. One of the greatest of these is enunciated in v. 15. Covetousness is as much a temptation of the poor man who is wronged as of his rich oppressor; and love for money will inevitably, in poor and rich, becloud the vision and disturb the inner peace. The worth of a man cannot be computed by the amount that stands to his credit. Not what you have, but what you are—*that* is your value in the eyes of God. Some men live to get; see to it that you live to be.

It is absurd to suppose that the soul can take its ease just because its barns are bursting with goods. Goods are not good! The soul cannot live on corn! Merriment cannot come to a heart that is smitten by remorse and shadowed by the remonstrances of an evil conscience! Besides, we cannot take with us our possessions when we cross the river. We can only take our character —our things pass into other hands.

LUKE 12:22-34

The Cure for Anxious Care. Notice this contrast between two kinds of men: the one cares for himself, is anxious for this life, worries about food and clothes and standing a cubit higher in the estimate of his fellows; the other is content to fill the niche and do the work assigned him by the Father. And he performs his life-task, not for the remuneration it will bring, but for the "Well done" of God—sure all that is needed, whether for his soul or body, will be provided by him who gave him being. The Father knows thy varied need; trust him!

Do not think of God as grudging! It is your Father's good pleasure to give. Nothing delights him more than to be able to "give good things to them that ask him." For him also "it is more blessed to give than to receive." Remember that the best investments are those we store, not in banks, but in the lives of others, for God himself guarantees the interest.

LUKE 12:35-48

Ever on the Watch. The Lord leads our thoughts on to his advent, when he will call his servants to account. The day may pass into the evening, the evening into the night, and the night may even begin to wear away to the morning, but the faithful servants keep their watch. Their loins are girt to serve, and the house is radiant with their trimmed lights. Presently he comes, and he raises his slaves to sit at his table! They are henceforth his friends—and his highly honored friends—whom he serves with his own hands. The grandeur of the reward seems to have been too much for Peter to grasp, v. 41. Surely it couldn't be for *all*. Yes, said our Lord in effect, to all who are faithful to their possibilities and use their position and gifts for others.

How abrupt and awful the contrast in vv. 45-48! The greater our responsibility, the greater our condemnation if we fail. Retribution is the inevitable penalty of infidelity to trust; but it will be precisely proportioned to our knowledge of the Lord's will. There are degrees or grades in retribution as in glory.

LUKE 12:49-59

The Great Divider. As Prometheus, in the old Greek fable, brought fire from above in a reed, so Christ brought the fire of the Holy Spirit in the frail lantern of his humanity. But first he had to pass through a baptism of tears and blood. He was under pressure to enter it, because impatient to get through with it. Here was the prelude of Calvary. And what was true of our Lord must be true of his Church. Always the sword, always strife, always division where the gospel begins to ferment like leaven in human hearts.

The signs of the time pointed to a climax of Hebrew history, for which most of his contemporaries were unprepared. The sands in God's hourglass were running out. This was the great requirement of the hour—*get right with God.* The warning is applicable to us all, but it was specially spoken of the brief interval which, like the silence that precedes a thunderstorm, preceded the fall of Jerusalem.

LUKE 13:1-9

Both Repentance and Fruitfulness Required. Our Lord did not hesitate to hang great lessons on passing events. It is a great art to lead men's thoughts from the outward and transient to the unseen and eternal. God often gives us texts in the happenings of his Providence, and when men's hearts are awed and softened there is a conspicuous opportunity for striking home.

We have no right to suppose that sudden disasters prove the presence of special sin in those who are involved in them. Sin is avenged in this life, but rather in the natural sequences than by some sudden "act of God." Accidents are not necessarily punishments, and we who witness the sad fate of others have no right to congratulate ourselves on our moral or spiritual superiority. Instead of judging others, let us look to ourselves and repent.

The parable of the fig tree, with its three years of effort to secure fruitfulness, was intended primarily for the Jewish nation favored with our Lord's three years of ministry. But it is of universal application. God is always seeking fruit; love is ever pleading, but sometimes may have to acquiesce in judgment.

LUKE 13:10–17

Good Work for the Sabbath. There was in this woman a noble principle which led her to persevere in attending God's house, although there was much to discourage her. Probably she was animated by a faith which made her specially susceptible to the healing word of Christ. Infirmity of any kind should drive us to the house of God. We shall meet Jesus there. When he says, "loosed," all the powers of hell cannot bind us down. "He breaks the power of cancelled sin."

The charge of Sabbath-breaking by these men was very unreasonable, because on that very morning each of them had unloosened his beast to lead him to the well. And if it was not wrong in their judgment to untie a beast, surely it would not be wrong to untie the knotted disease that bound this woman's head to her feet by an invisible thong! Great human needs must have precedence over the observance of details of ritual.

LUKE 13:18–30

The Penalty of Neglected Opportunity. Notice here the inward movement and the outward effect of the gospel, whether in the heart or in the world of men. The garden and the kitchen, the lives of men and women respectively yield the same lesson. Though the seed of the divine nature is sown in secret, it cannot remain secret, but works its way into manifestation. Man's method is from without inward; God's, from within outward. You cannot estimate the results when a little child receives the incorruptible seed, 1 Pet. 1:23.

But the entrance into the full power and blessedness of Christ is by a narrow way. The strait gate is open to all, but it means that we have to deny and leave behind all that is carnal, whether good or bad in the estimate of men, so that the divine life may have the entire field. Merely to eat and drink in Christ's presence betrays a self-indulgence which is foreign to his Spirit. You may sit at the Lord's Table and yet be a worker of iniquity! We may be first in privilege, but last in grace. Verses 29 and 30 remind us of Acts 10:34, 35 and Romans 2:11–13.

LUKE 13:31—14:6

The Lament for Those Who "Would Not." Our Lord was at that time in Perea, in the jurisdiction of Herod, who probably desired to get rid of him lest his presence should introduce political complications. Our Lord saw through and exposed his stratagem. How awful to be read by the light of divine purity! Jesus also kept his eye on his Father's will and knew that he was immortal till his work was done.

Jerusalem was clearly indicated as the scene of his death. The city was already so deeply dyed with martyr blood that it would hardly have been congruous for him to suffer anywhere else. Note that pathetic wail of disappointed love. God's brooding love desires to interpose between us and the hovering peril; but we have the awful power to neglect or reject the covering wings of the shekinah. See Ruth 2:12 and Ps. 91:4.

In 14:1–6 we have a specimen of Christ's table talk, which he continues through the 24th verse. Though he knew that he was being watched, nothing could stop his power and love. If men care for their beasts, how much more will Christ care for men!

LUKE 14:7–14

Lessons for Guests and Hosts. The word "rooms" should be "seats." We must, of course, guard against a false humility, which chooses a low seat in the hope of being invited forward. Let us seek it because we are absolutely careless of prominence except as it gives us wider opportunity. The unconscious humility and meekness of a little child are very dear to Christ. Dwell on your own defects and on the excellencies of others till you realize that you are the least of all saints! See Phil. 3:8.

Our Lord's words about invitations to our houses strike at the root of much of the so-called hospitality of modern society. Did not our Lord intend his words to be interpreted literally? They are imperative in their tone. He probably meant what he said. Some of us get so much thanks down here that there will be very little left to come to us at the resurrection of the just, when we shall stand before the judgment-seat of Christ to receive our rewards, 2 Cor. 5:10.

LUKE 14:15–24

The Slighted Invitation. In this parable the Master anticipated that the Jewish magistrates and

LUKE

leaders would repudiate his invitations, and that they would therefore be extended to the less likely masses to be found in the streets and lanes of the city, and to the Gentiles in the outlying world. What a preview is here of the suitableness of the gospel to all the world, and of the ultimate inclusion of all believing mankind under one roof, John 14:1, 2.

The excuses were obviously trumped up and invalid. Men see fields before buying them, try oxen before purchase, and can take their wives where they go themselves, if they wish to do so. They who are acute enough for this world are often slow and careless about the next, though that is the only world which really matters.

If thou art poor, maimed, blind, or lame, there is room for thee at God's table; and for thee "a great spoil" shall be divided, Isa. 33:23.

LUKE 14:25-35

The Cost of Discipleship. Here we have our Lord's use of the winnowing-fan. Amid the teeming crowds he knew that there were many light and superficial souls who had not realized the cost involved in discipleship. Mark the thrice-repeated words—"cannot be my disciple."

Our love must be greater than the ties of family affection, v. 26; must be greater than our love for our own way, which must be nailed to the cross, v. 27; must be greater than our love of possessions and property, v. 33. Christ has done more than any other teacher to cement the relationships of human love, but he always asks that they should be subordinated to the claims of God. Oh, for the love that Paul had! See Phil. 3:8.

What a comfort it is to realize that God counted the cost before he set about the task of redemption, whether of a world or of us as individuals. He knew all that it would cost, and surely he did not begin what he cannot complete!

LUKE 15:1-10

Seeking and Finding the Lost. They that have left the fold in which they were nurtured in early life, and have gone over bleak mountains and through tangled brush, find themselves in this exquisite picture; the Lord is on their track. He cannot abide happily with the rest, while one sheep is liable to be torn by beasts of prey or caught away by eagles. He goes after it till he finds it. Don't you think, mother, that the Lord loves that child of yours, now far away, as much as you do? Cannot you trust him to seek until he finds? Then he will ask you to rejoice with him. Jesus not only "receiveth" sinners, but "seeketh" them. Those who have always lived an outwardly correct life and who do not think themselves in need of repentance are the ninety and nine.

Some have the King's stamp on them, but have rolled away into the dark corner amid dust and shavings. Oh, that we were all more willing to go down on our knees to sweep the floor to find the lost! The nine links of a necklace are useless if the tenth is missing. Christ cannot be satisfied until the lost coin is found.

LUKE 15:11-24

The Son Who "Came to Himself" and to His Father. Here is the pearl of parables! Too often we desire God's gifts apart from himself. "A far country" is not far in actual distance, but in the alienation of the heart. You may be living in a pious home and yet be in "a far country." Sin is waste. "A far country" is always swept by famine, because our soul was made for God and cannot live on husks. Neither things nor people can really appease our awful hunger if we are away from God.

Sin is temporary madness. The first step to God is to come to ourselves. The prodigal's real nature stood face to face with the ruin and havoc of his sin. Never, not even for a moment, had the Father ceased to love and yearn. There was an instant response to the slightest indication of repentance. Love was quicker than words, understanding what the prodigal meant. The confession was therefore cut short. Note the profuse welcome, meeting every need —the robe of righteousness, the ring of reconciliation, the kiss of love, the shoes of a holy walk, the feast of fellowship.

LUKE 15:25-32

The Son Who Never Came to His Father. Notice the difference between the father's care for his elder son and the son's own estimate of his position, and you will see how easily you may miss the holy possibilities of your own life if you allow yourself to be blinded by jealousy!

"Ever with me"; life was meant to be irradiated and blessed by the constant sense of God's nearness. We were meant to live in God and God in us. "All that I have is thine"; such is our wealthy condition, in the purpose of God, that all his divine resources, stored in Jesus, await the appropriation of our faith.

But if we fail to recognize our brother in the penitent "thy son," if we shut ourselves out of the joy because of some fancied slight or Pharisaic pride, we miss our own truest

LUKE 16:1-13

The Right Use of Money. We are all stewards, but how much we waste! Well might our Master deprive us of our position and trust! The unjust steward used his opportunity of ingratiating himself with the tenants at the landowner's cost. He thus secured for himself a welcome to their homes, but his deceit came to light and he was dismissed. Our Master did not commend his fraud, but pointed out that the children of this world are singularly alive to their future and prepare for its contingencies. If they make a wrong use of money to provide for the future, how much more should Christians make a right use of it, so that when they die they may be welcomed to the eternal home by those whom they have benefited!

Money is described as unrighteous mammon, the name of the heathen god of wealth. It is so often associated with cheating that the adjective is most appropriate. Note also that money is "the least" and not "that which is our own," but God's, to be used by us as his servants and at his direction.

LUKE 16:14-31

A Look into the Future. Here was a flagrant case of heartless indifference, amid luxuries of every kind, to the daily spectacle of abject need. Most of us have at least one Lazarus at the gates of our life. The charge against the rich man was not that he had injured Lazarus, but that he had not helped him. Man condemns us for doing wrong, God for failing to do right.

Lazarus was translated to the realm of blessedness—the bosom of Abraham, bespeaking nearness to him at the great feast—not because he had been so poor and miserable, but because, beggar though he was, he possessed the faith of heart and the purity of motive that characterized his great ancestor.

Notice that memory plays a conspicuous part in the sorrow of Gehenna; that Christ gives no hope of changing the soul's habitation; and that we have in the Scripture a more certain agent of spiritual renewal than would be provided by even the apparition of the dead.

LUKE 17:1-10

"Take Heed to Yourselves." The world is full of stumbling-blocks. Men are perpetually placing them in each other's way, and especially before little children, the simple, and the weak. Let us take heed to ourselves and endeavor to make life's pathway easier for others. Let us spend lives of helpfulness and sympathy, full of love and forgiveness, of light and joy.

Do these precepts seem too difficult? Does a sevenfold forgiveness seem impossible? Then learn the lesson of the mustard seed, which opens its tiny door to the inflow of Nature's energy and is therefore enabled to produce what, to its unaided strength, would be impossible. Open your soul to God! His love through you will forgive and save to the uttermost!

But when you have done all, you have nothing to be proud of, and neither God nor man is under any obligation to you. Love is the elementary duty of the follower of Christ.

LUKE 17:11-21

The Man Who Was Grateful. Their common misery drew these poor outcasts together and made them forget the fierce national antipathies of Jew and Samaritan. When bidden to go to the priest before there were any outward signs of healing they started, and thus gave evidence of their confidence that they were healed. It was this faith that saved them, because faith like this lets in the whole tide of God's saving health. In the case of the poor alien, it was clear that he was not only healed, but saved, as his gratitude and worship indicated. Do we thank God, not only for his miracles, but for his daily Providence?

The best things are the quietest. The deepest work of God, in the individual and in the community, does not reveal itself to the newspaper reporter, but steals on the world like spring through garden and woodland.

LUKE 17:22-37

"The Days of the Son of Man." Clearly enough, our Lord foresaw the approaching dissolution of the Jewish state. There was no help for it, notwithstanding all that the Baptist and Christ himself had done. Suddenly and inevitably its doom must befall, as the Deluge in the old world and the overthrow of Sodom. The Roman eagles would gather round the devoted city and only instant flight would avail. The early Christian disciples were warned by these words, and escaped to Pella before Titus struck the last blow.

Since then other catastrophes have befallen, and finally the day of doom will break upon the world—to all of which the Master's words have been and are appropriate. In one sense, the advent of Christ took place at the fall of Jerusalem, the scenes of which were probably a miniature of the travail through which the new

LUKE

heavens and the new earth will be born. Let us not seek our own, but the things that belong to the kingdom; then all other things "shall be added," Matt. 6:33.

LUKE 18:1-8

The Lesson for Dark Days. There are three phases in our Lord's teaching about prayer—that of Matthew 6, this chapter, and the words of John 14 and 15. In Luke 18:1-8 he exhorts uniformity and urgency. There is an aspect of prayer that we are in danger of overlooking when the skies are blue and the sun is shining, and that is the need of holy persistence.

This lesson is taught, in the parable of this paragraph, by a striking contrast which may be stated thus: If an unjust and ungodly judge will finally grant a just petition, out of base and selfish motives and merely to save himself from being worried by a defenseless and oppressed woman, how much more shall the just and merciful God hear the cry and avenge the cause of those whom he loves. If answers to certain prayers, which we have offered in an agony of tears, are slow in coming, we may be sure either that the time is not ripe, or that he is going to do something better.

LUKE 18:9-17

Those Whom God Accepts. We are taught here the spirit in which we should pray. Too many pray "with themselves." The only time that we may thank God for not being as others is when we attribute the contrast to his grace, 1 Tim. 1:12-14. Let it never be forgotten that those who will be justified and stand accepted before God are they who are nothing in their own estimate.

To be self-emptied and poor in spirit is the fundamental and indispensable preparation for receiving the grace of God. "Be propitiated to me" (margin), cried the publican. "There is a propitiation for our sins," is the answer of Heb. 2:17. Each penitent counts himself *the* sinner, 1 Tim. 1:15. Bow yourself at the feet of Christ, and he will lift you to his throne.

We think that children must grow up to become like us before they are eligible for the kingdom. Nay, we must grow down to become like them—in simplicity, in humility, and in faith.

LUKE 18:18-30

The One Thing Needful. The young ruler was a man of irreproachable character. He might have said of himself all that the Apostle Paul says in Phil. 3:4ff. But he was restless and unsatisfied. He felt that Jesus had the key to a life deeper than he had experienced, and he longed to possess it. He was so much in earnest that he knelt in the crowded thoroughfare before the despised Nazarene, Mark 10:17.

He did not know himself. He thought he possessed that love which fulfils the Law, Rom. 13:10. Our Lord desired to prove to him that he was deficient in that love, and therefore could not have eternal life. He did this by suggesting that the young ruler should renounce all and accompany him in a self-giving for others that must end in a cross. But he shrank back. He dared not face a life of simple faith in God for the supply of temporal needs, and of absolute self-giving to a cross. For all who dare this, whatever is right and good is given back to be held and used under God's direction.

LUKE 18:31-43

The Reward of Faith. Our Lord knew what was awaiting him. He laid down his life voluntarily. But all the significance of his life and death was concealed from the apostles and others. Their eyes were blinded, till the glory of the resurrection morning had dawned and the day of Pentecost had fully come.

Our Lord's mind must have been filled with the anticipation of the momentous issues to be decided; but he was sufficiently at leisure from himself to hear the cry of distress from this blind beggar. How absolutely he placed himself at the disposal of those who needed his help! Human need and sorrow always commanded him. Each comer was able to draw all the grace he required, according to the measure of the bucket of his faith when let down into that infinite well. There is no reason why each of us should not be made whole and follow Christ, glorifying him. But we are blind without him.

LUKE 19:1-10

The Sinner and His Guest. For long, we may suppose, the better things had been striving against the worse in this man's character. John the Baptist had wielded great influence over Zaccheus' class and perhaps over himself. Zaccheus was a dissatisfied man. His dishonest acquisitions added to his wealth, but subtracted from his peace of mind. He knew that the least he could do would be to repay those whom he had robbed. But his soul required more, and longed for salvation such as only Jesus Christ could give.

The Lord knew this, and therefore halted beneath the tree and invited himself as a guest to the publican's home. The one man in all

Jericho who most needed the Savior was discovered by him and saved. The grace of God is ever in search of those who have gone as far as their light will carry them.

What a blessing it is that the Lord is willing to be our guest! See that he is welcomed to the guest room of your heart. Stand to serve him. He brings salvation for you and yours.

LUKE 19:11-27

Doing Business for God. In many respects this parable differs from that of the ten talents. In that, the servants are entrusted with different amounts; in this, the same amount is allotted to each. Obviously, the former deals with our powers and opportunities for service, which greatly differ; whereas the latter deals with those ordinary gifts which are common to all, and especially with the gift of salvation. All have the opportunity of using and enjoying the same bestowment of life which is in Jesus Christ for those who believe, Jude 3.

Some make the greatest possible use of "our common salvation." They increase its blessings by much prayer and faith and experience. They speak of it to others and spread the knowledge of the heights and depths of God's love. The more they do this, the more it grows on them. Others pass through life without realizing or enjoying Christ's gift of eternal life. They hope that they may be saved, but they have no deep experiential knowledge of his love. These are they who misuse their pound! What a contrast between such and Paul or Luther or Wesley!

LUKE 19:28-40

The Welcome of the King. This humble triumph is a further revelation of our Lord's character. The lowliness of it, which exposed him to the sneers and ridicule of scribe and Pharisee, greatly pleased the simple folk from Galilee, who recognized him as their own and were proud to identify themselves with him. See Matt. 21:11. It is thus that Jesus pursues his way through the ages; the princes of this world know him not, but his character is appreciated and his claims are recognized by babes, Matt. 11:25; 1 Cor. 2:8. Are you in the Master's procession?

Jesus' royalty is not of this world. It is based on character. It is ignored by the proud, but welcomed by the poor. It is fairest to those whose eyes are anointed to penetrate the veil and discern the eternal realities; and of their enthusiasm, praise to God is the irresistible expression. Note that their song is an echo of Luke 2:14. Oh, to glorify God to the highest degree!

The Lord's need is the master-motive. We can hold nothing back from his request, whether child or money or life. Let these words ring in our hearts: "The Lord hath need."

LUKE 19:41-48

The Doom of the Royal City. Our Lord loved the city of his race; and when it finally rejected his appeals, he knew that nothing could avert its downfall. Hence his tears! Each nation, city, and individual has one day which is the crisis of existence. We cross the equator without knowing it. There is one hour in each Godforsaken life when, as in the Temple before its fall, watchers hear the words, "Let us depart," and there is the rustle of wings! Notice that God visits us in mercy before he comes to us in wrath.

It was a startling act when Christ cleansed the Temple for the second time, John 2:13ff. If there had been daily papers in those days, they would have chronicled it in great headlines. Extraordinary that this meek and lowly man should break out so vehemently! But his zeal for God's house sustained and bore him along. Let us ask him to cleanse the temple of our heart.

These priests and scribes had vested interests to conserve, which blinded them to the beauty and glory of Christ. If we place a coin, however valueless, against the eye, it will blind us to the sun.

LUKE 20:1-8

The Unanswered Question. When anyone has received a divine commission, he does not need to prove it. His credentials are written large upon his life and message. It was so with John the Baptist. There was no need for him to argue his claims. The crowds in the Jordan valley, the multitudes in the baptismal waters were sufficient to attest him as God's servant. What he said about God and sin found corroboration in their hearts. So it was with our Lord. The masses of people that followed him and hung on his words had no doubt that he was the heir of the vineyard. The leaders professed to doubt it because, to use the language of the parable that follows, they were reluctant to surrender their claims to the ownership of the vineyard.

Probably sufficient stress has not been laid upon the supreme intellectual power of our Lord, which shone out so clearly in these conflicts with Hebrew casuists, and in which he always came off conqueror by the sheer force of his mind. "We have the mind of Christ!"

LUKE 20:9-18

"The Stone Which the Builders Rejected." The vineyard represents the privileges and blessings of the Hebrew race. The servants are evidently the prophets and others sent from God. Whatever our position in life, God expects a revenue from it. We are not owners, but tenants; not proprietors, but stewards. Are you sure that you are giving God the dues which he may justly claim?

Notice how our Lord severs himself from all human messengers, as the Son. When he said "my beloved Son," he anticipated John 3:16. The warm kiss of the Father's love was on his cheek. He realized that he was the heir, Heb. 1:2; Rom. 8:17.

It is said that in the building of Solomon's Temple, a valuable carved stone was cast aside and neglected till a part of the structure absolutely called for it. You may build society as you like, but there will come a time when Christ will be needed to give the finishing touch.

LUKE 20:19-26

Tribute to Caesar and to God. Fearing to touch him themselves, and finding no foothold against him according to the Mosaic law, his enemies sought to bring Christ into collision with the civil power. To do this, no hypocrisy was too mean.

So poor was our Lord that he must needs ask them to furnish the penny or drachma. Caesar has a certain claim on us. He has earned certain rights of homage and tribute by preserving the good order of society and the safety of our persons; but there his authority ends. When he intrudes into the realm of conscience, he is a usurper. In that kingdom he has no claims whatever.

We must give Caesar his dues. They can be paid in the coin of earth's mintage; but he has no claim on our conscience, faith, love. These bear the mint-mark of God, and to God they must be rendered. Ah, soul! Thou belongest to the great King; thou art stamped with his image and superscription! Give him thyself!

LUKE 20:27-40

The God of the Living. Here our Lord answers the materialism of his time. He speaks with the note of absolute certainty concerning the unseen, Heb. 11:27. Its inhabitants do not die or marry, nor are they subject to the conditions of our earthly life. These are "the children of the resurrection." What an inspiring title! May it be applied to us as in Col. 3:1-4! Too many are "the sons of this age," v. 34, margin! They adopt this transient earth as their foster parent! We cannot belong to both, though some, like Bunyan's waterman, row in one direction while they look in another.

How wonderful to find a proof of immortality in that passage about the bush, Exod. 3:6! The fact that Jehovah said, "I *am* the God of Abraham," proved that the patriarch was in existence somewhere at that moment. Those whom we describe as dead are living people who have died. Death is but a passage, a step. There is no break in the chain of existence. Yonder and here all live unto God, Rom. 14:8.

LUKE 20:41—21:4

David's Lord Testing Men and Women. It was the Master's turn to question. As man, he was David's descendant and son; as the Son of God, he was his Lord. Though it sealed his doom, our Lord tore the veil from before these hypocrites, that his followers might be warned against these sunken rocks, Jude 12.

We note the difference between the false teachers, who devoured widows' houses, and the true Leader and Teacher, who set so high a value on a widow's gift. Our gifts to God should cost us something, else they are not reckoned in the accounts of eternity. The real value of a gift is to be estimated by what is left behind. Remember that the fragrance and beauty of this act have lasted, while the stones of the Temple have crumbled to dust. Holy deeds are imperishable! Jesus is still sitting by the treasury, watching and estimating our gifts.

LUKE 21:5-19

Days That Try Men's Souls. When we ask speculative questions, the Master bids us take heed to ourselves. His predictions in this passage were literally fulfilled in the events which culminated in the siege and fall of Jerusalem, forty years afterward. "The whole creation groaneth and travaileth in pain together," and through these throes and agonies mankind steps up to a new level of experience. The devil will not surrender his kingdom, any more than the bodies of men, without a grievous rending first; but there is a mightier than he.

The Church is called to follow her Lord. No easier path than his may she choose. Where there is no outward suffering, there may be the inner cross and the death to all that the soul had once prized. Jesus has always stood beside his own wherever they have been called to witness for the truth; and the testimony given by his witnesses has reached the great ones of the earth and reverberated through courts and palaces. In suffering, our souls become searched as by fire. We learn to know ourselves and to come into possession of an experience and a self-knowledge with which only suffering could have endowed us.

LUKE 21:20–28

The Coming of the Son of Man in Glory. This paragraph clearly has its first reference to the fall of Jerusalem, which took place A.D. 70. The directions given by our Lord were of the greatest service to the Christian church, the members of which in large numbers fled to Pella, across the Jordan, and so escaped the horrors of the siege. But beyond this, each great event, such as the dissolution of the Hebrew state, the overthrow of the Roman Empire, the rise of the Reformation, the French Revolution, and so forth, is another stage in the advent of our Lord. He is always "coming in a cloud" so far as the eyes of men are concerned, but with the growing glory of clearer revelation and increased spiritual power. All these stages are leading up to his final unveiling at his Second Advent.

That generation did not pass away before these portents were fulfilled; but each great period or chapter of history closes with similar signs. It is as though Nature were as sympathetic to the experiences of the race as the body is to the motions of the soul. Again behold the travail-pangs of creation, through which the new heavens and the new earth are being born. See Rom. 8:22ff.

LUKE 21:29–38

The Need of Constant Watchfulness. The summer of the world is yet before us! This is but the springtide, when the seeds are beginning to sprout, but the winds are cold. Ah, peaceful days of unbroken summer glory, make haste to break!

In a limited significance, our Lord's words were fulfilled within forty years of their utterance; but we are still to see how much more is contained in them than has yet been realized. In the meanwhile let us beware of his warning. Note that "cares" endanger our soul's health equally with "surfeiting" and "drunkenness." It is impossible to live as we should apart from constant watching and prayer. The snare is so deftly laid that we may be entangled in it before we are fully aware. But, oh how great the honor to be one day accounted "to stand before the Son of man!" See 1 Kings 10:8.

These last hours of our Lord's ministry were very full. The days were days of activity, interspersed with snatches of blessed intercourse with the beloved group at Bethany, while the nights were spent on Olivet in prayer.

LUKE 22:1–13

Selling or Serving the Master. The world seemed in arms against the greatest Lover of souls that had ever trod earth's soil. Satan entered the heart of Judas, for it was his hour, and he gathered all his strength for one last prodigious effort to overthrow the Son of man and thwart his sublime purpose of redemption. Judas, one of the inner circle, did not hesitate to choose thirty pieces of silver rather than love, purity, compassion as they were incarnate in the Son of man. The religious leaders of the age also eagerly caught at their chance.

In the meanwhile the Lord girded himself for the conflict by gathering to his heart the remainder of the apostolic band, though none of them really understood. The arrangement of the man with the waterpot was evidently to elude arrest during the supper, as Judas could not inform his accomplices beforehand of the selected supper room. Remember that Jesus asks each of us for the guest chamber of our heart! Ask him, not to be as a wayfaring man who tarries for the night, but to abide always.

LUKE 22:14–23

The Feast of Love and Its Shadow. The human soul of Jesus needed this sweet fellowship with loyal friends to nerve it for its sorrows; and he desired to transmit it as a perpetual legacy for his Church. We may think of that Table being elongated till it reaches down the centuries to where we are seated. Look down the long vista and at the end, behold the Master himself!

These two allusions to the kingdom of God, vv. 16 and 18, point onward to the marriage supper when the full purpose of redemption will be consummated. As we partake of bread for our natural strength, so spiritual strength to suffer, to resist temptation, and to serve is possible only as we feed on Christ by meditation and appropriation. And let us never forget that the wine is the emblem of his blood, by which the new covenant was sealed. See Heb. 9:18. When therefore at the sacred feast we place the wine to our lips, we may quote the provisions of that covenant and hold God pledged to fulfill them. See Heb. 8:8ff.

LUKE 22:24–34

Disciples Who Grieve Their Lord. It is probable that this dispute about priority took place on their entering the supper room. It could hardly have taken place after the tender scene of John 13. But doubtless the irritated feelings which that contention engendered prepared the way for the testing, sifting, and ultimate fall of Peter. It is the little waves that eventually become the mighty billows which wreck the big ships and engulf human lives.

Satan cannot assail us until he has asked and obtained permission, v. 31. God does not tempt, though he permits us to be tempted, as in the case of Job; but with the temptation there is always a way of escape, if we wait on him, 1 Cor. 10:12, 13. How often does our Lord anticipate our trial hours by his prayers, v. 32! We owe it to them either that we do not fall, or that having fallen we turn back. This is the best use we can make even of our failures; they teach us humility, pity, and how to help others. How little do we know ourselves! See vv. 33, 34.

LUKE 22:35-46

Drinking the Cup for Others. Our Lord knew to what he was going. All lay naked and open before his eyes. He laid down his life of himself; but in this supreme act of love he suffered beyond words. It was not that he feared physical pain, but it was the horror of standing before the universe identified with the sin and sorrow of the world, as though these were his own.

In these instructions to his apostles, as to wallet, purse, and sword, we must understand that he meant them to realize that the storm was about to burst upon them with furious intensity.

Some think that our Lord prayed most of all that his body should not give way under his awful anguish. He feared lest he should die before he could reach the cross! See Heb. 5:7. O my Lord, thy chosen disciples failed thee in that hour; but so have we! What can we say! Help us to share thy vigil and thy prayer!

LUKE 22:47-53

"The Power of Darkness." It may have been about midnight when the lights and movement of feet indicated the approach of Judas and his band. The kiss of Judas was probably intended to hide his treachery from his fellow-disciples, but it did not deceive his Master, who even in that sad hour sought to touch his heart, v. 48.

When Malchus' ear was almost severed from the body, it was needful that our Lord should interpose, because if Peter had been arrested, the gaze of mankind would have been diverted from the spectacle of Christ's atonement, and a struggle might have ensued at the gate of the garden which would have justified the worst accusations of the high priest.

The quiet remonstrance with which the Lord met that ruffian band, reminding them of their cowardice in the daylight and amid the crowds, was followed by his submission to be led "as a lamb to the slaughter."

LUKE 22:54-62

The Disciple Who Denied His Lord. Peter loved Christ truly, but miscalculated his strength. Be very careful not to venture into the midst of temptation. If God leads you thither, that is another matter. We do well to remember Ps. 1:1-3. Let us beware of warming ourselves at the world's fires. It was the firelight falling on his face that revealed Peter, and his brogue that betrayed him.

If even at that hour, however, he had looked to God, a way of escape would have been found. "He delivereth and rescueth, and he worketh signs and wonders in heaven and in earth," Dan. 6:27. But Peter sought to save himself from the results of his folly and sin, only to land deeper and deeper in the morass.

What a look that must have been, v. 61! But even now, when we sin Christ looks at us from out of his holy Heaven with such mingled pity and love that these constitute the worst torment. There is no need of literal fire to make hell. Disappointed love is hotter than "coals of juniper."

LUKE 22:63-71

"Rejected of Men." This scene of mockery is very terrible. How difficult the twelve legions of angels must have found it to restrain themselves. See Matt. 26:53. Here we have an exhibition of the hidden evil of the human heart, which is drawn forth in contact with infinite purity as the stench of stagnant water is elicited by the summer sun.

Our Lord answered not a word to all the false accusations that were leveled against him. He left the false witnesses to refute each other. But as soon as his divine claims were challenged, he could not keep silence. It is very noticeable that in this Gospel, which lays such stress on Christ's pure humanity, Luke makes it so clear that the unwavering affirmation of his equality with God was the cause of his death, John 5:18. Is there not a sense in which the eye of faith always beholds him seated at the right hand of God's power?

LUKE 23:1-12

Silent under False Accusations. The Jewish Sanhedrin, hastily summoned at the hour of dawn, having elicited from Jesus the profession of his Messiahship and deity, and having agreed on the death sentence, set themselves to induce Pilate, the Roman governor, to concur in their verdict. In order to do this, they claimed that Jesus imperiled the Roman supremacy.

Pilate was accustomed to deal with men, and after careful examination was satisfied that there was no ground for the death sentence. "I find no fault." As God's Paschal Lamb, the Savior was searched to discover if there were spot, or blemish, or anything that could invalidate his claim to sinlessness. Only the sinless could save sinners. In his heart Pilate knew that our Lord should be acquitted, but his fear of the Jews deflected the verdict of his conscience. By sending the case to Herod, he hoped to get the right thing done, without incurring the odium incident to doing it.

LUKE 23:13-25

Barabbas or Christ? Herod's moral nature had become almost extinguished by a long course of immorality and cruelty. While the Baptist lived, Herod had done many things and heard John gladly; but when the beheading of this faithful witness on his own orders had taken place, the royal sinner went headlong to ruin. He treated this incident with Jesus with flippant levity. The gorgeous raiment, being an imitation of the royal apparel of the Jewish kings, may have suggested the inscription affixed to the cross.

By giving the people the alternative of Christ or Barabbas, Pilate expected that they would certainly choose the former. To his dismay, this second effort to salve his conscience without endangering his reputation failed. So he drifted and sold his soul for power. Each of us has to choose between Christ and Barabbas, between the self-surrender of the cross and brutal selfishness. Barabbas must have stolen to the cross in the afternoon and said, as he stood there, "He hangs where I should have been. I am saved by his death."

LUKE 23:26-34

"They Crucified the Lord of Glory." Simon's two sons are believed to have become Christians. See Mark 15:21; Rom. 16:13. Perhaps this strange interruption in his ordinary experiences led to the whole household becoming Christian. Jesus and he bore the cross together.

So later, Symeon of Cambridge, who was much reviled for his evangelical principles, loved to think that he and Christ were suffering together.

Ever more thoughtful for others than for himself, the Lord seemed to forget his griefs that he might address warnings and entreaties to these poor women, v. 28. He was the young green tree in the forest glade, consumed in the awful heat of divine burnings, while they and theirs were the dry wood which would soon crackle in the overthrow of their city.

On the cross our Lord became immediately the High Priest, pleading for the world and for his own, and he has never ceased since. See Heb. 7:25. Sins of ignorance are placed in a different category from those of presumption. See 1 Tim. 1:13; 1 John 5:16. The answer to that prayer, v. 34, was given on the day of Pentecost.

LUKE 23:35-46

Saving Others by Not Saving Himself. Rulers, soldiers, and malefactors all heaped their insults on the dying Lord, little realizing that they were all included in the great love which was pouring itself out as the propitiation for the sins of the whole world. It may be that we shall have to share the same reproach, if we drink of his cup and are baptized with his baptism. But God will do for us as he did for Jesus; he will not leave our soul in the grave, nor suffer his own to see corruption, Ps. 16:10.

The signs of renewal, wrought in the heart of the penitent thief, showed the sure work of the Holy Spirit. These were: the fear of God, the sense of justice in his suffering, the confession of evil deeds, the recognition of our Lord's sinlessness and dignity, and the anticipation of his coming kingdom. We may begin a day under the dull skies of earth and close it where there is no need of sun or moon. See Phil. 1:23; 2 Cor. 5:6. For the rent veil, see Heb. 10:20. Dying saints have often passed home with our Lord's last words on their lips, Ps. 31:5; Acts 7:59.

LUKE 23:47-56

Faith from Unexpected Quarters. God has his agents everywhere. They are not known to us, but are well known to him, and one word from him will bring them and their resources to his help. How many are unsuspected lovers of his kingdom! Who would have thought that Joseph was waiting for the kingdom of God, or that he would have identified its advent with the death on the cross!

The body of our Lord was well cared for. They who commit themselves to God will find

LUKE

that he will make himself responsible for the body, in life to feed and in death to honor. See Matt. 6:33; Deut. 34:6. The new tomb was so ordered that there could be no possible mistake in identifying the precious body, and that the resurrection should be beyond question. Love, which clings to last duties with tender solicitude, hastened to express itself with a devotion that braved the hatred of the rulers. Darkness and silence settled on the scene—but this was not the end.

LUKE 24:1-12

The Empty Tomb. The most perplexing question for those who deny Christ's resurrection is, "What became of his body if he did not rise?" If foes stole it, they would have produced it in disproof of the allegations of the apostles. If friends had taken it, they would certainly have borne it off wrapped in the garments of death; but these were left behind and wrapped together in such an orderly fashion that evidently there had been neither violence nor haste.

Notice the stress that the angels laid on Christ as "living." They had doubtless overheard that sentence of his spoken in Galilee and recorded in 9:22. Too many seek the living Christ amid the wrappings of ceremony and creed. He is not there. He has gone forth, and we must follow him where Easter is breaking.

Women were the first evangelist-messengers of the resurrection. The very ardor of their belief seems to have prejudiced their message; the apostles "believed them not," v. 11. But the orderly arrangement of the tomb proved to Peter that clearly it had not been rifled.

LUKE 24:13-27

Walking with the Risen Lord. This exquisite idyll of the resurrection is too lifelike and natural to have been invented. The sorrowful walk; the reasonings; the wonder that anyone could have been for ever so short a time in Jerusalem without knowing of the events that filled their souls; the lingering hope; the despair that the third day was waning and he had not come; the clue of the morning announcement which had not been followed up; the burning heart—all these touches are full of natural pathos.

How swiftly the seven and a half miles must have sped in such company; and what new light illumined the pages of the Old Testament! All the Bible is full of him, but we need to be shown its meaning. It is only through suffering that we shall come to the glory. But why should not life be one sweet walk of fellowship with One whom we cannot see, but whose presence fills our hearts with burning love until suddenly the veil shall part in twain! See 1 Pet. 1:8.

LUKE 24:28-35

"Abide with Us." Our Lord must be invited and constrained. He will not impose himself on an unwilling host; but how glad he is to enter where a welcome awaits! He turns ordinary meals into sacraments, common rooms into royal chambers, and the homiest things into symbols of the eternal. He sat with them, then vanished; but he was no less truly with them when he ceased to be seen—and all to teach them that when he had passed permanently from their sight, he would be nearer than ever.

When you have had a great vision of the Lord, be sure to tell it. Do not wait in the interior of your own chamber, hugging the joy and comfort of his presence. Hasten back to your fellow-believers. They also have much to tell. This appearance to Simon Peter is referred to by Paul in 1 Cor. 15:5. When men really love the Savior, they will love the ordinances of the Church, the fellowship of the brethren, and especially the holy Supper, where he makes himself known.

LUKE 24:36-43

"Peace Be unto You." Jesus himself is here! We need nothing else when we are terrified and afraid. You may be fearing the consequences of your sin; fearing the approach of your enemy; fearing the future with its unknown contingencies; but Jesus himself is the antidote of fear. He keeps the soul that trusts him within the double doors of peace. See Isa. 26:3.

This was not an apparition, but the clothing of the spiritual body, which evidently repeats the general outlines of the physical body, though in a rarer and more subtle substance. Does this incident not teach us that when we also are clothed in the spiritual body we shall not be wholly dissimilar from what we are today? We shall be recognizable by our beloved and they by us. See 1 Cor. 15:44.

What was it that made those hands and feet distinctly his own, except that the print of the nails was in them? See John 20:27. "In the midst of the throne . . . a Lamb as it had been slain," Rev. 5:6.

LUKE 24:44-53

"Witnesses of These Things." The risen Savior is the key to Scripture. The pages of Holy Writ need the illumination that falls from his face. Whenever you open the Old Testament, de-

scribed here under its customary Hebrew threefold division, be sure to ask him to open your understanding also!

Repentance is turning from sin. It is the act of the will. In remitting sin Christ not only forgives, but stands between the sinner and the consequences.

The "beginning" must be Jerusalem, because the Jew is first in the divine order, Rom. 1:16. But the end is the uttermost part of the earth. We are not called to be defenders, but "witnesses" of the truth. We speak what we know and testify what we have seen. Our fellow-witness is the Holy Spirit, Acts 5:32.

Those outspread hands have never been withdrawn. They are still extended over us in benediction and from Heaven itself rain down perennial blessing. Let us rejoice in him with great joy; may each lowly home be a temple full of praise!

THE GOSPEL ACCORDING TO
JOHN

JESUS IS THE CHRIST

PROLOGUE *1:1–14.*
   The Incarnation of the eternal Word.

I. THE WITNESS OF JOHN THE BAPTIST *1:15–51; 3:22–36.*
   "The voice of one crying in the wilderness"; "Behold the Lamb of God"; James, John, Andrew, Simon, Philip, and Nathanael meet Jesus; "He must increase but I must decrease."

II. THE WITNESS OF JESUS' MINISTRY *2:1—6:71.*
   First miracle, in Cana; cleansing of the Temple; visit of Nicodemus; talk with woman by Jacob's well and work in Samaria; nobleman's son healed; lame man healed by pool of Bethesda; feeding of the 5,000; Jesus walks on the sea; discourse on the bread of life.

III. THE WITNESS OF JESUS' CONFLICT WITH THE JEWISH LEADERS *7:1—12:50.*
   Jesus at the Feast of Tabernacles; dispute as to Jesus' origin; Jesus' claims contested by the Jews, "Before Abraham was, I am"; healing of man born blind; the Good Shepherd; raising of Lazarus; plot of the Pharisees to put Jesus to death; Jesus anointed in Bethany; Greeks meet Jesus; the voice from Heaven; the commandment of the Father.

IV. THE WITNESS OF JESUS' SUFFERINGS, DEATH, AND RESURRECTION *13:1—20:31.*
   The Feast of the Passover; Jesus washes the feet of the disciples; a new commandment; withdrawal of Judas; the Father's house; the Comforter; the true vine; the Spirit of truth; the high priestly prayer; the betrayal; trial before Caiaphas, before Pilate; the crucifixion; burial; visit of the women to the tomb; appearances of the risen Lord; purpose of the Gospel.

EPILOGUE *21:1–25.*
   Jesus' manifestation to his disciples by the Sea of Galilee; catching fish; special commission to Peter; author's final note.

INTRODUCTION

This is the "eagle" Gospel. It soars into the heavens with steady wing and searching gaze. The Church has attributed it with consistent tradition to the hand of the Apostle John. The style and spirit and method of thought are so evidently his. There was, indeed, no one else in the first century who could have written it and remained unknown.

Clement of Alexandria says that it was written by the apostle at the earnest solicitation of his friends, and that he was led by the Spirit of God to compose a Gospel which would unfold much that the Synoptic Gospels had omitted.

It was probably written during the last decade of the first century, at Ephesus. It is evident that Jerusalem had already fallen, and that Gnostic heresy was already rife. It fell to the lot of the apostle to give this last conclusive demonstration that Jesus was the Son of God, 20:31. It is interesting to study the development of the strife between faith and unbelief as they became more and more pronounced in respect to the Person of our Lord.

COMMENTARY

JOHN 1:1-13

Light and Life. The titles of our Lord are set forth in royal fashion. As speech reveals the hidden thoughts of men, so does our Lord utter the unseen God. God spake and it was done. His words preceded the act of creation, but Christ was the Word or utterance of God. He who created time preceded time, and that which is before time is eternal and divine. Christ is the organ or medium by which God goes forth in creation, Providence, and redemption. The life of God was stored in the human nature of Jesus, when the Word became flesh, that it might more readily pass into us. True life is always light, as the minute *infusoria* of the ocean are phosphorescent. When we receive Christ's life, we shine.

Men are still sent from God, as John was, to bear witness to Jesus; but there is also a witness to him in the breast of man. We call it conscience, or the inner light. The blinded world knew him not. Indeed, John 9 is a parable of mankind's condition, 2 Cor. 4:4. Believing and receiving are the same thing. Let Christ in, and you have instantly the right to call yourself a child of God, Gal. 3:26. Only God can impart to us the germ of that life, which we share with the Son himself, Jas. 1:18.

JOHN 1:14-28

The Voice of Promise. Note that the words "was made" can be translated "became," v. 14. Evidently Jesus had existed before this becoming; and evidently there was a process of self-limitation. "Dwelt" is "tabernacled." As the shekinah light was veiled by the curtain of the Tabernacle, so the divine essence in Jesus was veiled by his humanity, though it shone out at the Transfiguration. He was full of "grace," the unmerited love of God; full of "truth," coming to bear witness to it; full of "glory," that of the only begotten Son. There are many sons, but only one Son.

What a beautiful testimony John the Baptist gave! He was not the Christ, not Elijah (except in spirit), not the expected prophet, but just a voice, announcing the Christ and dying away. He was content to decrease before the greater whom he had been taught to expect and was sent to herald. There is a sense in which the preacher of repentance must always precede the Christ. There must be a putting away of known sin previous to the recognition of the Lamb of God. But how great must Christ be when so noble a man as the Baptist felt unworthy to unloose his sandals!

JOHN 1:29-34

Witness Borne to the Son of God. John's description of Christ gave answer to Isaac's inquiry,

Gen. 22:7. Let us not narrow the extent of the gospel. By the grace of God Jesus tasted death for every man, 1 John 2:2. Though they knew it not, the Messiah had stood on those banks, had mingled with those crowds, had descended into those waters, and was standing among them at that moment. But their eyes were blinded. The new era had already dawned.

The general reader of the story of our Lord's baptism probably supposes that the sign of the descending dove and the sound of the Father's voice were apprehended by all the crowd. This, however, was not the case. John had been previously informed that someday one, indicated by those signs, would come to his baptism. John was the porter of the door of the fold, and it was necessary to certify the true Shepherd when he appeared, John 10:3. To our Lord this was the beginning of his ministry. The heavenly powers were opened to him, which he was in turn to open to all who believe and cooperate with him for the regeneration of the world.

JOHN 1:35-42

How Jesus Wins Followers. On this third day John again looked eagerly and wistfully on Jesus as he walked. He spoke of him again as God's Lamb, and there was a significance in his words that was instantly detected by the two disciples —probably John and Andrew—who stood beside him. He intended to transfer their allegiance from himself to the Lord. Henceforth they were to behold *him.* So, at least, they understood it. We are told that they followed Jesus. As the preacher watched their retreating figures and realized that his work was done, he had no feeling of jealousy or regret. He was the Bridegroom's friend and rejoiced greatly to hear his voice, John 3:29. Notice how our Lord develops men. He invites them to his familiar friendship—"Come and see," and he looks deep down into their hearts, detecting capacities and possibilities that were hidden even from themselves, but which he helps them to realize: "Thou shalt be called Cephas," a "rock."

JOHN 1:43-51

The Doubter Becomes a Disciple. The apostles were attracted to the Master in different ways. Some came to him through preaching, as when John proclaimed his title and sacrifice. Others were brought through human relationships. The record does not say how many Andrew brought to Jesus, but we are told that he at least brought his own brother. Others were brought by the Master's direct personal influence—"he findeth Philip." Still others were brought by the call and ties of friendship, following on a long course of previous preparation. Philip had often crossed the hills that separated the lake from Cana, where Nathanael dwelt, and the two would earnestly discuss the signs of the time: the desperate straits of their country, the preaching of the Baptist, and the Messiah's advent. The guileless Israelite would sit beneath his favorite fig tree, pondering over the things which Moses and the prophets had written. It was not difficult to win such a man when Philip broke in on him with the news of their discovery.

Jesus is always showing us "greater things," v. 50. He leads his disciples onward and upward, for he is himself the ladder of ascent to God.

JOHN 2:1-11

Jesus Blesses Social Joys. The key word here is "miracles," or "signs," v. 11. They are windows into the eternal purpose. The Lord loved to join in simple human joys. "He came eating and drinking." He honored marriage by his first miracle. The wine had to fail, as the earthly and human always must, in order to make room for the eternal and divine. Like Mary, we are impetuous and would hasten the divine actions; but God is ever deliberate and waits for the exact hour before he interposes. It is hardly likely that our Lord made 130 gallons of wine; but as the servants drew and bore it to the table, the wondrous change was wrought. Our Lord did in a moment what he is ever doing, transforming dews and rain into the nutritive and gladdening juices of Nature.

Here was indeed a sign that the Master desired to sweeten and enhance human happiness, and that his influence could transform what was ordinary and common into the joyous and sacramental. It was his glory to show that religion is consistent with ordinary life, and to teach that God increases our joys from less to more, and still more. The best is yet to be.

JOHN 2:12-22

Right and Wrong Uses of God's House. This market was established in the Temple courts, and many evils were associated with it. The animals were sold at exorbitant prices, which made the dealers only the more covetous. The moneychangers made considerable profit in supplying Jewish coins—which alone could be offered in the Temple service—in exchange for Roman and Greek money. Our Lord's presence was august, his soul being aflame with the passion of zeal for his Father's honor. The consciences of those who offended were smitten by the contrast between that holy zeal and their own eagerness to barter.

Our Lord's reference to his body as the true temple is very impressive and interesting. The apostle refers to it in 1 Cor. 6:19. As Jesus cleansed the Temple, so he can cleanse our hearts. When he comes to dwell within us, he finds our hearts desecrated by unholy things which he quickly casts out. He sits as a refiner of silver; his fan is in his hand, and he thoroughly purges his floor. Our Lord's reference to the destruction of his body, by the act of the Jewish leaders, and to his resurrection, proves that from the first he had his sacrifice well before his eyes. In the next chapter this becomes the more apparent.

JOHN 2:23—3:8

New Life from Above the Need of All. A solemn question is suggested by v. 24. Can Jesus trust himself to us? We must show ourselves worthy of his trust. In Chapters 3 and 4 we have two remarkable instances of the Lord's intimate knowledge of the human heart.

Apparently Nicodemus had shrunk from identifying himself with John's baptism. He was one of the richest men in Jerusalem, and our Lord addressed him as "the teacher," v. 10, margin. He was willing to talk about systems of truth and schemes of philosophy. But the Master knew that more, much more, was necessary; there must be the emergence of his soul into the experience of an enlarged and fuller life. The phrase, "the new birth," the Jews always used for Gentiles, and it greatly startled Nicodemus to learn that there was needed for himself the same change as was required by Gentiles before entering the Jewish commonwealth. In speaking of water, our Lord probably refers to the baptism of John, in which men confessed their sins and expressed their desire to leave the past behind and to enter a fuller experience of the life of God. The new life begotten by the Spirit of God is as mysterious as the wind. That Spirit, bearing the germ of a new life, rejoices to enter each open casement and to fill each vacuum, wherever one allows it.

JOHN 3:9-21

Love's Great Gift: Received or Rejected. Though physically on earth, our Lord was spiritually in touch with the heavenly realities. He was living among them and bore witness to them. Notice that "must," v. 14. He was the Lamb slain from the foundation of the world, and the divine purpose of redemption would fail unless he fulfilled his part in the eternal compact. That which had been resolved upon before the foundations of the hills were laid must be carried out in all its terrible detail. He must be accounted as a sin offering, and go forth as a scapegoat. He must tread the winepress alone and pour out his soul unto death. Yet he was not rebellious, nor did he turn back. He rejoiced to do the Father's will. For the joy that was set before him, he endured the cross.

Redemption originated in God's great love. Notice the pairs in v. 16: "God" and the "Son"; "loved" and "gave"; "the world" and "whosoever"; "believe" and "have"; "not perish" but have "life." The judgment is already in process, and the turning point with each who has known the gospel will be his attitude toward the light he has enjoyed. Evil men avoid the light, as an inflamed eye the sun. No true heart fears Christ, and on coming to him it discovers that unconsciously it has been wrought upon by God.

JOHN 3:22-30

John Shows the Greatness of Humility. It is expressly stated in 4:2 that Jesus baptized through his disciples. This controversy arose with a Jew who was comparing the respective baptisms of John and the Lord. Perhaps he stirred John's followers with jealousy as he contrasted the crowds that gathered round the new teacher with the waning popularity of the old. But the Baptist had no sense of being aggrieved. His answer is one of the noblest ever made by human lips: "My work has been definitely assigned to me. It has been enough for me to fulfill it. The rapture of the Bridegroom and his success in wooing hearts is not for me. It is enough to behold his joy. He must increase, and I must decrease, but I sorrow not. Indeed, my joy is filled to the brim because of his success."

What a blessing it would be if we could enshrine in our hearts this immortal maxim: "A man can receive nothing except it be given him from heaven!" What we have is God's gift; let us hold it reverently. What another person has is God's gift to him; we have no right to find fault with his dealings with another of his servants. Our orbits are distinct; all we have to do is to shine our brightest where he has placed us, confident that he knows best.

JOHN 3:31-36

A Witness to Be Trusted. Let us all seek to live more habitually in Heaven, that is, in contact with the spiritual world. To do our best work in the world it is not necessary to be great in argument or rhetoric, but simply to bear witness of what we have seen and heard. It is true that the natural man will not receive our testimony. Paul found that out in later years, 1 Cor. 2:14. But where our witness is accepted by the spiritually-minded, another seal is placed upon it as being the truth of God. Notice also that when a man is sent on God's errand and speaks God's Word, he can count on the supply of God's Spirit without stint. There is no careful measurement of how much or how little. For long years and to any extent, he may count upon God.

Note the present tenses of the last two verses. They are as true today as when first uttered. Our eternity dates not from our dying moment, but from that in which we first trust in Jesus Christ. If you can do nothing else, be willing to trust him as soon as he is revealed to you, and in the meantime obey him; that path will bring you into the open.

JOHN 4:1-14

Satisfying an Eternal Thirst. Our Lord had no wish to precipitate the conflict with the Pharisee party until he had finished his ministry to the people. He was the last and greatest of the prophets, as well as the world's Redeemer. He therefore withdrew from the metropolis. Here is another "must," v. 4. There were three in the previous chapter and there are two in this. It was not necessary for Jesus to go through Samaria except for the purpose of mercy to one soul. Jacob's well is still visible, at the entrance of the green valley up which Sychar lay. "Thus," v. 6, that is, as a tired man would sit. It was noon. The time when women usually drew water was in the evening, but there were special reasons why this woman came by herself. The love of God overleaps narrow restrictions of sex, sect, and nationality. Two conditions, v. 10, precede our reception of God's best gifts: we must know, and we must ask.

The living water is not a stagnant pond or well, but leaps up from a hidden spring. The woman keeps referring to the "well," Jesus to the "spring" in the well. That alone can satisfy. Not the Word, but the Spirit in the Word. Not the rite, but the grace it symbolizes. Verse 13 might serve as the inscription on all places of worldly amusement. Ponder that word "be" or "become," v. 14. You first drink for your own need; then you help to meet the need of others.

JOHN 4:15-26

The True Worship of the Father of All. What a train of memories our Lord's words evoked! A spasm of remorse seized the woman as she remembered the grave within her heart where her first love lay buried, trampled down by the wild crew of later passion. But why awaken such memories? Why open the cupboard and bid that skeleton step down? It could not be otherwise! Christ was there not to enter into an argument, but to awaken the dormant conscience and save. The woman evaded the sword thrust, but she realized that she was dealing with a master hand in the spiritual realm. Hence her question about worship. This led to one of the greatest sayings ever uttered on earth—that God is spirit. That he is ever searching for true worshipers, that he is indifferent to places and nationalities and method, that we cannot worship until we live in the spirit realm and are willing to conform ourselves absolutely to truth—these thoughts have revolutionized the religious thinking of mankind. They have not yet fulfilled their mission, but they bear witness to the unique supremacy of the Christ.

JOHN 4:27-38

The Rewards of Service. As soon as Jesus opens the living spring within our hearts, we abandon our water pots. When we are saved, we must hasten with the tidings to those with whom we have sinned. First find Christ for yourself; then say, "Come and see." He who knows us with an unchallengeable knowledge cannot be other than the Christ.

The disciples were naturally astonished when they came upon this interview. They might have asked the woman what she was seeking, and the Master why he was talking to her. But they were silent; the awe of God was upon them. Their natural care for their beloved leader led them to press on him the provisions they had purchased, but they were destined to learn that the soul may be nourished in obeying the will of God. The whiteness of the harvest appeared in the crowds that were coming down the valley; but at harvesttime we are sometimes apt to forget the sower who passed home without seeing the result of his labor. That is not the divine method. The sower is rewarded for his share, as the reaper for his—they rejoice together.

JOHN 4:39-45

The Growth of Faith. There are many ways of coming to know Christ. In some cases he comes to us, as to the woman by the well, and reveals himself in a direct and illuminating manner, so that the soul can never afterward entertain a doubt as to his reality or its own experience. In other cases, the report of some associate or friend is the arresting and converting factor. Many Samaritans "believed on him for the saying of the woman." There was a light in her eyes, a radiance in her face, a strength and dignity in her bearing that convinced them. There was yet another section of the Samaritans who watched and listened as Jesus tarried with them. They heard him for themselves and were convinced that he was indeed the Savior, not of the Jews only, but of the whole world.

Our Lord could not remain among this interesting people, for his mission was primarily to his own nation. He therefore proceeded on his way to Galilee, not to Nazareth where he was so well-known, but as appears in the following paragraph, to Cana of Galilee, where he was welcomed because of the marked impression that he had already made in the metropolis.

JOHN 4:46-54

The Reward of Trusting Jesus' Word. The particular interest of this beautiful incident is in v. 50. The father had such faith in our Lord's promise that he started off at once on his homeward journey, needing no further assurance that all was well. It would appear, indeed, that he went to some inn or caravansary on his way back, because there would have been ample time between the seventh hour (one o'clock in the day) and nightfall to get from Cana down to Capernaum. Why should he hasten! The boy was living, doing well, since the Master had said so. He was sure of it and thanked God for it and gladly took the opportunity of a quiet night's rest, to sleep off the effects of long watching, intense anxiety, and the swift journey to Cana. When his servants met him with the news that the boy was healed, he inquired at what hour the change had taken place, merely to corroborate his own conclusions. What a happy family that was! This nobleman may have been Chuza, Herod's steward, Luke 8:3, or Manaen, Herod's foster-brother, Acts 13:1. Why should we not have the same simple faith in the word of God's promise!

JOHN 5:1-9

Weakness Made Strength. An interval of some months lies between the previous chapter and this, in which many of the incidents of our Lord's Galilean life took place. John does not touch on them, because they had been described in the Synoptic Gospels and because he wished to concentrate all his force on the great conflict which our Lord waged in Jerusalem, the stronghold of Jewish prejudice. He also chose the incidents which led to our Lord's discourses and served as the text of the Gospel.

The pool of Bethesda had medicinal properties. It was an intermittent spring. There must have been something in this man who lay at its brink which specially attracted Jesus. He saw that he had faith to be healed, and therefore made a direct challenge to the will of the sufferer. As soon as the appeal was made, the man opened his heart to Christ's power. Through his expectant faith new energy poured into his being.

Are you a withered soul? Healing and wholeness are in Christ for you. Receive from him the power that waits to flow through your wasted muscles. Believe that it is passing through you, and act accordingly. Spring to your feet, roll up your bed, and carry that which has so long carried you.

JOHN 5:10-18

Sabbath Work That Pleases the Father. In the foregoing incident our Lord not only healed the sufferer after thirty-eight years of deferred hope, but did so on the Sabbath, and bade him carry his bed home. This clashed with Pharisaic proscriptions; but the man was of course right to infer that he who would work so great a miracle was greater than either the Pharisee or mere ritual. The religious leaders of that time, like those of all time, could not tolerate the setting up of an authority superior to their own, by one who was outside their ranks; so they accused Jesus of Sabbath-breaking. His judges, however, were little prepared for his line of defense, which revealed the depths of our Lord's inner consciousness. First, he spoke of God as his own Father, making himself God's equal. See Phil. 2:6. Second, he said that God was working through his life and had energized him to perform that miracle of healing. It was not his own deed, but the Father's in him and through him. If, then, they condemned it, they were in direct collision with the Infinite One from whom the Sabbath law had originally come.

JOHN 5:19-29

The Father Working through the Son. The relationship of our Lord to the Father was such that he felt himself competent to fulfill all the functions of the Divine Being. Is it God's prerogative to raise the dead? It is also Jesus Christ's. "The Son quickeneth whom he will," v. 21. Is it the divine right to be the judge of man? It is also the Redeemer's right. See v. 22. Is it the peculiar attitude of God to be the fountain of life, so that life, inherent, underived, and perennial, is ever arising in his nature, sustaining here an angel and there a hummingbird? This is also an attribute of our blessed Lord. "So hath he given to the Son to have life in himself," v. 26. The entire sum of the attributes of Deity are resident in the nature of the Son of man. But though all divine attributes were his, and might have been called into operation, he forebore to use them, that he might learn the life of dependence and faith, the life which was to become ours toward himself. He did nothing apart from the Father, v. 19ff. No vine ever clung more closely to its trellis, and no child to its mother than he to the Father. See Gal. 2:20; Heb. 12:2.

JOHN 5:30-38

Jesus' Works His Sufficient Witness. The one desire and purpose of our Lord was to do God's will. We cannot penetrate the mystery of his ineffable being, but clearly, so far as his human nature was concerned, he had a will which could be denied and subordinated to the Father's. See 5:30; 6:38; Luke 22:42. It meant shame, a breaking heart, a soul exceeding sorrowful, the cry of the forsaken; but he never swerved. He clung to it as to a handrail down the steep dark staircase that led to Calvary. Let us live according to God's will. It feeds the spirit, 4:34. It clears the judgment, v. 30. It gives rest and tranquillity to the heart, Matt. 11:29. It is the key of certain and assured knowledge, 7:17. It introduces us into a great circle of others, who in the past and present, in Heaven and on earth, are living with the same purpose. Our Lord cites as allies John the Baptist, v. 36, the Scriptures, v. 39, and Moses, v. 45. Choose this life policy! There is no other way! Remember that God's will is goodwill, and that his love is endless and changeless.

JOHN 5:39-47

Willful Rejection of Truth Condemned. Our Lord was accused by the Jews of Sabbath-breaking. There were many grounds on which he might have claimed exoneration, but he forebore to use them. He dwelt on these things very lightly, lest he should direct men's attention to himself, his one aim being to bring glory to his Father. In utter self-oblivion, in distinct refusal to act on his own authority—that is, to come in his own name, with the one desire to reveal the inner source of his life, Jesus said, "I am come in my Father's name," v. 43. Let us learn not to be too careful of our own reputation, standing, or honor, but to live at firsthand, taking our orders and the power to fulfill them direct from Christ. Too often we consult this man's opinion and that person's whim, and our course becomes tortuous and uncertain. What new interest we should take in the Pentateuch if we really believed, v. 46.

JOHN 6:1-14

The Multitude Satisfied with Food. In this chapter we have a further illustration of John's method in selecting for his purpose the miracles which became the texts of our Lord's discourses. These multitudes had evidently gathered on their way to Jerusalem to celebrate the Passover. The imminence of that great festival, when the worshipers not only sacrificed but partook of the slain lamb, gave point to much that our Lord said after this memorable feeding of the multitude.

Christ often tests us to see what we shall say and do in the presence of overwhelming difficulty, but he always knows the way out. We at once begin to calculate our paltry resources and to confess their inadequacy. We come back to explain that when we have done our utmost, we can provide very little. Then he steps in, determined that everyone shall be "filled," with an ample supply left over. He makes his guests sit down in comfort on the grass, because there is plenty of time, as well as an abundance of food, for a happy and comfortable meal. We must bring him what we have, however slender; must enter into his great plan and arrange the people for the banquet; must distribute the food and gather up the broken pieces. The world is to be fed by the cooperation of Christ and his Church.

JOHN 6:15-21

Jesus Brings Peace to Troubled Hearts. The most conclusive proof that our Lord was no weak fanatic or enthusiast is afforded by the calm spirit which refused the eager impulse of the crowds to make him king. Here the temptation of the wilderness was repeated, and only one who was filled with the unwavering determination to do God's will could have refused this shortcut to the Messianic empire. Notice these withdrawals of our Lord to the calm of Nature's stillness and the bosom of God. If he needed such spaces of undisturbed meditation and communion, surely we do.

He knew when he pressed the disciples into the boat that the night would be full of storm, but he did not hesitate to expose them to its peril; he was conscious of his ability to turn that storm to the highest use by coming to their help. His advent is often delayed, but he always comes. Delays are not denials. He is as near in the storm as though already in the boat. The storm waves are his pathway. Be not afraid! The people hurried across the lake in the early morning, conveyed in the boats which had come to take them off; but as Jesus sorrowfully perceived, their object was to receive his gifts and not himself.

JOHN 6:22-29

Insincere Seekers of Truth. The mention in v. 23 of Christ's giving thanks recalls the vivid impression made by that solemn act, and the great importance which those who witnessed it attached to it. When the multitudes disembarking on the other side of the lake found Jesus there, though they knew that he had not accompanied his disciples in the one boat that left the farther shore on the previous night, his presence had the effect of an apparition. See v. 25. Our Lord's answer to the question of the crowd deals with the motive that dictated it. He exposed the spurious and carnal impulses that actuated them and contrasted the satisfaction of natural hunger, v. 26, with that true and effectual seeking which leads to the nourishment of the spirit, v. 27. What a difference between these people with their gross aspirations and carnal desires, and the spiritual Israel which could say with the psalmist, "My soul thirsteth for God, for the living God." All the labor described in v. 27 is to maintain a pure heart and exercise an appropriating faith. God sealed Christ by his declaration at the water of baptism and the miracles which were wrought through the Father's power, 14:10-12.

JOHN 6:30-40

The Father's Will Jesus' Law of Life. On the day following, our Lord had to encounter, first, the demand of the people for a continuation of the miracle of the preceding night, v. 25-40; second, the murmur of "the Jews," that is, their religious leaders, vv. 41-51; third, the growing heat of his opponents, vv. 52-59; and lastly, the failure of many of his disciples, vv. 60-71. But his mountain prayer had prepared him, v. 15.

The manna was only a type of his mission to meet the hunger of the human spirit for truth and love and hope. He is the true bread from Heaven, God's best gift (of the reality of which all material substances are but emblems), not only satisfying passing hunger but imparting life, and only waiting to be appropriated by any that will. Let us come to him, turning from all else. To come is to cease to hunger; to trust is to lose our thirst. Jesus suffices for Heaven; shall he not suffice also for earth? Note the identical clauses of v. 37. All whom the Father gives to Christ come to him; and all who come to him prove that they are included in the Father's gift, bestowed before the worlds were made. See 10:28, 29; 17:6.

JOHN 6:41-51

The Food of Eternal Life. That phrase, "the last day," was constantly on the Master's lips, vv. 39, 40, 44, 54; 12:48. It is an indefinite expression for those final scenes in which the history of our race is to be consummated through resurrection and judgment. Jesus lays great emphasis on his resurrection as completing his work for those who come to him. It is not enough to impart eternal life. That would bless the spirit, but leave the body untouched. And he cannot rest until the whole of our complex nature shares in the emancipation and fullness of his salvation. A transfigured manhood and a glorified body must be the crown of his service to his own. By his mighty power, he will raise them up in the likeness of his glory, that they may share his royal and exalted state. Nothing less will satisfy him, or undo the ruin that sin has introduced. Let us feed on Christ, by meditation on his words and by communion with himself, of which the sacred Feast of the Lord's Table is a perpetual reminder. Notice that every soul which is taught of God will recognize Christ, v. 45!

JOHN 6:52-59

Eat and Live. In v. 57 our Lord gives the secret of his inner life. At the beginning of his ministry he told the tempter that man did not live by bread alone, but by God's Word. Here he goes further and says that he lived not only by the words of God, but by God himself. There is also this other truth, that each of us is called to exercise toward Christ the same attitude and dependence that he exercised toward the Father. It is impossible by one illustration to set forth the eternal facts of the spiritual world. Metaphor has to be heaped on metaphor. Already our Lord had dealt with the symbol of manna and bread; he now goes further in order to emphasize the truth that the power to communicate life can only be acquired through death. Our Lord, therefore, describes the bread of the soul-life as his "flesh," which he would give for the life of the world. Obviously "flesh" is that which has passed through death. But it should always be borne in mind that the Christian soul does not dwell exclusively on the death of Jesus, but on the *life* of him who died. It is the risen and ascended Christ, who died for our sins but whom God exalted to his right hand, that should fill our thoughts.

JOHN 6:60–71

The Sifting of Jesus' Followers. The teaching of this chapter involves a deliberate act of Christ to arrest the revolutionary movement that was gathering around his person and making him its figurehead, v. 15. He therefore set himself to teach that these people had misconceived the meaning of his ministry, which was not intended to raise a standard of revolt against Rome, but to lead to a spiritual revolution. The effect of his words was precisely what he expected, and must have shattered any ambitions that had begun to stir in the hearts of his disciples. In v. 41 the men who the night before wished to crown him murmured at him. In v. 52 they strove among themselves. In v. 60 many of his disciples said that his sayings were hard to be understood, and still harder to be obeyed. In v. 66 many went back. And now as the shades of evening began to fall and the synagogue was almost empty, he was left alone with the little company of twelve, who had sorrowfully watched the overthrow of their hopes. Christ's pathetic question—"Will ye also go away?"—elicited from Peter a reply which proved that the inner meaning of his words had already broken upon their souls. "Thy words give us and nourish within us the eternal life."

JOHN 7:1–13

Known by Our Attitude toward Jesus. This feast was celebrated in October. Six entire months had elapsed between this and the preceding chapter. During the Feast of Tabernacles the people dwelt in tents made of boughs, on the roofs of the houses, and in the open places in or around Jerusalem. The rites of the fast recalled the miraculous interpositions of the Exodus. Water was poured forth each morning in the Temple to recall the smiting of the rock. Two candelabra, lighted each evening, represented the luminous cloud which lighted the Israelites by night. The brethren of Jesus are named in Matt. 13:55, of whom James afterward became chief pastor of the Jerusalem church. They could not deny his miracles, could not understand why he did not lead the popular movement that was ready to follow, and urged that he should at least give the authorities at the capital an opportunity of examining his claims. They felt that things had reached a point where there ought to be no standing still. Jesus could not explain the reasons that actuated him. He knew that his open challenge to Jerusalem would mean his death; but there was yet further work to be done before his time should come. Let us use our time according to the divine plan.

JOHN 7:14–24

How to Know the Truth of Jesus' Word. Jesus now went up to the feast, not because he was prompted by the worldly policy suggested by his brethren, but because he was led by his Father's will. We must be on our guard against unspiritual advisers, and must wait till the hour- and the minute-hands of the clock have reached the precise moment of the Father's appointment.

Here is an easy method of ascertaining whether our Lord's words about God, himself, and the future are merely the words of a human teacher or are really God's. Be willing to do as he says! Stand prepared to fulfill whatever is revealed to your mind and witnessed to by the inner Voice! Live with your face toward the dawn, for though it tarry long it will certainly break. See 3:21. Faith in the gospel does not come by logic, but as the result of obeying the highest truth that you know. Follow on and your path will lead you out to where Jesus stands, the revealed Son of God and the Savior of men. The old quarrel as to the miracle wrought at Bethesda on the Sabbath was still alive, vv. 22, 23. His critics did not hold that the Mosaic Law was violated if a child's submission to the Jewish initiatory rite was performed on the Sabbath. How foolish, then, to blame Jesus for an act of mercy and healing!

JOHN 7:25–31

The Unavoidable Christ. The freedom with which Jesus preached arrested the attention of the people in Jerusalem, and many wondered whether the cessation of hostility indicated a tacit admission on the part of the authorities that Jesus was what he claimed to be. But they were deferred in arriving at this final conclusion by the consideration that the origin of the Messiah would be unknown, v. 27. Jesus answered this objection in vv. 28 and 29. He says in effect: "What you say is true. The Messiah's origin is not known. But my origin is unknown, because it is from God, whom you, notwithstanding your profession, do not know. I know him, but to you he is only a venerable Name." The knowledge of the birth at Bethlehem and the lowly family of Jesus will not explain the mystery of his Person or the secret of his influence on men. All that can only be accounted for by his divine glory as the "only begotten" of the Father. His hearers immediately recognized the greatness of these claims, which appeared to them blasphemous, though to us they are the literal truth. While the adversaries of Jesus were strengthened in their purpose, his friends were confirmed in their faith. Verse 31 is a decided advance upon v. 12. See 2 Cor. 2:16.

JOHN 7:32-39

A Spring of Life-giving Water. "The natural man receiveth not the things of the Spirit of God." The truth of that saying clearly appears in the earlier part of this section. When the Lord spoke of returning to the Father, his hearers supposed that he was proposing to visit the Jews of the Dispersion. But how profound are these words of promise to those who come to him! He is not content with speaking of a river. He uses the plural—"rivers" shall flow from him. Add stream to stream, torrent to torrent, river to river, and these will barely suffice to set forth the freshness and abundance of life that shall proceed from the soul that previously had been thirsty for its own personal supply.

When our Lord ascended, he received from the Father the promise of the Holy Spirit, and then a new era broke on the world. The life of the believer was no longer only an imitation of obedience. It was the uprising and outpouring of the Holy Spirit from within. We become strengthened with might in the inner man, and Christ dwells in our hearts by faith. Thereupon we not only are infilled of the Spirit, but it is his gracious ministry to mankind through us that makes the desert rejoice and blossom.

JOHN 7:40-53

The Blindness of Prejudice. These short descriptions of the impressions made on his hearers by the discourses of Jesus indicate the double development which was resulting from his ministry. Those in favor spoke of "the Prophet" and "the Christ." Compare John 1:21; 6:14. Others raised objections, vv. 41, 42. Others again desired to take action, v. 44.

Though it was a holy day, the Sanhedrin was in session to receive the report of their officers. These, by their candid statement, unconsciously passed a strange criticism on the religious speakers to whom they were wont to listen. Compare v. 48 with v. 50 and Chapter 3.

How greatly Nicodemus had grown since his night visit to Jesus! And he was to advance still further, 19:39. The appeal to history was apparently true. Jonah is the only prophet who might have been quoted as an apparent exception, but he may only have been a resident in Galilee when the summons came to him. The reasoning of v. 52, however, was not conclusive. Even if none had arisen, it was the more likely that the Divine Spirit should choose the most humble origin, and the one most in keeping with the peasant birth of the manger bed.

JOHN 8:1-11

The Accusers Self-condemned. This passage has been the subject of much controversy, but there is no possibility of accounting for it except on the supposition that this incident really took place. It reveals in our Lord's character such tenderness, wisdom, hatred of sin, and insight into the heart of man that it is impossible to suppose that any evangelist could have invented the story.

The sinner's way of treating sin is to regard it as a case for curious speculation, and an opportunity for contrasting with it the immaculate virtue of the accusers. They take prurient pleasure in enumerating the terrible details, but give no sign of pity or shame for the sinner. *The Law's way of treating sin is to stone.* The executioner shows no mercy. The offender falls beneath the Law's curse and penalty. *The Savior's way of treating sin is to forgive.* In that bowed head and hidden face, v. 10, we learn how much sin costs him. But it is easy to hear his words of forgiveness, and to go forth from his presence with the assurance that "there is now no condemnation to them which are in Christ Jesus"; but we shall never know how much sin has cost him. That silent, averted gaze has made men bow their heads and beat upon their breasts.

JOHN 8:12-20

The Twofold Witness. On either side of the Temple court stood a huge golden candelabrum. On the first and each succeeding night of the week of the Feast of Tabernacles these were lit, and they poured a brilliant flood of light over the Temple and the city. It was to these that our Lord alluded in v. 12. They were symbolic and were intended to recall the pillar of cloud which led the pilgrim march through the desert, and at night disclosed a heart of illuminating fire. Our Lord compared himself to the manna in Chapter 6, to the smitten rock in Chapter 7, and to the cloud here in Chapter 8, v. 12.

What the pillar of cloud and fire was to Israel, Jesus will be to his Church and the individual soul. See Exod. 13:21; Num. 9:15-23.

The fire in the cloud was prophetic of his deity enshrined in his humanity. It was this consciousness of the union of the divine and human that enabled our Lord to speak as he did of himself. There was no egotism or self-assumption in his claim. It was the literal truth. He bare record of himself, because he could say nothing less, and knew whence he came and whither he went; and the miracles which he wrought in union with the Spirit of God ratified his witness.

JOHN 8:21–30

The Father Made Known in His Son. Our Lord was absorbed in acquiring glory for his Father. He was sent by the Father, lived by the Father, could do nothing of himself, and spoke only as the Father taught him, v. 28. He could dispense with all human help and stand alone, because the Father never left him, v. 29. To honor him, please him, work his works, live in his love was the passion of his life, vv. 29, 49.

There was a mystery in all this that baffled the men of his age. They were from beneath; they lived for worldly aims, were governed by earthly motives, and sought for the praise of men. His life was spent in fellowship with Heaven. But to us there should be no mystery. We, too, should aim to do the will of God as the supreme goal of life. Our aims and ends are too low. The conversion of the unsaved, the upbuilding of the Church are excellent, but they should be included in the sweep of a wider circle. Aim at the planet and you miss the sun; aim at the sun, and you include the planet. Our one intention should be that God be magnified in our bodies, both in life and death. But for this we must be willing to take up the cross and follow Jesus in his lifting up.

JOHN 8:31–38

The Source of True Liberty. Sin is not a necessary part of our being. "The servant abideth not in the house for ever." Your child is an integral part of the household; he has become one with it. However far he travels, he can never break the link of indissoluble connection. But it is different with a servant, especially under the provisions of the Levitical law. In like manner, a man may have served sin, but though tightly held, it has no necessary rights over him. The trumpet of Jubilee may sound, and he may go free. It is not freedom to do as we like. Jesus sets us free from the trap and birdlime, that is, from the unnatural conditions fastening and confining us from being what God meant us to be. The swallow would not thank you to be freed to live on carrion, but only to mount again into the sunny air.

Jesus frees us by the truth. The slavegirl will no longer serve in the house of her cruel oppressor, when she learns that the act of emancipation has passed and he has no longer any claim upon her. When we understand that we are accepted and triumphant because of our union with Christ, we begin to exercise our privilege and to draw upon the grace which he has made available. Thus we become free.

JOHN 8:39–47

The Test of Sonship. Godly ancestors and parents will avail nothing, unless we are animated by their spirit and do their works. There were in the old world two families that ran in parallel lines—that of Cain and that of Seth. See Gen. 4 and 5. The Cainites were citizens of this world; the Sethites were pilgrims of the eternal. The one family finally reached such a level of wickedness that they were swept away by the Flood, while the other furnished the world with an Enoch that walked with God and a Noah who was perfect in his generation.

This distinction has continued down the ages, and is not only accentuated by these words of our Lord but by 1 John 3:12, 15. In Eph. 2:2, those who walk according to the course of this world are walking according to the spirit that works disobedience in men's lives. It becomes us, then, to see to it that we are not deceived. We may never have plunged into such depth of sin as overwhelmed the men of that generation; and yet if our hearts are steeped in the love of this world, which is passing away, we betray our affinity to evil and not to good, to the devil and not to God, Eph. 2:2.

JOHN 8:48–59

The Eternal Christ. It is absolutely true that the Christian disciple does not see death as the king of terrors or as a grim monster. Jesus has robbed death of its sting; he has destroyed him that had the power of death. The moment of death is the moment of birth into a wider and happier existence. We are set free from this body of mortality and become possessed of the house not made with hands, eternal in the heavens. The grave is the vestibule of Paradise. We know that the iron gate opens into the city of God. Absent from the body, we are present with the Lord. The moment of transition is so desirable that it is only comparable to the falling asleep of the tired laborer.

The Father glorified his Son by the attestation given at the baptism and the Transfiguration, by the resurrection from the grave, by the exaltation to his right hand. Yet these are but stages in the glorification of our High Priest. The full outburst of his glory is yet future. We shall behold the glory with which the Father has rewarded his obedience unto death; nay, we are to share it with him. See John 17:22, 24. Notice the I AM of v. 58. Compare Exod. 3:14.

JOHN 9:1-12

Jesus Opens Blind Eyes. At the close of the previous chapter our Lord bore the contradiction of sinners against himself. The Jews had caught up the stones gathered to repair the Temple, in order to inflict the doom of the blasphemer; but Jesus passed through them unscathed and began to descend the great steps. To human gaze there was need for Jesus to hasten from his foes, 8:59; in *his* thought there was greater need to heal this blind beggar. In the most leisurely manner, therefore, he made clay and wrought this miracle of sight. His heart was at rest in God. No great thing is wrought by those who live in perpetual ferment. Through the quiet heart God works his own works, and there will be time enough to get them all done before "the night cometh, when no man can work," v. 4.

Our Lord perceived that beneath the unpromising exterior of this man were elements of nobility, which he set himself to elicit. The clay which the man found suddenly applied to his eyes awakened wonder, hope, expectation, and faith. It was a ladder by which he climbed from the pit of despair to the mount of joy. The walk to Siloam was a further venture of faith; but there were other steps to be taken ere he attained to the full stature of his discipleship. Some were forced on him by opposition; to others he was led by Christ himself.

JOHN 9:13-25

The Testimony of Personal Experience. The jealous Pharisees now set themselves to discredit the miracle and to throw suspicion upon the witness. But their hostility, prompted by jealousy and vindictiveness, forced the healed man to realize the moral majesty of Jesus. His eyes became opened to the true values of things, as well as to the world of Nature. In one day he had grown far away from the parents, who were simple people unaccustomed to the glare of publicity and very much afraid of these religious magnates.

It is marvelous to note this man proving himself more than a match for his opponents, and answering them with a simplicity and a majesty that confounded them. See Matt. 10:19. He needed, however, a touch that no human wisdom could impart, and this was given by Christ, who always seeks those whom man casts out and those who dare to live up to the truth they know. Notice the steps: "he is a prophet; he is not a sinner; he is from God; he worshipped him." None come in contact with Christ without being blinded or enlightened. Our guilt is proportioned to our refusal of the light.

JOHN 9:26-34

Willful Blindness. What a contrast between the opening and the closing of this chapter! The blind sees! The beggar is enriched! The outcast on the Temple steps is a worshiper in the temple of the spirit! And how vast a contrast to the deterioration at work in the hearts of these professedly religious men! From the mouth of a babe in the divine life God can elicit strength to quell the enemy and the avenger. "O God, our God, how excellent is thy name in all the earth!"

The man's judges cast in his teeth the lifelong deprivation from which he had suffered, as a conclusive evidence of his sins. This was the common Jewish interpretation of such a calamity, v. 2. Our Lord, however, taught that suffering is permitted to befall for wise and good reasons which are compatible with the character of God, and it provides a platform on which the grace and power of God may manifest themselves, each new phase of evil leading to a fresh manifestation of the power and love of God. How often he seems to say, when we are perplexed with the world's sin and sorrow, "These things are not unto death, but to manifest the works of God." Look not at the pain, but at its results! See what humility and patience God gives; wait to see the harvest of these sowings!

JOHN 9:35—10:6

"A Stone of Stumbling." In v. 35 we hear of Jesus finding the outcast whom the Pharisees had excommunicated. This story is appropriately followed by a picture of the true Shepherd as contrasted with the false. At night sundry flocks are brought to the Eastern sheepfold and committed to the care of the keeper or porter. In the morning the shepherds knock at the barred door of the enclosure, and the porter opens from within. Each separates his own sheep by calling their names, and when thus summoned the flock follows its shepherd, wherever he may lead.

The sheepfold in this parable holds the Jewish people. The stranger is the religious teacher who fails to speak in the familiar phrase of Moses and the prophets. The Pharisees and scribes are the thieves and robbers who have stolen God's glory and made profit of his flock. Note that whenever you are put forth, you will find Christ going before.

God has sent many true shepherds from his presence-chamber, to care not only for individuals or churches, but for nations.

JOHN 10:7-18

Jesus the Good Shepherd. He who came in by the door which John the Baptist opened has become the door. It stands open to all comers—"if any man." The salvation here mentioned refers to the entire process of soul-health: go "in" for fellowship; go "out" for service.

Wherever destruction is uppermost in speech or act, you may detect the presence of the great enemy of souls. Christ is ever constructive, saving, life-giving. Let us not be content until our life has become "abundant" life. Our life cost the Shepherd's life. He did not hesitate to interpose himself between the sheep and the wolf of hell. There is possible between our Lord and ourselves an intimacy of knowledge which can be compared to nothing less than that which subsists between the Father and himself.

Note how our Lord looked beyond the hurdles of the Jewish fold and thought tenderly of the Gentile sheep that were far away. In the revelation committed to the Apostle Paul he gave vent to his love, and through the succeeding centuries he has ever sought them. There may be many folds, but there can be only one flock. Men die because they cannot help it. Christ was born that he might die; he died because he chose to.

JOHN 10:19-30

Our Assurance of Safekeeping. Our Lord did not shrink from the avowal of his divine origin and glory, when there was need or when they were challenged. See John 4:26; Matt. 26:64. For the most part, however, he wished men to exercise their own faculties of discernment and to accept him, not because he told them what he was, but because they were inwardly convinced.

In v. 27 we have three characteristics of his sheep—to hear, to be recognized by him, and to follow; and in v. 28 there are also three privileges which they enjoy—to possess eternal life, never to perish, never to be snatched away by man or devil.

Note the safety of those who really belong to Christ. They are not only in his hand, but in the Father's, because the Father and he are one. "Your life is hid with Christ in God." Here is a double protection. They may wander far, lose joy and comfort, fall on dark and stormy times, but he is responsible for them, will seek them out, and bring them home. This also is true—that our relationship with Jesus involves our relationship with the Father. But if any should presume to live carelessly because of this divine grace, it is clear that such a one is not one of Christ's sheep.

JOHN 10:31-42

The Works of the Father. In the strongest terms known to the Jews, our Lord insisted on his oneness with God; and they understood his claims, threatening him with the penalty of blasphemy. This quotation from Ps. 82:6 was originally addressed to magistrates, and our Lord argued that if unjust judges were described by this phrase, because they exercised the divine prerogative of judgment, surely his opponents had no right to stone him when, as the Sent of God and sanctioned by God's witness in his works, he spoke of himself as the Father's equal and fellow. See Zech. 13:7 and Phil. 2:6. But their vindictive hate would brook no parley; and as his hour was not yet come, Jesus deemed it better to go beyond Jordan into hiding until the minute-hand should reach the exact figure on the dial.

There was a special reason why he was attracted to the region beyond Jordan. It was the place of John's early appearance. That ground had been black with crowds; those waters had witnessed countless baptisms. All that wonderful past trooped back to memory, and the people remembered John's words as they saw in Christ their precise fulfillment. We may work no miracle, but let us speak true words about Jesus Christ.

JOHN 11:1-16

Jesus Faces Death for His Friend. Sickness enters homes even where God is honored and loved. It is permitted because it affords an opportunity and platform for his delivering help. We should see to it that the Son of God is glorified in our physical weakness, either because of our patience and fortitude, which are ministered by his Spirit, or by the deliverances which he grants. See 2 Cor. 12:1-9.

There is a special emphasis on "therefore" in v. 6. Christ lingered because he loved. He allowed the worse to go to the worst, that the sisters (and the world through them) might receive a testimony to his saving power, which could be obtained at no less cost than their brother's death, vv. 9-11. As long as the heart is bathed in the light of God's presence and is conscious of living on his plan, it cannot be mistaken in its decisions and it will not stumble. Our Lord knew that he must go to Bethany, and that he would be safe because the hour of night had not arrived.

Since Jesus came to us, death has become a mere shadow of its former self and is to be dreaded no more than sleep. Had the Lord been beside his dying friend, he could not have borne the entreaty of the sisters; but now there was room for a faith-compelling miracle on his part.

JOHN 11:17-27

Jesus the Resurrection and the Life. His step may linger, but Jesus comes at length. While he seems to tarry, he knows each sigh, pang, and tear that escapes from the sufferer and his friends; and when he arrives, he does more than we asked or thought. He raises not the sick, but the dead. He makes the darkness of the tomb the background to set forth the resurrection glory. He turns tears into jewels, as the sun does with dewdrops. In later days the three would not have wished it otherwise. They would review it all, as we shall our life from the hilltops of heavenly glory, with the cry of "Amen, Hallelujah." "Amen" is the reverent assent of the will; "hallelujah," the glad ascription of praise. If we die before his Second Advent, we shall still live; if we live to see it, we shall be changed in a moment into his likeness.

Note that majestic consciousness of "I am," v. 25. None ever spoke like this. It is the crown of the eight "I ams" of this Gospel. He is unchangeably the same. All who have lived are living still in him. When you stand by the grave where your cherished hopes lie buried, still dare to affirm that he is the Christ, the expression of the love of God.

JOHN 11:28-35

The Sympathy of Jesus. It is not to be wondered at that the sisters and their friends wept as they stood beside the grave; but why did Jesus weep? He knew what he had come to do. He had come for the express purpose of turning their tears into joy. He wept for human frailty—that man's life is a handbreadth and his years as a tale that is told. He wept in sympathy with human sorrow, because he realized that the scene in which he was taking part was a sample of myriads more. He groaned, as in v. 33, as he beheld the evidences of death's grim power. Death had entered the world with man's sin, and Jesus felt the wrongfulness of Satan's usurpation. The anarchy that had invaded human life stirred his soul to its lowest depths. The wrong under which man bled wrought in him an anger which was without sin. He still stands among our groups of mourners, touched with the feeling of their sorrow; but they are not tears of weak sentiment, but of a noble pathos that hastens to help with a divine sufficiency. It has also been suggested that Jesus wept because he was calling a soul back from the land of glory to sojourn once more in the garments of mortality.

JOHN 11:36-44

Victory over Death. The Lord had been praying about this matter before he came to the grave: "Father, I thank thee that thou hast heard me." Notice that past tense. Perhaps he had done so when he first received the news of Lazarus' sickness. He had prayed and had received the assurance that his prayer was answered. When he started back across the Jordan, it was with the full assurance that Lazarus would be raised to life. He was conscious, also, of a life of unceasing prayer. There was unbroken and constant cooperation between him and the Father. He always did the things that pleased God, and God was always answering him. This, also, might be our constant experience. Christ made this prayer that those who stood around, as they saw the effect of prayer, should understand that prayer alone can work great miracles, which become the credentials of Christ and of all who love and obey him. His people similarily can do great miracles as missionaries, Christian workers, and philanthropists.

JOHN 11:45-57

The Innocent for the Guilty. The friends of the family who had come to lament with them were disposed toward Jesus and believed; but the mere spectators hastened with the news, to inflame the hatred of the Pharisees. The Romans dreaded the power acquired by permanent office, and often exchanged one high priest for another. Hence the expression, "being high priest that year." By his vote Caiaphas may be said to have appointed and sacrificed his victim, who in that memorable year was to bring in everlasting righteousness and to cause the sacrifice and oblation to cease. See Dan. 9:24, 27.

Caiaphas professed to fear that Jesus would presently gain such an ascendancy over the people as to lead a revolt against Rome, which would cause a deluge of blood in which the whole nation would perish. Therefore, he recommended that they should effect the death of Jesus. But, as the evangelist puts it, he spoke more wisely and truly than he knew, because the death of Jesus is gathering into one the children of God who are scattered abroad—that is, the heathen who were living up to their light, as in John 10:16—that of the twain, he might make one new man.

JOHN 12:1-11

Love's Fragrant Gift. Martha's service reminds us of Luke 10:41. The earlier Gospels (Matt. 26; Mark 14) do not mention Mary's name, probably because the whole family might have suffered for their intimate identification with Jesus; see v. 10. But when this Gospel was written, the beloved trio had been gathered home to God.

There was no value in the spikenard except to refresh and comfort, but this was sufficient to warrant Mary's act. We must not always be considering the utilitarian side of service. There are hours of holy ecstasy when we are lifted out of ourselves in the expression of our love to Jesus, in ways that to cold and calculating onlookers seem mere extravagance. In her absorption in him whom she loved, Mary has incited myriads to similar acts. But her love stirred up the evil in the heart of Judas, as summer's lovely sunshine extracts poison from stagnant ponds. Our Advocate will screen us from our dread accuser. He interpreted Mary's motive. She knew that her Lord would be crucified, and as she thought that there would be no opportunity for love to perform the last offices, she beforehand anointed him for the burial.

JOHN 12:12-19

The Tribute of the Multitude. This multitude of enthusiastic lovers of Christ were principally from Galilee. They had already reached the city, but hearing of his approach they went forth to meet and accompany him. They were proud to own him as their prophet, and were profoundly touched by the wonderful miracles he had wrought among them. It was a foretaste and glimpse of that yet gladder outburst when he shall be recognized as the King of men. The lowliness of Jesus' estate should have allayed the suspicion and hatred of his foes. What had they to fear from such a King! But the gladness of his followers maddened his adversaries, who saw with unconcealed vexation the spontaneous loyalty given by the crowds to Jesus, as contrasted with the strained obedience which was yielded to their prescriptions and exactions. Another element in the crowd was contributed by those who had witnessed the raising of Lazarus.

Religious jealousy is deplorable. It leads to murder, if not by the cross, by the lips. It embitters the heart, separates and divides those who ought to love, and hinders the coming of the kingdom. The cure of hatred and jealousy is the admission of Christ to the heart-citadel as king.

JOHN 12:20-29

Sacrifice—a Law of Life. These were genuine Greeks. The East came to the manger bed, the West to the cross. These men came to Philip, probably because of his Greek name. The inarticulate cry of the human heart, whether East or West, is for Christ.

The request of these representatives of Western civilization reminded our Lord of his glorious enthronement as the Savior and Lord of mankind; but he realized that the dreams of the prophets could be fulfilled, and the demand of the world met, only through his death and resurrection. There was no other way to the glory than Calvary and the grave. If his love for men was to bear much fruit, he must fall into the ground and die. Death is the only way to Saviorship. Death is the only cure of loneliness, and the necessary price of fruitfulness.

All through life we must be prepared to erect altars on which to sacrifice all that hinders our highest service to our fellows. The soul that dares to live in this way finds streams flowing from every smitten rock, and honey in the carcass of every slain lion. Day out of night, spring out of winter, flowers out of frost, joy out of sorrow, fruitfulness out of pruning, Olivet out of Gethsemane, life out of death. But through it all, our aim must be that the Father may be glorified.

JOHN 12:30-41

Belief May Become Impossible. The question of the Greeks led our Lord's thoughts to his death. He saw, too, the baptism of suffering through which his followers must pass. From all this that troubled him, he fled to the Father, asking only that all should converge to his glory. That request was immediately answered in the affirmative. Thus he was led to give this amazing interpretation of the events which were taking place, as viewed from the standpoint of Heaven. The age, not he, was being judged. It was standing before him for its verdict, not he before it. Caiaphas, Pilate, and the rulers of the age were passing before his judgment-seat and being judged as worthless. The prince of the age, Satan, not Christ, was being cast out, though the sentence might take long before fully realized. Little as they recognized it, the day of the cross was the crisis of the history of earth and hell, of men and demons. Then was settled the question of supremacy between darkness and light, between hate and love, between death and life. "Lifted up" recalls 3:14. The cross is the divine magnet, and our attitude with regard to it shows what we are. Learn from vv. 35, 36 the order of transfiguration into the sonship of light: believe in the light, walk in the light, and you will become "children of light."

JOHN 12:42-50

The Commandment of the Father. The fear of being cast out of the synagogue was a very real one, John 9:22; and the yoke laid on Israel by the Pharisees was a very crushing one. Only a very few, like Nicodemus and Joseph of Arimathea, could withstand it. Let us see to it that we set the promotion of God's glory above any thought of ourselves. We must "confess" Christ if we would experience his saving grace. See Rom. 10:10. To reject Jesus was nothing less to Israel than to reject God himself and his Word. Such a supreme act of rebellion could not fail to draw down unexampled judgment.

In vv. 48-50 our Lord unfolds to us the significance of his words. They will be the sole criterion at the day of judgment. He will apply to each of us the rule laid down in his teachings, which were purely and simply the reflection of his Father's mind. In every sentence he acted on the Father's mandate; hence his words were capable of quickening and regenerating his hearers. What a marvelous effect would be produced on the world if all ministers of Christ would utter what they had received!

JOHN 13:1-11

Jesus Glorifies Humble Service. In the Temple the laver preceded the brazen altar. It was kept filled with pure water for the constant washing of the priests, Exod. 30:18-21; Lev. 16:4. We cannot have fellowship with Christ at Calvary or on Olivet unless we draw near with our hearts sprinkled from an evil conscience and our bodies washed with pure water.

The Synoptic Gospels tell us that on their way to the feast, the disciples had yielded to contention and pride. It was needful that these should be put away, and our Lord's love was equal to the occasion. He loved them to the end of his life and to the end of love. Only such love could have made saints and apostles out of such material.

Jesus "began" a work which has never ceased, and which will continue "till all the ransomed Church of God be saved to sin no more." When we have contracted guilt, we have not to begin our whole life over again, but to go back to the place where we dropped the thread of obedience and begin there.

JOHN 13:12-20

The Master's Example. Notwithstanding his great humility, Jesus expects to be regarded as Master and Lord; do we so call and treat him? We must be as willing to obey him as a soldier to obey his commanding officers, even when the order conflicts with his comfort, convenience, or safety. We must also do for each other, in our poor measure, what he has done for us, taking on us the form and work of a slave, that we may remove from each other any stain that may have been contracted. It is only when we have stooped to the simplest and lowest humility that we are able to lift our brethren to a purer and nobler life. Let us watch over each other's souls, as those who must give an account.

What sorrow must have constantly weighed on our Savior's heart in knowing that all his love and care would be resisted by Judas, as the rock in a flower garden refuses to respond to the genial influences of spring! To "lift up the heel,"—that is, to kick—is emblematic of brutal malice. This treachery, foreseen by Christ, was transformed into a support of the disciples' faith. When the incident took place, as predicted, they knew that Jesus was all that he had declared himself to be.

JOHN 13:21-30

Kindness to the Traitor. In the circle of the twelve, Judas represented the carnal idea of the Messiah, which was directly opposed to the spirit just manifested in the washing of their feet. If he would not humble himself and renounce that spirit, Judas must depart; and a great sense of relief must have been experienced by our Lord, and to an extent by them all.

The people of the East lay rather than sat at table, each guest having his left arm on a cushion so as to support the head, the right being at liberty for eating. Thus the head of each was near the breast of his companion on the left.

Such was the place of John with regard to the Master at the Last Supper, and it was easy to whisper the inquiry of v. 25. In the course of the Paschal meal, the father would offer to the guests pieces of bread dipped in a sauce of fruit, representing the fruits of the Promised Land. It was a sign of special attention and was one more appeal to the conscience of Judas. He might yet have found pardon. But John saw, as his attention was attracted to him, a change pass over his features, which indicated that the traitor had finally cast the wavering balance on the side of Satan.

JOHN 13:31–38

The Sign and Seal of Discipleship. It was a relief when the traitor was gone. The Lord could now speak freely of his love and of his approaching glory, speaking at length about the shining tablelands, but not as yet revealing even to Peter the dark ravine which separated him from them, and the shadows which he was already entering. Peter was most anxious to be with Jesus wherever he was. Life without Jesus seemed impossible.

Peter relied upon his strong resolution to keep him faithful to his Master, but found it unavailing, as we have ourselves experienced many a time. Do not vaunt in self-confidence what you will or will not do, but seek strength from the living Lord. How little we know ourselves! Yet the time would come when this ardent spirit would be able to fulfill its vow through the Spirit of Pentecost, John 21:18; 2 Peter 1:14.

JOHN 14:1–11

Jesus, the Way, the Truth, and the Life. As he neared the end, our Lord could speak of little else than the Father. Heaven was his Father's house, where a prepared mansion awaits each of us, perfectly adapted to the peculiarities of our temperament. The yearning of the heart of man was truly set forth by Philip in his request to see the Father; but never before had it dawned upon human intelligence that the divine can find its supreme revelation in the simplicities and commonplaces of human existence. While Philip was waiting for the Father to be shown in lightning and thunder and the splendor of Sinai, he missed the daily unfolding of the life with which he dwelt in daily contact. To see Jesus was to see the Father. Nothing could more certainly prove the need of the Holy Spirit, by whom alone we can know the Lord.

JOHN 14:12–24

The Spirit of Truth. There is no adequate translation for the word *"Paraclete."* It may be rendered "interpreter," "comforter," "advocate," but no one word suffices. The Greek means, "one whom you call to your side in the battle or law-court." His advent depends upon the praying Christ ("I will pray the Father"), and upon the praying Church ("ye shall ask"). The Holy Spirit must be a person, or he could not be compared as "another" to Christ. It is characteristic of this dispensation that he shall be "in" us, and his indwelling brings with it that of the Father and the Son.

"We will . . . make our abode." That word "abode" is the same Greek word as is rendered "mansions" in the former part of this chapter. God prepares a mansion for those who believe in Christ, and asks in return that we shall prepare our hearts as guest chambers for him to dwell in. As he enters the loving, cleansed, and believing heart, we hear him say, "This is my rest for ever: here will I dwell; for I have desired it," Ps. 132:14. "My Father will love him." That he should love the world is wonderful, but that he should love us would be incredible, were he not infinite and did he not see us as in Jesus Christ our Lord.

JOHN 14:25–31

Christ's Gift of Peace. Our Lord gives the fourfold basis of his peace: (1) The vision of the Father. Throughout these wonderful chapters he seems able to speak of nothing else. If we lived in the thought and consciousness of God, our peace also would be as a river. Let us wrap that thought around us, as a man his overcoat on a stormy day. (2) Disentanglement from the world. We must stand clear of the ambitions of the world, of its fear and favor, of its craving for wealth and its fear of poverty. The world must have no charms for us. (3) A constraining love, as in v. 31. (4) Obedience to God's supreme authority. When we put the government on his shoulder, he sets up the inward reign as Prince of Peace.

What a contrast to the world's peace, which consists in the absence of untoward circumstances and the possession of material goods! Where the Holy Spirit is, there the peace of God rests. The world may be in arms, death may be imminent, and the prince of this world intent to injure, but the heart which reposes on the will of God is free from alarm and fear. The peace he leaves is that of forgiveness; the peace he bequeaths, that of his own indwelling. "Arise, let us go hence!"

JOHN 15:1-9

The Condition of Fruitfulness. The vine is not able to do its work in the world without its branches; they stretch far from the root, to bear its strength and sweetness to those who stand outside the wall, Gen. 49:22. We need the Lord Jesus, but he also needs us. Without us he cannot bless men as he would. What a sublime thought is here—that Jesus needs something which I can yield him! Service to God and man is possible only through abiding union in him. Let us yield ourselves to be pruned by the Word, that we may not need the pruning of awful sorrows. It is said that three out of five of the vine-berries are cut off that the remainder may attain their full size. How many of our own promptings have to be excised in order that our best fruit may be yielded!

We cannot be severed from Christ, our covenant head, when once we are truly united to him for salvation; but we may cease to abide in him for the supply of grace and power in ministry. Abide in me, says the vine to the branch; do not allow the aperture to become choked, and I will cause the sap to pulsate through thee. "Abide in me," says the Lord, "and I will be in thee strength in thy weakness, love in thy lovelessness, grace and beauty in thy uncomeliness." "From me is thy fruit found," Hos. 14:8.

JOHN 15:10-16

"I Have Called You Friends." We must estimate the Father's love to Jesus before we can measure his love to us. We are told to love one another with the same love, but enabling power is needed or we can never fulfill his command. Our love is not like his, unless it is prepared to sacrifice itself even unto death. "Not servants," but "friends." The first stage is that of the bond servant, who does what he is told not because he understands, but because he has no option. Friendship involves obedience on our part, and on his part the making known of the deep things of God. Even the Son learned obedience by the things which he suffered. It is by implicit obedience alone that we can pass into the closer intimacy of friendship and ultimately of sonship. There is no limit to what the Father will do for those whom his Son calls "friends."

JOHN 15:17-27

Suffering for Jesus' Sake. We have been appointed for the one purpose of bearing imperishable fruit, but our holy service to the world will never be appreciated. The world has its own god and religion. It hates without cause. The more Christlike we are, the closer we shall be identified with his sufferings. There is no limit to the hatred and persecution which the world will vent on those who have ceased to belong to it because of their identification with the Crucified. But through the pitiless storm, we must be glad; there must be no slackening of our love, which will as certainly conquer hate as tomorrow's sun the darkness, vv. 26, 27. In each Christian century there has been this double witness of the Spirit in the Church. The voice of the Church has testified to the living Christ, not arguing but attesting; and to each word of testimony the Holy Spirit has borne assenting witness. Christian apologetics are of less importance than the witness of obscure but Spirit-led lives.

JOHN 16:1-11

The Work of the Spirit. We gain by our losses. It was expedient for the disciples that the Lord should go, because the Spirit's presence was contingent upon his absence. The text needed to be completed before the great sermon could be preached. Christ's work must be finished before the Spirit could apply it. Every phase of human experience centers in him whom the Holy Spirit reveals. Whether it be conviction of sin, or faith, or hope, all of it begins and ends with Jesus. The chief sin of the present age is its rejection of Christ, and it is for this that men are condemned. The assertions of Jesus as to himself are vindicated, and his righteousness is established. His divine mission was proved by his resurrection and ascension. The cross was the scene of Satan's judgment. There the prince of this world was condemned and cast out. His power is broken, though he still does his utmost to intimidate and hinder the followers of Jesus.

The world comes to us first with her fascinations and delights. She comes next with her frowns and tortures. Behind her is her prince. He, however, exists only by sufferance. Meet him as a discredited foe. He has been judged and condemned. For the Church there awaits victory and freedom; for the world, the flesh, and the devil, hopeless defeat—the bottomless pit and the lake of fire. See Jude 7, 8.

JOHN 16:12-24

Looking beyond Present Sorrow. The disciples were terribly overwrought by the events of the last few days, the reversal of their cherished hopes, and the growing darkness and sorrow of the approaching cross. Their physical nature and their minds and affections could bear no more. Sorrow had filled their heart, and the Master declined to describe in further detail the valley of shadow through which they were still to pass. A comparison of the Gospels and epistles will indicate how much our Lord left unsaid. All this remained for the Spirit's teaching, to be communicated to the Church through the apostles. It is thus that Christ deals with us still, apportioning our trials to our strength, our discipline to our spiritual capacity. We long to know God's secret plans for ourselves, and for those whom we love. Where does the path lead which we are treading and which dips so swiftly and abruptly? How much longer will the fight be maintained between Truth on the scaffold and Wrong on the throne? What is the explanation of the mystery of evil, of the sorrow and agony of the world? Jesus says: "My child, you cannot bear to know now. Trust me. I will tell you as soon as you are able to understand." The blindness and limitation of the present time are not worthy to be compared with the glory that shall follow in God's own time. See Rom. 8:18; 2 Cor. 4:17.

JOHN 16:25-33

Good Cheer for Hours of Trial. God still speaks to us in proverbs. We could not understand or receive the perfect discovery of himself. These are but part of his ways, Job 26:14. But in a little while, when the entire mystery of his will has been fulfilled, we shall see him face to face, and he will speak to us plainly about the things that we do not now understand.

There is a close connection between prayer and joy. In the midst of a battle, when the soldiers are weary, if the general rides into their midst to cheer them with hearty words and to assure them that the key to the position is already taken, they fight with the inspiration of victory. So, down the line our Leader and Commander sends this encouragement. Let us carry his peace in our hearts and be of good courage, 1 John 5:4, 5.

JOHN 17:1-10

Jesus Prays for His Own. In Christ's own oratory we hear him pray. There is a tone of expectant faith in this marvelous prayer of assured trust, as if he knew that he was asking what was in his Father's heart and thought. The Lord speaks as if he had already passed through death and were pleading before the throne. He is glad to have authority, only that he may use it to give life.

The Father's gift to Jesus consisted in the men who followed him, the word he spoke, the works he did, the name he bore. How careful the Good Shepherd was of those who had been given to him! He prayed for them, he kept them, he entrusted them as his dying legacy to his Father's care. Though he did not pray directly for the world, he was doing his best for it, in concentrating all his solicitude on those who were to be the messengers of his gospel.

In v. 10 we are reminded of Luke 15:31. The very words which the father said to the elder brother are here appropriated by our Lord; and we are taught that we have the privilege of entering on the same inheritance of grace and power as our Lord had. He won for us, unworthy though we are, the privilege of saying, "All thine are mine." If only we believed this, and lived as children in our Father's house, how different life would become.

JOHN 17:11-17

In the World, But Not of the World. What is "the world"? The inspired definition is given in 1 John 2:16. Enumerating her three offsprings, the apostle goes on to say, "All that is in the world ... is not of the Father," that is, does not originate or proceed from him. We might reverse the proposition and say, "All that does not emanate from the Father, and which is inconsistent with perfect love and purity and truth, is of the world."

The spirit of the world permeates society. All its plans, aims, and activities belong to the present passing show. "Under the sun" is the suggestion of Ecclesiastes. The world has always been in collision with Christ, because his teaching reverses everything that the world prizes. In its beatitudes, its methods of pleasure and acquisition, its view and use of power, and its attitude toward God, the difference is wide as the poles. But its hatred is welcome to the followers of Christ, as proving that they are on the Master's track, and in his fellowship they are abundantly compensated.

JOHN 17:18-26

The Master's Commission. In John 10:36 we are told that the Father consecrated our Redeemer to the great work by which he brought nigh them that were far off, Eph. 2:13. What a scene that must have been when Jesus was set apart to destroy the works of the devil, bring in everlasting salvation, and gather into one family the scattered children of God! In that act we were included. We are bound, therefore, to a life of consecration and devotion to the world's redemption.

True unity is spiritual. When we abide in Christ, we abide in each other. Men do not recognize it, but the spiritual unity exists already. If we are one with our Lord, we must be one with all who are members of his mystical body. In different ages the Church has varied outward organization, but there has always been the unity of the one body, the one flock, the one temple. We cannot make that unity, but we must endeavor to keep it, always remembering it, especially when dealing with our fellow-believers. If we are one on earth, we must be with him forever.

JOHN 18:1-11

Jesus Accepts His Suffering. Our Lord went forth from the city and across the brook Cedron to Gethsemane, but not for the purpose of concealment, as the second verse clearly shows. How characteristic it was that he should meet the band and ask that he should be taken, while the disciples should be permitted to escape! Was not this what he was ever doing—meeting peril, temptation, and death, that the great company whom he was bringing to glory might be saved? What meekness and majesty are here! Meekness—that he should subject himself to the binding thong; majesty—that he should be able to use the unspeakable Name of God "I am," for the word "he" is not in the Greek.

"The cup" probably referred to the anguish caused to his holy nature in being numbered with the transgressors and bearing the sin of many. There was much in it from which his spirit recoiled, but he chose to do the will of God, however the flesh might start and shrink. Let us ever take the cups of life's pain and sorrow direct from the hand of God, not seeing Judas, but the Father.

Joseph told his brethren that it was not they who had sent him to Egypt, but God. David would not have Shimei silenced, because he felt that God had allowed him to utter his anathema. Here our Lord reposes absolutely on the Father, who loved him before the world was made.

JOHN 18:12-18

Fear Undermines Loyalty. Apparently a preliminary and private examination was held while the Sanhedrin was being hastily summoned. The other disciple was evidently John. It was a mistake for Peter to throw himself into such a vortex of trial. His foolhardiness and curiosity led him thither. While the Master was before one bar, Peter stood at another, but how egregiously he failed! In spite of his brave talk, he was swept off his feet—as we shall be, unless we have learned to avail ourselves of that power which is made perfect only in weakness. Peter's fall was due to his self-confidence and lack of prayer. Those who are weak should beware of exposing themselves in places and company where they are liable to fail. Do not warm yourself at the world's fires.

Three lessons emerge from Peter's failure: (1) Let us not sleep through the precious moments which Heaven affords before each hour of trial, but use them for putting on the whole armor of God, that we may be able to stand in the evil day. (2) Let us not vaunt our own strength. We need more than resolution to sustain us in the hour of conflict. (3) Let us not cast ourselves down from the mountainside, unless absolutely sure that God bids us to do so. He will not otherwise give his angels charge to keep us.

JOHN 18:19-24

Jesus before His Persecutors. Annas was the father-in-law of the high priest. For many years he had worn the high priest's robes, and though now he had nominally retired from his office, he still kept his hands on the reins. He was the most powerful factor in the high-priestly circles. He was awaiting the return of the expedition in the hall of his palace, and at once began a preliminary inquiry, in the hope of extracting something on which to base his case against our Lord. Jesus penetrated his crafty purpose, and referred Annas to the army of spies who had been always on his track. There was no anger in Jesus' heart. He desired simply to show how absolutely pure and true his words had been; that though he was exposed to searching scrutiny, yet this secret measure had to be resorted to by Annas to incriminate him. Jesus endeavored to bring his accusers and judges calmly to face their own consciences.

JOHN 18:25-32

Pilate's Weak Evasion. It may be that while Peter was thus denying his Lord, Jesus was passing from Annas to Caiaphas, and in doing so cast on the stumbling disciple that look of mingled sorrow and love which broke his heart. John does not dwell on the trial before Caiaphas, because the other evangelists have already described it, but passes on to tell more minutely of the vacillation and weakness of Pilate. The Roman governor first sought to rid himself of the responsibility of deciding the case. He refused to consider that it came within his jurisdiction, because it seemed connected with some religious dispute involving a technical knowledge which he did not possess. He suggested, therefore, that the Jewish leaders should deal with it under their own statutes. There was no apparent need for Roman law to interfere. When, however, the murderous intent of the high priests emerged, it became evident that their charges against Jesus were of a much more serious character, and Pilate was compelled to give his earnest attention to them. How little he realized the momentous issues to be decided that day!

JOHN 18:33-40

The King of Truth. There was a tone of satire in Pilate's question. "Thou poor, worn, tear-stained outcast, forsaken by every friend in this hour of need, are you a king?" Human ears have never heard more majestic words than our Lord's reply. But when he said, "My kingdom is not of this world," he did not mean that it had nothing to do with this world, but that it did not originate here. It has descended from Heaven and seeks to bring the inspiration, principles, and methods of Heaven into all the provinces of human activity. The one conspicuous proof of its absolutely foreign origin is its refusal to employ force. We do not fight, but sacrifice and suffer for its maintenance. Our Lord therefore hastened to show that his kingdom is based on the manifestation of the truth. There is no soul of man which is pure and true that does not recognize the royalty of Christ, as King of Truth, when it hears him speak.

JOHN 19:1-9

Jesus Endures Contempt. Pilate was convinced of our Lord's innocence, and he adopted several expedients to save his life; he did everything, indeed, except to act with absolute justice and discharge the case. If he had promptly and firmly refused to be a party to the unrighteous act to which the Jewish leaders were goading him, before they could further inflame the popular sentiment, the whole matter would have come to an end. But he let the golden moment slip, and every succeeding hour made it more impossible to retrieve it. The proposal to chastise Jesus; the endeavor to induce the people to ask for him rather than Barabbas; the scourging as an appeal to their pity—all such expedients failed to turn them from their purpose. The governor became more and more afraid. "Whence art thou?" Of human birth or more? Our Lord's silence was his answer. Had he been only of earth, he would never have let Pilate suppose that he might be of Heaven.

JOHN 19:10-17

The Rejection of the King. Pilate's pride was touched by that silence. In his reply our Lord refers to the relative responsibility of those who shared in his condemnation. It was as if he said, "Great as your sin is in forfeiting your position, it is less than the sin of those who have put me into your power." Pilate then became aware of the coil of evil in which he was caught. He was dealing with a matter that touched the unseen and eternal, but the threat to report him to Caesar suddenly brought him back to the earthly and human aspects of the case. With ill-concealed irritation he adopted the phraseology of the priests and cried, "Behold your King!" The Jews touched the lowest depth of degradation when, trampling under foot their national pride, they cried, "We have no king but Caesar!" Pilate signed the necessary documents and retired to his palace as having been himself sentenced.

JOHN 19:18-24

"They Crucified Him." Just outside the city gates, beside the main road, was a little conical eminence which from its resemblance to a skull was called in Aramaic, Golgotha, and in Latin Calvary. As we speak of the brow of a hill, they called the bald eminence a skull. The three languages in which the inscription was written stand for religion, government, and science. Note that every one of us is unconsciously writing his verdict about Jesus Christ; and when once it is written, there is no altering it. We may be forgiven, but the past cannot be obliterated.

The clothes of the crucified went to the soldiers. But Christ's were so poor that they were not worth keeping entire, except the inner tunic, the gift of someone's—it may well have been his mother's—love. What a contrast! Above, the consummate evidence of love working out the plan of eternity; below, the appeal of ignorance and brutality to chance.

JOHN 19:25-30

Jesus' Last Thought for Others. Love made Mary brave to encounter the tragedy of that scene. The sword, as Simeon had foretold, was piercing her soul, Luke 2:35. Jesus knew how lonely she would be. He had neither silver nor gold, but could at least secure her a home and tender care. As the cross was elevated but slightly from the ground, his words could easily reach the little group. He chose the title, "Woman," rather than "Mother," lest identification with himself should bring her insult.

It is to this paragraph that the soul turns when oppressed with the consciousness of guilt. The lighthearted world which has never known the terror of a sinful conscience turns from it as from a tragedy of woe and blood, but the repentant sinner presses from this vintage the wine of life. We stand beside thy cross, O Son of God, and worship in adoring love, as we behold thy tenderness to thy mother, thy devotion to Holy Scripture, and the majesty of thy last cry of victory. "It is finished"— the Savior's work of redemption and the ground of our salvation. What is there left for us, but to hide in the cleft of his pierced side, and to seek the cleansing of the water and the blood?

JOHN 19:31–37

The Pierced Side. How punctilious the Jewish leaders were to maintain each detail of their ritual! Remember that there is a religiousness which is not religion, but its counterfeit.

John solemnly attests the fact of the blood and water. "He knoweth that he saith true." It is referred to again in his epistle, 1 John 5:6, 8. Science tells us that the presence of those two elements was evidence that there had been heart rupture, and that our Lord literally died of a broken heart. But it was also, as devout souls have loved to remember, a symbol of the "double cure" which Jesus has effected: blood to atone; water to purify and cleanse. What a comfort it is that Jesus did not come by water alone! As we come to know ourselves better, we realize that only blood could meet our need. He bowed his head, that we might lift ours up to greet the eternal morning.

JOHN 19:38–42

Love-impelled Services. In that supreme hour Christ's secret disciples revealed their true heroism and carried him to the garden sepulcher. It had been written that the Messiah would make his grave with the rich, Isa. 53:9; that prophecy seemed unlikely of fulfillment until Joseph and Nicodemus stood forth, in the darkest hour, as confessors of their faith and reverence. There are more friends of Christ in the world than we know of. They sit in our legislatures, our councils, and we meet them day by day as we go about our work. Although they give no outward sign of love or loyalty, they are forming secret resolves in their hearts, and the time will come when the fires of their love will burn the bushel that hides it and they will avow themselves on the Lord's side. Let us plead with such, however, not to waste these precious years. How much Joseph and Nicodemus missed of Christ's inner fellowship by this long delay!

It was a royal burial. Love carried the body; sweet spices scented the air; a new-hewn grave received the precious treasure; and angels mounted guard. Remember that wherever the cross of Jesus is erected, whether in the soul for the daily crucifixion of the flesh, or in the life by self-sacrifice for others, gardens will inevitably bloom.

JOHN 20:1–10

The Witness of the Empty Tomb. In considering John's account of the resurrection, we should remember that it is largely supplementary to the other narratives. This Gospel having been written long after those were in circulation, the selection of incidents which are recorded is made for spiritual purposes. John's object was to show various instances of faith in the risen Christ, each one being typical and having its own lessons to teach.

It is Easter morning! What dismay there is in Mary's voice and what consternation in her face! What a mistake also she made, for who can take our Lord away from hearts where he is enshrined! The Greek word used to describe the disposition of the clothes is very remarkable. It convey's the idea that they had fallen together, as if that which they had covered had been suddenly withdrawn.

How much those two disciples missed! Had they only waited, they might have seen the Lord. Do not hurry with wanton haste from the mysteries of our Lord's grave; but learn that on the one hand he was declared to be God's Son, Rom. 1:4, and on the other we are taught the victory of faith even over death, John 11:26.

JOHN 20:11–18

The Joy of the Resurrection. Mary wept with hopeless sorrow, with no thought that Jesus was risen, and anxious only to secure the body of her dear Master and Friend. It is because we know so little of the inner meaning of events which are happening around us, under the hand of God, that we weep so bitterly. What we suppose we have lost is really close at hand, and what we count disastrous is part of the process designed to irradiate our lives forevermore.

In her grief Mary mistook Jesus for the gardener, but who shall say that she was greatly mistaken? Surely Jesus is the Keeper of the Church, which may fitly be compared to a garden. At that moment he had come into it to lift up one drooping flower. She recognized the intonation of his voice, for speech is ever a telltale. In the resurrection we shall hear again tones that we have not heard since childhood. In v. 17 women receive the highest authority for acting as evangelists. Let them tell out the glad news of a love that is stronger than death, and which passes through death undiminished and unchanged. Our beloved are waiting for us in the garden of Paradise. We shall hear and see them, and be with them forever.

JOHN 20:19-25

The Risen Christ Brings Peace. Evidently our Lord was clothed in the spiritual body of which the apostle speaks, not subject to the laws governing physical life. Twice he uttered the salutation, "Peace be unto you." The first time he accompanied his words with the indication of his wounds: "He shewed unto them his hands and his side." This was the peace of forgiveness, falling on conscience-stricken hearts as the dew distills on parched herbage. "Look at the wounds of Jesus!" cried Staupitz to Luther, and there is, indeed, no other sign which can give rest to the penitent. This is the peace of the evening hour, when we come back from the soil and fret of the world and need to have our feet washed and our heart quieted.

The second time the message of peace was accompanied by an injunction to go forth into the world, as he was sent from the Father, on the great errand of world evangelization. Then he breathed on them and said, "Receive ye the Holy Ghost," which shortly after was to descend as a rushing, mighty wind. There is no way of remitting sin but by preaching the gospel of reconciliation, with the Holy Spirit accompanying our message. This is the peace of the morning, when we go forth to our post of duty or danger.

JOHN 20:26-31

Overcoming Doubt. How great the anguish of Thomas during that week, as he tossed between hope and fear and saw on other faces the light which he might not share! At length Jesus came and suited himself to the needs of the perplexed disciple, complying with the conditions that his poor faith had laid down. Jesus was set on winning this one poor starving soul to himself and blessedness.

It is unlikely that Thomas availed himself of Jesus' invitation to reach forth his hand, that he might touch as well as see. Christ's evident knowledge of what Thomas had said, and his willingness to meet it, were sufficient. But as our Lord said, there is a greater blessedness than that which became his. When there is no star on the bosom of night, and no friendly voice in the solitude, to believe then is to get very near the heart of him who on the cross clung to the Father in the midnight darkness.

JOHN 21:1-9

The Miraculous Draught of Fishes. It would almost seem as if the apostles thought that the radiant vision of Christ was withdrawn forever; or did they think that they would glorify him best, and be most likely to encounter him, if they returned to the paths of ordinary toil? This miracle closely corresponds to that recorded in Luke 5, and proves that the methods of the risen Lord are not unlike those of his earthly ministry. Still he stands on the shore in the morning haze to comfort the hearts of discouraged workers, telling them where to cast their net and revealing the certainty of his help. The eyes that love as John loved are the quickest to descry his presence. He thinks not only of our spoils, but of us, and provides for our sustenance and comfort—not bread only, but fish and a fire. Is not this a picture of the believer's death? The plunge into the cold stream of dividing water; the welcome on the other shore; the discovery that Christ had expected and prepared; and the feast with the Lord himself as he girds himself to minister.

JOHN 21:10-19

"Lovest Thou Me?" Christ thrice questioned Peter's love, thus giving him the opportunity of canceling his threefold denial. There are two Greek words for "love." In his questions our Lord chose the higher, while Peter in his replies humbly chose the lower, till in his third question our Lord came down to Peter's level. Christ forecasted the hatred and opposition of the world, and suggested to Peter and the rest that the only way to combat and overcome was in the fervent love that they had for him. Only this could give them the necessary tenderness and delicacy in leading and feeding the flock.

JOHN 21:20-25

The Testimony of a Beloved Follower. Having cautioned Peter, our Lord seems to have moved away, bidding Peter follow—a mandate intended to convey a deeper meaning. John followed some steps in the rear. Hearing footsteps, Peter turned and was seized with curiosity to see how far the future experiences of John and himself would agree. At once, without gratifying his curiosity, our Lord explained that the life-plan of his servants is determined by his will—"If I will." It is equally certain that his arrangements for us are carefully adjusted to our nature, our special characteristics, and the service which we are best able to render. Peter was to be the apostle of the tried and suffering. John was to behold and declare the apocalyptic vision of the Living Church. The one, contrary to his native disposition, wrote the epistle of patient waiting; the other pictured the triumphant advent of the Son of God.

THE BOOK OF ACTS

"YE SHALL BE WITNESSES UNTO ME," 1:8

I. THE CHURCH IN JERUSALEM   *1:1—8:3.*

The ascension; day of Pentecost; Peter and John imprisoned; Ananias and Sapphira; martyrdom of Stephen.

II. THE CHURCH IN JUDEA AND SAMARIA   *8:4—11:18.*

Preaching of Philip; Simon Magus; The Ethiopian eunuch; conversion of Saul; Peter's visit to Cornelius.

III. THE CHURCH IN ANTIOCH   *11:19—13:3.*

The disciples first called Christians; The work of Barnabas; Peter's release from prison; death of Herod.

IV. PAUL'S THREE MISSIONARY JOURNEYS   *13:4—21:16.*

(1) With Barnabas, from Antioch through Asia Minor and return. (2) With Silas, through Asia Minor to Greece, returning to Antioch by way of Jerusalem. (3) Assisted by a number of disciples, through Asia Minor and Greece.

V. PAUL IN JERUSALEM   *21:17—26:32.*

Paul's speech to the people; Paul before the Sanhedrin; sent to Caesarea; before Felix; before Festus and Agrippa.

VI. PAUL SENT TO ROME   *27:1—28:31.*

The voyage and shipwreck; Melita; arrival in Rome; Paul's residence there, with continued missionary activity.

INTRODUCTION

The authorship, by the evangelist Luke, is established by a comparison of the address of his Gospel, v. 3, with Acts 1:1. Luke was eminently qualified for his task by his long and intimate association with the Apostle Paul. The place and hour of the commencement of their happy fellowship are fixed by the change in the pronoun in 16:10 from "they" to "we" and "us." Luke stayed with Paul to the end, 2 Tim. 4:11. During the long periods of Paul's imprisonment, his faithful friend and physician would have had ample opportunity for writing both the Gospel and this book.

The Acts is clearly a continuation of the life and ministry of the Redeemer. As the Gospel tells what he "began" to do and teach, so this treatise continues the story. There he wrought in a mortal body on earth, here in the body of his glory from Heaven. The book is also a commentary on v. 2. We are not specifically informed what the commandments were which our Lord enjoined upon the apostles, but are left to infer them from the ordering of the Church unfolded in these pages.

The division of the narrative is indicated in the enumeration of the widening concentric circles of v. 8: Jerusalem, chapters 1—7; Judea and Samaria, 8:1–12; the uttermost parts of the earth, v. 13 and onward to the end of the book, which has no formal termination, because the Acts of the Holy Spirit by the Church have continued throughout the Christian centuries and are not yet finished. There are some illustrious chapters still to be added by the pen of the angel scribes before the divine program is finished.

COMMENTARY

ACTS 1:1-14

Beginning Afresh. Luke informs Theophilus (the name means "a lover of God") that his Gospel told the story of what the Lord "began" to do and teach. Evidently this further book is a continuation of his deeds and words. It ought to be called "The Acts of the Ascended Christ." The Gospel tells of what Jesus did through a mortal body, and this book what he did through the Church, which is his body, "the fulness of him that filleth all in all." Here we learn that the time between the resurrection and the ascension was forty days; that our Lord issued commandments, no doubt about the ordering of the Church; and that he spoke with the apostles of the coming kingdom of God—that ideal society which is God's great objective through the ages. It would not be established by the sword of the soldier, but by the witness-bearing of the evangelist, v. 8.

Then the Lord rose before their eyes, and passed within a cloud which dropped like a curtain before him. He passed into Heaven, Heb. 9:24, to make intercession, to guide the course of his Church, and to sit at the right hand of the Father till his enemies should be made his footstool.

ACTS 1:15-26

Filling a Vacant Place. It may be that the apostles were acting upon Christ's directions when they proceeded to elect a successor to Judas. There was awe in Peter's voice as he described the traitor as the guide of the arresting band, although he had been numbered with the apostles and had obtained part in their ministry. It was as though Peter felt that it might have been himself. He and the rest had stood at the brink of the precipice over which Judas had flung himself.

Evidently there were favored and humble men who, though they did not belong to the brotherhood, had been allowed to company with the apostles and had been witnesses of the marvelous story as it had been unrolled before their eyes. They were thus able to give their testimony firsthand. What an honor had been theirs! And now one of them was summoned to take the place of Judas. His qualification was his ability to bear witness to the resurrection, v. 22. That was the salient point in the primitive evangel. But cannot we all bear witness to it? What but the resurrection of Jesus can account for the hot springs of religious fervor that arise in our wintry hearts!

ACTS 2:1-13

Speaking in Strange Tongues. The priests in the Temple were offering the first loaves of the new harvest, in celebration of the feast of Pentecost, when the Holy Spirit came as the firstfruits of our inheritance. Suddenly there was a sound that was heard throughout the city. There was no wind, but the "sound" of a rushing, mighty wind. Suddenly, as each looked on the rest, he saw their heads crowned with tongues of flame. Each, too, became suddenly aware of a drawing toward the Lord, of a longing to see him glorified, and of a vast enlargement and enhancement of spiritual joy and power.

When presently the vast crowd collected to know the meaning of the sound, each inspired soul gathered a little knot of hearers, to whom he discoursed of Jesus and the resurrection; and the hearers heard in their own tongue "the wonderful works of God." The Holy Spirit used telepathy of mind and heart, so that involuntarily the speaker clothed his thoughts in language borrowed from his hearer's vocabulary. This was the sign of Babel's undoing.

ACTS 2:14-24

The Outpoured Spirit. The exulting joy of these Spirit-anointed people was accounted for by some through charging them with drunkenness. Peter dismissed the charge as absurd, seeing that the day was yet young. With a readiness that the Spirit had inspired, he declared it to be a partial fulfillment of Joel's prophecy. "This is that," v. 16. Alas, we cannot say as much! This might be that; this shall be that—these are all that we can affirm. Shall we ever be able to say, "This is that"?

In pre-Christian times the Spirit was given to mountaintop saints, but from Pentecost onward sons and daughters, old and young, servants and handmaidens were to participate in his gracious influences. It is for the democracy of the Church, for the whosoevers who call on the name of the Lord, for the valleys as well as the hills.

Notice that God's determinate counsel and prearrangement did not take away the guilt that lay upon the murderers of the Christ. The hands that slew him were "wicked" ones, v. 23. But God vindicated Jesus by the resurrection, which reversed the judgment of men and proved him the Son of God with power, Rom. 1:4.

ACTS 2:25-36

David's Lord and Ours. When one considers the vast result of this address, one wonders at its simplicity. It is almost entirely a string of apt quotations. But what may not the Word of God do when it is wielded by the mighty Spirit! Our Lord might have chanted to himself vv. 26-28 when he descended, step by step, the dark staircase of death. God can never leave us in despair. At our lowest, he is nearest. There are ways up to life from the lowest deeps. David spake deeper than he knew, v. 30. Here is an illustration of 1 Pet. 1:11, 12.

In v. 33 we see the fulfillment of John 14:16. We can almost hear the Father asking what reward he should give the Son for his obedience unto blood, and our Lord replying, "Father, I want nothing for myself, but only that I may receive into my divine-human nature the same fullness of the Holy Spirit that I had with thee before the worlds were made." And it pleased the Father that the fullness of the Godhead should dwell in him bodily, Col. 2:9. Then, because he was united to man by his humanity, he was able to impart to him the fullness of Pentecost.

ACTS 2:37-47

Pentecostal Days. There were no exceptions in Peter's great appeal for repentance. "Every one of you!" he declared. "But I drove the nails into his hands." "Every one of you!" he insists. "But I pierced his side." "Every one!" says the apostle again. And from this motley crowd arose the primitive Church. Notice that those who had gone deep into sin are not required to serve a long novitiate between forgiveness and the gift of Pentecost. In v. 38 the two are combined. Notice also v. 39. Not only Jews, but far-off Gentiles—nay, as many as God shall call by his inward speech and grace are welcome to receive the fullness of the Spirit. Have you received it?

"Unto them," in v. 41, would better be, "unto him." The adding was primarily to Jesus Christ, 2 Cor. 8:5. From the teaching of the apostles these new believers stepped up into fellowship with them, because when we are joined to Christ we become one with all who are his. They still met in the Temple, standing there as one vast host and seeing a new significance in the ancient rites. Their homes and daily meals were also raised to a new level; and every day there were additions of those who had experienced Christ's saving power.

ACTS 3:1-10

Uplifting Power. Peter and John differed greatly in age, in gift, and in point of view. They had been rivals; now they walked together. It was at three in the afternoon that this incident took place. As they climbed the Temple steps, they must have spoken of the many times that the Master had walked at their side. But they realized, too, that he was still as near as ever; and so they became the means of linking this withered man to his glorious health-giving power. It was because Jesus went with them that the healed man was able to become the fourth of the group.

The gate was beautiful, but it could not heal. More is needed than beauty or art. We may have neither the silver of profound intellect, nor the golden speech of Chrysostom, but we must see that we have something to give to a paralyzed and perishing world. Let us so move among men as to lead them to expect that we have something to give, and then give them Jesus. The lame man needed strength, and this is the divine gift of the gospel. "It is the power of God unto salvation." The Savior makes us able to walk and leap in God's ways.

ACTS 3:11-26

Searching Words. Peter's sermon was delivered in the eastern colonnade of the Temple. It derived its name probably from the fact that Solomon's Porch had originally occupied that site. The apostle argued that the gospel which was given them to proclaim was only the flower of the revelations which had been given them through the prophets. How vast the change wrought in this man by the strength and illumination imparted to him at Pentecost! Why should we not seek to be similarly infilled!

How humble—not by their power! How daring—God had glorified him whom they slew! What glorious conceptions of Christ—Prince of Life, holy and righteous! What pity for the ignorance of the Jews! The times of refreshing which are to come on this distracted world depend on the repentance and restoration of Israel. The Jew has the first offer of the gospel, as the child of the covenant; but its wide provisions lie open to us all who by faith have become heirs of the promises made to Abraham. Christ begins his work of benediction for the soul by turning it away from iniquity. "Turn us, O Lord, and we shall be turned!"

ACTS 4:1-12

The Name above Every Name. The Sadducees are particularly mentioned, because they were the agnostics of the age and had no belief in the unseen and eternal. The fact of our Lord's resurrection was, therefore, especially obnoxious to them. The captain of the Temple, who was head of the Levitical guard, was probably their nominee. How weak man shows himself when he sets himself against God! All that they could do was to shut the apostles up; but they could not bind nor imprison the living Spirit or the speech of one saved soul to another, and so the numbers of disciples kept mounting up.

Peter must have contrasted this with his former appearance in that hall. Then he trusted his own power; now he was specially filled with the Holy Spirit for a great and noble confession. The name of Jesus stands for his glorious being. It was because the man had come into vital union with the ever-living Christ that disease was stayed and health restored. The name of Jesus rings through these chapters like a sweet refrain. Evidently he was living and at hand, or the streams of power and grace could not have poured forth to make desert lives begin to blossom as the garden of the Lord.

ACTS 4:13-22

Braving Men To Obey God. Do people realize that there is something about us which cannot be accounted for except that we have been with Jesus? Our company always influences us. A man is known by the company he keeps. Good manners are caught by association with the well-mannered. What, then, will not be the effect upon us, if only we live in fellowship with Jesus! Our faces will shine with a reflection of his purity and beauty; and the ancient prayer will be answered: "Let the beauty of the Lord our God be upon us," Ps. 90:17.

Our converts are our best arguments. "The man which was healed standing with them"—his face radiated the light of a new energy and hope. That fact answered all the sophistries of these Jewish leaders. It was as impossible to stay the effect of that miracle as to bid the sun cease shining. Note the exuberance of the life of God! "We cannot but speak," v. 20. When once we have got the real thing, we cannot and dare not be still; we must speak. As the swelling seed will break down a brick wall, so when the love of Christ constrains us, though all the world is in arms we must bear witness to our Lord.

ACTS 4:23-35

Help from on High. Like draws like; Judas went to his own place, and the apostles to their own company. The best answer to threats is prayer. The apostles' one petition just then was for boldness. They scorned to ask for their own safety; it was enough if Jesus was glorified.

What a note of jubilant triumph was in that glorious prayer, offered by this threatened little band! They realized that they were under the special protection of God, who had made the world, had spoken by the prophets, and was the Father of Jesus. They thought that more miracles of healing would promote their cause; but though they did not realize it at the time, their unity, love, hope, willingness to share their goods, coupled with their intrepid bearing, were their most potent arguments. Notice that in their consciousness, it was God's hand that was being stretched out to heal, though their hands were the immediate channel of its beneficent operations. They had been filled before, but they were filled again. It is our privilege to claim repeated infillings to make good our leakage and evaporation.

ACTS 4:36—5:11

Lying to the Holy Spirit. The Spirit of God is the source of generous and liberal giving. It is a poor substitute to set up bazaars, and fairs, and ice cream suppers. When the Church is filled with the Holy Spirit, her pockets will be easily emptied before his gracious, thawing presence. Let the sun arise in the heavens, and the frozen streams are instantly liberated and begin to sing on their way to transform wildernesses into gardens.

Mark the contrast between Ananias and Barnabas. The same phrases are applied to each. The sin of Ananias was not in keeping back part of the purchase money, but in pretending to have brought all to the apostle. He wished to pose as a saint, and at the same time to line his own nest. In the act of consecration, we must not allow one corner for Satan or selfishness to possess, because instantly we shall have to concede the right of way, and a thoroughfare will be opened along which all manner of contraband may be smuggled in. Peter had no doubt as to the personality of the Holy Spirit. You cannot lie to an influence! Note the interchange of "Holy Ghost" and "God" in vv. 3 and 4.

ACTS 5:12-26

Delivered To Testify. While the Holy Spirit works mightily within the Church, he cooperates with it in its outward operations by adding men and women to the Lord. None should be added to the Church roll who have not already been led into living union with Jesus. Through the Church, as his body, the risen Savior works such miracles as are here narrated, filling the hearts of the humble with love and joy, and exciting inveterate hatred in his foes.

The angel of God comes to open prison doors. Are you in sore trouble, from which there is no apparent deliverance? Are you imprisoned in the dungeon of doubt and despair? Are you being heavily persecuted? Oh, wrap around you the divine protection! Dare to believe that the doors will open as by unseen hands. Nothing can stay the purposes of God. Only use your God-given liberty to go forth to teach the people. The gospel is a message to the people. Let us preach to the hungry, needy crowds. Philosophers, scientists, the wise and prudent of the age may mock, but the people know the gospel when they hear it. Let us give it to them!

ACTS 5:27-42

Folly of Fighting Against God. The high priest and his party could not forget the imprecation of Matt. 27:25. It haunted them. Compare Peter's description of the cross as "the tree" with Deut. 21:23 and Gal. 3:13; also his own usage of the phrase in 1 Pet. 2:24. Notice in v. 31 the divine order—Jesus must be Prince if he is to be Savior. It is because that order is not observed, and men therefore seek to derive his benefits before they concede his rights, that he is unable to deliver them. Christ must be the enthroned Lord and Master of your life if you want to be saved to the uttermost. See Rom. 10:9. Repentance is his gift as equally as forgiveness. Mark that reference to the witness of the Holy Spirit, v. 32. Let us never stand in pulpit or class without being first assured that the truth we utter is such that he can endorse.

Gamaliel had been Paul's teacher. He was very astute and noncommittal. He said, "Let us wait and see; the truth will conquer." He expected that the new enthusiasm would die down if it were let alone. He knew that a draught of wind fans a fire. But he lived to see his mistake. We must be warned by v. 42 not only to preach Christ as king in the Temple, but also at home.

ACTS 6:1-15

Meeting Murmuring Within and Persecution Without. The Grecians here mentioned were Jews who had lived abroad and spoke Greek. There were as yet no Gentiles in the Church. It was regarded as an annex to Judaism, and people had to become Jews before they were admitted to its privileges.

What a glimpse is here afforded of the simplicity and fervor of the primitive Church! The daily ministration of relief; the choice of godly men to attend to secular details; the prime importance of prayer and the ministry of the Word; the recognition by the apostles of the rights of the people—all is so spiritual and so worthy of the era of the Holy Spirit. Alas, that so fair a dawn should ever have been overcast!

The Church must dedicate to God those whom she has chosen under the guidance of his Spirit. Stephen on the one hand, and Saul on the other, were the leaders of their respective

ACTS 7:1-13

Stephen's Defense: God's First Called-ones. There are several touches in this eloquent apology which deserve notice. Verse 2: "The God of glory." This chapter begins and ends with glory. See v. 55. Note that God appeared to Abraham in Ur, before he had come to Haran at the divine bidding. It is interesting to have this discrimination between the different appearances of God to the patriarch. Verse 3: We often have to leave our land before God shows us another. Verse 6: God's promises lighted up the weary bondage of Egypt. Verse 10: It is God that delivers us out of our afflictions and gives us favor with people.

The drift of the whole speech, which must be borne in mind as we read it, is that again and again the Chosen People had rejected their God-sent deliverers and prophets and had taken their own evil courses. The rejection of the Savior was only a parallel to that of Joseph by his brethren, and that of Moses by the nation. Israel had always been stiffnecked and froward, and ought not history to warn Stephen's hearers against taking a similar attitude toward Jesus of Nazareth? Might not Jesus prove to be as great a blessing in that generation as Joseph or Moses had been in his? The parallel will be complete when Jesus returns in power and glory.

ACTS 7:14-29

Stephen's Defense: The Deliverer from Bondage. Moses, we are here told, was "mighty in words"; that is, in eloquence as well as "in deeds." This confirms the statement of the Jewish historian, Josephus, that in the earlier part of his career, now lost in the oblivion of history, Moses led a very successful Egyptian expedition against Ethiopia. He complains to the Lord, in Exod. 4:10, of being slow of speech, but that probably refers to the habit of long disuse amid the silence and loneliness of the desert.

It is clear that stung by the sense of wrong, Moses at first interfered to deliver his people. He smote the Egyptian and tried to judge between his brethren. God had to bring him into the dust by repeated failure and rejection, that he might become an emptied and a broken vessel. God will not give glory to man. The treasure must be held in an earthen vessel, 2 Cor. 4:7. It is when we come to the end of ourselves that we arrive at the beginning of God. The world has ever to learn what God can do by those who are wholly emptied of self-confidence, but yielded to his hand.

ACTS 7:30-46

Stephen's Defense: Disobedience in the Wilderness. The Angel who appeared in the bush that burned with fire was the Angel of God's presence, who saved the Israelites and bare them and carried them all the days of old. See Isa. 63:9. Who could this be save our Lord himself? Only he could speak of himself as "I am." Remember the use our Lord made of that present tense, as carrying with it evidence that Abraham, Isaac, and Jacob were all of them living, though centuries had passed since their bodies had been deposited in Machpelah's cave. See Luke 20:38. It is very helpful to note that reference to the hand of the Angel in vv. 35 and 38. It reminds us of Acts 11:21. Would that in our service for God we were always conscious of the cooperating hand of the Savior!

The prophet referred to in v. 37 is, of course, our Lord, and the parallel between him and Moses is very apparent during our Lord's human ministry—for meekness, for reference in all things to the sending of God, for the work they did, as negotiating the Law from Sinai and the Mount of Beatitudes. But the difference in their posthumous ministry is emphasized in Heb. 3:1-6.

ACTS 7:47-60

A Martyr's Glorious Death. Words like these could not be forgiven. The growing irritation of the audience seems to have extorted those burning remonstrances and to have hastened the final scene. But the storm that burst around Christ's faithful confessor and first martyr could not disturb his serenity. His heart was fixed, trusting in God, Ps. 108:1. The peace of God garrisoned his heart and mind. At the moment when his foes were fiercest, the presence of Jesus, who had risen from sitting to standing in order to encourage and welcome him, was most vital. It will always be so. You will never know the completeness of Christ's comradeship till you have weathered a storm in his company.

They were particular not to violate the sanctity of the Temple, but not so in respect to the pure temple of the young martyr's body. The dying Stephen did not forget the Lord's prayer for those who crucified him, and he followed his Master's steps in this also. Amid the murderous flight of stones, he slept as a tired child on his mother's breast; and from that hour his patience, gentleness, and strength became as pricking goads in the heart of Saul of Tarsus.

ACTS 8:1-13

Fruits of the Scattered Seed. Evidently Stephen was beloved outside the precincts of the Church, for it would seem that the devout men who lamented his early death and carried his poor body to its burial were godly Jews who had been attracted by his earnest character. In the furious persecution that ensued under the leadership of Saul, neither sex nor age was spared. According to the subsequent statement of the arch-persecutor, the disciples of Jesus were dragged before the magistrate, thrust into prison, exposed to cruel torture, and compelled to blaspheme his holy name. During those terrible days, scenes were enacted which were destined to fill the heart of the future apostle with most poignant sorrow.

This persecution was overruled to scatter the Church, which had grown too prosperous and secure, and needed to be reminded of the Lord's injunction to go into all the world and preach the gospel to every creature. The light must be diffused; the salt must be scattered. How often God has to drive us by trouble to do what we ought to have done gladly and spontaneously! It was impossible to keep the deacons to the office of serving tables. Philip must needs go to Samaria, and that city welcomed what Jerusalem had refused. Here we enter upon the second circle of Acts 1:8.

ACTS 8:14-25

Confirming New Believers. Simon attracted people to himself; he posed as a man of power and mystery. The gospel fixes our thoughts exclusively upon Jesus. We preach him as Lord, and ourselves as servants for his sake. Simon's faith was spurious; he believed about rather than in Christ. John was sent with Peter to bring the fire of Pentecost to the very locality where formerly he and his brother had suggested that they should call fire from Heaven to destroy. See Luke 9:54. May we not learn from this mission that some are specially qualified to lead others into the enjoyment of Pentecostal blessing? In this service Peter used the power of the keys entrusted to him by the Master; and we may all do likewise when we lead others forward to claim that which awaits them in Christ Jesus.

Simon saw what an additional source of influence would accrue to him if only he could exert the same powers, but he had no idea of the spiritual conditions on which alone they could be obtained. "Simony" is the name for the practice of making gain by means of religion, 1 Tim. 6:5. "Perhaps" in v. 22 does not indicate a doubt upon God's side, but upon Simon's side—whether his treacherous heart would ever be able to conform to the divine conditions.

ACTS 8:26-40

Winning a Traveler. From the great city revival in Samaria Philip was led to the desert to minister to one seeking soul. It seems strange that God should be able to spare him from his busy and fruitful ministry in Samaria; but probably the comparative retirement was needed for soul and body after the strain of that successful campaign. How certain these Spirit-filled men were of the heavenly impulse! Every appearance suggested that this man of God was needed in the city, but the inner voice was the deciding factor, and his journey was so timed as to bring him in contact with a soul that was groping its way toward Christ.

The Bible is good as a traveling companion. Take it on your journeys. Read it as other men do their newspapers; not exclusively, but boldly. There are many war stories about bullets being stopped by pocket Testaments; and it is certain that many a desperate thrust of the devil has been warded off by the Word of God being hidden in the heart and worn as a breastplate. Live in touch with God, and he will put you in touch with souls. This conversion of a son of Ham was a worthy fulfillment of Isa. 56:3-8.

ACTS 9:1-9

Winning a Persecutor. A year had passed since 8:3. "The Way" had become the accepted phrase for the infant Church and its presentation of the truth, 19:9; 22:4. It may refer to the course of life the Christians pursued, or to their method of getting right with God—not by the deeds of the Law, but by their faith in Christ, Rom. 10:5-10. Compare with this narrative 26:13ff. and 22:6ff. Saul's companions saw the light and heard a noise, but did not see the Lord or distinguish what was said.

Mark how the Lord Jesus identifies himself with his suffering ones. Their sufferings are his, v. 5. To hurt them is to hurt him. The "pricks" are the ox-goad. The more the ox resists, the deeper the wound. Even from Heaven the Master speaks in parables. Evidently for a long time —perhaps from the death of Stephen—the persecutor had been fighting against conviction. When God needs captains for his army, he not unseldom takes them from the ranks of the enemy. The foremost persecutor became the foremost leader of the Church. The conversion of Saul was due to the personal interposition of the living Christ. It was the pierced hand that arrested and apprehended him.

ACTS 9:10-22

Opened Eyes. How graciously God makes use of prepared souls as partners in the work of salvation! It would have been easy for the risen Lord to have himself completed what he had begun; or he might have brought a Philip or an apostle upon the scene. But instead of this he called a comparatively obscure man who was to give Saul the help and counsel he needed. See to it that you are of such a temper that Jesus may commission you to heal the wounds with which he brings his predestined servants to the ground.

A little taper may be used to kindle a great light. Though not a great man, Ananias was preeminently a good man, 22:12. He had his suspicions about Saul, but laid them aside at the bidding of Christ. Take care not to entrench yourself too strongly in your prejudices. Be mobile to Christ's touch, while you are strong against all others. What a comfort v. 15 must have been to Paul in later days! Perhaps the sweetest part of these terms of his commission was "unto me." It was a noble act of faith for Ananias to call him "brother." Yet if the Master accepted, the disciple could not refuse. Note that a new convert was bidden in those days to seek the Pentecostal gift!

ACTS 9:23-31

Welcomed as a Brother. He who feeds on Scripture must wax strong. The new convert started at once to testify of the Savior. We have no right to keep to ourselves the great treasures that we have discovered, but must copy the lepers of 2 Kings 7:9. He probably showed, from a comparison between the predictions of the Old Testament and the facts of our Lord's life, that the key exactly fitted the ancient lock, and so proved its genuineness.

Those "many days" in v. 23 probably include the three years spent in Arabia, Gal. 1:17, 18. It was as though Paul wanted time and solitude for quiet thought. We may suppose that he went to Sinai, and there amid the silences of the school where Moses had studied before him, he received of the Lord Jesus that which also he was commissioned to pass on to the Church. From Arabia, he returned to Damascus; then happened vv. 24 and 25. Finally he came to Jerusalem, where he had the opportunity of comparing his teaching with that of the apostles, Gal. 1:18-24. A vision led him to leave Jerusalem, 22:17-21. While at Tarsus, he probably founded the churches in Cilicia, 15:23, 41.

ACTS 9:32-43

Strength and Life through Christ. Peter was now free for a visit of apostolic inspection, of which the two incidents here preserved are the only record. Lydda was a village on the great plain, abutting on the seaboard. The effect of the miracle of healing wrought upon Aeneas was profound. A general conversion of the agricultural population was the immediate result. They all turned to the Lord. The villagers had probably been prepared by the tidings of what had taken place, and a single spark sufficed to set the whole country in a blaze.

The little church at Joppa had sustained a serious loss in the death of one of its chief workers, a woman named Dorcas, vv. 36, 37. She is described as "a certain disciple." She had learned from Jesus Christ the great lesson that the love of God implies ministry to others, and she gave herself to practice it by quiet, feminine handiwork which she distributed among the desolate and friendless women of the town. Peter's prayer in the chamber of death was answered, and Dorcas was given back to her friends. Our Lord put his seal upon her work, and she has been crowned as the patron saint of women workers.

ACTS 10:1-16

Guidance for Men Who Pray. At this point the Church took a new departure, and the gospel broke over the walls of Jewish exclusiveness and was preached for the first time to pure-blooded Gentiles. Caesarea, built by the great Herod, was practically a Roman city, and the official seat of the Roman government in Judea. Cornelius was an officer of high rank and, it would seem, naturally of noble character. He had no sympathy with the religious fables and sensuous indulgence of his time and was attracted to the Jewish faith, which stood alone in the world for pure and undefiled conceptions of God. He adopted some of its characteristic features—its hours of prayer, its practice of fasting, and its almsgiving.

He had apparently set apart the whole of this memorable day for earnest inquiry as to the way of salvation, and as the sun was declining an angel brought the necessary indication of the steps that he should take. In the meanwhile God was about to prepare Peter to bring Cornelius into the perfect light. On the following day, as the messengers of Cornelius were nearing Joppa, the vision of a redeemed world from which Hebrew restrictions had vanished opened to the apostle a new and wider conception of God's purpose.

ACTS 10:17-33

Jew and Gentile Meet. It should be carefully noted that the mental impression which was produced by Peter's vision was corroborated by the fact of the knocking and inquiring group at Peter's door. This is God's invariable method. For us all, as we contemplate taking a new and important step in life, there is the urging of the Spirit, the impression or vision of duty, and the knock or appeal of outward circumstances.

Evidently Cornelius had gathered to his quarters in the barracks his kinsmen and a number of intimate friends, who were as eager as he to discover the will of God. They remained quietly waiting until the party from Joppa had completed their thirty-mile journey. Peter had taken the precaution of bringing with him six brethren, evidently with the expectation that the events of that day would not only create a new era, but would also be called into serious question.

The welcome that Cornelius gave was very significant. That a high-born Roman should prostrate himself before a Jewish evangelist was unprecedented, though it revealed the true reverence and humility of Cornelius's soul. But the noble simplicity of Peter's reply was also a revelation of the true greatness of the apostle, and ought to have more obviously influenced his would-be successors.

ACTS 10:34-48

Gentiles Receive the Holy Spirit. The address with which Peter answered the centurion's inquiry was largely a recapitulation of the great facts of gospel history. The ministry of Jesus in the power of the Holy Spirit was probably already familiar to his hearers. The story of the crucifixion was equally well-known. These things were not done in a corner. But the third division of the address, vv. 39-41, in which the apostle told of the resurrection and of our Lord's appearance to chosen witnesses, of whom he was one, was probably replete with new and startling tidings. Notice the implied invitation of v. 43 to them all to believe in Jesus for the remission of sin.

The Holy Spirit fell upon the audience, as on the day of Pentecost, v. 44. There must have been that wonderful stirring and moving among the people which we have beheld, in a modified form, in modern audiences when moved by the celestial wind, as a harvest field by the breeze. Peter never finished his sermon. It seemed as if the Holy Spirit put the apostle aside, saying, "You have spoken enough; leave the rest to me!"

ACTS 11:1-18

Following a Plain Course. It is very interesting here to find Peter on the defensive. We have always thought of him as masterful and strong, the born leader of men, whose authority was absolutely indisputable. But here we see him taken seriously to task by the mother church, and compelled to show the grounds of his unprecedented action. Here also appears the first clear indication of the rift which was, in due course, to develop in the Church between the converted Jews, who insisted that Gentiles must become Jews before becoming Christians, and those of more liberal views, who began to understand that in Christ Jesus neither circumcision nor uncircumcision availed anything, but a new creature, Gal. 6:15, and faith working by love, Gal. 5:6. This division was the cause of Paul's embittered and lifelong persecution.

But the first decision of those in the church in Jerusalem was a perfectly just one, v. 18. The facts compelled a favorable verdict upon Peter's action. They tacitly confessed that the seal of God's approval had been unmistakably affixed to his action, and that he had no alternative. When a man lives in union with the Spirit of God, crooked things become straight and rough places plain, Isa. 40:4.

ACTS 11:19-30

Knitting Together the Church. The development of God's plan is still further disclosed in the events recorded in this section, which describe the same phenomenon of Gentile conversion, but in different circumstances. In this case, it was not an apostle that was God's chosen instrument, but a few unknown and unrecognized disciples, who were fleeing north from persecution and had reached the pleasure-seeking city of Antioch. The hand of the Lord was with them, as it certainly had been with Peter, and large numbers of converts were gathered into a church. In this instance, also, the mother church felt bound to make inquiry, so "they sent forth Barnabas," v. 22.

Barnabas was a good man, and his unaffected piety enabled him to recognize at once that this movement was of God. All the signs of true conversion were present. He saw sure evidence

ACTS

of the grace of God, and pleaded with the new converts for tenacity and constancy. The secret of perseverance is in the phrase "cleave unto the Lord," v. 23. In addition to the other beautiful traits of his character, we must add the spirit of tender brotherhood that carried Barnabas to Tarsus to find Saul.

ACTS 12:1–12

Loosened Bonds. This Herod was the grandson of Herod the Great. He courted the goodwill of the Jews, though he was dissolute, cruel, and unscrupulous. How wonderful that God can spare from his work men like James, whom it has taken him so long to train! But doubtless other and higher service awaits them.

A quaternion numbered four. The total number of soldiers that guarded Peter, therefore, would be sixteen, exclusive of prison officials. But a praying household is stronger than the strongest precautions of human might.

God often delays his answers till the eve of our extremity; but Peter's sleep is typical of the quiet faith that can trust God absolutely, whether to live or die. When God bids us arise and obey, we must do so without considering the obstructions that confront us. It is our part to arise and gird ourselves; it is for him to cause the chains to fall off and the iron gates to open. What are iron gates to him who cleft a path through the Red Sea! The angel guides us supernaturally only so long as we are dazed and unable to form a judgment for ourselves. As soon as we are able to consider a matter, he leaves us to make use of our God-given faculties.

ACTS 12:13–25

Beyond Their Faith. Mark's mother was evidently a woman of property, as her house was large enough to receive the many who felt that prayer was the key to open Peter's prison. Rhoda's portrait has charmed every generation. It is so lifelike and natural. How good for every servant-maid to love the devotional meeting, and to be welcomed to it! Christianity had introduced a new spirit into the world. How often our deliverances seem too good to be true! These praying friends of Peter would not believe the maid, though she told them that their prayers were answered. This proves that while their faith was very imperfect, their request was granted. When we believe not, God remains faithful; he cannot deny himself, 2 Tim. 2:13. The James mentioned in v. 17 was the brother of our Lord, and afterward head of the church in Jerusalem, 15:13. See Jas. 1:1.

What a contrast between Peter's deliverance and Herod's death! Be not afraid of the reproach of men, for "the moth shall eat them up like a garment," Isa. 51:8. During these happenings Paul and Barnabas were in Jerusalem, and in later years their minds must often have reverted to them. Probably Paul's remembrance of this incident inspired his constant request for prayer in his own behalf, Eph. 6:18–20.

ACTS 13:1–12

Beginning a Missionary Campaign. This is one of the greatest chapters in the New Testament, making a new departure in the ministry of the gospel, which henceforth begins to pass out to the uttermost part of the earth, Acts 1:8. It is likely that the mother church at Jerusalem was too conservative to lend herself to the pressure of the Holy Spirit, urging worldwide evangelization, and that he had to employ the more mobile church at Antioch, which was more susceptible to the passion for humanity since it stood on the edge of the great heathen world, like a lighthouse on the shore of a desolate sea.

This momentous prayer meeting had apparently been convened to discover the Lord's will as to further developments. As the names indicate, it was composed largely of Hebrew Christians. Note that the Holy Spirit speaks with authority as Christ's Vicegerent, Acts 2:33. Modern missions are his work, and he selects his own agents. We should ever seek to cooperate with him in discovering and setting apart chosen men and women for his work.

ACTS 13:13–24

The Savior According to Promise. It was very natural that the missionary party should sail for Cyprus, partly because it was the first and nearest outpost of the great heathen world that lay to the west, and partly because Barnabas was a native of the island and had owned land there, which he had sold for the benefit of his poorer brethren in the church, Acts 4:36, 37.

In visiting a new city, it was the custom of the apostles to go first to the Jewish synagogue, where such was to be found. "To the Jew first, and also to the Gentile," was the divine order, Rom. 2:10. The journey from Cyprus to the mainland was easily made; but the journey up to this inland city of Antioch in Pisidia was very perilous, 2 Cor. 11:26.

Verse 16 gives us the apostle's favorite stance, 21:40; 26:1. "Ye that fear God" referred to the Gentile proselytes. This first address contained the seed-thoughts of the apostle's ministry. He loved to show that the gospel was the white flower that grew on the ancient stock of Judaism. Whatever his starting point, he was sure to come, by a direct path, to Jesus Christ. Observe throughout how Paul attributes all of the great events and movements of history to the direction and agency of God. God chose the fathers; God gave Saul; God brought unto Israel a Savior.

ACTS 13:25–37

Condemned by Men but Raised by God. For Paul the resurrection was always the keystone of faith. He had taken particular care to assure himself of the reality of that foundation fact. In 1 Cor. 15 he sets forth at length the testimony culminating in his own experience, on which he rested his belief. He had been allowed to see that blessed One and hear the word from his mouth. He quotes Ps. 2:7, Isa. 55:3, and Ps. 16:10. He makes unexpected use of the first of these quotations, teaching that it was fulfilled in the resurrection. This sheds new light on death. It is not death but birth, not an ending but a beginning. Our Lord was the firstborn from the dead. *We* say that a saint has died; angels say that he has been born.

Notice that great word about David, v. 36. He served God's counsel, or purpose, in his own generation. That should be the supreme objective of our lives. Not to succeed, or to make money, or to please ourselves, but to serve the will of God who sent us forth.

ACTS 13:38–52

Jews Reject, Gentiles Accept the Gospel. The doctrine of justification by faith, so closely associated with the work of Paul, is here stated for the first time. In Jesus there is forgiveness. For those who trust in him, past sins are absolutely put away, never to be named again, never to be brought up at any future judgment day. Our record is as clear as the sand which has been swept smooth by the ocean waves. We are not only forgiven, but justified. We are treated as though we had never sinned, and "are justified from all things." It is a present fact. You may not feel justified or forgiven, but if you are trusting in Jesus, you are at this moment as certainly and as fully justified as have been the saints in Heaven.

Pride, as well as jealousy of the Gentiles who were crowding into the fold, stirred the Jews to antagonism, but they could not eradicate the seed which had been so profusely scattered. Large numbers believed, and as they experienced salvation in Christ they discovered that they were in line with an eternal purpose. This is the meaning of "ordained" in v. 48. If with such slight opportunities, the disciples were filled with joy and the Holy Spirit, v. 52, should we not possess the same experience?

ACTS 14:1–13

Varying Treatment of the Message. From Antioch the apostles passed to Iconium, the capital of Lycaonia. It is most illuminating to note the source of their success: "The Lord . . . gave testimony unto the word of his grace." We must not expect success if that divine witness is absent. There is nothing more vital than this. The secret of joyful and successful service is the consciousness that in every sermon and address there is an unseen fellow-worker who is listening to each sentence and punctuating with his strong affirmation each utterance which magnifies the grace of God.

Lystra was situated in the highlands, amid a wild, mountainous country. In Paul's audience here he saw a cripple who had faith to be healed, vv. 8, 9. What quick insight God gives the soul that lives in fellowship with him! There was an old tradition that the gods had frequented this very region. Jupiter, the father of the gods, was the guardian deity of Lystra. There was, accordingly, a special reason for the excitement among these simple and untutored folk. Man has ever hoped there might be communication between Heaven and earth. Oh, that we were as quick to worship and adore the Son of God!

ACTS 14:14–28

Establishing the New Believers. In Paul's address we have distinct anticipations of the early chapters of the Epistle to the Romans. How fickle a mob is! Now, enthusiastic loyalty; again, disappointment and rejection. Today, "Hosanna"; tomorrow, "Crucify." "Cease ye from man, whose breath is in his nostrils."

It has been supposed by some that the trance of 2 Cor. 12 took place at the time of Paul's stoning in Lystra. It must have been sorrow indeed to awaken from such a vision to the suffering of his battered body. But that scene, no doubt, gave him the love and devotion of the young Timothy and his mother and grandmother. See Acts 16:1, 2. On Paul's next visit to Lystra, this son, whom he had begotten in the sore anguish of that hour, was to become his devoted attendant.

In spite of the treatment Paul had received, he returned to the city, v. 21. Back to the stones! Naught could stay his ardent spirit, if only disciples were to be won or confirmed in their

ACTS

faith for the Master, v. 22. Everywhere these intrepid missionaries found the blood-stained track of the cross, but they filled up to the brim the measure of their opportunity. This will be possible for us all only when we are such that God can cooperate with us as our fellow-worker and "open the door."

ACTS 15:1-11

One Way of Salvation for All. Paul and Barnabas were quietly resting in Antioch after their arduous toils, when these persons from Jerusalem stealthily commenced to undermine their influence. They contended that the way from paganism to Christ must be through Moses. They especially insisted that Gentiles must become Jews by submitting to the initial rite of Judaism. This insidious teaching followed Paul throughout his life, and extracted from him many of the noble arguments and appeals of his epistles. We can easily understand the vehemence with which he protested.

Finally it was determined to submit the question to the judgment of the apostles and elders in Jerusalem. The journey thither was a triumphal progress. The story of the seal that God had placed on all the labors of the two missionaries not only filled all hearts with joy, but was the conclusive answer to the Judaizing teachers who were the cause of all the trouble. The first great address at the solemn conclave was by Peter, who quoted his own experience at the house of Cornelius to prove that God at least made no difference between Jew and Gentile. Notice his statement that the believing heart is cleansed by receiving the Holy Spirit, vv. 8, 9.

ACTS 15:12-21

A Generous Conclusion. When their turn came to speak, Paul and Barnabas contented themselves with emphasizing the signs and wonders by which God had set his seal on their words and methods. Would he have done so if they had followed a wrong course? Notice the two prepositions that they used in describing their work. They first told of what God had done in cooperation "with" them and then of what he had done through or "by" them, 14:27; 15:4, 12. Consider also that remarkable phrase about God bearing witness, v. 8. See also 14:3 and Heb. 2:1-4.

James had a prominent position in the Jerusalem church, because he was the Lord's brother and a man of remarkable holiness and prayerfulness. He laid emphasis on the divine program, which moved forward from Jew to Gentile, from the rebuilding of the ruined Tabernacle of David to the seeking of the Lord by the residue of men. The implication was that though Jehovah dwelt in a special manner with his Chosen People, yet the Gentiles would come seeking him directly and without becoming incorporated with the Jews.

ACTS 15:22-41

"Confirming the Churches." This letter was a noble document and fitted for its immediate purpose, but it does not apply directly to us, as the circumstances which called it forth have long since passed away. It was explicit in denying that the rite of circumcision was needful for salvation. It bore ample testimony to the character and work of the two great missionaries whose action had been impugned. It denounced the false teachers whose intrusion had broken the peace of the Church, and laid down the principles which had been embodied in James's speech. Notice the association of the Holy Spirit with the persons who issued this letter, v. 28. Here is convincing proof that the Spirit of God is a Person, that he presides in the Church, and that he is willing to become our guide and teacher whenever we are perplexed.

The arrival of Judas and Silas, attesting by their presence the importance that the mother church attached to the question at issue, and the reading of the letter brought great relief to the believers at Antioch, and a blessed season of teaching and preaching ensued.

It is unpleasant to see the contention between the two leaders over John Mark, but God overruled it for good and Paul could later write to Timothy, "Take Mark, and bring him with thee; for he is useful to me for the ministry," 2 Tim. 4:11.

ACTS 16:1-13

Guided to New Fields. Paul had a wonderful influence over young men. Timothy, Titus, and Mark bore his impress. When circumcision was insisted upon, as in the previous chapter, no one opposed it more stoutly than Paul; when it conciliated Jewish prejudice, he was quite willing to concede it, since in itself it was a matter of perfect indifference. As the stoning of Stephen was the first step toward winning Paul, so his own stoning at Lystra on the former occasion, as we have noted, probably gave him Timothy.

Our path through life will often be indicated by the fact that the doors which lead off the straight track are barred and bolted, so that we have no option save to go on. Paul was blocked first on the left, that he should not go into the province of Asia; then on the right, that he should not go into Bithynia. Finally he reached Troas, and stood face to face with the ocean that lay between him and Europe.

Here he had a vision which made a deep impression upon him. He saw a man of Macedonia standing in an attitude of entreaty and saying, "Come over into Macedonia, and help us." Note that phrase, "assuredly gathering," v. 10. God often leaves us to infer our course. He does not ignore his own great gift of reason.

ACTS 16:14-24

Welcomed; Attested; Imprisoned. This was an epoch-making moment, but how quietly it is recorded. There was no heralding of the gospel which was to transform Europe. The need for it was unspoken and unfelt. It stole in like the dawn.

Paul's first experiences in Europe were not promising. In most cities there was a Jewish synagogue, but here only a small group of pious women in an arbor by the riverside. Let none despise the day of small things. What a contrast between Lydia, who had come over from Asia Minor and employed a number of hands in the dyeing trade, and the poor girl who was possessed by the demon! Yet each of them recognized the divine ministry of the newly arrived messengers. What a contrast, also, between the gradual response of Lydia's heart in the revelation of the risen Christ, to whom it opened as a flower to the sun, and the sudden awakening of the jailer!

When Christ touches the pockets of worldly men, he arouses their direct opposition. The world is troubled when it loses its gains; the saints are troubled when they see Christ's property being injured! See v. 18.

ACTS 16:25-40

Salvation in the Jail. Some, as we have seen, are converted by the gentle opening of the heart, others amid the convulsions of the storm. The first knowledge of salvation may have reached the heart of the jailer through the words of the possessed girl, v. 17. If only the heart is right with Christ, it can sing in the darkest night. The impression of those holy songs must have wrought still further upon the conscience of this rough Roman official, who had treated his prisoners with uncommon severity, v. 24. "The inner prison!" Perhaps some of our readers have been in it! They have come to an end of themselves and their feet are fastened!

But God has his own way of deliverance and never forsakes his own. Art thou in the stocks today? Then pray and sing praises! Choose, for instance, Ps. 103. God will be thy very present help. Thou shalt win thy jailer and become a monument of God's saving mercy. There is no course for the convicted sinner but to trust in the salvation wrought upon the cross; or still better, in him who wrought it.

Paul was perfectly justified in insisting upon his civil rights when he had the opportunity, v. 37. It made the way easier for his new converts.

ACTS 17:1-12

Persecution Spreads the Truth. Thessalonica: Slowly Paul made his way among the great cities of Greece. He was sowing seeds of which others would reap the harvest. His one theme was the risen Lord, whether amid the less or the more cultivated, vv. 3, 31. This is surely the true method of world evangelization—not to argue, but to proclaim the glorious personality of our risen Lord. Notice the distinction in v. 3 between the human name, Jesus, and the royal name, Christ. As Jesus, our Lord lived, ministered, and died; as Christ, he was raised from the dead, and as such he is the crowned King of men, v. 7. However loyal we may be to the civil government, our first allegiance is to "another king," v. 7.

Berea: True nobility consists in being open to any new truth that God may reveal to us from his Word. The one test of truth is Scripture as interpreted to the pure heart by the Holy Spirit; but we should examine the Scriptures "daily" as the Bereans did. It is not to be wondered at that many believed. If only our people would love the Bible, saturating their minds with it and teaching it to their children, what different results would follow the preaching of the gospel!

ACTS 17:13-21

Stirred by Idolatry. From the first, the gospel was baptized in the fire of persecution. How unutterable the loneliness and sorrow of the apostle as he reached Athens! Did doubt ever enter his mind as to whether he was on the appointed track? If it did, he at once dismissed it. His motto was to forget the things behind. When, in dependence upon God, you have once taken a path, dare to believe it is right whatever appearances there are to the contrary.

One purpose consumed the apostle. "One thing I do," was the thread on which the many beads of his experiences were strung. Persecuted and rejected today, he is at his favorite work tomorrow. How different this intense earnestness from the trifling of the so-called philosophers of Athens! The Epicurean made the pursuit of pleasure the main object of life. The Stoic, on the other hand, believed in the stern repression of Nature. All Greece was absorbed in the cultivation of art, architecture, eloquence, and intellectual brilliance. But here, as everywhere, Paul had but one message—Jesus and the resurrection. Oh, to be "pressed in spirit," 18:5, as he was, till our earnestness should compel our opponents to give us a serious hearing!

ACTS 17:22-34

The One Living and True God. The gospel preacher must avail himself of any circumstance in his surroundings that will enable him to arrest the attention of his audience. He must meet them where they are and take them with him to realms of thought with which they are not familiar. Paul was wise to begin with that altar "to the unknown god."

Around them stood the most exquisite temples ever reared by human genius, but these were not the home of God. He seeks the lowly and contrite heart, not of the Jew alone, but wherever man is found, and on whatever intellectual plane. Men, the world over, are brothers —"he hath made of one blood all nations." The arrangements of divine providence have been contrived to lead men to God. If they feel after him with reverence and true desire, he will be found of them. All men are his offspring, but only those who receive the Son of God into their hearts become really sons. Repentance is the act of the will, and therefore it may be commanded. God can overlook much that is hurtful and evil, because he loves the world and deals with men according to their light; and we may rejoice therefore that he will judge mankind by "that man."

ACTS 18:1-17

A Great Ministry in a Great City. Paul tells us in 1 Cor. 2:1-4 that he entered Corinth with fear and trembling and made no effort to attract by human wisdom or eloquence. From the first he preached "Christ and him crucified."

Similarity in trade discovered friends who were to be of the utmost assistance; nothing in our life may be attributed to chance. Sitting at their common toils, he won them for Christ.

"Pressed in the spirit," v. 5. The heart of the apostle yearned with irrepressible desire. God's Word was as a fire in his bones. The guilty city appealed to him and tugged at his heartstrings. So Jesus wept over Jerusalem. Do we participate in this soul anguish? Are our hands free of the blood of men? Are we prepared to suffer if only we may save others?

Gallio was a typical man of the world, intent upon matters of law and order, philosophical, and cultured. But when questions of religion were in debate, he was absolutely indifferent. How vast the contrast between him and Paul!

ACTS 18:18-28

New Helpers in the Gospel. In unimportant matters Paul was still amenable to Hebrew customs and rites, v. 18. Probably he desired to conciliate his Judaizing opponents so far as he could without surrendering vital principles. He took his newfound friends with him to Ephesus. Though none of them realized it, there was important work awaiting them in that mighty city. The plans of apostles, and of ordinary travelers as well, must be subordinated to the divine will. See 1 Cor. 4:19; Jas. 4:15.

Apollos combined the eloquence of the Greek with the religious instinct of the Jew. A student from the great university at Alexandria, a convert to the gospel, deeply conversant with the Old Testament, gifted with marvelous eloquence, he was a strong ally of the Christian forces of his age. But he needed to know of the death, resurrection, and ascended power of Christ, and to experience the Pentecostal gift. Into all these he was led by Aquila and Priscilla. How wonderful is that holy wisdom which the Spirit of God gives to simple and humble believers, so that they can become teachers of men who are intellectually their superiors!

ACTS 19:1-12

The Holy Spirit Working in Ephesus. Paul had planted good seed at Corinth and Apollos, in turn, had watered it, 1 Cor. 3:6. Large numbers became the latter's devoted followers. This, however, excited no jealousy in Paul. Apollos and he were only instruments through whom God was pleased to work.

Meanwhile, Paul had a ministry to fulfill in Ephesus. The twelve men mentioned had known only so much of the truth as had been revealed to the Baptist. They had felt the need of repentance and had heard of Christ as the Lamb of God; but of his resurrection and ascension and the gift of the Holy Spirit they were ignorant. Paul at once fixed on this lack as the source of their impotence. He seemed to say, "If you men had received the baptism of the Spirit, you would move this city."

It was wise on Paul's part to remove the disciples and his work to their own premises, which soon became famous throughout the city and indeed throughout the adjacent country. People who had come in to worship at the shrine of Diana gave themselves to Christ, and the Christian faith became disseminated through the province, Ephesus itself being mightily moved.

ACTS 19:13-29

The Power of Jesus' Name. Where God's Spirit is mightily at work, Satan is not far away. Here the enemy's emissaries were mean enough to use the name of Jesus to get themselves a few more shekels. But the name is useless apart from the living power of the Spirit. It is terrible when the very demons flout those who profess religion. "Who are ye?" meant, "You do not count." The demons knew Christ as the Holy One of God and Paul as his representative, but these exorcist Jews were hollow as sounding brass. Cast into the balances, they were altogether lighter than vanity, Ps. 62:9.

The outcome of all this was a mighty revival. The name of the Lord Jesus was magnified, and a searching work of grace led to the confession of sin and the cleansing of heart and life in many who had followed vain superstitions.

So deep was the work of God in that great city of Ephesus that the trade in charms and amulets, sold in the neighborhood of the temple, began to fall off. The crowd of worshipers in Diana's temple was also perceptibly less. People who came in from the seaboard would find their way to the apostle, who preached the gospel with a power that could not be withstood. Regenerated souls therefore, in turn, carried the gospel throughout the whole region.

ACTS 19:30-41

The Lawlessness of Selfish Greed. The theater of Ephesus still stands. I have spoken in its mighty enclosure, from the very spot where this town clerk—the model of officialism—must have stood to address and calm the frenzied crowd. Paul never knew the fear of man, and was with difficulty prevented from endangering his life in his desire to turn the occasion to account. He probably refers to this incident when he says that he fought with wild beasts at Ephesus, 1 Cor. 15:32. But he could have done no good in the face of such a turmoil. Be valorous, Christian soldiers, but be discreet! Do not throw yourselves from the mountain brow unless God clearly calls for it.

It is well to bear this scene in mind when the apostle tells us of a "peace that passeth understanding" which stands sentry over heart and mind. His was not the sequestered life of a religious recluse; he was continually battling his way through a stormy sea. But it is in the floods of great waters that we learn what our Lord can be. Dying outwardly and in human estimation, yet we live, 2 Cor. 4:16; the earthern vessel chipped and broken, but the heavenly treasure unimpaired, 2 Cor. 4:7.

ACTS 20:1-12

A Messenger of Truth and Life. The Second Epistle to the Corinthians should be read with the introductory verses of this chapter, as it reveals the apostle's inner mind at this time. He seems to have been less impressed with the imminent peril from which he had been rescued, and more solicitous as to the condition of the church at Corinth, to which he had addressed his first epistle during the early days of his Ephesian ministry.

Into how small a compass, v. 3, the evangelist crowds the three months' ministry in Greece, where he visited the scenes of his memorable first journey. In a few lines he enumerates the companions of his return journey, and before we know it we are back again in Troas and on our way to Jerusalem.

Notice that reference to the breaking of bread on the first day of the week, v. 7. This proves that the primitive Church was adopting the first day of the week for its characteristic meal; and as the Gentile element became predominant, it is easy to see how gradually and inevitably Sunday superseded Saturday as the rest day. See also Col. 2:16. It is possible that Eutychus was not already dead, although believed to be so. In that case, Paul's loving embrace and prayer restored him from the swoon that might easily have become death. Can we not imagine the theme of that talk which lasted till dawn!

ACTS 20:13-27

A Parting Message. The vessel had to stop at Miletus and Paul sent word to the Ephesian elders, urging them to come and see him. He spent the day in their company, and before parting delivered this pathetic and helpful address. There are many incidental touches revealing the nature of his work in the great city, of which there is little or no mention elsewhere in the Acts. For instance, we were not aware of his tears and trials through the opposition of the Jews, v. 19, nor of the labors of his toil-worn hands, v. 34. We hardly realized that his ministry was not simply the public proclamation of the gospel, but a visitation from house to house as well, v. 20.

The Greek word in vv. 20 and 27 for "kept back" and "shunned" is a nautical word which literally means "reefed up." It was so natural for Paul to use a nautical word which he must have been hearing every day. But notice how this heroic soul alludes to the lightness with which he held comfort and life, if only he might serve his Master perfectly and fulfill in full measure his opportunities. How Paul loved that great word "grace!" It was his perpetual theme, and as we come to know ourselves better and consider how little we have deserved from God, we also shall have but one theme. We are debtors to the sovereign grace of God, and have nothing to pay.

ACTS 20:28-38

Commended to God. Notice the change of the Revised Version in v. 28. The elder, whether presbyter or bishop, is not put "over" the flock; he is "in" it like the rest, needing redemption through the same precious blood. Notice also that remarkable expression, "the church of God, which he hath purchased with his own blood," v. 28. It clearly indicates Paul's view of the deity of our Lord.

The prediction of v. 30 was but too soon fulfilled, 1 Tim. 1:19, 20. Tears are thrice mentioned in this short passage: tears of suffering, v. 19; of pastoral anxiety, v. 31; and of personal affection, v. 37.

The builder was withdrawn before the edifice was completed, but he knew that God would continue, through other hands, to complete what he had begun, v. 32. We are in the company of God's heirs. Let us meditate on the word of his grace, as fellow-heirs with Christ and all his saints; let us enter into possession of our inheritance. In v. 35 we have the only saying of our Lord in the New Testament which is not preserved in the Gospels. The blessedness applies to our Lord as well as to ourselves. Let us not think that he is tired of our requests. Every time we ask for anything that he can give us, we add to his blessedness as well as to our own.

ACTS 21:1-14

Ready to Die for His Lord. The vessel coasted along Asia Minor, sighted Cyprus, sailed to the south of it, and so finally to Tyre. There the disciples were poor and obscure, and it took searching to find them; but they were very warmhearted. The whole community, including the children, who never forgot that incident, accompanied Paul to his ship. As they neared the vessel, they knelt on the shore to pray together, and so parted.

The journey from Ptolemais (Acre) to Caesarea lay along the edge of the plain of Sharon, at the season bright with the flowers of spring. The days Paul spent at Caesarea were the last happy days of freedom that he was to enjoy for two or three years. What blessed intercourse Paul and Philip must have had! They had both known Stephen. Agabus joined the happy party, with prophecies of peril ahead, but these only served to bring out the magnificent courage of the apostle. His purpose was inflexible. An unseen hand was beckoning; a Voice which only he could hear was calling. He had no doubt as to God's purpose and went straight forward, though he was not insensible to the love and sympathy of friends.

ACTS 21:15-26

Binding Together the Church. Mnason was an early disciple. He could remember the first days of the Church's story. It was good for Paul to have the society and care of this good man during those last troublous days. Notwithstanding all the efforts of the Judaizing elements in the Church, the splendid labors of the apostle were estimated at their true worth, and he was gladly welcomed by the brethren at Jerusalem. Note how careful he was to attribute all to God. Paul was only the instrument through whom the Almighty wrought for the glory of Jesus, v. 19.

The action here described, which was strongly recommended by the leaders of the Church, seems at variance with what Paul so clearly states in his Epistle to the Galatians, 2:3-5. Perhaps it would have been a wiser and stronger policy for him to have remained in quiet obscurity till the feast was over. But we must remember the deep coloring which the proximity of the Temple gave to church life at Jerusalem, and Paul was willing to be guided by men like James, in whose judgment he had full confidence. In addition, he was always willing to yield in cases which did not concern principle. He acquiesced in such matters for the sake of charity, so that he gladly became as a Jew to Jews, that he might save the Jews, 1 Cor. 9:20.

ACTS 21:27-40

Facing a Bigoted Mob. Four days passed and there seemed a hope that as the number of pilgrims grew less, Paul might escape recognition till his vow was fulfilled. In fulfilling it he was required to live with four paupers in a chamber of the Temple, to pay for sixteen sacrificial animals and the accompanying meat offerings on their behalf, and to stand with them while the priest offered lambs and rams on their behalf.

But as the ceremonies were approaching completion, he was recognized by Jews from Ephesus and other cities of Asia—perhaps Alexander the coppersmith was one of them— and a cry of hatred and horror was raised. They had seen the Ephesian Trophimus walking with him in the streets of Jerusalem, and supposed that Paul had taken him into the holy precincts. The punishment for that crime was death. They therefore seized him and forced him through the Beautiful Gate and down the fifteen steps, that they might kill him outside the Temple. This outburst attracted the notice of the Roman garrison in the neighboring Castle of Antonia, and Lysias with his soldiers forced his way through the throng, rescued Paul from his would-be murderers, and bore him beyond their reach. God had other work for the apostle yet to do.

ACTS 22:1-16

How His Life Was Changed. What a sermon Paul preached! His pulpit—the steps that ascended from the Temple level to the Castle of Antonia. His audience—the frenzied crowds who filled the court below him, but who were calmed to silence as they heard the venerable Hebrew speech, which was unintelligible to the Romans around them. His text—the real and personal interposition of the living Christ to arrest his course of persecution and convert him. Here was a fact which to the apostle was the greatest of all facts; namely, that he had seen Jesus Christ, and had been transformed by what he had seen and heard. No light thing could have revolutionized his life. His zeal for the old covenant and his persecution of the Christian sect were guarantees of his anti-Christian bias. He was not shallow or fickle, or likely to be moved by anything less than an imperative revelation.

We must obey a step at a time. God says much to us directly, but he loves to employ servants like Ananias, who live in immediate touch with him. Paul never forgot that salutation, "Brother." Be very careful how you treat young converts; they need the kindest and most sympathetic handling as they step out into their new life.

We are chosen of God for three things: to know his will; to see him; and to hear his voice, v. 14.

ACTS 22:17-30

Saved for Further Service. To the story of his conversion, as given in Acts 9, the apostle here adds a detailed account of that memorable interview in the Temple, when he questioned the advisability of the Lord's command that he should leave Jerusalem and received his final and irrevocable commission to go to the Gentiles. It is a great privilege to be permitted to overhear this dialogue! How close and intimate is the disciple's relationship with his Lord! God allowed Abraham, Moses, and Jeremiah to reason with him. He does not crush down our intelligence. It is his own word: "Come, let us reason together." But there is a point beyond which we may not go, when we must accept without question the final instructions of our Captain.

A freeborn Roman was Paul. More than once he had asserted his rights as a Roman citizen, as at Philippi. There are various social and political advantages which we can turn to account in our service of the gospel, but they cannot carry us very far, and ultimately we are better off if we step out upon the waters simply because Jesus says, "Come!"

ACTS 23:1-11.

Dividing His Persecutors. The behavior of the judge was quite unworthy of his office, but Paul's epithet cannot be defended. The best of men are but men at best. Paul was thrown off his guard by an insult which touched him to the quick; but nothing could have been finer than the grace and frankness with which he acknowledged his error. The adroit way in which Paul divided the Council probably saved the situation. If the body had been united, Lysias would doubtless have handed Paul over to them to deal with. But the fiery hatred that broke out gave the chief captain grave concern for the safety of this man with citizen-rights.

How timely and precious was the Savior's revelation on the following night! As Paul's heart was sinking amid the solitude of his cell, and he was beginning to think that perhaps the predictions of Agabus and others were about to be fulfilled, he suddenly became aware of the presence of his Lord. Do not trust in your own understanding; let your Master steer your course. Remember that in the darkest hour, as in the brightest, he is beside you. There will be made to you, at "the fourth watch of the night," revelations which will reassure your weary and despairing soul that you are not alone.

ACTS 23:12-24

Would-be Murderers Baffled. The Lord had told his servant that he was needed in Rome, but the conspirators said that he should not leave Jerusalem. There is only one conclusion when such a collision occurs—God's Word must stand, to the discomfiture of those who have sworn that they will neither eat nor drink till they have perpetrated their plan to the contrary.

These high ecclesiastics fell in with an infamous plot. What will not unscrupulous men do under cover of religion! It is a pleasing trait that the Roman officer took Paul's nephew by the hand and led him aside for a private audience. How proudly would the boy recount the whole story to his mother when he emerged from those grim walls. At nine o'clock that night there was a clattering of horses' hooves as seventy horsemen and 200 soldiers went through the stone-paved streets on their way to Caesarea. Already Paul had begun his journey to Rome. Often afterward, when it seemed as though his life would be forfeited, he must have rested on the Master's words, "So must thou bear witness also at Rome." What a lifebuoy that promise was! And if God had saved him from the mob at Jerusalem and given him the friendship of Lysias, what could God not do for him in the future!

ACTS 23:25-35

Sent to a Roman Tribunal. Antipatris was forty-two miles from Jerusalem. The escort and their prisoner made the forced march in a night. Next day the legionaries marched back to Jerusalem while the mounted soldiers rode forward to Caesarea, which was twenty-six miles farther on. The apostle therefore entered Caesarea in a guise different from that in which he had left it, 21:16. Philip and the other Christians must have been startled to see how soon their forebodings were fulfilled as the great missionary, from whom they had parted with so many tears, rode through the streets surrounded by soldiers.

When Felix read the letter which Lysias had sent explaining the case, he handed Paul over to a soldier, to be kept in one of the guardrooms of the old palace which now formed the stately residence of the governors of Judea. What mingled feelings must have filled the apostle's lion heart as he realized that while Rome had him in her power, all the artifice of his bitter foes would now be powerless to do him bodily harm. The psalms which he had sung at Philippi would come to mind with added force as he strengthened his soul in God.

ACTS 24:1-16

Truth against Slander. Paul was always on the lookout for the one ray of light in murky skies. He found a reason for counting himself happy in this dark hour, v. 10. He held himself with great dignity. He remembered that he was always God's ambassador, representing the court of Heaven amid the perverse courts of human government. As for the charge of sedition, he challenged his adversaries to prove it. He pointed out that as the nation was already divided into Pharisees and Sadducees, they could hardly find fault with him for belonging to a third sect—that of the Nazarenes. After the way which they called a sect or "heresy," v. 14, he worshiped God, but he had never stirred up strife in Temple or synagogue. He protested that it had been the aim of his life to keep a conscience void of offense toward God and man.

In 23:1 he had made a similar statement. Well would it be for us if only we would devote a few minutes at the close of each day to discover whether our conscience accused us of failure in heart, thought, or behavior. The Holy Spirit pleads in the court of conscience. We would be kept from many a fall if we would be more careful to watch against the little rifts.

ACTS 24:17-27

A Trembling but Mercenary Judge. The case had broken down. Paul's statement of faith and the absence of confirmatory evidence directly contradicted the only charge against him. Felix dared not hand over Paul as guilty, and he was equally unwilling to offend the high priest's party; so he postponed his decision. In the meantime Paul's custody was not to be severe. His friends might freely see him, and the long hours were doubtless lightened by visits from Luke and Aristarchus, Philip the evangelist, and other members of the local Christian community.

At first the governor was prepossessed in Paul's favor. He had some intimate knowledge concerning the tenets of the early Church, v. 22. He had studied it as an intellectual system, and enjoyed having opportunity for conversation with its foremost exponent. But his illicit union with Drusilla, whose husband was living, and his hope to receive a bribe from Paul's friends made him obtuse and dead to the claims of Christ. Paul, on the other hand, seemed oblivious to any thought of himself or of his dependence on the governor's whim, and used his one opportunity in seeking the salvation of this weak and sordid soul. It was in vain. Felix was anchored to a mudbank and would not avail himself of the rising tides of life about him.

ACTS 25:1-12

Granting Appeal to Caesar. How inveterately must these Jews have hated Paul, when after two years they still thirsted for his blood! It would never have done for the trial to be transferred to Jerusalem, as the Jews had requested. If Paul had been brought thither, many plots might have been set on foot for the purpose of ending his life, especially if Festus proved as amenable to a bribe as had his predecessor. Festus was quite prepared to humor the Jews by granting such a transference, and there was no way of averting it other than Paul's availing himself of his right as a Roman citizen to be tried by the Emperor himself.

The appeal was a great surprise. Festus himself was probably annoyed. It would not be agreeable to him to have his jurisdiction superseded on this the first occasion of holding a public inquiry. But there was no question that the appeal was admissible, and Festus had therefore no alternative. How strangely God was fulfilling his own word, "So must thou bear witness also at Rome!" Paul had always desired to visit the imperial city, to bear thither the message of the cross; but he never expected to go under the safeguard of Roman soldiers and at Roman expense. "Deep in unfathomable mines of never-failing skill" God fulfills his purposes.

ACTS 25:13-27

Seeking Charges against His Prisoner. Mark the difference with which these two men regarded our Lord. To the one, he was the supreme object of his affection and his life; to the other, he was "one Jesus." Notice also that Paul had made clear his belief that Jesus was alive. Evidently the risen Christ had been the burden of Paul's preaching. Even Festus had come to understand that, although he would not accept it as true.

The apostle's audience on the morrow was the most dignified and influential that he had addressed up to this point. As the Lord told Ananias that Saul had been chosen to bear his name before Gentiles and kings and the children of Israel, so it came to pass. See 9:15. There is no doubt that Paul was lifted far above the thought or fear of man by the awareness that the Lord was standing by to strengthen him, so that through him the gospel might be fully known. Let us view every circumstance in our experience as the lampstand on which to place the lamp of testimony. It is a good thing to ask, "How far will this promote my Lord's business?"

ACTS 26:1-11

Paul Permitted to Speak for Himself. Though Paul's defense before Agrippa is in substance the same as that from the castle stairs at Jerusalem, it differs in the extended description of the remarkable change which had passed over his life in consequence of the direct interposition of Jesus Christ. And in the opening paragraph he lays great stress on his determined opposition to the doctrine of Christ, as a proof that his conversion was trustworthy evidence.

Stretching out his hand, the apostle began by congratulating himself on the opportunity of laying his case before the great-grandson of Herod the Great, whose elaborate training in all matters of the Jewish religion made him unusually competent to deal with the matters in debate. He asked why it should be so hard to credit the attested fact of the Lord's resurrection. He granted that he himself had resisted the evidence when he had first heard it. Indeed, he had everything to lose if he accepted it. His fiery persecution of the Christians proved at least that he was an impartial witness. So he pleaded before that group of high and mighty potentates. What a contrast between their splendid robes and sparkling jewels, and the poor, worn, shackled prisoner! But they are remembered only because of this chance connection with Paul, while Paul has led the mightiest minds of subsequent ages.

ACTS 26:12-21

Obedient to His Heavenly Vision. Nowhere else is there such deliverance from the glare and lights of earth as is afforded by a vision of the face of Jesus, brighter than the sun at noon. To everyone there comes the opportunity of catching a vision of that face, sometimes reflected in a human one, as Paul first saw it in the countenance of Stephen. It confronts us when we go on forbidden paths, and summons us to arise and follow the life which is life indeed.

Verse 16: What we have seen is only a part of the great unveiling. He will show us other and greater things than these. Verse 17: We shall be delivered, even as we are sent. The Master holds himself responsible for our safety while we are engaged in his work. Verse 18: We have here an anticipation of Col. 1:13, 14.

We must not disobey the heavenly visions that visit us. When Paul in his dream beheld the beckoning Macedonian, he made a straight course for Europe. Sometimes, in obeying, the first appearances are discouraging, as when the missionaries on landing at Philippi met only a few women beside the little river; but the final results will justify the first stepping-out of faith.

ACTS 26:22-32

Convincing His Inquisitors. Paul was in his element. He was delivering to kings and governors the testimony which it was the constant object of his life to give, when suddenly he was stopped by Festus, who on hearing of the resurrection of the dead accused Paul of madness. Paul addressed him with perfect respect, and then turned to King Agrippa for support. But Agrippa did not choose to be entrapped in the discussion of these deep religious truths. With the contempt of a man of the world, he smiled at the enthusiastic earnestness of this man who fancied that a wearer of purple would embrace faith in a crucified Messiah. It was as if he said, "In a little while you'll be making me—a Christian!"

Paul immediately caught up his words. With evident sincerity he broke in with, "I would to God, that not only thou, but also all that hear me this day, were both almost, and altogether such as I am [here he must have raised his fettered hands] except these bonds." He was no common criminal, as his judges were glad to admit, and the proceedings of that day probably, under God, saved Paul's life, for Nero could hardly condemn to death a man who had been pronounced innocent by such hearers as these.

ACTS 27:1-13

On a Dangerous Voyage. The "we" indicates that the good physician, Luke, had rejoined the party. Separated from Paul by the apostle's imprisonment, he now accompanied him on the ship to Rome. The centurion was indulgently disposed toward Paul. He may have been one of the brilliant crowd who had listened to Paul's last address. It was a most merciful Providence that placed the apostle with such a man. He showed exceptional kindness in releasing Paul on parole at Sidon, that he might visit his friends and no doubt provide himself with basic necessities for the stormy and hazardous winter voyage.

The travelers were fortunate enough to find at Myra a large vessel carrying wheat from Egypt to Rome. There was room for the centurion, his soldiers, and the prisoners, as well as such others as chose to accompany them. It was toward the close of September, and perhaps at Fair Havens the apostle and any Jewish Christians on board may have observed the great Day of Atonement, the one fast of the Jewish calendar. The season for navigation with sailing vessels was drawing to a close and Paul counseled delay, but his words were unheeded. The man who knew God was wiser than the men who knew the sea.

ACTS 27:14-26

Savior of the Ship's Company. The crew, being greatly exhausted by severe exertion and want of food, were the more willing to listen to the apostle when he came to the front with his wise counsel and good cheer. They had previously ignored his advice, but were glad and wise enough to take it on this second occasion.

How calm faith makes us! We can sleep soundly amid the roar of the storm, and dream of angels when our hearts are stayed on God. His messengers can cleave their way through the murkiest skies and most drenching storms, to succor those who need their help. What a beautiful confession that was: "Whose I am, and whom I serve!" Can we all appropriate it? The first clause is literally true of us all. We belong to Christ by creation and redemption. But do we acknowledge his ownership and place our all in his service?

In the midst of the excitement, Paul was able to give thanks. Let not the good habit of grace before meals drop out of our practice or homes. What a magnificent sentence is this also—"I believe God, that it shall be even as it was told me." Yes, there is no peace outside of that faith. And it shall be, O believer, *your* happy experience!

ACTS 27:27-34

Safety Dependent on Obedience. Paul presents a noble picture, standing there in the gray dawn while the heavy seas are breaking over the ship. He seems to have become by force of character the commander of the entire company. Certainly the soldiers and passengers owed their lives to his sagacity in penetrating the purpose of the sailors in leaving the ship. Note that he said to Julius, "ye cannot be saved," not "we." The apostle was so sure of God that he had no shadow of doubt as to his own preservation, v. 24.

Once more he encouraged them, and urged them to take food. He himself set the example, giving thanks to God in the presence of them all. How brave and how inspiring was his behavior! They all began to be of good cheer. Men may say what they will about the impracticability of Christ's teachings, but let a man once begin to live by them, obeying them absolutely and trusting Christ utterly, and he becomes like a lion in courage. Through God we can do valiantly, for he treads down our enemies, Ps. 60:12.

ACTS 27:35-44

Saving Paul Saved Them All. The sailors endeavored to head the vessel toward the mouth of a creek that appeared before them, but she ran aground and stuck fast. It was here that a new and unexpected peril confronted Paul and his fellow-prisoners. The soldiers proposed to kill them, lest they should swim ashore and escape; but the centurion, perhaps out of gratitude to the man to whom they all owed their lives, forbade the soldiers and ordered everyone to endeavor somehow to get to land.

It was a drenched and shivering group that stood on the shore on that chill November day. Thank God, our condition will be very different when we emerge on the shore of eternity after crossing the cold waters. And as we stand on the beach of the glassy sea, all of us will render praise to him who has brought us safe home.

ACTS 28:1-10

Kindness Richly Repaid. It is pleasant to read of the kindness of these Maltese. In humanity everywhere there are kindly traits, and often there will be ready help for the really destitute.

Accidents are not punishments. The clinging of the viper to Paul's hand was not an evidence of the anger of God, but was permitted in order to give these simple-hearted people an evidence which they would appreciate of God's care for his own.

How changeable is human opinion, shifting in a moment from the highest to the lowest estimate of our fellows, and basing that estimate solely on the favorable or unfavorable aspect of outward circumstances! Let us not judge by appearance, but righteously. Because Paul cast off the viper, they accounted him divine; if he had died, they would have thought him a felon. Let us also shake off temptation. We cannot prevent its attacking us, but we need not take the viper into our heart.

Paul's unfailing influence for good shows what a blessing even one Christian man can be wherever he goes, if he lives in the power of God.

ACTS 28:11-20

Still Seeking His Own Kinsmen. Paul went toward Rome, as we have seen, under very different circumstances from those that he originally anticipated; but after all, they gave him the greatest opportunity of his life. The things that befell him were for the furtherance of the gospel. In no other way could he have approached or touched such men as the centurion, or the members of Caesar's household, or Publius, or Nero himself.

It was very good of Julius to give Paul seven days' rest in the lovely bay of Puteoli, at the foot of Vesuvius. The little towns of Pompeii and Herculaneum were not yet overwhelmed. What teaching and what happy fellowship the little church now enjoyed! Forty-three miles from Rome, at Appii Forum, a body of Christians awaited the apostle with greetings, and ten miles farther on, at the Three Taverns, was another group. If Paul had entertained fears about his reception, they were immediately dispelled. The apostle thanked God and took courage.

How he had longed to see mighty Rome! He was now suffered to live in his own house, chained to a soldier. In these circumstances he was secure from the hatred and plottings of the Jews, who in every city had endangered his life and impeded his labors.

ACTS 28:21-31

Preaching in the World's Capital. It was one of the earliest cares of Paul to summon the leading members of the Jewish community, that he might explain to them his position. He made clear that he had not opposed or injured his own people, and that he was suffering because of his devotion to the "hope of Israel," by which he obviously referred to Christ. The Jews replied cautiously, declaring that they had not as yet received the formal charge against him. But as they professed a wish for further information, he begged them to fix their own day and come. This they did in considerable numbers. All day long he set before them arguments from Scripture and the story of his own experience. A few were convinced; the rest disagreed. Probably the debate toward its close became somewhat stormy, and the apostle felt at liberty to quote Isa. 6:9, 10.

He thereafter turned to the Roman Christians, who had already been addressed in his memorable epistle, in the last chapter of which is a list of names of those whom he loved in Christ. They were constantly coming in to cheer his loneliness and to hear his words, while Tychicus, Epaphras, Epaphroditus, and others brought news, greetings, and gifts from the churches he had founded.

THE EPISTLE OF
ROMANS

THE REVELATION OF "RIGHTEOUSNESS BY FAITH"

INTRODUCTION   *1:1–15.*
- A. Salutation   *1:1–7.*
- B. Personal message   *1:8–15.*

THEME: THE REVELATION OF "RIGHTEOUSNESS BY FAITH"
1:16, 17.

I. THE UNIVERSAL NEED OF RIGHTEOUSNESS   *1:18—3:20.*
- A. By the Gentiles   *1:18—2:16.*
- B. By the Jews   *2:17—3:20.*

II. THE FREE GIFT OF DIVINE RIGHTEOUSNESS   *3:21—5:21.*
- A. Bestowed through faith in Christ   *3:21–31.*
- B. Promised in God's dealings with Abraham and David   *4.*
- C. Confirmed by Christian experience   *5:1–11.*
- D. The new creation compared with the old   *5:12–21.*

III. THE REFUTATION OF OBJECTIONS   *6, 7.*
- A. Salvation by grace means the overcoming of sin   *6:1–14.*
- B. Salvation by grace brings a higher obligation than that imposed by the Law   *6:15–23.*
- C. Salvation by grace accomplishes what the Law could only command   *7.*

IV. THE MINISTRY OF THE SPIRIT OF LIFE   *8:1–39.*
- A. No condemnation   *8:1–17.*
- B. No humiliation   *8:18–27.*
- C. No separation   *8:28–39:*

V. GOD'S PURPOSE FOR THE JEWS AND GENTILES   *9—11.*
- A. The falling away of the Jews   *9:1—11:12.*
- B. The calling of the Gentiles   *11:13–24.*
- C. The restoration of the Jews   *11:25–36.*

VI. THE CHRISTIAN'S CHARACTER AND CONDUCT   *12:1—15:13.*
- A. The Christian as a man   *12.*
- B. The Christian as a citizen   *13.*
- C. The Christian as a brother   *14:1—15:13.*

VII. PERSONAL MESSAGE AND GREETINGS   *15:14—16:27.*
- A. Paul's missionary program   *15:14–29.*
- B. His fellowship with the Romans in prayer   *15:30–33.*
- C. Salutations to his friends in the church at Rome   *16:1–23.*
- D. Benediction   *16:25–27.*

INTRODUCTION

This epistle, together with those to the Corinthians and the Galatians, is allowed by all critics save a negligible minority to have been the production of the Apostle Paul. It was written from Corinth during the three months that he spent in Greece, Acts 20:3, and before he started on his last journey to Jerusalem, to carry contributions to the poor Christians there, Rom. 15:19–25.

Though the apostle was personally unacquainted with the majority of those addressed, yet the list of personal messages in the closing chapter is very large. He felt, too, a special responsibility laid upon him to instruct them in Christian truth. No epistle has so many allusions to the Law of God, but this was in harmony with the method of thought that was congenial to this Christian church, situated as it was in the mighty city that laid the foundations of law and order for subsequent generations.

COMMENTARY

ROMANS 1:1-12

The Apostle's Burning Desire. Upon the threshold of his greatest epistle, Paul describes himself as a bond servant. Such humility as his qualified him to be the medium of God's wondrous revelations. How great must be the Master who has the absolute devotion of such a man! Paul was "called" to be an apostle; we are all "called" of Jesus Christ, and "called" to be saints, vv. 1, 6, 7. Note that emphatic reference to our Lord's dual nature, vv. 3, 4.

Long before Paul saw the faces of these Christians in Rome, he had been led out in prayer for them. He had won the battle before entering the battlefield. How noble it was on the apostle's part to say that his faith was strengthened by their faith, as theirs by his, v. 12. There is a wonderful give-and-take in the service of God. Each of us helps or hinders. None is neutral.

It is quite evident that prayer counted for much with the apostle. This journey of his was the subject of continual supplication. He knew that much was to be obtained through prayer which would otherwise be missed. Remember that your journeys must also be in the will of God, v. 10.

ROMANS 1:13-23

The Only Power of Salvation. We owe everything to our Lord, but since we can make him no direct return he has made men his legatees. We are to think of others as having a claim upon us for his dear sake. In helping them, we repay him. But note the apostle's humility—"as much as in me is," v. 15. Paul was not indifferent to the claims of intellectual culture. He had been thoroughly trained in Hebrew and Greek literature. The high culture of the Roman world was appreciated by the student of Gamaliel for what it was worth; but he was not ashamed to preach the gospel in its capital because it carried with it the divine dynamic. It was "power unto salvation." The Stoic, for instance, had a high ethical code, but it was ineffective for want of the driving power of Pentecost. The one condition is faith—"to every one that believeth," v. 16.

Every man born into the world has an opportunity of knowing right and wrong from the inner witness of conscience, and of learning something of God from his works. Men will be judged by their attitude toward these two luminaries. Notice, however, that sad, strong word! Too many "hold down the truth," v. 18, margin. They deliberately endeavor to throttle it.

ROMANS 1:24-32

From Gross Sins of the Flesh. Few men knew as much as did Paul of the unutterableness of human need. In terrible words he enumerates its various aspects. Truth would enter human hearts from God's work in Nature and from conscience; yet men pull down the blind and close the curtain. It is not that they do not know, but that they refuse to have God in their knowledge. They shun the thought of God, Ps. 10:4. They will not lift their happy faces toward him with filial confidence. Thus a heavy darkness steals over them and veils his presence.

The next downward step is uncleanness; and when once men have deliberately chosen the downward path, there is nothing to stop them. They go headlong from one point to another in their descent into darkness. When our hearts turn from the purifying presence of God, they become the haunt of every foul bird and noisome reptile. What a marvel it is that out of such material God can even create saints!

ROMANS 2:1–11

Leave Judgment unto God. In this chapter the apostle turns to address the Jews. His purpose is to prove that though they may deem themselves superior to the Gentiles and capable of judging them, they may be therefore liable to more severe judgment because, notwithstanding their superior knowledge, they commit the same sins. God will judge men, not by their professions but by their works. Those who are harshest in condemning others are often guilty of the same sins, though in their own case they manage to find some excuse which extenuates their shortcomings. Rid yourself of the beam in your own eye, that you may see clearly how to rid your brother of his mote, Matt. 7:5.

God's silence does not mean indifference, but the desire to give opportunity to repent. The Lamb is in the midst of the throne, Rev. 5:6. Our redemption is by his precious blood and that alone; but the rewards of the future, and the enjoyment of what God means by life, are conditioned upon our obedience. Glory, honor, and peace are within your reach if you will accept the reconciliation offered you in Christ, which will bring you into at-one-ment with God, and if you will live to do your Heavenly Father's will.

ROMANS 2:12–20

The Searcher of All Hearts. The apostle goes on to show that all men, whether Jews or Gentiles, will be judged by the same standard. For the Jew, that Law was written upon the pages of the Old Testament; but for the Gentiles, who possessed neither Moses nor Sinai, it was written on the tablets of the heart and known as "conscience." The difference between the two is comparable to that between the time of day indicated by the sun and by the watch which each man carries in his pocket. It is a blessed and profound truth, which makes all men amenable to God's judgment, that deep down in every man's soul he has engraven his holy Law.

How clearly Scripture bears witness to the eternal judgment! See Acts 17:31. The secrets of men are to be judged, v. 16. How thankful we should be that those who stand in Christ shall not come under condemnation! He has borne the curse of a broken Law for us, and is not ashamed to call us brethren, Heb. 2:11.

ROMANS 2:21–29

He Requires Heart Obedience. The Jew relied upon the position given him by the privileges and rites of Judaism, although his religious life as such had shrunk within these outward things, as a seed rattles in its pod. The apostle's argument is meant to show that personal irreligion and unbelief will neutralize all the benefit that outward rites might promise, while humble faith will compensate for any disadvantage which might result from heathen origin and environment.

The Jew will become as a Gentile, unless he have the spiritual counterpart to outward rites, while Gentiles will become as the Chosen People of God if they have that separation of soul and life which was set forth in the initial rite of the Jew. See Col. 2:11. The mere outward rite does not constitute sonship to Abraham; and he who has never undergone it, but by faith has put away all filthiness of flesh and spirit, is entitled to all the promises made to Abraham and his seed.

ROMANS 3:1–8

God Faithful Though Men Be Faithless. The Jewish people had a great treasure entrusted to them for the benefit of the whole world. This position as stewards for mankind conferred upon them very special privileges, but also exposed them to searching discipline if they should prove faithless. Some of these advantages are enumerated in 9:4, 5. But our failures cannot cancel God's faithfulness to his covenant promises, 2 Tim. 2:13. We may always reckon confidently upon his steadfastness to his commitments, whether to the individual or to the nation. It is wonderful, v. 5, how human sin has been a path for God's glory, eliciting qualities in his love which otherwise had been unknown; but this cannot excuse our sinfulness.

If this excuse were admitted, God would clearly have been unjust in punishing sin as he has done; and if that line of argument were maintained, it would be right to do evil, if good were always the outcome. Such an admission would open the door to all kinds of abomination, and the mere suggestion of such a conclusion to his argument ought to silence the objector and cover him with shame.

ROMANS 3:9-20

All Justly under Judgment. A number of quotations are advanced—mostly from the Septuagint or Greek version of the Old Testament—establishing the hopeless evil of man's condition. These apply, in the first place, to God's peculiar people, the Jews; but if true of them, how terrible must be the condition of the great heathen world! Every mouth will be stopped and all the world brought in guilty before God, v. 19. Various organs of the body are enumerated, and in each case some terrible affirmation is made of inbred depravity. What need for salvation! What can atone for such sin, or cleanse such hearts, save the redeeming grace of God?

"Law" here is obviously employed in the wide sense of conscience as well as Scripture. It is God's ideal held up before our faces, to show us from what we have fallen. The looking-glass is intended, not to wash the face, but to show how much it needs washing. You may commend your soap, and no one will use it; but if you reveal the discoloring filth, people will be only too glad to avail themselves of the cleansing power which otherwise they would neglect and despise. The way to fill the inquiry-room is to hold up the divine standard before men's consciences.

ROMANS 3:21-31

All Freely Justified by Grace. From the universal need the apostle turns to the all-sufficient remedy. The Law and the prophets hinted dimly at justification by faith, but did not unveil it. God's way of justification is to impute righteousness to the believer. He places us in that *position* in law, before proceeding by the Holy Spirit to bring us into the *condition* of holiness. The perfect day is imputed to the dawn, the perfect flower to the seed, the finished picture to the crude sketch. As soon as we trust in Jesus, we are viewed as standing in him and justified before the Law; but before us lies the great work of assimilation to his perfect likeness by the indwelling of the Holy Spirit.

It is sin to "come short," v. 23; and who among us has fulfilled his possibilities of god-likeness? See v. 24; Gen. 1:26, 27. Though justification costs us nothing but the sacrifice of our pride, it has cost Christ his own blood, v. 25. The basis of propitiation, the mercy seat, was the golden lid of the Ark which the high priest sprinkled with blood. See Heb. 9:5. Faith has no room in her household for vaunting and boasting, v. 27. The Law is best honored when the Lawgiver, dwelling within us, fulfills it through us.

ROMANS 4:1-8

Blessedness Follows Faith. In this chapter the doctrine of justification by faith is illustrated from the life of Abraham. It is evident that he was not justified because of his good works. Nothing is said of them, though he had crossed the desert in obedience to the divine command. No; he "believed God, and it was counted unto him for righteousness," v. 3. The life of God in the soul of man is one and the same in every age. The measure of light may vary from the twilight in Ur to the meridian glory of Patmos, but the attitude of the soul toward God must always be the same.

From the earliest times men have been justified by faith, Heb. 11:4. Faith has two invariable elements: attitude and receptiveness; that is, the right position toward God, and the power of receiving the full inflow of the divine nature. We are made "partakers of the divine nature," 2 Pet. 1:4. This was the case with the great Hebrew pilgrim—first of the pilgrim race. Rising above the rest of his contemporaries, he saw the advance gleam of the day of Christ and was glad, John 8:56. David also sings of the same grace which justifies the sinner and counts him as righteous, notwithstanding his iniquities and sins, Ps. 32:1, 2.

ROMANS 4:9-15

This Blessedness Is for All. In Abraham's case it is clear that he was justified when he was still a Gentile. The initial badge of Judaism was stamped upon him long after he had believed God. The apostle lays great stress on this order of time: first faith, then obedience, and afterward circumcision that made him the father and founder of the Jewish people. Justification is imputed to him in the first stage—not in circumcision, not even in obedience, but in the simple act of believing God, as we have it in Gen. 15:6. We do not hear of circumcision till Chapter 17.

Clearly, then, if we Gentiles have Abraham's faith, we may also claim the same justifying righteousness, though we have not received any outward rite. And also, we may be reckoned among his children. If we enter into the meaning of these earlier stages of the patriarch's life, we may claim the promises made to him in uncircumcision. Count them up; they are yours. We, too, may become heirs of the world; in us also, because we are his seed, all mankind may be blessed.

ROMANS 4:16-25

Following Abraham in Faith in God. Notice the remarkable alteration made by the RV in v. 19. The KJV suggests that Abraham refused to consider the physical disabilities which seemed to make the fulfillment of God's promise impossible; the RV says that he looked them all quietly in the face, as though taking into account all their significance and force. Then he looked to the promise; and after balancing one against the other, he decided absolutely and confidently that the Word of God must stand, however great and forbidding the difficulties in the way. He was fully persuaded that what God had promised he was able to perform.

Let us remember, then, that from the time we trust Christ—whatever may have been our frailties and temptations—we are reckoned as righteous in the sight of God. Yes, and in addition, we may count on absolute deliverance from the power of sin. Do not look down, brooding over your weakness! Do not look back upon your past, strewn with failure! Look up to the living Christ! All the promises of God are yea and amen in Christ Jesus, 2 Cor. 1:20.

ROMANS 5:1-11

Great Blessings through Christ. We stand in grace; we look for glory. Our standing is sure, although apart from our feelings or deserts. It is ours forever, through union with the living Christ. It is our admission to the home of God's elect. We have passed the threshold and have received, in the antechamber, the new white robe. But being in the house we find several stories or tiers of ascent. They are marked by the phrases "not only so" and "much more."

Starting from faith, the staircase mounts from peace, v. 1, to hope, v. 2; from hope to love, v. 5; from reconciliation to salvation and life and joy in God, vv. 9–11, so that whatever he does, as well as whatever he is, awakens in our hearts responsive admiration and glad consent. Stand on these successive terraces in the mountain climb to take your breath and behold the far-spread landscape. Let us not be content with the foot of the ladder when all these rounds of light invite us. Especially ponder v. 10, where the apostle distinguishes between reconciliation and salvation. What music there is in that wonderful phrase, "saved by his life." By his life *for* us in Heaven and *in* us by his Spirit.

ROMANS 5:12-21

Death through Adam; Life through Christ. This is the profoundest and most fundamental section of the whole epistle. It contains an insight into the deep things of God, 1 Cor. 2:10. We must read it slowly and thoughtfully many times in order to catch its drift. In these comments we can only skim in the most superficial manner across the surface.

We are here taught the unity of the race, not only in Adam, but in Christ. Adam's sin has affected the standing of every man; but the grace and the obedience of the "one man," Jesus Christ, have secured for all men the offer of the free gift. The guilt that lay upon the race by the sin of Adam has been removed from the race by the obedience of the Son of man to the cross. None, therefore, are condemned on account of that first transgression or doomed for that primal fall. In a sense, all are made righteous; that is, all stand before God on the basis of their individual, rather than their racial, responsibility. We are not condemned with Adam, but will be condemned if we refuse to avail ourselves of the grace of Jesus Christ. All that sin forfeited is put within our reach. Nay, we may reach higher heights than Adam, if we will only receive the abundance of the grace of Christ.

ROMANS 6:1-11

"Dead unto Sin, but Alive unto God." It is not sufficient merely to apprehend, however clearly, our standing in Christ; we must see to it that the doctrine issues in a holy life. Nothing is more hurtful than to hold a truth intellectually without giving it expression in character. Many who fight for the minute points of doctrinal accuracy are careless of the great demands of Christ for a life of Godlike love. Therefore, after the apostle's massive statements of doctrine, he now turns to discuss the way of a holy life. The work of Christ *for us* must lead to his work *in us* and deliverance from the power of sin.

All who believe in Christ are reckoned as having been included in his death. They did not make atonement for sin, but they died to the life of self-will, of self-pleasing, of subjection to the world-spirit, of citizenship in the earth-sphere, and passed with Christ into the life of resurrection glory. This is the significance of the rite of baptism. "Mark that seal!" cries the apostle. "You belong to the resurrection side of death. Live in union with the risen Redeemer."

ROMANS 6:12–23

"Sin Shall Not Have Dominion." Standing with Christ on the resurrection side of death, we must present our whole being to God for his use. We have left forever behind, nailed to the cross, the body of sin, Col. 2:14, and henceforth must see to it that every faculty shall become a weapon in God's great warfare against evil. Let your powers be monopolized by God, so that there shall be no room left for the devil, Eph. 4:27.

All serve some higher power, but which? Our real owner and master, whatever we may say to the contrary, is indicated by our life. We belong to the one whom, in a crisis, we obey. Service to sin leads to uncleanness, iniquity, and death. Service to God leads to righteousness, and that to sanctification, and that to eternal life. Run your life into the mold of holy precept, as the obedient metal into the cast, v. 17. We have our reward in the present enjoyment of the life which is life indeed.

ROMANS 7:1–13

The Law Makes Sin Known. To make his meaning clear, the apostle now enters upon a parable drawn from domestic life. He says that we are married to the Law as our first husband and seek, through union with it, to bring forth fruit unto God. Every convert earnestly endeavors, in the first impulse of the new life, to be good and to form, by incessant effort, a life that is pleasing to God. Like Cain, we bring the fruit of the ground, extorted from the soil by the sweat of the brow.

But we are soon disappointed in the result. Our laborious care ends in failure. Sinful desires are too masterful. As Luther said, "The old Adam is too strong for the young Melanchthon." Then we see that the cross has put death between us and our painful effort. We learn that the marriage contract which bound us to our first husband, the Law, has been dissolved. We are set free to enter into marriage union with the blessed Lord, and he, by his indwelling Spirit, effects in us what our own energies have failed to produce. We are joined to him that was raised up from the dead, and bring forth fruit unto God.

ROMANS 7:14–25

The Conflict Within. The apostle gives a further statement of his personal experience of the inability of the soul to realize the divine ideal which has been revealed to it as the norm and type of its attainment. Life does not run smoothly. There are effort, strain, failure, the consciousness of sin, the dazzling glory of sunlight on inaccessible peaks. Why is this? It is due to the lack of "power unto salvation." We are not strong enough to win any victory. We are weak through the flesh. There is a leakage through which our good desires vanish, as water through a cracked vessel.

Self is ever the difficulty. Before we find Christ, or are found of him, we try to justify ourselves, and afterward to sanctify ourselves. Notice how full these verses are of I, and how little is said of the Holy Spirit. As the corpse of a criminal that was, in the old barbarous days, hung around the neck of a living man, so the flesh is to us, with all its evil promptings. But this background of dark experience, ending in vanity, vexation, disappointment, and misery leads to the following chapter, which is saturated with Pentecostal power. The distant anticipation of this revives us, like the scent of land to animals sick with a long voyage; and we thank our God.

ROMANS 8:1–9

New Life in the Spirit. This may fitly be called "the chapter of the Holy Spirit." The apostle has carefully kept this great theme in the background till he has well prepared the ground, by showing us our inability to attain our ideals apart from reinforcements of divine energy. Here is the motive power to drive our machinery! Here is the life-giving power of spring, which shall cause the seeds buried within us to burst forth in the garden of the Lord! See Isa. 61:10, 11.

There is no need to live in perpetual self-condemnation. As the living bird, obeying the laws of flight, is superior to the down-pull of gravitation, so where the life of Jesus is wrought and sustained in the heart by the incessant communications of the Holy Spirit, victory is given us over the perpetual down-pull of sin. We can only hate the spirit that crucified our Lord. The believer reckons himself dead to it, but alive to each prompting of God's Holy Spirit. Life and peace and righteousness dwell in the temple within. A more perfect goodness is thus produced in us than any external obedience to Sinai's code could ever have achieved.

ROMANS 8:10–17

Children and Heirs of God. The Spirit here is of course the Holy Spirit, by whom Christ our Lord lives within us. It is wonderful that as the life which throbs in the heart beats also in the pulse, so the very life which is in Christ in glory is also in our hearts. Our main task is to put aside every barrier to its full expression. This is what the apostle means by putting to death the practices, stratagems, and lawless promptings of the body, which are ever calling for ease and self-indulgence. There is no stage of our earthly pilgrimage at which we can dispense with the power of the Spirit of God for deliverance from the deeds of the body.

But there is another most blessed function of the divine Spirit, v. 14. He is willing to lead us, to prompt our actions, to inspire our purposes, and to mold our characters. The more we yield to him, the deeper becomes our awareness of that filial relationship with God which is expressed in the cry, "Abba, Father." But note the wonderful climax, v. 17. If we yield to the Holy Spirit, he will conduct us into the divine treasure-house and bid us avail ourselves of the infinite resources which are there stored for our use, not in the next life, but in this.

ROMANS 8:18–30

Hoping for the Completed Redemption. Creation groans for freedom from the serpent's trail. Like a captive maiden, she sighs to be delivered from the curse which sin has brought upon her. The saints groan for the resurrection of the body and their full admission into the complete enjoyment of redemption. The Spirit also groans for the speedy accomplishment of God's purposes—the salvation of the lost, the unity of the Church, and the advent of the Father's kingdom. His yearnings express themselves through the prayers of the saints.

Sorrowful soul, take comfort from v. 28! All things are "working"; there is no stagnation. They are "working together," like the cogs of two wheels revolving in different directions. They are all "working together for good." The only condition is "love" on our part. Those who love God are loved by God, and all winds blow from the quarter of God's love. That love is a sure sign and token that they have been called; and if called, they may be sure that they are on the moving stairway which is bearing them up and on through successive stages to glory.

ROMANS 8:31–39

No Separation from Christ's Love. This is the close of the apostle's argument. He has shown that believers are dear to God because they are in Christ; that their every need has been anticipated and provided for; that their guilt has been canceled and provision made for their holy and victorious character; that the Holy Spirit is in them and with them forever; that sin is under their feet and Heaven over their heads —what, then, have they to fear?

Paul then goes on to show that the love of God is unaffected by even the most extreme changes of our condition—"neither death, nor life," v. 38. That it is undiverted from us by any other order of beings—"nor angels, nor principalities, nor powers." That it is universally present throughout creation. And finally, that this love is "in Christ Jesus our Lord." But in order to know and experience this love, we must be united to the Lord Jesus by a living faith. Then we shall be "more than conquerors"; that is, we shall not only be victorious, but shall get spoil out of the very things that have hurt us.

ROMANS 9:1–13

Longing for His Kinsmen. Our consciences should be continually bathed in the light and warmth of the Holy Spirit, v. 1, that the inward witness may be maintained in its integrity. We must love as Moses and Paul did, v. 3, before we can understand Exod. 32:32 and Gal. 3:10. The Hebrew nation was marvelously privileged by "adoption" as God's firstborn, by having the shekinah "glory," and by being called to maintain the witness of the Temple and its "services," v. 4. But these privileges were granted, not for the nation itself, but for the blessing of mankind. This is the meaning of election. There are elect races, elect nations, elect souls, that they may be able to impart what they have received and communicate whatever advantages have been intrusted.

The sorrowful admission must be made that a very large proportion of the Hebrew race had missed the privileges to which they were entitled, because they had regarded these merely as intended for their own comfort and enrichment, v. 6. This was the outstanding difference between Esau and Jacob. It is plain that the hatred in v. 13 means nothing more than relative repudiation, as it does in Matt. 6:24 and Luke 14:26. No personal animosity can obtain in the nature of the God of love except that he withholds from the recreant soul the full manifestation and outflow of his love.

ROMANS 9:14–24

The Righteousness of God's Choices. God desires to do his best for every man. But, as in the case of Esau who wantonly sold his birthright, and of Pharaoh who turned all God's revelations into occasions of aggravated resistance and stronger revolt, the Heavenly Father is sometimes compelled to cast away those who might assist in the execution of his purposes, and use inferior vessels made from common clay. In the earlier part of the conflict with the proud Egyptian monarch, it is said that *he* hardened his heart, and afterward that *God* hardened it, Exod. 8:15; 10:20. To the froward, God becomes froward; that is, the means that he takes to soften and save will harden, just as the sun which melts wax hardens clay.

The same power which was thwarted and resisted by the unbelief and stubbornness of the Chosen People has taken up us Gentiles, who have had none of their advantages. And what wonderful mercy has God shown to us! "Riches of his glory on the vessels of mercy," v. 23. What an argument for us all not to resist the grace of God, which strives with us so earnestly and continually! God can make saints out of the most unlikely material. Let us see that he has full opportunity.

ROMANS 9:25-33

Stumbling over the Cornerstone. There has been a notable transference of privilege from the Jew to the Gentile believer. This is not due to fickleness on God's part, but to a fatal defect in the Hebrew people. The vessel that was marred in the potter's hand suffered not from the clumsiness of the potter, but from some inherent flaw in the clay. The Chosen People stumbled over the law of faith and rejected their Messiah. The Gentiles, on the other hand, have exercised faith in him, and have thereby attained a justifying righteousness. There is no caprice with God, "neither shadow of turning," Jas. 1:17. Any apparent change in his dealings is determined by our attitude toward him.

Jesus is a stone of stumbling to the blind, but all who confide in him and rest on him shall not be put to shame. God has laid the foundation of our salvation deep in the waters of death and judgment. In the death of Christ he condemned sin in the flesh, and now we who are built into him, as a stone is clamped to the foundation, shall rest secure when the last great storms sweep over land and sea.

ROMANS 10:1-10

Missing God's Way of Salvation. How earnestly the apostle loved his own people! All their hatred of him could not extinguish the passionate devotion which he entertained for them. "Apostle to the Gentiles" he might be, but he was essentially "an Israelite, of the seed of Abraham, of the tribe of Benjamin," 11:1. The whole reason of their rejection of the gospel lay in their inveterate refusal to "submit," v. 3. Is not that the difficulty with us all? It is not that we cannot believe, but that we will not submit to God's way of righteousness, so humbling is it to our pride.

If only God would allow us to scale the heights or plumb the depths, to do some great thing, to make some vast sacrifice, we should be satisfied to be saved, and his help in the process would not be resented. But it is intolerable to our proud hearts to be told that our own efforts are useless, and that the exclusive source of salvation is God's grace.

Notice the distinction between "righteousness" and "salvation," v. 10. The one is objective; the other subjective. The first, our standing before God; the latter, the sanctification of our inner life, which not only depends upon the belief of the heart, but requires the confession that Jesus Christ has become Lord and King of the whole nature.

ROMANS 10:11-21

Needing Messengers of Good Tidings. The Chosen People chafed, not only at the freeness of God's justifying grace, but because there was no difference made, so far as salvation was concerned, between them and the Gentiles. Surely there ought to be a special doorway for them into eternal life, apart from that trodden by the feet of the ordinary heathen world! Were they not the children of Abraham, the friend of God? Here the apostle was compelled to withstand them. No, said he, it cannot be! There is no difference between Jew and Greek. All have sinned, and the same Lord is over all, rich to those who call upon him, of whatever nationality.

The guests for whom the marriage feast was prepared refused to come, and therefore it was decreed that the servants of the great King should preach the gospel to every creature, and scour the highways and byways of the world for guests. The remainder of the chapter, v. 14ff., therefore vindicates the apostle in his determination to preach the gospel beyond the limits of his own people; and in doing so, he was acting upon the old words of Deut. 32:21. God would provoke their jealousy by a no-people, as they had provoked his by no-gods, v. 19.

ROMANS 11:1-12

A Remnant Saved by Grace. In the worst days of Hebrew apostasy there was always an elect handful that did not go astray after other gods. It was so in the days of Elijah; and it was a comfort to the faithful heart of Paul to believe that amid the general opposition excited by the preaching of the gospel, there were many secret lovers of the cross who were true to the Messiah and his claims. Man can never count these quiet, unknown, holy souls who, like the sweetest wild flowers, can be detected only by the fragrance of their lives. But God counts them, to whose grace and care all that is good in them is due.

The few seek and find, because they stoop to seek in God's predetermined way and along his lines. But when men set themselves against these, they become hardened and overwhelmed by a "spirit of slumber," v. 8. When Scripture says that God gives them this, it simply means that such state of insensibility is the working out of an inevitable law. But the apostle cherished the secret hope that the avidity with which the Gentiles were accepting the gospel would, in the mystery of God's Providence, have the ultimate effect of bringing the Chosen People back to him whom their fathers crucified, v. 11.

ROMANS 11:13-24

Others Grafted in by Faith. Paul never abandoned the hope that ultimately Israel would come back to God in Christ. He believed that God's promises pointed in that direction and that though centuries might pass, those sure guarantees would be abundantly fulfilled. Notice his expressions: "how much more their fulness," v. 12; "what shall the receiving of them be, but life from the dead?," v. 15; "God is able to graff them in again," v. 23; "all Israel shall be saved," v. 26; "that he might have mercy upon all," v. 32. He realized, however, that Israel must temporarily make way for the ingathering of the Church, in which there is neither Jew nor Greek; and that when the Church has been formed and gathered to its Lord, then the time for the ingathering of the Jewish people will have arrived.

Let us see to it that we Gentiles understand our position as being permitted to partake of "the root and fatness of the olive tree," v. 17. Christ was the root of that tree, and it is from his rich nature that all the freshness and fatness, all the quickening and energy, all the love and grace of the Hebrew Scriptures and heritage of promises were gained. Whatever Israel had, we may have. Let us go up and possess the land!

ROMANS 11:25-36

That God "Might Have Mercy upon All." "Mysteries" are the reasons and principles of the divine procedure which are hidden from ordinary minds, but revealed to the children of God by the Spirit, who searches the deep things, 1 Cor. 2:10. We cannot tell how near the brim we are, or when the fullness of the Gentiles will fill the predestined measure. It may be much nearer than we suppose, and then the door will be closed, and the Hebrew nation will be grafted in to serve the divine program in the last stages of human history. They are still beloved for their fathers' sake, and the day is coming when all their sins will be forgiven and taken away.

We may go a certain distance in the devout understanding of the ways of God, but there is a point beyond which we cannot advance; and as we gaze down into the profound abyss of the divine dealings, we must cry, "O the depth," v. 33. The origin, the maintenance, and the ultimate end of creation, Providence, and redemption is God. To him must be the glory! In other words, we shall find that the whole story of sin, redemption, and salvation will unravel and reveal the nature of God, as the prismatic band of color the sunlight.

ROMANS 12:1-8

Devoting Self and Using Gifts. "Therefore" links this practical appeal to the whole of the sublime argument which reaches its climax in the previous chapter. It is easier to die once for God than to live always the surrendered life. But nothing so pleases God as daily surrender, the sacrificed and yielded will tied by cords to his altar. Such an attitude is the only reasonable one we can assume. If God be all we profess to believe, he is worthy of all we are. But we are reminded that the world is ever seeking to mold us to its will, and we need the renewing grace of the Holy Spirit, that we may withstand its baleful influence. We need to be transformed—that is, transfigured—by the renewing of our mind. Please God, and you will be pleased with the will of God.

Notice in v. 3 that God deals out according to the measure of our faith. Let us ask that it may be "pressed down and running over." In proportion as we are united to the Head, we are members of one another. We may not recognize each other, or be recognized by the world as one, but in his sight there is only one body, v. 5. Let each learn what he can do best, and devote his best to it. To give or rule aright is equally a gift with teaching.

ROMANS 12:9-21

Living as a Christian. In this section the apostle shows how the great principle of consecration must affect the details of conduct. It is most necessary to insist on these practical issues. At some impressive religious convention, where the vision of a surrendered and transfigured life is presented, sensitive souls are led to make vows and claim the plane of life which has been presented; but on their return to the common places, there is no perceptible improvement in their speech or tone or attitude. This induces shame and contempt. Hence the great wisdom of the apostle's particular teaching in this and the following chapters.

God has endowed us with faith as the receptive faculty, through which we may receive his blessed help. In the power of the Holy Spirit let us set ourselves to our common tasks, thinking humbly and soberly of ourselves, lovingly of our associates, and reverently of God. We are inspired to fulfill the obligations of our position, whether in giving money or in teaching the ignorant, whether in showing mercy or in exercising authority, because all is done as under the eye of the great Master of the household.

ROMANS 13:1-7

Rendering "to All Their Dues." Human government, like the existence of the family relationship, is a divine institution. It is part of the order of the world and rooted in the original conception of the race. It was never intended that we should live as individual units, but as members of family and state. It is evident, therefore, that the authority which is wielded by the ruler expresses, generally speaking, a divine principle. The comfort and well-being of society are better attained in that way than in any other, and the recognition of this principle carries with it the assent of our intuitive convictions. We must "render therefore to all their dues."

But it must be acknowledged, also, that there are limits beyond which imperial or legislative authority may not go. When Nero, according to tradition, bade the apostle to abandon his faith as the condition of liberty, Paul did not hesitate to say that the Emperor was intruding on a province to which he had no claim, and that he must obey God rather than man.

ROMANS 13:8-14

Love Fulfills the Law. The one debt which can never be discharged is love. Because we can never be out of debt to God, we are called upon to show unending love to man. So long as we love we cannot injure; and therefore the man who is always caring for others as much as, or more than, he does for himself (and this latter is the Christian ideal) is fulfilling that ancient law.

We resemble soldiers slumbering in their tents while dawn is flushing the sky. Presently the bugle rings out its awakening note. The long night of the world is ending, the dawn is on the sky, and all the malignity of men and demons cannot postpone it by a single hour. Let us put off the garments which only befit the darkness, and array ourselves in the armor of the day! What is that armor? In a word, it is Jesus Christ—his character and method, his unselfishness and purity—so that when men see us, they may involuntarily turn to him.

ROMANS 14:1-12

Consideration toward Brethren. The weak conscience needs further instruction. It is anemic and requires the hilltop, with its further view and bracing air; but in the meantime its owner must be guided by its promptings. A man must not take a certain course merely because others do so, unless he can justify their bolder faith and larger freedom. By thought and prayer and the study of God's Word, conscience becomes educated and strengthened and ceases to worry as to whether we should be vegetarian or not, whether we should observe saints' days, or adopt a specific method of observing the Sabbath. Some people are constantly wondering and questioning about such things, as though their eternal salvation depended on minute observances.

Such would have found but scant comfort from the apostle. He would have said, "Do the best you know, and when you have once adopted a certain method of life, follow it humbly, until some wider view is opened before you by the Spirit of God." The main principle for us all is to live and die to please our Lord. He is our Master, and it will be for him to allot our rewards. In the meantime let us not judge one another, but live in love, leaving each to work out the plan of his own life as his Master directs.

ROMANS 14:13-23

Yielding Rights for Others' Sake. We must be careful of one another's faith. Unkind criticism or ridicule, or the strong pressure of our arguments and reasons may impede the divine life in weaker natures by leading them to act in defiance of their own conscientious convictions. We must not flaunt our greater liberty or urge men to act against their conscience. We may, of course, temperately and lovingly explain why we are not held by minute scruples. We may show, as Paul did repeatedly, that Christ has called us to liberty; but we must not attempt the regulation of one another's conduct from without. The sanctuary of the soul must be left uninvaded. The Spirit alone may speak his oracles in the shrine.

Leave each disciple to his own Master, each plant to the Gardener, each child to the Father. In many things you may grant yourself a wider liberty than others allow themselves; but it must be used wisely, and you must refuse to avail yourself of it whenever those around you may be imperiled. We need not mind the censorious criticism of the Pharisee, but like the Good Shepherd with his flock, we must accommodate our pace to that of the lambs, Isa. 40:11.

ROMANS 15:1-13

Following Christ in Pleasing Others. This chapter is remarkable for its threefold designation of God: "the God of patience and consolation," v. 5; "the God of hope," v. 13; and "the God of peace," v. 33. Our character may be deficient in these things, but his fullness is there for us to draw upon. There is no stint or lack for those to whom he says, "Son, thou art ever with me, and all that I have is thine."

We must always be on the lookout for the weak, the heavy-laden, and the downcast. Let us help them with their burdens, anxieties, fears, and questionings—imparting to them something of our cheery hope, never pleasing ourselves, merciful to others, though merciless in the standard and criticism we apply to our own conduct, comforting ourselves with the Word of God, that we may be able to impart these divine consolations to others. Where such conditions are realized, life becomes a dream of Heaven actualized in flesh and blood. But we must fulfill the injunctions of vv. 9-13, rejoicing in praise and abounding in hope. The outlook on the earth-side may be dark and depressing, but uncurtain your windows toward God—see, the land is light.

ROMANS 15:14-21

A Preacher Who Found His Own Field. A superficial judge of the apostle's life at the time to which he refers might have supposed him to be a mere Jewish traveler, hurrying to and fro, under circumstances of extreme poverty and with no special results. But in fact he was laying the foundations of the Christian commonwealth. His one ambition was to present the Gentiles as a whole burnt offering to God; see v. 16. The phrase there is suggestive of the supreme sacrifice which was nobly realized in the strength of purpose that led those churches, shortly afterward, to yield holocausts of martyrs under Nero's persecutions.

All this was due to Christ working through the apostle. Anything that was not wrought through the power of the indwelling Christ was not worth recounting. The work which really mattered was not what Paul did for Christ, but what Christ did through Paul. It is noticeable how careful Paul was to break up new ground. This is especially characteristic of all the best and highest forms of work. It is a poor church which recruits itself from the labors of others, but has no power to secure converts from the world!

ROMANS 15:22-33

Ambitious to Render Service. The apostle felt that it was in the line of the divine will that he should visit Rome, 1:10. Relying as he did on the efficacy of prayer, it is not surprising to find him urging his Roman friends to unite with him in asking, as in vv. 30-32, that his way may be made plain. The prayer was not answered quite as he expected. He little thought that he would come as a prisoner, bound to a soldier, and at the expense of the Roman Empire. Yet he came with joy, and found refreshment and rest with the beloved circle of disciples whom he enumerates in the following chapter. How little do most of us know of this striving in prayer! But how near we get to absent friends when we pray like this! "Strive together with me."

"The love of the Spirit" is a very delightful phrase. It bears witness to the personality of the Holy Spirit, for love cannot be attributed to an influence. It also shows the confidence with which we may commit ourselves to his gracious indwelling and prompting. He is the *Holy* Spirit, but we need not shrink from him as an awful guest. It also reminds us how deeply he may be grieved. There is no grief so poignant as that which is suffered by love.

ROMANS 16:1-16

Personal Interest in Fellow-Christians. Here is a window into Paul's heart. He was apparently disowned by his own kindred, yet, as the Lord had promised, he had mothers, sisters, and brothers a hundred-fold. What a contrast there is between the spirit of this chapter and that of the mere disputant or theologian, the Stoic or monk. We see also the courtesy, purity, thoughtfulness, and tenderness of Christian relationships.

Women are here—Phebe, Priscilla, Mary, Junia, Persis, Julia, and others. The apostle realized the immense help that holy women could furnish in the ministry of the gospel. Men are here—old and young, fathers, brothers, and sons. Lovely titles are given with a lavish, though a discriminating hand—"succourer, helpers, beloved, approved in Christ, saints." How especially beautiful is the appellation, "the beloved Persis, which laboured much in the Lord." The kiss was the common mode of greeting, but there was to be a new sanctity in it, as though Christ were between. This church in Rome was a model for other churches. Would that we could realize the same spiritual unity that presided over the gatherings of these early saints!

ROMANS 16:17-27

Receive Helpers; Shun Hinderers. Those who cause divisions on obscure points of doctrine are to be avoided, lest they lead us away from the fundamentals. We need to be wise in heavenly wisdom and guileless in regard to evil. The pure, childlike heart is quick to discern right and wrong, because of the breath that evil leaves on its clear mirror.

In the case of each believer, however weak and helpless, God is pledged to fulfill to us Gen. 3:15. Not merely will he help us to do it, but he will do it for us. It is a remarkable conjunction; God against the devil, and peace "bruising."

These postscripts, from v. 17 on, were probably written by Paul's own hand. See 1 Cor. 16:21. We are not all, as were Gaius and Erastus, men of note and wealth, but we can all resemble Quartus, "a brother." The mystery or secret with which the epistle closes refers to the redemption wrought out by Jesus during his earthly ministry, 1 Tim. 3:16. But this was no new thing, as it had been in the mind of God from times eternal, Rev. 13:8.

THE FIRST EPISTLE TO THE CORINTHIANS

THE GOSPEL THE POWER OF GOD AND THE WISDOM OF GOD

SALUTATION   *1:1–3.*

I. TRUE AND FALSE WISDOM   *1:4—6:20.*
   A. Thanksgiving for the grace given to the Corinthians   *1:4–9.*
   B. The cause of and remedy for divisions in the Church   *1:10–31.*
   C. The basis of Paul's ministry   *2.*
   D. The function of the apostles   *3.*
   E. The labors of the apostles   *4:1–13.*
   F. Conditions which require Paul's presence at Corinth   *4:14—5:13.*
   G. Heathen and Christian life in contrast   *6.*

II. REPLY TO INQUIRIES FROM THE CORINTHIANS   *7—10.*
   A. Concerning marriage   *7.*
   B. Concerning things sacrificed to idols   *8, 10.*
      (Apostolic liberty)   *9.*

III. "A MORE EXCELLENT WAY"   *11—16.*
   A. The deportment of women in the Church   *11:1–16.*
   B. The observance of the Lord's Supper   *11:17–34.*
   C. Concerning spiritual gifts   *12.*
   D. The greatest gift   *13.*
   E. Speaking with tongues   *14.*
   F. The resurrection   *15.*
   G. The offering for the saints   *16:1–8.*
   H. Personal matters   *16:9–18.*

CONCLUSION   *16:19–24.*

INTRODUCTION

Corinth was an important and wealthy city. Having ports on two seas, it was a great trading center. Christianity was first introduced there by Paul on his second missionary journey. His continued labors were successful in building up a vigorous church. But on his leaving for other fields of labor, serious evils broke out among the members. Some countenanced immorality, idol feasts, lawsuits in heathen courts, and immodesty among women. As tidings of these evils were brought to Paul at Ephesus, he addressed this letter to the Corinthian church "with many tears," 2 Cor. 2:4. The letter was written about A.D. 57. Several features of special interest characterize this epistle—notably the gospel as the wisdom of God, the supremacy of love, and the doctrine of the resurrection.

COMMENTARY

1 CORINTHIANS 1:1-11

Enriched and United in Christ. It was pleasant to the church at Corinth to realize that one of their own number was associated with the apostle in his great ministry. Compare v. 1 with Acts 18:17. We have been sanctified in Christ in the purpose of God, but we must make our calling sure by living as saints. Note Paul's liberality—it was enough for him if men called on Jesus as their Lord. Such he could receive as brothers. There was no strain of narrow sectarianism in his nature.

If we would live a true life, we must draw on Jesus Christ. Our riches are in him, awaiting our claiming and use. The unsearchable riches of Christ are at our disposal, but we must appropriate and use them. Let us begin to live as God's heirs. Utterance and knowledge are ours through the Holy Spirit. We have looked into ourselves for them. That is the mistake! We must look up and reach down. God has called us into partnership with his Son. We share his sorrows, sufferings, and labors for a world's conversion; he bids us share in his grace. The perfecting of v. 10 is the weaving together of a rent garment. Paul's object in this epistle was the ending of the strife that had divided the Corinthian church.

1 CORINTHIANS 1:12-25

The Cross God's Saving Power. Apollos had gone straight from Ephesus to Corinth, Acts 19:1. A party gathered around him, especially attracted by his eloquence and intellectual brilliance. Cephas was Peter, and around his name the more conservative elements gathered. Christ stood for the promised glory of the Messianic kingdom. Paul was filled with dismay on hearing that a fourth division of the church called themselves by his name. He told the Corinthians that whatever any of their human teachers had done for them, they had contributed only different phases or viewpoints of truth, all of which service sank into absolute insignificance as contrasted with the death of Jesus Christ on the cross.

The "cross" here implies not only the doctrine of the Atonement, but the humble bearing of the cross in daily life. There are many who wear a cross as an article of dress, but who evince nothing of its pitying, self-immolating, sacrificial spirit. Everyone needs a Calvary in the heart. Note from v. 18, margin, that being saved is a process as well as an immediate experience. Oh, to have grace to know the cross, never to be ashamed of it, and to preach a crucified Savior in a humble, crucified spirit!

1 CORINTHIANS 1:26—2:5

God's Glory in Men's Weakness. Like the sons of Jesse before Samuel, so do the successive regiments on which the world relies pass before Christ. The wise, the mighty, the noble, the great, the things that are! And the King says, "I have not chosen these." The warriors with whom he will win the world to himself are the nobodies, the people who in the world's estimate do not count. Do not depreciate yourself, but give yourself to him; he will find a niche for you and make your life worth living. Notice that God has put you into union with Christ Jesus. Everything we need for life and godliness is in him; only let us make all that we can of our wonderful position and possessions.

Paul came to Corinth from Athens, where he had sought to win his hearers by a studied and philosophical discourse as best adapted to their needs. But as he entered Corinth, he appears to have deliberately determined that his theme would be the crucified Lord, expressed in the simplest phrases. When we speak the truth as it is in Jesus, the Spirit is ever at hand to enforce our testimony by his demonstration and power.

1 CORINTHIANS 2:6-16

God's Wisdom Spiritually Revealed. The perfect are those who are full-grown and mature in Christian experience. They need strong meat. For them there are blessed unveilings of the secret things of God, such as the profoundest thinkers of this world have never reached. The words in v. 9 must not be applied to Heaven alone; in their first intention they belong to us in this mortal life. The human eye that has seen the fairest of earth's things, and the ear that has heard the sweetest strains of human melody have never experienced the depths of enjoyment of those who have found the love of God in Christ. They who know Christ should not be content with the mere rudiments of the gospel, but should follow on to know those deeper things which evade men who are merely clever, but are revealed to those who are really good.

There are two types of men. There is the "spiritual" man, whose spirit is the temple and dwelling-place of the Spirit of God. He knows the thoughts of God, because he has a living union with the eternal Mind. And there is the "natural man," possessing merely the intellect and conscience of ordinary humanity.

1 CORINTHIANS 3:1-9

Prosperity Comes from God. In all relations with their fellowmen, Christ's followers must realize their obligations as members of one great family, with one God. A man may be "in Christ," truly regenerate and forgiven for his past sins, and yet be carnal; that is, according to Rom. 7:18, he may be ruled by me, I, self. The marks of this inward disposition are set out here. He is a babe who needs to be fed with milk, little and often, because unable to digest solid food. He is a sectarian, throwing contempt on those who do not belong to his own school of thought. He allows himself to be infected with jealousy and strife. Let us test our Christian life by these symptoms. Where are we? And if we are conscious that self has become enthroned as the governing motive of life, let us not rest till Christ takes its place.

It is not easy to learn that the planter or the waterer is just nothing at all, and that God is all. Let us think of ourselves only as God's instruments, and in a humble way as God's fellow-workers. It is a most helpful thought. Constantly when engaged in tilling the soil as evangelists or in building character as preachers and teachers, let us count on success because of the power of our great Partner. He must give the policy and direction; it is our part to conform wholly to his will and guidance.

1 CORINTHIANS 3:10-23

Build on the Sure Foundation. We are called upon to contribute our share to the building of saved souls which is rising through the ages, to be an habitation of God through the Spirit, Eph. 2:21, 22. But in addition, we must not neglect the building of our own character on the one foundation, which is Jesus Christ. God has placed him to be the foundation of every structure which shall stand firm in all the tests of fire through which we are destined to pass. We must needs go on building day by day. Whatever we do or say is another stone or brick. It is for us to choose which heap of material we take it from; whether from that of the wood, hay, or stubble, or from that of the gold, silver, or precious stones.

All things serve the man or woman who serves Christ. The lowliest life may be a link in a chain of golden ministry which binds earth and Heaven. Our Lord was constantly described in the Old Testament as the Servant of God. He said that he had come down to earth to do his Father's will. "I am among you as he that serveth." When we serve him as he serves the great purposes of God, then everything begins to minister to us. The extremes of existence, of creation, and of duration serve us.

1 CORINTHIANS 4:1-13

Stewards Responsible to Their Lord. At the most, the ministers or teachers of God's gospel are but stewards of the hidden things of God, according to Matt. 13:51, 52. They ought not to attract attention to themselves or to the way they purvey their Master's goods. Their prime object is to be faithful to their trust; to make much of the Master and as little as possible of themselves. Paul was not aware that he had violated his Master's confidence, but he could not be content till he had heard the Master's verdict on his lifework. Notice the four courts of appeal—my own judgment, your judgment, man's judgment, and Christ's. The Master will reverse many human judgments, but all will bear witness to the absolute justice of his verdict.

In vivid words the apostle shows how great was the difference between the ease and self-satisfaction of the Corinthian church and the sorry plight to which he and his fellow-workers were often reduced. Many regarded them as the captives in a conqueror's triumphal procession, who behind the triumphal car were being marched to death. But it mattered little to them so long as Christ was adored, loved, glorified, and his kingdom advanced.

1 CORINTHIANS 4:14-21

Teaching Converts Christ's Ways. The relationship between the apostle and his converts was very tender. They were his children. They might have instructors and tutors, but they could have but one father; and as father he might have to use the rod. Love can be stern and punitive. Spare the rod and spoil the child. It is not pure but selfish love that forbears to speak and act strongly when eternal interests are at stake. This is an aspect of God's love which is likely to be overlooked. If we escape chastisement, we are bastards and not sons. "What son is he whom the father chasteneth not?" (Heb. 12:7).

The beloved Timothy was sent to bring the recreant church back to its old love and faith. He was well fitted to represent the apostle till Paul could tear himself from his thronging duties at Ephesus. Notice that God's kingdom comes in power, not in word, v. 20. Is not this the reason why it comes so slowly? We treat it as though it would come through our much speaking, through eloquent and honeyed speech. But it is not so. It comes in the power of the Holy Spirit, and in that supremacy of the Divine Spirit over all other spirit forces. God, send us more of this great dynamic!

1 CORINTHIANS 5

Removing Germs of Evil. The sin referred to in this chapter had been condoned by the Corinthian church, and this proved that the prevalent standard of morals was low. A man had married his father's second wife—his father having probably died. Such an alliance could not be tolerated. A condemnation of the sin must be pronounced by the whole body of believers, acting in concert with the Holy Spirit resident among them. "It seemed good to the Holy Ghost, and to us," Acts 15:28.

Paul compares the Corinthian church to the children of Israel, who after sprinkling the blood kept the feast of joy within closed doors —a careful search having been made for any atom of leaven that had hitherto escaped scrutiny. So we should put away from our lives, homes, and churches everything that would offend the gracious Paraclete. Since Christ has been slain for us, we must daily feed on him with festal joy. Our loins must be girded as becomes those about to depart at a moment's notice. We must be ever on the alert to detect the summons for an exodus out of this dark Egyptian world into the world that is to come.

1 CORINTHIANS 6:1-11

Settling Differences between Brethren. The apostle was clearly of the opinion that it was wiser for a Christian to bear injustice and wrong than to go to law before a heathen tribunal. It would have been a happy solution of myriads of disputes if his advice had been followed. Where a course of lawless crime has to be arrested in the interests of the weak and defenseless, it *is* necessary to call in the law and police to vindicate and protect; but when our private, personal, and individual interests alone are concerned, we would be wise to submit our case to arbitration or suffer patiently.

Who are the heirs of the kingdom of Heaven, vv. 9-11? Do not inquire into their past history. There are pages in their lives that had better be obliterated and forgotten; or if remembered, they should be the background to set forth the matchless grace and love of God. Yes, that grace shall be our theme forever, when we recall the depths out of which it lifted us and the heights to which it raised us. Let us note that the Lord Jesus and the Holy Spirit are named together. It is by the Holy Spirit that we become possessed of the nature of our Lord, which takes the place of our old evil nature and empowers us to repeat his life.

1 CORINTHIANS 6:12-20

Keeping the Body Holy. It is interesting to compare v. 12 with 10:23. There are four clauses in each verse, three of which are similar, but the last ones differ. The two laws that should govern our life in doubtful things are: first, the arresting of oneself in the doing of anything which threatens to become our master; and second, the abstaining from anything which threatens to be a stumbling block in another's Christian life.

It is not enough to watch against temptation; we should be so filled with the Spirit of the risen Savior that the desires of the flesh shall have no fascination. The power that raised the body of Jesus from the grave is surely strong enough to raise our bodies from the bondage of corruption and to translate them to the resurrection plane. Let us keep joined to the Lord by one Spirit, that he may pour his own living energy into our nature. When he redeemed us, he undertook to save us wholly and entirely—spirit, soul, and body, 1 Thess. 5:23. Hand the keeping of your body over to him. Consider that it is the outer court of a temple, in the inner shrine of which the Holy Spirit lives; and as of old the glory of the Lord filled the whole structure, so trust the Spirit of Holiness to make and keep you whole.

1 CORINTHIANS 7:1-14

Marriage Bonds. The apostle first addresses the unmarried, v. 1. He speaks elsewhere reverently of marriage, Eph. 5:23. Forbidding to marry is in his judgment a symptom of apostasy, 1 Tim. 4:1-3. His recommendations here were evidently due to the special circumstances of that difficult and perilous time. The loftiest conception of marriage is the wedding of two souls, each of which has found its affinity. The apostle is treating here the only conception of marriage entertained by these recent converts from paganism. He deals with them on their own level, with the determination of ultimately leading them to view marriage from Christ's standpoint. It is often well to fast from lawful things, that we may surrender ourselves more absolutely to the Spirit of God.

In addressing the married, v. 10ff., Paul is not dealing with the formation of marriage ties; they are settled by 2 Cor. 6:14. He is deciding what course shall be followed when either a husband or a wife has become a Christian, the other remaining unchanged. He decides that the Christian should not separate, so long as the unbelieving partner is willing to continue their life together.

1 CORINTHIANS 7:15-24

Serve God in Your Calling. There was much unsettlement in regard to marriage in the church at Corinth. An unnatural asceticism was showing itself in some quarters and a lawless self-indulgence in others. Against these tendencies Paul resolutely set himself. While he held that marriage should be contracted only in the Lord, he also taught that where it had been consummated it should not be dissolved at the impulse of the Christian, though the wish of the unbelieving partner might be acceded to. Children, also, born when one of their parents was a heathen, might be reckoned clean.

The apostle refers both to vocation and to the Christian life as a divine calling, vv. 18-24. We are all called to our trade or profession as much as a student is to the ministry. It is interesting that a man will speak of his business as his "calling." God has a purpose for each of us and summons us to fulfill it. Unless we are specially led to do otherwise we should, on entering the Christian life, remain in the same calling in which our former life was spent. The only difference is that we are to stay in it with God, v. 24. In every service, however lowly, we should have an eye toward Christ. All may be done in him, with him, for him.

1 CORINTHIANS 7:25-40

Counsel for Times of Emergency. The "virgin" here referred to is probably the young woman who was engaged to be married, and the counsel is expressly defined to be advice, given only under the pressure of the times, when the dissolution of all things seemed at hand. It seemed wiser not to enter upon matrimony because everything was in flux, but no sin was contracted if marriage took place, so long as it was "only in the Lord," v. 39. As pilgrims we should hold all earthly things but lightly, v. 30.

The allusion of v. 31 is to the shifting scenery of a theater. The fashion of the age is like ever-changing film scenes that flash before the audience and cannot be arrested or brought back. Surely the unmarried among us should ponder carefully the recommendations of vv. 32-34, the first of which refers to the man and the second to the wife. Where both are Christians, however, surely there may be union in caring for the things of the Lord, that the great cause of his kingdom may be expedited rather than hindered. But everything in this chapter, as well as the general New Testament teaching, empha-

1 CORINTHIANS

sizes the absolute importance of marriage being "only in the Lord," v. 39.

1 CORINTHIANS 8

Consideration for Others' Weakness. It was the heathen custom of the time to present for blessing in the idol temples the food that was sold and bought in public marketplaces. A grave question arose, therefore, as to whether the Christian convert might partake of such food without blame. Paul took a broad and common-sense view of the situation. He declared there is only one God and that an idol is an absolute nonentity. Therefore, it was a matter of perfect indifference what the heathen butchers might have done before they exposed their meat for sale. At the same time, if some weaker brother were really thrown back in his Christian life by seeing his fellow-believer eating in a heathen temple, that in itself would at once be a sufficient reason why the stronger should abstain for the weaker brother's sake. There are many things which, so far as we personally are concerned, we might feel free to do or permit, but which we must avoid if they threaten to hinder the practice or divert the course of some fellow-Christian.

1 CORINTHIANS 9:1-15

Rights and Their Surrender. Paul's claim to an equality with Peter and the other apostles was violently disputed by his enemies at Corinth, because in several matters he differed from them. Unlike Peter, he had no wife to support; and he worked for his livelihood, instead of being supported by the churches. In this chapter he strongly asserts his rights in this particular; but he is equally strong in saying that he had refused to avail himself of his right, that he might influence a wider circle of men. He was a soldier, a vineyard-keeper, a shepherd, and could claim his maintenance. But he desired to be free from the slightest imputation of self-seeking. He knew that jealous critics were watching his every action and seeking to weigh his secret motives. These were the very men he desired to win, and for their sakes he voluntarily surrendered his undoubted rights.

What a lesson for all of us and especially for those who are called to be ministers of Christ's gospel! We must be above suspicion. If we do or permit anything that might prove a hindrance to the acceptance of Christ by others, we must forego it, though reasonable in itself, that we may win them to our Savior.

1 CORINTHIANS 9:16-27

Under Bondage to All. Paul's one aim was to "gain" men. He uses the word repeatedly. To gain one more for his Lord, he would forego comfort, compensation, and well-earned repose. He would allow no competitor for an earthly prize to supersede him in his sacrifices for this crown of rejoicing. He points to the denials, the hard training, and the severe discipline to which men who took part in the games subjected themselves. No one thought it strange that they should sacrifice so much for the chance of winning; why, then, should he be counted eccentric who sought the certain reward of gaining new lovers of his Master's cross?

He tells us that he lived in constant dread of becoming a castaway. He had no fear of being rejected from God's love; but he feared lest God, who had used him so wonderfully, should cease to do so, and should cast him aside in favor of someone more unselfish, more pliant, more free from that which would excite prejudice. If Paul was so eager to surrender his rights and bruise his body that he might attain the prize of soul-winning, the question arises whether for our failure in these respects God may not be obliged to cast us on the rubbish-heap!

1 CORINTHIANS 10:1-10

Learn from Bible History. Twice over we are told that the story of the Exodus was intended for our instruction, vv. 6 and 11. It becomes us, therefore, to study the account with the honest intention to obtain all the warning and suggestion that it is capable of yielding. The great lesson is human failure under the most promising circumstances. Here were people who had been brought out of the most terrible hardships and perils, who were under the greatest obligations to God, but who in the hour of temptation absolutely failed him.

Consider the privileges of the Chosen People. The cloud of divine guidance led them. The Red Sea, like a grave, lay between them and the land of bondage. They ate daily of the heavenly manna and drank of the water that gushed from the rock. But all these are types of spiritual blessings which await us in Christ. His grave lies between us and the world; his guidance is ours; we daily feed on his life and help. Let us take heed that we do not, like Israel, allow Moab to cast the witchery of sensual indulgence over us, lest we excite God's displeasure. Let us not tempt the Lord by murmuring or distrust. Let us ever live worthily of him who has called us out of darkness into his marvelous light.

1 CORINTHIANS 10:11-22

Have No Fellowship with Evil. By "the ends of the world" is meant the end of one great era and the beginning of another. The Jewish dispensation was passing, the Christian age coming. What gracious encouragement shines in v. 13! Our faithful God! The tempter must get permission before assailing us, Luke 22:31, 32. No temptation is unprecedented, and as others have conquered so may we, Heb. 4:15. The pressure of temptation is always accompanied by a corresponding store of grace, if only our eyes were open to perceive it.

To abstain from idol feasts was the clear duty of all Christians. By partaking of heathen sacrifices which were offered to demons, they became one with the demons and their followers, just as in the Lord's Supper we show our oneness not only with the Savior, but with each other. It was clear, therefore, that the Corinthian Christians could not consistently partake of idol feasts and the Lord's Supper. What an incentive is given here for frequent and reverent participation in the Lord's Supper! It proclaims our union with him and his people, and it gives us a distaste for all that is alien to its spirit.

1 CORINTHIANS 10:23—11:1

"Do All to the Glory of God." There seems to be a clear distinction in the apostle's directions between feasting in an idol temple on the one hand, and the acceptance of an invitation to a private house, as in vv. 25 and 27, on the other. The believer in Christ knew that an idol was nothing in itself, and the fact of food having been offered before a shrine did not make it better or worse. It was a common practice and meant nothing so far as Christian disciples were concerned. But if an unbeliever were to make the meal a test of faith, by reminding believers that in partaking of such food they were implicitly partners in heathen rites, then there was no course but to refuse and abstain.

In every meal and act we must so conduct ourselves that praise and honor may redound to God. The thankful enjoyment of God's gifts of food, which constitutes the essence of a Christian meal, must always be subordinated to our consideration of the religious scruples of others; and we must avoid doing anything which would blunt and injure their faith. Though our intelligence may give us a wide liberty in regard to personal conduct, we must allow a check to be placed on it by the thoughtfulness of Christian love.

1 CORINTHIANS 11:2-10

Covering the Head. No soul is complete in itself. The man is not complete apart from Christ, as the woman is not complete apart from man. As God is the head of the nature of Jesus on its human side, so must Jesus be head of man, and man of woman. But in each case the headship is not one of authority and rule, but of the impartation of resources of love, wisdom, and strength, without which the best cannot be realized. The covered head of woman as contrasted with the uncovered head of man is a sign and symbol of this interdependence.

But it is very interesting to notice that while the gospel so clearly insists on the divine order, it has elevated woman to be man's true helpmeet, and has caused her to be honored and loved as the glory of man. Neither society, nor family life, nor woman herself can be happy unless she attains her true position. On the one hand she finds her completion in man; on the other she is his queen and he ministers to her in all gentleness and tenderness and strength.

1 CORINTHIANS 11:11-22

Unity and Order in Public Assembly. The "power" on a woman's head in v. 10 probably refers to the veil or covering which the Grecian woman assumed at marriage as the sign that she was not free from the sacred ties and duties of wedlock. In Paul's thought of the matter, therefore, it was unseemly for the Christian matron to lay this aside. He conceded the absolute freedom and equality of male and female in Christ, and yet he stood for the observance of the best customs of the age, lest the gospel should be brought into disrepute. The women, therefore, must veil their heads in the Christian assemblies as the angels veil their faces in the presence of God.

The uncovered face of man is to the glory of God, but the covered face of woman recognizes that she finds her glory in her husband's love and care. Each is dependent on the other—the man on God, and the wife on her spouse. These precepts and reasons are somewhat foreign to modern thought, but at least we must notice that there was no subject too trivial—even the headdress—to be brought into subjection to Christ and related to the great principle of his supreme headship and lordship.

1 CORINTHIANS 11:23-34

Observing the Lord's Supper. There was much disorder in the Corinthian church, because the love-feast, which preceded the Holy Supper, was the scene of riot and conviviality, of ostentation and jealousy. In the love-feast of the early Church each brought his own supply of food, which was put into a common stock and shared by all alike; but at Corinth each family or group retained their own provisions, and a great distinction was thus made between rich and poor. This caused much heartache and was unworthy of Christians.

Note that the apostle received the words of institution by direct revelation. The Lord's Supper is intended not only to commemorate the supreme act of Calvary, but to enable us spiritually to incorporate into ourselves the very life and death of Jesus, so that we may truly be crucified with him and nevertheless live. "That I may know him . . . and the fellowship of his sufferings." We are liable to condemnation if we do not recognize the Body of Christ—that is, the Church—the unity of which is disturbed and obscured when there is dissension. If we judge ourselves, we escape the judgment and chastisement of the Almighty.

1 CORINTHIANS 12:1-11

Differing Spiritual Gifts. Each believer, being an heir of God, has the same amount of grace placed to his credit in the heavenly bank, on which he can draw in time of need. This is the parable of the pounds. Each servant received the same amount. But there are great diversities in the gifts with which we are endowed. Some have five talents, others two, and large numbers only one. A full enumeration of these gifts is made in vv. 8-11, and it is a comfort to learn that to everyone something is allotted, vv. 7 and 11.

Notice that the allotment is made by the Holy Spirit acting sovereignly as he will, v. 11. We are not informed when it is made—perhaps it is at the moment of our regeneration or adoption—but it is important to bear in mind that our gifts will probably correspond with our natural endowment. Hence our Lord tells us that to every man was given "according to his several ability," Matt. 25:15.

Mark the allusion to the Divine Trinity: "the same Spirit," v. 4; "the same Lord," v. 5; "the same God," v. 6. The Spirit directs, the Savior is the channel of supply, and the Father is the fountain of all.

1 CORINTHIANS 12:12-19

Many Members in One Body. The use of gifts must never be dictated by personal ambition or the desire for selfish gain. As every member of the physical body is united to the head by two sets of nerves—the afferent, which bring to the brain the slightest sense impressions, and the efferent, which bear to the extremities the commands of the mind—so is every member of the Church, even the feeblest and most distant, bound to his glorious Lord. The head of the swimmer is in one element—the air—and the members may be in another—the water. Yet the head is able to control and coordinate them. So it is with the unseen Christ and his visible Church on earth. He must direct and use us. We have nothing to do with the work he confides to others, and must concentrate on that which he wants to achieve through us. If this means cooperation with other members or service to them, if it means hidden obscurity or temporary disuse, we must be equally content. It is for him to do as he wills. There is no room for envy or jealousy; they must give place to loving fellowship and mutual help, and to the quiet peace and rest which come from recognizing the good pleasure of the Creator.

1 CORINTHIANS 12:20-31

Each Contributing His Part. The hand and the foot obviously stand in need of each other; but the same interdependence marks the feebler and humbler parts of our frame. Indeed, it would appear as if we bestow more abundant honor on them by covering them with clothes or ornaments. In this way the least important parts of our nature are leveled up and compensated.

The apostle's aim throughout this passage is to enforce the interdependence of believers. One gives to others that in which they are deficient, and he derives help from each of them in turn. The Christian Church is not an inert mass of mere learners and subjects who are to be authoritatively taught and ruled by a small fraction of its members. It is a great cooperative society, in which each is for all and all for each, and the object is to bring Christ into every department of our being and our fellowship, as the lifeblood nourishes the body of man. The word "solidarity" expresses the interdependence and mutual interests of men and nations; nothing could more aptly describe the apostle's ideal.

1 CORINTHIANS 13

The One Essential for All. With what wonder his amanuensis must have looked up as the apostle broke into this exquisite sonnet on love! His radiant spirit had caught a glimpse of the living Savior. Jesus sits for his portrait in these glowing sentences, and of him every clause is true. Substitute his name for "love" (or "charity") throughout the chapter, and say whether it is not an exact likeness. With Paul "love" stands for that strong, sustained, and holy subordination of self for others, which begins in will and act and is afterward suffused by emotion, as a cloud lying in the pathway of the rising sun. But if you want the divine love, you must get it after the manner of the bay which opens its bosom to the incoming tide. God is love, and if you would love, you must abide in him and he in you. Love is better than miracles, gifts, or philanthropy, vv. 1-3. Love is the parent of all that is most delightful in the moral sphere, vv. 4-7. Love is the best of all, because it is eternal. All else will perish. Our highest attainments will be as the babblings and playthings of childhood. But when we are in touch with the reality of things, love will be all in all.

1 CORINTHIANS 14:1-12

The Gift of Prophesying. The word "prophesy" is used here, as so largely in Scripture, not in the limited sense of foretelling the future, but of pouring forth Heaven-given speech. There was a strong tendency at Corinth to magnify the use of tongues; that is, forms of utterance which the assembly could not understand. The apostle rebukes this and says that it is far better to be able to speak to the edification of the hearers. Indeed, he directs that speech in an unknown tongue should be withheld, unless someone were present who could explain and interpret it.

The gift of tongues was a special sign intended for the convincing of that age, but it was not a necessary accompaniment of the filling of the Holy Spirit, and is certainly of inferior value. A mere blare of a trumpet, without note or modulation, conveys no meaning to the waiting ranks of soldiers; and the mere sound of an unknown tongue startles without teaching. Do not be content merely to make a sound; say something. Seeking to do actual service to others is one of the three directions suggested in v. 3. Edification is the building up of the soul in truth. Comfort is for the distressed and weary. Consolation is the heartening of the soul to fresh enterprise.

1 CORINTHIANS 14:13-25

Understanding Promotes Edifying. The apostle here gives two practical directions, in order to restore the rule of the understanding above the babble of incoherent sounds which was confusing the Corinthian church.

The first was that worship should be conducted in a form that the assembled congregation could understand. To utter prayer or thanksgiving to which the audience could give no assent, to utter sounds which were meaningless was inconsistent with the true nature of Christian worship. It was from this chapter that the Reformers drew their arguments against the practice of conducting the services of the Church in Latin. The second was that instruction was a most necessary part of worship, v. 19.

The effect of prophesying, that is, preaching, is set forth very forcibly and beautifully in the closing verses of our reading. We must always have in mind the unbelieving and the unlearned. If he hears the solemn voice of God speaking through human lips to his conscience, stirring its depths, moving it to repentance and faith, he will bear speedy testimony to the truth of what he has heard. We must seek to have in our assemblies the convincing power of God's Word, accompanied by the corroborating witness of the unhindered Spirit.

1 CORINTHIANS 14:26-40

Order of Church Services. Again the apostle sums up his directions in two simple rules: (1) "Let all things be done unto edifying"; that is, to building up individual character, and to fitting each member as a brick or stone into the rising fabric of the Church. Hence the stress laid on prophesying or speaking under the impulse of God's Spirit. All who had that gift should certainly have a chance to use it, because the whole Church would be thereby profited and enriched. (2) "Let all things be done decently and in order." "Decently," so as not to interrupt the dignity and gravity of the services; "in order," not by hazard or impulse, but by design and arrangement.

The apostle's ideal is that of the calm and simple majesty which should mark all solemn assemblies, as distinct from fanatical and frenzied excitement. Hence he discountenances the disuse of the Eastern veil (the badge of modesty), the speaking of women in public, and the interruption of speakers by each other. That the spirits of the prophets are subject to the prophets is a truth of universal application. It condemns every impulse of a religious character which is not under the intelligent control of those who display it.

1 CORINTHIANS 15:1-11

The Gospel: Christ Died and Rose Again. If the 13th chapter is a psalm of love, this chapter is a psalm of hope—a hope that cannot be ashamed. It is the most memorable argument in existence for the resurrection of the body.

Notice that the resurrection was primarily not a doctrine, but a fact. It is not necessary to argue it, but simply to say that Christ arose and therefore all will arise, because Christ is the Son of man. Other religions rest on foundations of philosophy and metaphysics, but the empty grave in Joseph's garden is the keystone of the arch. If that cannot be maintained, as it was in the primitive Church, the whole superstructure crumbles like a mass of clouds. But it can be maintained. There is more evidence for it than for any fact of modern history. Men may as soon refuse to believe in the battle of Waterloo as in our Lord's resurrection. The testimony of Paul is most important, because he knew all that could be alleged or argued against it by the Pharisees. Indeed, he had himself opposed it. Note that the words, "not I," v. 10, are also in 7:10 and Gal. 2:20.

1 CORINTHIANS 15:12-28

Christ's Resurrection Assures Ours. The argument here goes to show, first, that our resurrection is intimately connected with Christ's. There must be such a thing because he, as the representative of humanity, arose from the dead, in a human body which though more ethereal in its texture was easily recognizable by those who had known him previously. Mary recognized the well-known intonations of her Master's voice. Thomas was compelled to believe in spite of his protestations to the contrary. In fact, all of our Lord's friends were convinced against themselves. They credited the tidings of the risen Lord as idle tales. Therefore, says the apostle, it is far easier to admit that man will rise than to face the difficulties of a still buried Christ, a vain faith, a vain gospel, and a false testimony from so many accredited witnesses.

What a burst of music breaks forth in vv. 20-28! The first fruit is the forerunner and specimen of all the harvest. In Christ the whole Church was presented to God. Note the divine order in v. 23: first, Christ; then, his own; lastly, the end, when death itself shall be destroyed, all enemies conquered, and the kingdom of an emancipated universe finally handed back by the Mediator to the Father.

1 CORINTHIANS 15:29-41

This Body the Seed of a Glorious One. The anticipation of the final resurrection enabled the early Christians to endure incredible sufferings. As one rank fell martyred, another was ready to step into its place; young believers took the names of the martyrs, so as to perpetuate their testimony. With this hope in his heart, Paul himself had confronted at Ephesus the tumult of the infuriated mob, Acts 19. Belief in this sublime undoing of the last effects of sin was one of the chief features in the conquering power of Christianity.

In every seed there is the germ of a new and beautiful growth, more elaborate and yet identical. So in each of us there is something which has the capacity and potentiality of furnishing another body, through which the emancipated spirit will be able to express itself more perfectly than it can in this body, which is composed of coarser materials. It is not difficult to believe in this, when we have seen the caterpillar become the butterfly. The world is full of wonderful and beautiful things. God's inventiveness reveals itself in a myriad of differing organisms. It is by his will that the golden head of wheat is fairer than the little brown seed cast into the furrow; so it is his pleasure that the body which is to be shall surpass the present in glory.

1 CORINTHIANS 15:42-58

Victory over Sin and Death. Life on the other side will be as real and as earnest as here. We shall not dissolve into thin mist or flit as bodiless ghosts. We shall each be provided with a body like that which our Lord had after he arose from the dead. It will be a spiritual body, able to go and come at a wish or a thought; a body that will be perfectly adapted to its spiritual world environment. The last Adam, our Lord, will effect this for us. But we must in the meanwhile be content to make the best use of the discipline of mortality, keeping our body pure and sweet as the temple and vehicle of the Holy Spirit until we are born into the next stage of existence.

What triumph rings through those last four verses! As generations of Christians have stood around the mortal remains of their beloved, they have uttered these words of immortal hope. The trumpet's notes will call those who have died and the saints that are still alive on the earth into one mighty host of transfigured and redeemed humanity. Oh, happy day! Then we shall be manifested, rewarded, and glorified with Christ. All mysteries will be solved, all questions answered! Till then, let us abound always in the work of the Lord.

1 CORINTHIANS 16:1-12

Systematic Beneficence. It is remarkable that the apostle can turn from one of his sublimest displays of sacred eloquence to deal with so ordinary a matter as the collection. But, after all, there is no incongruity. The thoughts to which he has given expression should surely lead to some tangible response of Christian duty and activity, or they would injure rather than help. Nothing is more injurious to the Christian conscience than trumpet-sounding which leads to no response in action. If the foregoing chapter does not stimulate Christian generosity, nothing will.

Note *the time*—"the first day of the week," indicating the reverence with which the early Christians regarded that day. *The method*—the definite appropriation for God's work of a certain proportion of income, as it accrues. *The proportion*—as the giver may be prospered. Paul disliked vehement collection appeals and advised that we should give according to a system, and not merely by impulse.

Remember it is God who opens great and effectual doors before his servants. It is of no use to force them. Let us wait for the Lord Jesus, who has the key of David, to open them, for then none can shut. Our duty is to be prepared to enter when the moment comes and the door swings wide.

1 CORINTHIANS 16:13-24

Exhortations and Salutations. The apostle was careful to cultivate friendship, one of the priceless gifts of God; and he was very generous not only in his references to his friends, but also in his dealings with them. Because Timothy was deficient in virile strength, Paul was always contriving to make his way easier; and though Apollos had drawn away some of his converts, the apostle was desirous for him to visit Corinth again. Nor could he forget the household which had yielded him the firstfruits. His solitude had been greatly cheered by the advent of the Corinthian deputation. Human love is a revelation of the divine—an earthen pitcher which God fills with heavenly treasure, a chalice holding the wine of life.

Notice the flaming forth of Paul's passionate love for Christ. He felt that any who failed to love him must be accursed in disposition and soul and would be accursed at his coming, like the barren tree standing in the midst of an orchard of fruit trees, crowned with blossom or heavy with fruit. *"Maran-atha!"*—"our Lord cometh." He will put right the wrongs of time and crown his faithful servants with honor and glory. Hallelujah!

THE SECOND EPISTLE TO THE CORINTHIANS

THE GLORY OF THE MINISTRY OF THE GOSPEL

SALUTATION *1:1, 2.*

I. A CAREER OF TRIUMPH IN CHRIST *1:3—7:16.*
    A. Thanksgiving because of good news from Corinth *1:3-7.*
    B. Paul's deliverance from an affliction unto death *1:8-11.*
    C. His sincerity in all his dealings with the Corinthians *1:12—2:11.*
    D. The vindication of his authority *2:12—3:18.*
    E. The character of his ministry *4:1—6:18.*
    F. His good courage toward the Corinthians *7:1-16.*

II. THE OFFERING FOR THE CHURCH AT JERUSALEM *8, 9.*
    A. The liberality of the Macedonian churches *8:1-6.*
    B. "Complete the doing" *8:7-15.*
    C. Titus and Paul's other helpers *8:16-24.*
    D. The motive for and reward of benevolence *9.*

III. THE APOSTLE'S FINAL VINDICATION *10—13.*
    A. His standing with the Corinthians *10:1—11:15.*
    B. His labors, sufferings, and spiritual experience *11:16—12:13.*
    C. Announcement of a third visit *12:14—13:10.*

CONCLUSION *13:11-14.*

INTRODUCTION

Titus had been commissioned by the apostle to go from Ephesus to Corinth to enforce the instructions of the first epistle. See 2 Cor. 2:13; 7:6, 13; 8:6. For some reason his return had been delayed, a circumstance that caused Paul great anxiety. In the meanwhile the tumult at Ephesus had compelled the apostle to leave that city, and he went to Troas to await his friend. When Titus did not arrive, Paul went on to Macedonia, where they met.

On the whole, the report was encouraging. The majority in the Corinthian church had accepted Paul's instructions and had acted upon them. They were for the most part tenderly attached to him, though a party still resisted his authority, demanded letters of commendation from Jerusalem, accused him of vacillation, and boasted their pure Hebrew descent. It was largely for these that this epistle was prepared; but we may be thankful for the criticisms which called it into existence. It is an unrivaled revelation of tenderness, self-sacrifice, and triumphant hope.

COMMENTARY

2 CORINTHIANS 1:1-11

Sharing Comfort in Affliction. This was a circular letter, including in its scope all the scattered communities in the district. "Grace" was the usual salutation of the West, "Peace" of the East. Here they meet. All our mercies emanate from the Father's heart, and all comfort comes from the Comforter. When next passing through great sorrow and trial, notice how near God comes and what he says. Try to learn his methods, to get his secret. Remember that you are being comforted in order to comfort others. God is training you to be, like Barnabas, a "son of consolation." The gains of trial are immense, because they furnish the experience from which others may profit. Often God ministers comfort by sending a friend, 7:5-7.

Either through persecution or through severe illness Paul had been brought to the gates of death, v. 8. His recovery was little less than a miracle, but throughout his trust never wavered. Dare to believe, like Paul, that God has delivered, doth deliver, and will deliver, v. 10. Past, present, and coming deliverances blend in this sweet verse. What he hath done, he doeth now and will do. Only see to it that you have the sentence of death in yourself, and on yourself, and that you go out of yourself to God, in whom is all necessary help. In such hours we may also receive great help from the faith of our friends, v. 11.

2 CORINTHIANS 1:12-22

Sincere Like His Master. The apostle laid great emphasis on the witness of his conscience. See Acts 23:1; 24:16. As we pass out of this life and stand in the revealing dawn of eternity, it will be a blessed thing if we are able to say this much of ourselves.

Paul had thought of visiting Corinth on his way to Macedonia, and again on his return journey; but this purpose had been defeated. He was eager, however, that his friends should understand that the change was not due to vacillation on his part, for this would be unworthy of one who stood for the great certainties of the gospel.

Christ is God's attestation to his promises. All these have received their seal in the words, sufferings, and resurrection of our Lord. In Jesus God says "Yea" to the yearnings and prayers of human hearts, and "Amen" ("verily") to all the 10,000 promises of Scripture. He who rests on Christ stands in the focal point of certainty and assurance. Not one good thing shall fail him of all that has been promised.

Verse 21 is full of comfort. God alone can give us a settled and established position. He anoints us for service; seals us with his Spirit for safety, likeness, and authentication; and in this way gives us the earnest and foretaste of Heaven, as the grapes of Eschol were the pledge and foretaste of Canaan.

2 CORINTHIANS 1:23—2:11

Tenderhearted and Forgiving. In these opening words Paul evidently refers to the sin mentioned in 1 Cor. 5. His judgment had been strong and stringent, the Corinthian church had acted upon it, and the offender had suffered severely in consequence. But the result had been more than satisfactory. He had repented with great brokenness of spirit. Indeed, it seemed as if he would be "swallowed up with overmuch sorrow," v. 7.

The apostle desires the Corinthians to understand that he also had shed many tears over the case, v. 4. His was a very affectionate and tender disposition, which shrank from inflicting pain and yet was resolute at all costs to maintain truth. We get a sidelight here as to the heart of God. May we not believe that whenever he chastens us, it is with profound pity? Whom he loves he chastens; and whom he receives, he scourges. But when there is full and frank repentance, there should be forgiveness. The penitent offender was to be restored to church fellowship and received with brotherly welcome. The Savior himself speaks through forgiveness. It is his love that moves, his voice that declares, while an unforgiving spirit sets an open door to the entrance of Satan.

2 CORINTHIANS 2:12—3:6

The Savor of the Knowledge of Christ. Paul, in vv. 14–16, imagines himself as part of his Master's procession passing through the world. First he is a captive in Christ's conquering train; then he is one of the incense-bearers, scattering fragrant perfume; then he conceives of his life as being in itself that perfume. As the captives in a triumphal procession would be divided into two bodies, of which one company was doomed to die while the other was spared, so inevitably all who come in contact with Christ, either directly in the preaching of the gospel or indirectly in the lives of his people, are influenced either for evil or for good.

The apostle fancies himself challenged to furnish letters of commendation and he repudiates the claim. "No," he cries, "the lives and testimonies of those whom I have won for God are all the credentials that I require!" Every Christian should be a clearly written and legible tract, circulating for the glory of God. Men will not read the evidences for Christianity contained in learned treatises, but they are keen to read *us.* God alone can suffice us to sustain this searching scrutiny.

2 CORINTHIANS 3:7–18

The Veil upon the Heart. By a quick turn of thought, Paul passes from the idea of the fleshly tablets of the heart, where God writes his new name, to the Law graven on the ancient tables of stone, and to the Lawgiver, stern and veiled. He argues that if the glory which shone on the face of Moses was so beautiful, surely that of the gospel must be transcendently so. The one is transient, the other abiding; the one is reflected, the other direct.

Not only was Moses veiled, but the hearts of the Jews were covered with a thick covering of prejudice. They did not understand the inner significance of the Levitical Code; and when the Law was read, they listened to it without spiritual insight. Directly men turn to Christ, they see the inner meaning of Scripture. What liberty becomes ours when we live in Christ! We are free to love, to serve, to know, and to be. Note v. 18! We may gaze on the unveiled face of God in Christ. The more we look, the more we resemble. The more we endeavor to reflect him in doing what he desires, the more certainly and inevitably we become like him. Only remember that in all things we are deeply indebted to the gracious influence of the Spirit. He produces the Christ-life in us.

2 CORINTHIANS 4:1–6

God's Glory Reflected in Christ. The servant of Christ must never forget that he once needed and obtained mercy. This will sustain him in many an hour when heart and flesh fail. His weapon is the truth, his appeal to conscience. Others may vie with him in brilliant imagination, fervid enthusiasm, and intellectual force, but he has unrivaled supremacy in the realm of conscience. As Richard I of England, imprisoned in a castle dungeon, recognized the voice and song of his troubadour, singing outside the castle gate a strain familiar to them both, and responded note for note, so does conscience awaken and respond to the truth, which it recognizes as the voice of God.

Why, then, does the gospel fail? Not through any defect in itself, nor because of some arbitrary decree on the part of God, but because the god of this world has blinded the eyes of the heart by the glamour of worldly prosperity and success, or perhaps by the covering film or scale of evil habit, so that the light of the dawn, stealing over the world, is unable to penetrate the darkened life.

2 CORINTHIANS 4:7-18

The Inward Life Triumphant over Affliction. Few men have been more conscious of their weakness than was the apostle. The earthen vessel had become very cracked and scratched, but the heavenly treasure was unimpaired. As in the case of Gideon, when the pitcher was broken the lantern shone out. Paul here confesses that he was troubled, perplexed, persecuted, and cast down, always bearing the scars of Jesus, and being perpetually delivered over to death. But he gratefully accepted all these disabilities because he knew that they gave greater opportunities to Jesus to show forth, through him, his resurrection power. With the daily decay of the outward, there came the renewal of the unseen and spiritual. It is only in proportion as we are conformed to the sufferings and death of Christ that we begin to realize the fullness of what he is, and what he can be or do through us. Our one thought must always be the glory of Christ in the salvation of others.

Note the contrasts of v. 17. The affliction is light, but the glory of the future is fraught with radiant and satisfying blessedness. The one is transient, the other eternal. The one is the price of the other, though each is the gift of God. The comet which has gone farthest into the outer darkness returns closest to the central sun.

2 CORINTHIANS 5:1-10

"Present with the Lord." This mortal life is a pilgrimage and our body is a tent, so slight, so transitory, so easily taken down; but what does it matter, since there is awaiting us a mansion prepared by God? Often in this veil of flesh we groan. It cages us, anchors us down to earth, hampers us with its needs, obstructs our vision, and becomes the medium of temptation. How good it would be if our physical body could be suddenly transmuted into a glorified ethereal body like the resurrection body of our Lord! It would be sweet to escape the pull of death. But if not, then through death we shall carry with us the germ of the glorified body. That which shall be quickened will first die, but God will give it a body as it shall please him.

The gate of death may look gloomy on this side, but on the other it is of burnished gold and opens directly into the presence-chamber of Jesus. We long to see him and to be with him; and such desires are the work of the Holy Spirit and are the firstfruits of Heaven. But remember that just inside the door there is Christ's judgment-seat, where he will adjudge our life and apportion our reward. Prepare, my soul, to give an account of thy talents!

2 CORINTHIANS 5:11-19

Constrained by the Love of Christ. It was of small importance in Paul's eyes what his critics thought of him. He desired only to please his supreme Lord, whether he lived or died, whether he was considered cold and staid or hot and impassioned. He was overmastered by his love of Christ. This may have been the sense of Christ's love to his unworthy self, or the emotion that burned in his soul toward Christ, or the very love of Christ received into his heart, as a tiny creek on the shore receives the pulse of the ocean tide.

The apostle had arrived at the deliberate conclusion and judgment that the "all" who realized what Christ had done for them (and he among them) must live with as much devotion toward him as others toward themselves. A new world had been opened by Christ's resurrection. All things had become new. Let us live in daily touch with that world of faith and glory, refusing to be judged by the old standards. It is clear that the reconciliation of the world is as complete as God can make it, but it is for us to urge men to fall in with and accept God's proposals.

2 CORINTHIANS 5:20—6:10

Ambassadors for Christ. On God's side the work of reconciliation is complete. Everything has been done and is in readiness to make forgiveness and justifying righteousness possible as soon as a penitent soul asks for them. He only waits for us to make application for our share in the atonement of Calvary. Many as our trespasses have been, they are not reckoned to us, because they were reckoned to Christ. God wants this known, and so from age to age sends out ambassadors to announce these terms and urge men to accept them.

God sends none forth to entreat men without cooperating with them. When rain falls on a slab of rock, it falls in vain. Be not rock, but loam to the gentle fall of God's grace. Let none of us be stumbling blocks by the inconsistencies of our character, but all of us stepping-stones and ascending stairways for other souls.

The three marvelous series of paradoxes in vv. 4-10 deserve careful pondering. The first series enumerates Paul's sufferings on behalf of the gospel; the second, his behavior under them; the third, the contrast between appearance and reality, as judged respectively by time and eternity. The Stoic bears life's sorrows with compressed lips, the Christian, with a smile. Let us be always rejoicing, enriching many, and possessing all things.

2 CORINTHIANS 6:11—7:4

Separate from All Uncleanness. Paul's love failed to be appreciated by his converts because the channel of receptiveness, that is, of their faith and love, was so narrow. How often is this the case between Christ and us! Let us dredge the channel. Be ye enlarged! Open your mouth wide and he will fill it.

The best method of doing this is to be only, always, and all for him. We must not offer him only a share of our heart and devotion. There must be no division between him and others. Whenever iniquity, darkness, Belial, and unbelievers seek to share our nature with the Holy Spirit, and we permit the partnership, he withdraws. No idols must be permitted in any hidden shrine of the heart. The whole nature—spirit (that is, the Holy of Holies), soul (that is, the seat of our individuality), and body—must be the temple of the Eternal, who rules it from the shekinah, which is enthroned on the Ark of the Covenant. God still walks the world in those who love him and are wholly yielded to his indwelling. The loneliest spirit finds him to be father, mother, brother, sister, all. What an incentive to cleanliness, not only of flesh, but of spirit! See Heb. 10:22. The apostle concludes by expressing his intense thankfulness that his converts had not misunderstood the urgency of his former letter.

2 CORINTHIANS 7:5-16

The Joyous Effect of Godly Sorrow. After dispatching his first epistle, with the strong words of Chapter 5 and elsewhere, Paul's tender heart had been rent with anxiety lest the Corinthian church should resent its terms and be alienated from his friendship. But when Titus joined him in Macedonia, bringing the assurance of their deep repentance and unabated affection, he was profoundly comforted and gladdened. He felt also that their sorrow was of the true and genuine sort, which does not consist of mere mortification at being found out or the dread of punishment, but which implies a profound hatred of sin as grieving the Holy Savior and unworthy of his precious blood. This sorrow does not need to be repented of; these tears do not require to be cleansed. Godly sorrow accepts rebuke meekly, puts away the wrong, and with chastened steps comes again into the way of the sacred cross.

Titus had imbibed much of Paul's spirit. It is interesting to notice that though he was a companion and messenger of the apostle, even his spirit could be in need of refreshment, v. 13. Paul was pleased that his own anticipations had been realized in the response of his friends at Corinth. Here beats the heart of a true pastor, whose whole soul is wrapped up in the interests of his charge!

2 CORINTHIANS 8:1-15

Stimulating Liberality. Surely the plea for a generous gift of money toward the collection which Paul was making for the poor saints in Jerusalem could not have been more tenderly and convincingly urged than it is urged here. He begins by mentioning the generosity of the Christians in Philippi, Thessalonica, and Berea, who were very poor, the inference being that the wealthier Corinthians would make similar sacrifices. He quotes the example of the Lord Jesus, who made himself poor that they might be enriched and who for nineteen centuries since has had the joy of enriching myriads of souls. Paul reminds the Corinthians that a year ago they had resolved to make this gift. Finally he sketches his fair dream of reciprocity between church and church, so that wherever there was need the supplies of Christian benevolence should flow forth to meet it.

Notice, then, that Christian liberality originates in the grace of God, ministers abundant joy to those who give, is not staunched by deep poverty, begins with the consecration of the giver's soul to God, and does not wait to be entreated, because it demands the privilege of ministering thus to the lack of Christ's body.

2 CORINTHIANS 8:16-24

"Honest Things" with God and Men. Those who handle the gifts of the Church should be extremely careful that all their financing be above the slightest suspicion. The apostle shrank from handling these gifts himself, lest any should insinuate that he was appropriating them to his personal use. Even when we have no reason to accuse ourselves in the sight of the Lord, we should be careful of appearances in the sight of men; and whatever is intrusted to us should be administered by us to the glory of God.

In the present instance the apostle designated three brethren to attend to this matter: first, Titus, his partner and fellow-worker; next, the brother whose praise was in all the churches and who had been appointed for this very purpose; and thirdly, another brother, referred to in v. 22. Titus represented the apostle, and the others represented the churches themselves. These brethren are distinctly mentioned as "the glory of Christ," v. 23. It must be an encouragement to those who handle the financial matters of our churches that they also may promote Christ's glory and participate in its transfiguring beauty.

2 CORINTHIANS 9:1-7

"God Loveth a Cheerful Giver." Paul evidently had considerable anxiety about the collection at Corinth for the starving saints at Jerusalem. He had started the idea, not merely because of his affection toward his own people, but in order to promote and foster the unity of the Church of Christ. There could be no greater evidence of the transforming power of the gospel than that it should obliterate the strongly-marked differences between East and West, between Jew and Gentile, and make it clear that Christ is all in all. Paul does not, therefore, urge and entreat the Corinthians so much as he reminds them of his confidence in their response. No motive is so potent as the sense that a worthy response is expected of us by one whom we revere and love.

He likens money-giving to seed-sowing. What was placed in the collection box would assuredly return to the giver with large increase. Christians, therefore, should not give grudgingly, or of necessity, but freely, spontaneously, generously, as the farmer who does not hesitate to dip his hand deeply into his granaries, expecting, as he does, that every additional atom of grain scattered will come back to him augmented certainly to thirty-fold and perhaps to a hundred-fold. You will meet again somewhere and sometime every coin that you have given with a pure heart.

2 CORINTHIANS 9:8-15

Enriched unto Liberality. We are not really poorer by what we give away; and God will never starve his own givers. Note the comprehensiveness of v. 8. God's grace is like an ocean at full tide. Count the "alls": *"all* grace, *always, all* sufficiency, *every* good work," and twice the verb *"abound."* When you are going forth to sow, ask God to give you the seed. When after sowing you are hungry, ask God to supply you with bread. When you are discouraged at the results, ask God to increase the fruit. We sow the seed, whether of the gospel, or of money to aid its circulation, and lo! we reap a harvest of thanksgiving to God and of love to those who have given. But who can ever measure the thanks and love which are due to God for having given the Gift that includes all gifts! But have we accepted it? Do we use it?

Remember to look to God for your own supplies of spiritual nourishment, and specially for your seed of thought or money, of word or act. Leave the increase with him. Hold all that God has given you as a trustee holds property for others. Administer God's good gifts, giving people continual cause to glorify and praise him for your exhibition of the essential nature of his holy gospel.

2 CORINTHIANS 10:1-7

Mighty with Spiritual Weapons. Paul here makes his defense. Some who resisted his authority spoke disparagingly of his weak body and uneloquent speech. Why should they yield so absolute a submission to his words? Others suggested that he was little better than a schemer for his own ends, and that he walked after worldly maxims, v. 2. There is considerable comfort to others who are placed in the driving storm of adverse criticism to know that this great saint passed by the same road. Be of good cheer, comrade, if you are misunderstood and maligned! It is best to leave these reproaches with your Lord. He will shield and vindicate you. "No weapon that is formed against thee shall prosper; and every tongue that shall rise against thee in judgment thou shalt condemn," Isa. 54:17.

In reply Paul cites the spiritual results that have accrued from his ministry, and argues that they attest the purity and spirituality of his methods. He could not have attained to such great usefulness if his motives had been those which his enemies imputed. What a lesson v. 4 contains! In the gospel there are weapons which no human reasonings or workings can withstand; but we too often trust carnal methods and do not avail ourselves of this invincible arsenal.

2 CORINTHIANS 10:8-18

Enlarging One's Sphere of Influence. There is marvelous power in the weakest of men when governed by a single purpose and filled with the consciousness and the power of God. Weak and contemptible in themselves, they are often the chosen channels through which God pours his living water. Any child could have destroyed Raphael's brush, but in his hand it painted immortal pictures. Incidentally the apostle remarks that some who criticized him bore themselves proudly, because their standard was so low. A five-foot man thinks himself tall when he compares himself with a dwarf! Always compare what is worst in yourself with what is best in others, and you will be kept humble.

Paul was always pressing outward to the fields that lay beyond. These were vast unoccupied regions which he coveted to count as provinces in the kingdom of Christ. This is the supreme test of a man. It is comparatively easy to build on foundations laid by another Christian worker and to win away his converts. Such conduct is mean and cowardly. Open up new ground and show the stuff that's in you. The apostle was justified in making these affirmations, but he did so in the meekness and gentleness of Christ.

2 CORINTHIANS 11:1-9

"Godly Jealousy." As the Bridegroom's friend, Paul was eager to bring the Corinthian church to the Bridegroom of souls. But false teachers disturbed the purity and simplicity of their faith, as in Eden Satan perverted Eve. There would have been excuse if these false teachers had given his converts another and a better Savior or a greater Pentecost; but since these were impossible, he was well able to hold his ground, even though they were preeminent apostles in their own estimation. Paul was very conscious of the rudeness of his speech, of which apparently he had many reminders, but he was equally conscious of the direct knowledge that God had imparted to him.

He acknowledges that he had not taken their pecuniary support, which in itself was quite legitimate; but he altogether denies the inference which his enemies drew that therefore he admitted his inferiority to the other servants of the cross. He answers that insinuation by saying that he expressly refrained from accepting gifts because of his desire to rob his critics of their argument that he was evangelizing the world for the purpose of making money. That they should make such wanton suggestions proved that they were Satan's emissaries.

2 CORINTHIANS 11:10-21

Constrained To Silence Boasters. In vivid language, which proves how greatly he had been moved, the apostle contrasts the false teachers who were injuring his converts with himself. They brought their disciples under bondage, exalted themselves, and lived in self-indulgence. He did not hesitate to unveil their true character and to designate them as emissaries of Satan. Satan conceals his deeds under the guise of an angel clothed in light; and as it is with him, so with his instruments. As their deeds are, so will be their end.

In the succeeding category, vv. 16-21, Paul confesses freely that his words might seem in conflict with the humility that Jesus taught, and might savor of boastfulness and pride; but for the sake of the truth, he stooped to the level of these false teachers and adopted their own methods. Though he would not think of plundering or of smiting the disciples as these intruders did, yet he would meet the latter on their own ground. The proverb says, "Answer a fool according to his folly," and this is an exact description of the apostle's defense. This much at least was clear: that the motive of his life was absolutely pure and selfless, and was capable of lifting him to a career of unparalleled heroism.

2 CORINTHIANS 11:22-33

Preeminent in Labor and Suffering. It has been truly said that this enumeration represents a life which up to that hour had been without precedent in the history of the world. Self-devotion at particular moments or for some special cause had been often witnessed before; but a self-devotion involving such sacrifices and extending over at least fourteen years, in the interests of mankind at large, was up to that time a thing unknown. The lives of missionaries and philanthropists in later times may have paralleled his experiences; but Paul did all this, and was the first to do it.

The biography of the apostle, as told by Luke, comes greatly short of this marvelous description. Of the facts alluded to, only two—the stoning and one of the Roman scourgings—are mentioned in the book of the Acts; from which we gather that the book is, after all, but a fragmentary record, and that the splendid deeds of the disciples and apostles of that first age will be known only when the Lamb himself recites them from his Book. But even this enumeration omits all that the apostle suffered after the writing of this epistle, including, of course, the sufferings between his arrest and his appearance before Nero.

2 CORINTHIANS 12:1-10

The Secret of Strength. It is a sublime phrase—"a man in Christ." We reach our full stature only when we are in him. We are but fragments of manhood until the true man is formed in us. Of course the presence of Jesus is always with us, but its manifestation is reserved for special emergencies, when it is peculiarly needed. It is thought that this supreme revelation was synchronous with Paul's stoning at Lystra, Acts 14. While the poor body was being mangled, his

2 CORINTHIANS

spirit was in the third heaven, that is, in Paradise. What a contrast between being let down in a basket and being caught up into glory! How indifferent to the derisions of men is the soul that lives in God!

We do not know what this thorn, or stake, was—whether eye trouble, or imperfect utterance, or some deformity in appearance—but it was the source of much suffering and many temptations. At first Paul prayed for its removal, but as soon as he learned that its continuance was the condition of receiving additional grace, he not only accepted it, but even gloried in its presence. May we not believe that all disabilities are permitted to drive us to realize and appropriate all that Jesus can be to the hard-pressed soul!

2 CORINTHIANS 12:11-21

"I Seek Not Yours, but You." "The long burst of passionate self-vindication has now at last expended itself," says Dean Stanley, and Paul returns to the point whence he diverged at 10:7, where he was avowing his intention to repress the disobedience of those who still resisted his authority at Corinth. "Now," he says, "my folly is over. That I should have indulged in it is your fault, not mine." What a comfort it is that he lays such repeated stress on his weakness! Instead of complaining of it, he used it as an argument with Christ that he should put forth more grace, and as an argument with his converts that the results of his work had been granted as the divine endorsement of his apostolate.

Paul felt that his paternal relation to this church gave him the right to rebuke them, as a father rebukes his children. But he realized that they did not reciprocate his love, probably because they permitted the evil things enumerated in the closing verses. Often moral dullness accounts for the decline and failure of love. Among other things, they had even accused him of getting money, if not directly, yet through Titus. But there were worse things still that needed to be dealt with, vv. 20, 21. Would that we were more often humbled to the dust by the sins of our brethren!

2 CORINTHIANS 13:1-6

"Prove Your Own Selves." Once more Paul refers to the charge that his ministry was characterized by weakness. This deeply wounded him. He admitted that in his personal appearance and speech he might be all that his enemies averred, but he contended that weakness did not count when married to the divine. Was not Christ weak when he was crucified? Yet through that cross he has exerted his mighty saving power upon myriads! Through the weakness of death he passed to the right hand of power and bestowed the Pentecostal gift. Suppose, then, that the servant shared the weakness of his Lord. Might not the divine power work through his poor, weak nature as through the Lord himself? Let us not always be dwelling on our weakness and limitations; did not the divine fire tremble around the poor shrub of the wilderness?

Paul goes on to urge the Corinthians to prove —that is, to test—themselves by reminding them that unless they are reprobate, the Lord Jesus is truly and literally dwelling within them. This is the fundamental fact in a holy life. When we open our hearts, he enters and becomes in us the Life of our life and the Light of all our seeing.

2 CORINTHIANS 13:7-14

How To Be Built Up. None can really injure the truth or stop its victorious progress. One may as well try to stop the sunrise. We often help others most in our weakness, because then we rely most on the Spirit of God. It is the noblest end of life to build up others through our own expenditure, even to the draining of our strength and resources. The world is apt at destruction; and indeed not much skill is required for pulling down. But the divine work is to build; we have God's authority for that.

The closing address is very touching. "Be perfect," v. 11, is really "be adjusted," "properly jointed," "articulated." God desires to set us as a skillful surgeon sets a dislocated limb. Let him do it; let the Comforter comfort; let love and peace enter with the Holy Dove; and see that the inner atmosphere does not hinder the gracious healing work of the Spirit of God.

Note the threefold benediction, which maintains the doctrine of the Trinity, v. 14. The love of the Father is the fountain of all; the grace of the Lord Jesus is the channel for all; while the communion of the Holy Spirit brings us into partnership with the aims and resources of God. The salutation of the saints and the divine benediction are the worthy close of this noble letter.

THE EPISTLE TO GALATIANS

GOSPEL LIBERTY AND LEGAL BONDAGE

SALUTATION   *1:1–5.*

I. THE APOSTLE'S VINDICATION   *1:6—2:21.*
   A. The affront to his authority   *1:6–10.*
   B. His commission God-given   *1:11–17.*
   C. His recognition in the Church   *1:18—2:10.*
   D. His conflict with Cephas   *2:11–21.*

II. THE VINDICATION OF THE GOSPEL   *3—6.*
   A. The folly of reverting to legalism   *3:1–5.*
   B. The example of Abraham   *3:6–29.*
   C. The covenants contrasted   *4.*
   D. The conflict of the flesh and the Spirit   *5.*
   E. The law of Christ   *6:1–10.*

CONCLUSION   *6:11–18.*

INTRODUCTION

Galatia was a province, occupying a central position in Asia Minor. It derived its name from the Gauls (tribes of Celts), who came thither from Europe. Jews resided there in large numbers, attracted by the opportunities for trade. Paul visited this region on his third missionary journey, Acts 18:23. His converts, composed of Jews and proselytes, manifested great eagerness and affection at first; but soon after the apostle had left them, they fell an easy prey to the Judaizers, who wished to make the Mosaic ritual binding upon the Christian Church. These followed Paul's steps and made every effort to undermine his influence.

Their object in this was twofold: first, to convince Jewish converts that Paul's authority was inferior to that of Peter and others who represented the more conservative element in the Church; and second, to insist upon Gentiles submitting to the rites of the ceremonial law. On receiving information of this invasion of the young church that he had founded, Paul wrote this urgent letter to the Galatians from Ephesus in A.D. 54, to vindicate his authority and to insist upon the all-sufficiency of Christ's redeeming work.

COMMENTARY

GALATIANS 1:1–10

Danger from a Perverted Gospel. Note how strenuously Paul insists upon the genuineness of his call as an apostle. It had come directly from the lips of Christ. "Neither by man, but by Jesus Christ," v. 1. We who are redeemed have been lifted out of the present age, v. 4, into the next age, which may soon break forth in manifestation. It is now concealed, but it shall be unveiled. The age which preceded the fall of Jerusalem was notoriously corrupt. Speaking of the Jews at that time, Josephus says that they exceeded Sodom.

The false teachers who dogged Paul's footsteps suggested that he had only one side of the gospel, and that there was therefore abundant room for their statement of it. But this the apostle indignantly repudiated, v. 8. No, he said; there is no gospel other than that which you have heard from my lips. These are solemn questions that each of us should ask: "What has been the effect of the gospel upon *my* life? Have I been redeemed out of the world that passes away, into that unseen and eternal kingdom of which my Lord is center and Chief? Do I live according to the will of my God and Father?" See v. 4.

GALATIANS 1:11–17

The True Gospel a Revelation. When men belittle the apostle's teaching as being purely Pauline, we should recall these strong statements, which attribute his knowledge of the gospel to the direct revelation of the Lord. He received from Christ himself that which he delivered to the Church. See also Acts 1:2. It was this that made his message authoritative.

What intensity of interest must have gathered for him about Mount Sinai, which doubtless was the objective of his journey into Arabia! Moses and Elijah had been pupils before him in its majestic solitudes. As the apostle dwelt there, with unlimited opportunity for communion with God, his mind was turned in the direction of that massive system of thought which at once distinguishes his epistles and connects the New Testament with the Old. It is a profound discovery when God reveals his Son as resident in the believer's soul. That Christ is in each of us, if we be truly regenerated, is indubitable. See 2 Cor. 13:5. But it seems that in many cases a veil hides that blessed fact from our consciousness. We need a miracle of grace, similar to that which at the crucifixion rent the veil in twain, from the top to the bottom, Matt. 27:51.

GALATIANS 1:18–24

From Christ, Not from Men. Paul's first visit to Peter must have been of absorbing interest. Doubtless the two traversed together the holy scenes of the Lord's ministry, and Peter told the story of Gethsemane and Calvary with minute detail to ears that drank in every circumstance. How many inquiries would be addressed to the eyewitness of that sacred death and of the open grave! Paul was not ignorant of the facts, but wished to view them in the new light of faith and love. Such conversation as that which occupied these two souls gives us a glimpse of what may be expected when God's people are gathered into the many mansions of the Father's house.

The sudden termination of this visit to Jerusalem is described in Acts 9:28–30. Without delay Paul had to leave the city and start for his home in distant Tarsus, where he was to spend two or three years until the good Barnabas came to summon him to help in Antioch. See Acts 11:25, 26. Probably during this interval the apostle began to evangelize the regions named in 1:21. Let us see to it that *we* receive no glory from man, but that men see God in us and us in God. We are nothing; he is all, and to him be the glory, Ps. 115:1.

GALATIANS 2:1–10

Stand Firm for Truth. The great controversy in Paul's career was over the initial rite of Judaism. It would have been comparatively calm if he had been willing to admit that Christianity was a sect of Judaism, and that men must become Jews before becoming Christians. His contention was that the ceremonial aspect of the Law did not apply to converts from heathendom. Gentile sinners had the right to go directly to Jesus Christ for salvation, without traveling around the circuitous route of Judaism. When men insisted on the outward rite, he resisted it with all the fiery vehemence of his nature, vs. 3, 11, 12. But when his opponents were willing to admit that circumcision was not essential, he administered it to one of Jewish blood, as a concession to the weak and uninstructed, Acts 16:3.

What blessed intercourse the four men here named must have enjoyed together! James would tell of the earlier life of Jesus, in the home of Nazareth; Peter would dwell upon his own fellowship with Christ throughout our Lord's active ministry; John would unfold Jesus' inner life, as he afterwards did in his Gospel; Paul would tell of that revelation of the risen Christ on the Damascus road. Note that God must work in and for us if we are to succeed in the gospel ministry. See v. 8.

GALATIANS 2:11–21

Living by Faith in Christ. Evidently Peter had gone back from the clear revelation of Acts 10 and from his former practice, as stated in v. 12. The fear of the conservative party of the mother church had brought him into a snare. His example had a very unfortunate effect upon the rest of the Hebrew Christians, who took their lead from him. But Paul's remonstrance probably brought Peter back to his former and happier practice.

Paul goes on to show that the death of Christ has taken us altogether out of the realm of the ancient Law, with its restrictions and distinctions between clean and unclean, Jew and Gentile, vv. 15–19. If the conservative view was right and it was wrong to eat with the Gentiles, then all that Christ had done and taught was in vain. Indeed, he had become a minister to sin, v. 17, because he had taught his people to associate with Gentiles. But such a suggestion was, of course, unthinkable, and therefore Peter was wrong in withdrawing from Gentile fellowship.

Then the apostle breaks out into the memorable confession of the power of the cross in his own life, vv. 20, 21. It stood between him and the past. His self-life was nailed there, and this new life was no longer derived from vain efforts to keep the Law, but from the indwelling and uprising of the life of Jesus—the perennial spring of John 4:14.

GALATIANS 3:1–10

Righteousness Based on Faith. The strong tendency of the Galatian Christians to depend upon ceremonies or upon legal obedience, in addition to their faith in Christ, elicits in this chapter a magnificent demonstration of the simplicity and sufficiency of faith alone.

Faith had underlain the commencement of their Christian life, vv. 1–5. They had found peace with God through faith. Through faith they had received the fullness of the Holy Spirit. As they had begun, so let them finish!

Faith had been the means, too, of Abraham's acceptance with God, vv. 6 –10. From the first the gospel of faith had been proclaimed to him by the divine Spirit. Long before he had become a Jew by the initial rite of Judaism, he had been a humble believer in God's promise, on the basis of which he was reckoned righteous. Simple faith was the only condition that he had fulfilled, and the promise that all flesh should be blessed through him had been given when he was still a believing Gentile. Surely what had sufficed for the father of the faithful was good enough for his children! Let each reader see to it that he does not merely believe about Christ, but believes in him, so as to be no longer under the curse, but within the blessing.

GALATIANS 3:11-19

Inheritors of the Promise. We are not under ceremonial law, as contained in the precepts of Leviticus. Our Savior has perfectly fulfilled them. As to the curse that is uttered against everyone, whether Jew or Gentile, that offends against the moral code declared in the Ten Commandments at Sinai, our Savior has redeemed us from that by becoming accursed for us. There is nothing for us to do, but to trust in his finished work and to enter upon the same heritage of blessed service as was unfolded to Abraham in Gen. 12:1-3.

The Mosaic dispensation was a parenthesis in God's dealings with man. It was intended to produce conviction of sin. When God's ideal is held up before us, we become conscious of our deformities and our sins, and are driven to Christ. Let us see to it that we are truly united to him who is the predicted seed of Abraham; for as we stand in him, we become heirs to all the wealth of promise which is contained in the ancient covenant, made to the father of all who believe.

GALATIANS 3:20-29

The Law Leads to Christ. The Mosaic law was not designed to be the final code of the religious life, but to prepare the soil of the human heart to receive Jesus Christ in all the fullness of his salvation. It was the tutor of the Hebrew people, to enable them to become the religious teachers of mankind. It could not, therefore, take the place of the great covenant of grace, which had been initiated with Abraham before he had received the rite of circumcision, and when he thus stood for *all* who believe, whether Jew or Gentile. The mistake of those against whom Paul contended was that they treated as permanent a system which was temporary and parenthetic in its significance.

With many individuals now, as with the Hebrew race, there is often a period in which the conscience is confronted with the holy demands of God's Law, which men cannot keep; but when they discover the full grace of God in Christ, they no longer suffer at the hand of the schoolmaster, but become as children in the Father's home. They put on Christ and stand accepted in the Beloved, and understand that they are in unity with all who believe. Theirs are all the promises that were made to Abraham, and as his spiritual children they claim their fulfillment.

GALATIANS 4:1-11

Live as Sons, Not as Bondmen. The apostle often uses the word "elements" or "rudiments," vv. 3, 9; Col. 2:8, 20. High and holy as was the Mosaic legislation in itself, yet when it was imposed upon inquiring minds as necessary to salvation, Paul spoke of it as belonging to an age that had passed away and to a system that was already antiquated. The whole purpose of God in sending forth his Son was to redeem us from under the Law, that we might enjoy the liberty and joy of the Father's home. We are no longer infants under age, or servants, but sons and if sons, then heirs of God.

There is often a sense of failure among professing Christians that is sadly out of keeping with their rightful position in Christ. Do not be overanxious. Live in your Father's house in constant freedom of heart. Remember that you are under the same roof as Christ, and are therefore allowed to avail yourself of all his grace and help. Refuse no task, however irksome, that God sets before you; and do not worry about irksome rules or petty vexations.

GALATIANS 4:12-20

Truthful and Devoted Dealing. How great a loss is it when we allow ourselves to be diverted from the simplicity of faith to trust in ceremonies, rites, and a prescribed routine! Inevitably these bring us into bondage. Let us therefore not pay slavish attention to the outward, but seek to have Christ within, and from within he will become the energy and passion of a new life. Each time we yield to the prompting of his Spirit, there is less of self and more of him.

In v. 15 we perhaps have a hint as to the nature of Paul's thorn in the flesh. This reference has led many to suppose that he suffered from acute ophthalmia, or inflammation of the eyes. But nothing diverted him from his soul-travail on behalf of his converts, v. 19. What a beautiful analogy we may trace between the formation of Christ in the soul and the formation of a chick in the egg! At first the tiny germ of life is hardly discernible amid the viscous matter in which it floats; but day by day there is less of this and more of the tiny creature which is being formed. So in regeneration the life of Christ is implanted, which will continue to increase until all of sinful self will be lost in the one infilling Presence.

GALATIANS 4:21-31

"Children of Promise." In this allegory of Sarah and Hagar, it is important to notice that Paul is not dealing with the principle of evil within

our hearts, but with the attempt to mingle two dispensations or methods of religious experience—the Law and the gospel.

He says that the poor slave girl, Hagar, whom Abraham bought as a personal attendant for his wife, stands for Mount Sinai, the mountain of the Law, in the district of Arabia, from which she may have originally come. Hagar also stands for the Judaizers, whose headquarters were at Jerusalem while their emissaries everywhere dogged the apostle's movements, insisting that his converts must come under the old Levitical ceremonialism. Paul says that the Galatians must choose between their slavish observance of outward ritual and a simple faith in the finished work of Jesus. He exhorts them to cast out Hagar and Ishmael, which savor of the flesh, and to give themselves to the service of the Spirit, which stands for freedom, peace, and joy in God. Let us also guard against subservience to the outward, and cultivate a quick sensitiveness to the Holy Spirit.

GALATIANS 5:1-12

Hold Fast Your Freedom. We are free. The Son has made us free, and we are free indeed, though not free to disobey the dictates and promptings of our new nature. We are set free from minute prescriptions, from priestly rules and requisitions, from all that would cramp and hinder our spiritual development; but we are still under the law of Christ, who will see to it that the essential righteousness of the Mosaic Law is fulfilled in us "who walk not after the flesh, but after the Spirit," Rom. 8:1.

If the Mosaic Law is kept as a means of salvation, we must fulfill it all, v. 3. For himself, as "we" suggests, v. 5, Paul had an assured confidence that his hope could not be disappointed. Christ is ever calling us upward, v. 8. Be on guard against the ferment of false teaching, v. 9. The apostle shows the absurdity of supposing that he was in favor of circumcision, since, if that were the case, the long persecution of his life would cease, v. 11. These verses were in Bunyan's mind when he depicted Mr. Worldly Wiseman, of the town of Carnal Policy, as endeavoring to turn Christian out of the Way of the Cross to the house of Mr. Legality.

GALATIANS 5:13-26

Produce the Fruit of the Spirit. That Christ has freed us from the Law as a means of salvation does not free us from moral restraint, but brings us under the constraint of a higher law, the law of love. We do not keep this law to be saved; but being saved, we keep it out of love toward Christ. The power of the new life is the indwelling of the Holy Spirit. Unite yourself with his life that you find rising up within you. Live in the Spirit. As we live and walk in the Spirit, we are safe.

The Holy Spirit brings influences to bear which act upon the germs of sin as a disinfectant upon the germs of disease. If we yield ourselves to these influences and are filled with the Spirit of Jesus, we shall be delivered from the self-life, which the apostle describes as "the flesh." As Jesus is more and more formed in us, the new flower and fruitage of the risen life will appear, while the corrupt works of the flesh will shrink and drop away.

GALATIANS 6:1-10

Our Own and Others' Burdens. The spirit of the world gloats over sin; the Spirit of Christ leads us to restore the sinner. Our first thought should never be of revenge or contempt, or of the adjustment of our own claims, but rather of how to help our fallen brother to regain his old place in the love of God. The memory of our own temptations and failures should make us very pitiful and tender. The apostle does not speak, in this place, of premeditated sin, but of that by which we are entrapped and taken unawares.

The most spiritual men in the Church are needed for this holy work of restoration, and they must do it with great meekness and humility. It is thus that we bear one another's burdens; but there are some burdens that each must bear for himself alone, such as his own existence and personal accountability to God.

Life is a seedtime. It is the opportunity of preparing for heavenly harvests. The open furrows invite the seed, and every moment, in some form, we scatter seeds that we shall inevitably meet again in their fruition. Let us remember especially our obligations to God's own children.

GALATIANS 6:11-18

Glorying in the Cross Alone. Paul usually dictated his letters, but this was written with his own hand. The characters were large and clear, v. 11. Perhaps this was due to the trouble with his eyesight referred to in 4:15. But the apostle gloried in the scars that suffering had left upon his frame, because they seemed to him the brandmarks of the happy slavery of Jesus, v. 17. If Judaizing teachers gloried in their brandmarks, how much more did he in his! The cross had cut him off from the world. He was indifferent to worldly praise or blame; he took his marching-orders from Christ alone. This is the third time in his epistle that Paul names the influence of the cross. See 2:20; 5:24; 6:14. Compare v. 15 with 1 Cor. 7:19.

Notice the breadth of the apostle's benediction, v. 16. When we have been created anew in Christ's likeness and are walking by that rule, we find ourselves at once introduced into a family of kindred spirits, who have passed through the same radical change and are united beneath the gracious canopy of mercy and peace. Such are God's Israel. See 3:7.

THE EPISTLE TO EPHESIANS

"THE HIGH CALLING OF GOD IN CHRIST JESUS"

SALUTATION   *1:1, 2.*

PART ONE: CREATED IN CHRIST JESUS   1:3—3:21.

I. THE PRAISE OF HIS GLORIOUS GRACE   *1:3–14.*
   A. The work of the Father   *1:3–6.*
   B. The work of the Son   *1:7–12.*
   C. The work of the Spirit   *1:13, 14.*

II. THE FAITH OF THE EPHESIANS   *1:15–23.*
   A. Thanksgiving for their present faith   *1:15.*
   B. Prayer for their fuller enlightenment   *1:16–23.*

III. PAST AND PRESENT CONTRASTED   *2.*
   A. The former manner of life of the Ephesians   *2:1–3.*
   B. How they have been redeemed   *2:4–10.*
   C. The former character of the Ephesians   *2:11, 12.*
   D. How they have been transformed   *2:13–22.*

IV. PAUL'S SPECIAL MINISTRY   *3.*
   A. The Gentiles are fellow-heirs of the gospel   *3:1–13.*
   B. Prayer that the Ephesians may realize their privilege   *3:14–19.*
   C. Doxology   *3:20, 21.*

PART TWO: FOR GOOD WORKS   4:1—6:20.

I. THE CHRISTIAN IN THE CHURCH   *4:1–16.*
   A. Uniformity of Christian character   *4:1–6.*
   B. Variety of Christian service   *4:7–12.*
   C. Culmination of Christian development   *4:13–16.*

II. THE CHRISTIAN IN THE WORLD   *4:17—5:21.*
   A. Pagan living does not befit Christians   *4:17–24.*
   B. Points of contrast   *4:25–32.*
   C. Living in the light   *5:1–14.*
   D. Living in the Lord   *5:15–21.*

III. THE CHRISTIAN IN THE HOME   *5:22—6:9.*
   Duties of wives, husbands, children, parents, servants, masters *5:22–6:9.*

IV. THE GOOD FIGHT OF THE FAITH   *6:10–20.*
   A. The whole armor of God   *6:10–17.*
   B. Prevailing prayer   *6:18–20.*

CONCLUSION   *6:21–24.*

INTRODUCTION

Paul's first visit to Ephesus is related in Acts 18:19–21. The work commenced then was carried on by Apollos. On Paul's second visit he remained three years. Later, on his way to Jerusalem, he held a moving interview at Miletus with the elders of the Ephesian church. This epistle was addressed to that church about four years afterward, during the early part of his imprisonment at Rome, and immediately after that to the Colossians, to which it bears a close resemblance. The foundation, course, and destiny of the Church are the sublime subjects with which the epistle deals, and the style is of a correspondingly elevated character.

COMMENTARY

EPHESIANS 1:1-14

Our Riches in Christ. This has been called the "Epistle of In-ness," because it is so full of the preposition "in." "Saints" are flesh and blood like ourselves, and we may be saints. The word means "set apart." We are in Christ and he is in us, and any goodness we have is due to our giving room and scope to him to realize his own ideals. To be in the heavenlies, v. 3, means to live a spiritual life and to draw our reinforcements from the unseen and eternal world, which is focused in our Lord. We are in him so far as justification is concerned—that is our standing; and he is in us for sanctification—that is the source of a holy and useful life. The condition of a blessed life is the conscious maintenance of this oneness.

The source of all we are and have and hope to be, so far as salvation is concerned, is the will of God for us; but the stream flows to us through our Lord, and the end to which all things are moving is the summing-up of all in Christ. As he was the Alpha, so he will be the Omega. The sealing of the Holy Spirit is of incalculable advantage, because it means that we are stamped with the likeness of Christ and so kept inviolate among all the vicissitudes of life. See Esth. 8:8; John 6:27.

EPHESIANS 1:15-23

What the Heart May Receive. It is well to go over the successive links of this golden chain when we are in our secret chamber, appropriating them one by one and asking whether we have received a spirit of wisdom and revelation to know Christ, and whether the eyes of our heart have been enlightened to know the hope, the riches, the glory, and the greatness of his power. Insofar as we yield ourselves to the strength of God's might, he will raise us from the grave of selfishness and cause us to sit with Christ in the place of spiritual life and power.

Notice the emphasis with which the apostle affirms the supremacy of Christ's nature, vv. 21, 22. This is a psalm of ascension. We can almost follow his tracks, as all the evil powers which rule the darkness of this world drop far beneath him. The ascending Lord is high over all, and if we claim our right as members of his glorified body, we also shall stand above all our spiritual adversaries. It is easier to descend on an enemy from above him than to seek to assail him from beneath. Notice that Christ needs the Church as much as the head needs the body, because it is through the Church that he fulfills himself. Ask him to fill all of you with all of him.

EPHESIANS 2:1-10

What Grace Has Done. Evidently dead men may walk; that is, they may be dead to the eternal world but alive to this world, which is moving past like a moving picture. The death of the spirit is compatible with much active interest in "the course of this world." Behind the shifting scenes of the material world is the great enemy of souls. As the Spirit of God works in the obedient, so does the evil spirit work in the disobedient. Note this trinity of evil—"the course of this *world,*" "the lusts of our *flesh,*" and "the *prince* of the power of the air." If we desire to save men, we must be in living union with the all-conquering Spirit of Christ.

Notice, also, the past tense which describes the finality of Christ's work, vv. 5, 6. In the purpose of God we have been raised from the grave of sin and are seated with the risen Lord in the place of acceptance and victory. We were one with Christ when he lay in the grave and arose. In God's thought we have already taken our seat with the glorified Christ upon the throne; the pity is that we do not believe this or act as if we had done so. All this is the gift of God's unmerited love. By grace have we been brought into this position, and by grace are we maintained in it. We are of God's "making"; such is the Greek word for "workmanship," v. 10. We have been created for good works; they have been planned for us and we have only to walk in them.

EPHESIANS 2:11–22

Reconciled and United by the Cross. The state of the unconverted must be described by a series of negations. Shut the sun out of the world, love out of the home, liberty out of the state! The unsaved know not of their infinite loss; but if they could see what we inherit through union with Jesus, they could cease to wonder that we run not with them into the same excess of riot. Does a maiden need much persuasion to cast aside paste jewels when real ones are offered her?

There was no natural affinity between Jew and Gentile. This arose partly because of diverse nationality and genius; but in addition, the whole code of Jewish customs as to eating clean meats and ceremonial pollution prevented it. All these party walls of division were swept away by Christ. In him, as the cornerstone, two walls, running in different directions, met. Two sections of humanity, East and West, became united to each other, because each was united to him, and thus was formed a new unit of humanity.

What a noble conception is given of the Church and ultimately of the redeemed race, growing slowly through the ages and becoming God's dwelling-place! Notice the Trinity; through Jesus, the Eternal Father comes by his Spirit to dwell in the heart of man.

EPHESIANS 3:1–13

Gentiles Share "Unsearchable Riches." "Dispensation" should be rendered "stewardship." We are God's trustees for men. To each of us is given some special phase of truth which we must pass on to others by the force of our character or by the teaching of our lips. It was given to Paul to make known the great truth that Gentiles might enter the Church of God on equal terms with Jews. During the earlier stages of human education this secret had been withheld; but with the advent of the Son of man, the doors into the Church had been thrown open to all. Paul's insistence on this truth was the main cause of the hatred and opposition which checkered his life. "Fellow-heirs," fellow-members, and fellow-partakers! This truth was not the result of logical argument, but had been communicated by direct revelation, as was so much else in Paul's teaching. See Gal. 1:11ff.

The history of the Church—its genesis, growth, and development—is the subject of angelic study, v. 10. In the story of redemption there are presented and illustrated aspects of the divine nature which are to be learned nowhere else, and therefore heavenly intelligences bend with eager interest over human history from the viewpoint of the Church of Christ.

EPHESIANS 3:14–21

The Greatest of All Desires. The kernel of this prayer is in the clause that Christ may make his home in the believer's heart through faith. The previous petitions lead up to this. Note the apostle's attitude—with bended knee; his plea with God—he is the Father from whom all family love emanates; his measure—the wealth of God's glorious perfection; the necessary prerequisite to Christ's indwelling—the penetration of our inmost being with the strength of the Holy Spirit. And then note the outcome: The indwelling Christ intends that we shall be rooted and grounded in love. When this is the case, we shall understand his love; and when we experience and know Christ's love, we shall be as completely filled in our little measure as God is in his great measure.

A dying veteran in Napoleon's army, when the surgeon was probing for the fatal bullet, said, "A little deeper and you will find the Emperor." Faith opens the door to the Spirit; the Spirit reveals Christ; Christ fills the heart; the heart begins to understand love; and love is the medium through which we become infilled with God, for God is love. It is staggering to ask all this; but the God who works in us with such power is able to do more than we ask, more than we think—abundantly more, exceeding abundantly more.

EPHESIANS 4:1-10

Keeping the "Unity of the Spirit." Paul here admonishes lowliness in the presence of another's excellence; meekness in suffering injury; longsuffering under provocation; forbearance toward the trying mistakes and failures of others. Remember that the unity of the Church, as the Body of Christ, is already made; but it is for us to maintain it. We must avoid whatever in word or deed would break it. There are seven different bonds of unity, but of these the greatest is the nature of God, which is transcendent, "who is above all"; penetrating, "through all"; and immanent, "in all." Each saint has some grace or gift; use it. On the whole, after we reach maturity we had better center on what we can do best.

What a magnificent conception is given in vv. 8 and 9 of the ascended Christ! The original conception was supplied by Deborah in her noble song. Descending from her morning vigil on Tabor, she summoned Barak to lead captive the foe who for so long had held the land in captivity. But in Jesus' ascension, a long procession of yet mightier foes was led captive by him. Among them were death, the grave, and Hades, the underworld. It is from the hands of Jesus that even the rebellious may obtain their gifts. There is no depth to which Jesus will not go to save, no height to which he will not lift us!

EPHESIANS 4:11-19

Building Up the Body of Christ. Apostles, prophets, pastors, teachers, evangelists are the gifts of the risen Christ to his Church. There should be no rivalry among them. Each has his own work to do, as each cog in a watch has its special function. None can do the work of another, and none should try to do it. The apostles laid the foundations of the City of God, and the work of each is represented by a different stone. The pastor prepares the ground and sows the seed for the harvest which the evangelist reaps; but God will proportion the reward between them. The teacher is as much needed as the evangelist, but neither is so essential as God, who giveth the increase. Without that, all labor would be in vain.

We learn from v. 12 that the prime duty of all these agents is not to baptize, marry, and bury the saints, to comfort and console them, and to get them somehow into Heaven, as the Arab guides get travelers to the top of the Pyramids. Their duty is to "perfect," that is, to adjust, the saints for the work of ministry, that they may contribute to the building up of the Church. A minister is a failure if he does all the work himself. The people must all be at work—in the quarries, or shaping the stones, or fitting them into their places.

EPHESIANS 4:20-32

Putting on the "New Man." The Lord Jesus is our textbook and our teacher, the schoolhouse in which we are taught, and the object lesson in which all truth is enshrined. But all is in vain unless we definitely and forever put away the old man; that is, our old manners and customs insofar as they are contrary to the Spirit of Christ. With equal decision we are called upon to seek the daily renewal of our spirit and the outward conformity of our mode of life to the example of Jesus. But it should never be forgotten that the latter will be a dry husk unless it is energized from the true vine. There can be little of Christ *without* unless he dwells without rival *within*. But the Holy Spirit will see to this, if only we grieve him not.

What a transformation immediately ensues! Truth instead of falsehood, gentleness for anger, earnest toil for dishonesty, cleansed instead of filthy speech. If all believers were to live like this, the world would know that the Son of God has come. It is not enough that a man should believe to secure deliverance from the wrath of God; he must daily seek to attain to such resemblance of Jesus as shall make men recall him to mind.

EPHESIANS 5:1-12

"Walk as Children of Light." It is indeed a high calling to imitate God and to walk in love after the measure of Christ; but it will be impossible unless we open our innermost heart to the Holy Spirit. We must not only sacrifice ourselves for others, but there should be a fragrance in all that we do. "A sweetsmelling savor." Note carefully the injunctions of vv. 3 and 4, especially as they concern speech. It is by our speech that we betray the true condition of our hearts.

We must be as distinct from the world as light is from darkness. There should be no twilight in our testimony for our Lord, though there may be considerable obscurity in our views of truth. Whatever is unfruitful, whatever we should blush to have transcribed and read to the world, whatever would be inconsistent with the strong, clear light of the throne of God and the Lamb must be avoided. We must walk in the light of the Lord. Then we ourselves shall become luminous, as some diamonds do after being held in sunshine. People who love darkness will avoid and hate us; but their treatment may be only a cause for our own encouragement, as God becomes increasingly precious to us.

EPHESIANS 5:13-21

"Redeeming the Time." The earlier verses remind us of Isaiah 60. Awake, thou Christian soul; arise from the dust and put on thy beautiful garments! Stand on the mountain peak of prayer and Christ shall shine on thee as when morning gilds the highest Alps! The child of God must arise from among those who are yet in their graves, dead in trespasses and sins. He can have no complicity or fellowship with such. Is there effort in this, and cost? Christ will more than compensate. He will satisfy.

The opportunities of life are fleeting past; let us buy them up. They are most valuable, because they form the seed plot of eternity. In the other life we shall reap the harvests which we have prepared for here. Chrysostom, as a young man, kept silent for days together to break himself of a bad habit of criticism. But the apostle's method is better. Make room for the Holy Spirit. Be filled with him, and he will use heart and lip in the service of praise and thanksgiving. It is as much our duty to be filled with the Spirit as it is not to get drunk. Remember to give thanks "always" for "all" things. Whether you like the packing case or not, you may be sure that the contents are the very best that God could send you.

EPHESIANS 5:22-33

Love of Husband and Wife. The apostle has been urging us to be filled with the Spirit, and now proceeds to show how Spirit-filled people should act in their homes. He has been exhorting praise and joyfulness, and now urges that our lives, as well as our lips, should be attuned to music.

What a lofty ideal of wedded love is here! Chrysostom says, "Wouldest thou that thy wife obey thee as the Church doth Christ? Have care for her, then, as Christ for the Church." Our earthly relationships are similitudes and emblems of sacred realities, and the more we can import into the time sphere the inspiration and virtue of the eternal, the more transcendental and beautiful will they become. The Lord has taught us the utter renunciation of love. Men of the world reckon how much love they can get, the children of eternity how much they can give; but such giving always means getting back with compound interest. Notice those phrases about nourishing and cherishing. O wounded member of Christ's Body, he suffers in thee, and nourishes, cherishes, and will heal!

EPHESIANS 6:1-12

Children and Parents; Servants and Masters. Where our religion is true, it will affect every relationship in life. The love of Christ must find its manifestation in nursery and in kitchen, in workshop and in municipal chamber. But notice that its duties are reciprocal. We must give on our side, just as we expect others to give on theirs.

The first duty of children is obedience. They must be taught to obey because it is right, and their conscience bears witness to the rightness. Never plead with a child to do what is right, nor bribe him by a reward. Take your stand on that primeval sense of right and wrong, which is the foundation of morals and will be the stay of the child's whole after-life, when once its supremacy is established. But parents should help their children by removing irritation or passion from their own speech. Slaves formed a large proportion of the early Church. Their obedience must be explicit, and they were taught to believe that Christ took their faithful service to their earthly owner as service to himself. But masters must ever deal with their servants as liable to be called to account by the great Master of all. The center of all authority is Christ, and he will demand an account of our treatment of every servant he has sent into our homes.

EPHESIANS 6:13-24

"Finally, Be Strong in the Lord." Many would be strong, but fail because they forget that they can be effectively so only "in the Lord, and in the strength of his might." Paul had a very vivid conception of the powerful forces that are arrayed against the Church. He is not dealing here especially with our personal temptations, but with those hosts of wicked spirits that lie behind the evil of the world. It is probable that the vast systems which oppose the gospel—the philosophies, temples, and priests of false religions; the trade in strong drink, impurity, and like evils—are directly promoted and furthered by the agency of evil spirits in arms against God.

We must be pure and holy if we are to prevail against evil, and especially must we give ourselves to prayer. To prevail in this warfare we must diligently employ the weapon of "all prayer." Tychicus carried this letter. He was faithful to the end, Acts 20:4; 2 Tim. 4:12. The epistle closes, as it began, with uncorrupted, that is, pure and eternal, love. Alford says, "This is the only truth worthy to be the crown and climax of this glorious epistle."

THE EPISTLE OF
PHILIPPIANS
TO PRESENT EVERY MAN PERFECT IN CHRIST

SALUTATION *1:1, 2.*

I. A PASTOR'S REGARD AND CONCERN FOR HIS PEOPLE *1:3–11.*
   A. Thanksgiving for their cooperation *1:3–5.*
   B. Confidence that they share the same grace *1:6, 7.*
   C. Prayer for their spiritual enrichment *1:8–11.*

II. THE COMPENSATIONS OF PAUL'S IMPRISONMENT *1:12–26.*
   A. Testimony of his bonds throughout the praetorian guard *1:12, 13.*
   B. Increased boldness of the brotherhood in preaching Christ *1:14–18.*
   C. His hope of larger usefulness upon his release *1:19–26.*

III. THE LIFE THAT IS WORTHY OF THE GOSPEL OF CHRIST *1:27—2:30.*
   A. A life of courage in the face of conflict *1:27–30.*
   B. A Life of goodwill and helpfulness *2:1–5.*
   C. A life determined by the Spirit of Christ *2:6–11.*
   D. A life triumphant in an evil world *2:12–18.*

   (Illustrated by Paul's fellow-workers *2:19–30.* Timothy *2:19–24.* Epaphroditus *2:25–30.*)

IV. HUMAN AND DIVINE RIGHTEOUSNESS CONTRASTED *3:1—4:3.*
   A. Warning against those who glory in the flesh *3:1–3.*
   B. Paul's personal claim to legal righteousness *3:4–6.*
   C. His repudiation of all else for the righteousness of Christ *3:7–16.*
   D. Warning against the fleshly-minded *3:17—4:1.*

   (Personal message to Euodia and Synteche *4:2, 3.*)

V. THE FINAL EXHORTATION *4:4–9.*
   A. The place of prayer *4:4–7.*
   B. The need of purity *4:8, 9.*

VI. A PERSONAL MESSAGE *4:10–19.*
   A. The gift from the Philippians *4:10–14.*
   B. Their past assistance *4:15–17.*
   C. The divine acceptance of this service *4:18, 19.*

CONCLUSION *4:20–23.*

INTRODUCTION

The church at Philippi appears to have been one of the purest of the apostolic age, and called out the apostle's thankfulness and commendation beyond any other.

The occasion of the epistle seems to have been the return of Epaphroditus, who had brought a gift from Paul's friends in Philippi, but had been seized by a dangerous illness. Paul was a prisoner in his own hired house in Rome and was anticipating his trial before the Emperor.

There is nothing controversial in this letter. The peace of God keeps the apostle's mind and heart, and out of it pours a tide of deep and tender love. The hope of being alive at Christ's coming is still his guiding star. His citizenship is in Heaven, and all that he has forfeited of earthly wealth and joy is more than compensated for by what he has found in Christ.

COMMENTARY

PHILIPPIANS 1:1-11

Rejoice in Growth; and Seek Increase. It is exceedingly difficult to compress this epistle, which is the tenderest and most personal of them all. Every word merits consideration; every paragraph is full of linked sweetness long drawn out. In the opening verses we are taught that we may further the gospel, not only by direct efforts, but by helping those who, like the apostle, are devoted to its spread. From the early beginnings of their friendship, this church had never faltered in its loving gifts, which Paul sought to repay with prayers on their behalf. He regarded them as comrades fighting the same enemy, on the same field, and sharing in the same grace.

The apostle's confidence that whatever God begins will have its perfect end, v. 6, is very reassuring. This is what we need, though we must not take it for granted apart from faith and prayer. Each of the epistles has its "collect," its comprehensive prayer offered in the name of Christ. This one, vv. 9-11, is especially beautiful. Abounding love will lead to increased knowledge, and this to quicker discrimination between things that differ, however similar they may appear, and this, in turn, to freedom from blame and offense. And all will result in the fruit of a holy life, pleasing to Jesus and bringing glory and praise to God.

PHILIPPIANS 1:12-21

"To Live Is Christ, and To Die Is Gain." It was a matter of comparative indifference to Paul what happened to himself so long as the gospel progressed, because the extension of the gospel meant the growing glory of Jesus. He was quite content to be in bonds, if only by his chains he might gain access to new realms, hitherto untrodden, for proclaiming his Lord. He could even view with equanimity the envy and strife of some, if Jesus might be named to those who had never heard of him. He was prepared to live or to die, that Jesus might be magnified. He was willing to remain for a little longer outside of Heaven, if that would better serve the cause he loved. His main argument for consistency of life on the part of his converts was that the success of the gospel might not be impeded. It seemed good to suffer, if only it were on the behalf of Christ. Oh, that we might experience a similar absorption in the great interests of the gospel!

It is clear from this paragraph that death is not an unconscious sleep. It is "gain." It is a loosing from anchorage so that the soul may go forth on the broad ocean of God's love. It does not interrupt our conscious fellowship with the Lord. The moment of absence here is the moment of presence there. To die is therefore "gain."

PHILIPPIANS 1:22-30

Privileged To Suffer in Christ's Behalf. Our "manner of life" ("conversation," v. 27) is all-important. In the open day and in the hours of darkness it must be worthy of the gospel. We must show ourselves to be of a heavenly tone and temper, as citizens of that "city which hath foundations, whose builder and maker is God." Lady Powerscourt used to say that she dwelt in Heaven, but came down for a few hours each day to do her work on earth, returning home at night. Clearly, then, our dress, accent, and behavior should betray us as strangers and pilgrims who can well endure the discomfort of the inn or the troublous experiences of the place of our sojourn.

Notice that remarkable expression, "For unto you it is given in the behalf of Christ . . . to suffer," v. 29. This is an added honor conferred on us by our Lord. The King gives us the opportunity of lying in the stocks with him, of standing at the same pillory, and of being crucified on the same Calvary. But those who have drunk of his cup shall share his throne. When earth and sky shall pass away, his fellow-sufferers shall be his chosen bodyguard and attendants in a world where all shall love and honor him.

PHILIPPIANS 2:1-11

Following His Example of Self-Surrender. In all Scripture—indeed, in all literature—there is no passage which combines such extraordinary extremes as this. The apostle opens the golden compasses of his faith, placing one jeweled point on the throne of divine glory and the other at the edge of the pit, where the cross stood; and then he asks us to measure the vast descent of the Son of God as he came down to help us. Mark the seven steps: He was in the form of God, that is, as much God as he was afterward a servant; "being in the form of God . . . took the form of a servant." He was certainly the latter and equally so the former. He did not grasp at equality with God, for it was already his. He emptied himself; that is, refused to avail himself of the use of his divine attributes, that he might teach the meaning of absolute dependence on the Father. He obeyed as a servant the laws which had their source in himself. He became man—a humble man, a dying man, a crucified man. He lay in the grave. But the meaning of his descent was that of his ascent, and to all his illustrous names is now added that of "Jesus—Savior." This must be our model. This mind must be in us. In proportion as we become humbled and crucified, we, in our small measure, shall attain the power of blessing and rescuing men.

PHILIPPIANS 2:12-18

Lights in the World. The Apostle's sublime visions of the glory of the divine Redeemer are always linked with practical exhortation. Do nothing through pride and vainglory. Look on the things of others. Count others better than yourself. Work out what God is working in. Your heart is God's workshop! His Spirit is there, striving against selfishness, pride, impurity, and vanity, but you must consolidate each holy impulse in speech and act. Be careful of every such movement in your soul; it will become clearer and more definite as you yield to it, and it will be corroborated by outward circumstances, which God will open before you. But exercise fear and trembling, just as the young pupil of a great master will be nervously careful not to lose one thought or suggestion which the master may impart.

In this manner you will become as a lighthouse on a rockbound coast, shining with blameless and beneficent beauty among your companions. Light is silent, but it reveals. Light is gentle, but it is mighty in its effects. Light departs when the sun is down, but it may be maintained by various luminaries until dawn again breaks. As we shine, we shall be consumed, but the sacrifice will not be in vain.

PHILIPPIANS 2:19-30

Honoring Christian Messengers. The apostle nobly honored the younger men who wrought with him. He speaks of Timothy as his "son," and writes at length on the genuineness of Timothy's loving interest in each of his converts. He describes Epaphroditus as his "brother, companion in labour, and fellowsoldier." How tenderly he refers to Epaphroditus' sickness and recovery, as though God had conferred on himself special favor in giving back this beloved comrade in the great fight!

It is well worthwhile to ponder the remark that God does not add sorrow to sorrow, v. 27. He tempers his wind to the shorn lamb. He cautions the accuser that he must not take Job's life. With the trial he makes the way of escape. He keeps his finger on the wrist while the operation is in progress, and stays it as soon as the pulse flutters. Not sorrow upon sorrow! Note also that "hazarding" of life, v. 30, alternate translation. It was a common experience in those great days of Christ's suffering Church, Acts 15:26. How strange it is to watch the sacrifices that men and women will make in times of war, when a new spirit is stirring in the world and men adventure everything for liberty, righteousness, and fatherland, and then compare this extravagant expenditure of blood and treasure with what we have done for Jesus.

PHILIPPIANS 3:1-12

Losing All To Know Christ. Precept must be on precept, line on line. The false teachers who dogged Paul's steps insisted on rigid conformity to Judaism, with its rabbinical accretions, as the condition of being saved by Christ. Paul's answer was that he had gone through all the requirements of Judaism, but had found it absolutely unsatisfactory and inefficient to subdue the sin of his soul. But in Christ he had found everything he needed. What had been gain to him now seemed but dross. He had found the pearl of great price, and was only too glad to sacrifice all else to purchase and keep it, as the talisman of complete victory.

The essence of Judaism was not external but within. True circumcision was deliverance from the self-life, and that could only be gained by the cross of Christ. The "Israelite indeed," like Nathanael, had three traits of character—his worship was spiritual, he gloried in the Crucified, and he was delivered from reliance upon the self-life. Let us ask the Holy Spirit to teach us to know Jesus in the intimacy of personal fellowship, to feel the pulse of his resurrection-life, to experience the power of his death, and to realize the whole of his divine program. For this we might be more than content to trample on our boasted pride.

PHILIPPIANS 3:13-21

Pressing on "for the Prize." The nearer the saint comes to the perfect life, the farther he feels from it. It is only when we have climbed the foothills that we realize how lofty the mountain summits are. But there is no need for discouragement. We have eternity before us, the expanding landscape of truth is our inspiration, and the loving Spirit of God bears us upward on eagle's wings. Our Savior had a distinct purpose in view when he "apprehended" us. Its full scope was only known to him; let us strive to not fail to realize his ideal. We can do this best by forgetting past failures, past sins, and past successes, and pressing on toward the goal. Will not the prize be the Lord himself? Let us always remember that God's call is upward. This will help us when there seems collision between two duties.

Instead of judging another, let us walk together along the path of obedience. Those who leave the narrow track and still profess godliness are greater enemies of the cross than avowed antagonists. We are citizens of the skies, who come forth to spend a few hours each day on earth. This is our inn; yonder is our true home. Thence Jesus will come to complete the work of salvation by giving us a body like his own.

PHILIPPIANS 4:1-9

Inspiring Exhortations. What a strong and faithful heart was Paul's! Poor and despised though he was, he had both joys and crowns of which no hostile force could deprive him. He lived in the encompassing atmosphere of eternity, as we may. Surely these two Christian women could not have withstood this tender exhortation; and all his fellow-workers must have been heartened by the thought that their names were dear to Christ and entered in the birthday book of the twice-born.

Joy and peace are the subjects of the next paragraph. How wonderful that these struggling little churches were drinking of springs of which the princes and citizens of Greece and Rome knew nothing. Note the conditions. We must be moderate in our ambitions and gentle in our behavior. We must ever practice the presence of our Lord—he is always at hand. We must turn over all causes of anxiety to the Father's infinite care and leave them with him. We must thank him for the past and count on him for the future. While we pray, God's peace will descend to stand as sentry at our heart's door. But we must possess the God of peace as well as the peace of God—the one condition being that we must earnestly pursue all things that are true, just, pure, and lovely.

PHILIPPIANS 4:10-23

"My God Shall Supply All Your Need." The apostle had been glad to receive the gifts of his friends, because these evidenced their earnest religious life. It was fruit that increased to their account. On his own part he had learned one of the greatest of lessons—contentment with whatever state he found himself in. This is a secret that can only be acquired by our experience of life in the will of God. When once the soul lives in God and finds its highest ideal in the fulfillment of his will, it becomes absolutely assured that all things which are necessary will be added. All things are possible to those who derive their daily strength from God.

It is wonderful to hear Paul say that he abounded, v. 18, despite a prison, a chain, a meager existence! The great ones of the world would have ridiculed the idea that any could be said to "abound" in such conditions. But they could not imagine the other hemisphere in which Paul lived; and out of his own blessed experience of what Christ could do, he promised that one's every need would be supplied. God's measure is "his riches in glory"; his channel is Jesus Christ. Let us learn from v. 18 that every gift to God's children which is given from a pure motive is acceptable to him as a fragrant sacrifice. That reference in v. 22 shows that Paul was making good use of his stay in Rome!

THE EPISTLE OF
COLOSSIANS

"CHRIST IN YOU, THE HOPE OF GLORY," 1:27

SALUTATION   *1:1, 2.*

I. THE FAITH AND THE EXPERIENCE OF THE COLOSSIANS   *1:3—2:5.*
   A. Thanksgiving for the faith of the Colossians   *1:3–7.*
   B. Prayer for their growth in knowledge and grace   *1:8–11.*
   C. The preeminence of Christ   *1:12–20.*
   D. The experience of redemption   *1:21–23.*
   E. The ministry of redemption   *1:24—2:5.*

II. THE CHARACTER AND CONDUCT OF THE CHRISTIAN   *2:6—4:17.*
   A. False philosophies to be rejected   *2:6–15.*
   B. False practices to be avoided   *2:16–23.*
   C. The risen life and the old life in contrast   *3:1–4.*
   D. The scope of Christian obligation   *3:5—4:6.*
   E. Personal matters   *4:7–17.*

CONCLUSION   *4:18.*

INTRODUCTION

Colosse was an important city in Asia Minor, not far from Laodicea and Hierapolis. The church there had been planted by Epaphras, perhaps during Paul's residence at Ephesus. The apostle, apparently, had not visited it himself, 2:1, but was deeply interested in it through the report of his friend.

This epistle was written during Paul's imprisonment at Rome, 1:24; 4:18, and apparently about the same time as those to the Ephesians and Philemon; for the three letters were sent by the hands of the same persons, Tychicus and Onesimus, 4:7, 9; Eph. 6:21, 22. The church was suffering from the teaching of a false philosophy which combined oriental mysticism with Jewish ritualism, and turned the disciples from simple faith in Christ. The object of this epistle, therefore, is to set forth the majesty and glory of our Lord's Person and character.

COMMENTARY

COLOSSIANS 1:1–8

The Gospel Bearing Fruit. The saints are men of faith, for their holiness is derived from Christ, but they are also faithful men and will not betray their trust. "Grace" is the Greek and "peace" the Hebrew greeting. We can do a great deal with those whom we desire to correct or instruct if we begin by commending all that is worthy of being praised. Thus the apostle rejoices in the evidences of the trinity of Christian graces—faith, hope, and love. His prayers were filled with intercession. One marvels at the accomplishment of this extraordinary man, who in addition to his travels, labors, writings, and toil for his daily bread had time for such abundant prayerfulness.

There is a note of triumph in his reference to the reception given to the gospel in all the world. The handful of corn on the top of the mountains was already beginning to shake like Lebanon. It seemed as though victory was assured; if only the Church had possessed more men like him, the world would have been saved some sad experiences. Note the unaffected humility of the apostle in classing Epaphras with himself as his beloved fellow-servant in the household of God.

COLOSSIANS 1:9–20

Our Wondrous Privileges in Christ. Here is a paragraph which may rightly form part of our daily intercession for ourselves and others. We all need a quicker insight into God's will, and this is only acquired through the wisdom and understanding communicated by the Holy Spirit to our spirits. But that understanding is conditioned, as in v. 10, by a daily behavior which pleases God and bears fruit in every good work. It is as we slowly climb the ascent of consistent living that the landscape of God's nature expands around us. As character and knowledge grow, so will our spiritual strength; but notice that frequently such strength is needed not so much for great exploits, as for the patient bearing of the cross, v. 11.

In view of the fact that we are being qualified for an inheritance in light, there should be a song of perennial thanksgiving proceeding from us. What a wonder that the sons of ignorance and night can dwell in the eternal light, through eternal love! It is not enough to receive the forgiveness of sins; we must be conformed to the image of the Son, who is himself the image of the Father, v. 15. Notice the preeminence of Jesus—in creation, v. 16; in the Church, v. 18; in resurrection, v. 18; and in the great enterprise of reconciliation and restoration, v. 20. Let him be preeminent in us also!

COLOSSIANS 1:21–29

Laboring To Perfect the Church. How wonderful is God! His scheme of grace embraces the world of men, but he can concentrate on individual souls as unworthy as ours. "You . . . hath he reconciled." And he will never abandon his work until we arrive in his presence-chamber without spot or blemish or any such thing. But, of course, the putting forth of his power on our behalf is conditioned on our steadfast faith.

Paul drank deeply of the Master's cup. It seemed as if Jesus had trusted him with participation in the sorrows of Gethsemane and Calvary. And he was thus fitted for the stewardship of two great secrets, which it was his joy to unfold. In Eph. 3 he says that he was commissioned to show the Gentiles that they might become fellow-heirs, but here, v. 27, that they might experience the indwelling of Christ. Those who are conscious of that indwelling know its riches of power and joy and victory. Their hope of glory is dimmed by no fear, because they have the Christ in their hearts, and therefore Heaven in their hearts; so it follows naturally that their hearts will one day be with Christ in Heaven. Christ *in* us is "the hope of glory." Note the individual interest which the true pastor takes in his flock, as shown in the repeated use of "every man."

COLOSSIANS 2:1-12

Established in Their Faith. If you know Christ, you can lay your hand on the treasures of wisdom and knowledge. You know them, not by the intellect but by the heart. They are matters of daily experience. The apostle's aim in this chapter is to put his converts on their guard against those who might divert them from their simple faith in Jesus, and their sufficiency in him.

The first act of the Christian life is to receive Christ, and every moment afterward we must continue receiving him. The act must become an attitude. Breathe in the love and power of Jesus. Take deep breaths. Then we shall be rooted in him in secret, and built up in him in our outward walk and behavior. If we have Christ, we have all God's fullness. Like Jacob's ladder, he links us with God. What need have we for celestial beings, like those invented by the Gnostics, or for the rite of circumcision, as insisted on by the Jews? We have everything in Jesus. He has fulfilled the Law in all respects on our behalf. Let us put the waters of entire surrender and consecration between our past, our sins, and the world, and rise into his life, the life of resurrection-glory and power.

COLOSSIANS 2:13-23

Avoiding Errors. The reiteration of the prepositions "in" and "with" emphasizes our close identification with our Savior. Such we are in the purpose of God, and so we should be in daily experience. In union with him we have once and forever put away the sins of the flesh, have lain in his grave, have passed to the Heaven side of death, and are living under the blue sky of acceptance with God. Our Master's victory is potentially ours. He won it, but we may share its fruits. Yet faith must apprehend and affirm these blessings. The land of Canaan is ours by right, but every inch has to be claimed by faith. "Faith is an affirmation and act, that bids eternal truth be fact."

We must not allow our religious life to become a piece of outward ritual, vv. 16, 17, nor permit the supposed mediation of angels to obscure the supreme majesty of our Lord, vv. 18, 19. We who have died with Christ must not always regulate ourselves by the don'ts of the Law. Let us enter Christ's more intimate fellowship and live on the positive side. Ours should be the freedom of a full life and the ampler vision of the mountains. Nothing else really avails against the indulgence of the flesh.

COLOSSIANS 3:1-11

Seeking "Things Which Are Above." Let us repeat the glorious truth, which was doubtless the heart of Paul's teaching, that our old nature has been nailed, in Christ, to the cross and laid in the grave; and that our real self, in the second Adam, has entered the new world of resurrection. We belong to the world on the threshold of which Jesus said, "Touch me not, for I am not yet ascended." We must guard against the defiling touch of the world, of sin, and of the old self-life. We stand between two worlds; each solicits us. Let us yield to the influences that pull us upward, and not to those that anchor us to this sinful and vain world. Our eternal blessedness has begun; let us walk in it.

In Christ we profess to "have put off the old man," i. e., the habits of our former life, v. 9; now let us actually do so, in the power of the Holy Spirit. We profess to have put on the risen Christ, v. 10; now let us don the attire and habits of the new man. Too many Christians resemble Lazarus, quickened from his death-sleep, but still arrayed in grave-clothes. Too few array themselves in the radiant beauty of the risen Lord, which is the common heritage of all who believe in him, whatever their rank or nationality.

COLOSSIANS 3:12-17

Love, Peace, and Praise. The articles of the Christian's dress are enumerated here, and we need to refer to this list continually in order to be sure that none of them is missing from our spiritual wardrobe. We must not always live in the negative of avoiding wrong; the positive has a clear claim on us. And in each circumstance of trial or temptation, we must advance to meet it arrayed in Christ. As the Lord acted, so must we. We must partake of the family likeness. When a Christian friend manifests over the breakfast table some ugly feature of the old life, we may fairly urge him to return to his room and complete his dressing. Love is the girdle of the Christian attire.

Let the peace of Christ rule within. Let the word of Christ dwell in the innermost chambers of the soul. Let there be mutual love and wholesome glee, song in the life, and grace in the heart. Whatever is wrong will break into pieces like a glass when the name of Jesus is spoken over it. The thought of him is the touchstone of trial as well as the talisman of victory. A thankful heart makes for a victorious and attractive character.

COLOSSIANS 3:18—4:1

Home and Business Relations. From these high flights into the eternal and divine, Paul turns to the daily duties of the home, and demands that in the simplest domestic concerns the disciple should ever keep in mind the high claims of Christ. No act of life can be left outside the sacred enclosure of his everlasting love. As the moon affects the tides around the world, even in the smallest indentations of the coast, so must the power of Christ's resurrection make itself felt in the behavior of the servant and the child.

It is specially beautiful to notice the apostle's constant reference to the bond slaves, who formed so important an element in the early Church. There they learned that in Christ all souls were free, and that in him master and slave were brethren. Stealing out at night from the arduous labors of his lot, many a poor slave would return with new conceptions of his daily tasks, to be applied to the service rendered to his Lord. No angel in Heaven's high temple has more definite service to the King than any honest and industrious servant may daily render to Jesus. Here is the dignity of labor indeed! And, masters, remember *your* Master.

COLOSSIANS 4:2–9

Prayer and Daily Living. We must pray more. Our lives cannot maintain the Godward attitude without prolonged seasons of communication with him through the Word. This is so important that we must be ever on the watch against whatever might mar the life of devotion. Intercession will often unlock frostbitten lips and make our souls glow. "Withal praying also for us." If we are shut in and cannot perform active service, we can surely pray for those who are entrusted with the mystery of Christ; and let those who are called to active service be ready to step in when God opens the door, v. 3. The limitations of life are no excuse for idleness, v. 4.

It is not easy to walk in wisdom toward those that are without. But God will teach us how to buy up ("redeem," v. 5) opportunities and crowd each of them with good service. Our talk may sparkle like salt and purify as it does. Paul bound his fellow-workers to himself by the high estimate he placed on them. Love idealizes. Probably we should have thought some of these men to be very ordinary, but the apostle saw them in hues borrowed from his own heart. Onesimus, a runaway slave, recently converted, is described as "a faithful and beloved brother."

COLOSSIANS 4:10–18

Christian Greetings. What a noble group had gathered around the apostle in his enforced residence in Rome! That hired room of his must have been filled time after time with most interesting groups. Each friend was dear to the lion-hearted man of God and intent on some act of loving devotion. Aristarchus had been with him in the Ephesian riot; Mark was endeavoring to make good his former lapse of courage; Epaphras, who had come from Colosse, was remarkable for his soul-agony and prayer-labor on his friends' behalf; Luke, the beloved physician, was always on the alert to minister to malaria or other maladies that afflicted Paul; and Demas, of whom perhaps he had begun to have suspicions, 2 Tim. 4:10, was there also. Archippus is believed to have been a son of Philemon, and chief presbyter of Laodicea. Does the injunction, v. 16, imply that already the church there had begun to become lukewarm, Rev. 3:15? The closing words were probably written by Paul himself. The clumsy handwriting was accounted for by the weight of the fetters on the poor wrists; yet his heart was full of love and joy.

THE FIRST EPISTLE TO THE
THESSALONIANS
BUILDING UP ONE ANOTHER

SALUTATION   *1:1.*

I. FOUNDING AND GROWTH OF THE THESSALONIAN CHURCH   *1:2—3:13.*
   A. Fruits of the gospel in Thessalonica   *1:2–10.*
   B. Paul's missionary methods   *2:1–12.*
   C. Results of his labor   *2:13–20.*
   D. Visit of Timothy   *3:1–10.*
   E. Benediction   *3:11–13.*

II. THE WALK OF THE CHRISTIAN   *4, 5.*
   A. The need of purity   *4:1–8.*
   B. The need of love for the brethren   *4:9–12.*
   C. The return of Christ   *4:13–18.*
   D. How to be prepared   *5:1–8.*
   E. The will of God for the Christian   *5:9–22.*

CONCLUSION   *5:23–28.*

INTRODUCTION

Thessalonica stood on the seaboard and was the center of a large trade, which it shared with Corinth and Ephesus. It is the Salonika of today. It contained a large colony of Jews and a synagogue. The apostle visited it, as recorded in Acts 17:1-9. Probably he dispatched this epistle from Corinth; compare 1 Thess. 1:1 and 3:1 with Acts 18:1-5. It is the earliest of the epistles and more elementary than the later ones. An interesting study would be to trace the development of the apostle's thought to the fuller and deeper teachings of the epistles to the churches at Rome and Ephesus.

COMMENTARY

1 THESSALONIANS 1:1–10

Imitators and Examples. This chapter abounds in thanksgiving, and the apostle recites the many beautiful and hopeful traits of character and behavior by which the members of this Christian community had endeared themselves to him. Notice his favorite grouping of faith, hope, and love. We are taught to crave for these in our own soul-garden, and to rejoice to find them blossoming in others. Too often the gospel comes only in "word"; let us seek the other three accompaniments of v. 5. What a blessed thing it would be if our church life were so full of the Spirit of Christ that the ministers would not need to say anything! "By whose preaching," a lad was asked, "were you converted?" "By no one's preaching," was the reply, "but by my Aunt Mary's living."

There are three memorable steps indicated in vv. 9 and 10. Turn unto God: serve him as true and living: wait for the coming of the Son of man. The last phrase strikes the keynote of this epistle. The Church is encouraged to stand expectant at the window of hope. Behind her is the night from which she has been delivered, and on the bosom of the dawn shines the morning star.

1 THESSALONIANS 2:1–12

The Fruit of Unsparing Labor. Paul preached in great conflict of soul because of his passionate desire for the salvation of men. In this, many of the notable servants of God have shared; and we shall not attain to the great end of our ministry unless the seeds we sow are steeped in prayers and tears. The apostle viewed the gospel as a sacred deposit left with him by God on man's behalf, v. 4. Do we sufficiently realize that as Christ is our Trustee, entrusted with God's gift for us, so we are executors of his bequests to our fellowmen, who will have serious charges to bring against us if we hoard for ourselves what was meant for them? The questions which should sustain and quicken us are: "What does God think of my service? Is *he* pleased?"

Combined with Paul's strength of purpose there were the sweetness and tenderness of a nurse. Self-denying labor took from his eyes their needed sleep and was another proof of his sincerity and devotion. There was no harm in receiving gifts, but Paul was most anxious to do nothing that would invalidate his testimony or be unworthy of the Master he served. Here is an admirable example for us all!

1 THESSALONIANS 2:13–20

The Apostle's Glory and Joy. The Christian worker always should wait on God till he gets the word of the message. There is an essential difference between delivering a sermon or an address and delivering a message. The latter is direct, eager; you wait to be sure it is understood; you expect an answer. A gospel message "worketh in you that believe." That its ultimate effect will be to bring us into collision with the world-spirit goes without saying. For this conflict the Christian must be prepared in advance.

The separation between this true, strong, loving soul and his converts was a bereavement, though only for "a short time," and his heart longed to be with them again. He clung to them the more tenaciously because he had been cast out by his Jewish brethren, and also because he looked for a great revenue of joy and glory to accrue to the Savior's name. His one purpose seems to have been to accumulate garlands of saved souls, as children make garlands of flowers in Spring, that he might lay them at the feet of the Redeemer. Satan hinders, but Jesus helps and smiles his benediction.

1 THESSALONIANS 3:1-13

Awakening Thanksgiving and Intercession. At the outset observe that marginal reading by which Timothy is described as "a fellow-worker with God." What a wonderful phrase, and yet it is applicable to all true workers for God! Think what it must have been for a young artist to be permitted to collaborate with Michelangelo! No thought of his own comfort interfered with Paul's efforts for the young churches he had planted; he was only eager that they should be established and comforted amid the storm of persecution that swept over them. There is only one path for the followers of Jesus, and it is a path of blood.

Though the waters surged up to Paul's heart, he could bear anything, if only his work stood fast. What he suffered was as nothing compared with his joy at the stability of his charges. As he wrought day and night at his handicraft, so he prayed day and night for the believers. The stitches put into the tent cloth were accompanied by the holy threads of prayerful intercession. He only longed that Christ would make a straight thoroughfare to them, and would keep them blameless and strong.

1 THESSALONIANS 4:1-8

Called to Sanctification. The first paragraph of this chapter exhorts purity, the second industry, the third expectation of the Second Advent. But the three are closely combined, because those who wait for the Lord will instinctively wear white robes. The body is compared to a vessel, and we must keep it clean for the Master's use, walking day by day so as to please him. Before Enoch was translated, he had the testimony borne him that he had pleased God, Heb. 11:5. It is God's will that we should be holy; our redemption has this for its purpose. Therefore we ought to be holy, and if we ought we can, and if we can we must, and if we must we will! God gives his Holy Spirit for this purpose.

No one must come in between husband and wife to defraud either of the lawful love which should be received from the other. The home has been rescued and exalted by Christ, and the Christian Church must still be its custodian, not only inculcating the ideal, but revealing the sufficient power for its defense.

1 THESSALONIANS 4:9-18

United Now and Hereafter in the Lord. It is suggested that God himself is the Teacher of love. Others may teach the lower classes in the school of grace, but the highest is reserved for the Supreme Teacher. Note that recurring "more and more," 4:1, 10. Compare 3:12. The distribution of goods in the early Church may have led to abuses which the injunctions here given were intended to rectify. It is well to bring up every child to know one means of livelihood, and children are much more likely to grow up into noble and useful people if they are encouraged to work for their living. Do something in the world!

These disciples anticipated the speedy return of the Lord and feared lest those who had died would be worse off than they. The apostle bade them dismiss such fears, because they who remained alive until the coming of the Lord would have no precedence over others who had died. Paul assures them that they who had fallen asleep were with Jesus, and that they would accompany him when he came again. To those who needed to be raised, Jesus would be "the resurrection"; to those who were living, he would be "the life." They that believed in him, though they had died, would yet live; and they who lived till he came would never die.

1 THESSALONIANS 5:1-11

Ready for "the Day of the Lord." To the apostle "the day of the Lord" was near. He expected it in his lifetime, and if we remember that the Lord's words with reference to it were in part fulfilled when Jerusalem fell, it is clear that his expectation was not altogether vain.

The suddenness of the Advent was the theme of Jesus' reiterated assurances. See Matt. 24:38-44; Luke 17:26-30. The world spends its days in careless indifference (sleep), or in sensual enjoyment (drunkenness); but believers are bidden to be soldier-like in their attire and

1 THESSALONIANS

watchfulness. Ponder that wonderful word in v. 10. "Together" implies that Christians now living are closely united with those who have died. The state we call death, but which the apostle calls sleep—because our Lord's resurrection has robbed it of its terror—is as full of vitality as the life which we live day by day in this world. We "live together," animated by the same purposes—they on that side and we on this. Whether here or there, life is only possible "with him." The closer we live to him, the nearer we are to them.

1 THESSALONIANS 5:12-28

"Blameless" at His Coming. The remainder of the chapter is filled with brief sentences of exhortation, like cablegrams from our Heavenly Captain to his soldiers, who in the previous section are described as wearing the breastplate of faith and love. As we endeavor to put this into practice, we become conscious of a new and divine energy entering and quickening our nature. It is the God of peace who is at work, cooperating with our poor endeavors and sanctifying us wholly.

Each soul has a ministry to others, v. 14. A sketch is here given of the ideal believer, vv. 16-22: full of joy, constant in prayer, giving thanks in everything, loving with the unquenched fire of the Holy Spirit, willing to listen to any voice that may bear a divine message, testing all events and utterances with a celestial solvent, steadfast in good, and persistent against evil. This is a high standard, and impossible of realization apart from the indwelling of the Holy Spirit. But when the inner shrine is truly surrendered to him, he will possess the whole temple, even to our physical well-being. God is faithful and will never fail the soul that dares to be all that he wills.

THE SECOND EPISTLE TO THE
THESSALONIANS
THE SECOND COMING OF CHRIST

SALUTATION   *1:1, 2.*

I. The integrity of the faith and life of the Thessalonians   *1:3–12.*
II. The man of sin and the coming of Christ   *2:1–12.*
III. Prayer for the Thessalonians   *2:13–17.*
IV. A request for the prayers of the Thessalonians   *3:1–5.*
V. The Christian's manner of life   *3:6–15.*

CONCLUSION   *3:16–18.*

INTRODUCTION

This second epistle was probably written shortly after the first. The apostle appears to have heard of some who claimed to be acting on his authority and were announcing the immediate coming of the Lord. This had so excited and unsettled the disciples of Thessalonica that they were neglecting their means of livelihood. Writing from Corinth, where he was staying at the time, Paul endeavored to allay that spirit of unrest and to call these disciples back to their everyday duties.

COMMENTARY

2 THESSALONIANS 1:1-12

Faithful through Faith in a Righteous God. Notice the remarkable couplets of this chapter. Grace and peace, v. 2; faith and love, v. 3; faith and patience, v. 4; tribulation for those who trouble, and rest for those who are troubled, vv. 6, 7; know not, obey not, v. 8; the presence of the Lord, the glory of his power, v. 9; glorified and admired, v. 10; the good pleasure of his goodness and the work of faith, v. 11. Like mirrors that face each other, these words flash back and forth their depths of sacred significance.

What marvelous scenes the future conceals for believers! Rest for the weary, palms of victory for the defeated, glory for the name and cause of Christ, and above all, the revelation of that dear Presence with which we have been so constantly in touch. But how inexpressibly awful and terrible, on the other hand, is the fate of the willful rejecters of the love of God!

The final prayer has always been highly prized by God's people. If they shall ever be worthy of their high calling, it is for him to make them so. His being "glorified" and "admired" in his saints is not a far-off event, but one within the possibilities of the present hour; and the name of Jesus may be magnified here and now in us, as it will be finally and more perfectly. Compare vv. 10 and 12.

2 THESSALONIANS 2:1-12

Untroubled by Threatening Rumors. The apostle sets himself to correct certain erroneous impressions which had unsettled the church in Thessalonica. Notice how reverently he speaks of our Savior. Once and again he alludes to him as the Lord Jesus Christ. He is surely coming, and as surely will his saints be gathered to him as are drops of moisture drawn up from ponds and oceans to cluster in the clouds in radiant beauty around the sun.

But certain events must take place first. There must be a great apostasy and the unveiling of "the mystery of iniquity," which even at that time was already at work. First, the man of sin; then, the Son of man. First, he that set himself forth as God; then, God manifest in the flesh. First, the revelation of sin; then, the revelation of perfect salvation. Dan. 11:36 seems to have suggested Paul's words, which have been applied to Nero or Caligula, to Judaism or the papal church, and to some future manifestation of Satanic hatred toward the Church of God. But whatever form it may assume, the coming of Jesus will absolutely destroy this power of Antichrist. Let us be warned by the doom of those that are involved in this great apostasy, and ever cherish the love of the truth of Christ, that we may be saved.

2 THESSALONIANS 2:13—3:5

Held Firm and Guarded from Evil. This closing section is full of comfort and inspiration. Believers in Christ are the beloved of God; their salvation dates from his eternal love and choice, and his purpose for us is being wrought out in our characters by the Holy Spirit, who ministers to us through the truth. Our comfort is eternal and our hope is unfailing.

Paul was now preaching at Corinth, and he asks that the gospel "may have free course," 3:1. When unreasonable and wicked men try you, turn to the Lord, who is faithful to his promises and to his saints. The stronger the gales of opposition and hatred, the deeper should we become established and rooted in the truth. The word "direct" in v. 5 may be rendered, "make a thoroughfare through"; that is, we desire that our hearts should be a highway down which the love of God and the patience of our Lord may pass to a world of sin and fear. Let us ever connect the patience and kingdom of our Lord, as in Rev. 1:9.

2 THESSALONIANS 3:6–18

Separate; Industrious; Persevering. From his high expectations of the Advent, the apostle turns to the prosaic commonplaces of daily toil. There was need for this, because the expectation of the speedy return of Christ was disarranging the ordinary course of life and duty. People were neglecting the common round of daily tasks, and idlers were imposing on Christian generosity. Against these the apostle sets his own example of sitting far into the night at his tent-making. See 1 Thess. 2:9. The best attitude for those that look for their Lord is not in pressing their faces against the window to behold the chariot of their returning Master, but in plying their toil with deft hands and consecrated hearts.

Note that parting salutation, v. 16, and let us believe that the God of peace is causing peace for us at all times and in all ways. Even storms are forwarding our boat to its haven, and we shall be borne in with the floodtide of his mercy. Every wind is a home wind to the child of God, setting in from the quarter of God's love. Every messenger, however garbed, brings God's salutation and benediction.

THE FIRST EPISTLE TO
TIMOTHY

THE CHURCH AND ITS MINISTRY

SALUTATION *1:1, 2.*

I. THE CHARGE CONCERNING THE CHURCH *1:3—3:16.*
  A. The need of love, faith and a good conscience *1:3–20.*
  B. The conduct of public prayer *2:1–8.*
  C. The place of women in the church *2:9–15.*
  D. The appointment of bishops *3:1–7.*
  E. The appointment of deacons *3:8–13.*

EXHORTATION *3:14–16.*

II. "A GOOD MINISTER OF JESUS CHRIST" *4—6.*
  A. His ministry and teaching *4.*
  B. His bearing toward elders and widows *5.*
  C. His attitude toward slavery *6:1, 2.*
  D. Characteristics of false teachers *6:3–10.*
  E. The minister's personal life *6:11–16.*
  F. His charge to the rich *6:17–19.*

CONCLUSION *6:20, 21.*

INTRODUCTION

This epistle was written not long after Paul had left Ephesus for Macedonia; but it is a matter of debate as to when this was, some holding that it must have been about the time of the great riot which drove the apostle from the city, others that it was nearer the time of his second and last imprisonment at Rome.

Timothy is first mentioned as living at Lystra, Acts 16:1. His mother, Eunice, was a Jewess, 2 Tim. 1:5; his father was a Greek. He was early the subject of pious influence, 2 Tim. 3:14, 15. He was well spoken of by his fellow-believers, and became the intimate friend and companion of the apostle.

The epistle was designed to instruct him how to deal with false teachers, how to conduct public worship, and to urge him to cultivate all those qualities which would better equip him for the discharge of his important duties.

COMMENTARY

1 TIMOTHY 1:1-11

A Charge against Vain Talking. The relation of Paul to Timothy is an example of one of those beautiful friendships between an older and a younger man, in which each is the complement of the other, 1 Cor. 4:17; Phil. 2:22. Timothy was a lad of fifteen when converted at Lystra, and was probably about thirty-five years of age when this epistle was addressed to him. He was enthusiastic and devoted, but at times showed signs of timidity, and the apostle watched over him with tender interest.

In this chapter the young minister is warned against the Gnostic heresy, i.e., the heresy of the "knowing-ones," who pretended to give revelations about angels and their ministry and to bridge the gulf between man and God by a whole series of mysterious imaginary beings. Their teaching led from spiritual pride to sensuality, for they accounted the body as inherently evil. All this was contrary to "sound" or "healthy" doctrine. That word is peculiar to the pastoral epistles, 1 Tim. 6:3; 2 Tim. 1:13; 4:3; Titus 1:9; 2:1. It suggests a certain test of the various teachers who cross our paths. The question always is, Do these words of theirs promote the health of the soul, and above all "love out of a pure heart and a good conscience"?

1 TIMOTHY 1:12-20

An Example of Christ's Long-suffering. The apostle breaks off into expressions of heartfelt thanks to God for the abounding grace which had overcome his former obstinacy and blindness. Only his ignorance could palliate his outrage and insult toward Christ, who was now the beloved object of his entire surrender. He had been a blasphemer against Christ, Acts 26:9-11; a persecutor toward his fellowmen, Gal. 1:13; injurious, insolent, full of overweening pride. He felt that he had been the chief of sinners, because he had sinned despite having more knowledge and opportunity than others. It is only when we see God that we know ourselves and repent in dust and ashes. The apostle, however, comforted himself in this at least, that through coming time the most hopeless and abandoned sinners would take heart as they considered his case. He was a sample of mercy, a specimen of what Christ could do, an outline sketch to be filled in. Believe "on" Christ. Faith rests on Christ as foundation. Peter and John use another preposition, "toward" or "into"; i. e., they conceive of union with him, to which all else is preliminary. War the good warfare against sin. When men thrust away faith and a good conscience, they stab their pilot and make shipwreck. See 2 Tim. 2:17, 18; 4:14, 15.

1 TIMOTHY 2:1-15

Prayer and Modest Adorning. The apostle especially urged intercessory prayer, because it meant so much to himself. Three different words are used of prayer, because there are so many ways of approaching God. It is our duty to pray for those in authority and to seek after a calm and quiet life in all godliness and gravity. It was most important that Christians should not be suspected of revolutionary designs or civic turbulence. If they had to suffer, it must be only on account of their religious faith. The solidarity of our race is the reason for our wide-embracing supplications. The whole race is one in the creation of God and the ransom of Christ; we are therefore one with all men, and should express in prayer the common sins and sorrows of mankind.

The men were bidden to lead in public prayer and to see that the hands they uplifted were clean, while the women joined quietly after the Eastern fashion. There was nothing revolutionary in Paul's teaching. He was content, in minor matters, to conform to the usages of his age, though promulgating doctrines which would ultimately revolutionize the position of womanhood. A holy married life, with the bearing and training of children, is as a rule the appointed path for woman, and this will lead to their salvation through faith in the Holy One who was born in Bethlehem.

1 TIMOTHY 3:1-7

Fitness for Christian Leadership. One of Timothy's most urgent duties was to take care that those who held office in the churches were beyond reproach. The tone of a Christian community is largely that of its leaders. As the margin suggests, the bishop of the early Church was an overseer or presbyter. See Acts 20:28. God's minister must not only be irreproachable as far as the outside world is concerned, but exemplary in his domestic relations. Such was the facility of divorce among the Jews that it was a common thing for a man to have more than one woman living who had been his wife. But by Paul's ruling this would bar him from holding office, unless his divorce be for cause as provided in Matt. 19:9.

Notice how often the ideas of being grave, sober, and temperate occur in this chapter. The effect of a good sermon will be spoiled if a man yields to foolish levity or intemperate habits. Moderation, serenity of temper, freedom from love of money, a well-ordered household, an obedient and reverent family—these are signs that a man may aspire to the sacred work of the ministry. And these are the qualities which people should look for in candidates for pulpits, more than those of rhetoric, brilliance, or outward attractiveness.

1 TIMOTHY 3:8-16

Qualifications of Church Officials. Younger men, referred to as deacons, were appointed to subordinate tasks, especially the relief of the poor, Acts 6. Though their service was less important, their character must be of the highest quality. The strength of a church is as much in the godliness of those who fill subordinate offices as in its acknowledged leaders. The caretaker of a church should be a man of as high ideals as its chief pastor. Nothing is common or unclean, nothing trivial and unimportant where Christ's honor and glory are concerned. In the prophet's vision the very snuffers of the candlestick were of gold.

The women mentioned here are deaconesses, Rom. 16:1. Governor Bradford, describing the church of the pilgrim fathers, says of a deaconess: "She honored her place and was an ornament to the congregation. She did frequently visit the sick and weak, and would gather relief for them. She was obeyed as a mother in Israel."

The Church is the earthly dwelling-place of God. It lifts up and maintains the standard of truth in the midst of men; therefore it is hated. It is most necessary that Christians should bear witness to the truth, collectively as well as individually. The facts given us to witness to are enumerated, in v. 16, in the six clauses of an ancient antiphonal chant.

1 TIMOTHY 4:1-8

Reject False and Foolish Teaching. We have here the apostle's forecast of the last times; i. e., the condition in which men will find themselves as the age draws to a close. Notwithstanding all that Christ has done, the prevalence of evil will be enormous, not because of any failure in God, but because the Church has failed to be the organ through which his saving help could reach mankind. The symptoms are set forth with great clearness, such as demon spirits dwelling and working in men, error taught under the specious guise of excessive religious devotion, consciences seared, natural instincts thwarted and outraged. On the contrary, let us believe that the whole body, and all gifts that are natural and innocent, are to be cherished and used under three sanctions. (1) They must be accepted and enjoyed with thanksgiving to the Creator and Father. (2) They must be sanctioned by the Word of God. (3) Their use and enjoyment must not interfere with our prayer life.

The minister of Christ must be daily nourished by the words of Christian truth. If he is not fed on Christ's body and blood, his teaching will soon deteriorate, John 6. He must also exercise himself in godliness with as much care as the gymnast, who is continually exercising his joints and muscles so as to keep supple and alert. This is also God's purpose in the spiritual trials and discipline which he sends.

1 TIMOTHY 4:9–16

"Take Heed unto Thyself." In all Christian service we must set our hope on the living God. Nothing counts apart from God. Prayer implies that all our gifts and efforts cover only a small part of our efficiency. There are infinite resources in God, which he is waiting to employ in human affairs, and of which we fail to make use. The Christian worker, therefore, must not only labor and strive, but must hope in the living God, whose saving grace is at the disposal of our faith. The faith exercised by the average man results in obtaining only natural things; the supernatural is secured by the faith of those who have made profounder discoveries of God, and can therefore make demands on his resources which are hidden from the princes of this world.

In order to succeed, we must give ourselves wholly to our work for God. In answer to prayer great gifts had been communicated to Timothy, but he had to give heed to them, use them, and stir up the slumbering embers of the fire, kindled at his ordination. It is worthy of notice that the apostle's injunctions do not include a single allusion to priestly or sacramental service, but urge boldness of character, v. 12; diligent study, v. 13; rigorous orthodoxy, v. 16; and daily self-examination of the soul, v. 16. Take to heart the blessed assurance of the closing sentence of the chapter.

1 TIMOTHY 5:1–8

Wise Treatment of Young and Old. That minister of Jesus is happiest who introduces the tone and manner of family life into the church, vv. 1, 2. The attitude of son or brother to other men is peculiarly fitting. But he must always keep up the spiritual tone. It is so easy to descend to frivolity and familiarity. Remember that all intercourse with others must be governed by the words "with all purity."

The special references to widows evidence the early practice of the Church. Provision was made for godly women who had lost husbands by death, and who in return for the weekly gift from church funds gave themselves to Christian service. The apostle indicates the age and characteristics of those who might be eligible. It was his clear judgment, however, that, wherever possible it was becoming for children to make such provision as would place an aged mother or other relative beyond the reach of want or any need of claiming maintenance from church funds. The standard of Christian living here emphasized may well be pondered and prayed over by all Christian women, who should, as far as possible without fee or reward, consider church service only second to the claims of home.

1 TIMOTHY 5:9–16

Home-keeping Enjoined. The sphere of the younger woman must be in the home. This is the noblest work of all, and wherever it exists it has the prior claim; yet even during the years of early motherhood there may still be opportunities of offering hospitality to strangers, ministering to the children of God who need refreshment and comfort, and diligently assisting in good work. These forms of service, lovingly and humbly performed, will serve as a gracious opening for further ministries of the same description in the later period of life.

The apostle says nothing about remarriage in general, but simply refers to the fact that young women who have become widows are likely to accept the offer of a second marriage, and so abjure that "first faith" in which they had pledged themselves to the service of the church. Unless there is great watchfulness, the practice of going from house to house, ostensibly on church business, may degenerate into habits of gossip. Therefore, it was wiser not to put young women on the church service roll. If they did not marry a second time, they might at least work to assist others, widows like themselves, but less able to help themselves. There must be no idle hands.

1 TIMOTHY 5:17–25

Impartial and Kindly Supervision. A man of years was always to be honored, and if he were called to rule in the church, he was to be treated with double honor; but none should be appointed to that sacred office hastily or with partiality. Purity, gravity, and abstinence from alcohol were prime requisites in a Christian minister then, as they are now. It is clear from v. 23 that the apostles and their helpers practiced total abstinence, or there had been no need for that special injunction to Timothy.

It is clear also from vv. 17, 18 that the early Church was encouraged to support its ministers. The apostle quotes the words of our Lord to maintain this contention, Matt. 10:10; Luke 10:7. The character of a minister could not be lightly questioned. If anything had to be said, the informant must lodge his complaint in the presence of witnesses, who could be witnesses against him if the charge were found to be baseless and frivolous. But public wrongs must be met by public rebuke, that any suspicion of favoritism might be disarmed. No man, however, should be called to the sacred and responsible position of presbyter unless he had been tested and approved. In forming judgments of the fitness of men for office, we must not judge wholly by appearance, good or bad, vv. 24, 25.

1 TIMOTHY 6:1-10

Godliness Is True Gain. The apostle gives rules for the treatment of the slaves who rendered service in the households of that time. If the slave was in the household of a heathen master, he must honor and glorify Christ by being respectful and obedient; but if the master was a Christian, and therefore a brother in the Lord, the slave was still required to yield courteous and willing service. Service rendered for the love of God must not be inferior to that rendered from fear of man.

There were many false teachers in the early Church, the chief aim of whom was to make money. They were proud and ill-tempered, jealous and suspicious, juggling with words and given to splitting hairs. Godliness truly is great gain. It makes us content with what we have, and it opens to us stores of blessedness which the wealth of a Croesus could not buy. It is good to have just what is necessary. More than that breeds anxiety. Let us leave the provision for our needs with God. He is pledged to give food and covering, the latter including shelter. Not money, but the love of it opens the sluices and floodgates of the soul, through which wash the destroying waters of passion that drown men in destruction and perdition. Remember that you can carry nothing out of this world except your character.

1 TIMOTHY 6:11-21

"Fight the Good Fight of Faith." The poor need not envy the rich. Wealth makes no difference in the audit of eternity. A man cannot eat more than a certain amount of food and wear more than a certain amount of clothing. If we have enough, why envy others? The true wealth of life is in self-renunciation and beneficence. How different from the money-grabber is the man of God who flees such things and follows after righteousness, who fights the good fight against the world, the flesh, and the devil, and who never flinches from witnessing the good witness. If we suffer here with Jesus, we shall share in the glory of his manifestation. Notice the wealth of the apostle's ascription to Jesus! Here are life in its spring, light at its source, power and authority in their original fountain. Let us claim these blessings and enjoy them in our lives.

The charge to the rich is eminently sound. We must set our hope not on the attainment of fleeting things, but in God who loves to give and see his children happy. We hold all that we have, that we may be God's channels of communication to others. What we hoard we lose; what we give away we store. The life which is life indeed can be acquired only through death and self-giving.

THE SECOND EPISTLE TO
TIMOTHY

THE APOSTLE'S FAREWELL MESSAGE

SALUTATION *1:1, 2.*

I. THANKSGIVING FOR TIMOTHY'S FAITH *1:3–6.*

II. THE GLORY OF THE GOSPEL *1:7–14.*
   (False friends and true *1:15–18)*

III. "A GOOD SOLDIER OF JESUS CHRIST" *2:1–13.*

IV. "A WORKMAN THAT NEEDETH NOT TO BE ASHAMED" *2:14–26.*

V. GRIEVOUS TIMES IN THE LAST DAYS *3.*

VI. THE TRIUMPHANT CLOSE OF A GREAT CAREER *4:1–8.*

VII. PERSONAL INSTRUCTIONS *4:9–13.*

VIII. FINAL EXPERIENCES *4:14–18.*

IX. GREETINGS TO FRIENDS *4:19–21.*

CONCLUSION *4:22.*

INTRODUCTION

This is the last epistle of the great apostle, who was apparently awaiting sentence. He had already had audience with Caesar and escaped, 4:16, 17; but there could be no doubt as to the ultimate issue. When Paul composed these words he was imprisoned in the Mamertine dungeon, exposed to the chill ague of its damp walls, reeking with pestilence and recalling the miseries of generations of condemned criminals. There was one desire for the fulfillment of which he yearned. He longed to see once more the dear friend of earlier years, whom he had led into this life of stern suffering and whose spirit seems to have been somewhat overwhelmed by its severity. It was this that led Paul to dispatch this second letter, filled with advice and exhortation in case Timothy could not come, but specially full of desire that he should come before winter set in and traveling became difficult, 4:9, 21. There is no trace of despondency in this noble swan song. Though Paul had lost all things, he had gained Christ. "Glorious apostle! Would that every leader's voice could burst, as he falls, into such a trumpet-sound, thrilling the young hearts that pant in the good fight and must never despair of final victory!"

COMMENTARY

2 TIMOTHY 1:1-11

"Stir Up the Gift Which Is in Thee." Lonely and facing death, the apostle fell back on the bedrock of the will of God. If it were the divine plan that he should finish his lifework in that miserable plight, he was content that it should be so. But he longs to see his beloved son in the faith once more. He desires to stir up the dead coal of his ardor, in which there was fire and heat, but not enough flame.

Apparently the young evangelist was becoming daunted by the gathering difficulties of the time, and so Paul sets himself to encourage him. With this purpose in view he adduces his own example, v. 3, his fervent affection, v. 4, the memory of the sainted dead, v. 5, the solemn vows by which Timothy had bound himself at his ordination, v. 6, the divine donation of grace and power and love, v. 7, the eternal purpose which had received its fruition in the advent of Jesus, v. 9, the clear light which his resurrection had thrown on death and the hereafter, v. 10. Surely such a chain of arguments must have proved irresistible! God's soldiers must be brave and unflinching in meeting the opposition of the world. When once we realize that the stores which reside in God are at the disposal of our faith, we too shall be invulnerable and irresistible.

2 TIMOTHY 1:12-18

"Hold Fast the Form of Sound Words." How striking Paul's reference to the double committal, as if there had been an agreed exchange between his Master and himself! Paul had handed over to Christ as a sacred deposit all that concerned his well-being in time and eternity, and Christ had handed over to him the interests of his kingdom, which, by the grace of the Holy Spirit, he was required to maintain inviolate. It is a mutual exchange of which we all ought to know something. Give all to Christ and Christ becomes all to you. The proportion of your self-giving is the measure of your discovery of what Jesus will be to you.

Some of Paul's former friends shrank from identifying themselves with a suspect—the inmate of the condemned cell. It was no light matter to visit the bearer of a name which the world of that day detested, one who belonged to a sect accused of burning Rome. Demas, 4:10, and others forsook him, but the good Ephesian, Onesiphorus, set about seeking him through all the prisons of Rome, and was not ashamed of his chain nor content with a single visit. He "oft refreshed" his friend. Paul sends a grateful message to his family, 4:19. Perhaps there is here a gentle hint to Timothy. Compare vv. 8 and 16. Never shrink from taking your place beside Christ's prisoners!

2 TIMOTHY 2:1-9

"*A Good Soldier of Jesus Christ.*" *Soldier,* vv. 1-4: There is grace enough in Jesus for every need, but we must avail ourselves of it. We can expect nothing less than hardship, since life is a battlefield. Our one aim should be to please him who chose us to be soldiers. In order to be all that he would have us be, we must avoid entangling ourselves in the conditions around us. We must resemble a garrison in the town where it is quartered, and from which it may at any hour be summoned away. The less encumbered we are, the more easily shall we be able to execute the least command of our Great Captain. How high an honor it is to be enrolled among his soldiers!

Athlete, v. 5: Life is an amphitheater, filled with celestial spectators. Probably our worst antagonist is found in our own heart. If we win the crown, we must observe regulations as to diet, exercise, purity, 1 Cor. 9:24-27. *Husbandman,* v. 6: We ought to be working for God in his vineyard or harvest-field; but we are allowed to partake of the fruits. It is imperative that we should be nourished while we labor. In all these positions we must remember Jesus Christ, risen from the dead. We must draw upon the power of his resurrection, and to do this we must live on the Heaven side of the cross. "I am crucified with Christ: nevertheless I live," Gal. 2:20.

2 TIMOTHY 2:10-18.

"*Approved unto God.*" *The elect,* vv.10-13: The apostle sketches the experiences of the elect soul. It must endure, suffer, and die with Christ, that out of its surrender may come the truest, richest life, John 12:25. There is no path to lasting success save that of the cross and grave of Christ. It has been allotted to the redeemed in the divine program; each must tread it separately and with resolute purpose. But there is no doubt as to the sequel of a true life. The world of men may count it a failure, but God pledges himself that as the pendulum swings here in the dark, it shall swing equally in yonder world of light. Three things are impossible with God—to die, to lie, and to fail the soul that trusts him. Even when we cannot muster faith enough, his word of promise cannot be frustrated in the case of those whose faith is weak and trembling as the smoking flax.

The workman, vv. 14-18: The one anxiety with us all should be to stand approved before God. As the Revised Version margin suggests, we must hold a straight course in the word of truth. Our testimony should resemble an undeviating furrow. Let us construct in our life something which will be a permanent addition to the well-being of the world, so that at the last the Master may say that he is satisfied.

2 TIMOTHY 2:19-26

"*A Vessel unto Honour.*" Two men had been named whose teachings had overthrown the faith of some; but in contradistinction to this lamentable defection, Paul turns with thankfulness to the firm foundations of faith on which the Church is built. They stand firm because they rest on incontestable facts and are authenticated by the Christian experience of centuries. Medallion inscriptions were often placed on foundation stones. Here are two affixed to those of the Church—one between God and the believer, the other between the believer and the world. What a privilege to be known by God! What a responsibility to work worthily of him before men!

From the house the apostle proceeds to the vessels within. Each of us stands on one of those four shelves. But those to be honored and which are most often in the Master's hands are not necessarily the gold vessels, but the clean ones, of whatever material. Cleanliness counts more with God than cleverness. Do not be anxious about your service; be ready for the Master to use you. Lie like a silver cup in the trough of the fountain, v. 25. Repentance is God's gift, but there is a "peradventure" in it. Men are drunk with the world's drugs; they need to be recovered. Notice that we may rescue for God men whom the devil has entrapped.

2 TIMOTHY 3:1-9

A Dark Picture of Evil Men. The last days of the present age are to be black and sorrowful. Sinful rejection of Christ will come to a head. We must not be misled by the widespread profession of the forms of religion; this may coexist with the rankest apostasy. When women are conscious of sins against God, society, and themselves, they are very liable to the seduction of false teachers who promise peace and condone impurity.

Tares and wheat grow together unto the harvest. The devil has always set himself to counterfeit God's handiwork: the Holy City by Babylon; the Son of man by the man of sin; blessedness by the worldling's giddy merriment. Thus the Egyptian conjurers repeated the miracles of Moses by resorting to sleight of hand. So there is a pure gospel and a specious mimicry of it. Wait for the inevitable unfoldings of God's purpose. Time will show what is true and what is false. In the meantime, examine yourselves whether ye be in the faith.

2 TIMOTHY 3:10-17

Hold Fast to Inspired Scripture. The world does not love Christ or Christians any better than of old; and all who are minded to live godly lives will come inevitably to the cross in one form or another. To be without persecution should put us in serious doubt as to whether we are right. The spirit of the gospel is in absolute disagreement with the spirit of the world. But whatever the losses and trials, let the children of God abide in the things which they have learned, and walk in blameless purity and consistency. The conduct, purpose, and patience of this great and holy apostle gleam in front of us for our inspiration and guidance; and his experience will be ours—that there is no sorrow out of which we shall not be delivered, when we have learned the lesson it was sent to teach.

In the stern experiences of human life there is no stay that is comparable to the Holy Scriptures. The infinite variety of Scripture adapts itself to different states of the soul. Whatever our need, we can find its solace and remedy here. Thus we may live a complete life, finding in the Bible resources for all our emergencies. In this armory is every weapon for offense and defense; in this pharmacopoeia is a medicine and antidote for every wound.

2 TIMOTHY 4:1-12

The Victor's Final Charge. To the end Paul held to the appearing of Jesus, though he might not live to see it; and it was to precede and usher in the coming of the kingdom. The world of that time was sad and sick, and Paul's sole panacea was the preaching of the gospel. Verse 2: Do not only take opportunities, but make them. Verse 3: Make haste; such opportunities are closing in. "Sound" throughout these pastoral epistles means "healthy" and "health-giving." Note that striking phrase, "itching ears," which turn in every direction where they may obtain momentary relief. Verse 5: Be on the alert! "Make full proof of thy ministry"; that is, work to the edge of your pattern.

With what pathetic words Paul refers to his approaching death! He regarded his lifeblood as about to be poured out as a libation, v. 6, margin. The time had come for him to go on board the good ship which was waiting in the offing to sail at sunset for its port of glory. He was a veteran who had fought valiantly and successfully—keeping the faith as in the old Roman story the heroes kept the bridge. But he was soon to be relieved. The crown at the end of the course was already in sight. He was lonely—"only Luke is with me." He needed to be ministered unto—"take Mark, and bring him with thee." But his courage was unabated. Demas might forsake, but Christ failed not.

2 TIMOTHY 4:13-22

"The Lord Stood with Me." The winter was approaching, and the apostle wanted to have his cloak amid the damp of the Mamertine prison. Evidently his arrest under Nero's orders had been so sudden and peremptory that he was not allowed to go into his lodgings for this and other possessions, such as the books mentioned in v. 13.

He had made his first appearance before Nero, and was expecting a further appearance to receive his sentence. But the Lord was with him, and his comfort was that he had proclaimed the gospel to the highest audience in the world of his time. His one thought always was that the gospel should be heard by men, whether they would hear or forbear. If that were secured, he did not count the cost to himself. The "lion" may stand for Nero or Satan. See Luke 22:31; 1 Pet. 5:8. From v. 20 we gather that miraculous gifts of healing, which Paul possessed, may not be used merely for friendship's sake, but only where the progress of the gospel requires them.

THE EPISTLE TO
TITUS
THE WORK OF THE MINISTRY

SALUTATION *1:1-4.*

I. THE CHARACTER OF A BISHOP *1:5-10.*

II. THOSE WHO NEED REPROOF *1:11-16.*

III. TRAINING THE CHURCH TO BE ZEALOUS OF GOOD WORKS *2.*

IV. THE CHRISTIAN MOTIVE *3:1-11.*

V. PERSONAL MATTERS *3:12-14.*

CONCLUSION *3:15.*

INTRODUCTION

We know very little of Titus. Though never mentioned in the Acts, he seems to have been one of the most trusted and best beloved members of the noble little band of Paul's friends and disciples. As he was a Greek by birth, Paul took him to Jerusalem on that memorable visit referred to in Gal. 2:3. The bond between them was very close, 1:4. Titus was sent three times to Corinth on special embassies, during the troubles of that distracted church, 2 Cor. 7 and 8. The last mention of him is in connection with the visit to Dalmatia, during Paul's second imprisonment, 2 Tim. 4:10.

This epistle guides Titus in the right ordering of the churches in Crete, which may have owed their foundation to the Cretan Jews, who are mentioned as having heard Peter's Pentecostal sermon. Paul had evidently visited the island himself, but had been obliged to leave the consolidation of the work with his friend, 1:5. The epistle was warmly admired by Luther, who says: "This is a short epistle, but it contains such a quintessence of Christian doctrine, and is composed in such a masterly manner, that it contains all that is needful for Christian knowledge and life."

COMMENTARY

TITUS 1:1-9

Appoint Fit Men over the Churches. God's elect are known by their faith, and wherever they hear the voice of truth, which makes for godliness, they recognize and acknowledge it. They are also inspired by a great hope, and that hope cannot be disappointed because it is founded on the promise and oath of the God who cannot lie, Heb. 6:18. God's promise for us has been in his heart from all eternity, but it was hidden until the gospel was proclaimed in the power of the Holy Spirit. The germ-thought of eternity has been realized in Jesus and is unfolded in the gospel. Note the frequent recurrence in this epistle of the phrase, "God our Saviour."

The ordering of these early churches was very important. The presiding officers must be godly and consistent men, and able to commend the gospel by their lives. These traits of a holy man should be pondered and appropriated by us all; and we must all hold fast to the Word of God, which has been found trustworthy by countless myriads. Many are the seducing voices in the present day that counsel slackening faith and relaxing grasp.

> *If all the wiles that men devise*
> *beset our faith with treacherous art,*
> *We'll call them vanity and lies,*
> *and bind the gospel to our heart.*

TITUS 1:10-16

Reprove Those Whose Works Deny God. The Judaizing teachers, who insisted that men must become Jews before they could be Christians, were always on Paul's heels, visiting his churches and diverting his converts from the simplicity of the faith. Their motive in many cases was very largely self-aggrandizement. Such men were to be resisted to the uttermost and sharply rebuked. Where the work of grace is really commenced in the heart, a sharp rebuke will often turn the soul back to God. The gardener must not hesitate to use a pruning-knife if the well-being of the tree is at stake.

Note the marvelous power we possess of viewing things in the light or gloom cast upon them from our own temperament. We see life and the world in a glass colored from within. Oh, that we might possess that pure and untarnished nature that passes through the world like a beam of sunshine, irradiating all but contaminated by none! The true test of the knowledge of God is a holy life. These act and react. The better you know God, the more you will resemble him; compare Pss. 111 and 112. The more you are like God, the better you will know him.

TITUS 2:1-8

A Pattern for Old and Young. The supreme test of all Christian teaching and Christian work depends on whether they produce healthy characters, which are not contaminated by the noisome and germ-laden atmosphere around. Our teaching must be healthy and also health-creating.

The apostle's strophes are few but fine. In the briefest sentences he seizes the salient features of Christian character. The aged man is strong, calm, patient, full of faith and love. The aged woman is holy, reverent, beloved, honored, and obeyed by the younger women of the same household or church. So also with the young men and women. What a life is sketched here against which the tongue of slander is dumb!

But, after all, these results cannot be realized apart from the personal holiness of their minister and leader. He must furnish a pattern of good works. His attitude to things which are questionable and doubtful must be decided not by his own predilections or fancies, but by the consideration of the effect which his action is likely to have on the keen eyes that are carefully watching him.

TITUS 2:9-15

How We May "Adorn the Doctrine." The servants addressed in this tender and priceless paragraph were household slaves, employed in the most menial drudgery, but they were taught that even they might "adorn" the gospel as jewels adorn the brow of beauty. Their holy lives might display and set forth its loveliness. To please one's superiors in all things, so far as our loyalty to Christ permits, is to commend Christ to our households and win his approval. The grace of God has ever offered salvation, but in Jesus it was brought to our doors. In its first appearance, it came to teach; in its second appearance, it will bring us glory. Have we sat sufficiently long in the school of grace, that our gentle Teacher may instruct us how to live? It must be "soberly" in regard to ourselves, "righteously" toward others, and "godly" toward God. And we cannot realize any one of these unless we resolutely deny ungodliness and worldly lusts. This was the aim and purpose of Jesus in coming to die for us. He wanted to redeem us from all iniquity, purify us as his own, and use us in all manner of good works. It is a solemn question whether that supreme purpose has been realized in our own experience. If not, why not?

TITUS 3:1-7

Responding to God's Loving-kindness. Throughout this epistle, the apostle insists on good works. See 2:7, 14; 3:8, 14. The word "good" might be rendered "beautiful." We must not work to be saved, but being saved we must be "ready" to do every good work, and careful to "maintain" good works, v. 8. In this last phrase the apostle apparently refers to the trades and callings by which his converts were to earn their daily bread.

What singular beauty there is in this allusion to the appearance of "the kindness and love of God our Saviour." These appeared in the Person of Jesus, whose human nature alternately veiled and revealed them. The full outshining of God's love was curtailed by the veil of his humanity, but enough was shown to irradiate the life of humanity, if only men's eyes had not been blind. Paul speaks of the "laver of regeneration," v. 5, margin, because the new nature, which we receive when we are born again, is clean and cleanses the entire life from within outward. This is the result of the daily renewing of the Holy Spirit, whom God is ever pouring richly into our hearts. Is this your experience? Will you not claim an ever-increasing inflow? You have been born again; then, as an heir, enter upon the double portion of the firstborn, v. 7.

TITUS 3:8-15

Maintaining Good Works. It is wise advice that we should try to shun controversy and disputations. Small benefit accrues from such methods of advancing the truth. After all, the Lord's test is the true one for all teachings which are in question—What is their fruit? "By their fruits ye shall know them." Let us, therefore, cultivate the grace and beauty, the righteousness and purity of a holy life. Let us yield ourselves to Jesus to be wholly possessed and used by him; and let our one aim be to get glory for him and success for his kingdom. Then our views of truth will become clear and sound, and the beauty of our lives will have the most convincing effect on gainsayers. It is better to live a holy life than be a successful disputant. The best proof of orthodoxy is a Christlike life.

Paul, having been liberated from his first imprisonment, was itinerating in Asia Minor and Macedonia, accompanied by several friends. He was intending to winter at Nicopolis in Epirus, and was about to send Artemas or Tychicus to relieve Titus in Crete, so that Titus might join him in the winter sojourn. These plans were probably canceled by his own sudden arrest at Nero's instigation.

THE EPISTLE TO
PHILEMON
A PLEA FOR A RUNAWAY SLAVE

SALUTATION *1–3.*
I. PAUL'S PRAYER FOR HIS FRIEND *4–7.*
II. THE RETURN OF ONESIMUS *8–14.*
III. THE SIGNIFICANCE OF HIS ABSENCE *15, 16.*
IV. PAUL'S OFFER OF SECURITY *17–20.*
CONCLUSION *21–25.*

INTRODUCTION

The Epistle of Paul to Philemon is unique in that it is addressed to a personal friend regarding a private matter. No doubt Paul wrote many such personal letters, but this one alone has been preserved.

Philemon seems to have been a wealthy citizen of Colosse. He was a personal convert of the apostle's, and there were strong bonds of friendship between them.

Paul writes on behalf of a thief and a runaway. Philemon had suffered serious loss through the irregular conduct of his servant Onesimus, and might well be hesitant about trusting him again. Paul sees that it is the duty of the slave to return and of his master to receive him. By personal persuasion he had won over Onesimus to return, and by this letter he seeks to insure for him a welcome in his master's house. Onesimus goes back, not merely as a penitent but as a Christian. Paul pleads that he be received as a brother.

The epistle was written from Rome, the natural center of attraction for all fugitives, and is associated with the epistles to the Ephesians and the Colossians.

COMMENTARY

PHILEMON 1:1-14

A Plea for the Returning Slave. Onesimus had known the apostle well in the old days when Paul visited at the house of his master Philemon, who seems to have been a man of importance. His house was large enough for a church to assemble in it, and to accommodate the apostle and his traveling companions when they came to the city. Apphia, his wife, was also a Christian, and Archippus, their son, was engaged in some kind of Christian work in connection with the infant Christian community which they were nursing. Compare vv. 1 and 2 with Col. 4:17. It is beautiful to observe the apostle's humility in associating these obscure people with himself as fellow-workers.

Onesimus had been a runaway slave, and fleeing to Rome had been converted by the ministry of Paul—"whom I have begotten in my bonds." The converted slave had become very dear and useful to his benefactor, vv. 12, 13. The apostle now sends him back to his former owner with this letter, pleading that he be once more received into the household of Philemon.

PHILEMON 1:15-25

To Be Received as a Brother. The apostle's pleas for the restoration of Onesimus to his old trusted position in the household of Philemon are very touching. He suggests, first, that there may have been a divine purpose in it all, and that the former's flight had been permitted as a step in the entire renovation of the slave's nature. And, therefore, because Philemon and Onesimus were two Christians, their relationship had been transformed. "In the flesh, Philemon has the brother for his slave; in the Lord, Philemon has the slave for his brother." Then in v. 17 Paul identifies himself with Onesimus; and we are taught to think of our Lord identifying himself with us, because, as Luther says, "we are all Onesimuses." Further, in v. 18 Paul offers to assume all the losses which Onesimus had brought on Philemon, and signs the bond personally, as our Lord paid the great ransom price for us all. Finally, Paul delicately reminds his friend, in v. 19, that Philemon owed him a great deal more than a trifle of money; namely, his spiritual life. Does not our Lord address us in similar terms? We surely owe ourselves to him!

THE EPISTLE TO THE
HEBREWS

THE NEW AND BETTER COVENANT

I. CHRIST THE SURETY OF THE NEW COVENANT *1:1—6:12.*
   A. He is a divine Redeemer *1:1-4.*
   B. He is superior to angels *1:5-14.*
   C. He has accomplished redemption through suffering *2.*
   D. He is greater than Moses *3:1—4:13.*
   E. He is a great High Priest *4:14—5:10.*
   (Comment on the argument and direct appeal to readers *5:11—6:12.*)

II. THE RELATION OF THE TWO COVENANTS *6:13—10:39.*
   A. The promise to Abraham *6:13-15.*
   B. Its realization by us *6:16-20.*
   C. The unchanging priesthood *7:1-17.*
   D. The covenants contrasted *7:18—8:13.*
   E. The institutions of the old covenant fulfilled in the Person and work of Christ *9:1—10:18.*
   F. The greater privileges and responsibilities of the new covenant *10:19-39.*

III. FAITH, THE COMMON FACTOR OF THE TWO COVENANTS *11, 12.*
   A. The achievements of faith under the old covenant *11.*
   B. The summons to faith under the new covenant *12.*

IV. PRACTICAL ADMONITIONS *13:1-21.*

CONCLUSION *13:22-25.*

INTRODUCTION

This epistle was evidently written as the ancient Hebrew economy was passing away in the growing glory of the Christian Church. Perhaps Jerusalem had already fallen under the arms of Titus. It was addressed to Hebrew Christians who were settled in a definite locality. See 13:23. The writer is not certainly known. Luther thought that it was written by Apollos, and this view has had several learned advocates. But many ascribe it to the Apostle Paul, which was the opinion of the early Fathers. The object of this noble treatise is to counsel those to whom it was addressed to bear their persecutions with equanimity and to forego, with contentment, the external attractions of the Temple service, because of the transcendent glories of Christianity surpassing those of the Mosaic ritual. The penalties of apostasy would therefore be the more terrible as the claims of Christianity were the more compelling.

COMMENTARY

HEBREWS 1

God's Final and Supreme Messenger. Christianity is greater than the Mosaic dispensation because it has been given through the Son, whereas the Law came through angels. See Acts 7:53. The message of the gospel is connected speech; that of the Law was broken syllables.

The Son's intrinsic glory, vv. 1–4. Jesus is the channel of creation, Providence, and redemption. He is the far-traveled ray of Deity, but not one among many equals, for of him alone could it be said that his nature was coextensive with God's, as a seal with the die. He is on the throne not merely because of his original nature, but as the reward of his obedience unto death, Phil. 2:9, 10.

His superiority to angels, vv. 5–14. These quotations should be carefully studied as showing the deep inner meaning of the Psalms. Their fulfillment must be sought in Christ, and in them we overhear the voice of God. We must ever thank God for the ministry of angels. Note that their service to us is a liturgy of adoration to God; such is the force of the Greek words.

HEBREWS 2:1–9

The Author of Our Salvation. Drifting away, vv. 1–4. The Revised Version gives this solemn rendering. Unless we watch, the strong currents of the world will drift us away from God's great harbor of salvation; and sins against his offered love are even more to be dreaded than those under the ancient Law. To "neglect" is the equivalent of to "reject." Notice in v. 4 how God cooperates with his messengers. See John 15:27; Acts 5:32.

Jesus crowned, vv. 5–9. How can Jesus be greater than angels? He did for man what they could not do. It is through his death that humanity may be lifted to a supreme position in the universe of being. Man failed to realize his original *magna charta* in Gen. 1:26; but the divine purpose could not be frustrated, and there was a needs-be for the manger, the cross, and the ascension mount. As we look around, Psalm 8 seems a mockery; as we look up, we discover in Jesus the psalmist's dream more than realized. They who are one with him will share his glory and honor.

HEBREWS 2:10–18

"Made Like unto His Brethren." "Captain" reminds us of Acts 3:15. It means "file-leader." The Church follows its Leader, Jesus Christ, in single file through this world of the cross and the grave, to the glory. But notice that God himself is engaged in bringing us through, and he cannot lose one. See John 10:29. But he is not only our Captain, he is our Brother. We also are born of God. He is sanctifying us and we are being sanctified for a marvelous future, John 17:19. How great is his love, that he is not ashamed of us!

Our Elder Brother has encountered our foes and won deliverance for all who believe. Death remains, but its teeth are drawn and its power is annulled. We need not fear what men call death; to us it is only as falling asleep. He has taken hold of us with a grasp that will never let us go again, v. 17. He has been tempted that he might be able to succor us in our temptations. He has suffered that he might tread our darkened paths at our side. He has made reconciliation for our sins, and as our merciful and faithful High Priest pleads the cause of our souls.

HEBREWS 3:1-11

Superior to Moses. Dwell on those opening words: "holy," such is God's ideal for us; "brethren," by reason of our union with Christ and with one another in him; "partakers of the heavenly calling," God is ever calling upward and heavenward. Jesus comes from God as "Apostle" and goes for us to God as "Priest." In his human life, how humble and faithful he was; but he originally built the Jewish polity and commonwealth! He was and is as much greater than Moses as the architect than the foreman and the son than the servant.

It is not enough to begin the Christian race; we must hold fast our confidence and hope to the end. That was the point specially to be emphasized among these harried people. These Hebrew Christians missed the splendid ceremonial life of their ancient faith, and were suffering heavily from persecution and opposition. But was it not worthwhile to persevere, if only to be recognized as belonging to the household of God? Surely for them and for us the experiences of Israel in the forty years of wandering are full of warning. Be admonished by that wilderness cemetery!

HEBREWS 3:12-19

"Harden Not Your Hearts." There is a peril lest familiarity with God's words should beget indifference to them. The path may be trodden hard by the sower's feet. That story of the wilderness wanderings is for all time. Still men disbelieve and disobey; still they doubt that God is able; still they err in their hearts and therefore fail to understand with their heads; still they wander to and fro with weary souls and restless feet. But if they who failed to believe in words given by Moses were wrapped around by the blowing sheets of sand, what will not be the fate of those who refuse the words of Christ!

How wonderful it is that by just trusting we may be partners with our Lord of his rest, life, glory, and resources, v. 14! But we must listen to the inner voice, soft and low, speaking in the Horeb of our hearts, 1 Kings 19:12. Obey it, and you will enter into the rest of God; refuse it, and you will be as certainly excluded from the divine rest as they from Canaan.

HEBREWS 4:1-10

The Rest That Joshua Could Not Give. The good news of Canaan's rest was preached to Israel but availed nothing, because the hearers were destitute of faith. They said, Can God? instead of, God can! They thought of their enemies as giants and themselves as grasshoppers, because they left God out of account. Take God into account and we are giants and our enemies grasshoppers.

To all of us Christ offers "rest," not in the other life only, but in this. See vv. 3 and 11. Rest from the weight of sin, from care and worry, from the load of daily anxiety and foreboding. The rest that arrives from handing all worries over to Christ, and receiving from Christ all we need. Have we entered into that experience? In vv. 6 and 11, "unbelief" can read, "disobedience." If we disobey, we cannot believe; but when we believe we are sure to obey. In v. 10 we are directed to our risen Lord, who has finished the work of redemption and rests as God did when he pronounced creation to be "very good." When we understand what he meant by "It is finished," we too shall rest.

HEBREWS 4:11-16

Entered by Faith and Prayer. There is no escape for disobedience and unbelief, because we have to do with the omniscience of God. The conception of vv. 12 and 13 is of a victim appointed for sacrifice and thrown upon its back, that the keen edge of the knife may do its work more readily. The divine scrutiny is still sharper. There is so much of the "soul" in what we do; that is, of our opinions and activities. God distinguishes between these and those promptings of his Spirit which are really important and influential. Only what is born of the Spirit will stand the test of eternity!

Shall we not fail in that scrutiny? Will he not detect in us that evil heart of unbelief? We need not fear, because our High Priest has passed the veil that hides the invisible and eternal and has entered the divine presence. "Mercy and grace to help in time of need!" These will meet our supreme needs—mercy for our sins, grace for our helplessness and frailty.

HEBREWS 5:1-10

Our Divinely Appointed High Priest. Having to act for men, our High Priest must be man, acquainted with human conditions; having to do with God, he must be appointed by God. Is there one of us that is not conscious of habitual ignorance and wandering? We all evermore need the high priesthood of Jesus.

The Aaronic priests must needs make atonement for themselves, but our Lord was without sin. See Lev. 4:3. Verse 5 has reference to Christ's resurrection and ascension. See Rom. 1:4; Acts 13:33. His priestly service dates from the completion of his mediatorial work on the cross. No scene in our Lord's life fulfills v. 7 like that of the garden, when it seemed impossible for the human body to hold out under the stress of his anguish. He feared that he would succumb before he reached Calvary. He had to yield obedience unto death in order to learn what obedience really means. Thus as to his humanity he became perfected; and if only we believe and obey, he will effect a perfect deliverance for us from all evil. There is no sin so strong, no need so intricate that he cannot cope with it.

HEBREWS 5:11—6:8

Pressing on to Full Growth. The teacher has to suit his pace to his scholars. How much we miss because we are such inapt pupils! Milk is food which has passed through another's digestion. Many cannot get their spiritual nutrition direct from God's Word, but have to live on what others have obtained and have passed on in speech or book. Seek a firsthand acquaintance with the things of God. We grow by feeding and exercise.

We must leave the first principles as a builder leaves the foundation; he is never so much on it as when farthest above it. The third and fourth principles, v. 2, are the Jewish equivalents of the first and second, v. 1. Notice the marginal reading for "seeing" in v. 6—"the while." So long as men continue to tread the love of God under foot, they cannot repent and be restored. The failure, as with unproductive soil, is not on account of a failure of Heaven, but because the soil is hard and obdurate. If we are unproductive, it is due to our own hardheartedness.

HEBREWS 6:9-20

"The Hope Set before Us." The keynote of this passage is *patient continuance.* We should seek not only faith, but its accompaniments. It is not enough to manifest faith, hope and love, but to continue to do so "unto the end." Notice that the two conditions on which the promises are inherited are faith and patience.

These truths are enforced by the example of Abraham. He believed God and patiently endured. Your prayers cannot be lost, as ships at sea; they will make harbor at last, laden with golden freight. God's promise and oath are a double door behind which they who have fled for refuge are safe, a double window beyond which all noise dies down. The allusion is either to the cities of refuge, or to a ship safely riding out the storm. Hope is "sure," because the anchor has fastened in a sure ground; "steadfast," because its cable will not snap in the strain; and "entering," because it unites us to the unseen. Jesus has taken our anchor into the inner harbor and has dropped it down into the clear, still water there.

HEBREWS 7:1-10

A Priesthood Superior to Aaron's. Melchizedek was probably a literal king and priest in Salem. The blue smoke of his sacrifices rose morning and evening on the hill. Amid the turbulent lawlessness of those wild days, his realm was one of peace. Like him, Jesus meets us when flushed with success or wearied with some great effort, and therefore are peculiarly liable to temptation. Notice the order! It is invariable! First righteousness, then peace, Zech. 9:9.

The silences of Scripture are significant. In the case of this ancient priesthood no mention is made of parenthood. This was a matter of comparative indifference. So with our Lord. It is true that he did not come of the priestly family of Aaron, but this is quite unimportant. The one thing for us to notice is that Abraham paid tithes to Melchizedek, thus confessing him to be the greater. Levi was, so to speak, included in his grandfather's act, so that the Hebrew priesthood which sprang from Levi was confessedly inferior to Melchizedek's. If, then, Melchizedek is a type of Christ, we are taught that Christ's priesthood is evidently and eternally superior to all other priesthoods whatsoever.

HEBREWS 7:11-28

Our Ever-living and All-sufficient Intercessor. If, as we saw in our last reading, the Levitical priests have been superseded, clearly the whole order of things—that is, the Mosaic covenant under which these priests were appointed—has been superseded also. The law of the carnal—that is, the outward ritual—has passed away in favor of a new dispensation which deals with the heart and character. It served a temporary purpose, but we are living in an eternal order which is steadfast and abiding.

Our Lord's priesthood is unchangeable and indissoluble. His blood and righteousness, his mediation for us, his loving understanding of us will be a joy and comfort in the unending ages. We shall always be specially associated with him—the brethren of the King, the sheep of the Divine Shepherd. Each priest of Aaron's line had to vacate his office; but our Lord's priesthood will never pass to another; and therefore to the uttermost lapse of time and to the farthest demand of circumstance, he will save and help all that come to him. No infirmity weakens him, no stain or sin unfits him. Above the heavens and from the throne he exercises his ministry.

HEBREWS 8:1-13

The Mediator of the New Covenant. "*Such an high priest,*" vv. 1-6. He sits because his work is finished so far as his sacrifice is concerned. His place is at God's right hand—the seat of power. By faith we, too, may serve in the inner sanctuary. Before you start building, and while engaged in building, your lifework, see that your eyes are fixed on the divine ideal and pattern.

Such a new covenant, vv. 7-13. It is as superior to the former as Christ's priesthood is to Aaron's. A covenant is a promise, made on conditions to be fulfilled and attested by an outward sign, like the rainbow or circumcision or the Lord's Supper. The covenant under which we live is between God and Christ on behalf of those who belong to him. We have a perfect right to put our hand on every one of these eight provisions and claim that each be made good to us. We need not ask that God should do as he has said, but with lowly reverence expect that he will—especially when we drink of the cup of the new covenant at the Lord's Table.

HEBREWS 9:1-10

The Imperfect Way of Approach to God. With careful enumeration each item of the Tabernacle furniture is specified. For each, there is a spiritual equivalent in the unseen, spiritual temple to which we belong. The veil that screened the Most Holy Place and forbade entrance, save once a year, taught that fellowship with God was not fully open. Ignorance, unbelief, unpreparedness of heart still weave a heavy veil which screens God from the soul's gaze.

The altar of incense is here associated with the inner shrine, because it stood so near the veil. Its counterpart is seen in Rev. 8:4. The Ark was an emblem of Christ: the wood, of his humanity; the gold, of his deity. He holds the manna of the world, and is the ever-budding plant of renown, beautiful and fruit-bearing through death. There is one gateway in St. Peter's, Rome, through which the Pope passes only once a year; how glad we may be that our gates for prayer stand open day and night! Contrast the sadness of such passages as Ps. 51:3, 4 and Mic. 6:6 with the joy of Eph. 1:3-10.

HEBREWS 9:11-20

The Blood Which Sealed the New Covenant. We are led to consider Christ's high-priestly work. The scene for it is no edifice made with hands in this transitory world, but eternal and divine. His stay in the Holiest is not brief, hurried, and repeated year by year, but once for all he enters by virtue of his own blood. That blood cleanses not only from ceremonial guilt, but from moral and spiritual pollution. A will or testament comes into force when the testator dies; so the will of the eternal Father toward us has been made valid through the blood of Jesus.

Consider, then, "the eternal [or timeless] Spirit." What Jesus did on the cross was the doing of God through his Spirit. The Atonement was not wrought by the dying Sufferer to appease God, but to express God as reconciling the world to himself. *The timeless cross* belongs to no one age, but "towers o'er the wrecks of time," and is as near us as to the early Church. *The timeless Christ:* Cast yourself out of yourself and into him, out of the fret of the time sphere into the freedom and ecstasy of the eternal!

HEBREWS 9:21-28

The One Sacrifice That Puts Away Sin. Here are the three appearances of Christ: (1) He "appeared" once, at the ridge or meeting-place of the ages—where the first covenant and the second met—to put away the sin of the race; and he has done this for each of us. We are called on to believe this and to enter upon our inheritance without questioning or trying to feel it. Men are told clearly that God will not impute their transgressions unto them, unless they place themselves out of the at-one-ment by the deliberate repudiation of Christ. The one question for us all is not sin, but our attitude toward Christ, the Sin-bearer. See 2 Cor. 5:19.

(2) He "appears" in Heaven for us, as our Intercessor and Mediator, presenting our prayers mingled with the rich incense of his merit, and acting as the ground of our beseechings,

Rev. 8:3. (3) "He shall appear" the second time. There will be no sin-bearing then. His appearance will be "without sin." But then salvation will be perfected, because creation itself will share in the liberty and glory of the sons of God, Rom. 8:21.

HEBREWS 10:1-10

"Lo, I Come To Do Thy Will." When a heavenly body is in eclipse, it can be examined with even greater precision than when the astronomer's eye is directed toward its burning glory; so in Leviticus we can discover details of our Lord's atonement otherwise overlooked. This is notably the case in Lev. 1—4.

The key words of this chapter are "year by year" and "daily" as contrasted with "for ever." Repetition means imperfection. The ancient offerers of sacrifice could never be sure that they were finally accepted. Each year they had to go over the old ground. How different from us who have heard Jesus say, "It is finished."

The Spirit of inspiration offers to us the secret of our Savior's work in his voluntary identification with the divine purposes. It was not so much his outward anguish and blood-shedding that made reconciliation possible, as his cry, "Not my will, my Father, but thine." His attitude reminds us of the ancient custom of boring fast to the door the ear of the servant who desired never again to leave his master's service. "Mine ears hast thou bored." See Ps. 40:6, margin.

HEBREWS 10:11-25

The New and Living Way Open to Us. Note the contrast between the standing of the priests and the sitting of the Priest. The one indicated incompleteness, the other a finished work. All that needed to be done for our final and entire deliverance from sin was accomplished when Jesus returned to the Father. It is for us to make large demands and claims. The bank is full, but we must draw on it.

It is a great help, in the study of the Old Testament, to notice how explicitly the writer here attributes to the Holy Spirit the words spoken by one of the old prophets. What a comfort it is to know that God forgets our sins when we have confessed and forsaken them!

The way of prayer and faith was "new," for our Lord had just opened it, and "living, because only those alive in Christ can tread it. The rending of the Temple veil was emblematic of the open vision of God, given through Calvary. But we must be "true," believing, reliant on his death, and "pure" through his cleansing, John 13:5-8.

HEBREWS 10:26-39

Beware of Backsliding. The willful sin here referred to does not consist in isolated acts, but in a determined course of action, persisted in until the very desire for a better life wanes and dies out of the soul.

These strong remonstrances were needed in those days of sore persecution. Three considerations are adduced, urging steadfastness: (1) The certain punishment which must follow the rejection of the greatest gifts that God can make, so much richer than anything presented under the Mosaic covenant; (2) The sufferings already endured, the reward for which would be forfeited if these harried souls were now to draw back; (3) The near advent of the Christ, who would not fail to compensate his faithful servants.

Then we are reminded that the just—those who have been accepted in the Beloved—live; that is, they may derive all the reinforcements of soul-strength and patience that they require from the unseen and eternal world where Jesus waits to succor and uphold.

HEBREWS 11:1-10

Faith's Triumphs from Abel to Abraham. Faith is the sixth sense. It makes us as sure of unseen or future things, which we know about only through the divine Word, as we are of things which we can see and touch. When we are aware of the reality of these things, we naturally take them into account when we act. Rothschild laid the foundation for his fortune because he had news that the battle of Waterloo had been won, a day before anyone else in Britain. That fact enabled him to buy up all the depressed money-shares, which rose with marvelous buoyancy as soon as the news was universally disseminated. Faith does this for us!

Noah built the ark because he believed that the Flood would come. Abraham left his country because he realized that a Canaan would be his. The pilgrims and martyrs of all the ages have been derided by their companions, who would have acted similarly if only they had looked with faith into the unseen. And God never fails such. He always bears witness with his gifts.

HEBREWS 11:11-22

Seeking the Better Country. Faith has the twofold power, first, of making the unseen real; and second, of receiving the grace and strength of

God into the heart. Sarah, through faith, received strength to bear Isaac. By faith may come physical as well as spiritual strength.

The pilgrim life is possible only for those who have seen the city of God beckoning them from afar. Then they strike their tents and follow the gleam. By faith they so live that God is not ashamed to own them. They will discover, even in this life, that they have not trusted him in vain, and that the half has not been told. On the mere rumor that a new gold field is found, men sell everything in their mad rush. How many are disappointed! But none of those that trust God shall be left desolate.

Abraham was absolutely sure that Isaac would return with him, even though the lad might die beneath the knife. When leaving the young men at Moriah's foot, he said, "*We* will worship and come again." Had not God's voice definitely designated Isaac as his heir?

HEBREWS 11:23-31

Making the Far-seeing Choice. Faith—we cannot say it too often—is the direct vision of the soul. It doesn't reason, it doesn't ask for evidences, it doesn't seek the corroboration of spies sent forward to explore the land. It is to the spiritual world what the five senses are to things around us. It is even more than this; it is our power of deriving the help of the Unseen to carry out and complete the work of our life.

Moses "saw" him who is invisible, drew on God with a mighty faith that reckoned on him as being more real than Pharaoh, and secured his divine cooperation. First, he ascertained God's will at the place where the bush burned with fire, and then set about doing his part, depending upon God to do his. Of course, it brought him into collision with the whole might of Pharaoh and Egypt, but he didn't even fear it. The destroying Angel had no terrors for the blood-sheltered people. The waters lined up on each side to let them pass. Strongly built walls fell to the ground. Let us be sure that we are on the line of God's purposes, then trust him and fear naught.

HEBREWS 11:32-40

The Noble Army of Martyrs. Strong faith is consistent with very different views of religious truth. The conception that Abel, Enoch, or Noah had of so-called Christian truth was very slight; but the faith with which they grasped the scanty truth revealed to them was mighty, soul-transforming, and world-moving.

These persons were of every age and temperament—shepherds, statesmen, prime ministers, psalmists, poets, border chieftains, prophets, women martyrs—but they are all trophies of faith. The variety is extraordinary, but the unity is undeniable. The beads are many, but there is one golden thread uniting them all. Their circumstances and trials were widely different, but in all the talisman of victory was faith's watchword—"God is able." There is no kind of need, trial, persecution, experience for which faith is not the sufficient answer. It is the master key for every lock of difficulty. Fit your case into one of the clauses and what once was, shall be again.

HEBREWS 12:1-8

Persistently Press Forward. In one of Raphael's pictures the clouds, when looked at minutely, are seen to be composed of little cherub-faces; and those who have already witnessed and suffered for God gather around us as a great cloud, like the crowded amphitheaters in the old Olympian games. We are still in the arena; probably every blow and sigh are beheld and heard by the general assembly and church of the firstborn. What an incentive to lay aside all "cumbrances" or "weights"; that is, whatever in your life may be a hindrance, though hardly a sin! But above all, we must put away the sin of unbelief, which we can best do by looking unto Jesus.

The word "our" should certainly be eliminated in v. 2, not being part of the original text. Jesus began and finished his life-career by the same faith—"the faith of the Son of God"—which each of his children has to exercise. The light beyond the cross beckoned to him and so enamored him that he counted no cost too dear, if only he might realize the possibilities that gleamed before his vision of an elect Church and a transformed world.

HEBREWS 12:9-17

Endure Chastening; Seek Holiness. If we are God's children, we will not look on suffering as a punishment. Chastening it may be, but not the penalty of sin. It is administered by our Father. Don't look at the intermediary links in the chain, but remember that Satan could not go beyond the Father's limit in the case of Balaam or Job. See Num. 22:31; Job 2:6. It is only for the present; it will soon be over. It is intended to free us of dross and is therefore to profit; it will yield peace, and righteousness, and true holiness. Look on and up—the harvest will repay.

We are bidden, vv. 14-17, to watch each other's interests and to stay the first speck of corruption in the fruit, lest it spread. The corrupt soul infects all in its neighborhood. There are irrevocable acts in life. We cannot undo them, but we may be forgiven. Esau received all that this world could give and became a prince, but he never got back his spiritual leadership.

HEBREWS 12:18–29

Hearken to God's Latest Word. Sinai rocked with earthquake and burned with fire. None might touch it without incurring the death penalty. How much better our Christian heritage! Not a lonely mountain, but a city and commonwealth of holy souls. Not bands of worshipers gathered from the land of Canaan, but hosts of angels, the spirits of just men, and our blessed Lord himself. For the blood of animals, the blood of Jesus; for the old covenant, the new; for Abel's death beside his altar, the Savior's death on the cross.

Notice the writer does not say that we *shall,* but that we *"are"* come, v. 22. Already, in our holiest moments, we are part of that great throng to which so many of our beloved have gone. Around us the most stable structures are being tested and some are crumbling to the ground. As they fall, they show that their service was transient. But as the scaffolding is taken down, the true building—the city of God—emerges.

HEBREWS 13:1–13

Sanctify Daily Life. We may not like all the brethren, but there is something in each of them that Christ loves. Let us try to discover it, or love them for his sake. We can love people with our mind and think for them, or with our strength and serve them, even though the heart is somewhat reluctant.

Strangers and captives must never be forgotten, either in our prayers or our ministry. The love within the marriage tie must be unsullied, and we must watch against the insidious lust of gold. Why should we always be thinking of money when God has promised, with two negatives, never to fail us, v. 5? Thrice we are asked to remember those who bear office and rule in the church, vv. 7, 17, 24.

We are called to a holy crusade. It is not for us to linger in circumstances of ease and self-indulgence when our Master suffered without the gate! Let us go forth unto him, bearing his reproach! Has not the Church tarried in the city long enough, enervated by its fashions and flatteries?

HEBREWS 13:14–25

Praise, Prayer, and Peace. Notice that though the ancient sacrifices have been abolished, there is one which can never grow old—the "sacrifice of praise." This incense must ever ascend from the heart-altar. And to this we must add the sacrifices of doing good and distributing our goods.

Perfection in the closing paragraph, v. 21, means adjustment, the setting of a dislocated bone. We may be in the body of which Jesus is the Head, and yet be out of touch with him. We need setting; and this is work which God will delegate to no angel, however exalted. He will do it himself as tenderly and gently as possible, because he is the "God of peace." Do you doubt it? Did he not bring the Shepherd to glory, and is he not able to bring the sheep also? Never rest until you are in living organic union with Jesus, that he may be able to work his will through you to your own great joy and for the hastening of the kingdom.

THE EPISTLE OF
JAMES

THE MEASURE OF A CHRISTIAN

SALUTATION *1:1.*
I. TESTED CHARACTER *1:2–18.*
II. HEARING AND DOING *1:19–27.*
III. THE HYPOCRISY OF CLASS DISTINCTIONS *2:1–13.*
IV. THE EVIDENCE OF TRUE FAITH *2:14–26.*
V. THE UNRULY TONGUE *3.*
VI. THE GRACE OF HUMILITY *4.*
VII. THE CURSE OF ILL-GOTTEN WEALTH *5:1–6.*
VIII. THE NEED OF PATIENCE AND PRAYER *5:7–20.*

INTRODUCTION

The author of this epistle was probably the Lord's brother, mentioned with Joses, Simon, and Judah, and often seen in the Acts of the Apostles. See Mark 6:3; Acts 12:17; 15:13; 21:18. He was bishop, or president, of the church at Jerusalem, and this letter was probably written from that city. The emphasis laid on the nearness of our Lord's advent points to a date near A.D. 70. The epistle may have been written in Hebrew, and was addressed to the Hebrew section of the Church. It lays great emphasis on the sublime ideal of character which Christianity had raised, and to maintain which demanded the constant diligence of all professing Christians.

COMMENTARY

JAMES 1:1-11

Steadfast Faith. This epistle is marked by the austere features of the Jerusalem church, which refused to be affected by that wider contact with the Gentile world by which the life and teachings of St. Paul were so powerfully influenced. "Brother to Jesus" was the designation that James might have used, but he preferred the more modest title of "servant." The slaves of the King are nobles! The times were full of severe testing. Each believer had to face ignominy, loss, and death for his testimony to Jesus and his saving power. But James encourages these harried souls by the immense revenues that would accrue, more especially in the acquisition of patience. While patience is drawn out almost to the breaking-point, God is developing our characters with perfect beauty, so that no side is incomplete.

There are three urgent requirements for us all: (1) wisdom to act and speak wisely in the hour of trial; (2) faith that refuses to respond to the surging billows of doubt; (3) humility and contentment with God's dealings.

JAMES 1:12-18

God Rewards, Not Tempts. The word "temptation" may stand for trial and testing, without implying that there is any necessary impulse toward evil; or it may stand for the direct impulse of the evil one. Here, however, it is used in this latter sense. But of whatever kind the temptation is, whether upward or downward, whether of pain and sorrow at the permission of God, or of direct solicitation to evil at the suggestion of Satan, those who refuse to swerve from their high quest of nobility attain to higher levels of life. In the words of this paragraph, they receive the "crown of life" here and hereafter.

Notice the genealogy of sin, v. 15. Lust is the parent of sin, and sin when matured is the parent of death. How different to the blackness of this dark picture is the light and glory of our Father's home and realm! All the good things of our lives are from his good hand. He is not fickle and changeable. Even our sin cannot make him turn away. His sun still shines on the evil and the good, and his rain descends on the just and the unjust. See Matt. 5:45. We are his children; let us be sweet to the taste as the grapes of Eschol!

JAMES 1:19-27

Doers, Not Hearers Only. Keep your mouth closed when you are angry; the inner fire will die out of itself if you keep the doors and windows shut. In v. 18 we are taught that God's truth is the agent of regeneration; in v. 21 it is the means of deepening our consecration. It is a blessed thing, when not only the words, but the Word of God is engrafted on the wild stock of our nature.

The one and only way of making holy impressions permanent is by translating them into Christian living. It is not enough to see ourselves reflected in the mirror of God's Word; we must "continue," not as hearers who forget, but as doers that perform. Many appear to think that blessedness results from hearing and are always on foot to attend new conventions. No; the true blessedness accrues from *doing*. The heart of our Christian faith is purity, the stainless garb of the soul, and thoughtful ministration to the widow and orphan—but these are possible only through the indwelling of Christ by the Holy Spirit.

JAMES 2:1–13

Avoid Servility to the Rich. This sin of making distinctions in God's house is as rife today as ever; and wherever it is practiced, the divine Spirit departs. God's love is impartial, so far as outward appearances might affect it; and in his Church the only real differences must be those of humility, purity, and righteousness.

"Blessed are the poor in spirit," whether they be rich in this world's goods or not. But it is easier for a poor man to be rich in faith and an heir of the kingdom, because he can give more of his attention to the things of the Spirit.

The law of love must be supreme with us; and we must love our fellows, whatever their position or property, as ourselves, for Christ's sake. If we fail in this, we show that we have never entered into the heart of the Christian faith. A man may observe all the laws of health; but if he inhale one whiff of poison he may die; so we may be outwardly obedient to the entire Decalogue, but delinquency in love will invalidate everything.

JAMES 2:14–26

Deeds the Evidence of Faith. The apostle is speaking here of a faith that does not result in a changed life. It is the faith which believes *about* Jesus Christ, as distinguished from that which believes *in* him. We may believe about him as we do about Luther or Washington, but such faith will not avail, either here or hereafter. It can no more affect our condition than the pious wish that a shivering beggar may be warmed and fed will make him either one or the other.

The presence or absence of results in life and conduct is the real test of faith, as the green shoot of a living seed. James calls these results "works." We are justified by works, because they prove our faith to be the real faith. Real faith binds the soul to the living Christ, produces deep penitence and humility, and brings about an absolutely new sort of behavior—as when Abraham was willing to offer Isaac, and Rahab received and assisted the spies. To reckon on God is to be a friend of God.

JAMES 3:1–12

Bridle the Tongue. It is much easier to teach people what they should be and do than to obey our own precepts. Even the best of us stumble in many respects; but our most frequent failures are in speech. If we could control our tongues, we should be masters of the whole inner economy of our natures. The refusal to express a thought will kill the thought. Let Christ bridle your mouth, and he will be able to turn about your whole body. Let him have his hand on the tiller of your tongue, and he will guide your life as he desires.

A single spark may burn down a city. The upsetting of an oil lamp in a stable led to the burning of Chicago. Lighted at the flames of hell, the tongue can pass their poison on to earth. Man cannot tame the tongue, but Christ can. He goes straight for the heart, for, as he said long ago, the seat of the mischief is there. See Mark 7:14, 15; Ps. 51:10.

JAMES 3:13–18

Seek Wisdom from Above. The true wisdom is not the child of the intellect, but of the heart. It consists not only in what we know, but in what we are. It is in this sense that it is used in the early chapters of the book of Proverbs and in Job 28. Some who profess to be wise are jealous and factious, despising others and confident in their superiority. This spirit and temper are from beneath.

Notice this exquisite string of qualities—like a thread of pearls—that characterize true wisdom: First, pure; then peaceable—this is God's order, never peace at any price. First the holy heart, then the quiet and gentle one. Mercy and good works follow, "without partiality, and without hypocrisy"; and as the peace-loving soul goes through the world, dropping the seeds of peace, those seeds produce harvests of righteousness. Those that in peace sow peace shall reap a harvest of righteousness, the fruit of peace. Such a springtime! Such an autumn!

JAMES 4:1–10

"Draw Nigh to God." The apostle returns to the "bitter envying and strife" of the previous chapter, 3:14, and says that these evils are traceable to "lust," that is, to inordinate desire. The restless inward war is the prolific parent of failure in speech and act. If we would pray more

and better, we should soon find the inner fires dying down.

In v. 5, margin, we learn that God has placed his Spirit within us, and that he yearns for complete control over our hearts. He can best overcome inordinate desire and teach us how to pray. God wants more of us. His love is insatiable in its yearning for every room and cupboard of our inner life, and he is ever wishful to give more grace.

There are four conditions which we must fulfill if God is to have full possession: (1) We must be subject to the will of God, v. 7; (2) we must draw nigh to God, v. 8; (3) we must cleanse our hands and purify our hearts, v. 8; (4) we must humble ourselves in his sight, v. 10. Then God will fill the soul, the sluicegates of which are open to him.

JAMES 4:11-17

"If the Lord Will." When we speak evil of another, we usurp the functions of the only Lawgiver and Judge. If that other is endeavoring to model his life by the Law, to speak evil of him is to question not his action alone, but the Law he is trying to observe. Let us turn the light in upon ourselves and be merciless in self-criticism, while merciful to all others. When you see another doing wrong, always ask yourself whether the same evil is not hiding in your own character. Do not speak *of* men, but *to* them, when their faults confront you.

We are prone to make plans without reference to God's will. Life is so transient and brief that if we are to make the most of it, we should ask the divine Spirit to choose for and guide us. Our one endeavor must be to discover God's will and do it. If we are not constantly saying, "If the Lord will," the sentiment it expresses should always be uppermost with us. "Thy will be done" in me as in Heaven!

JAMES 5:1-11

Patiently Await the Lord's Coming. There are many among the rich who are using money as a sacred trust. Not against these does the apostle utter his terrible anathemas, but against those who make money by oppression and hoard it for their selfish ends. Riches which have not been gotten righteously ever bring a curse with them; and the rust of unused or misused wealth eats not only into the metal, but into the miser's flesh. In the light of this passage, it is as great a wrong to hoard up for selfish ends money entrusted as a stewardship as it is to obtain it unrighteously.

There is a sense in which the Lord is ever at hand and present. But he shall come again at the end of this age. Then all wrongs shall be righted and the oppressed avenged. Everything comes to him who can wait for it; do not judge the Lord by his unfinished work. Be patient till he unveils the perfected pattern in glory. Await "the end of the Lord."

JAMES 5:12-20

Effectual Prayer. In view of the judgment-seat, at which we shall have to give an account of our words, we shall do well to employ the simplest, plainest speech, Matt. 5:34; 12:36, 37.

How shall we act in any given situation? The apostle says in effect, be perfectly natural. The suffering should pray, the glad sing, the sick confess his sins and call for believing prayer. The oil is the symbol of the Holy Spirit. The body is the Holy Spirit's temple, and he is asked to bring it to the level of that spiritual wholeness which is his ideal. Where he initiates the prayer that can affirm and claim, there is no doubt that perfect health will result. But there is all the difference between human telepathy and divine healing, which is God's gift to faith.

Elijah became what he was by faith and prayer. Naturally he was subject to the same fears and failings as ourselves. There are two reasons why we should endeavor to convert men: (1) for their salvation, (2) for the arrest of their baleful influence.

THE FIRST EPISTLE OF
PETER

THE FELLOWSHIP OF CHRIST'S SUFFERING AND GLORY

SALUTATION   *1:1, 2.*

I. THE CONFLICT OF HOPE AND SUFFERING   *1:3–12.*
  A. The living hope born of Christ's resurrection   *1:3–5.*
  B. Trials and sufferings   *1:6, 7.*
  C. The triumph of hope   *1:8–12.*

II. A ROYAL PRIESTHOOD AND A HOLY NATION   *1:13—2:10.*
  A. The call to holiness   *1:13–17.*
  B. Christ's work of redemption   *1:18–21.*
  C. The believer's regeneration   *1:22—2:3.*
  D. The stone rejected by the builders   *2:4–8.*
  E. The people of God   *2:9, 10.*

III. CHRIST'S UNPARALLELED EXAMPLE   *2:11—4:19.*
  A. The obligations of the Christian life   *2:11–20.*
  B. The example of Christ   *2:21–25.*
     (His sinlessness.)
  C. The obligations of the Christian life   *3:1–17.*
     (Mutual forbearance of wives and husbands, brotherly love, pity, courtesy, overcoming evil with good.)
  D. The example of Christ   *3:18–22.*
     (His suffering for sin.)
  E. The obligations of the Christian life   *4.*
     (Living to God, watching, praying, hospitality, suffering as a Christian.)

IV. THE DIRECTION OF THE CHURCH   *5:1–9.*
  A. Duties of elders   *5:1–4.*
  B. Duties of young men   *5:5–9.*

CONCLUSION   *5:10–14.*

INTRODUCTION

This epistle was addressed primarily to Christian Hebrews, though it does not exclude Gentiles who, by adoption and faith, become members of the true Israel of God. The countries named are from northeast to southwest in Asia Minor. As might have been expected, the paragraphs glow with Peter's fervent zeal and ardent love. There is also a deep vein of patience and of desire to encourage those who were suffering. The fiery trial was the Neronian persecution, which the Emperor instigated to divert from himself the stigma of having set Rome on fire. The date, therefore, is about A.D. 65.

COMMENTARY

1 PETER 1:1-12

Our Imperishable Inheritance. "Scattered strangers." The designation is true of us all. Note the reference to the Trinity involved in the opening sentence. Our inheritance is prepared and kept for us, as we for it. We who believe may count on the guarding power of God. Not till our spirit is joined to a perfected body in the presence of Christ will our salvation be complete.

Trial is manifold. There is more or less of it in every true life. The best diamonds take longer in cutting and polishing. But, after all, compared to the eternity before us it is but short-lived, and there is a needs-be for all. Hope in v. 3, faith in v. 7, love in v. 8 blend in the joy that is unspeakable and full of the glory which is as yet hidden.

Notice that the prophets, angels, and apostles are represented as deeply interested in that glorious salvation which God has declared unto mankind in the gospel, and by which we have been redeemed.

1 PETER 1:13-25

Redeemed and Purified. The appeal for a holy life is enforced by considering the great cost of our redemption and the great hope which is opened before us. Ours must be the girded loins, lest our desires trail after forbidden things or be sullied by the mud on the road. We must be holy, as God is; and this can be realized only when we allow God, by his Holy Spirit, to pour himself into our natures.

There is no fear like that which love begets. We do not fear God with the fear of the slave or felon, but with the fear of the love that cannot endure the thought of giving pain to the loving and loved. Who can think of returning to Egypt when such a Passover lamb has redeemed us! Our redemption was not an afterthought with God. It is part of an eternal plan; let us not get entangled in the meshes of mere earthly ambition. Notice the familiar combination of faith, hope and love, vv. 21, 22. But these graces are only indigenous in those who have been twice-born by the Spirit through the Word.

1 PETER 2:1-10

Building on the Precious Cornerstone. It is easy to lay aside malice, guile, and evil speaking when we are constantly feeding on the unadulterated milk of spiritual truth. If you have tasted of the grace of Jesus, you will not want to sip of the wine of Sodom. Drink, O beloved, eat and drink abundantly, that we may grow, casting aside sinful and childish things.

The changing imagery of the next paragraph is remarkable. As we touch the Living Stone we live, and we touch others who are touching him, and so a temple begins to grow up. Then we become a holy priesthood in the temple, and finally the sacrifices which are offered within its precincts. If Christ is not that Living Stone for you, he will be your undoing.

All that God said of his ancient people may be realized by us in and through Christ. Compare v. 9 with Exod. 19:6. Thus songs of praise are ever ascending to him who has called us into his light.

1 PETER 2:11-17

The Christian Pilgrim's Walk. Strong desires must be kept under the stronger hand of the Christian soul—not extirpated, but turned into right directions as God's Providence points the way. Our desires ultimately rule our prayers and our life. We must therefore keep them above all else, for out of the heart are the issues of life. "Cleanse thou the thoughts of our heart by the inspiration of thy Holy Spirit, that we may perfectly love thee." God does not wish the extirpation of any element of our nature, but its consecration. We must not allow wrong things, and we must not allow the abuse or excess of right ones. The silent witness of a holy life or a well-ordered home is of incalculable worth. Oh, that people in contact with us may turn from us to glorify God! See v. 12.

Though we do not belong to this world, but are passing through it to our home, we should show ourselves willing to conform to the institutions and customs of the world around us, so far as we can do so without injury to conscience or betrayal of the rights of Christ.

1 PETER 2:18-25

Following the Shepherd of Souls. The argument from this point seems to be: Since you have been redeemed, live worthily of your heavenly calling in relation to your fellow-believers, to God, and to the state, v. 17; to your employers, v. 18; to husbands, 3:1; to wives, v. 7; to everyone, v. 8.

Some of the tenderest words in the epistles are addressed to household slaves, who constituted a very important part of the primitive Church. Masters and mistresses had absolute control over their chattels, and could put them to death without interference from the state. The apostle endeavors to cheer them while bearing their nameless wrongs. They were to bear all their sorrows patiently and silently, following in the footsteps of their Lord, certain that he would vindicate them.

Let employees remember that they have been placed as lamps on dark landings, in order to bear witness to Jesus by the simplicity and beauty of their conversation. The way of the cross is the only safe way for us all, if we would keep in touch with our Shepherd and Protector.

1 PETER 3:1-12

Christian Family Life. In the previous chapter the apostle had been urging the poor slaves of wealthy householders to submit quietly to wrongs, leaving God to vindicate. Here he turns to the wives of unbelieving husbands, showing that their chaste behavior, their meek and quiet spirit, their pleasant subordination of self are the greatest arguments for our religion. What we are is more important than what we say. Our life is our best sermon. If we would expend as much care on the hidden man of the heart as many do on the outer, what lovely characters would result! When Massillon had preached on this subject of the inner and outer man before Louis XIV, the king exclaimed as he left the church, "I know those two men!"

The same temper becomes us all. Let us be compassionate to the faults of others, even when they repay our good with evil and revile our blessing. God sends rain and sun irrespective of the character of the recipients. In this way we shall inherit the blessedness to which we have been called and see good days.

1 PETER 3:13-22

Following Christ in Bearing Injustice. It was said of Archbishop Cranmer that the way to make him a lifelong friend was to do him some disservice, and surely these words of the apostle have created many characters of the same type. The one aim and purpose of life should be to sanctify Christ as Lord; that is, to put him on the throne. Let all the powers of our nature stand around to do his bidding, as the courtiers of a royal sovereign.

Keep a good conscience! Remember you have to live with yourself! A good conscience is the best bedfellow! Paul exercised himself always to have a conscience void of offense toward God and man, Acts 23:1; 24:16. This is especially necessary when we are called on to give our witness for our Lord. We must not keep silent when we ought to speak, and when we speak we should do so reverently, simply, and without heat.

Our Lord seems to have carried the news of redemption through the world of disembodied spirits. The apostle compares baptism to the Deluge, because it lies between the believer and his old worldly life as Noah's Flood lay between the old world and the new which emerged from its waters.

1 PETER 4:1-11

The New Life in Christ. The apostle urges the disciples to make a clean break with sin. As our Lord's grave lay between him and his earlier life, so there should be a clean break between our life as believers and the earthbound life which was dominated by lawless passions. Sometimes God employs the acid of persecution or suffering to eat away the bonds that bind us to our past. Let us accept these with a willing mind. The one condition of reigning with the enthroned Christ is to submit to his cross. Of course, we must die to animal instinct, to the blandishments of the world, and to the temptations of the evil one; but it is quite as important to die to our self-life, whether it be clothed in white or black!

We are summoned to a life of prayer. But in order to promote fervency in prayer we must be sober-minded and self-controlled, v. 7; loving, v. 8; and faithful to our stewardship of all God's entrusted gifts, v. 10. Let us cultivate the invariable habit of looking up from our service, of whatever kind, to claim the ability to do it for the glory of God, v. 11.

1 PETER 4:12-19

Suffering as a Christian. We are called upon to share our Savior's sufferings—not those of his substitution, but his daily self-denial, the hatred of men, the anguish of his soul over the obstinacy and opposition of the world. The soldier who is nearest his leader, charging through the mêlée of the fight, is likely to get the same treatment as is meted out to his prince. It is not strange! It would be strange if it were not so, and if the traits in us that characterize our Lord did not win the same hatred they won for him.

The salvation of the righteous is a task of enormous difficulty. It requires Omnipotence. Nothing less will suffice than the infinite grace of the Father, the blood of the Son, and the patience of the Holy Spirit. What will be the fate of those who refuse these! Will they appear at the marriage-supper of the Lamb; and if not—where? What a beautiful closing verse! The committal of the soul, not only to the Savior, but to the "Creator." After all, he who made can best understand, adjust, and satisfy the nature which he himself has given!

1 PETER 5:1-7

Serving One Another. According to these words Peter, though he stood at a distance, must have been an eyewitness of the Savior's death. He is careful to speak of the "glory" in the same breath as the "sufferings," because if we endure the one we shall share the other. Positions of influence in the Church in those days involved grave risks, but the apostle believed that love to Christ would induce men to take the place of under-shepherds to the flock of God, and that they would use their power with gentleness, humility, and holy consistency.

The younger men may include the deacons, but the "all," v. 5, refers to the entire membership. They were to gird on humility as a slave his towel, that they might serve one another, John 13:4. Those who humble themselves in the profoundest loyalty toward God stand as rocks before their fellows. Remember Luther's "Here I stand, I can do no other." You cannot say, "Nobody cares what becomes of me." God cares, and with an infinite tenderness. He cared before you cast your care on him! God is linked to your little life by his tender regard and care for you.

1 PETER 5:8-14

Resisting the Devil. We hear of the adversary in Zech. 3:1. The enemy of Christ desires to hurt the Shepherd by injuring his flock. The hunger of a lion for his prey is an emblem of the insatiable desire of our spiritual foes for our undoing. "Walketh about"—temptation never assails us long from the same quarter. Perhaps the figure of a roaring lion suggests an outburst of persecution, which made timid people tremble. See 2 Tim. 4:17.

All grace is in God for every hour and need, v. 10. We too are called to his eternal glory through Christ. The path of suffering, and that path alone, leads to the world where suffering is unknown. The suffering is only for a little while. "Perfect," that nothing be lacking; "stablish," that we may not waver; "strengthen," that we may stand and withstand.

Silvanus is Silas, v. 12. He was a man to be trusted. Peter's theme was grace. So he began, so he finishes; and from the church in the literal Babylon, or in Rome, Rev. 14:8, where he and Mark were living and working, he sends this message of grace and love and peace.

THE SECOND EPISTLE OF
PETER

FAITH'S CONFLICT AND VICTORY

SALUTATION   *1:1, 2.*

I. FAITH IMPLANTED   *1:3–11.*
   A. Partakers of the divine nature   *1:3–7.*
   B. The Christian's security   *1:8–11.*

II. FAITH QUICKENED   *1:12–21.*
   A. The cultivation of Christian memory   *1:12–15.*
   B. The twofold witness to Christ   *1:16–21.*

III. FAITH ASSAULTED   *2.*
   A. The invasion of unbelievers   *2:1–3.*
   B. Warnings from past judgments   *2:4–10.*
   C. Bond servants of corruption   *2:11–22.*

IV. FAITH VICTORIOUS   *3:1–13.*
   A. The answer to mockers   *3:1–9.*
   B. The new heavens and earth   *3:10–13.*

CONCLUSION   *3:14–18.*

INTRODUCTION

This epistle was addressed to the same persons or churches as the former one, 3:1. But years separate the two, and the aged apostle was expecting to be called upon to seal his witness with his blood, 1:14. His purpose in this dying charge is to caution the Christian community against the dangers which were insidiously at work among them, and were more to be feared than persecution from without. His great argument to this end is the near advent of our Lord.

The genuineness of this epistle has been questioned; but it is contained in the list of canonical books put forth by the Council of Carthage in A.D. 397. There is so strong an identity in the use of words between these two epistles, and the testimony of the writer as an eyewitness of the glory of the Transfiguration is so unmistakable, that we need entertain no doubt as to the justice of its position among the accepted Scriptures. Compare 1:16, 17 with 1 Pet. 5:1.

COMMENTARY

2 PETER 1:1-11

The Rule of Christian Growth. The keynote of this paragraph is "these things," vv. 8, 9, 10. "Precious faith," v. 1, answers to "precious promises," v. 4. Notice that God has given us every provision for a godly life through the knowledge of Jesus, but that we must avail ourselves of it. The promises are great and precious, but we must appropriate and absorb them, if we are through them to partake of the divine nature. Our redemption has been secured by our Savior, but we must constantly advance and add to the golden links already securely stapled in faith.

In vv. 5-7 a choir with linked hands passes before us, each member of which leads another; or we may use another similitude and say that each grace, here mentioned, is contained in the next, as a series of Chinese boxes. To be deficient in "these things" is to be barren and unfruitful, v. 8, and to be shortsighted, v. 9. We may well desire the abundant entrance, v. 11, not like waterlogged vessels, but with every sail unfurled—not landing on the celestial shore unexpected and unwanted, but welcomed by those we have helped.

2 PETER 1:12-21

"Eyewitnesses of His Majesty." Peter could never forget what the Master had predicted of the apostle's death. See John 21:18, 19. Oh, that in our death, whatever be its mode, we may glorify God! The fulfillment of those words was already looming before Peter's eyes, but he had no fear. He describes his homegoing by the word used by Moses and Elijah when they spoke of the "decease" (lit., "exodus") which the Lord would accomplish. Compare v. 15 with Luke 9:31.

Then the whole scene of the Transfiguration rose before his mind. It seemed as if he were again on the holy mount, beholding the majesty of the Lord and hearing the Father's attesting voice. There are three infallible proofs of Christianity: (1) the witness of the apostles; (2) the light of prophecy as fulfilled in Christ; (3) the testimony of the Holy Spirit. These three burn in the dark night of the present, and we may count on them till we see the first glimmer of dawn. Then we shall need no candle, for the Lord God will give us light.

2 PETER 2:1-11

Doom and Deliverance. Already the early Church was threatened with destructive heresies introduced by men who desired only their self-aggrandizement. All the apostles give warning against such and point to character as the one supreme test of doctrine. The real drift of the heresies is to deny the Master who bought us as slaves in the market of the world. Of all the bidders, there is none who has bidden so high as he.

Many instances are quoted from the past to prove the fearful judgments which must overtake such false teachers. The angels who placed their self-will in antagonism to their Maker were cast down to *tartarus*—a Greek word used only here in the New Testament. The people who lived previous to the Flood, and they who afterward at Sodom disregarded the laws of purity and self-restraint, dictated alike by Nature and conscience, were overwhelmed in destruction. But even amid such judgments, God discriminates his Noahs and his Lots, preserves and delivers them, and numbers them among his jewels, Mal. 3:17. God has his eye on you and will succor you.

2 PETER 2:12–22

The Dark Way of Animalism. The description of these false teachers is terrific! They are slaves to their brute instincts. They are as abusive as they are ignorant. They destroy and will be destroyed. They feast daintily in the broad daylight, instead of leading abstemious and sober lives. With them, the very church feasts were occasions for self-indulgence. Their eyes never ceased from the sin against which the Lord warns us in Matt. 5:28. Balaam is an awful example of such, torn as he was between the celestial vision of his spirit and the sensual appetite of his soul.

The will of man, as in Balaam's case, is always poising itself between its knowledge of good and evil and its strong bias toward evil. Only the help of God can correct this. Let us "who are just escaping," v. 18, alternate translation, from the meshes of the world beware lest we be caught in the guiles and nets of false teaching, which would drag us back into the evils of the worldly life. It is in our heartfelt union with the Lord Jesus Christ alone that we can be permanently secure.

2 PETER 3:1–9

Longsuffering Delay. Peter does not hesitate to place the commandments of himself and the other apostles of Jesus on a level with "the words which were spoken before by the holy prophets," and he repeats his admonitions because of the urgency of the crisis then threatening the Church. Apparently there was a well-grounded fear that she would relax her attitude of expectancy and give credence to the materialistic philosophy of the age.

Men argued then from the appearances of things, and especially from the regular routine of cause and effect. They did not realize that from time to time there had been the intrusion of the divine personal will into the course of history, introducing a higher set of laws and arresting the ordinary succession of events; as for instance, the Flood and the miracles of Old Testament history. Why, then, should not the ordinary course of Nature be broken in upon by the Second Advent, when the Lord shall gather his saints about him and reign gloriously? What God has done, he can do again! There is a Person and a will behind the slight veil of the present life.

2 PETER 3:10–18

Holy Living and Godliness. How quickly the great European convulsion broke upon the world in the summer of 1914! Who expected such a sudden burst of the great storm! Such vast changes in the history of mankind point somewhat to the coming of "new heavens and a new earth," as mentioned in v. 13. The condition of the world calls on each of us to be holy, as the virgins in their pure dresses, with burning and well-filled lamps. See Matt. 25:1–13. This is the manner in which we may hasten the coming of the day of God. It is not enough to say, "Thy kingdom come." Each day we should move some pebble from its pathway!

In twenty-four hours God can do as much as all his servants at home and abroad could not accomplish in a thousand years. According to God's chronology, it was on the morning of yesterday that Jesus died. Be watchful. Christ's coming is certain, but not the hour. If we are blameless now, we shall be faultless presently. See Jude 24.

THE EPISTLES OF
JOHN

THE REDEEMING LOVE OF GOD IN CHRIST

INTRODUCTION *1:1–4.*
I. THE CHARACTER OF GOD REVEALED IN CHRIST *1:5—2:6.*
II. THE NEW COMMANDMENT *2:7–28.*
III. DIVINE SONSHIP TESTED BY LOVE *2:29—3:18.*
IV. THE GROUND OF ASSURANCE *3:19—4:6.*
V. "GOD IS LOVE" *4:7–21.*
VI. THE THREEFOLD WITNESS *5:1–12.*
CONCLUSION *5:13–21.*

Note: Because of their brevity, no outlines are included for 2 and 3 John.

INTRODUCTION

In addition to the Gospel, three epistles have come to us from the pen of the beloved apostle. Of these the first is the longest and most important. In form it is more like an essay or treatise than a letter; it bears no saluation nor signature. But if there were no other evidence, its similarity in phrase and thought to the fourth Gospel would decide the question of authorship. Whichever was written first, the relation between the two is perfectly clear and has been aptly expressed by Bishop Westcott: "The theme of the epistle is, the Christ is Jesus; the theme of the Gospel is, Jesus is the Christ." The bearing of the epistle upon practical living is also very plain. It shows that fellowship with the Father and the Son is realized in love of the brethren.

The second and third epistles are very brief, and are private and personal rather than doctrinal. They have been called by Jerome "twin sisters." In style and spirit, they markedly resemble the first epistle. There is the same emphasis upon love, truth, and obedience. While we are without exact information as to their date, they rank unquestionably among the latest documents in the New Testament.

COMMENTARY

1 JOHN 1:1-10

Fellowship in the Light. As the aged apostle began to write, he was living over again his first happy experiences with the Savior. He heard the voice, saw the Person, touched the very body in which Deity tabernacled. It was too great a bliss to be enjoyed alone, and John tells us that we may enter into the same close partnership with the Father and the Son. But no impurity or insincerity is permissible to those who enter that fellowship. Our one aim should be to maintain such a walk with God that union with God may be unimpaired. If there are still sins of ignorance, the blood of Jesus will continue to remove them. "Sin" differs from "sins," as the root from the fruit. God does not only forgive; he cleanses. He is faithful to his promises and just to his Son. Notice the "ifs" of these verses and in 2:1; they are a compendium of the blessed life.

1 JOHN 2:1-11

Keeping His Commandment of Love. It is clearly possible to be kept from known and presumptuous sin. We shall be tempted, for that is an inevitable experience of life in this world; but we may be perfectly kept by the indwelling Spirit. Yet if we should be overtaken by some sudden gust of temptation, let us not despair; our Advocate ever makes intercession for us. The evidence that we have a saving knowledge of our Savior is obtained, not by the memory of a rapturous experience, but because we are conscious of doing, for his sake, things which we should otherwise evade. Let us continue to do such things, because by the path of patient obedience we shall enter into the Paradise of perfect love. The outer walk is the best evidence to ourselves and others that there is an abiding union between us and Jesus. Light involves love; and love, light. Love and you are in light. Indulge hatred or ill will and you begin to grope in darkness.

1 JOHN 2:12-17

Transient Desires, Abiding Life. There are gradations in Christian experience—the child, the father, the young man. The note of the child is the glad sense of forgiveness; of the father, a deep knowledge of God; of the young man, victory over the power of evil. With all these is growth. The child, through forgiveness, also comes to know the Father; the fathers can only go on to know God more profoundly; and as the young men become stronger, they are more aware of the indwelling Spirit of power.

Distinguish between the world of Nature and the world of appearance, which is an illusion, the vain dream of human imaginings and boastings. It is the sphere of sense as contrasted with the sphere of spirit. It is the sum of all that the flesh lusts after, the eyes feast on, and the soul takes pride in. The Preacher gathers the world into one phrase, "under the sun," Eccles. 1:3. The world is passing as a movie, and the power to enjoy it is vanishing also. Only that which is rooted in God abides.

1 JOHN 2:18-29

Loyalty to Truth. The Holy One is surely the risen Savior, who has passed into the heavens, whence he bestows the Holy Spirit as a sacred chrism on meek and trustful souls. We can say with the psalmist, "Thou anointest my head with oil." Let us seek fresh anointings. "I shall be anointed with fresh oil," Ps. 92:10. Whenever we attempt to do God's work, we should be able to say, "The Spirit of the Lord is upon me, and he hath anointed me." The anointed soul understands things hidden from the wise and prudent, v. 27.

We must hold the Word of Christ by perpetual reiteration and meditation; only so shall we be able to abide in him. This abiding life involves not merely that we shall work for God, but that God will work through us. The abiding branch bears much fruit, because the energy of the vine is set free to work its will through its yielded channels. A life of abiding communion with Christ will never be ashamed in this or in any other world.

1 JOHN 3:1-12

The Marks of God's Children. This chapter opens with one of the astounding announcements of Scripture. Why God should have made *us* his children is incomprehensible, except to show forth the riches of his grace. See Eph. 2:7. That such we are is certain, but how marvelous! Yet even greater wonders await us, for we are to be like Jesus our Lord. He is the type to which we are being conformed, and on the other side we shall awake in his likeness.

"He is pure"; such is the verdict of one who lived in the closest possible association with him. We cannot think of Christ, or of the future to be spent with him, without desiring purity above all. Ask him to become in thee the fountain of purity! If he is thy constant study, the quality of his character will become thine. Presumptuous sin is impossible under such conditions. He will destroy the works of the devil in the individual and in the universe. That we are God's own children is proved by our integrity and love. They are the hallmark of God's ownership.

1 JOHN 3:13-24

Loving in Deed and in Truth. Love to the brethren is a sign that we have been born into the family. We may not *like* them all, yet we can *love* them. If we love, we live; and if we live in the deepest sense, we shall love. That is, we shall put others first, and our care for them will be tinged with the crimson of sacrifice. Love is not measured by the expressions of the lip or the emotion of the heart, but by the extent to which we will do or suffer.

The believer dares not affirm too much about himself, he is so unworthy and fickle; but God understands us and imputes to us what we would be. Mark in v. 22 the double condition of prevailing prayer. It is also clear from v. 23 that men can believe, if they will. God is prepared to impart to those who are wishful all that he commands. Augustine prayed thus: "Give what thou commandest, and command what thou wilt."

1 JOHN 4:1-11

The Token of God's Love. In those days the intense ferment of men's minds wrought many delusions and heresies which were fraught with temptation to young converts, and the apostle wished to give tests for determining which voice spoke from God. The confession of Jesus Christ as the Incarnate Word, a spirit of love and gentleness, and the willingness to abide in the doctrine of the apostles were signs that the speaker was commissioned by Christ.

Wouldst thou overcome the world? Let Christ enter, and the world will have no charms for thee. There is only one source of pure, divine love, and wherever that love is present you know that the possessor has found its source in God. God's love is absolutely selfless. He loves the unloving to make them love, putting away their sin and perfecting their union with himself.

1 JOHN 4:12-21

The Test of Our Love. If we are willing to be channels through which God's love flows to others, there need be no limit to the fullness of that holy current. In humility, selflessness, and gentleness it will become perfected. The vessel placed beneath the waterfall is filled to overflowing.

Through our Savior we know the Father who sent him, v. 14. See John 14:9, 10. We first venture on God's love by faith; afterward we know it. Dare to affirm that God is love. Love is the wafted fragrance of Paradise. If thou lovest, Heaven and earth will answer thee in terms of love. By strong, patient, selfless love thou wilt abide in unbroken touch with all pure and loving souls—whoever and wherever. Where love was crucified, there was a garden. Where there is love, lonely places blossom as the rose. Be not afraid! Love on! Love always! "This is the true God, and eternal life." But one thought of hatred or ill will will cause thy wholly happy experience to vanish.

1 JOHN 5:1-12

The Victorious Life. The "begotten" children of God are constantly referred to in this epistle. The word indicates the communication, in regeneration, of the divine nature, of which the first evidence is love. This love is not a weak sentimentality, but a strong, vigorous response to the motions of the divine love.

God's life in the soul also manifests itself in our faith; and as faith is the substance of the unseen and eternal world, it overcomes the fascination and glamor of this transient scene. Let your faith entwine around the risen Lord and you will be weaned from all else. Jesus must become all-in-all to you, else you will miss the crown!

We need not only the water of repentance, but also the blood of propitiation. When these two are admitted, the Holy Spirit will bear his secret witness to the soul. God is ever bearing witness to the Son by the eternal life that he gives to and maintains in those who believe. Eternity begins even here for those who have the Son as their indwelling guest.

1 JOHN 5:13-21

Ask According to His Will. We know that we have eternal life. The rope is in our hand bearing us onward, but its ends are hidden from view in the past and in the future. We also know that God hears us when we comply with the conditions of true prayer. We know, moreover, that we can become the medium through which the life of God passes to others. Thus the humblest child may have power with God and man.

The Only-Begotten keeps the begotten. Evil can no more touch them than blight could reach the bush in the wilderness that was bathed in the celestial fire. Who would go back to the world? Enumerate and press to heart these four items of positive knowledge; but beware lest what is legitimate and natural in itself may become an idol. Love, knowledge, abiding, conquering—these are the keynotes of this wonderful letter.

2 JOHN 1-13

Walking in Truth. This exquisite letter, a model of old-world correspondence, was probably written when the apostle was the guest of the nephews of the lady addressed. The epistle revolves around the two words "love" and "truth," which were the poles of his life. When Christ is in us, not only are we true in judgment and speech, but we recognize truth wherever it is to be found. No horizon bounds the vision of the true and truth-loving soul. Be true and loving, and you will have a rich heritage of grace, mercy, and peace. Love is best shown by obedience. Verse 8 shows a pastor's anxiety. Go on without Christ and you don't have God, v. 9. Remember that love can be stern, v. 10.

The letter reveals the strength, purity, and love of the primitive Church. Let us put into our letters thoughts which will make them worth receiving and keeping.

3 JOHN 1-14

The Apostle's Joy. Again we meet the words "love" and "truth." Transparency of speech and life is an essential condition of soul health. It would not be desirable to express the wish of v. 2 to all our friends, because if their bodies were to correspond to the condition of their souls they would suddenly fall into ill health. In an old legend, mirrors were blurred with mist when any approached who were out of harmony with truth, v. 4.

The Christian must always act worthily of God, especially toward strangers, vv. 5, 6. "For his name's sake," v. 7—as children we must maintain the family honor. Such hospitality makes us fellow-workers with the truth. There is a Boanergic touch in v. 10. The threefold witness to Demetrius should stir our desire to emulate his character. What will it not be when the dimness of earthly converse is exchanged for the face-to-face intercourse of eternity, v. 14.

THE EPISTLE OF
JUDE

"EARNESTLY CONTEND FOR THE FAITH,"
v. 3

SALUTATION   *1, 2.*
I. WARNING AGAINST TRAITORS   *3, 4.*
II. DEPRAVITY AND DOOM OF THE UNGODLY   *5–16.*
III. THE FAITH AND HOPE OF THE CHRISTIAN   *17–22.*
CONCLUSION   *24, 25.*

INTRODUCTION

The James mentioned in v. 1 is almost certainly the brother of our Lord, who was the well-known and universally revered leader of the mother church at Jerusalem and the writer of the epistle that bears his name. Jude, therefore, was also related to our Lord as brother; see Matt. 13:55; Mark 6:3. These two were probably with the apostles after the ascension, and finally engaged in evangelistic efforts. See Acts 1:14; 1 Cor. 9:5.

We have no certain information concerning him, but Eusebius states that when Domitian ordered all the posterity of David to be slain, "some of the heretics accused the descendants of Jude, as the brother of our Savior according to the flesh, because they were of the family of David, and as such were also related to Christ." It appears from the historian's subsequent statement that these people made a good confession before their persecutors.

The epistle was probably addressed to churches east of Judea, among whom Jude had labored, and was probably written about A.D. 66. There are remarkable similarities between this epistle and 2 Peter, indicating close communication between the two writers as they looked out on the heretical teachers of the age and the low state of prevailing morals.

COMMENTARY

JUDE 1-11

"Earnestly Contend for the Faith." "Kept" or its equivalent is the keynote of this epistle. It occurs in vv. 1, 6, 21, 24. Many evil doctrines and practices were intruding into the Church. Certain persons had crept in, who quoted the mercy of God as an excuse for immorality and practically disowned the teachings of the Lord Jesus.

In contrast with these were the disciples whom Jude addresses and who owned the Lord Jesus as their beloved "Despot," v. 4, R.V. They were kept for him, as the others were kept in chains. Let us also keep ourselves in the love of God, v. 21. It is much easier to live consistently in hours of storm than in hours of ease.

Let us be warned against drifting back from our first faith. Let us take heed from the fate of fallen angels, of Sodom and Gomorrah, of Cain and Balaam, of Korah and others. Let us watch and pray and "earnestly contend for the faith which was once delivered unto the saints," v. 3, bearing it through the world as the pilgrim host bore the sacred vessels in the days of Ezra. See Ezra 8:28.

JUDE 12-25

Beware of the Touch of the Ungodly. What traps and pitfalls beset us! How many have fallen who had as good or a better chance than we! The angels kept not their first estate; Adam, though created in innocency, fell; Cain was rejected; Balaam, who saw with open eyes, was slain; Korah, who had carried a censer filled with holy fire, was hurled into the abyss! How can *we* expect to stand! Be of good cheer! He "is able to keep you from falling, and to present you faultless," v. 24.

In the succession of terrible metaphors in vv. 12 and 13, notice that in each case there is promise without fulfillment and appearance without reality. Such is much of the Christian profession of the present day. And from time to time, as Enoch foretold, the day of the Lord comes, with its retribution for all such.

The four exquisite admonitions of vv. 20 and 21 are worth pondering. Keep yourselves in the main current of God's love. Build your character after the likeness of Christ. Pray in the Holy Spirit; keep at the oriel window of hope. Christ is able to keep, and when at last we are presented by him to the Father, we shall realize how much we owe him.

THE BOOK OF
THE REVELATION
THE FINAL CONSUMMATION

INTRODUCTION *1.*
I. THE MESSAGES TO THE SEVEN CHURCHES *2, 3.*
II. THE PERIOD OF STRUGGLE AND SUFFERING *4—7.*
    A. The throne in Heaven *4.*
    B. The book with seven seals *5.*
    C. The opening of the seven seals *6.*
    D. The sealing of the 144,000 *7.*
III. THE MESSIANIC CONFLICT *8—14.*
    A. The seven angels with trumpets *8—11.*
    B. The woman and the dragon *12.*
    C. The two beasts *13.*
    D. The heavenly proclamations *14.*
IV. THE MESSIANIC VICTORY *15—20.*
    A. The song of Moses and the Lamb *15.*
    B. The seven bowls of wrath *16.*
    C. The fall of Babylon *17:1—19:10.*
    D. The last judgment *19:11—20:15.*
V. THE MESSIANIC KINGDOM *21:1—22:5.*
CONCLUSION *22:6–21.*

INTRODUCTION

The book of Revelation completes the sacred canon. It sets forth in vivid figures the struggles and sufferings that precede the manifestation of "new heavens and a new earth, wherein dwelleth righteousness," 2 Pet. 3:13. The unveilings of the future which it contains were given to the beloved apostle on the island of Patmos, whither he had been banished by the Emperor Domitian in A.D. 94 or 95. The followers of Christ in those days were exposed to severe sufferings, and nothing could be more appropriate to their circumstances than this book, which is filled with consolation for those who are fighting the Lord's battles. Victory may be delayed, but it is sure.

To every believer this book is especially valuable, because it gives a view of our Lord's life on the other side of death, where he acts as Priest and is preparing to rule as King. His temporary subjection to death and his victory over it, his omnipotence and universal dominion, his reception of the adoration which his holy apostles refuse—these are the thoughts that are conveyed in the richest and most striking imagery.

Though many details of the book are difficult of interpretation its main teachings are perfectly clear, and some of its chapters rank among the greatest of all Scripture.

COMMENTARY

REVELATION 1:1–8

The Revelation of Jesus Christ. In his capacity as mediator, our Lord receives from the Father and transmits to his servants, that they may in turn transmit to the world of men, the great panorama of the future, known to him from before the foundation of the world. Let us not miss the special benediction which is attached to the patient reading and consideration of this wonderful book.

The seven churches represent the one Church under different phases and possibly in successive stages of its history; the letters addressed to them are therefore universally applicable. Notice the august reference to the Holy Trinity—the eternal Father, the sevenfold Spirit, and our Lord. Our Lord bore a faithful witness even to death; that death was a birth into the risen life, as ours may be. All kings are his vassals.

How wonderful it is to be told in the next verse that he loves us, and has not only washed, but loosed us. "He breaks the power of canceled sin." Jesus often comes with clouds. We cannot understand his dealings with us, yet those clouds are gold with his light. So he shall come at last. As Alpha he begins, but he never begins without carrying into full effect his purpose as our Omega.

REVELATION 1:9–20

From the Living Lord to the Churches. The tribulation and patience of Jesus are essential conditions of his kingdom. We cannot exert the divine energies of the latter unless we are willing to take our share of the former. There should be no Lord's day without our definite claim to be "in the Spirit"; and if we are "in the Spirit," every day is a day of the Lord. The seven churches are distinct in their several characteristics, but one in their blended light. Here is variety, but unity. Jesus was "in the midst" on the cross; he is "in the midst" where two or three are gathered; he is the Lamb "in the midst of the throne"; but he is also "in the midst" of the collective life of the Church in her earthly ministry and warfare.

The manifestation of his glory may overwhelm our mortality, but the touch of his pierced hand encourages the soul. His favorite assurance is, "Fear not." Here is life in its threefold aspect! In its original source, first and last. In its triumph over death—"I was dead." In its eternal reign—"I am alive for evermore." The things which John had seen are probably described in this chapter, "the things which are" in chapters 2 and 3, and the things which are to come to pass in the remainder of this book.

REVELATION 2:1-7

Renew Thy First Love. Each of these letters consists of three parts: (1) The introduction, specifying some characteristic from the vision of the preceding chapter which is appropriate to the need of the church addressed; (2) a description of the condition of the church; (3) a promise to the overcomer, following the successive revelations of God in the Old Testament, which begin with the tree of life and include the manna, the conquest of Canaan, the glory of the Temple, and the reign of Solomon.

We may go far in outward activity for the cause of the Redeemer and yet be threatened with the removal of our candlestick. We may be full of labor, opposed to wicked men and false teachers, persistently orthodox, not fainting in the day of trial; and yet, if love be wanting, nothing can compensate. Is the complaint true of us, that we have lost our first love? The exuberance of its emotion may have passed with the years, but has it been replaced by a deep, all-constraining, and masterful devotion to our Lord? It is the Spirit's prerogative to shed abroad his love in our hearts and to teach us to love him. But none of us can acquire that love without perpetually feeding on the tree of life, which is the emblem of himself, Gen. 2:9; Rev. 22:2, 14, 19.

REVELATION 2:8-11

"Be Thou Faithful unto Death." This epistle has a new pathos and significance if we connect it with "the blessed Polycarp," who almost certainly was the angel or chief minister of the church in Smyrna. He was the disciple of John. Irenaeus, who lived a generation later, tells how in early boyhood he had heard from the lips of Polycarp what John had told him of our Lord's Person, converse, and earthly ministry.

How sweet the comfort of this epistle must have been to him in the closing scene of his life, when at eighty-six he was sentenced to be burned! Notice how every line of it had a message for him, as for all who are called to follow in his steps. The Savior reminded him that beyond the suffering of this brief life a crown awaited him, which would abundantly reward his fidelity.

What music there is in those inspiring words! Even Peter's crown of glory and Paul's crown of righteousness seem to fade in comparison with this "crown of life." The thought of it enabled Polycarp to say at the stake, "I give thee hearty thanks that thou hast brought me to this hour, that I may have my part in the cup of thy Christ, unto the resurrection of eternal life, through the operation of thy Holy Spirit."

REVELATION 2:12-17

Beware of Evil Teachers. Notice the Lord's commendation of the church at Pergamos (from which we get our word "parchment"). He recognizes their peculiar dangers and their difficulties—"where Satan's seat is." It was an honorable thing to have held fast Christ's name under such circumstances. To hold fast his name is to be loyal to him in all circumstances. Not to deny his faith is to hold fast to the essential facts and doctrines of primitive Christianity, undeterred by the blandishments or threats of the world.

For the doctrine of Balaam, we must turn to Numbers 22—24, and then specially to 25:1 and 31:16. Balaam had failed to curse, but though he had thereby forfeited his prestige and payment, he won them back by advising Balak to corrupt the morals of Israel and so break their union with Jehovah. The Nicolaitans apparently promulgated similar tenets, and in their proud and wealthy city were prepared to admit orthodoxy of doctrine so long as it was combined with laxity of morals. But Christ cannot for a moment tolerate such a conjunction. His judgment sword must vindicate the purity of his Church.

REVELATION 2:18-29

"Hold Fast Till I Come." Note that Jesus does not hesitate to appropriate the sublime title, "the Son of God." His eyes penetrate profoundest secrets, and his advent leaves a trail of purity like fire behind him. He recognizes the many good qualities of his church at Thyatira, but accuses her of having raised no protest against the woman Jezebel. She had actually permitted the promulgation of soul-destroying error, with most disastrous results.

This Jezebel apparently taught that there were deep philosophies in the heathen system around them, and the result was that the professing servants of Christ were led into complicity with the outward corruption of heathendom. An evident attempt was being made to graft on to Christianity the mysteries of darkness, which were in direct antagonism to the purity of the teachings of Christ.

Notice the contrast between *her* works and "my works," vv. 22 and 26. The saints who are true to Christ shall be associated with him in his kingdom, but best of all they are made to possess the "morning star"; that is, they now stand with their Lord in the dawn of a new era.

Already the day has dawned and the day star has risen in their hearts, 2 Pet. 1:19.

REVELATION 3:1-6

"Strengthen the Things Which Remain." In other addresses to the churches our Lord began with commendation, but no such word is here. *He is* described in the fulness of his glorious nature, but *this church* is full of unfulfilled works. What a striking phrase and how true! We begin and do not finish, skirt the edges but do not penetrate to the heart, are superficial and fragmentary. How few can say with the Master, "I have finished the work"; and of how few it can be said, as by Paul of the Baptist, he "fulfilled his course," Acts 13:25.

There are four evidences of spiritual life. In a living church there will be growth, compassion, unity, and love; and the Lord missed all these and bitterly lamented their absence. Of what use was the fig tree to abate his hunger, when it bore leaves but no fruit? Amid all this disappointing formalism, there were a few live souls who fulfilled their works and did not defile their robes. Does not this suggest the Transfiguration? On the holy mount, the plain garments of Jesus shone with light; and so the inner purity of the saint shines through and glorifies his simplest acts. The holiness we love in this life shall be rewarded by the white robes, Christ's acknowledgment, and the deeds of heavenly citizenship.

REVELATION 3:7-13

Let No One Take Thy Crown. For those who have but a little strength, the Lord sets open a wide door. You may not be able to open the door, but you can enter it in his name. Once he opens the door, all the opposition you may be called upon to encounter will not avail to shut it; and if he shuts the door against your adversaries, all their craft and strength will beat against its exterior in vain. Get Christ to shut the door against the tempting thoughts that would allure you from your allegiance. His beloved may be sorely beset, but he will keep them in the hour of trial. They shall not miss their crown, but shall become permanent and important constitutents in the eternal Temple. We have often noticed the strength and stability of a pillar in an old church. It has looked unmoved on generations that have grown from youth to age at its base, and so shall Christ's saints endure.

It is marvelous how much Christ can make of our poor lives, if only we yield to him. It was said of a great statesman recently deceased, "He was a resounding example of what a great thing a great man may make of a life." But how much greater can Christ make a life, once a mere block of stone, but now inscribed with his own mystic handwriting and engraving!

REVELATION 3:14-22

"I Stand at the Door, and Knock." It is better to be cold than lukewarm, for in the latter case all that God's love can do for the soul has only produced a moderate result, while if we are cold our soul has yet to be tried. The gospel has a better chance with the openly profane and godless than with those who have been brought up under its influence and are so far unaffected. The mischief with men generally is that they do not know themselves, and do not want to know; and they are equally ignorant of the rich stores of blessedness that Christ waits to bestow. We think that we abound in gift and grace, when in Christ's eyes we are most pitiable. Yet, at this moment he is standing at the door, laden with the gifts of Heaven. Admit him, or at least lift the latch of the will, so that he may push the door back and enter. Do not attempt to deal with the squalor within; he will see to that, and cleanse, keep, and enrich. Do not try to provide supper; he will bring thee his own flesh and blood.

Ponder that last beatitude, which promises to all believers that if they share with him his age-long conflict against the evil of the world, they shall share his rule and power, which they shall use with him for the uplift and blessing of mankind. Complete and continually renewed self-surrender to Christ will admit into our hearts the royalty and power of Christ.

REVELATION 4:1-11

"A Throne Set in Heaven." The vision of the ascended Lord introduced the seven letters to the churches; so the visions of this and the next chapters introduce the seven seals. There is no form for the Divine Being. God is Spirit, and his glory can only be hinted at by appropriate imagery. His being should excite emotions in our spirit similar to those which these objects excite in our mind. The jasper with its transparent brilliance, the sardine or cornetian with its fiery red, the emerald with its refreshing beauty are laid to describe what cannot be described. The throne bespeaks majestic authority and power. The worship of the elders reflects that of Israel and the Church, 21:12, 14; the thunder, God's awful holiness; the seven lamps, the searching, cleansing purity of his Spirit; the glassy sea, the mystery of his ways;

the four living creatures, the homage of creation.

Here is the song of creation, v. 11. Originally all things did the will of God, and if creation is now subject to vanity, some day it will be delivered into the glorious liberty of the sons of God, and God's will will be done on earth as it is in Heaven. Notice that the will of God brought all things into existence, and that that will guarantees their ultimate redemption.

REVELATION 5:1-8

The Book with Seven Seals. This "book" is a roll of papyrus or parchment, written on each side to prevent unauthorized additions. Probably it contains the history of the successive steps to be taken to win the empire of the world for Christ. In other words, it tells of the successive stages of the coming of the kingdom of God. As the seals are opened, certain phenomena occur which in part reveal the mysteries hidden in the book, but the whole is in the hand of the Lamb of God. He alone knows the contents; he alone presides over their development. We must not weep because the future is unknown. "Jesus we know, and he is on the throne." We must trust our own future to Christ without fear or tears of foreboding. The Lamb who shed his blood to redeem may be trusted to order and perfect that which concerneth us.

What contrasts presented themselves! The apostle looked for a lion, and behold, a Lamb; for One who had overcome, and instead, One who had the appearance of having been slain; for One who had the majesty of a king, and instead, the emblem of humility. But in the Lamb were the seven horns of perfect power, seven eyes of perfect wisdom, and seven spirits traversing the world, denoting omnipresence. What homage can be offered worthy of this combination of Redeemer and Creator?

REVELATION 5:9-14

The One Worthy to Open It. Jesus is worthy to unroll the mystic scroll of history, because he loved and loves our race as no other has ever done; and he is equally worthy to open each new phase of our lives. When he came into the world he said, "In the volume of the book it is written of me." We need not fear those pierced hands. If we are his purchased property, he will provide for us. If we are priests and kings in his ideal, we may trust him so to arrange our life-plan as to secure the best exercise of those sacred functions.

Notice how the out-circling song of the redeemed reaches out in further and yet further response. It begins with the little group around the throne; then it spreads to the angels in their myriads; and thence it is borne forward and outward in concentric rings until the utmost shores of space are struck by the billows of song and it reverberates back to the living creatures and the elders. Heaven is full of the sacrificial side of our Savior's death. The heavenly beings describe themselves as his purchased people and stand closer to Christ than the angels.

REVELATION 6:1-8

The Riders on the Four Horses. The seals signify those events which prepare the way for the coming of the kingdom. The opening of the first seals is accompanied by the summons of one of the living creatures to the glorified Lord to hasten his advent. Come, glorious Redeemer, and bring about the wondrous consummation for which thy bride is waiting. The white horse signifies the victorious progress of the gospel; the red, war and its bloodshed; the black, scarcity and want; the pale or livid, pestilence and death. Compare with Ezek. 14:21 and Matt. 24:6-14. "Thus good and bad their several warnings give of his approach, whom none can see and live. Faith's ear, with awful, still delight, counts them as minute bells at night."

Many lines of interpretation have been adopted for these and the following mysterious utterances of this book. We shall not go into these questions, but present the main spiritual lessons which are generally accepted. That treasure is buried here none can deny; and the perpetual turning over of these sods to discover it has greatly enriched the Church.

REVELATION 6:9-17

"The Wrath of the Lamb." This imagery is very majestic; but we cannot really think that the holy martyrs desire to be revenged, except in love and grace. That their persecutors should be forgiven in Pentecosts of revival must be the highest conception of vengeance that they permit themselves to have. The striking command that they should rest, each enclothed in a white robe of acceptance and purity, until the full roll of martyrs is complete suggests that every age must yield its tale of those who love not their lives unto the death, because they love the Master so much more. We, too, have our daily martyrdoms, for it may be harder to live for Jesus always against continued opposition and scorn than to die once for him.

Verses 9 and 10 answer to Matt. 24:6, 7, verses 12 and 17 to Matt. 24:29, 30. Probably the words here refer, not to the final judgment, but to

REVELATION

those revolutionary changes which always accompany the closing of one era and the opening of another. See Heb. 12:26, 27.

REVELATION 7:1-10

The Multitude before the Throne. Before times of unusual trial God prepares for the safety of his people. See Gen. 7:1; 19:16; Exod. 12:13; Ezek. 9:3-5; Matt. 24:15, 16. What a majestic conception this is and how comforting the thought that the winds are controlled by angels, and that the storms which sweep earth and Heaven must obey the mandate of eternal love! God's people are not always saved from trial, but they are kept safe in it. We are "sealed" when the divine likeness is stamped on our character, Eph. 1:13. Those that have that likeness also enjoy the earnest of Heaven in their hearts, 2 Cor. 1:21, 22.

The definiteness of the number sealed indicates the perfectness and greatness of this firstfruit sheaf of souls. If the first sheaf be so full and heavy, what will not the harvest be! See 14:4. Beyond human count in number; representing every country under Heaven; spotless in character; victorious in their conflict with evil; ascribing all glory to the Lamb as the result of his travail of soul. The tribe of Dan is omitted, but perhaps reappears in 21:12. Does this mean that some will be saved as by firebrands plucked by the grace of God?

REVELATION 7:11-17

The Joyous Service of the White-robed Throng. No nation has a monopoly of saints. No tribe is unrepresented. No language is so rude that its children may not learn the speech of Heaven. The theology of Heaven attributes salvation to God as its source, through Jesus as its medium. Palm branches symbolize victory, and the white robes transfiguring purity. "His raiment was white," Luke 9:29. Thus it was spoken of the transfigured Christ. Notice that sevenfold doxology! The visions of the saved shall awaken new joy in the angelic hosts, but how much more in the heart of Christ!

When we stand face to face with an inexplicable mystery, how comforting it is to be able to say in perfect faith, "Thou knowest." Tribulation, whether it stands for our private afflictions or for some great crisis of martyrdom, is left behind forever. It should never be forgotten, however, that we are not saved by *our* sufferings, but by *his*. The blessedness of Heaven consists in the unveiled presence of God, in unbroken service, and in safety because God will spread his tabernacle over us. This exquisite description of the future life consists largely of negatives, because the positive defies human speech. No scorching trial, no fear, no want, no finality, because the Lamb will conduct our eternal progress deeper and deeper into Heaven.

REVELATION 8:1-13

The Incense of the Prayers of Saints. The seventh seal includes the seven trumpets. What a contrast that pause must have been to the jubilant songs of the great multitude! In the Jewish Temple, we are told, the musical instruments and chanting resounded during the offering of the sacrifices, which occupied the first part of the service; but at the offering of the incense a solemn silence was observed, Ps. 62:1. The people prayed quietly at the time of incense. What a glimpse is here afforded of the intercession of our great High Priest! The smoke of the incense of his great merit arises with the prayers of the saints. Pray on, believer, though your voice be feeble and so much imperfection mingles with your efforts to serve God. The incense of Christ's intercession is fragrant enough to make even you acceptable.

The four first trumpets include the devastation of natural objects. The dumb creation, and even the earth itself, suffers for man's sin. Think of the horses wounded in battle, dying in long agony; of vast countryside, once smiling, now becoming a wilderness; of the soil compelled to produce the ingredients of poisoning and intoxication. Poor Mother Earth! Goethe said that he could hear her sighing, as a captive yearning for redemption.

REVELATION 9:1-11

"Out of the Smoke of the Pit." This chapter reminds us of the prophet Joel who, under the imagery of a swarm of locusts, depicted the coming invasion of hostile nations. Whether these warriors are intended for barbarian hordes which swept over the Roman Empire previous to its fall, or whether they represent the Saracens, between whose appearance and the details of this vision there is much in common, is not within our province to determine. The point which specially concerns us is that only those escaped who had received the imprint of God's seal. Of old the destroying angel passed over the houses, on the lintels of which the blood was visible.

But there are spiritual foes, against whose invasion we must seek the sealing of God's Spirit. "Grieve not the holy Spirit of God, whereby ye are sealed unto the day of redemption," Eph. 4:30. What is marked with the royal seal is under special protection; and when temptation assails you, you may assuredly claim that divine protection, which shall surround you as an impenetrable shield. "The angel of the Lord encampeth round about them that fear him, and delivereth them," Ps. 34:7. We fight not against flesh and blood, but against wicked spirits in heavenly places, and only spiritual help can secure for us immunity against the spiritual.

REVELATION 9:12-21

Impenitent in Spite of All. "The river Euphrates" possibly stands for nations and hordes of men emanating from that region. These verses are held by a large number of expositors to foretell the invasion of Europe by the Turks, who have desolated and held the sacred places of the Jewish faith. The Church of that time was eaten through with idolatry. Image worship had become almost universal, and the invariable consequence of this relapse from the noble spiritual ideals of the Jewish and Christian dispensations was materialism, sensuality, and the greed of the priest. On the other hand, the Turks were fierce iconoclasts, and their progress everywhere was marked by the demolition of Christian emblems.

Demons contrive to get themselves worshiped under the effigies of idolatry, and murders, sorceries, fornication, and theft infest their temples. There is perpetual controversy between the spirit of truth and these perversities; and this conflict must continue, not only in the Church, but in the heart, until everything that opposes the reign of the Spirit is overthrown, and every thought is brought into captivity to the obedience of Christ, 2 Cor. 10:5. Is this supremacy of the Spirit secured for thee, my reader?

REVELATION 10:1-11

The Angel with the Little Book. If *one* of God's angels is so strong and glorious, what must the Lord of angels be! From the splendor of his retinue, we may estimate the wealth of the Prince. How exactly does this description of the little book suit the word of the cross, that is, the message of the gospel! Things are spoken to the saints which, as Paul says, no tongue can utter. They are sealed to the unbelieving, but opened to the children of God. Notice that magnificent description of the ever-living God, the Creator, the unfolder of the mystery of his dealings, vv. 6, 7. See also 1 Cor. 2:12.

The gospel is full of sweetness and delight in its first conception. The sense of peace with God, the consciousness of pardoned sin and acceptance in the Beloved are like the music of Heaven or the dew of Paradise. But the cross cuts deep into the self-life, as we carry the sentence of death in ourselves. We learn the necessity of being crucified with Christ if we would enter into his resurrection joys; and so the Word of God, which is sharper than any two-edged sword, penetrates lower and lower, dividing soul and spirit, the joints and marrow. Our Lord never concealed this from those who sought to be enrolled as his followers; but there is blessedness in the bitterness, as springs of fresh water arising amid the brine of the sea.

REVELATION 11:1-13

The "Two Witnesses." We cannot in this brief note indicate the various interpretations of this chapter, but certain great principles underlie it which are true of every age.

(1) During the darkest ages, men have been raised up to testify against the prevailing corruption of their time, and especially the corruption of the apostate church. Their opponents have endeavored to silence their voice and blacken their character, but God has ever vindicated them and given life out of death. (2) Always when the enemies of the truth have deemed themselves triumphant, there has been a rekindling of gospel testimony. A few years before Luther appeared, a medal was struck to commemorate the extinction of so-called heresy. (3) Such witness-bearing as is suggested by the comparison with Zechariah's vision is fed from the heart of Christ. He is the root of the martyr line; his Spirit is the life-breath of his witnesses. All through the centuries, commonly called Christian though generally very un-Christian, there has been an unbroken succession of pure and noble souls who have stood for Jesus Christ even unto death. Let us dare to stand with them and our Lord, that he may not be ashamed of us at his coming.

REVELATION 11:14—12:6

"He Shall Reign for Ever and Ever." The kingdom is even now Christ's, but it is hidden, even as he is. One day it will be manifested. For a long time David was the anointed king of Israel, but Saul sat on the throne until the predestined hour came when the tribes of Israel made David their chosen monarch. This surely is a type of that which will one day become apparent to the whole creation. The kingdom of the world will wholly and permanently become Christ's. Suffering and sorrow will then flee

away, as birds of ill omen at dawn. War will cease to the end of the world. The glad populations of mankind will walk in the light of life, and the long night and travail of Nature will be ended. It may be that each great era of human history ends with a scene of judgment; or that these series of visions are concurrent, viewing the earth-order from different standpoints.

What comfort is derived from this vision of the Ark of God's Covenant, which abides in the inner sanctuary! He is true to us. His word cannot alter, neither will he recede from his pledge to overthrow our enemies, to undo the devastation they have caused, and to realize his original purpose in man's creation.

REVELATION 12:7-17

Satan Cast Down from Heaven. The spirit of evil waits to destroy each birth of good in our world. As soon as Mary had given birth to our Lord, Herod sought to destroy him, and this is characteristic of all the ages. But God's care is always at hand to deliver his own. He has his prepared places, where he hides those who trust in him. He keeps them in the secret place of his pavilion, safe from the strife of men.

Sin has brought conflict, not on our earth only, but throughout the universe; but from the heavenly places it has been driven, and the last stand is made on our earth. There is but one talisman of victory. We overcome only insofar as we take shelter in the blood of the Lamb and wield as our weapon the Word of God. As darkness cannot resist the light, so evil cannot exist before the witness of the Church and the child of God, if only we care more for the honor and glory of Christ than for our own lives. To the end there must be war between the seed of the woman and the dragon, and there must be bruising. But the final outcome is sure. As Satan was cast out of Heaven, so he shall be cast out of earth, and Christ shall see of the travail of his soul and shall be satisfied.

REVELATION 13:1-18

The Beast and His Worshipers. The horns symbolize power; the heads, intelligence; and the beast, an earthly kingdom. The dragon must stand for Satan, who has wrought his greatest achievements through earthly potentates and systems. It is through the world power that the hatred of hell has been vented on the saints. What a comfort to know that the duration of such power is limited to forty-two symbolic months; that is, 1,260 days (or years). If you are enduring hatred and persecution, be of good cheer, for your name is written in the Lamb's book of life, v. 8. This may well compensate us amid the most violent opposition.

The beast arising from the earth, vv. 11-18, may represent the persecutions of papal Rome as contrasted with those of pagan Rome in the previous verses. Or this symbol may represent some of those modern devices by which men's hearts are turned from God, such as the new semi-religious schools of thought that strive for the empire of men's minds, or the customs of modern trade, v. 17. Be these as they may, the one outstanding lesson for us all is that the child of God is always in collision with the spirit of his age.

REVELATION 14:1-8

The Lamb's Chosen Worshipers. The blessed ones with whom this chapter opens are only the first-fruit sheaf from the great harvest field. Think of it! If one sheaf consists of 144,000, what will be the entire number of the saved? The characteristics attributed to them may be realized by us all now and here. We must bear the name—that is, the nature and character of Jesus—in our faces; we must be pure in heart and life; and we must go wherever he goes. If to Gethsemane, we must follow him; if to Calvary, we must take up our cross and go thither; if to Heaven, we shall be with him there also. It is thought by some that this first-fruit sheaf represents the dear children who have died in early life and have become the Savior's bodyguard and close associates. It may be so, but more likely it stands for the possessors of the child-heart.

In majestic procession, one after another, strong angels are seen issuing from the heavenly portals with their sublime announcements. Notice the phrase, "the everlasting gospel," v. 6. In other words, the gospel of the grace of God is no expedient brought in to patch up a program which has been seriously spoiled; it is as old as eternity and brings to men eternal joy and peace and hope.

REVELATION 14:9-20

The Winepress of God's Wrath. We cannot understand the torment of those who are depicted in vv. 9-12, except it be the remorse at having refused the love of the Lamb of God. Even Christ himself cannot save a soul from its self-condemnation. Note the emphasis of v. 13. The voice which pronounces the blessedness of the departed is "from heaven." The emphasis is on the word "henceforth." There is no pause in their onward progress, no dim and shadowy existence, no cessation in thought. "From henceforth," that is, from the moment of death, they are blessed who die in the Lord; and this announcement is endorsed by the emphatic "Yea" of the Spirit. It is a great matter to have that affirmation to our words, whether we preach or teach. What could better authenticate them than that deep co-witness to God's Word in the heart or in the Church? See Acts 5:32 and Heb. 2:4.

This harvest scene surely stands for the blessed revivals which have from time to time visited the world, and may especially be reckoned on in the last days of the present dispensation. Only when the harvest is gathered in will the vintage of woe and wrath commence. To which ingathering do *we* belong?

REVELATION 15:1-8

The Song of Moses and of the Lamb. The imagery in the magnificent scene with which this chapter opens is perhaps borrowed from Pharaoh's overthrow in the Red Sea which, as the rich lines of an Eastern dawn illuminated its waters, seemed like a sea of glass mingled with fire. So, beside the crystal sea of Time from whose surface all traces of storm will have been removed and on which the eternal morning will be breaking, we who by grace have overcome shall celebrate the final victory of God. We shall sing an anthem in which the Hebrew and the Christian, the children of the old dispensation and of the new, the souls who have seen through a glass darkly and those who have beheld face to face, shall rejoice together.

One day we shall see the rightfulness of all that God has done, v. 4. All his ways are just and true, whether our poor human sense detects this or not. Let us dare to affirm it even now. Ponder that great name—"King of the ages," v. 3, margin. He only is holy; we need the perfect cleansing and righteousness which he gives us, that we may dare to stand in his presence. From this radiant vision, we turn sadly to the fate of the godless, Christ-rejecting world. See vv. 5-8.

REVELATION 16:1-9

Recompense for the Blood of Saints. It makes us pause to hear that angels, who rejoice over one sinner that repenteth, are employed in these terrible judgments. It is very startling to hear their outspoken acquiescence in the plagues that spoil the earth, sea, springs, and sun. The angel of the waters insists that God has judged righteously, and the altar, beneath which are the souls of the martyrs, assents.

Our softer age shrinks from such conceptions of the divine judgments, but it is likely that our standards are weakened and warped by our daily contact with what is earthly and human. God's love is not soft and emasculated, but strong, vigorous, and righteous. Only when we reach the land of light and glory shall we understand the true horror of sin and the inveteracy of human apostasy. Then we also shall be able to take up those solemn words of endorsement in v. 7: "Even so, Lord God Almighty, true and righteous are thy judgments."

REVELATION 16:10-21

"The Battle of That Great Day of God." All these judgments apparently refer to the destruction of those great systems of falsehood and apostasy which set themselves against the truth and purity of God. The dragon, beast, and false prophet are the devil's mimicry of the divine Trinity. The dragon corresponds to God the Father in delegating his authority; the beast, like our Lord, is crowned with diadems, Rev. 13:1, 19:12; the false prophet directs attention to the beast, as does the Holy Spirit to Christ.

The mystery of iniquity will make one last effort to obtain the empire of the world, seeking to effect its purpose through a human confederacy. When that confederacy has reached its climax of effrontery, the coming of the Son of God is near; hence the need for watchfulness and purity, v. 15. Armageddon is the mountain of Megiddo, in the plain of Esdraelon. See Joel 3:2, 12, 14; also Zechariah 12:11. The great city symbolizes the apostate church, or professing Christendom. The true Bride is away from these judgments, awaiting the manifestation of her Lord.

REVELATION 17:1-18

The Great World City Overthrown. This scarlet-attired woman is that miserable attempt made in every age to counterfeit the true Church of the living God. Man does not like the religion of the cross, of faith, of self-denial, and each age has witnessed some false system from which all these objectionable elements are eliminated. Surely a false system has revelated itself successively in Babylon, Jerusalem, Rome, London, New York, and other great centers. Fashion smiles on it, wealth adorns it, human power unites with it, and in every age it has been intoxicated with the blood of martyrs.

Between this miserable travesty of the Church and the Church herself there has been perpetual conflict. But the ultimate victory has always remained with the Lamb, and if only we side with him, as the "called, chosen, and faithful" of v. 14, we also shall be more than conquerors. Human prestige and power shall not ultimately avail in the conflict against the all-conquering Savior. And finally the very world powers shall turn against the apostate and adulterous church, v. 16. Come out from her and be separate!

REVELATION 18:1-13

"Her Sins Have Reached unto Heaven." We have seen that the scarlet woman represents the false religion of human wit and fashion. It is found in every age. There is not a city, town, or village where it does not seek to allure men from Christ. The mischief is that so many really godly people are misled by it. In this they resemble Obadiah, who hid the prophets in a cave and fed them but was hand and glove with Ahab. To all such, who are endeavoring to keep in touch with the true Bride and with the apostate church, the summons of v. 4 has a very profound significance.

It was the unanimous verdict of the reformers that the great city here described, v. 10, was intended to represent Rome, as the seat of the great apostasy. If that be the case, the merchandise described here does not refer to literal commerce, but to the carnal delights which are often permitted and fostered by false religious systems to win the allegiance of the worldly and unclean.

REVELATION 18:14-24

Fallen Like a Stone into the Sea. This section delineates the utter desolation which will ensue when the judgments of God have finished their mission against professing but unfaithful Christendom. How near we are at the present hour to their fulfillment, we dare not say. But it often seems as if we are living in the last days of "the times of the Gentiles," and very near the fulfillment of all that is written in this book. It is the universal comment that all religious values are being altered. The church systems, as such, give signs that they are losing their hold on the vast masses of the people, while the heart of man cries out as eagerly as ever for the living God. We can only heed the Lord's command to watch, and see to it that we may be found of him in peace and standing patiently at our post. In the meantime, events in the distant East are symptomatic of the fig tree putting forth her leaves. See Matt. 24:32.

REVELATION 19:1-10

The Fourfold Hallelujah. One day we shall hear those four "Alleluias," vv. 1, 3, 4, 6. They will reverberate to the farthest limits of the universe. They will not be inspired by vindictiveness or revenge, but will be jubilant with the conviction that God has vindicated himself and has proved that right can conquer wrong; truth, falsehood; and love, hate. One of our chief anticipations when we think of the future is that God's character and government of the universe will be amply vindicated.

Contemporaneous with the fall of Babylon will be the marriage of the Lamb. Before he assumes, together with his saints, the task of governing the world, the union of supreme love will have been consummated, and the marriage supper will have been filled with guests. Note from v. 10 that the angels are our fellow-servants. They hail us as comrades on the condition that we never flinch from maintaining the testimony of Jesus.

REVELATION 19:11-21

"King of Kings, and Lord of Lords." Here is a sublime vision of Christ, as he comes to judge the beast, that is, the world power which has ever been in antagonism to the principles of God's kingdom. We must distinguish between it and the final judgment. This precedes, that follows, the millennial reign. Compare Matt. 24:27, 29, 37, 39. The blood in which his vesture is dipped is not his own, but that of his foes. See Isa. 63:2. Here at last is fulfilled Ps. 2:9.

Notice the attributes of Christ: He is "Faithful," because he will stand by us to the end. He is "True," never doing less but always more than he has promised. He is pure as flame. He is also in "many" realms, and "the Word of God," that is, the final utterance and complete revelation of the Most High. Let us follow him! But if we do, we must resemble him. His robes are naturally white, but we must wash ours, that we may have the right to the tree of life and to enter the city of God. Compare Ps. 110. This will be the time, also, to which our Lord referred in Matt. 13:41. God's whirlwind will scatter the chaff.

REVELATION 20:1-6

The Millennial Reign. In the preceding chapter the beast and the false prophet are depicted as meeting their punishment in the lake of fire. In this, the devil, death, and Hades are consigned to a similar fate. The imagery is apparently drawn from that fearful tragedy which left so deep an impression on the ancient world. See Gen. 14:10; 19:24; Jude 7. The last reference is especially interesting, because there the fate of the cities of the plain is quoted as an example of eternal fire. May it be ours to participate in the first resurrection! Let our loins be girded and our lamps trimmed, that we may be found of Christ in peace, at our posts, and prepare to enter with him into the bridal feast. This is a more solemn and critical consideration than the majority of Christians seem to suppose. In fellowship with their Lord, his people are to exert in a godly direction the same kind of influence over the affairs of men as the rulers of darkness in an ungodly sense now exercise. Thank God—every morning brings that blessed day nearer.

REVELATION 20:7-15

Before the Great White Throne. Gog and Magog take us back to Gen. 10:2; see also Ezek. 38 and 39. It would seem that this great confederacy of the northern nations against the beloved city, Jerusalem, will be led by Satan, and overwhelmed once and for all by the direct judgment of God.

The final judgment is depicted in vv. 11-15. God's people will not appear at that bar. All the human family will be arraigned, save those whose names are in the book of life, John 5:24. See Exod. 32:32; Dan. 12:1; Phil. 4:3; and Rev. 21:27. Death and Hades will surrender their contents. What a marvelous audience! The throne is "great," because of the destinies to be decided; and "white," because of the immaculate purity of the Judge, who will be none other than our Lord. See John 5:22; Acts 17:31. The books will surely include conscience, Rom. 2:15, 16; God's Word, John 12:48; and the tablets of memory, Luke 16:25.

REVELATION 21:1-8

"A New Heaven and a New Earth." Here is a vision of the new creation. This is the "restitution of all things" to which Peter refers in Acts 3:21, and the deliverance of creation from the bondage of corruption which Paul anticipates in Rom. 8:21. No words can portray in positive description what that universe will be, and even the inspired writer has to confine himself to negatives. All he does is to name various elements of terror and dread, saying: This shall not be there, nor that, nor the other, all of which are the fell brood of human sin. The one great positive blessing will be that which was given to Israel in type, but then will be the perpetual experience of the human family. Compare v. 3 and Exod. 25:8. Let us see to it that here and now the Lord Jesus is *the* Alpha and Omega, *the* A and Z of our life. If so, we may even in this mortal life begin to experience the life of the redeemed. We may now inherit all these things and know the intimacy of v. 7. But we must "overcome." Note that "the fearful," that is, the cowardly, who draw back in the face of opposition, are classed with the abominable and murderers.

REVELATION 21:9-27

"The Holy City." The "new Jerusalem" is the redeemed Church united with her Lord in the act of governing the whole world. This city is obviously the seat of imperial rule. In that blessed condition the saints will rule the earth as the powers of darkness rule it now. We shall enjoy the fellowship of the good and great of every age. In a literal sense we shall be fellow-citizens with the saints. All ages and dispensations will blend there. We see angels at the gates; the names of the twelve tribes and twelve apostles engraved in imperishable characters to indicate the blending of the dispensations; the differing stones, representing variety of character and function, but all blending in the light of the Lamb on the throne.

The happy throngs pour through the gates with never-ending rapture. Those gates, facing every quarter, stand always open; but none desire to go forth, except commissioned on some errand by the King. All the glory and honor of the world are gathered within those walls, because Jesus will be King over every department of human life. There will be room for all beauty, art, and culture in the city of eternal light and love.

REVELATION 22:1-9

"A Pure River of Water of Life." The first five verses of this chapter obviously belong to the preceding one, from which they should not be severed. The ever-flowing river of life proves that the whole life of the blessed depends on the life of God, resident in the enthroned Lamb and communicated through the Holy Spirit. In Eden there was one tree of life; in the new Jerusalem there is a grove with perennial fruit, not protected by a flaming sword, but standing freely in the main thoroughfare, that all who will may take. Observe the threefold description of the saints—they serve, they behold, and they resemble, vv. 3, 4. No night with its shadow; no rest is needed in the delightful service; no artificial, but underived and original light; no cessation of regnant power, for they shall reign forever and ever.

When the visions end, John is assured of the reality and truth of all that he has heard and seen. It appears that the Master himself

REVELATION

broke in with the assurance of his speedy advent; and who shall say that that assurance has failed, when we measure the flight of time with the years of the right hand of the Most High?

REVELATION 22:10-21

"Come, Lord Jesus." "Still," four times repeated, implies the crystallization and permanence of character. The rewards mentioned here are for the faithful service of Christ's stewards, as in Matt. 25:21. For the fourth time, he who began the book and closes it uses of himself the divine monogram of Alpha and Omega, 1:8, 11; 21:6. In the Authorized Version the way to the tree of life was opened to those who kept the commandments, but it is very comforting to read in the Revised Version that this blessed privilege is for those "who wash their robes." Notice the combination of various titles in Christ: David's Lord and David's Son; the Morning Star and the Sun of Heaven's Day; the Coming One, for whose quick return the whole creation waits; and the Water of Life, of which whosoever will may drink. The appeal of v. 17 is to our Lord, asking him to make haste to come, and it is answered in v. 20. But who shall tell whether that cry may not, sooner than we think, be answered by a spiritual transformation of the things seen and temporal, so that without a break, in the twinkling of an eye, the veil of matter may be rent and the whole imminent glory of the unseen and eternal swim into view! Let us be on the alert!